# CITIES IN
# A GLOBALIZING WORLD

# CITIES IN
# A GLOBALIZING WORLD
## GLOBAL REPORT ON HUMAN SETTLEMENTS
## 2001

KGQ020F   30cm   344pg

**United Nations Centre for Human Settlements (Habitat)**

EARTHSCAN
Earthscan Publications Ltd
London and Sterling, VA

First published in the UK and USA in 2001 by Earthscan Publications Ltd
for and on behalf of the United Nations Centre for Human Settlements (Habitat)

United Nations Centre for Human Settlements (Habitat)
PO Box 30030, Nairobi, Kenya
Tel: +254 2 621 234
Fax: +254 2 624 266
http://www.unchs.org

**DISCLAIMER**

The designations employed and the presentation of the material in this publication do not imply the expression of any opinion whatsoever on the part of the Secretariat of the United Nations concerning the legal status of any country, territory, city or area, or of its authorities, or concerning delimitation of its frontiers or boundaries, or regarding its economic system or degree of development. The analysis, conclusions and recommendations of the report do not necessarily reflect the views of the United Nations Centre for Human Settlements (Habitat), the Commission on Human Settlements or its Member States

HS/621/01/E

ISBN:     1 85383 806 3 paperback
          1 85383 805 5 hardback

Typesetting by PCS Mapping & DTP, Newcastle upon Tyne
Page design by S&W Design Ltd
Cover design by Susanne Harris
Printed and bound in the UK by Thanet Press, Margate, Kent

For a full list of publications please contact:

Earthscan Publications Ltd
120 Pentonville Road, London, N1 9JN, UK
Tel: +44 (0)20 7278 0433
Fax: +44 (0)20 7278 1142
Email: earthinfo@earthscan.co.uk
http://www.earthscan.co.uk

22883 Quicksilver Drive, Sterling, VA 20166-2012, USA

Earthscan is an editorially independent subsidiary of Kogan Page Ltd and publishes in association with WWF-UK and the International Institute for Environment and Development

A catalogue record for this book is available from the British Library

Library of Congress Cataloging-in-Publication Data

Cities in a globalizing world : global report on human settlements 2001 / United Nations Centre for Human Settlements (Habitat).
        p. cm.
    Includes bibliographical references and index.
    ISBN 1-85383-805-5 (hardback) — ISBN 1-85383-806-3 (pbk.)
    1. Human settlements. 2. Urbanization. 3. Urban policy. 4. Municipal services. 5. Urban poor. 6. Globalization. I. United Nations Centre for Human Settlements.
    [DNLM: 1. Urban Health-trends. 2. Urbanization-trends. 3. Housing economics. 4. Poverty. 5. Public Policy. 6. Sanitation. 7. Socio-economic Factors. WA 380 C5815 2001]

    HT65.C57 2001
    307.76—dc21

                                                                                                    2001002401

This book is printed on elemental chlorine-free paper

# FOREWORD

The world has entered the urban millennium. Nearly half the world's people are now city dwellers, and the rapid increase in urban population is expected to continue, mainly in developing countries. This historic transition is being further propelled by the powerful forces of globalization. The central challenge for the international community is clear: to make both urbanization and globalization work for all people, instead of leaving billions behind or on the margins.

Although globalization certainly affects rural areas, the impact of global economic change is largely centred on cities. Globalization is changing the structure of employment; it is altering the demographic make-up of cities; and it is introducing a strong international context to local concerns. At the same time, cities and their surrounding regions are themselves shaping and promoting globalization by providing the infrastructure and labour upon which globalization depends, as well as the ideas and innovation that have always emerged from the intensity of urban life.

The benefits of globalization are being spread unevenly. Cities present some of the starkest of these contrasts: homeless people living in cardboard boxes, next to skyscrapers occupied by corporations whose budgets exceed those of many countries; growing gaps between the salaries offered by labour markets and the housing costs determined by urban land markets; enormous levels of consumption alongside great pyramids of waste that threaten the environment and human health; and hitherto unseen patterns of segregation, with pockets of wealth at the centre and vast enclaves of poverty on the periphery.

The combined processes of urbanization and globalization have thrust additional responsibilities on city governments. Public administration and economic development are linked more and more to global markets and investment, but this is also an opportunity: to entrench democracy at the local level and to build new partnerships with the private sector, citizens' groups and other cities confronting similar challenges. National governments, for their part, will continue to play a key role in the governance of cities, not only in terms of finance, but also in overall strategic planning and in crucial matters such as justice, equity and social cohesion.

*Cities in a Globalizing World: Global Report on Human Settlements 2001* is a comprehensive review of conditions in the world's cities and the prospects for making them better, safer places to live in an age of globalization. I hope that it will provide all stakeholders – foremost among them the urban poor themselves – with reliable and timely information with which to set our policies right and get the machinery of urban life moving in a constructive direction. At the United Nations Millennium Summit in September 2000, world leaders pledged to achieve, by the year 2020, significant improvement in the lives of at least 100 million slum dwellers. As we strive to meet this target and to implement the Habitat Agenda adopted at the Istanbul conference in 1996, the United Nations system, including the United Nations Centre for Human Settlements (Habitat), will continue to place its unique services at the disposal of all the world's peoples.

**Kofi A Annan**
*Secretary-General*
*United Nations*

# INTRODUCTION

The *Global Report on Human Settlements 2001* chronicles human settlement conditions and trends since the second United Nations Conference on Human Settlements (Habitat II) convened in Istanbul in June 1996, emphasizing both progress made in the past five years and the issues that continue to confront a changing world. In addressing these issues, the structure of the report follows the two main strategic themes of the Habitat Agenda adopted by Habitat II: adequate shelter for all and sustainable human settlements development in an urbanizing world.[1]

The previous edition of the *Global Report on Human Settlements*, written prior to the Habitat II conference, contributed to worldwide understanding of the human settlements issues that became the focus of the Habitat Agenda. The 1996 report, entitled *An Urbanizing World*, characterized cities around the world as places of opportunity and presented a view of cities as engines of growth.

Today, the trend of urbanization continues, although intertwined with globalization. Like urbanization, globalization brings opportunities as well as problems, and its impacts are increasingly being observed worldwide, most clearly in the cities. The challenge is to develop solutions to problems associated with globalization, while at the same time strengthening its positive aspects. Human settlements can play a significant role in this process by fostering good governance and effective partnerships.

*Cities in a Globalizing World* acknowledges the positive consequences of globalization: facilitated diffusion of knowledge; facilitated spread of norms of democratic governance, environmental justice and human rights; increased city-to-city exchanges of knowledge, experiences, best practices and lessons learned; and increased awareness in both citizens and city managers of the potentials of peer-to-peer learning. The report also draws attention to many urgent and unresolved problems.

In Africa, only one-third of all urban households is connected to potable water. In Latin America, urban poverty stands at 30 per cent. In Asia Pacific, a mere 38 per cent of urban households are connected to a sewerage system. In Europe, processes of social exclusion marginalize many low-income and minority households, while urban crime and the decline of peripheral housing estates undermine the social cohesion of many communities. In North America, problems of residential segregation, discrimination in housing markets and affordability persist, particularly in the larger cities, despite recent economic growth. Worldwide, hundreds of millions of people live under conditions of abject poverty or experience highly unequal access to resources.

Studies presented in this report indicate that, while some population groups have improved their housing conditions, a disproportionate share of the world population has seen its situation deteriorate further. In many countries, real incomes have fallen, the costs of living have gone up and the number of poor households has grown, particularly in urban areas. Sixty countries have become steadily poorer since 1980. Many studies portray increasing economic disparities between nations, cities, neighbourhoods and households, revealing strong increases in polarization and growing global inequality.

The growing demand for public services in many countries is increasingly being met by local authorities and, in some cases, by the private sector, as these entities take on responsibility for functions previously ascribed to national governments. Furthermore, as civil society becomes more organized, effective and politically active, municipal institutions are becoming more democratic and adopting more participatory local structures.

Local political coalitions, together with representative groups from civil society, are attempting to shape their cities and towns in ways that help to maximize the opportunities as well as to minimize the social and economic disadvantages associated with globalization. Whether this involves campaigns against crime or plans to improve the local environment in order to attract tourists, or whether it involves strategies to reduce local taxes or develop more comprehensive educational or health systems, municipal officials and their partners are increasingly responsive to the potential benefits of competitive strategies.

As a result, and as pointed out in this report, many cities have experienced a shift in the policies of urban government from managerialism to entrepreneurialism. This entrepreneurial attitude views the city as a product that needs to be marketed. The emphasis on marketing underpins the restructuring of cities so that they appeal to global investors. By the same token, cities that do not always have the resources to attract outside interest and investment may find themselves even more bereft and impoverished. Local capacity building is essential to reducing the risk of global polarization. In this connection, it is encouraging that international cooperation in the form of city-to-city exchanges is rapidly growing in popularity. Public–private partnerships are also increasingly being broadened to include civil society groups and there is increasing evidence of the potential of community-based networks based on direct people-to-people interactions. The challenge at national and international levels is to create an enabling legal framework in which the various forms of community-to-community cooperation can be intensified and strengthened.

Considering the trends that are reshaping the world's urban structures, the report places emphasis on 'metropolization of the world economy'. It describes the archipelagic spatial structure of emerging global urban networks. Megacities, comprising urban cores and associated hinterlands, are theoretically able to address all kinds of technical problems, including urban service provision and environmental management. However, they are facing difficult governance challenges, owing to obsolete municipal political structures and inhabitants who are more and more concerned with only their immediate individual and local neighbourhood interests than with their common future as citizens of the same city.

Urban planners are inescapably caught up in this dynamic of the new urban political economy. Urban planning today is less codified and technical, and more innovative and entrepreneurial. It is also more participatory and concerned with projects rather than whole urban systems. Planning expertise is increasingly sought not only by states, but also by the corporate sector and civil society which seek to forge agreements through negotiation and mediation among contesting parties. Urban planning is no longer the prerogative of national and local governments, who previously claimed to possess privileged knowledge about the 'public interest'. As pointed out in the report, what is controversial is not urban planning per se, but how to reconcile its multiple goals of efficiency, equity and liveability.

Globalization not only increases competition but also fragmentation, with contradictory effects on cities. To compete effectively, cities must act as a collective unit. However, their growing social, political, economic and physical polarization hampers their capacity to build coalitions, mobilize resources and develop good governance structures. Given that metropolitan areas are the chief arenas for global competition, it is necessary to strengthen them by giving them greater authority and autonomy. However, the enabling and regulatory role of governments must be broader than just facilitating the functioning of markets. It must also include responsibility for social cohesion, equity and conflict resolution.

This report reflects the significance of human settlements for sustainable social and economic development in a globalizing world and focuses on key strategies to promote and facilitate the implementation of the Habitat Agenda, the main policy document and plan of action signed by 171 member states at Habitat II.

**Anna Kajumulo Tibaijuka**
*Executive Director*
*United Nations Centre for Human Settlements (Habitat)*

# Note

1    Report of the United Nations Conference on Human Settlements (Habitat II) (Istanbul, 3–14 June 1996). A/CONF.165/14.

# ACKNOWLEDGEMENTS

It is highly appropriate that the preparation of a work concerned with globalization was itself predicated on the global mobilization of specialized expertise from multiple disciplines and professions. Input contributed by members of overlapping international networks, in a very short period of time, was only possible thanks to a combination of modern information and communication technologies and strong personal commitments to the goals of social equity and environmental sustainability in human settlement development that are the concern of this report.

*Cities in a Globalizing World* was prepared under the general guidance of Daniel Biau, Director of the Global Division of UNCHS (Habitat), and the supervision of Nefise Bazoglu and Jochen Eigen, Urban Secretariat Chiefs. The Policy Analysis and Reporting Unit, headed by Jay Moor, had primary responsibility for the production of the report, with Iouri Moisseev coordinating its preparation. Pietro Garau, Axumite Gebre-Egziabher, William Cobbett, Paul Taylor and Farouk Tebbal provided strategic advice for its development.

Willem van Vliet– (University of Colorado, USA) was the main consultant and principal resource person for the preparation of this report. Alain Durand-Lasserve (Centre National de la Recherche Scientifique, France) and Yap Kioe Sheng (Asian Institute of Technology, Thailand) also provided assistance at the initial stage.

This publication reflects the contributions of numerous people. Regrettably, it is impossible to mention and do justice to them all, but it is in order that their roles at least be acknowledged.

On 12–15 April 1999, the United Nations Centre for Human Settlements (UNCHS (Habitat)) organized an Expert Group Meeting in Nairobi, Kenya. Participants representing major world regions and a variety of research and training institutes, NGOs and various international agencies worked with United Nations staff to develop an initial outline for the report. Those present included Sylvester Abumere, Koffi Attahi, Lamin G Barrow, Daniel Biau, William Cobbett, Cor Dijkgraaf, Yamina Djacta, Alain Durand-Lasserve, Selman Erguden, Richard Groves, Angela Hakizimana, Mathias Hundsalz, Inge Jensen, Guenter Karl, Kyung-Hwan Kim, Cecilia Kinuthia-Njenga, Ousmane Laye, Michel Lachambre, Sylvie Lacroux, Iouri Moisseev, Donatus I Okpala, Peter Ondiege, William Parmena, Catherine Parmentier, Markandey Rai, Akio Sasahara, Ann Schlyter, Shekou Sesay, Daniela Simioni, Diana Lee-Smith, Sabine Springer, Catalina Trujillo, Sampson Ik Umenne, Willem van Vliet– and Yap Kioe Sheng.

A number of authors were commissioned to write papers related to various themes taken up in this report (see Background Papers, page 252): Cecilia Anderson; Susan Clarke; Forbes Davidson; Alan Doig; Alan Gilbert; Stephen Graham; Trudy Harpham; Gareth A Jones; Jeff Kenworthy; Nadezhda Kosareva; Scott Leckie; Christian Lefevre; Peter Marcuse; Diana Mitlin; Sassy Molyneux; Caroline Moser; Peter Newman; Geoffrey Payne; Alexander Puzanov; Carole Rakodi; Saskia Sassen; David Satterthwaite; Ann Schlyter; Mona Serageldin; AbdouMaliq Simone; Mark Stephens; and Emiel A Wegelin. The willingness of these authors to give of their time, and their responsiveness to requests for revision at short notice, is much appreciated.

Many colleagues generously agreed to share their expertise pro bono. Those who summarized recent work or wrote papers especially for this report include Alex K Abiko, Tariq Alam, A Al-Gilani, Gerardo M Gonzales Arrieta, Hazel Ashton, Tency Baetens, Bruce P Baird, Marcello Balbo, Milica Bajic Brkovic, Paulo Camara, Sylvia Chant, Mou Charles, Louise Chawla, Rebecca Chiu, Katherine Coit, Mary C Comerio, Geoff Davis, Flavio DeSouza, Nick Emmel, Francisco Escobar, Yang Fan, M E Feeney, Sukumar Ganapati, Gerardo M Gonzales, J Green, Chaolin Gu, Matthew Gutmann, Yosuke Hirayama, Robert Hodgson, S S A Jafri, R Jenkins, Jerry Hunsinger, Olga Kaganova, Philip F Kelly, Stephen Kendall, Michael Leaf, James Lee, Haiyong Liu, Kosta Mathey, Brian Muller, Patrick Mullin, Yip Ngai Ming, Janusz Niemczynowicz, Philip Oxhorn, Diane Perrons, Bruce Podobnik, A Rajabifard, P S N Rao, Robert J S Ross, Fahriye Sancar, R Sandhu, Mara Sidney, William Siembieda, Rubenio Simas, Ken R Smith, Gale Summerfield, Andrew Thornley, David Thorns, Ulpu Tiuri, Mary Tomlinson, H R Trivedi, Robert S K Tucker, Norman J Waitzman, Edmundo Werna, Ian P Williamson, Talmadge Wright and Xiaopei Yan. A full listing of the titles of their invaluable contributions is given in the list of background papers (see page 252).

At UNCHS (Habitat) a number of people provided vital support by reviewing and commenting on background papers and taking leadership in drafting additional sections of the report. Among them are Pietro Garau, Joseph Maseland, Iouri Moisseev, Jay Moor, Naison Mutizwa-Mangiza, Cecilia Kinuthia-Njenga, Rasna Warah, Brian Williams and Christopher Williams.

Several professionals of UNCHS (Habitat) made other valued contributions. Graham Alabaster, Christine Auclair, Jean-Yves Barcelo, Marjolein Benshop, Liz Case, Andre Dzikus, Mohamed El-Sioufi, Selman Erguden, Szilard Fricska, Jorge

Gavidia, Mathias Hundsalz, Inge Jensen, Sylvie Lacroux, Diana Lee-Smith, Uwe Lohse, Guenter Karl, Dinesh Mehta, Reiner Nordberg, Laura Petrella, Kalian Ray, Wandia Seaforth, Ali Shabou, Sharad Shankardass, Soraya Smaoun, Tomasz Sudra, Catalina Trujillo, Rafael Tuts, Franz Vanderschueren, Susanne Wadstein, Rolf Wichmann and Nicholas You, in particular, kindly gave of their time amidst competing commitments.

The following colleagues from UNCHS (Habitat) were involved in the preparation of the Statistical Annex: Guenter Karl; Iouri Moisseev and Markandey Rai. Sabine Springer prepared the second revision of the unique UNCHS (Habitat) household projections data. The first household projections data, prepared by Gabriela Doblhammer, were published in the preceding *Global Report on Human Settlements 1996*. Phillip Mukungu and Mugabi Nsibirwa assisted in data processing and preparation of camera-ready copy, and Srdjan Mrkic of the United Nations Statistical Division assisted in data checking.

In addition, many other people were helpful in reviewing and commenting on drafts, making available unpublished reports, compiling data, preparing graphs, contributing information and in a variety of other ways. They include Judith Allen (University of Westminster, UK), Arjun Appadurai (University of Chicago, USA), Melissa Auerbach (Making Opportunities for Upgrading Schools & Education (MOUSE), USA), Oleg Baevski (Institute of Moscow City Master Plan, Russian Federation), Banshree Banerjee (Institute for Housing and Urban Development Studies, The Netherlands), Ted Baumann (Bay Research and Consultancy Services, South Africa), Erhard Berner (Institute of Social Studies, The Hague), Clara Braun (Fundación TIAU (Taller de Investigación y Acción Urbana), Argentina), Anne-Marie Brival (Organisation for Economic Co-operation and Development (OECD), Paris), Barbara Buttenfield (University of Colorado, USA), Goran Cars (Sweden), Manish Chalana (University of Colorado, USA), Gary Chapman (University of Texas, USA), Charles Choguill (Royal Melbourne Institute of Technology, Australia), Terry Clark (University of Chicago, USA), Peter Dale (University College London, UK), Baris Der-Petrossian (United Nations Office at Vienna (UNOV), Austria), John Doling (University of Birmingham, UK), James Dunn (Council of Canadians, Canada), Francisco Escobar (University of Melbourne, Australia), Peter Evans (University of California, Berkeley, USA), Marja Exterkate (Netherlands Interdisciplinary Demographic Institute (NIDI), The Netherlands), Susan Fainstein (Rutgers University, USA), Clarissa Fourie (McIntosh, Xaba and Associates, South Africa), Doug Gibson (Office of US Foreign Disaster Assistance (OFDA), USA), Wolfgang Glatzner (Goethe University, Germany), Assunta Gleria (Abaton Ltd, Italy), Mark Gross (Washington University, USA), Chaolin Gu (Nanjing University, China), Josef Gugler (University of Connecticut, USA), Geoff Davis (Harvard University, USA), Angela Hottinger (University of Colorado, USA), Mark Hudson (York University, Canada), Ray Hudson (University of Durham, UK), Jerry Hunsinger (Virginia Tech, USA), Ivo Imparato (Diagonal Urbana, Brazil), Fraderick Kailage (University of Dar es Salaam, United Republic of Tanzania), Brian King (University of Colorado, USA), Andrew Kirby (University of Arizona, USA), Sarah Krieger (University of Colorado, USA), Amitabh Kundu (Jawaharlal Nehru University, India), Tamara Laninga (University of Colorado, USA), Scott Leckie (Centre on Housing Rights and Evictions (COHRE), Switzerland), Tunney Lee (Massachusetts Institute of Technology (MIT), USA), Maurice Leonhardt (Asian Coalition for Housing Rights, Thailand), John Logan (State University of New York, USA), Amanda Lonsdale (International City/County Management Association (ICMA), Washington, DC, USA), Alan Mabin (Witwatersrand University, South Africa), Robert Marans (University of Michigan, USA), Kosta Mathey (Trialog, Germany), Caroline Michellier (Centre for Research on the Epidemiology of Disasters (CRED), Belgium), Faranak Miraftab (University of Illinois at Urbana-Champaign, USA), Diana Mitlin (International Institute for Environment and Development (IIED), UK), Patrick Mullin (Australian Housing and Urban Research Institute (AHUR), Australia), Mary Fran Myers (University of Colorado, USA), Kristopher Olds (University of Singapore), Meghann Ormond (University of Colorado, USA), Jose Ospina (The Wooden House, UK), Catherine Parmentier (Fédération Européenne d'Associations Nationales Travaillant avec les Sans-Abri (FEANTSA), Belgium), Sheela Patel (Shack Dwellers International and Asian Coalition for Housing Rights, India), Ann Pawliczko (United Nations Population Fund (UNFPA)), Janice Perlman (Mega-Cities Project, USA), Minar Pimple (Youth for Unity and Voluntary Action (YUVA), India), Graham Riches (University of British Columbia, Canada), Juanita Rilling (OFDA, USA), Natalia Rousakova (Moscow Institute of Architecture, Russian Federation), Jeff Rusler (World Bank, USA), David Satterthwaite (IIED, UK), Diana Shannon (University of Colorado, USA), Steven Strong (Solar Design, USA), Vladimir Storchevus (Habitat Executive Bureau in Moscow, Russian Federation), David Thorns (University of Canterbury, New Zealand), Irene Tinker (University of California, Berkeley, USA), Mary Tomlinson (Banking Council of South Africa), Netta van Vliet (Winston Foundation for World Peace, USA), Dahlia van Vliet (USA), Sandra Karina Vivona (Fundación TIAU, Argentina), Gilbert White (University of Colorado, USA), Shujie Yao (University of Portsmouth, UK) and Andreas Zehnder (European Federation of Building Societies, Germany).

The report also benefited from an invitation to its main consultant to attend a meeting of the Panel on Urban Population Dynamics of the US National Academy of Sciences, held on 24–25 February 2000 in Mexico City. The panel members shared generously of their expertise, and, in particular, the support of Richard Stren, co-chair of the panel, and Barney Cohen, Director of the Committee on Population, is much appreciated.

Several people and publishers graciously granted permission to use copyrighted work. Those kind enough to cooperate and their respective publishers, with source material in parentheses, include: David Satterthwaite, IIED (*Environment and Urbanization*); David Clark, Elsevier Publishers (*Habitat International*); Margaret Bergen, World Bank (*The Urban Age*); Charmaine Falcon-Steward, Homeless International; Donald Holton, International Housing Finance Union (*Housing Finance International*); Rajul Pandya-Lorch, International Food Policy Research Institute (IFPRI) (*Vision 2020*); Reggie Modlich (*Women and Environments International*); Rose Robinson, University of California Press (*Livable Cities: The Politics of Urban Livelihood and Sustainability* by Peter Evans); and Carol Bell, Fannie Mae Foundation (*Housing Facts and Finance*).

Nick Bain, Sriadibhatla Chainulu and Henk Verbeek of UNCHS (Habitat) and Josie Villamin and Joerg Weich of the United Nations Office at Nairobi (UNON) provided administrative support for preparation of the report. Secretarial support was provided by Mary Kariuki, Mary Dibo, Salome Gathu, Stella Otieno, Claver Rwabudariko and Florence Bunei of UNCHS (Habitat) and Esther Kimani and Valentine Musoga of UNON.

Anirban Pal (University of Colorado, USA) assisted with completion of the list of references. Jennifer Steffel (University of Colorado, USA) prepared the manuscript for production and developed the subject index.

Special thanks are also due to the people at Earthscan Publications Ltd, in particular its Publishing Director Jonathan Sinclair Wilson, Publishing Manager Frances MacDermott, copy editor Gillian Bourn and Akan Leander, Nim Moorthy, Richard Reid and Sara Bearman.

# CONTENTS

**PART IV**

**DEVELOPMENTS IN THE URBAN ENVIRONMENT AND INFRASTRUCTURE**

**PART V**

**ENSURING DEVELOPMENT PROSPECTS**

**PART VI**

**BUILDING A COMMON FUTURE**

**PART VII**

**STATISTICAL ANNEX**

# LIST OF BOXES

# LIST OF TABLES

# LIST OF FIGURES

# LIST OF MAPS

# LIST OF ACRONYMS AND ABBREVIATIONS

| | |
|---|---|
| AHUR | Australian Housing and Urban Research Institute |
| ARI | acute respiratory infection |
| ASEAN | Association of Southeast Asian Nations |
| ASNM | Agency for the Sustainable Development of the North Milano Area |
| BANANA | build absolutely nothing anywhere near anyone |
| BITs | bilateral investment treaties |
| BOOT | build–own–operate–transfer |
| BOT | build–operate–transfer |
| CBD | central business district |
| CBO | community-based organization |
| CBO | Congressional Budget Office |
| CCTV | closed-circuit television |
| CEDAW | Convention on Elimination of All Forms of Discrimination Against Women |
| CEES | Central and Eastern European States |
| CEO | chief executive officer |
| CID | common interest development |
| CILP | community infrastructure lending programme |
| CIP | community infrastructure programme |
| CIS | Commonwealth of Independent States |
| COHRE | Centre on Housing Rights and Evictions (Switzerland) |
| CPER | Contrats de Plan Etat-Régions |
| CRED | Centre for Research on the Epidemiology of Disasters (Belgium) |
| CRPC | Commission on Real Property Claims |
| DAC | Development Assistance Committee (of the OECD) |
| DALY | disability adjusted life year |
| DESA | Department of Economic and Social Affairs (United Nations Population Division) |
| DESEPAZ | Programa Desarrollo, Salud y Paz (Colombia) |
| DFID | Department for International Development (UK) |
| DHS | demographic and health surveys |
| EBRD | European Bank for Reconstruction and Development |
| EDURB | Empresa de Desenvolvimento Urbano Lda (Angola) |
| END | European Nuclear Disarmament |
| EU | European Union |
| FAO | Food and Agriculture Organization |
| FDI | foreign direct investment |
| FEANTSA | European Federation of National Organizations Working with the Homeless (Belgium) |
| FID | International Federation for Information and Documentation |
| FINDETER | Financiera de Desarrollo Territorial (Colombia) |
| FIRE | fire, insurance and real estate |
| GARNET | Global Applied Research Network |
| GATT | General Agreement on Tariffs and Trade |
| GDI | Gender-related Development Index |
| GDP | gross domestic product |

| GEF | Global Environment Facility |
| GEM | Gender Empowerment Measure |
| GESI | Global Environmental Sanitation Initiative |
| GIWA | Global International Waters Assessment |
| GKSS | Textile Workers Struggle Committee (India) |
| GNP | gross national product |
| GPI | genuine progress indicator |
| GSS | Global Strategy for Shelter to the Year 2000 |
| Habitat I | first United Nations Conference on Human Settlements (Vancouver, 1976) |
| Habitat II | second United Nations Conference on Human Settlements (Istanbul, 1996) |
| HDI | Human Development Index |
| HUDCO | Indian State Bank |
| ICDDR,B | International Centre for Diarrhoeal Disease Research, Bangladesh |
| ICLEI | International Council on Local Environmental Initiatives |
| ICMA | International City/County Management Association |
| ICPD | International Conference on Population and Development |
| ICTs | information and communication technologies |
| IDB | Inter-American Development Bank |
| IDP | internally displaced person |
| IDRC | International Development Research Centre |
| IEA | International Energy Agency |
| IFPRI | International Food Policy Research Institute (USA) |
| IHS | Institute for Housing and Urban Development Studies |
| IIED | International Institute for Environment and Development (UK) |
| ILO | International Labour Organization |
| IMF | International Monetary Fund |
| IMR | infant mortality rate |
| IRC | International Water and Sanitation Centre |
| IRS | Internal Revenue Service (US) |
| ISI | Institute of Scientific Information |
| ISI | International Statistical Institute (The Netherlands) |
| IUCN | World Conservation Union (formerly International Union for Conservation of Nature and Natural Resources) |
| IULA | International Union of Local Authorities (The Netherlands) |
| IWMI | International Water Management Institute |
| LGU | local government unit |
| LULUS | locally unwanted land uses |
| MBS | mortgage-backed security |
| MDF | Municipal Development Fund (Colombia) |
| MDHC | Mersey Docks and Harbour Company |
| MDP | Municipal Development Plan (Philippines) |
| MHT | Mahila Housing SEWA Trust (India) |
| MIC | municipal international cooperation |
| MIG | mortgage indemnity guarantee (UK) |
| MKSS | Worker and Farmer Power Organization (India) |
| MOSOP | Movement for the Survival of the Ogoni People |
| MSC | Multimedia Super Corridor |
| MOUSE | Making Opportunities for Upgrading Schools & Education (USA) |
| NATO | North Atlantic Treaty Organization |
| NDC | New Deal for Communities (UK) |
| NGO | non-governmental organization |
| NIMBY | not in my back yard |
| NIMTOO | not in my term of office |
| NSDF | National Slum Dwellers' Federation |
| NUREC | Network on Urban Research in the European Union |
| OCLC | Online Computer Library Center |
| ODA | Overseas Development Agency |
| OECD | Organisation for Economic Co-operation and Development |
| OFDA | Office of US Foreign Disaster Assistance (USA) |

| | |
|---|---|
| OFWAT | Office of Water (UK) |
| OPEC | Organization of Petroleum Exporting Countries |
| PPP | purchasing power parity |
| PROWWESS | Promotion of the Role of Women in Water and Environmental Sanitation |
| SAP | structural adjustment programme |
| SDI | Slum/Shack Dwellers International |
| SDI | spatial data infrastructure |
| SEWA | Self-employed Women's Association |
| SOEs | state-owned enterprises |
| SPARC | Society for the Promotion of Area Resources Centres (India) |
| SRB | Single Regeneration Budget (UK programme) |
| TB | tuberculosis |
| TI | Transparency International |
| TIAU | Taller de Investigación y Acción Urbana (Argentina) |
| TNCs | transnational corporations |
| TOADS | temporarily obsolete and derelict sites |
| UCDO | Urban Community Development Office (Thailand) |
| UI | Unemployment Insurance |
| UNCED | United Nations Conference on Environment and Development |
| UNCHS | United Nations Centre for Human Settlements (Habitat) |
| UNDP | United Nations Development Programme |
| UNECLA | United Nations Economic Committee on Latin America |
| UNEP | United Nations Environment Programme |
| UNESCO | United Nations Educational, Scientific and Cultural Organization |
| UNFPA | United Nations Population Fund |
| UNICEF | United Nations International Children's Fund |
| UNICRI | United Nations Interregional Crime and Justice Research Institute |
| UNIFEM | United Nations Development Fund for Women |
| UNON | United Nations Office at Nairobi |
| UNSD | United Nations Statistical Division |
| USAID | United States Agency for International Development |
| VDPA | Vienna Declaration and Programme of Action |
| WEDC | Water Engineering Development Centre (UK) |
| WMO | World Meteorological Organization |
| WSS | water supply and sanitation |
| WSSCC | Water Supply and Sanitation Collaborative Council |
| WTO | World Trade Organization |
| WUA | Water User Association |
| YUVA | Youth for Unity and Voluntary Action (India) |

# KEY ISSUES AND MESSAGES

To portray human settlements conditions and development trends is a challenging task for the Global Report series. *Cities in a Globalizing World* looks at the liveability of human settlements and their development prospects in the context of globalization. To encourage understanding of the dynamic nature of liveability, the following episode is presented.

On 11 July 2000, the collapse of a rubbish dump in Payatas, Manila, killed 218 people living in shanties at the bottom of the site and left another 300 people missing under the rotting garbage. The tragedy of their burial underneath the trash of a world city, off its edge and in the darkness of night, symbolizes the invisible, daily plight of innumerable poor people in today's globalizing world.

On 27 August 2000, the Housing Secretary of the Philippines and experts and slum dwellers from India, Indonesia and Sri Lanka joined 7000 residents from the Payatas dump site community for a week of meetings and activities, during which community leaders proposed plans for resettlement and showcased self-built model houses with details on construction costs and site plans. The successful gathering celebrated the competence and capabilities of the poor, evidenced the potential of international networks and demonstrated the enabling role of globalization-from-below.

The preceding episode captures in a microcosm several key findings of this report. First, and most obviously, the landslide, triggered by heavy rains, is an example of the death and devastation brought about by natural and human-made disasters. Those most affected are often the poor who live on steep hillsides, in low-lying riverbeds or other hazardous areas. Chapter 15 documents for the first time the enormous human impacts of such calamities across the world and reviews mitigating strategies and post-disaster reconstruction approaches.

At another level, the collapse of the Payatas garbage heap acutely illustrates what may happen when consumption patterns, made possible by globalization, produce waste that accumulates in unmanageable volumes to threaten environmental and human health. The scavenger families eked out a living from recycling the final discards of a global consumer culture. They dwelled daily amid fumes from synthetic decomposition whose toxicity prompted the cessation of emergency aid operations out of concern for the health of the rescue workers. This report stresses the importance of balancing the goals of globalization. It recognizes the importance of economic growth, but emphasizes that such growth must be guided by criteria of social justice and environmental sustainability.

Finally and perhaps most importantly, the Payatas experience illustrates the positive power of people living in poverty who adopt approaches that go beyond a confrontational face-off and who use astute initiatives to construct collaborative partnerships as a means to improve their living conditions. The disaster received much attention on television and in the printed media around the world. The initial response involved emergency aid and rescue actions. As bulldozers removed mangled corpses, shock and compassion for the survivors prevailed. However, soon after, official reaction declared the victims guilty. The Payatas residents countered this criminalization of their poverty with recriminations against the responsible authorities. Some survivors filed a US$22 million class-action suit against the local government and private waste contractors for gross negligence and flagrant violation of environmental laws, zoning and health regulations. More noteworthy and unusual, however, was the proactive response of other residents. Rather than getting trapped in a spiralling war of attrition, the families used insights about how poor communities can make choices. They strategically timed their invitation to the Housing Secretary to coincide with the ceremony for the prestigious Magsaysay award for International Understanding to Jockin Arputham, a founder and president of Slum/Shack Dwellers International. With the support of international networks, the slum dwellers created evidence of their own abilities, winning not only financial support but also earning official recognition as a legitimate partner in the joint development of long-term policy options.

This report highlights the vital contributions that people living in poverty can make to improve their situation. It acknowledges that lack of resources, insufficient institutional capacity and persistent corruption often greatly circumscribe the problem-solving abilities of governments. Parts V and VI underscore that, in light of these limitations, it is crucial that appropriate frameworks and strategies for cooperation are developed among governments, civil society and the private sector.

The Payatas episode illustrates the complexity of the message of this report. It is a message about poverty and prosperity – and the differences between them. It conveys despair about wasted and lost lives, but it also brings hope and raises expectations for the future.

When looking at human settlements around the world today, one can observe gains in wealth, made possible by globalization, in such forms as newly constructed luxury apartments, fashionable shopping malls, gleaming office towers, trendy restaurants, stylish department stores, modern airports and high-tech parks. On the other hand, various alarming trends must be of serious concern: in large regions, the number of poor people has increased and existing inequalities are getting worse. The negative effects of spatial segregation and social exclusion are becoming more and more evident. What are the implications of these contrasting developments for the planning, development and management of human settlements?

There is increasing evidence that present human settlements policies and programmes in many countries do not effectively address urgent problems of access to adequate housing, infrastructure and basic services, as documented in the chapters that follow. There is also greater recognition that many current developments are not only harmful to the poor but also detrimental to general economic growth and political health in the long run as well. The world cannot continue with 'business as usual' if it is to be successful in tackling the urban challenges of the new millennium. Support is growing for new approaches that hold more hope for the future. In particular, this report calls for better appreciation of policies that support the poor and help to develop their unrealized human capital potential, with benefits for the *whole* of society. The question then becomes, which strategies hold most promise?

This report examines this question within the context of globalization. It starts with the observation that globalization has brought valuable benefits, but that these benefits have been unevenly distributed. It stresses that this uneven distribution of benefits (and costs) is not coincidental but a function of the dominant logic that drives current globalization processes: the logic of market mechanisms, facilitated by advances in information and communication technologies and liberalization policies. Market mechanisms can be effective for some purposes and are often viewed as the best way to promote economic growth. However, market mechanisms do not perform well in several important respects. For example, markets do not respond well when household incomes are too low to translate need into effective demand or for providing universal access to public goods. Markets also tend to externalize costs to people living elsewhere or in future times, and they are ill suited to strengthen societal integration or to steer development according to a long-term vision.

This report develops the argument that globalization must serve other goals besides economic growth, particularly when this growth benefits some a great deal more than others. These other goals derive from the normative platforms that emerged from the plans of action formulated at the United Nations conferences of the 1990s, discussed in Chapter 3. They predicate provision of basic needs less on ability-to-pay and more on human rights. First and foremost, they accentuate social justice and strengthen support for sustainable development.

Human settlements are important in the realization of these goals in that they link economic globalization to human development. Cities can modulate the impacts of globalization and channel its associated processes to support development scenarios evolving from local democratic practices. They can play key roles in supporting a globalization-from-below to counterbalance present top-down processes. As constraints of geographical distance are becoming *less* important, the specific features of human settlements are becoming *more* important in the locational decision-making of businesses and households. This creates opportunities for local development choices. Rather than being at the mercy of global capital, cities can take advantage of their unique qualities as they seek to attract investment and develop employment markets. Therefore, far from exerting a deterministic, homogenizing effect, globalization can allow for local differentiation.

The capacity of cities to play a part in their own development, to exercise a degree of choice, makes them increasingly strategic sites for contesting alternative claims by stakeholders pursuing different and sometimes conflicting goals. In order to advance local urban agendas that give higher priority to social justice and environmental sustainability, urban policies should support the transition of cities' function as 'engines of growth' to their new important role as 'agents of change'. These changes require new political strategies for urban liveability and new forms of governance. Globalization has created new conditions for decision-making: interdependent, complex, loosely linked actors and institutions that may have shared purposes but no shared authority. Such governance requires that actors seeking mutual gains find ways to coordinate their efforts.

What is envisioned is not a precipitous transformation, but a slow, long-term process of incremental, cumulative changes that will increase the capabilities of citizens to address the problems they face. It is a process that involves a reconstituting of the relationships between the public and private sectors and civil society: the formation of broad-based cooperative partnerships. It is important that such partnerships are not restricted to ad hoc arrangements, set up just to realize a particular project, but are, instead, oriented to create lasting capacity for development.

It is also crucial that such partnerships include the poor as equal participants. This goal of inclusive capacity building can be assisted by the horizontal, community-based exchange of information, experience and support through transnational networks, as in the case of the Payatas community described above. The key roles played by women must be recognized, as women work to improve living conditions not just for themselves, but also for their families and communities. Finally, equitable ways to allocate funds that enable poor local communities to develop their own options have to be found.

From this background, several key points come to the fore, identified in the following summary and presented in greater detail in this report:

# The Uneven Distribution of the Benefits and Costs of Globalization

Without question, globalization has stimulated overall economic growth. However, the benefits and costs of this growth have been spread unevenly. In many countries, real incomes have fallen, the costs of living have gone up and the number of poor households has grown, especially in cities. Inequalities are getting worse, and high inequality sustains poverty, as smaller shares of total income reach those at the bottom. Inequality weakens the impact of growth on fighting poverty. Indeed, research shows that decreasing inequality can have as much impact on reducing poverty as increasing economic growth. The challenge is to share the fruits of globalization more equally.

# The Unbalanced Nature of Globalization

Advances in modern information and communication technologies (ICTs) have facilitated the opening of global markets. Market-led processes are geared to economic growth, and accumulation of wealth has dominated globalization. However, ICTs should also serve goals of social justice and environmental sustainability. This requires the strengthening of appropriate governance and planning mechanisms. The challenge is to balance the goals of globalization and to blend the roles of government, private sector and civil society in cooperative arrangements.

# Human Settlements Link Economic Globalization to Human Development

Globalization increases competition between, as well as fragmentation within, cities, with contradictory effects. Growing fragmentation hampers the capacity to build coalitions, mobilize resources and develop sufficient governance structures. Urban government has shifted from a managerial approach to entrepreneurialism that treats the city as a product to be marketed. This marketing approach, and the emphasis on restructuring the city so that it appeals to global business, has led to the dominance of economic interests in urban planning. The challenge is to develop enabling strategies that are not narrowly restricted to the economic functioning of markets, but that also include support for the exercise of citizenship – of 'the rights to the city', including the realization of housing rights.

# Decentralization and the Growing Role of Local Government

Decisions regarding development and management of infrastructure and services should rest with the level of government closest to the community that is able to deliver these services in a cost-effective and equitable way while minimizing the externalization of environmental costs. The extent of decentralization depends on the ability of central governments to devise appropriate regulatory frameworks for central–local relations and their willingness to provide local authorities with assets and intergovernmental transfers. Metropolitan areas are de facto pivotal arenas in today's processes of global competition. This requires that they be strengthened by giving them more political legitimacy, responsibilities and resources.

# Need for New Cooperative Frameworks

Governments have important roles, but limited abilities to address urgent challenges of shelter, infrastructure and services. They need to develop broad-based cooperative partnerships with the private sector and civil society. Integrated implementation of the Habitat Agenda adopted by the second United Nations Conference on Human Settlements (Habitat II) also requires effective, institutionalized coordination within the United Nations system. Further, it is necessary to strengthen the capacity of local governments and low-income communities to participate as equal partners in human settlements development. In addition, aside from the usual top-down decision-making, horizontal linkages through municipal international cooperation and community-based networks need to be reinforced. In these arrangements, people in poverty and women must be empowered to play key roles. In the end, the bottom line is a point that bears repeating: people living in poverty represent unrealized human capital potential, and the eradication of their poverty will bring benefits to the *whole* of society.

# Strengthening the Policy Development Process

Effective policies require careful monitoring and evaluation. Information and communication technologies facilitate the dissemination of such information through urban observatories and best practices databases. However, no matter how good the practices are, they can never be more than a reflection of what is possible under the current circumstances. Therefore, assessments of best practices against criteria derived from normative goals with measurable benchmarks are needed. Such information must be collected at the individual and local level to capture differences by gender, locality and other relevant dimensions. The transferability of approaches that work requires policy makers to distinguish between technical description of successful prototypes diffused through simple replication, on the one hand, and more analytical lesson-drawing based on prospective evaluations of differences in political, economic and cultural contexts, on the other.

# New Forms of Governance and Political Strategies for Urban Liveability

Governance strategies relying on market mechanisms to coordinate multiple, interdependent interests and shared resources and purposes ultimately fail to address critical governance tasks of steering and integration. The complementarity of civil society and government is at the core of good governance. Urban liveability depends on the state's capacity to perform as a public institution and deliver the collective goods and services that cities and communities need, but it depends in equal measure on the extent to which communities and civil society groups can build ties with people and agencies within the state who share the same agenda. Non-governmental organizations (NGOs) without a community base lack legitimacy, and communities that lack external ties are politically weak and parochial. Further, state agencies rely on political pressure from communities to enact legislation and implement policies. The challenge is to adopt approaches for working in interconnected, complementary ways in all aspects of human settlements development.

# HUMAN SETTLEMENTS IN A GLOBALIZING WORLD

In 1996, the United Nations Centre for Human Settlements (Habitat) produced its second Global Report on Human Settlements, characterizing cities around the world as places of opportunity. Aptly titled *An Urbanizing World*, it presented a view of cities as engines of growth. The report identified problems associated with urbanization but it also revealed cities as holding the potential for solving these problems.[1]

Today, the trend of urbanization continues[2] but, more so than five years ago, it is intertwined with globalization, a process whose salience is reflected in recent international events and publications, including the *Human Development Report 1999*[3] of the United Nations Development Programme (UNDP) and the World Bank's *World Development Report 1999/2000*.[4] An inventory of research literature since 1990 reveals an exponential growth of publications dealing with globalization. Figure I.1 illustrates this sharp rise during the last decade, showing a manifold increase.

In addition to the overall strong upward trend, it is noteworthy that the growth rate of publications on legal aspects of globalization is lagging behind that of publications on the subject in other fields (Figure I.1). The reason may be that the tradition of law tends to be reactive – rather than proactive – based on precedents which take time to establish. At any rate, the striking disparity is suggestive of an asynchronous and imbalanced relationship between the ongoing globalization of commerce and the delayed development of normative frameworks to guide its direction, generating pressing challenges with which *Cities in a Globalizing World* concerns itself.

Like urbanization, globalization brings opportunities as well as problems, both most clearly seen in cities. The challenge is to develop solutions to the problems associated with globalization, while at the same time realizing its positive prospects.[6] Human settlements can play a key role in this regard. Through good governance and effective partnerships, they can help eliminate poverty and reduce inequality. Their challenge is to function not only as engines of economic growth, but also as agents of social justice.

## A Globalizing World

Globalization is not a new phenomenon. The Silk Road is but one example of an early economic and cultural linking of diverse societies across large distances.[7]

---

Globalization is not a new phenomenon. However, what is new is the *speed*, the *scale*, the *scope* and the *complexity* of global connections today.

---

However, global connections today differ in at least four important ways. First, they function at much greater *speed* than ever before. Improved technologies enable much faster transportation of people and goods and the instantaneous transmission of information. Second, globalization operates on a much larger *scale*, leaving few people unaffected and making its influence felt in even the most remote places. Third, the *scope* of global connections is much broader and has multiple dimensions – economic, technological, political, legal, social and cultural, among others – each of which has multiple facets.[8] Linkages have proliferated to involve multiple, interdependent flows of a greater variety of goods, services, people, capital, information and diseases. Significant in this expanded scope is the growing globalization of human rights and the rule of law, which may conflict with established commercial routines and political practices. Fourth, the dynamic and often unmediated interactions among numerous global actors create a new level of *complexity* for the relationships between policy and practice.

It is important to acknowledge the positive consequences of globalization. Indeed, it would be short-sighted to ignore these benefits. Globalization has facilitated, for example, the diffusion of medical advances that have

**Frequency of 'globalization' in publication titles, 1990–1999**[5]

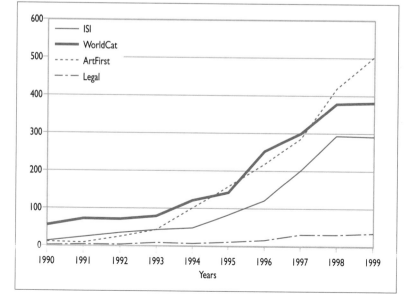

reduced mortality rates[9] and agricultural technologies that have boosted food production.[10] Globalization has also enabled the spread of norms of democratic governance,[11] environmental justice and human rights, helping to provide criteria against which the actions, policies and legislation of governments can be judged.[12] These valuable outcomes must be recognized and further encouraged.

The world welcomes these successes of globalization, but many urgent problems remain unresolved. In Africa, only one-third of all urban households are connected to potable water.[13] In Latin America, urban poverty stood at 30 per cent in 1997, and the estimated quantitative housing deficit for 19 countries with available data totalled more than 17 million units.[14] In Asia Pacific, a mere 38 per cent of urban households are connected to a sewerage system.[15] In Europe, processes of social exclusion marginalize many low-income and minority households,[16] while urban crime and the decline of peripheral housing estates undermine many communities.[17] In the United States, problems of residential segregation, discrimination in housing markets, and affordability persist, particularly in large cities.[18] Worldwide, innumerable people live under conditions of abject poverty or experience very unequal access to resources.

> *'The central challenge we face today is to ensure that globalization becomes a positive force for all the world's people, instead of leaving billions of them behind in squalor'* – Kofi Annan, *We the Peoples* (2000) p 6

It is clear that benefits attributed to globalization have not accrued to everyone alike. Indeed, studies indicate that, while the conditions of many have improved, others have seen their situation deteriorate. In many countries, real incomes have fallen, the costs of living have gone up and the number of poor households has grown, especially in cities. Sixty countries have been getting steadily poorer since 1980.[19] Many studies report increasing economic disparities between nations, cities, neighbourhoods and households.[20] The evidence reveals strong polarization, with inequalities getting worse.

> The world welcomes the successes of globalization, but, at the same time, important challenges remain. Pressing problems of poverty, inequity and polarization urgently demand action

This focus on social justice in an increasingly market-oriented world is consistent with Article 11 of the International Covenant on Economic, Social and Cultural Rights,[21] which 'recognizes the right of everyone to an adequate standard of living, including adequate food, clothing and housing, and to the continuous improvement of living conditions.'[22]

> The international community has universally recognized the right to an adequate standard of living, including housing, and the fundamental obligation of governments in the provision of shelter and the improvement of homes and neighbourhoods

It is also in accordance with the Istanbul Declaration on Human Settlements,[23] in which States announce that they will:

> *'intensify (their) efforts to eradicate poverty and discrimination, to promote and protect all human rights and fundamental freedoms for all, and to provide for basic needs, such as education, nutrition and life-span health care services, and, especially, adequate shelter for all'*

while committing themselves to the objectives, principles and recommendations contained in the Habitat Agenda[24] and pledging to attain its goals of adequate shelter for all and sustainable human settlement development in a urbanizing world.[25]

## Globalization and Human Settlements

In recent years, several publications[26] and public discourses[27] have focused attention on various questions of globalization and development. These reviews and discussions have mainly dealt with aspects of *macroeconomic* development and *human* development. The development of *human settlements* has received much less attention. This is unfortunate because the outcomes of economic and human development are strongly linked to conditions and processes in human settlements.[28]

The processes of globalization have a distinct spatial specificity. Their outcomes also show particular geographic patterns. Although globalization certainly affects rural areas,[29] global forces are centred in cities. It is in cities where global operations are centralized and where one can see most clearly the phenomena associated with their activities: changes in the structure of employment, the formation of powerful partnerships, the development of monumental real estate, the emergence of new forms of local governance, the effects of organized crime, the expansion of corruption, the fragmentation of informal networks and the spatial isolation and social exclusion of certain population groups.

> Human settlements form an important link in processes of globalization and their economic implications for human development

The characteristics of cities and their surrounding regions, in turn, help shape globalization; for example, by providing a suitable labour force, making available the required physical and technological infrastructure, creating a stable and accommodating regulatory environment, offering the bundle of necessary support services, contributing financial incentives and possessing the institutional capacity without which globalization cannot occur.[30]

Thus, urban settlements mediate the reciprocal relationships between globalization, on the one hand, and economic and human development, on the other.

# Making Choices: Globalization as a Purposeful Process

*'We know that the global dilemma of squalor amid splendour is a creature of human agency, and that it can be reversed by human agency'* – Kofi Annan, Address to the World Bank Conference on 'Global Knowledge '97', Toronto, 22 June 1997

Transportation and communication technologies are often seen as the driving forces behind globalization.[31] These technologies, however, are neutral tools that merely make globalization possible and that may be used to various ends.[32] Purposeful actors produce globalization as they develop and exploit technologies to their advantage. Among these actors, transnational corporations (TNCs) have been dominant. Motives of private gain have propelled their actions. Their chief purpose has been to maximize profit. Policies favouring market expansion have supported this purpose. Usually referred to as the neo-liberal platform, these include Structural Adjustment Programmes (SAPs) of the International Monetary Fund (IMF)[33] and World Bank, international financial rules of the IMF, trade rules of the General Agreement on Trade and Tariffs (GATT) and more recently the World Trade Organization (WTO),[34] and investment rules under Bilateral Investment Treaties (BITs).[35]

To date, objectives of economic growth have dominated the policy agenda. However, for development to be successful, economic growth must be pursued in the context of social justice and environmental sustainability.[36]

This sets up a conflict between the economic and social components of globalization and a dialectic on what the normative goals of globalization ought to be. There is little that is neutral about the content on either side as each seeks advantage by diminishing the effective power of the other.[37] The normative goals of globalization deserve and demand deliberate choices, informed by careful study of facts guided by agreed upon principles and standards of human living. The argument made in this report is that globalization strategies, which, up to now, have been dominated by economic interests, must give priority to the well-being and quality of life of the billions of people who are suffering increased hardship as a result of policies that have promoted, first and foremost, the global expansion of markets.

## Need for New Institutional Arrangements

During the era of industrialization, the introduction of new manufacturing technologies affected the physical, economic and social characteristics of human settlements. The beneficiaries were first of all the capitalist investors and owners of the means of production, seeking the accumulation of wealth. Millions of workers and their families provided the labour that produced this wealth. They lived in rapidly growing cities under abominable conditions that have been well documented.[38] Mobilization of various interest groups led to new roles for national and local governments, which assumed responsibilities for ensuring the public welfare; for example, by requiring a minimum living wage, proscribing the use of child labour, creating universal access to potable water, greatly improved provisions for sanitation (drains, sewers, garbage collection), basic health care and elementary education.

Similarly, during the present time of globalization, the widespread application of newly emerging transportation and communication technologies is reshaping the physical, economic and social fabric of cities everywhere. The benefits and costs of these changes are unevenly distributed. Homeless people are living in cardboard boxes next to gleaming skyscrapers occupied by corporations whose budgets exceed those of many developing countries. Just as in centuries past, industrialization brought in its wake advances and problems whose resolution demanded new institutional arrangements, so also does globalization at present.

> Just as in centuries past, industrialization brought in its wake advances and problems whose resolution demanded new institutional arrangements, so also does globalization at present

## The Role of Government

As global forces have increasingly asserted themselves, particularly in the form of TNCs, the sovereignty of national governments has declined. The gap in serving the public interest is being more and more taken up by local authorities and, paradoxically, by the private sector as these entities become responsible for functions previously ascribed to national governments. This 'hollowing out of the state' (upwards, sideways and downwards) can be observed, in various forms and to different degrees, in many countries around the world. However, this development does not render national governments impotent or irrelevant. In contrast, as shown in this report, important responsibilities remain and new roles are presenting themselves.[39]

These new roles must be given form under difficult circumstances. Not only do national governments face critical domestic issues, they are also constrained by major international interests that favour solutions thought to result from the workings of market mechanisms. The World Bank and the International Monetary Fund,[40] among others, have argued that the task of national governments should be to remove barriers that prevent the smooth functioning of markets. From their perspective, competition between cities and regions is something positive, leading to economic growth, which, in turn, is seen as the solution to poverty. According to this viewpoint, governments should eliminate regulations that hamper market dynamics and play an active role in 'levelling the playing field.'[41]

However, research reported in Chapter 1 shows that reducing inequality can have as much impact on reducing poverty as does increasing economic growth. Moreover, evidence, presented in this report and elsewhere, indicates that the notion of completely free markets is a myth. In reality, governments always shape market dynamics and outcomes; for example, through tariffs on trade, quotas for immigration, licensing requirements, taxation of income and property, anti-trust legislation and regulation of the supply of credit. An especially conspicuous contradiction is the renewed drive for stricter border controls to keep out immigrants and refugees, while at the same time lifting restrictions to create border-free economic zones.[42] Government intervention is often required to ensure that the strong centripetal tendencies of unregulated markets do not result in oligopoly or even monopoly that would adversely affect the leading indicators of market effectiveness: price and quality. These interventions reflect the influences of contending interest groups on policy,[43] and they produce outcomes that benefit some a great deal more than others.

Nor are 'open' markets a panacea. Indeed, there is growing recognition that opening new regions for expanding markets often creates or reinforces patterns of uneven development, as investors prefer some locations to others.[44] Acknowledging these concerns, the European Union, for example, created the European Regional Development Fund to promote infrastructure projects that enhance the productive capacity and strengthen the economy of disadvantaged regions. It also established the European Social Fund in support of vocational guidance and skill-improvement programmes to help young people and the long-term unemployed gain access to (better) jobs.[45] Debate exists about the adequacy of these initiatives, but research shows that different public policies can produce different living conditions in countries with similar experiences of globalization and technological change. It is clear that there will be a continuing need for strong government involvement.[46] This government role is shifting from that of provider to that of enabler, with an emphasis on the ability to act as a regulator, catalyst and partner. Markets, moreover, are not inclusive. Households with low incomes often cannot translate their needs into an effective market demand. It is not evident how profit-seeking suppliers can guarantee access to entitlements and assistance programmes without which such households are left to the mercy of market forces, unable to meet their basic needs for shelter, health care and food.

Markets also fail to generate solutions to serious environmental degradation, especially when powerful producers and consumers exploit distant natural resources. Economic calculations do not usually include the disruptions of ecosystems whose implications are far into the future or whose costs are borne by others rather than the profit makers.[47] Markets need to be regulated in ways that internalize such externalities and balance short-term private discount rates with long-term societal ones.[48]

The connection between the logic of the market and the logic of liveability is anything but automatic. The markets that shape cities are first of all markets for land, and land is a finite commodity.[49] More land cannot be produced in a particular place in response to increased demand. When demand for land exceeds supply, price increases are the likely result. Projection of a demand trend into a future without countervailing regulatory pressure results in the speculative valuation of land. A growing proportion of urban dwellers face an impossible disjunction between the wages generated by city labour markets and the housing costs generated by the market for urban land. At the same time, 'marketable' uses for land, like housing for affluent individuals and commercial space for corporations, drive out non-marketable uses, like parks and green space, making the city as a whole less liveable.[50]

## 'Glocalization', the Rise of Civil Society and the Changing Nature of Urban Planning

A recent analysis of spatial development patterns in Pacific Asia concludes that a strategy towards more resilient economies calls for policies that *localize* the potential for development across *national* space rather than global regions.[51] Just as national governments are not impotent onlookers on the global stage, but active participants with continuing responsibilities, so also can local governments play important roles. In fact, there is an inverse relationship between the significance of *distance* and the significance of *place*. As the constraints of geographical distance are becoming less important, the specific features of particular locales are becoming *more* important in the locational decision-making of businesses and households. Locational features impose certain restrictions but they also provide opportunities for local development choices that can be 'marketed'. Globalization necessarily materializes in specific institutional arrangements in specific places, many of which are in cities. 'Glocalization' is a term used to describe the dialectic interdependence of the local and global dimensions of economic, political and cultural processes. Local development is tightly linked to global forces, but not determined by machinations of international capital.[52] Therefore, far from exerting a deterministic, homogenizing effect, globalization processes allow for local differentiation. As will be argued later in this report, the outcomes of these processes reflect the claims that different interests make on urban places – more *or* less effectively. These interests include representatives of global capital that use cities as an organizational commodity to maximize profit, but they also include disadvantaged local population groups who need the city as a place to live. Cities are increasingly strategic sites in the realization of these claims. Against this background, the emergence of new forms of governance and the formation of civil society organizations in the interstices of existing arrangements reflect a 'globalization-from-below' whose articulation happens in transnational networks across urban nodes.[53]

The emergence of a new localism under globalization can be seen in three important ways.[54] First, we can observe a growing significance of organized civil society, particularly in countries of the developing world, but also in the north.[55] Civil society organizations and social movements emerged as central actors in Latin America during the 1960s and 1970s, when more direct forms of institutional demand making were not available. They left in their wake a strong NGO network that is increasingly working with municipal governments to improve services and participatory structures for the relatively disadvantaged majority. In the north, new attention to the local arises, to a considerable extent, from growing concerns about environmental risk and the consequences of uncontrolled urban development.[56] In Africa, where civil society and associational life has been slower to develop, with some exceptions, global forces have created an informal sector that fosters non-state initiatives at the local level in which women play prominent roles.

Second, as civil society becomes more organized and effective, municipal institutions have been democratizing. There is some connection between these trends in that more active civil society both requires, and responds to, more participatory local structures. Local elections with a choice among multiple parties have become increasingly common in Latin America, and in parts of Africa, South Asia and Southeast Asia. In many cases – such as South Africa, India and Brazil – this expansion of local democratic government has been reinforced by constitutional reforms. Although the full evidence is not yet in, there are encouraging signs that municipal performance is improving in response to democratization.[57]

Given an emerging civil society and democratic municipal institutions, a third element of 'the growing importance of the local' has to do with how communities make choices. Local political coalitions together with important groups from civil society are attempting to shape their cities and towns in ways that maximize what they consider the opportunities to be gained from globalization. Whether this involves campaigns against crime or plans to improve the local environment in order to attract tourists; or whether it involves strategies to reduce local taxes or develop a more comprehensive educational system in order to attract outside investment; in either case, municipal officials and their partners are increasingly alert to the potential benefits of competitive strategies.

As a result, in many cities there has been a shift in the policies of urban government from managerialism to entrepreneurialism. This entrepreneurial attitude views the city as a product that needs to be marketed. The emphasis on marketing underpins the restructuring of cities so that they appeal to global investors and favours the dominance of economic interests in urban planning. The particular historical character of a city tends to be subordinated in the quest for an international image, with local identity becoming a public relations artefact designed to aid marketing (see Chapter 2).

By the same token, cities that do not have the resources to attract outside interest and investment may find themselves even more bereft and impoverished. Local capacity building is essential to reduce the potential for such polarization. In this connection, it is encouraging that

international cooperation in the form of city-to-city exchanges is growing in popularity. Public–private partnerships are also being broadened to include civil society groups and there is increasing evidence of the potential of community-based networks based on direct people-to-people interactions. Decentralized cooperation further supports local choices in urban development. These developments are reviewed in Chapter 14.

Globalization not only increases competition but also fragmentation, with contradictory effects on cities. To compete effectively, cities must act as collective units. However, their growing social, political, economic and physical fragmentation hampers their capacity to build coalitions, mobilize resources and develop sufficient governance structures. Given that metropolitan areas are the chief arenas for global competition, it is necessary to strengthen them by giving them greater authority and autonomy in resource allocation. However, the enabling role of governments must be broader than facilitating the functioning of markets and also includes responsibility for social cohesion, equity and conflict resolution.

The term 'metropolization of the world economy' has been used to describe the archipelagic spatial structure of emerging global urban networks.[58] Megacities, comprising urban cores and associated hinterlands, are theoretically able to address all kinds of technical problems, including urban service provision and environmental management. However, they are facing difficult governance challenges, owing to obsolete systems tailored to traditional cities and inhabitants who are more concerned with their immediate individual and local neighbourhood interests than with their common future as citizens of the same city.[59]

Urban planners are inescapably caught up in this dynamic. The new planning is less codified and technical, more innovative and entrepreneurial. It is also more participatory and concerned with projects rather than whole urban systems. Planning expertise is increasingly sought not only by the state, but also by the corporate sector and civil society. Planners seek to forge agreements through negotiation and mediation among contesting parties. Planning is no longer lodged solely in urban government as a font of privileged knowledge about 'the public interest'. What is controversial is not urban planning per se, but its *goal*: whether it should be directed chiefly at efficiency, reinforcing the current distribution of wealth and power, or whether it should play a distributive role to help create minimum standards of urban liveability.[60]

As planning becomes more difficult to define as a state-based process of intervention, it finds expression in a greater diversity of forms, including the advocacy for and mobilization of community-based groups that seek to assert their rights to the city.[61] This development places marginality at centre stage. It stresses a notion of urban poverty that goes beyond monetary standards and consumption for basic needs. It offers insights from within households to show how poverty is a form of vulnerability and lack of power that is multidimensional and, further, how efforts at redress by households are not typically anti-systemic but oriented towards gaining benefits from more favourable inclusion in ongoing urban development processes.[62] These insights also provide a better understanding of the gendered nature of poverty and the important roles of women in attempts to eradicate it.[63]

Figure I.2 is a visual summary of how societal sectors interface at different scales vis-à-vis a range of issues. It indicates how actors in the public and private sectors as well as civil society, at all levels, may play a role in relevant approaches to those human settlement concerns that urgently demand attention. Foremost among these problems is the rapid growth of urban poverty and polarization. The challenges presented by these trends exceed the capabilities of governments. They require the formation of partnerships with the private sector as well as civil society. If such partnerships are to be effective, people living in poverty, and women among them in particular, must be empowered to deploy their unrealized potential as equal participants in the development of solutions to the problems that they experience first hand. It is clear, then, that appropriate capacity building and cooperative governing are vital elements of strategies to improve urban liveability for *all* people.

Whatever its merits as a representation of the multiple facets of human settlements development policies, Figure I.2 cannot capture the complex dynamics of real-world interactions, nor the distribution of resources and the real costs and benefits experienced by people. It is precisely these aspects that this report takes up.

## Purpose of this Report

The purpose of this report is to review human settlement trends in the context of globalization; to analyse their implications for poverty, inequity and polarization; and to develop recommendations for planning, development and management policies and practices in support of those most at risk

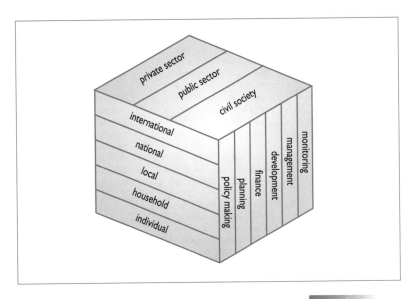

**Figure I.2**

**Interfaces of societal sectors**

Against this background, one aim of this report is to examine conditions and recent trends in human settlements around the world. In doing so, it concerns itself particularly with implications of globalization for poverty (the inability to maintain a minimum standard of living), inequity (poverty amid affluence and the unequal access to redress) and polarization (inequities becoming worse). It also makes recommendations from a perspective of advocacy on behalf of those at greatest risk: typically the poor, women, children, the elderly, the disabled, refugees, immigrants and minority groups. Although it is critical to give special consideration to these population groups, it is equally important not to restrict the focus to their particular characteristics which would have the effect of reifying them as *a priori* 'vulnerable categories'. Their vulnerability is not a given. It does not exist in a vacuum. This makes it essential to adopt contextual perspectives that direct attention to the factors that put these groups at risk. Without such perspectives, efforts will be misdirected at symptoms, rather than aimed at root causes.

## Notes

1   See UNCHS (Habitiat), 1996. For an earlier view of cities as engines of growth, see Klaassen et al, 1989.

2   Brockerhoff, 1999 reviews projected and actual urban growth rates in the developing countries since 1970. His analysis indicates a slow down of the anticipated urban transition. In the oft-cited case of Mexico City, based on simple extrapolation of a population increase from 5.4 million in 1960 to 13 million in 1980, the United Nations predicted a population of 31.3 million in 2000, whereas the actual number in that year was only about 18 million.

Brockerhoff's review indicates that observed trends warranting downward adjustments of urban growth rates are not limited to a few large cities, but are widespread in the developing world. These changed trends reflect the effects of relatively weak expansion of urban industries and price shifts unfavourable to manufactured goods, population ageing and migratory patterns.

3   UNDP, 1999.

4   World Bank, 1999a.

5   Data for Figure I.1 come from the following sources; ISI: Web of Science, Social and Behavioral Sciences, Institute of Scientific

Information (ISI) (www.isinet.com/); WorldCat: over 42 million cataloging records created by libraries around the world in 400 languages (available through Online Computer Library Center (OCLC) (www.oclc.org/oclc/menu/home 1.htm), used by over 36,000 libraries in 74 countries); ArtFirst: articles found in the table of contents of nearly 12,500 journals covering science, technology, medicine, social science, business, the humanities and popular culture (source: OCLC); and Legal: articles from legal journals,

yearbooks, institutes, bar association organs, law reviews and government publications originating in the United States, Canada, Great Britain, Ireland, Australia and New Zealand (source: OCLC).

6   Commenting on 'The Urban Revolution', Klaus Töpfer has described cities as 'home to a wealth of cultural diversity, political dynamism, immensely productive, creative and innovative', while, at the same time, noting that cities are 'breeding grounds of poverty, violence, pollution, and congestion' which 'for many millions of people, [have] become a nightmare',

thus creating a 'tale of two cities' (Töpfer, 1999).

7    See, for example, Foltz, 2000; Laut, 1990; Liu, 1998. The Silk Road is an interesting historical precursor of modern globalization; it has recently been used as the name for a proposed money system with low-cost electronic communication protocols, enabling small transactions, without a central bank, in an open system that supports network resource management, routing, interconnection with the internet and other information services, across trust boundaries with competing providers for all services (Hardy and Tribble, 1995). The Australian Department of Foreign Affairs and Trade similarly referred to the Silk Road in its recent report on facilitation of international trade through effective use of the internet (Australia, 1999); cf Bloor, 2000. For historical perspectives on economic globalization, see Henderson, 1999 and Chase-Dunn et al, 2000.

8    For example, economic globalization can include growth of international trade as well as increases in foreign investment. Likewise, political globalization can be seen in greater cross-border cooperation between national governments, but also in the 'twinning' of municipal governments (see Chapter 14) and in the rise of international networking of non-governmental organizations (NGOs) and civil society groups.

9    Especially important have been the benefits of antibiotics and vaccination. The best-known example is perhaps the eradication of the often fatal smallpox disease. Unfortunately, these gains stand along with setbacks resulting from new diseases, notably HIV/AIDS, which are taking their toll while patent protections limit the accessibility of medication on the basis of ability-to-pay, recently announced price cuts notwithstanding. For a recent examination of the link between globalization, urbanization and the spread of infectious disease, see Pirages and Runci, 2000. See also Lee and Dodgson, 2000 for a historical examination of cholera pandemics as a function of globalization. Aside from the spread of medication, noteworthy as well is the global work of organizations such as the 1999 Nobel Peace Prize-winning Médecins Sans Frontiers (www.msf.org/), an independent humanitarian medical aid agency, founded in 1971 with a commitment to providing medical aid wherever it is needed, regardless of race, religion, politics or

sex and raising awareness of the plight of the people in need.

10   A recent example is the development of high-yield, mosaic-disease-resistant cassava, the food staple of large numbers of households in East Africa. Optimism about these advances is tempered by concerns about unpredictable consequences of genetically engineered food products for environmental and human health.

11   According to the Institute for Democracy and Electoral Assistance (www.int-idea.se/index.htm), since the fall of the Berlin Wall, more than 50 countries around the world organized elections for the first time in their existence. See Karatnycky, 2000, for a historical review; cf Franck, 1992. The Press Freedom Survey 2000 (www.freedomhouse.org/pfs2000/) offers an assessment of recent changes in restrictions placed on printed and electronic media.

12   Hulchanski and Leckie (2000) provide a comprehensive chronology of United Nations activity concerning the human right to adequate housing. The Centre on Housing Rights and Evictions (COHRE) (www.cohre.org/), established in 1994 as a non-profit foundation, offers an informative web site with links to international organizations and data bases on economic, cultural and human rights; see also the web site for the Asian Coalition for Housing Rights (www.achr.net/). Castells (1996) has identified the growth of a diversified, worldwide women's movement as one of the most important grassroots developments under globalization. In this regard, see also Moghadam, 2000. For an excellent internet gateway to human rights, see www.hri.ca/. Adeola (2000) provides a discussion of a specific recent example of international environmental justice and human rights issues, highlighted by the Movement for the Survival of the Ogoni People (MOSOP) in Nigeria. See also Brooks, 2000, on the U'Wa people of the Colombian Andes, who have been fighting oil-drilling on their land by Occidental Petroleum.

13   UNCHS (Habitat), 1998.

14   See MacDonald and Simioni, 1999.

15   See note 13 supra.

16   European Commission, 2000 provides an in-depth study of social exclusion in ten urban neighbourhoods in eight countries. See also Lawless et al, 1998; Madanipour et al, 1998. For social exclusion specifically in relation to housing, see, for

example, Marsh and Mullins, 1998; McGregor and McConnachie, 1995; Ratcliffe, 1998; Somerville, 1998; Taylor, 1998.

17   Power (1997; 1999) provides a wide-ranging examination of 20 crisis estates in Britain, Denmark, France, Germany and Ireland. Krantz et al (1999) oriented a similar study to the social and physical dimensions of housing projects on the periphery of cities in Britain, Denmark, France, The Netherlands and Sweden. Hall (1997) offers a comprehensive review and analysis of regeneration policies for problematic outlying British housing estates.

18   For segregation, see, for example, Goering et al, 1997; Carter et al, 1998; Briggs et al, 1999. Schwemm (1990) and Yinger (1995) offer excellent coverage of fair housing and discrimination. See also the special issue of Cityscape; *Journal of Policy Development and Research* (1999) 4(3), commemorating the 30th anniversary of the Fair Housing Act. Treatment of affordability questions can be found in, for example, Joint Center for Housing Studies, 2000 and the *Journal of Affordable Housing and Community Development.*

19   See UNDP, 1999.

20   Chapter 1 of this report provides fuller discussion of trends in inequality.

21   Adopted and opened for signature, ratification and accession by General Assembly resolution 2200A (XXI) of 16 December 1966; entry into force: 3 January 1976, in accordance with article 27. Ratified by 142 states as of 15 May 2000. See www.unhchr.ch/html/menu3/b/a_cescr.htm.

22   This was a reaffirmation of article 25(1) of the Universal Declaration of Human Rights adopted in 1948.

23   See www.unchs.org/unchs/english/hagenda/ist-dec.htm.

24   See www.unchs.org/unchs/english/hagenda/haghome.htm.

25   The Habitat Agenda is discussed in Chapter 3 of this report, which also examines related policy platforms that have resulted from other United Nations summits. Chapter 16 reviews the human right to housing.

26   See, for example, Axtmann, 1998; Cosgrove-Sacks, 1999; Schuurman, 2000; Simmons, 1999; UNDP, 1999; World Bank, 1999a.

27   In the Spring of 2000, a six-week long internet-based discussion

(www.worldbank.org/devforum/forum_poverty.html) of the pre-publication draft of the 1999/2000 World Development Report, 'Attacking Poverty,' (World Bank, 1999a) (www.worldbank.org/html/extpb/wdr99.htm) attracted more than 1500 subscribers and participants from many countries, who frequently commented on aspects of globalization. A subsequent electronic forum on 'Globalization and Poverty', (www.worldbank.org/devforum/forum_globalization.html) held in May 2000, under the joint auspices of the World Bank (www.worldbank.org) and the Panos Institute (www.oneworld.org/panos/home/homepage.html), involved over 4200 participants from more than 120 countries, an estimated 30 per cent of them from the developing world. As well, the UK Department for International Development (DFID), jointly with OneWorld, conducted in Spring, 2000, an electronic consultation (www.oneworld.net/consultation/dfid/) to obtain feedback on the draft of a White Paper on the changes resulting from globalization and the opportunities and challenges this presents for faster progress in reducing poverty and promoting sustainable development in the poorest countries. This six-week forum solicited input from NGOs, academics, DFID staff, development workers, ICT and knowledge specialists, media and interested members of the public, in particular on information and communication technologies.

28   For example, see Burgers, 1996, for a study showing how national welfare state arrangements and specific urban histories are important mediating variables in the particular local outcomes of international economic restructuring.

29   For example, Structural Adjustment Policies have led to the growing of exportable products to substitute for subsistence farming, as in Ghana where cocoa has taken the place of plantain on a large portion of available arable land. Consequently, food now accounts for one-third of its imports, which has not helped that country's farmers (for a grassroots generated, sustainable alternative to help address problems related to imposed cocoa cultivation, found widely in West Africa, see work by the Lend-a-Hand-Foundation in Cameroon (www.lend-a-hand.org/index.htm). Globalization has also affected

peri-urban development; see, for example, Briggs and Mwamfupe, 2000, for a case study of an African city (Dar es Salaam). Losada et al (1998) review a Latin American city (Mexico City). Box 2.6 describes recent developments in the peri-urban zone of an Asian city, Manila. As another example of how globalization influences rural areas, modern information and communication technologies are increasingly harnessed in agricultural production and marketing (O'Meara, 2000). Farmers in Sri Lanka are using the internet to get information about produce prices in Colombo to negotiate better rates with brokers, increasing their income by as much as 50 per cent. In Papua New Guinea, the internet is being used to disseminate the knowledge of village elders, who can forecast storms weeks in advance by observing physical changes in plants and animals. In Africa, the internet is helping to avert famine by making farmers aware of the state of crops throughout particular regions or countries (Schenker, 1999). In Pondicherry, India, project staff of the Swaminathan Foundation distribute highly practical information in the local language (Tamil) through a village computer network, from the visiting dates of mobile medical clinics to warnings about wave height and wind direction for fishers in the Bay of Bengal, downloaded from a US Navy site (Dugger, 2000).

30 Although the focus in this report is primarily on cities, it is important to bear in mind that the rural–urban distinction is a fuzzy one and that there exist numerous economic, social and environmental connections; for example, through food production, migratory flows, kinship networks, wage remittances, production externalities, media and institutional infrastructure. Globalization tends to reinforce this functional integration, further illustrating earlier notions of the rural–urban continuum (Dewey, 1960; Duncan, 1957; Pahl, 1966) and the 'urban field' (Friedmann and Miller, 1965). The extent and the ways that globalization operates through a *hierarchical* urban pattern remains a largely empirical question (see, eg Douglass, 2000).

31 See for example UNDP, 1999, Chapter 2.

32 Globalization is *not* an autonomous process. It does *not* mechanistically 'run its course', as some have written. The literature is replete with

obfuscatory phrasing, denoting globalization as an independent variable and obscuring the significance of human agency. The following passage is characteristic:

*'Imagine a wondrous new machine … a machine that reaps as is destroys. It is huge and mobile, something like the machines of modern agriculture, but vastly more complicated and powerful. Think of this awesome machine running over open terrain and ignoring familiar boundaries. It plows across fields and fencerows with fierce momentum that is exhilarating to behold and also frightening. As it goes, the machine throws off enormous mows of wealth and bounty while it leaves behind great furrows of wreckage … no one is at the wheel. In fact, this machine has no wheel, nor any internal governor to control the speed and direction. It is sustained by its own forward motion … and it is accelerating,'* (Greider, 1997, p 11).

Most misleading is wording that inverts causality – for example, 'globalization unleashes forces' – found among proponents as well as detractors of globalization.

33 See www.imf.org/

34 See www.wto.org/

35 Barry Coates, Director of the World Development Movement. May 1, 2000. 'Globalisation, Development and Poverty: What Do We Know?' Introduction to the on-line debate on Globalization and Poverty organized by the Panos Institute and the World Bank Institute.

36 See Sen, 1999 and Evans et al, 2001 for compelling reasoning in support of this argument. Relatedly, in a historical examination of worldwide trade patterns, Chase-Dunn et al, 2000 have argued that 'economic globalization creates a demand for political globalization because markets are unable to resolve the problems of distributive justice and uneven development that they create', leading to a consideration of the role of hegemonic legitimacy (p 93). Fortunately, there is nothing deterministic about the ideological content of globalization or the aspiration(s) it serves. In principle, the same technologies TNCs use to further their private interests can also be used to advance public welfare. This point is eloquently argued by Falk, 1999. For a similar view, see Dirlik, 1998; Marris, 1998.

37 The proposed Multilateral Agreement on Investment

(MAI), for example, seeks to override social and environmental regulatory mechanisms where they may become barriers to commerce. For an analysis of the campaign against the MAI, including the role of the internet in mobilizing global opposition, see Wood, 2000.

38 See, for example, Booth, 1892; Engels, 1872; Riis, 1891; Veiller, 1910.

39 This is recognized even by proponents of classical liberalism, who see a minimalist role for national governments, upholding property and contract rules to provide a framework within which private actors interact freely on the basis of a decentralized world price mechanism (Sally, 2000).

40 See www.imf.org/.

41 See World Bank, 1999a.

42 See, for example, Sassen, 1999.

43 For example, labour unions seek protection against unfettered global competition that may threaten existing wage levels and global corporations lobby to prevent rival companies from cutting into their profit margins, while environmental interest groups press for regulations to safeguard natural ecosystems.

44 See Hudson and Williams, 1999, for a well-documented treatment of uneven development in the European Union and a persuasive case for the continuing relevance of national governments. See also Rodriguez-Pose, 1999. In a recent examination of the relationship between European economic integration and urban inequalities in Western Europe, McCarthy (2000) concludes that the prospects for reducing the already high income inequalities between cities by means of economic growth are not promising because many situational characteristics that are important for urban competitiveness and growth cannot be improved through the policy efforts of poorer local and national governments alone and the level of EU-funding is insufficient.

45 See Chapman and Murie, 1996; European Commission, 2000.

46 Further, while research has found a correlation between open markets and economic growth, the causality of this relationship has not been established. Successful economies may open themselves up to external trade, but open economies are not necessarily successful. Indeed, some of the better-performing countries have imposed their own terms on their participation in globalization processes (eg China, Singapore, South Korea).

47 For a good discussion of these points, see Hardoy, Mitlin and Satterthwaite (2001), especially Chapters 5 and 8. See also Haughton, 1999, for a discussion of principles and policy approaches in support of environmental justice and the sustainable development of cities, and Wirth, 2000.

48 For a fuller discussion of this point, see Evans et al, 2001, Chapter 1.

49 See Polanyi, 1957.

50 This, in turn, may force those seeking an affordable place to live and work to 'sprawl' into peripheral areas where land is generally cheaper.

51 See Douglass, forthcoming.

52 See Douglass, 1998.

53 See, for example, Cheru, 2000; Friedmann, 1998; Evans, 2000; Pile and Keith, 1997.

54 The following paragraphs draw on 'Urban Governance And Politics In A Global Context: The Growing Importance Of The Local', a paper by Richard Stren, University of Toronto, November 1998.

55 This is particularly seen through the environmental, women and human rights movements.

56 For example, it is at the local level that anxieties over unregulated toxic emissions are confronted by community groups attempting to influence municipal by-laws and regulations. This is the case in the developing as well as the more developed economies. See, eg Douglass and Friedmann, 1998; and Evans et al, 2001. In the US, Good Neighbor Agreements (GNAs) have emerged as a non-litigious method of dispute resolution among companies, their workers, environmentalists and local communities in the face of declining governmental power and rising corporate power. Facilitated by Right-to-Know legislation and databases (see www.rtk.net/), dozens of GNAs have been proposed and signed. For an analysis of the establishment of an enforceable, legally binding agreement that holds a transnational corporation accountable to a local community, see Pellow, 2000. Urban sprawl has also become a divisive issue in many local communities, producing a spate of citizen initiatives and counter-reactions by developers and builders. See, for example, the web site of the Sierra Club (www.sierraclub.org/sprawl/) and the Initiative and Referendum Institute (www.ballotwatch.org/).

57 Chapter 4 reviews newly emerging approaches to metropolitan government and the

challenges of democratization. Chapter 13 focuses on decentralized provision and management of urban infrastructure and services.

58 Veltz, 1996.

59 Barcelo, 1999.

60 Social welfare systems came about as attempts to address poverty through compensatory systems of distribution tied closely to employment status.

They are based on *individual* rights and take no account of community. Planning has become identified with place-based advocacy. See Marris, 1998.

61 See Douglass and Friedmann, 1998.

62 See Douglass, 1998.

63 On aspects of method and measurement, see, for example, Razavi, 1999a; Ruspini, 1999. The UNCHS (Habitat) has an

ongoing Women and Habitat Programme, which recently published a synthesis of individual country reports from Africa, Latin America and Asia on women's situation in human settlements development; see Miraftab, 2000. On women's roles in urban governance and democratization, see Razavi, 2000; Beal, 1996. On gendered impacts of globalization on

employment, population policy and exclusion, see Perrons, 1999; Pathak, 1995; Kuumba, 1999; Gray and Kevane, 1999. FEANTSA (Brussels, 2000) produced a series of country reports detailing homelessness among women in the European Union.

# THE DEVELOPMENT CONTEXT:
## CHANGES AND CHALLENGES

## PART I

The Prologue of this report presented a view of globalization as a process with positive as well as negative implications. It stressed that the distribution of the benefits and costs of globalization is neither even nor random. Building on these observations, Chapter 1 offers a review of trends that are a cause of alarm in cities worldwide. It provides evidence for widespread and growing poverty and pervasive patterns of worsening inequality, producing trends of heightened polarization with wealth and access to resources becoming more concentrated. It also describes several ways in which modern information and communication technologies (ICTs) tend to deepen existing economic and social divisions. However, while ICTs are an essential element of globalization, they do not predetermine its goals. Later parts of this report include a variety of examples showing how ICTs can also be used for more beneficial results. The trends of growing poverty and polarization form an essential perspective for gaining a better understanding of the implications of globalization for urban settlements, which is the subject of Chapter 2. It is in urban centres that global interests focus their activities and whence their influences on surrounding regions originate. Therefore, the second chapter examines implications of globalization more specifically for cities.

Human settlements are not powerless in the face of globalization, but, through good governance and in effective partnerships, can play an important part in mediating and directing its consequences for economic and human development in positive ways. The challenge is to develop and implement policies that support not only the function of cities as engines of economic growth, but also their role as agents of social change.

During the 1990s, a series of World Conferences held under the aegis of the United Nations helped to galvanize support for goals of social justice and environmental sustainability. These summits led to Programmes of Action that stressed rights-based approaches and democratic decision-making processes, and which gave special attention to the situation of women, children, the elderly, people living in poverty, minorities and others at risk. Chapter 3 concludes Part I of this report with a brief overview and assessment of the human settlement aspects of these action plans, including the Habitat Agenda in particular.

These agendas provide the outlines of a normative framework to guide the implementation of development policies that take advantage of the potential of globalization to eradicate poverty, reduce inequality and improve the liveability of human settlements.

# DEVELOPMENT CONTRASTS IN HUMAN SETTLEMENTS

## Highlights

### Contrasts in urbanization patterns

The world population is becoming predominantly urban.[1] While the population of industrialized countries is already largely urban, urbanization processes are still acute in developing countries. Today, 40 per cent of the population of developing countries already lives in cities. By 2020, that figure will have risen to 52 per cent. Latin America and the Caribbean already has 75 per cent city dwellers, while in contrast, only one-third of the population of Africa and Asia live in urban areas. The greatest challenge will present itself in Africa and Asia, where an explosive demographic change is expected in the next quarter century. By 2015, 153 of the world's 358 cities with more than one million inhabitants will be in Asia. Of the 27 'megacities' with more than 10 million inhabitants, 15 will be in Asia. There are even indications of forthcoming megacities with 20 or even 30 million inhabitants; urban agglomerations of a size never known before in human history, most of which will be in the developing countries.

Currently, three-quarters of global population growth occurs in the *urban areas* of developing countries, causing hypergrowth in the cities least capable of catering for such growth. The present decade's average annual population increase in developing countries' cities is estimated at 64 million, or 175,000 persons per day. Half of this increase is caused by natural population growth within these cities. Additionally, urbanization processes in the South do not merely recapitulate the past experience of the developed nations. Contemporary urban growth and rural–urban shifts in the South are occurring in a context of far higher absolute population growth, at much lower income levels, with much less institutional and financial capacity, and with considerably fewer opportunities to expand into new frontiers, foreign or domestic.

### Contrasts in the wealth of cities

The urbanization contrasts described above are accompanied by significant increases in the scale of poverty of urban populations. While urban poverty exists and is indeed growing in all cities of the world it characterizes aspects of the rapidly growing cities in the developing countries. There, urban poverty disproportionately affects women and children; fuels ethnic and racial tensions; and

---

**Box 1.1 En-gendering poverty**

According to a World Bank estimate, in 2000 there were 1500 million people living below the international poverty line of US$1 a day. A majority of them are women.[i] Although a large majority of people living in poverty is found in countries with developing economies, countries with a high GNP have not eliminated poverty among women. Over the last five years, the number of women in poverty increased in the US.[ii] In Canada, 19 per cent of adult women are poor, a figure that has been climbing steadily since 1980; 56 per cent of women heading single-parent households are poor.[iii] Clearly, strong economic performance is not sufficient.

Further, surveys of household expenditure tend to underestimate poverty among women because such studies are usually based on assumptions about per capita income without considering the (unequal) distribution of resources within households. Focusing on monetary income also excludes other aspects of poverty, such as women's roles in public and private decision-making, their access to food, education, health care, credit, transportation and jobs, and their rights to own and inherit housing and land.[iv]

Preoccupation with the incidence of poverty has outstripped consideration of a far more important question, namely how – through what social and institutional mechanisms – people slide into poverty and stay there. The gender analysis of poverty needs to explain how these mechanisms differ among men and women.[v] In addition, policy approaches must recognize and support the important work of international women's movements and empower women to participate fully in the development of their local communities.[vi]

**Notes:** i This is acknowledged even by critics of the oft-cited figure of 70 per cent; see Marcoux, 1998. ii US Women Connect (www.uswc.org/reportcards.html), 14 September 2000. iii Townson, 2000. iv See, for example, Kenworthy and Malami, 1999; Razavi, 2000; Beall, 1996; Tinker and Summerfield, 1999. v Razavi, 1999a. For a useful discussion of the feminization of poverty, see www.olin.wustl.edu/macarthur/working%20papers/wp-mclanahan3.htm#top. vi Noteworthy is, for example, the work of the Huairou Commission and the Gender Unit of UNCHS. See also the discussion of The Alliance in Chapter 14 and the Platform for Action adopted by the Fourth World Conference on Women, held in Beijing in 1995.

---

condemns large sections, and sometimes the majority, of urban dwellers to a downward spiral of marginalization, social and economic exclusion and unhealthy living environments. All of the above contribute directly or indirectly to increases in social unrest and urban violence. This situation also fuels aspirations to seek economic opportunity outside national borders. Thus, the 'urbanization of poverty' is one of the most challenging problems facing the world today.

### Contrasts in competitiveness

As a result of fading distinctions between traditional political spheres and other components of society, human settlements, and large cities in particular, have come out as a considerable actor in the global political economy arena. In response to this change, shifts have taken place in attitudes to urban governance: cities are now increasingly viewed as a product to be marketed at a regional and global scale. Information and communication technology (ICT) allows for internationalization of footloose investment funding, resulting in vast increases in the volume and speed of international capital flows of all types; ranging from foreign direct investment (FDI) to short-term banking activities. In such an environment, cities often have no option but to compete on a global stage for these investments, exploiting whatever comparative advantages they may have; at times even to their own detriment. This development has created a downward spiral of increased subjugation of domestic, economic and social needs to international competitiveness; an often painful phase after the massive socio-economic transformations that characterized the entire 20th century.

Globalization has thus placed human settlements in a highly competitive framework of inter-city linkages and networks with a geographical context limited only by planetary boundaries. This new constellation of globally networked cities is sometimes referred to as 'the urban archipelago'. It implies that a city may have more relations with some faraway place than with its hinterland and that such cities act as energy nodes in a global force field. These are processes with considerable potential, and the urban strategies of many governments are now gravitating towards providing an enabling environment for human settlements to compete on the international stage. Many cities now acknowledge that the current nature of funding flows and investment capital demands an international urban orientation over and above managing local issues. Since the supply of international investment funding is often driven by profit optimization through the identification of areas with lower labour costs and standards, and regulations that are more favourable for business, cities in the developing world risk becoming transient points of destination of predatory capital, with little or no prospects for a sustainable future.

## Contrasts in opportunities

Until recently, the success, decline and stagnation of cities and other settlements were strongly and often uniquely linked to territorial, geographic, resource or political features. This is the case of settlements at the intersection of important communication corridors, or facing waterways and harbours, or grown around the processing and/or commercialization of agricultural products or mining resources. In a globalizing economy, these factors are no longer the exclusive driving forces of urban economic growth. There are no classic locational factors that can explain the meteorical rise in prominence of 'e-regions' like Silicon Valley and Seattle in the United States, or Bangalore in India. The point is that location is not destiny. But an important corollary is that all booming regions require a minimum package of enabling conditions to develop and sustain themselves. These conditions, whether directly or indirectly, are shaped by the actions of central and local government. This mix will vary from place to place, but it is likely to contain incentives, tax expenditures, high-level

educational facilities, research centres and universities, coupled with well-functioning infrastructure and urban services, availability of housing, excellent communications, and efficient transport systems. All these factors are, of course, the foundation, the essential purpose and the product of good governance.

Although the paradigm of the urban archipelago reflects a very real urban evolution at the global level, the relationships between rural and urban areas still include a host of factors that do not necessarily depend on the international level. It is not simply the linkage to faraway places that defines the nature of the urban archipelago, but rather individual cities' ability to make efficient use of newly available links to resources and markets offered by networks of cities. Therefore, cities' responses to globalization are not to control this global phenomenon, but rather to manage their own resources within a new global context, including traditional links with the hinterland. Thus, good governance is not simply a desirable goal; it is a key prerequisite for taking advantage of new economic unfolding for all cities and urban regions.

## Contrasts in local and global priorities

As indicated in the Prologue, globalization is the end of territorialism: the condition whereby socio-economic and political space is reducible solely to territorial coordinates. It has created an apparent paradox whereby polity – the condition of civil order – is simultaneously becoming more global *and* more local. This concept captures the notion that the economic and information features of globalization are penetrating even the remotest corners of Earth and that each locality is now forced to participate in the new globalized world, while, at the same time, local concerns increasingly spring to the foreground as major social and political issues.[2]

On a more positive note, the world is no longer only a community of states, but also an increasingly borderless network of interconnected cities where power is being shared more evenly and where governance is becoming more democratic. Promising partnerships are evolving between the public sector, the private sector and civil society. There is a growing awareness of the needs and rights of women, the indivisibility of human rights and the need for participation and for social, economic and environmental stewardship.

In many localities, people are overwhelmed by changes in their traditional cultural, spiritual and social values and norms and by the introduction of a cult of consumerism intrinsic to the process of globalization. In the rebound, many localities have rediscovered the 'culture of place' by stressing their *own* identity, their *own* roots, their *own* culture and values and the importance of their *own* neighbourhood, area, vicinity or town. In political terms this has translated into demands for self-government, for effective participation in decisions affecting the community, and in locally led initiatives to improve the livelihoods for all. By this process, begun in the last decade but markedly apparent since Habitat II, civil society has become important in recasting national and local politics as a third-sector actor – distinct from state and market – shaping policies, norms and social structures. As is the case of all transformation processes, some deal better with these issues than others.

## Contrasts within countries and regions

A major impact of globalization has been the reinforcement of old socio-economic, and the emergence of new technology-based disparities within countries. Even nations whose economies are doing well, such as the United States, the UK and China, recognize growing disparities in economic performance and quality of life between booming regions and lagging regions, prosperous urban centres and cities in decline. This suggests a direct correlation between globalization and responses to urbanization processes. Most booming regions, such as those along the western seaboard of the United States, the south of England or the southeast coast of China, are the ones that have seized the opportunities provided by globalization and are indeed driving it. Invariably, and this is the crucial point in terms of human settlements development, they are also the regions that have invested most in physical infrastructure, environmental protection, housing markets, educational and health facilities and communication networks. The question of which factor drives the other may be the subject of a fascinating debate, but the close interconnection between investment in human settlements development and the opportunities offered by globalization, particularly in terms of economic growth, is incontestable.

## Contrasts within urban areas

One clearly manifest feature of growing disparity is the 'divided city'. Within cities in all regions of the world we almost invariably see the growth of disparities between the affluent and the dispossessed, exemplified by the coexistence of thriving business districts, affluent neighbourhoods and slums (in the case of most developing countries) or 'distressed neighbourhoods' and derelict quarters (in more affluent countries). This is the most visible trait of the divided city. What is equally disturbing is the presence of invisible barriers within the divided city. It is entirely possible for a modern business executive to spend months in any of today's 'world cities', as well as in the capital of a developing country, without ever coming into visual contact with a slum or a derelict neighbourhood. Similarly, affluent residents of virtually any city can spend years without ever needing to, not to mention wanting to, come into contact with less palatable sections of the city or their inhabitants.[3]

The remaining two parts of this chapter explore in more detail the issues raised above. First, as indicated in the Prologue, ICTs are important instruments used to advance globalization. It is important to be curious about how ICTs can help to reduce and eliminate the problems of poverty and inequality, especially within cities. Future approaches to urban development will be more effective when they are informed by lessons that enable us to avoid mistakes from the past. Therefore, it is also important to develop a keen awareness of the role that ICTs can play in worsening current conditions. This is the subject of the next section of this chapter.

Second, it is clear that human settlements are a product of broader socio-economic and political processes at the international, national and local levels, while being at the same time a source of some of these processes. When these processes manifest themselves in the physical structure of cities and towns, they reflect both successes and failures of the socio-economic and political strategies pursued by different countries. Thus, in order to develop a well-grounded understanding of conditions and processes in human settlements in general, and within cities in particular, it is necessary to gain insight into relevant trends in these broader contexts. Salient in this regard are changes in the extent and patterns of poverty, inequity and polarization in society at large. These changes are reviewed in the second half of the remainder of this chapter.

# Uneven Development: Impacts of Information and Communication Technologies on Human Settlements[4]

ICTs are often presented as 'liberating'; emancipating society from spatial constraints imposed by the limitations of yesterday's technologies. They enable businesses to develop global markets and allow people to form communities of interest ('Netvilles') that are based on shared values.[5] However, while ICTs bring enrichment to some, they leave others impoverished. Those who lack access are left behind. The following section of this report takes a closer look at how ICTs often worsen existing inequalities and patterns of uneven development. Subsequent parts of this report examine the positive potential of ICTs to help to eliminate poverty and reduce inequality.

## ICTs and contemporary urbanization: a critical nexus

Two major trends help to define contemporary human settlement development. The first is the most momentous process of urbanization in human history. The second is the extraordinarily rapid but highly uneven application of digital information and communications technologies; these technologies diffuse to connect growing portions of urban economies, societies and cultures 'on-line' and in 'real time'.[6]

Closer inspection reveals that these two trends are closely interrelated. Against the widespread assumption that electronic communications will undermine large metropolitan regions, evidence suggests that the two are in fact mutually supporting. Both are constitutive elements of modern industrialization and globalization. In the developed North and the developing South, as well as in newly industrializing and post-communist states, the application of ICTs within and between cities, while an intensely uneven process, constitutes a critical nexus in the current development of human settlements.

ICTs are intensifying global urbanization in three major ways. First, ICTs allow specialist urban centres, with their high value-added services and manufacturing, to extend their powers, markets and control over ever-more distant regional, national, international and even global hinterlands. ICTs support the accelerating and spiralling contacts, transactions, communication flows and interactions that help bind, integrate and add economic dynamism to the vast, extended and multi-centred urban settlements, corridors and regions of our age. Second, in a volatile global economy, the growing speed, complexity and riskiness of innovation in all sectors – even those that can theoretically be developed entirely on-line – seems to demand a parallel concentration in the cities with the assets and 'innovative milieux' to sustain on-going competitiveness. This explains why the greatest planning problem in many emerging 'multimedia clusters' and digital growth centres in cities of the North and South is transportation and car parking. Workers still need to move their physical bodies to be 'in the thick of' the digital innovation process, even though their products are then instantaneously sent on-line to distant markets. Third, demand for ICTs – mobile and land line phones, satellite TVs, computer networks, electronic commerce, internet services – is overwhelmingly driven by the growth of metropolitan markets. Large 'global' cities, especially, are of disproportionate importance in driving ICT investment and innovation.[7] This is because of cities' cultures of modernization, their concentrations of capital, their relatively high disposable incomes and their concentrations of internationally oriented firms and institutions. As the economic product base of cities becomes increasingly mediated by flows of electronic information, with the progressive digitization of money, services, media, information, education and logistics, this critical nexus between cities and ICTs will only strengthen.

> **The complex intersection of human settlements and ICTs is helping to forge new landscapes of innovation, economic development, cultural interactions, political dynamics and social inequalities within cities and urban regions**

The complex intersection of human settlements and ICTs, defined as the dialectic between the 'space of flows' and the 'space of places', is helping to forge new landscapes of innovation, economic development, cultural interactions, political dynamics and social inequalities within cities and urban regions.[8] Traditional monocentric cities are giving way to an 'all-pervasive and ever-present urbanization' and urban culture, strung together by vast complexes of technological and communications systems.[9] The fabric of many cities and human settlements is now becoming so intertwined with ICTs and other technological systems that some now characterize them as 'cyborg cities'.[10] Others talk of the 'infinite city' made up of transnational urban corridors.

However, the societal diffusion of ICTs remains very uneven at all scales. It is in the contemporary city that this unevenness is starkest. Enclaves of 'superconnected' people, firms and institutions, with their increasingly broadband connections to elsewhere via the internet, mobile phones and satellite TVs and their easy access to information services, often exist cheek-by-jowl with much larger numbers of people with at most rudimentary access to modern communication technologies and electronic information. These spatial disparities are described more fully in the next chapter. The social and economic cores and peripheries of the global information 'age' are not only continents apart, but can now also be found geographically adjacent to each other within individual cities. Often, they are just a short distance apart, but separated by gates, walls and greatly unequal access to the crucial portals supporting participation in electronic domains. Thus, while dominant parts of the economic, social and cultural fabric of the world are now being mediated with ICTs at an astonishing pace, 80 per cent of the world has never made a phone call. And, while it is growing very rapidly, the internet remains the preserve of an elite of between 2 and 5 per cent of the global population.

## ● Challenges for urban analysis

The complex interconnections between cities and ICTs are evolving within a broader context set by political and economic liberalization, fast technological change, the changing nature of nation states and an internationalizing political economy. Together, these processes of change create enormous challenges to traditional ways of understanding cities. They particularly challenge customary views concerning land use, physical form, urban design and transportation; ways of thinking about industrial-age cities that have long neglected the importance of electronic communications and technologies in urban life.[11]

In response to such challenges, urban research on ICTs is beginning to grow rapidly.[12] Still, many questions at the intersection of ICTs and human settlements remain largely unaddressed by urban researchers. How, for example, do digitally mediated economic flows articulate with city economies and urban systems in different places and sectors within developed, developing, newly industrializing and post-communist economies? What are the relationships between the application of ICTs and broader processes of social and geographical polarization, discussed earlier in this chapter? How can urban analysis and policy making grapple meaningfully with invisible and intangible domains of electronic flow and real-time exchanges at multiple geographical scales? And how can the policy worlds of the city be brought together with those of cyberspace and ICTs to foster creative policy initiatives that harness the power of new technologies for positive urban social and economic development?

> **Far from ushering us towards societies of reduced inequality, ICTs often support new extremes of social and geographical unevenness within and between human settlements, in both the North and the South**

The remainder of this chapter demonstrates that dominant trends in ICT development, far from ushering us toward societies of reduced inequality, often support new extremes of social and geographical unevenness within and between human settlements, in both the North and the South. Other parts of this report will explore the prospects that such stark 'urban digital divides' might be ameliorated through progressive and innovative policy initiatives. Boxes 4.3, 4.4, 14.6 and 17.5 provide a range of examples in a variety of contexts.

## Not the 'death of distance': why the dominant logic of ICT-based development supports urban polarization

Why is the application of ICTs supporting social and geographical polarization within and between the world's cities and human settlements? At first sight, it might appear that new computing and communications technologies offer tantalizing possibilities for transcending traditional social and geographical barriers. Advertisements and magazine articles endlessly suggest this, with their portrayals of ICTs, and especially the internet, as a value-free technological panacea offering instant, limitless access to some entirely separate and disembodied on-line world. In this 'death of distance' or 'end of geography' scenario, an intrinsically equitable, decentralized and democratic world is seen to be emerging. Within this, everything within the global economic, cultural and social space becomes equally accessible or 'one click away'.[13] 'Cyberspace' is cast as a single, unitary and intrinsically unifying electronic space. It is a space, moreover, that has somehow overcome in our 'collective imagery', the familiar social, economic, cultural and geographical segmentations and inequalities of the 'off-line', urbanizing world.

The reality, however, is very different and quite alarming; there is growing evidence that the main trends surrounding the application of ICTs support processes and practices that intensify urban polarization. This is occurring at every scale across the globe. The dominant logic of ICT-based change seems to reinforce urban polarization, the 'disembedding' of dominant economic, social and cultural activities, and the social and technological distancing of the powerful from the less powerful. There are four reasons why this is so. ICTs, as currently applied, tend to:

1   extend the reach of the powerful;
2   underpin intensified unevenness through tying together international divisions of labour;
3   allow socio-economically affluent groups to selectively bypass their local environment; and
4   be culturally and economically biased, especially in terms of the wider development of the emerging 'international information marketplace'.

### ● New technologies tend to extend the reach of the economically and culturally powerful

The explosion in the use of ICTs overwhelmingly represents an extraordinary extension in the social, economic, cultural and geographical powers of those groups and organizations that are best connected, most highly skilled and most able to organize and configure the on-line shift to their own advantage. It is those particular groups, organizations and places that are orchestrating the instantaneous and often international mediation of money, work, service distribution, transport, leisure and media access. So far, they are the key beneficiaries of the so-called 'information revolution'. Far from being a universally liberating stampede on-line, 'the changed mobility and, hence, power patterns' associated with new information technologies 'may negatively affect the control over place of some while extending the control and power of others'.[14]

### ● Urban polarization and the internet

A case in point is the relationship between the extraordinary growth of the internet and global urban polarization. The internet is the fastest diffusing medium in history. But the UNDP still characterizes it as a 'global ghetto' encompassing only 2 per cent, or 250 million, of the most privileged and powerful individuals of the global population, over 80 per cent of whom live in Organisation for Economic Co-operation and Development (OECD) nations.[15] In 1999, this global 2 per cent tended to be wealthy: 90 per cent of users in Latin America came from upper income brackets; 30 per cent in the UK had salaries over US$60,000. They were highly educated: globally 30 per cent had at least one university degree; in China the respective figure was 60 per cent, in Mexico 67 per cent and in Ireland almost 70 per cent. Male users dominate: 62 per cent in the US, 75 per cent in Brazil, 84 per cent in Russia, 93 per cent in China and 94 per cent in the Arab States. Internet users also tend to be young: under 30 as an average age in the UK and China, 36 in the US. Finally, dominant ethnic groups lead internet use, as do English speakers: in 1999, 80 per cent of all global web sites were in English while only 10 per cent of the world's population spoke the language.[16]

The internet tends to extend the power of the already powerful while further marginalizing the less powerful within the same geographical areas – a logic of growing polarization. As the UNDP observes:

> 'The Internet is creating parallel communications systems: one for those with income, education and – literally – connections, giving plentiful information at low costs and high speed; the other for those without connections, blocked by high barriers of time, cost and uncertainty and dependent on out-dated information. With people in these two systems living and competing side-by-side, the advantages of connection are overpowering. The voices and concerns of people already living in human poverty – lacking incomes, education and access to public institutions – are being increasingly marginalized.'[17]

More concretely, the global majority not connected to the internet is disadvantaged by not having access to the services and applications that depend on it. This is especially so as electronic means of access to services are growing progressively more dominant, leading to the downgrading or curtailment of traditional, face-to-face, physical or paper-based ways of delivering them. People without internet access can therefore face extra costs and barriers. They tend to lack the skills, knowledge, equipment, infrastructure access, capital, money, electricity and telephone access necessary to access and fully exploit the on-line resources. Even when the internet service itself is 'free' – as is often the case these days in developed nations – users still need a phone line, a computer, a modem, electricity supply, software, skills and money to pay for phone and electricity.

Urban societies are becoming more separated into the 'on-line' and the 'off-line' in complex tapestries of inclusion and exclusion. Such trends are multiple, superimposed and complex. They are clearly starting to affect the physical, technological, social and economic structures of human settlements in very important ways. Consider, for example:

- The position of people who remain stranded in the worlds of physical cash or the informal economy, while dominant service providers and consumers in many cities migrate into electronic forms of conducting transactions (often withdrawing or restructuring their physical offices and service-points in the process).
- The ways in which some roads in cities such as Toronto, Melbourne and Singapore have become commodified, rendering them accessible only to those who have electronic transponders in their cars.
- The landscapes of booming high-tech cities in the South, such as Bangalore (India) and Bintan Island (Indonesia). In such cities, huge efforts are being made to configure industrial and technology parks and elite housing areas with the best possible infrastructural connections to distant places. At the same time, many nearby informal settlements struggle to access payphones, paved roads, sewerage or electricity.

### ● The internet and the restructuring of US cities

In the cities of the North, it tends to be low-income and ethnic minority communities that are most excluded from the internet.[18] In the US, for example, in 1997, 24 per cent of whites had on-line access in major cities whereas only 7 per cent of blacks did. Fifty per cent of city residents earning over US$75,000 a year had internet access but only 6 per cent of those earning less than US$10,000 did so.[19] It should be remembered that telephone access, too, remains highly uneven, even in the US. Only 50 per cent of female-headed households living at or below the poverty line, and 43.5 per cent of families who depend totally on public assistance, have access to even this basic technology.[20]

It has been estimated that at present 60 per cent of US jobs require skills with technology and that 75 per cent of all transactions between individuals and the government – including such government aid services as delivery of food stamps, social security benefits and Medicaid information – take place electronically. Increasingly, people without technology skills or access to electronic communications will be at a disadvantage.[21]

It is certain that 'the rich are going to be getting richer in terms of information'; the concern is that 'the information poor will become more impoverished because government bodies, community organizations, and corporations are displacing resources from their ordinary channels of communication on to electronic ones'.[22] Inner-city communities, especially, face a concentration of poverty and the deconcentration of opportunity; that is, there is a ghettoization of non-connected groups within central cities at the same time that ICTs are helping to support the decentralization of growing information industries to 'edge cities'.

The internet is therefore much more than an unevenly diffused medium of communication and expression. In a complex relation of reciprocal dynamics, it now plays a direct role in the restructuring of the same cities that support its development. Certain urban areas, especially in 'world cities' of the North, are emerging as dominant powerhouses of global internet production: New York, San Francisco and London to name but three.[23] A new type of economic enclave is emerging in such cities: the gentrifying 'cyber' district. Such areas now propel the production of internet services, web sites and the digitization of design, architecture, gaming, CD-ROMs and music.

San Francisco's so-called 'Multimedia Gulch' district is a prototypical example. It is a fast-growing media and internet cluster in the City's 'SOMA' area. Here, downtown neighbourhoods have been refurbished to sustain the clustering demands of interlocking micro-, small- and medium-sized firms in digital design, advertising, gaming, publishing, fashion, music, multimedia, computing and communications. Over 2200 such firms now provide over 56,000 jobs in these sectors, up by 105 per cent between 1996 and 1998, as capital has moved north from Silicon Valley.[24] This development set off a spiral of gentrification, attracting investment from restaurants, retailers, property firms, 'loft' developers and infrastructure companies, leading to escalating rents and the eviction, displacement and exclusion of lower income groups from this new 'high-end' area. Somewhat ironically for an industry whose products can be sent on-line anywhere on Earth, parking shortages have become critical.

Urban social and political conflicts have emerged as 'dot.commers', with their extraordinary wealth, along with real estate speculators, have colonized selected districts. Under the banner 'The Internet Killed San Francisco', one description lists the following 'symptoms': commercial real estate rates went up 42 per cent between 1997 and 1999; the median price apartment was US$410,000 by August 1999; median rental for an apartment was US$2000 per month; and homelessness rates were rising fast.[25] Landlords, backed by the relaxation of rent controls and tenant protection laws by the City Council in the 1990s, have instigated a steep rise in evictions. The result is a severe housing crisis, the expulsion of poorer people from downtown, and accentuated landscapes of social and geographical polarization, with pockets of the city being repackaged as places of work, leisure or living for internet-based businesses and entrepreneurs.[26]

## ● ICTs as supports to the restructuring of human settlements: integrating international divisions of labour

*Digital capitalism is now free to physically transcend territorial boundaries and, more importantly, to take economic advantage of the sudden absence of geopolitical constraints on its development.*[27]

There is a close connection between ICTs, global urban polarization and the power of transnational corporations to shape urban development. Against the rhetoric that 'cyberspace' is a purely virtual and disembodied world, the radical growth of ICTs is closely related to the restructuring of real places at all geographical scales.[28]

*ICT networks and the exploitation of geographical differences.* ICTs offer unparalleled choice and flexibility to mobile firms and socio-economic groups, enabling them to exploit differences between places. This is done through the construction of highly elaborate divisions of labour, which can then be integrated in 'real time' through ICTs. Currently, international telecommunications tariffs are collapsing, technological capabilities are growing exponentially and mergers, alliances and acquisitions in telecom and media industries are beginning to allow firms to offer global 'one-stop shops' for international corporate ICT users.

---

Current trends enhance the capability of international firms to separate their manufacturing, financing, marketing and other operations, locating them in cities and towns across the world according to the most advantageous local environmental regulations, tax laws, labour conditions and costs, while maintaining overall control

---

These trends enhance the ability of corporations to separate out the various functions within their operations (eg finance, manufacturing, marketing) to cities and towns across the world, while maintaining close control and coordination. Transnational corporations and their affiliates can thus now benefit from the seamless and instant integration of plants located in globally spread networks of specialized and very different urban sites, with very different environmental regulations, tax laws, labour conditions and costs. Broadly, ICTs are being used to tie together:

- research and development centres in suburban technopôles of the North and, to a lesser extent, South;[29]
- corporate headquarters and financial service houses in select 'global' cities;[30]
- cultural, media and multimedia sectors in the emerging 'digital clusters' of some Northern and a few Southern cities;[31]
- cheap, mobile manufacturing plants on the peripheries of Northern cities and in the newly industrializing cities of the South;[32]
- decentralized call centres, data processing and e-commerce management centres in newly emerging

e-commerce enclaves across the world (including the Caribbean, Philippines, Ireland, India, northern and western UK);[33]
- electronically integrated resource extraction activities in minerals, forests, oil and fisheries; and
- the logistics, seaport and airport hubs that serve as the point-of-transfer and export processing zones that 'lubricate' internationalization.

The construction of ICT systems to support intensifying divisions of labour is further supported by the growth of local efforts to 'package' areas and zones with subsidies, labour forces, infrastructures, services and security to tempt mobile investment. Urban development agencies strive entrepreneurially to configure their spaces with the right local–global (or 'glocal') infrastructural connections to allow them to emerge as a valued node in international corporate networks. These efforts create a close nexus between the local production of infrastructure and urban space and globalizing networks of electronic and physical flow (see, for example, Boxes 2.1, 2.2 and 2.3 on Sydney, Singapore and London).

*The global liberalization of telecommunications and the 'cherry picking' of urban markets.*

---

Mosaics of growing inequality mark city regions, as providers seek to 'cherry pick' only the most lucrative business and professional customers from across the urban landscape

---

In the most liberalized telecommunications regimes, such as the US and UK, city regions are marked by mosaics of growing inequality, as providers seek to 'cherry pick' only the most lucrative business and professional customers from across the urban landscape.[34] Upper income areas and buildings with high computer ownership and communications expenditures are targets of vast, competitive, investment in broadband infrastructure and services. In mid-1999 about 86 per cent of all broadband internet delivery capacity in the US was concentrated in the prosperous suburbs and business areas of the 20 largest cities.[35] It is becoming clear that:

*The private sector builds where the high volume and the money is. In most communities the fibre-optic rings circle the business district. If you're in a poor suburban neighbourhood or the inner city, you're at risk. What's more, providers that have spent years building their infrastructures don't come back and fill in the underserved neighbourhoods. That may be a shrewd financial strategy. But the social impact could be devastating.*[36]

Such dualization is underpinned by the widespread shift from standardized marketing by emerging telecom and media conglomerates, to marketing targeted precisely at socio-economically affluent groups and areas. AT&T, for example, has recognized that it makes 80 per cent of its US$6000 million annual profits from 20 per cent of its customers.[37] This targeting of innovation and investment towards richer groups and areas is also supported by the attempts of cross-media alliances to take advantage of technological 'synergies' in offering high-value customers whole baskets of services on a single contract.[38] In the US, for example, the CEO of MCI recently stated that 'we're going to change our focus from being omnipresent to the entire market to talking to the top third of the consumer market that represents opportunities in cellular, Internet and entertainment'.[39]

As profit-driven mergers between telecommunications and media transnationals direct the global roll-out of ICT infrastructure, investment concentrates on the market 'hot spots': the downtown business districts, high-tech areas, media clusters and upper income residential districts of prosperous, internationally oriented and 'global' cities. The concentration of information, communications and knowledge infrastructures and industries creates a very strong demand in the business cores of such cities: in 1999, both New York and Tokyo had more telephones than the whole of Africa (14 million).[40] This focused demand drives a frenzy of competitive activity and investment by communication and media suppliers. The centres of global cities like New York and London now have six or more separate fibre-optic grids, offering the most capable, reliable, competitive and cost-effective electronic connections anywhere.

Driven by new start-ups that do not seek to serve whole cities, regions or nations, many of these new city-level fibre networks are limited to demand-rich parts of the main business cities. Such networks are connected seamlessly to each other via new transoceanic and transcontinental fibre and satellite networks, creating a global–local logic that bypasses both poorer parts of global cities and the areas between them.

Reflecting and reinforcing the 'global archipelago' of city cores, small high-capacity networks can mediate large portions of global economic flows. For example, in 1998, the WorldCom/MCI metropolitan network in London had only 180 km of fibre. But it had already secured fully 20 per cent of the whole of the UK's international telecommunications traffic.[41] Building similar networks in the major cities of the US, Europe, Asia and Latin America, along with dedicated transoceanic lines to connect them, WorldCom/MCI and similar firms are able to bypass incumbent carriers.[42]

Developing cities such as Mexico City, Beijing and São Paulo often face a competitive disadvantage in global telecommunications links. They tend to be more dependent on monopolistic, state-owned providers that are more expensive, less innovative and offer a more limited bundle of services. Global liberalization is changing this situation and cities like Mexico City are rapidly, but unevenly, being wired by Western telecommunications firms.[43]

Meanwhile, poorer parts of cities of the North – for example low-income, African American and blue-collar neighbourhoods in US cities – suffer from underinvestment and deteriorating service quality, and are being disproportionately affected by the rising relative costs of local

communications.[44] Within the context of liberalized markets and entrepreneurial planning and with the withdrawal of local monopolies, infrastructure providers do not target new investment, marketing and innovation in poor communities and marginalized neighbourhoods; places that already tend to face exclusion from formal financial services, insurance, retailing investment and other utilities.[45]

Marketing and infrastructure development strategies reflect the patchwork geographies of fragmented cities. The situation of Bell Atlantic in New Jersey is typical. By 1997, it had rolled out high-capacity fibre-optic links and broadband internet services to 'suburban business parks and large corporations' and 'set a schedule for suburban neighbourhoods'. But it had 'not yet made specific plans for the thousands of poor people who live in the state's largest cities'. Nor had it wired the Enterprise Zones that the New Jersey City Council was developing in the hope of attracting new corporate investment. Worse still, it had 'let its network deteriorate in parts of Brooklyn and the Bronx, where corroded wires led to scratchy lines and service outages'.[46] Physical offices, used by many poor people without bank accounts to pay bills, have also been routinely closed by US telecommunications firms, while rates for directory assistance and local call charges have been dramatically hiked to reflect 'cost-reflective pricing' and the withdrawal of social cross-subsidies.[47] In a context where bandwidth and connectivity are the lifeline of many businesses, these practices prevent new on-line and e-commerce-oriented small enterprises from competing within less prosperous, peripheral towns and marginalized inner-city areas.[48]

## ● ICTs, urban polarization and restructuring in developing cities

*New communication technologies and a metropolitan transportation system allow people to stay selectively in touch with those individuals/groups that they want to, while disconnecting from the city at large.*[49]

ICTs allow affluent urban groups to overcome the barriers of local geography by extending their access to distant places and resources. Increasingly, such groups also use ICTs to avoid real or perceived urban nuisances and dangers; for example, traffic congestion and crime. ICTs like the internet help their users to connect, without risk or fear, to people, services and resources across local, national or international boundaries. At the same time, ICTs make possible the selective dissociation of affluent groups from exposure to differences arising from social mixing in more traditional streets and neighbourhoods. Other phenomena, like the car, the mobile phone, the CCTV system, the privatized shopping mall and the gated community, discussed in the next chapter, further reinforce this fragmentation.[50]

ICTs thus facilitate a global economic system whose dominant logic has had a fracturing and polarizing effect on human settlements and cities. As Manuel Castells has demonstrated, intensifying global connections between the valued and powerful parts of cities, and the groups and organizations who control and inhabit them, are combined with a growing partitioning and disconnection at the local scale within cities.[51]

The uneven growth of ICTs and 'cyberspace' thus has important implications for the restructuring of real urban space. Walls, ramparts, security fences, electric fences, armed guards and defensive urban design are the physical manifestations of this urban restructuring in both Northern and Southern cities. Once again, ICTs support the formation of enclaves through 'smart' home technologies, intelligent utility metering, electronic finance and consumption systems, and help to secure their safety through CCTV systems, electronic alarms, movement and face-recognition sensors, electronic gates and electronically tolled 'smart' highways that filter out the vehicles of the poor.

> Cities are not only sources of innovation and the transactional hubs of the modern, knowledge-based economy. They are also the places where the contradictions of ICT-mediated change are most salient. The rapid expansion of cyberspace liberates the privileged to take advantage of globalization. At the same time, it reinforces the stark reality of spatial barriers for those left behind

As cities across the world are restructured in this manner, the common development model of the South – high-value enclaves surrounded by landscapes of marginalization – is re-emerging in the North.[52] Cities, then, are not only sources of innovation and transactional hubs of the modern, knowledge-based economy. They are also the places where the contradictions of ICT-mediated economic, social and cultural change are most salient. The rapid expansion of cyberspace liberates the privileged to take advantage of globalization. At the same time, it reinforces the stark reality of geographical barriers for those left behind.

*Telecommunications and restructuring in developing cities.* A similar logic of global connection and local disconnection is evident in developing, newly industrializing and post-communist cities, where personal internet and telephone access is much more limited than in cities in the North. In the near future at least, such personal connections are likely to remain beyond the reach of a large majority of households in the developing world. Infrastructure networks, too, are much less well developed, with many national phone systems falling into a state of disrepair and obsolescence. Even in late 1998 in over 70 developing nations, no internet access existed at all. In many others, text messages were the limit of the systems; multimedia and even Web access were impossible.[53]

When services do exist, they tend to be much more expensive than in the North. In Lima, for example, despite increased diffusion after the liberalization of telecommunications in 1990, less than half of all households have a telephone and less than a fifth of the poorest 20 per cent of the city's households have access to a phone.[54] When it comes to computer access, the average is 7 per cent, with large differences between the richest fifth (50 per cent) and poorest fifth (1 per cent) of households. With internet costs at over US$40 a month, the diffusion of the internet is restricted to the very rich. Thus, the issue of public internet booths becomes critical.

> In many developing cities, high-quality ICT infrastructures are being packaged through entrepreneurial planning, public subsidies and defensive urban design, into industrial parks for international firms and 'Euro-American' style gated residential enclaves for social and economic elites

In many developing cities, high-quality ICT infrastructures are being packaged through entrepreneurial planning, public subsidies and defensive urban design, into industrial parks for international firms and 'Euro-American' style gated residential enclaves for socio-economic elites. Consider the following examples:

- In Thailand – a rapidly developing nation which has more cellular telephones than the whole of Africa[55] – the installation of fibre optics in the so-called 'intelligent corridor' along the major arterial ring road of Bangkok is reinforcing the linear expansion of the city into exurban areas.[56] A 'leap frog' strategy 'provides households and firms with fibre-optic services in high-income and high-value industrial areas' at the expense of the wider city.[57]
- In São Paulo, Brazil, patterns of investment in advanced telecommunications are starkly uneven. Fortified enclaves around the Murumbi district of the city are designed to meet the demand of growing middle- and upper-income groups for perceived security, thus supporting their withdrawal from their surroundings.[58] Offering integrated areas for residence, work and consumption, these inward-looking, insular communities turn their backs on the public street while relying on veritable armies of service personnel, the automobile, dedicated energy and water connections and the most sophisticated telecommunications links available in Brazil. Such enclaves have benefited from investment strategies that have concentrated on the 'supply of sophisticated infrastructural services for top income groups in São Paulo',[59] while the collapse of public planning for energy, water and telecommunications infrastructure, and the concomitant withdrawal of cross-subsidies has left households of lesser means in situations of disadvantage or worse.
- In the export-oriented 'flagship' manufacturing enclaves of Johor (Malaysia) and the Riau islands of Batam and Bintan (Indonesia), Singaporean capital is equipping each new development with the requisite packages of infrastructural connections. The parks are 'conceived of as self-contained industrial townships'; 'each of these investment enclaves offers linkage to the Singaporean economy while minimizing dependence on the wider Indonesian

environment'.[60] For example, direct lines connect into Singapore's state-of-the-art telecommunications infrastructure, completely bypassing Indonesia's poor-quality telecommunications infrastructure. As a result, telephone calls from these enclaves across the national border to Singapore are classed as 'local'; those beyond the enclave walls to the rest of Indonesia, however, are classed as 'international'.

- The US$20,000 million Multimedia Super Corridor (MSC) in Malaysia is a giant among the emerging urban planning initiatives that engineer new industrial and multimedia areas. Here, at the heart of the Association of Southeast Asian Nations (ASEAN) block in Southeast Asia, a whole national development strategy has been condensed into a single plan for a vast new urban corridor. The aim of the MSC is nothing less than to replace Malaysia's manufacturing-dominated economy with a booming constellation of services, IT, media and communications industries by turning a vast stretch of rainforest and rubber plantations into 'Asia's technology hub' by the year 2020. The MSC starts at the centre of the capital, Kuala Lumpur, and ends 30 miles south at an immense new international airport, strategically placed on the routes to Singapore. As well as tax incentives, favourable cost structures and high-quality made-to-order infrastructure, Malaysia has developed custom-tailored laws for the MSC. Incoming transnational firms will have free in-migration for 'knowledge workers' from all over the world. A special set of 'cyber laws' surrounding intellectual property rights has also been created to ensure that firms can recoup their on-line investment costs.

  However, there are dangers that the MSC will result in a two-tier society with the workers providing the low-value added support for sealed-off corporate zones operating in global networks. There are also major questions over the fate of peripheral regions and Kuala Lumpur's marginalized urban areas, outside the MSC. The prevailing discourse implies that the whole country will benefit equally. However, the construction of the MSC is displacing plantation communities while developing new communities for the corporate elite and their families, able to afford the new, privately developed 'wired' homes. Low-skill, low-wage service staff – cleaners, security guards, gardeners – are being brought in from outside the corridor. These disparities have prompted criticism in the national press.

- Within Bangalore – 'India's Silicon Valley'[61] – the heightened wealth inequalities associated with high-tech growth have created a highly fragmented and polarized urban structure. This situation reflects 'participation in the information-intensive global economy by a core elite, and non-participation by the masses'.[62] At the Electronics City complex, for example, three-quarters of a mile from the centre of Bangalore, several hundred acres of 'offshore' technology campus have been configured to house companies like Texas Instruments, IBM, 3-M and

Motorola. The Indian firm Wipro, another major presence, exploits advanced communications as it uses India's low-wage software programmers to service computers worldwide remotely from Bangalore. All these firms 'are insulated from the outside world by power generators, by the leasing of special telephone lines, and by an international-style work environment'.[63]

Singaporean capital has also constructed an Information Technology Park on the outskirts of Bangalore, equipped with dedicated satellite ground stations, broadband telecommunications, uninterrupted power supplies, back-up generators and private water, sanitation and waste-disposal services. Because of the poor quality of the regional telecommunications infrastructure, the park also serves as a regional hub link to global markets: 'companies within 30 km of the park can simply point their microwave antennae and connect by satellite to clients anywhere in the world'.[64] The park is integrated with highly luxurious residential and leisure facilities, setting it even further apart from the poverty in the shanty towns that house most of the city's migrant population, over 50 per cent of whom are illiterate.[65]

Initiatives like Bangalore's technology parks compound the polarization caused by the gradual withdrawal of social and geographical cross-subsidies used by public telephone monopolies.[66] The present trend towards privatization appears to be ending all such subsidies. In the absence of effective regulation, privatization will likely result in efficiency gains and better service for those who already have or who can afford to get connected to the existing services. The urban poor, however, will be further marginalized.[67]

While most public infrastructural investment in Bangalore focuses on securing the new parks locally and linking them globally, the municipality has bulldozed 'illegal', self-built housing in the name of a civic modernization 'clean-up' programme. Conditions in the shanty town are deteriorating and many residents have no or very limited access to piped water, communications, energy, paved roads and motorized transport; a sharp contrast to the modern landscapes of the new technopolis parks, right in their midst. Indeed, a broader infrastructure crisis is emerging for the poor: power outages are common and a water shortage is looming. Thus, it is clear that 'the recent internationalization of Bangalore has had a negative impact on the poor'.[68]

## ● Cultural and economic biases of the international information marketplace

Dominant applications of ICTs are heavily biased culturally. Electronic power is being concentrated by a small number of people, institutions and places, which dominate global flows of technology, capital, infrastructure and intellectual property rights, transcending the traditional authority of nation states.[69]

This process raises questions about geo-political relationships, accountability, democracy, global citizenship, the ownership of information and the means of cultural expression. This is especially important given the extreme asymmetries of North–South relations. In many developing nations and cities, TV and internet media provide an overwhelmingly Anglo-Saxon content as US culture in particular is extended through the growth of electronic connections.[70] The United States, as the world's 'information super power', aims to extend and intensify its supremacy in telecommunications, internet backbone infrastructure, e-commerce, multimedia, biotechnology, education, research and development and digital content: an industrial development strategy that has been called 'bandwidth colonialism'.[71] Many nations now have better and lower cost internet connections to the US than to adjacent nations and regions.

The capital, technology, skills and finance of the North thus play a dominant role in supporting the liberalization and consolidation of telecommunications, media and technology. Encouraged by the WTO and similar organizations, these processes are meant to 'open up' and integrate international trade and finance systems. They are also going hand-in-hand with the creeping privatization of scientific research, allowing corporations to control intellectual property rights over matters ranging from media content through software, information and knowledge, to human genetic sequences and bio-engineered life forms.

This trend has caused concerns that 'the dynamic of the economic model of globalization may lead to a 'ghettoized' world organized around a few megacities in the North, but occasionally in the South, serving as the nerve centres of worldwide markets and flow.[72] A further worry is that a few media giants are structuring ICTs towards commercial consumption in ways that hamper other applications. Users are relatively powerless in the configuration and roll-out of digital media and communications systems. 'Vertical' communications back to the supplier and the associated e-commerce affiliates tend to outweigh opportunities for engaging in 'horizontal' communication within the community, and beyond, in support of 'digital democracy'.[73]

### Bridging the urban digital divide

The preceding discussion has reviewed how dominant applications of ICTs tend to worsen urban polarization. These trends are important. They provide useful insights for efforts to use ICTs in support of equitable urban development. However, the picture is by no means all gloomy. ICTs are *inherently flexible* technologies. The ways in which they are configured, diffused and applied are not set in stone. The remarkable powers of ICTs for supporting new types of information flow, communication, transaction and cultural experience can be mobilized and shaped in ways to greatly benefit people's quality of life. 'It is this enabling capacity of ICTs – the fact that they allow the user, whether individual or community, to take advantage of them in ways that the individual or community chooses – that gives these technologies their democratic and empowering potential'.[74]

The history of communications is not a history of machines but a history of the ways in which new media help to reconfigure systems of power and networks of social relations. Communications technologies are certainly produced within particular centres of power and deployed with particular purposes in mind but, once in play, they often have unintended and contradictory consequences.[75]

Beyond the dominant application of ICTs, many efforts are now emerging at the local, urban, regional, national and international levels, which seek to exploit these capabilities in support of development models that are more equitable, democratic and sustainable. As diffusion of ICTs widens, many more efforts to work 'against the grain' of commodification and polarization become possible. Given the linkage between places and information flows, social diversity, with its plurality of values and interests, is transforming the logic of the 'space of flows', making it a contested space – a plural and diversified space, with a blossoming of initiatives.[76] These progressive initiatives in, and political contestation of, urban space are taken up in subsequent parts of this report.

# Human Settlements in a Polarizing World: Poverty and Inequity

There are many reasons why inequity and poverty occupy centre stage in this 2001 issue of the *Global Report on Human Settlements*. One of them is that poverty has increasingly become the focus of multilateral and bilateral development organizations, as well as of United Nations member states. But there is one reason that is uniquely important to people living in human settlements and cities. This reason is strikingly simple: Today, poverty is more central than ever to the human settlements discourse, for the plain fact that decent housing and basic services are no more provided by the public sector, but have increasingly become a commodity to be accessed in the marketplace. Hence, people's (in)ability to pay market prices is absolutely crucial.

In today's world, globalization is the most significant socio-economic phenomenon, shaping the economic fortunes of both nations and cities. In spite of globalization, and sometimes because of it, extreme poverty has persisted and inequality deepened in many countries. In such countries, globalization has tended to fragment production processes, labour markets, political entities and societies. The main features of poverty today include falling incomes, rising costs of living, especially within urban areas, and inadequate access to basic services such as water and sanitation. Poverty is also increasingly becoming an urban phenomenon. The increase in the number of the world's poor has been accompanied by rising inequality and polarization, between nations, within nations and within cities. Most of these features of poverty are not limited to the developing world, but also apply to more developed countries.

### Decreases in income and increases in cost of living

In recent years, the number of poor people has risen worldwide. In some regions, the proportion of the poor has also risen. The total number of people subsisting below the international poverty line of less than US$1 a day has risen from 1200 million in 1987 to 1500 million in 2000 and is projected to grow to 1900 million in 2015. These increases have taken place particularly in Latin America, South Asia, the Middle East and North Africa.[77] In many countries, low-wage earners have experienced declines in real disposable income.

> *'Millions are experiencing globalization not as an opportunity, but as a force of disruption or destruction: as an assault on their material standards of living, or on their traditional way of life. And those who feel marginalized in this way are growing more and more numerous'* –
> **Kofi Annan, Address to the General Assembly, New York, 21 September 1998**

World Bank estimates of poverty show that very little progress has been made in reducing income poverty levels over the last decade. The Asian financial crisis partially undid improvements made in East Asia and, compared with 1993, conditions have worsened in Eastern Europe, Central Asia, Latin America, the Caribbean, South Asia, sub-Saharan Africa, the Middle East and North Africa. Indeed, in the aftermath of the crisis, the number of people living on less than US$1 a day has risen. The new figures in Tables 1.1 and 1.2 show that:

- The decline in the numbers of the poor in Asia is almost exclusively due to a reduction in the number of poor people in East Asia, most notably in China. But progress was partly reversed by the crisis, and stalled in China.
- In South Asia, the incidence of poverty (the share of the population living in poverty) did decline moderately through the 1990s but not sufficiently to reduce the absolute number of the poor. The actual number of poor people in the region has been rising steadily since 1987.
- In Africa, the percentage of people living in poverty declined but the actual numbers increased. The new estimates indicate that Africa is now the region with the largest share of people living below US$1 a day.
- In Latin America the share of poor people remained roughly constant over the period, but the numbers increased.

- In the countries of the former Soviet bloc, poverty rose markedly – both the share and the numbers of poor people increased.

At the same time, the costs of living have increased as subsidies on basic goods have been reduced or eliminated and interests rates have risen.

> **In many countries, real incomes have fallen, the costs of living have gone up, and the number of poor households has grown, especially in cities**

Further, the spread of user fees means that the poor now frequently have to pay for services, including health care and education, that previously were provided for free or at nominal cost. It is important to recognize that women and children disproportionately bear the burdens of poverty (see Box 1.1).

## The urbanization of poverty

Poverty should not be seen narrowly in terms of income in relation to costs of living. The ability to maintain a minimum standard of living also depends on access to basic services such as health care, safe drinking water, garbage collection and sewerage. About 220 million urban dwellers, 13 per cent of the world's urban population, do not have access to safe drinking water, and about twice this number lack even the simplest of latrines.[78] Women suffer the most from these deficiencies (see Chapter 10). Conceptualized in terms of security by the Human Development Report 1999,[79] poverty also includes exposure to contaminated environments and being at risk of criminal victimization (Chapter 17). Poverty is closely linked to the wide spread of preventable diseases and health risks in urban areas, labelled as an 'urban penalty' (Chapter 9). Further, within policy frameworks aimed at 'enabling', being poor means the lack of options, the absence of opportunities for meaningful participation and inadequate support for capacity development by low-income communities.[80]

Relevant as well is the concept of 'housing poverty', introduced by UNCHS (Habitat) *Global Report on Human Settlements 1996*, that is '…individuals and households who lack safe, secure and healthy shelter with basic infrastructure such as piped water and adequate provision for sanitation, drainage and the removal of household waste'. The shortage of affordable housing for low-income urban household in developing countries has resulted in a proliferation of slums and squatter settlements. One-quarter of the urban housing stock consists of non-permanent structures, while more than a third does not comply with local building regulations. Large numbers of people live in unsafe housing. In addition, hunger is increasingly becoming an urban problem, and the supply and distribution of food is placing higher demands on cities (see Box 1.2). However, urban housing poverty, food insecurity and malnourishment are not restricted to the developing world. Indeed, it is important to recognize that economic growth and prosperity do not guarantee their elimination: several

**Table 1.1**

**Population living on less than US$1 per day in developing and transitional economies, selected years, 1987–1998**

| Region | Number of people (million) | | | | |
|---|---|---|---|---|---|
| | 1987 | 1990 | 1993 | 1996 | 1998 (est) |
| East Asia and the Pacific | 417.5 | 452.4 | 431.9 | 265.1 | 278.3 |
| (excluding China) | 114.1 | 92.0 | 83.5 | 55.1 | 65.1 |
| Eastern Europe/Central Asia | 1.1 | 7.1 | 18.3 | 23.8 | 24.0 |
| Latin America/Caribbean | 63.7 | 73.8 | 70.8 | 76.0 | 78.2 |
| Middle East/North Africa | 9.3 | 5.7 | 5.0 | 5.0 | 5.5 |
| South Asia | 474.4 | 495.1 | 505.1 | 531.7 | 522.0 |
| Sub-Saharan Africa | 217.2 | 242.3 | 273.3 | 289.0 | 290.9 |
| Total | 1,183.2 | 1,276.4 | 1,304.3 | 1,190.6 | 1,198.9 |
| (excluding China) | 879.8 | 915.9 | 955.9 | 980.5 | 985.7 |
| Number of poor at $2 per day | 2,549.0 | 2,718.4 | 2,784.8 | 2,724.1 | 2,801.0 |

**Source:** The World Bank; Poverty Fact Sheets. Accessed on 31 May 2000, at www.worldbank.org/html/extdr/pb/pbpoverty.htm.

million people are homeless in Europe and North America (see Chapter 16).

All of these poverty-related problems tend to be more prevalent in urban areas than rural areas.

More and more people in the developing world are living in the cities. By 2020, the number of people living in developing countries will grow from 4900 million to 6800 million. Ninety per cent of this increase will be in rapidly expanding cities and towns. More than half the population of Africa and Asia will live in urban areas by 2020. Already more than three-quarters of the poor in Latin America live in cities.[81] In short, in the years to come, policy makers need to reckon with an urbanization and feminization of poverty whose extent and severity should not be underestimated (see Box 1.3).

## Inequality and polarization

Although absolute poverty is bad enough, it is worse when it occurs amid conditions of plenty. Relative poverty mirrors inequalities that raise important questions of equitable access to rights and resources. Polarization happens when these inequalities worsen over time and inequities become accentuated and magnified. Inequality across nations has steadily increased since 1980. The widening gap between rich and poor countries is easily seen in the coefficient of variation of per capita gross domestic product (GDP), shown in Table 1.3.

The growing inter-country inequalities that hinder development and human settlement planning are compounded by serious disparities that exist within countries. Research has revealed a close relationship between the degree of domestic inequality and the prospect of eliminating poverty.

*Research shows that decreasing income inequality can have as much impact on reducing poverty as does increasing economic growth*

Over the past decade, the amount of poverty reduction resulting from a given rate of national economic growth has varied in step with national income distribution. Decreasing income inequality can have as much impact on reducing poverty as does increasing economic growth. Analysis of data for the 1990s shows that, on average, an economic growth rate of 10 per cent reduced the percentage of people living on less than US$1 a day by 9 per cent in countries where income was fairly evenly distributed. However, in countries where income was more unequally distributed, a growth rate of 10 per cent reduced the poverty headcount by only 3 per cent.[82]

Some of the greatest domestic inequality exists in the less developed and transitional economies of, respectively, Latin America and Eastern Europe, impeding

| Region | Percentage of poor | | | | |
|--------|------|------|------|------|-----------|
| | 1987 | 1990 | 1993 | 1996 | 1998 (est) |
| East Asia and the Pacific | 26.6 | 27.6 | 25.2 | 14.9 | 15.3 |
| (excluding China) | 23.9 | 18.5 | 15.9 | 10.0 | 11.3 |
| Eastern Europe/Central Asia | 0.2 | 1.6 | 4.0 | 5.1 | 5.1 |
| Latin America/Caribbean | 15.3 | 16.8 | 15.3 | 15.6 | 15.6 |
| Middle East/North Africa | 4.3 | 2.4 | 1.9 | 1.8 | 1.9 |
| South Asia | 44.9 | 44.0 | 42.4 | 42.3 | 40.0 |
| Sub-Saharan Africa | 46.6 | 47.7 | 49.7 | 48.5 | 46.3 |
| Total | 28.3 | 29.0 | 28.1 | 24.5 | 24.0 |
| (excluding China) | 28.5 | 28.1 | 27.7 | 27.0 | 26.2 |
| Percentage of poor at $2 per day | 61.0 | 61.7 | 60.1 | 56.1 | 56.0 |

**Source:** The World Bank; Poverty Fact Sheets. Accessed on 31 May 2000, at www.worldbank.org/html/extdr/pb/pbpoverty.htm.

**Table 1.2**

**Percentage of people living on less than US$1 per day in developing and transitional economies, selected years, 1987–1998**

---

### Box 1.2 Feeding the cities: urban food supply and distribution

Urban expansion and issues of food supply and distribution to and in the cities have four major consequences for urban food security. The first is the competition between demands for land needed for housing, industry and infrastructure and land needed for agricultural production within and around cities. Agriculturally productive lands are likely to be lost in this competition.

The second consequence is the increasing quantities of food that must be brought into cities and distributed within the expanding urban areas (see table). This means more trucks coming into cities, contributing to traffic congestion and air pollution. It also means additional stress on existing food distribution infrastructure and facilities, most of which are already inefficient, unhygienic and environmentally unfriendly.

The third consequence is the modification of consumption habits and food purchasing behaviours. Consumers in urban areas – who generally pay up to 30 per cent more for their food compared with their rural counterparts – have less time to spend preparing food. Therefore, the demand for more convenience and processed meals increases, raising issues of food quality and safety in terms of the use of appropriate inputs, particularly safe water, in food processing.

The final consequence for urban food security is the likelihood that low-income urban households will reside further and further away from food markets, often in slums that do not have water, roads or electricity. Since these households are also less likely to have refrigerators, they face additional time and transport costs in accessing food daily.

As urban expansion continues apace, the overall cost of supplying, distributing and accessing food is likely to increase further and, with it, the number of urban households that are food-insecure. The challenge of feeding cities therefore lies in facilitating consumer access to food and ensuring that required investments are forthcoming for increasing food production, processing and distribution capacities and services under hygienic, healthy and environmentally sound conditions.

**Expected level of food consumption in selected cities, 2000 and 2010 (1000 t)**

| City | 2000 | 2010 |
|------|------|------|
| Yaoundé | 3,030 | 5,752 |
| Nairobi | 4,805 | 7,984 |
| Isfahan | 13,000 | 20,500 |
| Karachi | 41,800 | 63,900 |
| Lima | 19,276 | 24,567 |
| Port-au-Prince | 2,934 | 4,450 |
| Managua | 2,782 | 4,075 |

**Source:** Food and Agriculture Organization of the United Nations, FAOSTAT and Food into Cities (2000).
**Note:** Data are based on national food consumption averages.

**Source:** from a publication of the International Food Policy Research Institute (IFPRI) 2020 Vision for Food, Agriculture, and the Environment (www.ifpri.org/2020/welcome.htm) – an initiative to feed the world, reduce poverty and protect the environment (Argenti, 2000).

---

**Box 1.3 The underestimation of the scale and nature of urban poverty**

Most national and international estimates of the scale of poverty underestimate the scale and depth of urban poverty, because of unrealistic assumptions about the income level that urban inhabitants need to avoid poverty. Most estimates for the number of 'poor' people or people living in poverty are based on defining a poverty line (an income level that is said to be sufficient to meet a household's consumption needs) and then seeing how many households have incomes below this line. Thus the number of 'poor' people is greatly influenced by the income level at which the poverty line is set and governments and international agencies can increase or decrease the number of 'poor' people by changing this income level.

Many nations still have one poverty line that is applied to all areas within the nation. This assumes that the income needed to avoid poverty is the same everywhere, whether it is in rural areas, small urban centres or large cities. But in many urban settings, especially in the larger or more prosperous cities, the income needed by an individual or household to avoid poverty is higher than in most rural areas or in less prosperous smaller centres, especially where official provision for water, sanitation, education, health care and public transport are very inadequate and where the cost of buying, building or renting housing is particularly high (which is often linked to bureaucratic constraints on increased supply of land for housing).

The criteria used to define the poverty line often also fail to recognize the income needed to pay for *non-food* items. Income-based poverty lines are generally based on estimates of the cost of an 'adequate' diet with some minor additional amount added for non-food expenditures (for instance a 20 to 30 per cent upward adjustment from the cost of a 'food-basket' which is considered to constitute an adequate diet). This greatly underestimates the income needed to avoid many of the deprivations that are part of poverty including the income needed for secure and adequate quality accommodation with adequate provision for water, sanitation and garbage collection and also to meet the costs of transport, health care and keeping children at school. In many cities, renting a room takes 20–30 per cent of poor households' income, even though the quality of the accommodation may be inadequate. For city households who seek to keep down housing costs and live in informal settlements in peripheral locations, fares on public transport can take up 10–20 per cent of their income. Many households have such inadequate access to water and sanitation that paying vendors and paying for 'pay as you use' toilets takes up 5–20 per cent of income.

Most poverty lines also do not recognize the income needed to cover costs of education and health care. They often make no allowance for these costs, since they assume that there is free public provision. Yet keeping children at school can represent a high cost for low-income households; for instance having to pay for private provision when there is no public provision; or the payments that have to be made even when entry into a government school is free; for instance the cost of uniforms, school meals, school books and exam fees; or the informal payments often required from parents because public school funding is inadequate. Costs of access to health care and medicines can take up a significant proportion of low-income households' income, especially where public provision of health care is non-existent or of poor quality. And perhaps not surprisingly, poverty lines do not take into account the income needed for the bribes that so many low-income households have to pay to prevent their houses from being demolished or the goods they are selling on the street or in informal (illegal) stores being confiscated.

International poverty lines – such as the World Bank's US$1 a day poverty line – are even more misleading in that these imply that the income needed to avoid poverty is not only the same in all locations within a country but also the same across countries. This leads to a large underestimation as to the scale of 'income-poverty' since the income level needed to avoid poverty is much higher than US$1 a day in most large and/or prosperous cities.

A reliance only on income-based poverty lines to measure poverty also means that many other aspects of urban deprivation get missed or underestimated, including the following:

- *Inadequate, unstable or risky asset bases* (although with a recognition that there are different kinds of assets that help people to avoid poverty or its effects including assets that are important for generating or maintaining income, assets that help low-income people to cope with economic shocks or natural disasters – and avoid the need to take on onerous debt burdens – and assets that are important for limiting environmental hazards that can have serious health and economic costs).
- *Limited or no right to make demands within the political system or to get a fair response:* 'voicelessness and powerlessness' (often within a framework that does not guarantee civil and political rights – for instance the right to have representative government, the right to organize and to make demands and to get a fair response, the right to justice – which includes protection against forced eviction and corruption).
- *Poor quality/insecure housing and lack of basic infrastructure* including insecure tenure and inadequate provision for safe and sufficient water, sanitation and drainage (with the immense health burden that this imposes and the high economic and other costs this also brings); although higher incomes generally allow households to find more secure and better quality accommodation.
- *Inadequate basic services* including good quality education, health care, emergency services and protection from crime and violence.
- *Discrimination* in, for instance, labour markets and access to services, political representation and justice. This includes the discrimination that women face in labour markets and access to property, credit and services. It also includes the discrimination faced by certain groups based on their race or caste.

**Source:** Satterthwaite, background paper.
**Notes:** See for example Kanji, 1995; Pryer, 1993.

---

economic growth and the reduction of poverty. Table 1.4 summarizes information from the World Bank Development Indicators. The Gini Index is a commonly used indicator of inequality.[83] Although it presents an overall picture, it is less effective in conveying what is happening at the extremes of the distribution. Therefore, additional information is provided by figures showing the proportion of income received by the highest and lowest deciles of the population.

The indicators in Table 1.4 confirm the generally high levels of inequality found in countries in Latin America and the Caribbean. Inequality is high, as well, in many African nations and in the Russian Federation. In so far as data permit, the next section further examines trends observed in various world regions.

● **The developing countries**

Data on poverty and inequality trends in the developing world are scarce and incomplete. However, the information that is available indicates, on the whole, little improvement or worsening of conditions. A recent study of the distributional effects of IMF programmes in 39 developing countries found a significant sharpening of income inequality and a deterioration of incomes of the poor in the countries most in need of external financing to address prior balance of payments problems.[84]

In Latin America, a quarter of all national income is received by a mere 5 per cent of the population, and the top 10 per cent own 40 per cent of the wealth. Income distribution, which had become more equal during the 1970s, worsened considerably in the 1980s and remained stagnant in the 1990s, despite positive growth rates throughout the decade.[85] The region's income distribution is the most inequitable in the world, with the poorest 20 per cent earning a mere 3.5 per cent of total income. The figure is 5.2 per cent in Africa and 8.8 per cent in Eastern Europe and Southeast Asia.[86] Data from the United Nations Economic Council for Latin America (UNECLA) show that while the proportion of the urban poor in Latin America and the Caribbean fell during the 1990s, in 1997 the proportion of urban households in poverty and in extreme poverty was still higher than it was in 1980 and the absolute number of poor people living in cities increased. Over the last 20 years, the number of the poor has risen by 40 million to 180 million, equalling 36 per cent of the population. Of those, 78 million live in extreme poverty, unable to afford even a basic daily diet. The poverty rate is 80 per cent among the region's 30 million indigenous people, who are concentrated in Bolivia, Ecuador, Guatemala, Mexico and Peru.[87] During the 1990s, the Gini coefficient for urban household income inequality increased in 12 Latin American countries and declined only in Bolivia, Honduras and Uruguay.[88]

Many African countries are also characterized by very high levels of inequality. The continent faces difficult development challenges. It is the poorest region in the world, with an average income per capita of US$315 in 1997.[89] More than 40 per cent of Africa's 600 million people live below the internationally recognized poverty line of US$1 per day.[90] Deteriorating economic conditions during the 1970s brought about declines in urban incomes. Subsequent Structural Adjustment Policies (SAPs) served to further impoverish a majority of urban households and to newly impoverish a new class of junior public sector employees. At the end of the 1990s, African output per capita was lower than it was 30 years before.[91] During this period, its share of world trade fell to just 2 per cent. Most African countries are still exporters of primary commodities and are deeply indebted, with foreign debt representing more than 80 per cent of GDP in 1997.[92] Investment and savings per capita have declined since 1970, averaging 30 per cent of GDP in the 1990s.[93] Declining wage levels and increasing prices of food and services have combined to result in a widespread deterioration in standards of living. However, the pattern is not uniform across Africa. Broadly speaking, the countries of tropical sub-Saharan Africa have experienced the severest declines, but in some of these countries, drought and wars have been as or more important than economic policies. About one in five Africans live in countries formally at war or severely disrupted by conflict.[94] The mortality rate is increasing and now stands at 165 per 100,000, compared with 107 in 1970.[95] AIDS is

expected to reduce life expectancy by up to 20 years in the most affected countries.[96] Recession and adjustment seem to have had less dramatic effects on Northern and Southern African countries.[97]

Recent data on income distribution in Asian countries are scarce. An IMF study of trends in selected countries from the early 1970s through the early 1990s showed some improvement in Indonesia, the Philippines and Malaysia, but found considerable increases in income inequality in Sri Lanka, Bangladesh, India, Singapore, Thailand and Pakistan.[98] A recent analysis of the impacts of structural adjustment reforms in Pakistan reveals persistent poverty and inequality and moribund social safety nets.[99] These findings pre-date the Asian financial crisis at the end of the 1990s, which has thrown existing inequalities into sharper relief.

Since 1978, China has implemented influential economic reforms. For example, export firms were allowed to retain a proportion of foreign exchanges, which were previously entirely controlled by the central government. After 1980, Foreign Direct Investment (FDI) grew about 35 per cent per annum, making China in 1996 the second largest recipient of FDI, after the United States. In 1998, China's foreign exchange reserve was more than US$140,000 million, second only to that of Japan. The export-oriented development strategy articulated by Deng Xiaoping led to rapid economic growth. GDP more than quadrupled. Per capita disposable incomes more than tripled in the cities and almost quadrupled in the rural areas.

However, rapid economic growth also brought about growing income inequality, which slowed down poverty reduction. Before the economic reforms that started with the open-door policy in 1978, China was one of the most egalitarian economies in the world.[100] But between 1981 and 1995, the Gini coefficient, a widely used measure of inequality, increased from 28.8 to 38.8.

### ● The countries with economies in transition

In the formerly centrally planned economies, ownership of assets was concentrated in the state, earnings inequality in the dominant state sector was low and public policies were designed to limit income differences.[101] Inequality did exist, based not on market dynamics but as a function of differentially privileged positioning in channels of bureaucratic resource allocation; the party cadre, the leading intelligentsia, the upper echelon of the military and top security officers, managers of large state enterprises and elite

| Year | Coefficient of variation |
|------|--------------------------|
| 1980 | 0.7575 |
| 1985 | 0.7867 |
| 1990 | 0.8083 |
| 1995 | 0.8291 |
| 1996 | 0.8294 |
| 1980s | 0.7789 |
| 1990s | 0.8210 |

**Source:** Kanbur and Lustig, 1999.

**Table 1.3**

**Coefficient of variation of GDP per capita across countries**

| Country | Gini Index | Lowest 10% | Highest 10% | Survey year |
|---|---|---|---|---|
| Slovakia | 19.5 | 5.1 | 18.2 | 1992c,d |
| Belarus | 21.7 | 5.1 | 20.0 | 1998a,b |
| Austria | 23.1 | 4.4 | 19.3 | 1987c,d |
| Denmark | 24.7 | 3.6 | 20.5 | 1992c,d |
| Japan | 24.9 | 4.8 | 21.7 | 1993c,d |
| Belgium | 25.0 | 3.7 | 20.2 | 1992c,d |
| Sweden | 25.0 | 3.7 | 20.1 | 1992c,d |
| Czech Republic | 25.4 | 4.3 | 22.4 | 1996c,d |
| Finland | 25.6 | 4.2 | 21.6 | 1991c,d |
| Norway | 25.8 | 4.1 | 21.8 | 1995c,d |
| Croatia | 26.8 | 4.0 | 21.6 | 1998a,b |
| Slovenia | 26.8 | 3.2 | 20.7 | 1995c,d |
| Luxembourg | 26.9 | 4.0 | 22.0 | 1994c,d |
| Italy | 27.3 | 3.5 | 21.8 | 1995c,d |
| Romania | 28.2 | 3.7 | 22.7 | 1994c,d |
| Bulgaria | 28.3 | 3.4 | 22.5 | 1995a,b |
| Egypt | 28.9 | 4.4 | 25.0 | 1995a,b |
| Rwanda | 28.9 | 4.2 | 24.2 | 1983–85a,b |
| Germany | 30.0 | 3.3 | 23.7 | 1994c,d |
| Lao PDR | 30.4 | 4.2 | 26.4 | 1992a,b |
| Hungary | 30.8 | 3.9 | 24.8 | 1996c,d |
| Pakistan | 31.2 | 4.1 | 27.6 | 1996–97a,b |
| Canada | 31.5 | 2.8 | 23.8 | 1994c,d |
| Korea, Republic of | 31.6 | 2.9 | 24.3 | 1993a,b |
| Latvia | 32.4 | 2.9 | 25.9 | 1998c,d |
| Lithuania | 32.4 | 3.1 | 25.6 | 1996a,b |
| Spain | 32.5 | 2.8 | 25.2 | 1990c,d |
| Ukraine | 32.5 | 3.9 | 26.4 | 1996a,b |
| The Netherlands | 32.6 | 2.8 | 25.1 | 1994 |
| France | 32.7 | 2.8 | 25.1 | 1995c,d |
| Ghana | 32.7 | 3.6 | 26.1 | 1997a,b |
| Greece | 32.7 | 3.0 | 25.3 | 1993c,d |
| Poland | 32.9 | 3.0 | 26.3 | 1996c,d |
| Switzerland | 33.1 | 2.6 | 25.2 | 1992c,d |
| Mongolia | 33.2 | 2.9 | 24.5 | 1995a,b |
| Burundi | 33.3 | 3.4 | 26.6 | 1992a,b |
| Uzbekistan | 33.3 | 3.1 | 25.2 | 1993c,d |
| Bangladesh | 33.6 | 3.9 | 28.6 | 1995–96a,b |
| Republic of Moldova | 34.4 | 2.7 | 25.8 | 1992c,d |
| Sri Lanka | 34.4 | 3.5 | 28.0 | 1995a,b |
| Australia | 35.2 | 2.0 | 25.4 | 1994c,d |
| Algeria | 35.3 | 2.8 | 26.8 | 1995a,b |
| Estonia | 35.4 | 2.2 | 26.2 | 1995c,d |
| Kazakhstan | 35.4 | 2.7 | 26.3 | 1996a,b |
| Israel | 35.5 | 2.8 | 26.9 | 1992c,d |
| Portugal | 35.6 | 3.1 | 28.4 | 1994–95c,d |
| Ireland | 35.9 | 2.5 | 27.4 | 1987c,d |
| United Kingdom | 36.1 | 2.6 | 27.3 | 1991c,d |
| Viet Nam | 36.1 | 3.6 | 29.9 | 1998a,b |
| Jamaica | 36.4 | 2.9 | 28.9 | 1996a,b |
| Jordan | 36.4 | 3.3 | 29.8 | 1997a,b |
| Indonesia | 36.5 | 3.6 | 30.3 | 1996c,d |
| Côte d'Ivoire | 36.7 | 3.1 | 28.8 | 1995a,b |
| Nepal | 36.7 | 3.2 | 29.8 | 1995–96a,b |
| India | 37.8 | 3.5 | 33.5 | 1997a,b |
| United Republic of Tanzania | 38.2 | 2.8 | 30.1 | 1993a,b |
| Mauritania | 38.9 | 2.3 | 29.9 | 1995a,b |
| Uganda | 39.2 | 2.6 | 31.2 | 1992–93a,b |

| Country | Gini Index | Lowest 10% | Highest 10% | Survey year |
|---|---|---|---|---|
| Morocco | 39.5 | 2.6 | 30.9 | 1998–99a,b |
| Yemen | 39.5 | 2.3 | 30.8 | 1992a,b |
| Mozambique | 39.6 | 2.5 | 31.7 | 1996–97a,b |
| Ethiopia | 40.0 | 3.0 | 33.7 | 1995a,b |
| Guyana | 40.2 | 2.4 | 32.0 | 1993a,b |
| Tunisia | 40.2 | 2.3 | 30.7 | 1990a,b |
| Trinidad and Tobago | 40.3 | 2.1 | 29.9 | 1992c,d |
| China | 40.3 | 2.4 | 30.4 | 1998c,d |
| Guinea | 40.3 | 2.6 | 32.0 | 1994a,b |
| Cambodia | 40.4 | 2.9 | 33.8 | 1997a,b |
| Kyrgyztan | 40.5 | 2.7 | 31.7 | 1997c,d |
| Turkmenistan | 40.8 | 2.6 | 31.7 | 1998a,b |
| United States | 40.8 | 1.8 | 30.5 | 1997c,d |
| Senegal | 41.3 | 2.6 | 33.5 | 1995a,b |
| Thailand | 41.4 | 2.8 | 32.4 | 1998a,b |
| Turkey | 41.5 | 2.3 | 32.3 | 1994a,b |
| Bolivia | 42.0 | 2.3 | 31.7 | 1990c,d |
| Uruguay | 42.3 | 2.1 | 32.7 | 1989c,d |
| Saint Lucia | 42.6 | 2.0 | 32.5 | 1995c,d |
| Ecuador | 43.7 | 2.2 | 33.8 | 1995a,b |
| New Zealand | 43.9 | 0.3 | 29.8 | 1991c,d |
| Kenya | 44.5 | 1.8 | 34.9 | 1994a,b |
| Madagascar | 46.0 | 1.9 | 36.7 | 1993a,b |
| Peru | 46.2 | 1.6 | 35.4 | 1996c,d |
| Philippines | 46.2 | 2.3 | 36.6 | 1997a,b |
| Costa Rica | 47.0 | 1.3 | 34.7 | 1996c,d |
| Gambia | 47.8 | 1.5 | 37.6 | 1992a,b |
| Burkina Faso | 48.2 | 2.2 | 39.5 | 1994a,b |
| Malaysia | 48.5 | 1.8 | 37.9 | 1995c,d |
| Panama | 48.5 | 1.2 | 35.7 | 1997c,d |
| Dominican Republic | 48.7 | 1.7 | 37.8 | 1996c,d |
| Russian Federation | 48.7 | 1.7 | 38.7 | 1998a,b |
| Venezuela | 48.8 | 1.3 | 37.0 | 1996c,d |
| Zambia | 49.8 | 1.6 | 39.2 | 1996a,b |
| Nicaragua | 50.3 | 1.6 | 39.8 | 1993a,b |
| Mali | 50.5 | 1.8 | 40.4 | 1994a,b |
| Niger | 50.5 | 0.8 | 35.4 | 1995a,b |
| Nigeria | 50.6 | 1.6 | 40.8 | 1996–97a,b |
| Papua New Guinea | 50.9 | 1.7 | 40.5 | 1996a,b |
| El Salvador | 52.3 | 1.2 | 40.5 | 1996c,d |
| Honduras | 53.7 | 1.2 | 42.1 | 1996c,d |
| Mexico | 53.7 | 1.4 | 42.8 | 1995c,d |
| Lesotho | 56.0 | 0.9 | 43.4 | 1986–87a,b |
| Guinea-Bissau | 56.2 | 0.5 | 42.2 | 1991a,b |
| Chile | 56.5 | 1.4 | 46.1 | 1994c,d |
| Zimbabwe | 56.8 | 1.8 | 46.9 | 1990–91a,b |
| Colombia | 57.1 | 1.1 | 46.1 | 1996c,d |
| Paraguay | 59.1 | 0.7 | 46.6 | 1995c,d |
| South Africa | 59.3 | 1.1 | 45.9 | 1993–94a,b |
| Guatemala | 59.6 | 0.6 | 46.6 | 1989c,d |
| Brazil | 60.0 | 0.9 | 47.6 | 1996c,d |
| Swaziland | 60.9 | 1.0 | 50.2 | 1994c,d |
| Central African Republic | 61.3 | 0.7 | 47.7 | 1993a,b |
| Sierra Leone | 62.9 | 0.5 | 43.6 | 1989a,b |

**Source:** Data selected from World Bank Development Indicators 2000. Countries not shown were excluded for lack of data.

**Notes:** a Expenditure shares by percentiles of population. b Ranked by per capita expenditure. c Income shares by percentiles of population. d Ranked by per capita income.

**Table 1.4**

**Income inequality by country**

athletes were known to receive preferential treatment.[102] However, levels of income inequality were significantly lower than in OECD countries.[103] Given the initial conditions at the start of the transition, it is not surprising that liberalization and the introduction of market processes would lead to greater income inequality.[104] However, not all countries follow the same trend.

The transition economies in Central and Eastern Europe have experienced contrasting outcomes regarding income distribution since the late 1980s. Some, like

Slovakia, have maintained the relatively equal income distributions that were present at the beginning of the transition with government policies offsetting unevenness in wages. Others, like Russia, have seen dramatic increases in income inequality, which have combined with declines in total output to raise poverty rates sharply.[105] Causes of growing inequality include:

- asset redistribution, chiefly through privatization;
- liberalization of prices and, in some contexts, redistribution resulting from inflation tax and macroeconomic instability;
- liberalization of wage setting, tolerance of unemployment and changes in labour market institutions;
- shifts in the level and structure of public spending, including spending on transfers, education and health;
- tax reforms, generally a reduction of tax rates, aimed at raising incentives for firms and individuals; and
- trade liberalization, exposing technological obsolescence and associated lack of skills among workers.[106]

Recent studies of transition economies found that income inequality is positively correlated with the share of output in the informal economy, although the causality of this relationship may operate in both directions. An increasingly large informal economy may contribute to greater inequality due to weakened social safety nets eroded by falling tax revenues. This greater inequality wears away solidarity and trust, which may lead people to hide formal economic activities from the government to avoid onerous regulations, evade taxes, to engage in bribery, or other criminal activities that undermine the legitimacy and functioning of the system.[107] At the same time, trade liberalization and technological change have affected the relative demand for types of labour. In this light, policies aimed at increasing adaptability – for example, improving skills acquisition and the quality of the educational system – become more important in dampening wage inequality. However, developments in the Central and Eastern European States (CEES) are in the opposite direction, pointing to the probability of persistent inequality in the future.[108]

## ● The industrialized countries

A comparison of wage inequality in OECD countries during the 1980s and 1990s shows divergent patterns. The US and the UK experienced sharp increases in inequality. There was also a pronounced increase in inequality in New Zealand, following substantial deregulation of that country's product and labour markets. There were modest rises in inequality in Canada and Japan and declines in Sweden and Germany.[109] Various studies indicate that inequality in earnings income among Australian households increased during the 1980s and 1990s. However, research also suggests that these increases in inequality in the distribution of market income over this period were fully offset by increases in the progressivity in the tax/transfer system.[110]

The pattern of demand shifts for more skilled workers appears to be relatively similar in more developed economies, although not all OECD nations have experienced sharp increases in wage dispersion and educational wage differentials similar to the US since the end of the 1970s. Declines in the growth of relative skill supplies have been more pronounced in countries with the largest increases in educational wage differentials and overall wage inequality (the US and the UK). Differences in labour market institutions have also influenced the recent pattern of wage inequality changes in OECD countries.[111] Countries where unions, employer federations and government agencies play a larger role in wage determination had smaller increases in inequality than the US. A comparison with Canada is instructive because the labour market impacts from changes in trade and technology have probably been similar to those in the US. The decline of relative skill supply in the US, but not in Canada, offers a partial explanation for the larger increases in wage inequality seen in the former. In addition, the US has experienced much more deunionization. The relationship between the decreasing influence of wage-setting institutions and increasing wage inequality is also apparent in the UK (declining unionization in the 1980s), Sweden (shift from peak-level bargaining to more company- and industry-based settlement in the mid-1980s), and Italy (end of government intervention in wage setting through the *scala mobil*, ensuring automatic cost-of-living adjustments, in the early 1990s).[112]

The reason for the rise in inequality in the developed countries is not a simple one. In general, there has been an increase in the demand for skilled labour, relative to unskilled labour. The underlying cause of this shift involves aspects of globalization and technological change. In this connection, greater opening up of trade can lead to greater disparities. Many traded goods are intermediate inputs that substitute for unskilled labour more readily than for skilled labour, so that when trade lowers their prices, the demand for unskilled workers falls relative to that for skilled workers. Inequality is also increased by technological change that raises the quality of capital goods and the complementary need for skilled labour.[113]

*The Human Development Report 1999*[114] ranks Canada first among 174 countries included in its Human Development Index,[115] while the US is tied for second place.[116]

> During the recent period, the US and Canada have experienced strong economic growth. However, this economic growth happened at the same time that poverty increased and existing inequalities deepened

Both countries fare very well according to most indicators used to calculate the index. During the recent period, both countries have experienced strong economic growth. However, this economic growth happened at the same time that poverty increased and existing inequalities deepened.[117] Thus, both countries are also examples of how aggregate numbers may reveal little and obscure much about large differences underlying the summary statistics. Because the US strongly influences the policies of other countries, it is of interest to examine its own domestic situation in some detail.

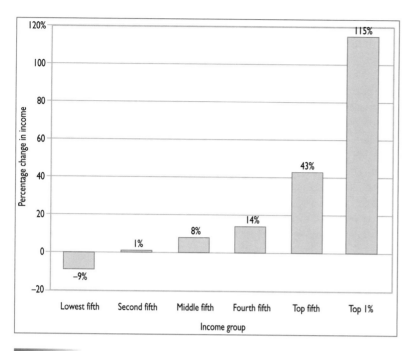

**Figure 1.1**

**Percentage change in after-tax income, 1977–1999 (US)**

**Source:** CBPP Analysis of CBO Data. 1999 data are projections

- In 1995, the wealthiest 1 per cent of households owned 39 per cent of the nation's wealth. By contrast, 1 per cent of US households with the highest incomes received about 13 per cent of the nation's after-tax income. The share of the nation's wealth possessed by the top 1 per cent is thus three times as large as their already large share of national income.
- The wealthiest 20 per cent of households owned 84 per cent of the nation's wealth in 1995. By comparison, the 20 per cent of households with the highest incomes receive a little more than 50 per cent of the national after-tax income.
- The bottom 80 per cent of households owned only 16 per cent of the nation's wealth, significantly less than half of what the wealthiest 1 per cent of the population possessed.
- Wealth was more concentrated among the top 1 per cent and top 20 per cent of households in 1995 than at any time since the Depression.

The concentration of wealth and after-tax income is shown in Figure 1.2.

The Center on Budget and Policy Priorities[118] is a leading non-partisan research organization and policy institute that conducts studies of a range of government policies and programmes in the US, with an emphasis on those affecting low- and moderate-income households. In a recent report, *The Widening Income Gulf*,[119] analysing data from the Congressional Budget Office (CBO),[120] the Center observes that the after-tax income gaps between those with the highest incomes and other households have widened sharply since 1977 and reached the widest point in recent decades (Figure 1.1).[121] The average after-tax income of the richest 1 per cent of the population more than doubled between 1977 and 1999, rising 115 per cent after adjusting for inflation. But the average after-tax income for households in the middle of the income scale increased by only 8 per cent over this 22-year period, an average real gain of less than 0.5 per cent per year, while the average income of the poorest fifth of all households fell. The analysis found that the richest 1 per cent of households had as much after-tax income in 1999 as the 38 per cent with the lowest incomes.

The report also examined data on wealth in US society and found that its distribution is even more skewed than that of income.[122] For example:

Data from different sources produce similar findings on income and wealth inequality, including a study by the US Congress's Joint Committee on Taxation,[123] and from two recent reports by the nonprofit organization 'United for a Fair Economy'[124] entitled *Shifting Fortunes: The Perils of the Growing American Wealth Gap*[125] and *Divided Decade: Economic Disparity at the Century's Turn*.[126]

What is noteworthy about the US situation is that a strong economic expansion has gone hand-in-hand with persistent poverty as well as widening economic disparities. This is significant in that the US is greatly influential in shaping international approaches to development. It is of interest to review recent Canadian trends, which show several similarities, but also important differences compared with the developments in the US.

*Falling Behind: The State of Working Canada 2000*,[127] a report by the Canadian Centre for Policy Alternatives,[128] highlights the following long-term socio-economic trends in Canadian society, ranked first in the United Nations Human Development Index:[129]

- Real, personal, disposable (after tax) income per person fell by an average of 0.33 per cent per year in the 1990s; in 1999, real, personal, disposable income per Canadian was 3.3 per cent lower than in 1989.
- Between 1981 and 1995, only the top 10 per cent of male earners experienced any increase at all in their real annual earnings (up 6.2 per cent over the entire period). The real annual earnings of the bottom 90 per cent of men fell, and they fell the most for lower earners, with the real annual earnings of the bottom 10 per cent of men falling by 31.7 per cent.
- Between 1980 and 1996, because of flat or falling wages and rising unemployment, lower income families came to rely more on transfer payments from governments (unemployment insurance, social assistance, public pensions, etc). Transfer payments

**Figure 1.2**

**Shares of after-tax income versus shares of wealth (US)**

**Source:** Wolff wealth data and CBPP analysis of CBO after-tax income data

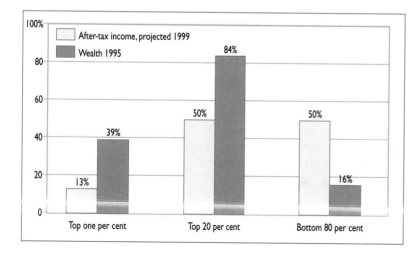

made up 59 per cent of the income of the lowest income 20 per cent of Canadian families in 1996, up from 46 per cent in 1980; and 25 per cent of the income of the next 20 per cent of families in 1996, compared with 14 per cent in 1980.

- Transfer payments make a huge difference to income inequality. In 1997, the most affluent 20 per cent of Canadian families had 21 times the income of the bottom 20 per cent when only pre-tax 'market' income (wages, salaries and investment income) is considered, but just five times as much income after taxes and transfers had redistributed income.
- The overall poverty rate in Canada rose from 16 per cent in 1980 to 17.5 per cent in 1997. However, this was the combined result of declining rates of poverty among the elderly (down from 34 per cent to 19 per cent) because of improvements to public pensions, and of increasing poverty rates for younger families with heads aged 25 to 34 (up from 12 per cent to 19 per cent). As a result, the child poverty rate also rose, from 16 per cent to 20 per cent. Child poverty rates have remained stubbornly high even during the 1990s recovery because of deep cuts to social assistance and unemployment insurance benefits.
- Job growth in the 1990s was, until very late in the decade, heavily tilted towards 'precarious' jobs. Between 1989 and 1998, the total number of self-employed workers grew by 40 per cent, part-time paid jobs grew by 16 per cent, and full-time paid jobs grew by just 2 per cent; 70 per cent of the increase in self-employment was in 'own account' businesses with no employees.
- Between 1989 and 1997, the average 'market' income of Canadian families from wages, salaries, self-employment earnings and investments (adjusted for inflation) fell from Can$53,937 to Can$50,672, and average family income after taxes and government transfers fell by 5.6 per cent from Can$48,311 to Can$45,605. Poorer families experienced the most serious decline in both market and after-tax/transfer incomes. The real after-tax/transfer incomes of the least well-off 40 per cent of families with children fell by 12 per cent over this period.
- Between 1990 and 1998, private health care spending per person rose by 19.6 per cent to Can$733, while public health care spending per person fell by 5.1 per cent to Can$1680. As a result, the private share of all health care spending rose from 24 per cent to 30 per cent. Over the same period, undergraduate tuition fees rose by 126 per cent.

The richest 1 per cent of the US population now own more personal wealth than the bottom 95 per cent combined. Responsible Wealth is a network of over 450 business people, professionals, investors and other affluent top income earners and asset holders, affiliated with United for a Fair Economy, a nonprofit organization concerned about growing inequality. In 1997, they pledged the proceeds of their capital gains tax cut to support groups working for a fairer tax system and economic justice and developing initiatives that improve access to health care and education as well as programmes to help low-income households build assets that will enable them to own a home or small business.

Since 1990, average worker pay increased 28 per cent, just slightly above inflation, while CEO pay rose 481 per cent. In 1999 alone, average CEO compensation jumped 23 per cent, while average, full-time worker pay increased a mere 3 per cent. Members of Responsible Wealth have also embarked on a campaign filing shareholder resolutions to bring about a fairer distribution of wages:

- Linking CEO and average worker pay according to a maximum ratio to reduce growing disparities.
- Freezing CEO pay during periods of downsizing and cost cutting.
- Conducting pay equity audits to identify and correct violations of pay equity legislation, exposing discriminators to adverse publicity and legal liabilities.
- Broadening ownership by increasing the number of shares held by employees, which has been associated with both faster economic growth and lower worker turnover, and which will help bridge the wage gap.
- Reforming corporate governance by holding real elections with multiple candidates for board positions, including representatives from employees and the community.
- Publishing corporate lobbying expenses and listing political contributions in order to respect the shareholders' right to know how their money is spent.
- Disclosing corporate welfare by reporting the extent and ways that a company's profits are tied to tax abatements, below-market financing and other government subsidies.

**Source:** Responsible Wealth (www.responsiblewealth.org), a project of United for a Fair Economy (www.ufenet.org/).

As can be seen from Table 1.5, unlike in the US, the rise in Canadian family income inequality is not due to an increase in the earnings of the highest paid, but reflects a sharp drop in incomes among the lowest quintile.

Table 1.6 presents a comparison of the overall distribution of disposable (after-tax and transfer) income for a number of advanced industrialized countries for the most recent years for which data are available.[130] The US clearly emerges as the most unequal society, with the top decile of households having incomes almost six times greater than the bottom decile. By this same measure, the Scandinavian and Benelux countries stand at the high-equality end of a wide income distribution spectrum, with the UK and the US standing at the other end. The US and the UK also have a relatively much less well-off middle class. Further, the table shows similar dramatic differences in the child poverty rate, ranging from 2.7 per cent in Sweden to 22.7 per cent in the US.

| | 1973 $ | 1984 $ | 1990 $ | 1996 $ | % change 1973–90 | % change 1990–96 |
|---|---|---|---|---|---|---|
| **Bottom 5th** | | | | | | |
| Decile 1 | 5204 | 2062 | 2760 | 435 | –47 | –84 |
| Decile 2 | 19,562 | 14,930 | 16,599 | 11,535 | +15 | +31 |
| **Top 5th** | | | | | | |
| Decile 9 | 71,611 | 79,628 | 88,426 | 86,497 | +23 | –2 |
| Decile 10 | 107,253 | 123,752 | 134,539 | 136,737 | +25 | +2 |

**Source:** Statistics Canada *Survey of Consumer Finance* data from Armine Yalnizyan, *The Growing Gap*, Centre for Social Justice, October, 1998.

Table 1.5

**Average Canadian family income before transfers, 1973–1996; families with children (Can$1996)**

| | Top/bottom decile | Bottom as % middle | Top as % middle | Child poverty rate (%) |
|---|---|---|---|---|
| US | 6.44 | 34 | 219 | 22.7 |
| Canada | 3.93 | 47 | 185 | 13.9 |
| UK | 4.56 | 46 | 210 | 17.9 |
| Germany (W) | 3.84 | 46 | 177 | 8.7 |
| France | 4.11 | 45 | 185 | 7.5 |
| The Netherlands | 3.05 | 57 | 173 | 4.1 |
| Sweden | 2.78 | 57 | 159 | 2.7 |
| Industrial country average | 3.53 | 52 | 181 | na |

**Source:** Luxembourg Income Study data in Timothy Smeeding. 'Income Inequality: Is Canada Different or Just Behind the Times?' Paper presented to the 1999 meeting of the Canadian Economics Association.

**Table 1.6**

**National income distributions compared**

The distribution of income and poverty in countries is determined by two main forces: the primary distribution of income by the market and the subsequent reshaping of this distribution by governments through taxes and income transfers. Table 1.7 provides an indication of the different roles played by the tax/transfer system in different countries. It shows the proportion of the population who fall below the poverty line, defined as half the median income, before and after transfers. In the US, the poverty rate of all households is reduced by less than one-third. However, in Canada, the poverty rate is cut in half by transfers, from 22.9 per cent to 11.2 per cent. In Germany, France and Sweden, the transfers are even more significant, reducing poverty rates by 75–80 per cent. Similar or more striking reductions occur in families with children (Table 1.7). The pattern of rising wage inequality in the US is not offset by changes in non-wage compensation favouring low-wage workers.[131]

## Assessment of trends

The data just presented are important. They illustrate a key point: public policies can produce quite different living conditions.

> The record shows that different public policies produce different living conditions in countries with similar experiences of globalization and technological change

All of the countries considered above operate in similar contexts of globalization, including increased capital mobility, competition and trade liberalization. They all experience more or less the same pattern of technological change. Yet, as societies, they have created very different outcomes for their citizens. Clearly, globalization is not a mechanistic

**Table 1.7**

**National poverty rates: before and after the impact of transfers**

process with predetermined consequences. Greater inequality is not a foregone conclusion. Our task is to channel the potential of globalization towards the elimination of poverty, the reduction of inequality and the protection of our natural environment. To date, market-led approaches have failed to attain these goals. Elsewhere in this report, reasoned arguments make clear that the prospect that markets will be effective in the future is bleak at best.

> New forms of governance must take advantage of the combined capabilities and strengths of governments at various levels, market mechanisms and civil society networks. Such governance will not pit the poor against the rich, but develop the unrealized productive potential of the poor and recognize that policies supporting people living in poverty also benefit the rest of society

What we need, instead, are new forms of governance that take advantage of the combined capabilities and strengths of governments at various levels, market mechanisms and civil society networks. Such governance will use strategies that do not pit the poor against the rich, but that develop the unrealized productive potential of the poor and recognize that policies supporting people living in poverty also benefit the rest of society. People living in poverty have shown that they have the capacity to establish their priorities, mobilize resources and negotiate the terms and direction of local development with external public and private interests. Our first priority must be to support this capacity, especially by strengthening poor people's security of land and housing, assisting them in mobilizing these assets, and by improving their access to basic services such as safe water supply and sanitation.[132]

The World Bank estimates that the economies of developing countries will grow at 4 per cent per capita per annum until 2015. What are the implications of this growth rate for meeting the OECD's Development Assistance Committee (DAC) income-poverty target? As Figure 1.3 shows, if the 4 per cent growth rate is accompanied by low income inequality then the DAC target is easily met, and poverty is halved by 2006. If, on the other hand, high income inequality accompanies growth then the DAC target is not achieved. The 4 per cent growth rate forecast is optimistic to begin with.[133]

Higher rates of growth help, but only to a limited extent. The same figure shows that shifting from a high inequality to a low inequality growth path has a greater effect on poverty reduction than adding an extra 1 per cent to the growth rate. In fact, in the high-income inequality scenario it would require an extra 5 per cent growth (to make a total rate of 9 per cent) per capita per annum to meet the target. This growth rate would be without historical precedent. Even the Southeast Asian economies only grew 5.5 per cent per annum between 1965 and 1997.[134]

Recent econometric studies also appear to invert the conventional wisdom that inequality is good for growth. A review of this research develops the argument that inequality is bad for growth for three reasons. To begin with,

| | All households | | Two-adult working families with children | |
|---|---|---|---|---|
| | Before | After | Before | After |
| US | 25.3 | 17.7 | 15.4 | 12.7 |
| Canada | 22.9 | 11.2 | 12.6 | 6.4 |
| Germany | 22.1 | 5.5 | 3.1 | 1.5 |
| France | 34.5 | 8.2 | 18.7 | 2.1 |
| Sweden | 33.9 | 6.5 | 9.6 | 1.4 |

**Source:** OECD Economics Department Working Paper 189 Income Distribution and Poverty in Selected OECD Countries (1998). Tables 5.4, 5.7. Poverty defined as income less than half median.

conditions of inequality restrict the opportunities for productive investment by the poor, especially in human capital, more than they increase such opportunities for the rich. Inequality also discourages effort by poor borrowers. Finally, it creates credit cycles that amplify macroeconomic volatility.[135] The same viewpoint was recently expressed by World Bank president James Wolfensohn who stated that:

*'Growth did not reduce poverty (in Latin America and the Caribbean), and had little impact on inequality. High inequality sustains poverty, as smaller shares of total income reach those at the bottom. Inequality weakens the impact of growth on fighting poverty.'*[136]

**'High inequality sustains poverty, as smaller shares of total income reach those at the bottom. Inequality weakens the impact of growth on fighting poverty' – James Wolfensohn, Address to Western Hemisphere Finance Ministers Meeting, Cancun, 3 February 2000**

Chapter 15 in Part V discusses approaches to fight poverty and inequality. However, it is important here to make several observations to set the stage for later discussions. These observations include the incontrovertible facts that

- today, large numbers of people live in abject poverty and squalor;
- unprecedented economic growth has done little to reduce their number; and
- in many places, inequalities have sharply increased.

We cannot continue with business as usual if we are serious about tackling the root causes of poverty and inequality.

**We cannot continue with business as usual if we are serious about tackling the root causes of poverty and inequality. For the development of human settlements, the implication is that we must broaden our view of cities as engines of economic growth to include and emphasize a perspective that sees cities as agents of social change**

The preceding discussion has been concerned with providing a general socio-economic background within which to situate the more urban-focused analyses of subsequent chapters. It identified a number of significant trends relevant to poverty within cities which are highlighted by the following points:

- In many countries, real incomes have fallen, the costs of living have gone up and the number of poor households has grown, especially in cities. It is clear that future urbanization in developing countries will

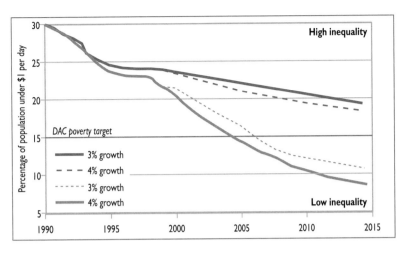

**Global poverty in 2015: effects of growth and inequality**

**Source:** Maxwell and Hammer, 1999

be accompanied by a shift in the concentration of poverty from rural to urban areas, a phenomenon which has been described as the 'urbanization of poverty'. Already, more than three-quarters of the poor in Latin America live in cities; other developing world regions are likely to follow the same path.

- Poverty should not be seen narrowly in terms of income in relation to costs of living. The ability to maintain a minimum standard of living also depends on access to basic services such as safe drinking water, sanitation and waste collection and disposal, all of which have important effects on health. Millions of urban dwellers do not have access to these services. In view of this, it is clear that the effectiveness with which urban infrastructure and services, and human settlements in general, are managed has significant implications for poverty eradication.
- Urban poverty, including food insecurity and malnourishment, are not restricted to the developing world. Therefore, it is important to stress that economic growth does not guarantee their elimination. Despite a booming economy, hunger and homelessness in the US have increased. Research has shown that decreasing income inequality can have as much impact on reducing poverty as increasing economic growth.

For the development of human settlements, the implication of the above trends is that we must broaden our view of cities as simply engines of economic growth to include and emphasize a perspective that sees cities as agents of social change. Such a perspective entails first the articulation of appropriate new normative agendas. The United Nations world conferences of the 1990s, reviewed in Chapter 3, were an important catalyst in this regard. Now is the time for *implementation* of these agendas.

# Notes

1 Today, more than 47 per cent of the world's population lives in cities. The actual transition to 50 per cent urban is expected to occur in 2007, while projections show that 56 per cent of the global population will be urban by 2020. Figures from United Nations, Population Division, 2000, pp 1–3 and Table A.2.

2 A detailed critique of this assumption is contained in the second part of this chapter.

3 For a detailed treatment of the impact of ICTs on the divided city, see further on in this same chapter.

4 The following section draws on a paper prepared by Stephen Graham, University of Newcastle (see Background Papers).

5 See Wellman, 1999.

6 Castells, 1999a.

7 Graham and Marvin, 1996.

8 Castells, 1996; 1998; 1999a.

9 Skeates, 1997.

10 Picon, 1998.

11 See Graham and Marvin, 1996, Chapter 2.

12 See, for example, the recent synthesis by Wheeler et al, 2000.

13 Graham, 1998.

14 Swyngedouw, 1992, p 322.

15 UNDP, 1999, p 63

16 Ibid, p 62.

17 Ibid, p 62.

18 Goslee, 1998.

19 NTIA, 1999.

20 Ibid.

21 Goslee, 1998.

22 Cited in Goslee, 1998.

23 See Braczyk et al, 1999.

24 Rothstein, 1998.

25 Borsook, 1999.

26 Concerns about the impacts of the growth of high-tech businesses are not restricted to San Francisco. See, for example, Boxall, 2000.

27 Schiller, 1999, p 205.

28 See Sussman and Lent, 1998.

29 Castells and Hall, 1994

30 Graham, 1999

31 Graham and Marvin, 2001

32 Sussman and Lent, 1998

33 See Wilson 1998.

34 Woodbury and Thompson, 1999.

35 Lieberman, 1999.

36 Ibid.

37 Schiller, 1999, p 54.

38 Including, for example, land line phone, mobile phone, cable TV, broadband internet, and corporate networks.

39 Such consumers or 'power users' have been described as 'high value residential customers who spend lavishly on a basket of telecommunications and information services, typically including (on an annualized basis) US$650 on cellular; US$500 on local wireline phone service; US$400 on long distance telephony; US$375 on cable, pay-per-view and video-on-demand; US$250 on paging; as well as hundreds of additional dollars on online access, newspapers, magazines, and fiction'. (Schiller, 1999, p 54).

40 Smith, 1999.

41 Finnie, 1998.

42 'On both sides of the Atlantic, newly established transatlantic submarine cable facilities and urban business networks will allow MCI/Worldcom to link directly some 4,000 business buildings in Europe with 27,000 such buildings in the United States' (Schiller, 1999, p 63).

43 Finnie, 1998.

44 Schiller, 1999, p 55.

45 See Speak and Graham, 1999 'Many communities and areas are not perceived as having a large enough customer base to attract a [telecommunications or internet] company to offer a service, let alone multiple companies' (Hallgren, 1999, p 1).

46 Schiller, 1999, p 56.

47 Schiller, 1999, p 57.

48 Woodbury and Thompson, 1999.

49 Castells, 1999a, p 15

50 Graham and Marvin, 2001.

51 Castells, 1996; 1998.

52 Chomsky, 1993

53 Everard, 1999, p 33.

54 Fernandez-Maldonado, 1999.

55 UNDP, 1999, p 62.

56 Hack, 1997, p 11.

57 Kaothien et al, 1997, p 14.

58 Caldeira, 1996b.

59 Ramos-Schiffer, 1997, p 10.

60 Grundy-Warr et al, 1999, p 310. See also Box 2.2 for a fuller detailing of Singapore's ICT-based development strategy.

61 Wetzler, 2000

62 Madon, 1998, p 232.

63 Madon, 1998, p 234.

64 Rapaport, 1996, p 105.

65 Unlike the rags-to-riches 'luck-and-pluck' stories from popular juvenile literature of days gone by, 'You won't see many Horatio Algers leaping from the shanty towns to work stations in Bangalore's infotech firms' (Wetzler, 2000, p 166).

66 Schiller, 1999.

67 Kalbermatten 1999, p 15.

68 Madon, 1998, p 236.

69 Everard, 1999.

70 In a telling example, 'it is far easier for a Russian language speaker with a computer to download the works of Dostoyevsky translated into English to read than it is for him to get the original in his own language'. Cited in Everard, 1999, p 38.

71 Neil, 1999.

72 Mattelart 1996, p 304. Ricardo Petrella, an ex-EU commissioner, is even more pessimistic. To him, current logic on the centralization of wealth and power on key cities in the technological core of the global economy risks a 'new Hanseatic phase in the world economy, ridden by a stark techno-apartheid' (Petrella, 1993).

73 Calabrese and Borchert, 1996.

74 Souter, 1999, p 412.

75 Murdock, 1993, p 536

76 Castells, 1999a, p 301.

77 See World Bank, 1999a.

78 See World Bank, 1999a.

79 See www.undp.org/hdro/99.htm

80 A simple monetary definition of poverty is problematic for several other reasons. For example, it tends to overestimate poverty in rural areas, where the economy is less monetarized, and it underestimates urban poverty because in cities the costs of food and services tend to be higher (see, eg, UNCHS (Habitat), 1999). A reliance on household income also makes questionable assumptions about equal intra-household distribution of and access to resources. The literature provides full discussion of these and other aspects of poverty (see, eg, Hill, 1999; Razavi, 1999; Zheng, 1997; UNCHS (Habitat), 1999). See also Box 1.1 on the gender-related aspects of poverty measurement methods. For excellent coverage of the characteristics, causes and consequences of urban poverty, see the special issue of *Environment and Urbanization* 7(1) April, 1995.

81 Address by James Wolfensohn, World Bank President (Wolfensohn, 2000).

82 See Maxwell and Hammer, 1999.

83 The coefficient measures the percentage of area under a Lorenz curve of perfect equality that lies between it and the actual Lorenz curve of a society, with higher Gini coefficients indicating greater inequality (Rosser et al, 2000).

84 See Garuda, 2000.

85 See Karl, 2000.

86 Address by James Wolfensohn, World Bank President (Wolfensohn, 2000). See also Londoño and Székely, 1997.

87 Address by James Wolfensohn, World Bank President (Wolfensohn, 2000).

88 UNECLA, 1998, pp 285–286. See also Tardanico and Menjivar, 1997.

89 World Bank, 2000, p 7.

90 Ibid, p 10.

91 Ibid, p 8.

92 Ibid, p 9. One striking comparative example of the continent's lagging development: in 1965, income and exports per capita were higher in Ghana than in Korea. Korea's exports overtook Ghana's in 1972 and its income overtook Ghana's in 1976. Korea's exports increased by 400 times between 1965 and 1995, whereas Ghana's increased only four times.

93 World Bank, 2000, p 9.

94 Chapter 14 documents the human impacts of armed conflict across the world, including homelessness; the data show that Africa's population is most heavily affected.

95 World Bank, 2000, p 10.

96 World Bank, 2000, p 11.

97 See Jamal and Weeks, 1993; Potts, 1997.

98 Ke-youn Chu et al, 2000.

99 Zaidi, 1999, pp 2943–2951.

100 As measured by the Gini coefficient (28.8). At the regional level, only Eastern Europe was more egalitarian (25.0). The highest level of inequality was found in Latin America and the Caribbean (49.8). See Yao, 1999.

101 Aghion and Commander, 1999.

102 See, for example, Szelenyi, 1983; Daniel, 1985; Alexeev, 1999. Cf. Fung, 1987 for China.

103 See Atkinson and Micklewright, 1992.

104 See Nee and Peng, 1996.

105 See Rosser et al, 2000; Forster and Toth, 1997; Speder, 1998.

106 See Aghion and Commander, 1999, pp 277–278.

107 See Rosser et al, 2000, pp 157–158.

108 See Aghion and Commander, 1999; Alexeev, 1999; Commander, Tolstopiatenko and Yemtsov, 1999; Milanovic, 1999.

109 See Katz and Autor, 1999.

110 See Harding, 1997b; Johnson, Manning and Hellwig, 1998. Nonetheless, this trend is expected to have important consequences for skill acquisition in the labour force and to put pressure on the social security system (Borland, 1999).

111 See Katz and Autor, 1999.

112 For a fuller discussion, see Katz and Autor, 1999.

113 Aghion and Williamson, 1998.

114 See www.undp.org/hdro/99.htm

115 The Human Development Index (HDI) has been constructed every year since 1990 to measure average achievements in basic human development in one simple composite index and to produce a ranking of countries. It includes indicators of life expectancy, educational attainment, and income. The Gender-related Development Index (GDI) and Gender Empowerment Measure (GEM) are composite measures introduced in 1995 to capture changes in gender inequalities in human development at the national level.

116 See UNDP, 1999, pp 134–137.

117 Although economic growth and monetary income can be an important indicator of living standards, it fails to include important aspects of well-being. There have been attempts to develop alternative and additional measures, not captured by Gross Domestic Product. Examples are the Genuine Progress Indicator (GPI), the Index of Social Health, and the Index of Economic Well Being (Jackson et al, 2000). Broader measures of well-being include the level of poverty and inequality, conditions of work, the level of security, quality of housing and community life, availability of services, and environmental sustainability. See also Sen, 1999.

118 See www.cbpp.org/

119 See www.cbpp.org/9-4-99tax-rep.htm

120 The data, which cover every other year from 1977 to 1995 and include CBO projections for 1999, are generally regarded as the most reliable and comprehensive data available on the distribution of after-tax income in the United States. They include various forms of income that standard Census Bureau data miss, such as capital gains income and income from the Earned Income Tax Credit.

121 See Shapiro and Greenstein, 1999. See also Morris and Western, 1999 for a more historical analysis showing a decline in median income over the past three decades and a marked increase in the inequality of income distribution in the United States. See Waters and Eschbach, 1995 for a review of the ethnic and racial aspects of US inequality.

122 Findings reported by Wolff, 1995, based on Federal Reserve Board Surveys of Consumer Finances.

123 See Shapiro and Greenstein, 1999.

124 See www.ufenet.org/

125 See Collins, Wright and Sklar, 1999b.

126 See Collins, Hartman and Sklar, 1999a, www.ufenet.org/press/divided_decade.html

127 See Jackson et al, 2000.

128 See www.policyalternatives.ca/

129 See UNDP, 1999, pp 134–137.

130 The data are from the Luxembourg Income Study and have been adjusted to account for differences in family composition and other factors.

131 See Katz and Autor, 1999, p 1468.

132 This perspective is a basic tenet of the Recife Declaration of 1996, which resulted from a meeting that brought together 128 participants from governments, United Nations agencies, municipalities, foundations, NGOs and CBOs from 35 countries of all regions of the world. The gathering produced a set of recommendations for fighting urban poverty in preparation for the Habitat II Conference held in Istanbul later that year (see www.unchs.org/unchs/english/suphome/finalrec.htm). Chapter 17 elaborates commensurate strategic approaches.

133 See Maxwell and Hammer, 1999.

134 Ibid

135 See Aghion and Williamson, 1998. Further analysis in a related vein points to the replacement of physical capital accumulation by human capital accumulation as a prime engine of economic growth. In the present situation, given conditions of credit constraints, equality enhances economic growth and the adoption of skill-biased technologies increases the return on human capital, further reinforcing economic growth. (Galor, in press; Galor and Moav, 2000.)

136 Address by James Wolfensohn, World Bank President (Wolfensohn, 2000).

# 2

# URBAN IMPACTS OF GLOBALIZATION

## Globalization, Urban Planning and Democracy[1]

There are two strands to the argument regarding the relationship between economic globalization and urban planning. First, decision-makers in cities take a view of globalization in which they see cities as competing for globally footloose investment and hence requiring particular priorities in urban policy. Second, their response results in a concentration of power in a city elite and a lack of local democracy. As argued in this report, a less deterministic approach to globalization will provide better opportunities for greater local political choice and participation, leading to a wider discussion of priorities in urban planning.

Globalization is a contested concept. The view that has provided the dominant paradigm over the last decade, and the context for much thinking about urban policy, is sometimes referred to as the 'hyperglobalist' perspective.[2] Those holding this view, largely informed by management and business schools, tend to believe that the increasing globalization of the economy is inevitable. They also consider that globalization is beneficial and that it will eventually have advantages for all parts of the world. This is the 'trickle down' concept on a global scale. In this scenario, the nation state is seen as losing its role in a world that chiefly involves interactions between transnational business and city or regional governance. Economic globalization is seen as a natural process and city government should ensure that its citizens derive the maximum benefit from it. Cities should adapt their policies to conform to the imperatives that the process demands.

However, there are other views of globalization. Some see the concept as an ideological construct to give neo-liberalism greater spatial dominance, and consider that there is nothing fundamentally new in the way that the world economy operates. This perspective provides a useful corrective in stressing the ideological potential of the 'hyperglobalist' stance, although it underplays the changes in both intensity and spatial penetration that have taken place in the world economy.

There is a third view that accepts such changes but does not agree that they have a natural, inevitable, dynamic of their own.[3] In this third view, it is claimed that there are choices to be made about whether to enhance, block or mediate these global economic forces. The nation state is considered still to have some role in determining policy over such matters. However, the nation state itself is seen as undergoing restructuring as part of the globalization process. Some of its functions are moving upwards to supranational regional levels (eg the European Union), while others are decentralizing to subnational regions or cities. The result can be described as a multilayered system of governance, which interacts in different ways with the processes of economic globalization, which is itself multifaceted. This more complex interpretation allows local variation in the response of the different political actors to broadly shared global contexts.

> In many places, there has been a shift in the attitudes of urban government from a managerial approach to entrepreneurialism. This entrepreneurial stance views the city as a product that needs to be marketed. This marketing approach, and the emphasis on restructuring the city so that it appeals to global business, has led to the dominance of economic interests in the decision-making process of urban planning

In recent years, city governments have been adapting to their new global environment. For example, in Sydney, Singapore and London (three cities that are examined in Boxes 2.1, 2.2 and 2.3), it has been assumed that to gain comparative advantage it is necessary to beat their competitors in the game of attracting investment from the leading sectors of the new globalized economy. In many places, there has been a shift in the attitudes of urban government from a managerial approach to entrepreneurialism.[4] This entrepreneurial stance views the city as a product that needs to be marketed. For economically advanced cities, this marketing effort is aimed at attracting the headquarters or regional branches of international companies, particularly in the financial sector. This city marketing approach adopts the 'hyperglobalist' view of the globalization process, accepting its imperatives and adapting city policy in order to compete and survive. This results in several consequences: a particular form of city decision-making, specific urban planning priorities and projects, and social polarization.

This marketing approach, and the emphasis on restructuring the city so that it appeals to global business, has led to the dominance of economic interests in the decision-making process of urban planning. A coalition

**Box 2.1 Globalization in a regional capital: Sydney**

The major cities of Australia have a long history of competing with each other. This tradition has provided a foundation for the wider geographical competition of recent years. Sydney has now established itself as the leading Australian city. It is the major international air hub and the most important financial centre in the country. During the growth in Asian economies, it has extended its role to become a location for many transnational corporations wanting to service Southeast Asia. The State of New South Wales undertakes the strategic planning of the Sydney metropolitan region.

In 1988, a Liberal–National coalition won the state election. It formed a government with an ideology of limited government, cuts in state finances and privatization. The new state government was keen to attract global activities to Sydney but found it difficult to provide infrastructure and tax concessions, as the main revenue-raising powers were held by the Federal Government. As a result, the major tools available to the state government to attract global investment were its land holdings and urban planning and development powers. In 1995, the state government produced a new metropolitan strategy called *Cities for the 21st Century*. It was heralded as a new approach to strategic planning that was more broadly based and more flexible: 'as we move into an age of more rapid change and diverse global influences, a metropolitan planning strategy needs to be dynamic rather than rigid'.[i] One of its policies was 'the promotion, nationally and internationally, of central Sydney as a corporate headquarters and financial centre and also as a tourism centre, and the development of planning and management in support of these roles'.[ii]

Thus by the mid-1990s, Sydney was orienting its land use strategy towards a global market, orchestrated by the state government. Part of this strategy involved the identification of key sites for world city functions. However, the state met reaction from the local authority level, which was not always happy to accept such decisions. The City of Sydney was subject to local community pressures and opposed many of the ideas for the development of the CBD, particularly when this involved the demolition of buildings with heritage value. It is, therefore, interesting to see how the state government sought to implement its globally oriented policy in the face of adverse local views.

The first important tool at its disposal was the planning power to intervene in any development decision that had strategic significance. The state used this power on numerous occasions during the 1980s and 1990s. In some cases, it contravened the controls agreed in the local plans of the City of Sydney. In order to try and circumvent these democratically formulated local plans, a special Central Sydney Planning Committee was established in 1988, dominated by state appointees. This committee had responsibility for the preparation of local plans for the City and for decisions on all developments with a value of over Aus\$50 million. Another ploy adopted by the state was to change the boundary of the City of Sydney to try and ensure a local council sympathetic to global city development. A further example of the bypassing of local opposition took place around the state's decision in the early 1980s to develop Darling Harbour as a major recreation and convention centre with a linked mono-rail. This had to be built in time for the 1988 bicentennial year, but the requirement to conduct an environmental impact assessment created an obstacle in this tight timetable. So, the state passed a special act of parliament to give planning powers to a new Darling Harbour Authority that would not be subject to local council controls or planning laws. When professional and community opposition developed over the proposed mono-rail, these special powers were extended to also cover this aspect of the project.

In 1995, the Labor Party returned to control the state. It judged that the *Cities for the 21st Century* strategy did not sufficiently explore the international context and so it commissioned a new study. In the foreword to the study report, entitled *Sydney as a Global City*, the Minister for State and Regional Development says 'we must ensure that planning for Sydney supports a competitive and efficient economy ... planning for new and efficient road and rail networks, supporting existing employment locations and providing a continuing supply of sensibly located land are key elements in this focus'.[iii] The report presents a thorough analysis of the factors that influence Sydney's potential as a world city and the implications for planning. In 1997, the state produced a new review of strategic planning, called *A Framework for Growth and Change*.[iv] It adopted many of the approaches of the previous plan and had an expanded section on fostering a competitive and adaptable economy, drawing on the work in *Sydney as a Global City*. New roads and airport expansion were proposed. *A Framework for Growth and Change* pointed out that the state would continue to use its powers to make decisions over major projects as this helped to attract major inward investment and 'encouraged major companies to locate regional headquarters and facilities in the region'.[v]

In 1997, a new body was established called The Committee for Sydney, officially launched by the Premier of New South Wales. It comprised business and community leaders and was chaired by the director of the successful Olympic bid. Its major aim was to give Sydney a higher international profile and it argued that 'we have to think smarter, work harder and plan better if we are to build a viable future for our city in an intensely and increasingly competitive regional and world economy'.[vi] It placed considerable emphasis on the need for a plan or vision and said that 'many of the world's major cities – such as Barcelona, Berlin, London, Paris, Rome and Venice – are showing the way, having developed clear visions of their future and applying long-term strategic plans to realise them'.[vii] It clearly implied that Sydney was falling behind in the competitive urban development game and that existing strategic plans were not sufficient. So it was no surprise that, in 1998, they commissioned a study entitled Sydney 2020 to 'determine what is needed to develop and enhance Sydney's future as a world city'.[viii]

The main instigator of the planning strategy in this example has been not the City of Sidney, but the State of New South Wales. The collaboration between the state and the Committee for Sydney with its strong business representation has strengthened the global orientation. Changes in political party have had no effect on the direction of the strategy. Meanwhile, the resultant projects, in the shape of new office developments in central Sydney and the conference- and casino- oriented Darling Harbour development, met with local opposition. To deal with this, the state used a number of instruments to bypass the local democratic process. The Sydney example shows how important the global environment has become in the strategic planning of the city. Competition, not only with other cities in the same country, but with cities across the world, has become the motivating force.

**Source:** Thornley, 2000.
**Notes:** i Department of Urban Affairs and Planning, 1995, p12; ii Ibid, p92; iii Searle, 1996, pv; iv Department of Urban Affairs and Planning, 1997; v Ibid, p59; vi Committee for Sydney, 1997, pp1–2; vii Ibid, p 5; viii Committee for Sydney, 1998.

## Box 2.2 Globalization in a city-state: Singapore

The British founded Singapore as a trading post early in the 19th century. Until its independence in 1965, these trading interests dominated the government of the city. In 1965, the new state was cut off from its hinterland and set about pursuing a survival strategy. Communication based on trade provided a useful foundation. It was decided that industry needed to be developed to secure a sound economic future. The state took the lead in organizing this economic strategy. New institutions such as the Development Bank of Singapore were created to facilitate, develop and control the foreign direct investment. The Jurong Town Corporation developed the new industrial estates. Further, one of the most important bodies was the Economic Development Board (EDB), an arm of government that developed strategies to attract potential investors. Thus, from this early period, the Singapore government was actively involved in deciding the city's economic role and promoting it.

By the 1980s, the limits on the size of the work force and the restricted land area, made the government realize that it was becoming increasingly uncompetitive in labour-intensive industry. An Economic Committee was established to advise the government on a new direction. It concluded that Singapore should focus on developing as a service centre and seek to attract company headquarters to serve Southeast Asia, develop tourism, banking and offshore-based activities. The government set up a specific initiative, the Operational Headquarters Program, to attract regional offices of multinational corporations.

In 1990, the Deputy Prime Minister stated that 'Singapore seeks to be a hub city for the region and the world in a growing interdependent global economy'. The land provision for this new orientation had already started in the early 1970s when the government realized that it lacked the banking infrastructure for a modern economy. A new banking and corporate district, known as the 'Golden Shoe', was planned, incorporating the historic commercial area.[i] This became the location for the major international companies and various government financial agencies. Major expansion has also taken place at the airport to make it one of the hubs of world air traffic. Recently, the government has seen its neighbouring cities, such as Jakarta and Kuala Lumpur, develop as financial and office centres. It believes it needs to keep one step ahead of trends and is now promoting Singapore as the 'intelligent island' with a focus on computer and telecommunication technology. Thus, since independence, the economic role of Singapore has been very consciously planned.

The centrally planned state economic strategy is closely linked to land use and development planning. The EDB has a key influence on the strategic land use plans that are prepared by another arm of government, the Urban Redevelopment Authority (URA). The private sector is also involved in the planning process. It is invited to give its opinions in the committees set up to advise these government boards. In preparing its plans, the URA responds to the views of the various advisory committees and the boards and ministries of government, in which the EDB plays an important agenda setting role. The URA translates these discussions into land use and development terms through its preparation of the Concept Plan, a strategic plan for the whole island.

The latest Concept Plan, completed in 1991, is clearly and openly oriented towards the attraction of business. It seeks continued economic growth through 'restructuring the city', ensuring that the facilities needed by future business are planned; this includes transport and telecommunication infrastructure, land and environmental quality. After conducting studies of other world cities, a major extension of the existing financial district is planned through a land reclamation scheme. This attempts to replicate the vitality of other cities with waterside central areas such as Sydney and San Francisco. Part of this area has already been developed as a conference and exhibition zone and the rest will be used for CBD expansion, housing and entertainment.

One of the new features of the latest plan is a broader conception of what contributes to economic success. This conception includes high quality residential areas, a good environment, leisure facilities and exciting city life. Thus, there is more provision for low-density housing, often in waterfront communities linked to beaches and recreational facilities. Another major land reclamation scheme is planned for these functions, stretching from the CBD to the airport. The environmental policy is oriented to the 'beautification' of Singapore; for example, creating green zones between settlements and along transport corridors. It is linked to the prime objective of assisting in attracting business through the provision of golf courses, beaches and pleasant setting for luxury housing. As a one-party city-state, Singapore has a particular ability to take a positive and coordinated approach to city planning. A major role of government has been to determine the economic strategy for the city, which has moved from industry through regional office headquarters and financial services to computing and technology. Throughout, these strategies have been formulated within a conscious understanding of the city's relationship with the rest of the world. Global communications and networking have been a central feature. This dominant role by state government has been supported by strong interaction with the business community through various advisory mechanisms.

Once the economic vision has been established, the land use and development strategy is expected to translate this into physical reality by creating the necessary sites and infrastructure. Local democracy has not played a major part in this decision-making approach. Rather, the support of citizens is sought through high quality, subsidized, social provisions, such as in housing, public transport and health. A majority of people live in housing built by the state but privately owned. This combination allows the state to determine the nature of the housing and its allocation while generating the stakeholding characteristic of ownership. The state's control of allocation has been used to bring about ethnic and social mix in each housing area, thus avoiding social polarization and gentrification, but also impeding the formation of shared interest groups, with the potential of mobilizing dissenting voices. In so far as integration has been achieved, it has happened not through local democracy, but through the provision by a benevolent state of high-quality material and social conditions. An interesting question for the future will be whether this approach can be maintained with the growing stress on quality of life, individual choice, limited low-density housing, and an economy built on education and the 'information age'.

**Source:** Thornley, 2000.
**Note:** i Chua, 1989.

**Box 2.3 Globalization in a world city: London**

London was a relative latecomer to the business of city promotion, handicapped by its lack of any city-wide government after the abolition of the Greater London Council (GLC) in 1986. The only strategic policy for London after the GLC was produced by national government. In tune with the non-interventionist ideology of the Thatcher period, the central government strategic guidance for London in 1989 was only a few pages long and merely set out the main parameters, such as supporting the private sector, within which the local authorities should operate.

As a result of the ideology of neo-liberalism and institutional fragmentation, very little London-wide thinking took place. The 33 local authorities within London had a joint committee, the London Planning Advisory Committee (LPAC), which produced strategic policies, but these had a very limited impact on central government.

Earlier, in 1980, central government had established the London Dockland Development Corporation to undertake the regeneration of a large area of land left unused after the move downstream of the London Docks. The Corporation was a body appointed by central government and it took over the responsibility for the area from the local authorities. The communities living in that area therefore lost their local democratic procedures, producing considerable local resentment. The Corporation was given the brief to promote the area and attract investment from the private sector. It took over land that previously belonged to the local authorities and was given the finances to provide infrastructure. Tax breaks were offered and planning constraints removed. One of the results of this approach was the development of the Canary Wharf office project.

However, from the early 1990s there was increasing pressure for a more concerted approach. The City of London, a small local authority covering the financial district and having unique institutional arrangements based on a medieval charter that privileged the business community, had been active in commissioning reports. One of the conclusions of such work was that London needed a single voice in order to promote itself. A similar conclusion was expressed in a consultant's report entitled *London: World City Moving into the 21st Century*, which surveyed leading international business opinion on how London could retain its competitive position.

In 1992, central government set up the London Forum to promote the capital, which, the following year, merged with London First, a similar body set up by the private sector. This set the pattern of private sector leadership with central government backing that was to dominate strategic thinking in London over the next five years. In 1994, the central government announced another initiative, London Pride, involving the orchestrating of a vision for London that would help the city to be more successful in its competition with other world cities, and the preparation of a prospectus of future priorities and action to coordinate the public, private and voluntary sectors. Its aim was the consolidation of London's position as the only world city in Europe. It sought to achieve this through three interrelated missions: a robust and sustainable economy drawing on a world-class workforce; greater social cohesion; and a high-quality provision of infrastructure, services and good environment. The main emphasis was on measures to support business and attract inward investment, such as adequate provision of good sites, telecommunication facilities, a suitably trained labour force, promotional activity, improved access to the airports and better public transport.

Meanwhile, central government had become more directly involved in strategic planning for the city, as the problems of fragmentation continued. It established a Minister for London, a Cabinet Sub-Committee for the capital, the Government Office for London which coordinated the different Ministries with interests in London, and produced a new enhanced *Strategic Guidance for London Authorities* that extended to 75 pages.[i] In 1995, it also established the Joint London Advisory Panel to advise the Cabinet Sub-Committee. This new body consisted of the same membership as the London Pride Partnership, and was again led by London First. This arrangement illustrates once more the close working relationship between central government and the private sector. The priorities of the partnership had a significant influence on central government thinking through the Joint London Advisory Panel and its input into the revised strategic guidance for London. This new guidance stated that 'the promotion of London as a capital of world city status is fundamental to government policy'. It warned that rival cities such as Paris, Frankfurt, Barcelona and Berlin were 'fighting harder than ever to attract investment and business opportunities'.[ii]

The London case shows that the fragmentation of decision-making that was a feature of the neo-liberal policies of the 1980s meant that London was poorly placed to promote itself in the globalized economy. This led to pressure, particularly from the business world and local authorities representing strategic development locations, to create some kind of leadership to promote the city. Many suggestions were made at the time but in the end the lead was taken by central government in partnership with the business-led London First organization. The London Pride Partnership created a vision document and the local authorities and training agencies were drawn into this, as the implementers. This vision then influenced central government's strategic guidance for London and local authorities were statutorily obliged to follow it.

However, in 1997 a major change took place in British politics when the Labour Party under Tony Blair won the national election after 18 years of Conservative rule. This outcome had a significant impact on the institutional context for strategic planning in London. A completely new political arrangement, the Greater London Authority, was devised. For the first time in history, this included an elected mayor for the whole of London. The elections for the mayor and a Greater London Assembly took place in May 2000.

A major theme for the new authority is the coordination and integration of policy. It is responsible for drawing up a new plan for the coordination of land use and development across the whole city. It is also required to produce an integrated transport strategy, an air quality management strategic plan, a waste management strategy, regular state of the environment reports, a strategy for culture, media and leisure, and an economic development strategy. This economic development strategy, the focus for promoting competitiveness and attracting inward investment, will be produced by the new London Development Agency.

A second theme of the new authority is to foster transparency of decision-making. This will be achieved through the elected mayor, the debates in the Assembly and an annual public hearing. It remains to be seen how this new arrangement, with its greater local democracy, will affect the priorities for the planning of the city. Previously, these were dominated by a coalition between central government and the private sector in an institutional environment that was highly complex and difficult to penetrate. In theory, the new situation should generate debate and discussion as the various strategies are formulated. The priority to pursue competitiveness and inward investment will be advocated by the London Development Agency but this will be one voice among many within the purview of the mayor. A more open debate could occur with opportunities for citizens to express their opinions. The result may be a less deterministic reaction to the imperatives of globalization.

**Source:** Thornley, 2000.
**Notes:** i Government Office for London, 1996; ii Ibid, p3.

develops between externally oriented economic interests and elements of city government that benefit from the attraction of 'world city' functions. The economic interests include international companies, financial organizations and sectors with a global reach such as computing or tourism, while the government elements represent strategic locations such as the central business district (CBD), new areas with potential for 'world city' functions or airports. These interests can be viewed as forming a new kind of elite dominating the agenda of city governance. The concept of the 'growth machine' has been developed to designate a particular coalition of economic interests dominating city governance in the US.[5] Such coalitions centre on real estate owners but may also include city politicians, media, utility companies and academia. Over the years, this concept has been further developed, particularly through cross-national research, and made more sophisticated, for example in 'regime theory'.[6] If we extend this work and broaden the economic interests in the coalition accordingly, focusing on those with global concerns, many aspects of the growth machine formulation retain their relevance. The overriding push for growth still provides the stimulus for the coalition, the highly focused goal leads to the formulation of a sympathetic elite, and the other agencies are drawn in because of the need for infrastructure and legitimacy.

However, as suggested by recent 'regime theory' literature and shown in the case studies of Sidney, Singapore and London, city governance is not confined to the local level. Higher level political actors also play a significant role in this new 'global growth coalition'. This role becomes particularly relevant when, as in Sydney, the political boundaries hinder the development of consensus behind the coalition. The importance of supra-city politics supports the third view of globalization, which suggests that, in our global world, governance is undergoing a process of restructuring in which the distinction between the previous political levels is becoming more complex. It runs counter to the 'hyperglobalist' view, which suggests that the nation state is becoming redundant.

The 'global growth coalition' will seek to push the policies of the city in a particular direction. This will be given legitimacy by arguing that the forces of globalization are inevitable and that the city, if it is to survive in an environment of competition with other cities, has to create a strategy to maximize its ability to benefit from global economic forces. This approach usually involves the formulation and propagation of some kind of 'vision' for the future of the city, oriented to reassuring potential investors that their needs will be met. The aim is to ensure that this vision informs other policies of the city, including the strategic land use plan, and expenditure priorities.

The global city's orientation places much emphasis on communications, including airport expansion and links to strategic office locations. The desire to attract global companies leads to the provision of attractive, well-serviced and favourably located sites for state-of-the-art office development. In the top world cities, this approach has produced New York's Battery Park, London's Canary Wharf and

Tokyo's Waterfront. Smaller versions can be seen in many cities around the world. Luxury housing, dining establishments, and entertainment amenities are also required to attract the professional personnel for these global activities. Tourism, whether for business or pleasure, and leisure have also become major economic growth sectors in the global economy. As a result, many of the recent urban projects have included trade centres, conference centres, hotels, casinos, urban theme parks and sports complexes. Development projects oriented to these global activities not only provide physical needs, but also contribute to the 'image' of the city. This is important in marketing any product and can help in advertising and making the product visible. In the case of a city, an exciting and dynamic impression can be given through the use of spectacular architecture. The Sydney Opera House provided an early example. In more recent years, there has been a proliferation of eye-catching buildings from the Guggenheim Museum in Bilbao[7] to London's Millennium Dome.[8]

Evidence suggests that global cities around the world have become increasingly polarized in recent years. The 'Dual City' label has been used to describe the disparities between rich and poor. As shown later in this chapter, contemporary social dynamics are more complex than such a bi-polar division and the variations in the social programmes of local and national states also generate diversity. Nevertheless, a great deal of research links the processes of economic globalization to social polarization.[9]

---

**The influx of global organizations into a city can create a highly paid workforce whose standard of living and salary levels are determined by global comparisons. On the other hand, the workers who service them through such activities as cleaning, providing food or routine office work, are typically poorly paid**

---

The influx of global organizations into a city tends to create a highly paid workforce whose standard of living and salary levels are determined by global comparisons. On the other hand, the workers who service this workforce through such activities as cleaning, providing food or routine office work, are typically poorly paid. Government hopes for the higher productivity and efficiency of foreign-owned companies to 'rub off' on local industries have been questioned by research. For example, a recent study based on data from UK companies in the first half of the 1990s found that on average there were no wage and productivity spillovers to domestic firms as a result of foreign presence, seriously calling into doubt one of the justifications for the huge packages of financial assistance and tax breaks that have been offered by successive British governments.[10]

These economic and social differences have a geographical dimension and concentrations of rich and poor have become increasingly evident. The process of gentrification is much in evidence, as the wealthy look for distinctive urban locations, often displacing existing residents. Such disparities can produce resentment, social instability and conflict. The kind of projects described above can also generate alienation, as many local people find little for themselves in luxury shopping centres, casinos and convention centres. Indeed, many of the new projects may worsen the city residents' quality of life through increased noise or congestion, or the loss of the opportunity to use the limited supply of key urban sites for other uses. Scarce public resources may be allocated in support of mega-projects intended to project a positive city image but with little value in the residents' daily lives. In many cases, the projects create islands of activity, oriented to those of means, surrounded by areas of poverty. This phenomenon has been called the 'bubble effect'.[11] Many of the people who visit these sites are tourists or visitors from wealthier residential areas, often in the suburbs. In a related vein, growth promoters put pressure on and support cities to host international mega-events with uncertain benefits at best for a majority of the urban population.[12]

> New projects may worsen the city residents' quality of life through increased noise or congestion, or the loss of opportunity to use the limited supply of key urban sites for other uses. Scarce public resources may be allocated in support of mega-projects intended to project a positive city image but with little value in people's daily lives

A recent review of such hallmark spectacles suggests that displacement of poor households should be viewed as an expected result of this form of urban restructuring as these glamorous events are used to bring new people, new facilities, and new money to cities at a rapid pace; these goals are rarely evaluated in an open, democratic manner.[13]

There is considerable debate over the causal factors behind social processes. Cities have always contained rich and poor areas. A case can be made, as with globalization more generally, that the speed of change, its pervasiveness, and greater public awareness, now create a situation significantly different from the past. However, the important point is that globalization, and the response of city government, can have variable impacts on different groups of citizens. Urban decisions are highly political.

> If a consequence of the local response to globalization is to restrict the determination of priorities to a small elite, then there is little opportunity for the political issues to be discussed and decided through local democracy

> An important message of this report is that there are encouraging examples of countervailing trends that reveal cities as active agents, attentive to concerns of social justice and environmental sustainability

If a consequence of the local response to globalization is to restrict the determination of priorities to a small elite, then there is little opportunity for the political issues to be discussed and decided through local democracy, as illustrated by the case studies of Sydney, Singapore and

London. In the longer term, this lack of accountability can be a threat to the social sustainability of the city. An important message of this report is that there are encouraging examples of countervailing trends that reveal cities as active agents, participating in processes of globalization while attentive to concerns of social justice and environmental sustainability.

## Physical Reflections of Globalization[15]

The changing relationship between manufacturing and service sector activities is sometimes taken as a hallmark of globalization. Its impact on settlement patterns is obvious and profound: cities that had been the hub of bustling manufacturing enterprises in the period of rapid urbanization have been losing their industrial employment base, and instead are becoming the seats of concentrated clusters of commercial financial and management activities; FIRE, finance, insurance and real estate are prominent among them. Manufacturing plants have been moved to the suburbs, sometimes to rural regions, and to a significant extent away from older, industrially more developed countries to less developed ones. Where the move has been to less developed economies, the direction of development

---

### Box 2.4 Globalization of land and housing markets: the Mexican experience

Most studies have linked the 'global' real estate cycle of the late 1980s to the source of net capital outflows in developed countries (especially Japan) and an international switching of portfolio investment that has targeted real estate investment in the US, Europe and Australia.[i] While the 'emerging markets' of Latin American finance have become closely tied to the global economy, there are insufficient data for a definitive assessment of how Latin American countries have been drawn into this cycle; no research has systematically looked into how Latin America's major cities are linked to international property markets.

However, data on the destination of foreign direct investment (FDI) flows to Mexico show that only 1.1 per cent is destined for the construction sector, suggesting that 'deterritorialization' of land and housing markets may still be some way off. Nevertheless, closer linkages are signalled by new workings of the real estate markets.

The peso crisis of 1994–1995 and its 'solution' provide the first insight into the globalization of real estate in Mexico. The devaluation of the peso against the US dollar, caused by the inability of the Salinas administration to allow the value of the peso to slide in an election year, with an economy vulnerable to foreign portfolio investment and rapid credit expansion, was occasioned by a loss of confidence among institutional investors.[ii] In order to prevent currency free-fall, domestic interest rates were sharply increased. As the Salinas reforms had sought to develop a secondary mortgage market and pension-based financial instruments, and middle-income households had borrowed large sums over the previous few years and invested in real estate, the results were catastrophic.[iii] Some reports had households attempting to give property away rather than service the debt. Prices and turnover in the formal segment of the market appear to be increasingly sensitive to events on the 'domestic' stock markets and to fluctuations in real interest rates, which are themselves more sensitive to events in New York and London.

**Source:** Gareth Jones, 2000 (see Background Papers).
**Note:** i see Renaud, 1997; ii see Burki and Edwards, 1996. Portfolio investment was negative during the 1980s but rose sharply to account for about 80 per cent of foreign investment during the 1990s, becoming negative US$10,000 million in 1995. FDI has increased more steadily; iii in 1994 there was a glut of secondary and prime property in Mexico City and prices had reached a plateau from a threefold increase in dollar prices from 1989. A number of stock-real estate funds that could have smoothed for fluctuations in one market had only just been set up.

is ultimately often similar to that in older countries: São Paulo, for instance, the relocation target of major automobile plants 50 years ago, is now seeing them leave for regions in the interior of Brazil and instead is watching its cluster of internationally oriented commercial high-rise office buildings proliferate. The Asian Tigers (for example, Hong Kong, Singapore and South Korea) are similarly facing competition for industrial labour from other less developed Asian economies and are seeking to maintain their position by shifting towards higher tech production as a matter of deliberate policy to develop human capital reservoirs as a means for propelling economic growth (for example, see the case of Singapore, described in Box 2.2).

> The shift from manufacturing to services only in part represents technological progress. The total amount of manufacturing activity in the world is increasing, not decreasing, whether measured in value or in employment

These developments are not the simple consequences of technological advances. They are in large part determined by changes in the organization and concentration of wealth and the policies of government, which in turn determine how (and where) new technology will be used. The shift from manufacturing to services, for instance, only in part represents technological progress. The total amount of manufacturing activity in the world is *in*creasing, not *de*creasing, whether measured in value or in employment. Its relocation from older cities – often the locus of past worker organizing efforts, strong trade unions and high wages – to other areas where greater profits can be made with a cheaper work force and less restrictive regulations is not a function of technology, but of the quest for higher profits. Advances in communications technology facilitate, but do not mandate, centralization of command functions. The particular constellation of power dictates the use of these technologies, rather than something inherent in these technologies themselves.[16]

> It is the complex intertwining of technological capabilities, economic resources and political power that produces the consequences of globalization

It is the complex intertwining of technological capabilities, economic resources and political power that produces the consequences of globalization that this report identifies as important concerns. On the other hand, these factors also provide the potential for positive outcomes brought about by processes of democratic governance informed by our accumulating knowledge of constructive models of urban development.[17]

Cross-border activities can have unfavourable effects that are easily seen. The impact of increased air traffic, for instance, is one of the most visible consequences of globalization. It has resulted in serious noise and air pollution in those cities near airports. Where airports are further from the city, as in New York City or London, problems of traffic congestion are heightened. Equally important are the implications of the growth of air commerce on regional forms of habitation. The clusters of 'airport cities' that have sprung up around major hubs, such as Frankfurt or Dallas/Fort Worth, have siphoned off business activity, and with it commercial life, from many downtown areas and severed connections of these activities from the fabric of urban life. The ability to develop mega-projects, such as the skyscrapers that are becoming an essential component of the image of any city that wishes to call itself global, would not be possible in most cases without cross-border financing.[18] In further pursuit of that image, many cities produce a uniform architecture, aspiring to a standard of international stature but often more characterized by plushness and pretentiousness than by its aesthetic quality.

## Inequality and the quartering of urban space

The previous chapter documented the deepening inequality associated with current globalization. The process leading from globalization to inequality is clear; it results from the use of advanced communications and transportation technology to enable the concentration of wealth in the hands of a few, to the comparative, and often absolute, detriment of most. The increasing mobility of capital, and the increasing span of control that is newly possible, have resulted in an increasing concentration of wealth at the top, and an increasing gap between the holders of that wealth and the poor of the world. The poorest 20 per cent of the world's population has seen its share of global income decline from 2.3 per cent to 1.4 per cent in the past 30 years, while the share of the richest 20 per cent increased from 70 per cent to 85 per cent.[19] Social welfare policies significantly affect the level of inequality; thus the states traditionally associated with such policies, from Sweden and The Netherlands to Singapore, show lower levels of inequality than more market-based societies, but even in these countries the gap between rich and poor is increasing.

These two major aspects of globalization, the restructuring of manufacturing and services, and widening inequality or polarization, have their reflections in the shape of cities and the activities they harbour. An especially striking urban concomitant of globalization is the expression of inequality in patterns of segregation of people and land uses. The most fundamental of these is in the quartering of urban space.

## Box 2.6 Planning to prevent 'unbalanced' development in Manila's mega-urban region

In Southeast Asia, much developmental effort has been focused on establishing attractive venues for foreign direct investment in manufacturing, services and infrastructure. Global capital flows, however, tend to concentrate within national core regions, mainly in and around capital cities that represent the principal nodes of connectivity between national and global economic spaces.

One result of this spatially differentiated integration into the global economy has been the reworking of urban cores, as office towers and middle-class landscapes of consumption emerge according to globally recognizable templates. A second consequence has been the development of extended metropolitan regions. Dense populations in wet-rice cultivating areas preclude the need for urban agglomerations to provide labour supply and market access. Studies of these mega-urban zones areas have emphasized their dynamism as the key engines of national economic growth.

Recent research in the extended region around Manila, however, suggests that tensions exist within such landscapes, creating a dynamic that leads to the domination of urban land uses over residual agriculture, rather than their juxtaposition and co-existence. Like other Asian cities, Manila and its surrounding regions command the lion's share of global investment in the national economy.

The consequence of this pattern of investment is that much of the Philippines' national economic dynamism in the last decade has been focused on the urbanizing region around Manila, creating exactly the mixed-use landscape described elsewhere in Southeast Asia. In particular, the landscape of neighbouring provinces is becoming a patchwork of residential subdivisions, industrial estates, commercial developments, golf courses and theme parks, all existing within what was, until recently, an almost exclusively agricultural economy.

Planning frameworks for the greater Manila region have tended to emphasize the need to maintain agricultural activities alongside industrial development, for reasons of both food security and the relatively universal access to employment in farming sectors. Planning documents too have aimed to foster 'balanced' agricultural and industrial growth.

While such goals are laudable, the social dynamics of development in mega-urban regions suggest that residential and industrial land uses and their associated socio-cultural implications are in conflict with agricultural production and rural life. Four sources of tension can be identified: economic, environmental, social and political.

- Economic tensions arise due to changes in labour and land markets in urbanizing contexts. The absorption of labour by urban and industrial activities has pushed up agricultural wages to a point where rice farming becomes barely profitable. Frequently, agricultural labour demand can only be met through engaging migrant bands of workers from other provinces. Land conversion, meanwhile, has presented tenant farmers with tempting compensation packages to entice them to surrender their tenancy rights.
- Environmental conflicts arise around issues of water supply and waste disposal. Irrigation canals may be silted up by eroded soil from nearby construction sites. After construction is completed, where waste disposal from new residential estates is inadequate, household refuse frequently finds its way into irrigation channels, again blocking and contaminating the water supply to remaining farmland.
- Social changes in urbanizing contexts present the perennial problem of keeping the younger generation 'down on the farm'. New employment opportunities arise in factories, offices and even overseas. There is often little interest in following the parents' footsteps in agricultural employment even when they are without work. Furthermore, because of household cash incomes boosted by waged employment or overseas remittances from other family members, there is less necessity to take such 'undesirable' work.
- All of the circumstances above encourage farmers to get out of agriculture and sell their tenancy rights. While legislation is designed to prevent fertile irrigated farmland from being lost in this way, local politics frequently facilitates the circumvention of such legal provisions. At one level, pressure from the owner to sell the land is difficult for tenant farmers to resist. In a broader sense, the vested interest of local politicians in land conversion means that zoning and planning regulations are frequently circumvented.

Thus residual farmland is placed under great pressure from advancing urbanization in the extended metropolitan region. For individual farmers there is little incentive to continue cultivating when economic, environmental, social and political pressures are all pushing towards the conversion of land. Indeed, such conversion often occurs well ahead of actual demand for residential or industrial land, as landowners seek to remove tenant farmers and secure convertible land for speculative purposes.

The corollary on the regional scale is that unless careful planning and zoning rules are implemented, the extended metropolitan region will not remain a mixture of agricultural and urban land uses, and will instead see the gradual 'squeezing out' of agriculture and the creation of a diffuse urban agglomeration. Retaining agricultural activities on the other hand would provide for a diversified economic base and labour market at a local level in urbanizing villages and, at a national scale, ensure food security for urban populations.

**Source:** Kelly, 2000a.
**Note:** For additional references, see Kelly, 1999; 2000b.

The link between inequality and urban space is not so much the division of society into two simple parts, that of the rich and that of the poor, as in the 19th century, but the quartered, divided or partitioned city of today. It is the indirect, but essential, product of current globalization. Inequality, in this broader sense, has been extensively documented as a worldwide phenomenon known as polarization.[20] It has four distinct aspects: an increase in the relative numbers of those who are rich and those who are poor; an increase in the financial distance between them; a greater differentiation among the groups between the richest and the poorest, so that one may speak of a four- or five-part division of classes rather than a simple division into two; and sharper differentiation among the groups from each other.

The four aspects of this process of polarization are reflected in the physical space of cities, particularly in the partitioning of the residential areas of cities, in a pattern we may call quartering. The *enclave*, whether as citadel of power, gentrified neighbourhood, exclusive suburb or immigrant quarter, is the most typical form of quartering. Harking back to the origin of the term in the enclaves of the imperial powers in the colonies, the enclaves accompanying globalization similarly represent the effort to wall some in and keep others out.

> There is growing evidence of five, increasingly separate *residential cities* – one mobile, four in separate quarters – each with a parallel *city of business and work*

The resulting residential pattern consists of five *residential cities*: one is 'non-spatial' in the sense that it floats freely[21] in multiple locations in and outside the city; the other four are based on traditional neighbourhood quarters. Each residential city has its source in a parallel (although not always congruent) *city of business and work*. This economic differentiation is induced by globalization, and each type of city has its own form of separation from the others, and its own dynamics of development. For business, the spatial patterns include areas in which people of many occupations, classes and levels of status live in many different residential areas, but work in close proximity. These five formations of parallel residential and business cities include:

- the luxury city and the controlling city;
- the gentrified city and the city of advanced services;
- the suburban city and the city of direct production;
- the tenement city and the city of unskilled work;
- the abandoned city and the residual city.

## ● Mobile citadels of wealth and business

The *luxury areas of the city*, the residences of the wealthy, while located in clearly defined residential areas, are at the same time not tied to any quarter of the city. For the wealthy, the city is less important as a residential location than as a location of power and profit. The restructuring of cities has led to an increased profitability of real estate, from which the already wealthy disproportionately benefit. They profit from the activities conducted in the city or from the real estate values created by those activities; they may also enjoy living in the city, but have many other options. If they reside in the city, it is in a world largely insulated from contact with non-members of their class, with leisure time and satisfactions carefully placed and protected. Some 75 per cent of the chief executives of corporations with their headquarters in New York City have been estimated to live outside the city.[22] This pattern is repeated throughout the world.

The *controlling city*, the city of big decisions, includes a network of high-rise offices, brownstones (three-storey, upper middle class townhouses) in prestigious locations and old colonial mansions of the imperial powers in developing countries. It includes yachts for some, the back seats of stretch limousines for others, aeroplanes and scattered residences for most. It is less and less locationally circumscribed, but it is not spatially rootless. Its activities take place somewhere, secured by walls, barriers and conditions to entry.

The controlling city tends to be located in the high-rise centres of advanced services, because those at the top of the chain of command wish to have at least those who work below them close at hand and responsive. Citibank in New York City wants its next level of professionals directly accessible to its top decision-makers; credit card data entry operations may move to South Dakota but not banking activities that require the exercise of discretion. Those locations, wherever they may be, are crucially tied together by communication and transportation channels which permit an existence insulated from all other parts of the city.

The controlling city parallels the luxury areas of the residential city in many ways, but not necessarily in physical proximity. When together, they form an age-old phenomenon, now in its market incarnation: the citadel. In the citadel, the mobile luxury residential city and the controlling city of business come together in space. Here also the phenomenon of walling (in and out) is at its most extreme.

> The citadel is where those at the top of the economic hierarchy live, work, consume and recreate in protected spaces of their own

The citadel[23] is where those at the top of the economic hierarchy live, work, consume and recreate in protected spaces of their own. For many years its residents have sought to protect their separate space in the city by public instruments such as zoning.[24] Today, private, high-rise condominiums all have their own security, and elsewhere real walls and gates protect the enclaves of the rich from intrusion. A growing number of such citadels are found from New York City to Tokyo, Vancouver to Shanghai, Johannesburg to London and Paris to Moscow.

## ● The quarter of gentrification

The *gentrified city*[25] serves professionals, managers, technicians, yuppies in their 20s and college professors in their 60s: those who may be doing well themselves, yet work for others.

> Gentrified areas are chosen for their environmental or social amenities, for their quiet or bustle, their history or fashion and their access to white-collar jobs

The frustrated pseudo-creativity[26] of their actions leads to a quest for other satisfactions, more related to consumption of specific forms of 'urban' culture, devoid of original historical content, than to intellectual productivity or political freedom.[27] The residential areas they occupy are chosen for environmental or social amenities, for their quiet or bustle, their history or fashion, their access to white-collar jobs; gentrified working class neighbourhoods, older middle class areas and new developments with modern and well furnished apartments, all serve their needs. Locations close to work are important because of long and unpredictable work schedules, the density of contacts and the availability of services and contacts they permit.

The *city of advanced services* parallels the characteristics of the gentrified residential city. It consists of professional offices tightly clustered in downtown areas, with many ancillary services internalized in high-rise office towers, and is heavily enmeshed in a wide and technologically advanced communications network. It is the most rapidly growing quarter of cities on an international level. The skyscraper centre is the stereotypical form. It is located at the edge of the city centre, as in Frankfurt/Main; outside the city, as in Paris at La Defense, outside Rome or the Docklands in London; or scattered both inside and outside a city with good transportation and communications, as in Amsterdam. Social, 'image' factors also play a role; the 'address' as well as the location is important for business. Whether in only one location or in several in a given city, there will be strong clustering, and the city of advanced services will be recognizable at a glance.

## ● Suburbanization inside and outside the city

The *suburban city* of the traditional family, suburban in tone if not in structure or location, is sought out by better paid workers, blue and white collar employees, the 'lower middle class' and the petite bourgeoisie. It provides stability, security and the comfortable world of consumption. Most prefer owner-occupancy of a single family dwellings (depending on age, gender and household composition), but cooperative, condominium or rental apartments can be adequate, particularly if subsidized and/or located close to transport. The home as a symbol of self, exclusion of those of lower status, physical security against intrusion, political conservatism, comfort and escape from the work-a-day world (thus often incorporating substantial spatial separation from work) are characteristic. Because the home functions as financial security and inheritance as well as residence, the protection of residential property values is important.

The *city of direct production* parallels, but is not congruent with, in either space or time, the residential suburban city. It includes not only manufacturing but also the production aspect of advanced services, government offices and the back offices of major firms, located in clusters and with significant agglomerations, in varied locations within a metropolitan area. These locations are not arbitrary or chaotic; they are positioned to enable clients to be in quick and easy contact, preferably in inner-city locations. Examples in New York City include the industrial valley between Midtown Manhattan and the Financial District for the printing industry, or between Chinatown and the Garment District for textile production.

For mass production, locations will be different. Here the pattern has changed dramatically since the beginning of the Industrial Revolution. At first, factories were near the centre of the city; indeed, to a large extent they led to the growth of the city around them, as in the industrial cities of England or the manufacturing cities of New England. But more modern manufacturing methods require vastly more single-storey space, with parking for automotive access rather than paths for workers coming on foot, and many more operations are internalized. Land costs have become more important than local agglomeration economies, and suburban or rural locations are preferred.

## ● The old working class quarter and the immigrant enclave

The *tenement city* serves as home for lower paid workers, workers earning the minimum wage or little more, who often have irregular employment, few benefits, little job security and no chance of advancement. Their city is much less protective or insular than the suburban, gentrified and luxury cities. In earlier days, the residents of these so-called slum neighbourhoods were perceived as unruly and undisciplined; they often were the victims of slum clearance and 'urban renewal'. Today, they experience abandonment, displacement, service cuts, deterioration of public facilities, and political neglect.

> Because low-paid workers are needed for the functioning of the city as a whole, they have some ability to exert political pressure

However, because they are needed for the functioning of the city as a whole, they have some ability to exert political pressure to get public protections: for example, rent regulation and public housing exist largely because of their activities. However, when their quarters are wanted for 'higher uses', they are frequently moved out, by urban renewal or by gentrification. The fight against displacement, under the banner of protecting their neighbourhoods, has given rise to some of the most militant social movements of our time. Urban protests in Paris in the 1960s received broad recognition, and anti-displacement activities, whether in San Francisco, New York City, Toronto, Frankfurt, Capetown or Hong Kong, have been worldwide. They were a major focus of attention at Habitat II in Istanbul in 1996 and a concern included in the current UNCHS Global Campaign for Secure Tenure. Relatedly, 'Cities Without Slums' is an ambitious initiative to improve the living conditions of millions of people living in poverty through a joint effort of UNCHS (Habitat) and the World Bank in partnership with cities and major development organizations.[28]

The *city of unskilled work* includes the informal economy, small-scale manufacturing, warehousing, sweatshops, technically unskilled consumer services and immigrant industries. These are closely intertwined with the cities of production and advanced services and thus located near them, but separately and in scattered clusters.[29] Their locations are determined in part by economic relations, and in part by the patterns of the residential city. Because the nature of the labour supply determines the profitability of these activities, the residential location of workers willing to do low-paid and unskilled work has a major influence. Thus, in New York City sweat-shops locate in Chinatown or the Dominican areas of Washington Heights, in Miami in the Cuban enclave, and generally in the slums of cities throughout the world.

The economic city of unskilled work parallels the tenement city. In the more industrialized countries, residence is separate from work. For older 'smokestack' industries, that is also true in developing countries. Major automobile plants in Brazil and China draw on pools of workers from various residential areas, often from large informal settlements and squatter colonies, located near the factories. For other types of work, such as textiles and forms of light manufacturing, home work is again coming into vogue as a cheap and flexible form of production, combining place of residence with place of work and avoiding the necessity of investing in a separate workplace entirely.[30] The ensuing separation of such workers from the core of the city is thereby further accentuated.

### ● Abandonment and the new ghetto of exclusion

The *abandoned city* is the place for the very poor, the excluded, the never employed and permanently unemployed and the homeless. In older industrialized countries, it will have a crumbling infrastructure and deteriorating housing. The domination by outside impersonal forces, direct street-level exploitation, racial and ethnic discrimination and segregation and the harassment of women are everyday reality. The spatial concentration of the poor in such areas is often reinforced by public policy. For example, public housing becomes more and more targeted at the poorest of the poor, turning into ghettoized housing of last resort. In some countries, they are the worst units, left after the better part of the stock has been privatized. Drugs and crime are concentrated here, education and public services neglected. In less industrialized countries, the excluded live on the fringe of the city, often in informal accommodations. They often lack proper sewerage, water supply or other basic infrastructure, and often subsist without protected legal tenure.

> Whether in developed or less developed countries, the residential areas of the excluded are abandoned by the formal structures of government and denied the public services considered normal in other parts of the city

Whether in developed or less developed countries, the residential areas of the excluded are abandoned by the formal structures of government and denied the public services considered normal in other parts of the city.

Here is also, in economic terms, the *residual city*, the city of the less legal portions of the informal economy. In the developing countries, it will overlap with the abandoned city: its residents derive income from marginal and illegal work. In industrialized countries, it is the city of storage where otherwise undesired facilities, such as manufacturing buildings are located. Many of the most polluting and environmentally detrimental components of the urban infrastructure, necessary for its economic survival

but not directly tied to any one economic activity, are located here: sewage treatment plants, incinerators, bus garages, AIDS residences, shelters for the homeless, juvenile detention centres, jails. Recognition of the resulting equity problems is evident in the adoption by several cities and regions of so-called fair share regulations to help ensure a more equitable distribution of what has been described by various acronyms: LULUS (locally unwanted land uses), TOADS (temporarily obsolete and derelict sites), NIMBY (not in my back yard), BANANA (build absolutely nothing anywhere near anyone) and NIMTOO (not in my term of office). Although a step forward, the enforcement of such regulations leaves considerable room for improvement.

Social exclusion is a characteristic of the abandoned and residual city in more industrialized countries. The excluded ghetto is widespread in the US.[31] Two separate streams of analysis have contributed to the discussion, differing in their starting points and emphases, but not necessarily inconsistent with each other. One places the central emphasis on race, the other on economic change and class. The former has been developed, logically enough, in the US;[32] the latter has greater linkages to European experience. The term 'underclass' stresses the role of economic change and its relationship to class; however, the structural underpinnings of this concept have been weakened by the imputing of behavioural connotations. Substitution of the term (new) 'ghetto poor' for 'underclass'[33] suggests the linkage between race and class and their spatial components.[34]

The ostracized marginal settlements and the apartheid township are the older parallels in the developing economies. The presence or absence of the excluded ghetto, or the apartheid township, is in significant part a function of the social and economic policies of government. Thus, although residents from the former Dutch colony of Surinam tend to cluster in certain areas in Amsterdam, and distinct immigrant quarters exist in Stockholm, while Turkish is the dominant language in certain sections of Frankfurt, the local and national policies in these countries preclude the type of ghettoization found in the US,[35] which strongly isolates poor, inner-city African Americans.[36] The Index of Similarity in European cities will hover around 0.35, whereas in the US this measure of isolation more typically is in the 0.5-and-up range. Census data show an ID of 0.68 for Hispanics in Newark, New Jersey, for example, and 0.83 for African Americans in Milwaukee, Wisconsin. The dangers of this pattern are visible around the globe, but they are recognized and countered with much greater will and effort in some countries than in others.

Putting the lines of residential and business division together, a general pattern emerges in which the lines of separation are more or less congruent, and the social, economic, political and cultural divisions largely (but not completely) overlap. One may thus speak of five distinct cities co-existing within the single 'city' of municipal boundaries.

The lines of separation in this five-part division are complex. In the less desirable areas, both in the residential city and the economic city, there is a disproportionately large number of immigrants and households headed by women whose access to better areas is closed off because of discrimination or costs.

> Urban patterns of residential differentiation are not simply a function of 'lifestyle' preferences or 'special needs', but reflect positions in a hierarchy of power and wealth in which some decide and others are decided for

Race, class, ethnicity and gender create overlapping patterns of differentiation: invidious differentiation, for there is no doubt that the differences are not simply a function of 'lifestyle' preferences or 'special needs', but reflect positions in a hierarchy of power and wealth in which some decide and others are decided for. The lines of division, and the spatial and physical reflection of economic polarization, are sharpest and most visible at the two extremes of the scale: the citadel and the ghetto. For example, in São Paulo, the separation of citadels of business into high-rise clusters connected by helicopter to the gated and patrolled residential communities both within and increasingly far outside the city, and the favelas of the poor confined to the far outskirts of town and to little ghettos within it, increasingly characterize a partitioned city.[37] In Shanghai, the shining international skyscrapers of Pudong, designed by and housing global firms, stand in stark contrast to the small ground-level homes of the poor local households that are being replaced. How sharp and how visible such lines of division become in cities around the world will depend both on the intensity of the impact of globalization and on the extent to which the various actors, in government and without, move to counter their negative features.

## ● Walls between the quarters

The poor are walled in by social convention – the stigmatization of their neighbourhoods, often subsidized housing, which has become more and more housing of last resort for the very poor. In large cities around the world, the rich wall themselves in, forming gated communities and walled enclaves in high-tech protected high-rises in security zones in the central cities.[38] For the poor, the demarcation of boundaries may be along the lines of streets, slopes of hills, freeways or open (usually deserted or undermaintained) spaces; they may be artificial or natural barriers (highways or railroad tracks, hills or rivers), or architectural barriers and indicators (the forms of housing, the placement of public facilities). The meaning of the walls of both the wealthy and the poor are recognized by all sides.

In between, the residents of the enclaves of the gentry, the middle class and the working class of the formal labour market also seek to separate themselves out from 'the others', each from those below them, and all from the very poor and excluded. In the US, gated communities and (aptly called) Common Interest Developments (CIDs) for affluent households now constitute the fastest growing segment of the housing market.

> By imposing fines and attaching liens to residents' homes, the governments of 'privatopias' enforce restrictions regarding property and codes of conduct that are rigid and often repressive. They seek to eradicate any behaviour that might conceivably pose a threat to property values, creating regulatory nightmares

These 'privatopias' house more than 32 million people in more than 150,000 such projects across the country. Their residents are required to belong to homeowner associations, pay monthly fees and live under the rule of private residential governments. These governments perform functions that are ordinarily the province of local government: police protection, waste collection, street maintenance, snow removal, landscaping and lighting. By imposing fines and attaching liens to residents' homes, they enforce restrictions regarding property and codes of conduct that are rigid and often repressive. These private governments can regulate people's daily lives in great and personal detail. They are known to have banned spouses below a certain age, pets above a specified weight and children altogether. They have cited a grandmother for kissing a friend goodbye at her front door and ordered a family to stop using their back door because they were wearing an unsightly path. They have forbidden children from playing with metal toys because the rules prescribed wood and they have levied fines for displaying election signs (although this was overruled by the Supreme Court). Appeals are heard by boards whose members may be the very same people who report the alleged violations; a blending of prosecutor and judge unacceptable in democratic society. Although the US constitution protects individuals against state action, the court views homeowner associations as voluntary, private organizations. In this vacuum, they seek to eradicate any behaviour that might conceivably pose a threat to property values, and they have become regulatory nightmares.

A recent study of these types of privatized quarters warns of the residents' diminished sense of civil responsibility to the larger community. Thus residents have organized as interest groups demanding tax refunds from local and state government on the grounds that they are already paying for the privately provided services. These developments further accentuate existing patterns of segregation.[39]

The new architecture of shopping malls, skywalks, and policed pedestrian malls is an additional striking physical mirror of social separation. Downtown skywalks, for instance, symbolically and physically permit the men and women of business and shoppers with money to spend to walk over the heads of the poor.[40] The market serves as the desired stratifying force. Thus retailing is geared to the different market levels of each quarter, and public services such as schools also reflect the characteristics of their locale. For example, schools in locally funded districts with higher revenue bases can purchase better equipment (eg computers), offer enriched curricula and attract more and higher qualified staff by paying higher salaries. However created and walled, the movement towards the hardening of boundaries between the quarters of the city is visible everywhere and can be mapped; for example in newspaper accounts showing the curfew lines after the civil unrest in Los Angeles or in ads showing the security zone around the office clusters in the centre of Johannesburg.

The awareness of this process has led several governments to attempt counter-measures, sometimes with significant success. In The Netherlands, the upgrading of areas with high concentrations of poverty has been a deliberate policy, as it has in other welfare states in Western Europe. The danger, of course, is that the upgrading may lead to gentrification and its concomitant displacement. This concern now pervades Harlem in New York, for example, where the goal – neither ghetto nor gentrified enclave – remains elusive.

### The debasing of the urban cultural environment

> The particular historic character of a city often gets submerged in the direct and overt quest for an international image and international business. Local identity becomes an ornament, a public relations artefact designed to aid marketing

The particular historic character of a city often gets submerged in the direct and overt quest for an international image and international business. From Shanghai to Johannesburg, from Buenos Aires to Melbourne, from Hanoi to St Petersburg, an international business class fashions downtown offices, stores, hotels, resorts and condominiums in its own image. Local identity becomes an ornament, a public relations artefact designed to aid marketing. Authenticity is paid for, encapsulated, mummified, located and displayed to attract tourists rather than to shelter continuities of tradition or the lives of its historic creators. Cultural critics speak of the international 'Disneyfication' of entertainment and recreation, but the process affects the built form of cities as well. Ubiquitous fast food franchises with their trademark architecture, malls of greater and greater scale, chain stores and international franchises dot the urban landscape, in the suburbs as well as downtown areas.[41] In fact, there is convergence in the cultural suburbanization of the central areas of cities, proceeding in parallel with the urbanization of the periphery, to change regional form from concentric to multi-centric to shapeless, while remaining dependent on a single centre for key financial, governmental and control functions.

Such developments have both favourable and unfavourable sides. The favourable ones are perhaps more obvious: McDonald's brings fast food and pleasure to many people, and the success of the Disney stores indicates a market for what they sell. The unfavourable aspects are found in what is lost by this addition to the range of choice: a submergence of identity, a loss of cultural traditions, and a feeling of powerlessness that has contributed to the growth of 'identity politics' around the world.[42] The line between reclaiming identity and separatism akin to tribalism is a thin one.

> Local governments must seek a meaningful multi-culturalism between submergence of identity in assimilation to the majority, on the one hand, and primacy of separate identity in enclavization, on the other

Many governments recognize this, and there is an ongoing quest for a meaningful multi-culturalism between submergence of identity in assimilation to the majority, on the one hand, and primacy of separate identity in enclavization on the other. Several decades ago, the Indian government sought to present the new town of Chandigarh as a showcase to the world, worthy of foreign investment. 'Unfettered by traditions of the past', in Nehru's words, it built a modern city planned by Western experts. But something went wrong. Neighbourhoods planned to be self-contained with one of each of different kinds of stores now have many stores carrying the same merchandise because residents in Chandigarh like to do comparative shopping and bargain; cattle lounge in the middle of the streets, even though it is illegal for most residents to own them; sidewalk vending is outlawed, yet you cannot walk on one without stumbling over peanut vendors, shoe repairmen and turban washers; and there is an expansive park, called 'Leisure Valley', yet few people take their leisure there.[43] In a more recent example of the relationships between local cultural aspects and larger economic considerations, in Ho Chi Minh City, blighted tracts within the inner city were unwelcome sights because it was feared that they would deter international investment by undermining the image of an economically strong and healthy modern city that officials wished to project.[44] A recent case study of two communities in Viet Nam and China offers further insight into peri-urban development under the influence of economic globalization.[45]

### The declining public orientation of the state and the distortions of land use by the market

While the economic aspects of globalization explain a great deal of the patterns just described, these developments could not happen without the support of state policies which reflect the political balance of power that influences as well as mediates globalization.

> The emphasis on the 'competitiveness of cities' has the effect of apotheosizing the private market

The emphasis on the 'competitiveness of cities' (as if a 'city' were competitive, rather than just particular businesses and other stakeholders), that is taken as essential for a city's ability to thrive in a global age, has the effect of apotheosizing the private market. The private market will naturally segregate; it abandons brownfield sites, wastes land in speculation, pollutes, sprawls, builds four petrol stations at one road junction, creates deserted malls all over and dead centres in the middle. Only with effective government action can such wasteful results be avoided. It takes public action to produce a measure of equality in the use of urban space, but public policy working in that direction is less and less evident. This was shown in the case studies of Sydney, Singapore and London, presented earlier.

> What is controversial is not urban planning, per se, but rather the *direction* of local governmental activity. Should it be directed solely at efficiency, reinforcing the current distributions of wealth and power, or should it play a redistributive role, creating a minimum standard for quality of life for *all* of its residents?

The extent of government's role in shaping cities is an ideologically controversial topic. The fact that without a very active governmental role, cities could not exist is hardly in issue: traffic could not move, the danger of fires would be uncontrolled, health hazards would multiply, cities would be unliveable. What is controversial is rather the *direction* of local government activity: whether it should be directed solely at efficiency, reinforcing the current distributions of wealth and power, or whether it should play a redistributive role, creating a minimum standard for quality of life for *all* of its residents. Attacks on public planning, epitomized by the policies of the Thatcher and Reagan administrations, often question the redistributive aspects of such planning, rather than the planning itself.

In response, the tendency is to call for the separation of planning from (potentially redistributive) politics, to technocratize it, place it in the jurisdiction of a specialized bureaucracy and remove it from public scrutiny. There are planners who resist this trend, individually or collaboratively, and seek to occupy a professional crossroads to mediate the global and the local.[46] However, the matter is first of all a political one. It is important to recognize local and community-based protest in the name of equality and of democracy, with varying effect depending on the issues involved in different countries. The move to greater local initiative and greater local participation, strongly encouraged by Habitat, in general supports the redistributive direction of governmental action. It is critical that this role of government is also explicitly emphasized in models of good practice identified by Habitat.

## The residualization of social housing

> In no country in the world does the market provide adequate housing for those unable to make payments for it at the prevailing rates of return; nor would the market be expected to do so

The place of social housing in cities may be taken as a litmus test for the extent of inequality in its residential structure. In no country in the world does the market provide adequate housing for those unable to make payments for it at the prevailing rates of return; nor would the market be expected to do so. This is true regardless of globalization. However, globalization has added to the

perennial problem of translating need into demand: an increase of inequality and a process of exclusion have made the plight of those at the bottom of the economic ladder even more difficult. Governmental action is thus needed to protect those the market does not serve. In the years immediately following the Second World War, most governments took energetic action to secure adequate housing for their populations, the extent varying with resource availability. Whether for returning war veterans or in devastated communities, the need was dire, and acknowledged. In many countries, the dominant force in housing construction was public, and broad sections of the population were eligible for government supported housing. Today, that situation is still true only in a handful of countries. The pattern is rather that of privatization of social housing, the reduction of government's role in housing provision. This trend is most strikingly evident in the formerly state socialist countries of Eastern Europe, where the income gap is also growing rapidly, but it can be seen as well in most other countries. The result has been a residualization of social housing in the developed countries and a stratification of its occupants in less developed countries. The unwillingness to subsidize 'unproductive' investment in housing is a consequence, at least in part, of the pressures felt by governmental leaders from perceived global competition; it has led to heightened segregation and inequality in housing provision around the world.

In summary, major unfavourable urban impacts of globalization include an increase in inequality, and its reflection and reinforcement in the quartering of the spatial structure of cities. Alongside this rise in spatial separation are other unfavourable consequences: the restructuring of central business districts, creating mismatches between job and housing markets; the debasing of older cultures with homogenization of new culture; and the residualization of social housing, as part of the general movement away from the use of government in a socially redistributive capacity towards a more technocratic and efficiency-oriented mode. However, there are also countervailing trends.

# Countervailing Favourable Trends

## The democratization of decision-making

> The single greatest positive feature of the development of cities in the last 30 years has been the increasing participation of their residents in decisions concerning their future

The single greatest positive feature of the development of cities in the last 30 years has been the increasing participation of their residents in decisions concerning their future. Citizen participation in planning and local government has been on the increase almost everywhere in the world. It has rightly been a major thrust of Habitat's efforts over the years. Participation, of course, is not necessarily the same thing as influence, and certainly not the same thing as decision-making; yet it is an essential element in each. How far participation will develop to change decision-making depends on the existing relationships of power, which, in many ways, globalization has served to reinforce. But the movement is undeniably there.

Decentralization of powers from national governments to cities, a characteristic policy of many countries, is ambiguous in this regard: since the resource base of national economies is not effectively tapped at the local level, if responsibility is devolved without a parallel devolution of resources, decentralization may increase inequality more than reduce it.

> Since the resource base of national economies is not effectively tapped at the local level, if responsibility is devolved without a parallel devolution of resources, decentralization may increase inequality more than reduce it

The impact of globalization on resident participation is still unclear. Two opposite tendencies can be discerned. On the one hand, the domination of a mass media, increasingly multinational in its ownership, homogeneous in its content and centralized in its control, permits a manipulation of popular opinion that the established holders of power are well able to exploit. On the other hand, the speed and ubiquity of communications technology facilitates the organization of social movements, helps citizens' groups to hammer out agendas, makes possible better coordination of protests and, above all, enables the distribution of the information necessary for effective action. By the same token, while the mobility of capital far exceeds that of labour, the internet has provided a channel of communication worldwide that has allowed local groups, organized around particular local problems, to share information with other groups having encountered similar problems. It also permits citizens' protest to be organized on a global basis, and a global public opinion to be formed that may exert a countervailing influence to globally organized established power. A case in point is the successful mobilization of support for the boycott of cargo originating from Liverpool by dockworkers in ports around the world, acting in solidarity with British colleagues. The Liverpool dockworkers were on strike to protest against deregulation and the introduction of more casual and less secure working conditions by Mersey Docks and Harbour Company, who were seeking an edge over global competitors.[47] Another example is the effective collaboration of activists in India and the US in opposition to the opening of a DuPont Nylon factory, resulting in the project being scrapped after disclosure of shortcomings in its environmental record.[48]

Three social movements go well beyond individual cities, but have strong local implications. The women's movement, movements of ethnic groups organized around issues of civil rights and environmental movements, all have supra-urban bases but important impacts on cities. The women's movement has put in the forefront the question of the impact of urban developments of globalization generally on human welfare, with disproportionately negative implications for women. Not only are women's pay scales still substantially below those of men for equal work, and not only is much of women's work still entirely unpaid and unrecognized, but also, in the distribution of public facilities and urban services, women's needs tend to be subordinated to those of the business community and the men who dominate it. Issues of child care, of security in the streets, of accessibility – of rights to the city – have all been effectively raised by women.

Globalization heightens the salience of urban identity politics, alluded to above. An important factor is the flow of immigrants into cities, which is expected to continue given labour market requirements and demographic trends and augmented by refugees requesting political asylum. These urban influxes often comprise minority populations without citizenship rights. Because inequality in income, education and political power is so often directly related to ethnicity and race, campaigns against discrimination are in general also campaigns for greater equality. Affirmative action, long a progressive slogan in the US, may be on the defensive there, but elsewhere it is increasingly recognized as a necessary accompaniment to efforts to reduce inequality. The forms it should take are matters of discussion in most of these places, but it involves explicit recognition of ethnicity and race as bases of inequality.

The environmental movement has probably most explicitly dealt with the unfavourable consequences of globalization, both in natural areas and in cities. Environmental quality and human equality are closely connected: pollution, lack of clean water, inadequate sewage disposal, polluting industries and lack of green space are all more typically characteristics of poor communities. The escape of the rich to environmentally more friendly suburbs in protected enclaves only reinforces the inequality in the distribution and location of environmental detriments and benefits. This relationship between environmental concerns and inequality has been clearly brought into focus, on a global basis, by various international meetings, including the Habitat conferences in 1976 and 1996. Figure 2.1 illustrates the role of these events in bringing these issues to the fore.[48]

The figure shows how the number of legal publications concerned with environmental justice increased significantly after the United Nations Conference on Environment and Development (UNCED), held in 1992 in Rio de Janeiro. The legal output on environmental justice then dropped off, only to rise again after UNCED+5.

Although these data are but a limited indicator of impact, they seem to signal that the United Nations global summit meetings help to crystallize and concentrate professional awareness and activity on selected key issues.

> United Nations global summit meetings help to crystallize and concentrate professional awareness and activity on selected key issues

## The advance of knowledge

At the beginning of the third millennium, the technical knowledge exists to deal with the unfavourable urban manifestations of globalization that have been described above. The social knowledge to put that technical knowledge into practice also exists. We have the scientific knowledge to avoid and to control environmental degradation; we have the planning competence to improve housing, to plan cities well, to equalize educational opportunity and to open the doors to a better quality of life for all of the residents of cities throughout the world. Globalization has significantly increased both our technical and our social know-how. More and more, this knowledge is being shared, allowing learning about, if not transfer of, successful policies and programmes. Habitat has provided the lead in the documentation of best practices.[50]

> Best practices often illustrate only the best that can be done under *existing* national policies and decision-making processes; what is further needed is a set of 'best policies' and 'best decision-making processes' for wide dissemination. Elaboration of normative 'first' principles will allow 'audits' or assessments of how well practices conform to stated goals and how they might be improved

The development of such databases produces valuable resources that help to build a cumulative body of knowl-

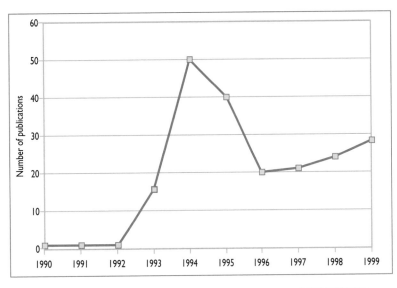

Figure 2.1

**Legal publications on environmental justice, 1990–1999**

edge. But best practices often illustrate only the best that can be done under existing national policies and decision-making processes; what is further needed is a set of 'best policies' and 'best decision-making processes' for wide dissemination. Elaboration of normative 'first' principles will also allow 'audits' or assessments of how well practices conform to stated goals and how they might be improved. In a related vein, with private and public sector support, UNCHS (Habitat) has established the Global Urban Observatory Programme[51] to put in place a reporting system for urban indicators meant to assist in the monitoring of policy implementation. However, inequalities of power, magnified by contemporary globalization, hamper the uses of that knowledge and information for beneficial public purposes. In more cases than not, interests favouring accumulation of private wealth prevail over groups that give greater priority to social justice and environmental sustainability. Fortunately, there are encouraging examples of more positive outcomes.[51]

> Globalization has significantly increased both our technical and our social know-how. More and more, this knowledge is being shared, allowing learning about, if not transfer of, successful policies and programmes. However, inequalities of power, magnified by contemporary globalization, hamper the uses of that knowledge for beneficial public purposes. It is important to identify ways to channel globalization into alternative and more positive forms

Although it is important to start this report by recognizing the pressing problems of human settlements associated with current globalization, it is equally important to identify ways for channelling globalization into alternative and more positive forms. Doing so will help to inform and guide the future development of our cities around the world. It is to this task that the remainder of this report now turns.

# Notes

1  This section is adapted from 'Globalization, Urban Planning and Local Democracy', a paper prepared by Andrew Thornley, London School of Economics.

2  See, for example, Held, 1999.

3  See, for example, Giddens, 1990; 2000.

4  See Harvey, 1989.

5  See especially Molotch, 1993; Ferman, 1996; Jonas and Wilson, 1999.

6  For a good account of this work, see Judge, 1995.

7  See Plaza, 1999; McNeill, 2000.

8  The ill-starred dome venture, with it slavish start-up budget, was pushed past a sceptical cabinet and treasury opposition, and has become a political albatross (Sunday Times, 2000).

9  These developments have been documented in many analyses, notably in the work of Saskia Sassen, for example:Sassen, 1998; 2000a, b.

10  It cost the equivalent of £19,000 per employee to attract Samsung, the South Korean electronics company, and £30,000 to attract Germany's Siemens to build plants in north-east England (Adams, 1999).

11  See, for example, Judd, 1999.

12  For example, for the World Soccer Championships in 1998 France spent $US500 million on the Stade de France (not counting the cost of such extras as new subway and commuter rail stations), a state of the art sports stadium located in what has been described as the most disadvantaged district of France with an unemployment rate of 15 per cent among a largely immigrant population living in deteriorated housing, lacking public services and facing multiple, serious neighbourhood problems (Le Figaro, 1998, pp 1, 8, 9; see also Swardson, 1998, p C6).Toronto's bid for the 2008 Olympic Games has caused concern among a coalition of groups, aptly named Bread Not Circuses (http://www.breadnotcircuses.org/home.html).

13  See Olds, 1998.

14  The following section is drawn from Jones, 2000.

15  The following discussion is drawn from 'Implications of Globalization for Cities', a background paper prepared by Peter Marcuse, Columbia University.

16  The greater facility at creating forms of entertainment and distributing them widely could as well be used to support a proliferation of diverse cultural experiments as a homogenization of culture; however, as an example, the domination of US movies on international television is not a function of the medium, but of the messengers.

17  Significant in this regard is the development of best practices databases and research on policy transfer, see www.bestpractices.org

18  See Olds, 1998.

19  From UNDP, 1996a.

20  See, for example, Demissie, 1998; Ha, 1998; Lee and Murie, 1999; Murdie and Borgegard, 1998; Musterd et al, 1999; Withers, 1997; Auyero, 1999; Caldeira, 1996a. A recent special issue of Progress in Planning 52 (1999) includes an examination of divided cities from an historical perspective. See also Harris, 1984.

21  Manuel Castells (1996) has coined the phrase 'space of flows' as non-place based spaces. However, as Saskia Sassen (1994) has pointed out, those spaces need to be based in specific places (she argues global cities, but all cities are to some extent globalizing) and what we here call the luxury city and its business correlate, the city of control, are among those places. Possible locations are limited, but the mobility available to them is far more extensive than for the activities in other parts of the city.

22  Steven Brint, in Mollenkopf and Castells, 1991, p 155.

23  The term was first used in this context by John Friedmann 30 years ago.

24  Toll, 1969.

25  The term is used here, not in its narrower sense, as a portion of the city in which higher class groups have displaced lower class (see definitions in Marcuse, 1985), but in the broader sense of areas occupied by, or intended for, the professionals, managers and technicians, and thus may include newly constructed housing as well as housing 'gentrified' in the narrower sense of the word.

26  The reference here is not to creative artists, to what in earlier days would have been called Bohemians, who cannot generally afford the prices of the gentrified city, and are more likely to live somewhere between the abandoned and the tenement city. To the extent that they tend to congregate in specific neighbourhoods, they may serve as precursors of gentrification (see Rose, 1984, who differentiates sharply among different categories of gentrifiers).

27  Häusermann and Siebel, 1987. See also Marcuse, 1991.

28  See www.worldbank.org/html/fpd/urban/cws/cwoslums.htm.

29  See, for instance, Sassen, 1989, with brief but provocative comments on intra-city spatial aspects of these trends.

30  See, for example, the CARDO International Project on home-based enterprises at http://buildnet.csir.co.za/hbe/Default.htm

31  For a recent discussion, see Marcuse, 1996.

32  See Massey and Denton, 1993. See also Goldsmith and Blakeley, 1992; Bullard et al, 1994.

33  Wilson, 1991.

34  Waquant and Gans have recently argued that overuse of the term 'ghetto' has made it a conceptual passepartout that insufficiently differentiates between the types of situations it originally denoted and the conditions described by its more recent usage.

35  See Burgers, 1996 for a study of undocumented immigrant workers in The Netherlands. See also the recent special issue of Urban Studies ((1999), 14(5)) on 'Divided Cities' in Europe.

36  See, for example, Massey and Denton, 1993; Goering et al 1997.

37  See also Caldeira, 1996a.

38  See intimidating walls at Chacara Flora in São Paulo, and walls at Courtyard Village, Rua Conde D'Eu, of Coelho da Fonseca. Even the name gives it away.

39  For an in-depth study of these privatopias, see McKenzie, 1994. See also Ross, 1999, for a study of Celebration, Florida, the new town owned and run by the Disney Corporation.

40  See Marcuse, 1988; Barnett, 1989.

41  Several US (small) towns have passed or are discussing enactment of local ordinances (a Community Vitality Act) prohibiting the opening of new commercial establishments that are part of (inter)national chains, such as certain fast food outlets, coffee shops, clothing and do-it-yourself stores. Proponents argue that this measure helps to retain local revenue and preserves local character; detractors oppose it on the grounds that it unfairly restricts competition, allowing local business to charge higher prices.

42  See, for example, McNeill, 2000, for a study of the tension between Basque national identity and globalization represented by the establishment of the Guggenheim museum in Bilbao, Spain.

43  See Brolin, 1972.

44  International Development Research Centre and Hanoi Architectural University, 1997.

45  See Leaf, 2000.

46  See, for example, Wright, 1998.

47  See Lavalette and Kennedy, 1996, for a vivid account. In brief, the dispute started when five dockworkers were sacked in a disagreement about overtime. Eighty of their co-workers responded by setting up a picket line to protest against the dismissals. The dispute intensified when 400 dockers employed by the MDHC refused to cross the picket line and were fired en masse. MDHC was able to take advantage of Britain's Thatcherite labour laws designed to prohibit traditional forms of working class resistance such as secondary strikes, also making it possible to sack workers without any right of redress and to replace them with casual, scab labour. British port employers engaged in a concerted drive to employ workforces that would be fully utilized, low cost and available on a just-in-time or 'as needed' basis. They wanted to employ only atomized workers who were isolated from each other, competed with each other for work and could be called to the docks at short notice, a system allowed by deregulation and facilitated by modern information and communication technologies. However, the strikers used the same technologies to mobilize support among fellow dockworkers around the world who recognized the similarity between their respective struggles. Detailed information on the emergence of the international dockworkers movement and their effective use of modern communication technologies can be found on the web at www.labournet.net/docks2/other/dockhome.htm

48  See Jenkins and Goetz, 1999.

49  Articles from legal journals, yearbooks, institutes, bar association organs, law reviews and government publications originating in the US, Canada, the UK, Ireland, Australia and New Zealand. Available through Online Computer Library Center (OCLC) atwww.oclc.org/oclc/menu/home1.htm, used by over 36,000 libraries in 74 countries.

50  See http://www.bestpractices.org/.

51  See http://www.urbanobservatory.org/.

52  See, for example, Evans et al, 2001 for a series of fine case studies of struggles for progress.

# 3

# FRAMING NORMATIVE POLICY PLATFORMS

*'Ultimately, global society will be judged on how well –
or how poorly – it treats its weakest and most disadvantaged. With one-tenth of humanity living at the margin
of survival, our record is not one that can be celebrated.
We must change it. We must act collectively and
decisively to bring about this change'* – Kofi Annan,
Address to the Eighth Annual Ministerial Meeting of
the Least Developed Countries, New York, 28
September 1998

The troubling trends reviewed in the preceding two
chapters have elicited responses from United Nations
organizations. A number of them held summit meetings
during the 1990s, and each resulted in political consensus
on, and adoption of, a global plan of action. Table 3.1 lists
those conferences whose themes are significant in relation
to human settlements and which are reviewed in
subsequent sections of this chapter.

What emerged from these conferences are the
contours of a normative framework for development
policies that take advantage of the potential of globalization as a tool to attain goals of social justice and
environmental sustainability. The crucial question now is:
How can this potential be better realized?

> What emerged from the United Nations conferences
> are the contours of a normative framework for devel-
> opment policies that take advantage of the potential
> of globalization as a tool to attain goals of social
> justice and environmental sustainability. The crucial
> question now is: How can this potential be better
> realized?

## Antecedents and Context

The normative frameworks that the global conferences of
the 1990s helped to establish did not come about in a
vacuum. A brief background of the historical antecedents
and context of the emergence of these new norms is of
more than just passing historical interest. Insights and
understanding in this regard will assist us in their
implementation in the future.

Global conferences were not unique to the 1990s.
Indeed, many of the subjects addressed – human rights,
population, women – had been the subject of international
conferences during previous decades. These precursors

offered valuable fora to discuss and search for global accommodation and consensus when the two superpowers had
stopped meaningful communication with each other for
extended periods. Although these earlier conferences helped
to spread new ideas, their momentum dissipated during
'the lost decade' of the 1980s, overshadowed, if not
hamstrung, by the Cold War, structural adjustment policies
and conservative political realignments, as pursued by the
Reagan and Thatcher administrations. Also, notwithstanding important progress, further advances stagnated, as
participating countries remained mired in blocs.

The Helsinki Accords of 1975 were followed by a
period of detente during which many Western Europeans
travelled to the Eastern Bloc, realizing there was no threat
of a communist invasion but also seeing first-hand evidence
of Soviet denial of human rights and the oppression of
dissent. NATO's decision to deploy a new generation of
nuclear missiles in Europe in the early 1980s met with
popular protests on a massive scale.

These unprecedented public actions stressed the link
between peace, democracy and human rights. Millions took
to the streets of the capital cities and signed the European
Nuclear Disarmament (END) Appeal, which called on its
signatories not to 'be loyal to East or West, but to each
other'. The end of the Cold War signalled new opportunities to engage major issues of the time by collaboration
across national boundaries. Willingness to create and use
those opportunities was stimulated by forms of
transnational civil society that had emerged from a dialogue
between peace movements in Western Europe and human
rights movements in Eastern Europe.[1]

The global conferences of the 1990s were
qualitatively different from their predecessors. These recent
summits were truer world conferences in the sense that
they were driven more by awareness of a single world that
shared pervasive common problems. These later conferences
helped to promote global cooperation on a less confrontational basis and yielded frameworks for problem solving
based more on principles of joint responsibility.[2]

> In the aftermath of the Cold War, the international
> community began to reconceptualize security more
> in terms of security of people, and less of states

After its civil war, in 1952, Costa Rica redefined its national
security as it abolished its army, deciding that the best
interests of its population would be better secured by

**Table 3.1**

Characteristics of
selected United
Nations conferences,
1990–1996

| Year | Title | Location | Participating governments | NGO presence | Principal themes | Resulting documents |
|------|-------|----------|--------------------------|--------------|------------------|---------------------|
| 1990 | World Summit for Children | New York, USA | 159 | 45 | Goals for the year 2000 for children's health, nutrition, education, and access to safe water and sanitation | World Declaration and Plan of Action on the Survival, Protection and Development of Children |
| 1992 | United Nations Conference on Environment and Development | Rio de Janeiro, Brazil | 172 | 2400 | Environment and sustainable development | Agenda 21, the Rio Declaration on Environment and Development, the Statement of Forest Principles, the United Nations Framework Convention on Climate Change and the United Nations Convention on Biological Diversity |
| 1993 | World Conference on Human Rights | Vienna, Austria | 171 | >800 | The promotion and protection of human rights | The Vienna Declaration and Programme of Action |
| 1994 | International Conference on Population and Development | Cairo, Egypt | 179 | 1500 | Population, sustained economic growth and sustainable development | Programme of Action of the ICPD |
| 1995 | World Summit for Social Development | Copenhagen, Denmark | 186 | 4500 | Social development with three core issues: eradication of poverty, expansion of productive employment and reduction of unemployment, and social integration | Copenhagen Declaration on Social Development and Programme of Action |
| 1995 | Fourth World Conference on Women | Beijing, China | 189 | 2100 | The advancement and empowerment of women in relation to women's human rights, women and poverty, women and decision-making, the girl-child, violence against women, and other areas of concern | The Beijing Declaration and Platform for Action |
| 1996 | Second United Nations Conference on Human Settlements | Istanbul, Turkey | 171 | 2400 | Sustainable human settlements development in an urbanizing world; adequate shelter for all | Habitat Agenda, Istanbul Declaration on Human Settlements |

**Source:** United Nations Department of Public Information, 1997.

investments in national health care and education than by military expenditures. Similarly, in the aftermath of the Cold War, the international community began to reconceptualize security more in terms of security of people, and less of states, acknowledging that there were also many people at risk in secure states. Although the North–South divide remained as salient as before, there was an increased realization that characteristics of the South are also found in the North, and vice versa. There are sections in New York with child mortality rates worse than in many developing nations, homeless people in London unable even to afford the cheapest local housing, and in Latin America, where poverty is widespread and increasing, there are people who rank among the world's most affluent elite.[3]

The emergence of global norms through the United Nations summits cannot be traced to a single factor. It involved the mobilization of civil society, the political will of governments and the initiative of private sector interests; not necessarily agreeing on the contents of the norms, but jointly moving in the *direction* of greater global discourse and action. This movement was facilitated by the same information and communication technologies used by owners of capital to enlarge their wealth. The process entailed negotiations that did not proceed without interruption. Certainly, progress was slow and non-linear, and results did not happen overnight.

> The articulation and implementation of new global norms is a slow and long-term process, involving contestation by multiple actors in governments, civil society and the private sector

The articulation of new global norms involves contestation and claims by multiple stakeholders, and their implementation advances through disputes and arguments. And just as the evolution of norms is a long-term process, their implementation will also take time. These realizations about past developments can help to inform future approaches.

The rest of this chapter develops a fuller understanding of this background, the more substantive aspects of which are elaborated in Parts II, III and IV. The insights thus provided guide the discussion of prospective developments and policy options in Parts V and VI. Before considering the priorities and outcomes of selected United Nations summits during the 1990s in relation to human settlement development, it is appropriate first to review briefly a major prior UNCHS initiative, developed during the 1980s: The Global Strategy for Shelter to the Year 2000.

## Global Strategy for Shelter to the Year 2000[4]

In 1988, the United Nations General Assembly adopted the Global Strategy for Shelter to the Year 2000 (GSS).[5] This action marked a major shift in housing-related policies of the United Nations as well as those of other multilateral and bilateral development assistance organizations. By the end of the 1970s, it had become clear to housing policy makers that simple replication of model projects did not work, and that they had to seek new ways to increase the scale in the provision of housing, whether through public or private sector efforts or some new combination of the two. What became the new policy focus and why was there a change?

Before the 1980s, human settlement policies almost exclusively focused on providing housing for the poor. Most international aid agencies and national governments concentrated on squatter settlement upgrading, and sites and services programmes to help the poor obtain housing. According to nearly all accounts, the 'housing-for-the-poor' strategy had not worked. Administrative and financial problems had thwarted the widespread replication of squatter settlement upgrading programmes. Sites and services programmes had fared no better, with only a few examples for which the output of the programmes had come close to matching the housing needs of the poor. Problems with replicability and implementation, as well as the sheer scale of housing needs of the poor, had revealed the limitations of the housing-for-the-poor strategy.[6] The GSS called for a scaling up of housing programmes, going beyond the traditional pilot project approach.[7] It further noted that investments in housing sector development are important productive contributions to economic growth.[8]

> The GSS replaced sites and services and squatter upgrading policies with the 'enabling approach', focused on reforms to improve the efficiency and effectiveness of housing markets

The GSS replaced sites and services and squatter upgrading policies with a totally different policy initiative referred to as the 'enabling approach'. This new directive, articulated by the United Nations, the World Bank and other multilateral and bilateral agencies concerned with housing, focused on implementing reforms to improve the overall efficiency and effectiveness of housing markets. Instead of direct interventions to improve squatter housing conditions or provide sites and services, the enabling approach was introduced to revise or eliminate policies or regulations that impeded the provision of housing. Overly restrictive land and housing development regulations were seen to prevent housing supply from responding to demand pressures. It was argued that many land use planners did not consider the cost and affordability implications of the master plans, zoning ordinances and subdivision development controls. If standards were set too high, low- and middle-income households would be forced into the informal housing sector, where housing development is unregulated.

According to the GSS, as the basis of a workable housing strategy, governments should review existing legislation and regulations and their impact on shelter production and improvement, and remove those that clearly appeared to be pointless and largely unenforceable. Governments should deploy their own resources in strategic areas such as the provision of trunk infrastructure, the development of land, the regulation of construction and the promotion of a variety of housing finance institutions.[9] GSS placed greater reliance on private and individual initiatives to produce housing. It also argued for integration of women's needs and roles in housing and human settlement development.[10] As a result, international development assistance agencies began to concentrate on providing technical assistance and policy-based lending to developing countries aimed at enabling housing markets to work better.

For example, in sub-Saharan Africa and parts of Latin America, land titling and land registration systems are often absent or non-functioning, making it extremely difficult and expensive to obtain land with secure title. Without secure titles, owners cannot obtain financing for the construction or upgrading of housing and are reluctant to invest personal resources. Also, without a well-developed housing finance system, it is difficult for housing markets to work efficiently. In response to these policy and institutional impediments, the GSS encouraged governments in developing countries to undertake a range of institutional reforms, including:

- Clarifying and strengthening property rights related to the ownership and transfer of land and real property.
- Developing housing and construction finance institutions to mobilize and disperse capital for housing construction and purchase.
- Rationalizing subsidies for housing and infrastructure to make them more transparent, better targeted and affordable.
- Improving the provision of infrastructure by better coordinating service delivery, rationalizing financing and cost recovery, and targeting service delivery to underused and vacant parcels in existing urban areas.
- Reforming land and housing development regulations to better balance costs and benefits.
- Promoting competition in the housing construction and building materials industry.
- Developing a market-oriented institutional framework for implementing enabling reforms that combine public, private and non-governmental actors.

The main objective of GSS was to facilitate adequate shelter for all by the year 2000, a target date chosen to be close enough to command immediate action but also sufficiently far away to allow enough time for the implementation of necessary changes and reforms.[11] The United Nations General Assembly designated UNCHS (Habitat) as the agency responsible for the coordination of implementation of GSS. UNCHS was to monitor progress on a continuing basis according to rigorous global indicators. Although progress has been made, as later chapters of this report make clear, many millions remain without adequate shelter or lack any shelter at all.

> The enabling approach represented an important shift in international housing policy. It stressed the role of the market, not the government, in housing delivery, and it focused on regulatory and institutional reform, not on direct housing production. Current strategies have introduced more rights-based approaches

The enabling approach characteristic of the Global Strategy for Shelter to the Year 2000 represented an important shift in international housing policy. It emphasized the role of the market, not the government, in housing delivery, and it focused interventions on regulatory and institutional reform, not on direct housing production. It sought a blend of state and private sector roles in housing provision oriented to deregulation so as to enable markets to work and to enhance market efficiency.[12] Its genesis, and more so its implementation, were linked to liberal development approaches geared to opening markets, such as those advocated by the World Bank and the IMF in their Structural Adjustment Policies, and were part of the dominant orientation of economic globalization, discussed in the Prologue of this report.

In comparison, current strategies, as advocated in this report, favour more rights-based approaches, while taking advantage of the potential of housing markets. This new strategy, as stated in a recent report of the Secretary General, promotes globally relevant norms and standards on secure land tenure and adequate housing and services, using an integrated approach of complementary action of research on norms and standards, capacity building, and direct intervention through field projects at the national and local levels.[13] These elements receive attention in subsequent parts of this report. This chapter now turns to a brief discussion of the major United Nations conferences of the 1990s, concluding with Habitat II in Istanbul in 1996.

# Human Settlements Policy Issues in United Nations Development Agendas in the 1990s

The United Nations development agendas of the 1990s have direct and indirect implications for the development of human settlements. These implications are reflected in the declarations and plans of action endorsed by summits and world conferences, which were held with active and wide participation of governments and non-governmental organizations (Table 3.1). In relation to the central concerns with human settlements in this report, two themes are especially pertinent. They focus on the urgency of eradicating poverty and reducing inequality, and the articulation of new policy approaches based on human rights to develop solutions to these problems. In addition, the summits centred attention on related issues of empowerment and gender equality.[14]

### The focus on poverty and human rights

Poverty and inequality were important in all of the United Nations conferences of the 1990s. The first of these, the *World Summit on Children*, held in 1990, focused on children, who represent not only a significant proportion of the overall population, but make up more than 50 per cent of the population in many of the world's poorest communities and are at greater risk from the adverse effects of poverty, such as those resulting from malnourishment, inadequate sanitation, unsafe water, environmental contamination and homelessness.[15] The first to specify measurable goals for the next decade, this summit adopted the Declaration on the Survival, Protection and Development of Children and a Plan of Action with goals for improving child survival;

protection from disease, death, unsanitary conditions and exploitation; and development. Its precursor, the 1989 Convention on the Rights of the Child is 'the world's most rapidly and widely ratified human rights instrument'.[16] The principles contained in this Convention directly relate to human settlements, offering the world 'a vision of … children and adolescents living in stable and nurturing homes and communities where, with adult guidance and protection, they have ample opportunities to develop the fullness of their strengths and talents, and where their human rights are respected'.[17] The Convention stressed equal rights and opportunities for all children, including street children.[18]

The *United Nations Conference on Environment and Development* of 1992 adopted Agenda 21 as 'a wide-ranging blueprint for action to achieve sustainable development worldwide'.[19] It included a chapter on combating poverty, which noted that 'the eradication of poverty and hunger, greater equity in income distribution and human resource development remain major challenges everywhere' (para 3.1). It set broad goals for action, many of which emphasize local-level action to enable the poor to achieve sustainable livelihoods. Despite the noble objectives, Agenda 21's five-year review concluded that poverty was increasing in many places and that poverty eradication had to be understood as an overriding goal. It stated that 'The enormity and complexity of the poverty issue could endanger the social fabric, undermine economic development and the environment and threaten political stability in many countries' and it established several goals related to human settlements:

1   Improving access to sustainable livelihoods, entrepreneurial opportunities and productive resources.
2   Providing universal access to basic social services.
3   Progressively developing social protection systems to support those who cannot support themselves.
4   Empowering people living in poverty and their organizations.
5   Addressing the disproportionate impact of poverty on women.[20]

The Vienna Declaration that came out of the *World Conference on Human Rights* of 1993, recognizes that human settlements provide a context in which human rights are both exercised and abused. Part I relates the physical environment of human settlements to human rights when it states that the dumping of toxic and dangerous products and waste threatens the rights to health and to life (para.11). It also invokes social aspects of human settlements in its condemnation of extreme poverty as inhibiting the enjoyment of human rights (para. 14,25,30). It further urges states to cease any measures that impede the realization of human rights, 'in particular the rights of everyone to a standard of living adequate for their health and well-being, including food and medical care, housing and necessary social services' (para 31).

In the aftermath of the Vienna Conference, some officials expressed disappointment with the Vienna Declaration and Programme of Action (VDPA), which failed to specify the right to housing. In particular, the Special

Rapporteur on housing rights, appointed by the Commission on Human Rights, stated that

> 'as fundamental as housing is in any society to the well-being of citizens, to the security and health of the population as a whole and even to the economy, very often housing rights are forgotten within the human rights domain'.[21]

The NGO forum that accompanied the World Conference issued a report that dealt extensively with the human right to housing and the practice of forced evictions.[22] Five years later, the follow-up review did mention protection of the right to adequate housing (para. 32).[23] It also condemned an 'economic growth-centred approach to development' (Part IV, para. 29), and noted the risk for many of being marginalized and effectively excluded from the benefits of globalization (Part IV, para. 29).

The Programme of Action adopted at the *International Conference on Population and Development* (ICPD) of 1994 offered a number of recommendations concerning poverty with implications for human settlements, including steps to promote the integration of the urban poor into the formal economy (para. 9.15) and the financing of infrastructure and service provision in an equitable manner (para. 9.16).[24] It also praised the work of local community-based organizations, which 'are rooted in and interact with constituencies that are poorly served' (para. 15.2). It advocated that grassroots movements be given greater recognition, including at the local level, as valuable partners for implementing the programme of action (para. 15.4). Consistent with these recommendations, the five-year follow-up review of 1999 urged governments to improve service delivery and to ensure adequate financial resources for meeting the needs of all citizens, including the urban poor, while continuing to promote collaboration with community-based organizations.[25]

The eradication of poverty was one of the core issues at the *World Summit for Social Development* of 1995. Its Programme of Action observed that:

> 'urban poverty is rapidly increasing in pace with overall urbanization. It is a growing phenomenon in all countries and regions, and often poses special problems, such as overcrowding, contaminated water and bad sanitation, unsafe shelter, crime and additional social problems' (Chapter 2, para. 21).

Government leaders committed to focusing on the root causes of poverty and ensuring that the poor have equal access to productive resources, including credit, land, education and training, technology, knowledge and information, as well as to public services, and the opportunity to participate in decision-making. The summit's policy recommendations expressed support for community development projects, and the involvement of the poor in setting the goals, implementing and assessing such projects (paras. 26h, 28a, 28f). Recommendations also stressed the importance of establishing and strengthening financial and technical assistance for community development projects, and the local groups who undertake them (28f, 31f).

Additional recommendations urged actions to increase the quality and availability of transport, communication and energy in poor communities, especially in isolated or marginalized settlements; improve opportunities for productivity and income generation (31a); promote public and private investment in housing, water and sanitation; and improve the supply of affordable and adequate shelter (34c, 36m). The report also identified several distinct populations of the urban poor whose needs should be addressed, including the displaced, the homeless, street children, single mothers, people with disabilities and older persons (34h, 39e) and encouraged cooperation by a range of actors in urban planning and development (34g).

Critics of the Summit's outcomes rejected its endorsement of free market forces, the priority it accorded to economic growth, the undemocratic nature of structural adjustment policies, and the failure to recognize the primacy of human rights.[26] Various international NGOs and activist networks drafted the Copenhagen Alternative Declaration,[27] which criticized the official Declaration, pointing out the contradictions of its underlying agenda and suggesting alternatives that they considered more equitable.[28]

The official Declaration resulting from the follow-up in 1999 re-affirmed the anti-poverty objectives stated five years earlier and pledged to halve extreme poverty by 2015. However, critics pointed to the lack of firm commitments and argued that support for a market-led development model, as advocated by the IMF and the World Bank, would benefit wealthy elites and multinational corporations rather than ensure provision of basic services for the poor. United Nations Secretary-General Kofi Annan warned that 'a backlash against globalization' would emerge 'if the needs of people in developing countries are not addressed'.[29]

The *Fourth World Conference on Women* of 1995 focused on gender-related issues in 12 areas of concern, with the feminization of poverty foremost among them. It extensively and explicitly considered the causes and types of poverty among women, including unequal access to resources and discriminatory rules, laws and practices regarding property. Although giving little attention to specific aspects of housing and human settlements, the Platform for Action produced numerous recommendations for ameliorative policies and programmes.[30]

## The emphasis on empowerment and gender equality

The emphasis that the summits of the 1990s placed on rights-based approaches to problems of poverty brings into focus the importance of participatory processes. This significance is evident in official documents:

- *The World Summit for Children* portrayed children as 'active and involved bearers of rights' rather than 'passive recipients of protection'.[31]
- *The United Nations Conference on Environment and Development* led to the goal of 'empowering people living in poverty'.[32]
- *The World Conference on Human Rights* emphasized the critical role of NGO and grassroots organizations in

implementation of the right to development.[33]
- *The International Conference on Population and Development* heralded the work of community-based organizations and grassroots movements and urged governments to integrate these partners in their decision-making.[34]
- *The World Summit for Social Development* expressed support for community development projects and the involvement of the poor in setting the goals for implementing and assessing such projects.[35]
- *The Fourth World Conference on Women* built on a series of prior declarations to re-affirm women's equal rights to resources, including access to housing, land, inheritance, credit and technical assistance.[36]

The summits of the 1990s also considered the gender-related aspects of the issues that were taken up. At times, mention of women seems perfunctory, listing them as one of a larger number of population groups meriting 'special' attention, including 'children, minorities, the disabled, the poor, and the elderly'. Nonetheless, there was increased recognition of the implications of intra-household dynamics for measuring poverty; the feminization of poverty; the seriousness of violence against women, from domestic assault to international trafficking in women and prostitution of girls; and the significance of women's roles in family functioning, community development and governance. International women's movements were instrumental in gaining a place for these issues on the conference agendas.

Almost needless to say, there are significant disparities between the words that emanated from the world conferences and the actions that have followed them. The rhetoric has often fallen far short of the deeds. None the less, the agreed-upon language contains elements that, over time, have begun to cohere as a narrative that shows the outlines of a new normative policy platform. This platform builds on core commitments to eradicate poverty and reduce inequality; it also highlights problem-solving approaches that are based on human rights and that empower people living in poverty as full participants, while recognizing and supporting women as equal partners.

> **The new normative policy platform, emerging from the United Nations summits of the 1990s, builds on core commitments to eradicate poverty and reduce inequality; it also highlights problem-solving approaches that are based on human rights and that empower people living in poverty as full participants, while recognizing and supporting women as equal partners**

A consistent theme throughout the declarations and programmes of action, adopted at the summits, has been an acknowledgement that the scale and severity of extant problems exceed governments' capabilities and resources. This acknowledgement has prompted calls for the development of enabling policies, capacity building and broad-based partnerships with the private sector and civil society.

> **A consistent theme throughout the declarations and programmes of action, adopted at the summits, is the acknowledgement that the scale and severity of extant problems exceed governments' capabilities and resources. This acknowledgement has prompted calls for the development of enabling policies, capacity building and broad-based partnerships with the private sector and civil society**

These elements were shown in the Key Issues and Messages and Prologue in this report and characterize the main conclusions emerging from the chapters that follow. They also form the background for the final section of this chapter, which briefly reviews the lead-up to the United Nations Conference on Human Settlements of 1996, describes some distinguishing aspects of the event itself, and evaluates the Istanbul Declaration and Habitat Agenda it produced.

# United Nations Conference on Human Settlements (Habitat II) (Istanbul, 1996)[37]

The Habitat I (Vancouver) Conference of 1976 achieved nominal consensus in five areas: land, water, transport, shelter and institutions. The main principles then articulated concerned equity, social justice and solidarity. The Deputy Secretary-General of that Conference stressed the need for a radical change in local government structure and in the system of flows of resources and services between different levels of government. He also emphasized the importance of participation to mobilize human resources.

The idealism that characterized the Vancouver Conference in 1976 was subsequently tempered by world events and field experience with shelter and urban development programmes over two decades. Despite the discussion of important issues at Habitat I, the level of governments' commitment to its recommendations for national action was minimal.

In 1996, the Secretary-General of the Habitat II Conference recalled the principles on human settlements that came out of the Vancouver conference and noted that there was little that unified them. Most were prescriptive and patronizing in tone. They resulted from a 'vigorous negotiating process which may be inimical to the very idea of globality', reflecting less than universal values.[38]

It is perhaps not surprising, therefore, that in the intervening 20 years, the principles adopted at Habitat I did not lead to decisive policy action. No country had an explicit national policy on human settlements and none could be expected to endorse one, given that policies respond to the interests of economic and political power and given the 'grotesque contrasts between extremes of wealth and poverty, between concentrated power and repression'.[39]

After the Vancouver Conference of 1976, human settlements problems not only remained but also multiplied manifold in size and scope. In an attempt to progress beyond past inadequacies, Habitat II framed the issues differently, with draft declarations and platforms featuring civil engagement, sustainability and equity.

Habitat II took place in Istanbul, Turkey, on 3–14 June 1996. In addition to representatives from 171 governments and some 2400 NGOs attending the conference, the parallel NGO Forum attracted about 8000 people. Also known informally as The City Summit, the event was the last in the series of major United Nations conferences held during the 1990s. It brought together many of the main themes taken up in these conferences in a blueprint for future policies and practices concerning human settlements. The Habitat Agenda, resulting from the summit, was meant to provide not just a vision for sustainable human settlement development but a practical roadmap for the years ahead, taking into account linkages with the natural environment, human rights, social development, demographic trends, population groups at risk and other issues.

> The Habitat Agenda was meant to offer a vision and a practical roadmap for sustainable human settlement, taking into account linkages with the natural environment, human rights, social development, demographic trends and population groups at risk

## Innovations

Habitat II presented several innovations in its format. While most of the earlier summits gave NGOs access to the conference process, Habitat II also involved NGOs, local authorities, the private sector and other groups in the deliberations for the eventual plan of action. Negotiations in the Conference Committee among national governments received recommendations from the 'Partnership Committee' which considered reports from more than 500 mayors and key municipal leaders (organized in the World Assembly of Cities and Local Authorities), as well as input from the World Business Forum, the Professionals and Researchers Forum, the Parliamentarians Forum, the Labour Unions Forum and the Forum on Human Solidarity, among others.

Habitat II also stressed the importance of building cumulative experience with problem-solving approaches by providing opportunities for exchanging information. In particular, it showcased 'best practices': initiatives and programmes that had proved to be effective in areas such as poverty eradication, managing the urban environment and providing access to land, shelter, finance and community infrastructure and services.

## The Istanbul Declaration and Habitat Agenda

Two documents resulted from the Conference. In the first, the Istanbul Declaration on Human Settlements, governments agreed to address seven priorities:[40]

1   unsustainable consumption and production patterns, particularly in industrialized countries;
2   unsustainable population changes;
3   homelessness;
4   unemployment;
5   lack of basic infrastructure and services;
6   growing insecurity and violence;
7   increased vulnerability to disasters.

Although expressing concern about the deteriorating situation of human settlements in most parts of the world, governments subscribed to the widely embraced view that cities and towns are centres of civilization, generating economic development and social, cultural, spiritual and scientific advancement. They acknowledged the need for concerted action in development financing, external debt, international trade and transfer of technology and agreed to strengthen the institutional and financial capacity of local authorities to implement the Habitat Agenda. They also agreed to seek the participation of public, private and non-governmental partners to ensure legal security of tenure, protection from discrimination and equal access to housing, and called for urban policies that expand the supply of affordable housing by enabling markets to perform efficiently in a socially and environmentally responsible way.[41]

The second document, the Habitat Agenda,[42] was intended as a call for action at all levels. It contains a statement of goals and principles, a set of commitments to be undertaken by governments and strategies for implementation.

### ● Goals and principles

The goals and principles cover a broad spectrum of issues related to human settlements. They interface significantly with concerns addressed at the earlier world conferences:

* equitable human settlements where all have equal access to housing, open space, health services and education, among others;
* poverty eradication in the context of sustainable development;
* the importance to quality of life of physical conditions and spatial characteristics of villages, towns and cities;
* the need to strengthen the family as the basic unit of society;
* citizens' rights and responsibilities;
* partnerships among all countries and among all sectors within countries;
* solidarity with disadvantaged and vulnerable groups;
* increased financial resources;
* health care, including reproductive health care and services to improve quality of life.

### ● Commitments

The conference resulted in over 200 commitments organized into the following categories:[43]

1   *Adequate shelter for all.* Within the overall context of the enabling framework, this includes governments' obligation to take appropriate action in order to promote, protect and ensure the full and progressive realization of the right to adequate housing (para 61). Adequate, in this connection, means more than a roof over one's head: it also includes adequacy regarding privacy, space, physical accessibility, safety, security of tenure, structural stability and durability, lighting, heating and ventilation, basic infrastructure such as water supply, sanitation and waste management facilities, environmental quality, health-related factors and location with respect to work and basic facilities, all of which should be available at affordable cost (para 60).

2   *Sustainable human settlements.* The high density of urban life worsens environmental threats to the quality of air and water and problems of waste disposal. Recognizing these problems, governments committed themselves to objectives that combined concerns regarding the carrying capacity of natural ecosystems and stimulating economic growth. The latter would require job creation and better access to work and services by improved public transport.

3   *Enablement and participation.* This commitment includes the goals of democratic rule, effective governance, decentralization of authority and resources, and ensuring availability of education.

4   *Gender equality.* Governments agreed to integrate gender perspectives in human settlement legislation, policies and programmes, and to strengthen policies and practices to promote the full and equal participation of women in human settlements planning and decision-making.

5   *Financing human settlements.* Based on the recognition that housing is a productive sector of the economy, governments committed themselves to developing innovative approaches for strengthening financial management at all levels and promoting equal access to credit for all people.

6   *International cooperation.* This commitment includes participating in multilateral, bilateral and regional programmes to further the goals of the Agenda; promoting exchange of appropriate technology; striving to fulfil the agreed target of 0.7 per cent of GDP of the developed countries for official development assistance to developing countries; and promoting international cooperation between public, private, non-profit, non-governmental and community organizations.

7   *Assessing progress.* Governments agreed to monitor progress towards attaining the Agenda's goals in their countries.

## ● Strategies

The Agenda describes several strategies to attain the agreed goals and commitments. They fall into the following categories:

- *Adequate shelter for all.* The cornerstones of this are policies that enable effective and efficient shelter delivery systems, interdependent with macroeconomic, environmental and social development systems. While having to address increasing demand for housing and infrastructure, such policies should also emphasize increased use and maintenance of the existing housing stock through ownership, rental and other tenure options; encourage and support people who individually or collectively act as producers of housing; and respond to the diverse needs of disadvantaged and vulnerable groups (paras 60–98).

- *Sustainable human settlements in an urbanizing world.* Broad-based strategies are required, aimed at 'economic buoyancy, social vibrancy, and environmental soundness' (para 101). These include planning for sustainable land uses based on social and environmental impact analyses; eradication of poverty, creation of productive employment and social integration; consideration of the implications of demographic developments for sustainable human settlement development; elimination of unhealthy living conditions; prevention of environmental degradation and mitigation of the effects of disasters, among others (paras 99–176).

- *Capacity building and institutional development.* Strategies in this category are seen to be interrelated with those in other areas and refer, for example, to decentralization; combating corruption; establishment of systems for effective information sharing and frameworks for cooperative actions; popular participation and civic engagement; and human settlements management training programmes (paras 177–193).

- *International development and cooperation.* This requires an enabling context with additional financial resources and higher priority for human settlement issues, especially in the developing countries; promotion of technology transfer and information exchange; and greater technical and institutional cooperation (paras 194–211).

- *Implementation and follow-up.* It is recognized that the impact of the commitments made by governments will depend on action at all levels. Performance evaluation will require regular monitoring based on appropriate indicators and documentation of best practices. The United Nations Centre for Human Settlements was assigned responsibility for providing assistance with the development of guidelines for monitoring and evaluating the implementation. Capabilities for the collection and analysis of data were to be strengthened, especially at the local level (paras 212–241).

## Evaluation

The official follow-up review and appraisal of progress in implementation of the Habitat Agenda will occur during a

Special Session of the United Nations General Assembly scheduled in June 2001. Country reports have been prepared according to a universal format developed by UNCHS (Habitat). In advance of the overall review, a comprehensive assessment is not possible but several observations can be made.

To begin with, among the positive contributions of Habitat II is a broad conceptualization of the issues, attentive to their interrelationships and wider context, rejecting the narrow sectoral perspectives that have proven to be unproductive in the past. The Summit also stressed the importance of decentralized and democratic decision-making; the need to put priority on vulnerable population groups; the need for coordinated action involving broad-based partnerships; and the potential of information and communication technologies. It came out in favour of the right to adequate housing and highlighted questions of poverty and inequity across gender, race, ethnicity, economic status, age and other relevant dimensions. The conference produced recommendations for action towards a wide range of goals. It set out a comprehensive and very ambitious agenda.

> The Habitat Agenda presented a broad conceptualization of the issues and recommended a range of actions that stressed the importance of decentralized and democratic decision-making, promoted coordinated action, highlighted the needs of vulnerable groups and the potential of ICTs, while reaffirming the right to housing

There is great value in the bold conceptualization of goals and the proposing of innovative means towards achieving those goals. Indeed, official declarations aside, Habitat II succeeded admirably in bringing together important stakeholders, opening up communication channels and encouraging partnerships among them, and suggesting a cooperative vision of future urban development that combines mediation and negotiation with the use of technical expertise guided by norms resulting from democratic and inclusive discourse. Its presentation of 'best practices' was a valuable stimulus to foster learning about problem-solving experiences. All this was no small feat. However, the same comprehensiveness and ambitiousness of the Habitat Agenda, by their very nature, inevitably raise some issues that are controversial and that, therefore, were largely skirted at the Summit in the interest of attaining consensus.

Further steps must be based on more explicit recognition that human settlement development is not a 'grab-bag' of goodies. The Agenda repeatedly states that human settlements must be 'economically buoyant, socially vibrant, and environmentally sound'; few will disagree. However, when seeking to translate these and other lofty goals into specific actions, decision-makers often face the need to make hard choices between competing options. Their task is not helped by the internal inconsistency of a dominant paradigm that favours competition in the economic realm but does not welcome as readily the political contestation

of alternative goals through democratic processes. The tenor of prevailing policy outlooks favours a kind of openness that paradoxically is mostly closed to open discourse on competing normative frameworks for development. This situation is conducive to ambiguity from which the Habitat Agenda cannot escape.

For example, the Agenda supports public transport as a means of decreasing pollution, conserving environmental resources and increasing people's access to jobs and services. What the Agenda does not engage, however, is the implications of this stance for changes in policies affecting investments in systems that are currently greatly dependent on the production and use of private cars (see Chapter 11).

In a similar vein, the Agenda champions the cause of decentralization, recommending 16 actions in paragraph 180, all of them relevant but none of them addressing basic questions of resource transfer. If it is important to advocate appropriate devolution of authority and democratic decision-making, then it is inevitably important that the next step involves a concern with the resources required to carry out the responsibilities for which authority is being devolved. Decentralization must proceed within an agreed normative framework, as proposed by the draft World Charter of Local Government, discussed in Chapter 14.

Likewise, the Agenda identifies the needs of population groups at risk as high priorities. In this connection it notes that 'vulnerability and disadvantage are mainly caused by *circumstance*, rather than inherent characteristics' (para 93, emphasis added). This is a very important observation to prevent bad policies that, based on false *a priori* assumptions, reinforce the perception of certain population groups as reified categories, whereas in fact, it is specific structures and processes in society that create them. The Agenda does not, however, take the next step to pursue an analysis of what these abstract 'circumstances' are and how they come about, an exercise bound to be somewhat controversial. As well, the Agenda urges the stepping up of efforts to combat discrimination, but it does so without probing the aetiology and dynamics of market-based and institutional discriminatory practices.

In short, the Agenda does address urgent problems, but its coverage more often offers extensive description of the manifestation of these problems than trenchant analysis of their causes and resolute prescription for their solutions. The suggested way forward is characteristically seen to arise from a perspective of enlightenment, based on the assumption that progress follows first from eliminating ignorance; whether due to biases of, unequal access to or the absence of information. When properly enlightened, policy makers would become concerned enough to propose and implement rational actions to redress bad situations. The root causes of problems are usually couched in notional categories. The Agenda is perceptive in its description of what 'is;' it is also forward-looking in its articulation of what 'ought to be;' but it did not sufficiently realize opportunities for greater specification of ways to get from the former to the latter. Hence, the ensuing recommendations remain chiefly limited to referencing necessary but insufficient ameliorative actions. The Agenda did not focus on, but leaves room for, demonstrating future leadership in evolving approaches that give more attention to the potential of communicative and related planning methods to arrive at decisions and action on development scenarios that can emerge as negotiated outcomes through informed and broad-based participatory processes.

> *'You have succeeded brilliantly in encouraging States to accept new norms of international behaviour. Now we need to see those norms implemented'* – Kofi Annan, Keynote Address to the Millennium Forum, 22 May 2000

Formulation of the Habitat Agenda was a noteworthy accomplishment. However, in the end, its value stands or falls with its implementation. In this regard, progress is hampered by three constraints. First, the commitments made by governments are non-binding. There are no implications of failure to make satisfactory progress towards the agreed goals. In fact, in many cases, it has been difficult even to obtain national reports on implementation of the Habitat Agenda. We need to guard against the danger that follow-up activities, institutionalized through the +5 and +10 processes, will become inconsequential routines and pro forma rituals that merely drain resources and create inertia, when the challenges facing us demand daring and dynamic approaches.

Second, the absence of a mandate and mechanism for enforcement of the Habitat Agenda is made worse by the lack of adequate provisions to ensure critical evaluation of reported progress. Certainly, the emphasis on monitoring and best practices is a significant step in the right direction. However, no matter how good, best practices are still limited in the sense of never being more than a reflection of what is possible under the current circumstances. What are also needed are *assessments* of best practices against criteria derived from normative frameworks that include goals with measurable benchmarks projected into the future. Indicators facilitate but do not guarantee such evaluations; their application has remained largely restricted to use as a descriptive tool. This should be expanded so they can also serve as an aid in analysis and assessment. Broadening the scope of best practices to include good policies, legislation, and plans of action will help as well.

> **No matter how good, best practices are never more than a reflection of what is possible under the current circumstances. We also need *assessments* of best practices against criteria derived from normative frameworks that include goals with measurable benchmarks**

Finally, implementation of the Habitat Agenda has been impeded by the lack of an effective institutionalized arrangement to ensure coordinated actions. Such coordination is crucial, between United Nations agencies and with other relevant partners, because the issues are multi-sectoral: the right to an adequate standard of living and right to development; access to basic services; social integra-

tion and social equity; gender and equality; and environmental sustainability.[44] These issues cut across the jurisdictional boundaries of established organizations and go beyond existing governmental arrangements. This cross-cutting becomes amplified through globalization. In the words of United Nations Secretary-General, Kofi Annan, 'problems without passports require blueprints without borders'.[45] Just as today's issues are shaped in new ways, so also must our approaches be innovative. Fresh challenges demand creative approaches. Effective strategies will require more extensive cooperation and new forms of governance.

> **In today's globalizing world, problems without passports require blueprints without borders**

The point is not to criticize current approaches, but to build on recognition of their limitations in order to establish the structures and processes necessary for the implementation of stated policy goals. Part IV of this report returns to these important points when it takes up questions of cooperative frameworks and emerging forms of governance.

> **Implementation of the Habitat Agenda will require an effective institutionalized arrangement to ensure coordinated actions**

## The Habitat Agenda in broader context

> **It is essential to consider human settlements as a crucial context for the principles and goals formulated at the United Nations conferences of the 1990s. The Habitat Agenda offers the potential for integrating their diverse but interrelated elements**

Situating the Habitat Agenda vis-à-vis the sequence of United Nations conferences and their broader background is important for three reasons. First, human settlements are the necessary environments for people's day-to-day lives – where they socialize, play, work and teach – in homes, streets, markets and other public spaces, factories and sweatshops, schools and clinics, offices and shops. Human settlements provide the stage where these lives are enacted and where problems become apparent. They also form a very important context that shapes attempts to solve these problems. The thematic frameworks of the United Nations conferences of the 1990s guided the formulation of many principles and goals that concern human settlements but without due consideration of their interrelationships in this essential context.

Second, the Habitat II Conference of 1996, the year that concluded the series of United Nations world conferences begun in 1990,[46] was to provide an opportunity for actions to improve living conditions in human settlements across sectoral lines and was seen as a vehicle for turning many of the principles and resolutions that emerged from these conferences into reality.[47] Habitat II and its Plan of Action thus provide the potential to help to integrate the contributions of the global conferences whose significance is seen to arise from:

- increasing public awareness of pressing problems shared by countries around the world;
- mobilizing national and local governments and non-governmental organizations to take action on major global problems;
- establishing international standards and guidelines for national policy;
- serving as a forum where new proposals can be debated and consensus sought;
- promoting the development of long-term frameworks for international cooperation;
- setting in motion a process whereby governments make commitments and report back regularly to the United Nations.

*'A normative agenda is probably the best protection that the United Nations can offer the urban poor'* – Klaus Töpfer, First Substantive Session, Preparatory Committee Istanbul + 5, Nairobi, 8 May 2000

Third, a key theme on the Habitat Agenda, adequate shelter for all, is essentially founded on governments' commitment to the full and progressive realization of the right to adequate housing and official recognition of governments' obligations in this regard. This rights-based approach

reflects the globalization and growing influence of the values and practices espoused by human rights movements. It also resonates with the emphasis on human rights permeating other United Nations summits.[48] Further, it is consistent with Habitat's mandate for setting normative standards.[49] The Global Campaign for Secure Tenure is Habitat's strategic angle on fulfilment of the right to adequate housing.

The other major initiative of the UNCHS, the Global Campaign for Urban Governance, is likewise anchored in the Habitat Agenda and is closely linked to a continuing worldwide push for decentralization, democratization and more participatory forms of urban governance; goals that also feature prominently in the Programmes for Action emanating from the other world conferences held under the aegis of other United Nations organizations.
Habitat II thus helped to crystallize important themes cross-cutting the other summits and brought into focus the critical need to develop normative frameworks and strategic foci for coordinated policies and actions.

Habitat II helped to crystallize important themes cross-cutting the other summits and brought into focus the critical need to develop normative frameworks and strategic foci for coordinated policies and actions

# Notes

1 Contributing to these movements in Eastern Europe were Solidarity, and Freedom and Peace in Poland, Charter 77 and the Independent Peace Association in Czechoslovakia, Democratic Opposition and the West-East dialogue group in Hungary, and Swords into Ploughshares in East Germany.

2 See Deutsche Stiftung für Internationale Entwicklung, 1996.

3 United Nations Research Institute for Social Development, 1995.

4 The following section draws on Dowall, 1998, Pugh, 1994a, b, and United Nations Centre for Human Settlements (Habitat), 1990.

5 Global Strategy For Shelter To The Year 2000; 43rd Session, December 20, Agenda Item 12; Document Number: A/RES/43/181.

6 Dowall, 1998.

7 UNCHS (Habitat), 1990, p 12.

8 UNCHS (Habitat), 1990, pp 18–19. See also Pugh, 1994a, b.

9 UNCHS (Habitat), 1990, p 13.

10 UNCHS (Habitat), 1990, p 9.

11 UNCHS (Habitat), 1990, pp 4, 7.

12 It also contained elements that have become more prominent in recent years, including the mainstreaming of gender and the promoting of tenure security.

13 See United Nations General Assembly, 2000, p 7.

14 The foci selected here are not the only ones relevant to human settlements. For example, the Summits also brought threats to environmental sustainability and the pervasiveness of violence to the fore as major urban issues, as well as health, the provision of infrastructure, and local capacity building. Various of these issues are taken up in different parts of this Report, where they are linked to aspects of poverty and inequality.

15 See UNICEF/Carol Bellamy, 1999.

16 By 1996, 187 governments had ratified the Convention. United Nations, 1997c.

17 UNICEF, 2000.

18 See Chawla, 2000; Bartlett et al, 1999

19 United Nations, 1997a.

20 United Nations, Economic and Social Development, 1999.

21 Hulchanski and Leckie, 2000.

22 Hulchanski and Leckie, 2000.

23 United Nations High Commissioner for Human Rights, 1998.

24 Report of the International Conference on Population and Development.

25 Proposals for key actions for the further implementation of the Programme of Action of the International Conference on Population and Development, May 1999.

26 See United Nations Research Institute for Social Development, 1995, pp 17–19.

27 Critics included Third World Network, the International People's Health Council, Development Alternatives with Women for a New Era, and Environmental Development Action in the Third World, among others. The alternative declaration is available at www.millenniumforum.org/html/docs/Copenhagen_Alternative_De

claration.htm and www.globalsolidarity.npaid.org/altngo.html. One-quarter of the participating NGOs signed the alternative declaration in Copenhagen; within nine weeks their number had grown to nearly 10,000 organizations from nearly every country in the world, sending a powerful message from the world's civil society; see United Nations Research Institute for Social Development, 1995, pp 17–19.

28 Poverty issues dividing the Summit were symbolized when the leader of Malawi declared he could not afford to attend a conference about poverty alleviation. See D Todd, 1995.

29 Social Summit +5: Advancing the Social Development Agenda, *Geneva Press Kit, Release 1.* www.un.org/esa/socdev/geneva2000/media.

30 See the background paper prepared by Ann Schlyter (2000).

31 The World Summit for Children of 1990 followed adoption of the Convention on the Rights of the Child by the United Nations

General Assembly in 1989. The wording quoted here is taken from the language of the Convention.

32 United Nations, Economic and Social Development, 1999.

33 United Nations High Commissioner for Human Rights, 1995.

34 Report of the International Conference on Population and Development.

35 Programme of Action, paragraphs 26h, 28a, and 28f.

36 See the background paper prepared by Ann Schlyter (2000).

37 Background literature for the following sections is available in the following sources: Cohen, 1996; Garau, 1996; Leaf, 1997; Leaf and Pamuk, 1997; Okpala, 1996; Pugh, 1997a; 1997b; Strassmann, 1997; Tosics, 1997; Wakeley, 1996.

38 Preparatory Committee for the United Nations Conference on Human Settlements (Habitat II), 1995.

39 Preparatory Committee for the United Nations Conference on Human Settlements (Habitat II), 1995.

40 See paragraph 4; the full text of the declaration is available at www.unchs.org/unchs/english/ha genda/ist-dec.htm

41 United Nations Department of Public Information, 1997.

42 See www.undp.org/un/ habitat/agenda/.

43 See Habitat Agenda, Chapter III, available at www.unchs.org/unchs/english/ha genda/index.htm.

44 See United Nations General Assembly, 2000, p 7.

45 Keynote address to the Millennium Forum, 22 May 2000; SG/SM/7411 GA/9710.

46 As is apparent from the review in this chapter, there is an institutionalized process for follow-up of the initial summits at five- and ten-year intervals to appraise progress in implementation of the agreed plans of action.

47 Preparatory Committee for the United Nations Conference on Human Settlements (Habitat II), 1995.

48 The Children's Summit of 1990, following the adoption of the Convention of the Rights of the Child in the previous year; the Human Rights Conference of 1993; the exercise of reproductive rights at the Population Conference of 1994; the rights to an adequate standard of living and development at the Social Summit of 1995; women's rights as human rights at the Beijing Conference of 1995; the right to housing at the City Summit of 1996; and the right to adequate food at the World Food Summit of 1996.

49 See United Nations General Assembly, 2000, p 6.

# EMERGING APPROACHES TO URBAN GOVERNANCE AND POLITICS

The rapid growth of urban poverty and deepening inequalities in cities are the chief concerns permeating this report. Market mechanisms are ill-suited to redress these problems without effective regulation. Effective regulation requires good governance. Solutions to today's urban problems, therefore, call for good urban governance and appropriate political strategies, whether the issues concern infrastructure, housing, service provision, environmental quality or violence. Under globalization, urban governance faces new challenges and opportunities.

Contemporary governance involves multiple stakeholders, interdependent resources and actions, shared purposes and blurred boundaries between the public and private, formal and informal, state and civil society sectors, greater need for coordination, negotiation and building consensus. Consequently, three key tasks involve coordination, steering and integration of diverse and sometimes conflicting interests. To these ends, governance arrangements draw on market-based strategies arising from the private sector, hierarchical strategies articulated by the public sector and networking strategies emerging from the public sector.

Many national governments have devolved responsibilities that they had traditionally assumed to lower levels of government, while seeking to enhance the competitiveness of cities. The increased competition that characterizes globalization is accompanied by urban fragmentation, producing two conflicting trends: to compete effectively, cities must act as a collective unit; however, growing social exclusion, spatial segregation and economic polarization are divisive and hamper the ability of cities to build coalitions, mobilize resources and develop good governance.

Given that metropolitan areas are the chief arenas for global competition, it is necessary to strengthen them by giving them greater authority and autonomy in resource allocation. However, the enabling role of governments must be broader than facilitating the functioning of markets and also includes responsibility for social cohesion, equity, conflict resolution and support for citizenship in the sense of rights to the city.

The success of initiatives and reforms in government at the subnational level is closely linked to the ways and extent that national systems embrace and incorporate democratic processes. In this connection, it is important that a government grants its citizens political rights by permitting them to form political parties that represent a significant range of voter choice and whose leaders can openly and safely compete for, and be elected to, positions of authority in government. It is also important that governments uphold their citizens' civil liberties by respecting and protecting their religious, ethnic, economic, linguistic, gender, family and other rights, including personal freedoms and freedoms of the press, belief and association. The vital

PART II

importance of these links between good governance and democratic practices is well-illustrated by recent experience in Latin America, reviewed in Chapter 4, but of broader interest to developments elsewhere as well.

Globalization necessarily materializes in specific institutional arrangements in specific places, many of which are in cities. 'Glocalization' is a term used to describe the dialectic interdependence of the local and global dimensions of economic, political and cultural processes. Far from exerting a deterministic, homogenizing effect, globalization processes allow for local differentiation. The outcomes of these processes reflect the claims that different interests make on urban places and the power they can wield to advance those claims. These interests include representatives of global capital that use cities as an organizational commodity to maximize profit, but they also include disadvantaged local population groups who need the city as a place to live. Cities are increasingly strategic sites in the realization of these claims.

The withdrawal of the state and limitations on institutional demand making have combined to create new spaces for political contestation. This development signals emerging opportunities for civil society to engage government and the private sector in new forms of cooperation that enable the low-income communities to participate as empowered partners. More broadly, this development is about authentic citizenship, meaning the rights and responsibilities of the urban citizenry.

Low-income communities, taking advantage of modern communications technologies and less bound by local constraints, have begun to reconstitute themselves as overlapping, sometimes transnational networks with shared interests. The unlocking of their unrealized potential through participation in shared governance is essential to improving urban liveability for *all* people.

# 4

# THE CHANGING CONTEXT AND DIRECTIONS OF URBAN GOVERNANCE[1]

The *Human Development Report 1999* concerned itself with the uneven outcomes of globalization. It urged careful attention to appropriate governance to eliminate poverty and reduce the inequality associated with processes attendant to globalization.[2] Human settlements, and cities in particular, are important nodes in the new forms of governance that are currently emerging. These forms of governance are being developed in the context of globalization processes that create new conditions under which decisions must be made; interdependent, complex, loosely linked actors and institutions with shared purposes but no shared authority. This requires that actors seeking mutual gains find ways to coordinate their efforts.

To this end, this chapter first describes the key tasks of governance and the repertoire of basic governance strategies. This discussion stresses that the different strategies serve different goals. It points to the need for blending the supplemental roles of the public and private sectors, as well as civil society, in broad-based partnerships to build the capacity required to address today's urgent urban problems. (Chapter 14 further develops the theme of capacity building and forming partnerships.) The discussion then shifts focus to the paradox, associated with globalization, that cities are increasingly operating as territorial units in competitive processes (and are encouraged to do so by current development dogma), while at the same time cities are becoming more and more fragmented: socially, economically, physically and politically. Cities thus face two contrary developments whose management requires effective governance. Against this background, this chapter describes four newly emerging forms of government and offers six recommendations for policies that enable local areas to capitalize on their special strengths. The concluding section argues that the success of initiatives and reforms in government and governance at the subnational level is closely linked to the ways and extent that national systems embrace and incorporate democratic processes. In this regard, it examines the recent experience of Latin America with a view to the lessons it may hold for other parts of the world.

## The Repertoire of Governance Strategies[3]

Today, governance involves multiple stakeholders, interdependent resources and actions, shared purposes and blurred boundaries between the public and private, formal and informal, state and civil society sectors, greater need for coordination, negotiation and building consensus.[4] It must address three key tasks:

1   *Coordinating* a more complex and fragmented government landscape.
2   *Steering* interdependent activities through new bargaining systems and institutions such as public–private partnerships or regional confederations in order to achieve desired outcomes – specifically, public goods – by bringing the necessary actors to the table and then moderating differences and negotiating cooperation.
3   *Integrating* and managing diverse networks rather than focusing primarily on internal affairs.

---

Governance processes address three key tasks:
1   Coordinating
2   Steering
3   Integrating

---

To this end, the repertoire of strategies for distributing the costs and benefits of making and carrying out decisions includes *markets*, *hierarchies* and *networks*.[5] These three strategies have typically been associated with, respectively, the private sector, the public sector and civil society.

In a global context, none of these strategies can be presumed to be privileged or outdated; all three are viable governance strategies, depending on the shared problems and purposes at stake. In different ways, they reduce the costs of making decisions while increasing the capacity to act. The question of *'how'* governance is exercised is crucial:[6] the choice of governance strategies influences who is likely to be included or excluded. Thus it should be asked: Under what conditions do different governance strategies work effectively and for which purposes?

---

The repertoire of governance strategies includes *markets*, *hierarchies* and *networks*

---

### Markets

*Markets* use price competition as a central coordinating mechanism. Under many conditions, this is an effective means of coordinating decisions if not generating cooperation. But in a globalizing context of interdependence, relying on market mechanisms controlled by the private sector is often inadequate. As argued in the Prologue of this report, governance through market strategies tends to lead to short-term and ad hoc responses rather than the long-term strategic guidance necessary when dealing with multiple stakeholders, public goods, tangled networks and the need for negotiated decisions.

Governance strategies relying on market mechanisms to coordinate multiple, interdependent interests and resources and shared purposes ultimately fail to address critical governance tasks of steering and integration. In particular, they fail to integrate 'at-risk' groups into global society and to draw on their human capital potential. For markets to be more effective under the new global conditions, they need more responsive institutional structures in which to operate. The regulation of market conditions becomes a crucial task.

> Governance strategies relying on market mechanisms to coordinate multiple, interdependent interests and shared resources and purposes ultimately fail to address critical governance tasks of steering and integration

### Hierarchies

*Hierarchies* rely on rule setting, norms and institutional design to ensure cooperation and to coordinate decisions. The capacity to create hierarchical strategies rests in the public sector even though the governance arrangements created by these strategies need not be limited to public actions. They provide the traditions, norms and practices that shape or constrain policy alternatives. Bureaucratic hierarchies are familiar mechanisms for coordinating through administrative practices that balance competing values of efficiency and equity.

Hierarchical, top-down governance strategies continue to be important in a global era. For example, the use of rules and creation of new rule-setting bodies at different regional and transnational scales, such as international agreements on ocean resources or bi-national environmental commissions in North America, internalizes the costs associated with making decisions under contemporary conditions. Similarly, decentralization policies and 'direct democracy' provisions require formal government changes that create new sub-authorities and allow for referenda and initiative procedures. Although governance through hierarchy retains a significant role in a global era, it is criticized for lacking flexibility and adaptability.

### Networks

*Networks* use informal coalitions, trust, reciprocity and mutual adjustment to produce cooperation and coordinate decisions. These processes are rooted in civil society although they are shaped as well by public and private sector configurations. Historically, these processes were labelled as 'community' and were presumed to be defined and circumscribed by territorial boundaries. In a global era,

modern information and communication technologies facilitate the formation of coalitions and networks from the bottom up, forming non-territorial communities centred on shared problems and purposes. It is such networks, rather than governments or markets, that increasingly link global and local processes.

## The Globalization Paradox

Globalization is changing the scale of international regulation, not only at the global level, but also at the subnational level. A few decades ago, before globalization accelerated and intensified, the nation state was the main pilot of societal change. Today, its place at the centre of society is being challenged by several developments. First, increasing globalization sets the regulation level of society at various scales, the state or national one being only one among others. Second, decentralization is pulling the regulation level downwards (to regional, municipal and intra-municipal levels). Third, regionalization at the sub-world level is pulling regulation upwards; the growing importance of the European Union is a good example of this phenomenon.

In that context,[7] cities are emerging as new territories of regulation, that is, as territories relevant to address crucial issues, notably the increasing territorial competition that globalization entails.[8] However, to regulate does not mean to govern.[9] Cities are at the forefront of competitive processes whose successful management requires an effective capacity to govern a territory. Cities must work as collective actors; that is, they must mobilize their economic, social and political resources in order to develop their assets and to reduce their weaknesses; what is commonly described as building coalitions and regimes.[10]

> Globalization increases competition as well as fragmentation, with contradictory effects on cities. To compete effectively, cities must act as a collective unit. However, their growing fragmentation hampers their capacity to build coalitions, mobilize resources and develop good governance structures

However, several studies[11] have cast doubt on the capacity of cities to function as collective actors. This scepticism is based on evidence that urban territories are becoming more and more heterogeneous, as a result of the growing social and economic differentiation of urban society.[12] This phenomenon is better indicated by the expression 'fragmented city'.[13]

To begin with, social fragmentation is increasing. This is readily demonstrated by the growing socio-spatial inequalities in urban areas. Also politically, the fragmentation of power is growing. Many countries are witnessing the breaking up of traditional political parties into a greater number. Moreover, political parties seem to be less and less capable of acting as mediators between civil society and the political powers that be. Where political parties do serve as channels of mediation, they do so in ways that are more sectoral, more issue-oriented and more linked to specific segments of society (eg related to gender, ethnicity, religion, etc).

Institutional organization is also becoming more fragmented and more complex. Almost everywhere the number of local authorities and ad-hoc bodies in functional metropolitan areas is increasing. The issue of territorial solidarity, previously largely taken care of by the state, is seriously challenged by local structures as shown by the difficulties of establishing cooperation at the area-wide level and the desire for local communities to secede. In many nations and cities, the declining role of the state in its traditional areas of responsibility has increased the importance of NGOs and the voluntary sector, but in the process there has been a dramatic increase in the fragmentation of the capacity for collective action.

There is also a trend of economic fragmentation. The traditional structures of representation of economic interests (chambers of commerce, local business associations, etc) are being contested because they do not represent the emerging economic interests such as the small- and medium-sized firms and those of the 'new economy'. Further, they are usually organized in ways that are less and less effective in territorial competition. Therefore, while some traditional bodies are being reformed (like the chambers of commerce in Italy or in France), new associations of business are created, adding to the already complex systems through which economic interests represent themselves.

In consequence, cities face a paradox. On one hand, they must act as a collective unit since they are more than before confronted with competition and less able to rely on higher levels of government to assist them in that process. On the other hand, they are encountering increasing difficulties in mobilizing their resources, which hampers their capacity to build the necessary coalitions of actors or structures of governance. This is all the more damaging in places where changes are dramatic and require more control, more anticipation and greater decision-making capacity, as is the case in many metropolitan areas of the developing countries.

# Emerging Elements of Governance

Among the various changes that have occurred in the last decade to address the 'globalization paradox', we can identify four emerging elements of governance:

1    Decentralization and formal government reforms.
2    Participation of civil society.
3    Multi-level governance.
4    Process-oriented and territorially based policies.

Some of these elements are not new or innovative, such as decentralization or metropolitan government reform, but their rationale differs from earlier periods.[14] These emerging elements of governance do not necessarily replace more traditional arrangements (eg top-down, hierarchical schemes with a strong presence of the state). Their relative importance in decision-making processes also varies greatly among countries.

## Decentralization and formal government reform at the area-wide level

Decentralization is devolution of power – responsibilities, resources and legitimacy – to subnational levels, ranging from regional bodies to intra-municipal structures.[15] One major reason for decentralization is so-called 'governing failures',[16] meaning that the state is no longer able to diagnose and solve problems so that these problems and issues are better dealt with at the local level. In some countries, decentralization is viewed negatively as a way for the state to shift away the responsibility for developing solutions to intractable problems, typically without a corresponding transfer of resources required to address the issues. Decentralization trends now occur in most countries, including regionalization in the UK (eg devolution given to Scotland and Wales and creation of regional development agencies in England), Italy and Spain (the so-called regionalist states of Europe), the strengthening of municipalities in many Latin American and some African countries (eg South Africa) and the establishment of intra-municipal levels of government like the neighbourhood councils in Amsterdam and Bologna. Chapter 13 reviews recent developments regarding decentralization more specifically in relation to urban infrastructure management capacity. The draft World Charter of Local Government, discussed in Chapter 14, is an initiative to develop and gain acceptance of a constitutionally anchored framework for local self-government on the basis of internationally recognized principles.

There have also been attempts at formal government reforms at the metropolitan level. The general purpose of these reforms has been to create new governmental structures with area-wide responsibilities in strategic planning, economic development, management of services (notably networks like public transport, water systems, etc) and, more recently, the environment. The rationale for these reforms has changed since the 1970s. The logic of functionalism remains; that is, for instance, the metropolis is still considered to be a relevant functional territory for infrastructure building and the provision of urban services. However, additional rationales, like the necessity to develop and implement policies regarding environmental protection, social inclusion and the fight against violence, are now the dominant reasons for creating these new entities. Examples of such reforms abound. They range from the creation of strong local government units, such as the new Greater London Authority, the Verband Regio Stuttgart and Metro Toronto, to less powerful authorities like the recent metropolitan structures in South Africa.[17] The process is still unfolding in many places in Europe (eg Italy, The Netherlands) and Latin America (eg Bolivia, Venezuela).[18]

New governmental forums can increase the voices of marginalized groups, particularly where ethnic minorities are geographically concentrated. Implementation of the Popular Participation Law in Bolivia, for example, created municipal councils where Quechua and Aymara representatives now play a role in allocating resources

**Box 4.1 The Digital City: an electronic forum for citizen interaction**

Amsterdam's Digital City (http://www.dds.nl) was launched in January 1994 to place information about the city and its services within direct reach of the people, to stimulate political discussion among citizens and to explore the possibilities and limitations of a local virtual community.

Amsterdam has a strong tradition of community activism. In the early 1990s, the municipal government was troubled by signs of increasing political apathy and cynicism among the city's voters. On the eve of local elections in 1994, the Amsterdam City Hall decided to support the Digital City as a 10-week social experiment to stimulate the interest and involvement of citizens in local public affairs. Within a week, the network's 20 phone lines were overloaded around the clock and the new 'city' had more than 3500 'residents' and thousands more visits by 'tourists'.

Five years later, the Digital City is a growing network of small virtual communities with more than 100,000 regular participants and tens of thousands of tourists. The project, which has received no public funding since 1995, has influenced the extension of not-for-profit internet access throughout The Netherlands, has been replicated by other cities throughout the country, and has spawned many imitators in cities across Europe.

The Digital City is constructed in the image of a real city with 'squares' corresponding to different themes or areas of interest (the environment, government, art, sports, Europe, alternative lifestyles, women's issues, music, etc). Each square offers space for a fixed number of 'buildings' which can be rented by businesses, nonprofit organizations or other information providers. The squares also feature billboards (advertisements), cafés (chat rooms and specialized discussion groups), kiosks (collections of on-line newspapers and magazines related to the square's theme) and side roads (related links).

Although most of the Digital City's contents are in Dutch, anyone is welcome to visit. Each resident has a free email account, the right to participate in discussion groups and space to create a 'home', or personal Web page. The homes are situated in residential areas between the squares and may not be used for commercial purposes.

The 'city' metaphor reinforces the idea of the Digital City as a public domain, a forum where citizens can meet and express themselves freely. This metaphor was also chosen to make the Digital City easier to navigate: citizens intuitively grasp that they must stop in at the post office to send and receive (electronic) mail or visit the City Hall for information on political affairs. Although the Digital City does not correspond to the layout of the real Amsterdam, its structure lets it easily accommodate all aspects of life there. A digital bike path was added so that biking enthusiasts can meet and exchange information, reviews of newly released films can be found at the cinema square and a cemetery has even been added for the commemoration of loved ones.

Despite the project's autonomy from political influence, the 'city' metaphor also makes explicit the political dimension that its founders have wanted for the project from the start. The government neighbourhood is one of the Digital City's most popular areas, and visitors there can read the fine print of proposed laws and upcoming referenda, email city officials directly and argue with their elected representatives on the issues of the day. Subjects such as a controversial plan to extend Schipol Airport, upkeep of the city's parks, whether to ban cars from the city centre, the proposed conversion of Amsterdam from city to province and other local political issues have been debated. Politicians frequently participate in more structured discussion formats as well.

The Digital City has become a true city, dynamic and creative, where houses, buildings and squares are constructed, demolished or abandoned every day. And it is this organic quality that distinguishes Amsterdam's Digital City from many of its counterparts elsewhere. Digital city projects in the United States, for example, tend to be more rigidly structured and primarily serve as clearinghouses of information for the city and its service providers. The organizers of Amsterdam's Digital City see their project more as an 'open city' than as an organized virtual community. In the Digital City, residents are not passive consumers of information and services but interacting and participating citizens. The successful Clean Clothes campaign against the local sale of clothes produced by child labour in Asia is one example of how ordinary citizens in Amsterdam have been able to use the format provided by the Digital City to inform their fellow citizens and bring about change on both local and global levels.

The political results of the Digital City are, however, still far from the electronic democracy for which its founders were hoping. The real influence of virtual debates on traditional politics has been minimal. Most visitors are young, well-educated and highly computer-literate, a profile which corresponds to only a relatively small segment of society. Although the project's direct political impact is not yet what its planners envisioned, the Digital City has helped bring Dutch citizens on-line, enabled them to find other citizens with similar interests or concerns and provided them with a format for exchanging information and taking action.

**Source:** adapted from Del Vecchio, 1999.

Strategies creating new governmental forums can increase the voices of marginalized groups, particularly where ethnic minorities are geographically concentrated. Implementation of the Popular Participation Law in Bolivia, for example, created municipal councils where Quechua and Aymara representatives now play a role in allocating resources.[19] In 1993, India passed a Constitutional Amendment reserving seats for women in local government. But even supporters agree that more women in government may not be enough. Mandating representation of women in new governmental forums appears to increase their inclusion but not necessarily their voice: despite mandated representation, empowerment of women is often constrained by traditional gender relations.[20]

> Despite mandated representation, empowerment of women is often constrained by traditional gender relations

## Civil society participation in policy making

> Civil society participation infuses policy making with greater legitimacy and helps to compensate for failures of central governments to provide basic infrastructure and services

Participation by civil society may be direct (eg through the electoral process) or indirect (notably through the participation of community-based organizations in policy making). In most countries and cities there is growing support for greater involvement of civil society. There are several reasons. First, as in the case of decentralization, there are governing failures at the national and local levels. Resident participation is necessary to elaborate and implement policies in ways that are more responsive to local problems and needs. In this regard, the internet can facilitate citizen involvement in local public affairs (eg see Box 4.1) and help nform voters (eg see Box 4.2). In addition, civil society participation helps to legitimize local policy structures of government and consequently would make public policies more efficient, especially in cities where people have had to organize because of the inability of public institutions to provide basic services like water and sewers (see, for example, Box 10.4 on Dar es Salaam).[21]

There are numerous examples of civil society participation. In more developed countries, most government programmes to fight social exclusion and induce economic development now require the involvement of communities, such as the Single Regeneration Budget (SRB) and the New Deal for Communities (NDC) programmes in the UK, and most of the Policy for Cities programmes in France. In the developing world, the involvement of civil society is more significant since governing failures are more frequent and salient. Therefore, community participation often occurs in planning (eg the Rebuilding and Development Programme in Cape Town), water production (eg Haiti and Yaounde), environmental issues (eg implementation of Local Action Agenda 21 programmes in Uganda and Bolivia)[22] or budget setting (eg Porto Alegre). Chapter 14 brings out the importance of civil society capacity building to enable effective participation by community-based groups in development initiatives.

## Multi-level governance and partnerships

Multi-level governance is a commonly used term to describe a whole set of joint practices: partnership, contractualization, institutional forms of negotiation procedures, co-funding, etc. They may involve public institutions as well as private entities at various levels. In some countries (eg France and Italy) multi-level governance is mostly restricted to public institutions, while in others (eg UK and India) the voluntary sector, NGOs and the private sector are frequently included.

Where multi-level governance is limited to public institutions, the origin of this restriction derives from historical traditions in these countries, according to which central and local government are considered to be the only actors able to represent the general interest and act on its behalf. The emerging need to involve various levels of government in policy making is explained by the increasing overlapping of responsibilities among these levels of government. Further, there is a need for co-financing services, projects and programmes, related to decentralization and the implementation of a matching fund system in, for example, the US, and in Europe related to the increasing importance of the European Union.[23] Good examples of this type of multi-level governance are the Italian *accordi di programma*, which involve the state, the regions, the provinces, the municipalities and their relevant public companies, and the French 'Contrats de Plan Etat-Régions' (Programme Agreements between the State and the Regions), which involve the EU, the state, the regions, *départements* and municipalities in the field of territorial development at the regional and metropolitan levels (see Boxes 4.3 and 4.4).

In many countries and cities, multi-level governance also includes non-public actors. Often the private sector is

---

> **Box 4.2 Politicking on the Web**
>
> In a time when many candidates who are running for office have little chance of being elected if they are unable to capture their policy platforms in sound bites of less than 30 seconds, voters are increasingly turning to the internet to read speeches, peruse past voting records and examine position statements. Political hopefuls are responding by setting up listserves and web sites to provide information, to sell campaign products and to elicit financial contributions, raising millions of dollars on-line. Others are establishing commercially sponsored sites that offer news and analysis.
>
> On one site, www.selectsmart.com, each day some 30,000 people take a quiz that matches their answers with those of the candidates to questions on issues ranging from abortion to taxes and then calculates a suggested candidate whose views align best with those of the quiz taker. Voxcap.com, recording more than 300,000 visits a month, aims to promote personal activism through nonpartisan commentary and a series of links to advocacy groups, think tanks, elected representatives and government agencies. It has also created an electronic clipping service and email newsletters. Further, it set up an e-drive to raise funds for hunger prevention, matching Oxfam International and other nonprofit organizations with donors who can make contributions via real-time secure credit card transactions.
>
> Although the internet holds potential for increasing political engagement among citizens, there are undisclosed biases of 'infomercials' and 'decoy' web sites that hinder the transparency necessary for constructive discourse. There are also serious concerns about the ways in which increased reliance on the internet for informed democratic functioning reinforces existing patterns of social exclusion (see Box 4.1).

---

involved because of privatization policies (for example, the water systems in many African countries). Community-based organizations may be involved because of their legitimacy in representing people and because of their knowledge of local problems. NGOs can also play an important role because of their knowledge of programme management or an implicit transfer of responsibilities from the state. Multi-level governance is very often the result of practical situations but is increasingly considered as a new way of policy making. The UK experience of public–private partnership is probably the most extreme example of partnerships becoming new institutions,[24] with many urban and regional policies now carried out by public–private–voluntary sector partnerships (eg the new Regional Development Agencies; see also Box 2.3 on London).[25] But the same logic is also being applied in developing countries such as the Philippines (eg the Urban Basic Services Programme of Cebu City)[26] and India (eg the Slum Networking Project of Ahmedabad),[27] among others. Partnerships are more fully discussed in Chapter 14.

## Decision-making structures

> The emerging polycentric governance forms, with multiple actors, need to establish legitimacy for their policies through new processes for building consensus according to appropriate procedures

Today's governance takes place in a more polycentric system of actors in which the state is less dominant than before. The multiplicity of actors complicates policy making since no single actor is legitimate enough to direct societal change. Consensus is no longer a given by virtue of

## Box 4.3 The Agency for the Sustainable Development of the North Milano (ASNM) area and the involvement of civil society: lessons from a failure?

The ASNM was created in 1996 to produce sustained development in an area of industrial decline in Northern Italy. To that end, the Agency created a development forum from the members of ASNM (four municipalities, the Province of Milan, the Lombardy Region, the Chamber of Commerce and the industrial companies owning the area's brownfield sites) and parts of civil society (various associations of firms, unions and co-ops). Despite some significant success for the ASNM, notably in professional training and in the development of an economy centred on SME in the 'new economy' sectors, the development forum never took off. Two major reasons have been put forward to explain this failure:

1. Civil society was not very interested in ASNM problems; although ASNM had excellent access to resources in the Milano area, it dealt with firms and employees on issues that concerned the whole metropolitan area, rather than just the ASNM area. Consequently, civil society members did not participate actively in the forum.

2. The private sector was too fragmented for ASNM to develop a dialogue with it. There was no clear interlocutor representing the private sector; instead, there were various leaders, representing different and sometimes competing interests. Without a common voice on behalf of the private sector, it was difficult to evolve a coherent economic development strategy.

The ASNM example holds two lessons. First, participants of civil society should represent organizations that identify with a particular area, although they may not have many resources, rather than organizations that, although rich in resources, see their interests elsewhere. Second, it is important to have an effective structure of interlocutors; in their absence, development agencies should develop such a structure.

legitimacy granted to the state's action, but must be socially constructed. This requires alliances, coalitions and compromises. It also requires negotiation, debates and discussion, which, in turn, requires appropriate procedures. It is a new way of achieving decisions in which policy content is, at least in part, a function of the decision-making process itself.

These new forms of collective action cannot take place at the central level anymore. Territorial regulation has replaced national regulation because of the limited ability of the state to solve problems and address issues at lower levels and because of the increasing integration of diverse elements that efficient public policies require. This is a major reason for the development of so-called area-based initiatives.

This development is well illustrated by most European Union programmes regarding territories in general and metropolitan areas in particular. The objective of 'Territorial Pacts', for instance, is to produce territorial development. In order to get funding, national and local actors must work together and produce a set of priorities and specific actions arrived at after a long process of negotiation and debate. The same operational logic exists in the Rebuilding and Development (RDP) programme of Cape Town,[28] in some social programmes in Latin America[29] and in spatially smaller programmes in various Western countries (eg the US, UK and France) where urban areas are divided according to specific funding procedures and socio-economic features.

# Lessons and Analyses

Globalization is often seen as a one-way process, homogenizing people's way of life, their problems, as well as appropriate 'remedies' such as deregulation, privatization and decentralization. However, there is now growing acknowledgement that the specific territorial characteristics of each region and country are important. There is no single functional response to globalization because, for example, the national and local political history and culture help to shape public–private relationships and decision-making processes. Therefore, globalization should also be analysed as a heterogenizing process, especially since territorial competition accentuates the differences between locales. It is possible to base several recommendations for strengthening urban governance on the recognition that it is important to enhance the particular development advantages and assets that are local to a given area.

## Formal public institutions are crucial actors in urban governance

Public institutions must remain responsible for issues that concern society as a whole

Despite some failures of governmental initiatives and policies, despite the difficulties of metropolitan government reforms and despite the slowness of area-wide authority building, public institutions must remain the central element in the governance of cities. In many developing countries, and to a degree in some developed countries, public institutions have explicitly or implicitly transferred several of their responsibilities to civil society, especially to NGOs in sectors such as education, health and welfare. Deregulation and privatization policies have given more importance to the private sector in urban governance. However, civil society cannot deal with several vital issues that are essential responsibilities of legitimate, public (ie democratically elected) institutions. The setting up of long-term urban agendas, strategic planning, sustainable development, social cohesion and so on, are issues and actions that concern the future of societies and metropolitan areas. As such they must be the subject of debates and decisions made by entities representing the population as a whole: that is, public institutions whose legitimacy derives from a territorially based population.

Only governments have the legitimacy and capability to steer and integrate the activities of multiple stakeholders by acting beyond single purposes. Steering entails bringing the necessary actors to the table and then moderating differences and negotiating cooperation. Integrating tasks includes managing diverse interests to ensure that wider public goals are met by putting more narrowly defined interests in a larger context. Priorities set by new decentralized units, for example, may compete with those in other areas or conflict with national goals. Achieving leverage over a complex, fragmented system with expertise in the small units involves a process of setting and implementing appropriate norms.[30]

## New key role for the state in urban governance

Notwithstanding observations about the so-called 'hollowing out of the state', central government remains an important, even essential actor in the governance of cities. It still holds crucial powers, not only in terms of economic and financial resources but also in terms of normative legitimacy. By tradition, it still generates the cognitive framework for most local collective action and policy making. Of course, this presence of the state varies greatly from one country to the other, between strong states and weak states, unitary and federal states; in some developing countries, the state may seem almost nonexistent. Also, in many situations, the state is fragmented, especially in the policy sector, and unable to speak with a single voice. None the less, it would be misleading to assert the demise of the role of the state in urban governance.

Globalization, however, does imply a change in the role of the state.[31] Even in countries where the state is still strong, as in France and the UK, it no longer has the political and economic resources needed to carry out its traditional functions of societal governance on its own. In the 1980s, the Thatcher government in the UK described its changed role by applying to itself the label of 'enabling authority'; other countries have used similar expressions like 'facilitating authority' or 'animating state'. Whatever the terms employed, the idea remains the same: the new role for the state has become to create frameworks and to facilitate collective action, rather than to intervene directly.

> The enabling role of national governments must be broader than the facilitating of market functioning and include responsibility for social cohesion, equity, conflict resolution and support for the exercise of citizenship – of 'rights to the city'

It does not diminish the significance of recent decentralization policies to point out that local actions can rarely solve major urban problems. The state must retain a major role, giving coherence to local actions and mediating between local actors and between supra-national and subnational levels, thus giving a much broader meaning to 'enabling' than merely facilitating market functioning.[32] The state has a legitimate intervention role, first, in matters of national interest and, second, in local matters when they affect wider interests or when local actors prove too incapable or dysfunctional.

## Partnerships cannot be a comprehensive form of urban governance

> Partnerships can be effective to help address urban management problems, but they are inappropriate for addressing issues whose resolution requires democratic decision-making

Partnerships, whatever their forms and their membership, cannot be full-fledged solutions to the governance problems of urban areas. Too often, their action is piecemeal and

contributes further to the already existing fragmentation of the territory, either because they focus on a specific area, or because they concentrate on a single policy sector, or both. They cannot effectively assume responsibility for the tasks that fall within the purview of public institutions (see above). There are several reasons for this. The partnerships are often short-lived and have a fluctuating membership. Private enterprises frequently opt out of participation.[33] Civil society is often not a stable partner, with changing representation through community-based organizations that tend to represent particular interests and lack the knowledge, skills, or motivation to view the city as a single collective entity. Partnerships also pose a problem of democracy since they are very often characterized by a lack of accountability and oversight by the population itself or by elected officials.[34] In short, partnerships are useful and necessary, but they are more appropriate for solving management problems (in urban services for instance) than for addressing issues that require democratic decision-making.

## Area-based policies and actions are not a panacea

Area-based approaches seem the logical solution when the state can no longer deal with issues on a comprehensive basis. However, this newly popular form of territorial policy can have negative impacts on urban governance. First, as noted, it worsens existing fragmentation because it typically operates on the basis of discrimination according to the distinguishing characteristics of different areas, such as their ethnic, social, cultural or economic composition, rather than what they share in common. Second, area-based approaches may stigmatize a neighbourhood and its residents.

Area-based policies do have obvious positive aspects as they focus on the specific local manifestation of problems. However, to address these problems effectively, they must also connect to a comprehensive development strategy at the metropolitan level.[35] The specific form for such strategic vertical integration will necessarily vary from country to country and there exists no magic formula that can apply universally.

## Political leadership is a key element of governance

The mere presence of governance is certainly not an automatic cure-all to redress problems arising from globalization. Some metropolitan areas function more ably as collective actors than others. One key element is political leadership. It is essential because governance is not a process free of conflict. Globalization changes political power arrangements. It supports the emergence of new political elites whose strategies and norms are different from the traditional elites.[36] These new political elites rely less on clientelism and party politics. Rather, their legitimacy derives more from their capacity to act, than their allegiance to a traditional ideology or political constituency. Globalization represents an opportunity for these emerging elites: first, because it opens the political system to new actors and, therefore, challenges the incum-

---

**Box 4.4 The French 'Contrats de Plan Etat-Régions' (CPER) and metropolitan areas**

Established in 1986, CPER are the instruments for regions and the state for the joint planning and financing of regional infrastructure and services in France. They receive about one-third of their funding from the European Union. The 1999 Act on National Planning and Environment established that urban areas of more than 50,000 people could get funding from the state only if they present an area-wide strategic plan that considers social inclusion and sustainable development. Once approved, the urban authority signs an 'agglomeration agreement' (*contrat d'agglomération*) with the state, describing the various elements to be financed during a six-year period. In order to avoid potential conflicts between the priorities of the regions and of the state at the regional level and between the priorities of local governments and the state at the local level, such 'agglomeration agreements' must be signed within the CPER framework. This means that they will have to be discussed and approved also by the region and other local authorities, but on a subsidiary basis. As an example, the Region Nord-Pas de Calais has used this process to implement actions against social exclusion in poor neighbourhoods.

---

bent elite; second, because it brings with it a change in the issues to be addressed and in the ways of addressing them.

It is the responsibility of the state and also international organizations to support these emerging urban elites because this strengthening is a condition for effectively addressing the new challenges that globalization produces. However, this support must be cautious (see below) and based on the development of structures and procedures to ensure local democracy because the accountability of these new political elites cannot be taken for granted.[37]

### The political strengthening of metropolitan areas

Globalization has increased the role of metropolitan areas by placing them at the forefront of territorial competition. They have become an essential place for the regulation of relations between the local and the global. This makes it necessary and legitimate to strengthen them politically,[38] granting them the responsibilities, resources and political legitimacy they require to function as strong governmental units.

> Metropolitan areas are *de facto* pivotal arenas in today's processes of global competition. This requires that they be strengthened by giving them more political legitimacy, responsibilities and resources

This strengthening of the economic and political roles of metropolitan areas and emerging political elites, discussed above, raises questions concerning power relationships at the subnational level: that is, regions versus metropolitan areas. In this regard, when providing political legitimacy and allocating national resources, the state (and supranational entities) must avoid creating imbalances. To this end, multi-level governance can serve as a useful framework for articulating all levels of government in subsidiary ways, as illustrated by the 'Contrats de Plan Etat-Régions' in France (see Box 4.4).

## The Democratic Challenge: Insights from Latin America[39]

Chapter 1 situated current trends in poverty and inequality in the context of globalization. Solutions to these problems require good governance and good governance is inextricably linked to human settlements.[40] It is important to recognize that the success of initiatives and reforms in government and governance at the subnational level is closely linked to the ways and extent that national systems embrace and incorporate democratic processes. In this connection, it is important that a government grants its citizens political rights by permitting them to form political parties that represent a significant range of voter choice and whose leaders can openly and safely compete for and be elected to positions of authority in government. It is also important that governments uphold their citizens' civil liberties by respecting and protecting their religious, ethnic, economic, linguistic, gender, family and other rights, including personal freedoms and freedoms of the press, belief and association.[41] The vital importance of the links between good governance and democratic practices is well illustrated by developments in Latin America, where effective political rights are more widespread today than at any time in its history. With few notable exceptions, national governments are chosen through relatively free, fair and competitive elections. Moreover, as attested by the short-lived (lasting just a few hours) military coup in Ecuador in January 2000, and the failed attempt by Peruvian President Alberto Fujimori to win the first round of presidential elections through undemocratic means in April 2000 (and his subsequent flight and resignation in November 2000), efforts to subvert democratic electoral processes are likely to be met by significant national and international pressure. This reflects the fact that current democratic regimes are the result of political struggles involving considerable levels of popular mobilization and organization during the 1970s and 1980s.[42] Not surprisingly, regional public opinion surveys have found that political democracy enjoys an unprecedented level of legitimacy.[43]

> It is important to recognize that the success of initiatives and reforms in government and governance at the subnational level is closely linked to the ways and extent that national systems embrace and incorporate democratic processes

Despite these undeniably positive trends, recent research shows that the region's democratic regimes will remain fragile unless political inclusion is broadened and reinforced by efforts to address other forms of exclusion that still predominate throughout Latin America.[44] This reflects the particular kind of democracy that has emerged in the region: *neopluralist democracy*.[45] Notwithstanding its own particularities, the present situation in Latin America is also of broader interest, considering the oft-assumed (causal) relationship between open economic systems and open political systems. A careful examination of developments in Latin America suggests that this relationship is not a simple one.

## Neopluralist democracy

Neopluralism revolves around the belief that the best balance of interests and values within a given polity is produced by competition among individuals in the rational pursuit of their self-interest. Ultimate political authority is decided on through a free market of votes. But once elected, officials have few checks on their power and frequently bypass representative democratic institutions

Neopluralism is a market-centred pattern of political incorporation. It has replaced the state-centred pattern of incorporation associated with corporatism and the developmentalist state that dominated Latin America through the 1970s, and is closely associated with current market-based economic policies emphasizing free trade, open markets and a minimal role for the state in both the economy and society. The pluralist aspect of neopluralism revolves around 'the belief that the best balance of interests and values within a given polity is produced by some form (however limited) of free competition among individuals in the rational pursuit of their self-interest'.[46] What distinguishes neopluralism from the more traditional pluralist model[47] is its marked authoritarian bent. Ultimate political authority is essentially decided on through a free market of votes. But once elected, officials have few checks on their power and frequently bypass representative democratic institutions.[48] Moreover, a variety of unelected (and unaccountable) power holders, particularly the military, exercise control over key state decisions.[49]

Three aspects of Latin America's neopluralist democracy highlight the nature of the region's democratic challenge:
1  economic insecurity
2  crime rates and the dominant responses to them
3  fragmentation of civil society

Three aspects of Latin America's neopluralist democracy highlight the nature of the region's democratic challenge. The first is increased economic insecurity. This is a direct result of neopluralism's reliance on the market for determining the best allocation of resources and opportunities for all members of society. Labour codes throughout the region have been modified to generally make it easier for firms to hire temporary workers and fire current employees. Governments increasingly informalize themselves vis-à-vis their own laws in their quest for even more foreign investment by creating special production zones that exempt foreign firms from labour legislation and taxation policies applicable in the rest of the nation.[50] Where remaining workers' rights are not taken away outright, their systematic violation is often ignored.

Labour movements, the principal representatives of the lower classes in Latin America, have been weakened throughout the region. Workers in the informal sector and most free trade zones are only rarely organized.[51] Declining union membership and organizational fragmentation have combined to reduce the collective bargaining power of organized labour, independently of legal changes designed to have a similar effect.[52] Increasingly, organized labour has become a narrowly self-interested actor, competing with other groups in civil society in the pursuit of the particularistic interests of its reduced membership. Labour leaders have often bargained with elected governments over concessions to preserve their own individual status and institutional position in exchange for labour's acquiescence to legislative changes curtailing organized labour's effective power.[53] This has further weakened organized labour and contributed to a growing distance between the union rank-and-file and their leaders.

The consequences of this have been significant. Latin American economies grew approximately 15 per cent in the first half of the 1990s, yet unemployment also rose and real wages fell. This is in part because 90 per cent of all new jobs created in the 1990s were in the informal sector.[54] Poverty levels have remained steady at approximately 35 per cent of the population, or roughly 150 million people. Moreover, economic inequality has remained stagnant after sharply increasing during the 1980s, making Latin America the most unequal region in the world.[55]

'An educated electorate is a powerful electorate ... An informed citizenry is the greatest defender of freedom ... An enlightened government is a democratizing government' – Kofi Annan, Address to the World Bank conference 'Global Knowledge '97', Toronto, 22 June 1997

All of these are reflected in the region's problematic educational system.[56] Teachers and administrators remain largely unaccountable to the communities they serve. Educational systems have become skewed in favour of imposing uniformity and rewarding mediocrity rather than encouraging innovation. In many countries, more than 90 per cent of total educational budgets goes towards salaries, reflecting the continued strength (and self-serving nature) of many teachers' unions. The result is generally poor quality education at a relatively high cost. The poor quality of education, in turn, makes it a less attractive alternative to entering the labour market for young people from low-income families. While school attendance during the early years of schooling is comparable to other regions in the world, Latin America stands out due to its high and more rapid dropout rates among the poor. This creates highly stratified educational systems which 'do not constitute a mechanism for social mobility, or for reducing income differences, as is true in other areas of the world'.[57]

Rising crime rates and the predominant responses to them are a second aspect of neopluralism threatening existing democratic regimes. Crime rates, in part fed by growing economic insecurity, have risen substantially in almost every country in the region.[58] To deal with rising crime rates, the poor are often targeted by police efforts to control crime in what amounts to criminalizing poverty.[59] Despite recent transitions to democracy and a substantial reduction in the systematic violation of human rights by the state (with the exceptions of Peru and Colombia due to ongoing civil wars), the overall level of state violence has generally not declined. Instead, it has undergone a qualitative change, as it is no longer directed against the political opposition, but the poor. In some cases, the criminalization of poverty is even formalized to law.[60] For example, the dramatic rise in the crime rate after the transition to democracy in El Salvador led to the passage of the Emergency Law Against Delinquency (Ley de la Emergencia Contra la Delincuencia) and the Law for Social Defence (Ley para la Defensa Social) on 19 March 1996. The laws, portions of which were eventually declared unconstitutional, stipulated that individuals were to be considered potential criminals subject to imprisonment and the loss of basic rights simply because of their appearance. The unemployed, the poor, young people or simply people who dressed differently were targeted by laws that ignored the equally serious (but largely white-collar) problems of organized crime and official corruption.[61] Yet because the poor are also the principal victims of crime, these laws enjoyed overwhelming popular support.

Repressive responses to crime often receive widespread support among the poor.[62] This is in part due to the fact that the poor remain the principal victims of crime. It is also due to a very low level of public confidence in legal institutions. This lack of confidence reflects not only the continued distrust of state institutions caused by high levels of abuse under authoritarian regimes, but also the fact that such practices often do not end with the transition to democracy. People become accustomed to pursuing extra-legal remedies for their grievances and are reluctant to cooperate with law enforcement agencies. This lack of cooperation leaves few alternatives to applying more violence because effective law enforcement and crime prevention are dependent on community involvement. Yet repressive police measures ultimately do little to improve the image of law enforcement agencies, threatening to create a vicious circle.

The criminalization of poverty and resort to repressive police methods also reflect the widespread marketization of the rule of law. Basic civil rights are in effect allocated according to people's 'buying power'. Although equal protection under the law exists on paper, the poor cannot access it because of their limited economic resources. The state is incapable (because of corruption and its own lack of resources) of filling the void. Instead, legal systems serve to further reinforce structural problems of inequality and social exclusion.[63] At the same time, there is an increasing privatization of law enforcement throughout the region as the relatively well-off purchase personal security by contracting private police forces. For those who lack the economic resources to hire armed guards or pay corrupt judges and police, taking justice into one's own hands in the form of vigilantism or 'popular justice' is a growing phenomenon.[64]

Third, neopluralist democracy has contributed to the fragmentation and atomization of civil society. Popular sector organizations often remain small and dependent on external (state and/or non-governmental agencies) largesse. Their efficacy thus remains severely circumscribed. This fragmen-

tation reflects a variety of factors associated with neopluralism, including the demobilization of popular sector organizational activities during democratic transitions.[65] Efforts to reform both the state and society to conform more closely to market principles have often exacerbated this problem. Social welfare reforms, for example, emphasize helping people to participate in the market by targeting those most in need for assistance until they can resolve their situation through participation in the labour market. This can generate political apathy as people's efforts increasingly are devoted to finding even low paying jobs, and they have less time and perceived need to become politically active. State agencies frequently play popular organizations off against one another in a competitive scramble for limited resources, particularly when social welfare budgets remain tight, in order to curtail government spending.[66] Decentralization of social welfare services can further fragment social movements, restricting popular sector organizational activity to narrowly circumscribed communities.

---

Recent public opinion polls show that only 27 per cent of Latin Americans have confidence in existing democratic institutions

---

Together, these various aspects of neopluralism contribute to a very low level of citizen satisfaction with how their democratic regimes actually function. For example, recent public opinion polls show that only 27 per cent of Latin Americans have confidence in existing democratic institutions.[67] Apart from voting, which on average 53 per cent of respondents felt allowed them to influence political outcomes, the majority of Latin Americans had little sense of political efficacy according to *Latino barómetro* survey data from 17 countries in the region collected in 1996.[68] Only 43 per cent of respondents felt that the political tendency with which they most identified was as likely as other tendencies to assume power. Even more serious, an average of just 14 per cent of respondents felt that politicians offered solutions to their problems. These statistics reflect widespread perceptions of exclusion from political power and alienation from formal politics. Political elites seem disconnected from society.

## The need for inclusion

Latin America in many ways faces an opportunity that is historically unique: the unprecedented importance of democratic elections throughout the region offers the possibility that structural problems of socio-economic exclusion can be addressed. At the same time, this 'opportunity' carries a real danger: if democratic governments prove incapable and/or unwilling to address the principal concerns of their citizens, democracy itself risks becoming irrelevant as people search for ways to create better lives for themselves.[69] If democratic institutions can effectively address the increasingly obvious limits of neopluralist democracy, a type of democracy that is more faithful to its own underlying normative justification may be able to consolidate itself in a region long known for often violent authoritarian rule. But if today's democratic institutions fail, Latin America may again fall into a spiral of social polarization and violence.

---

To realize its democratic potential, Latin America needs to become more inclusive, allowing the electoral process to define fiscal responsibilities in social terms.
Policies to this end will require:
- effective law enforcement and judicial processes, especially legal reform
- compliance of work environments with international labour laws
- strengthening of social safety nets
- support for educational reform

---

To realize its potential, Latin America will need to become more inclusive. While such a development inevitably will require some redistribution of national resources towards disadvantaged groups, it is not a question of returning to the overly intrusive developmentalist states of the past, with their fiscal and monetary excesses. In contrast, what such social change would entail is a reinterpretation of the so-called 'Washington Consensus' to encompass *socially defined* fiscal and monetary responsibility as determined through democratic electoral processes.[70]

As part of this process of change, state policies should be directed towards four priority areas:

1   The investment of more resources in *effective law enforcement and judicial processes, particularly legal reform*. The criminalization of poverty and marketization of the rule of law must be reversed. Only through the effective enforcement of civil rights can electoral democracy realize its potential to empower disadvantaged groups. Moreover, it is essential for the effective regulation of markets,[71] and is perhaps the most effective way to regulate workplace environments in order to minimize abuses in Latin America.[72]

2   The *regulation of workplace environments* can also be strengthened through effective compliance with labour market norms embodied in various International Labour Organization (ILO) conventions. Critics of 'globalization' all too often neglect the positive aspects of international structures for addressing employment concerns in developing countries. Enforcement of existing ILO norms regarding, for example, workplace environments and collective bargaining rights can help to empower workers. The ILO can also provide a forum for expanding the collective rights of workers, helping to compensate for the inherent advantages enjoyed by business interests in the international economy.

3   *Social safety nets need to be strengthened* in order to cushion workers from the inevitable periodic economic dislocations that flexible labour markets and expanded exposure to international trade

entail.[73] This should include unemployment insurance. Just as Chile provided a model for many of the market-based social policies currently favoured by policy makers, its current unemployment insurance project, to be funded by employee and employer contributions, may provide a model.

4   Finally, *education reform* must be viewed as the principal long-term basis for greater inclusion. Additional resources in many cases will be less important than ensuring that existing resources are used more effectively. To achieve this, educational reforms should focus on increasing the accountability of teachers and local school administrators to parents and local communities who have an interest in ensuring that children are well educated.[74] Bolivia's current programme of educational reform, emphasizing increased community involvement and introducing a multi-ethnic dimension to the curriculum, offers a particularly useful model for improving educational quality and reducing class dropout rates.[75]

Beyond these basic policy priorities, what is perhaps most important is the need to recapture the momentum of mobilization that began during transitions. This involves taking advantage of the potential of existing democratic institutions to empower civil society by providing institutional mechanisms to pursue the expansion of basic rights and government accountability. It is a challenge to adapt the organizational experiences developed in many countries as part of the struggle against authoritarian rule to a democratic context, where there is no dictator to mobilize against and other socio-economic trends make organizing more problematic. The organizational capacity of disadvantaged segments of Latin American societies needs to be strengthened in order to overcome civil society's atomization.

As a starting point, the possibility of utilizing the national and international human rights apparatus that emerged during the period of authoritarian rule to help to secure effective civil rights and build stronger civil societies under democratic rule should be explored. 'Human rights' might even be best understood as citizenship rights in a democratic context. Past efforts to curtail state political repression could be redirected towards curbing police and judicial abuse. The expertise gained in organizing the myriad of human rights groups under dictatorships similarly could be applied to help distinct groups within civil society to organize themselves so that they can begin to define and defend their interests through democratic institutions.

The state has an important role to play here, too. One obvious role is in providing material and technical assistance to emerging groups within civil society. Only the state has the necessary resources to enable society's disadvantaged to participate effectively. What is often needed, aside from political will, is the necessary imagination to devise strategies by which the state can play the same kind of role in Latin America that it has historically played in the West in helping to build civil society's organizational capacity.[76] A less obvious role for the state is in identity affirmation, particularly to counter the largely negative images of disadvantaged groups in the mass media. Efforts need to be undertaken systematically at the grassroots level to begin to empower people by helping them to be proud of who they are regardless of their social class, gender, ethnicity, religion and so on. Studies have demonstrated the success that such efforts can have in overcoming people's symbolic exclusion.[77]

The challenge facing Latin America is clearly a large one, with very high stakes for all concerned. Yet the opportunity provided by existing political rights and the organizational experiences gained through the political struggles to achieve those rights mean that it is by no means an impossible or utopian challenge. Moreover, although the specifics differ from place to place and there are no easy formulas, it is a challenge faced by all nations seeking to strengthen their democratic processes by making them more inclusive of population groups that frequently are marginal to political and economic decision-making.

> Although the specifics differ from place to place and there are no easy formulas, the challenge facing Latin America is shared by all societies seeking to strengthen their democratic processes by making them more inclusive of population groups that are marginal to political and economic decision-making

# Notes

1. Unless indicated otherwise, this chapter draws in the main from 'Urban governance in the context of globalization: a comparative analysis', a background paper prepared by Christian Lefevre, University of Paris 8, France.

2. UNDP, 1999. The UNDP has defined governance as 'the exercise of political, economic and administrative authority in the management of a country's affairs at all levels. It comprises the mechanisms, processes and institutions through which citizens and groups articulate their interests, exercise their legal rights, meet their obligations and mediate their differences', while:

   'Urban governance is the sum of the many ways individuals and institutions, public and private, plan and manage the common affairs of the city. It is a continuing process through which conflicting or diverse interests may be accommodated and cooperative action can be taken. It includes formal institutions as well as informal arrangements and the social capital of citizens'. (UNDP, 1997, pp 2–3)

   Chapter 17 sets out the norms guiding the Global Campaign for Urban Governance initiated by UNCHS (Habitat).

3. The following section draws on 'Newly emerging forms of governance in an era of globalization', a background paper prepared by Susan Clarke, University of Colorado.

4. See Stoker 1998, pp 17, 22; Rhodes, 1996; Jessop, 1998; Rosenau, 1992;

5. Cox, 1997.

6. DiGaetano and Klemanski, 1999.

7. Cox, 1995; Harding and Le Galès, 1997.

8. Gordon and Cheshire, 1996.

9. Governing stresses political aspects of collective action having to do with the direction and goals of societal development, whereas regulation deals more with management of the processes needed to attain those goals. See Warin, 1993.

10. Molotch, 1993; Harding, 1997a.

11. Savitch and Thomas, 1991, for the United States; Jouve and Lefèvre, forthcoming, for Europe; Prévôt-Schapira, 1999, for Latin America.

12. Rodriguez and Winchester, 1996.

13. Prévôt-Schapira, 1996; May et al, 1998.

14. Lefèvre, 1998a, b.

15. Decentralization is thus different from 'deconcentration', which is the transfer of responsibilities within the state apparatus from the central (national) to local levels, a trend also seen in various countries (UK, France, Ghana, Bulgaria).

16. Mayntz, 1993.

17. N Dewar, 1999.

18. UTUI, 1999.

19. Blair, 2000.

20. Blair, 2000. See also an excellent report by Razavi (2000).

21. Ministry of Cooperation and Development, 1998.

22. Wacker et al, 1999.

23. For example, the European Union created the European Regional Development Fund to promote infrastructure projects that enhance the productive capacity and strengthen the economy of disadvantaged regions. It also established the European Social Fund in support of vocational guidance and skill-improvement programmes to help young people and the long-term unemployed gain access to (better) jobs. The probability of success in obtaining assistance from EU sources is usually greater when applicants form effective partnerships.

24. Harding, 1997a.

25. Department of the Environment, Transport and the Regions, 1998.

26. Etemadi, 2000.

27. Dutta, 2000.

28. N Dewar, 1999.

29. Prévôt-Schapira, 1996.

30. Rhodes, 1996, p 664.

31. Wright and Cassese, 1997.

32. Cochrane, 1993.

33. Hirschmann (1970) has termed this 'exit' behaviour.

34. Guy Peters, 1997.

35. See Pastor Jr et al, 2000, for recent case studies in support of this point.

36. Jouve and Lefèvre, forthcoming.

37. Lefèvre, 1998b.

38. Lefèvre, 1998b.

39. The following section is based on 'Latin America's democratic challenge', a background paper prepared by Philip Oxhorn, McGill University.

40. See Chapter 17 for extensive discussion of ways to strengthen new forms of governance, including the UNCHS (Habitat) Global Campaign for Urban Governance. Chapter 14 reviews the proposed draft of the World Charter of Local Government and the Epilogue discusses political strategies for urban liveability. The Human Development Report 1999 similarly emphasizes the importance of governance to spread the benefits of globalization more equally (UNDP, 1999).

41. See Karatnycky, 2000.

42. O'Donnell et al, 1986; Diamond et al, 1999; Foweraker and Landman, 1997; Eckstein, 1989; Oxhorn, 1995.

43. Lagos, 1997.

44. Oxhorn and Ducatenzeiler, 1998; Agüero and Stark, 1998; Chalmers et al, 1997.

45. Oxhorn, 1998.

46. Oxhorn, 1998, p 201.

47. See Dahl, 1961.

48. Weffort, 1998; O'Donnell, 1994.

49. McSherry, 1999.

50. Portes, 1994, p 168.

51. OIT, 1996.

52. OIT, 1993.

53. Zapata, 1998; Murillo, 1997.

54. Vilas, 1999, p 15.

55. Karl, 2000; Lora and Londoño, 1998.

56. Inter-American Development Bank, 1998.

57. Ibid, p 49.

58. Neild, 1999; NACLA, 1996.

59. Méndez et al, 1999; Neild, 1999; McSherry, 1999.

60. Oxhorn, 1997.

61. Proceso, 16, p 702 (27 March 1996).

62. Neild, 1999; Méndez, 1999.

63. Pinheiro, 1999.

64. Neild, 1999.

65. Oxhorn, 1998.

66. Piester, 1997; Gay, 1990; Cardoso, 1992.

67. New York Times, 25 March 1998, A7.

68. Lagos, 1997.

69. Garretón, 1999.

70. Williamson, 1990.

71. Marshall, 1950.

72. Portes, 1994.

73. Graham, 1994.

74. Inter-American Development Bank, 1998.

75. Contreras, 1998.

76. Walzer, 1999; Cohen and Rogers, 1995; Schmitter, 1995.

77. Fleury, 1998.

# 5

# POLITICS OF THE GLOBAL CITY: CLAIMING RIGHTS TO URBAN SPACES[1]

Each phase in the long history of the world economy raises specific questions about the particular conditions that make it possible. One of the key features of the current phase is the ascendance of information technologies, the associated increase in the mobility and liquidity of capital, and the resulting decline in the capacities of nation states to regulate key sectors of their economies. This is well illustrated by the case of leading information industries, finance and advanced corporate services; these industries tend to have a space economy that is transnational and to have outputs that are hypermobile, moving instantaneously around the globe.

The master images in the currently dominant account of economic globalization emphasize precisely these aspects: hypermobility, global communications, the neutralization of place and distance. There is a tendency in that account to take the existence of a global economic system as a given, a function of the power of transnational corporations and global communications. But the capabilities for global operation, coordination and control contained in the new information technologies and in the power of transnational corporations need to be *produced*. By focusing on the production of these capabilities we add a neglected dimension to the familiar issue of the power of large corporations and the new technologies. The emphasis shifts to the *practices* that constitute what we call economic globalization and global control: the work of producing and reproducing the organization and management of a global production system and a global marketplace for finance, both under conditions of economic concentration.

A focus on practices draws the categories of place and production process into the analysis of economic globalization. These are two categories easily overlooked in accounts centred on the hypermobility of capital and the power of transnationals. Developing categories such as place and production process does not negate the centrality of hypermobility and power. Rather, it brings to the fore the fact that many of the resources necessary for global economic activities are not hypermobile and are deeply embedded in place.

Further, by emphasizing that global processes are at least partly embedded in national territories, such a focus introduces new variables into current conceptions about economic globalization and the shrinking regulatory role of the state. That is to say, the space economy for major new transnational economic processes diverges in significant

ways from the global/national duality presupposed in much analysis of the global economy. The duality of national versus global suggests two mutually exclusive spaces: where one begins, the other ends. This is fundamentally incorrect.

By necessity, the global materializes in specific places and institutional arrangements, a good number of which, if not most, are located in urban territories. 'Glocalization' is a term commonly used to describe the hybrid economic, political and cultural structures and processes associated with the growing interdependence of local and global dimensions.[2] This condition, in turn, creates the possibility of a new type of politics of the global: a grassroots politics that localizes in the network of global cities. Recapturing the geography of places involved in globalization allows us to recapture people, workers, communities and, more specifically, the many different work cultures, besides the corporate culture, involved in the work of globalization. The global city is a nexus where these various trends come together and produce new types of politics.

An important background condition that strengthens the possibility of these new types of politics and political actors is that globalization has had the effect of unbundling some of the components of power of the nation state. This in turn has created voids/openings where these other types of actors can emerge.

---

By necessity the global materializes in specific places and institutional arrangements, a good number of which, if not most, are located in urban places. This condition creates the possibility of a new type of politics: a grassroots politics that localizes in a network of global cities

---

## Nation States and New Political Actors

One of the impacts of globalization on state sovereignty has been to create operational and conceptual openings for other actors and subjects. Various, as yet very minor, developments signal that the state is no longer the exclusive subject for international law or the only actor in international relations. Other actors who become subjects of adjudication in human rights decisions are increasingly emerging as subjects of international law and actors in international relations. These non-state actors can gain visibility as individuals and as collectivities, and come out of the invisibility of aggregate membership in a nation-state exclusively represented by the sovereign. More generally, the ascendance of a large variety of non-state actors in the international arena signals the expansion of an international civil society.

> The ascendance of a large variety of non-state actors in the international arena signals the expansion of an international civil society

There is an incipient unbundling of the exclusive authority over territory and people we have long associated with the nation state. The most strategic instance of this unbundling is probably the global city, which operates as a partly de-nationalized platform for global capital and, at the same time, is emerging as a key site for the most astounding mix of people from all over the world, including immigrants, refugees and minorities.

There are two strategic dynamics here: (a) the incipient de-nationalizing of specific types of national settings, particularly global cities; and (b) the formation of conceptual and operational openings for actors other than the nation state in cross-border political dynamics: in particular, the new global corporate actors and those collectivities whose experience of membership has not been subsumed fully under nationhood in its modern conception, eg minorities, immigrants, first-nation people and many women.[3]

The national as container of social process and power is cracked.[4] This cracked casing opens up possibilities for a geography of politics that links subnational spaces. The large city of today emerges as a strategic site for these new types of operations. It is one of the nexus where the formation of new claims materializes.

One question this engenders is how and whether we are seeing the formation of a new type of transnational politics that localizes in these cities. One instance of this is the variety of networks around women's and immigrant issues now operating across borders. For example, the Asian Coalition for Housing Rights,[5] started by under-privileged women in slums fighting for housing, has gone beyond Asia and incorporates a growing number of cities, including cities in Latin America and South Africa.[6]

## Recovering Place

Including cities in the analysis of economic globalization is not without consequences. Economic globalization has mostly been conceptualized in terms of the national–global duality where the latter gains at the expense of the former. And it has largely been conceptualized in terms of the internationalization of capital and then only the upper circuits of capital. Introducing cities in this analysis allows us to reconceptualize processes of economic globalization as concrete economic complexes situated in specific places. Place is typically seen as neutralized by the capacity for global communications and control. Also, a focus on cities decomposes the nation state into a variety of subnational components, some profoundly articulated with the global

economy and others not. It signals the declining significance of the national economy as a unitary category in the global economy.

> Recovering 'place' in our analysis of globalization allows us to see the multiplicity of economies and work cultures in which the global information economy is embedded

Why does it matter to recover place in analyses of the global economy, particularly place as constituted in major cities? Because it allows the recovery of the concrete, localized processes through which globalization exists and to argue that much of the multiculturalism in large cities is as much a part of globalization as is international finance. Further, focusing on cities allows the specification of a geography of strategic places at the global scale, places bound to each other by the dynamics of economic globalization. This is a new geography of centrality. Is there a transnational politics embedded in this centrality of place and in the new geography of strategic places that cuts across national borders and the old North–South divide?

In so far as economic analysis of the global city recovers the broad array of jobs and work cultures that are part of the global economy (though typically not marked as such), it allows us to examine also the possibility of a new politics of traditionally disadvantaged actors operating in this new transnational economic geography. This is a politics that arises out of actual participation as workers in the global economy, but under conditions of disadvantage and lack of recognition.

> The centrality of spatial location in global processes produces openings for the formation of new, transnational economic and political claims to cities. These claims are made by interests representing global capital, using cities as an organizational commodity, but also by disadvantaged local population groups who need cities as a place to live

The centrality of spatial location in a context of global processes makes possible a transnational economic and political opening for the formation of new claims and hence for the constitution of entitlements, notably rights to place. At the limit, this could be an opening for new forms of 'citizenship'. The city has indeed emerged as a site for new claims: by global capital which uses the city as an 'organizational commodity', but also by disadvantaged sectors of the urban population, whose presence is frequently as international as that of capital. The de-nationalizing of urban space and the formation of new claims by transnational actors, raise the question, Whose city is it?

This is a type of political opening that contains unifying capacities across national boundaries and sharpening conflicts within such boundaries. Global capital and the new migrant workforce are two major instances of transnationalized actors that have unifying properties internally and find themselves in contestation with each other inside global cities. Global cities are the sites for the over-valorizaion of corporate capital and the devalorization of disadvantaged workers.

The leading sectors of corporate capital are now global in their organization and operations. And many of the disadvantaged workers in global cities are those whose sense of membership is not necessarily adequately captured in terms of the national, and indeed often evince cross-border solidarities around issues of substance. Both types of actors find in the global city a strategic site for their economic and political operations.

Immigration, for instance, is one major process through which a new transnational political economy is being constituted, one which is largely embedded in major cities, in so far as most immigrants, whether in the US, Japan or Western Europe are concentrated in major cities. It is one of the constitutive processes of globalization today, even though not recognized or represented as such in mainstream accounts of the global economy.[7] The ascendance of international human rights illustrates some of the actual dynamics through which this operational and conceptual opening can be instituted.[8] International human rights, while rooted in the founding documents of nation-states, are today a force that can undermine the exclusive authority of the state over its nationals and entitles individuals to make claims on grounds that are not derived from the authority of the state.[9]

# A New Geography of Centrality and Marginality

**The global economy can be seen as materializing in a worldwide grid of strategic places, uppermost among which are major international business and financial centres**

The global economy can then be seen as materializing in a worldwide grid of strategic places, uppermost among which are major international business and financial centres.[10] This global grid can be seen as constituting a new economic geography of centrality, one that cuts across national boundaries and across the old North-South divide. It has emerged as a parallel political geography, a transnational space for the formation of new claims by global capital.

This new economic geography of centrality partly reproduces existing inequalities but also is the outcome of a dynamic specific to the current forms of economic growth. It assumes many forms and operates in many terrains, from the distribution of telecommunications facilities to the structure of the economy and of employment. Global cities are sites for immense concentrations of economic power and command centres in a global economy, while cities that were once major manufacturing centres have suffered inordinate declines.

The most powerful of these new geographies of centrality at the inter-urban level binds the major international financial and business centres: New York, London, Tokyo, Paris, Frankfurt, Zurich, Amsterdam, Los Angeles, Sydney and Hong Kong, among others. But this geography now also includes cities such as São Paulo, Buenos Aires, Mumbai, Bangkok and Mexico City.[11] The intensity of transactions among these cities – particularly through the financial markets, in services and investment – has increased sharply, and so have the orders of magnitude involved. At the same time, there has been a sharpening inequality in the concentration of strategic resources and activities between each of these cities and others in the same country.

The growth of global markets for finance and specialized services, the need for transnational servicing networks due to sharp increases in international investment, the reduced role of the government in the regulation of international economic activity and the corresponding ascendance of other institutional arenas, notably global markets and corporate headquarters: all point to the existence of transnational economic processes with multiple locations in more than one country.

Alongside these new global and regional hierarchies of cities is a vast territory that has become increasingly peripheral, increasingly excluded from the major economic processes that fuel economic growth in the new global economy. A multiplicity of formerly important manufacturing centres and port cities have lost functions and are in decline, not only in the less developed countries but also in the most advanced economies. This is yet another meaning of economic globalization.

Also within global cities we see a new geography of centrality and marginality.[12] The downtown areas of cities and key nodes in metropolitan areas receive massive investments in real estate and telecommunications while low-income city areas and the older suburbs are starved for resources.[13] Financial services produce superprofits while industrial services barely survive. These trends are evident, with different levels of intensity, in a growing number of major cities in the developed world and increasingly in some of the developing countries that have been integrated into the global financial markets.[14]

The new urban economy is problematic. This is perhaps particularly evident in global cities and their regional counterparts. It sets in motion a whole series of new dynamics of inequality. The new growth sectors – specialized services and finance – contain capabilities for profit making vastly superior to those of more traditional economic sectors. Many of the latter remain essential to the operation of the urban economy and the daily needs of residents, but their survival is threatened in a situation where finance and specialized services can earn superprofits and bid up prices.[15] Polarization in the profit-making capabilities of different sectors of the economy has always existed. But what is happening today takes place on another order of magnitude and is engendering massive distortions in the operations of various markets, from housing to labour.

The dynamic of valorization is increasing the distance between the valorized, indeed overvalorized, sectors of the economy and devalorized sectors, even when the latter are part of leading global industries. This devalorization of growing sectors of the economy has been embedded in a massive demographic transition towards a growing presence of migrants in the urban workforce.[16]

Large cities in the more highly developed regions of the world are the terrain where a multiplicity of globalization processes assume concrete, localized forms. A focus on cities allows us to capture, further, not only the upper but also the lower circuits of globalization. These localized forms are, in good part, what globalization is about. Cities with growing shares of disadvantaged populations can be seen as strategic sites for conflicts and contradictions associated with the internationalization of capital.

# 'Glocalization': The Localization of the Global

**Economic globalization needs to be understood in its multiple localizations. The global city can be seen as a dominant instantiation of such multiple localizations, creating a strategic terrain for local and global stakeholders, all claiming rights to the city**

Economic globalization, then, needs to be understood also in its multiple localizations, rather than only in terms of the broad, overarching macro-level processes that dominate the mainstream account. Further, we need to see that many of these localizations do not generally get coded as having anything to do with the global economy. The global city can be seen as one strategic example of such multiple localizations.

Many of these localizations are embedded in the demographic transition evident in such cities, where a majority of resident workers today are immigrants and women, often women of colour. These cities are seeing an expansion of low-wage jobs that do not fit the master images about globalization, yet are part of it. Their embeddedness in the demographic transition evident in all these cities, and their consequent invisibility, contribute to the devalorization of these types of workers and work cultures and to the 'legitimacy' of that devalorization.

This can be read as a rupture of the traditional dynamic whereby membership in leading economic sectors contributes conditions towards the formation of a labour aristocracy; a process long evident in Western industrialized economies. 'Women and immigrants' come to replace the Fordist/family wage category of 'women and children'.[17] One of the localizations of the dynamics of globalization is the process of economic restructuring in global cities. The associated socio-economic polarization has generated a large growth in the demand for low-wage workers and for jobs that offer few advancement possibilities. This, amid an explosion in the wealth and power concentrated in these cities; that is to say, in conditions where there is also a visible expansion in high-income jobs and high-priced urban space.

'Women and immigrants' emerge as the labour supply that facilitates the imposition of low wages and powerlessness under conditions of high demand for those workers and the location of those jobs in high-growth sectors. It breaks the historic nexus that would have led to

empowering workers and legitimates this break culturally.

Informalization, which is another form of localization that is rarely associated with globalization, re-introduces the community and the household as an important economic element in global cities. Informalization in this setting is the low-cost (and often feminized) equivalent of deregulation at the top of the system. As with deregulation (eg as in financial deregulation), informalization introduces flexibility, reduces the 'burdens' of regulation and lowers costs, in this case especially the costs of labour. Informalization in major cities of highly developed countries – whether New York, London, Paris or Berlin – can be seen as a downgrading and devaluing of a variety of activities for which there is an effective demand in these cities. There is enormous competition in informal sectors given low entry costs and the ability to produce and distribute goods and services at a lower cost and with greater flexibility. Immigrants and women are important actors in the new informal economies of these cities. They absorb the costs of informalizing these activities.[18]

> Going informal is one way of producing and distributing goods and services at a lower cost and with greater flexibility. This further devalues these types of activities. Immigrants and women are important actors in the new informal economies of these cities. They absorb the costs of informalizing these activities

The reconfiguration of economic spaces associated with globalization in major cities has had different impacts on women and men, on male-typed and female-typed work cultures and on male- and female-centred forms of power and empowerment. The restructuring of the labour market brings with it a shift of labour market functions to the household or community. Women and households emerge as actors that should be part of the theorization of the particular forms that these elements in labour market dynamics assume today.

These transformations contain possibilities, even if limited, for women's autonomy and empowerment. For instance, we might ask whether the growth of informalization in advanced urban economies reconfigures some types of economic relations between men and women. With informalization, the neighbourhood and the household re-emerge as sites for economic activity. This condition has its own dynamic possibilities for women. Economic downgrading through informalization creates 'opportunities' for low-income women entrepreneurs and workers, and therewith reconfigures some of the work and household hierarchies in which women find themselves. This becomes particularly clear in the case of immigrant women who come from countries with rather traditional male-centred cultures.[19]

Recent studies show that immigrant women's regular wage work and improved access to other public realms has an impact on their gender relations. Women gain greater personal autonomy and independence while men lose ground. Women gain more control over budgeting and other domestic decisions, and greater leverage in requesting help from men in domestic chores. Also, their access to public services and other public resources gives them a chance to become incorporated in the mainstream society; they are often the ones in the household who mediate in this process. It is likely that some women benefit more than others from these circumstances; we need more research to establish the impact of class, education and income on these gendered outcomes. Besides the relatively greater empowerment of women in the household associated with waged employment, there is a second important outcome: their greater participation in the public sphere and their possible emergence as public actors.

There are two arenas where immigrant women are especially active: institutions for public and private assistance, and the immigrant/ethnic community. The incorporation of women in the migration process strengthens the settlement likelihood and contributes to greater immigrant participation in their communities and with the state. For instance, one study found that immigrant women come to assume more active public and social roles which further reinforces their status in the household and the settlement process.[20] Women are more active in community building and community activism and they are positioned differently from men regarding the broader economy and the state. They are the ones that are likely to have to handle the legal vulnerability of their families in the process of seeking public and social services for them. This greater participation by women suggests the possibility that they may emerge as more forceful and visible actors and make their role in the labour market more visible as well.

On the one hand, the women in global cities described above constitute an invisible and disempowered class of workers in the service of the strategic sectors constituting the global economy. This invisibility keeps them from emerging as whatever would be the contemporary equivalent of the 'labour aristocracy' of earlier forms of economic organization, when a low-wage worker position in leading sectors had the effect of empowering that worker, that is, the possibility of unionizing.[21] On the other hand, the access to (albeit low) wages and salaries, the growing feminization of the job supply and the growing feminization of business opportunities brought about with informalization, do alter the gender hierarchies in which they find themselves. Another important localization of the dynamics of globalization is that of the new professional women stratum.

## A Space of Power

What makes the localization of these processes strategic and potentially constitutive of a new kind of transnational politics, even though they involve powerless and often invisible workers, is that these same cities are also the strategic sites for the valorization of the new forms of global corporate capital.

Global cities are centres for the *servicing* and *financing* of international trade, investment and headquarter operations. The multiplicity of specialized activities present in global cities are crucial in the (over)valorization of leading sectors of capital today. And in this sense they are strategic production sites for today's leading economic sectors. This function is reflected in the ascendance of these activities in their economies. What is most important about the shift to services is not merely the growth in service jobs, but the growing service intensity in the organization of advanced economies: firms in all industries, from mining to wholesale, buy more accounting, legal, advertising, financial, economic forecasting services today than they did 20 years ago. Whether at the global or regional level, urban centres – central cities, edge cities – are adequate and often the best production sites for such specialized services. When it comes to the production of services for the leading globalized sectors, the advantages of location in cities are particularly strong.

The rapid growth and concentration of such services in cities signals that the latter have re-emerged as significant 'production' sites after losing this role in the period when mass manufacturing was the dominant sector of the economy. Under mass manufacturing and Fordism, the strategic spaces of the economy were the large-scale integrated factory and the government through its Fordist/Keynesian functions.

> The rapid growth and concentration of global production services in cities signals that the latter have re-emerged as significant 'production' sites after losing this role in the period when mass manufacturing was the dominant sector of the economy

Further, the vast new economic topography that is being implemented through electronic space is one fragment of an even more vast economic chain that is in good part embedded in non-electronic spaces.[22] There is no fully dematerialized firm or industry. Even the most advanced information industries, such as finance, are installed only partly in electronic space, as are industries that produce digital products, such as software designers. The growing digitization of economic activities has not eliminated the need for the physical accommodation of major international business and financial centres and all the material resources they concentrate, from state-of-the-art telematics infrastructure to brain talent.[23]

> The growing digitization of economic activities has not eliminated the need for the physical accommodation of major international business and financial centres and all the material resources they concentrate, from state-of-the-art telematics infrastructure to brain talent

It is precisely because of the territorial dispersal facilitated by telecommunication advances that agglomeration of centralizing activities has expanded immensely. This is not a mere continuation of old patterns of agglomeration but, one could posit, a new logic for agglomeration. Many of the leading sectors in the economy operate globally, in uncertain markets, under conditions of rapid change in other countries (eg deregulation and privatization), and are subject to enormous speculative pressures. What glues these conditions together into a new logic for spatial agglomeration is the added pressure of speed.

A focus on the work behind command functions, on the actual *production process* in the finance and services complex, and on global market *places* has the effect of incorporating the material facilities underlying globalization and the whole infrastructure of jobs typically not marked as belonging to the corporate sector of the economy. An economic configuration very different from that suggested by the concept 'information economy' emerges. We recover the material conditions, production sites and place-boundedness that are also part of globalization and the information economy.

# Making Claims on the City

> **The shrinking of distance and of time that characterizes globalization finds one of its most extreme expressions in the formation of new, electronically based communities of shared interests – individuals and organizations from all around the globe interacting in real time**

These processes signal that there has been a change in the linkages that bind people and places and in the corresponding formation of claims on the city.[24] Today the articulation of territory and people is being constituted in a radically different way from past periods at least in one regard, and that is the speed with which that articulation can change. One consequence of this speed is the expansion of the space within which actual and possible linkages can happen.[25] The shrinking of distance and of time that characterizes the current era finds one of its most extreme forms in electronically based communities of individuals or organizations from all around the globe interacting in simultaneous real time, as is possible through the internet and kindred electronic networks.

Another radical form assumed today by the linkage of people to territory is the loosening of traditional sources of identity, such as the nation or the village. This unmooring in the process of identity formation engenders new notions of community of membership and of entitlement.[26]

> **The global grid of cities is both place-centred in that it is embedded in particular and strategic sites; and it is transterritorial because it connects sites that are not geographically proximate yet intensely connected to each other**

The space constituted by the global grid of cities, a space with new economic and political potentialities, is perhaps one of the most strategic spaces for the formation of transnational identities and communities. This is a space that is both place-centred, in that it is embedded in particular and strategic sites, and is transterritorial because it connects sites that are not geographically proximate yet intensely connected to each other. It is not only the transmigration of capital that takes place in this global grid, but also that of people, both rich (ie the new transnational

professional workforce) and poor (ie most migrant workers); and it is a space for the transmigration of cultural forms, for the reterritorialization of 'local' subcultures. An important question is whether it is also a space for a new politics, one going beyond the politics of culture and identity, though likely to be partly embedded in these.

Yet another way of thinking about the political implications of this strategic transnational space is the notion of the formation of new claims on that space. Has economic globalization at least partly shaped the formation of claims?[27] There are indeed major new actors making claims on these cities, notably foreign firms who have been increasingly entitled to do business through progressive deregulation of national economies, and the consequent large increase in international businesspeople. These new city users have profoundly marked the urban landscape. Their claim to the city is not contested, even though the costs and benefits to cities have barely been examined. These claims contribute to the incipient de-nationalization dynamics discussed in the previous section which, though institutional, tend to have spatial outcomes disproportionately concentrated in global cities.

City users have made an often immense claim on the city and have reconstituted strategic spaces of the city in their image: there is a *de facto* claim to the city, a claim never made problematic. They contribute to change the social morphology of the city and to constitute the metropolis of second generation, the city of late modernism. The new city of 'city users' is a fragile one, whose survival and successes are centred on an economy of high productivity, advanced technologies and intensified exchanges.[28]

On the one hand, this raises a question of what the city *is* for international businesspeople: it is a city whose space consists of airports, top-level business districts, top-of-the-line hotels and restaurants, a sort of urban glamour zone. On the other hand, there is the difficult task of establishing whether a city that functions as an international business centre does in fact recover the costs involved in being such a centre: including the maintenance of a state-of-the-art business district and all it requires, from advanced communications facilities to top-level security and 'world-class culture'.

Perhaps at the other extreme of conventional representations are those who use urban political violence to make their claims on the city, claims that lack the *de facto* legitimacy enjoyed by the new 'city users'. These actors are struggling for recognition, entitlement and to claim their rights to the city.

There are two aspects in this formation of new claims that have implications for the new transnational politics. One is the sharp and perhaps sharpening differences in the representation of these claims by different sectors, notably international business and the vast population of low-income 'others'.[29] The second aspect is the increasingly transnational element in both types of claims and claimants. It signals a politics of contestation embedded in specific places – global cities – but transnational in character. At its most extreme, this divergence assumes the form of: (a) an overvalorized corporate centre occupying a smaller terrain with sharper edges than, for example, in the ost-war era characterized by a large middle class; and (b) a sharp devalorization of what is outside the centre, which comes to be read as marginal or even criminal (cf the criminalization of being homeless in a number of large cities).

There is something to be captured here: a distinction between powerlessness and a condition of being an actor even though lacking power. In the context of a strategic space such as the global city, the types of disadvantaged people described here are not simply marginal; they acquire presence in a broader political process that escapes the boundaries of the formal polity. This presence signals the possibility of politics. What this politics will be will depend on the specific projects and practices of various communities. In so far as the sense of membership of these communities is not subsumed under the national, it may well signal the possibility of a transnational politics centred in concrete localities.

Global capital has made claims on nation states and these have responded through the production of new forms of legality.[30] The new geography of global economic processes, the strategic territory for economic globalization, has to be produced; it is created both in terms of the practices of corporate actors and the requisite infrastructure, and in terms of the work of the state in producing or legitimating new legal regimes. These claims are very often over the city's land, resources and policies. Disadvantaged sectors which have gained presence are also making claims, but these lack the legitimacy attached to the claims of global capital.

There are two distinct issues here. One is the formation of new legal regimes that negotiate between national sovereignty and the transnational practices of corporate economic actors. The second issue is the particular content of this new regime, one that often contributes to strengthen the advantages of certain types of economic actors and to weaken those of others.[31] There is a larger theoretical and political question underlying some of these issues which has to do with which actors gain legitimacy and which ones lose legitimacy.

## A Politics of Places and Cross-border Networks

Globalization is a contradictory process; it is characterized by contestation, internal differentiation and continuous border crossings. The global city is emblematic of this condition. Global cities concentrate a disproportionate share of global corporate power and are one of the key sites for its overvalorization. But they also concentrate a disproportionate share of the disadvantaged and are one of the key sites for their devalorization. This joint presence happens in a context where: (a) the globalization of the economy has grown sharply and cities have become increasingly strategic for global capital; and (b) marginalized people have found their voice and are making claims on the city as well. This joint presence is further brought into focus by the sharpening of the distance between the two. The centre now concentrates immense power, a power that rests on the capability for global control and the capability to produce superprofits. And marginality, notwithstanding

little economic and political power, has become an increasingly strong presence through the new politics of culture and identity, and an emergent transnational politics embedded in the new geography of economic globalization. Both actors, increasingly transnational and in contestation, find in the city the strategic terrain for their operations.

Cities are very complex and multifaceted. They are sites for extreme exploitation of masses of people; but they are also sites for new types of politics, new ways in which the powerless can engage power in a way they may not be able to in rural areas or in small towns. And they are also sites where the many different cultures of resistance, subversion and contestation of power can become present to each other, aware of each other, in a way they cannot on a plantation or in a small town where the diversity and critical mass are lacking. Cities have become international spaces for a diversity of actors and subjects. They have, of course, always been so, though perhaps differently and a bit less than today. Cities are new frontier zones where actors from many different types of struggles and national origins can come together.

Cities are a space for a far more concrete politics than that of the nation state. Cities make possible the formation of informal political subjects: various types of activists around the rights of the homeless, the rights of immigrants, the rights of lesbians and gays; direct action politics against capital; squatters; anarchists; anti-racism and police brutality struggles; and others. The protests against the WTO in Seattle in 1999 illustrate how mobilization can happen because at some point the global economy must materialize in specific places: it becomes a concrete event in the form of 132 trade ministers in a city. Similar mobilization occurred with the IMF/World Bank meetings in Washington, DC in 2000.

Cities are a key site for the feminization of survival, profit making and the development of a new type of grass-roots politics around global issues. Nowhere are there such vast concentrations of women in the strategic economic sectors at the top of the system and in the infrastructure of low-wage jobs, and nowhere do the conditions of trafficking in women materialize so clearly as a mechanism for illegal profit as in these cities. The strategic nature of all these dynamics and the vast concentrations of women from different countries and socio-economic backgrounds, signals the possibility of a variety of concrete politics of resistance, contestation and implementation by women. Because these cities have women from so many different countries, one effect could be to strengthen the formation of existing coalitions, while also leading to new cross-border networks. The cross-border network of global cities is a space where we are seeing the formation of counter-geographies of globalization that contest the dominant economic forms the global economy has assumed.

---

Cities are strategic sites and will become even more so – sites for global interests seeking to maximize profit, but they are also sites where local grassroots and civil society develop new claims and assert their rights to liveable urban places

Cities are strategic sites and will become even more so – sites for global interests that seek to maximize profits, but they are also sites where local grassroots and civil society develop new claims and assert their rights to liveable urban places. They are about a new type of politics that has to do with engaging the global in the localized site that is the city. It is here that diverse interests coalesce around and contest goals of economic growth, social justice and environmental sustainability.

# Notes

1   This chapter is drawn from 'Politics of the global city: claiming rights to urban spaces', a background paper prepared by Saskia Sassen, University of Chicago.

2   See, for example, Robertson, 1994; Swyngedouw, 1997; 'National Governments, Cities and Society: The Habitat Conference II, Istambul (sic) 1996'. European Union National Committees Meeting, Madrid, November 1995 (available at http://habitat.aq.upm.es/rech/a004.html); Shelton, 1996; Brenner, 1998. Glocalization takes on special significance given the growing salience of the principle of subsidiarity under current decentralization processes (see Chapters 4, 13 and 17) and the importance of supporting participation by civil society (see Chapter 14).

3   These two arguments are developed at length in in Sassen, 1996 and 1998b.

4   Taylor, 1995; Shachar, 1990; Sassen, 1996; Allen, 1999 in Allen et al, 1999.

5   See http://www.achr.net/.

6   Face to Face 2000, see http://www.achr.net/; Copjec and Sorkin, 1999.

7   For a full examination of these issues, see Sassen, 1998a, Part One.

8   Jacobson, 1996.

9   See also Franck, 1992.

10   Abu-Lughod, 1999; Knox and Taylor, 1995; Friedmann, 1995; Smith and Kim, 1999; Stren, 1996; Sassen, 2000a.

11   Sassen, 2000b.

12   Fainstein et al, 1993; Kloosterman, 1996; Sassen, 2000a; McDowell, 1997; Allen, 1999 in Allen et al, 1999.

13   See, eg *Journal of Urban Technology* 1995.

14   Cohen et al, 1996; Sassen, 2000b.

15   Sassen has shown how these new inequalities in profit-making capacities of economic sectors, earnings capacities of households and prices in upscale and downscale markets have contributed to the formation of informal economies in major cities of highly developed countries (see Sassen, 1998a). These informal economies negotiate between these new economic trends and regulatory frameworks that were engendered in response to older economic conditions.

16   See also Peraldi and Perrin, 1996; McDowell, 1997; Eade, 1996.

17   Sassen, 1998a, Chapter 5. This newer case brings out the economic significance of these types of actors more brutally than did the Fordist contract, which veiled or softened the significance through the provision of the family wage.

18   See Sassen, 1998a, Chapter 8; Tabak and Chrichlow, 2000.

19   The downside of this situation is also readily seen in insecure and unfavourable conditions of employment. See, for example, Perrons, 2000 (see Background Papers) and Chang, 2000.

20   Hondagneu-Sotelo, 1994.

21   See Sassen, 2000c, Chapter 9; McDowell, 1997; Eade, 1996.

22   See Sassen, 2000c, Chapter 9; McDowell, 1997; Eade, 1996.

23   Castells, 1996; Graham and Marvin, 1996; Sassen, 1998a, Chapter 9; Sassen, 2000b. Telematics and globalization have emerged as fundamental forces reshaping the organization of economic space. This reshaping ranges from the spatial virtualization of a growing number of economic activities to the reconfiguration of the geography of the built environment for economic activity. Whether in electronic space or in the geography of the built environment, this reshaping involves organizational and structural changes.

24   Copjec and Sorkin, 2000; Clark and Hoffman-Martinot, 1998.

25   Martinotti, 1993; *Futur Anterieur*, 1995; Rotzer, 1995; Bonilla et al, 1998.

26   Sassen, 1998a, Chapter 1; Suro, 1998; Eade, 1996.

27   For a different combination of these elements see Dunn, 1994; *Wissenschaftsforum*, 1995.

28   Martinotti, 1993.

29   King, 1995.

30   Sassen, 1996, Chapter 2.

31   There are many issues here, from the question of the legitimacy of the right to economic survival, to the question of human rights and the question of the representativity of the state. See, for instance, discussions as diverse as Cohen et al, 1996; Franck, 1992; Jacobson, 1996; Reisman, 1990. See also Sassen, 1996, Chapters 2 and 3, for a fuller discussion of these issues.

# CHANGES IN HOUSING FINANCE AND SHELTER DELIVERY SYSTEMS

Housing is an essential component of human settlements. At its most elemental level, it addresses basic human needs by serving as shelter, offering protection against excessive cold and heat, rain, high winds and other intemperate weather. If housing is inadequate because of dampness, vermin, overcrowding and other substandard conditions, it undermines individuals' health and well-being. Housing also protects people against street crime. If housing costs are excessive, this affects people's ability to meet other basic needs such as food and health care.

At the household level, housing also fulfils important functions. It provides a physical enclosure for domestic behaviour: a place for daily activities, where people cook, eat, socialize and rest, away from the public realm, and a place where, in many cultures, they are born and die. At the same time, through its location, housing forms the basis for activities in the community and larger outside world, such as interactions with neighbours, work, school and shopping.

In the wider community context, the design and location of housing can denote a household's affiliation with a particular cultural or religious group, serving to reinforce the social bonds among its members. But, these same housing characteristics can also reflect segregation from other population groups and reinforce unequal access to jobs, schools, services and life chances generally. In this sense, housing is inextricably connected to questions of redistributive justice and, thereby, to political and economic processes.

It is not only to its occupants that housing is important. Aside from the residents, there are land developers, lenders, investors, design professionals, unions and government agencies at various levels. Each of these groups has its own particular interests. In market-based societies that treat housing foremost as a commodity, to be produced and traded for profit, the interests of these groups typically revolve around obtaining and regulating financial gain. Treatment of access to housing as a function of ability-to-pay contrasts with a view of housing as a right.

At the policy level, governments use housing to attain various other objectives. Chief among them are economic ones. Internationally, housing investments constitute between 2 and 8 per cent of gross national product (GNP), between 10 and 30 per cent of gross capital formation, between 20 and 50 per cent of accumulated wealth and between 10 and 40 per cent of household expenditure. Residential construction has numerous backward linkages (eg building components) and forward linkages (eg furniture). Using this multiplier effect, governments can stimulate new construction to boost employment. Alternatively, during times of high inflation, governments may seek to slow new building, for example by limiting credit supply. On the other hand, housing is significantly affected by many *non*-housing policies, for example those concerning trade, employment, public finance, social welfare and transport.

PART III

Globalization affects these and other aspects of housing in different ways and degrees. There are, for example, effects on patterns of population segregation (Chapter 2) and the right to housing (Chapters 3 and 16). This part of the report reviews recent changes in shelter delivery mechanisms and in particular housing finance. As in all else, it is difficult to make generalizations and individual countries differ in, for example, foreign direct investment, debt service, trade barriers, fiscal pressures to keep budgets under control, demands for greater transparency and technological capability. While recognizing these differences, the three chapters that follow focus on the developing countries, the countries with economies in transition and the industrialized countries.

In the developing countries, a vast majority of households use their own or informal savings. Globalization has increased the informal economy, and formal sector commercial financial institutions do not meet the housing loan needs of people living in poverty. Many informal settlements also house a large number of renters whose needs are often overlooked. Government programmes do not reach enough people and do not reach the lowest income groups. There is a need for governments to support innovative approaches involving a range of micro-finance schemes and partnerships with local communities. Keys to success are access to land, secure tenure and income generation to reduce poverty. Women play crucial roles in this regard.

In the countries with economies in transition, globalization has led to deregulation of an elaborate system of rules and laws, decentralization of a strong state apparatus, increased residential mobility and the slow emergence of local housing markets. Widespread privatization of the state housing stock, with deep discounts on the sale of units to existing tenants, and the lifting of rent controls, have brought issues of inequity, although affordability has not so far become a major problem. However, there has been a sharp decline in housing investment and new construction, while lack of maintenance and repair is also a fast-growing cause of concern. There exists a significant challenge in the development of a private capital market and institutional mechanisms as well as legislation to construct more functional housing markets while protecting access of low-income households to adequate housing.

In the industrialized countries, globalization has several implications for housing finance. Most obvious are the vastly increased mobility of capital and the greater integration of housing finance with more general circuits of finance. Coupled with deregulation, this means that local lenders and individual homeowners are increasingly competing for capital in the same pool as the richest multinational corporations. At the same time, globalization is associated with widening, skill-based wage inequality with the effect of reinforcing existing patterns of segregation. In many industrialized countries, there are also continuing concerns about tenure polarization and residualization of the social rented sector. Governments tend to play a diminishing role, in part, as a result of their lesser ability to tax mobile capital, thus putting a downward pressure on housing subsidies. However, they fulfil important functions as regulators, catalysts and partners.

# 6

# THE DEVELOPING COUNTRIES[1]

## Housing Finance: Needs and Capacity

For the urban poor, there are four significant potential sources of housing finance.[2] The first is investments by the urban poor themselves, using their own monies and the informal savings and lending institutions that are immediately available to them. The second is government-supported housing finance, either through direct construction or through the provision of subsidized loans. The third source is formal sector commercial financial institutions. The final source is micro-finance institutions that have emerged from primarily NGO-led development innovations.

### Direct investment by low-income residents

> The biggest investors in low-income housing are the poor themselves

The biggest investors in low-income housing are the poor themselves. With only limited assets, many of the urban poor find land in the city, invest in housing, negotiate for services and secure land tenure, often in that order. This is the reverse of the formal process of housing development, in which land is purchased, infrastructure installed and housing constructed. In the informal sector, infrastructure comes last.

These processes are illustrated by numerous accounts from residents throughout the world, including the *posseiros* in Brazil[3] and the 'slum' dwellers in India.[4] Two points need to be highlighted in the context of the following discussion. First, the sources of finance are varied and include savings, contributions from friends and relations and/or borrowing from informal moneylenders. However, these are rarely sufficient to complete a house, and improvements take place over several years. Second, investments are not limited to housing improvements but may include land purchase and infrastructure improvements.[5] Box 6.1 gives an indication of the significance of housing investment for low-income urban citizens in India.

More generally, it is difficult to estimate the scale of direct investment in urban areas that is not supported by formal institutions, either public or private. The squatter populations in cities are indicative of this scale, but many ex-squatter areas have been brought into formal residential areas, either by state decree or by negotiation with private landowners. The number of squatters, therefore, is an underestimation of those who have been and are currently investing in their own housing and neighbourhoods. However, the global scale of finance is undoubtedly substantial, and most squatters have invested upwards of several hundred dollars in their housing.

### State investment programmes

In a few countries, the state is an investor in low-income housing, first, by being directly involved in construction. As discussed below, the impact of development policies over the last two decades has tended to reduce the role of the state. Nevertheless, state agencies (at national, provincial and local level) still take part in housing construction. For example, in the Philippines, the National Housing Authority as a developer is building about 5000 units a year. In Brazil, the federal state has recently launched a new house-building programme that will offer 15-year leases with an option to purchase at the end of this period. Typically, the limited scale of these programmes and the high subsidies involved mean that they are attractive to middle-income groups and that it is difficult to reach their official target group, the poor.

Second, the state may implement housing subsidy programmes. In both South Africa and Chile, for example, there are extensive housing programmes financed by the national government that provide a full or partial capital subsidy for both low-income and lower middle-income housing.[6] For the most part, these programmes are implemented by private construction companies but they also include options for community-managed housing development. A problem with such programmes is the limited scale due to their high cost for the national budget.

---

**Box 6.1 Estimates of citizen direct investment in housing in India**

The huge variety of standards within illegal and designated 'slum' settlements makes it difficult to estimate the scale of existing investment. Drawing on a number of cost estimates from the 1980s and 1990s, a finished house in an informal settlement requires an investment of approximately Rs.20,000–30,000 (when valued today) and an unfinished house at least one-quarter of this amount. This suggests a private investment in India's illegal and designated 'slum' settlements equal to at least Rs.350,000 million, but probably several times this figure.

**Source:** Acharya, 2000.

Third, there are a number of state programmes that provide subsidized housing finance through reduced interest rates. These programmes are invariably limited by the amount of finance that is made available. They include the Unified Home Lending Programme in the Philippines and funds managed by HUDCO in India. These institutions target an income group above the very poor because the finance they offer is used (in the vast majority of cases) for the provision of completed formal housing rather than investment in incremental housing.

Despite special measures to reach low-income target groups, such as a partial capital subsidy and/or interest rate subsidies, these programmes have faced many problems. The scale of the schemes is likely to be small if they have to fit in with existing rules and regulations. Furthermore, the programmes often do not provide lasting support to those they seek to reach as in the case of Visakhapatnam, India, where the poorest beneficiaries were selling their houses.[7] Similar problems are seen in subsidy programmes that target the poor – in South Africa, for example.[8] Some

micro-finance programmes and NGO interventions seek to avoid such problems by providing more integrated and holistic support, with lending for income generation and emergency loans.

Fourth, there have been some attempts to provided subsidized funds for community-based housing initiatives through a number of innovative government schemes, particularly in Asia. Such programmes typically offer loans to community groups at subsidized interest rates and with a support programme for borrowers that involves technical assistance and institutional support from NGOs. For example, in the Philippines, the Community Mortgage Programme offers funds at 6 per cent to community groups. The high land costs, particularly in Manila, mean that most loans have been simply for land purchase with community residents constructing their own housing. In Thailand, the Urban Community Development Office provides collective loan finance for a range of activities including land purchase and housing construction. Fonhapo in Mexico produced about 15 per cent of the public sector assisted supply with 9 per cent of the budget.[9] In South Africa, the South African Homeless People's Federation builds houses that are regularly 20–40 per cent larger than units provided by commercial producers for the same funds, and additional scale is sometimes achieved when residents add more of their own finance. However, bureaucracy, high cost, limited funds and a lack of technical assistance have limited such programmes.[10]

At the same time, governments have begun to recognize the importance of micro-finance, an approach that has emerged from a group of civil society agencies working, particularly, to provide loans for small enterprise development. Micro-finance seeks to work directly with the poor through adopting terms and conditions for lending that do not discriminate against those working in the informal sector and living in informal settlements. Many micro-finance initiatives for enterprise development have been targeted at women although there are many exceptions to this general orientation. In the case of housing, some initiatives are explicitly targeted at women while others seek to ensure that women are not excluded. Box 6.2 discusses how the loan fund of the South African Homeless People's Federation seeks to ensure that women's access to housing improvements is central. The South African government supported this fund with a R10 million contribution in 1995 (then worth approximately US$1.5 million). Inevitably, situations differ for legal and cultural reasons. Whoever the target beneficiaries, many micro-finance programmes for housing investment are concerned with incremental development because a lack of capital restricts big loans and there are concerns over affordability by those borrowing money.

---

**Box 6.2 Housing improvements, women and empowerment**

The Alliance of *uMfelandaWonye* (South African Homeless People's Federation) and People's Dialogue (its NGO partner) seeks to support a process by which the urban poor reclaim their power to choose their development options. Its activities are oriented towards urban poverty reduction and it seeks to target those who are most in need. The programme has developed around several key components including a loan fund to support housing development, as working with women quickly identified housing as a priority.

Very early on, the network of homeless poor that was to become the Homeless People's Federation realized the importance of access to credit. While the homeless poor possess energy, initiative, skill and experience, they lack the material resources to transform their situation. The Alliance decided, in 1993, that the only way around this problem was for the People's Dialogue to assist the Federation in becoming directly involved in managing its own loan fund. The *uTshani* Fund began operations in January 1995 (*uTshani* means grassroots in Zulu), since when it has given over 5000 loans for housing to Federation members.

In South Africa, the dual focus on savings and housing has resulted in a high participation by women:

*'Because the focus has been placed on housing, with a particular stress on savings for housing, women who generally feel a greater need for decent secure housing tended to play a leading role. Men, as typical organizational leaders, have been willing to create the space for women's central participation because savings for housing is regarded as "a woman's skill". Women's central participation in the Federation is a practical issue. The process through which the poor and excluded can obtain housing is difficult. Inevitably, those who are most committed to improved housing will come to the fore, it is this non-random social selection process which has resulted in the central participation of women.'*[i]

The high profile of women is a significant change from the situation that prevailed within most community organizations prior to the establishment of the Federation. Previously, such meetings were dominated by male participation and the discussions had little to do with the practical problems faced by most women (see also Box 14.4). At the first meeting of community leaders that launched the People's Dialogue, over 60 per cent of the delegates were men. Women now make up 85 per cent of the Federation's members and their presence is particularly strong at the lowest level of Federation activity, namely, the Housing Savings Schemes (see also the discussion of the Alliance in Mumbai in Chapter 14).

Note: i People's Dialogue, 1995.

---

Governments have begun to recognize the importance of micro-finance, supporting the poor by adopting terms and conditions for lending that do not discriminate against those working in the informal sector

Throughout, it is important to recognize the gender dimension. In many societies, the provision of a clean and healthy home is the woman's responsibility. Investment in housing is likely to assist women directly, as they manage their multiple roles as income earners and care-takers. Many women work in the informal sector both due to gender discrimination and because of the frequent need to combine income activities with child rearing. A good home and neighbourhood often help with the prosperity of such activities.[11] Investing in housing is important for all women but particularly important for the significant number of women who head their households and who are solely responsible for a number of dependants.

## Formal financial sector

The formal financial sector does not provide finance to low-income housing and communities on any scale. There are many reasons for the reluctance of commercial banks to lend to the poor (including high administrative costs, lack of collateral or regular employment of borrowers and lack of experience and familiarity); these are well documented in a number of studies of micro-finance initiatives.[12] The programmes that exist often only fund formal housing and hence are too expensive for the poor, even if they do qualify for inclusion. This holds true whether they are commercial, state-supported or joint state/private sector ventures.[13]

There have been a small number of initiatives that have sought to link the formal financial sector with the urban poor. These have been initiated by development agencies seeking to improve these links rather than by the commercial enterprises themselves. In India, for example, Northern NGOs have had to provide guarantees in order to encourage the formal financial sector to lend to the poor. The Society for the Promotion of Area Resources Centres (SPARC), a leading NGO working in urban poverty and housing, has had guarantee funds from both SELAVIP and Homeless International in order to secure loans from HUDCO in India. Homeless International also offered guarantee funds to the Youth Charitable Organization and found that it had to guarantee 109 per cent of the loan. Similarly, the Asian Development Bank recently gave a soft loan of US$300 million to the housing finance sector in India. The inability of the formal financial sector to use these funds in innovative ways to reach the poor resulted in a one-year programme to link interested formal financial institutions with community-based financial institutions.[14]

## Micro-finance institutions

There has been a growing interest in micro-finance throughout the world. In the main, this focus has been on financing income generation rather than on housing and associated investments. However, in a number of cases, the development of these programmes has resulted in the extended provision of credit for housing, for example, in some Latin American countries,[15] including El Salvador,[16] and in India.[17]

Perhaps the largest example is the Grameen Bank, which has lent for shelter development to over 300,000 of its members. However, this case is somewhat unusual as it includes the provision of an agreed package of materials for housing construction. Unlike the enterprise loans given by the bank, housing loans are provided at a subsidized interest rate. The funds for housing loans are provided by the government and are part of a larger programme of government lending for housing development. Excluding this example, most micro-finance institutions lending for housing have rarely exceeded 10,000 loans, with a substantial number falling into the 5000–10,000 bracket.

There are two distinct approaches to micro-finance for housing.[18] The first is the extension of traditional micro-finance programmes for enterprise development into housing. This approach seeks to overcome the constraints placed on the informal sector due to the reluctance of formal financial institutions to lend to the poor. Hence, it bases its development intervention on the need to improve financial markets. Micro-finance institutions such as the Self-employed Women's Association (SEWA), for example, have extended lending to housing because of the demand from their members.

The second approach has emerged from within the housing and urban development sector itself. This approach seeks to understand how better to address urban poverty and identifies a number of advantages to micro-finance initiatives based around savings and loans. The South African Homeless People's Federation's *uTshani* (see Box 6.2) illustrates the benefits of a revolving loan fund; savings help to build strong community organizations based on trust and have a capacity to manage funds:[19]

- the poor have a capacity to invest in their own housing, and loans (although subsidized) help the poor to improve their choices and improve their situation;
- micro-finance initiatives may also be an important source of finance, in particular when they manage to tap into formal financial flows.

**Revolving loan fund savings help to build strong community organizations, based on trust and with a capacity to manage funds**

# Housing Finance and Globalization

The following discussion of the implications of globalization and its associated trends on housing finance cannot be comprehensive but is limited to a few major issues. Broadly speaking, the provision of housing finance is influenced by:

- changes in demand for, and the supply of, housing investment funds due to the nature and extent of economic growth and the related scale and nature of poverty;
- changes in the supply of finance due to changes in

state investments and state regulation of financial markets and the financial services industry;
*   changes in the capacity to demand and use finance due to the changing nature of low-income urban communities.

## Poverty

The importance of communities' own funds in housing investment means that the level and nature of poverty is an important determinant of housing finance. A number of very general comments can be made about recent trends:

*   The increasing informalization of the labour force has implications for citizens who seek to acquire finance from formal institutions, either state housing loan companies or commercial enterprises. As more and more of the urban poor are drawn into informal employment, it is increasingly difficult for them to access formal finance. At the same time, lower-middle and middle-income families may lose access to loan finance as they shift from being formal to informal workers.
*   Informal sector incomes tend to be more volatile than formal sector wages. This makes it more difficult to meet regular repayments that may be required by formal financial institutions for existing loans or by informal sector moneylenders (who often expect to be repaid within a short period of time).
*   The shift to more complex forms of mixed livelihood (including livelihoods that cross the traditional urban and rural sectors), combined with the difficulties of securing land tenure may reduce households' commitment to urban areas and therefore reduce the likelihood of housing investment in urban areas.

In most towns and cities, two further elements emerge as critical, namely, the availability of credit and, perhaps most important of all, the availability of land. These factors are discussed below.

## Credit

Among the characteristics of globalization are floating exchange rates and fewer government currency restrictions, facilitating greater capital mobility. While some capital is investment funds, as much as 82 per cent of it has been estimated to be in the form of speculative flows.[20] In the absence of alternative controls, interest rate policy is used by governments to assist with foreign reserves management. Hence, interest rates may be high simply to reduce speculative flows and may be significantly above inflation in the short to medium term. If these rates are passed on to homeowners, the consequences for housing finance at all income levels may be severe. For example, in 1997 and 1998, the economic situations in Asia and then Latin America caused interest rates for housing loans in South Africa to rise to 23 per cent. Throughout this period, inflation remained at less than 10 per cent.

## Land

Globalization, together with related trends, has also affected urban land in a number of ways (although, it is important to recognize that individual cities are affected differently and some may not be affected at all). The freer currency and financial investment markets have created a growing tendency towards speculative investments. Land markets are no exception. In some Asian cities in particular, high land prices, caused by speculative investment, have resulted in increased difficulties for the urban poor. Squatters have been evicted from well-located land that previously was of little value. Even where construction does not take place, there may be increased pressure for eviction.[21]

There have been attempts to address such inequities. For example, in Thailand, widespread concern about the inequality of access to the benefits of economic development and an acknowledgement that rising land prices have increased the difficulties of the urban poor resulted in a new government initiative in the early 1990s, namely, the Urban Community Development Office.[22] This initiative manages a loan fund, capitalized with a grant worth US$50 million from the Thai government, aimed at assisting the urban poor to purchase land and develop housing. The office lends money to the members of savings groups for income generation, land purchase and housing development. As another example, in Cebu, the Philippines, land sharing arrangements between a group of inner city squatters and the private owners of the land on which they are located have been realized, with an offer of alternative land. The landowners wanted to secure their land from squatters quickly and peacefully due to its high value. A local NGO, the Pagtambayayong Foundation, has been assisting the community.[23] Without such institutional intervention, globalization appears to increase the probability of land speculation and, therefore, of increased land prices, thus causing greater difficulties for the urban poor, particularly in capital cities and secondary cities of global significance.

> Without institutional intervention, globalization appears to increase the probability of land speculation and, therefore, of increased land prices, thus causing greater difficulties for the urban poor

A further factor affecting the availability of land is privatization. The growing relaxation of trade barriers and of restrictions on market activities is associated with the privatization of state assets. Many state companies had considerable land holdings that could be sold together with the rest of the company. In some countries, such state companies had relatively lax attitudes towards squatters but these attitudes are not necessarily shared by the new private owners whose interests are to develop or re-sell the land for profit.

Another related aspect is the liberalization of the banking sector that has taken place in many countries. As more financial institutions are created and existing ones are given more freedom of action, it might be anticipated that some would seek to reach the poor with financial services. However, despite considerable diversity in circumstances, there exists very little interest in doing so. Many commercial enterprises are reluctant to enter this market for the same reasons that have encouraged the growth of micro-finance institutions. When they do venture in, it is generally alongside an NGO (see Boxes 6.3 and 6.4).

The deregulation of the financial sector has been accompanied by an attitude towards housing finance by development agencies that can be typified by the World Bank's approach. A recent discussion paper reviewing the experience of the World Bank emphasizes the importance of housing finance in order to improve residential dwellings and support the construction industry.[24] It argues the importance of positive interest rates being charged in order to ensure the continuing viability of the lending institution and adds that private sector involvement should be encouraged (as has been the case in many World Bank projects) in order to ensure efficient administration. It does not rule out subsidies but it is not clear as to how they can best be introduced into such programmes in order to reach the poor. As has been argued elsewhere, it emphasizes that past subsidies have often not reached those most in need.

There is evidence that it is increasingly difficult for programmes that target the lowest-income residents to be effective without subsidies.[25] Moreover, for the reasons given above, private sector collaboration is likely to formalize the programme and thereby reduce its outreach to the poor. As is the case with micro-enterprise lending, formal financial institutions wish to give larger loans to literate individuals who offer acceptable collateral and who will repay at regular intervals through formal sector banking processes.

> There is evidence that it is increasingly difficult for programmes that target the lowest-income residents to be effective without subsidies

## State funds

In general, globalization has also been associated with a reduction in state funding for basic services and infrastructure. Consequently, there is less money for public funding to reach and support people's own investment. However, while recognizing the significance of the general constraint, experiences in a number of countries suggest that where governments are willing to address the needs of the urban poor, and where there is a lobby for such innovative funds, it is possible to secure government support.

Hence, a contradiction in policy making emerges. Commonly accepted orthodoxy emphasizes the reduced role of the state. In this context, the inability of the state to address the needs of the poor through direct policy measures is stressed. The orthodoxy argues that it is the role of the government to manage the macroeconomy to enable the market to address the needs of the poor.

However, in practice, even where the government has adopted such policies, equity and political pragmatism help to justify measures that support the poor. As Perez

---

**Box 6.3 Partnerships to provide housing finance for the poor**

The Unit Trust of India was anxious to explore reaching low-income citizens. It teamed up with SPARC, an Indian NGO working in 22 cities in India with two community organizations, the National Slum Dwellers' Federation and *Mahila Milan* (a federation of women's collectives), to launch the Interval Fund, especially for Federation members. Together with SPARC, it worked out how to reduce administrative costs by only accepting deposits five days each month. Thus the bank can access the savings of the poor while the poor can obtain higher interest rates of 12–14 per cent. When land is obtained, the savings are moved to the housing finance agency (generally HUDCO) to pay the necessary deposit. Previously, most low-income households could only secure 4–6 per cent for their savings in ordinary accounts, equal to or below the rate of inflation. Factors such as these make it hard to save and access formal loan finance for housing.

---

Montiel and Barten[26] argue in the case of Leon in Nicaragua, despite the 'reduction in social expenditures and a strengthening of the private sector and the market economy … there would appear to be more scope for local political action'. They describe an innovative city

---

**Box 6.4 The changing Mexican loan market for housing finance**

Private developer interests in housing provision for lower middle-income groups evolved from earlier investment in rented accommodation in the 1950s to the large-scale home-ownership public housing projects of the 1970s and 1980s. Throughout this period, because of the virtual non-existence of private mortgage capital, savings and loans associations and the like, the expansion of speculative housing development was severely limited.

The short-lived liberalization of mortgage funds from commercial banks in 1989, closely followed by the radical reforms to the payroll funds that privatized some financial investment, gave an additional boost to the housing development industry. Housing developers increasingly expanded from or into the contracting business, landed property and the financial sector. By 1994, the National Federation of Industrial Housing Promoters (PROVICAC) had over 900 members which, by then, were responsible for almost all formal housing production in the country. While most of these developers were only active in one town or city, some extended their operations to various cities all over the country and beyond, including California and Chile. These developers started building massively, often with projects for over 10,000 units at a time, in most of Mexico's major cities.

The re-privatization of banks, coupled with the influx of short-term speculative investment, resulted in the rapid growth of financial services between 1990 and 1993. For the first time in Mexico, there were mortgages available to middle- and upper middle-income groups to acquire new and reconditioned housing. This created a building boom of condominiums and, hence, escalating land prices in many cities. By 1993, many of these interest-capitalized mortgages were unpayable, even under the relatively stable prevailing inflation and interest rates. After the crash of December 1994, mortgagees were facing unpayable debts combined with acute negative equity as the market plummeted. In 1996, a special programme to restructure mortgage debts was set up as part of the more general scheme to bail out the banks.

Catering essentially to the lower middle-income market, housing developers continue to produce housing paid for by subsidized credits provided by FOVI (with World Bank loans) and the payroll housing funds. The lower end of their market is approximately four times minimum wage, thus excluding about 50 per cent of the urban population. However, a lowering of standards and increased efficiency is enabling some developers to reach lower-income brackets, replacing the better-off segments of the informal sector. Yet, at present, none of the housing loan schemes in operation can offer a completed dwelling to families with irregular or very low incomes, who are still obliged to resort to the informal sector: an impoverished 'self-build' syndrome of the irregular settlement.

**Source:** Connolly, Cilla (2000) Universidad Autonoma Metropolitana-Azcapotzalco, Mexico City.

programme with state resources and changes in local government practices and procedures to ensure basic needs including improvements to water supply, literacy and waste removal as well as housing. In some Brazilian cities, municipal reforms have similarly enabled additional funds to be raised, helping to finance participatory budgeting and leading to improved infrastructure in low-income settlements.[27]

Similar trends appear in Asia. In the Philippines, NGOs and community-based organizations have succeeded in increasing the allocation to the Community Mortgage Programme to P2000 million in 2000 (US$47 million) from P240 million in 1999. This represents a significant increase in previously available funding (see also Box 14.10 and Chapters 13 and 14 on the importance of partnerships in infrastructure development). Not only can local institutions successfully negotiate an increase in available government funds, they can also provide a useful challenge through which available donor funds can be used in programmes that are considered to have a lasting impact. Thus, in Thailand, the economic recession resulted in social investment funding from the World Bank and other donors. One-quarter of the funds destined for reducing poverty (Baht 250 million) has been routed through the Urban Community Development Office which has made it possible for the Office to extend its work and address the difficulties faced by its members.[28] Much of the remaining monies is allocated to macroeconomic support.

Hence, it is not clear that the reductions in public expenditure have resulted in an inability of the state to support housing finance where the institutions of local government and civil society are strong enough to demand resources, and demonstrate the effective use of such resources.

## Institutional responses

An analysis of the ways in which globalization is affecting investments in housing the poor should not ignore institutional responses to this social and economic context. Three types of institutions must be considered in particular.

### ● Local government

First, the role of local government is increasingly significant. Just as there has been a consensus about the need for central government to play a reduced and more focused role, there has also been an equal consensus in favour of the decentralization of responsibilities to lower levels of government and, particularly, to local authorities.[29] While local authorities may have been made responsible, they have struggled to meet these responsibilities. For the most part, they are not able to offer even basic services to many of the citizens living within their area of jurisdiction. Some have sought to support the urban poor with land availability. In a few cases in Latin America, municipalities have provided subsidized loans for housing upgrading (see, for example, the *mutairo* programmes of São Paulo and Fortaleza in Brazil.)[30] State funds have been made available, with those receiving support repaying a proportion of the

monies and loan repayments as a fixed proportion of the minimum wage.

### ● NGOs

> NGO activities range from helping squatters to obtain land tenure to the provision of low-cost sanitation and direct loan finance

Second, NGOs have sought increasingly to address the needs of the urban poor. On the one hand, there has been a growing interest among international NGOs to consider issues of urban poverty.[31] On the other hand, local NGOs have become increasingly pragmatic about securing effective development interventions.[32] Together, these organizations are anxious to increase the capacity of local communities to improve their housing. Their activities range from helping squatters to obtain land tenure to the provision of low-cost sanitation and direct loan finance. In some countries, such as Pakistan, major multilateral and bilateral development agencies have been interested in ensuring that such initiatives can assist state agencies to address their obligations (see, for example, World Bank support to extend the work of the Orangi Pilot Project in Pakistan).

> The limitations of approaches that try to address the housing needs of the poor through market mechanisms is becoming increasingly evident

Alongside NGOs, there has been a range of micro-finance institutions, many of which owe their origin to voluntaristic activity.[33] However, the limitations of approaches that try to address the housing needs of the poor through market mechanisms is becoming increasingly evident. Agency studies of micro-finance agencies in Bangladesh echo more general concerns.[34] Micro-finance institutions are finding that the not-so-poor are the easiest clients to reach. Hence, there may be a group of residents in low-income settlements that are not supported even by the more innovative NGO and government programmes. Both NGO and micro-finance efforts are too small and may not be reaching some of those most in need.

### ● Civil society groups

> Through networks such as the Shack/Slum Dwellers International, low-income communities have been able to learn from one another to increase the effectiveness of their housing strategies and practices

Third, and at a more local level, there have been a host of citizen-to-citizen exchanges that have been sponsored by groups such as Oxfam. The communications revolution has enabled like-minded groups to identify each other and connect more easily. Thus, low-income market women in Senegal have been able to link up with groups facing similar housing development issues in South Africa.[35] Repeated eassurances by the women of the South African Homeless People's Federation assuaged the visitors' worries, and first-and observation of the South Africans making bricks and designing plans convinced the Senegalese women that they too could acquire 'professional skills'.[36] The Senegalese also enjoyed the Federation women's down-to-earth explanation of technical issues.[37] Through networks such as the Shack/Slum Dwellers International, low-income communities have been able to learn from one another to increase the effectiveness of their housing strategies and practices.[38]

The failure of many institutions, and in particular of both the market and the state, to address poverty, may have been one of the major reasons behind the search for partnership solutions. A partnership between multiple stakeholders, including the state, financial institutions, communities and NGOs can offer much: state agencies can provide land and the financial institutions can provide credit. Communities can repay the loans and provide the required local management skills. NGOs can help to bridge the gap between the formal world (state and commercial enterprise) and the local neighbourhoods in which the poor develop housing (see Chapter 14 for a fuller discussion of partnerships). The scope of joint programmes to address the need for housing finance is evident in a number of cases. However, it is important to recognize that participation in such programmes is still not an option for many of the urban poor.[39]

# Implications for Policy

What are the policies that will assist the poor to obtain access to the finance that they need to invest in housing? The strategic focus should be concentrated to promote rental housing, both private and informal and to upgrade slums.

## Land and secure tenure

> State agencies seeking to assist the poor need to put in place policies that facilitate their access to land with reasonably secure tenure

Land is critical. State agencies seeking to assist the poor need to put in place policies that facilitate their access to land with reasonably secure tenure. Once tenure is secure, the poor themselves invest in their own homes and neighbourhoods. For reasons discussed above, the land situation in some cities may become more difficult as a result of globalization and its associated processes. Hence, it becomes even more important for state, provincial and local government to address the need for land.

## Access to credit

> There is a need for government to support a variety of non-formal financial institutions in order to facilitate housing investment and reduce poverty

Credit for land purchase and housing development can help those with low incomes to invest quickly and effectively. Many formal financial institutions are not well suited to dealing with the needs of the poor. A range of micro-finance institutions provide models and mechanisms for doing it better. In some countries, the formal financial sector may perceive a potentially lucrative market and be willing to work in partnership. In general, however, there is often a great reluctance to be involved. In this context, there is a need for government to support a variety of non-formal financial institutions in order to facilitate housing investment and reduce poverty. Based on recent experiences, as illustrated by the cases mentioned above, such initiatives can be wholly managed by government, as with the Urban Community Development Office; they can be government funds drawn down by community organizations with the support of an NGO, as is the case with SPARC and the National Slum Dwellers' Federation, who use funds from the state bank, HUDCO; or they can be independent loan funds managed by communities with appropriate professional assistance, as is the case with *uTshani* Fund of the South African Homeless People's Federation.

Credit can also be used to assist in infrastructure development, and state support for financing initiatives to improve housing should take into account the likely need for infrastructure improvements. Moreover, many of these initiatives are flexible enough to include finance for income generation.

Successful initiatives share common characteristics. Funding is provided to groups needing home improvements rather than to individuals. This means both that administrative costs are lower and that the group can support members who are in need of assistance. Savings prior to loan delivery helps to strengthen trust and mutual confidence within the group, helps the group to develop experience in financial management, and generates additional development resources. Few such initiatives charge market rates of interest and, hence, most involve a subsidy of some kind.[40] Without a subsidy to help repayments, housing improvements are likely to take a considerable time. This is particularly true in high-inflation situations. While generally the adopted macroeconomic policies have resulted in reduced inflation, sudden devaluations can cause inflationary shocks to domestic economies.

## Partnerships with local communities

The state funds that exist for housing sector support and poverty reduction can be put to greater effect (whether as loans or grant funds) if they are used by agencies in partnership with local communities. A number of innovative programmes to date suggest that:

- state agencies can bring money, relief from existing regulations and can gain effective interventions;
- communities can bring money (in repayments), local organizing capacity (to reduce administrative costs) and they gain housing improvements;

**Box 6.5 Housing plus: the Urban Community Development Office**

The Urban Community Development Office was established by the Thai government in 1992 in order to provide support to the development of the urban poor. While the Thai economy was booming, urban land prices were rising, evictions were increasing and there was little prospect for squatters to find adequate alternative accommodation. The Office was placed under the National Housing Authority with a loan fund of US$50 million. However, from the beginning, there were two unusual features. First, it offered loans for small revolving funds to help communities to address the immediate small-scale needs of their members for credit, and it offered loans for income generation. Second, the Office is managed by a board of 12: four government officials, four community representatives and four independent professionals.

For several years, the Office built up a loan portfolio in housing (60 per cent of total lending) and other areas, assisting thousands of the urban poor who were organized into savings groups in order to access the funds. In 1998, the Thai economic crisis resulted in difficulties for all sectors of society, including the poor. The Urban Community Development Office saw loan repayments fall from almost 100 per cent to 93 per cent. In response to this situation, the Office sought to strengthen the groups in two ways. First, network loans were offered that encouraged savings schemes to work together in larger groups, thus reducing their vulnerability and strengthening their ability to manage through increasing their access to local skills and capacities. Second, reconstruction loans were offered at 1 per cent a year to groups that needed to restructure loans and restart their repayments. A proportion of donor funds designated for poverty relief was allocated to the Office. The loan funds of the Urban Poor Development Office were augmented by additional monies, including 250 million Baht from the Miyazawa Programme and grant aid from the Japanese government.

At the same time, DANCED, the Danish aid fund, wanted to support infrastructure improvements in low-income settlements. It approached the Office with a request to work together and a programme was agreed. DANCED funds are managed at the city level by committees on which the community has majority representation. The other participants are the local authority, NGOs and additional institutions involved in urban development. The committees allocate small grants to communities that are affiliated to the Urban Community Development Office. The communities must themselves provide 20 per cent of the cost of the improvement. Communities bid against each other for the funds and those that are successful manage the monies themselves.

By 2000, the Office was supporting housing investment in numerous ways. For example:

- direct loans for housing;
- loans for land;
- network strengthening to help groups to negotiate for land;
- infrastructure grants to increase neighbourhood quality and enhance enterprise development;
- loans for enterprises to increase income;
- support for savings to increase local and community assets and to assist private investment.

- local authorities can bring land and relief from existing regulations, and they have an improved local environment;
- commercial agencies can bring funds and they can reach a market that they previously considered to be high risk.

The Urban Communities Environmental Activities Project in Thailand is a good demonstration of how interested parties can work together effectively for mutual benefit in a wider context of globalization (see Box 6.5).[41]

The need for housing finance in the developing world is as acute as ever. The vast majority of the urban poor manage to obtain this finance themselves and they continue with the difficult process of urban development. Many government housing programmes reach too few people and often they do not reach the poorest. Looking beyond housing, more and more of the labour force is joining the informal economy, and globalization has done nothing to reduce the gap between the formal and informal sectors. Because formal commercial financial institutions do not meet the needs of the poor for housing loans, it is important for the state to give greater support to innovative initiatives that bridge this divide and that reach the poor.

The greatest challenge for the 21st century is poverty reduction. Support for housing can play a significant role in this regard. At the level of the household, limited family income can be allocated more efficiently with less spent on repairs. Better quality housing reduces the burden of disease and injury and a death in the family. Income generation opportunities emerge through rental income. Houses are assets that often attract further investment. For the community, housing developments that are managed through community collectives can do much to strengthen local organizations, thus helping to secure further development. And improving neighbourhoods increases the demand for local enterprises. As illustrated by the Urban Community Development Office (UCDO) (Box 6.5) and demonstrated also by various other innovative approaches in different countries, facilitating greater investment by local residents in the housing and neighbourhoods of low-income settlements is one answer to improving the condition of the urban poor.

*Facilitating greater investment by local residents in the housing and neighbourhoods of low-income settlements is one answer to improving the condition of the urban poor*

## Notes

This chapter is based on 'The implications of globalization for the provision of and access to housing finance in developing countries', a background paper prepared by Diana Mitlin, IIED, London.

This chapter focuses on the needs of the poorest citizens, and most of the references and information relate to the housing situation of the urban poor rather than their rural counterparts. This focus is justified partly because securing housing in rural areas appears to be easier for two reasons. First, land for housing may be easier to obtain and, second, in many countries, easily available traditional materials are used in rural areas. This means that the financial needs are less than in urban areas, where families have to purchase construction materials on the open market. However, in the case of those rural families that need to secure land and/or purchase building materials, many of the following arguments apply.

3 Barbosa et al, 1997.

4 For a recently published study see Baken and Smets, 1999.

5 See, for example, Bolnick et al, 1997 for a discussion of community investment in water supplies in South Africa, Pakistan and the Philippines.

6 See Beall et al, 2000, and Rojas and Greene, 1995, respectively.

7 Baken and Smets, 1999, pp 107–109.

8 As noted by Basil Davidson, director of housing for Cape Metropolitan Council, 1999.

9 Pezzoli, 1995.

10 Mitlin, 1997.

11 Albee and Gamage (1996) discuss and illustrate these synergies in the context of the Women's Bank in Sri Lanka. The Women's Bank is an example of a micro-finance institution that has moved from income generation to finance and has found that a better home and neighbourhood increases the demand for goods and services.

12 See, for example, Hulme and Mosley, 1996.

13 See Ferguson, 1999, for a recent discussion of the situation in some Latin American countries, and Klak and Marlene, 1999, for a discussion of a housing institution facing these problems in Jamaica.

14 Narayan, Asian Development Bank, April 1998.

15 Ferguson, 1999.

16 Cosgrove, 1999.

17 Mehta, 1994.

18 Mitlin, 1997.

19 Bolnick and Mitlin, 1999.

20 In 1996, the Federal Bank of New York estimated the daily value of transactions in foreign exchange in the New York, Tokyo and London markets alone at US$650 million dollars. Other estimates have ranged up to US$1 million million. About 18 per cent of these transactions are the result of international commerce and investments. The other 82 per cent was speculation, aimed at making a profit from the fluctuation of exchange rates. See De Angelis, 1996.

21 See http://www.cohre.org/forced-evictions/# for extensive information on eviction on the web site of the Centre for Housing Rights and Evictions.

22 Boonyabancha, 1996.

23 Francisco Fernandez, personal communication.

24 Buckley, 1999, pp 46–7, 54.

25 Siembieda and Lopez Moreno, 1999.

26 Perez Montiel and Barten 1999, p 25.

27 Souza, 2000, p 8.

28 See Boonyabancha, 2000.

29 McCarney, 1996.

30 Denaldi, 1994, and Cabannes, 1997, respectively.

31 Hall et al, 1996.

32 Anzorena, 1996.

33 Hulme and Mosley, 1996.

34 Johnson and Rogaly, 1997.

35 Ndella Dieng, chairperson of a savings and loan cooperative in Senegal, exclaimed at the end of her visit to the South African Homeless People's Federation (see Box 6.2): 'We've experienced a "mirroring" effect through our contact with the Federation. We hear the Federation women talk and we feel like we're still in the midst of a meeting in Senegal, since the same vocabulary is used: "mutual learning processes" (rather than training); "network of community-based schemes" (as opposed to pyramid structure); "opportunity-driven approach" (rather than problem-based); "facilitator" (rather than technician or professional)'.

36 Abdul-Hamid, 1999.

37 For example, Aminata Mbaye claimed: 'When I asked the technician (who works with us in Dakar) to show us how layout plans are designed, he used such a sophisticated jargon that I barely understood a word he said. In Protea South, during our last evening, we asked a woman to draw us a plan. When she explained house modelling, I understood and felt that I too could do it.'

38 Patel et al,2001.

39 Mitlin, 1997.

40 Mitlin, 1997.

41 Boonyabancha, 1999.

# 7

# THE COUNTRIES WITH ECONOMIES IN TRANSITION[1]

A distinctive feature in the development of transition economies is the double influence of globalization and the formation of market-based relations in sectors of the economy that were traditionally managed by administrative and planning instruments of the state. However, the main trends in the housing sector in Western countries during the past two decades – reduction of the public rental sector in favour of the private sector, development of loan instruments for construction and purchase of housing and implementation of targeted assistance programmes to the poor – almost fully coincide with the tasks also faced by the East European countries during their transition to market economies.

Comparative analysis of the reform progress is available in several publications.[2] This chapter presents an overview of some important processes occurring in the transition economies. In doing so, it offers a regional perspective, and individual country situations are described by way of illustration. The discussion is organized with respect to aspects of marketization, deregulation and decentralization.

## Marketization

### Housing privatization

The 1990s saw major structural changes in the ownership of the housing stock of transition countries, with the most dramatic changes occurring in the former Soviet Union. Table 7.1 illustrates the changes in several East European countries. The share of the public sector decreased and, in most countries, increases occurred in the share of the private housing stock. In Poland and the Czech Republic, little quantitative change in housing ownership was seen because the state in these countries did not actively support privatization.

In the Russian Federation and other countries of the CIS (Commonwealth of Independent States) transforma-

tion of the housing stock had its own specifics. First, an overwhelming majority of units in these countries were privatized free of charge. It was expected that in this way the state would create some starting capital for the solution of housing problems under market conditions for a population that had been unable to accumulate substantial saving because of rigid income controls in the planned economy. Second, and of no less importance, was the state's desire to speed up the process of divesting its responsibility for the maintenance, repair and renovation of the huge public housing stock. Third, ownership changes were stronger than in Central Europe. In the Russian Federation, by 1999, after 45 per cent of the eligible units had been privatized, private housing made up 59 per cent of the housing stock, against just 33 per cent in 1990 (including cooperatives).

This shift led to an increase in intra-urban population mobility. According to the available estimates, the mobility rate in major cities of Russia has more than doubled since 1992. Broad population groups were given the opportunity to deal more efficiently with their housing problems: 1.5–2 per cent of all apartments in private ownership are transferred annually. At the same time, housing privatization merely simplified the options that were already de facto available to tenants in social housing, who enjoyed extremely broad rights under the housing law in the planned economy (most of these laws still remain in effect).

Privatization in the Ukraine proceeded at a similar pace. In Central Asia and the Caucasus (Kazakhstan, Kyrgyzstan, Armenia), the state and municipal housing stock was almost completely privatized by 1996. Although officially the process was voluntary, privatization in these countries proceeded under substantial administrative pressure. Kazakhstan has created associations of housing owners (cooperatives) in a majority of multi-family buildings, but their activities are mostly nominal. Maintenance and repair work is usually not performed, and most of the buildings are falling into decay.

> For most housing owners, privatization was a formal procedure that failed to foster an owner-occupier mentality

In practice, for most housing owners privatization was a formal procedure that failed to foster an owner-occupier mentality. According to current legislation of the Russian

**Table 7.1**

**Changes in tenure, 1990–1994**

|  | Slovakia | Czech Republic | Estonia | Hungary | Poland | Latvia | Lithuania |
|---|---|---|---|---|---|---|---|
| Public rental 90 | 31.6 | 29.6 | 65 | 22 | 29.7 | 64 | 51.4 |
| Public rental 94 | 8.9 | 27.6 | 56 | 13 | 25.4 | 54 | 12.9 |
| Private rental 90 | 3.0 | 0.9 | 0 | 0.5 | 5.2 | 0 | 0 |
| Private rental 94 | 4.7 | 4.7 | 5 | 1 | 5.2 | 5 | 8.5 |
| Owner occupied 90 | 65.4 | 40.3 | 35 | 77.5 | 40.2 | 22 | 39.2 |
| Owner occupied 94 | 87.7 | 42.2 | 30 | 86 | 41.7 | 39 | 78.6 |

**Source:** USAID, 1996.

Federation, fees for maintenance and utility services have remained the same for both tenants in municipal housing and owners of privatized units, in an effort to stimulate privatization. Maintenance and management decisions for the properties, including common elements, are still made by the 'balance holders', represented mainly by state enterprises or local self-governments. Thus the goal of conveying multi-family buildings and common grounds into the genuine management by apartment owners remains unmet.

It was expected that with enactment of supporting legislation in the mid-1990s the number of condominiums in Russia would grow dramatically. However, to date this has not happened. Condominium associations in Russia number just over 3200, or less than 1 per cent of the total housing stock of multi-family buildings; they are created mainly in newly constructed buildings. Land is also not being conveyed into ownership of condominium members, as required by the law.

Reasons for the slow progress in the formation of condominium associations include the following:

- Owners of housing do not fully understand the benefits of forming an association and using the rights granted to them by the law. It may be that with the increase in the cost of maintenance services, apartment owners will be more willing to play a role in the decision-making and control over use of the money they pay for maintenance of the housing.
- Lack of a market for professional property managers.
- Lack of transparency about the costs of both management and maintenance companies makes it difficult for the owners to evaluate the economic effect of independent management of the building versus the use of the current municipal subsidy.
- In a majority of municipalities, the position of the local authorities ranges from lack of support to open opposition. This is revealed in overcomplicated registration requirements and discrimination against condominium associations in the allocation of subsidies from the municipal budget as compared with similar municipal housing.

Existing associations have an economic efficiency. Their buildings' maintenance cost per square metre is 29 per cent lower than in similar municipal housing. However, professional management of the housing stock remains undeveloped in the CIS. In countries where the law permits the privatization of apartments only after a condominium association is in place, such as Hungary and Czech Republic, professional management services have developed and are now provided by both municipal and private companies. Most of the associations are yet unable to manage the housing at a high professional level, but they maintain minimum operating standards.

> In buildings managed by condominium associations, maintenance cost per square metre is 29 per cent lower than in similar municipal housing

## Formation of the rental market

Privatization has resulted in a strengthening of the private rental sector which before 1999 did not exist in the Baltic States and played a much less important role in other countries, except Poland (see Table 7.1). Private rentals have developed slowly in most CIS countries, primarily because of limited demand for such units as a result of highly subsidized rents in state and municipal housing. Housing units owned by private individuals are actively leased out and, according to some estimates, make up to 5 per cent of the total housing stock. However, because of defects in the legislation, most of the deals are closed on the shadow market, resulting in very little protection for both the landlord and the tenant.

Economic restructuring is closely tied to increases in population mobility and migration. This is particularly important for the CIS countries where structural distortions from the planned economy produced vast depressed areas where potentially mobile and able households are trapped in chronic poverty. Despite the dynamic development of markets for sale and purchase of urban housing, inter-urban migration remains extremely low. The essential condition for improvement in this area is ready availability of municipal or private units for rent rather than purchase.

## Structural changes in the construction market

> Direct budget financing of new construction is a thing of the past for most countries of the region

Direct budget financing of new construction is a thing of the past for most countries of the region. With just a few exceptions, none of the Baltic countries subsidizes building companies and developers for the construction of new housing. In CIS countries, there is a steady trend to deep reductions of direct budget financing of housing construction as compared with the period preceding reforms. In the Russian Federation, at present, private developers play the principal role in housing construction. The share of housing constructed by the state and municipal enterprises went down from 80 per cent in 1990 to 20 per cent in 1998.

Fundamental changes have occurred in the system of housing finance: state budget sources no longer play an important role, with 40 per cent of construction financed by individual developers. Construction of multi-family buildings involves the broad use of private investment, including household savings, but bank loans are still definitely a minor source.

Substantial changes have also occurred in state participation in housing finance. Priority is now given to down payment subsidies for the purchase of housing to households needing improvement in their living conditions. At the federal level, this policy is implemented within the framework of a targeted programme, 'State Housing Certificates'. During 1998–1999, more than 28,000 households acquired housing under this programme. None the less, to date, Russia, along with most other transition countries, has failed to stabilize the volume of new housing construction after it plummeted in the early 1990s.

## Formation of the housing market: availability and affordability

Owing to the sharp drop in overall housing investment, total new housing constructed by enterprises and organizations of all ownership types in the Russian Federation in 1998 equalled merely 30.7 million m², or 387,700 units. As a result, only 5 per cent of the households on the waiting lists were provided with a new unit, as compared with 11 per cent in 1991. At the same time, during 1990–1997 the waiting list for improved housing decreased by 3.5 million households, or 35 per cent. Meanwhile, average housing consumption increased substantially, by 2.1 m² of total floor space, reaching 18.9 m² per person (as of 1 January 1999). This was accompanied by an increase in the level of comfort in terms of such indicators as: percentage of housing space with hot water supply (from 51 to 58 per cent); water supply (from 66 to 73 per cent); and central heating (from 64 to 71 per cent).

Thus there is a paradox that housing conditions improve when state and municipal investments for the housing sector and the volume of new housing construction are on a decline. The explanation is that households have mobilized their own resources to address their housing problems, which is confirmed by changes in the structure of financing of housing construction projects. Today, households with purchasing power have no incentive to register on the waiting list for improved housing because the waiting time is unacceptably long.

In the second quarter of 1999, the per-metre price for an existing apartment equalled 4.6 months of average per capita income, which means that a household with an average income would need 6.9 years of income to be able to buy an apartment of the 'standard size' (the norm is 18 m² per person) at an average market price. At the beginning of the reforms, the comparable average figure for Russia was close to 10 years. In particular, in Moscow, the housing affordability index has fallen from 13.8 years in 1993 to 2.5 years in 1997.[3] This positive trend, observed since the mid-1990s, was stopped by the 1998 crisis and has started to recover only recently. Housing affordability is still characterized by strong geographical differentiation, although high affordability levels are found both in high-income cities and depressed areas with low population income where housing is extremely cheap. In other countries of the region, the housing affordability indicator ranged from 3.7 years in Estonia to 12.8 years in Bulgaria.[4]

> Mixed and market allocation mechanisms are increasingly replacing administrative housing allocation

In 1997, more than one-half of all households in Moscow could afford to purchase a market apartment (of the social norm corresponding to household size) using the sale of their existing unit, savings, loans and state subsidy funds.[5]

Further, by the mid-1990s, only 18 per cent of relocating households in Moscow acquired their new unit through the municipal waiting lists. These data suggest that mixed and market allocation mechanisms increasingly replace administrative housing allocation and reallocation. However, the greater reliance on markets does not necessarily imply the absence of affordability problems.

## Development of financial markets

There is a sharp distinction between Central European countries and the CIS. The governments of the four Visegrad countries (Poland, Hungary, the Czech Republic and Slovakia) were the first in Central and Eastern Europe to declare their intention to access the European Union and have made substantial capital investments to create water supply and wastewater collection systems that meet EU requirements. The work was partly financed by external borrowings (World Bank and the European Bank for Reconstruction and Development (EBRD) loans) and partly by introduction of environmental impact taxes (Poland). In the future, public infrastructure in these countries will have an important source of finance in the structural adjustment grants available from the European Union. In addition, these countries widely use bank loans and bond issues for investments in public infrastructure (Hungary, Poland, the Czech Republic). There are also many examples of cooperation with foreign investors on the basis of concession agreements (see also Chapter 13 on decentralization of infrastructure management).

> Most local governments in the CIS are unable to finance infrastructure investments from current budget revenues

In contrast to Central Europe, in the CIS the search for investment capital is a widespread problem. Basically, the responsibility for capital investments for public infrastructure rests with local governments, rather than utility companies, and most of them are unable to finance investments from current budget revenues. Bank loans and bond issues are quite limited, partly because of low transparency of local governments' tariff setting and payment systems to service providers.

# Deregulation

## Changes in the state's social mandate in the housing sector

Reduction of the state obligation to provide housing to selected population groups is a goal of the new housing policies of almost all CIS countries. In Russia, the constitution defines eligible groups as 'low-income households and several other categories stipulated by the law'. In the Central Asian republics, they include 'certain categories of state employees'. However, the volume of the remaining social housing stock in these countries is insignificant.

Even in countries where social housing still makes up an important share of the housing stock (such as Russia and the Ukraine), it does not yet perform its designated function of targeted housing provision: to serve first low-income households as guaranteed by the constitution. Slow progress in this area is explained by the prior obligations to households on the waiting lists for improved units on the one hand, and the rights of sitting tenants in the state and municipal housing stock, on the other. Socially acceptable mechanisms should be developed to encourage households with purchasing power to use market methods of improving their living conditions, and to implement new principles for allocation of social housing to the poor. Rent increases play a key role in this connection.

> Even where social housing still makes up an important share of the housing stock, it does not yet perform its designated function of targeted housing provision to low-income households as guaranteed by the constitution

## Termination of state rent control

In almost all countries of Eastern Europe and CIS, the rents charged in the private sector are driven by the market without state control. Poland is an exception in this regard. However, three patterns are evident for rents in public rental housing:[6]

1   *Full coverage of service costs by the tenants.* Estonia and the Ukraine are examples of countries following this model. The new policy was designed and implemented within a relatively short time: from two to three years. Notably, in some instances subsidies have been retained for power supply: utility service producers were sold resources below world prices, and sometimes the price does not include capital costs.

2   *Full coverage of energy costs, partial coverage for other communal services and full coverage of the cost of housing services subject to insubstantial rate increases.* This trend is typical for most countries of the region. The state has lifted energy price controls and consumers have already felt the impact. Armenia, Poland, Hungary and Bulgaria are examples here.

3   *Gradual increases in charges for housing and communal services to achieve full cost recovery.* The Russian Federation adopted this model as have the Czech Republic and Slovakia, although less explicitly.

In a majority of the countries under consideration, the charges for housing services in the municipal stock are based on a fixed rate without differentiation for housing quality and location. Thus the process may be classified as 'deregulation' but with strong reservations. Moreover, in cases of the third option above, it has become necessary to create a series of additional regulatory mechanisms to manage the transition to full coverage of operating costs by the households.

> Lifting of rent controls in the Eastern European and Baltic States dramatically increased the share of housing expenses from 3–10 per cent to 15–25 per cent of household income. Housing payments in the lowest income groups have risen up to one-half of household income

Lifting of rent controls in the Eastern European and Baltic States in the early 1990s resulted in dramatic increases in the share of housing expenses: from 3–10 per cent to 15–25 per cent of total household income. As a result, housing payments in the lowest income groups reached up to one-half of household income. CIS countries initiated a similar process in the second half of the 1990s. In particular, Russia started the transition to self-sustaining operation of the public economy by reducing budget subsidies and the cross-subsidizing of consumers by charging industry higher prices for public services. Price liberalization in 1992–1993 did not include prices for housing and public services; shortly afterwards, households covered about 2 per cent of service costs. However, at present, households cover about 40 per cent of such costs. As a result, on average, housing payments as a share of household income rose from a fraction of a per cent to more than 4 per cent. In the Ukraine, where households cover 80 per cent of the service cost and incomes are much lower, housing expenses require more than 10 per cent of average household income.

The impact of the above processes on the poorest households largely depends on the implementation of targeted social support programmes. Most countries in the region have introduced housing allowances (subsidies) for rent and utility payments. The effectiveness of these programmes is related to the readiness of the authorities (at the national or local level) to assume the financing obligations associated with housing allowances; and the scale of rent increases.

Russia, Ukraine, Poland, Estonia and Kazakhstan have developed broad programmes of targeted social assistance for low-income households in the form of subsidies for housing and utility payments. At present, about 7 per cent of the poorest Russian households benefit from the programme, over 8 per cent in urban areas. In the Ukraine, about 20 per cent of all households receive this subsidy, and in Estonia the figure is about 16 per cent. The size of subsidy is tied to the recipient's income; on average, it covers from one-third to one-half of the payments due. The magnitude of the household's maximum contribution rates varies from 12.5 per cent of household income in several Russian regions to 30 per cent in Estonia and Kazakhstan.

This subsidy arrangement has cushioned the impact of rent increases on the low-income households, provided a guaranteed standard of housing services, and stabilized the public reaction to higher rents. However, Latvia, where the burden of payments for public services was the highest, did not implement such a social assistance programme. In general, housing allowances have not been implemented in countries where the decision rests exclusively with the local authorities and where there have been no dramatic rent increases, for example in Hungary. Several other countries (eg Slovakia) have just started to introduce housing allowances because the first rent increases occurred only recently.

> Where housing allowances were implemented, they covered only a portion of the population with household incomes below the official subsistence level

In all countries where housing allowances were implemented, they covered only a portion of the population with household incomes below the official subsistence level. The share of such households varies in CIS countries, from about 25 per cent (Russia before the 1998 crisis) to more than 60 per cent in Kyrgyzstan and Tajikistan. Within this group, housing allowances are targeted to those with the largest utility expense burden, mostly the urban population.

Several countries (eg, Armenia, Kyrgyzstan) have rejected the idea of a housing allowance programme because they implemented unified family assistance programmes. However, most of the unified benefit recipients belong to the poorest households who consume few public services (eg in Kyrgyzstan most of the unified monthly benefits go to rural areas where often the only utility consumed is electricity). On the other hand, the low-income working groups such as teachers and doctors are dependent on heating and water supply systems which they cannot individually give up for cheaper substitutions. They are not among the poorest and therefore might not be covered by family assistance programmes. However, they may face a much higher burden of housing expenses. This situation may eventually result in 'de-urbanization' of important professional groups and unprecedented changes in the social structure of urban society.

### Regulation of local natural monopolies

At the beginning of the transition, in nearly all countries of the region, regulation of tariffs and financing of water supply, sewerage and central heating services were placed within the authority of local governments. With respect to tariff regulation, greater progress was achieved in Central Europe, particularly Hungary and Poland, but even there, activities of the local authorities failed to expand beyond a very limited scale. In CIS counties, little has changed from the pre-reform period; providers of communal services still operate without clear contracts with the local governments.

> The replacement of state monopolies in public service provision by new monopolies of private service providers is hurting the poor

As a result of the delay in the formation of a tariff regulation system, the monopoly of the state has been replaced by a more dangerous monopoly of private service providers. When housing stock managers relieve themselves of the obligation to secure public services, and resource providers enter into direct contracts with individual households, the latter are left without any recourse to protect their rights both in terms of reasonable tariff rates and volume of

service (for the majority of services, no metering/controlling equipment is available). As in other situations, the poorest households find themselves in the worst position.

### Growing income dependence of housing consumption rates and housing segregation

The socialist planned economy did not do away with income-dependent housing consumption, nor did it eliminate housing segregation. By the end of the 1980s, this dependence was pronounced even in cities, where a state or municipal unit allocated according to a single standard was the only officially mandated means of improving living conditions. Moreover, for some population groups a free unit served as compensation for a low income. High-income groups improved their living conditions by exchanging units with a semi-legal bonus and through special access to allocated housing, particularly elite units. Construction of elite housing was usually concentrated in selected districts, dividing cities into 'prestigious' and 'non-prestigious' residential districts resulting in housing segregation. Neither of these phenomena developed to the extreme, but they were visible enough to be documented in the literature of the period.[7]

The result of the transition to market-oriented functioning of the housing sector changed the relation between income and living standards. Changes in the income status of selected social and occupational groups early in the transition were too fast for an adequate response from the housing market. But surveys conducted during the same period in other Russian cities (eg Nizhni Novgorod, Barnaul) revealed a stronger link between income and housing consumption. This may signify that in medium and small cities, changes in the relative status of different groups were smaller and that the 'new' elite formed mainly from the 'old' one.

> The accessibility and quality of occupied housing has grown increasingly dependent on household income, but no fundamental changes have yet taken place

More recently, the accessibility and quality of occupied housing has grown increasingly dependent on household income, but no fundamental changes have yet taken place. For example, while the median housing consumption in cities of Khabarovsk krai in 1998 was about 19 m², it was less than 14 m² for the 10 per cent of households in the lowest-income group, and over 24 m² for households in the top decile. The trends and scale of the problem are typical for all transitional economies. For example, median housing consumption in Kyrgyzstan is about 15 m² per person (14 m² in Bishkek), whereas households below the poverty level have 13 m² on average (9 m² in Bishkek).[8]

The dispersion of household incomes is not the only factor that shapes the complicated patterns of housing dynamics. Another important factor is the relatively high housing consumption among single pensioners. In the past, the powerful but slow-moving machine of centralized housing allocation created a system in which households in eed of better housing were often provided with a unit meeting their needs not long before the children moved out. As a result, the regular relationship between housing consumption and income has been distorted by a strong peak of disproportionately high housing consumption by single pensioners who are well represented among the poorest population groups (Table 7.2).

The situation is typical for other countries of the region that pursue a policy of phased rent increases. The burden of housing payments is not an incentive for households to move to smaller units, and thus the state is effectively subsidizing certain households at levels that exceed the official standards. This has a negative impact on the efficiency with which the existing housing stock is used and also creates inequities in the allocation of state assistance.

Thus in general one may state that, so far, the development of market relations in the housing sector has not yet produced a significant increase of housing segregation, but the possibility of deepening inequality in housing remains. A new class of rich households has moved to new elite residential complexes and suburban residences, but the number of such households is still too small to affect the overall picture. One of the most important constraints is the uniformity of the housing constructed during the period of the planned economy, which still makes up a great majority of the housing stock, as well as the strong inertia of the construction industry that continues to produce 'standard housing units'. To date, there are no examples of housing being constructed specially for the poor in countries of the former Soviet Union, although discussions of the prospect take place from time to time.

# Decentralization

## Increased role of local authorities and the burden of housing payments

> Most municipalities now have the authority to establish rents and utility rates, normative usage for these services and social safety net parameters. As a result, there are large local differences in housing cost burdens

Under the system of the centrally planned economy, nearly all decisions concerning people's living conditions were taken at the federal level. The political reforms have given a greater role to municipalities. In Russia and most other countries of the region, municipalities now have the authority to establish the rates for rent and utility services, normative usage rates for these services and basic social safety net parameters. In particular, they set maximum levels of household expenses for housing and utilities. As a result, the burden of housing-related payments differs strongly depending on location.

For example, in Russia the greatest protection from undue housing burdens is provided in Moscow, the city with the highest income levels. Muscovites are entitled to a subsidy if housing costs exceed 12.5 per cent of their

| Income group | Excess over social space standard, %* | | | | |
|---|---|---|---|---|---|
| | 0 | Up to 10% | 10–20% | 20–30% | Over 30% |
| Bottom quintile (20% of lowest-income households) | 57.6 | 11.3 | 6.7 | 8.0 | 16.4 |
| City average | 65.7 | 11.9 | 6.6 | 5.0 | 10.8 |

**Note:** Excess space was not counted in communal apartments and one-room apartments.
**Source:** Moscow, 1995.

Table 7.2

**Households with units exceeding social space standards, by income group**

income, while in most other cities the threshold is 18–20 per cent. However, housing costs in Moscow account for less than 5 per cent of average household income, while in such regions as Ivanovo, Chita and Kurgan they exceed 10 per cent. As a rule, local authorities try to postpone the inevitable but unpopular rent increases and enact them only if there is an acute budget crisis. These attempts to alleviate social tension and avoid inequality only make the problems worse. In addition, these practices undermine the principle of equal protection of citizens' rights, including the right to housing.

## The danger of accelerated decay

> Capital repairs in the housing stock have either dropped sharply or ceased entirely

In the past decade, the trends of a decaying housing stock and decreasing reliability of a crumbling public infrastructure have not been reversed. As a result, there is an increasing number of accidents and sickness caused by the collapse of buildings, disruption of heating services, lower quality of tap water, etc. An important reason is lack of adequate financing for maintenance of housing and public infrastructure. While households show strong payment discipline (average collection in Russia stays at about 90 per cent), actual payments are only half of the needed budgets. The situation is worst with capital repairs and replacement of depreciated equipment. The slowing pace of capital repairs is of special concern. In 1992, in Russia such repairs were made in about 22 million m$^2$ of housing; in 1998 this figure had fallen precipitously to only 4.9 million m$^2$. In a majority of CIS countries the situation is even worse: capital repairs in the housing stock have almost completely stopped.

# Concerns and Challenges

- The search for a speedy transition to a market-based housing sector under a weak market infrastructure has forced the leadership of transition countries to create 'substitute' non-market mechanisms. These include subsidizing privatized housing, excessive licensing systems, certification and supervision of management, maintenance of housing and public infrastructure, and other, more complicated, administrative procedures for setting the rents and fees for housing and public services. Many of these measures were initially intended to protect the housing rights of the citizens but with time have turned into instruments of bureaucratic control and corruption.

- Deregulation and decentralization have changed the form of relationships in the housing sector rather than their essence. Households have generally failed to take advantage of the potential benefits of globalization. However, the associated risks (primarily, polarization and segregation) are also less evident than in other countries. On the positive side, some observers suggest that the reforms have mobilized some private resources and intensified utilization of the material wealth already accumulated in the housing sector. These additional resources may help to maintain the living standards created in the planned economy in many of the countries of the region, despite the dramatic declines in housing production and household incomes. They may also help to avoid drastic decisions that would affect the population at large and could have particularly negative consequences for low-income groups.

**The reforms have mobilized private resources and intensified utilization of the existing housing stock**

- At present, the lack of stability of the 'status quo' is a major issue. The continuing dilapidation of the housing stock and deteriorating infrastructure in almost all countries of the region foreshadow serious problems in the years to come with potentially disastrous consequences for public service provision and a dramatic transformation of basic elements of the housing sector.

**The continuing dilapidation of the housing stock and deteriorating infrastructure foreshadow serious problems**

# Notes

1  This chapter is based on 'The implications of globalization and privatization for the provision of and access to housing and urban development in the transition economies,' a background paper prepared by N Kosareva and A Puzanov, Institute for Urban Economics, Russian Federation.

2  See for example, Struyk, 1996; 1997.

3  Nozdrina and Sternik, 1999.

4  USAID, 1996.

5  Struyk, 1997, Table 9.9.

6  'Public' means state or municipal housing provided under a lease in the economic sense, which in Russian law corresponds to a *naim* or lease contract.

7  See, eg Szelenyi, 1983; Daniel, 1985; Alexeev, 1988. See also Kosareva, 1992; Hamilton, 1993.

8  See also Chapter 1 for discussion of inequality in the transition economies.

# CHAPTER 8

# THE INDUSTRIALIZED COUNTRIES[1]

This chapter examines the impacts of globalization on the housing finance systems of the more advanced economies. The impact of housing finance instruments on whole housing systems is examined within their social and economic context. The framework adopted draws on some of the typologies of housing systems that were developed in the 1990s. These attempts move beyond descriptive tenure-based comparisons in order to capture the dynamics of housing systems. Two schemas are most notable. The first is the application of Esping-Andersen's typology of welfare states to housing systems, and the second is Kemeny's parallel 'unitary'/'dualist' dichotomy.[2] The countries that fit the social democratic and corporatist categories in the Esping-Andersen schema roughly parallel with Kemeny's 'unitary' rental systems. In unitary systems the market and cost rental[3] sectors form part of the same market. Further, Esping-Andersen's 'liberal' category parallels with Kemeny's 'dualist' category, in which the cost rental sector is residualized and owner-occupation is the tenure of choice. Unitary/social democratic/corporatist systems are associated with countries in northwest Europe, such as Germany, The Netherlands and Sweden. The dualist/liberal systems are associated with English-speaking countries, such as the US, Australia and the UK. It is more difficult to categorize Japan, and to a lesser extent France.

Housing finance comes from three principal sources: loans from intermediaries, households and governments. The globalization of trade and finance has implications for each of these sources of housing finance:

- *Loans from intermediaries.* Perhaps the most tangible aspect of globalization is the much greater freedom of movement of finance, as legal barriers to movement are reduced or removed and technology reduces the cost of movement.
- *Households.* Globalization has been associated with widening wage inequality as demand for less skilled labour in advanced economies falls, while the most skilled are able to bid up their wages.
- *Government.* The mobility of tax bases makes taxation more difficult, so there is downward pressure on government spending.[4] While some tax bases are clearly more mobile (eg multinational corporations), the mobility of labour is greatly exaggerated (note the variations in tax rates within the European Union), although electoral resistance to rising taxes is a common phenomenon.

Further, globalization has an important effect on the economic context for the provision of finance:

- *Macroeconomy.* The free movement of capital makes it more difficult for countries to run high-inflation economies. There has been a significant convergence of monetary economic variables between the advanced economies since the early 1980s.

Since the impacts of globalization on housing finance are complex, three areas require special consideration:

1  The way in which the liberalization of finance flows affects access to housing finance for owner-occupation.
2  The ways in which globalization affects the government's role in housing finance, particularly in the provision of social rented housing.
3  The impact of globalization on individuals' ability to pay for housing.

## Housing Ownership

Most people in the industrialized countries live in owner-occupied housing. Nevertheless, the tenure patterns vary greatly between countries (Table 8.1).

In the so-called 'liberal' or 'dualist' housing systems, between 64 and 72 per cent of households are in owner-occupation. In the US and Australia, owner-occupation expanded very quickly in the 1950s, reflecting government programmes that promoted it, but owner-occupation has been relatively stable since then. Japanese home-ownership rates have been similarly stable since at least the 1960s, albeit at a somewhat lower level than in these countries. Owner-occupation rose more gradually in the UK, until the 1980s when it was boosted by discounted sales of social rented housing to sitting tenants. In many countries, owner-occupation has strong cultural connotations. Home ownership was and still is a key part of the 'American Dream'. The US government attaches great importance to edging up ownership levels by even a few percentage points.[5] The British aspire to a 'property owning democracy', while the Belgians are said to be born 'with a brick in their bellies'. These cultural attributes of owner-occupation have not been established independently of a long-term financial advantage associated with owner-occupation. But it is clear that owner-occupation plays a

| | Owner occupation[i] | Rental[ii] | Mortgage debt as % GDP[iii] | GDP per capita (OECD = 100)[iv] |
|---|---|---|---|---|
| Australia | 71.6 (1990) | 28.4 | 25.1 (1994) | 111.9 |
| Canada | 64.1 (1993) | 35.9 | 41.2 (1994) | 115.8 |
| EU-15 | 56.0 (1990) | 44.0 | 36.0 (1997) | 99.0 |
| France | 54.5 (1997) | 45.5 | 21.0 (1997) | 98.4 |
| Germany | 38.0 (1990) | 62.0 | 51.0 (1997) | 107.0 |
| Italy | 68.0 (1990) | 32.0 | 7.0 (1997) | 99.3 |
| Japan | 61.0 (1988) | 38.7 | – | 111.9 |
| UK | 67.3 (1997) | 32.7 | 57.0 (1997) | 100.8 |
| USA | 66.8 (1999) | 33.2 | 53.8 (1994) | 150.4 |

**Notes:** i Tenure figures are often outdated due to the timing of the census. ii Includes both market and social renting. iii For the non-EU countries these are estimates derived from Lea, 1995. For the EU countries the source is the European Mortgage Federation (EMF). However, problems arise in figures due to difficulties in distinguishing between tenures and occasionally between residential and commercial real estate. Sometimes lending by institutions not affiliated to EMF lead to underestimates. iv Purchasing Power Parities, 1999.
**Sources:** European figures: Maclennan et al, 1998, and national sources; non-European figures from Lea and Bernstein, 1995, except US from HUD web site www.hud.gov/.

**Table 8.1**

**Housing tenure and mortgage debt**

crucial role in housing these populations independently of any perceived cultural advantage.

> The cultural attributes of owner-occupation have not been established independently of a long-term financial advantage associated with owner-occupation

Equally fundamental is the role that housing finance plays in enabling households to enter home ownership. In the social democratic/corporatist countries with unitary rental systems, owner-occupation is at much lower levels, notably in Germany where fewer than 40 per cent of households own their own home. Owner-occupation levels are typically under 55 per cent in these countries which include Austria, Denmark, Switzerland, Sweden and The Netherlands. The fact that this group includes many of the world's richest countries demonstrates that home-ownership levels cannot be taken as a symbol of national prosperity.

> The fact that many of the world's richest countries have a large rental sector demonstrates that home-ownership levels cannot be taken as a symbol of national prosperity

**Table 8.2**

**Mortgage terms**

| | Loan to value ratio (%) | Duration of mortgage (years) | Interest rate adjustment |
|---|---|---|---|
| Australia | 90–100 | 20–25 | 90% reviewable; some renegotiable after 1–2 years |
| Canada | 95[i] | 30 | renegotiable after 5 years |
| France | 70–80 | 15–20 | 80% fixed |
| Germany | 60–80 | 25–30 (Bauspar = 10) | 20% fixed (Bauspar); 40% renegotiable; 40% reviewable |
| Italy | 40 | 15 | 60% fixed; 40% variable |
| Japan | 80[ii] | | mixed |
| UK | 100 | 25 | 70% reviewable; 30% renegotiable |
| USA | >90 | 30 | mix of fixed and variable |

**Notes:** Fixed: fixed for duration of mortgage. Renegotiable: fixed for at least 1 year, but less than period of loan. Reviewable: adjusted at discretion of lender. Variable: adjusted automatically according to reference index. Bauspar: loan from a Bausparkassen (a type of specialist housing-savings institution found in Austria and Germany). i The minimum deposit on a NHA loan was dropped to 5 per cent in 1992. ii Valuations are extremely conservative, being based on construction costs, hence actual LTVs are reduced to 50–60 per cent.
**Sources:** Lea and Bernstein, 1995; Maclennan et al, 1998; personal communications.

Indeed, some of the highest levels of home-ownership among the advanced economies are found in some of the less prosperous countries, as the southern European countries demonstrate. Italy and Portugal have owner-occupation rates in the 67–68 per cent range, and Spain and Greece have levels approaching 80 per cent. These countries are omitted from the unitary/dualist typology and have only been tacked on to the housing version of Esping–Andersen where they have been characterized, with a somewhat ethno-centric view of welfare, as 'rudimentary' because much welfare and significant amounts of housing finance in these countries are arranged within families on an inter-generational basis.[6] With the decline of the extended family, owner-occupation in these countries will become more reliant on formal systems of intermediation.[7]

> With the decline of the extended family, owner-occupation in southern Europe will become more reliant on formal systems of intermediation

Intermediation is not the sole factor in explaining levels of owner-occupation, but it is an important one. Globalization might be expected to facilitate a convergence in intermediation systems, as investors become reluctant to accept poor rates of return and intermediaries are exposed to greater competition. Its likely impacts are examined in the next section.

In the English-speaking 'dualist' systems globalization might be expected to have the least impact. These countries generally opened up their finance systems in the 1980s and experienced a shift from non-price to price rationing, which helped to expand the supply of mortgage finance. This manifested itself in more generous loan terms, and hence an improved access to mortgage finance (Table 8.2).

The English-speaking countries are notable for high loan-to-value ratio loans of a long duration. These factors, which by definition imply a wide level of access to housing finance, are derived in part from competition between lenders, but more fundamentally by the way in which risks are passed on from intermediaries to borrowers or third parties. Loan insurance is provided by a variety of mechanisms. In Australia the Housing Loan Insurance Corporation protects lenders against losses made on mortgages. In the UK, lenders are protected against losses arising from loan default, normally by mortgage indemnity guarantees (MIGs) paid for by borrowers on high loan-to-value loans. In Canada and the US, the governments insure some mortgages (Table 8.3).

These are purchased by government-sponsored enterprises which in turn issue mortgage-backed securities. This passes interest rate risk on fixed rate mortgages on to the investor. Intermediaries in Australia and the UK pass interest rate risk on to borrowers by using variable rate mortgages, although interest rate swaps have been used to provide fixed rate loans of limited duration (up to five years). Access to finance in these countries is enhanced by valuation systems that normally are based on the current market value of the property (cf Germany and Japan) and foreclosure laws that allow for relatively quick repossessions (cf France and Italy). Nevertheless, important institutional differences exist between these countries. For example, defaulters in the US can limit their liability by voluntary repossession, but in the UK the liability continues, even after a house has been repossessed and even if the loan was covered by a MIG. However, the similarities between these countries mark them out from those in the other groups.

### The owner-occupation market tends to be more volatile in financially deregulated countries

The social and economic significance of high levels of owner-occupation is increased by the framework of a liberalized financial system. The owner-occupation market tends to be more volatile in financially deregulated countries, with periodic speculative house price booms and busts. Owner-occupiers carry more risk, manifested by the rise in default and foreclosure rates in countries such as the US and the UK following mortgage market liberalization.[8] Important debates in Australia and the UK have taken place concerning the role of government and private insurance in protecting borrowers against the loss of earnings. While the situation of marginal owner-occupiers is an important one, the proportion of arrears cases is low, and the vast majority of owner-occupiers gain from their ownership. The significance of housing wealth is enhanced since liberalized systems make it more liquid, with equity release instruments being used to boost consumption, and sometimes, in the case of the elderly, to enhance pension income or pay for long-term care. The ability of owner-occupiers to enjoy untaxed imputed rental income and capital gains is important in providing owner occupiers with these benefits.

### The economic advantages of home-ownership increase the divide with renters

The economic advantages of home-ownership increase the divide with renters, who generally do not benefit from imputed rental income or capital gains. This may explain why so much effort in the US is devoted to increasing access to mortgage credit for groups, particularly some ethnic groups, through an education and counselling programme (see Box 8.1).[9] Technology has already widened access to mortgage credit among higher risk groups by enhancing risk assessment through credit scoring, and has led to the growth of sub-prime lending, especially, but by no means exclusively, in the US. Some commentators predict the further development of this trend as automatic underwriting systems measure risk more accurately and distinguish between risks once thought to be similar (and priced the same).[10] As risk assessment is improved, the rigid division between prime and sub-prime lending could disappear, leading to a marginal widening of access to mortgage credit, albeit with a wider range of prices. Further competitive gains may arise from internet origination as pricing becomes more transparent, although there are significant barriers to on-line originations, notably fraud.[11]

US banking literature often emphasizes the possibilities of further developing mortgage-backed securities (MBS)

| | Agency | Role |
|---|---|---|
| Canada | Canada Mortgage and Housing Corporation (CMHC) | Provides insurance on National Housing Act (NHA) mortgages |
| | | Issues mortgage-backed securities (MBS) on NHA loans |
| | | Little direct lending |
| Japan[i] | Housing Loan Corporation | Provides low-interest loans via postal savings scheme |
| | | Main provider of mortgage finance |
| USA | Federal Housing Authority (FHA)/ Dept. Veterans Affairs | Mortgage insurance |
| | Government-sponsored Enterprises (FNMA, GNMA) | Purchase insured loans and issue MBS |

**Note:** i Under the Administrative Reform Act (1998) the postal savings scheme will be transferred from the post office to a new agency, the Postal Service Agency sometime in 2001–2003. Traditionally post savings have been automatically transferred to the Ministry of Finance's Trust Fund Bureau for distribution to state-favoured programmes, but this will cease to be the case (see OECD, 1998).

**Table 8.3**

**Mortgage public sector agencies**

markets as risk assessment allows other risks to be passed on to increasingly globalized capital markets. However, while securitization has developed elsewhere, particularly as legal frameworks have been put in place, the extent of securitization in the US arises from special circumstances, not least the existence of government-sponsored enterprises. Outside the US, the conditions for securitization are less favourable: there are fewer credit-constrained institutions and seldom are there government-supported enterprises. More significant restructuring of mortgage industries is occurring, partly through the rise of new entrants using new technology to originate loans, without carrying the legacy of expensive branch networks. Consolidation in the industry is common, and Australia and the UK have seen the decline of mutual building societies that have often converted into banks (Table 8.4). But these revolutions in mortgage delivery systems have not fundamentally altered the nature of mortgage products or access to mortgage credit.

### Convergence in monetary indicators produces mixed signals for borrowers. Lower and more stable interest rates reduce risk, but lower inflation also slows down the rate at which the real value of debt declines

#### Box 8.1 Capacity building in mortgage finance

In order to increase the number and role of minority professionals in mortgage finance in the US, the Fannie Mae Foundation established the Community Colleges Initiative. It supports the development of mortgage finance training programmes at community colleges to prepare minority students for mortgage finance jobs. Such programmes have been started in Cleveland, Miami and Los Angeles. The curricula offer an array of courses in mortgage lending, fair housing and diversity awareness. Through a comprehensive internship, full- and part-time students gain direct, hands-on professional experience. The community college programmes are supported by an active local industry collaborative that involves a committee with representatives from mortgage banking and finance. These groups support and guide the development of the programmes. Their members form an essential linkage between the academic programme and the local housing finance sector by mentoring students and providing internship and job opportunities. Many graduating students have found jobs in the field or improved their position as a result of completing the certificate programme.

**Source:** Fannie Mae Foundation, 1999.

|  | Principal intermediaries | Comment |
|---|---|---|
| Australia | >80% commercial banks (est. 1999) | Market share is concentrated between four banks. There was widespread building society demutualization in the early 1990s |
| Canada | 85% chartered banks (1998) | Chartered banks allowed entry to market in 1969, since when they have swallowed up the trusts |
| France | 70% commercial banks, savings banks and mutual co-ops<br>10% mortgage banks (1995) | The loss-making state mortgage bank (Crédit Foncier) was sold to the savings banks in 1999 |
| Germany | First mortgages: mortgage and savings banks<br>Second mortgages: Bausparkassen | Germany operates a system of packaged loans Commercial banks tend to own mortgage banks and Bausparkassen |
| Italy | 100% commercial banks | There is still a tradition of direct (inter-generational) lending in Italy |
| Japan | > 50% public banks<br>35–45% Housing and Loan Corporation (1999) | The government-owned Housing and Loan Corporation has the largest mortgage loan book in the world |
| UK | 70% commercial banks<br>30% building societies (1999) | Widespread building society demutualization from 1995 |
| USA | 50% mortgage banks<br>25% commercial banks<br>20% thrifts | Widespread use of securitization |

**Note:** Intermediary – an institution that collects funds from savers and converts the savings into loans. Savings may be obtained either from many individuals ('retail' funds) or from institutions, such as pension funds, that purchase bonds issued by the intermediary ('wholesale' funds).

**Table 8.4**

**Mortgage intermediaries**

There is simply less scope for developments in intermediation to make much difference to the access to mortgage credit in systems that have already liberalized and already supply long-term mortgages with high loan-to-value ratios. Two other aspects of globalization should not be neglected. Convergence in monetary indicators produces mixed signals for borrowers. Lower and more stable interest rates reduce risk, particularly when mortgages are at variable rates, but lower inflation also slows down the rate at which the real value of debt declines. The long-term impact of these contradictory factors on the user cost of capital is not yet clear, but it is possible that the relative attraction of owner-occupation might be altered.

> **The overemphasis on mortgage delivery systems leads to a conflation of the related issues of access to mortgage credit and access to housing**

The overemphasis on mortgage delivery systems also leads to a conflation of the related issues of access to mortgage credit and access to housing. The two are related, but there are clear limits to the ability of easy access to mortgage credit to be translated into access to owner-occupation. If house prices cease to be affordable, then access to owner-occupation is diminished. For example, Australia's home ownership rate is sustained by demographic ageing which masks falling home ownership rates in younger age groups and shows up in the diminishing proportion of owner-occupiers with mortgages.[12] There are several possible explanations for this trend, but the most likely is that house prices are now less affordable, meaning that issues of land supply and income inequality are equally important.

Globalization might be expected to have a greater impact in the countries with social-democratic housing systems and in the countries with 'rudimentary' systems. Globalization of capital might lead to greater competition in

these countries, broadening the access to mortgage credit by shifting to price rationing in countries such as Germany while leading to a greater role for intermediation in countries such as Italy (which has a strikingly low mortgage debt:GDP ratio; see Table 8.1). However, Europe demonstrates that, ironically, the internationalization of finance has comparatively little impact on mortgage systems.

> **Europe demonstrates that, ironically, the internationalization of finance has little impact on mortgage systems. Great diversity remains in types of intermediary and the terms of mortgage products are similarly diverse**

The members of the European Union have passed legislation that is designed to facilitate greater competition in banking, as part of the Single Market programme. Since 1993, all credit institutions must meet basic prudential criteria (modelled on the Basle accord), but can operate throughout the EU on the basis of a home country passport. Free movement of capital was also introduced, and currency fluctuations were limited by the Exchange Rate Mechanism. Since 1999, 11 of the 15 members of the EU have been members of the single currency with a single interest rate set by the European Central Bank. Despite all this, mortgage credit systems have remained stubbornly divergent.[13] Great diversity remains in types of intermediary, and the terms of mortgage products are similarly diverse.

Part of the reason why the types of intermediary have remained unchallenged by cross-border competition is that some lenders, particularly retail lenders, often enjoy regulatory privileges and privileged access to funds. For example, French retail banks enjoy access to tax-exempt savings which are used to subsidize housing loans, and which place wholesale and cross-border lenders at a disadvantage. German *Bausparkassen* have the monopoly over contract-savings schemes that enjoy tax privileges and provide subsidies to lower income home buyers. These commonly form part of a 'packaged' loan, which is provided by either banks or mortgage banks that own the *Bausparkasse*. The structure of the mortgage market and the conditions attached to establishing a *Bausparkasse* makes the system extremely robust. Attempts at cross-border lending have been small scale, frequently loss-making, and often brief. They have had negligible impacts on mortgage system convergence. The advent of the euro is likely to see some diminution of the privileges enjoyed by some retail lenders, since small investors can now look abroad for more competitive savings rates. Yet, it is important not to assume that systems that produce conservative loan terms are necessarily inefficient. For example, German mortgage banks are among the most successful financial institutions in Europe, and the *Pfandbrief* is a viable alternative to US mortgage-backed securities on the international capital markets, especially since their liquidity has been improved.

> **The unique feature of mortgages is that the most mobile factor of production (global capital) meets the least mobile factor (local property/land)**

To understand fully why mortgage systems do not easily converge, one must look beyond the financial part of a mortgage (the loan) to the legal part (secured on property). The unique feature of mortgages is that the most mobile factor of production (global capital) meets the least mobile factor (local property/land). It is the factors affecting a loan's security that lead to distinct mortgage products. Valuation systems vary between countries, and can be rudimentary or conservative. An example of a conservative valuation can be found in Germany where the 'mortgage lending value' approach to valuation is used. This attempts to establish the 'long-term' value of a property, which is generally lower than the 'market value' approach used in many English-speaking countries. In Japan, construction costs are used as the basis of valuation, which has a similarly depressing effect on loan sizes. While loan-to-value ratios are limited by law in Germany (to 60 per cent for loans funded by mortgage bonds), in other countries, loan-to-value ratios are restricted by foreclosure systems that offer poor security for a loan. In France it can take five years to repossess a property, in Italy it can take up to seven years. While from the outside it is tempting to attribute conservative loan criteria to inefficient intermediaries, the reason is often a good one: it is too risky to lend more.

For these reasons, European mortgage systems may see some equalization of funds between lenders, so the risk and option adjusted price of loans might be equalized over time, but important differences will remain in mortgage products, and hence access to mortgage credit will continue to vary between countries. This has some interesting social and economic implications. Restricted access to mortgage finance implies artificially constrained levels of owner-occupation. Of course, restricted access to mortgage credit provides only a partial explanation for home ownership levels. After all, Sweden has a liberalized mortgage system, but a low level of owner-occupation, partly because flats can be owned only through a company, and partly because renting is more attractive than in many liberal countries. The German tax system has encouraged people to postpone house purchasing while private renting has been treated more favourably than elsewhere. In countries where access to mortgage credit is limited, there seems to be less scope for house price volatility, which has both social and economic benefits, especially within the context of a single currency zone.[14]

---

**Lower levels of owner-occupation facilitate less polarized housing systems because the larger rental sectors contain a broader band of the national income distribution and are therefore less residualized**

---

Further, lower levels of owner-occupation facilitate less polarized housing systems because the larger rental sectors contain broader bands of the national income distribution and are therefore less residualized.

| | Tax on imputed rent | Mortgage interest tax relief | Capital gains tax |
|---|---|---|---|
| Australia | ✗ | ✗ | ✗ |
| Canada | ✗ | ✗ | ✗ |
| France | ✗ | ✔ | SPEC[i] |
| Germany | ✗ | ✗[ii] | SPEC[i] |
| Italy | ✔ | ✔ | ✗ |
| Japan | ✗ | ✗ | ✔[iii] |
| UK | ✗ | ✗[iv] | ✗ |
| USA | ✗ | ✔ | ROLL OVER[v] |

**Notes:** i Capital gains may taxed if property is resold within a short period. This is to discourage purely speculative behaviour that might disrupt the market. ii Mortgage interest tax relief was applied 1991–1994. Germany's principal tax concession has been an eight-year depreciation allowance. iii Described as 'very high'. iv The UK phased out mortgage interest tax relief in the 1990s, with abolition in April 2000. v Roll over relief applies. This means that capital gains are not taxed provided that they are re-invested in another property. The exemption from capital gains tax also applies to older people making their final sale.

**Sources:** Europe: Maclennan et al, 1998; USA: *Housing Statistics of America*; Australia: Yates, 1997; Canada and Japan: personal contacts

**Table 8.5**

**Tax treatment of owner-occupied housing**

# Globalization and the Role of Government in Housing Finance

Governments have intervened in three ways in order to widen access to owner-occupation. First, some countries have had formal subsidy programmes that either lowered the construction cost of housing or the interest rate on loans. These schemes, such as grants for home owners that are provided under the Australian Commonwealth and State Housing Agreement and the subsidized PAP loan programme in France, are very much in retreat. Second, governments often treat owner-occupation favourably in the tax system. Imputed rental incomes are commonly untaxed, as are capital gains on owners' principal homes, although there are exceptions. Mortgage interest tax relief is available in some countries, but not others, and was phased out recently in the UK (see Table 8.5). Third, governments provide loan insurance in some countries, including the US, Australia and Canada.

A possible reason for the retreat of government from direct and indirect financial support to owner-occupation is the general climate of fiscal austerity. This is often attributed to globalization, which has increased the mobility of tax bases. However, when one considers that levels of taxation and spending vary greatly between countries, but that spending levelled out in the 1980s, internal resistance to higher taxes seems to provide a more convincing explanation for fiscal austerity. Nevertheless, globalization seems to have made large government deficits less acceptable, and in Europe the limitation of government borrowing has been formalized first by the Maastricht convergence criteria for countries wishing to join the single currency, and second by the Growth and Stability Pact.[15]

---

**Perhaps one-third of households in advanced economies cannot access housing of an acceptable standard without state assistance**

---

Perhaps one-third of households in advanced economies cannot access housing of an acceptable standard without

| | Size of social rental sector (%)[i] | Type of landlord |
|---|---|---|
| Australia | 7 | Public housing authority |
| Canada | 5 | Public housing authority |
| EU–15 | 18 | – |
| France | 17 | Local authority companies; trade union/ employer companies |
| Germany | 26 | Municipal housing companies, trade union/employer/church companies; co-ops |
| Italy | 6 | – |
| Japan | 8 | – |
| The Netherlands | 38 (1995) | Housing association |
| UK | 23 (1995) | Mainly local authority; housing association |
| USA | 1–2 | Public housing authority |

**Note:** i Around 1990, unless stated otherwise.

**Table 8.6**

**Table 8.6 Social rented housing**

state assistance. In many countries, governments have intervened to lower the cost of rental housing, usually by means of some form of 'social' rented housing. Among the advanced economies, the largest stocks (proportionately) of social rented housing are found in northwest Europe and Scandinavia, where the sector accounts for around one in five dwellings. The sector is much smaller in southern Europe and in the English speaking countries, other than in the UK. Nevertheless, even when social rented housing provides only a small proportion of the total stock, as in the US, in some urban areas there are some very big landlords. For example, the New York City Housing Authority owns 181,000 units housing 535,000 tenants, while it uses the Section 8 program to assist another 77,000 tenants living in private housing.[16] Social rented housing in the English-speaking 'liberal' countries tends to be 'residualized', that is, primarily for the poor, whereas it serves a wider client base in the social democratic/corporatist countries (Table 8.6).

In the 'liberal' countries, such housing has traditionally been provided directly, mainly by the state or by state agencies, such as Public Housing Authorities in the US, Canada and Australia, and local authorities in the UK. In the social democratic countries a more pluralist view has been adopted, with a variety of landlords including municipal housing companies, housing associations, trade unions, employer and church companies, cooperatives and, in the case of Germany, private landlords.

Government support in the form of finance has been in long-term retreat. In the 1980s, state loans often disappeared. They are now almost unheard of, although they are still used in France and Finland. Landlords wishing to build new stock now depend more heavily on private finance, usually raised through the banking system, but sometimes through capital markets. Government subsidies for new construction have declined in virtually all countries and in recent years there has been no support at all from federal or central governments in several countries including Australia, Canada, the US and The Netherlands.

Three examples point to ways in which governments have attempted to maintain the ability of social landlords to provide new, affordable accommodation:

*The Netherlands.* The Netherlands has the largest social rented sector of any of the advanced economies (36 per cent). It is almost exclusively owned by housing associations. State loans were withdrawn in the 1980s. From 1995, the government wrote off the sector's outstanding state loans, but phased out new subsidies by the year 2000. Two institutions have been put in place to assist the newly marketized sector: a guarantee fund helps to reduce the cost of private finance, while a mutual guarantee fund exists to provide loans to distressed associations. So far, the new regime has led to a rapid consolidation of the sector with the average size of landlords growing and their areas of operation expanding.[17]

*Finland.* In Finland, a semi-autonomous Housing Fund was established in 1990 through which government subsidized (ARAVA) loans are channelled to the social rented sector, which is composed of municipal housing companies and other non-profit companies. From the mid-1990s, tranches of low risk ARAVA loans that had been transferred to the Housing Fund were securitized using a Special Purpose Vehicle established in Ireland (for legal reasons). The money raised from securitization has been used to support future subsidized housing. This was the first example of securitization applied to loans secured on social housing loans.[18]

*United Kingdom.* In the UK, non-state housing associations were adopted as the main providers of new social rented housing beginning the late 1980s. Private borrowing by housing associations, in contrast to local authorities, does not score as public spending. In the 1990s, many local authorities with housing stocks that were worth more than outstanding debt transferred their entire stocks to new housing associations which were able to refinance the stock and improve the housing. Unfortunately, the worst housing conditions are found in urban areas, where housing stocks are often worth less than the outstanding debt. However, government debt write-offs and loan servicing are being used to transfer big city stocks of up to almost 100,000 properties to housing associations (subject to tenant ballots) and to lever in private finance to renovate the housing.

> Rents have commonly risen in the 1990s, which, combined with the rise in unemployment, has increased dependence on housing allowances

These examples indicate that it is not correct to characterize governments as simply washing their hands of housing. However, rents have commonly risen in the 1990s and, combined with the rise in unemployment during the first half of the 1990s, dependence on housing allowances has risen. This has prompted some governments, notably Sweden, to restrict eligibility in order to reduce costs.

# Globalization and the Ability to Pay for Housing

Housing outcomes are determined not only by housing policies, but also by contextual factors, such as labour markets and social security systems. Globalization has been associated with increased wage inequality. One explanation s that the demand for skilled labour, relative to unskilled labour, rose in the 1980s and early 1990s, and in countries where there are few corporatist institutions in the wage-setting process, an increased pay differential emerged. OECD data confirm that wage inequality in the English-speaking countries rose markedly in the 1980s. Smaller increases in inequality were experienced in Japan, Austria and France, but in many of the social democratic countries, inequality actually declined in this period. In the 1990s, corporatist wage structures were in decline in some of these countries (such as Sweden and The Netherlands) and it is possible that wage differentials will begin to widen in these countries too (Figure 8.1).

However, the social democratic countries also do more to counter wage inequality through the tax and social security system. These countries tend to rely much more heavily on systems of social insurance that deliver generous benefits in relation to previous earnings. For example, the replacement ratio provided by Swedish unemployment benefit is 80 per cent of previous earnings. In contrast, the 'liberal' welfare states rely much more heavily on means-tested social assistance benefits that generally provide very basic incomes. These differences are reflected in pre- and post-transfer Gini coefficients (Table 8.7).

At first sight, these differences seem likely to be reflected in housing outcomes. Not only are the poor more likely to exercise market choices in housing in the social democratic countries, but they are less likely to be dependent on means-tested housing allowances. Further, because social security benefit income is above subsistence levels, it is possible to retain housing price signals even when the housing allowance is being claimed.

However, the cohesiveness of housing systems in some social democratic countries is being weakened by unemployment, which neo-liberal economists often attribute to inflexible labour markets, the non-wage costs of labour (social security taxes) and the impact of generous benefits on the reservation wages of (particularly) unskilled workers. As a result of higher- and longer-term unemployment, dependence on social assistance benefits and housing allowances rose in the 1990s, although there have been some reductions in housing allowance dependence as unemployment has fallen. However, The Netherlands stands out as a country that has retained a generous welfare state, but also has some of the lowest levels of unemployment among the advanced economies. The link between welfare states and unemployment is certainly not as straightforward as is sometimes assumed.[19]

## Countries with liberal/dualist housing systems

The English-speaking countries have attained high levels of owner-occupation, but there seems to be an upper limit of around 70 per cent. Owner-occupation is the tenure of choice, and this results in polarized housing systems. Globalization is unlikely to make fundamental differences to the access to housing finance, since intermediation systems are already producing long-term loans with high loan-to-value ratios. Other policies, such as assistance for

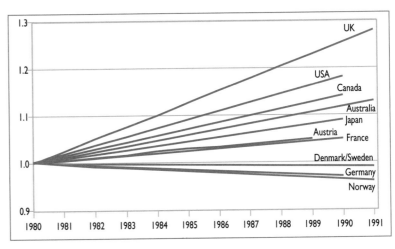

marginal owner-occupiers or counselling programmes, may make a marginal difference, but the sustainability of home ownership levels is more likely to be shaped by labour market developments. A key challenge faced by these countries is the residualization of the social rented sector, which can be seen as the flip side of achieving high levels of owner-occupation. Polarization of housing outcomes is also promoted by income inequalities arising from flexible labour markets and a reliance on social assistance for income transfers.

## Countries with social democratic housing systems

These countries enjoy relatively cohesive housing outcomes. While commentators in these countries have detected adverse trends, there is a great deal of 'safety' room in these systems before they move into the 'liberal'/'dualist' category. Relative cohesion in the social rented sectors arises in part from the way in which finance systems, and other features of the housing system, limit access to owner-occupation among middle income groups. The greater diversity among renters, and less sharp divisions between the social and market rental systems also contribute to cohesion. Globalization may have a limited impact on access to mortgage credit, since key features of mortgage products are derived from regulation, valuation systems and property rights. The cohesiveness of housing

**Figure 8.1**

Changing wage inequality

**Table 8.7**

Income inequality before and after taxes and transfers (Gini coefficient)

| | (1) Before taxes and transfers | (2) After taxes and transfers | (3) % changes due to taxes and transfers (2)/(1) – 1 |
|---|---|---|---|
| Australia 1994/94 | 46.3 | 30.6 | –33.9 |
| Belgium 1995 | 54.5 | 29.9 | –48.4 |
| Canada 1994 | – | 28.4 | – |
| Denmark 1994 | 42.0 | 21.7 | –48.3 |
| Finland 1994 | 42.0 | 21.7 | –48.3 |
| France 1994 | 39.2 | 23.1 | –41.0 |
| Germany 1994 | 43.6 | 28.2 | –35.3 |
| Italy 1993 | 51.0 | 34.5 | –32.4 |
| Japan 1994 | 34.0 | 26.5 | –22.0 |
| The Netherlands 1994 | 42.1 | 25.3 | –39.8 |
| Sweden 1995 | 48.7 | 23.0 | –52.9 |
| USA 1995 | 45.5 | 34.4 | –24.5 |

**Note:** The lower the Gini coefficient, the more equal incomes are.
**Source:** OECD (1999) *Economic Surveys Sweden*, p 112.

systems has not been undermined by the rapid growth in wage inequality seen in the liberal economies, and social insurance provides more generous support for the unemployed, sick and elderly. However, cohesiveness is often challenged by unemployment. Much will depend on developments in the labour markets in these countries. Further, reductions in subsidies to social housing, which arise partly from the global tendency towards fiscal austerity, might be expected to undermine cohesion in the longer term.

## Countries with 'residual' housing systems

These countries have some of the highest levels of owner-occupation, despite the weakness of intermediation systems in some countries and the lack of reliable valuation systems and security. Again, globalization might be expected to have limited impacts on access to mortgage credit. However, given the weakening of the extended family in southern Europe, considerable welfare gains might be derived from a reform of valuation systems and foreclosure rules when these inhibit intermediaries from providing long-term, high loan-to-value ratios.

## Notes

1  This chapter is based on 'Implications of globalization for the provision of and access to housing finance in the advanced economies', a background paper prepared by Mark Stephens, University of Glasgow.

2  Esping Andersen, 1990; Kemeny, 1995.

3  Kemeny uses the term 'cost-rental housing', although the term 'social rented housing' is more commonly used to refer to rental housing that is allocated administratively at sub-market rents.

4  This argument is proposed by Tanzi (2000).

5  Former President Clinton initiated the founding of a Partnership, under the leadership of the HUD Secretary, to promote home-ownership, which aims to 'Make the American Dream a Reality in the 21st Century'. It aimed to increase the level of owner-occupation from 66.8 per cent (in 1999) to 67.5 per cent by the end of 2000.

6  Barlow and Duncan, 1994.

7  There are parallels between the southern European countries and the housing systems emerging in Central and Eastern Europe. The sale of state-owned rental housing to tenants at discounts has raised the level of owner-occupation, but often a strong mortgage system has yet to be created to sustain the levels of owner-occupation. Inheritance and informal transfers are likely to become important features of these systems.

8  The proportion of loans in foreclosure in the US rose from 0.68 per cent in 1984 to around 1 per cent in 1987 (figures from van Vliet, 1998, p 195). In the UK, foreclosures rose from 0.17 per cent of all loans in 1984 to a peak of 0.69 per cent in 1992,

falling to 0.3 per cent in 1997 (Council of Mortgage Lenders).

9  Housing America Update, 2000.

10  Glenn, 1999.

11  Beidl, 1999.

12  Yates, 1997.

13  Lea et al, 1997; Stephens, 2000. See *Financial Times*, 2000. See also Driver, 1998.

14  Maclennan et al, 1998.

15  See Butti at al, 1998.

16  See http://www.nyc.gov/html/nycha/.

17  Boelhouwer, 1997.

18  See Tulla, 1999.

19  See Nickell, 1997.

# DEVELOPMENTS IN THE URBAN ENVIRONMENT AND INFRASTRUCTURE

Earlier parts of this report noted that current economic globalization is dominated by the logic of market mechanisms. The argument was developed that markets can be effective for some purposes but that they do not perform well in other situations. For example, they tend not to be effective in guaranteeing universal access to public goods. Among these public goods are the urban environment and infrastructure. Inadequate regulation permits environmental degradation and engenders unequal access to services to meet basic needs. The solution is not to centralize responsibilities for environmental management and infrastructure development in government. What is needed is the development of broad-based partnerships that comprise not only the public and private sectors, but also civil society and in particular low-income communities. There is a growing number of examples of such partnerships that attest to the potential of this cooperative approach in redressing environmental problems, deficient urban infrastructure and inadequate service provision.

Official statistics greatly overstate the extent to which urban populations are served with safe water and adequate sanitation. Among those classified as 'adequately served' are the inhabitants of settlements where hundreds of people have to share a single standpipe and others who have access to standpipes that are poorly maintained or contain contaminated water. The burden of hauling water disproportionately falls on women, and evidence indicates that this task has become more arduous. Likewise, households are counted as having adequate sanitation if they share access to a public latrine, even if it is shared with 100 or more people and when maintenance and cleaning is so poor that using the latrine is a major health hazard and people avoid using it.

These conditions are especially worrisome in cities where they help to spread easily preventable diseases that affect particularly women and children. Research shows very large income-based differences in mortality and morbidity rates related to unequal access to piped water and adequate sanitation. Improvement requires policies that integrate human settlement programmes with programmes that bridge the provision of safe water, the collection and disposal of human excreta and hygiene education.

Inequalities are also evident in urban energy consumption where they are becoming a source of economic and political tension. The wealthiest 20 per cent of the world's population consumes 68 per cent of the world's commercial energy, whereas the lowest quintile uses less than 2 per cent. In recent decades, the developing economies have been transferring energy resources to the more developed economies at an increasing rate. Per capita energy usage in the US is more than five times the global average. Car-dependent cities have particularly high levels of energy consumption and associated pollution problems. Worldwide, more than 1 thousand million people are estimated to live in urban settlements where air pollution levels exceed health standards. Low-income communities are disproportionately located in proximity to pollution generated by energy plants and road traffic.

Needed policies must promote public transit and non-motorized forms of transport and must substantially reduce the massive subsidies for conventional fossil fuel and nuclear power, which benefit large industrial producers and consumers, rather than people living in poverty. In many metropolitan areas, Agenda 21 and other coalitions are spearheading energy reforms. It is only when local civil society and business interests participate in developing and implementing these innovative agendas that efforts to achieve sustainability can succeed.

Recent experience shows that the shift in responsibility for service provision and management of infrastructure to the local level is not always supported by a commensurate transfer of resources and authority to develop the requisite tax base. The implications have been serious deficiencies, total system collapse and loss of physical assets as a result of overload and insufficient maintenance. The success of decentralization depends greatly on the ability of central government to institute an appropriate regulatory framework for central–local relationships and its willingness to provide localities with assets and intergovernmental transfers rather than budget allocations.

Democratic local governance is essential if decentralization of infrastructure management is to be effective. Recognizing the empowering role of infrastructure, micro-finance institutions and community-based organizations have initiated programmes that provide low-income households with access to land and needed services to improve their earnings capacity and living conditions. Urban policies and international development agencies should be directed to support these initiatives.

# URBAN HEALTH IN THE DEVELOPING COUNTRIES[1]

Globalization has affected human health in complex ways with positive as well as negative implications. Through trade and military conquest, native populations were exposed to communicable diseases previously unknown to them, sometimes intentionally, which in some regions decimated the autochthonous inhabitants.[2] The HIV/AIDS pandemic is a contemporary example with particularly devastating effects on the economies, communities and households in sub-Saharan Africa. In a different vein, the global expansion of a consumerist culture has brought with it an increase in lifestyle-related diseases and industrial pollution, while chemical contamination associated with agricultural mass production, and toxic waste dumping have had worldwide health impacts. On the other hand, globalization has made possible the spread of medical and pharmaceutical advances, leading to the eradication of some diseases and the diminished incidence of others. Likewise, there have been widespread gains in food production as a result of the development of more disease-resistant and more nutritious strains, and tele-medicine has made available diagnostic tools previously unavailable in remote areas. To be sure, these benefits have not been equally shared; however, the reasons for this inequality are political and economic, rather than inherent in globalization. Finally, also in association with globalization, new organizations and programmes have been established whose missions of health promotion are explicitly international in scope. A good example in the context of human settlements is the Healthy Cities Programme of the World Health Organization.[3]

The focus in this chapter is on human health in the developing countries and, within this context, the discussion concentrates on cities. This orientation is in keeping with the continuing urbanization in these countries, but it is not to negate the importance of health issues in rural areas; indeed, as noted in the conclusion of this chapter, the two are often linked.

When considering urban health patterns it is useful to distinguish four phenomena. First, urban health patterns are different from those in rural areas because urban populations are leading the 'epidemiological transition': a shift from communicable to non-communicable diseases. Second, there are still some communicable health problems that dominate in urban areas (eg HIV/AIDS), particularly among children (eg infectious respiratory diseases). Third, low-income urban populations suffer the 'worst of both worlds' in terms of

both communicable and non-communicable diseases. Fourth, the health burden of the urban poor can only be fully understood in terms of inequity within the city as a whole. These four issues are dealt with in turn below.

## Urban Populations Lead the Health Transition

Empirical evidence from the Americas indicates that the 'epidemiological transition' is taking place fastest in countries with the highest levels of urbanization, and that the transition generally occurs first in urban areas.[4] This pattern is supported by studies in other developing countries that demonstrate higher rates of malaria, malnutrition, maternal mortality and respiratory diseases in rural compared with urban populations,[5] and higher risk factors for and rates of diabetes, cardiovascular disease, cancers, coronary heart disease and accidents in urban areas.[6]

---

By the third decade of this century, depression, traffic accidents and heart disease are predicted to become the leading disease burdens in developing countries, as opposed to respiratory disease, diarrhoea and perinatal conditions at present

---

The reasons for the differences in rural and urban health profiles are complex and relate to dramatic environmental, socio-economic and cultural changes brought about by urbanization. Interrelated factors such as relatively low fertility rates, better immunization coverage and better access to and 'appropriate' use of health facilities in urban areas have contributed to a decrease in communicable diseases and a concomitant child survival advantage associated with urban compared with rural residence.[7] Non-communicable diseases (including 'diseases of affluence') and diseases associated with social instability, have therefore gained in relative importance, particularly among urban adults.[8] The dramatic and growing impact that mental ill-health, violence, accidents and chronic disease will have on developing countries is illustrated in disability adjusted life year (DALY) predictions. By the third decade of this century, depression, traffic accidents and heart disease are predicted to become the leading disease burdens in developing countries, as opposed to respiratory disease, diarrhoea and perinatal conditions, which are leading at present.[9]

A growing body of empirical work over the 1990s has contributed to and supported these predictions, and demonstrated their importance as emerging urban health issues. Work on injuries, mental ill-health and 'lifestyle' diseases is particularly illuminating and is considered below.

## Injuries

Violence is a major cause of injuries. Much of the empirical work on violence has been carried out in the world's most violent region: Latin America and the Caribbean. Latin America has the world's highest burden of homicides, at a rate of 7.7 per 1000 individuals, compared with the world average of 3.5 per 1000. Approximately 30 per cent of all homicides are among adolescents between 10 and 19 years old, and males are the most affected.[10] Violent crime is particularly prevalent in the regions' large cities, and within them, among men living in low-income urban areas.[11]

Analysis of data collected between 1991 and 1993 in São Paulo, Brazil, showed that males aged 15–24 living in low-income areas were over five times as likely to become victims of homicide compared with their counterparts resident in higher-income areas.[12] Higher rates of homicide in low-income areas are the outcome of multiple factors:

> 'concentrated poverty, urban deterioration, racism and other forms of social discrimination, lack of opportunities of employment and formal education, lack of policing … emphasis on violent behaviour as a way of resolving personal conflicts … easy access to fire-arms, the increasing consumption of drugs (such as crack and marijuana) and alcohol abuse… The correlation between living conditions and structural violence [violence arising from a social system that produces gender, race and age discrimination, as well as inequalities of social class] is not a linear or mechanical relation… [Also involved are] cultural traits and aspects of personal relationships in some segments in the population.'[13]

Traffic accidents are another major cause of death and injury in cities and towns.[14] Causes of motor vehicle crashes are many, but necessarily involve the interaction of three pre-crash factors: people, vehicles and the road environment.[15] The higher density of each of these in urban areas puts urban populations at greater risk than rural populations. Although this has been supported with empirical data,[16] higher rates – at least of injuries – have also been found in rural areas.[17] Furthermore, research in Latin America and the Caribbean has documented a strong negative correlation between the number of vehicles per 1000 persons and the death rate per 100,000 vehicles.[18] Broader factors influencing the rate of traffic accidents are alcohol consumption, a country's capabilities to invest in roads, legislation and control. According to a recent report, the fatality rate on South African roads fluctuated around 11 persons killed per 100 million vehicle miles. This rate is lower than that of some other African countries, but compares unfavourably with, for example, Zimbabwe (3.3) and Zambia (3.0) as well as the US (1.1) and Australia (1.8).

More than 40 per cent of the fatalities were pedestrians.[19] A recent review of research on road traffic injuries in developing countries found that casualty rates per 10,000 varied widely, from 3.0 in Saudi Arabia to 301.9 in Haiti.[20] In all 73 studies, rates were at least twice as high among men than women; the outcome of greater exposure and possibly – to a lesser extent – behaviour. Adolescents and young adults are particularly high-risk groups. Of interest for urban planners is that traffic-related injuries account for between 30 and 86 per cent of all trauma admissions (15 studies), with the mean length of stay 20 days (11 studies). Given that the majority of trauma facilities are located in urban areas, these statistics suggest that accidents not only pose an enormous mortality and morbidity risk to urban residents, they also are a significant burden on urban health systems.

Accidents other than those involving traffic have been less carefully documented, but include accidental falls, drowning, poisoning and fire. Some unintentional injuries are more common in urban areas because of factors such as overcrowding.[21] Although precise statistics are not available, it is known that what passes for a domestic accident is, in reality, often an instance of spousal abuse; a fact that throws women's disproportionate health risks into further relief.

## Mental ill-health

By 2020, depression is predicted to become the leading disease burden in developing countries. Community-based studies of mental health in urban areas of developing countries have documented prevalence rates of between 12 and 51 per cent.[22] Prevalence of anxiety and depression is typically higher among women than men, and among lower-income communities, with variations reflecting differential exposure and vulnerability to diverse risk factors, including control over resources, marriage patterns, cultural ideology, long-term chronic stress, exposure to stressful life events, coping strategies and social support.[23] Social support – 'the degree to which a person's basic social needs are gratified through interaction with others' – has been estimated to account for between 5 and 10 per cent of variance.

> The chronic stress of poverty and stressful life-events can have very negative direct and indirect effects on physical and mental health

Emotional support (love, empathy, companionship) and practical support (goods, services, information) are key resources drawn upon to cope with or to 'buffer' the potential mental (and physical) health effects of chronic or short-term stress.[24] Urban environments, and low-income urban environments in particular, are characterized by harsh physical and social environments, poor-quality housing and service provision and reduced employment and income generation potential.[25] Day-to-day life in these contexts can amount to chronic stress. The strategies that low-income households employ to cope with such stresses re numerous, including working longer hours, depending more heavily on women's earning capacities, deploying children into income-generating activities, fostering out children to rural relatives (and adopting other forms of multi-location households), circular or permanent migration by household members for employment, exploring new niches in the informal sector and maximizing the use of the meagre resources available. These strategies point to the creativity and resilience of low-income groups. Nevertheless, the chronic stress of poverty and stressful life-events can have very negative direct and indirect effects on physical and mental health. Urbanization has also been associated with a reduction in social support linked to the breakdown (or at least reorganization) of extended families, increase in single parent households, reduced fertility and participation in work outside the home.[26] Clearly this has implications for the coping strategies themselves, and for physical and psychological well-being.

Current knowledge gaps concern the interrelationships of mental illness with social support, and with community-level factors such as high levels of violence or low levels of social cohesion.[27] Regarding the latter, an ecological variable that may play a role is social capital, or 'the density and nature of the network of contacts or connections amongst individuals in a given community'. Strong social capital has been linked with reduced mortality at the state level in the US. As the coping ability of low-income urban households decreases and community trust breaks down, social capital weakens; it is also eroded by violence (see Chapter 17).[28]

### Chronic or 'lifestyle' diseases

Chronic or 'lifestyle' diseases such as heart problems and cancers will become an increasingly heavy health burden in developing countries. Risk factors include potentially toxic emissions such as carbon dioxide, sulphur dioxide, nitrogen oxides and suspended particulate matter, and lifestyle factors such as increased smoking, alcohol consumption, increased fat intake, reduced fibre intake and reduced exercise. Risk factors for and rates of diabetes, obesity, cardiovascular disease, cancers and coronary heart disease have been documented to be higher in urban than in rural areas. Research has amply documented that sources of pollution are disproportionately located near low-income communities and minorities,[29] raising questions of environmental justice that are also in evidence at the global level. In this connection, the Basel Action Network (BAN) is a global network of individuals and non-governmental, non-commercial organizations working to stop the globalization of the toxic chemical waste crisis and to support ratification of the Basel Convention, which bans the export of hazardous wastes from OECD countries to the developing countries.[30] People living in poverty are also more exposed to toxic and hazardous environments in their daily work activities, dramatically illustrated by the lives (and deaths) of the scavengers in the Payatas community in the Philippines.[31]

In Latin America, there is an upward trend in specific types of mortality, such as cancer of the lung, gall-bladder

and breast.[32] Circulatory disease is the second most important cause of death among 15–44-year-olds in Accra, Ghana, and São Paulo, Brazil, and the principal cause of death of 45–64-year-olds.[33] Community-based studies among the elderly have also documented high rates of mortality and morbidity due to chronic and lifestyle diseases.[34] These diseases are primarily adult health problems, and the changing demographic structure, as well as prevalence and increase of risk factors in urban populations support the DALY predictions that they will become increasingly important sources of mortality.

## Emerging Evidence of an Urban Penalty?

The term 'urban penalty' or 'le handicap urbain' was prompted by analysis of mortality data in England from the Industrial Revolution of the 19th century, which revealed that urban mortality rates (particularly from tuberculosis) were much higher than rural rates.[35] In continental Europe, at the same time, infant gastrointestinal disease accounted, for example, for one-third of all deaths in Prussian urban communities in 1887.[36] Rural–urban differences were stark. In 1875, the infant mortality rate (IMR) in rural Prussia was 190 compared with 240 in urban areas.[37] Public health measures such as supply of clean water and sanitation plus socio-economic changes led to a decline in urban IMRs after around 1893.[38]

---

**Since 1970, infant mortality rates in sub-Saharan cities have increased**

---

Recent analysis of urban demographic and health survey (DHS) data from 43 countries has demonstrated a much slower decline since the 1970s in levels of early mortality of residents in large cities than in those in smaller towns and villages in all regions of the developing world (with the exception of Southeast Asia). It is particularly disturbing that infant mortality rates had actually risen substantially in small and medium-sized cities in sub-Saharan Africa, in many cases including the capital city.[40]

In addition to sustained recession, persistent urban growth, deteriorating physical environments and strained management capabilities, the HIV/AIDS epidemic is contributing to the sub-Saharan African urban penalty. There is substantial evidence of higher HIV prevalence in large urban areas compared with smaller urban and rural areas.[41]

The current narrowing of rural and urban child health differentials, in Africa and elsewhere, is more likely to be the outcome of changes in patterns of traditional diseases of poverty rather than emerging epidemics. Regarding food security and malnutrition, for example, in 12 out of 16 countries of the WHO Global Database on Child Growth and Malnutrition, the absolute number of underweight children in urban areas is increasing, and at a faster rate than in rural areas. As noted in Chapter 1, the locus of malnutrition is shifting from rural to urban areas.[42]

Given the well-known synergies between malnutrition and infectious disease,[43] and evidence of growing poverty, inequity and environmental degradation within urban communities, this pattern is reflected in other 'diseases of poverty'. The next chapter of this report details the health risks resulting from lack of access to safe water and adequate sanitation, burdens that are borne first and foremost by the poor and, among them, women, children, and the elderly.

> Despite major advances in reducing communicable diseases in the cities of developing countries, such diseases continue to be a major cause of mortality

A plethora of studies over the 1990s have demonstrated that despite major advances in reducing communicable diseases in developing countries, and particularly in urban areas, such diseases continue to be a major cause of urban mortality. The burden is particularly heavy for young children. For example, infectious and parasitic diseases are the main cause of death for under-15-year-olds in Accra, Ghana.[44] In São Paulo, Brazil, respiratory diseases are the chief cause of death in under-five-year-olds, while infectious diseases are the second most important cause of death. Child mortality due to communicable disease is significantly higher in more deprived areas in both cities.

Studies of low-income urban communities demonstrate the importance of preventing neonatal death, diarrhoea, non-specific fever, malaria, acute respiratory infection (ARI), tuberculosis (TB) and measles to reduce child mortality and morbidity.[45] Significant associations between these diseases, and with HIV infection, have also been documented. The interaction of multiple risk factors in an urban environment is illustrated by those factors associated with acute respiratory infection:

> 'Acute respiratory infections tend to be endemic rather than epidemic, affect younger groups, and are more prevalent in urban than in rural areas. The frequency of contact, the density of the population and the concentration and proximity of infective and susceptible people in an urban population promote the transmission of the infective organisms. Poor groups ... are much more at risk because of the greater proportion of younger age groups, limited health and financial resources, and over-crowded households in congested settlements with limited access to vaccines and antibacterial drugs. The constant influx of migrants susceptible to infection and possible carriers of the new virulent strains of infective agents, together with the inevitable increase in household numbers, foster the transfer of nasopharyngeal microorganisms.'[46]

Non-communicable diseases gain in relative importance as urban populations age. But communicable diseases continue to be an important cause of adult mortality. In Dar es Salaam, Tanzania, HIV is the primary cause of death among urban males, and HIV and maternal mortality are the primary killers of urban women.[47] Noteworthy in this rural–urban comparison, 10.8 per cent and 19.2 per cent of

the adult deaths recorded in the two rural study sites were urban residents who had returned to the rural area after becoming ill. This pattern of return urban–rural migration of sick adults is a common characteristic in developing world regions where rural–urban ties are maintained, and may lead to underestimates of adult mortality rates in urban community surveys.

Before the HIV/AIDS epidemic, TB was the leading cause of death among adults in developing countries, killing an estimated 3 million people in 1995.[48] The interaction between HIV and TB, and the spread of multi-drug-resistant strains of TB, has increased concerns about a global resurgence of TB. Given that socio-environmental conditions (particularly high levels of crowding) are risk factors for TB,[49] and that there is higher prevalence of HIV in many urban populations, TB will become increasingly prevalent in many urban areas. High-density, low-income populations are particularly at risk. The socio-environmental conditions in these areas have also led to the emergence or re-emergence of vector-borne diseases, including malaria, filariasis, dengue, Chagas' disease, plague and typhus.[50]

## Low-income Urban Populations: The Worst of Both Worlds?

Is an urban penalty a risk for entire urban populations, or only for a specific sub-population? More precisely, does evidence suggest 'a penalty for the urban poor' rather than an urban penalty? A principal contribution of the last major urban health review[51] was to bring together studies highlighting intra-urban inequities in morbidity and mortality in developing countries.[52] Together, these studies suggested that the urban poor suffer the 'worst of both worlds': a 'double burden' of both 'old' and 'new' epidemiological profiles. Much of the research reviewed above demonstrates the high burdens of disease suffered by low-income populations and therefore supports the hypothesis. However, more systematic explorations into intra-urban health differentials are necessary to answer the question. This gap has recently been filled by research on urban nutrition by the International Food Policy Research Institute (IFPRI).[53]

DHS data from 11 developing countries show that the ratio of stunting prevalence between poorer vs. wealthier quintiles is greater within urban than within rural areas, and that intra-urban differences (between socio-economic groups) are greater than urban/rural differentials. Urban poor households have worse nutritional status than rural poor households, contributing to greater ill-health related to nutrition. Malnourishment, hunger, dietary excess and obesity often co-exist in urban populations. FAO 1999 data for 133 low-income countries show that more urbanized countries have a higher consumption of sweeteners and fats:

> 'a shift from 25 per cent to 75 per cent urban population in very low income countries is associated with an increase of approximately four percentage points of total energy from

*fat and an additional 12 percentage points of energy from sweeteners'.*[54]

Although this pattern is often considered to apply only for the urban rich, research in urban Brazil and South Africa has found that the more educated are less likely to be overweight than the less educated.[55]

Additional analysis of DHS data found socio-economic status, short birth intervals, young maternal age, parental education and in-migration of mothers from rural areas powerful predictors of infant survival in cities with populations of over 1 million.[56] Possible explanatory factors include the threat of new infectious disease agents, temporary residence in particularly poor housing environments on arrival, changes in care-giving practices, a termination of breastfeeding, a decrease in income and incomplete immunization due to lack of familiarity with services. Overwhelming empirical evidence from all developing regions now links poor housing conditions in urban areas to childhood disease and injuries.[57]

Particularly insidious is Chagas' disease (American trypanosomiasis), a parasitic infection that afflicts between 18 and 20 million people in Mexico, Central and South America. It leads to an estimated 50,000 fatalities annually and debilitates many more, making it the leading cause of death just after ARIs, diarrhoeal diseases and HIV/AIDS. Although the disease is also passed on through blood transfusions and breastfeeding, its main vectors are nocturnal beetles (*Triatoma reduvii* and *Rhodnius prolixus*) whose bites transmit a parasite (*Trypanosoma cruzi*). These beetles breed in cracks in the walls of homes, in thatched roofs and in spaces between wooden boards. They thrive in dark, poorly ventilated, humid environments. Currently, there is no cure and attempts to control the disease involve preventive measures. Fumigation is temporarily effective but long-term intervention requires home improvements, using locally available, low-cost materials. Education is important as well. Because the disease is often asymptomatic for 15–20 years and mainly affects poor people with more immediate survival concerns, awareness-raising efforts must accompany schemes aimed at upgrading the housing environment.[58]

> A key message is that disposable household income and the way it is spent are not the sole or even most important determinants of the health of urban children, which is affected significantly by their wider social and physical environment

Studies of 0–15-year-olds in Ghana, Brazil, Egypt and Thailand found major socio-economic disparities in health and mortality within the urban sector of all four countries. The differences reflect the interrelated effects of socio-economic status, access to health services and environmental conditions. The relative importance of each, and the size of intra-urban differentials in child health, are related to overall national income and the particular histories of economic and urban development of each country. A key message therefore is that disposable household income and the way it is spent are not the sole or even most impor-

tant determinants of the health of urban children, which is more significantly affected by their wider social and physical environment.

An influential analysis of routinely collected urban data on socio-economic status, indicators of environmental quality and mortality from Accra, Ghana, and São Paulo, Brazil, has demonstrated enormous disparities between the health status of urban populations living in the most deprived areas compared with the least deprived areas.[59] The most deprived areas not only suffer relatively high mortality rates due to diseases of the respiratory system, and infectious and parasitic disease, but also due to diseases of the circulatory system. In São Paulo, deaths due to external causes (homicides and traffic accidents) were three times higher in the most deprived compared to the least deprived areas. Figures for homicide were particularly striking in São Paulo: there was an 11-fold mortality differential between rich and poor neighbourhoods. With a similar socio-economic and environmental profile, 55 per cent of the deaths in the most deprived zones could have been prevented. In Accra, adult mortality in the poorest three zones was 67 per cent higher than in the city's best areas.[60] The research on environmental urban health inequalities in Accra, São Paulo and Jakarta is summarized in Box 9.1.

The work on intra-urban inequalities highlights the diverse experience in different countries and communities, but in general provides evidence that the urban poor die disproportionately of both infectious and chronic degenerative diseases. Extant research also underlines the importance of disaggregating urban data *within* cities by gender, income and age.

---

**Box 9.1 Environmental health inequalities in Accra, Jakarta and São Paulo**

It is often assumed that the worst physical environments are in megacities where it may be difficult for even the affluent to avoid the worst environmental hazards: industries and transport systems pollute the ambient air that most residents breath as well as other public environments. But many of the most serious environmental health hazards are in people's homes and workplaces. Here the patterns of inequality are different, and relate more closely to poverty than to city-size and industrialization. Illustrative patterns of inequality at the household level are provided in Tables 9.1 and 9.2 and are based on representative surveys of 1000 households in Jakarta and São Paulo, coordinated by the Stockholm Environment Institute.

In Accra, the smallest and poorest of the three cities, by far the highest share of households are exposed to what could be considered health-threatening living environments. Jakarta, in turn, has a higher share than São Paulo, the largest and most affluent city (Table 9.1). However, there are also appreciable inequalities within Accra where some of the most significant differences arise among poor households and neighbourhoods (Table 9.2). Table 9.3 relates environmental health risk factors to child diarrhoea. Among households facing two or less of these risk factors, only 2 per cent reported diarrhoea incidents, among those facing three or four risk factors the percentage rose to 14, and among those facing more than four risk factors the percentage rose to 39. Generally, the deeper in poverty, the more risk factors a household faces. Children's health (indicated by both diarrhoea and acute respiratory infections) is clearly affected by the environmental correlates of poverty. Whether the children were girls or boys was not found to be significant. However, the respiratory health of women is related to risk factors associated with their gender roles, such as cooking food and spraying for insects.

**Source:** McGranahan et al, 1999; Jacobi, 1999; Surjadi et al, 1994.

| Environmental health indicator | Accra | Jakarta | São Paulo |
|---|---|---|---|
| Water: no water source at residence (%) | 46 | 13 | 5 |
| Sanitation: share toilets with > 10 households (%) | 48 | 13 | 3 |
| Solid waste: no home garbage collection (%) | 89 | 37 | 5 |
| Indoor air: main cooking fuel wood or charcoal (%) | 76 | 2 | 0 |
| Pests: flies in kitchen (%) | 82[i] | 38[i] | 20[ii] |
| Number of households | 1000 | 1055 | 1000 |

**Notes:** i As observed by interviewer. ii As perceived by respondent.
**Sources:** McGranahan et al, 1999; Jacobi, 1999; Surjadi et al, 1994.

**Table 9.1**

Household environmental indicators in Accra, Jakarta and São Paulo

# Shifting the Focus from the Urban Poor to Urban Inequity

**Studies reveal enormous intra-urban inequity in housing conditions, income earned, sanitation, drainage, piped water, environment, access to services, morbidity and mortality**

Much of the research attention in urban health continues to be directed towards the urban poor rather than on intra-urban inequities. However, studies reveal enormous intra-urban inequity in housing conditions, income earned, sanitation, drainage, piped water, environment, access to services and morbidity and mortality.[61] These disparities, and particularly those supporting the double burden of communicable and non-communicable disease faced by low-income urban groups, could be used to support a continued focus on the urban poor. However, these findings could equally justify a shift in attention away from the urban poor in isolation towards *relative* poverty and *whole* urban populations. Box 9.2 dramatically highlights the interrelatedness of low- and high-income groups, the importance of psycho-social forces in the mental and physical health of low-income groups and, ultimately, of all urban residents.

**The fallacy of focusing on the urban poor as opposed to inequity is that individuals and households come to be perceived as the ones to solve problems, rather than a societal responsibility to alleviate poverty**

The fallacy of focusing on the urban poor as opposed to inequity is that individuals and households come to be perceived as the ones to solve problems, rather than a societal responsibility to alleviate poverty. It leads to descriptions of physical and socio-economic deprivation and how this affects health, rather than focusing on the mechanisms that have brought about and maintain such

**Table 9.2**

Household environmental indicators in Accra, by affluence of neighbourhood

| Environmental health indicator | Poor | Middle class | Affluent |
|---|---|---|---|
| Water: no water source at residence (%) | 55 | 14 | 4 |
| Sanitation: share toilets with > 10 households (%) | 60 | 17 | 2 |
| Solid waste: no home garbage collection (%) | 94 | 77 | 55 |
| Indoor air: main cooking fuel wood or charcoal (%) | 85 | 44 | 30 |
| Pests: flies in kitchen (%) | 91 | 56 | 18 |
| Number of households | 790 | 56 | 18 |

**Source:** Benneh et al, 1993.

deprivation.[62] Intra-urban analysis of wealth and health suggests the opposite: it places the importance of governance, municipal management and the genuine empowerment of low-income communities at the centre of urban health:

> 'In many instances, it is not people's poverty which drives the illness but the incapacity or unwillingness of government institutions to provide them with the means to prevent ill health – in part through basic services. This in turn is related to unrepresentative political structures where the poor majority have little power and influence over public actions ... it is the poor's lack of influence on government policies and institutions and their lack of protection from the law that explain a significant part of the deprivation they face ... [and] ... governments will not address urban poverty and its underlying causes unless the poor have more political influence.'[63]

This shift towards intra-urban inequalities in health, and towards the empowerment of low-income groups through socio-political change, is also supported by analysis of historical data from the UK. What was important in determining the changing relationship between economic growth and health was poorer sections of the community having an effective political voice. And having an effective political voice required more than voting rights: the leadership, the relationship of the poor with elements of other, more privileged, social groups, and the latter's ideologies were the critical factors in determining the consequences of voting.

# Beyond the Rural–Urban Divide

The complex picture of urban health presented in the previous sections is matched by a complex array of health-care providers. The urban health 'system' is increasingly pluralistic with traditional practitioners, central and local government facilities, NGOs, private for-profit practitioners, telemedicine and retail outlets for self-medication. Increasing quality of care within and coordination between this array of providers in the urban scene is a priority of researchers and governments, but there are few models to use as examples. Practices of good governance are important but offer no panacea. For example, health sector reform in Brazil built the Unified Health System according to a dense corpus of administrative instruments for organizing decentralized service networks and routinizing complex decision-making procedures. The intent was to increase regional equity in terms of the distribution of funds and the use of health services. However, research shows that access remains extremely unequal across income, employment status and level of education.[64]

Our understanding of urban health dynamics, like other aspects of urban development, also needs to be more informed by the extent of rural–urban links. Official boundaries between rural and urban populations are often too rigid and may not reflect the perceptions or realities of the people living in either. Populations and activities described either as ral' or 'urban' are more closely linked across space and ·ctors than previously assumed. The strength of rural–urban teraction and interdependence is illustrated by large umbers of multi-spatial households and enterprises, with nkages maintained through temporary and long-term circu- atory mobility, remittances and exchanges of goods and information. These linkages can be far more than simply motional and symbolic; they can be important household rategies aimed at maximizing the benefits and minimizing he hardships in both areas. At the household level, divisions f labour and power according to gender, age and relation- hips to other household members, affect the propensity and reedom of different individuals to engage in rural–urban migration in the first place. The extent, frequency and mportance of rural–urban ties therefore vary considerably ver space and time, and according to the strategies adopted y numerous different types of households.

The importance of rural–urban links in health is most frequently illustrated in the transmission patterns of HIV/AIDS and other infectious diseases. In some contexts he interaction between rural and urban populations ontributes to low-income rural and urban populations haring similar disease patterns and risk factors for disease. or example, detailed mobility and treatment-seeking urvey work was carried out with 248 lifelong rural esidents and 284 low-income urban resident mothers in coastal Kenya.[65] Indicators of strong rural–urban ties ncluded:

- 32 per cent of lifelong rural resident mothers had husbands resident elsewhere, most commonly (80 per cent) in an urban area.

| Factor | Odds ratio | 95% confidence interval |
|---|---|---|
| Use pot for storing water | 4.3 | 1.7–11.1 |
| Water interruptions are common | 3.1 | 1.4–6.6 |
| Share toilet with >5 households | 2.7 | 1.2–5.8 |
| Purchase vendor-prepared food | 2.6 | 1.1–6.2 |
| Open water storage container | 2.2 | 1.1–4.3 |
| Outdoor defecation in locality | 2.1 | 1.1–3.9 |
| Many flies in food area | 2.1 | 1.1–3.8 |
| Do not always wash hands before preparing food | 2.0 | 1.1–3.8 |
| Number of observations = 500 | | |

**Source:** Songsore and McGranahan, 1998.

- 33 per cent of urban resident mothers had spent at least 10 per cent of nights in the year preceding the interview (or since migration into the current house- hold of residence) elsewhere, primarily in rural areas.
- 10 per cent of lifelong rural resident mothers had spent at least 20 per cent of nights over the previous year with urban residents (through their own visits and through visitors in their households), and 14 per cent of urban residents had spent at least 20 per cent of nights with rural residents.
- 61 per cent of urban resident mothers reported regularly assisting at least one individual resident elsewhere, with most assisted people (90 per cent) resident in a rural area.
- 74 per cent of urban resident mothers stated that they wished to 'retire' in a rural area.

The importance of moving beyond the rural–urban divide is likely to influence the next decade of research and policy concerning urban health.

**Table 9.3**

**Relative risk of diarrhoea among children under six in Accra**

---

### Box 9.2 Inequalities in health: absolute versus relative poverty

On the basis of a review on inequalities in health at a national level, Richard Wilkinson stressed that the most egalitarian societies had lower national mortality rates. He suggested that the pathway between low income and poor health outcomes revolved around psychosocial factors; that knowledge of 'how the other half lives' affects psychosocial well-being and therefore overall health status. Regarding the importance of *relative* and *absolute* poverty to health outcomes in developing countries, he suggests that prior to a society's (or city's) epidemiological transition, absolute standards of living have an important impact on health: infectious and parasitic diseases are widespread and access to clean water, adequate food, sanitation facilities and good quality housing are essential in maintaining good health. The importance of relative poverty at this stage is the unequal power relations that enable some to gain access to these features, while others are deprived. During and after the epidemiological transition relative standards of living become more important: people's access to basic necessities of life *and* the subjective experience of the circumstances in which they live impact on health. At this stage, poor groups living in unequal societies suffer both the direct material effects of deprivation (absolute poverty) and its indirect psychoso- cial consequences (relative poverty).

*'From the point of view of the experience of people involved, if health is being damaged as a result of psychosocial processes, this matters much more than it would if the damage resulted from the immediate physical effects of damp housing and poor quality diets... To feel depressed, cheated, bitter, desperate, vulnerable, frightened, angry, worried about debts or job and housing insecurity; to feel devalued, useless, helpless, uncared for, hopeless, isolated, anxious and a failure: these feelings can dominate people's whole experience of life, colouring their experience of everything else. It is the chronic stress arising from feelings like these which does the damage. It is the social feelings which matter, not exposure to a supposedly toxic material environment. The material environment is merely the indelible mark and constant reminder of the oppressive fact of one's failure, of the atrophy of any sense of having a place in a community and of one's social exclusion and devaluation as a human being.'*[i]

Wilkinson proposes that relative inequalities in income lead to a breakdown in a society's social cohesion, creating chronic psychosocial stress with both direct and indirect negative influences on both physical and mental health. The deterioration of community life and subsequent rise in violence and crime have a detrimental impact on all members of society, not just the poor. It is the proximity of the urban poor to what are frequently some of the richest people in the world that has been linked to much of the tension and social unrest characteristic of urban areas.

**Source:** Summary of Richard Wilkinson's work on inequalities in Blue, 1999.
**Note:** i Wilkinson, 1996, p 215, cited in Blue, 1999, p 21.

## Box 9.3 Promoting health: more than medicine

Globalization focuses on a narrow definition of health as the absence of disease. It emphasizes the improved opportunity for the transfer of medical technologies to address health problems. The bulwarks of modern medicine – immunization, antisepsis, antibiotics and other essential drugs, anaesthesia and analgesia – alongside the knowledge to use these rationally, are, of course, important. But, the biomedical view largely ignores the overwhelming evidence that health improvement is brought about by more than just the introduction of modern medical technology. Biased by technological optimism, it fails adequately to grasp the wider social, economic and political environment within which health is improved and health care is delivered. Health improvement needs development as well as medical technologies.

In the North, mortality from the diseases that now cause the greatest disease burden in the South were already in decline long before the medical technologies were available to cure them. Tuberculosis kills 26 per cent of the adult population of the South today.[i] It affected a similar proportion of the population in the North in the 19th century. The decline in mortality from this deadly disease was brought about through improved nutrition and a more equitable distribution of income. This, in turn, led to improved host resistance to this deadly mycobacterium.[ii] Better health requires more than the delivery of better health technologies. It must also encompass poverty alleviation, public health services and the meeting of basic civil rights.[iii]

One of these civil rights is the equitable delivery of international public goods, including medicines and health care. However, the new institutions and rules of the global market do not facilitate their equitable delivery. For instance, South Africa, where 50 per cent of antenatal women carry the HIV virus,[iv] cannot afford to buy essential drugs to prevent the transmission of HIV from mother to new-born child because it must adhere to World Trade Organization-initiated patent legislation, the Trade and Intellectual Property Rights (TRIPS) agreement and is unable to buy the generic form of the anti-AIDS drug AZT from India at a price five times lower than the same drug marketed by a multinational pharmaceutical company. South Africa has been threatened with sanctions by the United States if it buys the cheaper generic drug.[v] A price cut in HIV/AIDS drugs, announced by five major pharmaceutical companies in the spring of 2000, was a step in the right direction, but was expected to have little impact in sub-Saharan Africa, where 70 per cent of the world's 33.6 million HIV-infected people live. Aside from costs, there are additional barriers to the health improvements of this population. The effectiveness of the drugs depends on a balanced and adequate diet, which is often impossible because food is unavailable or too expensive. In addition, AIDS treatment typically requires a strict regimen of medication that must be taken according to a set schedule, which may not be possible in more rural areas where roads may be cut off by floods, delaying critical deliveries. Further, many people who are HIV-positive die from other causes, such as pneumonia, because they lack the medicines to fight these curable diseases that attack their weakened immune systems. A careful series of studies of diarrhoeal disease among children in Bangladesh found that the single greatest determinant of reduction in associated mortality were increases in the level of education among women.[vi]

Clearly, effective promotion of health requires the availability of required medicines and commensurate know-how. However, within the panoply of human settlements considerations, these elements are only part of a broader approach that also includes strategies to eliminate poverty, improve education and develop physical and organizational infrastructure.

**Source:** The material for this box is drawn from 'Globalization, Polarization and the Poor', a paper prepared by Nick Emmel, The Nuffield Institute for Health, The University of Leeds, Britain.
**Notes:** i Farmer, 1997; ii McKeown et al, 1975; iii Sen, 1999b; iv Walker, 1999; v Bond, 1999; vi see Muhuri and Menken, 1997.

# Notes

1 This chapter draws heavily on 'Urban health in the context of poverty, inequity and polarization trends in developing countries', a background paper prepared by Trudy Harpham and Sassy Molyneux, which is based on material originally prepared for the US National Academy of Sciences' 'Panel on Urban Population Dynamics'.

2 A sad example from the annals of American history is the spread of smallpox among Native Americans, promoted by Europeans like the British commander Sir Geoffrey Amherst, who in 1763 wrote 'You will do well to innoculate the Indians by means of blankets [contaminated by smallpox] as well as to try every other method that can serve to extirpate this exorable race'. See Thornton, 1987.

3 See www.who.int/hpr/cities/index.html. A recent review describes the origin of the Healthy Cities Programme and presents case studies from Egypt, Pakistan and Brazil, while examining the roles of international agencies, local government and grassroots organizations in the long-term sustainability of schemes established under the programme; see Werna et al, 1999. See also Kenzer, 1999. Both articles are part of a special issue on 'Healthy Cities, Neighborhoods and Homes'.

4 PAHO, 1998a; Tanner and Harpham, 1995.

5 Mbizvo et al, 1993; Mock et al, 1993; McCombie, 1996; Fawcus et al, 1995, 1996; Root, 1997.

6 Reviews by Beevers and Prince, 1991; Muna, 1993; Walker, 1995, Walker and Segal, 1997; Walker and Sareli, 1997; and studies by McLarty et al, 1996; Steyn et al, 1996; Ceesay et al, 1996; Delpeuch and Maire, 1997.

7 Bah, 1993; Bahr and Wehrhahn, 1993; Taylor, 1993; Fawcus et al, 1995; Brockerhoff, 1994; 1995; Brockerhoff and Brennan, 1998; Gould, 1998.

8 Feachem et al, 1990.

9 WHO, 1996.

10 Frenk et al, 1998; PAHO, 1996; 1998a, cited in Grant, 1999.

11 Barata et al, 1998; Grant, 1999. See Chapter 17 for a more extensive discussion of aspects of violence.

12 Grant, 1999.

13 Barata et al, 1998, p7.

14 Mock et al, 1999; Kayombo, 1995; Byarugaba and Kielkowski, 1994.

15 Odero et al, 1997.

16 Mock et al, 1999.

17 Odero, 1995.

18 Grant, 1999.

19 See Road Traffic, available at www.transport.gov.za/docs/greenp3e.html; accessed on 17 July 2000.

20 Odero et al, 1997. The OECD collects regular road accident data from the member and associate countries of the European Conference of Ministers of Transport; see www.oecd.org/cem/index.htm.

21 Bartlett et al, 1999; Mock et al, 1999; Knobel et al, 1994.

22 Sixteen studies reviewed by Blue, 1999.

23 Harpham, 1994.

24 Thoits, 1995.

25 Ekblad, 1993; Fuller et al, 1993; Satterthwaite, 1993; 1995.

26 Harpham, 1994; Parry, 1995; Harpham and Blue, 1995.

27 Blue and Harpham, 1998.

28 Moser and Shrader, 1999.

29 See, for example, Evans et al, 2001; Hardoy et al (2001).

30 For more information, see www.ban.org/.

31 See the Key Issues and Messages at the beginning of this report.

32 Timaeus and Lopez, 1996.

33 Stephens et al, 1994.

34 Bella et al, 1993; Allain et al, 1997.

35 Kearns, 1988; 1993.

36 Vögele, 2000.

37 Vögele, 2000.

38 Szreter, 1997.

39 Brockerhoff and Brennan, 1998.

40 See Gould, 1998.

41 Boerma et al, 1999.

42 See Haddad et al, 1999.

43 Fonsesca et al, 1996.

44 See Stephens et al, 1994.

45 See, for example, von Schirnding et al, 1991; Mock et al, 1993; Molbak et al, 1992, 1993; Ekanem et al, 1994; Fonesca et al, 1996; Mahalanabis et al, 1996; Mirza et al, 1997; Byass et al, 1995; Awasthi and Pande, 1998; Molyneux et al, 1999; Sinha et al, 1999; van Rie et al, 1999.

46 WHO, 1992, cited in Satterthwaite, 1993.

47 Kitange et al, 1996.

48 Boerma et al, 1998.

49 van Rie et al, 1999.

50 Knudsen and Slooff, 1992.

51 Bradley et al, 1992.

52 Such inequities have been well established for more developed economies, in particular the US. See 'Polarized communities, unhealthy lives: the effects of inequality and economic segregation on mortality in metropolitan America', a background paper by Waitzman and Smith, University of Idaho. A recent examination of data using the Luxembourg Income Study found that greater income inequality was related to premature mortality in 14 OECD countries; Lobmayer and Wilkinson, 2000. For a recent review of the relationships between health inequalities and housing, see Dunn, 2000.

53 Published in a special issue of *World Development* (November 1999), and by Brockerhoff, 1994; 1995; Timaeus and Lush, 1995; Stephens, 1996; Stephens et al, 1994.

54 Popkin, 1999, p 1908.

55 See Monteiro et al, 2000; South Africa Department of Health, 1998.

56 Brockerhoff, 1994; 1995.

57 Brockerhoff, 1993, p10, cited in Stephens, 1996.

58 See, for example, de Arias et al, 1999, and 'Improved Housing and Spraying to Fight the Spread of Chagas' Disease'. International Development Research Centre , Canada, available at http://voyager.idrc.ca/nayudamma/chaga_67e.html. For a recent longitudinal study of health effects of housing in the context of a more developed economy, see Marsh et al, 2000.

59 Stephens et al, 1994; Stephens, 1996.

60 Stephens et al, 1994; Timaeus and Lush, 1995.

61 Mitlin et al, 1996; Mutatkar, 1995; Wang'ombe, 1995; Atkinson et al, 1996; Todd, 1996; Harpham, 1997.

62 Mitlin et al, 1996.

63 Mitlin et al, 1996, pp 5–6.

64 See Almeida et al, 2000.

65 Molyneux et al, 1999.

# 10

# ASSESSMENTS OF THE URBAN ENVIRONMENT: WATER SUPPLY AND SANITATION SERVICES

In 1900, only one in ten people lived in cities but today half of the world population – well over 2900 million people – lives in urban areas. Already, 19 cities – 15 of them in the developing world – have populations exceeding 10 million. The result is that during the last century, the combined municipal and industrial use of water worldwide grew 24 times while agricultural use of water increased only five times.[1]

Only 1 per cent of the world's water resources provides the fresh water necessary for agriculture, industry and human consumption. To meet the present urban demand for water, more than half of Europe's cities, for example, are already overexploiting groundwater reserves and many countries report groundwater pollution. Mexico City has sunk more than 10 m over the past 70 years because of excessive withdrawal of water from groundwater sources. Bangkok is facing the problem of intrusion of saltwater into aquifers. The city of Johannesburg draws water from over 600 km away, from the Lesotho highlands. Despite these efforts, it is estimated that currently over 20 per cent of the world's population faceswater shortages. Furthermore, the constant search for freshwater for cities is a potential source of international conflict and water wars.

The problem of water in cities has not only been affected by the rapid process of urbanization but also by the unprecedented urbanization of poverty. It is estimated that over a thousand million people live without adequate shelter and access to basic services such as clean running water. In many countries, the poor pay exorbitant prices to private vendors for clean water. Paradoxically, as the poor struggle for water, in many cities up to half of the water supply is lost through leakages and illegal connections. Such inefficient and inequitable mechanisms for the delivery of water increase the likelihood of conflict within cities. Water supply and sanitation are of critical importance in the equitable and sustainable development of human settlements.

This part of the report reviews documents, databases and research of the past five years to identify important accomplishments, gaps and implications for addressing water and sanitation issues in human settlements programmes. The next section briefly reviews how water and sanitation issues were addressed in 1996 at Habitat II. It then updates that perspective with a brief survey of issues, accomplishments and data presented at The Hague conference.

## From Habitat II to The Hague World Water Forum: Global Patterns and Trends[2]

Habitat II followed the International Decade of Water Supply and Sanitation (1980–1990) which established many of the international organizations and programmes in this field. The Decade was also followed by critical appraisals of what was and was not accomplished.[3] Most notably, an international advisory group, the Water Supply and Sanitation Collaborative Council (WSSCC) was established, and the International Water and Sanitation Centre (IRC), the Global Applied Research Network (GARNET) and the United Nations agencies WMO, UNESCO and UNICEF expanded their information services. New research centres, for example the Water Engineering Development Centre (WEDC) at Loughborough University, were also established.

The second Global Report on Human Settlements, *An Urbanizing World*, included coverage of water and sanitation issues based mainly on country data, self-reported as percentages of urban and rural populations with access to safe water supplies and adequate sanitation services. City data were also self-reported as numbers of persons served for a selection of 160 cities.[4] Technical papers, newsletters and other materials presented in Istanbul provided a wealth of additional information, perspectives and examples of water and sanitation projects. *An Urbanizing World* did not indicate which water and sanitation problems were most acute or how they have been addressed. Similar types of data have been presented in annual reports of the World Bank and other United Nations agencies.

Many countries report 100 per cent access to safe water and sanitation. However, even in the US, regular government surveys find a percentage of homes that lack indoor plumbing, safe water supply and basic sanitation.[5] And those results do not include homeless persons or temporary migrant workers. Curiously, international reports often devote more attention to national than city-level data, though the latter present a more promising strategy for two reasons. First, urban units of analysis are more clearly specified, verifiable and relevant to policymaking. Second, urban-level data offer opportunities for comparative analysis (eg cities of comparable size, economic activity, governance structures and environmental context). Indeed, one clear recommendation is that information should be disaggregated to the local level.

As elaborated in the Water Supply and Sanitation Collaborative Council report for Vision 21 at The Hague in 2000, there are serious and recognized problems with data on the provision of safe water and adequate sanitation. Definitions and standards of 'access' vary across countries, data are not comparable over time, there is no independent collection or verification of data quality, and the sample design for estimating national levels of access is unclear.[6] Recent data suggest that international data seriously overstate urban access to safe water supplies and sanitation.[7]

### The Hague Water Vision 21: Water for People

The World Water Forum's 'Water for People' component of Vision 21 produced a report titled, *A Shared Vision for Hygiene, Sanitation, and Water Supply, and A Framework for Mobilisation of Action*. In contrast with previous reports, it did not reproduce national data tables on the percentages of populations *with* access to water. Instead, it produced graphs of the numbers of people *without* access to water and sanitation. Although subject to the reservations mentioned above, these graphs suggest that the number of people without safe drinking water has increased in Africa but declined significantly in Asia and the Pacific and in the world overall between 1980 and 1994. However, the number of people without adequate sanitation appears to have increased worldwide between 1980 and 1994 to almost 3000 million. The report discussed problems with those data and went on to present a qualitative discussion of the issues. It made 13 points ranging from the assertion of a human right to water (comparable to claims for a human right to housing) to increased emphasis on hygiene and sanitation, gender and institutions. The framework for action set targets for 2015 and 2025 and for improving monitoring strategies. Some organizations questioned whether sufficient emphasis was given to sanitation and its links with water and development.[8] In a speech to symposium delegates, Klaus Töpfer, Executive Director of the United Nations Environment Programme (UNEP), emphasized better urban governance as the key to the conservation of water. He called on cities and city authorities to adopt a six-point integrated strategy for managing urban water resources. The first step is for local authorities to carry out city-wide water audits. Second, policies need to be introduced to stop the pollution of water sources and to protect watersheds. Third, local authorities must use new technologies to minimize the amount of water lost through leakages and illegal connections. Fourth, socially sensitive pricing policies should be introduced which neither protect nor penalize the poor but remove any opportunity for profligate use. Fifth, city authorities must involve industrialists and community groups in the design of innovative ways of recycling wastewater. Sixth, each city needs to set up an integrated strategy for demand management. This includes launching city-wide campaigns to change people's attitudes towards freshwater conservation.[9] UNCHS and UNEP also organized a session on water problems in megacities and contributed to other sessions. However, overall, The Hague conference did not feature a comprehensive appraisal of water and sanitation in the context of human settlements development.

## Persistent and Emerging Gaps

One way to address water and sanitation problems in human settlements is to focus on key 'gaps': gaps between different kinds of water problems; gaps between places or people that are well served and those that are poorly served; gaps between previous objectives and actual accomplishments; gaps between what is known and unknown, and so on. Six such gaps and responses to them over the past five years are highlighted below.

### Gaps between water supply and sanitation

The gap between access to safe water supply and adequate sanitation has been recognized for decades, but appears to persist. Sanitation is deemed to be a key determinant of vulnerability to water-related disease, and the 'sanitation gap' may indicate where investment in water supply should be redirected towards sanitation and hygiene improvements. Data from *An Urbanizing World* indicate that many countries report large gaps between access to safe water and sanitation. Provision of improved water supplies, without adequate sanitation, can aggravate unhealthy drainage and disease vector problems. Additionally, hygiene behaviour may be as or more important than wastewater connections.[10] Some countries report no sanitation gap, or even a higher level of sanitation than water service. If these data are accurate, they should be examined either for possible lessons or to identify cases of severe water scarcity.

The Second World Water Forum concluded that the sanitation gap has persisted. Some 3000 million people are estimated to lack adequate access to sanitation, more than twice the number of persons who lack access to safe water supplies. The world sanitation gap and associated water-related disease vectors are especially worrisome in rapidly urbanizing regions. In response, an international Global Environmental Sanitation Initiative (GESI),[11] begun in 1997, was re-launched in 2000 to underscore its importance. Proposed sanitation programmes call for bridging between wastewater treatment, hygiene education, human waste disposal and collection and solid waste management.[12]

> Some 3000 million people lack adequate access to sanitation, more than twice those without safe water. The associated water-related diseases are especially worrisome in rapidly urbanizing regions. We need programmes that bridge between wastewater treatment, hygiene education, human waste disposal and collection and solid waste management

While some progress has been made in linking water supply and wastewater treatment, these water sector activities remain weakly linked with solid waste management. At the same time, the past five years have witnessed continuing advances in innovative sanitation initiatives such as the Orangi Pilot Project in Karachi, Pakistan,[13] and Sulabh

International in India.[14] Recent research has been extended to address the politics of sanitation and wastewater treatment.[15] The experience is not uncommon that water supply comes first and that sanitation comes later with more money and education.

In each case, there has been increasing recognition of the importance of sanitation in urban settlements, and of the importance of community-based schemes for empowerment of often-stigmatized and exploited social groups. Sulabh International, for example, began with the aim of improving the social status, as well as health and livelihood, of sweepers in India.[16] Discriminatory service based on ethnicity, particularly in situations and periods of violent conflict, is reported but rarely analysed. In cases where waste disposal involves toxic chemicals, the gap shifts from environmental equity to environmental justice,[17] bringing into focus interrelationships that need additional attention.[18]

### Gaps in gender equity and empowerment

Questions of equity and justice are also central to concerns about women's access to safe water and sanitation. The International Decade on Water Supply and Sanitation and the Dublin International Conference on Water and Environment (1992) succeeded in concentrating attention on women's heavy responsibilities for household and farm water management, and issues of equity, abuse and empowerment. Following the Decade, the IRC in The Netherlands has compiled and distributed a wealth of research and training material advancing the participation and empowerment of women.[19] The PROWWESS Project is dedicated to the Promotion of the Role of Women in Water and Environmental Sanitation. The Hague conference in 2000 also included papers on gender equity in household and farm water management; described the 'mainstreaming' of water and gender issues by IRC, the International Water Management Institute (IWMI), IUCN and the United Nations Development Fund for Women (UNIFEM); and it called for the establishment of a Gender Water Alliance.[20]

To what extent have these efforts eased women's burdens of village water carrying and vulnerability to urban water and sanitation inequities? The Women's Environment and Development Organization[21] analysed 18 case studies where women's activism has made a difference in water resources equity and environmental quality.[22] Research on women and water has also expanded in scope and depth.[23] However, research on water and gender continues to document cases of the greater vulnerability of girls to water-related diseases and lower levels of medical attention for diarrhoeal disease.[24] These inequities also translate into, and are compounded by, inequities in other social sectors, notably education.[25] On the one hand, mothers' coping strategies and resources for dealing with water-related disease episodes may have expanded with oral rehydration (ORS), hygiene and women's education programmes. Women are more effectively organizing at local to international scales on water issues ranging from village water systems to dams that threaten to inundate villages. On the other hand, many infrastructure programmes continue to exclude women from planning and implementation decisions. These inequities are compounded in other regions by changing household structures and outmigration of male family members for work, which can increase women's responsibilities and coping pressures in the home. Reports presented at The Hague 2000 conference indicate that community-level research and projects continue to advance, but it is not clear how those projects 'scale up' to larger metropolitan levels where male roles are more dominant.[26] International programmes have tended to equate 'gender' with women, failing to direct attention to how the changing roles of men in water management (eg in urban water utilities, flood control, irrigation and environmental engineering) affect equity and livelihood from the household to metropolitan scale.

### Gaps in institutional and financial restructuring

As in many sectors, the 1980s and 1990s were a period of institutional experiments and restructuring in water resources management. Institutional changes included increasing roles for non-governmental and activist organizations as well as changes in bureaucratic, legal and market institutions. The Dublin and Hague water conferences called for expanding social participation, devolution of authority, reform and coordination of bureaucratic organizations, and capacity building at all levels of governance. For example, Vision 21 called for the establishment of regional sanitation resource centres to expand programmes of training, education and access to technical information.[27]

Institutional experiments have focused on community-scale water and sanitation initiatives, several of which are featured in the UNCHS Best Practices database. Successes at the community level have sometimes proved difficult to 'scale up' to metropolitan, regional and national policy levels.[28] Weaknesses in municipal and state water bureaucracies have contributed to pressures for financial reforms, which range from improved billing practices to water pricing, marketing and, in some cases, full privatization of water and sanitation utilities. The 1992 Dublin Conference called for treating water as an 'economic good'. In the late 1990s, the World Bank, World Water Council and other organizations went further in testing and reporting on water pricing, marketing, property rights and privatization experiments in South America and elsewhere.[29] In these experiments, water is treated as an article of commerce and the utility as a business.[30]

### ● Privatization and commodification of water

In 2000, the World Water Commission also called for treating water as an economic good with targeted subsidies for the poor, but the conference was disrupted by protestors on precisely these points of privatization and water marketing. At about the same time as The Hague Conference, a 'water war' erupted in Cochabamba, Bolivia over privatization and pricing of domestic water services (see Box 10.1). Resistance to water marketing and privatization has arisen in many

**Box 10.1 Cochabamba's water war: organized protest against privatization of a public resource**

In April 2000, a coalition of peasant unions, student groups, working class unions and ultimately much of the general population as well as segments of the national security forces, joined to protest against the privatization of the public water system in the Bolivian city of Cochabamba, with a population of half a million.

The proposed sale, promoted by the World Bank, would transfer control of Cochabamba's water system from local authorities and the Bolivian government of Hugo Banzer to Aguas del Tunari, a multinational consortium of private companies that would 'dollarize' and sharply raise rates, in some cases to US$20 a month. The monthly minimum wage in Cochabamba is less than US$100.

In response to the announcement, a new organization, Coordinadora de Defensa del Agua (Coordinators in Defense of the Water) formed and a four-day general strike shut down the city. The government announced a reversal of the new water rates, but when it failed to abide by its promise, the Coordinadora called for public protest. The president sent thousands of heavily armed anti-riot police, who clashed violently with the unarmed protesters, resulting in more than 175 injured civilians. Forced by public anger, the government and water company again promised cancellation of the rate increases. However, with popular sentiment against the sale of the water system growing, Cochabamban residents demanded that the whole contract with Aguas del Tunari be cancelled and that the move towards privatization itself be reversed. A survey of about 60,000 residents showed that 90 per cent opposed privatization.

The people of Cochabamba went back to the streets and called for another general strike, which brought the city to a standstill. Coordinadora got the support of the peasants' union that was fighting a parallel struggle against the privatization of water provision in the countryside and against the Land Reform Law that would benefit big landowners. Thousands of peasants organized road blocks in six of Bolivia's nine districts. On 6 April, residents stormed the local city hall and surrounded the building where talks were taking place between the Coordinadora and the authorities. The government arrested all 15 leaders of the Coordinadora.

After massive demonstrations of peasants and Cochabamba residents, the protest leaders were released a day later and the archbishop announced that the government had agreed to cancel the contract to privatize the water system. However, soon after, the national government reversed this decision, claiming that regional authorities had made it without their permission. Next, the regional governor was replaced by a military officer, and the Banzer government declared a State of Emergency. It suspended basic rights, prohibiting strikes and gatherings of more than four people, while permitting legal use of the army to prevent civilian unrest.

The army arrested 22 union leaders in house-to-house searches, as the protests in Cochabamba grew into widespread discontent throughout the country. In the next few days, the military responded to separate disputes in Sucre where university students had gone on a hunger strike and in the Southern District of Tarija where the president had been declared a 'persona non-grata'. The army killed two people in an attack on 2000 peasants who were blocking a road 95 km from the capital La Paz, while military actions caused additional fatalities in ongoing protests in Cochabamba and Lahuachca.

Rather than quell popular discontent, the State of Emergency declaration further antagonized a population already upset with the government's attempts to privatize Cochabamba's water system and its wider disregard for basic needs that the sale represented. A call by rural teachers for a general national strike was joined by students and the main trade union. About 20,000 peasants marched to Cochabamba and the miners' union warned that its actions were just the beginning of the struggle against the Banzer government's acquiescence to sale of the country's resources to international companies. Aguas del Tunari announced that it was withdrawing from the deal.

Coordinadora called off the strikes when it became clear that the privatization of water provision in Cochabamba and in the countryside would not occur. The government agreed with peasant unions to pay 'compensation' to the families of the people who had been killed in the police violence. However, in April 2001, there were renewed tensions throughout the nation.

Although the immediate cause of the unrest had been removed, the continuing actions in Cochabamba reflect growing popular discontent with attempts to privatize the country's public resources, seen also elsewhere. Ecuador, for example, early in 2000, suffering a precipitous decline of living standards, 60 per cent rate of inflation and an economic depression after a decade of enforced structural adjustment policies during the 1990s, experienced massive protests by Indian peasants, urban workers, junior military officers and lower clergy. A few months later, Costa Rica also saw widespread turmoil, when a general strike by electricity, water and oil company workers, teachers, public hospital employees and city and federal government employees shut down the entire city of San Jose and demonstrators blocked major highways throughout the country, demanding cancellation of plans to privatize the national telecommunication and power industries. A Gallup poll showed that 64 per cent of the population opposed the proposed bill, which the national Constitutional Court declared to be unconstitutional.

These and similar episodes illustrate the emergence of broad-based coalitions acting in opposition to the dominant impacts of translocal, profit making and private accumulation.

**Source:** Netta van Vliet.

regions.[31] Although private water utilities are a relatively small proportion of all utilities in 2000, pressures for privatization are increasing worldwide. If this trend continues, access to safe water will increasingly become a human rights issue.

Proponents of privatization argue that sound financial management can benefit the poor who are less likely to be served by underfinanced and deteriorating infrastructure.

Squatter settlements often rely on water vendors at tens to hundreds of times the cost of water supplied by properly financed private or quasi-public utilities.[32] Critics stress the lack of private accountability to public needs and regulation; higher risks of disconnection and reduced service for the poor; market segmentation and formation of 'dual systems' where some are served at higher, and others lower, levels; and failure to follow through with proposed subsidies for the poor.[33] Some utilities and legislatures object to requiring higher-income customers to subsidize low-income customers on grounds of equity.[34]

Research has also examined the impacts of commodification in the UK, which privatized all of its regional water utilities in 1990. British water companies were subjected to regulatory oversight by the Office of Water (OFWAT).[35] Concerns about the effects of privatization on the poor ranged from disconnections to financial distress and increased water-borne disease.[36] Initially, disconnections for non-payment increased dramatically. Increased public regulation and enforcement of those regulations by OFWAT followed, to the point where British water utilities now have fewer disconnections than before privatization. Strong public regulation and a parliamentary threat of banning disconnections altogether were key factors in reducing social impacts; but concerns persist about long-term consequences for the poor. The US National Research Council (NRC) is currently studying privatization of water provision in the US.[37] In rural areas, 'small systems' that serve towns receive less technical and financial assistance from public sources than larger cities, and there is concern that they would receive even lower service from private utilities.[38]

Although the number of case studies is increasing, they often employ different methods and are rarely comparable across the full range of impacts of concern.[39] Clear conceptualization of 'access' to safe water and sanitary conditions (eg as compared with 'rights' to such resources) is important for increasing the comparability of case studies.[40] More research is also needed on customer access and exclusion under different water rate, tariff and billing practices.[41]

Political analyses of water and sanitation institutions and economies have broadened in the past five years to ask persistent questions about which social groups are, and are not, served;[42] about the evolving roles of water vendors, entrepreneurs, sanitation workers and microfinance organizations;[43] about the special problems of restructuring in borderland regions;[44] and about emergency water and sanitation needs in areas of conflict and post-disaster reconstruction.[45] The coming decade will see broad institutional experimentation in the provision of water and sanitation that will require rigorous evaluation.[46]

## Gaps between water infrastructure and environmental management

Water and sanitation have often been viewed as 'infrastructure and services' programmes, while broader links with and implications for urban ecosystems are neglected. Urban withdrawals from streams and aquifers have long-term consequences for sustaining human benefits from natural hydrologic, aquatic and riparian ecosystems. Even well-sewered cities can discharge untreated wastes into urban watercourses, polluting drinking, bathing, washing and fishing waters.

The Istanbul+5 *Guidelines for Country Reporting* address several water and sanitation indicators under the heading of 'Environmental Management' (indicator 13: water consumption; indicator 14: price of water; and indicator 16: wastewater treated) along with urban population, transport, air pollution, solid waste disposal and natural hazards mitigation.[47] The relationships between these environmental indicators are not yet entirely clear, but some research has begun to link water supply and sanitation variables to measures of 'ecosystem services' and 'ecosystem health', which are in turn related to economic and human health benefits.[48] Other projects have employed concepts of 'sustainability' or 'carrying capacity' from environmental management to address issues in infrastructure planning.[49]

More immediately pertinent to the water and sanitation sector are emerging programmes in 'ecological sanitation'.[50] Ecological sanitation employs biological methods of waste treatment, disposal and reuse (eg wastewater lagoon and ponding systems) and seeks to link infrastructural development with environmental restoration. 'Ecological sanitation' encompasses a broad range of linkages between water use, land use, wastewater management, and urban agriculture.[51]

---

Ecological sanitation employs biological methods of waste treatment, disposal and reuse and links infrastructural development and land use with environmental restoration

---

In Japan, for example, the UNEP International Environmental Technology Centre (1999) is focusing on urban water supply in ways that reduce eutrophication in lakes.[52] In a related vein, some organizations have sought to rediscover and adapt traditional water management systems to new urban and rural settlements. An outstanding example is the Centre for Science and Environment's study entitled, *Dying Wisdom: Rise, Fall and Potential of India's Traditional Water Harvesting Systems*.[53] Urban environmental hazards have implications, often little examined, for water supply and sanitation. In this connection, UN Disaster Information Briefs often cite disruptions of, and need for, emergency freshwater supplies and infrastructure restoration. Similarly, the World Bank has recently sought to link project lending with disaster mitigation, and the International Development Research Centre (IDRC) has launched a water demand management programme in North Africa and the Middle East.[54]

To be effective over the long term, these efforts must be integrated with urban ecosystem processes, including those most closely related to water supply and sanitation. Cities should begin to monitor key ecological variables along waterfronts, river corridors, riparian habitats, wetlands and floodplains. Urban riverfront restoration programmes, which are increasingly promoted (eg on the Sabarmati River in Ahmedabad, India[55]), should include baseline measurement and monitoring to assess their actual vs. planned benefits. This theme of baselines, or benchmarking, and *ex post* evaluation is elaborated opposite.

## Gaps between first principles, best practices and ex post evaluation

The past five years have shown increasing attention to defining first principles and best practices of water and sanitation management. The 1992 Dublin Water Conference identified four principles:

1   water is a common, shared resource;
2   water should be managed at the lowest practicable level of governance;
3   women's roles in water management should be recognized and empowered;
4   water should be treated as an economic good.

Since Dublin and Habitat II, there have been increasing calls for recognizing a 'human right' to water, comparable with arguments that housing is a human right.[56] The legal and ethical basis for a human right to water in domestic law is strong in some societies; for example the 'right of thirst' for humans and animals in Islamic law, and weak in others; for example US water law.[57] There is growing support for such claims in international law (eg in the United Nations Convention on the Rights of the Child; see also the ascendancy of human rights-based approaches reviewed in Chapter 3).

The prospects for a 'rights-based' approach should be explored. Although some countries do not recognize a strong 'natural right' to water, they may enforce 'moral duties' to provide water or allow access in certain circumstances. Excluded social groups (especially indigenous groups) may have 'paper rights' to water, which are never transformed into the 'wet water' needed for economic development.[58] Arguments for treating water as a human right need not conflict with valuation of water as an economic good. But the complex relations among such views have not been resolved in theory or on the ground.

It seems crucial to have more detailed ex post evaluations of urban water and sanitation experiments. While there are many assessments of proposed projects and policies, there are few detailed ex post evaluations or post audits of the actual impacts that completed projects have on people and places.

> There are few detailed ex post evaluations or post audits of the actual impacts that completed projects have on people and places

A detailed post audit is one that is comprehensive, integrated, long-term, cumulative, participatory and adaptive.[59] A comprehensive evaluation encompasses social, economic, environmental and political impacts. An integrated evaluation considers the interactions among those diverse impacts. Long-term means evaluation on timescales from years to decades. Participatory and cumulative assessments are important in the urban water and sanitation field where thousands of household and neighbourhood actions contribute to aggregate urban impacts. Finally, post audits should be adaptive, contributing directly to the adjustment

of policies, projects and programmes as new evidence of their impacts becomes available through monitoring.

Few evaluations fit these criteria of ex post evaluation. An important exception is the re-examination of an influential study of water supply in East African villages and towns titled, Drawers of Water: Domestic Water Use in East Africa.[60] This restudy of the same villages, 30 years later, represents the most detailed longitudinal examination of community water systems to date.[61]

Preliminary findings indicate which areas have maintained or improved water supplies, and which places have lost ground. Overall, piped water systems appear to have been less well maintained than unpiped systems over the past 30 years. Other excellent experiments – such as the Lahore Old City Cultural Heritage and Infrastructure Upgrading Project in Lahore, Pakistan – have not had adequate baseline documentation or monitoring to determine whether and where the project has met its objectives.[62]

The UNCHS Best Practices Database incorporates a measure of ex post evaluation. It includes some 20 projects that focus primarily on water and sanitation, as well as many other projects that have water resources components. They range from innovative sewer construction technologies in industrialized countries to low-income water and sanitation programmes, and from watershed protection to water conservation and wastewater treatment. Some examples from the 1998 database are listed alphabetically in Table 10.1.

The diversity of these water-related projects is striking, and the database helps to facilitate comparison by classifying projects by scale (from village to global), ecosystem, and region as well as by subject category. For the most part, the descriptions of these cases are brief and self-documented. They become icons for replication, but their database entries are not necessarily updated to reflect monitoring results, nor are the limits of replicability discussed. Several other examples of best practices in the water and sanitation field stand out.

**Table 10.1**

**UNCHS Best Practices Database: water resource examples, 1998**

| | |
|---|---|
| Australia | Southwell Park Wastewater Recycling Pilot Scheme |
| Australia | Western Australia Sewerage and Wastewater Quality Program |
| Austria | Sewer construction/the Viennese Approach |
| Colombia | The Community as Drinking Water Provider in a Low Income Area |
| Egypt | National Public Scheme for Conservation of Drinking Water |
| Egypt | The Aqueduct Area Project: Urban Environmental Management |
| Honduras | Empowering Poor Communities in Tegucigalpa: Water Supply |
| Japan | Fukuoka: Water Conservation Conscious City |
| Kenya | Maina Village Community Water and Sanitation Project |
| Kenya | Water for Work Project |
| Malawi | Piped Supplies for Small Communities in Malawi |
| Papua New Guinea | Building of Water Tank and House Using Indigenous Materials |
| Romania | New Technologies for the Water Treatment Plant in Slobozia |
| Senegal | Community Based Environmental Sanitation and Hygiene Project |
| Senegal | Women Run Waste Management and Recycling Programme |
| Spain | Navarra, Water and Waste Management |
| Spain | Zaragoza: A City Saving Water |
| Sudan | Rural Towns Water Supply Project in South Darfur State |
| Sudan | Upgrading of the Water Supply System in Nyala and El Geneina |
| United Republic of Tanzania | The Health through Sanitation and Water (HESAWA) Programme |
| USA | Integrated Watershed Management: Government and NGO Partnership |

**Source:** http://www.bestpractices.org/.

The Orangi Pilot Project in Karachi, Pakistan, has had detailed documentation, monitoring and adaptation over the course of more than two decades, conducted by project participants as well as professional planners.[63] For water-borne diseases, the International Centre for Diarrhoeal Disease Research, Bangladesh (ICDDR,B) has conducted long-term health and demographic monitoring at its Matlab and Dhaka sites to evaluate and adapt interventions in diarrhoeal disease reduction, including oral rehydration therapies and hygiene behaviours.[64]

In a recent study of a best practices case, the Indore Slum Rehabilitation project has been critically re-evaluated.[65] This project had developed a concept of slum networking to guide investment in waste collection, stormwater drainage, tree planting and park development. An independent survey of slum residents raised questions about the level, effectiveness and sustainability of these programmes.[66] Project leaders responded with a rebuttal of the criticisms.[67] The example points to the potential for developing innovative methods of critical project evaluation.

The main point here is that *ex post* evaluation is rarely undertaken to determine whether, in fact, people and the places where they live are better or worse off after adopting various first principles or best practices.

> *Ex post* evaluation should be undertaken to determine whether, in fact, people and the places where they live are better or worse off when adopting first principles or best practices

In addition, there have been few comparisons of best practices by city size, subsector or regional context. How different are the problems of historic centres, peri-urban areas and secondary cities? How different are the peri-urban problems of different cities?[68]

For larger urban water utilities, the World Bank has developed a benchmarking and indicator system.[69] Its *Water and Wastewater Utilities Indicators* include operational and financial variables. Major classes of operational variables are water consumption, distribution, unaccounted for water, wastewater piping and flows, wastewater treatment, personnel and equipment. Financial indicators focus on efficiency, leverage, liquidity, profitability and ratios with operational variables. These indicators address utilities management issues. However, they do not yet include the outcomes or impacts of water and wastewater treatment services for the people and their environments.

> Existing indicators measure aspects of utilities management, such as efficiency, leverage, liquidity, profitability. They should also include impacts of water and wastewater treatment services for people and their environments

The International Decade for Water and Sanitation (1980–1990) monitored project inputs and activities. Participating organizations, such as the Water and Sanitation for Health project assessed the 'Lessons Learned'

from scores of local projects in different regions.[70] Most of those lessons were supported by qualitative and expert judgement, as detailed project baseline data and monitoring designs were rare.

Following the International Decade, three international organizations have maintained continuing programmes of evaluation, documentation and information dissemination concerning water and sanitation. Among universities, the WEDC at Loughborough University has made a sustained commitment to applied water and sanitation research in developing countries.[71] It organizes bi-annual conferences on water and sanitation around the world, and it also supports the GARNET,[72] an electronic database of applied research on water and sanitation.[73] The IRC International Water and Sanitation Centre[74] in The Netherlands is the leading global repository for research and training material on water and sanitation. Together with the WSSCC, it publishes *Source*, a newsletter that reports on case studies as well as new publications and meetings. The WSSCC serves as a consultative and coordinating organization for multilateral and non-governmental organizations working in the field of water and sanitation, and it prepares position papers (eg the Water for People statement for The Hague Vision 21 meetings). Further, a new initiative is underway to manage global water information systems, which may include archiving of *ex post* evaluations and an international strategy for information management.[75]

## Gaps between water, sanitation and human settlements policy initiatives

The preceding discussion indicates a need for stronger coordination between water, sanitation and settlement policies. Water and sanitation programmes cannot be properly planned or evaluated without taking into account the structure and dynamics of the settlements they serve. The quality of life in human settlements depends in significant measure on their water and sanitation services.

> There is a need for stronger coordination of water, sanitation programmes and human settlement development policies

The programmes mentioned above recognize these connections, but in practice gaps persist between these subsectors of municipal governance. The Habitat Agenda does not make strong links between water and sanitation and other aspects of human settlement. Similarly, the World Water Forum gave limited attention to human settlements issues, programmes and policies. The Hague 'Water for People' documents did not cite UNCHS publications on water for cities,[76] while the vision document for water and sanitation, *A Shared Vision for Hygiene, Sanitation, and Water Supply, and A Framework for Mobilisation of Action*, lacked an explicit analytical approach appropriate to human settlement questions.

Representatives from WSSCC and IRC made important contributions to Habitat II in 1996, and UNCHS and

UNEP made important contributions on 'Water and Megacities' at The Hague. But five years after Habitat II, it is worth asking whether water, sanitation and settlements programmes are adequately integrated, or coordinated, with one another. Evidence indicates that this is not the case.

A case where integration of water, environment and human settlements development policies seems promising is the joint UNCHS/UNEP Managing Water for Cities in Africa.[77] Established in 1999 as a follow-up to the Cape Town Declaration of 1997, this programme is being implemented in seven demonstration cities: Abidjan (Côte d'Ivoire), Accra (Ghana), Addis Ababa (Ethiopia), Dakar (Senegal), Johannesburg (South Africa), Lusaka (Zambia) and Nairobi (Kenya). These rapidly growing cities plan to jointly investigate approaches to water demand management, water supply expansion and environmental protection. Their objective is to promote an integrated approach to managing urban water resources (see Box 10.2). They also plan to compare the applicability of technical, behavioural and financial innovations in other regions of Africa. Ideally, the design of this regional programme will be subject to critical feedback and comparison with urban water programmes in other regions of the world.

Further, recognizing that urban demands for water can affect people in neighbouring regions or countries, UNEP has been working on transboundary water-related issues through the Global Environment Facility (GEF) and the Global International Waters Assessment (GIWA) aimed at developing a comprehensive strategic assessment to identify priorities for remedial actions in international waters.

## Implications

This review of water and sanitation in human settlements points towards several overarching implications for an appraisal of progress in implementing the Habitat Agenda. These implications cut across the six gaps discussed above. This discussion concentrates on three such implications.

### Focus on gaps

The first implication of this review is that it is important to 'focus on the gaps', rather than broadly review conditions of water and sanitation infrastructure. This review identified six gaps and some promising approaches to address them. The Vision 21 process at The Hague also sought to identify water and sanitation goals for the next quarter-century. However, that process did not give as detailed attention to the settlement context of those gaps and goals as is warranted. The Istanbul +5 process could help to supplement, refine, contextualize and thereby advance those long-term goals.

### Improve data, analytical tools and historical reviews

A second implication concerns the utility of international water and sanitation data and the analytical tools needed to monitor and guide human settlements programmes. Questions are increasingly raised about the reliability and

---

**Box 10.2 Conserving water must start in cities**

Only 1 per cent of the world's water resources is freshwater available for human use. This limited resource has to provide a thirsty world with all its needs for agriculture, industry and human consumption. As urban growth continues, many regions of the world are already experiencing severe water stress. Aside from the unnecessary death and suffering that results from lack of safe water, economic development is seriously hampered, food production becomes expensive and many production and service industries become dysfunctional. Urban water demands have a serious environmental impact on water resources, both by overexploitation of fragile freshwater reserves and unacceptable disposal of wastes and toxic substances.

UNCHS (Habitat) and UNEP have recently initiated a project to assist African cities to manage water more effectively. Funded by the Turner Foundation, the project will address issues of water conservation and demand management as well as protection from the effects of urbanization, and is meant to become an example for other regions of the world.

The project has three components: (1) an information and awareness campaign to sensitize all stakeholders to the need for conserving precious resources; (2) a water demand management programme that will demonstrate the benefits to be gained from progressive water tariffs, low-cost water saving technologies and repairing of leaks; and (3) a programme on protecting water quality through policies and planning concerning effluent treatment and discharge from polluting sources.

Promoting good policies and building capacity to manage water more effectively is necessary both to avert a crisis and to reduce the debt burden of developing nations by delaying or reducing the need for large capital investments.

**Source:** Adapted from 'World Water Day: Conserving Water Must Start in Cities', United Nations Centre for Human Settlements (Habitat); released 18 March 1999.

---

utility of national water and sanitation data. National data cannot be made useful, it seems, without major expenditure to refine, standardize and implement scientific sampling designs and techniques, and to provide for independent scientific review. As water and sanitation are generally municipal responsibilities (supported to varying degrees by national financing), it seems more promising to focus on improving urban data. Although urban water statistics face increasing criticism as well, they can be more readily verified and corrected.[78] The development of indicators by UNCHS (Habitat) is also an attempt to improve the availability of data to allow regular monitoring and evaluation as a basis for policy.[79]

In addition to improving the quality of urban water data, the analytical basis for making comparisons and drawing inferences needs attention. At present, comparative studies often employ qualitative case study methods.[80] Even in qualitative studies, greater emphasis is needed on the analytical aims and logic of case study selection, comparison and analogies used to frame policy recommendations. Indeed, it is worth asking: when and how do comparative studies make a practical difference for urban water, sanitation and settlement programmes? For example, during the 1990s when South Africa looked around the world for water policies that worked in other regions, it needed a framework for assessing experiences elsewhere.[81] The UNCHS Best Practices Database provides a useful tool for organizing comparative analyses, in part through its classification of cases by region, scale, ecosystem, and category. As these best practices are subjected to more detailed *ex post* evaluation, they may become even more valuable for comparative research.

Likewise, as urban-scale data improve, quantitative analysis of urban datasets should more effectively complement case study research. In comparison, the observational networks for weather and hydrology are more sophisticated than those for monitoring urban water use and problems. The global urban observatory of UNCHS (Habitat), the water and wastewater utilities indicators of the World Bank and the Large Cities Statistics Project (LCSP) of the International Union of Local Authorities (IULA), the International Statistical Institute (ISI), the Network on Urban Research in the European Union (NUREC), United Nations Statistical Division (UNSD) and UNCHS (Habitat) are useful starts, but they need to go further.[82] Quantitative monitoring of water and sanitation should encompass long-term social and environmental 'impacts' (ie health, livelihood, equity, human development and ecosystem indicators) as well as project 'outputs' (eg length of pipe and number of taps).

> **Monitoring of water and sanitation programmes should encompass long-term social and environmental impacts on health, livelihood, equity and ecosystems, as well as project outputs in terms of number of taps and length of pipe**

Finally, there are few historical studies of international urban water and sanitation programmes. Recent research on irrigation and forestry, in contrast, makes increasing use of historical and cultural geographic research to help to explain current problems and to evaluate alternative solutions to those problems. One of the great accomplishments of many cities in the 20th century was the provision of relatively inexpensive, widely accessible, high-quality urban water supplies and municipal and industrial wastewater treatment systems. How did it happen? And how did water and sanitation innovations diffuse through national and international urban networks? Urban historians have attributed the establishment of modern public water supplies not so much to altruism as to broad civic concern about fires and communicable diseases that crossed class boundaries in late 19th- and early 20th-century cities.[83]

> **Urban historians have attributed the establishment of modern public water supplies not so much to altruism as to broad civic concern about fires and communicable diseases that crossed class boundaries. Universal access is in the interest not just of the poor, but of the whole of society**

Universal access is in the interest not just of the poor, but of the whole of society. As urban spatial structure and environmental hazards change, will the commitment to uniform public water standards give way to segmentation of water and sanitation services based on ability to pay? Other historians have reasserted the importance of ethics, altruism and philanthropy in public water systems ranging from Baroque Rome to Victorian England and Ottoman Istanbul.[84] These historical, cultural and geographical perspectives enrich our understanding of current water and sanitation problems.

## Develop clear objectives for coordinating water, sanitation and human settlements programmes

The 'gaps' discussed in the preceding review all imply that some kind of integration is needed – integration of water and sanitation, water and gender, infrastructure and environment, institutions and finances, monitoring and evaluation, and so on. Although integration is often desirable, differences and resistance to integration are sometimes warranted. For example, it has been stated that:

> *'Women do not want to be mainstreamed into a polluted stream. We want to clean the stream and transform it into a fresh and flowing body – One that moves in a new direction – a world at peace, that respects human rights for all, renders economic justice and provides a sound and healthy environment.'*[85]

Resistance can help to identify pressure points and new directions of development.

# Basing Policies on Inaccurate Data? The Importance of Critical Scrutiny[86]

International statistics and many national statistics greatly overstate the extent to which urban populations are adequately served with water and sanitation in light of many detailed city studies that show far worse levels of water and sanitation provision.[87] This disparity is important because it appears to bias priorities in the allocation of support, failing to target resources to areas in greater need.

> **Current statistics greatly overstate the extent to which urban populations are adequately served with safe water and adequate sanitation**

This section of the report compares official statistics on provision for water and sanitation in urban areas at a global, regional (continental) and national level with statistics drawn from more detailed city studies. It also questions the criteria used by governments and international agencies to define what is 'access to safe water' and 'access to sanitation' since it is often the inappropriateness of these criteria (rather than the actual statistics) that underlie the inaccuracy of national statistics.

## The problem of inaccurate data

Official statistics suggest that problems with provision for water and sanitation in urban areas affect only a minority of urban dwellers. For instance, statistics for 1994 suggested that only 300 million urban dwellers were not served by water supplies in Africa, Asia, Latin America and the Caribbean,[88] which implies that 80 per cent of the urban population is served. UNDP's *Human Development Report 1996* states that by the early 1990s, 87 per cent of the urban population of 'developing countries' had access to 'safe' water and 72 per cent had access to sanitation.[89] This same source also included a table, suggesting that a considerable proportion of low- and middle-income countries had 80–95 per cent of their urban populations adequately served both by safe water and sanitation (see Table 10.2).[90] It even suggested that 63 per cent of sub-Saharan Africa's urban population had safe water and that 56 per cent had provision for sanitation.

Official statistics also suggest that there has been considerable progress in improving provision, especially for water, and that urban inhabitants are far better served than rural inhabitants. There has indeed been great progress in some countries and particular cities, and there are cities in Latin America and Asia where virtually all households now have water piped into their home.

However, official statistics greatly overstate the extent and quality of provision. There are two main reasons why this occurs. The first is the use of inappropriate criteria to define what is 'adequate' and 'safe'. The second is that governments often provide inaccurate statistics and the international agencies who publish these do not publicly question their accuracy.

International agencies such as the World Bank, the World Health Organization or the United Nations Development Programme are 'inter-governmental bodies' with governing boards made up of representatives of national governments. This makes it difficult (or impossible) for them to openly question the validity of what their member governments report.[91]

> Data on water and sanitation provision are often deficient because the statistics are inaccurate and because inappropriate criteria are used to define what is safe and adequate

## ● Water provision

In regard to the criteria used for assessing provision, for water supply to be 'adequate', it must be: of good quality, readily available, piped to the house (or at least very close by), and affordable. But many governments include in their official statistics of people 'adequately' served all households with access to public standpipes or with some form of water-supply infrastructure within 100 m of their home.

Thus, among those classified as 'adequately served' are the inhabitants of settlements where hundreds of people have to share each standpipe, and even if the public standpipes are poorly maintained or contain contaminated water. Households are still classified as served by piped systems, even if water is only available in the piped system intermittently, or as little as one or two hours a day – or even only once a week or fortnight. For instance, in Mombasa, Kenya, there are many households who have water pipes that extend into their homes but who have seen no water in these pipes for years.[92]

> Among those classified as 'adequately served' are the inhabitants of settlements where hundreds of people have to share a single standpipe and others who have access to public standpipes that are poorly maintained or contain contaminated water

Perhaps the strongest evidence for the inaccuracies in official statistics comes from comparing official statistics for provision in urban areas with data from detailed city studies.

> Evidence for inaccurate statistics comes from comparisons of official data on urban provision with data from detailed city studies

Table 10.2 shows figures for the proportion of some urban populations, allegedly having access to safe water and sanitation, according to UNDP's *Human Development Report 1996* and the World Bank's *World Development Indicators 2000*. According to the UNDP Report, 99 per cent of the urban population of Zimbabwe and Bangladesh had safe water by the early 1990s; for Pakistan, it was 96 per cent, for India 85 per cent, and for the Philippines 93 per cent. The World Bank's *World Indicators 2000* suggests more modest figures for urban Bangladesh and Pakistan but it gives similar figures for Zimbabwe, the Philippines and India. Both publications also suggest that many African nations other than Zimbabwe have urban populations that are relatively well served.

It is difficult to reconcile the figures for India in Table 10.2 with the profiles of provision for water and sanitation for many cities in India, which show that much less than 85 per cent of their population is adequately served with 'safe water' and much less than 70 per cent has adequate sanitation.[93] Similarly, it is difficult to reconcile the official statistic of 96 per cent of Pakistan's urban population with safe water in the UNDP Report (or the lower figure of 77 per cent in the World Bank report) with the documented lack of water provision for Karachi and Faisalabad since these two cities contain a sizeable proportion of Pakistan's total urban population. It is similarly difficult to see how 70 per cent of Ghana's urban population can have had access to safe water in the early 1990s, given the levels of water provision documented in Kumasi and Accra.

One particular example of unreliable statistics comes from Kumasi, Ghana's second-largest city. The official

**Table 10.2**

**Proportion of the urban population reportedly having 'access to safe water' and 'access to sanitation' in selected countries, 1990–1996**

| Country | Statistics from the UNDP *Human Development Report 1996* | | Statistics from the World Bank's *World Development Indicators 2000* | |
|---|---|---|---|---|
| | % of urban population with access to safe water | % of urban population with access to sanitation | % of urban population with access to safe water | % of urban population with access to sanitation |
| Bangladesh | 99 | 75 | 47 | 77 |
| Burkina Faso | na | 42 | | 8 |
| Ethiopia | 91 | 97 | 90 | n d |
| Ghana | 70 | 53 | 70 | 53 |
| India | 85 | 0 | 85 | 46 |
| Indonesia | 79 | 73 | 78 | 73 |
| Jamaica | na | 100 | 92 | 89 |
| Nigeria | 63 | 40 | 63 | 61 |
| Pakistan | 96 | 62 | 77 | 53 |
| Philippines | 93 | 79 | 91 | 88 |
| Sudan | 84 | 79 | 66 | 79 |
| United Republic of Tanzania | 67 | 74 | 65 | 97 |
| Uganda | 47 | 94 | 47 | 75 |
| Zimbabwe | 99 | 9 | 99 | 99 |

**Note:** The World Bank figures are said to be the most recent year available in the period 1990–1996.

## Box 10.3 The burden of water collection

Obtaining water often involves significant inconvenience in the time spent in collection, the physical effort required and negative health effects. In many ways, the burden of water collection for unpiped households seems to have increased during the last 30 years. These findings emerge from a follow-up on the first large-scale assessment of domestic water use and environmental health in Africa.[i] The study looked at the use of water for consumption, hygiene and amenities in household life. It also examined the cost of water in monetary terms as well as, less readily measured, amount of energy and time spent. It recorded information on per capita and total household water use, while identifying factors influencing variations in use and effects on health.

### Who bears the burden?

As was the case 30 years ago, women bear primary responsibility for water collection. However, some changes have occurred. For example, there has been an increase in child drawers as well as in the number of males, notably teenagers, collecting water for commercial purposes.

Neither has the principal mode of transport changed. Women and children continue to walk to and from the source, carrying water on their heads using jerrycans and saucepans. As a consequence they are prone to experiencing health problems such as headaches, general fatigue and pains in the chest, neck and waist.

However, to a large extent, the mode of transporting water depends on the sex of the drawer. Among males there has been an increase in the use of bicycles and hand-driven carts. These are the principal modes used by vendors (75 per cent), enabling them to transport large quantities of water.

### How many trips are made?

On average, the daily number of trips for water made per household increased from 2.6 in 1967 to 3.9 in 1997. This is largely due to the increase in water use by unpiped households.

### How far are the sources?

Drawers can travel considerable distances to obtain water. On average the distance covered to collect the daily water for one household decreased slightly from 428 to 405 m. This decrease is in part due to the improved accessibility of protected sources such as hydrants, standpipes and wells. It also reflects the increase in vendors supplying water direct to the house. However, the decrease is not uniform. At some sites, households reported that sources that were previously available had dried up and as a consequence they had to walk longer distances to the next source.

**Note:** i White et al, 1972.
**Source:** Thompson, 2000.

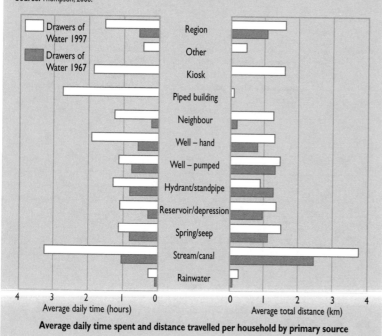

**Average daily time spent and distance travelled per household by primary source**

figures suggest that 99 per cent of its population are adequately served with water.[94] However, a recent report states that although three-quarters of the Kumasi population is served with piped water, large numbers only have access through shared taps or standpipes; long waits and queues are common. Even where there is a piped network, water pressure is often inadequate and the service not continuous. Only 10 per cent of households have indoor plumbing. Water provision is particularly poor on the urban periphery where there is rapid urban growth.[95]

Often, a high proportion of those reported as having access to piped water have access only to public standpipes. Where water is only available at a public place – for instance a communal well or public standpipe – the quantity used by each household will be influenced by the time and energy needed to collect and carry water back to the home. Collecting water this way can be very time-consuming. It is common for 200 to 500 persons to share a standpipe and many government agencies regard this as 'adequate'. In one part of Dakar, Senegal, a survey in the late 1980s found that there were 1513 persons per tap.[96] In Nouakchott, Mauritania, only 179 standpipes were installed to cover the entire urban area, which meant an average of only one standpipe for around 2500 inhabitants.[97] In many areas of Luanda, Angola, there is one standpipe for 600–1000 persons.[98]

> In one part of Dakar, there were 1513 persons per tap, while in many areas of Luanda there is only one standpipe for 600–1000 inhabitants. In Nouakchott, Mauritania, there was one standpipe for every 2500 residents

For those reliant on standpipes, the difficulties in getting the water are often much increased by the fact that water is only available a few hours a day; or water pressure is very low, so it takes a long time to fill up each person's water containers. It also requires much physical effort to carry water any distance. If a household keeps its water consumption down to only 160 litres a day (well below the minimum recommended level), this still means carrying a total weight of 160 kilos of water each day from the standpipe (or well) to the home. A recent study found that for many households in East Africa the burden of collecting water had increased over the last 30 years (Box 10.3).[99]

The assumption that households with piped water supplies are adequately served can also be questioned for many cities. Many piped water systems do not have water in them for much of the time. For instance, in Zaria (Nigeria), a survey in 1995 found that 11 per cent of those who had piped water received water one day in two, while 4 per cent received it once a week or once a fortnight, and 12 per cent rarely or never received water.[100] In Mombasa (Kenya), very few parts of the city have a continuous water supply (on average, it is available for only 2.9 hours a day); some parts of the city have had no water in the pipes for several years.[101] The availability of water supplies in several Indian cities, including Chennai/Madras and Hyderabad, deteriorated during the long drought of the early 1990s to the point where water was available for only two hours in very 48. In Madras, the situation deteriorated further in 1993 to the point where water was only available every third day.[102] Even in India's capital city, Delhi, water supplies are intermittent for large sections of the population, including one-fifth that receives water for less than four hours a day.[103] Data on water provision from water utilities in 50 cities in Asia and the Pacific during the mid-1990s highlighted how many provided water for only a few hours a day including Karachi (four hours), Chennai (four hours), Mumbai/Bombay (five hours), Bandung (six hours), Kathmandu (six hours) and Faisalabad (seven hours).[104] In 26 of the 50 cities, the utilities claimed to provide water 24 hours a day but consumer surveys, drawing from 100 randomly selected customers in each city, suggested that the water utilities overstated the time for which water was available.[105]

> Water provision in 50 cities in Asia and the Pacific was often for just a few hours per day, even though the utilities in 26 of these cities claimed to provide water around the clock

Thus, it is likely that tens of millions (and perhaps hundreds of millions) of urban dwellers, classified in official statistics as having 'safe water', still face great difficulties in obtaining clean and sufficient water for good health.

## ● Sanitation

A comparable gap between reality and official statistics is also evident for sanitation. Official statistics suggest that by 1994, more than half the urban population in Africa had adequate provision for sanitation, as did two-thirds of the population of Asia and close to three-quarters of the urban population of Latin America and the Caribbean.[106] However, these figures cannot be taken at face value. For example, 100 per cent of Jamaica's urban population was said to have had sanitation by the early 1990s, but a report on Kingston, Jamaica's largest city, indicates that only 18 per cent of the population are connected to sewers; 27 per cent have soakaway pits, 47 per cent use pit latrines and 8 per cent report no sanitary facilities at all. Similarly, one cannot but wonder about the credibility of statistics showing high levels of sanitation provision in urban populations by the early 1990s in Zimbabwe (99 per cent), Uganda (94 per cent) and Ethiopia (97 per cent).

Some 97 per cent of Tanzania's urban population is said to have had access to sanitation by the early 1990s. However, this statistic cannot be reconciled with the many reports that detail the inadequacies in provision for sanitation in Dar es Salaam (see Box 10.4) which contains a considerable proportion of the national urban population. Likewise, the statistic for the Philippines cannot be reconciled with reports on provision for sanitation in Manila and Cebu.

One possible reason why official statistics exaggerate the extent of provision for sanitation is because they include any household that in the census or some household survey is said to have access to a public latrine as having 'adequate sanitation'. Thus, they include those who have to compete with 100 or more other people for access

to each latrine and where maintenance and cleaning of public latrines is so poor that using the latrine itself is a major health hazard and many people avoid using it. For instance, 40 per cent of Kumasi's population is dependent on public latrines and thus officially classified as served with sanitation, even if many defecate in the open because they cannot afford the wait or the fee, or avoid the use of poorly maintained facilities.

In a low-income settlement in Nairobi (Mukuru village), before two public latrine blocks were constructed in 1996, there was only one latrine per 1000 persons.[107] In a low-income settlement in Kumasi, Atoinsu, there are 360

---

**Box 10.4 Water supply and sanitation in Dar es Salaam: self-help and sustainable technology**

Trunk and distribution losses from the city's water supply amount to about 60 per cent of pumped water. An additional 50 per cent is lost as tap losses and spills, resulting in a general water delivery shortage. Pipe breaks cause erratic water supply in several areas. Due to fast urban development, pipes are often installed in shallow trenches *after* the development of housing. They are often broken during road and house construction, causing ponding on the surface, which leads to destruction of roads by erosion and creation of swampy mosquito breeding areas where drinking water and sewerage from loose pipes are mixed, thus polluting surface water and groundwater. Many house connections are performed illegally with inappropriate technology and bad materials.

Only between 5 and 10 per cent of the population is served with sewerage. The system is very old and some sewers have collapsed due to lack of maintenance. About 75 per cent of the population uses on-site sanitation, consisting of pit latrines, septic tanks with soakaways, cesspits, soak pits, ventilated pit latrines or French drains. The adoption of modern sanitation models in the rapidly growing urban areas of Dar es Salaam has not been successful.

Dar es Salaam is a 'garden city' where many people grow vegetables in urban and peri-urban agriculture. Pollution of soil is, thus, another important problem threatening health.

Finding both central authorities technically and economically unable to improve water supply and sanitation, local citizen groups look for affordable ways of improving the necessary infrastructure. Local communities have formed organizations with elected members, such as the Kijiotoyama Development Community (KIJCO). Negotiations between KIJCO and the City Authority resulted in a Community Infrastructure Programme within which residents received assistance in construction of two deep wells as an alternative water source. Through self-help residents also provided technical input in the design and provision of the road and water network. Improvement of the water supply resulted in a reduction of the distance to water taps for most households.

In order to secure a sustainable water supply for the growing population in Dar es Salaam urgent steps should be taken towards pollution prevention of surface water, groundwater and soil. In order to make progress it is very important to establish better cooperation between water authorities and citizen action groups.

Local water authorities and citizen groups urgently need support in their actions, first of all in the form of information about alternative solutions. Water-borne sanitation is not the only or best option. Its costs exceed national economic capabilities, aside from the additional expense of constructing treatment plants. In Dar es Salaam freshwater resources are very limited and vulnerable, so it is important to introduce technologies that require much less water than traditional sanitation. Dry sanitation solutions, and especially separation sanitation, might save about 70 per cent of households' water use and would also recycle nutrients.

It is necessary to educate construction workers on proper installation technology and to provide house owners with information on proper use and maintenance. Community groups also need help in developing methods for the utilization of human excreta as fertilizer. Successful demonstration of the benefits of the dry- and nutrients-recycling sanitation approach will be good for the environment and improve the health of the population.

**Source:** Janusz Niemczynowicz, 2000 (see Background Papers).

**Box 10.5 Women building toilets and government–community partnerships**

In cities around India, communities within the National Slum Dwellers' Federation /Mahila Milan Alliance are building toilets, with a clear cost-sharing formula: communities design, build and maintain common toilets, while cities pay for building materials and provide sewer and water connections.

The Sabzi Mandi toilet project was a groundbreaker. For the Federation, it was a chance to test its toilet paradigm within the context of the Gomti project partnership. For the government, it was a chance to test the idea of community contracts.

Sabzi Mandi is a vegetable market just off the Pata Nala. To one side is a tiny settlement of 11 houses, clustered around a broken-down public toilet, whose crude, half-century-old plumbing channelled soil right into the *nala* (sewer lines). The toilet's location made it potentially useful for both community and public, but it needed rebuilding and the women were determined to do it. The Sabzi Mandi toilet was the project partnership's first community toilet contract.

With help from Mumbai Mahila Milan and funds for building materials from the British DFID, the Sabzi Mandi community demolished the old toilet, and built a new one in its place, with full sewer and water connections, 20 seats (including 10 special children's latrines) and 4 bathrooms. At Rs.5000 (about US$110) per seat, the toilet worked out to less than one-fifth what most cities spend building public toilets. The immaculate facility is managed by the women on a pay-and-use system, and has become a popular pit-stop for vendors, labourers and market-goers.

**Source:** SPARC, Mahila Milan and the National Slum Dwellers' Federation In India, 1998.

persons per squathole.[108] In most Indian cities, a considerable proportion of low-income households have no provision for sanitation in their home. A survey in Pune (India) found that in the worst-served settlements, there was just one toilet stall per 2500 inhabitants.[109] In Delhi, a 1990 survey showed that the 480,000 families in 1100 'slum' settlements had access to only 160 toilet seats and 110 mobile toilet vans.[110] Tenements, cheap boarding houses or other forms of cheap rented accommodation often have the worst provisions for sanitation or no provision at all. It is difficult to get landlords to invest in sanitation, especially where their tenants have very low incomes and the landlords' profits come from squeezing as many tenants as possible into rooms within shacks that required very little investment to build. Households with no provision for individual or shared sanitation within their homes have only three possibilities: public toilets, defecation outside or defecation into some container which is then thrown away (what in some cities is called 'wrap and throw' or 'flying toilets'). Among the cities where open defecation is reported to be common for significant proportions of the population are Accra, Addis Ababa, Ahmedabad, Bangalore, Bhilwara, Cebu, Colombo, Dhaka, Kingston, Kumasi and Ouagadougou, as well as large sections of the population in other cities in India.[111] For instance, in Ahmedabad, an estimated half a million people defecate in the open.[112] These sorts of conditions have given rise to community-based toilet building projects (see Box 10.5) that in the case of the Alliance in India have been inaugurated in 'Toilet Festivals' (*sandas mela*) that are at once carnivalesque and empowering and help to direct attention to much needed sanitary improvements.[113]

Thus, there are strong grounds for doubting the accuracy of official statistics on provision for sanitation in urban areas, as well as for water. If our concern is to significantly reduce the health burden associated with inadequate provision for water and sanitation, then the criteria as to 'what is adequate' need to be changed. There is some research on which to draw; for instance, a study of the association between health and provision for water and sanitation in Betim (Brazil), which emphasized how it was not only the availability of water and sanitation infrastructure that influences health but also water quality, per capita consumption, regularity of supply, extent of indoor plumbing and provision for drainage.[114]

> It is not only the availability of water and sanitation infrastructure that influences health, but also water quality, per capita consumption, regularity of supply, extent of indoor plumbing and provision for drainage

The difficulties plaguing official statistics on urban provision also means that existing 'rural–urban' comparisons should be questioned. If the extent of provision for urban populations is greatly overstated, the magnitude of the rural–urban gaps may in fact be much less. In addition, urban households lacking provision for sanitation may face a significantly higher health burden because higher densities and larger populations make it more difficult to dispose of excreta and wastewater in ways that ensure no possibility of human contact. It is also more difficult to safeguard local water sources from contamination. Urban populations may face much greater difficulties than rural households in getting access to a communal standpipe because there are far more people competing with them for access to that standpipe. Defecation in the open may be less problematic in rural areas as places are available for open defecation that limit the risk of human contact with the excreta and that pose less threat of harassment for women. Urban populations may be more willing and able to pay for improved provision than rural communities for several reasons. Many urban populations have higher monetary incomes, they face larger direct and indirect costs of inadequate provision, and because efficient water and sanitation providers can take advantage of economies of scale to reduce the costs of individual house connections. While water supply is both a rural and an urban issue, sanitation is primarily an urban issue.

It is clear that provision for water and sanitation is also very inadequate for much of the rural population. Further, it may be that official statistics for rural areas also exaggerate the quality and extent of provision. However, the discussion of priorities for water and sanitation should not turn into a fight between rural and urban proponents. What need to be recognized are key differences in rural and urban contexts and their implications for forms of water and sanitation provision that best meet people's needs.

> We must recognize key differences in rural and urban contexts and their implications for forms of water and sanitation provision that best meet people's needs

# Notes

The introduction to this chapter draws from *Water & Megacities*, jointly released by UNEP and UNCHS (Habitat) on 19 March 2000, on the occasion of the second World Water Forum and Ministerial Conference, 'From Vision to Action', held in the The Hague, The Netherlands, 17–22 March 2000. See www.worldwaterforum.org/.

This part and the following chapter sections on gaps and implications are adapted from a background paper prepared by James L Wescoat Jr (2000), University of Colorado.

2 eg Black, 1998; Cairncross et al, 1990; WASH, 1993.

3 UNCHS, 1996, Table 16.

4 US Department of Housing and Urban Development, 1999.

5 Gleick, 1998a, b.

6 Jonsson and Satterthwaite, 2000.

7 IRC, Source, April 2000.

8 *Water & Megacities* (see Note 1, supra).

9 Boot and Cairncross, 1997.

10 See www.irc.nl/index.html.

11 Srinukoon, 1999.

12 Hasan, 1992; 1993; 1997a, b; Khan, 1994.

13 Pathak, 1999.

14 Chaplin, 1999; Michel, 2000.

15 Pathak, 1999.

16 Race, *Poverty and Enviroment*, 1992.

17 Pulido, 1996.

18 Eg the GENPAK information package; Wijk-Sijbesma, 1998.

19 Hemmati and Leigh, 2000.

20 See www.un.org/esa/sustdev/wedo.htm.

21 WEDO, 1998.

22 Halvorson, 2000; Jordan and Wagner, 1993; Wijk-Sijbesma et al, 1996; Wijk-Sijbesma, 1998.

23 Halvorson, 2000.

24 Mitchell, 1998.

25 For exceptions, see Venkateswaran, 1996; Hasan, 1997a, b; Hasna, 1995.

26 IRC, 2000.

27 Hasan, 1993; 1997a, b.

28 Alfaro et al, 1998; Bauer, 1998; Briscoe, 1997; Crane, 1994; Katakura and Bakalian, 1998; Rees, 1998; World Bank, 1999d.

29 Dinar and Subramaniam, 1997.

30 Barlow, 1999.

31 Briscoe, 1997.

32 Beecher, 1994; Burns et al, 1995; Drakeford, 1997; Johnstone, 1997; Middleton and Saunders, 1997; Perchard, 1992; ID21, 1998.

33 AWWA, 1991; Saunders, et al, 1998.

35 Bella S Abzug quote; OFWAT, 1995.

36 Huby, 1995; Lister, 1995; Mara and Schweiger, 1996.

37 Cf. NRC, 1997.

38 US Department of Agriculture, 1998ab; US Environmental Protection Agency, 1998.

39 Eg Marino and Kemper, 1999; cf Swyngedouw, 1995.

40 Daniere and Takahashi, 1999.

41 Colten, 1992; NCLC, 1991; Saunders et al, 1998; Wescoat and Halvorson, 2000. A recent paper offers a detailed discussion of criteria that must be considered in plans for privatized provision of water and sanitation in ways that best meet the needs of low-income households, particularly in informal settlements; see Hardoy and Schusterman, 2000.

42 Chaplin, 1999; Heller, 1999.

43 Solo, 1999; Wegelin-Schuringa and Kodo, 1997.

44 Ingram et al, 1995.

45 de Veer, 1997.

46 See *Habitat Debate*, special issue on Water (October 2000), available at www.unchs.org.

47 Other water and sanitation variables [eg per cent access to water and sanitation] are addressed under the heading of 'economic development'.

48 Costanza et al, 1992.

49 Eg Joardar, 1998; McGranahan and Kjellen, 1997.

50 Simpson-Hebert et al, 1998.

51 Smit and Nasr, 1992.

52 UNEP/IETC, 1999.

53 Agarwal and Narain, 1997.

54 Brooks, Rached, and Saade, 1997; cf Dietz and Ranton, 1996; cf in Asia, ESCAP, 1998; Esrey et al, 2000.

55 Environmental Planning Collaborative, 1998.

56 Gleick 1998a, b.

57 Wescoat, 1995.

58 An early essay by Gilbert White (1974) explored these views of water as a 'right' or 'good'.

59 Wescoat and Halvorson, 2000.

60 White et al, 1972.

61 Thompson, 2000. See also Box 10.3.

62 Wescoat, 1993.

63 Orangi Pilot Project, 1998.

64 Arifeen and Mahbub, 1983; Hoque et al, 1994.

65 Verma, 2000.

66 Verma, 1999; 2000.

67 Anon, 2000.

68 Le Jalle, 1999.

69 World Bank, 1999e; Yepes, 1996.

70 WASH, 1993.

71 Cotton and Haworth, 1995.

72 See http://info.lboro.ac.uk/garnet/.

73 Eg WEDC, 1999.

74 See www.irc.nl/index.html.

75 IRC, 2000.

76 Eg UNCHS (Habitat), 1996 (Beijing), and 1997 (Cape Town)

77 UNCHS/UNEP, 1999.

78 Jonsson and Satterthwaite, 2000.

79 See www.urbanobservatory.org/indicators/database/pdf/infrast.pdf.

80 Eg Audefroy, 1995; Kjellen, Bratt and McGranahan, 1997; and Sandelin, 1994.

81 See Goldblatt, 1996; and Macy, 1999 for a broader discussion of southern Africa.

82 UNCHS 2000; Yepes, 1996. NUREC is a nonprofit-making international association of institutional organizations and individual members. Its home page is www.uni-duisburg.de/duisburg/nurec.htm

83 Anderson, 1988; Melosi, 1994; Rosen and Keating, 1991.

84 Eg Davies, 1989.

85 See Women's Environment and Development Organization, www.un.org/esa/sustdev/wedo.htm.

86 The rest of this chapter is drawn from the paper, 'Overstating the Provision of Safe Water and Sanitation to Urban Populations: A Critical Review of the Quality and Reliability of Official Statistics and of the Criteria Used in Defining What is "Adequate" or "Safe"' prepared by A Jonsson and D Satterthwaite of the International Institute for Environment and Development (IIED), London, for presentation at a meeting of the Panel on Urban Population Dynamics of the National Academy of Sciences, 5 May 2000, Washington, DC.

87 This point was discussed in Cairncross, et al 1990. It was also developed in Satterthwaite, 1995b.

88 WHO and UNICEF, 1994.

89 UNDP, 1996a, pp 152–153.

90 Ibid.

91 The development of internationally standardized indicators is an attempt to deal with this difficulty, although agreement in this regard is by no means a guarantee that the data, thus collected and reported, will validly represent actual conditions.

92 Rakodi et al, 2000.

93 See for instance UNICEF (1995-6) 'Multi indicator cluster surveys in India 1995-96, urban slums and the right to privacy: Individual toilets, bathing area'. *Urban Poverty*, April-June 1997, page 11. (Article from Women and Sanitation: 'The Urban Reality Experiences of Government Programmes/NGOs/CBOs'. R Khosla, Training Co-ordinator, NIUA National Workshop on Women, Children & Sanitation, 10–11 April 1997, New Delhi.)

94 Living standards survey quoted in Devas and Korboe, 2000.

95 Korboe et al, 2000.

96 Ngom, 1989.

97 Azandossessi, 2000.

98 Development Workshop (1995) *Water Supply and Sanitation and its Urban Constraints: Beneficiary Assessment for Luanda*.

99 See also Thompson et al, 2000.

100 Centre for African Settlement Studies and Development (CASSAD) (1995) 'Urban Poverty in Nigeria: Case Study of Zaria and Owerri, Cassad, Ibadan'.

101 Rakodi et al, 2000. The 1993 estimate was from UNCHS (Habitat) (1997) *Analysis of Data and Global Urban Indicators Database 1993*, UNCHS Urban Indicators Programme, Phase 1: 1994-6, Nairobi. The results of the household survey came from African Medical Relief Fund (AMREF) and Office of the Vice-President/Ministry of Planning and National Development (1997) *The Second Participatory Assessment Study – Kenya Vol. 1*, Nairobi. As part of the national study, Mombasa district was selected for in-depth assessment as an example of an urban district. Other data drawn from Gibb (Eastern Africa) Ltd (1995) *Sewerage, Drainage and Sanitation Studies Strategy Study, Appendix E, Sanitation Options and Strategies*, Report for the National Water Conservation and Pipeline Corporation as part of the Second Mombasa and Coastal Water Supply Engineering and Rehabilitation Project, Nairobi, p E/2.

102 Giles and Brown, 1997.

103 Ibid.

104 Asian Development Bank, 1997.

105 Ibid

106 WHO and UNICEF 1994.

107 Wegelin-Schuringa and Kodo, 1997.

108 Devas and Korboe 2000.

109 Shelter Associates (1999) *Primary Survey*, Pune.

110 Chaplin, 1999.

111 Multi Indicator Cluster Surveys in India 1995-96, Urban Slums, UNICEF.

112 Dutta, 2000.

113 See Appadurai, 2000. See also Hobson, 2000, and Chapter 14.

114 Heller, 1999.

# CHAPTER 11

# IMPACTS OF RECENT TRENDS ON URBAN TRANSPORT[1]

Cities have always competed regionally and globally with one another. What is new is the extent to which a city's economy can contribute to globalization, and how much of a city's economy can be oriented to that bigger arena. The transport component of human settlements influences the course and outcomes of globalization but is itself affected by globalization as well. These reciprocal impacts can only be understood by better insights into the changing priorities of urban form and infrastructure in relation to globalization processes.

## Transport and Urban Form

Historically, transport system developments have helped to shape urban form.[2] For example, in many of the more developed economies, dense, mixed-use 'walking cities' predominated to the mid-19th century, corridor-based 'public transport cities' emerged from the industrial revolution, and dispersed 'automobile cities' grew with the car from the 1940s. Now, as we enter the new economic era of the global knowledge economy where ICTs are increasingly dominant, the question is how these changes will impact on cities and their transport priorities.

Simplistic notions about global information technologies, first put forward during the 1960s, suggested that the impact on cities would be to create 'community without propinquity', to disperse people into 'non-place urban realms' or exurbs, where they only needed to telecommute.[3] With a growing awareness that telecommuting is not significantly replacing travel,[4] the complex role of ITCs in shaping cities has been assessed in a more subtle and nuanced way. Modern information technology, like the telephone before it, reduces the need for face-to-face interchange in some activities but cannot replace many of the quality human interactions critical to economic and cultural processes.[5] 'The new world of information technology will largely depend, as the old world did, on human creativity; and creativity flourishes where people come together face-to-face.'[6]

Various theories have emphasized that 'local milieux' of the global economy will emerge,[7] that local culture will be strengthened as globalized information makes national borders less relevant,[8] or that the importance of face-to-face contact will ensure centres emerge as critical nodes of information-oriented production.[9]

Information technologies could be associated with the concentration of urban activities into nodal centres,

rather than leading to the dispersal of cities, based on a combination of:

- The shifting of intrusive industrial production out of urban centres to allow clustering of information-oriented jobs.
- The need for integration of specialized disciplines to solve most global economy issues, encouraging face-to-face interaction between professionals for critical phases of any project.
- Easy access to the purchase of the extra choices provided in quality urban environments by those with the wealth created by being part of the global economy.

Whether such places will be in central/inner city centres or edge city centres[10] becomes an important consideration. The future city will probably be multi-nodal, organized around information technologies, and have distinct sub-centres with a particular cultural and economic identity. The city with just one major centre (CBD) will become less and less prevalent. Other agendas like social justice, sustainability and particularly automobile management, in urban areas, need to be assessed in the light of these likely changes in urban form and function. In this regard, recent studies[11] indicate the following trends in transport sector developments.

## Wealthy Cities are Slowing Down in Car Use

In the late 1980s, regional scientists began to speculate that the sprawling US and Australian cities would begin to stabilize growth of car use.[12] This was expected due to dispersal of work to the formerly residential suburbs leading to a reduction or stabilization of journey-to-work distances. This stabilization was seen as the 'self-regulation' of the car-based city, and therefore old ideas about public transport could now be discarded. The conclusion that low-density sprawl, particularly random suburbanization of workplaces, may lead to reduced car use, was used to justify the continued sprawl and lack of public transport options in these cities.

Similar patterns of slower car growth are observable in Canadian cities and in the European cities where reurbanization is also apparent. For example, Stockholm had a per capita decline in car use (229 km) between 1980 nd 1990. Its per capita public transport use grew by 15 per cent in this period and at the same time, it increased its density in the city centre, the inner area and the outer suburbs through various innovative compact developments. Table 11.1 shows the growing share of the developing countries in the world's total fleet of motor vehicles.

# Public Transport is Growing Nearly Everywhere

The data show considerable differences in commitment to public transport. The limited data on trends indicate that the US and Canadian cities were virtually static in public transport use and system growth during the 1980 to 1990 period, while Australian cities grew a little. Meanwhile, European cities showed 15 per cent growth from their already high levels, and in wealthy Asian cities the growth figure was 11 per cent. Zurich, for example, grew by 171 trips per capita in the 1980s to reach a level of 515 trips per person per year. The average total trips per capita in Australian cities is 92. In fact, the average public transport trips per capita *growth* in European cities from 1970 to 1990 is more than the *total* per capita public transport use in US cities and is similar to the total trips per capita in Perth, Adelaide and Brisbane. Growth in public transport in European cities has increased at an accelerating rate.

Although some commentators have suggested that the world of ICTs would somehow leave public transport behind as an old technology that is part of another era,[13] transit systems remain a vital part of any city in the new global economy. In fact, ICTs can be used to upgrade transit systems. With the maturation of 'intelligent transport system' technologies, reliable and responsive public transport services are ever more possible. Mass transit vehicles can deviate to carry people to their door at night, request times for service by those with disabilities can be shortened and so on. The possibilities are many and agencies around the world are increasingly sharing their successes.[14]

# Transport and Social Exclusion

## Cities in the more developed economies

Recent evidence shows that most wealthy cities which are part of the global information age are reconcentrating around urban centres. Not only are many cities now increasing in density (after a century of declining densities), but it is also becoming apparent that the more global the city's economy, the more it is concentrating into these nodes.

This process has led to an urban renaissance in the old central areas of many cities. The reurbanization process is evident in Canadian and European cities, as well as in the US, despite significant job and population loss in American cities in previous decades. The reurbanization of US cities is also underway, but the next decade will show if this fully follows the more global trend to reconcentrate the city. The

| Year | Low- and middle-income countries | | High-income countries | | Total motor vehicle fleet |
|---|---|---|---|---|---|
| | (millions) | (%) | (millions) | (%) | (millions) |
| 1995 | 164 | 25 | 487 | 75 | 651 |
| 2000 | 209 | 27 | 565 | 73 | 774 |
| 2010 | 340 | 31 | 759 | 69 | 1,099 |
| 2020 | 555 | 35 | 1,020 | 65 | 1,575 |
| 2030 | 905 | 40 | 1,370 | 60 | 2,275 |
| 2040 | 1,470 | 44 | 1,840 | 56 | 3,310 |
| 2050 | 2,400 | 48 | 2,475 | 52 | 4,975 |

**Source:** American Automobile Manufacturers Association, 1996.

transport impacts of this process, as shown above, are generally favourable as it can reduce car use per person and favour public transport, but it can also leave large suburban areas excluded from the new economy and its services.

Strategies to deal with the new economic geography of wealthy cities need to include:

* ways of bringing jobs of the global economy to the suburbs through urban design of centres that create the interchange networks required by the new economy;
* new rapid transit that can link the suburbs and the new centres;
* social housing near places of employment to reduce the need for travel by lower-income groups.

## Cities in the developing economies

The development of new economic opportunities and new technologies in many cities worldwide are widening social and economic inequalities (see Chapter 1). This situation is even worse in the metropolitan areas of developing countries, where the labour market is mainly located in the core and many of the poor live in peripheral areas. Even if participating in the labour market, either formally or informally, travelling can still be a significant time and financial burden (up to four hours a day may be spent commuting, and up to a third of poor workers' earnings may be spent just on commuting costs). Economic exclusion often leads to the spatial segregation of social groups in areas with inferior housing, lack of educational opportunities, health care, leisure and amenities and isolation from other areas. Those most likely to be isolated socially are those without access to good transport.

A majority of the world's population does not have access to a private car. Car-dependent systems also isolate the young, the elderly, many women and anyone else who does not drive or have access to a car. Public transport still remains the principal means by which motorized travel takes place in most cities worldwide – the bus accounts for 80 per cent of all trips in Bogota, 75 per cent in San Jose, 61 per cent in Tunis. In cities with rapid rail transit the bus share is lower: London, 23 per cent; New York, 14 per cent; Paris, 8 per cent; and Tokyo, only 6 per cent.[15]

The world's 5850 million person population shares a total vehicle fleet of approximately 500 million cars, or 11 people per vehicle on average. However, the most mobile

**Table 11.1**

**Projected growth of global motor vehicle fleet by national income level, 1995–2050**

countries have a ratio of only two to three people per vehicle (EU, US and Japan). In the rest of the world, the ratio is around 35 people per car, but the figure can be as high as 500 to 1000 people per car in countries such as Malawi, Burkina Faso or Ethiopia.[16]

This inequality in levels of motorization and public transport provision has major implications; it reflects conditions and policies that provide some segments of society with access to jobs and facilities, while excluding others from employment and services needed for a good quality of life.

Lack of access to transport can lead to four types of social exclusion, which tend to reinforce each other: spatial, temporal, personal and economic.

- *Spatial* exclusion usually occurs in low(er)-density areas where public transport operation is not financially viable, or in urban peripheral areas where services are less frequent or demand for services is often higher than supply. In developed countries, this is mostly felt in rural areas, many of which have no link by public transport at all, making the car the

only feasible mode of transport. However, spatial exclusion may also affect low-income urban populations as found in distressed inner-city areas in the US and run-down peripheral housing estates in European cities.
- *Temporal* exclusion refers to the problems faced by travellers mainly late at night or very early in the morning and often at weekends when service is nonexistent or infrequent.
- *Personal* exclusion is based on individual characteristics such as gender, age, ethnic background and religion, illness or disability that may constrain people's mobility and access to transport, whether private, public or non-motorized forms such as walking and cycling.
- *Economic* exclusion refers to the inability of people to pay for transport costs.

In developed countries, spatial, temporal and personal exclusion may be more common among its citizens; in developing countries the main source of exclusion lies in spatial segregation and the inability of individuals to pay for transport. These last two factors can combine to create a spiral of exclusion that will eventually include temporal and personal exclusion as well.

Social exclusion in a broader context is much more than just poverty, deprivation and inequality. Social exclusion is the short-hand term for what can happen when people or areas suffer from a combination of inter-related problems such as unemployment, poor skills, low incomes, poor housing, high crime, bad health and family breakdowns.[17]

## Poorer Cities are Being Trapped in Traffic

Most cities in the developing world moved dramatically from being dense, mixed-use walking cities into the era of the automobile, and now into the era of ICTs. This transition happened so quickly that few developing country cities had an opportunity to build a public transport city base as did the cities of the industrial world. These cities remain very dense apart from a few wealthy suburbs on the fringe, but now have traffic levels which, although small on a per capita basis, are very high in terms of the available space. This means they tend to be plagued by the worst levels of air pollution and road accidents in the world. Mitigation of the daily impact of traffic in such cities presents difficult urban development challenges.

Many Asian cities are more than ten times denser than, for example, US and Australian cities and so cannot be considered auto-dependent in the same way as the dispersed cities of the West. However, the poorer cities of Asia are saturated with automobiles and have a kind of auto-dependence that is based on the lack of adequate alternative modes of transport. Despite being seven times less wealthy, the newly industrializing Asian cities actually have a slightly higher level of car use than the wealthy Asian cities; further, they do not have nearly the same level

---

**Box 11.1 Eliminating gender inequality in transport**

Men have better access than women to superior transport modes, whether this is more regular use of the family car or more disposable income to ride a bus instead of walk. This 'gendering' of transport results from women's greater domestic responsibilities coupled with their lesser access to household resources. Transport deprivation may take the form of women forced to use inferior modes; their journeys having multiple purposes (unlike those of males who more typically just commute to work); customary or legal restraints on their rights to travel or to use a particular mode of transport; or physical harassment (see Box 11.2).

Many families have to make difficult choices about who will make the more expensive motorized trips and who is relegated to cheaper and less convenient modes of transport. As any decision of this sort reflects existing power relations in a family, its outcome is often determined by age and sex. Quite frequently, the male head of household will travel by public transport leaving female household members to walk. The inequality in this arrangement is heightened because in many cultures women are prohibited from riding a bike or using other non-motorized modes of transport, although doing so would ease their travel burden.

Women tend to have shorter journeys between work and home but they make many more trips than men to serve the needs of children, the elderly and other household members. In every age and income group, women make more of the shopping and other family business trips. In lower-income households where only one car is available, men tend to use the family car for work trips while women are dependent on public transport. Yet, complex household and caretaking responsibilities usually force women to make multiple stops. This also often makes travel more costly since they must pay for multiple single-fare tickets.

Despite the now almost universal recognition that women's domestic load, often in combination with low paid or unpaid work off the peak, leaves women both time- and resource-poor, the implications of this situation for transport and travel have largely been ignored. Transport planning, transport infrastructure design and transport management have historically been geared to servicing peak demand during rush hours, catering to more regular travel patterns to and from places of work. Development projects all too frequently ignore women's lack of mobility, which also hinders women's participation in project planning and design. Improving women's access to resources not only reduces gender-based inequities, but also has broader economic implications. The removal of impediments in women's daily travel needs is an important component of poverty eradication strategies.

**Notes:** For a series of case studies and projects concerning gender and transport, see the World Bank web site www.worldbank.org/gender/transport/. For a recent review of gender-related issues in transport and mobility in more developed economies, see R Law, 1999.

of public transport use, which in the wealthy Asian cities satisfies over 60 per cent of all the motorized transport needs. The Asian cities with successful public transport systems have retained their compactness and channelled their transport needs into this form of transport. They also have relatively high levels of walking and cycling (eg Tokyo's residents make 42 per cent of total daily trips by non-motorized means).

The newly industrializing Asian cities are becoming dominated by their traffic problems and tend to invest in large roads in an attempt to solve them. The belief that they can build their way out of congestion, rather than building public transport systems appears to be fostered by the advice they are given, which is predominantly a globalized transport policy that currently does not favour mass transit.[18] This was also the case with cities like Singapore, which built its mass transit system in the late 1970s and early 1980s against advice from the World Bank. Its success has helped to enable them to plan a multi-centred city suitable for the new economy. Many poorer cities now face the challenge of determining how to best use their limited capital to solve their transport problems while not harming their economies as they battle to attract investments from around the world.

There are three reasons for a renewed emphasis on mass transit systems in these cities. First, their urban form lends itself to public transport: not only are these cities compact, they are also invariably developed along very dense corridors that are ideal for rapid transit. Thus investment in rail systems could produce dramatic improvement to their traffic situations. Their urban forms are also characterized by mixed land use patterns, which favour high levels of non-motorized local trips. However, the traffic and environmental problems in these cities, as well as lack of investment in non-motorized infrastructure, are forcing pedestrians and cyclists off the streets. In China and many other developing nation cities, there is a conscious policy of exclusion of cyclists and rickshaws from certain areas on the grounds that they are a congestion nuisance. Additionally, there may also be gender-based discrimination, prohibiting women from riding bikes.

Second, an alternative commonly presented is that incremental improvement in bus fleets will be a better investment than a rail system. However, this is often compared with very expensive above- or below-ground metro systems rather than surface rail systems. Further, data from around the world show that only public transport systems with a speed advantage can compete with private car use.

The traffic speeds in the poorer Asian cities are very slow but their bus-based transit systems are much slower (Table 11.2). In Bangkok, the traffic averages a mere 13 kmph but the bus system averages only 9 kmph. Buses stuck in traffic do not offer a solution to these cities for their traffic problems. Bus systems must be upgraded, but by not allowing mass transit financing in poorer cities, the global transport policy community is condemning these cities to a future of car dependence where they cannot compete to attract global capital.

---

**Box 11.2 Buses for women only in Bangkok**

In May 2000, the Bangkok Mass Transit Authority (BMTA), a state-run bus operator in the Thai capital, began service for what was dubbed 'The Lady Bus'. The initiative came in response to numerous complaints by women about safety. Women, reacting to sexual harassment and crimes while commuting, had been demanding a safer travel option during rush hours. The Lady Bus accepts only women as passengers, except for accompanying sons aged less than 15 years. Bus drivers and fare collectors on the Lady Bus will be male because the BMTA wants them to protect passengers in case of emergencies.

The Lady Bus runs as every third bus on ten routes on the 30th, 31st and 1st of each month, between 4 pm and 9 pm. BMTA chose the evening and night trips during salary payment dates for introductory services because these are the riskiest times for women passengers to become crime victims. The ten introductory routes run past crowded business centres in the Thai capital, including Victory Monument, Maboonklong and Siam Centre. The number of routes and frequency of service will be increased if the BMTA finds that the project works.

**Source:** *Japan Economic Newswire; Kyodo News Service*, 30 May 2000.

---

**Box 11.3 Urban transport and poverty**

Within one generation, the developing world's urban population will double in size. Population growth translates into increased numbers of motor vehicles. Thus, during the past decade, the growth rate of motor vehicles has been very high in the urban areas of developing countries and it is expected to be higher in the years to come. For the urban poor, issues of urban transport are becoming of critical importance. Transport is an essential component of urban life, but it is often a major physical burden for the poor because it can account for a large part of their monetary income and time. The complex urban transport problems in many developing countries are triggered by a number of interrelated trends: urban population growth; land use mismatches; and underinvestment in non-motorized transport (NMT).

In Asia, most of this growth stems from increases in the number of two- or three-wheeled motorized vehicles. The mobility and affordability advantages of such vehicles are diminished by their pollution disadvantages. The environmental, social and financial impacts of current transport trends are significant: Motorized transport produces more air pollution than any other human activity and in congested city centres traffic can be responsible for 80–90 per cent of nitrogen oxides and hydrocarbons and a large portion of the particulates. In the cities of many developing countries, ambient lead levels greatly exceed health standards.

The development of the urban form is a second factor at the heart of many transport problems around the world. Increasing urban sprawl is disadvantaging public transport supply and reducing access, especially to those forced to peri-urban settlements outside the range of existing urban facilities. Transport problems have a disproportionate impact on the urban poor, while poor women are especially badly affected. Women often carry the lion's share of poor families' transport burden, and services at convenient times and at prices they can afford rarely exist. This reduces their productivity and capacity to meet their families' needs. As a result, everyone suffers: economically, physically and socially. Adequate transport is a necessity but not the panacea to poverty reduction. More transport does not necessarily result in less poverty. However, inadequacy of transport and infrastructure and misguided transport interventions will almost invariably affect the poor most and encourage social segregation and a spiral of exclusion.

The third factor is that NMT, although the main mode of transport in many developing countries, it is often associated with poverty and economic failure and therefore seen as something that countries should aim to develop out of rather than cultivate and improve. Thus, planning for NMT frequently sacrifices the needs of the poor in favour of planning for a faster flow of vehicles. However, the majority of the world's population does not have access to motorized private transport and probably never will. NMT will therefore remain prevalent and should be viewed as a highly viable option if there is a suitably high population density, sufficient NMT infrastructure and a mixed land use development pattern.

| Cities | Average speed (km/h) | | | Relative speed of transit to traffic |
|---|---|---|---|---|
| | Car | Train | Bus | |
| New York | 38 | 39 | 19 | 0.89 |
| Sydney | 37 | 42 | 19 | 0.91 |
| Vancouver | 38 | 42 | 20 | 0.67 |
| Zurich | 36 | 45 | 21 | 1.24 |
| Tokyo | 24 | 40 | 12 | 1.58 |
| Bangkok | 13 | 34 | 9 | 0.70 |
| Seoul | 24 | 40 | 19 | 1.07 |

**Source:** Newman and Kenworthy, 2000.

**Table 11.2**

**Average speed by mode and relative speed of public transport to traffic in selected cities, 1990**

Third, cities' economic problems will only be aggravated by the policy of creating higher capacity roads. Car-based 'solutions' to urban transport favour the urban elites over the many who do not own a car. It is often the highway construction and car lobbies that are behind the building of the roads.[19] Although this may bring some investment into the automobile industry, it does not advance fundamental solutions to urban transport problems and worsens sustainability problems of environmental quality and limited non-renewable resources, while also exacerbating existing inequalities in access to jobs, schools, shops, services and community facilities.

# Reducing Car Dependence

The patterns reveal that those cities with the most automobile dependence have the highest overall costs for their transport systems. They spend the most on roads, have the most heavily subsidized public transport systems, face the highest indirect costs from factors like transport deaths and pollution, and overall must commit a higher proportion of their city wealth for the non-productive purpose of passenger transport.

Still, many commentators on global city urban form have expressed a belief that car dependence is unavoidable for a city to be competitive. They argue that the trends in such cities indicate an overwhelming dependence on the private car and thus public transport will only be able to service a shrinking proportion of total trip demands.[20]

The evidence shows, however, that there is no techno-economic imperative for a city in the new global economy to be more car-dependent. The capacity of traffic systems and road space is reaching the saturation point in many cities. Average journey speed for motorized individual traffic is nearly down to that of pedestrians in some places. The goal of future development should be decoupling: that is, maintaining economic growth but with less car dependency.[21] If this can be achieved, economic growth could be maintained without the burden and the negative impacts caused by growth in motorization levels and road traffic.

Technology and information may well play a key role in reducing travel demand, or at least its rate of growth. In the more developed economies, there is some potential to replace motorized travel by activities that can be done from people's homes. For example, shopping through the internet is growing by leaps and bounds, which may decrease the number of trips people make to stores. Telemedicine schemes like 'First Help' facilitate self-diagnosis, which may

reduce the need for visits to clinics.[22] Likewise, telecommuting may help to ease traffic congestion. For example, according to a recent estimate, the number of telecommuters in Tokyo will grow to between 9 and 14 million by 2010, reducing pressures on roads and public transport systems with associated cost savings of up to 25 per cent of annual spending on public transport.[23] However, as reviewed in Chapter 1, such changes will be restricted to more affluent population groups and further marginalize excluded groups.[24] By and large, these developments are also immaterial to the situation in the developing countries.

A major global challenge is the mismatch between supply and demand for transport due to population growth as well as urban sprawl. In developing countries in particular, population growth rates have been higher than the growth of transport provision, especially public transport. However, a slowing down of car use and increase in public transport use is occurring. Cities in the new global economy may indeed be able to assist the sustainability agenda, but only if infrastructure priorities enable them to progress in less car-oriented ways.

Promoting bicycling and walking transport policies can play a useful role in promoting individual health, decreasing pollutant emissions, reducing accident rates and easing traffic congestion. Yet, in most countries, the modal share of the bicycle is still low; for example, on average only 5 per cent of all trips within EU-member states are made by bike. The proportion is lower still in the US, Canada, Australia and other automobile dependent countries.

However, in some countries the modal share of bicycle trips is much higher. For example, it is 18 per cent in Denmark and 27 per cent in The Netherlands; the average Dutch person cycles 850 km a year. In the provincial capital of Groningen, 50 per cent of all trips in the city centre are made by bicycle. In China, non-motorized transport still remains a predominant means of personal mobility. In Shanghai, public transport and bicycles are the two main modes of transport, with a fleet of some 6500 buses and trolleybuses distributed over a city-wide network of 327 routes handling an annual ridership of 5700 million passengers. At the same time, 3.5 million bicycles are in circulation in the urban area, accounting for 40 per cent of all commuting trips (an equivalent of one bicycle for every 2.2 inhabitants); the car accounts for only 3.5 per cent of all journeys.[25] In Beijing, 71 per cent of all daily trips are on foot or bicycle.[26]

Increasing safety and convenience is key for encouraging more cycling and walking. Cycle use has been boosted significantly in European cities such as Basel, Graz, Hannover, Münster and Delft, after traffic conflicts were minimized through the implementation of traffic calming schemes and dedicated bike lanes. Short automobile trips are the most frequent and most polluting, and many could be easily shifted to cycling or walking. For example, in the UK, 72 per cent of all trips are made by car, of which 59 per cent are less than 8 km. Further, some places in the US have seen increased bicycle use after the installation of bike racks on city buses, allowing commuters to combine cycling and public transport on longer trips.

Globalization is creating different transport challenges in the poorer cities of the world. They are filling rapidly with cars as their urban elites begin to be international consumers, but their urban forms were not designed to cope with the growing demands of traffic. Further, despite having dense population corridors well suited to support mass transit, they are being discouraged from investing in these systems by the global transport policy community, which instead advocates high-capacity roads. The lack of an adequate public transport system will keep poorer cities trapped in traffic with little chance of competing for global capital. However, it is possible that a new alignment will emerge between globalization, information technology and reduced car dependence. The solution will require more visionary and integrated transport planning and financing.

# Notes

1 This chapter is based on a synthesis prepared by Brian Williams, UNCHS (Habitat), based on 'Impacts of globalization on urban transportation', a background paper by Peter Newman and Jeff Kenworthy, and 'Transport in the 21st century', a background paper prepared by Paulo Camara, Maunsell Transport Planning, Birmingham, UK.

2 Newman and Kenworthy, 1999.

3 Webber, 1963; 1964; 1968.

4 Hodge et al, 1996.

5 Castells, 1989; Castells and Hall, 1994; Sassen, 1991; 1994.

6 Hall, 1997b, p 89.

7 Willoughby, 1994.

8 Ohmae, 1990; Naisbett, 1994.

9 Winger, 1997.

10 Garreau, 1991.

11 Newman and Kenworthy, 1999 and Kenworthy et al, 1999.

12 Gordon and Richardson, 1989; Gordon et al, 1989; Gordon, Richardson and Jun, 1991; Brotchie, 1992.

13 Analysed by Vuchic, 1999.

14 Hodge et al, 1996.

15 Hussmann, 1995.

16 UNCHS (Habitat), 1996.

17 Local Transport Today, 1999. See Chapters 1 and 2 for more extensive discussion of this point.

18 Ridley, 1995; Allport and Thomson, 1990; Mohan and Tiwari, 2000.

19 See, for example, Feagin, J (1983) 'Rites of way'. In The Urban Real Estate Game. Prentice-Hall, Englewood-Cliffs, chp 6.

20 Stimson, 1995, p 2.

21 Banister, 2000.

22 Medical experts have routinized diagnostic algorithms used by trained personnel when answering hotline calls placed by people who are experiencing symptoms about which they seek to consult a doctor. A veterinarian parallel initiative in the US was called 'First Yelp'.

23 See Mitomo and Jitsuzumi, 1999.

24 For example, in 1999, Allstate Insurance Corporation announced a major restructuring that will eliminate 4000 jobs to save money that it plans to invest in call-in technology. The new system will allow customers to use the internet and the telephone to buy insurance policies, eliminating the need to go through the company's sales agents (St Louis Post-Dispatch, Business Section, 11/11/1999). See Chapter 1 for a fuller discussion of how digital technologies work to deepen existing societal inequalities. See Boxes 4.3 and 17.5 for attempts to bridge the digital divide.

25 Godard, 1994.

26 Newman and Kenworthy, 1999.

# 12

# ENERGY DEMANDS AND CONSUMPTION[1]

As the world moves into the 21st century, energy-related dilemmas are certain to become increasingly intense. Energy challenges have already grown quite severe in cities throughout the world, in countries at all levels of development. From Beijing to Calcutta, from Tehran to Mexico City and from Moscow to Los Angeles, city residents are exposed to unhealthy levels of energy-generated pollution. Urban emissions are also having regional impacts, reducing crop yields and forest integrity in wide areas across North America, Europe and eastern Asia. Furthermore, the greenhouse gas emissions generated in the course of providing power to the world's cities are contributing significantly to the problem of global climate change.

---

At the same time that the negative environmental impacts of urban energy consumption are manifesting themselves on local, regional and global levels, the demand for energy continues to grow

---

At the same time that the negative environmental impacts of urban energy consumption are manifesting themselves on local, regional and global levels, the demand for energy continues to grow. This relentless growth in demand for modern energy resources is understandable in cities throughout the developing world, where per capita consumption rates remain startlingly low. Unfortunately, the environmental externalities generated by conventional energy systems are eroding the health and productivity of citizens in many developing country cities, and so new paths towards more efficient and sustainable patterns of energy consumption must be pursued in these areas. However, expanding demand for energy in developed countries, where per capita consumption rates are already very high, is less defensible.

---

In a context of tightening resource and environmental constraints, persistent global energy inequalities are becoming a source of economic, political and social tension

---

Indeed, in a context of tightening resource and environmental constraints, persistent global energy inequalities are becoming a source of economic, political and social tension. It is clear that leaders and citizens of the developed world must redouble their efforts to reign in excessive energy consumption, and support the diffusion of new technolo-

gies capable of providing power while reducing the environmental damage created by modern patterns of energy consumption.

This chapter explores the dilemmas posed by energy consumption patterns in urban areas throughout the world. It begins by describing the inequalities embedded in the modern world energy system. It then proceeds to examine the human and environmental constraints created by contemporary energy consumption patterns in cities in both developed and developing countries. Following this delineation of fundamental problems, the discussion turns to an analysis of new energy technologies and policy initiatives that may provide options for reducing the severity of urban energy problems. In particular, the fuel cell is highlighted as a system with the flexibility to ameliorate pressing environmental problems in cities throughout the world.

## Historical Patterns of Energy Production and Consumption

---

The world energy system has at least two problematic features that threaten to undermine economic and social progress in cities across the globe. The first involves the system's over-reliance on hydrocarbon resources, and the second involves the inequalities embedded in the system

---

The world energy system has at least two problematic features that threaten to undermine economic and social progress in cities across the globe. The first involves the system's over-reliance on hydrocarbon resources, and the second involves the inequalities embedded in the system. It has been estimated that about three-quarters of the world's commercial energy is consumed in cities.[2] More specifically, over 75 per cent of carbon emissions from fossil fuel burning and cement manufacturing, and 76 per cent of industrial wood consumption, occur in urban areas.[3] A primary function of the world energy system is to provide urban settlements with massive quantities of electricity, petrol and heat for use in commercial, transport and residential sectors.

As a whole, global reliance on hydrocarbon resources has increased exponentially throughout the modern era. Today, coal, oil and natural gas resources combined provide pproximately 90 per cent of all world commercial energy requirements. The non-hydrocarbon industries of nuclear energy and large-scale hydroelectric power together provide most of the remaining 10 per cent. All alternative energy technologies combined (small hydro, geothermal, wind, solar, tidal) currently provide less than 1 per cent of the world's commercial energy; a sobering statistic for those concerned about the environmental viability of modern society.[4]

Over-reliance on petroleum is a particularly worrisome feature of the energy system, especially where urban centres are concerned. Oil products currently provide around 40 per cent of the world's commercial energy. This share has grown since the mid-1980s, as consumers in the developed and developing worlds have taken advantage of lower petroleum prices offered by OPEC producers. A long-term trend of increasing reliance on imported petroleum, which had been temporarily contained in the 1970s, has therefore reasserted itself.

> In recent decades, the nations of the global south have been transferring energy resources to wealthier nations at an increasing rate

It is important to note that the nations of the global south have been transferring energy resources to wealthier nations at an increasing rate in recent decades. By the end of the Second World War the industrialized world was almost totally self-sufficient in energy. Since then, however, regions such as the Middle East and Latin America have exported ever-larger amounts of petroleum to the economies of North America, Western Europe and Japan. These transfers reflect the fact that the Middle East, Central Asia and Venezuela collectively contain over 70 per cent of the world's proven oil reserves. As a result, North American consumers have come to rely on imports for about 10 per cent of their energy supplies, while the import ratio is around 30 per cent for Western Europe and 80 per cent for Japan. Moreover, recent decades have seen significant growth in demand for petroleum resources in countries throughout the developing world.[5]

> It would be shortsighted to construct urban infrastructure that is predicated on false assumptions about the availability of cheap and secure oil imports, given these widely acknowledged resource constraints

Overall, cities throughout the world are growing increasingly dependent on petroleum resources imported from a small number of regions. A number of oil-exporting countries have achieved impressive levels of economic growth on the basis of this trade. However, the broader effects of this trend are highly problematic. For instance, cities are exposing themselves to substantial economic vulnerability by turning towards heavier reliance on imported oil supplies. Urban planners need to recognize that the world's production of oil is likely to reach its apex sometime in the next decade or two, and once this occurs petroleum prices will become increasingly volatile.[6] It

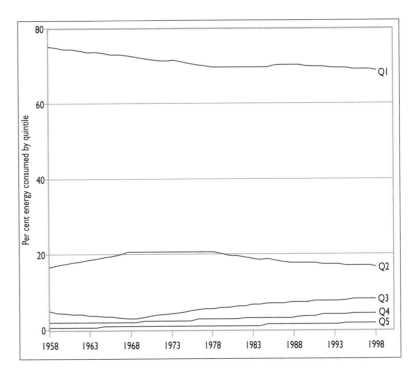

would be shortsighted to construct urban infrastructure that is predicated on false assumptions about the availability of cheap and secure oil imports, given these widely acknowledged resource constraints.

In addition to concerns about financial exposure, it is also important to highlight the extremely unequal levels of energy consumption between more developed and developing countries. The average citizen in the United States, for instance, consumes roughly ten times as much energy as a typical person in China and over 20 times more than a resident of India (see Figure 12.3). Even in such major oil-exporting nations as Venezuela and Iran, per capita consumption of commercial energy resources is less than one-third and one-fifth of the US average, respectively. Overall, per capita commercial energy consumption in the United States is more than five times higher than the global average. Meanwhile, it is estimated that around 1600 million people in the developing world have no regular access to commercial energy products at all.[8]

> Per capita commercial energy consumption in the United States is more than five times the global average. Meanwhile, around 1600 million people in the developing world have no regular access to commercial energy products at all. The wealthiest 20 per cent of the world's population consumes approximately 68 per cent of the world's commercial energy, whereas the lowest quintile consumes less than 2 per cent

These unequal patterns of consumption show little sign of easing. Their persistence can be demonstrated through an analysis of commercial energy consumption by quintile group.[9] As shown in Figure 12.1, in 1998 the top quintile (containing the wealthiest 20 per cent of the world's population) consumed approximately 68 per cent of the world's commercial energy, while the lowest quintile

**Figure 12.1**

**World commercial energy consumption by quintiles, 1958–1998**[7]

**Sources:** see Appendix A

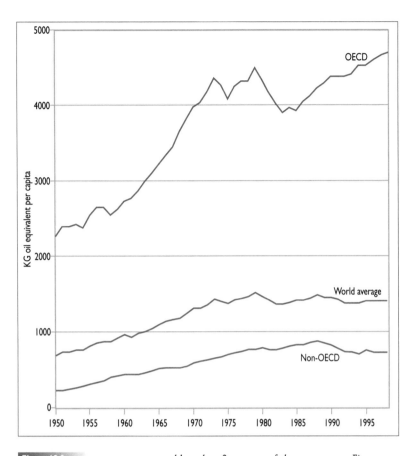

**Figure 12.2**

**Per capita commercial energy consumption, 1950–1995**

**Sources:** see Appendix A

consumed less than 2 per cent of these resources. Figure 12.1, which graphs the quintile distribution over the period 1958–1998, also shows that during the post-1978 period the top quintile has seen its share of world energy consumption remain steady. The second quintile, meanwhile, has seen its share diminish, while the third quintile has increased its share modestly. The bottom two quintiles (containing the poorest 40 per cent of the world's population) have seen virtually no increase in their consumption of the world's commercial energy resources. In sum, though there has been a slight change in the relative share of the world's commercial energy resources going to the second and third quintiles, inequalities have remained fundamentally unaltered in the post-1958 period.[10]

---

Global energy inequalities have remained fundamentally unaltered since 1958

---

While many people in the developing world struggle to gain access to modern energy technologies, citizens and companies in the global north are generally consuming energy resources at an unsustainable rate. The high levels of energy use found in wealthy countries are the source of most of the greenhouse gases emitted into the atmosphere today.[11] In contrast, most citizens in the global south, because of poverty, produce relatively little energy-related greenhouse emissions. Compare the very different rates of greenhouse gas emissions found in particular countries. The energy used annually by an average US resident generates over 20 times as much carbon dioxide as a typical Indian, over seven times as much as a typical Chinese and over five times as much as the global average. Since these gases

remain in the atmosphere for long periods of time, it should also be noted that nations of the developed north have emitted most of the total greenhouse gases accumulated in the atmosphere over the last two centuries.

At the same time as the environmental problems of conventional patterns of energy consumption are becoming manifest, there is growing need for modern forms of energy in the developing world. To put the challenge in perspective, consider that during the period 1970–1990 approximately 40 million people per year gained access to modern energy services. Given the number of people currently in need of service, combined with expected population growth, almost 100 million people would have to be connected to modern energy systems each year in order to achieve universal access by around 2020.[12] This is certainly a daunting task, especially given tightening resource and environmental constraints.

Many of the people in direst need of access to modern energy systems are located in rapidly growing urban settlements throughout the developing world. With diminishing traditional sources of fuel, the citizens of medium and large cities often face escalating energy prices while they are forced to contend with the pollution generated by conventional energy industries. Residents of cities in the developed world, meanwhile, are increasingly experiencing problems associated with overconsumption of energy resources. The next section of this report explores these energy dilemmas in cities across the globe in more detail.

# Development Constraints Created by Urban Energy Consumption Patterns

Historically, cities throughout the world have been arenas of tremendous economic and social development. The higher densities of people and material resources found in urban areas allow significant gains in productivity to be achieved, while reducing human impacts on natural ecosystems. These higher densities also make it easier to provide basic services to citizens, and as a result urban areas also have the potential to offer better health, education, sanitation and electrical services than are found in most rural areas.[13] From both a human development and environmental point of view, therefore, it makes eminent sense to encourage the continued growth of high-density population centres – provided underlying developmental problems can be addressed.

Many of the most severe challenges confronting cities originate from the manner in which energy resources are produced and consumed. While energy is a key input for urban development, virtually every type of power generates varying levels of environmental problems. Some of these impacts are experienced outside city limits. The harvesting of wood for use by impoverished city residents in Asia and Africa, for instance, has led to extensive deforestation around numerous urban areas.[14] The mining of coal and uranium, and the construction of large-scale hydroelectric dams – activities required for the provision of the bulk of he electrical power consumed in cities – have also led to widespread disruption of ecosystems and rural communities throughout many regions of the world.[15] Within cities, meanwhile, intensive levels of energy consumption are leading to unprecedented, spatially concentrated forms of pollution.

> More than 1000 million people throughout the world live in urban settlements where air pollution levels exceed health standards. The health costs of urban air pollution approach US$100,000 million annually

It has been estimated that more than 1000 million people throughout the world live in urban settlements where air pollution levels exceed health standards. The human consequences of this energy-generated pollution can be quite significant. In the United States, for instance, it is thought that at least 28 per cent of the urban population is exposed to harmful levels of particulates; a level of exposure that causes the premature death of an estimated 40,000 US residents each year. Meanwhile, 46 per cent of the US urban population is exposed to unhealthy levels of ozone, which exacerbates respiratory and cardiovascular diseases in a growing portion of the population. In European cities conditions are equally bad, with high levels of energy-related pollution causing elevated cases of chronic pulmonary disease and mortality. In the developing world, conditions are even more extreme. In Mexico City, high levels of pollution are estimated to cause over 6500 deaths each year. Meanwhile, over 52,000 people in 36 Indian cities are thought to have been killed by air pollution in 1995 alone. And in China, air pollution is estimated to cause anywhere from 170,000 to 280,000 deaths each year. On top of the human toll registered in these figures, there are growing financial costs as well. In developed countries, air pollution is estimated to cost around 2 per cent of GDP; in developing nations such pollution can cost anywhere from 5 to 20 per cent of GDP. On a global scale, the health costs of urban air pollution are thought to approach US$100,000 million annually.[16]

> Severe manifestations of energy-related urban problems in the developing world have the potential to overshadow the fact that it is cities in the industrialized world that contribute the most to global environmental problems

Severe manifestations of energy-related urban problems in the developing world have the potential to overshadow the fact that it is cities in the industrialized world that contribute the most to global environmental problems. Before examining the challenges faced by urban residents in developing nations, therefore, it is worthwhile to highlight the damage being wrought by overconsumption in wealthy nations.

Cities in the United States have particularly high levels of energy consumption and its attendant pollution problems. In a study of 47 metropolitan areas across the world, US cities emerged as being by far the most energy-intensive.[17] The sprawling, low-density cities that have

proliferated in the United States in the post-Second World War era have been predicated on the extensive use of private automobiles, which is the least efficient form of transport available. This structural foundation has made it difficult to develop viable public transit systems, and many suburbs are also poorly served by pavements and bike lanes. Over-reliance on private cars has translated into problems of traffic congestion and ambient pollution. Moreover, the vast car parks and road systems required by this mode of transport have contributed significantly to the urban heat island effect, which causes city residents to use air conditioners more frequently and further increases the consumption of energy. Citizens of lower classes in these cities are often underserved by systems that depend on private cars, while they are typically exposed to the brunt of the pollution effects that are generated.[18] Given these multiple consequences, this model of urbanization is undermining the quality of life and economic efficiency of cities such as Atlanta, Denver, Los Angeles, the San Francisco Bay Area, Seattle and Washington, DC.[19]

> Cities in the United States have particularly high levels of energy consumption and its attendant pollution problems. Though the problems inherent in low-density, automobile-reliant cities are increasingly in evidence, this model of urbanization is being replicated in many other developed countries

Though the problems inherent in low-density, automobile-reliant cities are increasingly in evidence, this model of urbanization is being replicated in many other developed

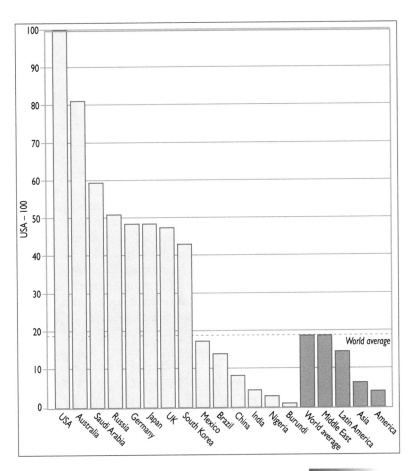

**Figure 12.3**

**Per capita commercial energy consumption relative to US, 1998**

countries. Numerous cities in Canada, for instance, are exhibiting patterns of urban sprawl that have long been the hallmark of US cities. Again, this form of urban organization translates into high levels of energy consumption and pollution. Indeed, it has been estimated that almost 40 per cent of total anthropogenic carbon dioxide emissions from North America comes from 50 metropolitan areas.[20] Many Australian cities are also evolving in this pollution-intensive direction.[21]

While the infrastructural characteristics of cities in the developed world heavily condition the energy consumption options of residents, it is also clear that affluent populations in these metropolitan areas are often encouraged by private corporations to make choices that exacerbate such problems. In a context of low energy prices during the mid-1990s, for instance, large numbers of North American consumers were to purchase extremely inefficient sports utility vehicles and energy-intensive homes. This behaviour is beginning to be mimicked in parts of Western Europe.

> **In recent years, energy efficiency gains have slowed or even been reversed in numerous developed nations**

The result has been that energy efficiency gains have slowed or even been reversed in some transport and residential sectors in numerous developed nations in recent years.[22]

> **The primary responsibility for reducing impacts of energy-related environmental problems should rest on those living in the wealthiest regions of the world economy**

As a result of these dynamics, the largest per capita contributors to energy-related environmental problems continue to be affluent citizens living in cities throughout the developed world. The primary responsibility for reducing such impacts therefore should rest on those living in the wealthiest regions of the world economy. Still, there are also serious energy-related problems emerging in cities in the developing world. The following brief analysis of dilemmas emerging in metropolitan centres in poorer regions will make clear that significant developmental constraints are being generated by conventional energy systems there as well.

While cities in the developed world confront problems originating primarily from overconsumption, metropolitan areas in the developing world face a much more complex set of energy dilemmas. On the one hand, the vast majority of urban residents in cities throughout the Southern hemisphere suffer from inadequate access to modern energy systems. On the other hand, even at low per capita levels of consumption many of these cities are generating very intense forms of pollution. There are a number of factors that are producing this unfortunate combination of low per capita consumption rates and high aggregate urban emissions throughout the developing world.

First, there is the issue of population increase. The rapid growth of cities in Latin America, Africa and Asia has generated such high densities of people that even modest levels of energy consumption at the individual level can translate into severe environmental problems. Unlike in large cities in the Northern hemisphere, local municipal agencies in the Southern hemisphere are rarely able to mobilize sufficient resources to cope with these growth-related challenges. In fact, budgetary pressures have forced many cities throughout the developing world to reduce environmental expenditures in general, and energy management in particular, even as the scale of the problems continues to expand.[23]

> **The fact that certain large cities in the Northern hemisphere have had some success in confronting energy-related challenges indicates that population pressures can be managed**

The fact that certain large cities in the Northern hemisphere have had some success in confronting energy-related challenges indicates that population pressures can be managed. High population densities in the Southern hemisphere, while certainly posing a significant challenge, are clearly not the sole factor leading to problematic outcomes.

> **While privileged classes in the South often replicate the modern, energy-intensive lifestyles found in North America, numerous impoverished urban inhabitants depend on heavily polluting resources such as wood and coal. Public policy often exacerbates these inequalities**

Of at least equal importance as population pressures are the severe social inequalities found in cities throughout the developing world. While privileged classes in the Southern hemisphere often replicate the modern, energy-intensive lifestyles found in North America, substantial numbers of impoverished urban inhabitants are forced to subsist on heavily polluting resources such as wood and coal.[24] Public policy often exacerbates these inequalities. For instance, the limited subsidies for energy products provided in many developing countries have been shown to benefit wealthier residential or industrial groups, while the truly impoverished typically pay high unit costs for resources purchased in informal markets.[25] In short, affluent urban consumers generally contribute disproportionately to pollution problems while poorer residents are again subjected to higher levels of exposure to energy-generated pollution throughout the developing world.

A final factor that contributes to energy-related difficulties in less affluent cities has to do with technological inadequacies found in their energy sectors. Electrical power plants currently in operation in the developing world, for instance, are estimated to be between 20 and 40 per cent less efficient than plants typically found in industrial countries. Transmission losses, meanwhile, are thought to lead to losses of another 20 per cent. This means that more than half the energy that is normally put to use in developed countries is often lost in the developing world, though he environmental externalities are still being generated.[26] In the case of transport sectors, huge efficiency losses are again incurred because of old vehicles and congested roads. More seriously, the continuing use of leaded petrol in many developing country cities is causing neurological, cardiac and other health problems in urban residents.[27]

Technological upgrading is sorely needed in energy sectors throughout the Southern hemisphere. The dilemma is how this can be achieved. Some analysts believe that the development process itself will inherently address these issues. For instance, it has recently been suggested that a bell-shaped, Kuznets-type curve describes the relationship between local pollution and levels of economic development.[28] At very low levels of development, poverty appears to limit the ability to pollute and so emissions rates tend to be low. As industrialization and urbanization begin to accelerate, however, larger quantities of resources are often consumed in relatively archaic, unregulated conditions and air quality tends to worsen. It is generally thought that only once a city or country has reached higher levels of affluence, and social demands for better qualities of life have been articulated, that resources will be mobilized to improve technological systems and counteract the impact of pollution.

While the potential existence of this Kuznets curve has led some to assume that development automatically cures underlying environmental problems, the fact that the majority of the world's urban residents are located at the beginning of the curve has troubling implications. Unless concerted efforts are made to bypass the curve, through proactive policies of technology transfer and careful regulation, the human and environmental damage generated by urban energy consumption will escalate dramatically.

The combined effects of energy overconsumption in affluent cities and inadequate energy sectors in developing cities, are clearly producing serious pollution problems on local and regional levels. Though the causal connections are less obvious, it is also known that urban settlements are contributing significantly to the problem of global warming. Cities themselves are thought to be particularly vulnerable to the consequences of climate change. It is expected that infectious diseases will proliferate in a warmer world, especially in dense urban settlements. Regional temperature rises will foster more urban smog. Changes in precipitation will adversely affect urban water supplies. An increase in extreme weather events will cause damage to urban infrastructure, and a rise in sea levels will begin to threaten coastal cities throughout the world.[29]

Given the likely consequences of climate change, urban managers throughout the world are facing a closing window of opportunity in which to undertake proactive strategies of damage control. As the financial costs of global warming begin to mount,[30] fewer and fewer cities will have the resources to foster the diffusion of new energy technologies that could reduce environmental impacts. The time for concerted action is clearly upon us. But are there alternative energy technologies that could provide solutions to the energy-related developmental constraints that are emerging in both affluent and impoverished cities? A growing body of evidence suggests that the answer to this question is a tentative yes. The following section examines the energy technologies that may have the capacity to ease these constraints in urban settlements throughout the world.

## Sustainable Energy Technologies Appropriate for Urban Applications

Advances in a variety of new energy technologies offer considerable promise for reducing pollution, increasing efficiencies and broadening the resource base of urban energy sectors in countries at all levels of development. The new energy systems that hold the most promise for enhancing sustainability include small-scale hydroelectric, wind, solar, modern biomass and fuel cell technologies. While the literature on these new energy systems has generally highlighted the potential for their utilization in rural areas, it is becoming clear that they can make a significant contribution in urban energy sectors as well.

A few of these new energy technologies are locationally restricted, but they could provide power to urban areas via long-distance transmission. Small-scale hydroelectric stations, for instance, offer one of the most benign forms of energy production available to the world. In contrast to disruptive large-scale hydroelectric projects, small-scale systems allow electrical power to be generated without significantly altering the flow of rivers. Wind systems offer similarly benign options for electrical generation in areas surrounding cities. And large-scale solar arrays have been shown to be capable of generating electricity that can then be fed into utility grids.[31]

> With the support of development agencies, governments and corporations, more environmentally sustainable energy systems can begin to bring electricity to urban communities throughout the world

If development agencies, governments and corporations begin supporting such alternative energy systems, a more environmentally sustainable network of facilities can begin to bring electricity to urban communities throughout the world in the coming decades.

> Urban areas have long benefited from preferential energy provision. Inadequate access to modern energy services in rural areas is one factor prompting migration to cities in many regions of the world. It is therefore important for policy makers to ensure that the benefits of new energy technologies are equitably shared by rural and urban settlements

Urban areas have long benefited from preferential treatment in terms of energy provision. Indeed, inadequate access to modern energy services in rural areas is one factor prompting migration to cities in many regions of the world. It is therefore important for policy makers to ensure that the benefits of new energy technologies are equitably shared by rural and urban settlements alike. Moreover, it is crucial that cities begin reducing their burdens on rural areas by generating their own power. Urban-based solar, biomass and fuel cell technologies offer opportunities to improve the self-reliance of urban energy sectors.

Solar thermal and photo-voltaic systems designed for use in metropolitan areas have received increasing attention in the last decade. In part this continued growth is the result of public support. In the US, for instance, the Million Solar Roofs Programme has helped to foster the diffusion of solar thermal and photo-voltaic systems in numerous cities.[32] In Japan, the New Earth 21 programme has aggressively promoted solar system construction in urban areas.[33] In Western Europe, publicly funded programmes have supported the proliferation of photo-voltaic roofs and building facades.[34] Smaller government programmes in South Korea, Mexico, Brazil, India and China have fostered solar systems for domestic use and export as well.[35]

> Recent trends show fast-growing private investment in solar systems by sophisticated companies with access to the capital required to fully commercialize needed technologies

Of crucial importance, meanwhile, has been recent growth in private investments in solar systems. Indeed, major multinational energy corporations are increasing their participation in solar power sectors.[36] While there are still many small manufacturing companies in solar sectors, the trend is towards greater involvement by sophisticated, high-technology companies with access to the capital required to fully commercialize solar technologies. All of these initiatives are increasing the usable electricity and heat generated by built structures in cities throughout the world.

Another strategy for expanding city-based energy production involves the utilization of modern biomass technologies to turn waste materials into sources of useful power. The huge volumes of solid and liquid waste generated by metropolitan areas throughout the world are replete with combustible resources. Urban waste contains large amounts of organic material, while landfills and sewage tailings spontaneously generate methane gas: a powerful greenhouse gas. These solid and gaseous materials can be fed into a variety of incineration systems, thereby simultaneously reducing the volume of wastes while generating heat and electricity from inexpensive, plentiful urban resources. Given this combination of advantages, waste-to-energy projects have proliferated throughout North America, Western Europe and Japan.[37] Similar projects are underway in developing countries such as Brazil, Chile, South Africa, Hong Kong, Indonesia and China.[38]

Greater use of urban-based solar and biomass technologies provides options to increase the efficiency and reliability of local electrical grids that supply power to residential and commercial locations. But these systems

cannot directly serve the energy-intensive transport sector, which generates a great deal of pollution. The fuel cell, however, can be used to power automobiles, as well as residential, commercial and energy-to-waste systems. Given its remarkable flexibility, the fuel cell is emerging as a new energy technology with tremendous potential applications in urban settings.

Fuel cells resemble common batteries, in that they rely on chemical reactions to produce electricity. In their most environmentally pristine form, fuel cells are injected with hydrogen and oxygen which, when exposed to a catalyst, react to generate electricity. In hydrogen-powered fuel cells, pure water is the only by-product generated by this electrochemical reaction. Recent engineering innovations have also permitted the use of fuels such as methanol methane and petroleum in fuel cell systems; these fuel cells do generate some carbon dioxide emissions. But because fuel cells can attain much higher efficiency rates than conventional engines, their emissions levels are greatly reduced even when they are powered with gases derived from fossil fuels.[39]

Fuel cells can be assembled in stacks of different sizes, from systems small enough for use in electronic devices to systems large enough to generate electricity in grid-connected power stations. Numerous companies have already begun manufacturing fuel cells for use in laptop computers, roadside warning signs and other small electronic components.[40] Meanwhile, firms such as Analytic Power and Plug Power are developing medium-sized fuel cell systems for use in residential homes.[41] And corporations such as General Electric, Mitsubishi, Tokyo Electric Power, Toshiba, United Technologies and Westinghouse have begun manufacturing large fuel cells designed to generate electricity for commercial buildings and utility grids.[42] The competitive race to bring fuel cell-powered products to the consumer market has become particularly intense in the automotive industry. The current leader in the effort to mass-produce fuel cell vehicles is a partnership between the Ballard Power, DaimlerChrysler and Ford corporations. Meanwhile, General Motors and Toyota have teamed up to develop their own fuel cell cars. Similar efforts are being undertaken by Honda, BMW and Mitsubishi Motors.[43]

The first generation of commercial fuel cells will be powered primarily by methanol and natural gas mixtures. Although still generating some pollution, these fuel cells will significantly increase the efficiency with which conventional hydrocarbon resources are consumed. Petroleum corporations such as ARCO, British Petroleum, Nippon Oil, Royal Dutch Shell and Texaco have already begun developing refining and distribution systems to provide methanol, natural gas and hydrogen to consumers using fuel cell systems.[44]

> It is possible to operate fuel cells on methane gas collected from sewage systems and municipal landfills, thereby reducing the emission of an extremely harmful greenhouse gas while providing a useful source of energy

t is also possible to operate fuel cells on methane gas collected from sewage systems and municipal landfills, thereby reducing the emission of an extremely harmful greenhouse gas while providing a useful source of energy.[45]

The widespread use of fuel cell systems is certain to occur first in affluent cities. Indeed, the first large deployment of fuel cell vehicles is scheduled to occur during the period 2000–2005 in California metropolitan areas. Cities in Japan and Western Europe, meanwhile, are aggressively pursuing commercialization as well. But the diffusion of fuel cells need not be restricted solely to cities in the developed world. Indeed, studies currently underway in cities such as São Paulo, Delhi, Hong Kong and Beijing suggest that fuel cell-powered buses, motor scooters and stationary power generators could help to ease environmental problems in cities in developing countries as well.[46]

A variety of new energy technologies have clearly attained the engineering maturity required for use in many different urban settings. Researchers at the World Bank, the World Energy Council, the International Energy Agency and the US Department of Energy have also gathered evidence indicating that numerous alternative energy systems are approaching the price competitiveness required for large-scale commercialization.[47] As shown in Figure 12.4 and Table 12.1, comparative cost information gathered on different kinds of electrical generation systems reveal a closing price gap between conventional and new energy systems. It should be noted that, for a variety of reasons, these data on electrical generation costs must be treated with caution. To begin with, these cost estimates are averages from many regions of the world and they are based on facilities with widely varying technologies and operating histories. Second, it is difficult to account for the effects of subsidies on generation costs. Since it has been well documented that conventional power sectors receive extensive subsidies throughout the world, it is likely that the generation costs shown for these sectors underestimate true costs. Similarly, it is hard to factor in externality costs for conventional energy systems, again resulting in an underestimation of true conventional energy costs. Even given these price distortions, however, it is clear that wind, biomass, solar and fuel cell systems are approaching commercial viability in many markets throughout the developed and developing worlds.

> Given relatively moderate levels of public support, alternative energy systems could be providing 20 per cent of the world's energy by the year 2100

The world commercial environment appears set at last to foster the expansion of new energy systems. Although it is impossible to predict how quickly new energy technologies can spread, it nevertheless appears that they are in a strong position to begin processes of rapid diffusion in the coming decades. Indeed, in a recent analysis published by the World Bank[48] it was argued that, given relatively moderate levels of public support, alternative energy systems could be providing 20 per cent of the world's energy by the year 2100.

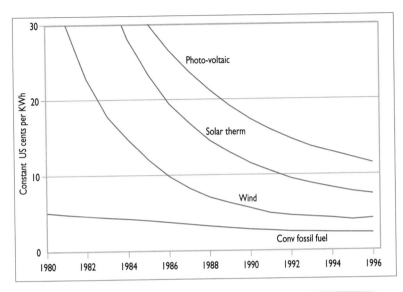

**Figure 12.4**

**Average US electricity generation costs**

**Sources:** Weinberg, 1994; US EIA, 1997c

The final section of this discussion turns to an analysis of strategies that could accelerate this diffusion of new energy systems in urban areas throughout the world. When combined with efforts to more effectively organize energy sectors in cities at all levels of development, these new technologies may provide opportunities to ease the constraints that are increasingly hindering economic and human advancement in many metropolitan areas.

## Strategies for Achieving Reform in Urban Energy Sectors

As the world enters the 21st century, the long-term viability of urban energy sectors throughout the world is increasingly being called into question. If new generations of city residents are to be provided with access to vital energy systems, and urban environments are to be simultaneously improved, at least three underlying developmental challenges must be addressed. First, existing urban energy systems must be reorganized in order to enhance efficiencies. Second, new energy technologies, which minimize urban pollution, must be made widely available to cities throughout the world. And third, the inequalities embedded in the world energy system must be reduced.

Before examining the prospects for achieving these objectives, it is necessary to highlight the institutional context within which attempts at urban reform are most likely to succeed. Extensive experience has revealed that

**Table 12.1**

**Estimated global average costs of grid-connected electricity, circa 1995**

| Technology | 1990 US cents per kWh |
|---|---|
| Average electrical costs in urban areas | 8.0–10.0 |
| Coal-powered utilities | 2.5–4.0 |
| Natural gas-powered utilities | 2.5–5.0 |
| Wind-powered systems | 4.5–8.0 |
| Modern biomass systems | 7.0–12.0 |
| Solar-thermal systems | 8.0–20.0 |
| Fuel cell systems | 9.0–15.0 |
| Photo-voltaic systems | 20.0–70.0 |

**Sources:** See endnote 20.

lasting changes in local city environments are most reliably achieved through the combined efforts of grassroots groups, government officials and private enterprises. National and multilateral development agencies certainly have an important role to play in fostering sustainability, but these agencies have to work closely with local groups if reforms are to be actually carried out.[49]

It is only when local civic organizations and business interests participate in designing and implementing reform agendas that efforts to achieve sustainability have a reasonable chance of success.

> **It is only when local civic organizations and business interests participate in designing and implementing reform agendas that efforts to achieve sustainability have a reasonable chance of success**

Fortunately, it would appear that policy reformers are taking these lessons to heart. Indeed, in the field of urban management there has been a proliferation of programmes intended to foster public–private coalitions and enhance cooperation between local, national and international organizations. Given innovative efforts such as the International Council on Local Environmental Initiatives[50] (ICLEI) Cities for Climate Protection Campaign, the Clean Cities Programme and the Local Agenda 21, among others, it appears that the institutional environment is at last favouring participatory approaches to reform. The achievements of some of these coalitions will be highlighted as we turn to a review of contemporary initiatives that are underway to improve urban energy sectors.

> **Low-cost strategies have resulted in improved transport efficiencies and lower rates of urban pollution in Curitiba**

Although this discussion has emphasized the key role that new energy technologies can play in improving urban sustainability, energy efficiencies can also be enhanced at the city level by reorganizing urban services and directing growth in specific directions. Perhaps the best example of this strategy can be found in the city of Curitiba, Brazil. Urban planners, working in close consultation with local residents and businesses, began by designating a number of transport corridors that ran along the axes of the city as open only to authorized buses. These corridors substantially improved the efficiency and reliability of public transport, resulting in a very high level of usage. Furthermore, this coordinated planning allowed real estate developers to build new properties in specified locations, with the confidence that the public would have easy access to their commercial and residential areas on the transit lines. These low-cost strategies have resulted in improved transport efficiencies and lower rates of urban pollution in Curitiba.[51] Many other cities, including Copenhagen, Portland, Singapore, Surabaya, Toronto and Zurich, have pursued similar strategies of reorganizing existing urban areas in order to improve transport efficiencies.[52]

It is also possible to upgrade energy systems, thereby achieving higher efficiencies and lower environmental impacts. For instance, emissions from urban transport sectors can often be reduced by shifting to alternative fuels such as compressed natural gas, liquefied petroleum gas and ethanol.[53] This is precisely the strategy that will be pursued in Hong Kong, where extremely high levels of ground-level pollution prompted taxi and truck drivers to organize a protest in which they demanded that city officials accelerate conversion to liquefied petroleum gas.[54] In another example of system upgrading, existing electrical power plants can often be transformed into cogeneration systems that make more effective use of the large amounts of heat generated in the process of producing electricity.[55]

The virtue of these strategies of system upgrading is that they can often be carried out by local municipalities, at quite moderate cost. Consider, for instance, the achievements of the ICLEI. The ICLEI consists of over 300 cities in all regions of the world that are committed to reducing their carbon dioxide emissions. At the 1997 Kyoto Climate Change Summit, the ICLEI reported that these cities had together succeeded in reducing carbon emissions by more than 41 million tons. Moreover, it was shown that in nearly every case these reductions were associated with an improvement in the local economy.[56] Many other urban coalitions, including the US Clean Cities Programme and the European Energie-Cités project, are having similar success in improving efficiencies and reducing energy-related pollution at little or no cost.[57]

In addition to upgrading existing energy systems, it will also be necessary to accelerate the diffusion of new energy technologies to urban areas throughout the world. As discussed in the previous section, a variety of innovative energy systems have reached the engineering maturity required for successful utilization in metropolitan regions. The challenge now is to foster commercial expansion in new energy sectors.

> **Opening utility grids to small-scale electricity producers would reduce one institutional barrier that has inhibited the expansion of alternative energy sectors**

To accomplish this, fair market conditions must first be introduced into energy industries. Currently, decentralized energy providers are generally prevented from connecting to power grids. Opening utility grids to small-scale electricity producers would reduce one institutional barrier that has inhibited the expansion of alternative energy sectors in many countries.

More importantly, the massive subsidies provided to conventional fossil fuel and nuclear power sectors must be substantially reduced.[58] While removing subsidies is often politically difficult, it is important to note that these subsidies tend to benefit large industrial producers and consumers rather than the truly impoverished.[59] Once the commercial playing field is levelled in these ways, private-sector dynamics can begin to foster the expansion of new energy systems in cities throughout the world.

---

Massive subsidies for conventional fossil fuel and nuclear power must be substantially reduced. These subsidies tend to benefit large industrial producers and consumers rather than the truly impoverished

---

There are other, market-based mechanisms that are likely to provide additional support to environmentally friendly energy systems. For instance, emissions trading schemes are already encouraging private companies to invest in domestic acid rain-reduction technologies in North America.[60] Similar agreements show promise on the international level. The Prototype Carbon Fund, an emissions trading system administered by the World Bank that focuses on renewable energy systems, attracted more private investments in its first six months of operation than had been expected for its entire first year of operations.[61] The Joint Implementation and Clean Development Mechanisms, meanwhile, should facilitate the international transfer of new energy systems; under the provisions of these agreements companies headquartered in developed countries will be able to get credit for emissions reductions they achieve by investing in new energy ventures in developing countries.[62]

While these market-based strategies are certain to be important components of any global effort to accelerate the diffusion of new energy technologies, by themselves they are not likely to represent a sufficiently robust policy response. In part this is because emissions trading mechanisms may allow cities that are currently over consuming resources to purchase relatively inexpensive permits and thereby continue such behaviour.[63] What is needed as well is an influx of public and private investments that can finance the construction of new energy infrastructures. Unfortunately, at present, the level of funding for new energy projects does not appear to be adequate to the task.

Since the economic crisis of 1997–1999, governments throughout the world have sharply scaled back public funding for energy infrastructure development.[64] In place of public financing, it has been hoped that energy sector restructuring would prompt private companies to increase their investments in energy projects. While a few countries in Latin America have seen modest growth in private investments, the vast majority of cities throughout the world have been forced to contend with declining public and private energy sector investments.[65]

Given this difficult context, an increasing number of countries have turned to multilateral development agencies such as the World Bank Group for assistance in upgrading existing energy sectors and expanding new energy systems. However, while the World Bank has publicly acknowledged the need to increase financing for new energy projects,[66] reforming its own investment practices has proved to be difficult. For instance, during the period 1995–1999 the World Bank Group's total portfolio of lending commitments to energy projects amounted to US$13,500 million. Just over US$1000 million of this financing, or about 7 per cent of the total, went to renewable energy projects. In comparison, over US$3600 million, or 27 per cent of the total, went directly to oil, gas and coal projects. The remainder went to large-scale hydroelectric and utility grid development. Though the World Bank has made great strides in publicizing the potential benefits of new energy technologies, its lending portfolio clearly still favours conventional, environmentally problematic energy technologies. Moreover, during the period 1995–1999 annual World Bank lending for energy projects has actually declined, even as its own studies highlight the need for greater commitments to improving energy systems across the world.[67]

While a contraction in energy-related investments by national governments, private companies and multilateral development agencies has been occurring in recent years, it is expected that this trend will eventually reverse itself and a new round of financing will become available for energy development projects. Once this occurs, it is likely that a substantial portion of these new resources will be utilized to expand sustainable energy systems. A variety of international mechanisms, such as the Global Environment Facility and the Clean Development Mechanism, are now available to utilize capital resources more effectively.[68] National governments, under moderate pressure from the Kyoto Accords, are also committing themselves to pursuing emissions-reduction strategies that favour new energy technologies.

And city-level coalitions such as the ICLEI and Local Agenda 21 have proved to be capable of spearheading innovative energy reforms in many metropolitan regions. In short, the policy environment appears to be at last set to favour true changes in urban energy industries in urban centres throughout the world.

---

City-level coalitions such as the ICLEI and Local Agenda 21 have proved to be capable of spearheading innovative energy reforms in many metropolitan regions

---

There still remains, of course, uncertainty regarding how to reform the severe inequalities in energy consumption that are embedded in the contemporary world energy system. As shown earlier, high-income nations consume a disproportionate share of the energy resources available for human use. These consumption practices cannot be universalized without causing rapid environmental crises at regional and global levels.

Instead of supporting the replication of these unsustainable consumption practices in the less developed economies, international policy priorities should focus on reducing energy consumption rates in affluent nations. Unfortunately, there is little indication that the political will exists to begin addressing this most intractable development constraint.

---

Instead of supporting replication of unsustainable consumption practices in the less developed economies, international policy priorities should focus on reducing energy consumption rates in affluent nations

It is possible that a grim future lies in store for urban settlements throughout the world. The impacts of global warming, which are already beginning to become manifest, are likely to hit metropolitan regions particularly hard. The window of opportunity to take proactive steps to reduce local and global environmental threats will narrow, as the effects of climate change begin to take their toll on municipalities in affluent and impoverished nations. What is needed in the current era is the creation of a coalition – involving grassroots organizations, national governments and multilateral organizations – which has as its central goal the reduction of overconsumption in developed nations. The work of the United Nations Development Programme, which has attempted to document and counteract growing inequalities in the world economy, may provide a model upon which to build in this regard.[69] For in the field of energy policy, as in most other spheres of development, it will only be by fundamentally redefining the agenda of development – to focus on reducing overconsumption – that true sustainability has a chance to be attained.

## Appendix A: Energy Data Sources and Conversion Procedures

The quantitative data on energy production and consumption presented in this report come from the following

sources: (1) for the period 1950–1995: United Nations (1997); and (2) for the 1996–1998 period: US Energy Information Administration (1999). Since particular energy resources have different quantities of useful energy per volume unit, it is necessary to convert each distinct resource into comparable units before data aggregation or comparison is undertaken. For this report, volume units of measurement have been converted into *oil equivalencies* using conversion factors published in the United Nations (1997) source.

## Appendix B: Methods Used to Calculate Energy Consumption Quintiles

To calculate energy consumption quintiles, countries were first ranked according to their per capita energy consumption in each individual year. Once ranked in this way, countries were then grouped into 20 per cent portions of the world's population. In cases where countries fell across the 20 per cent dividing line, they were divided proportionately between the respective quintile groups (ie the same proportion of the country's population and energy consumption were placed into the appropriate quintiles). Given these calculations, it was then possible to determine what proportion of the world's commercial energy was consumed by each quintile in each given year.

## Notes

1 This chapter is drawn from 'Urban energy dilemmas in a globalizing world: Implications for economic growth, social justice and environmental sustainability', a background paper prepared by Bruce Podobnik, Lewis and Clark College.

2 This estimate, which comes from the OECD, 1995, p 20 should be seen as a very rough approximation of urban energy consumption. Few efforts have been undertaken to gather city-level energy consumption information, though the data collection project currently being carried out under the auspices of the United Nations Urban Indicators Programme (UNCHS, 2000) should begin to remedy these gaps in empirical information.

3 O'Meara, 1999, p 7.

4 See Appendix A for a full description of the sources of the quantitative data presented in this report.

5 Import ratios come from the energy data described in Appendix A. For similar figures,

see Bairoch, 1993, p 59; the World Energy Council, 1995; International Energy Agency, 1996. For an analysis of rising demand for petroleum in developing countries, see Gately and Streifel, 1997.

6 For analyses of global petroleum reserves and estimates on when world production will peak, see WEC, 1995, p 13; IEA, 1996, p 31; US EIA, 1997a, Table 11.3; MacKenzie, 1997, pp 25–27; Campbell and Laherrere, 1998.

7 To calculate energy consumption quintiles, countries were first ranked according to their per capita energy consumption in each individual year. Once ranked in this way, countries were grouped into 20 per cent portions of the world's population. Given these calculations, it was then possible to determine what proportion of the world's commercial energy was consumed by each quintile (20 per cent portion of world's population) in each given year. So, for instance, in 1998 the top quintile consumed around 68 per

cent of the world's commercial energy.

8 World Energy Council, 2000.

9 See Appendix B for a description of the methods used in calculating energy consumption quintiles.

10 It should be noted that within-nation inequalities are often severe as well. For studies documenting inequalities within nations, see Barnes, 1995; Parikh et al, 1997.

11 See the data sets made available by the Carbon Dioxide Information Analysis Center (CDIAC, 2000) for further information on greenhouse gases. Its web site is http://cdiac.esd.ornl.gov/home.html.

12 WEC, 2000.

13 However, see the discussion of water supply and sanitation provision elsewhere in this report for a critical examination of rural–urban comparisons.

14 WRI, 1996, p 63.

15 McCully, 1996; O'Meara, 1999.

16 For the United States, see US EPA, 1997; for Europe, see EEA, 1996; for Mexico, see Eskeland,

1992; for India, see Kumar, et al, 1997; for China, see Florig, 1997; for the economic estimates, see Leitmann, 1999, pp 15–16.

17 See Kenworthy and Laube, 1999, and Newman and Kenworthy, 1999, for detailed information on this international study of urban areas.

18 Harvey, 1996.

19 See Firestone, 1999 and Stoel, 1999, for analyses of US transport problems attendant with processes of suburbanization.

20 Gatlin, 1995.

21 Kenworthy and Laube, 1999.

22 IEA, 1998; Bradsher, 1999.

23 Sheng, 1997.

24 For studies documenting energy inequalities in the developing world, see Parikh et al, 1997; Reddy, 1997; Karekezi, 1999; Tomlinson, 1999.

25 Barnes, 1995; Alam et al, 1998.

26 Pearson and Fouquet, 1996, p 142.

27 Bartone et al, 1994, p 29.

28 World Bank, 1995; Nordstrom and Vaughan, 1999.

29 See publications by the

Intergovernmental Panel on Climate Change (IPCC, 1995; 1997) for best-guess estimates on the likely consequences of global warming.

30 See World Bank, 1999a, p 97, for tentative estimates of the cost of climate change in developed and developing nations.

31 For reviews of the market-potential of small-scale hydro, wind, and solar energy systems, see World Energy Council, 1994; IEA, 1999; US EIA, 1998; World Bank, 1999b.

32 US GAO, 1999.

33 Murota and Yano, 1993.

34 O'Meara, 1999.

35 US EIA, 1998.

36 IEA, 1999.

37 OECD, 1995, p 203.

38 Johannessen and Boyer, 1999.

39 The following sources provide useful descriptions of fuel cell systems: Elliot, 1997; Geyer, 1999; Fuel Cell Commercialization Group, 1999.

40 Eisenberg, 1999.

41 Jimenez, 1999.

42 For overviews of investments in fuel cell systems made by established electrical manufacturing corporations, see Hojo, 1995; Saito, 1995; Tokumoto, 1995; Moore, 1997; Siemens, 1999; Wald, 1999.

43 For information on the DaimlerChrysler–Ford–Ballard partnership, see Jewett, 1999; for the GM–Toyota partnership, see Brown, 1999; for fuel cell investments by other auto companies, see Ball, 1999; Burt, 1999; Evarts, 1999.

44 See Law, 1999; Siemens, 1999; Yomiuri, 1999.

45 Roe et al, 1998; Revkin, 1999;

Trippel et al, 2000.

46 For information on the São Paulo fuel cell study, see Mattos, 1999; on India, see Perumal, 1998; TERI, 1998; Matur et al, 1999; on China, see Cannon, 1998, pp 13–14; on the potential viability of fuel cell powered motor scooters, see Lin, 1999.

47 For cost estimates, see: Grubb et al, 1992; OECD, 1997a; US DOE, 1997; Anderson, 1999; World Bank, 1999b. For the fuel cell cost estimate, see Technology Transition Corporation, 1995.

48 World Bank, 1999b.

49 See OECD, 1995, p 24; 1996, p 112; World Bank, 1999a, p 49; for acknowledgment of the critical need for public–private cooperation in reform efforts.

50 ICLEI was launched in 1990 as the international environmental agency for local governments under the sponsorship of UNEP, the International Union of Local Authorities (IULA), and the Center for Innovative Diplomacy. ICLEI's mission is to build and support a worldwide movement of local governments to achieve and monitor tangible improvements in global environmental conditions through the cumulative impact of local actions. It maintains a formal association with IULA and has official consultative status with the United Nations through which it advocates the interests of local government before international bodies. It works with local government constituents and partners in more than 55 countries. Its web site is www.cities21.com/la21/map/iclei .htm.

51 See Bartone et al, 1994, p 54, and Leitmann, 1999, p 328, for descriptions of the innovative policies pursued in Curitiba, Brazil.

52 World Bank, 1999a, p 150.

53 Pearson and Fouquet, 1996, p 154; WRI, 1996, p 97.

54 Associated Press, 2000a.

55 OECD, 1995, p 131.

56 ICLEI, 1997; Newman and Kenworthy, 1999, p 62.

57 OECD, 1995, p 24.

58 For analyses of subsidies provided to nuclear and fossil fuel sectors, see Michaelis, 1996; OECD, 1997b; World Bank, 1999a, p 90.

59 Barnes, 1995; Alam et al, 1998.

60 Burtraw, 1998.

61 Associated Press, 2000b.

62 Both the Clean Development Mechanism and the Joint Implementation Programmes were created under provisions of the Kyoto Protocol. They are managed primarily by the United Nations, but with significant input from the World Bank. The Clean Development Mechanism is one of the key entities through which emissions credit trades will be carried out. Under the process of credit trading, industrial countries are to get emissions credits by helping developing countries lower their emissions. The Clean Development Mechanism is one of the entities through which officially sanctioned trading can occur. The Joint Implementation Programme is essentially the same thing. It also was created as part of the Kyoto Protocol, and it is another programme through which emissions trading

schemes can be carried out. Both of these schemes are new, and few trades have yet been made. Still, they are likely to become the key organizations in emissions trading in the coming years. One useful source that describes recent activities of these programmes is: World Bank, 1999a pp 42, 94, 100–101.

63 US EIA, 1997b, p 46.

64 OECD, 1996, p 149; Martin, 1999.

65 Izagirre, 1998; Bacon, 1999.

66 See Ahmed, 1994, Anderson and Ahmed, 1995, and World Bank, 1999b, for examples of studies published by the World Bank calling for greater support of alternative energy systems.

67 World Bank, 1999c.

68 The Global Environment Facility (GEF) is a programme managed by the World Bank (with significant participation by the United Nations). The GEF provides grants and concessional funds to projects which focus on four target areas: biological diversity, climate change, international waters, and depletion of the Earth's ozone layer. It tries to encourage private companies to carry out these kinds of projects, by providing supporting financing. Although initially a World Bank entity, the GEF has recently become the one of the organizations through which projects from the Convention on Biological Diversity and the UN Framework Convention on Climate Change are managed. One useful source that describes recent activities of this programme is: World Bank, 1999a pp 42, 94, 100–101.

69 UNDP, 1999.

# 13

# DECENTRALIZATION AND URBAN INFRASTRUCTURE MANAGEMENT CAPACITY[1]

## Overview

This chapter reviews a range of infrastructure initiatives implemented since the early 1990s in different economic, social and cultural settings. It assesses recent trends and presents innovative approaches. In each case, the challenges faced and the context within which infrastructure problems had to be addressed determined the range of options and the choice of strategies. The discussion also highlights noteworthy results achieved by Best Practices with a special focus on the ingredients underlying their success.

### Decentralization and infrastructure policy

Since the late 1970s, countries in different regions of the world have pursued their own path towards decentralization. These paths have been shaped as much by historical legacy and cultural tradition as by their contemporary administrative structure, political system and economic opportunities. Despite these differences, there is a degree of convergence among the stated objectives underlying the decentralization process:

- reducing disparities among regions, with a special emphasis on rural development in Asian and African countries;
- providing flexibility to respond to the different local and regional problems and opportunities;
- improving local governance through increased autonomy and better accountability;
- mobilizing private resources for local development;
- empowering people in the development of their communities.

Infrastructure plays a key role in achieving these objectives. Regional particularities, ethnic diversity, democratic local governance and the inability of central governments to reach the very poor are driving communities to demand a stronger voice in their own development. In many ways, these same forces are also driving the decentralization of infrastructure services as a critical component of local economic development and the key to improving local conditions.

> In the early stages of the decentralization process, an appropriate balance among administrative, political and fiscal aspects has rarely been achieved

Decentralization entails fundamental changes to the structure of intergovernmental relations, involving a shift away from vertical hierarchies to a differentiation of roles and the reallocation of functions among actors operating in the same sector or territory. Political pressures, rather than economic considerations, are driving the pace and degree of devolution. In the early stages of the process, an appropriate balance among administrative, political and fiscal decentralization has rarely been achieved. In Eastern Europe, political autonomy preceded economic decentralization and control over expenditures preceded control over revenues. In Latin America and Africa, political autonomy was granted prior to fiscal decentralization. In this respect, South Africa is a particularly interesting case having institutionalized in 1994 a policy of comprehensive administrative, fiscal and financial decentralization granting a high degree of autonomy to provincial and local governments.

> The extent of decentralization depends primarily on the ability of central government to devise an appropriate regulatory framework for central–local relations and its willingness to provide localities with assets and intergovernmental transfers rather than budgetary allocations

Institutions are affected by changes in the macro- and micro-environments within which they operate. Worldwide, since the early 1990s, these contexts have undergone rapid and profound changes. The extent of decentralization depends primarily on the ability of central government to devise an appropriate regulatory framework for central–local relations and its willingness to provide localities with assets and intergovernmental transfers rather than budgetary allocations. These same factors are shaping infrastructure policies and programmes.

### Decentralization of infrastructure services

> The reallocation of functions related to planning and management of infrastructure typically has been guided by the concept of *subsidiarity*: decisions regarding services should rest with the entity of governance closest to the community that is able to deliver these services in a cost-effective way while minimizing the externalization of environmental and social costs

The reallocation of functions related to planning and management of infrastructure typically has been guided by the concept of *subsidiarity*: decisions regarding services should rest with the entity of governance closest to the community that is able to deliver these services in a cost-effective way while minimizing the externalization of environmental and social costs.

Technological advances in the infrastructure sector have improved the efficiency of providing services for smaller jurisdictions and market areas, thus allowing for a greater degree of decentralization than was possible a few decades ago. This has made it easier for local entities, including private operators and NGOs, to participate in the delivery of infrastructure services. They are now better equipped to respond to community needs, priorities for services and preferences for technology and service standards, thus creating a more direct link between the incidence of benefits and costs.

Decentralization has usually led to increases in public expenditures on infrastructure. Size, diversity, wealth, mobility, income inequality and social exclusion have all been viewed as determinants of increased demand. Issues relating to efficiency, equity, competition and performance are addressed in depth in publications on the economic aspects of infrastructure and decentralization, particularly in current working papers by international and bilateral development aid organizations and other specialized institutions.[2]

The general approach to infrastructure management in decentralized institutional settings is to unbundle service provision in terms of decision-making and management in accordance with the particular characteristics of each service and to allocate responsibilities accordingly. These include the following: network planning, system design, choice of alignments, service standards, project priorities, construction of physical plant and operation and maintenance of services. Regulating, financing and undertaking each of these functions for the different services are important aspects of decentralization and need not be the responsibility of a single actor. The assignment of these functions varies among countries according to institutional and policy frameworks, and also between jurisdictions and communities in response to need, means and the various actors from the public, private and NGO sectors operating at the local level. Coordination among decision-makers and providers concerned with primary, secondary and tertiary infrastructure is intended to ensure the productivity of investments.

## Expanding the scope of private sector involvement

Entrepreneurial skills, efficiency in management and the ability to perceive, assess and capitalize on the opportunities created by the decentralization of infrastructure are increasingly prompting the private sector to participate in financing, implementing and managing infrastructure services. The adoption of creative business solutions and innovative financial packages have combined cash flows and negotiated incentives (tax abatements, financial guarantees and concessions) to ensure the profitability of these undertakings.

---

**The government role has shifted from provider to enabler, with an emphasis on the ability to act as:**
- **regulator**
- **catalyst**
- **partner**

---

The privatization of infrastructure has in no way diminished the public role in the sector. At all levels of government, this role has shifted from provider to enabler, with an emphasis on the ability to act as:

- *regulator*, monitoring service quality, ensuring equitable access and limiting monopolistic pricing;
- *catalyst*, providing incentives and streamlining procedures regulations;
- *partner*, contributing to project finance directly or through incentives and credit enhancements.

Partnerships or project-based joint ventures range from outsourcing design and/or construction to private firms; to contracting management of existing systems or granting operating concessions to specialized enterprises; to privatizing new service delivery through build-operate-transfer (BOT) and build-own-operate-transfer (BOOT) agreements; to outright sale of assets to private companies. In contexts of limited public sector resources, BOT and BOOT schemes are increasingly used to finance and build infrastructure (eg dams, national highways, bridges, airports, power plants, sewage treatment plants, bulk water supply and even parking structures). The choice between BOT or BOOT depends on the nature of the infrastructure facility, particularly the feasibility of private ownership and the source of capital cost recovery. Under a BOOT contract, private sector firms are responsible for financing and building a specific infrastructure project. In return, they own and operate the facility through a franchise agreement for a specific period of time. The operating period is typically long enough to allow investors to recoup their capital investment and realize a reasonable rate of return through agreed user-charges. At the end of the period (10–30 years on average), the ownership is transferred back to the government.

## A growing role for NGOs and civil society

Pervasive difficulties in securing financing for infrastructure investments and in building the capacity of local governments to deliver services in many parts of the developing world have prompted poorer households to seek access to services through collaborative action at the community level. This situation is leading to a gradual shift towards partnerships between local governments, NGOs and CBOs. In many ways, these partnerships are the hallmark of the infrastructure projects highlighted in this report and constitute the cornerstone of successful local development initiatives.

## Challenges in the decentralization of infrastructure

Paralleling the common features outlined above are recurrent challenges which central and local governments in different countries and regions have to address:

- Overcoming a tradition of centralized administration entrenched through state control, colonial rule and centralized planning systems. This legacy is reflected in regulatory and fiscal controls, which can still be rigid enough to constrain local government's ability to exercise statutory powers. In particular, the reluctance of central governments to devolve control over revenues and the allocation of resources has adversely affected infrastructure services.
- Balancing the emphasis placed on economic growth and industrialization guided by central agencies with concerns for social equity and inclusion, which are best addressed at the local level.
- Tempering the priority given to managing the macroeconomy, especially in the aftermath of debt or financial crisis, to give localities a space for innovation and creativity. Even in decentralized systems, monetary and fiscal policy has tended to reinforce central oversight through targeted transfers, curbs on borrowing, caps for particular categories of expenditures and limits on discretion to reallocate funds among budget categories. All of these policy measures affect local capacity to implement infrastructure projects.[3]
- Addressing problems of coordination among public agencies, private enterprises, NGOs and CBOs delivering services within the framework of integrated local development programmes.
- Reinforcing the capacities of local governments and communities to discharge the responsibilities devolved to them as their role expands in a decentralized institutional setting.
- Building awareness among local representatives and community leaders of the broader economic, social and environmental issues which are affected by infrastructure decisions.
- Putting in proper perspective concerns regarding the ability of local leaders and officials to pre-empt or influence resource allocation decisions to serve their own private interests. These concerns should not be allowed to overshadow the fundamental role of civil society in defining priorities, allocating resources and managing services at the community level.

Most localities in developing countries are ill-equipped to address these challenges. Demographic pressure in South Asia, sharp fluctuations in the domestic economy and urban violence in Latin America and political instability and civil strife in Africa are exacerbating deficiencies in infrastructure, inequities in access to services, environmental degradation and the lack of funds for capital investments.

Several recent initiatives addressing these challenges are described in the following sections, grouped under three main themes:

1  Decentralized institutional frameworks, participatory processes and capacity building.
2  Financing investments in infrastructure: the expanding scope for intermediary institutions and public/private partnerships.
3  Equitable access to infrastructure and the empowerment of poor and marginalized communities.

# Decentralized Institutional Frameworks, Participatory Processes and Capacity Building

Development banks, international and bilateral organizations and donors have been the traditional source of funding for large infrastructure projects in developing countries and transitional economies directly or through financial intermediaries, particularly municipal finance institutions. These organizations have had and continue to have a major influence on decentralization, infrastructure policies and municipal development programmes. Funding is often linked to reforms in fiscal and administrative policies affecting intergovernmental relations and the promotion of market-oriented approaches to infrastructure provision and delivery of urban services. These organizations have displayed a marked preference for the creation of special institutional arrangements and entities to oversee implementation of agreements if not directly implement projects.

Working outside the existing framework of agencies allows the programmes they sponsor to proceed unencumbered by bureaucratic red tape and interference. It also insulates the special purpose entities from the politics and activities of other actors operating within the same geographic or sectoral territory. The special status these entities often enjoy hampers their integration into existing institutional frameworks, thereby compromising their efficiency and viability in the longer term.

> Bi- and multilateral organizations have reoriented their approaches to include a range of institutional arrangements emphasizing the role of intermediary institutions capable of managing programmes that meet international guidelines, procedures and scrutiny

As they have moved away from sectoral to integrated approaches promoting sustainable development, and poverty alleviation and environmentally sound management of natural and cultural resources, international and bilateral organizations have sought improved performance and accountability in governance, increased participation by the private sector, and a larger le for civil society in the development process. They have gradually reoriented their approach to include a range of institutional arrangements emphasizing the role of intermediary institutions capable of managing programmes that meet international guidelines, procedures and scrutiny. These new approaches focus on building the capacity of local government and encouraging participatory processes.[4]

## The role of regional and intermediary institutions

Worldwide, infrastructure programmes of significant scale have highlighted the need for partnerships among the different levels of government, intermediary institutions and community-based organizations. Strengthening the role and capacity of regional entities enhances their effectiveness as sponsors, partners, catalysts and facilitators in local development and infrastructure programmes.

The Municipal Development Project in Sindh, Pakistan, built up the role of the provincial government to provide an enabling environment for fragile municipalities which have to rely on their own resources to finance their development expenditures. Alarming deficiencies in infrastructure hindered the implementation of local development programmes, resulting in a marked decline in the region's GDP. By streamlining operations to improve the efficiency of public expenditures and discontinuing the practice of overdrafts to finance operating deficits, the provincial government redirected resources towards the long-term finance of productive infrastructure. In Karachi, water supply projects involved local elected representatives in decision-making and enlisted their efforts to reach out to their constituencies. This strategy increased willingness to pay for services, as the quality of these services improved. Collection rates have increased despite a fourfold increase in the average water charge over five years.

In the face of mounting deficiencies in its infrastructure services, the municipality of Bauan in the Philippines decided to participate in the national Municipal Development Programme (MDP) to build its capacity to deliver services and access financing. Prior to seeking funding for specific projects, the municipality opted to first build its institutional capacity and adopt effective managerial and fiscal procedures meeting MDP criteria. Participation in the MDP enabled the municipality to engage in sound investment planning for the effective expansion and upgrading of its infrastructure. A demand-driven approach to project selection ensured responsiveness to local needs and priorities, greater impact on the local economy and high levels of performance by the local government units (LGUs) responsible for preparation and implementation of the selected projects.

The commitment of stakeholders was crucial to success. A participatory approach to local governance allowed LGUs to prepare investment proposals reflecting local needs and priorities. Rather than pre-selecting projects likely to be financed by the MDP, only those projects prepared by the LGUs were submitted for funding. Improved distribution of piped water supply reduced the incidence of water-borne diseases. Improved roads, drainage

and flood control systems resulted in greater accessibility and increased property values. Market facilities and stalls were upgraded, enabling vendors to expand their activity. The rate of return for the project exceeded the 10 per cent lower bound established by MDP and reached close to 14 per cent for the public market component.[5]

## Strengthening local government leadership and initiative

Decentralization has given local governments the discretion and scope they need to take a lead role in responding to the challenges of economic downturn, degradation of the urban environment and social hardship. They institute bold initiatives and innovative practices. Western European nations have put in place sophisticated frameworks to provide local governments with technical and financial assistance. The European Union supplements these national programmes with coordinated assistance aimed at promoting economic development, assisting distressed localities and fostering social inclusion. Infrastructure is an important component of these programmes.[6]

In Jerez de la Frontera, Spain, strong local government leadership and active community participation were key to implementing an integrated plan involving urban planning, infrastructure and economic development. Despite its location in an industrialized province, Jerez' economy relies on wine production which, in recent years, has been declining. Weak community participation, inadequate infrastructure, poor accessibility to regional resources and an unskilled labour force compounded the effects of massive job cuts in the wine industry. To address these problems, Jerez launched a new strategy for economic recovery in 1993, shifting the emphasis from seeking to attract investments from sources outside the municipality to fostering local integrated development.

The 1993 integrated plan calls for economic diversification, and improved infrastructure and communications. The strategy seeks to capitalize on the development of an airport, logistics hub and railway terminal, and improve existing roads connecting Jerez to Cadiz to facilitate access to the region's resources. With regard to economic development, the project focuses on the development of cultural tourism and the promotion of entrepreneurial activities.

> Access to structural funds for economic reconversion from the European Union enabled Jerez, Spain, to implement an integrated development strategy, improving infrastructure and enhancing the local environment. Unemployment fell by 8000, the number of tourists increased to 120,000 and 4600 jobs were created.

Access to structural funds for economic reconversion from the European Union allowed Jerez to implement an integrated development strategy, improving infrastructure and enhancing the local environment. Unemployment fell by 8000 from 1991 to 1992, the number of tourists has increased to 120,000 and 4600 jobs have been created in the small business sector. Underlying Jerez' success are seven key factors:[7]

1   A dynamic local government leadership.
2   A coherent strategy, acted on with determination.
3   A healthy climate of cooperation with business.
4   Local government's investment initiatives to jump-start the stagnant economy.
5   Creative use of EU funds to implement local policy.
6   Efficient municipal administration.
7   Coherent links between urban planning, infrastructure and economic development.

## Partnerships between municipalities and NGOs

Partnerships with municipalities have provided the best channel for the participation of communities in the organized delivery of public services and paved the way for the growing role of NGOs and CBOs in this sector in urban and rural areas and different regions of the world.[8]

Albania, one of the smallest and poorest countries in Eastern Europe, has experienced a transition marked by sharp economic swings and periods of civil strife. The early phases of decentralization witnessed the transfer of political autonomy, and limited administrative and fiscal authority to local governments. Inadequate legislation outlining central/local responsibilities, scarce financial resources and deficient infrastructure strained the capacity of local governments to manage urban services. In Tirana, sustained population growth since 1991 led to rapid expansion of the urbanized area, resulting in the proliferation of informal settlements. With an estimated population of 575,000 in 1997, 6500 families were seeking new housing each year. Local government, even with central transfers, could accommodate only 5 per cent of the demand for new infrastructure.

In the absence of fiscal resources to improve infrastructure in urban and rural areas, the government, with donor assistance, initiated community-driven development strategies to provide infrastructure services based on a cost-sharing formula and to set up participatory management structures. In January 2000, the government promulgated a national Strategy for Decentralization and Local Autonomy, which includes laws to strengthen the autonomy of local governments and increase their capacity to manage local infrastructure and services. Supported by donor assistance and international and local NGOs, the city initiated a community-based development strategy in the informal settlement of Berglumasi in Tirana. The programme brought together local government teams, NGOs and residents to formulate a development plan for the neighbourhood, define priorities for improvements and determine equitable cost-sharing formulas to finance infrastructure. This partnership led to the upgrading of roads and electrical networks, the construction of community buildings and schools, improved public spaces and programmes for youth. Clarifying the legal status of residential land and formalizing an urban plan resulted in the sufficient leveraging of community and household resources to provide infrastructure and build new housing.

In 1997, the experience was expanded to a city-wide effort and was subsequently funded by the World Bank. As the local government teams and NGOs gain experience and residents begin to trust the local government, the Tirana Land Management Programme is scaling up and expanding to other formal and informal residential zones in Tirana.[9]

Similar community-based initiatives were structured in rural areas in Albania. As part of an IDA-funded Irrigation Rehabilitation Project, 250 Water User Associations (WUAs) were created to manage irrigation and drainage systems. In 1997, the government permitted the transfer of primary system management responsibilities to WUAs on a pilot project basis. To date, three pilot projects involving 31 WUAs have been implemented. Service has improved and cost recovery increased through cost sharing. An effective local leadership has emerged, capable of managing water resources and ensuring equity in the allocation of water rights. Building the capacity of the WUAs and allowing them to set irrigation charges restored trust in partnering with government. Finally, the engagement of senior government officials in the dissemination of project information secured commitment among communities and farmers. By mid-1999, the project had positively impacted agricultural production and increased rural incomes by an estimated US$400 to 600 in the average annual income of a farm family.

In the more challenging context of sub-Saharan Africa, Tanzania's Local Government Reform Act of 1996 granted local governments a high degree of autonomy with some control over financial resources. Donors are funding 96 per cent of the cost of the reform through a centrally administered Common Basket Fund channelling resources to local authorities. However, the inability to generate local revenue has undermined the effectiveness of local government. To address this challenge, the city of Dar es Salaam has adopted a 'Two-Point Strategy', incorporated in the Community Infrastructure Programme (CIP):

•   to work closely with community-based organizations so as to enhance their capacity to participate in development programmes and strengthen the city council's capacity to respond to requests from communities;
•   to adopt a new approach to environmental planning and management based on capacity building.

The CIP upgraded infrastructure, enhanced participation and built the capacity of CBOs and stakeholders. The CIP strengthened institutional capacity by establishing programme offices in each community, forming steering committees made up of representatives from all stakeholder groups and formalizing institutional links between the relevant partners and communities through memoranda of understanding. Adequate and transparent information for decision-making and monitoring of performance among the stakeholders altered attitudes and understanding of roles and responsibilities. Communities have agreed to earmark part of their incomes towards the improvement of infrastructure. Involving CBOs and other stakeholders as artners in urban development ensures the sustainability of these assets.[10]

## Community-based approaches to infrastructure services and neighbourhood revitalization

---

**Democratic local governance is a prerequisite to the meaningful decentralization of infrastructure management**

---

Democratic local governance is a prerequisite to the meaningful decentralization of infrastructure management. When people participate in defining visions for sustainable development for their communities, in formulating strategies for equitable access to services and resources and in setting priorities for action, they readily commit to support the activities they have endorsed. Participation also sharpens their awareness of the interrelations between economic, social and environmental issues. This is a highly significant feature of infrastructure programmes and carries important implications for local development.

Poland is viewed as the flagship of Eastern Europe with regard to decentralization. In 1990, Poland passed the Law on Local Self-Government, granting autonomy to local governments. Specifically, the law transferred to municipalities the authority over housing, health services, social assistance, energy and heat, local transport systems, water supply and sanitation, kindergarten and primary education, public order and fire protection, land use and environmental protection. Sustained political pressure and the demonstrated capacity of municipalities to manage their responsibilities were the driving forces for local administrative and fiscal autonomy. Initial assessments suggested that decentralization did improve the quality of service delivery and foster a new, user-oriented attitude, facilitating the transition from a centrally planned to a market economy. In 1998, Poland adopted a set of reforms to enhance regional development and democracy through the creation of new regional and subregional entities and the reassignment of responsibilities and roles. Sixteen regions and 272 counties were established as a coordinating framework for the 2489 municipalities. These reforms increased the proportion of public funds controlled by democratic local institutions from 20 per cent to 60 per cent.

The creativity and commitment of municipal councils and staff since 1990 is demonstrated in the experience of Lublin, Poland. Two lower-income neighbourhoods – Bronowice and Kosminek, housing a population of 6000 – had suffered progressive deterioration. Dwindling central transfers and tight budgets necessitated the mobilization of community resources to improve the urban environment, a new approach in Eastern Europe. The main objective was to build a new working relationship between residents and city officials, based on a shared vision of the future and 'a lasting trust'. Because the districts had been designated as urban renewal sites, residents in the older zones could not upgrade their infrastructure and households in the unserviced extensions could not connect to existing networks. Repairs to buildings were also prohibited, except in the case of roof

leaks. This state of affairs lasted over 30 years, resulting in resentment and distrust of municipal authorities.

In 1992, the city's Urban Planning Unit decided to initiate a participatory process to rehabilitate and revitalize the districts. The process required an extensive outreach effort, involving consultations with every household. Regularly scheduled public meetings were held and, gradually, residents became aware of the role they could play in shaping the future of their neighbourhood. The city council subsequently adopted a new strategy to stimulate local investment in infrastructure and buildings based on partnership between the city and the residents. The Act for Support of Local Investment committed the municipality to cover 50 per cent of the cost of water, sewerage and power lines, 70 per cent of the cost of roadbeds and sidewalks and 100 per cent of the cost of drainage and street paving. The cost-sharing formula could be modulated to take into consideration issues of equity and cost burden. As an incentive to private rehabilitation of buildings, investors were granted a three-year exemption from property taxes.

The partnership between the municipality and the residents was institutionalized through the Local Initiatives Programme to ensure its continuity as a city-wide development strategy. The key features of the programme are:

- introducing participatory planning and community-based development processes through neighbourhood development committees and street representatives working in partnership with the city;
- creating an enabling environment for private investment;
- empowering citizens to pursue their own self-improvement;
- promoting privatization of the housing stock and fostering the development of micro-enterprises;
- ensuring the sustainability of activities initiated; and
- promoting the replicability of successful initiatives.

As of 1998, 391 existing houses have been partially or fully renovated and 87 new ones have either been completed or are in advanced stages of construction. Only six shops existed in the neighbourhoods before regularization; today, 123 shops are operating in rehabilitated buildings. The changing image of the area is attracting private developers and investors interested in vacant parcels close to the city centre.

Lublin's Local Initiatives Programme demonstrates that community-based development processes adapted to the dynamics of the local economy can ensure the sustainability of infrastructure upgrading and economic revitalization efforts through strategic public investments, partnership with the community and empowerment of residents.[11]

In Latin America, widespread inequities in access to land and infrastructure have contributed to the proliferation of unserviced settlements, uncontrolled squatterization in hazardous zones and encroachments of environmentally sensitive areas. Widening disparities in the distribution of income and wealth are aggravating poverty and exacerbat-

In 1996, the first Indian elected official in Cotacachi Canton, Ecuador, initiated a citizen participation process to promote equitable and sustainable economic development, fight poverty and improve standards of living. The Canton Unity Assembly was established as a forum to bring together the different stakeholders from urban and rural areas to discuss problems, propose strategies, define priority actions and prepare a 'Canton Development Plan' with technical assistance from the Urban Management Program in Latin America (PGU/LA). The first Assembly met in September 1996 and brought together around 250 participants, representing the different interest groups in the Canton.

At its annual meeting, the Assembly elects the Canton Development and Management Council, responsible for monitoring compliance with guidelines set by the Assembly and updating the Development Plan. The Assembly also evaluates performance, defines policy guidelines for each budget year, and assigns roles and responsibilities among the different participants, including the municipality and the different community groups, with an emphasis on citizens' contribution.

In the initial phase, the stakeholders discussed the problems and challenges facing their Canton and classified them in four categories. Infrastructure was a key aspect in each category. *Social problems* included illiteracy, worsening health conditions, out-migration, fragmentation along ethnic lines and isolation due to deficiencies in infrastructure, all of which created a lack of social cohesion and a deep sense of insecurity. *Economic problems* affecting productivity included small indigenous farm-holdings, limited production and marketing capacity, lack of access to credit and deficiencies in infrastructure. The latter affected living and working conditions, particularly in rural areas, and hampered the potential for environmental and cultural tourism. *Environmental problems* included river pollution and inadequate river basin management, deforestation and deficient solid waste management in populated centres. Finally, *administrative problems* included lack of technical capacity, low level of citizen participation and inadequate municipal resources. Workshops and zonal meetings, held over an eight-month period, built the consensus needed to prepare the Cotacachi Canton Development Plan. The document is a strategic framework guiding action and it is constantly updated with contributions from the different sector committees.

Five committees, referred to as 'Sector Harmonization Tables' were structured to work on priority sectors: health and education, tourism and production, environmental and cultural resources management and community organization. The five committees present proposals and priority actions to be incorporated in the Development Plan. Their inputs resulted in the implementation of several development projects. The participatory process has been institutionalized, and the Canton Unity Assembly was legalized by a Municipal Ordinance enacted in January 2000.

Equitable participation of the different stakeholders is ensured, with a special emphasis on the representation of women, rural people, marginalized groups and children and youth. Women's participation was 40 per cent in the Assembly and 20 per cent in the Development and Management Council membership. Historically marginalized groups, such as the *mestizo* and black communities, are equitably represented in the Assembly and Sector Committees, as are geographically isolated inhabitants of remote rural parishes. Finally, a special 'Children and Youth Table' has been formed and the Canton's First Children's Congress is being organized.

The size of the municipal budget doubled as international organizations and, more importantly, the community itself contributed funds for social investment projects. At present, municipal funds cover 57 per cent of the total budget, support from international organizations 27 per cent, and community contributions 16 per cent. A large proportion of the resources are being allocated for priority infrastructure projects to improve living conditions. The participatory process succeeded in building consensus on issues of cost and quality, and potable water rates were increased to improve the service. In 1997, sanitation was declared a primary concern and resources directed towards investments in sanitary improvement and community health programmes. Most recently, ecology came to the forefront and additional resources have been allocated for the sustainable management of natural resources.

In June 2000, the Cotacachi initiative received international recognition through the UNCHS/Habitat Best Practices and Local Leadership Programme as one of 10 Best Practices worldwide in improving the living environment.

ing the marginalization of vulnerable segments of the population. In this context, access to infrastructure services is a critical component of strategies fostering poverty alleviation and social inclusion.

The Cotacachi Canton ranks among the three poorest zones in Ecuador, with 80 per cent of the Canton's population of 35,000 living below the poverty line, mostly in rural parishes and scattered remote settlements. Lack of access to land and the ongoing process of fragmentation of family holdings have led to widespread poverty, prompting out-migration. To meet these daunting challenges, the Canton democratized its planning and management procedures. This process allowed the Canton to build consensus, prepare a development plan, allocate municipal funds equitably, leverage additional resources and improve infrastructure and living conditions. The participatory municipal management process was institutionalized, ensuring representation of women and marginalized groups (See Box 13.1).

# Financing Investments in Infrastructure: The Expanding Scope for Intermediary Institutions and Public–Private Partnerships

> Devolving the management of infrastructure to local governments without granting them an adequate tax base to support the associated costs has led to serious service deficiencies or total collapse of the systems and loss of physical assets as a result of overload and lack of maintenance

Devolving the management of infrastructure to local governments without granting them an adequate tax base to support the associated costs has led to serious service deficiencies or total collapse of the systems and loss of physical assets as a result of overload and lack of maintenance. Similarly, decentralizing services, requiring high levels of expenditures on operation and maintenance, can burden municipalities with demands exceeding their managerial, financial and technical capabilities. Furthermore, integrated local development programmes require municipalities to simultaneously implement several projects, which can overwhelm local institutional capacity, compromising sustainability of development efforts.[12]

Partnership for joint service provision by different levels of government, combined with capacity building and resource management programmes, is a viable strategy in the shorter term. It allows for a progressive increase in the local component and in the involvement of communities. Assurance of commitment and leverage from higher levels of government encourages the private sector, including commercial banks, to participate in project financing. Central and provincial support to municipalities has usually taken the form of capital grants for specific infrastructure rojects or particular categories of capital expenditure. To ttract private investment, tax incentives, credit enhancenents and guarantees have been widely used.

Feasibility studies for larger projects usually include an ssessment of life cycle costs. Operation and maintenance mplications can then be matched with the revenues which ntities assuming responsibility for the service can realistially be expected to generate. When revenues fall short of overing the recurrent expenditure on operation, naintenance and debt service (if any), central or provincial governments have to fill the gap at least in the short term. This situation, allowed to continue over prolonged periods, as cumulatively led to increased national budget deficits, rompting curbs on the fiscal discretion of local government. A resource mobilization strategy has to be put in place to ensure continuity in the delivery of services and sustainabily of the infrastructure assets.

## Public–private partnerships to finance infrastructure

Public–private partnerships have come to the forefront as an effective mechanism to attract private investment and mobilize local resources. In China, decentralization has allowed localities to experiment with different infrastructure financing schemes, backed by liberalizing legislation of the water sector. Decision-making powers have been reallocated across the five layers of government: national, provincial, prefectural, county and community. Regulatory and planning authority has remained with higher levels of government responsible for capital investments. Management and maintenance are assigned to the lower levels (counties currently manage 77 per cent of all projects). The Water Policy Act of 1988 regulated use rights and payment and maintenance responsibilities of users. The Water Industry Policy Act of 1997 offered incentives to private businesses to participate in the water sector, thereby enabling the establishment of financially independent utilities through public–private partnerships.

The City of Chengdu has taken advantage of these liberalizing acts to finance badly needed investments to the water supply system. Sponsored by the Asian Development Bank, the Chengdu water supply project is the first BOT project in China. CBDEM, a joint-venture company between the French Compagnie Générale des Eaux-Sahide and Manubeni Corporation of Japan, will design, build and operate the system (See Box 13.2).

Partial government guarantees reduce the financial risks perceived by private sector institutions. In fragile economic and institutional settings, they are an effective instrument to induce the private sector to enter into partnerships with public agencies.

Sub-Saharan African nations face a growing imbalance between the demands for services required by population growth and rapid urbanization, and the financial resources they are able to mobilize. Infrastructure deficiencies have adversely affected economic development and are particularly acute in urban centres where large concentrations of poor households live in slums and squat-

---

**Box 13.2 Public–private partnerships in Chengdu, China**

With 3 million urban residents, Chengdu is the political, cultural, financial and educational centre of southwest China. Located between the Fu and Nan Rivers, Chengdu relies on both the Duijiangyan Irrigation System and Yangtze River System for its water needs. During the 1990s, increasing agricultural and urban demands on water, arising from rapid growth, liberalization and industrialization, transformed Chengdu into one of the most polluted cities in southwest China. Industrial effluent, raw sewage and intensive water usage created severe shortages, undermined water quality and caused widespread environmental damage. Squatter settlements on the river banks exacerbated the situation.

Chengdu adopted the 'Fu and Nan Rivers Comprehensive Revitalization Plan' in 1993 to strategically guide the use of water to meet social, environmental and economic objectives. A major section of the river has been rehabilitated through the renovation of bridges, drainage channels and dykes and improved oversight of more than 1000 polluting enterprises. Affordable housing has been provided to resettle 30,000 squatter households. Thirteen new public parks have been created along the river banks, transforming the banks into recreational open space.

In a first phase, the municipality earmarked a substantial portion of its annual budget to meet the project's cost of US$360 million. It established partnerships with public organizations, schools, education and research institutions, neighbourhood associations and private investors, including real estate developers and construction companies. In the second phase, the municipality is experimenting with the first BOT project in China. Sponsored by the Asian Development Bank, the project involves the construction of a water treatment plant. CBDEM, a joint-venture company between the French Compagnie Générale des Eaux-Sahide (a member of the Vivendi Group) and the Manubeni Corporation of Japan will design, build and operate the plant which will increase Chengdu's potable water supply by 40 per cent. The distribution network will be expanded beyond the 1.8 million people currently served.

The utilization of local resources and the participation of stakeholders in project development and implementation were seen as crucial to its success. The municipality established a framework for the participation of representatives from the planning, construction, land administration and environmental protection departments, business enterprises, schools, neighbourhood committees, scientists, community organizations and residents in the development of a vision for a sustainable future. In all, more than a million people participated through 188 neighbourhood committees and 1291 enterprises and institutions. The city then strategically deployed its own resources to ensure financing of the infrastructure services it required.

In June 2000, Chengdu was selected as one of 10 Best Practices worldwide to receive an award for excellence in improving the living environment under UNCHS/Habitat Best Practices and Local Leadership Programme. Separately, the International Council for Local Environmental Initiatives (ICLEI) presented Chengdu with the 'Local Initiatives Award for Excellence in Freshwater Management'.

---

ter settlements. The challenge is to increase the very low current rates of mobilization and leveraging of local resources, and use available funds effectively to promote local development. Investment in upgrading and expansion of infrastructure systems as well as operation and maintenance of urban services are critical to the success and sustainability of this development effort.

In Angola, the population of Luanda has grown from 470,000 inhabitants in 1975 to more than 3 million today at an annual rate of 7 per cent. The living environment deteriorated for lack of infrastructure, urban services and housing. Chaotic urbanization degraded the natural environment and endangered the health and safety of the inhabitants. The scarcity of financial resources made it very difficult to address these mounting problems.

In 1993, an innovative partnership between government agencies Empresa de Desenvolvimento Urbano Lda (EDURB), the private sector and the community, referred to as the Luanda Sul 'Self-Financed Urban Infrastructure Programme', was established to finance and implement badly needed infrastructure services in Luanda. The concept is to grant concession of titles to land and use the private funds mobilized to finance the infrastructure (primary, secondary and tertiary) needed to service the sites. A special Achievement and Management Fund capitalized by receipts from land sales was set up to finance servicing costs.

Laws were enacted to privatize and restitute land formerly held by the state. The provincial government issues land titles in coordination with EDURB, which manages the programme. In turn, EDURB relies on the technical expertise and entrepreneurial skills of its private partners (Odebrecht and Prado Valldores) who prepared the programme's financing strategy and business plan and are

managing and coordinating land disposal and development in the different sectors of the city.

The strategy was to start by serving the affluent clients capable of prepaying their serviced parcels. The surplus profits after payment of developers' fees and return on investment are used to finance servicing of plots for lower-income households who do not have accumulated savings to contribute. The combination of legal guarantees regarding title to land offered by the state and a sound business plan submitted by the private developer convinced oil companies to prepay the purchase of serviced parcels to house their employees, experts and managers. This prefinancing provided the programme with start-up capital. Bulk infrastructure had to be constructed to service the selected sites and the developer had to contribute supplementary funding to complete the water supply system. The infrastructure included access roads, potable water, electricity, storm water drainage and sanitary sewerage to support development at the standards demanded by the clients.

The social component of the programme started with a pilot scheme to resettle 860 families living in shacks in hazardous areas and security zones in downtown Luanda. Today, over 2700 families have been resettled. Service charges for water and electricity are deposited in a Replacement Fund to ensure sustainability of the services provided.

In December 1999, contracts totalling US$85.6 million had been signed and US$96.3 million in infrastructure investments committed, of which US$16.4 million were allocated to the programme's social component. Eight million square metres have been fully serviced, 4000 jobs were created and local tax revenue has increased. The urban environment is improving through planned urban expansion, revitalization of the city centre, rehabilitation of public spaces and protection of the natural landscape and vegetation. Most importantly, the programme created a formal, private real-estate market which was nonexistent in Angola. It then capitalized on the dynamics of this market to valorize the public land assets it held and to leverage funds based on the future value of the serviced land.[13]

## Box 13.3 FINDETER, Colombia: an innovative municipal development fund

Financiera de Desarrollo Territorial (FINDETER) partially rediscounts loans granted by commercial banks to municipal borrowers. The banks can borrow from FINDETER up to 85 per cent of the value of loans they extend to municipalities and other sub-national entities. FINDETER's intervention allows commercial lenders to balance the maturity of assets and liabilities and enhances their liquidity. However, the banks assume the credit risk associated with their municipal borrowers since FINDETER does not purchase the loans but rather recapitalizes the institution with liabilities having appropriate maturities. In addition to second-tier lending, FINDETER manages the national government's matching grant programme for infrastructure projects including water, roads and schools.

FINDETER, which inherited the staff, experience and project pipeline of its predecessor MDF, has reached close to two-thirds of Colombia's 1000 municipalities in its first three years of operation. It has refinanced loans for the rehabilitation, improvement or expansion of urban infrastructure and services including water, sewerage, roads, traffic management, environmental protection, drainage and flood control, solid waste, slum improvement, education and health facilities. Water, sanitation and roads account for 75 per cent of loan disbursements, institutional development 8 per cent, and schools 6 per cent. Projects must meet specific criteria regarding developmental and environmental impacts to be eligible for FINDETER refinancing.

In addition to its own capital consisting of retained earnings, loan repayments and borrowing from international institutions such as IBRD and IDB, FINDETER issues bonds on the domestic capital market to raise funds and has to offer competitive yields. Despite owning 86 per cent of FINDETER's shares, the national government does not guarantee the bonds. In addition, unlike its predecessor FFDU, local governments and financial intermediaries are not compelled to buy FINDETER bonds by regulation or in order to obtain borrowing privileges.

FINDETER loans carry a variable interest rate and borrowers are charged a service fee. The institution fully covers its operating costs, foreign exchange and credit risks, and produces a positive return on investment. Several measures substantially reduce risk. Commercial banks are liable to FINDETER if their borrowers default, and municipal revenue, pledged as loan guarantee to the banks, can be used to repay FINDETER. Furthermore, the percentage of municipal revenues which can be pledged is capped and lower bounds are set on debt service coverage ratios. Municipal infrastructure loans cannot exceed a maximum loan-to-value ratio of 70 per cent, and a municipality which defaults on a FINDETER-backed loan cannot access new funding through FINDETER.

While the dependence of larger municipalities on FINDETER has decreased as they manage to access competitive financing from commercial banks, FINDETER's mission remains critical to small- and medium-size municipalities. Given its development mandate, FINDETER offers technical assistance on project design, including the development of business plans, financial forecasts, loan application requirements, and implementation, particularly with respect to contracting and procurement. Larger and fiscally stronger municipalities have managed to secure financing with competitive spreads. To protect the smaller municipalities, FINDETER sets a ceiling on the maximum interest rate banks can charge on the loans it refinances.

## The role of intermediary institutions in infrastructure finance

In Latin America, decentralization has fostered creative initiatives involving intermediary institutions and NGOs. In Colombia, decentralization has given municipalities strong revenue generation powers. Conversely, they have assumed the responsibility for urban services including water and sanitation, streets, education and health. Despite improvements in the volume of local revenue and large increases in central transfers and in the local share of national taxes, municipalities are unable to access long-term credit for capital investments on the domestic capital market. Financial intermediaries holding mostly short-term liabilities are reluctant to provide long-term financing, especially to municipalities with no track record of administering long-term debt. To address this problem, in 1990 Colombia restructured its Fund for Urban and Infrastructure Development (FFDU) which operated from within a mortgage bank and established a Municipal evelopment Fund (MDF), known as FINDETER *inanciera de Desarrollo Territorial*), sponsored by the Inter-merican Development Bank (IDB) and the World Bank.

FINDETER differs from conventional MDFs, through hich central government channels subsidized credit to ocalities, in that it does not lend directly to municipalities. is a second tier lender operating through the banking ector by partially rediscounting loans granted to municipal orrowers (See Box 13.3).

## Privatization of infrastructure services: ublic utility companies

Decentralization and privatization are integral components f the process of transition from a centrally planned to a narket economy. In Eastern and Central European ountries, local autonomy has been a fundamental principle f governance since 1990. Public assets and enterprises are eing privatized and the scope for private participation in he infrastructure sector is further enhanced by the progres-ive dismantling of central regulatory controls. Unlike ransitional countries in the Commonwealth of ndependent States (CIS), Central European nations have nvested heavily in their infrastructure. Despite these ubstantial investments, their infrastructure needs to undergo serious modernization and renovation to enable hem to compete effectively in the global marketplace. Privatization is being increasingly used as the choice instru-ment to improve efficiency in the management and operation of services and leverage the financial resources needed to upgrade the quality of the physical plant.

In Romania, public service corporations were trans-formed into commercial utility companies and public subsidies are being phased out. Privatization has compelled the public utilities to seek more efficient and cost-effective approaches to service delivery and establish partnerships with various stakeholders.

The city of Brasov in Central Romania had to deal with ageing infrastructure and artificially low utility rates which did not cover maintenance and operation costs. Changes in operation and management of water and waste-water services were needed to gradually move towards European environmental quality standards. A utility company, the Regii Autonome, was created to manage the services. Technical modifications to water filtration increased water production, and wastewater treatment was improved by the installation of a low-cost aeration system meeting national environmental standards. Monitoring and planning is supported by a computerized water evaluation system. Finally, changes to the organizational structure improved administrative efficiency.

The success of the Regii Autonome is attributed to the partnerships established among various stakeholders in planning for the improvement of services. The Brasov County Council, the Brasov Prefecture, other municipalities within the region, government departments and agencies, the University of Transylvania, public-owned societies, business representatives and the Chamber of Commerce and Industry participated in the planning of improvements.

The European Bank for Redevelopment and Reconstruction, local finance institutions and intermediary NGOs provided technical and financial support. An open communication channel facilitated the implementation of an operational plan requiring the city to approve significant increases in utility rates.

# Equitable Access to Infrastructure and the Empowerment of Poor and Marginalized Communities

Access to land and infrastructure is a powerful empowering mechanism, enabling impoverished and marginalized citizens to improve their income and their living conditions through self-reliance

Access to land and infrastructure is a powerful empowering mechanism, enabling impoverished and marginalized citizens to improve their income and their living conditions through self-reliance.[14]

Rural development programmes were among the first to focus on the economic and social impacts of infrastruc-ture. These programmes have included infrastructure services crucial to the development effort, starting with water supply and electrification and extending to education and health facilities. Decentralization has resulted in greater involvement of rural populations. In India, the process has included the devolution of administrative and financial powers to the units of governments closest to the people. Despite the slow pace of change, local public officials have started to pay greater attention to the needs of the rural poor.

Indonesia's Kampung Improvement Programme has, over the course of 25 years, upgraded 11,000 ha of unserviced slums and improved the living conditions of 15 million people

Among urban programmes, the most widely recognized is Indonesia's Kampung Improvement Programme which, over the course of 25 years, upgraded 11,000 ha of unserviced slums and improved the living conditions of 15 million people. A programme of similar magnitude has been launched in 1996 in South Africa where overcoming the legacy of apartheid is a daunting challenge. These initiatives are in line with a new initiative, 'Cities Without Slums', being carried out by a broad-based coalition of partners headed by UNCHS (Habitat) and the World Bank.

South Africa's geographic size, ethnic diversity and differences in development levels among regions and locali-ties made decentralization the best approach to ensure responsiveness to local needs and opportunities. Local governments can legally set rates for user charges and property taxes, and leverage resources by entering into partnerships with the private sector. Redistribution policies

## Box 13.4 The South African Government's grant-funded municipal infrastructure programme

The South African municipal infrastructure programme, launched in 1996, is one of the largest and most ambitious in the world. The programme's mission is to 'ensure that all communities have access to at least a basic level of service'. The government views municipal infrastructure as a critical component of local development, and the most effective mechanism by which poor and marginalized communities can be empowered. The aim is to promote five key objectives:

1    upgrading the living environment;
2    promoting social equity;
3    integrating former apartheid cities and towns;
4    enhancing economic opportunity;
5    fostering partnership to leverage inputs.

The government made a strategic decision to create a grant-funded programme in order to reach the poorest 20 per cent of the population. The programme serves urban and rural communities and is structured as a partnership between the state, the provinces and the municipalities to ensure community-driven delivery of services. Decentralized programme management was necessary on political and technical grounds to cope with the large number of geographically dispersed and typically small projects.

Despite the overriding priority placed on delivery, the programme sought to ensure community participation and structure a constructive interface between communities, municipalities, provincial governments and central authorities. Communities submit project proposals to their municipality for approval, assistance and support. The municipality prepares business plans for the projects and submits them to the Provincial Cabinet for approval, possible additional funding and mobilization of grant funds. Funds for the project meeting the programme's criteria are channelled from the national government to the provinces. In turn, the provinces make the funds available to the municipalities and monitor project implementation.

As of March 2000, 48 per cent of MIP funds were allocated to water supply, 22 per cent to roads, 17 per cent to sanitation, 6 per cent to storm water drainage, 5 per cent to community facilities and 2 per cent to refuse collection. To promote integration and development, the programme supports the government's housing scheme by providing bulk infrastructure to new extension zones. Most recently, the MIP has been reoriented to allow for the rehabilitation of existing systems.

Impacts on the ground are impressive. Improvements to water supply systems have promoted economic activity and diminished the incidence of water-borne diseases. New and upgraded roads have fostered the development of micro-enterprises and created jobs.

Extensive community involvement is critical to successful project implementation. Communities define priorities, also develop plans and elect committees to serve as a link to municipal and provincial governments. Several have structured creative financial packages through private–public partnerships and have managed to maximize local resource mobilization. In general, willingness to pay for services increased as the quality of the services improved.

By March 2000, the programme had provided employment totalling 3.7 million person days through the use of labour-intensive construction methods and local materials. An impressive total of 272,000 person days had been devoted to training workers, thus enabling them to perform 90 per cent of construction activities. At present, a special emphasis is placed on the employment and training of women.

Lack of capacity at the local level has emerged as the single most critical constraint impeding programme performance and undermining the sustainability of achievements. The government had at first earmarked 5 per cent of MIP project funds for capacity building and training of emerging contractors and workers. This allocation has recently been increased to 10 per cent to provide adequate funding for building up local governments' technical and managerial capacity to operate services and maintain infrastructure assets.

By March 2000, South Africa's municipal infrastructure programme had implemented 1496 projects for a total expenditure of over US$350 million. MIP funds have provided water supply to 9.3 million rural and urban residents, sanitation to 5.1 million, storm water drainage to 1.7 million, access roads to 3.8 million, community lighting to 1.1 million and solid waste disposal to 0.9 million.

In 1998, MIP was recognized as a Best Practice under UNCHS/Habitat Best Practices and Local Leadership Programme.[i]

**Note:** i The Centre for Urban Development Studies at Harvard University undertook a detailed evaluation of the programme funded by the World Bank and UNDP, in collaboration with public officials and PDG Consultants. The Centre also provided capacity building to the programme management team at the central and provincial level, and conducted training courses on infrastructure and local development. These activities were funded by USAID and the government of South Africa.

channel targeted central transfers to both provincial and local governments based on prevailing levels of poverty and the state of the rural economy. A major effort is underway to improve living conditions, provide infrastructure to unserviced and underserviced communities, build up the capacity of smaller and weaker municipalities and provide them with technical and financial support to enable them to develop economically and socially (See Box 13.4).

## Community-based financing of infrastructure projects

Recognizing the empowering role of infrastructure, shelter advocacy groups and microfinance institutions have initiated programmes to enable the poor to access the services they badly need to improve their living conditions recognizing the empowering role of infrastructure, shelter advocacy groups and lately microfinance institutions have initiated programmes to enable the poor to access the services they badly need to improve living conditions in both urban and rural settings.

A leader in this field is the Self-Employed Women's Association (SEWA), established in 1972 in Ahmedabad, India, as a trade union to empower low-income women working in the informal sector (which accounts for 96 per cent of employed women). SEWA has established two institutions: SEWA Bank, a cooperative bank fully owned by SEWA shareholding members, and the Mahila Housing SEWA Trust (MHT) which provides members with legal and technical assistance to improve their shelter and access infrastructure services. By the end of 1999, SEWA had a membership of 220,000 and SEWA Bank had close to 13,000 depositors and 36,000 borrowers with a working capital of just over US$6 million.

Parivartan – a city-wide Slum Networking Project initiated by the Ahmedabad Municipal Corporation (AMC) involves SEWA, SEWA Bank and MHT. The project aims to provide families in underserviced slums with infrastructure services, including individual water supply, underground sewerage, individual toilets, solid waste disposal service, storm water drains, internal roads and paving, street lighting and landscaping. Acting respectively as financial and technical intermediaries, SEWA Bank and MHT motivate families to contribute US$48 towards an infrastructure improvement package ranging between US$333 and US$345. In addition, families are required to contribute US$2.30 towards the cost of maintenance, which will be assumed by the community. Local industry matches the family contribution with US$48 and the balance is covered by the municipality, which also provides all Parivartan participants with written documents ensuring security of land tenure for a minimum period of ten years. To help participants to meet their contribution, SEWA Bank provides loans of up to US$37 to each family. Loans can be repaid in monthly instalments of US$2.30 or as a lump sum, and carry an interest rate of 14.5 per cent. At this time, 18 slum communities are participating in the programme.

For the three settlements where infrastructure improvements have been completed, an evaluation documented an average increase of US$1.15 per day in net household earnings. Fruit and vegetable vendors are able to wash their produce at home and do not have to wait in long queues at public water points. This allows them to get to the market at 6 a.m. and spend more time selling produce. Health problems and serious illnesses, including typhoid, malaria, diarrhoea and skin disease, have been reduced by 75 per cent. In addition, the success of the project prompted members of SEWA Bank to take out a collective loan providing each household with US$575 for home improvements.[15]

Similar approaches fostering access to services by marginalized communities are being initiated in many parts of the developing world. In Guatemala, 61 per cent of inhabitants live in rural areas, the highest proportion among Latin American countries. The vast majority are indigenous groups living in poverty. Inequitable access to land and infrastructure services perpetuates this situation. It is estimated that less than 30 per cent of the rural population has access to infrastructure. INEG, the state-owned enterprise in charge of rural electrification, requires communities to form a committee, submit an application for the service, specify the contribution they are able to make towards the cost and secure a state or municipal subsidy to cover the remainder of the cost. Construction is then undertaken by a private contractor supervised by INEG. To obtain water supply, communities must additionally pay for a report on the quality of local water sources, and commit to maintaining the system. Rural communities, lacking financial resources to meet their cost-sharing obligations, political power to leverage adequate co-funding and organizational skills to manage the process, are unable to obtain services without the assistance and support of intermediary NGOs.

Genesis Empresarial was established in 1988 to improve living conditions for low-income rural communities by providing microcredit to finance community-based delivery of infrastructure. The Community Infrastructure Lending Programme (CILP) provides technical assistance and financing to help communities to obtain electrification and water supply. A government matching grant still has to be secured by the community. Genesis loans are not subsidized. Interest rates reflect the costs associated with different sources of capital. Current rates range from 21 per cent on funds from the Central American Bank for Economic Integration (BCIE) to 30 per cent on funds from commercial banks and Genesis' own funds.

By mid-1998, 8700 households in 189 communities had received loans for electric connections under the electrification programme, launched in 1993, and 1820 families in 21 communities had received loans for water connections under the water supply programme initiated in 1995. A prerequisite for participation in the programme is that at least 90 per cent of residents must agree to the provision of infrastructure. The project is then administered through groups of four to twelve families sharing similar socioeconomic characteristics. Loans range from US$120 to US$450 per household.

Collective liability and submission of a documented land title held by one household in each participating group are the only conditions for eligibility. Loan amortization periods range from one to four years, according to the group's income. Repayments are monthly with an option to pay after harvests available for agricultural labourers. In 1998, the CILP repayment rate was just over 92 per cent.

Genesis provides assistance in organizing borrowers, registering the project committee, preparing the technical report and cost estimates, filing applications for matching grants, structuring affordable repayment terms, filing applications for credit, dealing with contractors and managing the group loan accounts. Despite the financial burden of technical assistance, CILP managed in 1998 to achieve a positive return on investment of 1.2 per cent.

The initiatives presented here illustrate the particularities and shared features of decentralized provision of infrastructure services across countries and regions. The experiences of outstanding programmes and best practices highlighted in the preceding sections provide ample evidence that dynamic local leadership, sustained outreach, civic engagement, creativity and sound financial manage-ment are important ingredients of success. These ingredi-ents allow localities to overcome constraints, ensure delivery of infrastructure services, promote sustainable loc development and foster social inclusion in very challengin contexts.

## Notes

1   This chapter is based on 'Decentralization and urban infra-structure management capacity', a background paper prepared by Mona Serageldin, Suzanne Kim, and Sameh Wahba, Harvard University.

2   See, for example, Asian Development Bank; Besley and Coate, 1999; Bird et al, 1995; Burki et al, 1999; Centre on Integrated Rural Development for Asian and the Pacific, and Division of Human Settlements Development of the Asian Institute of Technology, 1991; World Bank, *Decentralization and Infrastructure*; UNDP, *Draft Report on Global Workshop on UNDP/MIT Decentralized Governance Research Project*; Estache, 1995; Estache et al, 1995; Fisman et al, 2000; Fukasaku et al, 1999; Halperin, 1998; Humplick et al, 1996; Litvack et al, 1998; Manor, 1999; Mody and World Bank, 1996; Rojas, 2000; Roy and Mackintosh, 1999; Shah, 1997.

3   In 1997, OECD and other inter-national organizations voiced concern over the potential impacts of fiscal decentralization on China's capacity to manage its macro-economy and to finance large investments in productive infrastructure.

4   For a fuller discussion of capacity building, see Chapter 14.

5   In 1997, Bauan received interna-tional recognition as a Best Practice in Urban Infrastructure Development at the Second International Expert Panel Meeting on Urban Infrastructure sponsored by the United Nations Centre for Regional Development (UNCRD) and the Urban Management Programme-Asia (UMP-ASIA). In 1998, the municipality of Bauan was also selected as a Best Practice under UNCHS (Habitat) Best Practices and Local Leadership Programme.

6   See Chapters 4 and 17 for a fuller discussion of changes in and strengthening of local govern-ment.

7   Jerez received recognition for its achievements from the OECD as one of three Best Practices under the Local Economic and Employment Development Programme (LEED).

8   See Chapter 14 for discussion of public–private partnerships, as well as broad-based partnerships including civil society partners.

9   The Center for Urban Development Studies at Harvard University provided technical assistance and training for this initiative funded by the World Bank and USAID.

10  In 1998, the Community Infrastructure Programme was recognized as one of ten Best Practices worldwide to receive an award for excellence in improving the living environment under UNCHS (Habitat) Best Practices and Local Leadership Programme.

11  In 1996, Lublin's Local Initiatives Programme received international recognition when it was selected as one of ten Best Practices worldwide to receive an award for excellence in improving the living environment under UNCHS (Habitat) Best Practices and Local Leadership Programme. The Center for Urban Development Studies at Harvard University provided Lublin with technical assistance and training funded by USAID.

12  See Chapter 14 for a discussion of local capacity building.

13  In June 2000, the Luanda Sul programme was selected as one of ten Best Practices worldwide to receive an award for excel-lence in improving the living environment under UNCHS (Habitat) Best Practices and Loc Leadership Programme.

14  The UNCHS Global Campaign for Secure Tenure, referenced in Chapter 16, is an important initiative in recognition of this point.

15  In 1996, SEWA received interna-tional recognition when it was selected as one of ten Best Practices worldwide to receive an award for excellence in improving the living environment under UNCHS (Habitat) Best Practices and Local Leadership Programme.

# ENSURING DEVELOPMENT PROSPECTS

Lack of resources, insufficient institutional capacity and persistent corruption often greatly circumscribe the problem-solving abilities of governments. In recognition of this constraint, a major conclusion at the Habitat II conference in 1996 concerned the need for capacity building, particularly at the local level.

Capacity building goes beyond the training of individuals to the strengthening of the institutions and frameworks within which they work. In this connection, Chapter 14 is especially oriented to ways of supporting the growing responsibilities of local government, including decentralized arrangements as promoted through on-going attempts to seek finalization of the proposed world charter of local self-government. Based on internationally recognized principles, these efforts aim to provide a constitutional anchoring of local self-government for assisting the effective and sustainable implementation of the Habitat Agenda and the strengthening of local democracy. This chapter also discusses two other major aspects of capacity building: the formation of public–private partnerships and the broadening of cooperative arrangements to include civil society groups as full partners in decision-making. It considers as well the implications of these trends for the funding priorities of international development agencies.

Capacity building has often been conceived of as happening in a top-down manner, involving designated agencies and training institutes. High-level experts and consultants play key roles. The process is characteristically hierarchical and relies on vertically structured relationships. However, there is increasing recognition of the importance and potential to foster capacity building through horizontal processes. Such relationships can link sectoral agencies of different local governments in exchange and information sharing schemes. A good example of this approach is municipal international cooperation (MIC). Widespread decentralization has increased interest in MIC: point-to-point municipal knowledge exchange across international borders, designed to build institutional capacity and to improve municipal responsiveness and service delivery. MIC is more likely to produce sustainable results, going beyond merely the sharing of technical information, if the public agencies involved are transformed into 'learning organizations'. Modern information and communication technologies facilitate such learning processes.

Based on growing experiences of cooperation between the public and private sectors, partnerships are now evolving from single-purpose, project-oriented ad hoc agreements between government and business interests to more institutionalized arrangements concerned with a range of interrelated long-term goals, involving multiple partners that include civil society. For these arrangements to be successful in meeting the needs of low-income households, public regulations must lower the profit margins of private sector operations without jeopardizing their commercial viability.

At the same time, low-income communities, taking advantage of modern communications technologies and less bound by local constraints, have begun to reconstitute themselves as overlapping, sometimes transnational networks to access and share information, material resources and solidarity. This development signals new opportunities for civil society to engage government and the private sector in new forms of cooperation that enable the poor to participate as empowered partners.

The formation of transnational civil society networks, aimed at social justice and environmental sustainability, represents a 'globalization-from-below' whose goals offer alternatives to the priority accorded to economic growth under the globalization processes that are currently dominant. Slum/Shack Dwellers International (SDI) is a good example of such a network. The Alliance in Mumbai is an active member of SDI and its work plays a crucial part in informal, horizontal capacity building at the community level, involving the active and direct participation of people living in poverty. The Alliance is committed to methods of organization, mobilization, teaching and learning that build on what the poor *themselves* know and understand. The first principle of this model is that 'no one knows more about how to survive poverty than the poor themselves'. Its politics is one of accommodation, negotiation and long-term pressure rather than of confrontation or threats of political reprisal.

The experiences of SDI illustrate the promise of efforts to forge broad-based cooperation among partners that in the past have often opposed each other. However, the fulfilment of this potential requires a strong commitment, including changes in the use of existing resources. It is not so much that large amounts of funding are needed but that a reliable flow of assistance is required, so that each action can build on the experience of the previous one. There is also a need to develop new channels for technical advice and direct funding of community-level initiatives where decisions about support are made locally and where accountability is to local institutions and citizens. Necessary innovations face a key institutional and political challenge: any real decentralization implies decentralization of power, while governments must at the same time remain responsible for regional equity.

Chapter 15 concerns itself more specifically with capacity building in the context of post-disaster recovery. It first documents the astounding human costs of natural and human-made disasters, including armed conflict and civil strife. The burdens of rebuilding lives and communities disproportionately fall on women. Often, the vulnerability of people at risk is also made worse by their poverty, their state of health, their food supply, the condition of their housing, insecure tenure and the physical and social infrastructure of their community. Although natural disasters cannot usually be prevented, the severity of their consequences can be reduced by human settlements development, including effective land use planning, enforcement of appropriate building regulations and non-discriminatory legal provisions to safeguard women's rights to property and inheritance.

Disaster recovery and mitigation have evolved into a global enterprise involving multiple transnational relief agencies and the increasing use of special assistance programmes. There is a trend to include community development and social and economic rehabilitation in post-recovery efforts. Networks established by the informal and non-governmental sectors furnish frameworks for more inclusive models of institutional recovery following disasters. Such models can help to prevent a repeat of past experiences, where post-disaster recovery policies have reinforced previously existing inequalities. Disaster mitigation activities provide unique opportunities for local governments to enhance planning and management capacity in support of greater liveability for all citizens.

# 14

# BUILDING CAPACITY

The Habitat Agenda identifies capacity building and partnership development as one of the requirements for reaching its two main goals of adequate shelter for all and sustainable human settlements development in an urbanizing world. Chapters 16 and 17 review selected aspects of progress towards those goals. This chapter concerns itself with capacity building and the development of partnerships. The discussion is especially oriented to the greater role of local government and the broadening of cooperative arrangements to include civil society groups as full partners.

> Capacity building goes beyond the training of individuals to the strengthening of the institutions and the frameworks within which they work

As a concept, capacity building goes beyond the training of individuals to the strengthening of the institutions and the frameworks within which they work (see Figure 14.1). This chapter will first consider capacity building in the context of the decentralization processes through which national governments devolve functions to local authorities. Effective decentralization requires, among other things, that the transfer of responsibilities to municipal governments be accompanied by a parallel transfer of resources and the creation of necessary revenue-generating capacity (see Chapters 4 and 13). It also requires appropriate institutional, legal and financial frameworks for development and management tasks. By implication, it is necessary to strengthen the capacity of local governments (see pp 162–165; see also Chapter 4). Decentralization and strengthening of local authorities are also mandated by the Habitat Agenda.

> There is increasing recognition of the importance and potential to foster capacity building through horizontal processes

Capacity building has typically been conceived as happening in a top-down manner, involving designated agencies and training institutes. High-level experts and consultants play key roles. The process is characteristically hierarchical and relies on vertically structured relationships. However, there is increasing recognition of the importance and potential to foster capacity building through horizontal processes. Such relationships can link sectoral agencies of different local governments in exchange and information

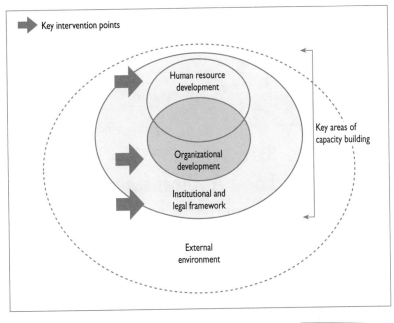

sharing schemes. A good example of this approach is municipal international cooperation (see pp 163–165).

Capacity building usually involves developing partnerships, largely between the public and private sectors (see pp 165–171). However, there is increasing evidence of the effectiveness of more broad-based partnerships that also include participants from civil society. To maximize the potential of these more inclusive cooperative arrangements, more and more community-based organizations are establishing direct interactions among themselves, as illustrated by the Face-to-Face[1] initiatives developed with the support of Shack/Slum Dwellers International.[2] This chapter describes the operations of the Alliance in Mumbai as a good example of such informal, horizontal capacity building at the community level. This discussion includes consideration of the formation of transnational civil society networks; their goals of social justice and environmental sustainability inspire a 'globalization-from-below' as an alternative to the priority accorded to economic growth under the globalization processes that are currently dominant. Chapter 4 more fully articulates the complementary roles of the public, private and civil society sectors in evolving and implementing new political strategies and forms of governance for urban liveability. The concluding section of this chapter considers implications of capacity building for development funding priorities.

**Figure 14.1**

**Capacity building concept**

**Source:** Davidson (Background papers)

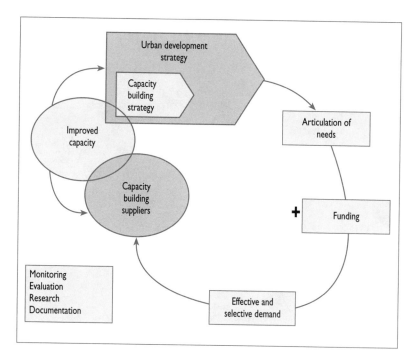

# Strengthening Capacity of Local Authorities and their Partners[3]

Local governments, taking on a broader range of responsibilities, should not only be efficient, but they also need to be effective in carrying out programmes that tackle the main challenges of equitable and sustainable development. Doing so requires the ability to analyse social, environmental and economic situations across sectoral boundaries, as well as the ability to develop creative solutions with partners and to communicate effectively with decision-makers. Decision-makers further need the knowledge and ability to set priorities and to work for medium- and long-term as well as short-term objectives. This means that training must be aimed at local council members as well as government agency officials, and must encompass local government as well as its partners.

The discussions on Capacity Building for Better Cities held during the City Summit (Habitat II) in Istanbul in 1996 produced the following recommendations:

- Develop capacity building strategies, particularly locally, which are integrated with urban development and management strategies.
- Commit resources necessary for capacity building.
- Undertake capacity building activities in a manner that integrates human resource development, organizational change and improvement of institutional, legal and financial frameworks.
- Introduce measures to widen the supply of capacity building services and encourage them to become more responsive to demand.
- Coordinate activities of institutions charged with capacity building so as to strengthen linkages between actors in urban development and ensure

complementarity, increased choices and productive competition.
- Give high priority to monitoring, evaluation, impact assessment and research in terms of improving tools and ensuring dissemination using traditional and new media.

A major conclusion from the Habitat II discussions was that capacity building strategies should be developed at the local level to ensure relevance and to obtain the institutional support that local decision-makers require. In related vein, two main areas need to be stimulated. One is the articulation of new needs by existing and new actors. This can be difficult, as there is often no awareness that anything needs to change. Conservative behaviour is the hallmark of many bureaucrats. Second, it is necessary to clarify new needs to the suppliers of capacity building services, who also may be rather conservative, and to make them more responsive to changing situations.

Capacity building also involves training for new roles that demand new knowledge, skills and attitudes. To make this more concrete, it is useful to look at the example of urban planning (Figure 14.2). Here, the focus of activity has moved from land use planning and development control to more participatory forms of action and strategic planning. In these emerging approaches, there is more emphasis on developing creative approaches and innovative partnerships comprising several parties that can jointly commit the necessary resources. For these approaches to work, it is essential that those involved maintain positive attitudes towards cooperation, coordination and shared interests. Skills in communication, interpersonal relationships and negotiation become critical. Such qualities are often alien to the culture of governmental organizations, and fostering them will require sustained effort.

## Drafting a world charter of local self-government[4]

At the Habitat II Conference, governments committed themselves to the objectives of decentralizing authority, responsibilities and resources, enabling local leadership and promoting democratic rule (para 45 of the Habitat Agenda). Governments further underscored this commitment in the Istanbul Declaration on Human Settlements, by which they recognized local authorities as their closest partners and essential to the successful implementation of the Habitat Agenda. In order to achieve those ends, in the Declaration they reiterated the need to promote decentralization through democratic local authorities and to strengthen their institutional and financial capacities (Istanbul Declaration, para 12).

These formal commitments by governments reflected a broad consensus at Istanbul for the international community, in partnership with the representative associations of local authorities, to take steps to draw up a worldwide charter of local-self government as an internationally agreed, adaptable framework for the practice of local autonomy and decentralization. Such a charter was seen as a vital contribution to the improvement of people's lives, to local democracy and to national and global economic progress. Inspired by the successful experience of the European Charter of Local Self-Government, a proposal for a global charter was subsequently submitted to the Habitat II Conference.

It was envisaged that the charter would provide a framework of rights and responsibilities of local government, but would also be flexible and adaptable enough to apply to different national and regional particularities, socio-economic settings and historical experience.

In attaining the goals of the charter, national governments would need to consider practical means for increasing the capabilities of local governments to plan, programme and operate the systems and services that would be added to the local portfolio of responsibilities.

These decisions and recommendations of Habitat II opened the way for continuous dialogue and closer partnership between the United Nations and all the major associations of local authorities and cities, under the coordinating umbrella of the World Associations of Cities and Local Authorities Coordination (WACLAC), formed in 1996 as the interlocutor of the local authority movement with the United Nations.

This charter remains to be negotiated by national governments as an international instrument to guide national legislation on decentralization and the role of local authorities.

## Funding to strengthen municipal capacity[5]

> Many development agencies have shifted a significant part of their funding from urban projects to capacity building of local authorities and supporting 'good governance'

International development agencies have shifted a significant part of their funding from urban projects to strengthening the institutional capacity of urban governments and supporting 'good governance'. The World Bank was among the first to sponsor improved urban administration, rather than specific urban projects, and it became the largest donor in terms of financial support for this purpose. This shift can be seen in the growing scale of loans specifically to increase the institutional capacity of recipient governments to address their own needs with regard to urban development and to enhance local capacities to install and maintain infrastructure and services.[6] Commitments to building the institutional and financial capacity of urban authorities totalled close to US$2500 million between 1983 and 1996 with close to three-quarters of this committed in the years 1988–1995.[7] The World Bank also provided an increasing number of loans to national or municipal institutions responsible for providing funding to local governments.[8] There are also examples of the Bank funding intermediary institutions that in turn fund projects, rather than the Bank funding the projects themselves, further illustrating the shift from 'retailing' to 'wholesaling' of urban development finance.[9] There have

been parallel changes in funding for water and sanitation sectors where the Bank has moved from support for the construction of infrastructure to funding the transformation of institutions within recipient governments to make them more responsive to low-income communities' preferences and willingness to pay.[10] A further implication is the Bank's increasing involvement in working with municipal governments and in changing central–local government relations.[11]

The growing interest among donors in municipal government capacity building led to the setting up of the World Bank/UNDP/UNCHS (Habitat) Urban Management Programme in 1986 and in 1999 to the establishment of the Cities Alliance.

## Municipal international cooperation (MIC)[12]

Some cities function like well-oiled machines, while others struggle to provide even basic services. Municipal international cooperation (MIC) matches cities whose engines are already humming with those that need priming. Through MIC strategies to create partnerships and networks of information exchange, cities can build local capacity and harness resources and knowledge that they might never muster on their own.

> Widespread decentralization has increased interest in MIC: point-to-point municipal knowledge exchange across international borders, designed to build institutional capacity and to improve municipal responsiveness and service delivery

MIC is an umbrella term for point-to-point municipal knowledge exchanges that cross international borders. Such exchanges are designed to build institutional capacity and to improve municipal responsiveness and service delivery. The worldwide trend of devolving power and resources from central to local authorities has generated more interest in using MIC. Cooperative initiatives typically involve bilateral arrangements between cities (eg sister cities and peer-to-peer learning), but the spread of information technology creates opportunities for multilateral cooperative systems to emerge.

MIC is becoming particularly favoured as a form of development assistance. In 1996, the Habitat II Conference called on local government to be a partner in international cooperation. For the first time, it was recognized that local sustainable development was more likely to take hold if local governments took part in development work. MIC is one strategy through which this can occur. MIC offers opportunities for 'smaller scale interventions targeted to specific problems or populations'.[13] Additionally, the concept of MIC emphasizes partnerships between cities, rather than the hierarchical relationship implicit in a funder/grantee arrangement.[14] The strategy is a flexible one, enabling partners to tailor the process in terms of 'the type of assistance to be provided, in timing and in the variety of person-to-person relationships established'.[15] Finally, MIC represents a relatively low-cost strategy.

Funding streams vary enormously from one MIC set-up to the next. Sometimes, exchange funding comes from municipal associations. Most major municipal associations operate through membership fees but receive programme assistance from their national development aid agencies. For example, the Institute for Housing and Urban Development Studies (IHS)[16] works closely with The Netherlands' Association of Municipalities, which handles exchange programmes on behalf of the Ministry for Development Cooperation. Municipalities and the ministry each put up 50 per cent of costs. National or supra-national agencies, such as the World Bank or United Nations agencies, also sponsor such work. Other players include international professional organizations such as the International Council for Local Environmental Initiatives (ICLEI)[17] and the International Union of Local Authorities (IULA).[18]

The Washington, DC-based International City/County Management Association (ICMA)[19] is a noteworthy MIC participant involved in urban issues worldwide through a broad array of partnerships. For example, through ICMA, business improvement districts in Baltimore, Maryland, and Orlando, Florida, joined counterparts in Jamaica to improve Kingston's cleanliness and safety. Homeless and poor residents were hired for various street-cleaning efforts, and 'public safety ambassadors' were trained to dispense information and watch for potential crime. The redevelopment began in 1995 and was partially funded by local Jamaican businesses. Information was shared with other Jamaican cities.

The Federation of Canadian Municipalities (FCM) backs both technical exchanges, such as the ICMA project just described, and grassroots democratization efforts, like the Kitchener (Ontario)–Windhoek (Namibia) partnership. Namibians' observations of diversity management in Kitchener's integrated human resources plan helped them to break down racial barriers in their home city, Windhoek.

### ● Evaluating MIC initiatives

Evaluating the success of particular MIC efforts is not a straightforward task. Questions arise about who benefits from a partnership, and whether the benefits will be sustained over time. The cooperation between city agencies in Toronto and São Paulo on emergency medical services and affordable housing offers a good illustration of these issues.[20]

First, the link between improvements in the quality and efficiency of municipal services cannot be assumed to benefit equally all citizens of a place.[21] Projects initiated through partnerships may also be limited in scope, and thus not help a significant number of people in need.[22]

Further, although 'receiving' countries will adapt programme ideas to their contexts, there is a risk that they may accept programmes from developed countries too uncritically. São Paulo adopted Toronto's density bonus programme to generate a funding stream for affordable housing, which has resulted in more than 53,000 new units over nine years. Experience reveals that North American urban development strategies have bred a host of problems for cities as well, from displacement and demolition of

vibrant neighbourhoods, to suburban–central city disparities, and more. The small-scale, site-specific nature of many MIC initiatives may actually limit the likelihood that participants will consider a programme's potential negative impacts within a larger context and time frame before adopting it as an appropriate solution.

Additionally, there is some controversy over the purpose or potential of MIC, and thus the nature of the benefits that the process should produce. Where some observers point to equipment acquisitions or changes in delivery systems as signs of success, others look for broader signs of organizational change. On the one hand, some suggest that MIC projects that work best have concrete, fairly technical goals; for example, a solid waste management department that wants to improve operations. This sort of management process can be communicated to a counterpart fairly easily. Yet even such narrowly defined, technically oriented projects face constraints. São Paulo's providers of emergency medical care wanted to stock their ambulances with the same array of equipment and supplies that their Toronto counterparts used, but they could not secure the resources to acquire the full range of equipment.[23]

> The transformation of a public agency into a 'learning organization' is more likely to result in sustainable changes and benefits to 'receiving' cities than mere technical information sharing

Others argue that organizational learning and change is the broader goal of MIC, and partnerships should be evaluated on these grounds. The transformation of a public agency into a 'learning organization' is more likely to result in sustainable changes and benefits to 'receiving' cities than mere technical information sharing. One way to promote institutionalization of learning is for employees of 'receiving' agencies to become trainers themselves, rather than simply learning skills from 'donor' agency personnel.

It is significant that recently there have been attempts to broaden conventional twinning arrangements to include more partners. For example, ICMA supports several 'triads' that involve a Serbian partner, a US partner and a partner from Eastern Europe.[24] There are also partnerships including a coalition of cities. In Arizona, US, for example, Tempe, Chandler and Pinal County were partnered with a larger city in the State of Jalisco, Mexico – an arrangement that has worked well because the US partners contribute complementary strengths (eg water treatment, urban finance) and can spread demands on staff resources. An ancillary benefit has been that the US cities now work more closely together.[25] On a larger scale, Eurocities is an association of 97 metropolitan cities from 26 countries that aims to improve the quality of life of the 80 per cent of Europeans living in cities by promoting the exchange of experience and best practice between city governments. It lobbies for an integrated European urban policy and facilitates the planning and implementation of transnational projects between cities. Within seven specialized committees, Eurocities builds up technical expertise in different fields.[26]

Likewise, METREX is a European network of practitioners, politicians, officials and their advisers with a common interest in spatial planning and development at the metropolitan level. It seeks to promote the exchange of knowledge on strategic issues and to support metropolitan planning at the European level.[27] In the Asia-Pacific region, CityNet acts as a focal point and facilitator by promoting the exchange of expertise and experience and by expanding bilateral relationships into a multilateral network. It stresses the need to enhance cooperation between local governments for the development of human settlements, and to promote consultation between these authorities and NGOs.[28] The spread of internet technology supports the development of these more broad-based exchanges and the formation of 'consortia'.[29]

> MIC is part of a broader arsenal of cooperative development and capacity building approaches. It cannot supplant local-to-(inter)national relationships and resources still need to come from beyond the local level

The recent development, just described, occurs in the context of efforts to build local capacity through the formation of partnerships. In many countries, local governments find themselves with greater responsibilities and fewer resources. As a result, there is a continuing and growing interest in seeking partners to deliver services and accomplish projects for which local capacities are insufficient. The intent is to leverage land, property assets, tax incentives, human resources and limited funds to enlist others that can contribute required supplemental resources to create 'win–win' situations. As discussed below, such partnerships are still predominantly with the private sector. However, a later part of this chapter will highlight the emergence of more broad-based partnerships with low-income communities, in particular, as invaluable participants. The development of partnership-based approaches is at the core of new strategies for sustainable capacity building.

## Capacity Building through Partnerships[30]

National and local governments have been increasingly unable to meet shelter and service needs of low-income and poor households, especially in the fast-growing cities of the developing countries. Conventional approaches based on direct provision by the public sector have been constrained by the heavy burden of necessary subsidies, bureaucratic management and inefficient production systems, resulting in housing, infrastructure and service provision that is often inadequate. As discussed earlier in this report, under processes of globalization, direct provision by the state has further diminished and relegated the vast majority of urban populations to options determined by market forces.

The increasing role of market forces has forced public sector agencies to review other options for meeting housing and urban development needs. More and more, governments have focused their efforts on influencing the private and nonprofit sectors and encouraging them to play a more active role in meeting the needs of the poor and not just affluent households.

However, there are several impediments to improved cooperation between the public and private sectors. On the one hand, many urban land and housing markets are often dominated by a small number of powerful companies who influence prices, restricting access to an affluent minority while excluding large numbers of poor people. The long-standing ethos of public sector agencies is that they should compensate for this failure of private housing markets by providing directly for those in need. On the other hand, from the developers' perspective, public sector agencies are often seen as incompetent, inflexible and corrupt. Official standards and procedures are often inappropriate for the varying levels of affordability, making it hard for private developers to meet social needs *and* conform to official requirements. Delays in processing proposals, and the cost of obtaining permissions, erode profit margins, prompting many developers to raise prices to stay in business.

> It is clear that neither the public nor the private sector alone can address the growing challenges of providing adequate and affordable housing and services to predominantly poor, urban populations

Changing policies is one challenge, but changing the ingrained habits, motives and practices of key stakeholders in both public and private sectors can take much longer. Recognizing this is the first step towards a wide range of innovative approaches by which the roles and relationships of the two sectors, together with third sector groups, such as NGOs and CBOs, are being radically transformed. Such broad-based partnerships are now being widely promoted as a pragmatic response to the constraints that the public sector faces in its efforts to make urban land and housing markets, as well as basic infrastructure and services accessible to the poor.

> Partnerships are evolving from single-purpose, project-oriented ad hoc agreements between the public and private sectors to more institutionalized arrangements concerned with a range of interrelated long-term goals, involving multiple partners that include civil society

Such partnerships are evolving from single-purpose, project-oriented ad hoc agreements between the public and private sectors to more institutionalized arrangements concerned with a range of interrelated long-term goals, involving multiple partners that include civil society. They are a key component of the Habitat Agenda.

Each of the examples in Boxes 14.1–14.3 entails relatively formal, public and contractual relationships between the partners. To date, these formal public–private partnerships have been limited in scale and have had only a modest impact at best on low-income access to land, services and finance.[31] However, when partnerships include community organizations (NGOs and CBOs) and custom-

---

**Box 14.1 Sharing land development benefits in Mumbai, India**

When the City and Industrial Corporation of Maharashtra (CIDCO) sought to obtain land for new urban development in Navi Mumbai, rural landowners did not want CIDCO to acquire their lands, since they had ample previous experience of receiving low compensation levels from public authorities.

To overcome their objections, CIDCO introduced a new approach whereby landowners received both monetary compensation and serviced plots in the new development. The land area returned was in proportion to the land area acquired, after the costs of developing it had been deducted. To discourage speculation, owners of the new plots were not permitted to transfer or sell them for ten years after allotment, though many residents transferred their plots by granting power-of-attorney. Regulations limiting the extent of plot development and the use of the plot were relaxed so that owners could maximize their investment potential within the site. The approach enabled CIDCO to plan and reallocate nearly 17 km² of land within the area designated for the new city and enabled many farmers to become affluent. However, benefits were not equally distributed. Because of the higher densities resulting from relaxing restrictions, CIDCO provided wider roads, but resources were insufficient to finance expanded infrastructure provision.

**Source:** Adusumilli, 1999.

---

**Box 14.2 Facilitating partnerships by requests for proposals in Bulgaria**

Following the tumultuous socio-economic and political changes that swept Eastern Europe in the late 1980s and 1990s, municipal authorities lacked resources to develop land. Technical assistance provided by USAID helped to introduce public–private partnerships in selected towns in 1993, following workshops attended by municipal officials and private developers.

The Requests for Proposals (RFPs) approach was adopted to increase access to desirable sites and as an alternative to the often complex and lengthy negotiations with private landowners. RFPs are intended to introduce or strengthen open, fair competition between developers, elicit proposals that provide a complete and detailed description of a developer's plan, allow for an assessment of a developer's ability to execute a proposed plan and protect the municipality's financial and legal interests. RFPs should include mandatory performance standards, clear conditions or terms under which the developer will operate, a time frame for construction and criteria by which the proposals will be evaluated.

A prerequisite is that municipalities must have a solid understanding of the local real estate markets. The RFP can then be prepared stipulating the development objectives and components that developers must provide, so that the proposal that generates the best public benefit can be clearly identified. The Bulgarian projects were designed to introduce the approach and encourage public officials to view the process of urban development from the perspective of the private developer. This enabled them to see the importance of site selection and the financial implications of official standards. It also emphasized the importance of soliciting the participation of developers in creating viable and sustainable partnerships.

**Source:** Lynch et al, 1999.

---

**Box 14.3 The Birmingham Heartlands Development Corporation, England**

The 1990s saw a major growth in partnership approaches to urban development in the UK. The Birmingham Heartlands was established by Birmingham City Council and five major construction companies to develop and implement a development strategy for the area and provide over 700 new homes, improve 350 existing ones and provide a range of environmental improvements as well as commercial, social and recreational facilities. The project reflected the ethos of 'city first, politics second' and regenerated large areas of derelict industrial land which benefited a large, mixed community.

**Source:** Archer, 1999a.

---

ary or traditional practices of the types listed above, together with other, less formal, associations, arrangements or relationships, the scale and reach of programmes increase considerably.[32] Therefore, it would be better to think in terms of more inclusive 'multi-stakeholder partnership' (MSP) arrangements, including informal relationships between the public and private sectors, consistent with the broad-based approaches advocated in the Habitat Agenda (see, for example, Box 14.4).

Examples of informal partnerships include the guided squatting approach, or incremental development concept, which has been adopted in Hyderabad, Pakistan and Conakry, Guinea.[33] Guided land development has been particularly effective in sub-Saharan Africa where it has helped to facilitate the development of customary lands. This was achieved by associating customary owners with all phases of the operation, from site selection to the development and sale of plots.[34] The approach has also been used in Lima, Peru. In Mexico, joint ventures between *ejidos* and the private sector have been implemented for many years.[35] One common practice involved private developers acquiring *ejido* land in return for private land of equal value elsewhere.[36] (See Box 14.5.)

The aforementioned examples do not imply that informal partnerships are preferable to formal ones. The informal sector provides as many examples of exploitation, manipulation and inefficiency as other forms of development. However, it exists largely because the regulatory frameworks that determine official standards, regulations and administrative procedures are often inappropriate to the social, cultural, economic and environmental realities that apply in developing countries. Under such conditions, the inability or refusal to reform such standards, regulations and procedures forces lower income households into the informal sector and leaves a range of informal arrangements or partnerships as the only viable means of development.

The essential quality that partnerships embody is that of complementarity, in which the relative strengths and weaknesses of each partner are offset against each other to produce developments that combine the best contributions of each. In practical terms, these developments are economically efficient, socially responsive and environmentally sustainable. However, partnerships mean different things to different people. To some, it may be a series of discrete projects and to others a way of doing business. While such variations are possibly necessary in winning support for the concept, it does present problems in defining and assessing examples.

## Issues involved in public–private partnerships

An approach that redefines the roles of the state and its relationship with private and third sectors raises several major issues. A central question concerns the reasons for pursuing partnerships. While self-interest is an essential element, beyond this, partnerships offer each party benefits that cannot be achieved when operating independently.

**Box 14.4 Women form partnership to upgrade 'Masese slum' in Uganda**

In the 'Masese slum' on the outskirts of Jinja, Uganda's second-largest city, destitute poverty and unemployment were the way of life until a few years ago. In a unique and inspiring partnership, citizens, governments and NGOs worked together in the Masese Women's Self Help Project. Its Housing and Human Settlement Upgrading Programme established a settlement and credit plan that enabled women to acquire secure land tenure and construction materials for housing. The project also developed a community infrastructure for employment, health and education services.

**Appalling conditions**

After British colonialism ended in 1962, Uganda went through periods of political upheaval. As a result of the civil strife during the Idi Amin rule (1971–1978), refugees had begun to squat in the Masese slum area. By 1989, about 2000 destitute people or over 600 families, many of them single mothers, widows and orphans, lived there in appalling conditions, without skills, training or access to jobs. Prostitution, liquor brewing and trading were widespread.

Housing consisted of mostly one-room mud huts with grass, or rusty corrugated iron roofs, without electricity or safe water supply. Absentee landlords rented out the dilapidated houses to people without other options. An average of six persons occupied the one-room dwellings. A woman with an 11-member family in a one room, grass thatched hut, commented: 'The room also doubles as a kitchen. There are no toilets. When it rains, water does not just leak through the roof, it streams in through the doors and floods the house.' A housing project to improve living conditions was essential. The goal of the Women's Self Help Project was therefore to: 'upgrade the settlement, improve security, develop social and economic infrastructure and guarantee sustainable incomes'.

**Women form partnership**

The Masese Women's Self Help Project was a partnership between non-govermental and government agencies. The Masese Women's Association (MWA) assumed responsibility for all major decision-making. The African Housing Fund (ARF) coordinated the project's on-site activities. The Ministry of Lands, Housing and Physical Planning (MLHPP) planned, designed and supervised the project. The Jinja Municipal Council (JMC) supplied land and electricity, and opened up the area with a network of roads. The Danish International Development Agency (DANIDA) provided most of the seed capital for equipment, materials and training. Three committees were organized: the Project Coordination Committee (meeting annually), the Project Organizing Committee (meeting quarterly) and the Project Implementation Team (meeting monthly). AU committees had ten elected community or MWA representatives and municipal, national, administrative or technical delegates.

**Obstacles to overcome**

The project had to overcome major obstacles. Motivating the community and explaining the project's objectives were important to overcome these difficulties. Illiteracy slowed the learning process and hampered project management, accounting and marketing. Improper financial management also created problems. Close supervision of financial transactions and continued on-the-job training helped to increase worker accountability. Business management training for the community is gradually changing these attitudes and building confidence.

Traditional thinking and practice in Uganda placed women into the private sphere. The head of the household owned land and property and was assumed to be a man. Beliefs that women are inferior to men and should not inherit property were the norm. Meetings were regarded as the men's domain and it was difficult to attract women to project meetings. Even when women attended, initially they often lacked the confidence and skills to participate. Illiteracy made them dependent on men. When the project was introduced as a women's project, the men were sceptical.

**Project implementation**

To change these attitudes, the national government adopted a housing policy that addresses the issues of women, shelter and discrimination in land ownership, construction jobs and other respects. It combined a strategy of legislation, education and awareness programmes to protect a woman's rights. National legislation, policies, strategies and local by-laws were adapted to make the project happen. The Masese slum was on municipal land for which the tenants had temporary occupancy permits. The area had originally been designated for middle-income residents and part of the land had already been surveyed for larger lots. To make the land affordable, plots were reduced to 250 m$^2$ and divided into 700 parcels. Private development on the land was stopped and those who did not want to be a part of the project, mostly absentee landlords, were compensated. The council also donated a large piece of land. The land then was transferred to the project so that it could in turn be assigned to community members. Building regulations were revised to allow the use of local building materials and reduce construction costs.

**Outcomes**

Compacted earth roads with storm water drainage were installed to be upgraded as the community accumulates more resources. Initial high-standard roads and services would have greatly increased the market value of the lots and encouraged low-income owners to sell these, only to return soon to another slum. Adopting this incremental upgrading allowed women and the poor to own property. Women also gained access to credit, assumed responsibilities in construction and development and demonstrated their abilities as good decision-makers and managers. Project results are highlighted overleaf. However, the biggest impact of the project has been its effect on public awareness, perceptions and acceptance of what women are capable of doing.

- 80 per cent of the community members who participated in the Masese Women's Self Help Project were women. Various women's committees managed the project and made all major decisions.
- The Masese women constructed and operate a concrete building products factory, which also supplies commercial markets. They opened carpentry workshops to produce doors, windows and furniture. The building material production and the carpentry workshops are a valuable source of income and have already generated more than 200 million Uganda shillings (US$200,000). Construction firms have hired some of the women.
- Another 150 community members, 130 of them women, have found steady employment through the project, as an important step towards achieving sustainability.
- Training programmes enabled women to construct 370 low-income, permanent houses with proper sanitation, roads and drainage. Some members rent out their houses, or parts of them, to repay their loans. Land title deeds were prepared for 274 women-headed households and 96 in joint titles.
- Jinja Council contracted women to build a 20-classroom primary school in Masese. A day care centre for 100 children opened. It shares its building with a health unit for simple ailments, immunizations and family planning services.
- An open-air market has spawned small-scale businesses and jobs for 56 women and men.
- Installing water wells in Masese has created jobs for eight women, who sell water for US$2 per 20 l.
- Since the project began, incomes have increased fourfold to an average of US$70 per month.
- A US$70,000 revolving loan fund, a small-scale credit scheme and other credit and savings opportunities benefit the community.
- Families are more stable; husbands – rarely permanent members of their households – are now becoming an important part of the community. Prostitution and drunkenness declined.
- Masese women have trained women in the Mbale and Arua districts of Uganda, in Kenya and in Rwanda, where similar projects have been initiated.

**Source:** Ochwo, 1999.

---

> The first step in forming partnerships requires actors from each sector to acknowledge each other's legitimate interests. Private developers have to accept lower profit margins and mixed developments that benefit lower-income groups. Public regulators must enable developers to meet the needs of lower-income groups while operating on a commercially viable basis

A first step in this process requires actors from each sector to understand and acknowledge the legitimate interests of the other. In this connection, government is responsible for protecting the wider public interest and particularly the needs of vulnerable households, unable to gain access to the legal land and housing market. The state is also expected to maintain an appropriate legal, policy and administrative framework within which other actors can operate effectively. Throughout, there is a potential conflict of interest since partnerships involve the state acting as a player as well as the referee.

The traditional tension between public and private sectors will require an adjustment on both sides; public sector agencies must become more market sensitive and the private sector must become more socially responsive. Formal private sector developers have to accept lower profit margins and mixed developments that benefit lower-income groups. At the same time, regulatory frameworks must enable developers to meet the needs of lower-income groups while operating on a commercially viable basis. Partnerships should not be seen, however, merely as a means of extending market forces, but rather a new way of producing social and environmental benefits.

While public sector staff may regard partnerships as a withdrawal of the state from its traditional roles, or as a threat to their authority, partnerships can, in fact, be a

means of maintaining and even increasing them. For partnerships to be effective, central government will need to create an appropriate policy, legal and administrative framework within which local authorities can create a range of partnerships to suit local conditions. This requires a better knowledge of how land markets operate.[37] Striking the right balance, and adapting it to changes in market conditions, will not be easy. Failure to adapt the administrative system would render partnerships more of a public relations exercise than a transformation of government roles in land development.

> Central government must create appropriate policy, legal and administrative frameworks within which local authorities can create a range of partnerships to suit local conditions

To date, the ability of the state to provide the necessary level and type of support at the scale required is, at best, unproven. Even if such investment is available, the value of the final development will have been increased to a level that either puts it out of reach of poorer households, or requires subsidies to ensure access, thus adding to market distortions. This issue is particularly relevant in cities where public authorities hold land in, or adjacent to, prime central locations. In such cases, should local authorities sell land at the full market price for private sector development and use the revenue generated for other projects targeted at low-income groups? Or, should it forgo such revenue in order to enable poorer households to live in central locations near employment areas, even though some houses may find their way onto the commercial market?

These questions do not necessarily apply equally or uniformly. In land and property markets, public–private partnerships encourage developments that maximize 'added alue', but also allow a proportion of speculative increase to accrue to the wider community. Incorporating the potential benefits of this approach will, however, require public sector agencies to reassess planning policies, particularly those relating to development control, and to revise them in ways that can facilitate a partnership approach. In services provision, concessions and other forms of private sector participation can offer efficiency gains, though they are less common in low-income areas. For finance and credit, it is more important that public sector subsidies (eg in interest rates) do not distort markets and discourage private and voluntary sectors from offering viable options.

Partnerships may not need to operate at all stages of the land development process, from site selection, planning, development, marketing, allocation and house construction. However, establishing mechanisms that can incorporate user groups, NGOs and CBOs at the appropriate stages, is an integral part of necessary changes and provides new opportunities for civic leadership. Although partnerships have been established practice in the UK for some years, there has been disappointment at the lack of a role for local residents and community organizations, a problem that is not unique to the UK.[38] Yet, partnerships will only flourish if they satisfy the primary needs and interests of *all* key stakeholder groups, especially the potential beneficiaries, community groups and, where appropriate, those involved in customary land allocation systems. This is another reason for broadening partnerships to include multiple stakeholders.

## Criteria for assessing partnerships

How should the success of partnerships be measured? Four basic assessment criteria focus on the extent to which partnerships:

1 increase the *supply* of urban land, services and finance for housing;
2 improve the *efficiency* of urban land, housing and finance markets;
3 improve *access* to land, services and finance for low-income groups;
4 provide the basis for a more productive *long-term relationship* between public, private and third sectors.

In meeting these criteria, successful partnerships will be those that possess or provide:

- an efficient way of identifying different and changing needs;
- adequate trust between the partners;
- clarity concerning the purpose of the partnership and individual roles within it;
- adequate leadership;
- the possibility for all partners to fulfil their role;
- adequate access by all partners to essential information;
- necessary financial and other resources;
- compatibility within the prevailing political and legal climate;

---

### Box 14.5 Public–private partnerships for housing finance

Across the developing world, formal institutions have been reluctant to offer financial services to low-income groups. The standard reasons are that transaction costs are too high, incomes are too erratic for long-term amortization schedules and groups have no redeemable sources of collateral. In order to acquire land and initiate housing construction, households have had to employ a range of financial mechanisms including use of savings, which are often the only safeguard against health emergencies or consumption crises, or use moneylenders or rotating credit schemes. To address this gap, in the past 20 years there has been considerable innovation in the provision of housing finance from Southern NGOs.

Among these NGOs, most reject what has become known as the 'minimalist' perspective that advocates the provision of full-cost non-subsidized finance. NGOs accept that the minimalist approach assures financial sustainability but argue that social development is important to the 'housing' process. In some cases, learning from the experience of micro-enterprise schemes, NGO housing finance has promoted savings to provide collateral to qualify for bank credit, expanded community-based credit rotation, disbursed donor subsidies and offered intermediation with local government and the provision of technical advice. The principal difficulties faced by NGOs are how to ensure financial sustainability *and* household affordability, *and* achieve scale given the larger capital requirements *and* maintain close community contact.

One approach has been to establish partnerships with government agencies. These arrangements have drawn on the comparative advantage of the NGOs in working with communities and target low-incomes groups, and have opened opportunities for NGOs to 'lock in' innovative models to local government. In Xalapa, Mexico, a community organization (UCISV-VER) and a national NGO (CENVI) worked with local government to have 80 irregular settlements recognized, set up training programmes and extend services. In 1993, a request was made to gain access to part of the government's land reserve and a modified rotating credit scheme (*tanda*) was set up.

Working with government has not been without its problems. Partnerships have suffered from a shortfall between people's expectations and the ability of parties to deliver, the lack of experienced NGO staff, changing government priorities with administration turnover, policies to restrict subsidy allocations and attempts at politicization. However, at the end of the tanda cycle CENVI loans each person one and a half times their savings, and the state government provides a sum equivalent to twice their savings in the form of building materials. The CENVI loan has to be repaid; the state government contribution does not. To date, the repayment rate is 100 per cent, and the programme has been extended to other settlements and other cities.

**Source:** Jones and Mitlin (1999) UNCHS (Habitat) Best Practices Database.

---

### Box 14.6 The role of information technologies in supporting partnerships

The dramatic and universal spread of the internet and the World Wide Web has spawned a range of networks dedicated to promoting innovative and participatory development processes.[i] These have enabled professionals in developing countries to obtain and disseminate information on urban development issues and mobilize support from colleagues around the world. The Urban Resources Centre in Karachi is one example of a group that seeks to build on the efforts of local communities to strengthen their influence in dealings with the authorities, developers and external professionals and create more inclusive forms of development. The Network-Association of European Researchers on Urbanization in the South (N-AERUS) is another group that links researchers in Europe and the South with similar objectives. These groups use the internet to disseminate examples of innovative partnership arrangements and shorten the previously lengthy process of 'public learning' by which new ideas were transmitted and adopted. Their strength lies in their accessibility, speed, informality and universality.[ii]

**Note:** i See Davidson and Payne, 2000 for details of selected networks; ii Archer, 1999a.

### Box 14.7 Evaluating partnership projects

**Land pooling/readjustment projects in Taiwan**

This approach is a technique for managing and financing the subdivision of selected urban fringe areas for planned urban development. In each project, a group of separate land parcels is consolidated for their unified design, servicing and subdivision into a layout of roads, utility service lines, open spaces and building plots, with the sale of some of the plots for project cost recovery and the distribution of other plots to the landowners in exchange for their rural land.

*Increasing the supply of urban land, services and finance for housing*

Up to 190 projects were completed by 1993 to produce 8379 ha of urban land.

*Improving the efficiency of urban land, housing and finance markets*

The approach has stimulated the supply of urban land and helped to reduce the pressure of land price inflation.

*Improving access to land, services and finance for low-income groups*

Only a small proportion of land was allocated for low-income groups.

*Providing the basis for a more productive long-term relationship between public, private and third sectors*

The approach is well understood and accepted by key groups, including municipalities, landowners and developers and forms the basis for a productive relationship between all key stakeholders.

**Source:** Archer, 1999b.

**The Islamabad New City project, Pakistan**

In Islamabad, a large area of land between the capital and the airport was scheduled for development as a major public–private partnership. The project was initiated in 1995, but was terminated a few years later after allegations of malfeasance.

*Increasing the supply of urban land, services and finance for housing*

About 1000 ha of land was designated for the project, to provide nearly 20,000 residential plots. Another 4000 ha was intended for later expansion.

*Improving the efficiency of urban land, housing and finance markets*

After the project was launched, accusations were made that it was a clandestine investment project by a senior politician. This raised suspicions among both sellers and potential buyers of plots.

*Improving access to land, services and finance for low-income groups*

Landowners raised the price of their land when they realized what its potential value was. This made it impossible to acquire further land for residential use, reducing potential access for all income groups, especially the poor.

*Providing the basis for a more productive long-term relationship between public, private and third sectors*

The scheme collapsed amid recriminations from all parties and an enquiry was launched into its financing. The prospects for other urban development partnerships suffered a severe setback.

- the potential for wider application.

This framework makes it possible to assess the organizational structure through which the partnership is to operate at each relevant stage and the roles of central, regional and local government, together with those of other stakeholders: from developers, landowners, NGOs, CBOs and local residents. It will require major changes in the outlook, working practices and capacities of each sector before partnership approaches can overcome generations of mutual suspicion. This will inevitably take time. Small practical steps on the ground are the best way to help build trust and confidence from which more ambitious initiatives can be developed. Because failure will discourage later prospects, initial partnerships should be modest in ambition.

> A key feature in the creation of more productive relationships will be political leadership, which is essential in approving enabling legislation and producing necessary administrative changes

A key feature in the creation of more productive relationships will be political leadership, which is essential in approving enabling legislation and producing necessary administrative changes. Increasing the authority and accountability of local government will also facilitate more flexible arrangements within which 'win–win' approaches can evolve and improve urban governance along the lines advocated by the Habitat Agenda. The efficient collection of tax revenues that reflect property values will enable the public sector to recover a proportion of the added value that its planning has helped to create. It will also provide the basis for a virtuous cycle of public investment in environmental improvements to raise property values that will generate more revenue for further improvements. By setting tax thresholds at rates that exclude the lowest property values, taxation can also be socially progressive and protect the poor. The obvious barrier to the implementation of such policies is the opposition that can be expected from those adversely affected: hence the need for decisive political leadership to break the mould of private affluence and public squalor.

On a professional level, staff working in the urban sector should be encouraged to broaden their perspectives by offering them incentives for moving between sectors rather than spending their whole careers on one side of the fence. Universities and training institutions should also encourage more multidisciplinary approaches to urban development than is usually the case. At the same time, private landowners, investors and developers must recognize that their social contribution to the wider community serves their own long-term economic interests. Indeed, a key point in this report concerns the need to recognize and realize the productive potential of people living in poverty. To this end, an important strategy involves processes that support horizontal capacity building through direct interactions between low-income communities, to which the discussion now turns.

## People-to-People Community-based Approaches

For poor people, globalization has often created new problems and made existing problems worse. Chapter 1 of this report, in particular, has focused attention on alarming trends that cause great concern. However, globalization also enhances the potential of poor communities to address these problems. In demographic terms, globalization increases the ranks of the poor by accelerating urbanization and by placing more people on the economic margins. Yet, globalization also facilitates the diffusion of values and norms that provide alternatives to the goals of economic growth and capital accumulation, which currently dominate globalization. Thus demands for democratization, human rights (including the right to housing, see Chapter 16), environmental sustainability and social justice could gain greater support thanks to globalization processes that have enhanced awareness and involvement across borders.

Global investors of capital seek to avoid volatility and prefer to operate under stable conditions. This need for stability, combined with larger numbers of people more conscious of and committed to alternative development scenarios, along with a withdrawal by governments from some of their traditional roles, has enabled the creation of new spaces for political contestation (see Chapter 5).

> Low-income communities, taking advantage of modern communications technologies and less bound by local constraints, have begun to reconstitute themselves as overlapping, sometimes transnational networks of connections comprising new channels to access and share information, material resources and solidarity. This development signals new opportunities for civil society to engage government and the private sector in new forms of cooperation that enable the poor to participate as empowered partners

Low-income communities, taking advantage of modern communications technologies and less bound by local constraints, have begun to reconstitute themselves as overlapping, sometimes transnational networks of connections comprising new channels to access and share

information, material resources and solidarity. This development signals new opportunities for civil society to engage government and the private sector in new forms of cooperation that enable the poor to participate as empowered partners. More broadly, this development is about authentic citizenship, meaning the rights and responsibilities of urban residents.

At the same time, the explorations of this new political space by low-income communities affect their internal organization and alter the roles of the poorest people; women in particular. The work of the Alliance in the city of Mumbai, in the state of Maharashtra, in western India provides an excellent illustration of these changes and their potential for bringing about progress. The following sections review its history, strategies and actions, and place its operations in the larger context of the formation of transnational advocacy networks as a way of community-based capacity building.[39]

### The Alliance

The Alliance, formed in 1987, consists of three partners, all with their historical base in Mumbai. SPARC[40] is an NGO formed by social work professionals in 1984 to work on problems of urban poverty. It provides technical knowledge and elite connections to state authorities and the private sector. The National Slum Dwellers' Federation (NSDF) is a powerful community-based organization established in 1974. It has contributed a new form of grassroots activism in a federation model, described below. Mahila Milan is an organization of poor women, set up in 1986, and now networked throughout India; it focuses on women's issues in relation to urban poverty and is especially concerned with local, self-organized savings schemes among the very poor. It brings the experience of having learned how to deal with the police, municipal authorities, slumlords and real-estate developers. All three organizations are united in their concerns with gaining secure tenure in land, adequate and durable housing and access to urban infrastructure, notably to electricity, transport, sanitation and allied services.[41]

### ● The setting

Mumbai is a city of at least 12 million in a country whose population has just crossed the 1000 million mark (one-sixth of the population of the world). About 5 million people live in slums or other degraded forms of housing; another 5–10 per cent are pavement-dwellers. This 40 per cent of the city's population occupies only 8 per cent of the city's land. It is a huge population of insecurely or poorly housed people with negligible access to essential services, such as running water, electricity and ration-cards for essential foods. These *citizens without a city* are, none the less, a vital part of the workforce of the city.[42]

Housing is at the very heart of the lives of this army of toilers. Their everyday life is dominated by ever-present risks. Their temporary shacks may be demolished. Their slumlords may push them out through force or extortion. The torrential monsoons may destroy their fragile shelters and their few personal possessions. Their lack of sanitary facilities increases their need for doctors to whom they have poor access. And their inability to document their claims to housing may snowball into a general 'invisibility' in urban life, making it impossible for them to claim any rights to such things as rationed foods, municipal health and education facilities, police protection and voting rights. In a city where ration-cards, electricity bills and rent receipts guarantee other rights to the benefits of citizenship, the inability to secure claims to proper housing and other political handicaps reinforce one another. Housing – and its lack – is the most public drama of disenfranchisement in Mumbai. Thus, the politics of housing is the single most critical locus of the politics of citizenship in this city. This is the context in which the Alliance operates. The following section sketches some characteristics of its strategies.

## ● The politics of patience

> The Alliance is committed to methods of organization, mobilization, teaching and learning that build on what the poor *themselves* know and understand

The Alliance has consciously evolved a style of pro-poor activism that departs from earlier models of social work, welfarism and community organization (akin to those pioneered by Saul Alinsky in the United States). Instead of relying on the model of an outside organizer who teaches local communities how to hold the state to its normative obligations to the poor, the Alliance is committed to methods of organization, mobilization, teaching and learning that build on what the poor *themselves* know and understand. The first principle of this model is that 'no one knows more about how to survive poverty than the poor themselves'. Drawing on a federation model of teaching and learning, the goal is for the poor to 'own' as much as possible of the expertise that is necessary for them to claim, secure and consolidate basic rights in urban housing.

A crucial and controversial feature of this model is its vision of *politics without parties*. The strategy of the Alliance is that it will not deliver the poor as a vote-bank to any political party or candidate. Instead of finding safety in affiliation with any single ruling party or coalition in the State Government of Maharashtra or in the Municipal Corporation of Mumbai, the Alliance has developed political affiliations with the various levels and forms of the state bureaucracy; including national civil servant bureaucrats who execute state policy at the highest state levels and run the major bodies responsible for housing loans, slum rehabilitation and real estate regulation. The members of the Alliance have also developed links to the quasi-autonomous arms of the federal government (such as the Railways, the Port Authority, the Bombay Electric Supply and Transport) and to municipal authorities that control critical aspects of infrastructure, such as regulations concerning illegal structures, water supply, sanitation and licensing of residential structures. Finally, the Alliance works to maintain a cordial relationship with the Mumbai police and at least a hands-off relationship with the under-

world, which is deeply involved in the housing market, slum landlording and extortion, as well as demolition and rebuilding of temporary structures.

> The politics of the Alliance is one of accommodation, negotiation and long-term pressure rather than of confrontation or threats of political reprisal

The politics of the Alliance is one of accommodation, negotiation and long-term pressure rather than of confrontation or threats of political reprisal.[43] This realpolitik is grounded in a complex vision about means, ends and styles that is not just utilitarian or functional. It is also based on ideas about the transformation of the conditions of poverty by the poor in the long run. This political horizon calls for patience. The mobilization of the knowledge of the poor into methods driven by the poor and for the poor is a slow process. The need for cumulative victories and long-term asset building is wired into every aspect of the activities of the Alliance. It informs the strong bias of the Alliance against 'the project model' that has underlain so many official ideas about urban change and that has guided the short-term investment logic, accounting, reporting and assessment of most international development and donor agencies. The Alliance has steadfastly advocated the importance of slow learning and long-term capacity building. This open and long-term temporal horizon is difficult to retain in the face of the urgency, and even the desperation, that characterizes the needs of Mumbai's urban poor. But it is a crucial normative guarantee against the ever-present risk, in all forms of grassroots activism, that the needs of funders will take precedence over the needs of the poor themselves. The politics of the Alliance is thus a politics of patience, constructed against the tyranny of emergency.

## ● Words and deeds

Experiences over 15 years have evolved several key norms. Central among them is the principle of *federation*: a uniting of political and material forces. The centrality of the principle of federation reminds all members, particularly the trained professionals, that the power of the Alliance lies not in its donors, its technical expertise or its administration but in the will to federate among poor families and communities. It is a reference to the primacy of the poor in driving their own politics, however much others may help them to do so.[44]

*Savings* is another key principle. Creating informal savings groups among the poor often builds on older ideas of revolving credit and loan facilities managed informally and locally, outside the purview of the state and the banking sector.[45] But in the life of the Alliance, 'savings' has a profound ideological, even salvational status. The idea of daily savings among small-scale groups is the bedrock and building block of every other activity of the Federation, something far deeper than a simple mechanism for meeting daily monetary needs and sharing resources among the poor. It is a way of life organized around the importance of daily savings, viewed as a moral discipline that builds a

**Box 14.8 The cooking pots …**

Once upon a time there was a very poor community where the people lived in need of even the most basic things such as food and clothes. Life was very hard and the occasional penny that was left over was so rare and such a small amount that it was hardly worth saving. After all, what use is one penny in a pot? But the people of this community did not mind being so poor because they thought they had a good, wise ruler who they knew would soon release them from their poverty and bring them all food, fine clothes and houses to live in. For many years, they believed this and watched as their wise ruler got on with running the country. They waited patiently for him to decide to give them their rightful share. As they waited and waited, their children grew stunted with hunger, their backs grew bent with the toil and their bodies grew weak with sickness. 'Soon', they whispered, 'soon we will be given what we have waited for for so long.' Year after year, season after season, they waited to be given what they deserved … until one day, the whisp of a thought, the spirit of an idea came and spoke to them. This idea said, 'Why wait to be given what you can create yourselves?' First, the people scoffed at this and said, ' Don't be so foolish! What can we do when we have so little? What use is one penny in the pot?' 'Ah!' said the idea, 'but you have each other; therefore you have unity and you have hundreds of pennies in your pot!' And so it was that this idea came to live with them.

A pot was placed in the shack of one of the families and each day the women of the community (for is it not always the women who watch the pennies?) came and put in anything they could spare, sometimes a penny, sometimes two, and sometimes nothing at all. As they met in the shack, they would talk. One would say, 'My little boy has grown out of his shoes and I don't know what to do.' To which another would say, 'My son has just grown out of a pair, which would fit your boy, you may have them!' A second woman would say the, 'The roof of my shack is leaking and I don't know how to mend it,' to which another would reply, 'I mended my roof last week. I'll come and show you how.' And so their knowledge and unity grew, as did the money in the pot. What had begun as one person's penny, alone in the bottom of the pot on the first day, soon multiplied and increased a thousandfold. When a woman came with a problem that could not be solved by the other women, she would be given money from the pot to pay for medicine or to buy food when she had been robbed, or whatever needed doing. She would pay the pot back little by little by saving more carefully or by working a little harder. The women trusted each other because they helped each other, and anyway they all knew each other, so that any betrayal of trust would not go unnoticed or be forgotten.

All this they had done themselves. They had created all the thousands of pounds in the pot, with the spark of an idea to set it going. But now it was time for the idea to speak again ' You have unity and knowledge and you have the power of the money in the pot. Perhaps it's time to give a little of that knowledge to your ruler; it seems he is sorely in need of it!' The people frowned at this and said, 'What can we possibly give our ruler that he already doesn't have?' 'Well,' said the idea, 'each time you ask for a proper home your ruler says that it cannot be done until more is found out about the scale of the problem and the shape of the solution. And this is the knowledge that only you have!'

So, the people went from shack to shack, counting how many people lived there and how much land there was. Then they realized that because it was their community they knew exactly the number of people who were in need and precisely how and where the solution could be built, so they took some money from the pot and gave it the people with the skills and said, 'Help us to build a house.' And with their knowledge of what materials were best suited to the type of land, and what the people from the community needed from a home, they built the perfect house; one that they would all be happy to live in if it were theirs.

Now, finally, the people went to the their ruler and asked for their homes to be built. The ruler listened because he had heard of these poor people who had saved many thousands of pounds, and money was the one thing he really respected. But, as usual he told them again, 'No, it's not that simple. We cannot just go ahead and built your houses, as we do not yet know the scale of the problem or the shape of the solution.' But the people replied, 'Oh but it is that simple. We know the scale of the problem and we know the shape of the solution.' They handed him their carefully tabulated statistics and their perfectly drawn-up plans, along with an invitation to come and view their beautiful new house. Well! What was the ruler to do when faced with a group of people who had already shown the work could be done? Suffice to say, the houses were built. I'm not going to say that the community lived happily ever after, because that would be just a fairy tale, and this is a true story. But the people now do have their own homes to live in.

**Source:** Adapted from D, a *Big Issue* poet and member of the Groundswell network. Homeless International, www.homeless-international.org.

certain kind of political fortitude and commitment to the collective, and creates persons who can manage their affairs in many other ways as well.

Mahila Milan, the women's group that is the third partner in the Alliance, is almost entirely preoccupied with organizing small savings circles. Thus, in putting savings at the heart of the moral politics of the Alliance, its leaders place the work of poor women at the very foundation of what they do in every other area (see Box 14.8).

The third key is *precedent-setting*: the poor need to claim, capture, refine and define ways of doing things in spaces they already control and then show donors, city-officials and other activists that because these 'precedents' are good ones, other actors should be encouraged to invest further in them. This is a politics of 'show and tell', but it

is also a philosophy of 'do first, talk later'. This principle also provides a linguistic device for negotiating between the legalities of urban government and the full force of the 'illegal' arrangements that the poor almost always have to make, whether they concern unauthorized structures or informal arrangements for water and electricity. It shifts the burden for municipal officials away from the strain of whitewashing illegal activities to building on legitimate precedents. 'Precedent' turns the survival strategies and illegal experiments of the poor into legitimate foundations for policy innovations by the government and donors. It is a strategy that moves the poor into the horizon of legality on their own terms (see also Box 14.10).

But the world does not change through language alone. Three organized practices are integral to the

Alliance's strategy: (1) self-surveys and enumeration; (2) housing exhibitions; (3) toilet festivals.

*Self-surveys and enumeration.* Censuses and various other forms of enumeration have been applied to populations by modern states throughout the world after the 17th century. Tied up by their nature with the state (note the etymological link to statistics), classification and surveillance remain at the heart of every modern state archive. Censuses are perhaps the central technique of modern governmentality. They are highly politicized processes, whose results are usually available only in highly packaged form and whose procedures are always driven from above. Against this backdrop, the Alliance has adopted a conscious strategy of *self-enumeration and self-surveying* by teaching its members a variety of ways of gathering reliable and complete data about households and families in their own communities. They have codified these techniques into a series of practical tips for their members and have thus created a new governmentality *from below*.

This kind of knowledge is a central part of the political capability of the Alliance and is a critical lever for their dealings with formal authorities.[46] Since the poor are by definition socially, legally and spatially marginal, they are by definition uncounted and uncountable except in the most general terms. By rendering them statistically visible, the Alliance controls an indispensable piece of any actual policy process (eg regarding tenure security, relocation or upgrading), namely the knowledge of exactly who lives where, how long they have lived there, how and where they make their livelihoods and so forth.[47]

*Housing exhibitions.* Housing exhibitions are the second organized technique through which the structural bias of existing knowledge processes is challenged, even reversed, in the politics of the Alliance. The general philosophy of state agencies, donors and even NGOs concerned with slums has been to assume that the design, construction and financing of houses has to be produced by various forms of expert and professional knowledge ranging from that of engineers and architects to that of contractors and surveyors. The Alliance has challenged this assumption by a steady effort to appropriate, in a cumulative manner, the knowledge required to construct new housing for its members.

Housing exhibitions are a crucial part of this reversal of the standard flows of expertise. The large, crowded, open events showing housing models built by the poor is a democratic appropriation of a middle-class practice that became popular in India in the 1980s: expos that were major venues for demonstrating new kinds of consumer goods (from detergents and washing machines to cookware and cleaning materials). They were occasions for socializing the urban middle classes into the products and lifestyles of contemporary urban life and for manufacturers to advertise and compete with one another.

Not only do these exhibitions allow the poor (and especially the women among them) to discuss and debate designs for housing best suited to their own needs, they also allow them to enter into conversations with professionals about housing materials, construction costs and urban services. Through this process, their own ideas of adequate space and of realistic costs are brought to the fore, and they begin to see that house-building in a professional manner is only a logical extension of their greatest expertise, which is to build adequate housing out of the flimsiest of materials and in the most insecure of circumstances. These poor families are enabled to see that they have always been architects and engineers and can continue to play that role in the building of more secure housing. In this process, many technical and design innovations have been made. These events are also political events where poor families from one city travel to housing exhibitions elsewhere, socializing with each other and sharing ideas. They are also events to which state officials are invited to cut the ceremonial ribbon and to give speeches associating themselves with these grassroots exercises, thus simultaneously gaining points for hobnobbing with 'the people' and giving legitimacy to poor families in the locality in the eyes of their neighbours, their civic authorities and themselves.

By performing their competences in public, and by drawing an audience of their peers and of the state, NGOs and sometimes international funders, the poor gain official recognition and technical legitimation, capturing civic space and pieces of the public sphere hitherto denied to them. This is a particular politics of visibility that inverts the harm of the default condition of civic invisibility characterizing the urban poor (see Box 14.10).

*Toilet festivals.* Chapter 10 reviews the horrendous sanitary conditions faced by many poor people in the developing countries, in particular those living in urban areas. Provisions for collection and disposal of human waste are often grossly inadequate. In the absence of proper sewer systems, running water, ventilation and privacy, defecation frequently occurs in public view, exposing people to humiliation and increased risk of disease. For girls and women there is the added fear and risk of sexual assault.

Toilet festivals (*sandas mela*), organized by the Alliance in many cities of India, seize on this degrading and unhealthy experience to focus the attention of the public on technical innovation, collective celebration and carnivalesque play with officials from the state and the World Bank, among others.[48] These toilet festivals revolve around the exhibition and inauguration *not of models but of real public toilets*, by and for the poor, with complex systems of collective payment and maintenance, improved conditions of safety and cleanliness, and a collective obligation to sustain these facilities (see Box 10.5).[49] These facilities are still small-scale and have not yet been built in the large numbers required for the urban slum populations of India's cities. However, like the house exhibitions, they are evidence of competence and innovation, turning humiliation and marginality into dignifying initiative and performance of technical accomplishment.

Each of these organized practices sustains the others. Self-enumeration and surveys are the basis of claims to new housing and justify the exhibition of models, while houses uilt without attention to toilets and fecal management ake no sense. Each of these three practices, refined over ore than a decade, uses the knowledge of the poor to verage expert knowledge, turns the experience of humilia- on into the politics of recognition and enables the eepening of democracy among the poor themselves. Each f them adds energy and purpose to the others. They rovide the public dramas in which the moral injunctions o 'federate', to 'save' and to 'set precedents' are made aaterial, tested, refined and revalidated. Thus key words nd deeds shape each other, permitting some levelling of he knowledge field, turning sites of shame into dramas of nclusion, and allowing the poor to work their way into the ublic sphere and visible citizenship without open onfrontation or public violence.

## The international horizon: globalization-from-below

The work of the Alliance is situated in the wider context of he emergence of transnational advocacy networks and the nternationalization of grassroots NGOs, creating a *global-zation-from-below*. Such networks have been visible for some ime in global struggles over the rights of women, refugees nd immigrants, sweatshop production by multinational corporations, indigenous rights to intellectual property, and popular media, among other issues. For example, the Habitat International Coalition is a broad-based, independ-ent alliance of more than 350 non-governmental and community-based organizations working in the field of housing and human settlements in more than 80 countries, which plays an active role in advancing housing rights and promoting a gender perspective in community development issues.[50] The Huairou Commission brings together six inter-national women's movements with links to grassroots organizations in low-income neighbourhoods to lobby around issues of women, homes and community. It partici-pated actively in preparations for the Beijing Fourth World Conference on Women and plays an influential role in international events and meetings on housing and human settlements through its links in all regions of the world.[51] In Europe, the Platform of European Social NGOs links over 1700 organizations throughout Europe to promote social inclusion agendas,[52] and the European Federation of National Organizations Working with the Homeless (FEANTSA) lobbies European institutions and national governments while also supporting NGOs that provide services to homeless people.[53]

The underlying questions for many of these movements and networks are: how can they organize transnationally without sacrificing their local goals? When they do build transnational organizations, what are their greatest assets and their greatest handicaps? At a deeper political level, how can the mobility of capital and the potential of the new information technologies be used to serve the goals of local democratic projects? These questions are briefly taken up in the remainder of this section.

Counter-hegemonic globalization-from-below takes advantage of the ability of transnational networks to support

communities in 'thinking locally' and 'acting globally'. They do so, for example, by disseminating information and invok-ing global norms that help to build new alliances and by projecting local struggles onto wider arenas to create extra-local leverage.[54] However, local organizing must precede global action and must persist to achieve its goals. Transnational networks are not a substitute but a catalyst that enable local efforts to become more efficacious.[55]

The Alliance in Mumbai, for more than a decade, has been an active part of Slum/Shack Dwellers International (SDI): a transnational network with federations in 14 countries on four continents, concerned with 'horizontal learning' through sharing and exchanging. Links between federations of the poor in South Africa, India and Thailand have been especially instrumental in the gradual building of these grassroots exchanges (see Box 14.9 ). Key are visits by small groups of slum or shack dwellers to each others' settlements, regionally or internationally, to share in on-going local projects, get and give advice and reactions, share in social and life experiences and exchange tactics and plans. The model of exchange is based on the idea of 'seeing and hearing', rather than teaching and learning, of sharing experiences and knowledge rather than seeking standard solutions. Visits usually involve immediate immersion in the on-going projects of the host community, such as scavenging in the Philippines, sewer-digging in Pakistan, women's savings activities in South Africa or housing exhibitions in India.

These horizontal exchanges function at several levels. By visiting and hosting other activists concerned with similar problems, communities gain a comparative perspec-tive and obtain a measure of external legitimation for local efforts. Thus activist-leaders who may still be struggling for recognition and space in their own localities may find themselves able to gain state and media attention for local struggles in other countries and towns, where their very presence as visitors carries a certain cachet. The fact that they are visiting as members of some sort of international federation further sharpens this image. Local politicians feel less threatened by visitors than by their own activists and sometimes open themselves to new ideas because they come from the outside.

Second, the horizontal visits arranged by the federa-tions increasingly carry the imprimatur of powerful international organizations and funders, such as the World Bank, state development ministries and private charities

---

**Box 14.9 Face-to-face community exchanges**

Increasingly, communities of people living in poverty are making direct connections with each other. Groups are visiting other communities in their city, elsewhere in the region and in other countries. The Asian Coalition for Housing Rights has been supporting these exchanges for more than a decade. After some years of experimentation, this method of sharing and learning became so successful that it was formalized into a training process.

Along with involvement by SPARC, India, and the People's Dialogue, South Africa, community exchanges now extend to an international network among poor communities. *Face-to-Face* (www.achr.net/face_to_face.htm) is a newsletter that informs about the process and outcomes of its activities.

In August 2000, the Housing Secretary of the Philippines and slum dwellers from Sri Lanka, India and Indonesia attended a meeting of about 7000 people from the Payatas Dumpsite community in Manila and the Philippines Homeless People's Federation, organized in collaboration with Shack/Slum Dwellers International and the Asian Coalition for Housing Rights. The meeting started off a week of activities involving more meetings with the Housing Secretary and a meeting with President Estrada who agreed to participate in the forthcoming Philippine launch of the Secure Tenure campaign. The communities proposed alternative resettlement plans, and nine model houses were set up with details on construction costs, land sites and plans. Agreements were reached on land, relocations and site development.

The meeting also resulted in:

- an allocation by the President of 15 million pesos for the Manila Homeless Peoples Federation to establish an urban poor fund;
- a promise to contribute a similar amount to the Federation's funds in the other six cities in which it operates;
- a promise to fast-track and help facilitate relocations of poor communities to identified government-owned land as well as on-site upgrading.

Impressed with the constructive spirit of the gathering and the solid alternatives and viable solutions presented, the Housing Secretary responded positively to the ability of the savings federation to offer partnership with, rather than make demands on, government and invited Federation representatives to further meetings.

**Source:** Asian Coalition for Housing Rights, http://achr.net/philsecten.htm.

from Europe, the UK, the US and Germany, and increasingly include political and philanthropic leaders from other countries as well. These visits become signs to local politicians that the poor themselves have cosmopolitan links, which increases their capital in local political negotiations (see Box 14.10).

Finally, the occasions that these exchanges provide for face-to-face meetings between key leaders in, for example, Mumbai, Cape Town and Thailand actually allow them to progress rapidly in making more long-term strategic plans for funding, capacity building and what they call scaling up, which is now perhaps their central aim. That is, having mastered how to do certain things on a small scale, they are eager to find ways of making a dent on the vast numerical scope of the problem of slum dwellers in different cities. In parallel, they are also deeply interested in 'speeding up', or shortening the times involved in putting strategies into practice in different national and urban locations.

For the latter goal, it may be necessary to build a large transnational funding mechanism that would reduce dependence on existing multilateral and private funding sources and put long-term funding under control of the SDI to allow for the best alignment of its activities with the goals of the urban poor. The issue of development funding along these lines is more fully discussed later in this chapter. This approach builds on the capacities of the poor to create large-scale, high-speed, reliable mechanisms for improving their conditions. However, this is not only a new vision for equalizing resources. This report emphasizes that it is also a vision of developing the unrealized potential of human resources, producing benefits not just for the poor

but for the whole of society. It is an approach that is socially just and economically sound.

Among the many varieties of grassroots political movements, at least one broad distinction can be made: between those who seek armed, militarized solutions to their problems of exclusion and marginality and those that have opted for a politics of partnership; cooperation between partners that in the past have often opposed each other, such as states, private corporations and workers.

The Alliance and the transnational network of which it is a part have consciously decided to opt for partnerships in order to gain secure housing and urban infrastructure for the urban poor. This choice is based on the conviction that the poor are the best managers of solutions for the problems of poverty and that the poor themselves will prove to be the most capable, once mobilized and empowered by such partnerships, to 'scale up' and 'speed up' their own disappearance as a global category. This perspective is consistent with insights concerning newly emerging forms of governance (Chapter 4) and broader political strategies for urban liveability (Chapter 5). These convergent developments have implications for directions of development funding, which are reviewed in the final section of this chapter.

# The Role of Development Agencies in Capacity Building[56]

Lessons drawn from four decades of development experience demonstrate that solutions to many local problems require the involvement of local institutions. Local governments' capacity to ensure adequate provision and maintenance to all their populations of water supply, sanitation, health care, education, drainage and garbage collection, is essential but involves complex political changes. Effective and accountable local government may imply substantial institutional changes. For instance, most governments in Asia remain highly centralized and approach planning as a political process, whereas it is precisely the highly centralized power structures that are least able to provide support to local institutions.[57] The same is true for much of Africa, with national power struggles often impeding the development of competent and accountable local authorities.[58]

> We must make better use of existing resources to increase the capacity of local governments and channel more funds directly to community-based organizations and local NGOs

Each city needs to develop its own urban development programme, based on a careful evaluation of its own problems and of the resources it can mobilize. Even if current levels of international aid to urban development were multiplied many times, urban centres would still not receive more than a useful supplement to their own resources. What is needed is to place a far higher priority on the better use of existing resources to increase the capacity

| Box 14.11 The most important aid project characteristics from two different viewpoints | |
|---|---|
| **Characteristics of many successful projects** | **Project characteristics that make implementation easy for funding agency** |
| • Small scale and multi-sectoral: addressing multiple needs of poorer groups | • Large scale and single sector |
| • Implementation over many years: less of a project and more of a longer-term continuous process to improve housing and living conditions | • Rapid implementation (internal evaluations of staff performance in funding agencies often based on volume of funding supervised) |
| • Substantial involvement of local people (and usually their own community organizations) in project design and implementation | • Project designed by agency staff (usually in offices in Europe or North America) or by consultants from funding agency's own nation |
| • Project implemented collaboratively with beneficiaries, their local government and certain national agencies | • Project implemented by one construction company or government agency |
| • High ratio of staff costs to total project cost | • Low ratio of staff costs to total project cost |
| • Difficult to evaluate using conventional cost-benefit analysis | • Easy to evaluate |
| • Little or no direct import of goods or services from abroad agency's own nation | • High degree of import of goods or services from funding |

of local governments and channelling more funds directly to community-based organizations and the local NGOs with whom they choose to work.

Interventions by aid agencies and development banks that seek an efficient implementation of 'their' project may inhibit innovative local solutions that are cheaper and more expensive but less effective than solutions designed by foreign consultants. Although international agencies stress the need to ensure that the capital projects they sponsor continue to function, their mandated need to spend their funding often conflicts with more 'sustainable' solutions that keep down costs, maximize the mobilization and use of local resources and minimize the need for external funding. In addition, international agencies rarely stay and continue a local presence to guarantee the maintenance and expansion of a new water or sanitation system or health-care facility that they helped to fund. Box 14.11 contrasts the characteristics of many successful projects with the characteristics that make implementation easier for external funding agencies.

Basic infrastructure and services for water, sanitation, health care and education cannot be adequately provided without effective local institutions. Yet many aid agencies and development banks still operate on a 'project by project' basis when what is needed is a long-term process to strengthen institutional capacity, overseen by democratic governance. There may be potential for private sector enterprises to provide needed improvements in particular kinds of infrastructure and services. However, after at least a decade in which privatization has been strongly promoted by many international donors as one of the key solutions for improving the environmental infrastructure and services, the documented successes are more modest and less numerous than hoped for. Much of the literature on privatization overstates its potential and ignores that effective privatization requires strong, competent and representative local government to set the conditions, oversee the quality and control prices charged (for an

example, see Box 10.1; see Chapters 4 and 5 for analysis of, and recommendations concerning, appropriate political strategies and governance forms in this context).

## 'Going to scale' in supporting community initiatives

International agencies seek to ensure that their funding reaches a significant proportion of those in need. However, there is a need for more institutional innovation among the official bilateral or multilateral aid agencies about 'going to scale': how to channel technical and financial support to the many hundreds of community or neighbourhood level actions where the inhabitants and their organizations are allowed a significant influence in what is funded. Or to go beyond this and fund a diverse, continuous and coherent transnational programme of support for community-directed initiatives within many different low-income nations. Most decisions about what is funded still remain largely centralized in international agencies whose own funding criteria may not match local neighbourhood priorities. Many international agencies also retain cumbersome procedures for funding applications. This means long delays before a particular community knows whether it can go ahead with an initiative it has planned and for which it had sought funding.[59] Further, international agencies need to strengthen support for the institutional processes by which low-income groups organize and develop their own plans and programmes: for instance, through funding the salaries of community organizers and the staff of local NGOs to whom they turn for support.

It is not so much that large amounts of funding are needed in each settlement but that a reliable flow of assistance is needed, so that each action can build on the experience of the previous one

In general, international funding agencies must recognize better the need to support a constant development process in most low-income neighbourhoods. Unfortunately, many withdraw support from a community after completing one 'successful' project, just when this should have laid the basis for expanding the scale and extending the scope of their work. It is not so much that large amounts of funding are needed in each settlement but that a reliable flow of assistance is needed, so that each action can build on the experience of the previous one. Supporting a neighbourhood programme that involves the local inhabitants and that works in ways suited to local circumstances often takes a long time. But once momentum has been built up, one successful community-based action tends to lead to another and then another. Most poor settlements have many problems that have to be addressed. In addition, the capacity of their residents to work together grows with each successful intervention and this also allows more complex and ambitious actions to be undertaken. It is support for this continuous process that fosters people's capacity to cooperate effectively and to participate competently in partnerships and negotiations with other actors in the public and private sector.

As a rule, international funding agencies pose limits on the time they provide support to a particular community. Or, they will only support one project and assume that their role ceases when the project is completed. It is crucial to acknowledge that developing effective community responses to a lack of piped water, sanitation, drainage, street lighting, schools, health care, child care, play facilities and so forth, is a long-term process over which the inhabitants themselves must have influence and which involves recurring costs. Virtually all development assistance agencies seek to be participatory, but frequently, aid recipients have little influence on agency priorities and funding conditions. New approaches must be found if aid is to be effective in supporting a diversity of community-level initiatives that permit low-income groups to address their self-chosen priorities.

## Working with NGOs and civil society groups

International agencies need local implementors for the work they fund

The shift in thinking from 'government' to 'governance' has helped to highlight the critical role of civil society in ensuring and developing appropriate responses to development problems. It has also encouraged external agencies to consider how they can support 'civil society' groups. International agencies need *local* implementors for the work they fund. They typically oversee the implementation of projects to which they contribute funding,[60] but it is not their staff that dig the ditches, install the water pipes and provide the connections to households. The scope and potential success of any international agency's projects are thus dependent on the quality and capacity of their local implementors.

The international aid and development assistance structure from the late 1940s onwards was set up on the assumption that capital and technical advice made available to national governments would deliver 'development'. The emphasis was on the product rather than the process of development. The limitations of this approach became apparent as most 'recipient' governments were ineffective implementors or promoted other priorities. Such limitations have long been recognized in the debates about the failure of aid to reach poorer groups and support social development, going back at least to the late 1960s. None the less, it has proved very difficult to change the institutional structure of development assistance. It is also difficult politically for the official aid agency of a government from a high-income nation to steer aid to non-government local 'implementors' without the approval of the recipient's government. The same applies even more for multilateral agencies, which are part-'owned' by recipient governments; for such agencies as the World Bank, the regional development banks and the various bilateral agencies that provide loans, it is the national government client that has to repay the loans. No national government is going to sanction increasing aid over which they have little control, or funding citizen groups or NGOs that do not support or even oppose them. Even where external funding is intended for other government bodies – especially local governments – national governments are not greatly enthusiastic about relinquishing control over which localities and which sectors receive funding. Nor are they eager to have international donors fund local authorities governed by opposition parties.

Development depends on good governance, which requires a political, legal and institutional framework that guarantees citizens civil and political rights and access to justice

Development depends on good governance; not only in what national, regional and local governments fund and regulate but also in how they encourage and support the efforts and investments of households, citizen groups, NGOs and the private and nonprofit sector. This, in turn, requires a political, legal and institutional framework that guarantees citizens civil and political rights and access to justice. Considering that many national governments have yet to embrace the trend of supporting more effective and accountable local government, it would be a mistake to continue channelling virtually all external support through national governments whose interventions have failed to produce solutions to many of the most serious problems and sometimes have made them worse. It is low-income households and communities working outside of government that have been responsible for building and upgrading most new housing units and for a large proportion of investments in infrastructure and services.

Current trends do not allow us to continue as usual. We must explore innovations in governance, cooperative liveability strategies, multiple stakeholder partnerships and horizontal capacity building

As stressed earlier, current trends do not allow us to continue as usual. We must explore innovative approaches,

uch as those concerning newly emerging forms of governance, cooperative liveability strategies, multiple
takeholder partnerships and horizontal capacity building,
discussed in other sections of this report.

One key question concerns which institutional structures can considerably increase the proportion of
development assistance going directly to low-income households and communities. The most common response is to
look for local NGOs. However, some care is needed in
channelling support to local NGOs, which may have
agendas that do not accord with the needs and priorities of
low-income groups. Indeed, if they represent the priorities
of middle- and upper-income groups, they may be promoting the same distorted priorities as international NGOs
from high-income nations. Many opportunistic NGOs have
been formed within recipient countries to tap into the
greater enthusiasm from donors for funding NGOs. Even
where they have 'pro-poor' agendas that appear to address
pressing problems such as inadequate water and sanitation,
they may operate in ways that are unaccountable to low-
income groups and their community organizations. NGOs
are often insensitive to political and power struggles within
communities and may find it convenient to support traditional leaders who do not reflect the needs and priorities of
many community members.[61] They are often reluctant to
delegate power and responsibility to community organizations. They may also impose their own professionally
driven means of addressing problems and their own implementation timetables. If these NGOs rely on international
donors, it is often difficult for them to avoid doing so, since
this is in part the result of them having to follow the procedures and meet the criteria of the donor agencies and
having to generate enough funds to cover their staff
salaries. This difficulty is discussed more fully in Chapter 4
which considers the roles of NGOs in the broader context
of other political actors in governance processes.

New channels of international support must be
developed and linked directly to community-based action.
This would usually mean support to associations formed by
low-income groups, including savings and credit groups,
self-help groups and neighbourhood associations. Although
there are many examples of highly cost-effective projects in
squatter settlements funded by external agencies, the scale
of the support remains small and generally ad hoc. By and
large, decisions about what to fund and who to fund are
still made in the capitals of North America, Europe and
Japan. The scale of funding and the conditions under which
it is available are usually more influenced by the accounting
procedures of the institutions providing the funding than
the needs of those to whom it is provided.

> There is a need to develop new channels for techni-
> cal advice and direct funding of community-level
> initiatives where decisions about support are made
> *locally* and where accountability is to *local*
> institutions and citizens

There is a need to develop new channels for technical
advice and direct funding of community-level initiatives

---

**Box 14.12 A city-based fund for community initiatives**

If the scale of funding to support community-level initiatives is to increase substantially, new institutional channels are needed. Existing funding agencies cannot cope with a large increase in requests for small projects. One possibility would be a fund for community initiatives set up within each city, accepting funds from external donors but managed by a small board made up of people based in that city. These people would have to be acceptable to community groups and would usually include some NGO staff that were already working with low-income groups and community organizations. It could include some locally based staff from external donors.

*Functioning of the fund:* Low-income groups could apply for funding for projects and also for support for developing projects. The procedures by which application has to be made for funds and the decision-making process has to be kept simple, with a capacity to respond rapidly. These would also have to be completely transparent with information publicly available about who applied for funds, for what, who got funded, how much and why. For funding provided as loans, the loan conditions and their repayment implications would have to be made clear and explicit, including repayment period, grace period (if any), interest rate and subsidy.

*Kinds of projects that could be supported:*
- *Health* (eg support for the construction of sanitary latrines or improved water supplies; campaigns to promote personal and household hygiene and preventive health measures, including mother and child immunization; the setting-up or expansion of community-based health centres);
- *Education* (eg special programmes for children or adolescents who left school early; literacy programmes);
- *Housing* (eg building material banks, loans to community-based savings and credit schemes through which members could access loans to upgrade their homes or purchase land and build their own home);
- *Environment* (eg site drainage, improved water supplies);
- *Employment* (eg support for micro-enterprises, local employment exchanges, skill train-ing etc).

*Funding:* Between US$2000 and US$50,000 available to any group or community organization formed by low-income households. The first loan provided would generally be small, with further loans available if the project (and any planned cost recovery) proceeds to plan. Some level of counterpart funding would generally be expected (although this could be in the form of labour contribution).

*Terms:* Total or close to total cost recovery sought where feasible – with allowance made for inflation and for the cost of borrowing funds – with funding recovered shown publicly to be recycled back into supporting other community initiatives. For most projects, a short grace period would be permitted before the loan repayment had to begin (typically 3 months to a year) so that income generated or expenditure savings are partially realized before repayments begin. The fund for community initiatives would also provide a range of support services; for instance, assistance to community organizations in developing proposals, and technical and managerial support in project implementation. Grants or soft loans could be made available for certain specific interventions where cost recovery is difficult to achieve (either because funding cannot easily be collected or because incomes are too low).

---

where decisions about support are made locally and
where accountability is to local institutions and
citizens.[62] Even the most flexible institutional structure
within an external donor cannot support hundreds of
community-based initiatives if all decisions about funding
and all monitoring and evaluation are concentrated in the
donor's headquarters.

> Necessary innovations face a key institutional and political challenge: any real decentralization implies decentralization of power, while governments must at the same time remain responsible for reducing regional inequities

The necessary innovations in funding models face a key institutional and political challenge: any real decentralization implies decentralization of power. A fund for community initiatives can only work if decisions about what is to be supported are made locally in ways that respond to the priorities of low-income groups and that are accountable to the local population (see Box 14.12). At the same time, as argued in Chapters 4 and 13, decentralization may increase the potential for inequities between cities and regions. Hence, national governments must develop policy strategies that combine genuine decentralization with continued responsibility for equity.

# Notes

1 See www.dialogue.org.za/ sdi/default.htm.

2 See www.sparcindia.org/ netsdi.html.

3 The following paragraphs have been adapted from 'The implications of globalization and polarization for capacity building', a background paper prepared by Forbes Davidson of the Institute for Housing and Urban Development Studies.

4 Material for this section was drawn from 'The role of local authorities, other partners and relevant United Nations organizations and agencies in the review and appraisal process'. Progress report on the preparations of the proposed world charter of local self-government, presented to the Preparatory Committee for the special session of the General Assembly for an overall review and appraisal of the implementation of the Habitat Agenda, First session, Nairobi, 8–12 May 2000. HS/C/PC.1/CRP.7.

5 This section is drawn from 'The role of donor and development agencies in combating poverty, inequity and polarization in a globalizing world', a background paper prepared by David Satterthwaite, IIED, London.

6 The World Bank made over 50 project commitments during the period 1970 to 1996 to building the institutional and financial capacity of urban governments or to institutions that support urban development. All but two were made since 1983. Although some of the World Bank's urban projects have long had institution building components relating to urban government and many 'integrated urban development' projects have strong institution building components, it was only in the 1980s that project commitments were made specifically to institution building for urban areas, training in urban management, local government finance and urban planning.

7 One reason for this change may stem from a recognition by the World bank of the unsustainability of many of its previous urban projects. Another reason for strengthening the capacity of urban authorities is that this will increase the capacity of recipient governments to manage and invest in infrastructure and services, and thus increase their demand for World Bank funding.

8 For example, loans to support the work of the Cities and Villages Development Bank in Jordan, the Autonomous Municipal Bank in Honduras and the Fonds d'Equipement Communal in Morocco. Other loans to Zimbabwe and Brazil have provided credit direct to certain urban authorities.

9 See Kessides, 1997.

10 Ibid.

11 See Tjønneland et al, 1998.

12 The following section draws from Peltonen, 1999, and material prepared by Mara Sydney with additional information gathered by Jennifer Steffel.

13 Hewitt, 1999.

14 Jones and Blunt, 1999.

15 Askvik, 1999.

16 See www.ihs.nl/.

17 For a list of partnerships set up under the Local Agenda 21 Charters Project, see www.iclei.org/la21/charters.htm.

18 See www.iula.org/.

19 See http://icma.org/ (for resource cities: http://icma.org/go.cfm? cid=1&gid=3&sid=229).

20 Hewitt, 1998.

21 Hewitt, 1999.

22 Ibid.

23 Ibid.

24 The reason for setting up the partnership this way was a prohibition not allowing US citizens to travel to Serbia during the regime of President Milosevic. A third party from Eastern Europe was brought in to host the exchange visits, which serendipitously led to a strengthening of working relationships between the host city and the Serbian partner. Personal communication, Amanda Lonsdale, ICMA, 25 October 2000.

25 Personal communication, Amanda Lonsdale, ICMA, 25 October 2000.

26 See www.eurocities.org/; the site has extensive links to Eurocities members, European Union institutions, and local government organizations.

27 See www.metrex.dis.strath.ac.uk/ en/intro.html.

28 See www.iclei.org/la21/map/ citynet.htm.

29 See, for example, www.flgr.bg/indexen.htm for innovative local government reform in Bulgaria undertaken in the context of international urban cooperation; see www.lmp.org.ph/ for municipal networking in the Philippines.

30 This section draws extensively on Payne, G (ed) (1999) Making Common Ground: Public-Private Partnerships in Land for Housing. Intermediate Technology Publications, London. Although the discussion here is primarily oriented to aspects of housing and land provision, many of the same issues are relevant as well to partnerships that involve the provision of services and infrastructure, in particular water and sanitation (see Chapter 13).

31 See, for example, PADCO, 1991, p 32; UNCHS, 1993, pp 60–61; United Nations Centre for Human Settlements (Habitat), 1993.

32 See, eg Payne, 1999.

33 See Durand-Lasserve, 1996, p 63.

34 Ibid, p 65.

35 See Varley, 1985; Jones and Ward, 1998, p 15.

36 See D Dewar, 1999.

37 See Durand-Lasserve, 1996, p 52.

38 See Gore, 1991, p 215.

39 The remaining sections of this part of the chapter are drawn from 'Deep democracy: Urban governmentality and the horizon of politics', an unpublished paper by Arjun Appadurai, University of Chicago, June 2000. The full text of this paper is can be accessed at www.dialogue.org.za/sdi/. Examples of TANs are 'issue-based' (eg environment, child-labour, anti-AIDS) networks and 'identity-based' (eg women, indigenous peoples, gays, diasporic) networks.

40 See www.sparcindia.org/.

41 The Alliance has also strong links to Mumbai's pavement-dwellers and to Mumbai's street children, who it has organized into an organization called Sadak Chaap (Street Imprint), which has its own social and political agenda. Of the six or seven non-state organizations working directly with the urban poor in Mumbai, the Alliance has by far the largest constituency, the highest visibility in the eyes of the state, and the most extensive networks in India and elsewhere in the world.

42 Many are 'toilers', including children, engaged in temporary, menial, physically dangerous and socially degrading forms of work.

43 This pragmatic approach makes sense in a city like Mumbai where the supply of scarce urban infrastructure (housing and all its associated entitlements) is embroiled in an immensely complicated set of laws governing slum rehabilitation, housing finance, urban government, legislative precedents and administrative laws that are interpreted differently, enforced unevenly and almost always with an element of corruption in any actual delivery system.

44 There is a formal property to membership in the federation and members of the Alliance have on-going debates about slum families, neighbourhoods and communities in Mumbai that are not yet part of 'the federation'. In effect, this means that they cannot be participants in the active politics of housing, resettlement, rehabilitation and the like which are the bread-and-butter of the Alliance.

45 See Chapter 6 for a discussion of related aspects of micro-lending.

46 This of particular relevance to places like Mumbai, where a host of local, state-level and federal entities exist with a mandate to rehabilitate or ameliorate slums. But none of them knows exactly who the slum dwellers are, where they live or how they are to be identified. This is of central relevance to the entire politics of knowledge in which the Alliance is perennially engaged. All state-sponsored slum policies have an abstract slum population as their target and little or no knowledge of its concrete, human components.

47 At the same time, the creation and use of self-surveys is a powerful tool for internal democratic practice, since the major mode of evidence used by the Alliance for claims to actual space needs by slum dwellers is the testimony of neighbours, rather than other forms of documentation such as rent receipts, ration-cards, electric meters and other civic insignia of occupancy that can be used by the more securely housed classes in the city. Social visibility to each other is essential to the techniques of mutual identification used for locating and legitimizing slum dwellers.

48 See also Hobson, 2000.

49 See also UNCHS, 1996, p 385.

50 See Habitat International Coalition, http://home.mweb.co.za/hi/hic/.

51 See Huairou Commission, www.huairou.org/.

52 See www.socialplatform.org.

53 See www.feantsa.org.

54 See Keck and Sikkink, 1998; Evans, 2000; Boxes 16.5 and 14.10; endnote 47 in Chapter 2 on the role of the international dockworkers movement in the Liverpool port dispute; Jenkins and Goetz, 1999a; 1999b.

55 Jenkins and Goetz, 1999a. In the US, Good Neighbor Agreements (GNAs) have emerged as a non-litigious method of dispute resolution among companies, their workers, environmentalists, and local communities in the face of declining governmental power and rising corporate power. Facilitated by Right to Know legislation and databases (see www.rtk.net/), dozens of GNAs have been proposed and signed. For an analysis of the establishment of an enforceable, legally binding agreement that holds a transnational corporation accountable to a local community, see Pellow, 2000.

56 The remainder of this chapter is drawn from 'The role of donor and development agencies in combating poverty: Inequity and polarization in a globalizing world', a background paper prepared by David Satterthwaite, IIED, London.

57 Douglass, 1992.

58 Rakodi et al, 2000, illustrate this, in regard to Mombasa.

59 It dampens initiative when a low-income community has developed a plan for improving local conditions through, for instance, a communal water tank or building a small day-care centre, but then has to wait many months, or even years, to find out whether the few thousand dollars they requested will be granted.

60 There are some exceptions, especially in disaster relief, but this generalization holds true in most instances.

61 Mitlin, 1999.

62 Recently, there has been some experimentation with ways of supporting local funds for community initiatives; for instance the loan programme of the Thai government's Urban Community Development Office and its small-grants programme, supported by funding from DANCED (Boonyabancha, 1996; 1999). The UK Department for International Development is likewise experimenting with a fund for community initiatives. UNDP has sought to support local environmental initiatives through its LIFE programme.

# 15

# STRENGTHENING POST-DISASTER RECONSTRUCTION OF HUMAN SETTLEMENTS

The cyclone that hit Orissa, India, in 1999, caused the total collapse or destruction of 742,143 housing units.[1] About 1 million people were reported as homeless after the earthquake in Turkey that same year, including 70 per cent of the population of Izmit.[2] These disasters are not isolated episodes, but merely examples of similar catastrophes that occur year after year. They result in damage and loss of housing and urban infrastructure with devastating effects on the lives of those affected. Sustainable human settlements development cannot often prevent disasters from happening, but it can help to mitigate their impacts. This chapter first briefly documents the human impacts of natural and human-made disasters, before examining what can be learned from these experiences and reviewing approaches to support post-disaster recovery.

## Consequences of Armed Conflict, Natural and Technological Disasters

Discussions and policies concerning homelessness in the context of human settlements have typically focused on factors such as lack of affordable housing, stagnating earnings, erosion of social safety nets, curtailment or elimination of welfare benefits, deinstitutionalization and rapid urbanization. Very rarely do disasters receive attention as a cause of homelessness that demands the attention of those with responsibilities for human settlement development. This inattention is unfortunate because natural as well as human-made disasters result in very large numbers of homeless people.

Table 15.1 shows the number of people made homeless by disasters worldwide from 1990 to 1999. The data distinguish between natural disasters and human-made disasters (ie technological disasters and armed conflict). During this period, more than 186 million people lost their homes due to a disaster. Parties engaging in armed conflict were responsible for making almost 100 million people homeless. A large majority of these conflicts took the form of civil strife. Natural disasters such as floods, landslides, droughts, hurricanes, cyclones and earthquakes caused more than 88 million people to become homeless during the 1990s.[3] These numbers are greatly deflated because they only count the people who had homes to begin with but lost them. Armed conflict and disaster recovery have additional impacts which worsen homelessness, because they divert resources away from the construction of housing for those who already are homeless and thus extend their homelessness. Technological disasters were relatively much less significant in the 1990s, making 164,156 people homeless as a result of chemical spills, explosions, fires and a variety of industrial and transport accidents.

Table 15.2 contains comparable information for the total number of people affected by disasters, excluding homeless people but including those killed. Those 'affected' are people who require immediate assistance during a period of emergency (ie help in meeting basic survival needs such as food, water, shelter, sanitation and urgent medical assistance).[4] The data in Table 15.2 show that from 1990 to 1999 more than 2000 million people were thus affected by disasters: most of them (1800 million) by natural calamities; many in the course of armed conflict (163 million); and a relatively smaller but still significant number were affected by so-called technological factors (600,000).[5]

Tables 15.1 and 15.2 make clear that the impacts of disasters are distributed unevenly and, further, that the distribution of impacts across world regions differs according to the type of disaster. Almost two-thirds of homelessness resulting from armed conflict during the past decade occurred in Asia. However, when prorated according

**Table 15.1**

**Homelessness resulting from armed conflict, natural and technological disasters, 1990–1999**

| Continent | Type of disaster (N) | | | Type of disaster (%) | | |
|---|---|---|---|---|---|---|
| | Armed conflict | Natural disasters | Technological disasters | Armed conflict | Natural disasters | Technological disasters |
| Africa | 30,171,903 | 3,604,340 | 63,850 | 30.7 | 4.1 | 41.6 |
| America | 415,850 | 2,814,214 | 36,910 | 0.4 | 3.2 | 24.0 |
| Asia | 61,364,400 | 80,802,494 | 48,459 | 62.4 | 91.9 | 31.5 |
| Europe | 6,387,500 | 449,265 | 4,401 | 6.5 | 0.5 | 2.9 |
| Oceania | 0 | 249,091 | 36 | 0 | 0.3 | 0 |
| Total | 98,339,653 | 87,919,404 | 153,656 | 100 | 100 | 100 |

**Source:** Centre for Research in the Epidemiology of Disasters, Université Catholique de Louvain, Belgium. Table compiled by Sarah Krieger.

| Continent | Type of disaster (N) Armed conflict | Natural disasters | Technological disasters | Type of disaster (%) Armed conflict | Natural disasters | Technological disasters |
|---|---|---|---|---|---|---|
| Africa | 101,553,666 | 101,181,011 | 84,705 | 62.0 | 5.4 | 14.0 |
| America | 7,249,029 | 54,600,922 | 111,791 | 4.4 | 2.9 | 18.5 |
| Asia | 45,216,161 | 1,677,789,948 | 318,778 | 27.6 | 89.7 | 52.9 |
| Europe | 9,582,061 | 18,416,100 | 72,965 | 6.0 | 1.0 | 12.1 |
| Oceania | 70,025 | 18,022,672 | 14,841 | 0.0 | 1.0 | 2.5 |
| Total | 163,670,942 | 1,870,010,653 | 603,080 | 100 | 100 | 100 |

**Source:** Centre for Research in the Epidemiology of Disasters, Université Catholique de Louvain, Belgium. Table compiled by Susan Krieger.

Table 15.2

Total number of people affected by armed conflict, natural and technological disasters, 1990–1999

to population size, armed conflict as a cause of homelessness was much more prevalent in Africa: nearly 400 persons per 10,000 of the population were affected, more than double the rate of Asia's population and more than four times that found in Central and Eastern Europe (Table 15.3). On the other hand, natural disasters did hit Asia hardest, both in absolute terms (81 million homeless during the 1990s) and as a share of the total (92 per cent); see Table 15.2. These spatial patterns are visualized in Maps 1, 2 and 3.

When comparing the impact of the various types of disasters on homelessness across regions, taking into account population size, the chief cause of homelessness during the 1990s was armed conflict in Africa (causing 394 of every 10,000 people to lose their homes). Next are natural disasters (222 per 10,000 of population) and armed conflict (169 per 10,000 of population) in Asia. Overall, Africa was hit hardest with nearly 450 homeless people per 10,000 of the population, followed closely by Asia (390 people). The numbers for Europe (93), Oceania (83) and the Americas[6] (40) are much lower (see Table 15.3).

Many more people were affected by loss of basic infrastructure and services which, together with shelter, are key components of human settlements.

Considering the astounding human costs of disasters, it is important that planners, designers and policy makers involve themselves in mitigation efforts. Granted, natural disasters cannot usually be prevented but the severity of their consequences can be reduced by, for example, effective land use planning and the development and enforcement of appropriate building regulations. Municipal authorities and international relief organizations have also used urban livelihood strategies to diversify the asset base of low-income households as a means to lessen impacts from disasters.[7] Much can be done as well to reduce technological hazards, particularly those related to transport, toxic waste and pollution. Selected aspects of technology-related hazards are taken up in other chapters in the context of transport, energy and health. Armed conflict has severe

impacts, ranging from hunger to ill health to homelessness among resident and refugee populations, affecting especially women and children.[8] The rebuilding of war-torn societies and communities falls heavily on women, as men are often absent; killed, injured or engaged in continued fighting. However, because of discriminatory customary laws concerning ownership and inheritance of property, many returning women find that they have little or no access to land and housing left behind. These issues raise broader questions that go beyond the competence of human settlement development, although there have been coordinated efforts with other organizations.[9]

The following two sections of this chapter examine the experience of recovery from natural disasters and seek to draw lessons from it with a view to improving future interventions.

## Post-disaster Recovery: Learning from Recent Experience[10]

The previous section showed the severe impacts of natural disasters on human settlements and their populations. The Bangladesh cyclone in 1990; the Chinese river floods in 1991, 1995 and 1998; Hurricane Andrew in Miami, Florida in 1992; the Maharashtra, India, earthquake in 1993; the Northridge earthquake in Los Angeles, California in 1994; the Kobe, Japan earthquake in 1995; Hurricane Mitch[11] in Central America in 1998; the earthquake near Istanbul, Turkey[12], the cyclone in Orissa, India[13] and flooding and mudslides in Venezuela in 1999; and the flooding in Mozambique in 2000[14] are just a few examples of natural disasters that have wreaked havoc in the last decade. Most of these events have caused numerous fatalities and tremendous devastation in urban areas where there are large concentrations of people with a heavy dependency on infrastructure and services. Although it is impossible to

Table 15.3

Homelessness and total affected by armed conflict, natural and technological disasters (per 10,000 of population), 1990–1999

| Continent | Homelessness (P/10,000) as a result of: Armed conflict | Natural disasters | Technological disasters | Total affected (P/10,000) as a result of: Armed conflict | Natural disasters | Technological disasters |
|---|---|---|---|---|---|---|
| Africa | 394 | 47 | 0.83 | 1325 | 1320 | 1.10 |
| America | 5 | 34 | 0.45 | 89 | 667 | 1.37 |
| Asia | 169 | 222 | 0.13 | 124 | 4617 | 0.88 |
| Europe | 88 | 6 | 0.06 | 132 | 253 | 1.00 |
| Oceania | 0.00 | 83 | 0.01 | 23 | 6004 | 4.94 |
| Total | 165 | 147 | 0.28 | 274 | 3128 | 1.01 |

**Source:** Centre for Research in the Epidemiology of Disasters, Université Catholique de Louvain, Belgium; United Nations Population Division, Department of Economic and Social Affairs, 1999. Table compiled by Tamara Laninga.

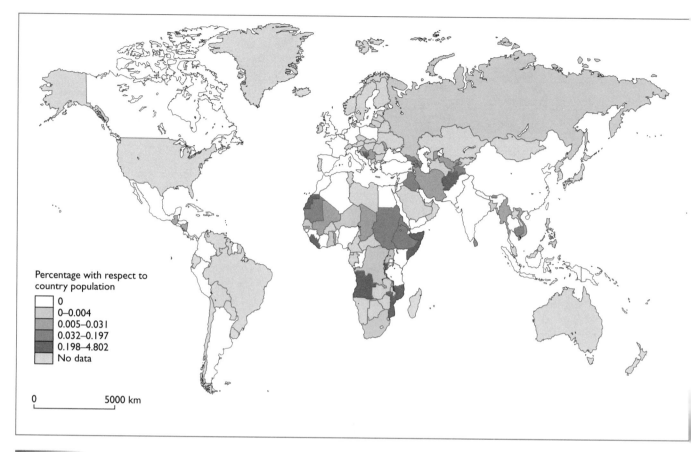

Percentage with respect to
country population

- 0
- 0–0.004
- 0.005–0.031
- 0.032–0.197
- 0.198–4.802
- No data

0          5000 km

**Map 1**

**Distribution of homelessness due to armed conflict (1990–1999)**

**Source:** Map created by Francisco Escobar at the Centre for GIS and Modelling, Department of Geomatic Engineering, University of Melbourne, using the quantile method for interval breaking in Arcview (ESRI). Data from the Centre for Research in the Epidemiology of Disasters, Université Catholique de Louvain, Belgium.

prevent such hazards from occurring in the future, it is possible to examine these experiences to see if we can learn from them so that we can reduce their effects when they strike again.

Three issues dominate any discussion of disasters and human settlements:

1   Increased urbanization in high hazard areas around the globe has led to increased vulnerabilities.
2   Governments and charitable organizations, whether local or international, cannot by themselves provide adequate relief or recovery assistance to victims.
3   The poor will suffer most in any natural disaster.

For the first time in human history, we are approaching a moment when more people worldwide live in cities than in rural areas, and many of those cities are located in areas prone to earthquakes, hurricanes and other natural disasters. The globalization of businesses in manufacturing and information services combined with the deregulation of international trade has changed growth and development patterns, creating expansion of existing urban areas and encouraging the growth of new communities. Clothing and tennis shoes designed for the US market are produced in Southeast Asia and Latin America. Information for the Silicon Valley computer industry is often produced, or at least processed, in Bangalore, India. Ensuing land pressures precipitate development of disaster-prone areas.

> As urban growth follows business development, the concentration of people and economic value in areas exposed to natural hazards is also growing

As urban growth follows business development, the concentration of people and economic value in areas exposed to natural hazards is also growing. Hence, it is not surprising that the impact of natural disasters is on the rise. It has been estimated that the number of major natural disasters in the last ten years was four times as high as in the 1960s. Economic losses were six times as high and insured losses no less than 14 times as high.[15] The 1990s saw the two most damaging years ever in terms of insurance losses owing to natural disasters: US$33,000 million in 1992 and US$29,000 million in 1999. Total damages, insured and uninsured, exceeded a staggering US$100,000 million in 1999 alone.[16] Indeed, the United Nations 'International Decade for Natural Disaster Reduction' from 1990 to 1999 was well timed. Current trends of globalization and population growth, which define our urban reality, assure that natural disasters will increase in number and severity. This prospect requires us to seek better practices that lessen disaster impacts and speed disaster recovery.

The condition of the world's cities has often been described in terms of 'urban crises', implying complex problems, frequent breakdowns in services and a general lack of policy, programmes or funding. In developing nations, problems are commonly associated with rapid growth, social inequalities, volatile flows of corporate investment, demographic change and environmental neglect. In developed countries, problems are associated with deindustrialization, dilapidation of old physical infrastructure and changing markets.[17] Natural disasters simply exacerbate the existing social, physical and economic problems.

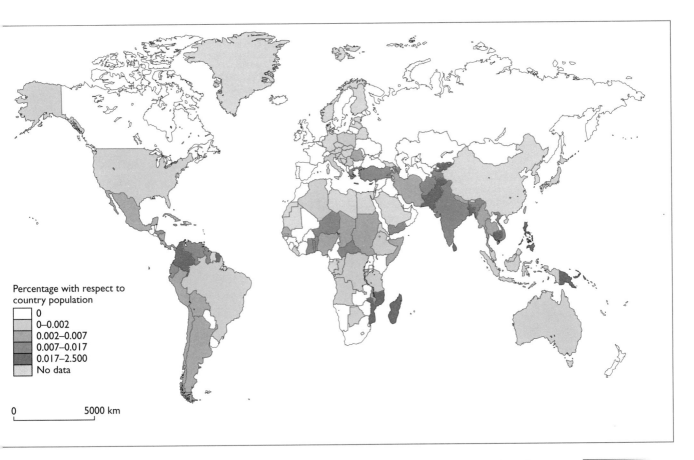

Percentage with respect to
country population
- 0
- 0–0.002
- 0.002–0.007
- 0.007–0.017
- 0.017–2.500
- No data

0          5000 km

Recent experiences in Los Angeles, California, and Kobe, Japan, demonstrate the relationship between existing problems and disaster recovery. The earthquakes experienced by both cities had significant impacts on housing. In the 1994 Northridge earthquake, the damage was heavily concentrated in the San Fernando Valley, a suburb northeast of downtown Los Angeles. Fifteen neighbourhoods were dubbed 'ghost towns' where 40–90 per cent of the housing was uninhabitable. Post-earthquake inspections tallied about 60,000 units as severely damaged and 400,000 with minor damage, most in apartments. Because Los Angeles was in a deep recession at the time of the earthquake, rental housing vacancies were over 9 per cent, and earthquake victims were easily rehoused, all within their same postal code. Three years later, it became clear that there was also costly damage to about 300,000 single-family homes. The information on these damages only became evident as insurance claims were added to the loss estimates. In this circumstance, there was no sheltering crisis because of the available housing in the market, but the financial crisis resulting from a total of US$13,000 million in insured losses continues to have repercussions throughout California and the US.

Private insurance companies were shocked by the losses, not only from the Northridge earthquake, but also from similar losses in Hurricane Andrew in Miami, Florida in 1992. Most companies in California, Florida and Hawaii no longer offer disaster insurance along with a traditional homeowner insurance policy. State-run mini-insurance programmes have tried to fill the gap, but typically these have high premiums, high deductibles and limited coverage. Fewer than 20 per cent of Californians carry earthquake insurance, and federal aid will never take the place of insurance in helping victims to repair housing losses in a major urban disaster.

In Japan, the epicentre of a 7.2 magnitude earthquake was directly beneath the city of Kobe (1995), and 6000 people died in the event. The damage to buildings and infrastructure dwarfed the losses in the Northridge earthquake. Port facilities, freeways and railroads were extensively damaged. About 4000 commercial, industrial and public buildings were heavily damaged or collapsed. In total, approximately 400,000 housing units in 190,000 buildings were uninhabitable. Another 400,000 units were damaged. The total losses were estimated at US$89,000 million.[18]

The displaced population lived in shelters for nearly a year, and about 100,000 were transferred to 48,000 temporary housing units assembled by the government and placed in parking lots and open sites outside central Kobe. Some portion of the population was rehoused in the larger metropolitan area, but the shelter crisis was long term. Japan was also in a major economic recession at the time of the earthquake, and government invested heavily in the repair of the port and transport infrastructure. Although the government issued a three-year plan to build 125,000 housing units, government funds were used for only about 30,000 units of public housing. The remaining recovery efforts were left to the private sector. Because disaster insurance is virtually unavailable in Japan, individuals who lost their homes had to rely on savings and land value to finance any rebuilding.

More than half of the Japanese government's expenditures went for the provision of temporary shelter. Despite

**Map 2**

**Distribution of homelessness due to natural disasters (1990–1999)**

**Source:** Map created by Francisco Escobar at the Centre for GIS and Modelling, Department of Geomatic Engineering, University of Melbourne, using the quantile method for interval breaking in Arcview (ESRI). Data from the Centre for Research in the Epidemiology of Disasters, Université Catholique de Louvain, Belgium.

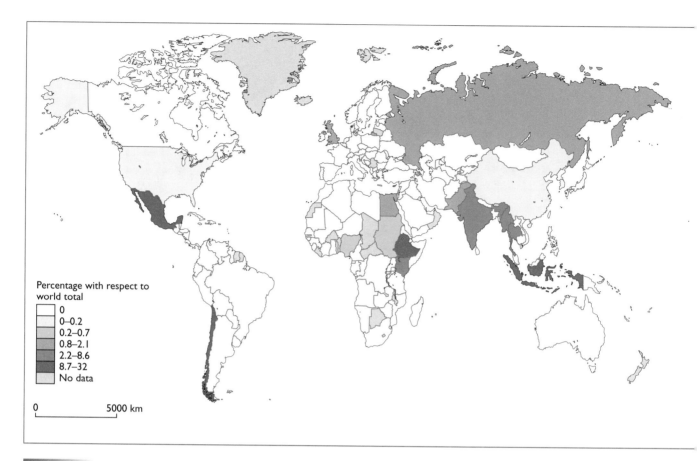

**Percentage with respect to world total**
- 0
- 0–0.2
- 0.2–0.7
- 0.8–2.1
- 2.2–8.6
- 8.7–32
- No data

0          5000 km

**Map 3**

**Distribution of homelessness due to technological disasters (1990–1999)**

**Source:** Map created by Francisco Escobar at the Centre for GIS and Modelling, Department of Geomatic Engineering, University of Melbourne, using the quantile method for interval breaking in Arcview (ESRI). Data from the Centre for Research in the Epidemiology of Disasters, Université Catholique de Louvain, Belgium.

the obvious need, the temporary units costing US$40,000 each may not have been the best use of limited government funds. Government programmes rebuilt 20,000 units in Los Angeles, and 30,000 units in Kobe, but in both cases reconstruction was largely a private sector initiative. By contrast, in most developing nations, housing aid comes from international agencies and charities, and temporary shelters often serve long-term housing needs. See Table 15.4 for a comparison of the earthquakes in Mexico City, Kobe and Northridge.

> The vulnerability of residents of poorly built housing is made worse by their poverty, their state of health, their food supply and their physical and social infrastructure

Research on more than 30 cases of post-disaster problems in developing countries has documented that their populations are vulnerable not only because their housing and buildings tend to be poorly built, but also because their vulnerability is increased by their poverty, their state of health, their food supply and their physical and social infrastructure.[19] In the last decade, much has been done to try to overcome or minimize the problems often associated with relief and aid. Many researchers have found disincentive effects associated with disaster aid and have shown the interdependence of development aid and disaster relief.

Two examples document the changing approach to disaster aid and housing recovery. In 1985, an earthquake devastated the centre of Mexico City. The official estimate of 76,000 housing units lost is probably low. The initial government response was to move earthquake victims to

new communities on the outskirts of the city but, when victims protested, the Federal District government undertook an innovative plan to quickly shelter victims in tin sheds in the streets, and then built 100,000 replacement units in two years. Half the units built were in new buildings on vacant lots, and half were in renovations of damaged structures. The programme was funded with aid from the International Monetary Fund and loans based on federal government debt-restructuring. The building process was managed by a central government agency created for the building programme and disbanded after its completion, using hundreds of local architects and contractors to carry out the work.

In the Maharashtra earthquake in India in 1993, over 8000 people were killed and 1 million residents were rendered homeless. Approximately 67 villages were completely destroyed and there was extensive damage in 1300 villages in the Latur and Osmanabad districts. The condition of housing in the area prior to the earthquake was extremely poor, and the government of Maharashtra committed to a massive rebuilding programme that included a commitment to improving the living standard of those affected. The scale of the losses dictated the use of a variety of approaches. In areas which bore the brunt of the devastation, villagers were too traumatized to undertake rebuilding themselves. Here contractors were used to build new houses in relocation villages. In other areas, NGOs were involved in the reconstruction, but the largest component of the programme was an owner-builder programme, designed to allow individual work and choice. Housing funds (largely provided by the World Bank) accounted for 58 per cent of the programme's budget and included relocaion of 52 villages, reconstruction of 22 villages and in-situ strengthening of houses in 2400 villages. The remainder of the budget was dedicated to infrastructure, economic and social rehabilitation and technical assistance, training and equipment.[20]

> There is a trend to include community development and social and economic rehabilitation in post-recovery efforts

Both the urban example of Mexico City and the rural example of India demonstrate the trend to localizing services and investing in community development as part of disaster relief. In both cases, housing is better and safer as a result of the effort.

Given the increased urban vulnerabilities and the increased cost of relief, it is important to recognize that no governments or relief organizations can make disaster victims whole. The best these agencies can do is to understand the local development needs and help the local governments and victims decide housing strategies that can improve rather than hinder future local development. Research indicates that, in this connection, national governments can have an important role in fostering local adoption and enforcement of seismic provisions of building codes.[21]

In any disaster, urban or rural, in a developed or a developing country, the old, the young and the very poor suffer disproportionately. Successful disaster aid should use a variety of organizations to manage construction, employing local engineering and construction methods, local leadership and community participation. This multipronged approach will expedite and lower the cost of recovery and can be combined with reducing future vulnerability and enhancing sustainable development.

It is important to take into account the wider context within which such efforts are undertaken. The Marmara earthquake of 1999 provides a good example. Given that, during the 1990s, three other major urban earthquakes in Turkey preceded this disaster, the experience of this country offers an opportunity to examine the lessons learned. In this regard, some observers have pointed to corruption and lack of professional training as reasons behind inadequate enforcement of building codes.[22] Be that as it may, there is a wider context as well, relating to patterns of urbanization in Turkey and the country's economic policies in the context of globalization. In the years before 1980, the Turkish government adopted prevailing IMF and World Bank guidelines, prescribing privatization of its policies in support of public transport, health care, education, housing and economic development. Concomitantly, some 60–70 per cent of urbanization occurred illegally on lands surrounding new industrial centres, many of them in earthquake-prone areas. All planning functions were transferred to the local level and between 1983 and 1991 there were eight amnesties for illegal residential and commercial development. Land became a major commodity; in 1998, land speculation and rent amounted to 30 per cent of GNP, equal to the national budget. Municipalities used master plans as an instrument

| | Mexico City September 1985 | Kobe January 1995 | Northridge January 1994 |
|---|---|---|---|
| Magnitude | 8.1 | 7.2 | 6.8 |
| Deaths | 7,000 | 6,000 | 57 |
| Total damage value (US$) | 12,500 million | 150,000 million | 40,000 million |
| % housing loss | 33% value 64% buildings | 50% value 99% buildings | 50% value 90% buildings |
| Housing units lost | 76,000 | 400,000 | 60,000 |
| Total units damaged | 180,000 | 800,000 | 500,000 |
| % multi-family | 100% | 30% | 80% |
| % uninhabitable | 50% | 50% | 1% |
| Vacancy rate | ~1% | ~3% | 9% |
| Short-term recovery | 50,000 temp. housing | 48,000 temp. housing | Minimal sheltering |
| Long-term | 46,000 new units, 42,000 repaired with govt. funds in 2 years 7,400 units by NGO | 29,200 public sector units complete 9/97; est. 70,000 private sector units built in the region | 20,000 govt. funded units built; earthquake insurance for homeowners |

**Source:** Comerio, 1998; Tomiko, 1997.

**Comparison of housing loss and recovery: Mexico City, Kobe and the Northridge earthquakes**

to realize financial profits and had no incentive to undertake rational planning in the public interest.[23] In a different context, the US experience in the flawed local adoption and enforcement of building codes also points to an important role of national government in disaster mitigation.[24]

# Enhancing the Classical Post-disaster Recovery Model

> Disaster recovery and mitigation has evolved into a global enterprise involving multiple transnational relief agencies and the increasing use of special assistance programmes

Disaster recovery and mitigation have evolved into a global enterprise involving multiple transnational relief agencies and the increasing use of special assistance programmes. Traditional transnational efforts are crucial to any national recovery framework where resources are transferred from developed to less developed countries, and much of this work is now carried out by NGOs. Although the logical stages of disaster recovery – from emergency response through restoration and replacement – appear to be orderly and sequential, experience clearly demonstrates that these stages are not so easily 'governed'. Each stage acquires a momentum of its own which must be understood in process terms before any useful post-disaster planning can be done. Each country has its own history of tension between central government efforts at risk prevention and local and regional needs to address urbanization pressures while promoting risk mitigation measures. Thus it is essential to understand the catastrophic consequences of the risk-sharing formula in each country.[25]

The following section examines the 'classical post-disaster recovery model' and suggests additional elements that take into account the growing realities of citizen participation and new leadership roles being played by grassroots organizations and NGOs. A new, enhanced model then focuses attention on how to utilize disasters to empower local authorities and civil society to rebuild in ways that are constructive for all segments of society, and which help to prepare for the next disaster. After disasters, especially in developing countries where central governments often do not have the resources to sustain strong preparedness organizations, the non-governmental sector and the informal sector actually furnish *de facto* governance of the long-term recovery process. The classical model needs some adjustment to accommodate these realities.

## The institutional framework: globalization and disaster recovery

The notion of 'single, high-level institutions as the best means of controlling human settlements' supported at Habitat I, the first United Nations Conference on Human Settlements, convened in Vancouver in 1976, and upheld as a framework for governance, now seems oddly anachronistic. To the extent of their abilities, centralized governments can and must provide a channel for foreign assistance and some general policy guidance or technical expertise.

> Networks established by the informal and non-governmental sectors furnish the framework for a more inclusive model of institutional recovery following disasters

But as the process of transnational globalization continues, the networks established by the informal and non-governmental sectors furnish the framework for a more inclusive model of institutional recovery following disasters. As urban services to support globalization (especially transport and communications infrastructure) become more sophisticated, response at the community level fosters self-help, local governance and the introduction of appropriate technologies to serve various constituencies.

A framework for disaster recovery has evolved in which stakeholder groups mobilize to serve their defined interests alongside traditional, centralized government relief programmes. In this context, new linkages will develop, joining groups not previously allied. A good example of this organizational adaptation following a major disaster occurred in Central America in the aftermath of Hurricane Mitch (October–November 1998). The tracking of international relief supplies defaulted to the 'stovepipe' model (see below), with major NGOs such as CARE, Red Cross and humanitarian religious groups taking over direction of their own field efforts in the absence of effective national coordination. Institutional improvisation and unplanned adaptation took place alongside very limited national-level organization, forging alliances among stakeholder groups and village leaders in Honduras and Nicaragua which are now serving to facilitate allocation of long-term recovery resources.[26]

In Honduras, the Public Law, which authorizes disaster functions at the national level, was amended six months after Mitch to reconstitute the lead disaster agency, COPECO, as a civilian group operating independently of military authority for the first time in the country's history. This action was observed by one executive staff member to be a move towards the 'municipalization of emergency services' which will enhance local stakeholder involvement in administering disaster programmes during future emergencies. A marked increase in participation by municipalities and NGOs in flood hazard-prone areas of the country is taking place in areas such as the Aguan and Choluteca River valleys, supported by grants from international organizations like the Pan American Development Foundation and Peace Corps, which have strategic importance for reducing vulnerability to future disasters.[27] This experience suggests that it is useful to reconsider the classical disaster recovery model.

## The classical recovery model defined

The recovery/reconstruction classical model includes four overlapping periods,[28] as illustrated in Figure 15.1. The time required for reconstruction is a function of economic or other trends, which were already in place before the disaster occurred. What exists in terms of social class and economic conditions in society prior to the disaster will define to a great extent the shape of long-term recovery. The four periods of recovery are:

1   the *emergency period* covering the first few days following the disaster when services are disrupted and response is organized regionally, nationally and internationally;
2   the period of *restoring major urban services*, combined with debris clearance;
3   the *replacement period* when homes, jobs and major civil and commercial activities are restored;
4   the *developmental reconstruction period*, when improvement of previous public and private production and distribution systems occurs as part of future growth and expansion.

These periods do not necessarily follow in perfect stepwise sequence, and their application can be uneven. Political, technical, institutional and class factors intervene to direct the placement and delivery of recovery services. For example, an affluent neighbourhood with more direct access to outside assistance usually recovers faster than a heavily damaged, and largely ignored, lower-income neighbourhood.

The classical model is useful to disaster planners in marking the points at which various kinds of relief and reconstruction assistance can be channelled to local governments from state and federal sources. For example, under US federal disaster statutes, reimbursement for emergency protective measures, such as sandbagging operations, are paid from different categories of assistance from debris clearance or rebuilding of transport infrastructure. In defining the stages of recovery, the model establishes a 'sender–receiver' relationship between levels of government during recovery. This is done to facilitate the administration of disaster relief based on clearly established categories. At the international level, these would be defined as 'sectors' such as housing, transport and water systems,

upported by transnational donor institutions. The model
eeds enhancement, however, in defining how completion
f recovery actions actually led to preparation for future
isasters and in identifying the 'sustainable' elements for
ommunity participation at each stage.

## Enhancing the classical model

ased on experience in Asia and Latin America, the classical
ecovery model can be improved by adding to it other kinds
of activities, which occur sequentially. Three general areas
f effort are: mitigation measures and risk assessment;
pecial donor groups; and a period of logical planning.
These efforts are described below and illustrated in Figure
5.1.

1. *Mitigation measures and risk assessment* can be simultaneously carried out in the emergency and restoration
   periods, instead of later in the recovery. Such an
   enhancement would capitalize on the engineering
   and damage assessment resources which are on-site
   immediately following disasters, rather than delaying
   such studies until later, when crucial data or observations may be lost. Among the most useful examples
   of these immediate actions directed at reducing
   future losses is the post-Hurricane Mitch evaluation
   report prepared by the US Geological Survey, the
   Army Corps of Engineers and the University of
   South Carolina in January 1999, just two months
   following the disaster.[29] The report analysed the
   suitability of selected sites for housing reconstruction
   in seven municipalities, including evaluation of
   landslide and flooding risk, and water supply and
   access issues. Both short- and long-term recovery
   decisions were made using the report's technical
   findings, which were available in Spanish and English
   on the World Wide Web.
2. Identification and support of *special donor groups*
   which serve as expedient conduits for disaster relief,
   often operating independently of the central government's effort. This phenomenon is sometimes
   known as 'stovepiping', a descriptive term which
   suggests stakeholder organizations acting in a vertical
   fashion to nurture their own constituents' interests,
   linking headquarters policies and priorities directly
   with in-country field elements.
3. Finally, the classical model can be enhanced by an
   overarching effort to combine mitigation, risk assessment and the issues articulated by special donors
   into a new national programme for integrated disaster preparedness, driven by special legislation,
   emergent leadership and support from international
   financing institutions. Going beyond the replacement
   and reconstruction periods of the existing model, and
   building on them, this *new period of 'logical planning'*
   represents an expression of national application of
   post-disaster recovery activities. These activities are
   designed to empower local authorities to develop and
   implement reconstruction plans, which incorporate

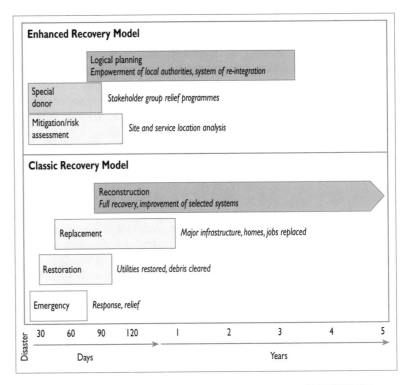

**Figure 15.1**

**Classical and enhanced recovery model**

**Source:** Siembieda and Baird (Background Papers)

local realities and allow for full expression of participation and voice by stakeholders. This logical
planning phase provides a space for new actors to
participate. This certainly was the case in Kobe,
Japan where the Machizukuri process of town
design, building and citizen participation was implemented as a result of the catastrophic 1995
earthquake.[30]

Coordination is essential in all aspects of the enhancements
described above. What varies, however, is the extent to
which regional and local governments are furnished with
the authority and resources to direct and influence the
work of donor groups, and to allow civil society to participate. The long-term risk assessment as is advocated here
will require coordination between units of government and
all agencies, including sharing of information and technology at appropriate levels.

## Opportunities for local capacity building

Post-disaster activities provide unique opportunities
for local governments to build new planning capacity
in preparation for the next disaster

Post-disaster activities provide unique opportunities for
local governments to increase planning capacity in preparation for the next disaster. This may require changes in
national law (as was the case in Japan and Honduras) and
will certainly require new resources such as training and
technology. The continued integration of transnational
assistance organizations at the local level is occurring. In
Honduras, United Nations and Organization of American
States-sponsored projects are providing mayors and regional
preparedness staff with the resources needed to strengthen

local capacity. Cooperatives have formed in the post-Mitch environment to acquire parcels of land and engage in self-help activities with the assistance of small-scale donors. The Honduras experience mirrors many others in the developing world. From it, we see a need for spatially bounded functional operations and transcending administrative boundaries, allowing for much stronger pre-event planning and service provision. It should also be recognized that a 'return to normality' is difficult to achieve in countries with wide income and class differences. A good example is the housing recovery policy that followed the Hanshin Great Earthquake of 1995. Before the earthquake, urban restructuring had been generating growing socio-economic polarization and geographical disparities in housing conditions in the city of Kobe. A detailed analysis of housing

recovery policies during the three years following the disaster showed that these policies simply reinforced pre-existing inequalities, with the result of further isolating low-income and elderly households.[31] In a related vein, a series of recent studies analyses disasters as socially constructed events, with gender-based actions that endure amidst and after severe disruptions. There are, however, examples of disaster recovery efforts that have sought to empower women, converting disaster relief into development work supportive of women's needs.[32] Thus, public policies need to promote a 'betterment of normality' approach, based on the enhancements outlined in the classical recovery model, which alone can address the reality of institutional change and capture whatever benefits globalization can give to post-disaster recovery efforts.

# Notes

1   See www.un.org.in/dmt/orissa/shelter.htm.

2   See www.who.int/eha/emergenc/turkey/index.htm. See also 'Reflections on the 1999 earthquakes in Turkey', a background paper by Fahriye Sancar, University of Colorado.

3   See also Key Issues and Messages in this report for the disaster that hit the Payatas dumpsite community in the Philippines in the Spring of 2000.

4   This definition was approved in September 1992 in a workshop that brought together representatives from OCHA, IDNDR, IFRC, UNEP, CRED, USAID, WHO and WFP (Personal communication from Caroline Michellier, Centre for Research in the Epidemiology of Disasters (CRED), Ecole de Santé Publique, Université Catholique de Louvain, Belgium, 25 January, 2000).

5   This number is, however, greatly deflated since it does not include, for example, accidents with fewer than ten people affected, thus excluding injuries and fatalities resulting from most domestic and traffic accidents. Nor does this figure include the large numbers of people who are displaced or whose experience of home is otherwise adversely affected by exposure to air, water and land pollution.

6   Difficulties in data compatability across different sources did not permit a regional breakdown of the Americas.

7   See Sanderson, 2000.

8   According to UN estimates, women and children make up 70–80 per cent of refugees and internally displaced persons.

9   For example, UNCHS (Habitat), UNIFEM, UNDP, and UNCHR have worked with the Women for Peace Network (www.unchs.org/unchs/english/feature/peace.htm), and The Global Campaign for Secure Tenure has produced a report,' Women's rights to land and property during conflict and reconstruction' (www.unchs.org/tenure/Gender/Woman-land.htm). In Kosovo, UNCHS created a Housing and Property Directorate and Claims Commission as part of a larger strategy to restoring housing and property rights that includes also the development of a cadaster and land information system and capacity building to re-establish municipal administration and the basic functions of local government. These efforts have led to the proposal of similar support in East Timor and Sierra Leone (see 'Rebuilding municipal government in Kosovo', CHS/00/15 (www.unchs.org/press2000/chs15.htm) and 'Successful creation of

Kosovo Housing and Property Directorate and Claims Commission leads to similar proposals for other post-conflict zones', CHS/00/02 (www.unchs.org/press2000/chs2.htm). See also 'Housing and property in Kosovo: Rights, law and justice' in Leckie, 1999.

10  The following sections draw heavily from 'Natural hazards and human settlements: Issues and lessons from recent experience', a background paper prepared by Mary C Comerio (University of California, Berkeley) and 'Who governs reconstruction? Enhancing the classic post-disaster recovery model', a background paper prepared by William Siembieda (California Polytechnic State University) and Bruce Baird (California Governor's Office of Emergency Services).

11  See www.who.int/eha/emergenc/mitch/index.htm.

12  See www.who.int/eha/emergenc/turkey/index.htm. See also 'Reflections on the 1999 earthquakes in Turkey', a background paper by Fahriye Sancar, University of Colorado; Ozerdem, 1999.

13  See www.un.org.in/dmt/orissa/shelter.htm.

14  See www.who.int/eha/emergenc/mozamb/index.htm.

15  Boulle et al, 1997.

16  Swiss Reinsurance Company (Zurich) (14 March 2000), cited in Emergency Preparedness News. Business Publishers Inc, Silver Spring, MD, p 51. During the same decade, the US experienced 460 presidentially declared disasters, including the costliest in its history, the 1994 Northridge earthquake with total damages estimated at over US$40,000 million.

17  Jacobs, 1997.

18  See Comerio, 1998. See also Hirayama, 2000.

19  See Anderson and Woodrow, 1989.

20  See EERI, 1999.

21  See Burby and May, 1999.

22  See, for example, Ozerdem, 1999.

23  See Sancar, 2000.

24  See Burby and May, 1999.

25  Burby et al, 1999.

26  Olson et al, 1999.

27  Pan American Development Foundation, 2000.

28  Schwab et al, 1998

29  United States Geological Survey, US Army Corps of Engineers and University of South Carolina, 1999.

30  Topping, K C 'Urban planning during rebuilding: The Machizukur experience' (unpublished manuscript).

31  See Hirayama, 2000.

32  See Enarson and Morrow, 1998.

# BUILDING A COMMON FUTURE

In 1996, Habitat II emphasized two themes of global importance: 'Adequate shelter for all' and 'Sustainable human settlements development in an urbanizing world'. These themes are central to the worldwide responsibility for building a common future and form the subject of the two chapters making up the last part of this report.

Chapter 16 focuses on selected aspects of adequate shelter for all. Attempts to arrive at a universal definition of adequate shelter are fraught with difficulty because standards and norms vary considerably according to cultural, climatic and political factors. Hence, there are also differing perceptions of the need for action and the types of approaches that would be appropriate. However, there is no disagreement about the need to do something about the complete lack of any shelter at all for a growing number of people. Homelessness represents the most obvious and severe manifestation of the unfulfilment of the distinct human right to adequate housing.

It is important to recognize the different needs of particular homeless populations, whether they are migrants, transients, substance abusers, mentally ill people, battered women, street children or others. However, it is also important not to stigmatize these groups and to avoid concentrating on individual characteristics without directing attention to the broader structural factors that underpin homelessness. Homelessness cannot be severed from its wider economic, political, cultural and social contexts. Strategies to combat its root causes, rather than its symptomatic expressions, must necessarily deal with these contexts, which vary internationally.

The experience of the US, Canada and Japan illustrates that high levels of affluence do not preclude – and indeed, can easily hide – homelessness. Chapter 16 stresses that markets have not eliminated and cannot be expected to eliminate homelessness. This chapter describes a range of policy approaches in relation to the causes behind homelessness. In the developing economies, these causes include rapid urbanization and household formation that produce a demand for housing that exceeds existing production capabilities. In addition, structural adjustment policies have curtailed subsidies on basic services, eliminated public assistance programmes and contributed to migration, eroding existing social safety nets and undermining family cohesion. Forced evictions also continue to be a source of homelessness, posing a particular problem to women in countries where they possess unequal property and inheritance rights. Women are also more at risk of violence and abuse when rendered homeless.

In more developed countries, the causes of homelessness include lack of affordable housing, gentrification, cutbacks in welfare budgets, stagnating and falling real earnings, the rise of part-time and insecure jobs, erosion of job benefits, lack of afford-

able health care and deinstitutionalization of people afflicted by mental illness. Further, discriminatory practices based on race, ethnicity, gender and family status remain widespread, part of processes of social exclusion in which lack of access to housing plays a key role. These problems are often compounded by spatial mismatches between housing and job markets.

In all parts of the world, but particularly in Africa and Asia, natural and human-made disasters – including wars and civil strife – are major causes of homelessness.

Globalization has played an ambiguous role concerning the right to housing. The number of people living in inadequate shelter, or no shelter at all, appears to have increased as a result of the expansion of market processes associated with contemporary globalization. However, at the same time, modern information and communication technologies have helped to spread norms deriving from the right to housing, facilitated the exchange of information about model legislation and supported cooperative action to counter violations of housing rights. Thus, housing rights *in law* have advanced, even if *in practice* they have not. Housing rights provide clear and consistent criteria against which the actions, policies, practices and legislation of states can be judged. In this regard, the Global Campaign for Secure Tenure is a major initiative to guarantee a justiciable right of access to and use of property. Secure tenure is also important because it stimulates investments by people in their own homes.

Within the context of tenure, an overall shelter strategy must necessarily be concerned not only with strengthening security of tenure, but also with developing and supporting appropriate forms of tenure. In this regard, cooperative housing offers advantages because it pools resources to lower individual housing costs; fosters collective action and self-help; increases the creditworthiness of low-income households; and limits or prevents speculation.

The second principal theme of the Habitat Agenda, sustainable human settlements development, has many aspects. Chapter 17 emphasizes the importance of supporting governance to create more inclusive cities and eradicate poverty, corruption and violence. The Global Campaign for Urban Governance promotes the establishment of legal frameworks and policy reforms to enable decentralized, democratic approaches for addressing these challenges. This chapter also insists that the eradication of poverty must be recognized as a public good because people living in poverty represent unrealized human capital potential with benefits for the *whole* of society. Given the failure of market forces to invest in people who are poor, governments have a key role that includes support for the informal sector.

Corruption undermines good governance. People are more susceptible to corruption when they have the monopoly over a good or service, the discretion to decide who gets that good or service and are not accountable for that decision. Privatization has increased the incentives for multinational companies to offer bribes in order to secure profitable concessions and contracts. Corruption tends to be reduced by separation of power, checks and balances, transparency, a good justice system and clearly defined roles, rules, responsibilities and limits. Corruption tends not to thrive where there is a democratic culture, competition and good systems of control, and where people have rights to information and rights of redress. Transparency and accountability are central o good democratic governance. Often, the performance of urban government can only be effectively audited at the city level where people's expertise about local events, people and places can be brought to bear.

Urban violence is not primarily a spontaneous occurrence, but above all, the product of societies characterized by inequality and social exclusion. Measures that protect urban communities from deprivation, unemployment, homelessness, illiteracy, injustice and social disintegration will ultimately also protect them from crime and violence.

Conflicts between neighbours and communities often revolve around scarce resources. Shared water is a major cause of violence, and may be exacerbated by privatization. With deregulation, interpersonal violence is also increasingly linked to cut-throat competition in informal sector activities. The availability of firearms, facilitated by worldwide organized crime groups, multiplies the risks of urban violence and represents a fundamental threat to security.

In the urban context there has been a broad shift from approaches that focus on the control of violence, to those that concentrate on prevention, to more recent perspectives that aim to rebuild social capital. Two further approaches, commonly at national level but with important urban focuses, are peaceful conflict resolution through negotiation and legal enforcement of human rights. Cities need integrated frameworks to coordinate these approaches.

# 16

# ADEQUATE SHELTER FOR ALL: STRATEGIC FOCI

## Combating Homelessness

*'Homelessness represents the most obvious and severe manifestation of the unfulfilment of the distinct human right to adequate housing'*[1]

*'In many cities in the developing countries, an increasing proportion of the population lives in substandard housing or on the streets. In Mumbai alone, more than 5 million residents live in slums and the number of pavement dwellers has been estimated at over 1 million.'*[2]

*'When 43-year-old Yette M Adams froze to death at the doorstep of the US Department of Housing and Urban Development headquarters in Washington, DC, her death riveted public attention on a persistent and egregious problem in a country where it is possible to find 4 x 8 foot plywood dog houses at US$500 a piece, designed to house homeless people, as well as a US$15,000 miniature Victorian mansion for a Dobermann pinscher, with a redwood cathedral ceiling, Italian porcelain tile flooring, solid brass fixtures, cedar shake roof, double pane windows, pool and rock garden.'*[3]

*'In Tokyo, in the entrails of Shinjuku subway station, in front of an office window displaying an advertisement for a life insurance company, a homeless person finds shelter in a carton box – previously used by Microsoft, epitome of globalization, owned by the richest person on earth, with a net worth of over US$60,000 million*[4] *– within a stone's throw from the Welfare Office, housed in the Metropolitan Government building whose price tag of 157,000 million yen earned it the nickname of "the Tax Building".'*[5]

The citations above succinctly capture several important points about homelessness worldwide. First, housing is now universally recognized as a human right and pervasive homelessness demonstrates clearly that efforts to implement this right must be strengthened and accelerated. The International Year of Shelter for the Homeless (IYSH) in 1987 helped to direct public attention to the extent and severity of homelessness and spurred a plethora of reports,[6] but subsequent policies have not diminished the problem. Second, although data are sparse and scattered, it is clear that the scale of urban homelessness in the developing countries is enormous. The situation in Mumbai, with

more than 1 million pavement-dwellers, is not unusual. Lack of adequate shelter is common. In comparison, problems of homelessness in the more developed economies are neither as widespread nor as severe.

However, the two vignettes from the United States and Japan illustrate a third point: high levels of aggregate affluence do not preclude – and indeed, can easily hide – homelessness. In 1998, the US and Japan ranked in the top among countries worldwide in terms of per capita GNP,[7] yet neither country has eliminated homelessness.[8] This point is further demonstrated by the situation in Canada, another member of the world's economic elite, where, in an unprecedented action, the Toronto City Council by a vote of 53 to 1 adopted a resolution requesting that homelessness be declared a national disaster requiring emergency relief.[9]

> High levels of aggregate affluence do not preclude – and indeed, can easily hide – homelessness

In varying degrees, these three advanced economies have systems of housing provision that rely on market mechanisms. In such systems, access to housing is predicated on people's ability to pay the price resulting from the dynamics of supply and demand. If demand does not generate sufficient profit, suppliers will make rational business decisions to seek higher returns on their investments elsewhere. Hence, households without adequate incomes, who cannot translate their real housing needs into an effective market demand, find themselves at risk of homelessness. Interests that have pushed for economic globalization, with its attendant emphasis on competitive processes, privatization of public provisions and curtailment of social programmes, even as more and more people live in poverty, have undoubtedly contributed to a rise in homelessness.[10] It is clear that markets have not eliminated and cannot be expected to eliminate homelessness.

> Markets have not eliminated and cannot be expected to eliminate homelessness

### The diversity of homelessness

Homelessness is a complex problem. It has a variety of causes and consequences. The definitions of and approaches to it are many, shaped by political ideologies as much as

---

**Box 16.1 Houselessness and inadequate shelter: seeking clarification**

People *sleeping rough* – meaning in the street, in public places or in any other place not meant for human habitation – form the core of the 'homeless'. Those *sleeping in shelters* provided by welfare or other institutions can also be considered as a part of this population. Persons or households living under these two types of circumstances can be categorized as being 'houseless'. This definition avoids cultural and regional variations. An individual with no access to housing will be considered as houseless all over the world.

*Concealed houselessness* is another aspect of what is commonly grouped under homelessness as well. This category includes people living with family members or friends because they cannot afford shelter by themselves (eg doubling up). Without this privately offered housing opportunity they would be living in the street or be sheltered by an institution of the welfare system. This phenomenon is extremely difficult to enumerate, especially in countries where the extended family takes care of its members if necessary. Further, new strategies of sharing housing units are emerging as pressures on housing markets increases (eg in Eastern Europe), making enumeration of these situations even more challenging.

Others living under the threat of houselessness are those facing eviction or expiration of the lease, with no prospect for alternative housing. People being released from institutional settings with no place to go fall into this category of being at 'risk of houselessness'.

People living in inadequate, *substandard housing* should also be included in studies and policies concerned with houselessness because such housing often is an antecedent condition, as well as a temporary situation for those seeking to escape houselessness. Households with insecure incomes are likely to live in such housing units.

The three last categories are overlapping, but none includes the whole of the others. Someone can live in the house of a relative (concealed houselessness) and the house may (but need not) be substandard. And the relative may or may not be liable to eviction (at risk of houselessness).

Figure 16.1 visually organizes these mutually non-exclusive types of situations under the label 'inadequate shelter', which is central to the concerns of the Habitat Agenda. In contrast to the above definition of houselessness, this classification of inadequate shelter is subject to multiple interpretations, owing to differences in climatic conditions, historic traditions, legislative contexts and culture-based variations. For example, a house without heating can be seen as adequate in a country with a mild climate, whereas it would be substandard in areas with cold winters.

For technical reasons the definition of inadequate shelter has to be restricted to measurable elements: a housing unit without a roof and/or walls that does not allow privacy; without adequate space, adequate security (legal and physical), adequate lighting, heating and ventilation and adequate basic infrastructure such as water supply, sanitation and waste-management facilities; without environmental quality and safeguards against health threats, and with housing costs that are not reasonable.

Figure 16.1 clarifies the relationships between the different categories of houselessness. Houselessness is part of the inadequate shelter situation, forming its bottom end. The introduction of the term 'houselessness' is meant to help the statistical analysis of movements in and out of houselessness.

There are several reasons for this refining of the conventional notion of homelessness. First, the categories correspond to different spheres of action by policy makers. Emergency action is required for the houseless part of the population, whereas those in inadequate shelter must be targeted for actions that prevent a worsening of their situation and that assist them in the transition to adequate and secure housing. Second, while the incidence of different forms of inadequate shelter can be established by census counts or surveys based on housing units, this is by definition not possible for the houseless population. The enumeration of houselessness and concealed houselessness will require the development of new methods. Third, the implementation of approaches to eliminate homelessness requires a proper understanding of the underlying causes that lead to each of the different forms of inadequate shelter. Each of these forms may demand a different approach. Finally, the conceptual distinctions make it possible to adopt *houselessness* as a global, universally acceptable category, while maintaining *inadequate shelter* as a category that can be sensitive to regional variations as to what constitutes substandard housing.

**Source:** Adapted from Springer, 2000.

---

dispassionate analysis. A voluminous literature reveals a great variety in conceptualizations of homelessness. Much of this literature concentrates on specific population groups: the unemployed, (im)migrants and transients, substance abusers, mentally ill people, racial and ethnic minorities, battered women, people infected with HIV/AIDS, war veterans, runaway youth, street children and so forth. Studies of this kind can be helpful in providing a close-up view of the experiences of homeless people.[11] However, the problem with these perspectives is that they centre on subjective experiences and implicate the personal characteristics and backgrounds of individual people, risking their stigmatization and failing to bring into focus the broader structural factors that underpin homelessness.[12]

There would be considerable merit in having an unambiguous definition of homelessness that applies uniformly, making possible consistent monitoring and comparative assessment of ameliorative approaches. At the global level, this seems an elusive goal in light of the diverse structural causes of homelessness, the range of consequences, the diverse cultural norms and national standards and the particularities of the groups most affected. There have, nevertheless, been various attempts to develop such universal definitions. For example, a recent effort proposes use of the term 'houselessness' to denote various forms of inadequate shelter (see Box 16.1 and Figure 16.1). An advantage of this particular conceptualization is that it distinguishes between one component about which there can be no disagreement (ie those without any form of housing are houseless) and another component that flexibly allows for various interpretations (inadequacy), thus accommodating a range of regionally and culturally appropriate standards. However, its contribution remains on the conceptual level and the potential of its immediate practical applicability is limited.

There exist other conceptualizations of the multiple dimensions of inadequate housing. For example, the notion of 'housing poverty' includes qualitative deficiencies of the dwelling as well as the neighbourhood infrastructure, insecure tenure of the dwelling and the land, and excessive costs.[13] In a related vein, the concept of 'shelter poverty' captures the trade-off relationship between housing expentures and the costs of meeting other basic needs, providing a useful method of measuring housing affordability (see Box 16.2).

The diversity of conceptualizations and operational definitions, combined with political influences on and practical difficulties in data collection, have led to measurements that show considerable range in the extent of homelessness. Measurement methods vary a great deal across countries, data collection is frequently incomplete at best, and the prospect for improvement in this regard is not promising[14] (Box 16.2). Bearing these caveats in mind, the number of people who are homeless or residing in inadequate housing conditions has been estimated at more than 1000 million.[15]

There exist contexts where accurate figures are important. At disaggregate levels of policy making and programme implementation, it matters how many households fall into specific categories of homelessness. In this regard, self-enumeration by pavement dwellers and slum dwellers, as carried out successfully through the Society for the Promotion of Area Resource Centres (SPARC) and Mahila Milan in Mumbai, India, are an empowering alternative to conventional counting methods.[16] However, for the purpose of the present global discussion, an undue preoccupation with the elusive precision of statistics is a misplaced pursuit of exactitude. There is a bottom line regarding homelessness worldwide whose veracity is not in doubt. While we may be not be sure about exact figures, we can be certain about one thing: the number of homeless people is a *very large* number. What are the reasons?

The causes of homelessness are many and diverse. They vary across countries and across population groups. In many cities of the developing countries, the suppliers of housing cannot keep pace with the increasing need for housing resulting from rapid urbanization and new household formation. Aside from questions of affordability, there also exist serious quantitative and qualitative deficits. For example, ECLAC reports an absolute housing shortage of 17 million housing units (18 per cent) for Latin America and the Caribbean.[17] Another 21 million units (22 per cent) are considered inadequate but repairable.[18] Table 16.1 shows a more detailed breakdown of the region's total housing deficit of 40 per cent, including Brazil ( 45 per cent), Colombia (43 per cent), Mexico (35 per cent) and Peru (53 per cent). Further, in most countries, the deficits are steadily growing (see Box 16.3).

In India, depending on criteria, the country's housing shortfall has been estimated at between 30 and 70 million units, up to 46 per cent of the stock required to house the national population[19] (see also Box 16.4).

The contribution of precarious housing situations to homelessness is exacerbated by breakdowns of social safety nets and family units related to IMF-imposed structural adjustment policies that have curtailed subsidies and eliminated public assistance programmes, inducing migration, fomenting domestic violence and contributing to the rise in street children.[20] Although a gross violation of human rights, forced evictions also continue to be a cause of homelessness, posing a particular problem to women in

countries where they possess unequal property and inheritance rights. The actions of the Railway Slum Dwellers in Mumbai, India, are an example of effective community organizing to resist displacement, turning a crisis into a situation of advantage (see Boxes 16.5 and 16.6).[21] In the East European and Baltic states, the lifting of rent controls under liberalization policies dramatically increased the share of housing expenses from 3–10 per cent to 15–25 per cent of household income. Housing payments in the lowest income groups have risen up to one-half of household income.

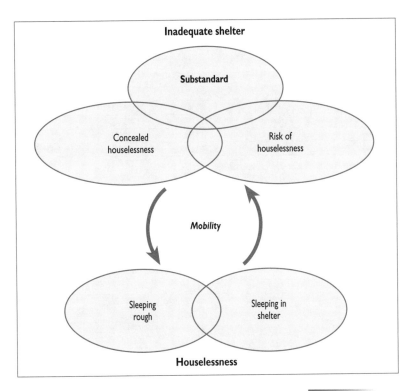

**Figure 16.1**

Conceptualizing homelessness: inadequate shelter and houselessness

**Box 16.2 Measuring shelter poverty**

Affordable housing plays an important role in many situations of homelessness. There exist a variety of ways in which to conceptualize affordability (see, eg Hulchanski, 1995) and each can be measured in more than one way. Careful comparative studies of affordability measures and subsidy mechanisms amply illustrate this point (see, eg Haffner, 1998; Haffner and Oxley, 1999; Kemp, 1997 for the European Union). A common rule of thumb in many countries expresses households' housing cost burden as a percentage of household income. However, this approach is problematic because the adequacy of residual income varies widely as a result of household size, level of income and other living expenses. The recently developed concept of shelter poverty addresses this difficulty (see Stone, 1993). It calculates how much income is left for housing after accounting for the known costs of 'basic (non-shelter) necessities' for households of given sizes. If the remaining income is insufficient to cover local housing costs, households are considered 'shelter poor'. Measuring housing affordability as shelter poverty introduces an opportunity for coordinating national policies. It makes it possible to agree on a common goal (ie preventing shelter poverty) within a shared policy framework that is responsive to variations in key variables among countries. Thus a single measure of housing affordability could accommodate national and regional differences in essential non-housing cost-of-living expenditures and household size. It would permit a better comparative assessment of housing affordability across countries and cities. However, as with the conceptual refinement of 'houselessness', implementation of policies based on the concept of 'shelter poverty' would require data that are simply not available in most countries.

| Country | Year | Total households | Quantitative deficit [b] | % of total deficit | Qualitative deficit [c] | % of total deficit | Total deficit [d] | % of all households w/deficit |
|---|---|---|---|---|---|---|---|---|
| Argentina | 1991 | 9,380,204 | 1,449,783 | 49.2 | 1,496,212 | 50.8 | 2,945,995 | 31.4 |
| Bolivia | 1992 | 1,614,995 | 406,979 | 55.4 | 327,844 | 44.6 | 734,823 | 45.5 |
| Brazil | 1991 | 35,517,542 | 5,881,221 | 36.7 | 10,145,712 | 63.3 | 16,026,933 | 45.1 |
| Chile | 1992 | 3,365,462 | 609,255 | 62.8 | 361,212 | 37.2 | 970,467 | 28.8 |
| Colombia | 1985 | 5,824,857 | 1,098,711 | 43.6 | 1,423,095 | 56.4 | 2,521,806 | 43.3 |
| Costa Rica | 1984 | 527,299 | 71,073 | 37.9 | 116,386 | 62.1 | 187,459 | 35.6 |
| Cuba | 1981 | 2,350,221 | 395,472 | 60.7 | 256,100 | 39.3 | 651,572 | 27.7 |
| Ecuador | 1990 | 2,136,889 | 424,833 | 55.8 | 336,834 | 44.2 | 761,667 | 35.6 |
| El Salvador | 1992 | 1,091,728 | 402,410 | 69.0 | 180,461 | 31.0 | 582,871 | 53.4 |
| Guatemala | 1994 | 1,591,823 | 328,978 | 31.7 | 709,911 | 68.3 | 1,038,889 | 65.3 |
| Honduras | 1988 | 808,222 | 137,026 | 41.9 | 189,767 | 58.1 | 326,793 | 40.4 |
| Mexico | 1990 | 17,394,368 | 3,323,847 | 55.3 | 2,687,615 | 44.7 | 6,011,462 | 34.6 |
| Nicaragua | 1991 | – | 289,994 | 56.8 | 220,992 | 43.2 | 510,986 | – |
| Panama | 1990 | 541,704 | 103,688 | 58.9 | 72,366 | 41.1 | 176,054 | 32.5 |
| Paraguay | 1992 | 873,694 | 161,227 | 45.3 | 194,889 | 54.7 | 356,116 | 40.8 |
| Peru | 1993 | 4,762,779 | 1,207,483 | 47.7 | 1,323,828 | 52.3 | 2,531,311 | 53.1 |
| Dominican Republic | 1993 | 534,827 | 8,570 | 4.1 | 199,266 | 95.9 | 207,836 | 38.9 |
| Uruguay | 1985 | 902,300 | 120,045 | 53.4 | 104,553 | 46.6 | 224,598 | 24.0 |
| Venezuela | 1990 | 3,750,940 | 763,413 | 70.8 | 315,359 | 29.2 | 1,078,772 | 28.8 |
| Latin America and the Caribbean | | 92,969,854 | 16,544,477 | 44.5 | 20,662,402 | 55.5 | 37,206,879 | 40.0 |

**Notes:** Percentage of the 1990 population of Latin America and the Caribbean covered: 96.15%.

a ECLAC, Human Settlements: The Shelter of Development. b Quantitative deficit: number of households – number of adequate and repairable dwellings. c Qualitative deficit: number of repairable dwellings. d Total deficit: quantitative + qualitative deficit.

**Source:** MacDonald, 1998 135, pp 25, 54.

**Table 16.1**

**Latin America and the Caribbean (19 countries): housing situation in the 1990s[a]**

Forced evictions continue to be a cause of homelessness, posing a particular problem to women in countries where they possess unequal property and inheritance rights

In more developed countries, the causes of homelessness include lack of affordable housing, gentrification, cutbacks in welfare budgets, stagnating and falling real earnings, the rise of part-time and insecure jobs, erosion of job benefits, lack of affordable health care and deinstitutionalization of people afflicted by mental illness. In addition, discriminatory practices, based on race, ethnicity, gender and family status remain widespread, part of processes of social exclusion in which lack of access to housing plays a key role.[22] These problems are often compounded by spatial mismatches between housing and job markets. It is not uncommon to find a strong demand for low- or moderate-income workers who cannot afford housing on the local market, while there are high vacancy rates in other places where jobs are hard to find.

Natural and human-made disasters, including wars and civil strife, are much overlooked causes of homelessness. During the 1990s alone, more than 186 million people lost their homes as a result of disasters of one kind or another. Although it is often difficult to prevent disasters from happening, appropriate planning of human settlements can sometimes reduce their probability and mitigate their effects (see the discussion on sustainable development in Chapter 15).

## Framing policies to overcome the limits of market mechanisms

Just as there are a variety of structural and personal antecedents of homelessness, so also are there a variety of strategies to combat homelessness. These strategies span a wide spectrum. They vary between countries and cities. They also change over time and official government reaction has ranged from educational approaches to mass shootings at railway stations, reflecting the leanings of different political regimes.[23]

Current strategies are wide-ranging as well. They include criminalization of homelessness in some cities and measures that may eliminate its local manifestations but that simply displace homeless people to elsewhere; narrowly focused programmes that address the most immediate concerns of the homeless, such as night shelters and free meals; intermediate support programmes such as mental health services, substance abuse counselling and transitional housing; and long-term approaches such as support for low-cost permanent housing and poverty eradication.

---

**Box 16.3 Housing deficits in Latin America and the Caribbean**

The countries of the region suffer from significant housing shortfalls. Only 60 out of every 100 households have adequate housing, while 22 require improvements and 18 need a new home or to rebuild the one they are now occupying. Taking both qualitative and quantitative aspects into account, the current deficit is at least 38 million units. This figure is increasing by more than 2 million each year as new households are formed. A great majority of the countries are not even managing to construct enough housing for the new households that come into being each year, so their shortfalls are steadily growing. The rate at which the housing stock is growing obsolete is also high, due to a lack of housing maintenance and repair programmes; this in turn is contributing to a worsening of the deficit, as it means that high rates of replacement are needed.

**Source:** ECLAC, *Human Settlements: The Shelter of Development.*

> Homelessness cannot be severed from its wider economic, political, cultural and social contexts. Strategies to combat the root causes of homelessness, rather than its symptomatic expressions, must necessarily deal with these contexts

The problems of homelessness cannot be addressed in isolation. Homelessness does not occur in a vacuum. It cannot be severed from its wider economic, political, cultural and social contexts. Strategies to combat the root causes of homelessness, rather than its symptomatic expressions, must necessarily deal with these contexts. This report emphasizes a rights-based approach. Most of the remainder of this chapter is dedicated to a review of recent and prospective developments concerning the right to housing. UNCHS's Global Campaign for Secure Tenure is a major initiative developed within this context. However, other strategies are important as well, including the eradication of poverty, increasing affordability of housing, enhancing construction capacity, facilitating access to land and elimination of discrimination. Although some of these strategies can take advantage of market mechanisms when developed with appropriate regulatory provisions, they all require intervention by government, often with participation by civil society groups. The most appropriate combination and operationalization of strategies will differ from one country to another.

In high-income countries, there has been a shift in public policy regarding homelessness from remedial treatment and control towards a more preventive approach.[24] In support of this change, there is now more interagency collaboration than a decade ago, and programmes have become more targeted to the specific needs of homeless people. There is a frequent distinction between two, sometimes overlapping groups: those in crisis poverty and those suffering from chronic disabilities. A common model includes a two-pronged general strategy:

- to take emergency measures aimed at bringing those who are currently homeless back into mainstream society;
- to prevent the occurrence of homelessness by addressing the structural needs for housing and social infrastructure for the very poor.

> The trend towards more individualized programmes and services requires the combination of resources across a variety of agencies and professions

The trend towards more individualized programmes and services requires the combination of resources across a variety of agencies and professions. This network style of management moves away from large-scale bureaucratic public agencies towards more collaborative organizational structures.

In the United States, programmes to remedy the homeless problem are often viewed along a 'continuum of care'. This approach has three distinct components: emergency shelter assessment to identify an individual's or family's needs; transitional or rehabilitative services for

---

**Box 16.4 Housing need in India**

In India, rapid urbanization and the deteriorating financial conditions of urban local bodies, coupled with an increase in urban poverty have resulted in inadequate provision of shelter, amenities and services in urban areas. In most Indian cities with populations of more than a million, one in four inhabitants live in illegal settlements, which are growing twice as fast as the rest of the city. In big Indian cities such as Ahmedabad, Mumbai and Calcutta, the percentage of households in designated slum settlements ranges between 40 and 60 per cent. Estimates of the percentage of the total urban population living in designated slum and squatter settlements vary between 20 and 25 per cent. In total, 350 million people are now estimated to be living in urban areas, suggesting that between 70 and 85 million people are in designated slum and squatter areas.

The Indian government recognizes that the need for housing investment is acute. Indian government agencies estimate that the housing stock increased from 93 million in 1971 to 148.1 million in 1991, while the number of households increased from 97.1 million to 153.2 million during the same period, increasing the housing deficit by 5.1 million units. Other sources estimate a housing shortage by 2001 of 30 to 41 million units, one-third of which is in urban areas and two-thirds in rural areas. The Ninth Plan (1997–2002) estimates that about 9 million new units are required in urban areas and 7.7 million in rural areas, while an additional 7.5 million units in urban and 20 million units in rural India require upgrading.

**Source:** Mitlin (background paper) compiled from information in Acharya, 2000.

---

those who need them; and permanent or supportive housing arrangements for every homeless individual and family. These ideas currently emphasize social improvement for the poor. Their overemphasis on social dependence as the problem has encouraged the use of shelters and social programmes to change individuals and households rather than improvement of kind and amounts of affordable housing in mixed residential communities, including low-rent single room occupancy.[25]

In several countries in Western Europe, a similar idea of the 'staircase of transition' as a means for re-integration into society has been gaining ground in national policies. In 'dwellings for training' homeless people are to make gradual improvements in their housing, in terms of quality, privacy and control over the home. Step-by-step, the service providers reduce support and control until the once homeless person becomes an independent tenant. However, this system may turn out to be a 'staircase of exclusion'. Landlords have no incentives for converting a transitional contract or a 'dwelling for training' into an independent tenancy. Thus, the 'final step' for the client may be postponed or even removed. At the same time, social authorities can use referral to lower steps of the 'staircase' as negative sanctions, resulting in downward mobility.

In the transition economies, policies differ according to the state's recognition of homelessness. There tend to be three stages:

1. The number of homeless people grows dramatically. There is economic breakdown, closure of workers' hostels, the appearance of a 'real-estate mafia' and surging utility prices. Owing to weak economic performance, a social housing policy is not an affordable solution, so shelters are established.
2. The number of homeless people begins to stabilize as the additions are offset by high mortality among

**Box 16.5 Empowerment by partnerships: relocation of the railway slum dwellers in Mumbai, India**

Rural poverty has fuelled rapid migration to urban centres in India, as in most developing countries. As India's largest commercial centre, Mumbai attracts thousands of new residents every day from across the country. Finding work is relatively easy for the migrants, but finding shelter on this cramped island city is not. The open real estate market offers little affordable housing, and nearly half of the city's 11 million residents live in slums. These informal settlements have sprung up on private lands (about 50 per cent of the slum population), state- and city-owned lands (about 25 per cent) and lands owned by the central government (about 25 per cent). These last include more than 30,000 families living in rows of shacks 1.5 to 30 m from the three major suburban railway lines.

Living conditions in the railway communities are generally worse than in other Mumbai slums, comparable only to those of pavement dwellers. In slums on private and state-owned land, over time the city government has extended basic services such as water and sewerage. However, the land along the tracks is the property of Indian Railways (IR), a subsidiary of the central government, which argues that providing services will encourage more illegal settlement. Residents of the railway shanties have no clean water, electricity, sewerage or trash removal. They are vulnerable to extortion, since by living where they do they are technically breaking the law. Living so close to the tracks, the slum dwellers also risk being hit by one of the frequent trains, which kill an average of three slum dwellers a day. Trains travelling through the railway slums must slow down from their normal 50 km/hr to about 15 km/hr, thus extending the daily commute of 4.5 million people and increasing tensions. The relocation of the railway slum dwellers, described below, is an example of how people in poverty managed to improve their living conditions by forming and participating in a broad alliance of community-based partners.

In the late 1980s, a coalition of three NGOs emerged as advocates for the railway slum dwellers: the National Slum Dwellers' Federation (NSDF), and its Mumbai branch the Railway Slum Dwellers Federation; Mahila Milan (Women Together), founded to help poor urban women organize local savings schemes; and the Society for Promotion of Area Resource Centres (SPARC), a group of professionals dedicated to various issues of welfare and the urban poor in Mumbai. In 1988, these three groups conducted a census of the railway slums and published it as *Beyond the Beaten Track*. The alliance generated a new sense of power within the slum dweller community; women especially began to push for relocation. For the next decade, the alliance approached the central government and the railways with proposals for relocation; it argued that the government should contribute to the effort, since the slum dwellers had added so much to the economy over the years and yet received so few services. However, little progress in negotiation was made during this period.

A shift occurred in 1996 when the state government of Maharashtra and the railways began negotiations with the World Bank for the Mumbai Urban Transport Project II (MUTP-II). This project was designed to ease Mumbai's traffic problems by expanding and updating the rail network and by constructing new roads. The former would require the relocation of many of the slum dwellers. Years of international attention on the negative consequences for the poor displaced by past World Bank projects led the Bank to make comprehensive rehabilitation plans mandatory for MUTP-II and many other loans. The alliance of NGOs was invited to participate in the negotiation process. By 1999, the World Bank had approved a US$500 million loan to the Mumbai Metropolitan Regional Development Authority (MMRDA), an agency of the state government, which included a plan for the rehabilitation of 14,000 households to be directed by SPARC with money from MUTP-II. The World Bank also made it clear that if slum dwellings were demolished without a resettlement plan, it would review the loan to MMRDA.

However, projects of MUTP-II's size take years to get through their initial negotiation and planning phase. In the meantime, tensions on the ground increased between commuters, slum dwellers and the railways. Commuter anger at delays and breakdowns of trains precipitated the damaging of railway property. Train accidents also led to violence by the slum dwellers against the passengers. Frustrated, concerned commuters founded two groups, Citizens for a Just Society and the Suburban Railway Passengers Association, to lobby for the clearance of dwellings near the tracks. As tensions increased, the railway safety commissioner promised to stop trains unless buildings near a critical section of track were removed. In February 2000, the railway authorities began to bulldoze structures along two of the lines. The alliance and the state government tried to block the demolition by invoking a state law prohibiting the destruction of any building more than five years old. After reminders that the operation was also clearly jeopardizing the MUTP-II project, the demolitions were stopped. By that time, over 2500 families had been made homeless, including some who had been living there for over 30 years. With the months passing and the MUTP-II relocation remaining in the pipeline, tensions grew once again, and in September 2000, the central government undertook another demolition that rendered several thousand more people homeless. Again, they were stopped by the alliance of NGOs and the state government, which feared the loss of the World Bank funds.

By the end of 2000, the MUTP-II relocation process was finally underway. Of the 14,000 originally designated households, 1800 had moved into new formal housing constructed by the state housing authority (MHADA) and purchased with MUTP-II funds. Another 2500 had moved into transitional houses constructed under the supervision of the NGO alliance; 2000 more families were expected to move into permanent homes procured by the state in the suburb of Wadala by mid-2001; 5000 additional transitional houses were being built by a private developer in the Mankhurd area in exchange for development rights elsewhere in the city. By the middle of 2001, more than 11,000 of the 14,000 families will have moved away from the tracks. The experience of the slum dwellers illustrates how the participation of poor people in a broad coalition of partners can empower them to create better living conditions.

**Source:** Prepared by Manish Chalana, University of Colorado, based on information from the following sources:
Appadurai, 2000;
Beattie and Merchant, 2000;
Burra, no date;
Marquand, 2000;
*Indian Express*, 2000;
Patel, Sheela, personal communication, 5 January 2001;
RSDF website: www.dialogue.org.za/RSDF\index.htm;
SPARC website: www.sparcindia.org.

existing homeless people. At this stage, a system of shelters is often established. Discussions start on how policies should try to re-integrate homeless people into society. However, regulations tend to be confusing and there tends to be deep distrust so it is very unlikely that homeless people receive all the benefits to which they are entitled.

3   The transformation to a market economy is almost complete but rising prices are not compensated through higher wages, and the social security regulations target only those most in need. The number of homeless people grows dramatically.

Developing countries are still at a stage where changes in policies affecting housing supply have the greatest impact on the incidence of homelessness and the means for redressing the problem. The most important have been the structural adjustment programmes of the last two decades, frequently resulting in greater hardship and worsened housing conditions among the poor. The Global Strategy for Shelter to the Year 2000 and the Habitat Agenda aimed to provide an enabling environment for the construction of housing through the private sector, alone or in partnership with the public sector and non-profit organizations (see Chapter 3). In practice, however, there has been no increase in the supply of affordable housing to reduce the number of homeless people. It is necessary to bridge the gap between the amount of income that people in poverty can afford to spend on housing and minimum housing costs. This may involve reducing the standard of the minimum dwelling, or regulating its cost, or increasing people's ability to pay (eg by raising wages or subsidies such as housing allowances), or all of these.

> It is necessary to bridge the gap between the amount of income that people living in poverty can afford to spend on housing and minimum housing costs

Emerging strategies to combat homelessness often contain the following elements:

- Outreach, education, training and health care services for homeless people and street children that are inclusive and relevant to street life and built around their needs. There is a great need to modify the training of professionals who deal with vulnerable people. Homeless people, particularly street children, should be regarded as potential assets rather than burdens to society.
- Shelters that assist survival in the short term and provide a locus for services aimed at re-integrating homeless persons back into mainstream society. They tend to be the first response to the issues faced by homeless people but they must not be the main or only response. It is vital to ease the paths of homeless people into a sustainable lifestyle, anchored in social relationships and a supportive network of welfare services. Health services are required both for prevention and cure. For street children and young people, there is a need to provide basic information about nutrition and hygiene.
- A holistic approach towards homelessness through cross-sectoral collaboration. There is an increasing role for voluntary or not-for-profit organizations in promoting problem solving through cooperation across professional fields, as well as public, civil and private spheres of society. It is of particular importance that financial and other resources are allocated to these organizations proportionate to their given tasks and responsibilities.
- Policies towards homeless people that are inclusive and offer services near the areas where they live. People with health conditions may need special assis-

---

**Box 16.6 Eviction, exclusion and resistance**

Evictions have been a long-standing feature of Latin American cities. To some extent, international pressure, democratization and better training of planners has prevented the worst excesses. Eviction has not disappeared, however, and new pressures to enhance the productivity of cities have motivated governments to regain strategic sites for commercial and tourism use, and to market an image of order. What has also changed is the ability of groups resisting eviction to draw upon global networks of NGOs, discourses and declarations of human and indigenous rights.

*Dominican Republic:* The attempt by the Balaguer government to evict 30,000 households between 1986 and 1992, mostly without compensation, was reminiscent of the same president's attempts during the 1960s to 'sanitise' Santo Domingo through mass removals. During the 1990s, however, the government had to recognize the voice of NGOs, community and religious groups. The violence of the evictions and their ambiguous legal legitimacy brought condemnation from the United Nations Human Rights Commission. The construction of the Lighthouse Monument served as a focal point to 'think-ins' such as the '500 Years Eviction Forum', attracting global media attention. Groups resisting eviction also drew upon political and financial support from the Dominican community in the United States.

*Mexico:* In 1990 the governor of the State of Puebla attempted to expropriate 1082 ha from four *ejido* communities on grounds of 'public utility' to construct 21,014 houses, 13,731 sites-and-service plots and an ecological park. The communities opposed the expropriation as two-thirds of their land would be lost and compensation was set at a rural rate when documents revealed that the government had sold the land at commercial rates to developers. Housing built on illegally occupied land was bulldozed and threats were made against other settlements even though these were in process of an earlier legalization programme. The *ejidos* and occupiers responded by issuing legal writs against expropriation and dispositions were made to the Supreme Court and the Commission for Human Rights. Resistance also questioned the right of the Mexican state to acquire land from what were now represented as indigenous groups; approaches were made to Rigoberta Menchú and the Mexican Council for 500 Years of Indian, Black and Popular Resistance. The legal resistance strategies failed to prevent the evictions but raised the compensation. The land was eventually sold for a private university and hospital, shopping malls and elite residential areas.

**Sources:** Everett, 1999; Jones, 1998; Morel and Mejía, 1998.

---

tance in obtaining access to appropriate housing. Policies must create opportunities for paid employment and guarantee minimum wages sufficient to pay for low-cost housing. Programmes that provide work through renovating housing to be used as supportive shelter assist with the development of job skills and earnings capacity

## Supporting the Realization of Housing Rights

Experience has shown that the private market does not respond well, if at all, to the needs of the poor. If access to and tenure of adequate shelter are restricted to those with the ability to pay, the needs of those with incomes too low to generate profit will go unmet. On the other hand, experience has also shown that most governments lack the resources to meet the housing needs of low-income households.

In response, a variety of community-based and self-help approaches have come about, within or outside the context of legal protections. In the resulting arrangements, security of tenure has emerged as a key issue. It is the focus of the Global Campaign for Secure Tenure, which is discussed later in this chapter. Questions of tenure security are situated within the broader framework of housing rights. The following sections review recent developments in this regard and recommend actions to help to implement the human right to housing.

### Recent developments[26]

> Housing rights *in law* have certainly advanced, even if housing rights *in practice* have not

While the number of people living in inadequate housing (or no housing at all) appears to have increased during the era of contemporary globalization, paradoxically, *the legal prominence* of the human right to housing has improved dramatically. Housing rights *in law* have certainly advanced, even if housing rights *in practice* have surely not. In this light, globalization is an ambiguous influence with respect to the human right to adequate housing. What are the implications of the relationship between these two areas?

Globalization, if defined as the freeing of market forces, reducing economic regulation and the increased inter-connections in the world economy, is invariably more detrimental than supportive to the enjoyment of housing rights to the one-quarter of humanity that do not yet have their housing rights met. For as markets become less regulated, as public expenditures decline and as the trade of goods and services across national borders becomes increasingly unfettered, the natural assumption is that the implementation of rights requiring some form of governmental intervention will suffer as a result of the renewed dominance of profit over people.

However, if we define globalization not purely in economic terms, but view this process within additional political, social and legal contexts, the negative impact of globalization on housing rights is by no means comprehensive. It is true that the economic dimensions of globalization can and clearly do yield negative socio-economic results for the most vulnerable groups throughout the world due to increases in housing costs, forced evictions to acquire prime land, reductions in social housing construction, privatization of the housing stock, exclusion of the poor from policy consideration and so forth. However, great strides have been made during the globalization era relating to the recognition, enforceability and seriousness accorded to housing rights. Granted, this may have come about in response to the overall decline or stagnation in housing and living conditions, but arguably the advancements that have been made with respect to the law relating to housing rights can, at least in part, be attributable to the increased openness and access by popular groups, civil society and individuals to institutions that were previously the exclusive domain of states. The emergence of civil society as an influential political force, whether implicitly or explicitly as a side-effect of globalization, has manifested in ways that are favourable to changing laws, policies and procedures to strengthen rather

than undermine economic, social and cultural rights, including housing rights.

> Housing rights provide clear and consistent criteria against which the actions, policies, practices and legislation of states can be judged

While the past two decades have been correctly criticized as a period of declining housing and living standards for many, this same historical period was witness to unparalleled advances with respect to the treatment of housing as a human right. It is now widely accepted that housing rights provide clear and consistent criteria against which the actions, policies, practices and legislation of states can be judged.

> Housing rights provide citizens with legal procedures and mechanisms to ensure implementation of housing rights and compensation in the event of violations

Housing rights are also an important means of providing citizens with legal procedures and mechanisms designed to ensure the implementation of the right to adequate housing and the receipt of compensation in the event of violations. Further, viewing housing through the looking glass of human rights creates a systematic, common and universally applicable framework for developing appropriate legal and other measures leading to the full realization of housing rights. Most actors have now understood that the pursuit of housing rights as human rights promotes good governance, governmental accountability, transparency, democratic decision-making, popular participation and international cooperation.

During the 1990s, many important advances were made with respect to housing rights. The work of the United Nations Special Rapporteur on Housing Rights (1992–1995),[27] the publication of a Housing Rights Strategy by the UNCHS (Habitat) in April 1995,[28] the United Nations Housing Rights Programme (UNHRP), a joint programme between UNCHS (Habitat) and the United Nations Office of the High Commissioner for Human Rights that will seek to provide overall United Nations-wide guidance on housing rights issues,[29] the launching by UNCHS (Habitat) of the Global Campaign for Secure Tenure in 2000 and the appointment by the United Nations Commission on Human Rights of a Special Rapporteur on Housing Rights in 2000 all represent key strides forward.

These and other positive developments are noteworthy in many respects, not the least of which is the recognition of the important role played by the law as a means of securing adequate housing for all. The relative permanency of legislation provides a valuable assurance that the acceptance of housing as a human right will not be subject to the whims of differing political administrations. Enshrining housing rights standards in national legal frameworks may be the only manner of ensuring equitable access to adequate housing resources by disadvantaged groups and protecting the rights of economically marginalized populations. The incorporation of housing rights provisions in law ncourages governmental accountability to citizens and provides tangible substance to what are often vague international commitments by a particular state. Housing rights laws can be important determinants for equality of treatment. It is on this basis that the Committee on Economic, Social and Cultural Rights have emphasized that 'policies and legislation should not be designed to benefit already advantaged social groups at the expense of others'.[30]

## Property restitution

> Refugees and IDPs have not only a right to return to their countries of origin, but *to the actual homes they lived in at the time of their initial flight*

Another recent housing rights advancement has been the attention given to the issue of housing and property restitution and compensation for refugees, internally displaced persons (IDPs) and others who lost housing or property during periods of exile from their original homes, particularly during the past decade. The United Nations Sub-Commission on Prevention of Discrimination and Protection of Minorities (now the Sub-Commission on the Promotion and Protection of Human Rights) adopted resolution 1998/26 on *Housing and Property Restitution for Refugees and Internally Displaced Persons* which reaffirms the rights of refugees and IDPs to 'return to their homes and places of habitual residence in their country and/or place of origin, should they so wish'. This and other similar pronouncements recognize that refugees and IDPs have not only a right to return to their countries of origin, but *to the actual homes they lived in at the time of their initial flight*.

While many factors have influenced the renewed emphasis on housing and property restitution, much is due to the changing nature of the origins and manner by which displacement has taken place in recent years, in particular 'ethnic cleansing', forced evictions and the growing scale of housing and property destruction resulting from armed conflicts. Ensuring the *reversal* of ethnic cleansing and violent forced evictions has probably contributed more than any other factor to strengthening the rights associated with housing and property restitution. Moreover, it has been widely recognized that ensuring these rights prevents refugees from being penalized or losing their homes and properties purely on the grounds that they fled their homes due to forces beyond their control. Implications in this connection follow from the right to adequate housing and other internationally agreed human rights: the right to property and the peaceful enjoyment of possessions, the right to privacy and respect for the home, the right to freedom of movement and to choose one's residence, and the legal doctrines of reasonableness, proportionality and fair balance.

Institutions designed to promote the rights of persons to return to their original homes have been established in many settings. In Bosnia, the Commission on Real Property Claims (CRPC) was established under the Dayton Agreements to settle outstanding disputes and facilitate residents' return,[31] and in Georgia work is underway towards

the creation of a Housing and Property Claims Commission to ensure restitution to refugees and IDPs forced from their homes in the early 1990s. In Kosovo, the United Nations Mission in Kosovo (UNMIK) established a Housing and Property Directorate (HPD) in mid-November 1999 to facilitate the regularization of the highly complex housing and property situation in the territory, while the United Nations Transitional Authority in East Timor will shortly create the East Timor Land Dispute Mechanism (ETLDM).

## Addressing forced evictions

> The United Nations Commission on Human Rights has declared forced evictions as 'gross violations of human rights, in particular the human right to adequate housing'

International standards addressing the practice of forced evictions grew in scope in the 1990s, and began consistently to equate forced evictions with violations of human rights, in particular housing rights. The United Nations Commission on Human Rights has declared forced evictions as 'gross violations of human rights, in particular the human right to adequate housing' (Res. 1993/77); a perspective echoed on numerous occasions by various United Nations human rights bodies and other human rights institutions.[32] In one of the first of what have become regular pronouncements on forced evictions, the United Nations Committee on Economic, Social and Cultural Rights declared in General Comment No. 4 (1991) that

> '*instances of forced evictions are* prima facie *incompatible with the requirements of the Covenant [on Economic, Social, and Cultural Rights] and can only be justified in the most exceptional circumstances, and in accordance with the relevant principles of international law*'.

In the past few years, a number of governments have been singled out for their poor eviction records and criticized accordingly by United Nations and European Human Rights bodies.

In 1997 the Committee adopted what is now widely seen to be the most comprehensive decision yet under international law on forced evictions and human rights. General Comment No 7 on Forced Evictions significantly expands the protection afforded to dwellers against eviction, and goes considerably further than most previous pronouncements in detailing what governments, landlords and institutions such as the World Bank must do to preclude forced evictions and, by inference, to prevent violations of human rights.

General Comment No 7 asserts that 'the State itself must refrain from forced evictions and ensure that the law is enforced against its agents or third parties who carry out forced evictions' and requires countries to 'ensure that legislative and other measures are adequate to prevent and, if appropriate, punish forced evictions carried out, without appropriate safeguards by private persons or bodies'. Thus, in addition to governments, private landlords, developers and international institutions such as the World Bank and any other third parties or non-state actors are subject to the relevant legal obligations and can anticipate the enforcement of law against them if they 'carry out forced evictions'.

The role of an appropriate domestic legal framework as a means of securing protection for people against forced evictions is a pervasive theme throughout General Comment No 7, which notes that 'legislation is an essential basis upon which to build a system of effective protection'. Governments that wish to act in good faith with their housing rights obligations and comply with the sentiments expressed in the Comment, therefore, should consider adopting laws expressly prohibiting forced evictions and developing proper legal procedures that can be drawn upon by evictees to secure the prosecution and punishment of 'persons or bodies' who may have carried out illegal evictions.

---

**Women are especially at risk of and impacted by eviction, given discrimination in property rights, including homeownership, and their vulnerability to violence and sexual abuse when they are homeless**

---

While extending protection to all persons, the Comment gives special consideration to groups that suffer disproportionately from forced evictions, including women, children, youth, older persons, indigenous people and ethnic and other minorities. With respect to the rights of women, the text asserts that

> 'women in all groups are especially vulnerable given the extent of statutory and other forms of discrimination which often apply in relation to property rights (including home ownership) or rights of access to property or accommodation and their particular vulnerability to acts of violence and sexual abuse when they are rendered homeless'.

General Comment No 7 declares that 'evictions should not result in rendering individuals homeless or vulnerable to the violation of other human rights', thus making it incumbent on governments to guarantee that people who are evicted – whether illegally or in accordance with the law – are to be ensured some form of alternative housing.

## Security of tenure

Of all elements of the right to housing, it is the right to security of tenure (and increasingly the 'right to security of place') that forms the most indispensable core element. When security of tenure – the right to feel safe in one's own home, to control one's own housing environment and the right not to be arbitrarily forcibly evicted – is threatened or simply nonexistent, it jeopardizes the full enjoyment of housing rights. Secure tenure derives from a justiciable right of access to and use of land and property, underwritten by a known set of rules that may be anchored in constitutional and legal frameworks, social norms or cultural values.

---

**Secure tenure derives from a justiciable right of access to and use of land and property, underwritten**

---

**by a known set of rules that may be anchored in constitutional and legal frameworks, social norms or cultural values**

---

While it is true that all human rights are premised on principles of equality and non-discrimination, treating security of tenure as a human right (rather than as an exclusive by-product of ownership or the comparatively rare cases of strong protection for private tenants) expands the legal protection afforded by human rights not merely to all who can afford to buy a home, but to *all people of all incomes and in all housing sectors*. In this regard, it is important to note that securing tenure for a household does not necessarily secure tenure for women and children; gender equality is a fundamental principle underpinning the Global Campaign for Secure Tenure. Considering security of tenure in terms of human rights allows an approach to housing that treats all persons on the basis of equality.

In general, the rights associated with ownership of housing offer considerably more security of tenure, and protection against eviction or other violations of housing rights than those afforded to renting tenants or those residing in informal settlements (where perhaps one-quarter of humanity resides). Therefore, the right to security of tenure raises the baseline – or minimum core entitlement – guaranteed to *all* persons who possess housing rights based on international human rights standards, irrespective of housing tenure. In recognition of the central place of security of tenure to the rights of dwellers (just as everyone is a citizen, so too is everyone a dweller) as well as to the important role it can play in promoting individual and family investments in the improvement of their own homes, international human rights standards increasingly approach security of tenure in terms of human rights.

General Comment No 4 on the Right to Adequate Housing (E/1992/23), approved in 1991 by the United Nations Committee on Economic, Social and Cultural Rights, is widely considered to be the single most authoritative international legal interpretation of what the right to housing actually means in terms of international law. It gives security of tenure particular prominence. In defining the nature of adequate housing under the Covenant on Economic, Social and Cultural Rights, legal security of tenure is addressed in the following manner:

> 'Tenure takes a variety of forms, including rental (public and private) accommodation, co-operative housing, lease, owner-occupation, emergency housing and informal settlements, including occupation of land or property. Notwithstanding the type of tenure, all persons should possess a degree of security of tenure which guarantees legal protection against forced eviction, harassment and other threats. States parties should consequently take immediate measures aimed at conferring legal security of tenure upon those persons and households currently lacking such protection, in genuine consultation with affected persons and groups.' (para 8(a))

> With secure tenure, people will begin investing in their own homes

This right is also inexpensive to confer and is viable in all countries regardless of overall levels of human development. The conferral of secure tenure is particularly important to slum dwellers, squatters, residents of housing owned or controlled by exploitative landlords, and others threatened by insecure housing situations and most likely to be evicted. When security of tenure is squarely in place, people are legally protected from most forms of forced eviction and consequently (even in the worst of slums) will begin investing in their own homes, and in the process augmenting the enjoyment of housing rights through personal efforts. While there are obvious distinctions between the systems and structures in which tenure security is generated, the universal importance of secure tenure is clear. Its significance is recognized by the Global Campaign for Secure Tenure, an important new partnership initiative launched by UNCHS (Habitat) in 2000.[33] The Campaign is aimed at furthering the realization of the right to housing as part of a more encompassing strategy to provide all people with access to adequate shelter. It spearheads a new, more pragmatic and affordable approach to implementing the Istanbul Declaration and the Habitat Agenda, adopted at the City Summit of 1996, with less emphasis on conferences, meetings of experts and ritual reporting of progress by national bureaucracies and with more emphasis on partnerships and decentralization.

## Focusing further actions

It is abundantly obvious that despite the many legal gains made during the initial phases of globalization, much more needs to be done to ensure the implementation of housing rights. The bulk of such activity needs to take place at the local and national level. In terms of international actions, however, several undertakings would be particularly timely and potentially effective in securing housing rights for all.

### ● Reappraising housing rights standards

Serious consideration should be given to further entrenching international standards relating to the human right to adequate housing. Although the standard-setting process is long, arduous and not free of risk, several initiatives are underway to create new international standards on the right to housing. For instance, a draft International Convention on Housing Rights was prepared by the then Special Rapporteur on Housing Rights in 1994,[34] while the Office of the High Commissioner for Human Rights has given some attention to the drafting of guidelines for the planning of international events, designed to persuade states to take appropriate measures during the preparation of large-scale events such as the Olympic Games to ensure that mass forced evictions so often associated with such events are prevented.[35] A set of *Comprehensive Human Rights Guidelines on Development-Based Displacement* was adopted at a United Nations expert seminar in 1997 and is

currently pending approval by the United Nations Commission on Human Rights.[36] The adoption of each of these three draft standards will assist in further strengthening housing rights norms.

### ● Creating a global property registry

> Comprehensive and regular housing, property and land registration systems are a crucial element of housing rights

While the specific methods of registering land and property differ greatly between nations, the importance of updated, transparent and secure housing, property and land records is widely recognized.[37] It is through such records that homes can be bought and sold, housing markets developed, property developed to increase economic value and land used for whatever purposes zoning or planning laws may have determined. It is also through such records that rights to housing and property can be defended against the aims of ethnic cleansers. As the ethnically driven, forced displacement in Bosnia-Hercegovina, Croatia, Yugoslavia, East Timor and elsewhere have made clear, removing people forcibly from their homes, confiscating personal housing and property documents, destroying housing and property and cadaster records have been the hallmarks of ethnic cleansers in their attempts to perpetually alter the ethnic composition of a territory and permanently prevent return. While little positive emerged from the Balkan wars of the past decade, the international community was not ambivalent about the need to reverse ethnic cleansing and ensure the right to housing and property restitution for everyone displaced during the conflicts in the region. The difficulties of protecting rights to return to one's original home, however, have been considerably augmented by the loss, destruction, fraudulent alteration and illegal confiscation of records needed to prove ownership, occupancy and tenants rights. Intractable political considerations aside, were such records available to the institutions tasked with resolving land, housing and property disputes and promoting voluntary repatriation, fairly determining housing and property rights would be far more fluid. Indeed, comprehensive and regular housing, property and land registration systems are a crucial element of housing rights. Through registration systems the conferral of legal security of tenure is made possible, a public record of ownership and dweller rights exists and all rights relating to housing can be protected. Without such a system, tenure may be partially protected but only through informal means or based on political or organized crime patronage.

If the United Nations were to coordinate the establishment of a *global property registry* – a worldwide digital database containing the housing, property and cadaster records of all countries – an independent source of this invaluable information could serve to deter governments from attempting to solidify ethnic cleansing by destroying such records. In addition, a global property registry would promote the use of advanced technology to assist governments in the mapping of as yet unmapped areas, in the regular updating of housing, property and land records, and ultimately promoting the right to security of tenure for all inhabitants of the planet.

### ● Developing housing rights indicators

Of all the internationally recognized economic, social and cultural (ESC) rights, indicators relevant to housing rights are probably the most sparse and unreliable. Few governments collect the type of data required to establish the degree to which housing rights are enjoyed in given countries. The highly personal nature of housing processes, coupled with the fact that a high proportion of persons reside in unregulated circumstances and communities for which data collection is more difficult, have contributed to a paucity of international statistics.

While the development of a composite *housing rights index* will require extensive discussion, ten key areas that could be incorporated into such a measurement tool include:

1    public expenditure on housing as a percentage of national budgets;
2    percentage of population with access to potable indoor running water and electricity;
3    percentage of population legally protected with security of tenure rights;
4    average household expenditure on housing as a percentage of income;
5    percentage of population residing in informal or irregular housing and the total number of homeless persons;
6    legal status of housing rights;
7    access to affordable and impartial judicial and other remedies;
8    number of persons forcibly evicted per year;
9    access to remedies for housing rights violations;
10    protection against discrimination for women.

The Women and Habitat Programme of the United Nations Centre for Human Settlements (Habitat) is an ongoing effort to gather information on the situation of women in human settlements.[38] A recent synthesis of individual country reports includes an examination of women's empowerment indicators, several of which cover gender-related aspects of housing rights.[39]

### ● Improving complaint mechanisms

---

**The provision of effective remedies is an indispensable element of any housing rights strategy**

---

The right to an effective remedy has been recognized as a key element of international human rights law since the adoption of the Universal Declaration on Human Rights. The provision of effective remedies is an indispensable element of any human rights strategy, including those designed to promote and protect economic, social and cultural rights, including housing rights. The right to a remedy, in turn, raises the related issue of the form of such remedies. If housing rights are to be subject to 'effective remedies', then these rights must also be seen as capable of

judicial consideration and to be sufficiently precise to command clear decisions by courts of law or through non-judicial routes of action geared to protect housing rights.

The United Nations Committee on Economic, Social and Cultural Rights has emphasized the importance of ensuring that domestic legal remedies are available to all beneficiaries of housing rights, in particular with respect to illegal evictions or discrimination in access to housing. In its General Comment No 4, the Committee stated that it

*'views many component elements of the right to adequate housing as being at least consistent with the provision of domestic legal remedies. Depending on the legal system, such areas might include, but are not limited to: (a) legal appeals aimed at preventing planned evictions or demolitions through the issuance of court-ordered injunctions; (b) legal procedures seeking compensation following an illegal eviction; (c) complaints against illegal actions carried out or supported by landlords (whether public or private) in relation to rent levels, dwelling maintenance, and racial or other forms of discrimination; (d) allegations of any form of discrimination in the allocation and availability of access to housing; and (e) complaints against landlords concerning unhealthy or inadequate housing conditions. In some legal systems, it would also be appropriate to explore the possibility of facilitating class action suits in situations involving significantly increased levels of homelessness.'* (para 17)

---

**An international housing rights legal aid fund to provide legal assistance and advocacy to communities and households unable to access lawyers and thus judicial remedies would be a valuable resource in support of housing rights**

---

There is nothing inherent about housing rights that makes these rights incapable of judicial consideration. The compatibility of housing rights standards and the capacity of making complaints, however, is by no means automatic. In numerous countries not only is an independent and impartial judiciary lacking, but even more so are rights to legal aid and assistance for lower-income groups. Even where legal aid programmes do exist, the right to counsel is generally reserved for criminal cases, leaving persons pursuing civil matters (as most housing rights cases would be), without rights to a lawyer. Such circumstances are by no means reserved for developing countries. Many housing groups and other community-based movements struggling against pending evictions and towards other housing rights objectives find it impossible to access affordable lawyers to represent them and assist in adjudicating their cases. The establishment of an *international housing rights legal aid fund* to provide legal assistance and advocacy to communities and households unable to access lawyers would be a valuable resource in support of housing rights.

# Strengthening Appropriate Forms of Housing Tenure

**Within the context of tenure, an overall shelter strategy must necessarily be concerned not only with strengthening security of tenure, but also with developing and supporting appropriate forms of tenure**

Secure tenure is but the first component of the progressive realization of the right to housing; a necessary but insufficient condition for a successful shelter strategy that will lead to further economic and social benefits. Within the context of tenure, an overall shelter strategy must necessarily be concerned not only with strengthening security of tenure, but also with developing and supporting appropriate forms of tenure. A broad distinction is often made between owner-occupied housing and rental housing. The latter is frequently divided between private and public rental. For economic and political reasons, housing policies typically are not 'tenure neutral', but seek to promote home ownership through a variety of means. Prominent among them are highly regressive tax benefits to owners.[40]

## Recognizing the diversity of relevant tenure forms

The common tripartite tenurial classification, mentioned above, with its emphasis on private home ownership, is a simplification that does not do justice to the greater diversity of tenure forms that exists and that is needed to accommodate the varied needs of different households. Housing policies must recognize the range of relevant tenure alternatives and provide each with appropriate support. The following review identifies several major categories of tenure that are recognized in the Campaign for Secure Tenure and deserve careful consideration in the formulation of housing policies.

### ● Rent

Rent is a form of leasehold, in terms of which access to a property and the use thereof is governed by a legal agreement of fixed duration. Agreements are normally governed by law. Rental agreements operate either in the private domain, as contract between private citizens and corporate bodies, or in the public domain, wherein the rental is provided by a public body, such as a local authority, as part of a social housing policy. It is common, in formal rental agreements, for the lessor to assume some responsibility for the maintenance of the property. It is the form of secure tenure least likely to lead to capital investment by the lessee (and, some may argue, by the lessor).

However, in many countries, for low-income families, rental – which is the most used form of tenure – is seldom formal or regulated. Agreements are arrived at informally, with little or no recourse to legal advice, and the agreements are enforced in a non-legal manner. Indeed, a major part of the Campaign will have to address the urban-poor segment of the rental sector, and the tension that exists between secure tenure for tenants and sub-tenants, and the property rights of the owners. Both in percentage and in policy terms, addressing the informal rental sector will be one of the most significant challenges for the Campaign, and one which will have the most impact for the urban poor.

### ● Leasehold

Leasehold conveys the right of beneficial occupation to land or property, but such occupation is circumscribed both by a finite period of time, as well as the specific conditions of the lease. The lessor retains ultimate control over the property, through the stipulated time limit and conditions. Upon expiry of the lease, the lessor may automatically reassume occupation, reallocate the lease to another person or body, or extend the lease of the occupant. For the period of the lease, which may be very long (eg 99 years), and subject to compliance with the terms of the lease, the occupant does enjoy secure tenure.

### ● Freehold

Freehold is the form of tenure which confers on the title-holder the maximum control and discretion over the land, normally only circumscribed by law and/or planning and zoning restrictions. It provides for the land (and improvements) to be used as collateral and mortgaged, it may be transferred or bequeathed in the discretion of the title-holder, and is free from any time restrictions; it is title in perpetuity. It is the form of tenure most associated with investment and, indeed, speculation. Ideologically, it is most favoured by the proponents of the free-market and individualist conceptions of society.

### ● Conditional freehold: 'rent-to-buy'

A hybrid of leasehold and freehold, this is effectively a lease that may be converted to freehold upon the fulfilment of stipulated conditions, which ordinarily include the payment of the lease (or 'rent') for a period of time. Another form of this approach is found in the term 'contract-for-deed'. However, it is all too often the case that the equity does not accrue in terms of the contract, and that even one or two months of missed payments – not unusual for this segment of the market – can lead to all previous payments being forfeited, and the renter being forced to start the repayment process from the beginning.

### ● Communal tenure

One of the defining features of communal tenure is that it is common for the community to have a long and common history and cultural identity, such as a tribe or clan. Access to such land may be governed by custom, and include the right to use and to occupy, but not to transfer or alienate, which would be determined by the community as a whole. Under Islamic tenurial systems, *musha* refers to a collective land holding, whereas *Waqf* is a category of land held in perpetuity by a religious institution, and is effectively removed from market mechanisms.

## ● Forms of collective tenure

There are a variety of methods of enjoying full security of tenure within a collective framework. The principle relates to the sharing of access to a property on the basis of an agreement, which specifies the terms and conditions of such access. This may take the form of the creation of a corporate body, such as a condominium or a private company, or a housing association or cooperative. What all of these forms of tenure share is the need for a relatively high level of common interest, and the skills and capacity to administer the arrangement, which generally requires quite a high level of organizational ability and commitment. The remainder of this chapter reviews housing cooperatives as a particular form of collective tenure with the potential to provide low-income households with improved access to adequate housing.

## Housing cooperatives

Housing cooperatives are democratically governed nonprofit corporations whose members jointly own residential developments consisting of multiple units. Cooperatives resemble rental housing in that residents usually pay a monthly fee in return for the occupancy of a dwelling that they do not own. These fees buy down the collectively held mortgage, pay for operating expenses and capitalize reserve funds. Cooperatives also resemble homeownership in that residents own shares in the total property; enjoy the security, control and tax advantages of homeownership; and are responsible, usually through a mechanism of elected resident representatives, for maintenance and management. But, they are unique in being collectively owned and governed.

There are different types of housing cooperatives. Market equity cooperatives allow shares to be traded at market value as if housing units occupied by members are individually owned. Shares may also reflect individual unit characteristics such as size, layout and siting. On the other hand, limited-equity cooperatives restrict the amount of return on the sale of a share to the amount of equity accrued during occupancy, sometimes adjusting for inflation, interest or improvements. Members of leased cooperatives do not own their units but hold long-term leases from a community land trust, mutual housing association, or similar organization that grants them particular rights.[41] The discussion that follows concerns itself with cooperatives that loosely conform to characteristics of the limited-equity and leased cooperatives, both of which lend themselves to providing and maintaining long-term affordable housing. However, the specific forms of cooperative housing differ from country to country.

## ● Advantages for low-income housing[42]

Two governance principles of cooperatives are central to their institutional potential for low-income housing: collective ownership and democratic management

Two governance principles of cooperatives are central to their institutional potential for low-income housing: collective ownership and democratic management. In collective ownership arrangements, members jointly own the resources of the housing cooperative. Members collectively pool their investment resources for achieving a common housing objective (eg finance, construction, management and maintenance). Their investment is often in the form of share capital, but it can also be in the form of material inputs, labour or land. Collective management entails collective participation of members in monitoring and managing the cooperative. Decisions are made in a democratic way, based on a 'one member, one vote' principle, regardless of the number of shares owned by each member.

These two features of the cooperative are advantageous for low-income housing in at least four ways. First, pooling of resources in the collective lowers the individual housing costs that each household would otherwise incur. Such pooling offers economy of scale on several fronts: land, building materials, construction, financing, maintenance, management and service provision.[43]

The second rationale – partly related to the first – is that of community organization and participation among low-income households. In this context, cooperatives foster collective action and self-help. For example, in cities such as Mumbai, NGOs have helped to organize informal cooperatives to mobilize slum dwellers and pavement dwellers for collective action. In some cases, women's participation, in particular, has been encouraged by organizing cooperatives focused on their particular housing needs and their potential to contribute to community leadership and action.[44] Some have argued that self-help strategies would be more effective if they were based on collective initiatives and collective democratic decision-making rather than individual households' efforts.[45]

Third, the collective pooling of resources increases the credit worthiness of low-income households. Low-income households typically have little access to formal housing finance due to lack of collateral and meagre or unstable income (see Chapter 6). By and large, they depend on informal credit or personal savings. Pooling their limited resources in a cooperative increases their collective asset value. Group lending and micro-finance programmes usually require formation of a cohesive network of households for lending to be sustainable. In this regard, cooperatives may function better than conventional banks for two reasons. First, enduring cooperatives avoid asymmetric information between the lender and the borrower due to local knowledge about each other's assets, capabilities and character traits; thus they lower transaction costs of screening.[46] Second, members have incentives for repayment through group-based social sanctions that help to enforce savings discipline: all members will be deprived of future borrowing in case of default. Such social sanctions are typically not available in the context of conventional bank loans.[47] Peer monitoring among borrowers can also be more effective because they have better information about each other's borrowing capacity.[48]

Fourth, cooperatively owned housing can more readily help to prevent or contain speculation and gentrification. Collective ownership of land, for example, limits the ability of individual households to sell land in the open market. This restriction can be especially beneficial in slums where granting of private land tenure to households on an individual basis can result in upward filtering.[49] Cooperative land banks have also been proposed as a means of limiting speculation through collective ownership.[50] In this arrangement, common areas in buildings, as well as land and infrastructure, belong to the cooperative. Individual households have perpetual leases to the unit and the number of shares owned by each household is proportional to the area occupied by it. When a household sells the housing unit, the cooperative appropriates a part of the value of land, infrastructure and common areas, while the household obtains the rest of the value, including the value of the housing unit. Speculation is limited through such sharing of value.

---

Cooperative housing offers four advantages to low-income households:

- pooling of resources lowers individual housing costs
- it fosters collective action and self-help
- it increases their creditworthiness
- it limits or prevents speculation

---

### ● Potential problems

Given these advantages of cooperatives, why are they not used on a larger scale for low-income housing? While collective action does have its advantages for low-income housing, it is not achieved easily. First, cooperatives are seldom formed spontaneously. Low-income cooperatives typically emerge from the mobilization of low-income households into a group by some catalytic agent. Usually an organization such as a trade union, local authority, commercial enterprise or the government is the moving force behind the cooperative.[51] Second, self-management in housing cooperatives can be problematic due to lack of managerial, legal or financial expertise of members. This is especially so in low-income housing cooperatives where members have not (yet) acquired the skills and knowledge and lack resources for obtaining technical assistance.[52]

Third, collective action and management entail costs for participating households. Low-income people face opportunity costs between being involved in the collective and other productive income earning activities. Households will participate only if benefits from the collective outweigh the costs of participation. In addition, collective action problems (such as free-riding) can arise. For example, some households may reap the benefits of the collective without paying their dues or without contributing in other ways. Small group size and imposition of selective incentives are crucial for overcoming free-riding.[53] Some have argued that, since costs of monitoring and sanctioning can be high, the degree of the cooperative's success depends on mechanisms developed by the group to minimize such costs.[54]

### ● Government policies

In the past, if governments supported cooperatives, it was usually on an ideological basis. Any consequent policies typically involved extending special benefits to them in terms of subsidies, allocation of land and so on. Unfortunately, such preferential treatment does not help cooperatives in achieving their potential for low-income households. Rather, it encourages rent-seeking and in many instances bogus cooperatives emerge. More fundamentally, such policies do not address collective action problems inherent in cooperative arrangements.

---

Policies should provide enabling institutional structures to support the establishment and operation of housing cooperatives

---

Policies should rather be directed towards setting up a supportive institutional structure that can reduce these problems, while enhancing the potential of cooperatives. A supportive institutional structure can act as an enabling mechanism. Such structures can help in mobilizing housing finance for cooperatives. They can also channel technical, administrative, legal, accounting and financial assistance to them; such assistance is crucial to the functioning of cooperatives composed of low-income households. In addition, they can help to resolve disputes within cooperatives.

A concurrent advantage with the setting-up of institutional support structures is that it reduces transaction costs in the formation and functioning of housing cooperatives. Lowering such costs (for example by routinizing legal incorporation procedures) means making more efficient use of the time and effort that low-income households can contribute, an advantage that applies to inner-city neighbourhoods in industrialized countries[55] as well as communities in the developing countries.[56]

---

# Notes

1  UNCHS (Habitat), 1999.

2  See Appadurai, 2000.

3  See van Vliet–, 1997; 1993.

4  *Forbes Magazine*, www.forbes.com/tool/toolbox/billnew/. As of 21 August 2000.

5  Personal observation, 1994; construction costs of TMG building provided by Kyoko Dohnomae, librarian of the International House of Japan,

Roppongi, Tokyo (13 April 1994), referenced in *Tokyo: The Making of a Metropolis*.

6  See, for example, *Third World Planning Review*, 1987; Dear and Wolch, 1987; Friedrichs, 1988; Burt, 1992; Watson with Austerberry, 1986; Glasser, 1994; Bingham et al, 1987; Jamshid, 1989; An examination of the Social Sciences Citation Index reveals that between 1988 and

1993, the annual number of articles on homelessness increased from 78 to 200, rising further to 309 in 1997, after which a levelling off seems to occur (see van Vliet–, 2000).

7  World Development Indicators database, World Bank 8/2/2000; Purchasing Power Parity in international dollars (www.worldbank.org/data/databytopic/GNPPC.pdf).

8  Estimates based on survey research suggest that 14 per cent of the US population (26 million people) have been homeless during their life; see Link et al, 1994; recent data from Japan indicate that the homeless population of Tokyo has grown by more than 70 per cent since 1994; see Matsumoto, 2000.

9  The text of the resolution read: 'That the provincial and federal

governments be requested to declare homelessness a national disaster requiring emergency humanitarian aid and be urged immediately to develop and implement a National Homelessness Relief and Prevention Strategy using disaster relief funds, both to provide the homeless with immediate health protection and housing and to prevent further homelessness' (City of Toronto: Housing in the City, www.city.toronto.on.ca/housing/winter98.htm).

10  These trends are reviewed in Parts I and II of this report. At the same time, as argued in later in this chapter, globalization has also contributed to the spread of support for the human right to housing and, therefore, has played an ambiguous role in pursuit of the goal of adequate shelter for all, adopted at the Habitat II conference.

11  See, for instance, ethnographic studies such as reported in the *Journal of Social Distress and the Homeless*. Examples, from this source and other places, include Vance, 1995; Anderson, 1996; Cress and Snow, 1996; Conover et al, 1997; Roschelle, 1998; Lyon-Callo, 1998; Baldwin, 1998; Miller, 1998; Wardhaugh, 1999.

12  Note the wording in the title of *Journal of Social Distress and the* **Homeless** (emphasis added).

13  See UNCHS (Habitat), 1996c.

14  On diversity in legal definitions and measurement approaches, see, for example, Daly, 1996; Helvie and Kunstmann, 1999; and a recent UNCHS (Habitat) report (2000) 'Strategies to combat homelessness', which distils the following numbers from the available literature: US: 1.5–2.5 people per thousand population use shelters; Canada: 130,000–260,000 homeless people; Japan: 19,500; Korea: 3000; Western Europe: between 4 and 12 per cent is homeless in Germany, France and the UK, and less than 2 per cent in other countries; Eastern Europe: 500,000–700,000 homeless people of which 100,000 in Russia; Hungary: 30,000–50,000; India: 1.2–2.3 million; Nigeria: 15,700; South Africa (Johannesburg, inner city): 7500. For the reasons mentioned, the meaning of these numbers is not clear and they must be treated with great caution.

15  The Commission on Human Settlements 16th session, Nairobi, 28 April–7 May 1997.

16  See www.sparcindia.org/documents/alliance.html and www.dialogue.org.za/sparc/City watch.htm#survey. See also Chapter 14.

17  Total number of households minus the combined total of

adequate and repairable dwellings, MacDonald et al, 1998, p 25, Table 4.

18  Ibid.

19  About half of this total consisting of inadequate housing; see Sandhu, 2000 (Background Papers).

20  A review of studies of street children in 15 countries in Africa, Asia and Latin America found that poverty was a major and often the main reason cited as the cause for homelessness. Domestic violence was the next most significant cause (Cohen, 2000).

21  See the Centre on Housing Rights and Evictions for current and detailed information concerning evictions, www.cohre.org.

22  See, for example, European Federation of National Organizations Working with the Homeless, 1998; Marsh and Mullins, 1998; McGregor and McConnachie, 1995; Ratcliffe, 1998; Somerville, 1998; Taylor, 1998.

23  See Stolee, 1988.

24  The remaining paragraphs of this section have been adapted from the UNCHS (Habitat) report 'Strategies to Combat Homelessness' (2000).

25  See Hoch, 2000.

26  The following sections are drawn from 'The implications of globalization for the human right to housing: Recent developments and actions for implementation', a background paper prepared by Scott Leckie, COHRE, which contains appendices with full source documentation on the points reviewed in this discussion.

27  Reports of the United Nations Special Rapporteur on Housing Rights, Justice Rajindar Sachar, include: *Final Report* (UN doc. E/CN.4/Sub.2/1995/12); *Second Progress Report* (UN doc. E/CN.4/Sub.2/1994/20); *First Progress Report* (UN doc. E/CN.4/Sub.2/1993/15); and *Working Paper on the Right to Adequate Housing* (UN doc. E/CN.4/Sub.2/1992/15).

28  UNCHS (Habitat) (1995b).

29  UN doc. HS/C/17/INF.6 (30 March 1999).

30  General Comment No 4 (paragraph 11).

31  For analysis of the CRPC, see: UNHCR, the Office of the High Representative (OHR) and the CRPC (1999) *Property and Housing Issues Affecting Repatriates and Displaced Persons in Bosnia and Herzegovina*.

32  The United Nations Committee on Economic, Social and Cultural Rights *General Comment No 2 on International Technical Assistance Measures*, adopted on 2 February 1990 at

its fourth session, addresses the obligations of the World Bank and IMF concerning the financing of projects involving evictions. In particular, para 6 of General Comment No 2 draws the attention of the international financial institutions, in particular the World Bank and IMF to the view of the Committee that:
*'International agencies should scrupulously avoid involvement in projects which, for example … promote or reinforce discrimination against individuals or groups contrary to the provisions of the Covenant, or involve large-scale evictions or displacement of persons without the provision of all appropriate protection and compensation… Every effort should be made, at each phase of a development, to ensure that the rights contained in the Covenant are taken duly into account.'*

33  For more information on the Global Campaign for Secure Tenure, see www.unchs.org/tenure/.

34  E/CN.4/Sub/21994/20, pp 27–35 (Draft International Convention on Housing Rights). See also: Leckie, 1994.

35  *Guidelines on International Events and Forced Evictions* (Report of the Secretary-General), E/CN.4/Sub.2/1995/13. See also Olds, 1998.

36  E/CN.4/Sub.2/1997/7.

37  See also 'An integrated Geo-Information System (GIS) with emphasis on cadastre and Land Information Systems (LIS) for decision makers in Africa'. Paper prepared for UNCHS by Clarissa Fourie, November, 1998; and 'Conclusions from a research study based on best practices analysis on access to land and security of tenure', a paper prepared by Clarissa Fourie for the International Forum on Urban Poverty (IFUP), 3rd International Conference on 'Social integration and security for the urban poor; Towards Cities for All'. 12–14 October 1999, Nairobi, Kenya, UNCHS.

38  See www.unchs.org/unchs/english/women/womenbody.htm.

39  See 'Women's empowerment indicators: Synthesis of the women and habitat indicators process'. Report for UNCHS prepared by F Miraftab (2000) See also www.unchs.org/unchs/english/women/content.htm.

40  These benefits often include write-offs from personal income taxes in the form of interest paid on mortgage loans and property taxes, and exclusion from capital gains tax realized on the sale of one's home. In the US, the total tax expenditure for the mortgage interest deduction alone exceeds US$60,000

million annually. The lowest earning 14 per cent of owning households filing itemized tax returns receive less than 0.5 per cent of this total housing subsidy, whereas the richest 18 per cent get over 70 per cent. The lowest income owners, who do not itemize deductions, and renters, do not benefit from this policy, which profits most those who need it least. A theoretical justification for the policy lies in the assumption that it will encourage construction at the upper end of the housing market, stimulating vacancy chains through which units will filter down to lower-income households. Segmentation and distortion of housing markets set severe limits to the practicability of this model.

41  These brief characterizations are discussed more fully in Silver, 1998.

42  The following sections draw from Ganapati, 2000 (see Background Papers).

43  Cost sharing may or may not benefit low-income households depending on local real estate market. For example, under high housing demand conditions, land or housing costs may be so high that cost sharing may still not make housing affordable for low-income households.

44  See Moser, 1992; also Chapter 14.

45  For example, Marcuse, 1992.

46  See Wenner, 1995.

47  Besley and Coate, 1995.

48  Varian, 1990; Stiglitz, 1990.

49  See, for example, Johnson, 1987.

50  For example, Turnbull, 1983.

51  Lewin, 1981, p23.

52  See Vakil, 1996 for leadership and management issues in five housing cooperatives in Zimbabwe.

53  See Olson, 1965.

54  For example, Hechter, 1990.

55  See, for example, White and Saegert, 1997.

56  See, for example, Vakil (1996) for case studies in Africa and Latin America and Ganapati, 2000 (see Background Papers) for a conceptual model and empirical examination of the internal and external variables that are critical to the success of housing cooperatives in India. For a study finding community-based, cooperative regularization of squatter settlements more effective than an individually oriented approach, see Glenn et al, 1993. Habitat (UNCHS) is currently engaged with the International Cooperative Alliance in a research project assessing the contributions of the cooperative sector to shelter developments in eastern and southern Africa.

# 17

# SUSTAINING HUMAN SETTLEMENT DEVELOPMENT: STRATEGIC FOCI

The World Bank estimates that the number of urban poor will almost treble to 1500 million by the year 2025.[1] At least 600 million people, most of them poor, already live in health- and life-threatening situations in decaying urban environments. A third of all city dwellers live in substandard housing. At least 250 million urban residents have no ready access to safe piped water, and 400 million do not have adequate sanitation.

Many urban centres are beset by such problems as rising poverty, violence, unsustainable environmental practices and social exclusion of the poor and minority groups. Corruption in city government often reinforces the control held by elites, contributing to the disenfranchisement of many city residents.

Sustainable urban development will depend largely on the capacity of cities to manage efforts to redress these problems, which is closely linked to the functioning of urban governance and the active participation of citizens in it. Therefore, this last chapter first examines the critical role of governance and discusses the contribution of the Global Campaign for Urban Governance to making cities more inclusive. It then reviews ways in which urban management can help to eradicate poverty. The last two sections focus on approaches to combating corruption and violence as two major urban problems that affect especially people living in poverty and other marginalized population groups.

## Supporting the Governance of More Inclusive Cities[2]

The Habitat Agenda committed to 'institutionalizing a participatory approach to sustainable human settlements development and management, based on continuing dialogue among all actors involved in urban development' and to 'enabling local leadership, promoting democratic rule, exercising public authority and using public resources in all public institutions at all levels ... conducive to ensuring transparent, responsible accountable, just, effective and efficient governance of towns, cities and metropolitan areas'.

In this connection, urban governance refers to the complex set of values, norms, processes and institutions by which citizens and governments interact to organize the functions, activities and space that make up the urban environment. Good urban governance works to make cities more efficient, equitable, safe and sustainable. Systems of urban governance that are based on transparent and accountable processes can go a long way in making cities more inclusive. This not only involves the state and local governments but also civil society groups. Good urban governance results in economic efficiency, social equity, gender-aware policies, overall sustainability and, ultimately, improved living conditions of not only the urban poor but *all* city residents.

At the city level, there has been a tendency to see urban governance in terms of urban management: the operation and maintenance of infrastructure and services from the viewpoint of financial accountability and administrative efficiency. However, cities are located in wider regional, national and international economies, environmental and political systems and socio-spatial relationships. Inter-governmental relations encompass such joint activities as negotiations, dispute resolution, cooperative ventures among public and private parties and the fiduciary responsibilities of government. In addition, it implies bottom-up decision-making, decentralization and broad-based participation. Indeed, participatory decision-making is essential to good urban governance. A solely managerial perspective fails to consider these wider contexts within which urban governance is conducted and ignores the essentially politicized nature of governance. Good urban governance is not merely a matter of efficient management; it also has political dimensions related to democracy, human rights and civic participation in decision-making processes. Participation and human rights are, therefore, critical in governing cities well, concentrating attention on those who are excluded and denied access to the social, economic and political resources of the city.

> Good urban governance is not merely a matter of efficient management; it also has political dimensions related to democracy, human rights and civic participation in decision-making processes

### The growing importance of good governance

Systems of urban governance should:

- ensure that the regulatory frameworks and infrastructure provision of cities work efficiently to provide for and capitalize on the local opportunities for economic development in an increasingly global economy;

- promote economic development that leads to employment generation and poverty eradication;
- develop and maintain decision-making processes that are transparent and accountable to all citizens;
- include all sectors of the community in participatory decision-making and implementation processes;
- ensure that the particular needs of all citizens are identified and taken into account in developing and implementing policy;
- meet the increased demand for housing and urban services through broad-based partnerships and enabling policies;
- protect the health, safety and security of all citizens;
- preserve the urban environment and the cultural and historical heritage of cities;
- implement the fiduciary responsibilities of the present generation of residents to future citizens through rational planning.

## Poverty eradication at the local level

Among these tasks, the elimination of poverty must be a central concern. Although the causes of poverty may lie largely outside municipal jurisdiction and control, good urban governance can make an important difference.

> The elimination of poverty must be a central concern of urban management because the extent and level of poverty directly affect its operational ability and viability

Poverty reduction programmes have tended to operate at two levels. First, at the macro level, where they involve interventions defined and implemented by central government, including aspects of investment, subsidy, pricing and credit. Second, at the local level, which involves working directly with community groups in supporting a variety of activities including the provision of credit, basic infrastructure and slum upgrading, micro-enterprise development and strengthening community participation. Traditionally, the macro level has been more targeted by the international agencies and development banks working with national governments, while the local level has been supported more by NGOs and CBOs working with donor agencies. However, international agencies, regional development banks and bilateral aid agencies increasingly recognize the importance of local capacity building (see Chapter 14) and have begun supporting poverty reduction activities at the city level.[3] To some extent, the growing emphasis on NGOs and community networks also stems from a focus among development organizations on strengthening civil society as a precondition of democratic society.

Local government thus has opportunities to combat poverty by systematically enacting policies that improve access to housing and basic urban services through regularization of land tenure, extending access to credit for micro-enterprise and housing finance, supporting urban upgrading, creating jobs and support to the informal sector.

Local government action may be constrained by financial and political dependence on central government, a lack of clarity of functions and responsibilities or lack of a coherent policy for addressing urban poverty. These considerations, as well as possible changes in responsibilities of local government and its authority to act as a financial intermediary, as well as the need to generate and increase access to financial resources may also require changes in local government powers (see Chapters 4 and 13).

However, local government action to eliminate urban poverty does not necessarily require a change in mandate; it may also not require additional funding, as is illustrated through some of the examples of possible action noted below. Particularly if a participatory approach is used that works in partnership with local communities and NGOs, existing resources can be more efficiently used to reduce poverty.[4] In this regard, the single greatest resource is the potential of poor households themselves, in the informal sector, discussed next.

### ● The informal sector

The extent and impact of poverty on urban populations, as well as on urban and national economies would be much greater were it not for the informal sector. Variously described as unregulated, largely self-employed and small-scale activities, this largely 'hidden' or 'unrecognized' part of the economy often provides employment, goods and services for as much as 60 per cent of the urban population.

Research shows that the informal sector is better integrated with and recognized by the formal sector than its title would suggest. It is far more buoyant and elastic in generating jobs for an increasing urban labour force than the formal sector. It has a number of other advantages as well. Its small scale of operations and low levels of capitalization greatly lower the costs of creating employment, and it also produces jobs that require fewer skills and less training than the formal sector may demand. Coupled with a lack of regulation and controls, the ease of entry makes the informal sector well suited to the absorption of rural–urban migrants and other newcomers to the urban labour market. Many enter the informal sector during economic crisis, as a survival strategy of last resort. Women often find domestic and other service employment, while men more often seek self-employment. When local economies have been impacted by globalization in general and structural adjustment in particular, it has been mainly the informal sector that has provided a safety net and a source of income for those made redundant or unemployed.

However, the informal sector has its problems and limitations. First, the low-productivity nature of the sector and its lack of bargaining power mean that household incomes are generally lower than in the formal sector. Second, the very nature of the sector makes earnings more intermittent. The more erratic pattern of earnings tends to disqualify households in the informal sector from access to formal credit mechanisms. Third, the irregular and often illegal nature of many of its activities makes informal sector operators subject to official harassment or persecution as well as prone to mafia-style protection rackets. Fourth, the unregulated nature of the informal sector makes it difficult, and often impossible, to obtain access to services and supports necessary for increasing earnings and moving out of poverty. Fifth, the informal nature of many of the activities makes it difficult to protect those who are engaged in them, whether as paid workers or as unpaid family members. One much-publicized example is that of child-labour where the 'rights of the child' conflict with the survival strategies of the family. Another common situation concerns lack of protection against environmental contaminants and other hazards in the work setting.[5] Sixth, informal sector jobs do not have associated with them health insurance and other common fringe benefits. This affects particularly women and migrant workers.[6] Seventh, informal sector jobs do not produce government revenues to support welfare policies and can, thereby, erode safety net programmes and increase societal inequalities, as seen in the transition economies.[7]

● Investing in the poor[8]

One of the myths of globalization is that it pits elites and poor people against each other. To the extent that poverty reduction can be construed as a public good, the interdependence of better-off and poor groups gains prominence, and mobilization of broader constituencies becomes more feasible and benefits for poor people more likely. Doing so also sets a moral tone and political platform capable of mobilizing a broad range of citizens around common, even prosaic, interests.[9]

> Poverty reduction must be recognized as a public good because people living in poverty represent unrealized human capital potential with benefits for the *whole* of society

Poverty reduction must be recognized as a public good because people living in poverty represent unrealized human capital potential with benefits for the *whole* of society.[10] Market-based governance strategies exacerbate poverty and social disparities, most significantly by under-investment in human capital. Current policy recommendations target human capital resources as the key to generating wealth and maintaining competitiveness.[11] Underinvestment in this strategic asset is an inefficient use of an important source of potential future wealth and international competitiveness.[12]

Opportunities for carrying out initiatives to ensure the realization of human capital are enhanced by partnerships (see Chapter 14). The Casa Pia de Lisboa project, for example, brings together public and private agencies, labour unions, business organizations and universities to move Cape Verde families into the political and economic mainstream. One goal is to legalize the families' situation in order for them to gain access to social and employment rights. Casa Pia also provides 'customized', on-the-job vocational training as well as support for small business start-ups. Casa Pia is affiliated with IGLOO (Global Integration Through Housing and Jobs),[13] itself a joint initiative set up by three European NGO partners (FEANTSA, CECODHAS-ICAP, ETUC-CGIL) as a platform to encourage projects integrating housing, social support, training and employment initiatives.

Given the failure of market forces to invest in human capital, there is an important government role. In turn, this requires more articulated policy and financial frameworks for identifying and assessing human capital needs as well as for negotiating with the many public and private actors involved in enhancing this potential. For poor people, their inability to take advantage of new economic opportunities stems from a lack of information, skills and credit as well as the marginalized opportunities of a volatile informal economy.[14] An institutional commitment to investing in human capital is a necessary but not sufficient strategy for overcoming the systemic barriers that perpetuate social exclusion.

A key to poverty eradication lies in productive employment and income generation. Once a local government is ready and able to develop and implement appropriate programmes, the following options should be considered:

*Employment generation through municipal works.* In a number of countries such as Pakistan, Egypt, Colombia, Jamaica and Sri Lanka programmes of community-based, small-scale public works and contracts have been successfully implemented. Some cities have made the generation of jobs an explicit criterion for assessing and evaluating all bids for municipal contracts. The participation of women, especially as managers, supervisors, storekeepers, etc must be ensured. Box 17.1 describes a programme along these lines, developed in Senegal with the help of the national government.

*Support for informal sector activities.* Local government must recognize the contribution that the informal sector makes to employment and income generation and should remove regulatory impediments limiting the opportunities for informal sector operators such as hawkers, traders and waste recyclers to enhance the productivity of their activities. Municipalities can review and adjust land use and

---

**Box 17.1 Creating jobs that benefit urban infrastructure and services**

In 1989, the government of Senegal created the Agency for the Implementation of Public Interest Work (AGETIP) with support from various bilateral and multilateral donors. Its objectives were to create significant numbers of jobs in urban areas while increasing the productivity of the labour force through their employment on socially useful tasks. It works through a network of commercial companies and contracting authorities. During the first eight years, it has given 228,000 contracts in the building and civil engineering sector, which includes 7.7 million working days or 3000 permanent jobs. A total of 17,500 million CFAs have been spent on the labour component of these contracts with the total investment of the agency equalling 70,000 million CFAs. A third of its funds went to urban environment projects (including sanitation, water supplies, drainage, electrification and roads), 24 per cent to education and 22 per cent to health.

**Source:** MELISSA Program, 1998.

## Box 17.2 The hidden significance of urban agriculture

In the next 20 years, urbanization will intensify in Latin America and the Caribbean, but Africa and Asia will witness the most explosive urban growth. Countries that are urbanizing the most rapidly are also among the least well prepared to satisfy their food needs, and many already depend precariously on food aid and imports.

Urban agriculture bolsters city food supplies while also increasing the incomes of the poor. Urban agriculture uses resources, products and services found in and around the urban area and, in turn, often supplies resources, products and services to that area.

### Magnitude of urban agriculture

The United Nations Development Programme estimates that 800 million people are engaged in urban agriculture worldwide, the majority in Asian cities. Of these, 200 million are considered to be market producers, employing 150 million people full time. Urban agriculture is thus an important supply source in developing country urban food systems, a critical food-security valve for poor urban households. It productively uses open urban spaces, treats and recovers urban solid and liquid wastes, generates employment and income, adds value to products and manages freshwater resources more sparingly.

Urban agriculture complements, rather than supplants, rural supplies and imports of food. Cities will continue to depend largely on rural agriculture for bulkier, less perishable foodstuffs. But urban agriculture can provide significant amounts of food at small scales and for specific items. It can generate goods valued at tens of millions of dollars in any given major city. By growing their own food, cities lower their food deficits and obtain an important source of fruits and vegetables and livestock products, including dairy. Urban agriculture provides an estimated 15 per cent of all food consumed in urban areas and is likely to double that share in the next couple of decades. Cities with more advanced urban agriculture sectors, particularly in Asia, have become largely self-sufficient in higher-valued, nutritious perishables. Some cities even export surpluses.

Urban agriculture is also integral to city life, a vibrant part of urban economic and ecological systems. Urban farmers use urban land, public services, inputs and even urban wastes in production. They then sell to local markets and often reinvest profits into goods produced or sold at local city outlets.

Urban agriculture can also be an important supplement to household income. In Cairo, the rearing of small livestock, practised by over a quarter of households, provides more than 60 per cent of household income. In Dar es Salaam urban agriculture is the second-largest employer. High-valued speciality foods (for example, mushrooms) and non-food crops (such as ornamental flowers) that require little space for production are especially good for providing needed cash.

Still, the great majority of urban farmers are poor and grow food mainly for their own subsistence, with little support or protection, on small plots that they do not own. These households can secure food from urban agriculture that they could not afford otherwise. Studies in Harare, Kampala and Nairobi found that urban agriculture can improve nutritional status of household members, as measured by caloric and protein intake, meal quality or children's growth rates.

Many surveys indicate that women predominate in urban agriculture, enabling them to earn income, improve household diets, perform household chores and exert greater control over household resources, budgets and decision-making.

### Risks and constraints

The poor can be constrained from doing well with urban farming for many reasons, including lack of access to land, credit, water and other inputs or legal obstacles arising from concerns about public health. Urban farmers often use public spaces, and if they lack title to the land they use, they cannot be assured they will actually reap the benefits of their investment. Without title, the majority of low-income urban producers cannot get formal loans that require assets as a guarantee nor can they get support from national farmers' unions, whose members' activities must be legally sanctioned. Women may be denied aid by extension or credit services that distrust or disregard their knowledge of crops, input combinations and cultivation methods.

Aridity, unreliable supplies of piped water and violent rainfalls can all critically constrain production systems. If improperly managed, urban agriculture can contribute to environmental degradation, including soil erosion, loss of vegetation, siltation and depletion of water resources.

Public health concerns stem from misuse or mishandling of agrochemicals; the application of untreated or improperly treated wastes to food crops; the exposure of crops to air, water or land pollution, including possible contamination from heavy metals; and unsafe disposal of vegetable and animal wastes. Some threats, such as those from agrochemicals, are less prevalent than commonly believed because the poor usually cannot afford inorganic inputs. Consequently they grow crops or raise livestock organically. However, the poor often have no option other than to grow their crops in hazardous conditions, and threats from authorities may only deter them from investing in safer production methods.

### Policy and practice

To improve urban agriculture and make it more sustainable, farmers must use better practices and governments must promote or better manage it through more informed policies. NGOs can support these efforts.

Legitimizing urban agriculture can help its low-income practitioners to gain access to land, needed services and credit. Governments can provide land for urban agriculture in city master plans, support greenbelt projects and set up a network of input and service centres. They can engage directly in urban agricultural production by leasing out public land; assigning undeveloped, public land to farmer organizations; partnering with producers; or becoming producers themselves. Urban laws and regulations can be revised to be compatible with people's survival options, as in Kampala, where bylaws now allow for certain kinds of farm production in certain zones. Governments can also tolerate urban agriculture as interim land use in public housing schemes or incorporate it as a way to productively manage open urban spaces. Some development banks in South Africa and Tanzania have also provided credit by supporting revolving funds for cooperatives of urban farmers. Farmers' organizations can also help to legitimize the sector and organize access to credit, inputs and markets.

There is enormous potential for reducing risks to public health by educating and empowering urban producers, as opposed to ignoring or harassing them. Farmers can reduce environmental risks and gain financially by making appropriate choices about what crops to grow.

Producers can be taught to avoid the use of contaminated organic or chemical fertilizers on specific crops or to draw water from wells instead of rivers. Urban farmers can have mutually beneficial contracts with municipal waste-disposal services, and non-food urban agriculture can be used to rehabilitate contaminated water bodies and soils, generating income in the process. NGOs can help to determine the scale of composting that would be both cost-effective and environmentally suitable. Cities can treat and recirculate wastewater.

Challenges to urban agriculture remain to be addressed from the community up to the national level. Governments must apply the wealth of local experiences to creating institutional structures for implementing urban agriculture policies. Overall, experience shows that prohibition of urban agriculture has been ineffective. Governments now should move beyond accommodation and into issue resolution: multiple-stakeholder governance so far seems to be the best approach to creating a sustainable urban agriculture.

Experience also has shown that urban agriculture is most viable where it is mainstreamed into robust strategies for land use, poverty alleviation, economic development and sound environmental management. Outside Asia, few national food policies seek synergies between rural and urban production or guide integrated urban agricultural programmes. Land use and regulatory systems must be designed and enforced for fairer access to land, water and markets. Agricultural extension must be adapted to the needs of urban producers. Agricultural research stations and urban planning departments must collaborate. Model health and land use codes need to be developed. Regional and global networks are developing, but national and local networks must also be created and supported. Public policy should also acknowledge women's knowledge, constraints and opportunities and act on them to enhance women's citizenship.

**Source:** from a publication of the International Food Policy Research Institute (IFPRI) 2020 Vision for Food, Agriculture, and the Environment (www.ifpri.org/2020/welcome.htm), an initiative to feed the world, reduce poverty and protect the environment (Mougeot, 2000a).
**Note:** For further reading see Mougeot, 2000b; UNDP, 1996b.

zoning regulations and infrastructure provision to facilitate marketing, manufacturing and employment generation activities. Support for informal sector activities can also include revising inappropriate construction standards to allow for lower cost building materials and to encourage self-help and gradual upgrading. In many cities in the developing countries, urban agriculture is growing fast as a source of food and earnings. Local governments can provide support by, for example, appropriate land use planning, extending credit and technical assistance concerning the use of fertilizers and choice of crops (see Box 17.2)

*Establishing credit for small scale and micro-enterprises.* Local government should support credit for small scale and micro-enterprises, preferably through providing funds for lending to NGOs and CBOs, or by providing guarantees for them to financial institutions. Biases against women either as borrowers or as entrepreneurs should be removed.

*Mitigating the impact of economic shocks.* Emergency credit facilities (small, very short-term loans available on a fast-track basis, triggered by general rather than particular circumstances) should be made available to reduce the vulnerability of low-income households and businesses to withstand economic shocks and fluctuations in market conditions. These local actions should occur in the wider context of strengthening international institutions to manage the volatility of global capital markets.[15]

*Provision of marketing advice and information support.* Credit schemes and facilities should be linked to market information and advice centres to support business networking and exchanges between micro-enterprises as well as vertically with other up- and down-stream enterprises. This will facilitate enterprises to move up the value-adding ladder through joint, collaborative or cooperative initiatives. Local government can also assist in the formation of 'chambers of micro-commerce', through which it can have a direct channel of communication and feedback on its employment generation and poverty eradication programmes.

*Support for training and capacity building.* Local government should provide or support vocational and other practical training and capacity building courses. These efforts should include initiatives to help bridge the 'digital divide' by developing skills in modern ICTs, in conjunction with creating professional jobs and the application of ICTs in support of affordable housing and neighbourhood development (see Boxes 17.4; 17.5; 17.6 ; and 17.7 ). It is particularly critical to encourage the participation of women in these programmes by meeting their needs for childcare and transport.

*Provision of security of land tenure.* Providing security of tenure to 'owner-occupiers' in illegal settlements greatly increases the value of their assets and their ability to access credit.[16] It also reduces the risks of eviction, thereby encouraging investment in property and equipment, associated with manufacturing, repair and assembly. Awarding secure tenure to women, rather than men, often has a greater multiplier impact on improvements and income generation.

*Access to urban services and land.* The poor, like other urban dwellers, need access to municipal services, as this directly influences their living conditions and, particularly, their health status. Further, well-serviced housing with secure land tenure plays a vital role in the survival of poor households.[17] However, low-income neighbourhoods are usually

---

**Box 17.3 Using ICTs to franchise access to information**

In Dhar district, one of India's poorest, in the state of Madhya Pradesh, a model computer project provides residents with access to commonly needed state records and daily crop prices. The service is provided by young people with at least a 10th-grade education, picked by the state and given a franchise to sell the information for a small fee from the state's computer network. For 25–35 cents, people can buy immediate print-outs of documents that they might otherwise have spent days trying to get from local bureaucrats: land records, caste certificates, proof of income, etc. For another 25 cents, any citizen can send a complaint to the state by email and the state guarantees a reply within a week. The service provider will write out the grievance for those who are illiterate. Since the project was started in January 2000, 22 villages have each bought a computer, a modem, a printer and a battery for $1500 with their own money and agreed to provide a small booth to house the set-up. It is expected that this sort of revenue-generating project will spread more quickly than those dependent on scarce public funds. The arrangement is also thought to counteract a tendency among low-level officials to demand bribes before furnishing information.

**Source:** Dugger, 2000.

The City Design Center at the University of Illinois at Chicago is establishing the first internet Affordable Housing Design Catalogue. 'Design Matters: Best Practices in Affordable Housing' will document exemplary functional and innovative affordable housing projects for a range of building types, site planning and technology practices across the US. With financial support from several national and local foundations and individual donors, the catalogue will take advantage of the internet technology to provide universal, free access to professionals, community groups, developers, builders, consumers, policy makers, researchers, educators and students worldwide.

The Affordable Housing Design Catalogue will help to demonstrate that 'design matters' in affordable housing and that it does not have to cost more. The catalogue will include all types of affordable, 'permanent' housing for independent living, constructed between 1980 and 1999. In addition to affordability considerations, economic, social and formal criteria will be used to catalogue projects that:

- minimize construction and life cycle costs;
- support household and neighbourhood fit;
- are adaptable to household changes;
- are universally accessible;
- meet high aesthetic standards;
- maximize energy and resource efficiency;
- promote healthy indoor environments;
- support physical safety and security.

Browsers will be able to search the database for photo-images and plans, location, architect, developer, project description (eg building and construction type, construction practices, number and type of units, building construction costs), 'target' residents (eg income, type of household), tenure, strategies to achieve affordability, and priority design objectives. In addition, the catalogue will offer information and resources for each of the design objectives, both in print and on the internet, as well as contacts for follow-up.

**Source:** Roberta M Feldman, Director, City Design Center at the University of Illinois at Chicago, personal communications, 15, 16 and 20 June 2000.

not the first targets for road upgrading, water supply, sewerage, drainage or municipal waste collection. Typically, women and girls bear the brunt of these deficiencies (see, for example, Chapters 9 and 10). Cities must be actively involved in efforts to decentralize the provision of urban infrastructure and services, preferably by forming enduring partnerships with the private sector and civil society groups (Chapters 13 and 14).

# Combating Corruption

*'There is increasing evidence that corruption undermines development. It also hampers the effectiveness with which domestic savings and external aid are used in many developing countries, and this in turn threatens to undermine grassroots support for foreign assistance'* – James D Wolfensohn, President of the World Bank (http://www1.worldbank.org/publicsector/anticorrupt/)

Corruption is the misuse of office for personal gain. It means charging an illicit price for a service or using the power of office to further illicit aims. Corruption can entail acts of omission or commission. It can involve legal activities or illegal ones. It can be internal to the organization (eg embezzlement) or external to it (eg extortion). While some acts of corruption are 'freelance', others are more systematic. Systematic corruption generates (a) economic costs by distorting incentives and discouraging investment; (b) political costs by undermining institutions; and (c) social costs by redistributing wealth and power towards the undeserving. Overall, corruption has effects that vary widely, including sometimes net social benefits, but it usually leads to inefficiency, injustice and inequality.

In October 1996 the World Bank's President James Wolfensohn launched the Bank's campaign against 'the cancer of corruption' indicating that the Bank was willing to address the problem overtly and systematically. This followed a realization that political corruption and inefficiency are detrimental to economic growth as well as a growing concern over waste resulting from corruption-prone Bank projects.

## Corruption within municipalities: What can be done?[18]

One of the key challenges facing municipalities today is how to reduce corruption. Corruption negatively affects the provision and maintenance of urban services and deprives taxpayers of the right to these services.

### ● A preventive strategy

*People are more susceptible to corruption when they have the monopoly over a good or service, as well as the discretion to decide who gets that good or service or how much anyone gets, and are not accountable for that decision*

People are more susceptible to corruption when they have the monopoly over a good or service, the discretion to decide who gets that good or service and are not accountable for that decision. Therefore a key to successful prevention of corruption lies in making changes in the policies and systems that put people into office rather than hunting for culprits after the deed. When public officials are paid meagre salaries without being rewarded for performance, and when penalties against corruption are rare and mild, we can expect corruption to flourish. A successful strategy against corruption focuses on corrupt systems, not just corrupt individuals.

Corruption tends to be reduced by separation of power, checks and balances, transparency, a good justice system and clearly defined roles, rules, responsibilities and limits. Corruption tends not to thrive where there is a democratic culture, competition and good systems of control, and where people have rights to information and rights of redress.

Fighting corruption should not be viewed as an end in itself because the economic costs of reducing corruption may outweigh the benefits. For example, setting up expensive monitoring systems may have little or no impact on corruption. Eliminating corruption can provide a lever for urban financial recovery, the reform of service delivery and

**Box 17.5 MOUSE: building partnerships to bridge the urban digital divide**

Founded in 1997 by a group of concerned and motivated individuals from New York City's Silicon Alley, MOUSE (Making Opportunities for Upgrading Schools & Education) is a nonprofit volunteer organization that provides New York City public schools and their extended communities with technology resources, expertise, access and support by linking them with professionals from the local high-tech industry. It has provided schools with an estimated $5 million worth of equipment, technical expertise and support. MOUSE's core roster of 1500+ volunteer tech professionals have spent more than 40,000 hours working hands-on in the public schools building networks and solving technology problems. In 1999, volunteers put 50,000 teachers and students on-line.

MOUSE is currently managing programmes in 38 New York City public high schools. MOUSE selects partner schools based on the following criteria: strong administrative interest and support; short and long-term curricular goals utilizing technology; a dedicated and interested corps of teachers; community partners, corporate partners, PTA and alumni groups; and a willingness to let the students take part in creating and maintaining the technology.

In addition to the school-based technology programmes, MOUSE and its various partners are also involved in outreach programmes that include:

- a large-scale *computer donation programme* for 14 elementary and middle schools in in Central Harlem. An internet company has donated more than $500,000 worth of hardware distributed equitably throughout the district and installed and maintained via MOUSE's volunteer manpower. In addition to setting up 14 school networks, MOUSE coordinates staff development and student programmes as well as parent workshops to help schools begin to utilize the technology in meaningful ways.
- a three-year US$1.1 million grant from the US Department of Education to set up a *community technology centre*. The centre fulfils the vital need of providing access to information technology for one of the poorest congressional districts in New York. Providing free access to families, students and teachers beyond school hours of 8 a.m. to 2:30 p.m. is an important step in narrowing the digital divide that exists in this city.
- an *annual two-day conference* which brings together over 350 teachers from high schools in Manhattan to share their experiences regarding 'best practices' on using technology in the classroom.
- an *On-line Student Designed Newspaper Contest* designed to give public high school students the opportunity to learn first hand about creating an on-line newspaper, web site design and programming, as well as to develop their critical and creative thinking skills as they gain experience in the field of journalism. Winning sites appear on *The New York Times* web site and winning teams are awarded laptop computers.
- a new programme that encourages young women in local high schools to get involved in the world of new technology. Called 'The NYC Young Women's Technology Club', the project brings New York City high school girls together with professional women in the new media industry to learn technology skills through building an on-line magazine. Project content is driven by the interests of participating students, and the mentors provide skills workshops, brown bag lunches and one-on-one interaction.
- an *Interactive Internship and Learning Programme* designed to prepare highschool students for the jobs of the future. MOUSE partnered with local high-tech and new-media firms to place students in paid summer internships. The year-round programme provides them with the skills necessary to be successful in today's high-tech workplace. Participating students attend monthly hands-on workshops taught by industry professionals and bi-monthly meetings with advisers.

The MOUSE volunteer network comprises a wide array of multimedia professionals: network designers, planners and architects, programmers, web site developers and designers, database managers and content providers. Approximately 75 per cent of MOUSE volunteers come from new technology companies. The remainder work for traditional media and other volunteer-minded corporations.

It works in partnership with dozens of private sector companies which provide funding, equipment, expertise and labour to the organization and its projects.

**Source:** Melissa Auerbach, Communications Director, MOUSE, personal communication, 6 June 2000.

the involvement of citizens – reflecting and reinforcing good governance.

## ● Assessing corruption

Corruption comes in many varieties. A good start for analysing corruption is to unbundle it. Citizens and government officials themselves can help to diagnose the extent of, and damage caused by, various kinds of corruption by simple methods:

*Participatory diagnosis.* The first task is to demystify corruption. This can be done by analysing a case study of a successful anti-corruption campaign in another city or country. Analytical frameworks can be provided to help participants to realize that corruption is not (just or primarily) a problem of evil people but of corrupt systems. Participants can then move on to a diagnosis of their own situation. This method can produce a deeper understanding of corruption in general and its specific local manifestations, and lead to a plan of action.

*Technical studies and experiments.* Studies can be useful to gain a better understanding of how corrupt systems work (or, rather, do not work). Clients are encouraged to share their knowledge without fear of recriminations, for example, through anonymous surveys or group work involving anonymous written contributions that are then discussed. Employees are then centrally involved in the subsequent design and eventual evaluation of experiments with new ways of providing information, incentives and accountability.

*Implementing reform.* Campaigns against corruption need some entity to be in charge. However, because no single agency can do everything in the fight against corruption and a coordinated effort is required, the anti-corruption 'body' must, above all, facilitate joint action and mobilize the resources of many government agencies. The first question facing a government wishing to fight corruption is what sort of coordinating authority it requires. It may choose to set up a 'super-agency' that combines investiga-

---

**Box 17.6 Using the internet as a tool for improving urban neighbourhoods and preserving affordable housing**

Despite the booming economy and the unprecedented wealth being generated by high tech, US cities face serious problems with housing, especially in low-income neighbour-hoods. An interesting project at UCLA, with an impressive array of local and national partners, is using the internet to do something positive about housing in Los Angeles.

Neighbourhood Knowledge Los Angeles (NKLA) is a web site (http://nkla.sppsr.ucla.edu) aimed at improving and preserving neighbourhoods. Offered in two languages (English and Spanish), it is an on-line tool that provides easy access to a vast collection of data about properties and neighbourhoods that are in danger of falling into urban blight.

The conditions the project and its partners are trying to fix are sobering. The Los Angeles Citizens Committee on Slum Housing found that the number of LA-area rental units occupied by tenants living below the poverty level grew from 217,200 in 1989 to 422,500 in 1995, a 95 per cent increase over six years. The Census's *American Housing* Survey reported in 1995 that in the Los Angeles–Long Beach area there were 154,400 substandard apartments in need of major repair, 107,900 units infested with rats, and 131,700 units without working toilets. Such grim statistics are the product of severe pockets of poverty.

Leaders of the NKLA project, based at UCLA's School of Public Policy and Social Research and funded by the City of Los Angeles Housing Department, Fannie Mae and the US Department of Commerce's Telecommunications and Information Infrastructure Assistance Program, use computer data from a variety of public sources to look for 'early warning signs' that properties in Los Angeles are headed for unliveable status. One of the best predictors of housing abandonment is tax delinquency. Property tax delinquency is often followed by building code violations and tenant complaints, then by abandonment of the property. Slum landlords 'work the system' by buying a building and milking the tenants for rent without paying for maintenance or taxes, then disappear when the government threatens legal action.

The NKLA project and similar community data projects in other cities are good examples of two phenomena made possible by the internet. The first is that the internet tends to blur the boundaries between institutions; in the case of NKLA, between a university, the city and county governments and community activist organiza-tions. This blurring is common in the private sector but is only beginning to emerge in the public and civic sectors. The second phenomenon is that NKLA shows what can be done with what would otherwise be underutilized public information. UCLA researchers use public data to serve specific ends, particularly community development. Importantly, NKLA enables new technologies to be used in ways that give people left out of the high-tech boom real hope, when those technologies are used as tools for solving specific, concrete problems.

The NKLA site and its on-line databases allow citizens and housing activists to look for properties with tax problems, code violations or other difficulties, such as tenant complaints or fire violations, that could be precursors to abandonment, neighbourhood deterioration and urban decline. The web site offers searchable databases by zip code or other parameters and shows individual properties on interactive maps of Los Angeles.

NKLA researchers also work with grassroots community organizations, tenant groups and activists to promote code enforcement by government officials. The NKLA project and its community partners played a role in developing the city's comprehensive slum housing ordinance, which mandates that all properties be inspected for code violations every three years. That, in turn, is having an effect on improving compliance by property owners.

One nonprofit community organization that finds the NKLA tools useful is Concerned Citizens of South-Central Los Angeles. This group is developing a land trust for housing in its community, which has the oldest housing in the city. The organization buys properties that are available because of tax delinquency or other problems, such as foreclosures, and then helps first-time homebuyers acquire the properties and refurbish them. All of this is made possible through information gleaned from public data.

**Source:** Chapman, 2000.

---

tion (like a police force), prevention (like a management consulting agency) and popular participation (like a community relations office). To be effective, it should have power and resources.

There is a simple rule for where to begin when combating corruption: 'Pick low-hanging fruit'. That is, select a type of corruption where visible progress might be made soon, without too great a cost. To generate political support, it makes sense first to attack the kinds of corrup-tion that are most obvious to citizens or are most hated by them. This advice runs counter to the tendency to tackle everything at once, in a comprehensive plan, or to take on the kind of corruption with the most serious costs, even if this would seem to be the best approach for improving urban finance.

Experience suggests that municipal leaders usually should not begin anti-corruption initiatives by attacking their own officials and agencies, even if these are known to be corrupt. Instead, it may be more effective if they take positive steps to reform corrupt bureaucracies by improving ways of obtaining information, enhancing performance incentives and promoting competition. However, when corruption has become systematic, it is necessary to remove perceptions that impunity exists. Such perceptions may arise when all that citizens and bureaucrats have seen are just a few minor prosecutions, making them cynical about the fight against corruption. Then it becomes necessary to break through this culture of impunity and 'fry some big fish'. Prominent culprits must be named publicly and punished so that a distrustful citizenry is persuaded that an anti-corruption drive is more than just words, more than just a campaign against one's political opponents.

## Corruption in the water sector[19]

Globalization and the associated processes of marketization and deregulation have been accompanied by encouragement of privatization of public services and infrastructure by the World Bank and other international development banks. At the same time, privatization has increased the incentives for multinational companies to offer bribes in order to secure profitable concessions and contracts.

---

Privatization of public services has increased the incentives for multinational companies to offer bribes in order to secure profitable concessions and contracts

One of the sectors most at risk is water and sanitation. The concessions invariably involve long-term monopoly supply of an essential service, with considerable potential profit. Significantly, the label of 'Blue Gold' has been used in the context of the commodification of water.[20] Often, major construction works are also involved, themselves a source of profit.

It is not just the developing countries where corruption is problematic. In recent years, leading politicians have been prosecuted and convicted of corruption in a number of Western European countries, including Austria, Belgium, France, Germany, Italy, Spain and the UK. In 1999, the entire European Commission, the highest political authority in the European Union, resigned over corruption allegations. Corruption also extends to business practices abroad, where it is so routine that British companies employ special agents to recover bribes that have failed to produce the desired result.[21]

In the field of public utilities, France pioneered the system of privatization by contracting out (*gestion déléguée* or delegated management). As a result, the major water multinationals are French. Therefore, many of the convictions or investigations on allegations of corruption concern French companies.[22] For example, in the city of Grenoble in 1996, a former mayor and government minister and a senior executive of a private water company both received prison sentences for receiving and giving bribes to award a water contract to a subsidiary of the company.[23] In March 2000, the city dismissed the water company, and brought the water service back under public control, a case of re-municipalization. Another major company was convicted of bribery to obtain water concessions in the town of Angoulême.

As privatization of water and sanitation has spread to other parts of the world, the European multinationals have been centrally involved. For example, in Lesotho, 12 multinational companies are being prosecuted for paying bribes in connection with huge water engineering contracts for a water supply scheme.[24] In Indonesia, Jakarta's water was privatized, with support from the World Bank, through a French and a British consortium both of which were in partnership with companies owned by Suharto's relatives and associates. The World Bank has since then introduced procurement regulations that provide for the indefinite banning from Bank projects of companies found to have paid bribes on any project.[25] Allegations surround many other privatized water schemes, on all continents. In India, for example, the state of Karnataka is reviewing a decision to grant a water project to a UK-based company after alleged irregularities in the tendering of the contract.[26]

> The World Bank has introduced procurement regulations, providing for the indefinite banning from Bank projects of companies found guilty of bribery

● **International initiatives**

Transparency International (TI) is an international NGO that produces corruption indexes and surveys which rank countries in terms of the degree to which corruption is perceived to exist in those countries. The TI Bribe Payers Index, for instance, ranks the leading exporting countries in terms of the degree to which their companies are perceived to be paying bribes abroad.[27]

In 1998, the OECD agreed to a Convention on Combatting Bribery in International Business Transactions. This initiative was an attempt to generalize the US Foreign Corrupt Practices Act (FCPA), under which it is an offence in the US for a company to engage in bribing officials of a foreign government.[28] This was seen as having put US companies at a competitive disadvantage, as their European competitors have had no such legislation to deter them from using bribery to obtain business.

Whether the Convention's adoption will produce the intended results will depend largely on whether the OECD countries will enforce such laws against their own companies. In practice, OECD governments and business associations have tended to be more concerned about protecting their companies' contracts than supporting action against corruption.

● **Country responses**

Developing countries can protect themselves against bribery in the water and sanitation sector by effective action that contains the following three elements:

- *Economic deterrents.* The most effective sanction against bribery among multinationals is to ban them from future contracts. Singapore, for example, banned five companies from bidding for any contracts for five years after an intermediary was convicted of handling bribes totalling US$9.8 million.
- *The public sector option.* The best economic defence against bribery in public procurement is to ensure that the option of public sector provision is always kept open. This was a key part of the historical rationale for placing services under municipal or national control. Water and sanitation services are still 95 per cent in public sector hands worldwide. Any acceptable privatization proposal should be justifiable in light of this option.
- *Democratic transparency.* Public availability of all documents relies on democratic practice as a basic safeguard against corruption. This is a real issue in the water sector; some multinationals insist that the contract documents themselves are kept secret, on grounds of commercial confidentiality, even from elected members of the municipality that awards the contract. Transparency is the best defence against corruption; as practised in Kerala, India, with its widely praised model of decentralized democracy, in which documents on beneficiary selection, reports and minutes of meetings and all documents on works undertaken through contractors, including bills and vouchers, are made public.[29] The following section examines this approach in greater detail.

---

**Box 17.7 The village internet programme: using ICTs to create jobs and stem urban migration**

The village internet programme (VIP), in operation since July 1999 in Madhupur, a village in Tangail district about 160 km away from Dhaka, Bangladesh, has as its main objectives to:

- Familiarize the village people, particularly the young generation, with the use of computer and the internet.
- Provide computer training for a minimal price, thus helping to build a computer literate generation.
- Create IT-related local job opportunities.
- Offer low-cost computing and printing facilities, previously unavailable in this rural area.
- Facilitate access to relevant market information, for example, prevalent market prices of specific products in different locations. This gives the village people a better bargaining capacity when selling their produce.
- Provide email facilities for families with relatives abroad.
- Provide free email services to teachers and students for educational purposes and to doctors and journalists for emergency purposes.

In order to fulfil these objectives, Grameen Communications has introduced the following commercial services, which cross-subsidize the free services provided for educational and medical purposes:

- Job training for students and unemployed youth in rural areas, including data entry and programming, at an affordable price.
- Courses on computer operating systems and application software, eg MS Word and Excel.
- Advertising and marketing facilities through email. Clients are offered free advertisement for the first two months, after which they can become members for a minimum fee.
- Page composition and printing for a fee of 5–15 takas (50 takas = US$1).

**Source:** Tariq Alam, Grameen Communications, personal communications, 14 and 15 February 2000.

---

### Reconceptualizing transparency: grassroots movements for accountability to the poor[30]

If globalization is as much about the flow of ideas as it is the movement of capital, then among its many manifestations has been the widespread diffusion of ideas about governance. Global institutions such as the World Bank have been crucial in disseminating the idea of good government, a notion that has come in for much criticism since its entry into the development lexicon at the beginning of the 1990s.

---

Transparency and accountability are central to good, democratic governance

---

Two concepts have been central to the idea of good (democratic) government: transparency and accountability. The former is, in theory, meant to help achieve the latter, though both are ill-defined. While increased transparency has indeed generated markedly higher levels of accountability in many parts of the world in recent years, the primary setting of this trend has been the private rather than the public sector: it is in the area of corporate governance that transparency has been taken furthest, in the form of stricter and more uniform disclosure norms that clearly have increased the capacity of shareholders to keep a vigilant eye on the performance of corporate managers.

These innovations have clearly influenced approaches by the public sector, especially the 'client focus' rhetoric, if not actual behaviour, of agencies throughout the world. But government bureaucracies have inherited a number of the shortcomings of corporate transparency as well.

The work of several activist groups in different parts of India illustrates the main deficiency of existing efforts, both within and beyond India, to promote transparency in the public and private sectors: their elite bias, and their consequent inability to rectify the information inequalities that characterize even today's globalizing world of free-flowing data. Just as importantly, they signal the radical possibilities of transparency, an idea in serious danger of withering from overuse and underspecification. The experiences of two groups serve as examples illustrating points of broader applicability. The first highlights problems and prospects in public sector, while the latter addresses issues relating to transparency and accountability in the private sector.

#### ● Local participatory auditing of the public sector

The Mazdoor Kisan Shakti Sangathan (MKSS), or Worker and Farmer Power Organization, is based in the northern state of Rajasthan. Over the past six years, the MKSS has held a series of 'public hearings', unofficial gatherings of ordinary people in villages and small towns. Prior to these hearings, MKSS activists obtain copies of government documents related to the planning and execution of local development projects. India's bureaucracy, still operating within the constraints of the colonial-era Official Secrets Act, is not keen to share these sensitive records, partly due to sheer force of habit and partly for fear of providing evidence of official misdeeds. But sympathetic (or sometimes naive) bureaucrats often provide the necessary documents. Sometimes direct action protests, such as a sit-in outside a local rural development agency office, are required.

The MKSS activists include a number of seemingly unlikely members of local society, such as semi-employed labourers, poor women and members of the lower strata of the Hindu caste hierarchy. Armed with documents indicating the amounts spent on each aspect of specific public works in the local vicinity, the technical specifications of the works and statements indicating payments to labourers, the MKSS goes about systematically auditing these projects. For instance, labourers on employment-generation schemes are shown official accounts, which show that the workers have been paid the minimum wage, and are asked to verify or dispute the amounts entered next to their names in the ledgers. Drivers of camel carts – a popular mode of transport in mainly desert-covered Rajasthan – report on how many bags of cement were actually delivered to specific work sites, in many instances calling into question the inflated figures listed in project documents.

At the public hearing itself, workers and others with relevant evidence that contradicts the statements contained within government records are invited to repeat their testimony. MKSS activists have read aloud (to the largely non-literate villagers) from employment registers that list ecent payments to people everyone knows are long dead. n one case, the public hearing was held in front of a dilapi-ated school which, according to official documents read ut at the meeting, had just been repaired at considerable xpense. A stream of satirical commentary combines with ublic outrage at the extent of fraud to create an tmosphere in which the trappings of power lose some of heir magic. Local politicians and bureaucrats, a surprising umber of whom actually attend the hearings, are asked to ccount for these discrepancies, as their signatures are to be ound on the documents certifying that construction was omplete, even when it manifestly was not, and that eneficiaries of anti-poverty programmes meet the eligibil-ty criteria, even when everyone knows they do not. In ome instances, officials have owned up to appropriating unds. In a small number of cases they have actually eturned ill-gotten loot.

The public-hearing process has allowed the MKSS to levelop a radical interpretation of the notion that ordinary itizens have a right both to know how they are governed nd to participate actively in the process of auditing their epresentatives in minute detail. Not only has the MKSS uilt a movement demanding the passage in Parliament of Right to Information legislation – a state-level act was passed in Rajasthan in mid-2000, and much-debated national legislation should be enacted by 2001 – it has managed to transform the popular understanding of freedom of information by showing its applicability to the concerns of the rural poor, for whom government programmes are a lifeline against the vicissitudes of (increasingly global) economic circumstances.

Public debate increasingly acknowledges the relation-ship between opacity and the perpetuation of everyday forms of corruption that afflict highly vulnerable people. Until the mid-1990s, the right to information had been most closely associated with the right to free expression. India thus followed international precedent, which tended to group the right to information with press freedom, as in the United States, where the Freedom of Information Act is associated with the press in general, and has received judicial affirmation under the free-expression provisions in the US Bill of Rights. The MKSS, in its grassroots organiz-ing and practical work, as well as in its own documentation, prefers to locate the right to information within the Indian Constitution's provisions guaranteeing the right to life and livelihood.

There are many implications of this case, but what needs to be emphasized in the context of this report is the extent to which the MKSS's grassroots work has breathed new life into an increasingly hackneyed term, transparency. Its skill in mobilizing ordinary people on very sensitive matters has exposed the hollowness of initiatives by public agencies in many parts of India to pass off bureaucratically controlled information-sharing activities as radical experi-ments in 'open government'. The type of 'information' that government departments pledge to provide is usually prospective rather than retrospective, thus avoiding the possibility of popular 'audit' and genuine accountability. Government initiatives on transparency often involve bureaucrats preparing promotional literature on existing

---

**Box 17.8 Sign the contract yourself!**

In the global rush to privatize property in developing countries, local specialists and foreign advisers assigned to survey land and grant titles most often treat the family as a unit. Because families change and women often do not receive explicit title to property, the practice increases disparities between women and men. The case of Laos illustrates the issues. Although a small country, Laos is particularly interesting because of the matrilineal tradition in rights to land among the lowland Lao (the majority group); it is also an example of transition from socialist planning to market-oriented reforms.

The reform period began in the mid-1980s. Forest and farmlands that were tradition-ally used by certain families have gradually been officially titled. The government also permits purchase of up to 15 ha of land per person (the limit is to prevent total domination by one or two wealthy families). The biggest problem is that typically the husband alone would sign a contract for the family's land. This amounted to a transfer of control of land from the wife and her extended family to that of the husband.

This constituted a windfall profit for the husband and his relatives. Divorce and abandonment have been increasing, though still low compared with Western experience. Even though most couples have stayed together, the transfer of control could be seen to affect land use and sale since the husband's family did not have long ties to that plot of land. The practice contributed to more rapid deforestation. In addition, the award of initial titles led some people to believe erroneously that they could sell their land and then get another title for a new plot from the government.

Specialists analysing gender aspects of land titling in Laos began to point out that women were losing their traditional rights and that courts might not recognize their share in land ownership if their names did not appear on the contracts. Local researchers managed to get the contracts altered so that they now have two lines for the signatures of both wife and husband. This has been useful, but problems continue in getting those witnessing the titling process to make sure that the wife also signs. Although this is just one part of addressing gender inequality in property rights, it can be beneficial and one of the simpler, win–win strate-gies in assigning rights to use and own property.

**Source:** Tinker and Summerfield, 1999.

---

schemes, or else promising to speed up the delivery of 'information services', such as delivery of a birth certificate for a citizen who needs documentary proof of age and residence for a government job. These kinds of initiatives are usually not only anodyne in content, but also seldom developed at local levels accessible to the poor.

The MKSS is fighting an uphill battle, not only because of the power and resources of state and private elites who would like to shield their activities from public gaze, but also owing to the suspicion with which critical public opinion in India has come to view the idea of trans-parency. The push for transparency is associated with multinational capital, which tends to discredit the idea to some degree among India's mainly left-leaning social activists. Their fear is that official multilateral agencies like the World Bank and transnational NGOs like Transparency International (founded by former World Bank staffers and funded by several high-profile multinational companies) promote transparency only to the extent that it can assist foreign firms in gaining access to the Indian market and exploiting India's natural and human resources. Thus, there is support for more transparent settlement systems on the Mumbai Stock Exchange; but no effort to promote access for members of the public to background documentation relating to Memoranda of Understanding between foreign firms and various public authorities.

### ● Private sector transparency that goes beyond disclosure of financial performance

Indeed, the elite-biased transparency initiatives pursued by government agencies in India are seen as a natural by-product of the form that corporate transparency has taken. The work of a trade union in Mumbai has highlighted the need for private sector transparency to shed its narrow preoccupations with those aspects of financial disclosure that concern, almost exclusively, capital markets. The Girni Kamgar Sangharsh Samiti (GKSS), or Textile Workers Struggle Committee, has sought to hold Mumbai's textile firms accountable for their commitments to workers. Ailing companies have taken large packages of state assistance, but have not been forced to account publicly for their use of the funds, which are supposed to assist in the revitalization of the mills, the preservation of jobs and the welfare of workers.

Unions such as the GKSS are hamstrung due to a lack of information. GKSS activists would like not only detailed information on what state-provided revitalization funds have been used for, but also (in those cases where companies have clearly not lived up to their side of the bargain) why government regulators have failed to take action. Thus, the GKSS has turned the spotlight on the lack of transparency in those regulatory bodies responsible for protecting the interests of highly vulnerable citizens from unaccountable exercises of corporate power.

That transparency in the regulatory bureaucracy – which implies transparency in corporations themselves to the degree that they must submit documentation to government agencies which is then available to the public – has not been a concern of either international bodies or Indian public authorities comes as no surprise to activists working among poor communities. The agenda, they argue, is being driven by the interests of domestic and international investors, whose interest extends almost exclusively to data on financial performance. Investors would, of course, care more about information relating to other regulatory functions were they convinced that, for instance, provincial Pollution Control Boards were likely to do their jobs effectively – that is, in ways that might impinge upon profits – rather than, as is all too often the case, with scant regard for proper procedure. The lack of transparency allows these and other regulatory agencies to get away with such lapses and the corruption that accompanies them.

### ● Lessons

Both the MKSS and the GKSS have participated, in collaboration with a range of other NGOs and people's movements, in protests against the process by which public authorities have vetted various business projects involving multinational corporations. It is in this sphere of activity that the lessons of these two organizations may have their most powerful reverberations. The opposition to multinationally financed industrial projects often takes the same locality-specific form that the MKSS has pioneered. This is logical. Just as government accounts can only be effectively audited at the local level (where people's expertise about local events, people and places can be brought to bear), claims by multinationals about the proposed project sites (their environmental characteristics, employment profiles and, most importantly, the opinions of local people about the desirability of such projects) are best verified at local levels.

> Government accounts can only be effectively audited at the local level where people's expertise about local events, people and places can be brought to bear

For this conception of accountability to take root, however, corporations must be obliged to supply information about their intentions not only to government regulators, but to citizens as well. While the main beneficiaries will be people residing in the vicinity of proposed projects, a larger range of actors from among the nation-wide network of civil society organizations will no doubt analyse and debate the implications of the information received; things like environmental impact statements and projections of employment creation, foreign-exchange requirements and all the other things that national laws require authorities to scrutinize before approving the establishment of such ventures.

Moreover, as a number of existing cases of local opposition to multinational projects in India have demonstrated, the information supplied will have to cover the global operations of the firms concerned. Only by studying in detail, on the basis of documentary evidence, the conduct and impact of a firm's previous and existing business ventures in other countries can an informed judgement on an investment proposal be made. Through just such means were activists in the western state of Goa made aware of shortcomings in the environmental record of the DuPont Corporation, which was at that time planning a nylon factory near Goa's famed beaches. Data obtained from activists in the United States highlighted several inconsistencies in the government of Goa's defence of the DuPont project, and the project was ultimately scrapped. This experience is also a good example of 'globalization-from-below', showing how civil society can take advantage of transnational networks to obtain relevant information to help mobilize necessary resources.

> People whose lives and livelihoods depend on the accountable exercise of corporate and governmental power should have official information available to them by right

People whose lives and livelihoods depend on the accountable exercise of corporate and governmental power should not have to rely on having to obtain official information informally by activists. It must be made available by right. For this to happen, governments must rethink transparency; both in terms of their direct interactions with poor and vulnerable people in development programmes, and perhaps more importantly, in the obligations they impose on private-sector actors to divulge details of their intentions and ongoing activities. Pension-fund managers in the North will only demand the degree of transparency necessary to protect their investments. To

rotect people, governments (and people themselves) are
he only solution.

# Reducing Urban Violence[31]

Violence, previously regarded as an issue of criminal pathol-
gy, is now recognized also as a development problem,
articularly in urban areas.[32] The incidence of crime,
obbery and gang violence, as well as gender-based domestic
iolence, undermines both macro- and micro-economic
growth and productivity of a country's development, as
well as societal and individual well-being.[33] In addition, the
umber of countries currently experiencing internal armed
onflict has escalated dramatically since the end of the Cold
War, with cities often at the centre of civil strife. Map 1 and
ables 15.1–15.3 in Chapter 15 showed the massive disloca-
ions and vast numbers of homeless people that result.

> 'The same technological means that foster globalization
> and the transnational expansion of civil society also
> provide the infrastructure for expanding global networks
> of "uncivil society" – organized crime, drug traffickers,
> money launderers and terrorists' – Kofi Annan,
> Renewal Amid Transition: Annual Report on the
> Work of the Organization, 3 September 1997

The globalization of crime through international rings – such
as Mexican and Colombian drug cartels, the Jamaican posses
and the Chinese triads – has reduced the significance of city
or national boundaries with some violence problems.[34] In
urban areas, the relationship between inequality, exclusion
and violence is increasingly acknowledged. Its impact on
human rights, governance and democratic political
procedures is now a global concern.[35] At the same time, there
is an alarming trend where safety and security are decreas-
ingly seen as a public responsibility and increasingly treated
as a private good, available to those with the ability to pay,
protecting those that are better off, while leaving the poor
more vulnerable and especially putting women at greater
risk. This worrisome trend is closely linked to the quartering
of cities, discussed in Chapter 2.

## ● Definitional issues

References to 'violent crime', 'criminal conflict', 'conflictual
violence' and 'violent conflict' illustrate how terms such as
violence, crime and conflict frequently are categorized
synonymously, despite important distinctions between
them.[36] Both violence and conflict are concerned with
power. The key difference refers to the fact that conflict –
power struggles over competing goals for scarce resources
between two or more parties[37] – does not necessarily inflict
physical or mental harm on others, while violence by its
very nature does.

> Conflict can be peacefully resolved through negotia-
> tion without recourse to force but becomes violent
> when it includes fighting and killing

Conflict can be peacefully resolved through negotiation
without recourse to force but becomes violent when it

includes fighting and killing. Violence by its very nature
includes 'an uninvited but intentional or half-intentional
act of physical violation'.[38] Finally, crime is an act (usually a
grave offence) punishable by law; that is, the breach of a
legal prohibition. Perceptions as to which crimes are violent,
or which types of violence are unlawful differ widely, determined less by objective indicators of degree of damage or
injury than by cultural values and power relations.

Violence can refer to the *nature of a violent act*[39]
(including the distinction between direct, indirect, repressive and alienating violence), or to the *organizational level*
(such as the distinction between organized [politically
motivated, organized in groups] and disorganized violence
[individual crime, delinquency, vandalism]).[40] Equally it can
be defined *by uneven distribution of power and resources in
society*, as in the concept of personal and 'structural
violence',[41] or in terms of *unequal access to justice* as in the
concept of 'institutional violence' as perpetrated by police
and other state institutions.[42] Given definitional complexi-
ties such as these, frequently it is virtually impossible to
distinguish the point at which violence ends and conflict
begins.[43]

## ● Measurements

The measurement of violence is fraught with difficulties.
The most common measures are based on mortality rates.
However, statistics are notoriously unreliable as they can
only reveal those cases reported, and are difficult to inter-
pret.[44] In addition, national and regional differences in data
collection methods recall periods and cultural definitions of
crime and violence make valid cross-country comparisons
hard to achieve, and only possible through global data sets
such as the International Crime Victimization Survey.
Other data sources commonly used to measure crime and
violence levels include victimization studies, official crime
statistics, homicide/ intentional injury statistics from
hospitals and undertakers, offender surveys and death
certificates.[45] More recently, qualitative participatory urban
appraisal techniques have been used for the study of
community perceptions of violence.[46]

## Categories of urban violence

The range of types of urban violence is both highly complex
and context-specific. In a participatory study in urban
Jamaica, local residents listed up to 19 types of violence in
one community including political, gang, economic, interpersonal and domestic disputes; in a similar study in
Guatemala, some 60 types of violence were identified.[47]
Therefore, it is important to clarify the complexity of
violence without oversimplifying the concept. Any categorization is, by its very nature, static since in the real world,
violence exists along a continuum with important reinforcing linkages between different types of violence.

Recent research has divided violence into three
categories: *political violence*, *economic violence* and *social violence*,
each identified in terms of the type of motivation that
consciously or unconsciously uses violence to gain or
maintain its power. Table 17.1 summarizes some of the

| Category | Definition | Manifestation |
|---|---|---|
| Political | The commission of violent acts motivated by a desire, conscious or unconscious, to obtain or maintain political power | Guerrilla conflict; paramilitary conflict; political assassinations; armed conflict between political parties |
| Economic | The commission of violent acts motivated by a desire, conscious or unconscious, for economic gain or to obtain or maintain economic power | Street crime; carjacking; robbery/theft; drug trafficking; kidnapping; assaults made during economic crimes |
| Social | The commission of violent acts motivated by a desire, conscious or unconscious, for social gain or to obtain or maintain social power | Interpersonal violence such as spouse and child abuse; sexual assault of women and children; arguments that get out of control |

**Source:** Moser and Shrader, 1999.

**Table 17.1**

**Categories of violence**

common types of violence for each category, in terms that are deliberately broad, and not necessarily mutually exclusive.

This categorization allows for integrated approaches, both conceptual and operational, that recognize the connections between the dynamics of different types of violence, based on the differing motivations of the perpetrators. This assists in explaining why interventions to reduce one type of violence may not yield results for other types of violence. For example, while community-policing programmes have been credited with a 43 per cent decline in New York City's economic crime rates, reports of police brutality in the city have increased by 41 per cent, a social problem.

## Causes of urban violence

Violence is complex not only because of its different categories, but also because of the multitude of causal factors. Empirical evidence shows that women and men, girls and boys, are not all equally violent, that communities vary in their levels of violent conflict, and that violence tolerance levels differ across societies. Circumstances relating to the individual, the family, the community and the broader national context all play a role in violence or victimization.

Despite the wealth of descriptive evidence on violence, theoretical analysis of specific causal factors of violence is both limited and fragmented. Analyses tend to reflect professional disciplines such as economics, biomedical sciences, criminology, epidemiology, psychology and sociology. Frequently they are compartmentalized and tend to perpetuate fragmented understandings of violence. The causes of violence can be identified at four interrelated levels: individual, interpersonal, institutional and structural.[48]

### ● Individual level

These are factors relating to personal history and biophysical make-up. Overcrowded conditions and a lack of privacy prevalent in low-income human settlements contribute to violent behaviour. Children's exposure to violence perpetrated by their parents, particularly gender-based violence, may influence their propensity to commit similar violence. In addition, severe mental ill-health, when aggravated by poor living conditions and lack of support, may increase a person's likelihood of committing violence.[49]

### ● Interpersonal level

> Conflicts between neighbours and communities often revolve around scarce resources. Shared water is one of the biggest causes of violence, and may be exacerbated by privatization. With deregulation, interpersonal violence is also increasingly linked to cut-throat competition in informal sector activities such as market stalls or informal transport

These are factors that involve interactions between individuals, including intimate or acquaintance relationships. In the urban context, this relates mainly to social violence, including high levels of street and bar conflict as a consequence of high levels of substance abuse, both of alcohol and of drugs.[50] In addition, availability of firearms is strongly related to the number of deaths resulting from crime.[51] Of critical importance are conflicts between neighbours and communities in resource scarce situations. In urban slums in cities throughout the world, shared water is one of the biggest causes of violence, and may be exacerbated by privatization.[52] (see Box 10.1). Equally with deregulation, interpersonal violence is increasingly linked to cut-throat competition in informal sector activities such as market stalls or informal transport systems.[53] In El Salvador, after the 1992 Peace Accords, the influx of return migrants from the US exacerbated the activities of US-modelled youth gangs, including drive-by shootings, high casualty gang warfare and daylight armed assaults.[54] Finally, lack of adequate infrastructure in informal settlements exposes people – particularly women – to greater risk when in situations such as accessing sources of fuel, eliminating bodily waste in shared toilets or open space, fetching water and walking in unlit areas.[55]

### ● Institutional level

Crime is also associated with factors at the level of social institutions, both informal and formal, associated with workplaces and local communities. Governance issues relating to local municipalities and their capacity to mediate conflict have critical implications for public security. Democratization processes, for instance, are often linked to shifts from political to other types of violence. In the wake of El Salvador's peace accords and a corresponding reduction in political violence, rates of homicide and economic crime increased. For example, the number of violent deaths in 1994 stood at 9135 and, despite a decline to 8047 in 1996, this still exceeded the annual average of 6000 violent deaths a year during the civil war.[56] In South Africa, police data show that violent crimes have increased substantially during the democratic transition from the apartheid system; especially since 1990 and particularly for murder and rape.[57]

> 'Our safety depends not only on the local police station, but on an environment safe from pollution, nuclear menace, drugs and terrorism' – Kofi Annan, Address to the World Television Forum, New York, 19 November 1998

The strength of the police and the judicial system increases the probability of apprehension and punishment, and reduces the incentive to commit crime. However, if past incidence of crime in society is high, and if policing is inadequate or corrupt (for example, involved in drug trafficking), crime and violence may rise.[58] In some contexts, informal community-level responses may include the creation of neighbourhood patrols to prevent criminal behaviour. More frequently, these become mechanisms of social cleansing that perpetrate 'rough justice' and lynching not only to offenders but also to members of marginal social groups, such as street children or homeless people.[59] Such vigilante behaviour is a negative manifestation of civil society, reinforced by municipal measures that criminalize homelessness.

## ● Structural level

> Inequality is now recognized as an important determinant of violence

This refers to the macro-level political, economic and social structure and policy environment, including cultural norms that permeate society. At the urban level, issues of inequality, poverty and exclusion are critical. While traditionally violence levels have been linked to poverty,[60] it is now recognized that violence is also linked to inequality. A recent global study showed that this is an important determinant of national homicide rates, after controlling for the distribution of education, poverty, ethnic and economic polarization, security services and social capital.[61]

> 'Urban violence is not a spontaneous occurrence, but above all, the product of a society characterized by inequality and social exclusion. Measures that protect urban communities from deprivation, unemployment, homelessness, illiteracy, injustice and social disintegration will ultimately also protect them from crime and violence' – Message of the Executive Director to the World Habitat Day, 5 October 1998

Structural causal factors associated with globalization relate to on-going processes of polarization and differentiation between those who are 'connected', and those who are not, increasingly overlapping with the spatial and economic segregation of disadvantaged groups, neighbourhoods or even cities. Those excluded from 'connectivity' to the dynamic new sectors (through lack of education or infrastructure) are more likely to turn to crime, violence and a drug culture.[62]

Organized criminal groups linked to global networks (ie mafia groups and drug cartels) are increasing, with a tendency to tap into other illegal activities such as extortion rackets, prostitution and trafficking in women, at times abetted by tourism promotion.[63] As drug syndicates become more aggressive, so, too, does violence, augmented by the free trade in firearms.[64] Drug production and drug possession crime rates correlate positively with homicide rates, because the illegal drug trade is usually accompanied by violent disputes for market shares between different

networks of producers and distributors.[65] The availability of firearms, facilitated by worldwide organized crime groups, multiplies the risks of urban violence and represents a fundamental threat to security.

> The availability of firearms, facilitated by worldwide organized crime groups, multiplies the risks of urban violence and represents a fundamental threat to security

## Characteristics of urban violence

Extensive research on urban violence, at both macro- and micro-levels, shows that violence has increased. For instance, a United Nations Interregional Crime and Justice Research Institute (UNICRI) report states that violent crime has increased in the majority of developing cities and accounts for 25–30 per cent of offences worldwide.[66] At the *global level*, crime and violence is generally much higher in Africa and Latin America than Asia. A UNICRI data set of 18 developing country cities[67] shows that Asia consistently ranks the lowest for all types of crime, while Africa and Latin America share first place for all types of crime.[68] Drawing upon World Health Organization data the report describes regional homicide rates (not based on exclusively urban data) across the world, and notes that in 1990 sub-Saharan Africa had a median homicide rate of 40 per 100,000 population, compared with 23 per 100,000 in Latin America.[69] Central and Eastern Europe and former Soviet bloc nations are substantially lower than this at approximately 9 per 100,000.

At the *country level*, the UNICRI 18 developing country cities survey (1998) shows that assault with force was highest in Zimbabwe and South Africa (around 6 per cent), followed by Botswana, Colombia, Bolivia and Argentina, with rates of approximately 3 per cent. The highest robbery rates (more than 10 per cent) were observed in Brazil and Colombia, followed by all the other Latin American countries and Tunisia with rates around 6 per cent. Again, the pattern remains the same whereby Asian countries score relatively low and African and Latin American countries compete for highest crime levels.

At the *regional level* urban violence measurements to date have focused principally on Latin America. The overall picture shows that homicide rates are not significantly related to city size, but crime in general is, as measured by victimization. A household living in a city of more than 1 million inhabitants is almost twice as likely to be victimized as a household living in a city of less than 20,000 inhabitants. The probabilities of victimization do not change much once the 1 million threshold is surpassed.[70] UNWCS data (1970–1994) indicate that urbanization level is not significantly associated with the homicide rate.[71] They do find a relation with the robbery rate, however, 'confirming the view that this type of property crime is more an urban phenomenon than homicide'. A study of 17 Latin American countries indicates that the probability of *victimization* increases with socio-economic status and *city size*; the probability of being a victim of crime is substantially higher in larger cities.[72] According to this study, this relates to the fact that larger cities have lower probabilities of arrests. Consequently, impunity and good governance emerge as critical issues.

*Intra-urban* economic differences and associated levels of violence have long existed in cities, particularly those with colonial or post-colonial origins[73] Upper income areas are well maintained and serviced with housing interspersed with public and private amenities like parks and shops. In contrast, poor marginal, informal settlements, far from major centres of employment on the periphery of cities, are marked by squalor and poverty, overcrowded, underserviced, lacking formal retail services and community and recreational facilities, particularly open space.[74] Violence and crime are widespread in these areas.

Turning to perpetrators and victims, global evidence shows that young men are the main perpetrators and victims of political and economic violence, and that men are the perpetrators and women and children the victims of social violence particularly rape and sexual abuse. Race is also a critical variable. In the US, black men are more likely to die of homicide than of any other cause, and male life expectancy in the Bronx, New York, is 30 years;[75] far lower than low-income countries such as Bangladesh.

## Costs and consequences of violence in urban areas

The economic and social costs of violence have been well documented. The direct costs and associated losses due to deaths, disabilities and 'transferrals' resulting from property crimes can be measured as percentages of GNP or GDP. In Mexico City, for example, the 1995 costs from violence were calculated as equivalent to US$2975 million dollars, worth 1.1 per cent of GDP or 4.2 per cent of the city's GDP in that year.[76] In Colombia, expenditures on protection and the associated direct and indirect costs arising from crime and violence might be as high as 13 per cent of GDP.[77] Similarly, the net accumulation of human capital in Latin America and the Caribbean had been cut in half because of the increase in crime and violence over the last 15 years.[78]

Despite decades of research, these remain difficult to measure. Expenditure assessments of the police, the judiciary, the penal system and even the armed forces are constrained by serious problems of access to information. Therefore, assessments of the impacts of violence on a city's capital and associated assets would give a better understanding of the true price of violence. In this connection, it is useful to distinguish between four types of capital: physical, human, social and natural (Box 17.10).[79] In each case, violence is erosive.

### ● The erosion of physical capital

Economic costs of violence are frequently associated with violent attacks on infrastructure such as electrical installations, roads and airports. However, a number of important sectors in the urban economy can be affected, directly or indirectly, by violence. For instance, the banking and taxation sectors can become linked to drug trafficking. Drug syndicates generate enormous amounts of cash that, to be useful, must pass through legitimate international banking or commercial channels; something that has been facilitated by current globalization processes. Where police and judicial institutions are weak, the increasing privatization of security is a mounting economic and social problem. In many developing countries, there are two to three times as many private guards as policemen. It is estimated that 10 per cent of Brazilian GNP is spent on private security including insurance, security gadgets, armoured cars and private guards.[80]

### ● The erosion of human capital

Violence reduces access to, and the quality of, education and health services. When teachers or health workers are threatened, attacked or even killed, schools and health posts can be abandoned. School dropout rates may increase because of neighbourhood violence, which can result from family conflicts, scandals, gang presence, drug use and prostitution. Dropout rates are also associated with domestic violence, and alcohol or drug use within the family. Night school dropout rates are increased by fear of street or public transport crime. Finally, violence creates an additional burden for the health sector, when trauma care consumes a significant portion of health resources.

### ● The erosion of natural capital

Scarcity of natural capital such as land and water can cause

xtreme levels of conflict between neighbours and commu-
ities alike. When displaced populations fleeing violence
low into urban areas, this can seriously exacerbate such
nvironmental problems as solid waste disposal and water
ontamination. Inappropriate land use and land degradation
sually become more severe when rural populations are
orcibly evicted or flee to escape violence. With the growing
ntensity of civil wars and cross-border disputes, the erosion
f natural capital in urban areas is largely invisible.

## The erosion of social capital

ocial capital is important because of its recognized contri-
ution to sustainable economic development; the size and
ensity of social networks and institutions and the nature
f interpersonal interactions significantly affect
evelopment processes.[81] Violence erodes social capital
when it reduces trust and cooperation within formal and
nformal social organizations that are critical for a society
o function.[82]

*ocial capital in formal institutions.* In contexts with human
rights violations and high impunity rates, violence often
rodes faith in the relevance and governability of formal
ocial institutions. When judicial, educational, health,
media and security institutions are no longer able to
function appropriately and transparently, the institution of
democracy itself is challenged. Violence-linked industries
ssociated with drugs, diamonds or other natural resources
can erode the state by corrupting institutions and dividing
the population. For instance, drug traffickers' systematic
threats and attacks against the communications media
effectively suppress 'the voice' of civil society institutions
to participate effectively and peacefully in political
decisions at community and national levels.

*Social capital in informal community-level institutions.* The
capacity for community-level organizations to function
depends on levels of cohesion and the ability to meet
locally; which hinges on personal safety issues. Sustained
violence often systematically creates fear and reduces trust
between neighbours and communities. Fear of crime is
higher where contact crimes are higher.[83] The response,
particularly for women, is frequently to avoid certain places
after dark. This restriction breaks community cohesion.
Fear increases urban fragmentation, resulting in a new
urban landscape made up essentially of 'fortified fragments'
from which the poor and marginalized are excluded[84] (see
Chapter 2).

Violence also contributes to the creation of 'perverse'
social capital.[85] A primary example of perverse social capital
is gang involvement, in which young people, bereft of strong
family and community support, form mutually reinforcing
groups. In many poor neighbourhoods, gangs form the main
context of socialization for children, who join as young as
age 12 or 13. Often gangs are at war with rival groups
involved in robbery, theft, drug distribution or consumption
and assaults. In some communities gangs protect their neighbours, committing crimes elsewhere; in others they prey on
their neighbours, creating a climate of fear.[86]

*Social capital in household relations.* Violence erodes
household relations when it reduces the capacity of households to effectively function as a unit. High levels of stress
in conflict zones, for instance, where many men join illegal
guerrilla or paramilitary groups, can seriously disrupt family
life. Many women identify a direct link between male
unemployment, alcohol abuse and increased domestic
violence. This may result in an increase in women-headed
households, which reduces violence but also household
assets.

## Interventions to reduce urban economic and social violence: 'good practice' examples

In recent decades, extensive and highly innovative interventions have been implemented to address and reduce
violence. However, like much of the analysis of violence
itself, interventions to reduce violence have usually been
dominated by a particular policy approach and its associ-

---

**Box 17.11 Shifts in policy approaches for violence reduction**

**Control of violence**
Most commonly associated with *criminal justice*, one of the most widely established approaches,
this focuses on deterrence and control of violence through higher rates of arrest, conviction
and punishment, facilitated by judicial, police and penal reform. More successful in reducing
economic crime than in reducing social and political violence, this top-down approach is
popular among politicians seeking short-term solutions to the symptoms of violence.

**Prevention of violence**
Linked to the well-established *public health* approach, it focuses on economic and social
violence at individual and interpersonal levels. This approach aims to prevent violence by
reducing individual risk factors. It draws on epidemiological surveillance – especially homicide
rates – and identification of risk factors to develop strategies for modifying individual behaviour, the social and physical environment, or both.

**Negotiation of peaceful conflict resolution**
This approach aims to rebuild the fabric of societies through the *resolution of conflicts*.
Influenced by international actors such as the United Nations, it addresses political and, to a
lesser extent, social violence through non-violent negotiation among conflicting parties, often
relying on third-party mediation.

**Legal enforcement of human rights**
A 'rights-based approach' to violence reduction, focuses on the role of the state in *protecting
citizens' rights* to be free from the threat or victimization of violence. Drawing on the documentation of abuse in relation to international human rights conventions, this approach addresses
political and social violence, mainly at the individual and structural levels. While early users of
this perspective were targeted towards governments that violated human rights, more recent
formulations have focused on other social actors denying or abusing rights.

**Rebuild social capital**
This is a new approach, still being formulated. It focuses on rebuilding *social capital* in informal
and formal institutions such as families, community organizations and the judiciary. Using
bottom-up, participatory processes, it seeks to create trust by building on community identification of needs, and focuses on the strengths and assets of communities affected by violence,
providing the potential for community needs to be scaled up to public sector interventions.

**Source:** Developed from Moser and Shrader, 1999.

Colombia's *Casa de Justicia* programme works within the criminal justice system to achieve binding resolutions, a first step in moving the judicial system towards a system that promotes conciliation rather than winners and losers. An additional objective of the *Casas de Justicia* is to facilitate access to the justice system in poverty-stricken communities with very high rates of violence.

A typical *Casa de Justicia* is the one created in 1994 in Bogotá's Ciudad Bolivar lower-income *barrio*. With support from USAID, the Foundation for Superior Education and the Ministry of Justice, the *Casa* includes a lawyer for consultations, a centre for conciliation, a family commissary, a police inspector, a forensic doctor, a defender of human rights and a prosecutor (attorney general). Various manuals on 'conciliation techniques' have been developed to support the programme. Based on an initial follow-up survey of cases attended, over 60 per cent of those who had used these services reported being satisfied with the result.

**Source:** Moser et al, 2000, p 25.

ated professional disciplines (such as criminology or epidemiology). Thus interventions have tended to prioritize a particular type of violence and focus on a particular level of causality and target group. Even when initiatives do address more than one type of violence or target multiple levels of causality, a lack of impact evaluation or cost-benefit analysis often severely hinders identification of 'best practices', reducing the chances of replicating successful interventions.

To provide an integrated framework for intervention, it is important to classify dominant violence reduction policy approaches in terms of both the categories of violence they address and the causal factors on which they focus. In the urban context there has been a broad shift from approaches that focus on the *control* of violence, to those that concentrate on *prevention*, to more recent perspectives that aim to *rebuild social capital*. Two further approaches, more common nationally but with important urban focuses, are *peaceful conflict resolution through negotiation and legal enforcement of human rights*. These policy

*El Programmea Desarollo, Seguridad y Paz* (DESEPAZ) was established by the Mayor's Office of Cali in 1992 to address the high rates of crime and violence in the city. Grounded in a public health approach, it was based on an epidemiological analysis of violence – primarily homicide rates – to identify specific risk factors for urban violence as well as community involvement in combating crime and violence. DESEPAZ and the Colombian Legal Medicine and Forensic Science Institute identified several key risk factors for homicide in Cali, which revolved around alcohol use, gun ownership and leisure time. They therefore restricted alcohol sales in public areas and initiated a disarmament programme, which appears to have had a beneficial effect on homicide reduction.

A key principle of DESEPAZ is that the prevention of crime and violence requires a commitment from all citizens. *Consejos Municipales de Seguridad* (Municipal Security Councils) were created in order to educate government officials; the mayor held weekly meetings with community leaders. Open to the public, participants suggest and agree on concrete solutions. This community-based approach has led to the creation of law enforcement, public education and social development programmes.

**Sources:** Ayres, 1998; Guerrero, 1998; Vanderschuren, 1996, cited in Moser et al, 2000.

approaches are 'ideal types' (see Box 17.11). More than one approach can be used simultaneously, and often well-established approaches are combined with more innovative ones.

> There has been a broad shift from approaches that focus on the control of violence, to those that concentrate on prevention and rebuilding social capital. Increasingly important as well, are peaceful conflict resolution through negotiation and legal enforcement of human rights

### ● Criminal justice approach

Historically, efforts to reduce violence have focused primarily on a *criminal justice* approach. In many developing countries, criminal justice systems are characterized by inefficiency, delays, high costs, lack of transparency, widespread corruption and political interference.[87] These factors prevent the justice system from constituting an effective deterrent and punishment body, and may result in impunity and citizens' lack of trust in the state. Judicial reform often includes harsher sentencing for felons, a shift to accusatory evidentiary procedures, and training for prosecutors and police. Other initiatives have addressed widespread corruption and impunity, and the training of judges. 'Community policing' – community-based surveillance strategies implemented by police departments – is designed to increase patrols in high crime areas and to train community leaders to monitor the number of crimes and victims per neighbourhood.

One of the biggest problems that poor urban populations experience is their lack of access to the judicial system. A recent, highly innovative intervention to address this issue in Colombia is the *Casas de Justicia* (Houses of Justice) programme (Box 17.12). This is a particularly valuable approach, as it provides different forms of conflict resolution. Rather than simply employing traditional judicial procedures, these are designed to improve poor communities' access to conciliation, legal and human rights services. Other innovations have introduced various types of conflict transformation tools and developed manuals based on 'Conciliation Techniques'. Educating low-income groups on human rights issues is also integral to the programme.

### ● Public health approach

The public health approach has also been important in relation to the reduction of both *economic* and *social violence*. Particularly useful from this perspective has been the use of the media, especially through campaigns to limit violence on television, and to promote public awareness of the causes of violence. Other significant public health initiatives include controlling situational precipitators such as drugs, alcohol and firearms. Many countries have made attempts to restrict the carrying of weapons, as well as the sale of alcohol in an attempt to reduce crime rates. Again in Colombia, one of the most important showcase public health interventions is DESEPAZ (*Programa Desarrollo, Salud y Paz*) in Cali (Box 17.13). It employs public health tools such as epidemiological surveillance, environmental maniplation and behavioural modification to achieve measurable reductions in homicide. It identifies risk factors, such as alcohol use and gun ownership, and then attempts to limit exposure to these risks. The DESEPAZ programme is notable in that it focuses on economic violence using a number of approaches to the problem. For instance, its emphasis on community-level solutions indicates that rebuilding community and social institutions is also important. In addition, some of its interventions have direct and indirect implications for social violence reduction.

## Conflict transformation approach

Interventions that draw on conflict transformation mechanisms such as mediation, arbitration and non-violent conflict resolution, have been developed only quite recently. The SERVOL programme in Trinidad and Tobago, for example, focuses on violence prevention by providing 'life skills' that include mediation and conflict resolution for youths (see Box 17.14). Life skills programmes are designed to overcome a culture of failure felt by many youths –which can lead to their joining gangs – and include elements of self-awareness and self-knowledge, anger management, conflict resolution, family planning and parenting skills.

## Human rights approach

A human rights approach is gaining greater recognition in terms of social violence, especially in relation to recent United Nations rights. These relate to such issues as children's rights and gender-based violence and are based on the Convention to Eradicate, Sanction and Prevent All Forms of Violence Against Women and the Declaration of the Rights of the Child. However, laws in many countries make it impossible to prosecute violence against women, especially violence perpetrated by an intimate partner. In Pakistan, for instance, four male Muslim witnesses must testify before a man can be convicted and subjected to the *hadd* punishment (the most severe) for rape.[88] The Law of Evidence considers women 'incompetent' as witnesses in cases of rape and grants their testimony only the status of corroborative evidence.[89]

Despite such constraints, a growing number of countries have passed laws or reformed their penal codes to criminalize domestic violence – including Malaysia, Puerto Rica and Barbados[90] – with women's NGOs adopting a rights-based approach to try to effect their enforcement. One of the best known urban initiatives has been the creation of women-only police stations that has greatly facilitated the reporting of abuse, although the tremendous demand by women for their services has meant this important innovation has had its problems (see Box 17.15).

## Social capital approach

Interventions aimed at building social capital often focus on youth. In many cities, youth clubs provide alternative recreational opportunities while building trust and cohesion. Such projects generally provide adolescents with a meeting place free from alcohol and drugs, where they are encouraged to engage in activities such as sports or music along

---

**Box 17.14 The SERVOL programme in Trinidad and Tobago**

SERVOL is an NGO that works in poor urban neighbourhoods, particularly with children who are not reached by the school system, aged 0–5 and 16–19. They run an early childhood intervention programme, a parent outreach programme and an adolescent development programme; all are community-based programmes. Father Pantin, the director, describes a culture of very high levels of psychological battering and physical abuse in families (including sexual abuse) that result in youth with low self-esteem who are 'conditioned to failure'. The adolescent development programme is an intense, full-time, three-and-a-half-month programme that teaches 'life skills' designed to overcome low self-esteem. The programme consists of courses in self-awareness and self-knowledge, anger management, nutrition, personal hygiene, parenting skills, family planning and public speaking, among others. After successful completion the students continue on a one-year to two-year skills training and apprenticeship programme in professional trades such as mechanics and nursing. Most graduates find a job in their field after completing the total programme.

SERVOL is an interesting example of community-based interventions directed at helping at-risk youth and preventing violence at the individual, family and community levels. Its success has led to its expansion to work with the Ministries of Social Development and Education.

**Source:** Moser and van Bronkhorst, 1999.

---

with making friendships and contacts. For many children and youth living in marginalized neighbourhoods – where the role models and heroes are gang members – joining a gang often seems to be the only way to achieve some status in the community and gain self-esteem. Successful programmes provide an alternative path.

An innovative example from Brazil, for instance, describes how a theatre group can give children an opportunity to take on responsibility and become 'someone' in an alternative way, while gaining important life skills (Box 17.16). Other examples of programmes that offer alternatives to gang and delinquent life and help to build self-esteem are based on cultural activities – on the rediscovery of black culture, for example, as in Olodum in Salvador – or on joint efforts to improve the community.

## Towards integrated approaches to urban violence reduction

Given the varied emphases and levels of interventions of different policy approaches, a more integrated approach to

---

**Box 17.15 Innovative government solutions to gender-based domestic violence: women-only police stations**

In South America the innovation of women-only police stations has spread from Brazil to Colombia, Uruguay, Peru, Costa Rica and Argentina. Data from Brazil show that this has greatly facilitated the reporting of abuse. In São Paulo reported cases went from 67 in 1985 (before they were opened) to 841 in 1990. This city has 96 of the country's 125 women's police stations.

While an important innovation, they have also had problems. May stations have been overrun by women seeking assistance that the stations do not provide, such as counselling and legal advice, while the female police officers assigned to the stations become easily demoralized because their male peers do not consider their job 'real police work'.

**Source:** Heise, 1994, pp 32–33.

**Box 17.16 Nos do Morro theatre group, Rio de Janeiro**

*Nos do Morro* (Us up the Hill) is a small community theatre group in Vidigal, one of the most violent *favelas* in Rio de Janeiro. Founded in 1986 by Guti Fraga, it has about 120 members (adults and children). The group has a small theatre and facilities in a school in Vidigal. They work as a collective with everyone expected to help with all the different tasks. This has inadvertently led to a change in gender roles and perceptions as boys become accustomed to doing work such as cleaning. The group has been very successful, and some of its members have gone on to work in cinema and television. They also have links with the Royal Shakespeare Company in London, members of which came to Vidigal to give workshops.

The plays are rotated between Brazilian classics and their own productions. The topics that surface most often during improvization and in the plays are school, sex, pregnancy, single parenthood and domestic violence. The subjects of violence and drugs and trafficking often come up in workshops but not in the official plays, as part of the gang 'code of conduct'.

The principal qualities of the project appear to be the way in which it provides an alternative path to gangs to build self-esteem and a sense of responsibility within the local community. As Guti Fraga says, by joining the group youth take a position. This position complicates their life; in their relationships with parents, siblings and peers they defy gender stereotypes. This transformation results in the acquisition of life skills that go far beyond those skills directly related to the theatre.

**Source:** Moser and van Bronkhorst, 1999, p 13.

intervention needs to be developed. This will allow policy makers to shift from menu-like checklists of single-sector interventions towards an interdisciplinary approach that

recognizes a spectrum of violence and addresses simultaneously the reduction of different types of violence. It will facilitate synergies between interventions at different levels. Such an integrated framework coordinates interventions that prevent and reduce violence with interventions that rebuild social capital.

> We need integrated frameworks to coordinate interventions that prevent and reduce violence with efforts that rebuild social capital

Since the causes and manifestations of violence are context specific, the particular details of integrated intervention frameworks need to be tailor-made to the requirements of different situations. Ultimately, in many cities, one of the biggest problems is not the multitude of interventions, but the lack of a coordinated approach to violence reduction. The impact of impressive menus of initiatives – implemented by government, the private sector and NGOs – is often limited by fragmented approaches to violence reduction with single-focused independent programmes. One of the most important priorities is the development of a cohesive policy that integrates and combines different objectives and instruments for reducing violence, develops monitoring indicators and undertakes rigorous evaluations.

# Notes

1. World Bank, March 2000 *Cities in Transition: A Strategic View of Urban and Local Government Issues.*

2. The following section is condensed from Taylor, 1999.

3. See for example: Asian Development Bank, Urban Sector Strategy, July 1999; World Bank, March 2000 Cities in Transition - A Strategic View of Urban and Local Government Issues. See also Chapter 14.

4. For a range of city-specific experiences along these lines see Special Theme Issues of *Environment and Urbanization* (1995; 2000).

5. See O'Rourke, 1999, cited in Evans, 2000.

6. See, for example, Perrons, 2000, (see Background Papers) and Chang, 2000.

7. See Chapter 1.

8. This section is drawn from 'Newly emerging forms of governance in an era of globalization', a background paper prepared by Susan Clarke, University of Colorado.

9. Moore and Putzel, 1999.

10. Clarke and Gaile, 1998.

11. Reich, 1991.

12. For example, McGregor, 1994; Hornbeck and Salamon, 1991.

13. In French: Intégration Globale par le LOgement et L'emplOi, see www.igloo-europe.org

14. www.worldbank.org/poverty/voices/listen-findings.htm.

15. See, for example, Rogoff, 1999.

16. An unintended side-effect of tenure regularization may be that land and housing will be appraised, with property taxes producing a hardship or the sale of property to generate one-time income during a crisis time, both of which cause displacement of poor households. See also Box 17.8.

17. Vanderschueren et al, 1996.

18. This section draws on a summary of the Urban Management Programme's Working Paper No 7, *A Practical Approach to Dealing with Municipal Malfeasance* by R Klitgaard, R MacLean-Abaroa and H Lindsey Parris (May 1996), jointly published by UNDP, UNCHS (Habitat) and the World Bank, prepared by Jyri Juslen, [Associate Expert with the Urban Management Programme (UMP) at UNCHS (Habitat)]; and material adapted from an article by Michael Lippe published in *Habitat Debate* 4(1). Michael Lippe is Urban Coordinator at Transparency International, an

international nonprofit organization based in Berlin, Germany, which focuses on corruption.

19. This section draws from David Hall 'Contracts, concessions and corruption in the water sector'. *Habitat Debate* **6**(3). That article is based on a paper, 'Privatization, multinationals and corruption', published in *Development in Practice* **9**(5), November 1999, available on the PSIRU website: www.psiru.org with permission of the publishers. This site contains regularly updated news on all aspects of privatization in public services, including corruption. David Hall is Director of the Public Services International Research Unit (PSIRU), based at the University of Greenwich in London, UK.

20. See Barlow, 1999. Chapter 10 offers further discussion of privatization of water provision.

21. 'Bribes', transmitted by BBC Radio 4 on 28 April 1996.

22. The French water system is critically appraised in a report by France's state auditor, the Cour des Comptes: La Gestion des Services Publics Locaux d'Eau et Assainissement (Paris, January 1997). This is available at www.ccomptes.fr/Cour-des-

comptes/publications/rapports/eau/cdc72.htm.

23. Reuters, 16 November 1995.

24. *Financial Times*, 5 June 2000. The trial began in Lesotho on 5 June 2000 and has yet to conclude. The World Bank, the European Union and the South African government have all offered assistance to the Lesotho government for what is expected to be a very complex and costly trial.

25. For the World Bank's anti-corruption web site, see www1.worldbank.org/publicsector/anticorrupt/.

26. *The Times* of India, 28 April 2000.

27. The Index does not name the private companies and multinationals involved in corrupt deals. For more information, see its multilingual web site, www.transparency.de/.

28. For more information, see www.oecd.org/daf/nocorruption-web/.

29. See *The Hindu*, 24 May 1999.

30. Drawn from Jenkins, 2000 (see Background Papers). Additional source information can be found in Jenkins and Goetz, 1999a; 1999b; Jenkins, 2000.

31. This section draws from a background paper by Caroline

Moser that is a highly abridged, and considerably adapted version of a Research Paper written for the National Academy of Science Panel on Urban Population Demographics (see Moser and Grant, 2000). The framework was developed by Caroline Moser when task manager of the Urban Peace Programme in the World Bank. For an earlier version see Moser and Shrader, 1999; for a gendered version, see Moser, 2000.

42 Ayres, 1998.

43 Fajnzylber et al, 1998; Heise et al, 1994.

44 Castells, 1998.

45 Fajnzylber et al, 1998; Moser and McIlwaine, 2000a.

46 As defined by the *Oxford English Dictionary*, for instance, 'Violence is (i) the quality of being violent; violent conduct or treatment, outrage, crying; (ii) by law, violence is the unlawful use of physical force; or intimidation by the use of this'. In contrast, '*conflict* is (i) a state of opposition or hostilities; fight or struggle; the clashing of opposed principles; (ii) the opposition of incompatible wishes or needs in a person; an instance of this or the distress resulting from this'.

37 Soley, 1996.

38 Keane, 1996. A recent US National Academy of Sciences Research Panel defines violence as 'behaviours by individuals that intentionally threaten, attempt or inflict physical harm on others' stating that death is the basis for defining the most serious crime: murder. They distinguish between *individual* behaviour causing fatal or non-fatal violent crimes, and *collective* violence identified as wars, state violence, riots and some activities of organized crime (Reiss and Roth, 1993, p 2).

39 Salmi, 1993.

40 Pecaut, 1997.

41 Galtung, 1985.

42 Peneiro, 1993.

43 McIlwaine, 1999.

44 Underreporting is particularly

prevalent in crimes such as sexual assault. The UNICRI (1998) report, for instance, shows that Bolivia, Brazil, Colombia and Costa Rica had the lowest average reporting rates for sexual incidents.

45 Glaeser, 1999.

46 Moser and McIlwaine, 1999.

47 Moser and Holland, 1997; Moser and McIlwaine, 2000b.

48 Since violence is frequently the result of a combination of factors, it may occur simultaneously at several levels; for example, factors at the structural level may also cause violence at the interpersonal level.

49 Hiday, 1995.

50 In the Manila metropolitan area, for instance, six out of ten women were widowed over a ten-year period as a consequence of their husband's involvement in violent bar fights (Moser, 1998). For a detailed description of the impact of alcohol on social violence in urban Guatemala, see Moser and McIlwaine, 2000b.

51 PAHO, 1998b.

52 For instance this is widespread in the 'yards' of urban Jamaica (Moser and Holland, 1997) and the urban settlements in Guatemala (Moser and McIlwaine, 2000b).

53 Anecdotal evidence from Cape Town describes the violent competition in the taxi car business between two ethnic groups: the Coloured population who control the business and the Black population attempting to enter the sector.

54 Rogers, 1999.

55 Shaw and Louw, 1998.

56 Pearce, 1998.

57 Louw, 1997. 'Since the election of Nelson Mandela's government in April 1994, political crime has fallen sharply. In its place has come an upsurge of common-or-garden criminal violence. At 110 per 100,000, Johannesburg (now including Soweto) has a higher murder rate even than Washington, DC' (*Economist*, 1995, 28).

58 Fajnzylber et al, 1998.

59 Paes Manso, 2000.

60 Rosenburg, 1999.

61 Lederman and Loayza, 1999.

62 Castells, 1998:144.

63 See Taylor and Jamieson, 1999; Wilson, 1997a; b; Barry, 1997, for recent discussions of this growing problem.

64 Vanderschueren, 1996.

65 Fajnzylber et al, 2000, p 24.

66 UNICRI, 1995.

67 UNICRI data set on crime in 18 developing country cities collected through the International Crime Victimization Survey (ICVS) constitutes the most detailed global data set on urban violence available. Crime was measured and categorized into five types: vehicle-related crime, break and enter crime, victimization experienced by the respondent personally (including robbery, theft of personal property, assault/ threat and sexual incidents), consumer fraud and bribery/ corruption (UNICRI, 1998). Data were collected in the largest city in each of the selected countries. Although it is not representative of the urban population in each country, it provides a starting point for regional comparisons of urban crime (bearing in mind issues of under reporting, etc).

68 UNICRI, 1998. When the 'contact crime' rate is analysed separately (broken down into incidents involving violence), Latin American cities outstrip African and Asian cities for sexual assault, with a rate of 5 per cent (compared with 2.4 per cent in the African cities and 1.6 per cent in the Asian cities). For assault with force, African cities show a rate of 3.1 per cent compared with 2.7 per cent in Latin America and 0.8 per cent in Asia; and for robbery, cities in Latin America have a rate of 8.1 per cent compared with 4.2 per cent in Africa and 1.4 per cent in Asia.

69 Gartner, 2000; However, Ayres, 1998 notes that Latin America

and the Caribbean has a regional homicide rate of approximately '20 per 100,000 inhabitants, which makes Latin America and the Caribbean the most violent region in the world'. It is not clear which data set Ayres is using, but these conflicting viewpoints reflect the lack of clarity surrounding the issue of homicide rates and the inadequacy of reliable data sources.

70 Gaviria and Pagés, 2000: 15.

71 Fajnzylber et al, 2000.

72 Gaviria and Pages, 2000.

73 Peneiro, 1998; Soares et al, 1998.

74 Stren, 1999.

75 Novello, 1991.

76 Inter-American Development Bank calculations cited in Mexican Health Foundation, 1999.

77 Moser, 1996, cited in Ayres, 1998.

78 Londoño, 1996.

79 This draws on recent work on sustainable economic, environmental, and social development (Serageldin and Steer, 1994; Serageldin, 1996) as well as on the asset vulnerability framework (Moser, 1996; 1998).

80 Ayres, 1998.

81 Putnam, 1993.

82 Moser, 1998; Moser and Holland, 1997.

83 UNICRI, 1998.

84 Caldeira, 1996a, p 63.

85 A useful distinction can be made between productive and perverse institutions. While productive institutions aim to provide benefits in order to improve the well-being of the community, perverse institutions benefit their members but are usually detrimental to the community or society at large (Rubio, 1997; Moser and McIlwaine, 2000a, p 78).

86 Moser and McIlwaine, 2000b; Rogers, 1999.

87 Ayres, 1998.

88 Human Rights Watch, 1992.

89 Heise et al, 1994.

90 Ibid.

# LIVEABILITY OF CITIES IN A GLOBALIZING WORLD

Forty years ago, Jane Jacobs wrote *The Death and Life of Great American Cities*, a fervent plea to create viable communities through urban planning.[1] Today, it is the death and life of the world's urban poor that are bound up with planning. More than anything else, the promise for improving urban liveability rests on freeing the potential of people living in poverty. Recognition of this important fact not only acknowledges the inability of the public and private sector to end urban poverty, but also welcomes marginalized and disenfranchised population groups as equal members of and participants in the world community, extending to them the full rights and responsibilities of urban citizens.

Against this background, this Epilogue first revisits the question: what is urban liveability? Next, it explores contexts for enhancing liveability and, finally, it highlights strategic directions for making human settlements better places to live.

## Questioning Urban Liveability

> To people living in poverty and squalor, the question of what constitutes urban liveability is simple enough. To them, it is not an abstract notion, but the real struggle for daily survival

Urban researchers have put much effort into the conceptualization of urban liveability. They have attempted to develop sophisticated measurement instruments, including multidimensional scales and weighted indices for use with advanced analytic techniques. Their work has resulted in 'quality of life'[2] classifications and the ranking of cities as places to live or work.[3] Experts continue to debate the pros and cons of these different approaches. There is undeniable merit in efforts to enhance methodological rigour when seeking to obtain valid, reliable and comparable data as a basis for urban planning and management. However, to those living in poverty and squalor, the question of what constitutes urban liveability is not complicated. To them, it is not an abstract notion in need of operationalization, but the real struggle for daily existence. They do not have the luxury of being able to consider methodological options; they toil to meet basic survival needs of food, shelter and safe water. They often lack access to adequate sanitation, health care and education.

One in four of the world's urban population is living below the poverty line. In many cities, confronted with rapid growth, environmental problems and slow pace of economic development, it has not been possible to meet the challenges of generating sufficient employment, providing adequate housing and meeting the basic needs of the citizens. These are real challenges for human settlements development and the world is facing unprecedented further growth of urban population in the developing world.[4]

In recent decades, there has been encouraging progress in improving the living conditions of many people around the world due to the efforts of national and local governments, which have the primary responsibility for the implementation of the Habitat Agenda through laws, policies and programmes.[5]

In many places, there have been impressive steps forward in increasing access to safe water and sanitation services and elementary education.[6] NGOs and community-based organizations have played more visible roles in bringing about these improvements. Progress notwithstanding, this *Global Report on Human Settlements 2001* documents the continuing prevalence of abysmal living conditions in cities where hundreds of people have to share a single public standpipe to obtain water; in cities where each resident has to compete with 100 or more other people for access to a public latrine, which itself is a major health hazard; in cities with governments that are corrupt and unable to deliver basic services to their citizens; in cities with too few jobs that pay a living wage and not enough affordable housing units; and in cities whose residents suffer from environmental contamination and fear for their safety.

From the perspective of these people, who make up a large number of the world's population today, the answer to the question: What are liveable cities? is simple enough. Liveable cities are places where residents can find jobs that pay a living wage. A liveable city provides its citizens with basic services, including safe water, adequate sanitation and transportation. The inhabitants of a liveable city have access to educational opportunities and health care. They are not at risk of forced eviction and enjoy secure tenure in affordable housing. They live in communities that are safe and environments that are clean. Liveable cities are void of discriminatory practices and governed through inclusive local democratic practice.

While it is relatively straightforward to specify the conditions that make cities liveable, it is more challenging to implement the processes that will help bring about

reater liveability. There are different views as to the strate-
ies most likely to be effective. This report has repeatedly
bserved that market considerations dominate current
rocesses of globalization, and it has emphasized the limita-
ions of market mechanisms in improving people's quality
f life. Further, it has made the argument that globalization
s occurring mainly in a top-down manner, driven by the
notivation of transnational corporations to maximize
rofit and accumulate financial wealth.[7]

This report has made the case for alternative goals
or globalization – goals that derive from newly emerging
iormative platforms, as articulated during the United
Nations world conferences of the 1990s.[8] These goals stress
he importance of social justice and environmental sustain-
bility. Attainment of these goals requires support for
globalization-from-below', through broad-based partner-
hips with full participation by civil society, specifically
ncluding women and low-income groups. Forming and
perating such coalitions, in turn, requires deliberate capac-
ty-building strategies.[9]

## Contexts of Urban Liveability

The increasing economic role of cities and towns in a
globalizing world has been well documented. Cities and
owns hold the potential to maximize the benefits and to
ffset the negative consequences of globalization. Well-
nanaged cities can provide an economic environment
capable of generating employment opportunities as well as
ffering a diversity of goods and services.[10]

Globalization has placed cities in a highly competitive
ramework of inter-city linkages and networks. These
globally networked cities act as energy nodes in a field of
global forces. In a volatile world economy, the growing
peed, complexity and precariousness of change in all sectors
eem to demand a parallel concentration in cities that have
he necessary assets to sustain ongoing competitiveness.

For cities to succeed in the competition for global
capital, they must provide a minimum package of enabling
conditions that will serve the forces of globalization. The
package varies from place to place, but includes incentives
such as well-functioning infrastructure and urban services,
a skilled labour force, excellent communications, efficient
transport systems, availability of affordable housing and
access to educational and recreational facilities. As global
forces increasingly mediate the economic base of cities, the
critical nexus between cities and globalization will only
strengthen.

Pro-growth policies are not necessarily pro-poor, as
the recent East Asian crisis has demonstrated. In that
region, the urban poor were worst affected when there was
a sudden decline in economic growth. Technology-driven
options for growth and development, which spur globalization, have a global and local downside: they lead to more
lines of stratification between places, people and groups.
The paradox associated with globalization is that while
cities need to increasingly operate as territorial units if they
are to compete effectively in the global economy, globalization has in fact led to increased fragmentation of cities –
socially, economically and physically.

The social and economic cores and peripheries of the
global information age and the global economy are not only
continents apart but can now also be found geographically
adjacent to each other within individual cities. In many
cities, the disparities between the affluent and the dispossessed are exemplified by the co-existence of thriving
business districts, affluent neighbourhoods and slums or
derelict inner-city quarters.

On the other side of the digital tracks, living conditions are not only worsening, but also becoming unliveable.
In many countries, real incomes have fallen, living costs
have gone up and the number of poor households has
grown. Real estate costs in certain cities have skyrocketed,
pushing middle- and lower-income groups to the fringes of
the city. A growing proportion of urban dwellers faces an
impossible disjunction between the salaries generated by
city labour markets and the housing costs determined by
the urban land market. This has led to the birth of enclaves
of poverty on the urban periphery and in the inner city,
showing a hitherto unseen pattern of spatial segregation.

However, the reality emerging from the world's
slums reveals that while the poor so far may have had little
influence over global economic forces, they are taking an
increasingly active role as agents of their own development.
Where banks do not lend to them, they save and lend to
each other; where no housing is available, they build their
own shelter; where no education is provided, they teach
each other. The poor are also getting more organized.
Federations of slum dwellers in some countries, for
instance, have managed to influence national and international policies by presenting a formidable political force and
by participating in cooperative national frameworks

Notwithstanding the so-called 'hollowing out of the
state', central governments remain important, even essential, actors in the governance of cities. They still hold
crucial powers, not only in terms of financial resources but
also in terms of long-term urban agendas, strategic
planning and sustainable development.

The state has a legitimate intervention role in the
process of decentralization, first, in matters of national
interest and, second, in local matters when they impact on
wider interests or when local actors prove to be incapable
or dysfunctional.

National government must act as a watchdog,
safeguarding the interests of vulnerable sections of society.
The state must also retain a major role in giving coherence to
local actions and mediating between local and international
actors. While national governments must facilitate the
functioning of global markets and forces, they must also take
responsibility for social cohesion, justice, equity and conflict
resolution in cities. In the long run, governments have the
ultimate responsibility of ensuring that globalization and
urbanization are positive forces of development.[11]

New forms of governance are required to manage
and mitigate the risks associated with globalization. The
combined processes of urbanization and globalization have
thrust additional responsibilities on city governments,
which find themselves suddenly having to deal with the
economic development of their local constituents vis-à-vis
the international community, while at the same time

having to shoulder the burden of ensuring social justice and equity within cities.

Local governments have to play a strategic role in facilitating decision-making and mediating the divergent needs of business and organized elements of civil society. Where local government has decentralized powers and where civil society is buoyant and organized, urban development can improve the life of every urban citizen.[12]

Globalization has created an apparent paradox where polity – the condition of civil order – is simultaneously becoming more global and more local. Globalization and localization, or 'glocalization' – the hybrid economic, political and cultural structures and processes associated with the growing interdependence of local and global dimensions – creates the possibility of a new type of grassroots politics that localizes within the network of global cities.

Such developments require empowering local authorities, NGOs and other Habitat Agenda partners, within the legal framework and according to the conditions of each country, to play a more effective role in shelter provision and in sustainable human settlements development. This can be achieved through effective decentralization of responsibilities, policy management, decision-making authority and sufficient resources, including revenue collection authority to local authorities, through participation and local democracy as well as through international cooperation and partnerships. In particular, the effective role of women in decision-making in local authorities should be ensured, through appropriate mechanisms.[13]

## Strategic Directions to Ensure the Liveability of Cities

The liveability of cities depends on a number of factors, one of which is their global competitiveness. Economic globalization has grown through the expansion of markets made possible by deregulatory policies that have lifted trade barriers and restrictions on capital mobility. While seeking to enhance the competitiveness of cities, many national governments have devolved responsibilities that they had traditionally assigned to lower levels of government. The increased competition that characterizes globalization is accompanied by urban fragmentation, producing two conflicting trends. To compete effectively, cities must act as a collective unit; however, growing social exclusion, spatial segregation and economic polarization are divisive and hamper the ability of cities to mobilize resources and govern their development in a sound and sustainable manner.

Given that metropolitan areas are the chief arenas for global competition, it is necessary to strengthen them by giving them greater authority and autonomy in resource mobilization and allocation. However, the enabling role of governments must be broader than facilitating the functioning of markets and should also include responsibility for social cohesion, equity and conflict resolution. Under globalization, urban governance faces new challenges, as well as new opportunities.[14]

Liveability of cities depends on political recognition that globalization necessarily materializes in specific institutional arrangements in specific places, many of which are in cities. Far from exerting a deterministic, homogenizing effect, globalization processes allow for local differentiation. The outcomes of these processes reflect the claims that different interests make on urban places and the power they can wield to advance those claims. These interests include representatives of global capital that use cities as an organizational commodity to maximize profit, but they also include disadvantaged local population groups who need the city as a place to live. Cities are increasingly strategic sites in the realization of these claims.[15]

Liveability of human settlements cannot be enhanced without recognizing the empowering role of infrastructure, micro-finance institutions and community-based organizations that have initiated programmes providing low-income households with access to land and services needed to improve their earnings capacity and living conditions. Urban policies and international development agencies should, as this report points out, be directed to support these initiatives.

Recent experience shows that the shift in responsibility for service provision and management of infrastructure to the local level is not always supported by a commensurate transfer of resources and authority to develop the requisite tax base. The implications have been serious deficiencies, total system collapse and loss of physical assets as a result of overload and insufficient maintenance. The success of decentralization depends greatly on the ability of central government to institute an appropriate regulatory framework for central–local relationships and its willingness to provide localities with assets and intergovernmental transfers rather than budget allocations. Democratic local governance is essential if decentralization of infrastructure management is to be effective.

Liveability of human settlements depends on a properly established and efficiently functioning legal system. Globalization, as the report points out, has played an ambiguous role concerning the right to housing.[16] The number of people living in inadequate shelter, or no shelter at all, appears to have increased as a result of the expansion of market processes associated with contemporary globalization. Such trends could bring considerable damage to cities' liveability if appropriate actions are not taken.

This report highlights that urban liveability depends on the efficacy of measures undertaken to protect the urban population from deprivation, unemployment, homelessness, illiteracy, injustice and social disintegration, as well as protect them from crime and violence. To enhance liveability in the urban context, there are further needs to search for new approaches that not only focus on the control of violence but concentrate on its prevention through peaceful conflict resolution, negotiation and legal enforcement of human rights.

Liveability of human settlements is heavily dependent on the housing situation. The report shows that if housing is inadequate because of dampness, vermin or overcrowded conditions, it undermines people's health and well-being. While a number of achievements are seen in housing policy formulation in many countries, it is neces-

...ry to undertake legislative and administrative reforms to ...pport the efforts of people, individually and collectively, ... produce affordable shelter, adopt proactive planning of ...nd supply, promote the efficient functioning of land ...arkets and administration, eradicate legal and social barri-...s to the equal and equitable access to land and to ensure ...at equal rights of women and men to land and property ...re protected under the law. There is a need to vigorously ...romote affordable shelter and basic services for the ...omeless, preventing forced evictions that are contrary to ...e law and facilitating access of all people to information ...n housing legislation, including any legal rights and to ...emedies where these laws are violated.[17]

Liveability of human settlements can be enhanced ...hrough capacity building that goes beyond the training of ...ndividuals to the strengthening of the institutions and ...rameworks within which they work. Traditional capacity ...uilding is characteristically hierarchical and relies on verti-...ally structured relationships. However, there is increasing ...ecognition of the importance of and potential for fostering ...apacity building through horizontal processes.

The drive for cities' liveability requires cooperation ...etween the public and private sectors. Partnerships are ...ow evolving from single-purpose, project-oriented ad hoc agreements between government and business interests to more institutionalized arrangements concerned with a range of interrelated long-term goals, involving multiple partners that include civil society.

*Cities in a Globalizing World* presents a view of globalization as a process with positive as well as negative implications. Human settlements are not powerless in the face of globalization, but, through good governance and in effective partnerships, can play an important part in mediating and directing its consequences for economic and human development in positive ways. It is necessary to intensify efforts for ensuring transparent, responsible, accountable, just, effective and efficient governance of cities and other human settlements. Good governance at all levels is essential in addressing the challenges of urban poverty and environmental degradation and to harnessing the opportunities offered by globalization. Cities need to improve governance, to plan and act strategically in order to reduce urban poverty and social exclusion and to improve the economic and social status of *all* citizens and protect the environment in a sustainable way.[18] The challenge is to develop and implement policies that support not only the function of cities as engines of economic growth, but also their role as agents of social change.

# Notes

Jacobs, 1961. In a scathing critique of existing urban renewal practices in the US, Jane Jacobs described four 'generators of diversity': mixed land use patterns; aged buildings; population density; and short blocks. Her emphasis on principles of physical planning invited accusations of advocating an approach premised on a naive belief in 'physical determinism' (see, for example, Gans, 1962).

2  See, for example, Grayson and Young, 1994.

3  Fisher, 1999

4  Draft declaration on 'Cities and other human settlements in the new millennium'. HS/C/PC.2/3/Rev.1, paragraph 3.

5  Ibid, paragraph 14.

6  It is significant that many of these improvements are the work of non-governmental and community-based organizations. For documentation of successful efforts, see, for example, the case studies reported in the journal *Environment and Urbanization* and the Best Practices database of UNCHS (Habitat) (www.bestpractices.org). See also data presented in the annual *Human Development Report*

(UNDP 1996a; 1998; 1999).

7  Detailed arguments are given in the Prologue and Chapters 2 and 5.

8  See Chapter 3 for details.

9  Chapter 14 presents detailed analysis of capacity building strategies.

10  Draft declaration on 'Cities and other human settlements in the new millennium' HS/C/PC.2/3/Rev.1, paragraph 12.

11  See Chapter 4 for trend analysis in urban governance.

12  Detailed analysis of decentralization and urban infrastructure management capacity is

presented in Chapter 13.

13  Draft declaration on 'Cities and other human settlements in the new millennium' HS/C/PC.2/3/Rev.1, paragraph 37.

14  Chapter 4 shows both new challenges and new opportunities for urban governance under globalization.

15  See Chapter 5 for additional arguments.

16  See Chapter 16 for details.

17  Draft declaration on 'Cities and other human settlements in the new millennium' HS/C/PC.2/3/Rev.1, paragraph 47.

18  Ibid, paragraph 49.

# REFERENCES

Abdul-Hamid, Y (1999) 'The Women's Savings and Loan Network in Senegal visit the South African uMfelanda Wonye, March 1999'. Enda-Graf, Dakar

Abu-Lughod, J L (1999) *New York, Los Angeles, Chicago: America's Global Cities*. University of Minnesota Press, Minneapolis

Acharya, S (2000) *Innovative Housing Finance for Low-income Groups*. School of Planning, University of Ahmadabad, India

Adams, R (1999) 'Overseas efficiency fails to translate'. *Financial Times* **4**, London

Adeola, F O (2000) 'Cross-National Environmental Injustice and Human Rights Issues: A Review of Evidence in the Developing World'. *American Behavioral Scientist* **43**(4): 686–706

Adusumilli, A (1999) 'Partnership approaches in India'. In G Payne (ed) *Making Common Ground: Public–Private Partnerships in Land for Housing*. Intermediate Technology Publications, London

Agarwal, A, and S Narain (eds) (1997) *Dying Wisdom: Rise, Fall and Potential of India's Traditional Water Harvesting Systems*. CSE, New Delhi

Aghion, P, and S Commander (1999) 'On the Dynamics of Inequality in the Transition'. *Economics of Transition* **7**(2): 275–298

Aghion, P, and J G Williamson (1998) *Growth, Inequality and Globalization: Theory, History and Policy*. Cambridge University Press, Cambridge

Agüero, F, and J Stark (eds) (1998) *Fault Lines of Democracy in Post-Transition Latin America*. North-South Center Press, University of Miami, Miami

Ahmed, K (1994) *Renewable Energy Technologies: A Review of the Status and Costs of Selected Technologies*. World Bank Technical Paper, Washington, DC

Ahmed, Q M (1997) Design of Intergovernmental Fiscal Relations and International Finance Institutions' Allocations for Rural Development. *Technical Consultation on Decentralization*

Alam, M, J Sathaye and D Barnes (1998) 'Urban Household Energy Use in India: Efficiency and Policy Implications'. *Energy Policy* **26**: 885–891

Albee, A, and N Gamage (1996) *Our Money, Our Movement: Building a Poor People's Credit Union*. Intermediate Technology Publications, London

Alexeev, A (1988) 'The effect of housing allocation on social inequality: A Soviet perspective'. *Journal of Comparative Economics* **12**: 228–234

Alexeev, M (1999) 'The Effect of Privatization on Wealth Distribution in Russia'. *Economics of Transition* **7**(2): 449–465

Alfaro, R, R Bradburn and J Briscoe (1998) 'Reforming Public Monopolies: Water Supply'. Chapter 10 in Birdsall, N, C Graham and R H Sabot (eds) *Beyond Trade-Offs: Market Reform and Equitable Growth in Latin America*. Inter-American Development Bank and Brookings Institution Press, Washington, pp 273–304.

Allain, T J, A O Wilson et al (1997) 'Morbidity and Disability in Elderly Zimbabweans'. *Age and Ageing* **26**(2): 115–21

Allen, J, D Massey and M Pryke (eds) (1999) *Unsettling Cities*. Routledge, London

Allport, R J, and J M Thomson (1990) *Study of Mass Rapid Transit in Developing Countries*. Report 188, TRL, Crowthorne, UK

Almeida, C, C Travassos, S Porto et al (2000) 'Health sector reform in Brazil: A case study of inequity'. *International Journal of Health Services* **30**(1): 129–162

Alvarado, O, and V Gouarne (1994) *FINDETER: Financing Municipal Investment in Colombia. Infrastructure Notes No. 7*. The World Bank, Transportation, Water and Urban Development Department, Washington, DC

Ambagtsheer, R (1998) 'The Social Health Atlas of Young South Australians: Monitoring the Spatial Distribution of Health and Welfare Amongst South Australian Children and Youth'. *Ninth National Conference of the Australian Population Association, University of Queensland*, St Lucia, 29 September–2 October 1998

American Automobile Manufacturers Association (1996) *World Motor Vehicle Data*. American Automobile Manufacturers Association, Washington, DC

Amin, J, L Hueston, D Dwyer and A Capon (1998) 'Ross River Virus Infection in the North-West Outskirts of the Sydney Basin'. *Communicable Diseases Intelligence* **22**(6): 101–102. www.health.gov.au/publhlth/cdi/cdi html.htm

Anderson, D (1999) 'Addressing Pollution Problems in Developing Regions'. In *Energy and Development Report 1999*. World Bank, Washington, DC, pp 65–68

Anderson, D, and K Ahmed (1995) *The Case for Solar Energy Investments*. World Bank, Washington, DC

Anderson, L (1988) 'Fire and disease: The development of water supply systems in New England, 1870–1900'. In: J A Tarr and G Dupuy (eds) *Technology and the Rise of the Networked City in Europe and America*. Temple University Press, Philadelphia, pp 137–156

Anderson, M B, and P J Woodrow (1989) *Rising from the Ashes: Development Strategies in Times of Disaster*. Westview Press, Boulder, Co

Anderson, R (1996) 'Homeless violence and the informal rules of street life'. *Journal of Social Distress and the Homeless* **5**(4): 369–380

Anon (2000) 'A slum free India within ten years'. www.globalideas bank.org/wbi/WBI1162.html

Appadurai, A (2000) 'Deep democracy: Urban governmentality and the horizon of politics'. University of Chicago. Unpublished paper. Available at www.dialogue.org.za/sdi/DEEPper cent20DEMOCRACY.html

Archer, P (1999a) 'Partnerships in the UK context'. In G Payne (ed) *Making Common Ground: Public–Private Partnerships in Land for Housing*. Intermediate Technology Publications, London

Archer, P (1999b) 'The potential of land pooling/readjustment to provide land for low-cost housing in developing countries'. In G Payne (ed) *Making Common Ground: Public–Private Partnerships in Land for Housing*. Intermediate Technology Publications, London

Argenti, O (2000) 'Brief 5 – Feeding the cities: Food supply and distribution'. In J L Garrett and M T Ruel (eds) *2020 Focus 3: Achieving Urban Food and Nutrition Security in the Developing World*. August. International Food Policy Research Institute (IFPRI), Washington, DC

Arifeen, S E, and A Q M Mahbub (1993) *A survey of slums in Dhaka metropolitan area – 1991*. UHEP. ICDDR,B, Dhaka

Asian Development Bank. *ADB's Experience and Lessons Learned. Water in the 21st Century: ADB's Evolving Role in the Changing Context*. Asian Development Bank. www.abd.org

Asian Development Bank. *Chengdu Générale Des Eaux-Marunbeni Waterworks Company Limited. PS: PRC 32912–01*. Asian Development Bank. www.abd.org

Asian Development Bank (1997) *Second Water Utilities Data Book Asian and Pacific Region*. A C McIntosh and C E Yñiguez (eds). ADB, Manila

Askvik, S (1999) 'Twinning in Norwegian development assistance: A response to Jones and Blunt'. *Public Administration and Development* **19**: 403–408

Associated Press (2000a) 'Drivers Stage Slow-Drive Protest for Help to Cut Pollution'. *Associated Press*, 7 May

Associated Press (2000b) 'Carbon Emissions Plan Finds Interest'. *Associated Press*, 21 April

Atkinson, A, and J Mickelwright (1992) *Economic Transformation in Eastern Europe and the Distribution of Income*. Cambridge University Press, Cambridge

Atkinson, S, J Songsore et al (1996) *Urban Health Research in Developing Countries: Implications for Policy*. CAB International, Wallingford, UK

Audefroy, J (1995) *15 Alternative Experiences in Drinking Water and Sanitation in Urban Communities: Case Studies Cross Analysis*. Habitat International Coalition, Mexico City

Australia Department of Foreign Affairs and Trade (1999) *Driving Forces on the New Silk Road: The Use of Electronic Commerce by Australian Businesses*. Barton, Australia Department of Foreign Affairs and Trade

Auyero, J (1999) '"This is a lot like the Bronx, isn't it?" Lived experiences of marginality in an Argentine slum'. *International Journal of Urband and Regional Research* **23**(1): 45–

Awasthi, S, and V K Pande (1998) 'Cause-specific mortality in under-fives in the urban slums of Lucknow, North India'. *Journal of Tropical Pediatrics* **44**(6): 358–61

AWWA (American Water Works Association) (1991) 'Discontinuance of Water Service for Nonpayment'. Adopted 1978, revd. 1982, and reaffirmed 1991

Axtmann, R (ed) (1998) *Globalization and Europe: Theoretical and Empirical Investigations*. Pinter, London.

Ayres, R (1998) 'Crime and Violence as Development Issues in Latin America and the Caribbean'. *Latin American and Caribbean Studies Viewpoint Series*. World Bank, Washington, DC

Azandossessi, A (2000) 'The struggle for water in urban poor areas of Nouakchott, Mauritania'. *WATERfront* 13, January. UNICEF, New York

Bacon, R (1999) 'A scorecard for energy sector reform in developing countries'. In *Energy and Development Report 1999*. World Bank, Washington, DC, pp 50–55

Bah, S (1993) 'Re-examination of recent trends in under-five mortality rates in Zimbabwe: Evidence from the ZDHS, 1988'. *Central African Journal of Medicine* **39**(9): 180–3. [published erratum appears in *Central African Journal of Medicine* (1995) **41**(8): 265]

Bähr, J, and R Wehrhahn (1993) 'Life expectancy and infant mortality in Latin America'. *Social Science and Medicine* **36**(10): 1373–82

Bairoch, P (1993) *Economics and World History: Myths and Paradoxes*. Harvester Wheatsheaf, New York

Baken, R J, and P Smets (1999) 'Better a "hut" on the ground than a castle in the air: Formal and informal housing finance for the urban poor in India'. In K Datta and G Jones (eds) *Housing and Finance in Developing Countries*. Routledge, London

Baldwin, D M (1998) 'The subsistence adaptation of homeless mentally ill women'. *Human Organization* **57**(2): 190–199

Ball, J (1999) 'Auto Makers are Racing to Market "Green Cars" Powered by Fuel Cells'. *Wall Street Journal*, 15 March, A1

Banister, D (2000) 'Sustainable urban development and transport – a Eurovision for 2020'. *Transport Reviews* **20**(1): 113–130

Barata, R B, M C Ribeiro et al (1998) 'Intra-urban differentials in death rates from homicide in the city of São Paulo, Brazil, 1988–1994'. *Social Science and Medicine* **47**(1): 19–23

Barbosa, R, Y Cabannes and L Moraes (1997) 'Tenant today, *posseiro* tomorrow'. *Environment and Urbanization* **9**(2): 17–41

Barcelo, J-Y (1999) 'Modern approaches for local development'. *Habitat Debate* (special issue on Rural–Urban Linkages) **5**(1)(March)

Barlow, J, and S Duncan (1994) *Success and Failure in Housing Provision: European Systems Compared*. Pergamon, Oxford

Barlow, M (1999) *Blue Gold: The Global Water Crisis and the Commodification of the World's Water Supply: A Special Report*. International Forum on Globalization, San Francisco

Barnes, D (1995) 'Consequences of energy policies for the urban poor'. *World Bank FPD Energy Note*, No 7, November

Barnett, J (1989) 'Redesigning the Metropolis: The Case for a New Approach'. *Journal of the American Planning Association* **55**(2): 131–135

Barry, K (1997) 'Prostitution of sexuality: A cause for new international human rights'. *Journal of Personal and Interpersonal Loss* **2**(1): 27–48

Bartlett, S, R Hart, D Satterthwaite, X de la Barra and A Missair (1999) *Cities for Children: Children's Rights, Poverty and Urban Management*. Earthscan, London

Bartone, C, J Bernstein, J Leitmann and J Eigen (1994) *Towards Environmental Strategies for Cities*. World Bank, Washington, DC

Bauer, C J (1998) *Against the Current: Privatization, Water Markets, and the State in Chile*. Kluwer Academic Publishers, Boston

Beal, J (1996) *Urban Governance: Why Gender Matters* (Accessed at www.undp.org/gender/resources/mono1.html on 5 May 2000). United Nations Development Programme, New York

Beall, J, O Crankshaw, and S Parnell (2000) 'Urban governance, partner-

ship and poverty: Johannesburg'. Urban governance, partnership and poverty working paper 12. International Development Department, University of Birmingham

Beattie, A, and K Merchant (2000) 'Bombay's rail scheme benefits slum dwellers'. *Financial Times* 6 November

Beecher, J A (1994) 'Water affordability and alternatives to service disconnection'. *Journal of the American Water Works Association* **86**(10): 61–72

Beevers, D G, and J S Prince (1991) 'Some recent advances in noncommunicable diseases in the tropics. 1. Hypertension: An emerging problem in tropical countries'. *Transactions of the Royal Society of Tropical Medicine and Hygiene* **85**(3): 324–6

Beidl, R A (1999) 'The Virtual Mortgage Bank: How Technology is Toppling Traditional Barriers'. Research Note. TowerGroup, Needham, MA

Bella, A F, O Baiyewu et al (1993) 'The pattern of medical illness in a community of elderly Nigerians'. *Central African Journal of Medicine* **39**(6): 112–6

Benneh, G, J Songsore, J S Nabila, A T Amuzu, K A Tutu, Y Yangyuoru and G McGranahan (1993) *Environmental Problems and the Urban Household in the Greater Accra Metropolitan Area (GAMA) – Ghana*. Stockholm Environment Institute, Stockholm

Besley, T, and S Coate (1995) 'Group lending, repayment incentives, and social collateral'. *Journal of Development Economics* **46**(1): 1–18

Besley, T, and S Coate (1999) *Centralized Versus Decentralized Provision of Local Public Goods: A Political Economy Analysis, Working Paper Series; 7084*. The National Bureau of Economic Research, Cambridge, MA

Bingham, R D, R E Green and S B White (eds) (1987) *The Homeless in Contemporary Society*. Sage Publications, Newbury Park, California

Bird, R M, R D Ebel and C Wallich (1995) *Decentralization of the Socialist State: Intergovernmental Finance in Transition Economies, World Bank Regional and Sectoral Studies*. International Bank for Reconstruction and Development/The World Bank, Washington, DC

Black, M (1998) UNDP/World Bank Water and Sanitation Program. Learning What Works: 20 Years Cooperation in Water and Sanitation

Blair, H (2000) 'Participation and accountability at the periphery: Democratic local governance in six countries'. *World Development* **28**: 21–39

Bloor, R (2000) *The Electronic B@zaar: From the Silk Road to the Eroad*. Nicholas Brealey Publishing, Naperville, Illinois

Blue, I (1999) 'Intra-urban differentials in mental health in São Paulo, Brazil'. PhD thesis, South Bank University, London, UK

Blue, I, and T Harpham (1998) 'Investing in mental health research and development'. *British Journal of Psychiatry* **172**: 294–295

Blunt, A C, and A Muziol-

Weclawowicz (1998) 'Improved management of the existing stock: the case of Poland'. *Housing Studies* **13**(5): 697–711

Body-Gendrot, S (1999) *Controlling Cities*. Blackwell, Oxford

Boelhouwer, P J (ed) (1997) *Financing the Social Rented Sector in Western Europe*. Delft University Press, Delft

Boerma, J T, A Nunn et al (1998) 'Mortality impact of the AIDS epidemic: Evidence from community studies in less developed countries'. *AIDS* **12**(Suppl 1): S3–S14

Boerma, J, M Urassa et al (1999) 'Spread of HIV infection in a rural area of Tanzania'. *AIDS* **13**: 1233–1240

Bolnick, J, and D Mitlin (1999) 'Housing finance and empowerment in South Africa'. In K Datta and G Jones (eds) *Housing and Finance in Developing Countries*. Routledge, London

Bolnick, J, S Cuff, A Dizon, A Hasan, D Mitlin and P Rahman (1997) 'Driven by need, learning by experience'. *Waterlines* **16**(2)

Bond, P (1999) 'Globalization, pharmaceutical pricing, and South African health policy: managing confrontation with US firms and politicians'. *International Journal of Health Services* **29**(4): 765–792

Bonilla, F, E Melendez, R Morales and M Torres (eds) (1998) *Borderless Borders*. Temple University Press, Philadelphia

Boon, S, and F de Jong (1999) 'Local government reform in Tanzania: A solid base or missing stones? A research into the expectations of success of decentralisation considering the extent to which factors affecting success are present in the Tanzanian context'. Master's thesis, The Hague

Boonyabancha, S (1996) 'The Urban Community Development Office'. IIED Human Settlements Programme

Boonyabancha, S (1999) 'The urban community environmental activities project and its environment fund in Thailand'. *Environment and Urbanization* **11**(1): 101–116

Boot, M T, and S Cairncross (1997) 'Actions speak: The study of hygiene behaviour in water and sanitation projects'. *Environment and Urbanization*, **9**(1): 271–272

Booth, C (1892) *Life and Labour of the People in London*. Macmillan, London

Borland, J (1999) 'Earnings inequality in Australia: Changes, causes and consequences'. *Economic Record* **75**(229): 177–202

Borsook, P (1999) 'How the Internet Ruined San Francisco'. Salom.Com, News Feature. www.salon/com/nes/feature/1999/10/28/internet

Boulle, P, L Vrolijks and E Palm (1997) 'Vulnerability reduction for sustainable development'. *Journal of Contingencies and Crisis Management* **5**(3): 179–188

Boyld, N, and A Kumar (1993) *Infrastructure Notes: Transportation, Water and Urban Development Department of the World Bank: Urban No FM-6*.

Boxall, B (2000) 'California And The West; Bay Area Cities Try To Stem Dot-Com Tide; Communities: Tech Firms Are Swallowing Up Office Space, Driving Up Rents And, In

Some Cities, Stirring Up A Backlash Among Those Who Fear Loss Of Small-City Atmosphere'. *Los Angeles Times*, 19 October, Part A, Part 1, p 3.

Braczyk, H-J, G Fuchs and H-G Wolf (eds) (1999) *Multimedia and Regional Economic Restructuring*. Routledge, London

Bradley, J, C Stephens et al (1992) *A Review of Environmental Health Impacts in Developing Country Cities*. Urban Management Program, Urban Management and the Environments, The World Bank, Washington, DC

Bradsher, K (1999) 'With SUVs More Popular, Fuel Economy Continues to Fall,' *New York Times*, 5 October

Brenner, N (1998) 'Global cities, glocal states: Global city formation and state territorial restructuring in contemporary Europe. *Review of International Political Economy* **5**(1): 1–37

Briggs, J, and D Mwamfupe (2000) 'Peri-urban development in an era of structural adjustment in Africa: The city of Dar es Salaam, Tanzania'. *Urban Studies* **37**(4): 797–809

Briggs, X, J Darden et al (1999) 'In the wake of desegregation: Early impacts of scattered-site public housing on neighborhoods in Yonkers, New York'. *Journal of the American Planning Association* **65**(1): 27–49

Briscoe, J (1992) 'Poverty and water supply: How to move forward'. *Finance and Development* **29**: 16–19

Briscoe, J (1997) 'Managing water as an economic good: Rule for reformers'. In M Kay, T Franks and L Smith (eds) *Water: Economics, Management and Demand*. E & FN Spon, London, pp 339–61

Brockerhoff, M (1994) 'The impact of rural–urban migration on child survival'. *Health Transition Review* **4**(2): 127–49

Brockerhoff, M (1995) 'Child survival in big cities: The disadvantages of migrants'. *Social Science and Medicine* **40**(10): 1371–83

Brockerhoff, M (1999) 'Urban growth in developing countries: A review of projections and predictions'. *Population and Development Review* **25**(4): 757–778

Brockerhoff, M, and E Brennan (1998) 'The poverty of cities in developing regions'. *Population and Development Review* **24**(1): 75–114

Brolin, B C (1972) 'Chandigarh was planned by experts, but something has gone wrong'. *Smithsonian* **3**(3): 56–63

Brooks, D B, E Rached and M Saade (1997) *Management of Water Demand in Africa and the Middle East: Current Practices and Future Needs*. International Development Research Centre, Ontario, Canada

Brooks, N R (2000) 'Activists Urge Occidental Petroleum Shareholders to Sell Their Stock'. *Los Angeles Times*, 29 April, Part C, p 1

Brotchie, J (1992) 'The changing nature of cities'. *Urban Futures* Special Issue **5**: 13–26

Brown, W (1999) 'GM, Toyota Team Up to Make Electric Cars'. *Washington Post*, 20 April

Buckley, R (1999) 'Housing finance in development countries: A review of the World Bank's experience'. In K Datta and G Jones (eds) *Housing and Finance in Developing Countries*. Routledge, London

Bullard, R D, E Grigsby III and C Lee (eds) (1994) *Residential Apartheid: The American Legacy*. Center for Afro-American Studies, University of California at Los Angeles, Los Angeles

Burby, R J, with T Beatley, P R Berke, R E Deyle, S P French, D R Godschalk, E J Kaiser, J D Karatz, P J May, R Olshansky, R G Patterson and R H Platt (1999) 'Unleashing the power of planning to create disaster-resistant communities'. *Journal of The American Planning Association* **65**(3): 247–257

Burby, R J, and P J May (1999) 'Making building codes an effective tool for earthquake hazard mitigation'. *Environmental Hazards* **1**(1): 27–38

Burgers, J (1996) 'No polarisation in Dutch cities? Inequality in a corporatist country'. *Urban Studies* **33**(1): 99–106

Burki, S J, and S Edwards (1996) 'Latin America after Mexico: Quickening the pace'. World Bank *Latin American and Caribbean Studies Viewpoints*

Burki, S J, G Perry and W Dillinger (1999) *Beyond the Center: Decentralizing the State, World Bank Latin American and Caribbean Studies Viewpoints*. World Bank, Washington, DC

Burns, R, J Beecher, Y Hegazy and M Eifert (1995) *Alternatives to Utility Service Disconnection*. National Regulatory Research Institute, Columbus, Ohio

Burra, S (no date) *Resettlement and Rehabilitation of the Urban Poor: The Story of Kanjur Marg*. Report produced by Society for the Promotion of Area Resource Centres (SPARC), Mumbai

Burt, M R (1992) *Over the Edge: The Growth of Homelessness in the 1980s*. Russell Sage Foundation, New York

Burt, T (1999) 'Car Makers in Fuel Cells Initiative'. *Financial Times* (London edition), 20 September

Burtraw, D (1998) *Cost Savings, Market Performance, and Economic Benefits of the US Acid Rain Program*. Resources for the Future, Washington, DC. www.rff.org/disc_papers/PDF_files/9 828rev.pdf

Butti, M, D Franco and H Ongena (1998) 'Fiscal discipline and flexibility in EMU: The implementation of the Stability and Growth Pact'. *Oxford Review of Economic Policy* **14**(1): 81–97

Byarugaba, J, and D Kielkowski (1994) 'Reflections on trauma and violence-related deaths in Soweto, July 1990–June 1991'. *South African Medical Journal* **84**(9): 610–4

Byass, P, M D Adedeji et al (1995) 'Assessment and possible control of endemic measles in urban Nigeria'. *Journal of Public Health and Medicine* **17**(2): 140–5

Cabannes, Y (1997) 'From community development to housing finance: From *Mutiroes* to *Casa Melhor* in Fortaleza, Brazil'. *Environment and Urbanization* **9**(1): 31–58

Cairncross, S, J E Hardoy and D Satterthwaite (1990) 'The urban context'. In J E Hardoy, S Cairncross and D Satterthwaite (eds) *The Poor Die Young: Housing and Health in Third World Cities*. Earthscan Publications, London

Calabrese, A, and M Borchert (1996) 'Prospects for electronic democracy

in the United States: Rethinking communication and social policy'. *Media, Culture and Society* **18**: 249–268

Caldeira, T (1996a) 'Building up walls: The new pattern of spatial segregation in São Paulo'. *International Social Science Journal* **147**: 55–65

Caldeira, T (1996b) 'Fortified enclaves: The new urban segregation'. *Public Culture* **8**: 303–328

Campbell, C, and J Laherrere (1998) 'The end of cheap oil'. *Scientific American* March: 78–83

Cannon, J (1998) *China at the Crossroads: Energy, Transportation, and the 21st Century*. INFORM, Inc., New York. www.informinc.org

Cardoso, R (1992) 'Popular movements in the context of the consolidation of democracy in Brazil'. In A Escobar and S Alvarez (eds) *The Making of Social Movements in Latin America: Identity, Strategy, and Democracy*. Westview Press, Boulder, pp 291–302

Carter, W, M Schill et al (1998) 'Polarisation, public housing and racial minorities in US cities'. *Urban Studies* **35**(10): 1889–1911

Castells, M (1989) *The Informational City: Information Technology, Economic Restructuring and the Urban–Regional Process*. Blackwell, London

Castells, M (1996) *The Information Age: Economy, Society and Culture. Volume I: The Rise of the Network Society*. Blackwell, Oxford

Castells, M (1998) *The Information Age: Economy, Society and Culture. Volume III: End of the Millennium*. Blackwell, Oxford

Castells, M (1999a) 'Grassrooting the space of flows'. *Urban Geography* **20**(4): 294–302

Castells, M (1999b) *The Culture of Cities in the Information Age*. Report to the US Library of Congress

Castells, M, and P Hall (1994) *Technopoles of the World: The Making of 21st Century Industrial Complexes*. Routledge, London

CDIAC (Carbon Dioxide Information Analysis Center) (2000) *Global, Regional, and National Fossil Fuel CO2 Emissions*. Oak Ridge National Laboratory, Oak Ridge, TN. http://cdiac.esd.ornl.gov/trends/emis/tre_coun.htm

Ceesay, M M, M W Morgan, M O Kamanda, V R Willoughby and D R Lisk (1996) 'Prevalence of diabetes in rural and urban populations in southern Sierra Leone: A preliminary survey'. *Tropical Medicine and International Health* **2**(3): 272–7

Centre on Housing Rights and Evictions (2000) *The Human Right to Adequate Housing: A Chronology of United Nations Activity, 1945 to 1999*. Geneva

Centre on Integrated Rural Development for Asian and the Pacific, and Division of Human Settlements Development of the Asian Institute of Technology (1991) *Impact of Decentralization on Rural Poverty: An Asian Perspective CIRDAP Study Series No. 136. HSD Proceedings No. 71*. September. Centre on Integrated Rural Development for Asia and the Pacific, Bangkok

Chalmers, D, C Vilas, K Hite, S Martin, K Piester and M Segarra (eds) (1997) *The New Politics of Inequality in Latin America: Rethinking Participation and Representation*. Oxford University Press, Oxford

Chang, G (2000) *Disposable Domestics: Immigrant Women Workers in the Global Economy*. South End Press, Cambridge, Massachusetts

Chant, S (1998) 'Households, gender and rural–urban migration: Reflections on linkages and considerations for policy'. *Environment and Urbanisation* **10**(1): 5–22

Chaplin, S E (1999) 'Cities, sewers and poverty: India's politics of sanitation'. *Environment and Urbanization* **11**: 145–58

Chapman, G (2000) 'UCLA Project harnesses cyberspace for improving living spaces in Los Angeles: Internet project logs housing units' (University of Texas-Austin). *CUP Report* **11**(11): 6, Spring (Rutgers University, Centre for Urban Policy Research, New Brunswick, USA)

Chapman, M, and A Murie (1996) 'Housing and the European Union'. *Housing Studies* **11**(2): 307–318

Chase-Dunn, C, B Brewer and Y Kawano (2000) 'Trade globalization since 1975: Waves of integration in the world system'. *American Sociological Review* **65**(1): 77–95

Chawla, L (2000) *Insight, Creativity, and Thoughts on the Environment: Integrating Children and Youth into Human Settlement Development*. Whitney Young College, Kentucky State University

Chekki, D A (1999) 'Poverty amidst plenty: How do Canadian cities cope with rising poverty?' *Research in Community Sociology* **9**: 141–152

Chen, Y, E Waters, J Green, R Andrews and F Escobar (1999) 'Geospatial analysis of pertussis in Victoria 1993–1997'. *Australian Population Association Conference*. Brisbane, September 1999

Cheru, F (2000) 'Transforming our common future: The local dimensions of global reform'. *Review of International Political Economy* **7**(2): 353–368

Choguill, C L (1997) 'Ten steps to sustainable urban infrastructure'. *The Urban Age* **5**(2): 22–23

Chomsky, N (1993) 'The new global economy'. In D Barsamian (ed) *The Prosperous Few and the Restless Many*. Odonian, Berkeley, pp 6–16

Chua, B H (1989) *The Golden Shoe: Building Singapore's Financial District*. Urban Redevelopment Authority, Singapore

Clark, T N, and V Hoffman-Martinot (eds) (1998) *The New Public Culture*. Westview Press, Oxford

Clarke, S E, and G L Gaile (1998) *The Work of Cities*. University of Minnesota Press, Minneapolis, MN

Cochrane, A (1993) *Whatever Happened to Local Government?* Open University Press, Buckingham, UK

Cohen, B (2000) 'Street and working children in cities in the developing world: A review'. Paper prepared for a meeting of the Panel on Urban Population Dynamics of the National Research Council, National Academy of Sciences, Mexico City, 24–25 February

Cohen, J, and J Rogers (1995) 'Secondary associations and democratic governance'. In E O Wright (ed) *Associations and Democracy: The Real Utopias Project*, Vol 1. Verso, London, pp 7–98

Cohen, M (1996) 'Habitat II and the challenge of the urban environment:

Bringing together the two definitions of habitat'. *International Social Science Journal* **48**(1): 95

Cohen, M A, B A Ruble, J S Tulchin and A M Garland (eds) (1996) *Preparing for the Urban Future. Global Pressures and Local Forces*. Woodrow Wilson Center Press, distributed by The Johns Hopkins University Press, Baltimore

Collins, C, C Hartman and H Sklar (1999a) *Divided Decade: Economic Disparity at the Century's Turn*. United for a Fair Economy, Boston

Collins, C, B L Wright and H Sklar (1999b) *Shifting Fortunes: The Perils of the Growing American Wealth Gap*. United for a Fair Economy, Boston

Colten, R D (1992) *Nonparticipation in Public Benefit Programs: Lessons for Energy Assistance*. National Consumer Law Center, Boston

Comerio, M C (1998) *Disaster Hits Home: New Policy for Urban Housing Recovery*. University of California Press, Berkeley

Commander, S, A Tolstopiatenko and R Yemtsov (1999) 'Channels of redistribution: Inequality and poverty in the Russian transition'. *Economics of Transition* **7**(2): 411–447

Committee for Sydney (1997) *A Better Future: It Is up to Us*. Committee for Sydney, Sydney

Committee for Sydney (1998) *Committee for Sydney Launches 'Sydney 2020' World Benchmark Study*. Media Release, 10 February

Conover, S, A Berkman, A Gheith, R Jahiel, D Stanley, P A Geller, E Valencia and E Susser (1997) 'Methods for successful follow-up of elusive urban populations: An ethnographic approach with homeless men'. *Bulletin of the New York Academy of Medicine* **74**(1): 90–108

Contreras, M (1998) 'La Reforma Educativa'. In J C Chávez Corrales (ed) *Las Reformas Estructurales en Bolivia*. Fundación Milenio, La Paz

Coopers and Lybrand Deloitte (1991) *London, World City Moving into the 21st Century*. HMSO, London

Copjec, J, and M Sorkin (eds) (1999) *Giving Ground*. Verso, London

Cosgrove, S (1999) 'Engendering finance: A comparison of two micro-finance models in El Salvador'. In K Datta and G Jones (eds) *Housing and Finance in Developing Countries*. Routledge, London

Cosgrove, W J, and F R Rijsberman (2000) *World Water Vision: Making Water Everybody's Business*. For the World Water Council, Conseil Mondial de l'Eau. Earthscan, London

Cosgrove-Sacks, C (ed) (1999) *The European Union and Developing Countries: The Challenges of Globalization*. Macmillan, London

Costanza, R, B G Norton and B D Haskell (1992) *Ecosystem Health: New Goals for Environmental Management*. Island Press, Covello

Cotton, A, and D Haworth (1995) Water Supply & Sanitation for Developing Countries: Directories of UK-Based Research Volumes I (1986–1992) and II (1992–1995)

Cox, K (1995) 'Globalisation, competition and the politics of local economic development'. *Urban Studies* **32**(2): 213

Cox, K (1997) 'Governance, urban regime analysis, and the politics of local economic development'. In M

Lauria (ed) *Reconstructing Urban Regime Theory: Regulating Urban Politics in a Global Economy*. Sage, Thousand Oaks, CA, pp 99–121

Crane, R (1994) 'Water markets, market reform and the urban poor: Results from Jakarta, Indonesia'. *World Development* **22**(1): 71–83

Cress, D M, and D A Snow (1996) 'Mobilization at the margins: Resources, benefactors, and the viability of homeless social movement organizations'. *American Sociological Review* **61**(6): 1089–1109

Cusimano, M K (ed) (2000) *Beyond Sovereignty: Issues for a Global Agenda*. St Martin's, New York

Cwiklinski, H K (no date) *New Institutional Arrangements for Regional Development in Poland: Their Impact on Local Economies and Interregional Cooperation*. Institute of Geography of the University of Tartu

Dahl, R (1961) *Who Governs: Democracy and Power in an American City*. Yale University Press, New Haven

Dale, P E R, S A Ritchie, B M Territo, K Hulsman and B H Kay (1998) 'Use of remote sensing to map intertidal wetland water distribution'. In A J McComb and J A Davis (eds) *Wetlands for the Future. Proceedings of INTECOL's V International Wetlands Conference*. Gleneagle Press, Adelaide, pp 581–595

Daly, G (1996) *Homeless: Policies, Strategies, and Lives on the Street*. Routledge, London

Daniel, Z (1985) 'The effects of housing allocation on social inequality in Hungary'. *Journal of Comparative Economics* **9**: 391–409

Daniere, A G, and L M Takahashi (1999) 'Poverty and access: Differences and commonalities across slum communities in Bangkok'. *Habitat International* **23**(2): 271–288

Davies, P (1989) *Troughs and Drinking Fountains: Fountains of Life*. Chatto & Windus, London

De Angelis, M (1996) 'The autonomy of the economy and globalization'. *Vis-à-Vis* **4**(Winter)

Dear, M, and J Wolch, Jr (1987) *Landscapes of Despair: From Deinstitutionalization to Homelessness*. Princeton University Press, Princeton, New Jersey

de Arias, A R, E A Ferro, M E Ferreira, and L C Simancas (1999) 'Chagas disease vector control through different intervention modalities in endemic localities of Paraguay'. *Bulletin of the World Health Organization* **77**(4): 331–339

Delpeuch, F, and B Maire (1997) 'Obesity and developing countries of the South'. *Médecine Tropicale* **57**(4): 380–8

Del Vecchio, D (1999) 'Amsterdam: The hooked up city', *Urban Age: The Global City Magazine* **7**(2)

Demissie, F (1998) 'In the shadow of the gold mines: Migrancy and mine housing in South Africa'. *Housing Studies* **13**(4): 445–469

Denaldi, R (1994), *Viable Self-Management: The FUNACOM Housing Programme of Sao Paulo Municipality*, IHS Working Papers No. 9, Rotterdam

Department of the Environment, Transport and the Regions (1998) *Building Partnerships for Prosperity*, White Paper. HMSO, London

Department of Urban Affairs and Planning (1995) *Cities for the 21st Century*. State of New South Wales, Sydney

Department of Urban Affairs and Planning (1997) *A Framework for Growth and Change*. State of New South Wales, Sydney

Deutsche Stiftung für Internationale Entwicklung (1996) *Entwicklungspolitisches Forum/Development Policy Forum; Evaluation of the UN World Conferences 1990–1996 from the Perspective of Development Policy: A Comparison of their Goals, Results, and Implementation Strategies*. Deutsche Stiftung für Internationale Entwicklung, Berlin

Devas, N, and D Korboe (2000) 'City governance and poverty: The case of Kumasi'. *Environment and Urbanization* **12**(1): 123–135

de Veer, T (1997) *Sanitation in Emergencies: Sanitation Programmes in Camps for Refugees or Displaced Persons*. IRC Report VO 1-E

Dewar, D (1999) 'South Africa: Two case studies of partnerships in the provision of land for housing'. In G Payne (ed) *Making Common Ground: Public–Private Partnerships in Land for Housing*. Intermediate Technology Publications, London

Dewar, N (1999) 'La transformation de la métropole du cap: Dynamiques de croissance et orientations politiques'. In J M Rennes (ed) *La Recherche sur la Ville en Afrique du Sud*. Anthropos. Paris

Dewey, R (1960) 'The rural–urban continuum: Real but relatively unimportant'. *American Journal of Sociology* **17**: 529–537

Diamond, L, J Hartlyn, J Linz and S Lipset (eds) (1999) *Democracy in Developing Countries: Latin America*, 2nd edition. Lynne Rienner Publishers, Boulder

Dietz, C, and J Ranton (1996) 'Targeted program for low income households'. *Proceedings of CONSERV '96, Orlando, Florida*, pp 755–759

DiGaetano, A, and J S Klemanski (1999) *Power and City Governance: Comparative Perspectives on Urban Governance*. University of Minnesota Press, Minneapolis

Dinar, A, and A Subramaniam (1997) *Water Pricing Experiences: An International Perspective*. World Bank Technical Paper no 386, Washington, DC

Dirlik, A (1998) 'Globalism and the politics of place'. *Development* **41**(2): 7–13

Douglass, M (1998) 'Beyond dualism: Rethinking theories of development in a global–local framework'. *Regional Development Dialogue* **19**(1): 1–18

Douglass, M (2000) 'The political economy of urban poverty and environmental management in Asia: Access, empowerment and community-based alternatives'. *Environment and Urbanization* **4**(2): 9–32

Douglass, M (forthcoming) 'Urban and regional policy after the era of naive globalism'. *Regional Development Dialogue*

Douglass, M, and J Friedmann (eds) (1998) *Cities for Citizens: Planning and the Rise of Civil Society in a Global Age*. John Wiley, New York

Dowall, D E (1998) 'Global strategy for shelter'. In W van Vliet– (ed) *The Encyclopedia of Housing*. Sage, Thousand Oaks, CA, pp 199–200

Drakeford, M (1997) 'The poverty of privatization: Poorest customers of the privatized gas, water and electricity industries'. *Critical Social Policy* **17**(2): 115–32

Driver, J (1998) 'UK and European mortgage securitisation: Trends and prospects'. *Housing Finance* **40**

Dugger, C W (2000) 'Connecting Rural India to the World'. *New York Times*, 28 May

Duncan, O D (1957) 'Community size and the rural–urban continuum'. In P K Hatt and A J Reiss (eds) *Cities and Society: The Revised Reader in Urban Sociology*. Free Press, New York, pp 35–45

Dunn, J R (2000) 'Housing and health inequalities: Review and prospects for research'. *Housing Studies* **15**(3): 341–366

Dunn, S (ed) (1994) *Managing Divided Cities*. Keele University Press, UK

Durand-Lasserve, A, assisted by Clerc, V (1996) *Regularization and Integration of Irregular Settlements: Lessons from Experience*. UMP Working Paper no 6

Dutta, P (2000) 'Partnerships in urban development: A review of Ahmedabad's experience'. *Environment and Urbanization* **12**(1): 13–26

Eade, J (ed) (1996) *Living the Global City: Globalization as a Local Process*. Routledge, London

Eckstein, S (ed) (1989) *Power and Popular Protest: Latin American Social Movements*. University of California Press, Berkeley

Economist Intelligence Unit (1998) *EIU Country Profile: Guatemala 1998/1999*

EERI (Earthquake Engineering Research Institute) (1999) *Lessons Learned Over Time: Innovative Earthquake Recovery in India*. EERI, Oakland, CA

Eisenberg, A (1999). 'Fuel Cell May Be the Future "Battery"'. *New York Times*, 21 October

Ekanem, E E, O T Adedeji et al (1994) 'Environmental and behavioural risk factors for prolonged diarrhoea in Nigerian children'. *Journal of Diarrhoeal Diseases Research* **12**(1): 19–24

Ekblad, S (1993) 'Stressful environments and their effects on quality of life in third world cities'. *Environment and Urbanization* **5**(2): 125–134

Elliot, D (1997) *Energy, Society and Environment: Technology for a Sustainable Future*. Routledge, London

Enarson, E, and B H Morrow (eds) (1998) *The Gendered Terrain of Disaster: Through Women's Eyes*. Praeger, Westport, CT

Engels, F (1872) *Zur Wohnungsfrage* (trans: *The Housing Question, 1935*). International Publishers, New York

*Environment and Urbanization* (1995) 'Urban poverty II: from understanding to action'. Special Theme Issue. *Environment and Urbanization* **7**(2)

*Environment and Urbanization* (2000) 'Poverty reduction and urban governance'. Special Theme Issue. *Environment and Urbanization* **11**(2)

Environmental Planning Collaborative (1998) *Sabarmati Riverfront Development*. VIKAS Centre for Development, Ahmedabad

ESCAP (1998) *Towards Efficient Water Use in Urban Areas in Asia and the Pacific*. United Nations, New York

Escobar, F, I P Williamson, J Green and E Waters (1998) 'The Use of the Internet in the Diffusion of GIS for General Practices in Victoria, Australia'. Internet and Society Conference, Geneva (Proceedings on CD-ROM). www.rch.unimelb.edu.au/CCCHAP/gis-in-health.htm

Escobar, F, J Green, E Waters and I Williamson (1999) 'Establishing an International Research Agenda on Geographic Information Systems for Public Health'. *GEOMED'99*, Paris, 22–23 December 1999

Eskeland, G (1992) 'The objective: Reduce pollution at low cost,' *Outreach* **2**. World Bank Country Economics Department, World Bank, Washington, DC

Esping Andersen, G (1990) *The Three Worlds of Welfare Capitalism*. Polity Press, Cambridge

Esrey, S, I Andersson, A Hillers, and R Sawyer (2000) *Ecological Sanitation: Closing the Loop to Food Security*. Report from an international workshop in Cuernavaca, Mexico, 17–21 October 1999. UNDP/SEED, New York

Estache, A (1995) *Decentralizing Infrastructure: Advantages and Limitations*, World Bank Discussion Papers; 290. World Bank, Washington, DC

Estache, A, S Sinha and World Bank Office of the Vice President Development Economics (1995) *Does Decentralization Increase Spending on Public Infrastructure?* Policy Research Working Papers 1457. World Bank, Washington, DC

Etemadi, F (2000) 'Civil society participation in city governance in Cebu City'. *Environment and Urbanization* **12**(1): 57–72

European Commission (2000) *Social Exclusion in European Neighborhoods: Processes, Experiences, and Responses*. Brussels, European Commission, TSER

European Environmental Agency (EEA) (1996) *Environment and Health, Volume 1: Overview and Main European Issues*. EEA, Copenhagen

European Federation of National Organizations Working with the Homeless (1998) *Europe Against Exclusion: Housing for All*. FEANTSA, Brussels

Evans, P (2000) 'Fighting marginalization with transnational networks: Counter hegemonic globalization'. *Contemporary Sociology* **29**(1): 230–241

Evans, P, et al (2001) *Livable Cities: The Politics of Urban Livelihood and Sustainability*. University of California Press, Berkeley

Evarts, E (1999) 'The refueling of America'. *Christian Science Monitor*, 22 April, p 13

Everard, J (1999) *Virtual States: The Internet and the Boundaries of the Nation-State*. Routledge, London

Fainstein, S, I Gordon and M Harloe (1993) *Divided City: Economic Restructuring and Social Change in London and New York*. Blackwell, New York

Fajnzylber, P, D Lederman and N Loayza (1998) *Determinants of Crime Rates in Latin America and the World*.

World Bank Latin American and Caribbean Studies Viewpoints Series, World Bank, Washington, DC

Fajnzylber, P, D Lederman and N Loayza (2000) *Crime and Victimization: an Economic Perspective.* The World Bank, Washington, DC

Falk, R (1999) *Predatory Globalization: A Critique.* Cambridge, Polity Press

Fannie Mae Foundation (1999) *A New Way Home* **3**(2): 4. Newsletter of the Fannie Mae Foundation, Washington, DC (available at www.fanniemaefoundation.org/prog rams/nwh.shtml)

Farmer, P (1997) 'Social scientists and the new tuberculosis'. *Social Science and Medicine* **44**(3): 347–358

Fawcus, S, M T Mbizvo et al (1995) 'A community based investigation of causes of maternal mortality in rural and urban Zimbabwe. Maternal mortality study group'. *Central African Journal of Medicine* **41**(4): 105–13

Fawcus, S, M Mbizvo et al (1996) 'A community-based investigation of avoidable factors for maternal mortality in Zimbabwe'. *Studies in Family Planning* **27**(6): 319–27

Feachem, R, R Kjellstrom et al (eds) (1990) *The Health of Adults in the Developing World.* World Bank, Washington, DC

Federal Ministry for Transport, Building and Housing of the Federal Republic of Germany (2000) Order of the Federal Ministry for Transport, Building and Housing of the Federal Republic of Germany *Urban 21.* Federal Ministry for Transport, Building and Housing, Berlin

Ferguson, B (1999) 'Micro-finance of housing: A key to housing the low or moderate-income majority?' *Environment and Urbanization* **11**(1): 185–200

Ferman, B (1996) *Challenging the Growth Machine: Neighborhood Politics in Chicago and Pittsburgh.* University Press of Kansas, Lawrence, Kansas

Fernandez-Maldonado, A (1999) 'Telecommunications in Lima: Networks for the networks'. (Available from a.fernandez-moldon-ado@bk.tudelft.nl)

*Financial Times* (2000) 'The German Pfandbrief: Report for Investors'. *Financial Times* (London edition), 24 May

Finnie, G (1998) 'Wired cities'. *Communications Week International,* 18 May, 19–22

Firestone, D (1999) 'Suburban Comfort Thwarts Atlanta's Plans to Limit Sprawl'. *New York Times,* 21 November

Fisher, A (1999) 'The best cities for business'. *Fortune* **12**(140): 102–108

Fisman, R, R Gatti and World Bank Development Research Group Macroeconomics and Growth (2000) *Decentralization and Corruption: Evidence across Countries.* World Bank Development Research Group Macroeconomics and Growth, Washington, DC

Fleury, S (1998) 'Política social, exclusión y equidad en América Latina en los años noventa'. Paper presented at the Conference *Política Social, Exclusión y Equidad en Venezuela durante los años 90 Balance y Perspectuva, Caracas, Venezuela,* May

Florig, H (1997) 'China's air pollution

risks'. *Environmental Science and Technology* **31**(6): 274–279

Foltz, R (2000) *Religions of the Silk Road: Overland Trade and Cultural Exchange from Antiquity to the Fifteenth Century.* Macmillan, Basingstoke, UK

Fonseca, W, B R Kirkwood et al (1996) 'Risk factors for childhood pneumonia among the urban poor in Fortaleza, Brazil: A case control study'. *Bulletin of the World Health Organization* **74**(2): 199–208

Förster, M F, and I G Tóth (1997) 'Poverty, inequality and social policies in the Visegrád countries'. *Economic Transitions* **5**(2): 505–510

Foweraker, J, and T Landman (1997) *Citizenship Rights and Social Movements: A Comparative and Statistical Analysis.* Oxford University Press, New York

Franck, T M (1992) 'The emerging right to democratic governance'. *American Journal of International Law* **86**(1): 46–91

Frenk, J, J Londono et al (1998) 'Latin American health systems in transition: A vision for the future'. In C Bezold, J Frenk and S McCarthy (eds) *21st Century Health Care in Latin America and the Caribbean: Prospects for Achieving Health for All,* pp 109–142

Friedmann, J (1995) 'Where we stand: A decade of world city research'. In P L Knox and P J Taylor (eds) *World Cities in a World-System.* Cambridge University Press, Cambridge, UK, pp 21–47

Friedmann, J (1998) 'The new political economy of planning: The rise of civil society'. In M Douglass and J Friedmann (eds) *Cities for Citizens: Planning and the Rise of Civil Society in a Global Age.* Wiley, Chichester, pp 19–35

Friedmann, J, and J Miller (1965) 'The urban field'. *Journal of the American Institute of Planners* **31**: 312–319

Friedrichs, J (ed) (1988) *Affordable Housing and the Homeless.* Walter de Gruyter, New York

Frontier Finance International (no date) 'Genesis Empresarial: Community infrastructure lending program in Guatemala. Analysis and strategic recommendations'. Unpublished internal report, Frontier Finance International

Fuel Cell Commercialization Group (1999) *What is a Fuel Cell?* Fuel Cell Commercialization. Group, Washington, DC. www.ttcorp.com/fccg/fc_what2.ht m

Fukasaku, K, L R de Mello, Organisation for Economic Co-operation and Development. Development Centre, and Escola de Administração Fazendária (Brazil) (1999) *Fiscal Decentralisation in Emerging Economies: Governance Issues, Development Centre Seminars.* Centre of the OECD, Paris

Fuller, T D, J N Edwards et al (1993) 'Housing, stress, and physical well-being: Evidence from Thailand'. *Social Science and Medicine* **36**(11): 1417–28

Fung, K K (1987) 'Surplus seeking and rent seeking through backdoor deals in Mainland China'. *American Journal of Economics and Sociology* **46**(3): 299–317

Galor, O (2000) 'Income distribution and the process of development'.

*European Economic Review* **44**(4–6): 706–712

Galor, O, and O Moav (2000) 'Ability biased technological transition, wage inequality and economic growth'. *Quarterly Journal of Economics* **115**: 469–498

Galtung, J (1985) 'Twenty-five years of peace research: Ten challenges and some responses'. *Journal of Peace Research* **22**(2): 145–46

Gans, H (1962) 'City planning and urban realities'. *Commentary* XXXIII, February, 170–175

Garau, P (1996) 'Parallel activities at Habitat II and the H@bit@t University: A call for takers'. *Environment and Urbanization* **8**(1): 273–279

Garreau, J (1991) *Edge City: Life on the New Frontier.* Doubleday, New York

Garretón, M A (1999) A social and economic transformations in Latin America: The emergence of a new political matrix?' In P Oxhorn and P Starr (eds) *Markets and Democracy In Latin America: Conflict or Convergence?* Lynne Rienner Publishers, Boulder, pp 61–78

Garuda, G (2000) 'The Distributional Effects of IMF Programs: A Cross-Country Analysis'. *World Development* **28**(6): 1031–1051

Gately, D, and S Streifel (1997) 'The demand for oil products in developing countries'. *World Bank Discussion Papers,* no 359

Gatlin, D (ed) (1995) *Climate Change Policy Workbook for Local Leaders.* The Climate Institute, Washington, DC

Gaventa, J (1997) 'Crossing the great divide: Building links between NGOs and community based organisations in North and South'. Paper prepared for the Conference on NGOs and Voluntary Organisations: North and South Learning from Each Other. Centre for Voluntary Organisations, London School of Economics, 18–19 September, 1997. Institute of Development Studies, Sussex

Gaviria, A, and C Pagés (2000) *Patterns of Crime Victimization in Latin America.* Inter-American Development Bank, Washington, DC

Gay, R (1990) 'Popular incorporation and prospects for democracy: Some implications of the Brazilian case'. *Theory and Society,* **19**(4): pp 447–463

Geyer, B (1999) *Developments in Fuel Cell Technology.* Fuel Cells 2000, Washington, DC. www.sustdev.org/journals/edition.01 /preview/1.103.shtml

Ghatate, S (1999) *Credit Connections: Meeting WSS Needs of the Informal Sector through Microfinance in Urban India.* Mahila Housing SEWA Trust and World Bank

Giddens, A (1990) *The Consequences of Modernity.* Polity Press, Cambridge

Giddens, A (2000) *The Third Way and its Critics.* Polity Press, Cambridge

Giles, H, and B Brown (1997) '"And not a drop to drink". Water and sanitation services to the urban poor in the developing world'. *Geography* **82**(2): 97–109

Glaeser, E (1999) *An Overview of Crime and Punishment.* Harvard University and NBER

Glasser, I (1994) *Homelessness in Global Perspective.* G K Hall, New York

Gleick, P H (1996) 'Basic water requirements for human activities: Meeting

basic needs'. *Water International* **21**: 83–92

Gleick, P H (1998a) 'The human right to water'. *Water Policy* **1**: 487–503

Gleick, P H (1998b) *The World's Water: The Biennial Report on Freshwater Resources.* Island Press, Covello

Glenn, D W (1999) 'Future trends in housing finance'. *Mortgage Banking,* April, p 37

Glenn, J M, R P Labossiere and J M Wolfe (1993) 'Squatter regularizatio – problems and prospects: A case-study from Trinidad'. *Third World Planning Review* **15**(3): 249–262

Glover, J, K Harris and S Tennant (1999) *A Social Health Atlas of Australia,* 2nd edition, vol 3. Public Health Information Development Unit, Victoria

Godard, X (1994) *Les Transport dans les Villes du Sud: La Recherche de Solution Durables, Karthala.* CODATU/INRETS, Cedex, Paris and Arcueil

Goering, J, A Kamely and T Richardson (1997) 'Recent Research on Racial Segregation and Poverty Concentration in Public Housing in the United States'. *Urban Affairs Review* **32**(5): 723–745

Goldblatt, M (1996) 'Making the cup run over: The challenge of urban water supply for South Africa's Reconstruction and Development Programme.' *Geojournal* **39**(1): 21–26

Goldsmith, W, and E Blakeley (1992) *Separate Societies: Poverty and Inequality in US Cities.* Temple University Press, Philadelphia

Gordon, I, and P Cheshire (1996) 'Territorial Competition and the Predictability of Collective (In)action'. *International Journal of Urban and Regional Research* **20**(3): 383–400

Gordon, P, and H W Richardson (1989) 'Gasoline consumption and cities: A reply'. *Journal of the American Planning Association* **55**: 342–346

Gordon, P, A Kumar and H W Richardson (1989) 'The influence of metropolitan spatial structure on commuting times'. *Journal of Urban Economics* **26**: 138–149

Gordon, P, H W Richardson and M Jun (1991) 'The commuting paradox: Evidence from the top twenty'. *Journal of the American Planning Association* **57**: 416–420

Gore, T (1991) *Public–Private Partnership Schemes in UK Urban Regeneration: The Role of Joint Enabling Agencies.* Butterworth/Heinemann, Cities

Goslee, S, and C Conte (1998) *Losing Ground Bit by Bit: Low Income Communities in the Information Age.* Benton Foundation and National Urban League, Washington, DC

Gould, W T (1998) 'African mortality and the new "urban penalty"'. *Health and Place* **4**(2): 171–81

Government Office for London (1996) *Strategic Guidance for London Authorities.* Government Office for London, London

Graham, C (1994) *Safety Nets, Politics, and the Poor: Transitions to Market Economies.* The Brookings Institution, Washington, DC

Graham, S (1998) 'The end of geography or the explosion of space? Conceptualising space, place and information technology'. *Progress in Human Geography* **22**(2): 165–185 raham, S (1999) 'Global grids of glass: On telecommunications, global cities and planetary urban networks'. *Urban Studies* **36**(5–6): 929–949

raham, S, and A Aurigi (1997) 'Virtual cities, social polarisation and the crisis in urban public space'. *Journal of Urban Technology* **4**(1): 19–52

raham, S, and S Marvin (1996) *Telecommunications and the City: Electronic Spaces, Urban Places.* Routledge, London

raham, S, and S Marvin (2001) *Splintering Urbanism: Networked Infrastructures, Technological Mobilities and the Urban Condition.* Routledge, London

rant, E (1999) *State of the Art of Urban Health in Latin America.* European Commission funded concerted action: 'Health and Human Settlements in Latin America'. South Bank University, London

ray, L, and M Kevane (1999) 'Diminished access, diverted exclusion: Women and land tenure in Sub-Saharan Africa'. *African Studies Review* **42**(2): 15–39

rayson, L, and K Young (1994) *Quality of Life in Cities: An Overview and Guide to the Literature.* The British Library, London. A selection from this publication is accessible at: www2.rudi.net/resrch/quality/qual_con.htm

reen J, E Waters, F Escobar and J Sneddon (1999) 'Evaluating a geographic information system in divisions of general practice: A work in progress'. *General Practice Evaluation Program Conference,* May 1999, Brisbane, Australia (peer reviewed conference poster)

reen J, F Escobar, E Waters and J Sneddon (2000) 'Geospatial information in the general practice sector: Development and evaluation of a geographic information system'. *Telehealth International* **1**(1)

reider, W (1997) *One World, Ready or Not: The Manic Logic of Global Capitalism.* Simon and Schuster, New York

rubb, M, J Walker, R Buxton, T Glenny, H Herring, B Hill, C Holman, W Patterson, J Procter and K Rouse (1992) *Emerging Energy Technologies: Impacts and Policy Implications.* Dartmouth Publishing, Brookfield, VT

Grundy-Warr, C, K Peachey and M Perry (1999) 'Fragmented integration in the Singapore–Indonesian border zone: Southeast Asia's "growth triangle" against the global economy'. *International Journal of Urban and Regional Research* **23**(2): 304–328

Gu, C, and H Liu (2000) *New Urban Poverty and Peasant Enclaves in Beijing.* Nanjing University, Department of Urban and Resource Sciences/ University of North Carolina, Department of Urban and Regional Planning, Nanjing/Chapel Hill

Guerrero, R (1998) 'Epidemiology of violence in the Americas: The case of Colombia'. In S J Burki, S Aiyer and R Hommes (eds) *Poverty and Inequality: Annual World Bank Conference on Development in Latin America and the Caribbean, 1996 Proceedings.* World Bank, Washington, DC, pp 95–100

Guy Peters, B (1997) 'With a little help from our friends: Public–private partnerships as institutions and instruments'. In J Pierre (ed) *Partnerships in Urban Governance: European and American Experience.* Macmillan, London

Ha, S K (1998) 'Housing problems and new-town policy in the Seoul Metropolitan Region'. *Third World Planning Review* **20**(4): 375–390

Hack, G (1997) 'Infrastructure and regional form'

Haddad L, M T Ruel and J L Garrett (1999) 'Are urban poverty and under-nutrition growing? Some newly assembled evidence'. *World Development* **27**(11): 1891–1904

Hall, N, R Hart and D Mitlin (1996) *The Urban Opportunity: The Work of NGOs in Cities of the South.* Intermediate Technology, London

Hall, P (1997a) 'Regeneration policies for peripheral housing estates: Inward- and outward-looking approaches'. *Urban Studies* **34**(5–6): 873–890

Hall, P (1997b) 'Reflections past and future on planning cities'. *Australian Planner* **34**(2): 83–89

Hallgren, M (1999) Personal communication, 17 March

Halperin, R A (1998) *Infrastructure Sector Strategy: Living by Serving: New Directions for the Transition Economies. Report No 18426ECA.* Europe and Central Asia Infrastructure Sector Unit of the World Bank

Halvorson, S (2000) 'The geography of children's vulnerability: Households and water-related disease hazard in a mountain community in northern Pakistan'. Doctoral dissertation. University of Colorado, Boulder

Hamilton, E (1993) 'Social areas under state socialism: The example of Moscow'. Submitted in partial fulfillment of the requirements for the degree of Doctor of Philosophy in the Graduate School of Arts and Sciences, Columbia University

Harding, A (1997a) 'Public–private partnerships in the UK'. In J Pierre (ed) *Partnerships in Urban Governance: European and American Experience.* Macmillan, London

Harding, A (1997b) 'The suffering middle: Trends in income inequality in Australia, 1982 to 1993/94'. *Australian Economic Review* **30**: 341–358

Harding, A, and P Le Galès (1997) 'Villes et etats en Europe'. In V Wright and S Cassese (eds) *La Recomposition de l'Etat en Europe.* La Découverte, Paris

Hardoy, A, and R Schusterman (2000) 'New models for the privatisation of water and sanitation for the poor'. *Environment and Urbanization* **12**(2): 63–75

Hardoy, J E, D Mitlin and D Satterthwaite (2001) *Environmental Problems in an Urbanizing World: Local Solutions for City Problems in Africa, Asia and Latin America.* Earthscan, London

Hardy, N, and E D Tribble (1995) 'The Digital Silk Road', Agorics web site, 29 April 2000. www.agorics.com/dsr.html

Harpham, T (1994) 'Urbanization and mental health in developing countries: A research role for social scientists, public health professionals and social psychiatrists'. *Social Science and Medicine* **39**(2): 233–45

Harpham, T (1997) 'Urbanisation and health in transition'. *Lancet* **349**(Suppl. III): 11–13

Harpham, T, and I Blue (eds) (1995) *Urbanisation and Mental Health in Developing Countries.* Avebury, Aldershot, UK

Harvard University Graduate School of Design (1996) *The New Planning Agenda: Proceedings of a Conference 7–8 April 1995.* Harvard University, Cambridge, MA

Harvard University Graduate School of Design's Center for Urban Development Studies (1999) *Review of the South African Government's Grant Funded Municipal Infrastructure Programs: Summary Document*

Harvard University Graduate School of Design's Center for Urban Development Studies and Development Alternatives, Inc (2000) *Housing Microfinance Initiatives: Synthesis and Regional Summary for Asia, Latin America and Sub-Saharan Africa with Selected Case Studies.* Harvard University, Cambridge, MA

Harvey, D (1996) *Justice, Nature and the Geography of Difference.* Blackwell Publishers, Cambridge, MA

Hasan, A (1992) *Manual for Rehabilitation Programmes for Informal Settlements based on the Orangi Pilot Project Model.* OPP-RTI, Karachi

Hasan, A (1993) *Scaling Up of the OPP's Low-cost Sanitation Programme.* OPP-RTI, Karachi

Hasan, A (1997a) 'Working with government: The story of the Orangi Pilot Project's collaboration with state agencies for replicating its low-cost sanitation programme'. *Environment and Urbanization* **9**(2): 321–322

Hasan, A (1997b) *Working with Government.* City Press, Karachi

Hasna, M K (1995) 'Street hydrant project in Chittagong low-income settlement'. *Environment and Urbanization* **7**(2): 207–18

Haughton, G (1999) 'Environmental justice and the sustainable city'. *Journal of Planning Education and Research* **18**(3): 233–243

Häusermann, H, and W Siebel (1987) *Neue Urbanität.* Suhrkamp, Frankfurt am Main

Hechter, A (1990) 'The attainment of solidarity in intentional communities'. *Rationality and Society* **2**(2): 142–155

Hegedus, J (1998) 'Transition in land and housing, Bulgaria, and the Czech Republic and Poland'. *Housing Studies* **13**(1): 139–141

Hegedus, J, and I Tosics (1998) 'Rent reform: Issues for the countries of Eastern Europe and the Newly Independent States'. *Housing Studies* **13**(5): 657–678

Heise, L, with J Pitanguy and A Germain (1994) *The Hidden Burden of Health.* World Bank Discussion Papers No 255. The World Bank, Washington, DC

Held, D (1999) *Global Transformations.* Polity Press, Cambridge

Held, D, A McGrew et al (1999) 'Globalization'. *Global Governance: A Review of Multilateralism and International Organizations* **5**(4): 483–496

Heller, L (1999) 'Who really benefits from environmental sanitation services in the cities? An intra-urban analysis in Betim, Brazil'. *Environment and Urbanization* **11**(1): 133–44

Helvie, C O, and W Kunstmann (eds) (1999) *Homelessness in the United States, Europe, and Russia: A Comparative Perspective.* Bergin & Garvey, Westport, CT

Hemmati, M, and V W Leigh (2000) 'NGO Women's Caucus, Position Papers: Freshwater. Women and Freshwater'. www.earthsummit2002.org/wcaucus

Henderson, D (1999) *The Changing Fortunes of Economic Liberalism: Yesterday, Today and Tomorrow.* Institute of Economic Affairs, London

Hewitt, W E (1998) 'The role of inter-national municipal cooperation in housing the developing world's urban poor: The Toronto–São Paulo example'. *Habitat International* **22**(4): 411–427

Hewitt, W E (1999) 'Cities work together to improve urban services in developing areas: The Toronto–São Paulo example'. *Studies in Comparative International Development* **34**(1): 27–44

Hiday, V (1995) 'The social context of mental ill health and violence'. *Journal of Health and Social Behavior* **36**(June): 122–137

HiFi News (1999) International Institute for Environment and Development, London

Hill, R P, and B Adrangi (1999) 'Global poverty and the United Nations'. *Journal of Public Policy and Marketing* **18**(2): 135–146

Hirayama, Y (2000) 'Collapse and reconstruction: Housing recovery policy in Kobe after the Hanshin Great Earthquake'. *Housing Studies* **15**(1): 111–128

Hirschmann, A (1970) *Exit, Voice and Loyalty: Responses to Declines in Firms Organizations and States.* Harvard University Press, Cambridge, Mass

Hitz, H (1995) *Capitales Fatales: Urbanisierung und Politik in den Finanzmetropolen Frankfurt und Zürich.* Rotpunkt Verlag, Zurich

Hobson, J (2000) 'Sustainable sanitation: Experiences in Pune with a municipal-NGO-community partnership'. *Environment and Urbanization* **12**(20): 53–62

Hoch, C (2000) 'Sheltering the homeless in the US: Social improvement and the continuum of care'. *Housing Studies* **15**(6): 865–876

Hodge, D C, R L Morrill et al (1996) 'Implications of intelligent trans-portation systems for metropolitan form'. *Urban Geography* **17**(8): 714–739

Hojo, N (1995) 'Fuel cell development by city gas industry'. *Japan 21st* November: 24–25

Hondagneu-Sotelo, P (1994) *Gendered Transitions.* University of California Press, Berkeley

Hoque, B A, M M Hoque, N Ali, S E Coghlan (1994) 'Sanitation in a poor settlement in Bangladesh: A challenge for the 1990s'. *Environment and Urbanization* **6**(2): 79–86

Hornbeck, D W and L M Salamon (eds) (1991) *Human Capital and America's Future: An Economic Strategy for the '90s.* The Johns Hopkins University Press, Baltimore

*Housing America Update* **1**(1), Spring 2000

Huby, M (1995) 'Water, poverty and

social policy: A review of issues for research'. *Journal of Social Policy* **24**: 219–36

Hudson, R, and A M Williams (eds) (1999) *Society and Territory*. Sage, Thousand Oaks, California

Hugo, G and R Ambagtsheer (1998) 'GIS equity and provision of services for a sub group: The example of residential care for the elderly in Adelaide'. *Second Symposium on GIS and Health, Developments in the Application of Geographic Information Systems Within the Health Sector.* Department of Geomatics, The University of Melbourne, Melbourne, Australia, 10 June. www.sli.unimelb.edu.au/HealthGIS98/presentations

Hulchanski, D, and J D Leckie (2000) *The Human Right to Adequate Housing: A Chronology of United Nations Activity, 1945–1999.* Centre for Housing Rights and Evictions, Geneva

Hulme, D and P Mosley (1996) *Finance Against Poverty: Volume 1.* Routledge, London

Human Rights Watch (1992) *Double Jeopardy: Police Abuse of Women in Pakistan.* Human Rights Watch, New York

Humplick, F F, A Moini-Araghi and World Bank Policy Research Department Environment Infrastructure and Agriculture Division (1996) *Decentralized Structures for Providing Roads: A Cross-Country Comparison.* World Bank, Washington, DC

Hussmann, H (1995) *The Bus Transit System and its Contribution to Promoting Mobility and Quality of Life.* 51st International Congress, UITP, Paris

ICLEI (International Council for Local Environmental Initiatives) (no date) *Brasov Region, Romania: From Industrial Past to Eco-Tourism, from Planned to Market Economy.* International Council for Local Environmental Initiatives. www.iclei.org/europe/economy/regions/braso.htm

ICLEI (no date) *Local Initiatives Award for Excellence in Freshwater Management.* International Council for Local Environmental Initiatives. www.iclei.org

ICLEI (1997) *Biennial Report 1996–1997: Sustainable Development Through Local Action.* ICLEI, Toronto. www.iclei.org/iclei/bien9697/

ID21 (1998) 'Pipe Dreams. Does Privatised Water Offer Poor Urban Neighbourhoods a Better Supply?' ID21, 26 October 1998. www.id21.org/static/2bgl3.htm

IEA (International Energy Agency) (1996) *World Energy Outlook.* IEA/OECD, Paris

IEA (1998) *Energy Efficiency Initiative, Volume 1.* International Energy Agency, Paris. www.iea.org/pub.htm

IEA (1999) *The Evolving Renewable Energy Market.* IEA, Paris

*Indian Express* (2000) 'MHADA scheme to resettle slum-dwellers'. *Indian Express* 19 August

Ingram, H et al (1995) *Divided Waters.* University of Arizona, Tucson

Inter-American Development Bank (1998) *Facing Up to Inequality in Latin America: Economic and Social Progress In Latin America, 1998–1999 Report.* Inter-American Development Bank,

Washington, DC

Intergovernmental Panel on Climate Change (IPCC) (1995) *Climate Change: The IPCC Scientific Assessment.* Cambridge University Press, Cambridge

Intergovernmental Panel on Climate Change (IPCC) (1997) *The Regional Impacts of Climate Change.* IPCC, New York

International Development Research Centre (IDRC), Canada, and Hanoi Architectural University, Vietnam (1997) *Shelter and Environmental Improvement for the Urban Poor: Summary Report.* October, p 82

International Water Resources Association. *IWRA Update Newsletter: October 1999.* International Water Resources Association. www.iwra.siu.edu

IRC (1994) Working with Women and Men on Water and Sanitation: An African Field Guide. OP 25-E

IRC (2000) 'FID Review: Key Issues in Water Information'. Double issue April 2000

IRC and WSSCC (2000) ' World Water Forum (5): Priority for Sanitation?' *Source Weekly.* www.wsscc.org/source/weekly/00124.html#sanitation

IRC, International Water and Sanitation Centre (2000) *Streams of Knowledge: The Role of Water and Sanitation Resource Centres in Closing the Gap on Unmet Needs.* IRC, Delft

Irwin, T (1997) 'Responsible investing for cities and taxpayers'. *The Urban Age* **5**(2): 4–7

Izagirre, A (1998) 'Private participation in the electricity sector: Recent trends'. *World Bank Research Note,* 154, pp 1–8

Jackson, A, D Robinson and C Wiggings, with B Baldwin (2000) *Falling Behind: The State of Working Canada 2000.* Canadian Centre for Policy Alternatives, Ottawa

Jacobi, P (1999) *Cidade e Meio Ambiente: Percepções e Práticas em São Paulo.* Annablume, São Paulo

Jacobs, B (1997) 'Urban crisis: Complexity and risk'. *Journal of Contingencies and Crisis Management* **5**(3): 127–130

Jacobs, J (1961) *The Death and Life of Great American Cities.* Random House

Jacobson, D (1996) *Rights Across Borders: Immigration and the Decline of Citizenship.* The Johns Hopkins University Press, Baltimore

Jamal, V, and J Weeks (1993) *Africa Misunderstood: Or Whatever Happened to the Rural–Urban Gap?* Macmillan, London

Jamshid, A M (ed) (1989) *Homelessness in the United States.* Greenwood Press, New York

Jenkins, R (2000) 'Globalization and corruption'. *WorldLink: The Magazine of the World Economic Forum* January/February

Jenkins, R, and A M Goetz (1999a) 'Accounts and accountability: Theoretical implications of the right-to-information movement in India'. *Third World Quarterly* **20**(3): 603–622

Jenkins, R, and A M Goetz (1999b) 'Constraints on civil society's capacity to curb corruption: Lessons from the Indian experience'. *IDS Bulletin* **29**(4): 2–16

Jessop, B (1998) 'The rise of governance and the risks of failure'.

*International Social Science Journal* **155**: 29–45

Jewett, D (1999) 'Venture Hopes for 50 Fuel Cell Cars'. *Detroit News,* 21 April, p B1

Jimenez, R (1999) 'A Power Plant in the Basement'. *Boston Globe,* 11 July

Joardar, S D (1998) 'Carrying capacities and standards as bases towards urban infrastructure planning in India: A case of urban water supply and sanitation'. *Habitat International* **22**(3): 327–337

Johannessen, L and G Boyer (1999) *Observations of Solid Waste Landfills in Developing Countries.* World Bank, Washington, DC

Johnson, D, I Manning and O Hellwig (1998) 'Trends in the distribution of income in Australia'. *Australian Journal of Labour Economics* **2**: 1–28

Johnson, S and B Rogaly (1997) *Micro-Finance and Poverty Reduction.* Oxfam, Oxford

Johnson, T E (1987) 'Upward filtering of housing stock'. *Habitat International* **11**(1): 173–190

Johnstone, N (1997) *Economic Inequality and the Urban Environment : The Case of Water and Sanitation.* International Institute for Environment and Development, London (Environmental Economics Programme discussion paper / IIED; DP 97-03)

Joint Center for Housing Studies (2000) *The State of the Nation's Housing: 2000.* Harvard University, Kennedy School of Government, Cambridge, Massachusetts

Jonas, A E G, and Wilson, D (eds) (1999) *The Urban Growth Machine: Critical Perspectives Two Decades Later.* State University of New York Press, Albany, New York

Jones, G A and P M Ward (1998) 'Privatizing the commons: Reforming the ejido and urban development in Mexico'. *International Journal of Urban and Regional Research* **22**(1): 76–93

Jones, M L and P Blunt (1999) '"Twinning" as a method of sustainable institutional capacity building'. *Public Administration and Development* **19**: 381–402

Jonsson, A and D Satterthwaite (2000) 'Overstating the provision of safe water and sanitation to urban populations: A critical review of the quality and reliability of official statistics and of the criteria used in defining what is "adequate" and "safe"'. Draft. IIED, London

Jordan, S and F Wagner (1993) 'Meeting women's needs and priorities for water and sanitation in cities'. *Environment and Urbanization* **5**(2): 135–45

*The Journal of Urban Technology* (1995) Special Issue: 'Information Technologies and Inner-City Communities', *The Journal of Urban Technology* **3**(1)

Jouve, B and C Lefèvre (forthcoming) *In Search for Urban Gargantuas: Power, Territories in European Metropolitan Areas.* Frank Cass Publishers, London

Judd, D (1999) 'Constructing the tourist bubble'. In D Judd and S Fainstein (eds) *The Tourist City.* Yale University Press, New Haven

Judge, D E A (ed) (1995) *Theories of Urban Politics.* Sage, London

Kalbermatten, J (1999) 'Should we pay for water, and if so, how?' *Urban*

*Age,* Winter: 14–16

Kanbur, R, and N Lustig (1999) *Why is inequality back on the agenda?* Paper prepared for the Annual Bank Conference on Development Economics. Available at www.worldbank.org/wdrpoverty/inequality.htm

Kanbur, R, and X Zhang (1999) 'Which regional inequality? The evolution of rural–urban and coastal–inland inequality in China from 1983 to 1995'. *Journal of Comparative Economics* **27**: 686–701

Kanji, N (1995) 'Gender, poverty and structural adjustment in Harare, Zimbabwe'. *Environment and Urbanization* **7**(1)(April): 37–55

Kaothien, U, D Webster and J Lukens (1997) 'Infrastructure investment in the Bangkok region'. Mimeo

Karatnycky, A (2000) 'A century of progress'. *Journal of Democracy* **11**(1): 187–200

Karekezi, S (1999) 'Access to modern energy: A view from Africa'. In *Energy and Development Report 1999.* World Bank, Washington, DC, pp 75–78

Kariuki, M (1999) 'WSS services for the urban poor'. Background paper for WSSCC

Karl, T L (2000) 'Economic inequality and democratic instability'. *Journal of Democracy* **11**(1): 149–156

Katakura, Y and A Bakalian (1998) 'PROSANEAR: People poverty, and pipes'. Working paper series. UNDP-WB WSP, Brazil

Katz, L F, and D H Autor (1999) 'Changes in the wage structure and earnings inequality'. In O Ashenfelter and D Card (eds) *Handbook of Labor Economics,* vol 3A. Elsevier, Amsterdam, pp 1463–1555

Kayombo, E J (1995) 'Motor traffic accidents in Dar es Salaam'. *Tropical and Geographical Medicine* **47**(1): 37–9

Keane, J (1996) *Reflections on Violence.* Verso, London

Kearns G (1988) 'The urban penalty and the population history of England'. In A Brandstrom and L Tedebrand (eds) *Society, Health and Population during the Demographic Transition.* Almquist and WisKELL International, Stockholm, pp 213–236

Kearns G (1993) 'Le handicap urbain et le déclin de la mortalité en Angleterre et au Pays de Galles 1851–1900'. *Annales de Demographic Historique* 75–105

Keck, M E, and K Sikkink (1998) *Activists beyond Borders: Advocacy Networks in International Politics.* Cornell University Press, Ithaca, New York

Kelly, P F (1999) 'Everyday urbanization: The social dynamics of development in Manila's metropolitan region'. *International Journal of Urban and Regional Research,* **23**(2), 283–303

Kelly, P F (2000a) *Undermining 'Balanced' Development in Manila's Mega-Region.* York University, Canada

Kelly, P F (2000b) *Landscapes of Globalization: Human Geographies of Economic Change in the Philippines.* Routledge, London

Kemeny, J (1995) *From Public Housing to the Social Market: Rental Policy Strategies in Comparative Perspective.* Routledge, London

Kenworthy, J and F Laube (1999) 'A global review of energy use in urban transport systems and its implications for urban transport and land-use policy,' *Transportation Quarterly* **53**(4): 23–48

Kenworthy, J R, F B Laube et al (1999) *An International Sourcebook of Automobile Dependence in Cities, 1960–1990*. University Press of Colorado, Boulder

Kenworthy, L, and M Malami (1999) 'Gender inequality in political representation: A worldwide comparative analysis'. *Social Forces* **78**(1): 235–269

Kenzer, M (1999) 'Healthy cities: a guide to the literature'. *Environment and Urbanization* **11**(1): 201–220

Kessides, C (1997) *World Bank Experience with the Provision of Infrastructure Services for the Urban Poor: Preliminary Identification and Review of Best Practices*. Transport, Water and Urban Development Department, TWU-OR8, World Bank, Washington, DC

Keynote address to the Millennium Forum, 22 May 2000; SG/SM/7411 GA/9710

Ke-youn Chu, H Davoodi and S Gupta (2000) *Income Distribution and Tax and Government Social Spending Policies in Developing Countries*. International Monetary Fund. WP/00/62

Khan, A H (1994) *Orangi Pilot Project Programs*. 3rd edition. OPP, Karachi

Khan, A H (1998) *Orangi Pilot Project: Reminiscences and Reflections*. OUP, Karachi

King, A D (ed) (1995) *Representing the City: Ethnicity, Capital and Culture in the 21st Century*. Macmillan, London

Kitange, H M, H Machibya et al (1996) 'Outlook for survivors of childhood in sub-Saharan Africa: Adult mortality in Tanzania'. Adult Morbidity and Mortality Project. *BMJ* **312**(7025): 216–20. [published erratum appears in *BMJ* 24 February 1996 **312**(7029): 483]

Kjellen, M, A Bratt, and G McGranahan (1997) 'Water supply and sanitation in low and middle-income cities: Comparing Accra, Jakarta and Sao Paulo'. *Environment and Urbanization* **9**(2): 342–343

Klaassen, L H, L van den Berg and J van der Meer (eds) (1989) *The City: Engine Behind Economic Recovery*. Avebury, Aldershot, UK/ Gower, Brookfield, Vermont

Klak, T, and S Marlene (1999) 'The political economy of formal sector housing finance in Jamaica'. In K Datta and G Jones (eds) *Housing and Finance in Developing Countries*. Routledge, London

Kloosterman, R C (1996) 'Double Dutch: Polarization trends in Amsterdam and Rotterdam after 1980'. *Regional Studies* **30**(5): 467–477

Knobel, H H, W S Yang et al (1994) 'Urban–rural and regional differences in infant mortality in Taiwan'. *Social Science and Medicine* **39**(6): 815–22

Knox, P L and P J Taylor (eds) (1995) *World Cities in a World-System*. Cambridge University Press, Cambridge

Knudsen, A B, and R Slooff (1992) 'Vector-borne disease problems in rapid urbanization: New approaches to vector control'. *Bulletin of the World Health Organization* **70**(1): 1–6

Konishi, T (no date) *Albania: Irrigation Rehabilitation*. World Bank Case Study, Washington, DC

Korboe, D, K Diaw and N Devas (2000) 'Urban governance, partnership and poverty: Kumasi'. Urban Governance, Partnership and Poverty Working Paper 10, International Development Department, University of Birmingham, Birmingham

Kos, D (1999) Environmental and housing movements: Grassroots experiences in Hungary, Russia and Estonia'. *Housing Studies* **14**(2): 270–272

Kosareva, N (1992) 'Housing market and social guarantees'. *Voprosy Prognozirovaniya* **1** [in Russian]

Krantz, B, E Oresjo and H Priemus (eds) (1999) *Large Scale Housing Estates in North West Europe: Problems, Interventions, Experiences*. Delft University Press, Delft

Kumar, P, et al (1997) 'Death in the air,' *Down to Earth*, 15 November

Kuumba, B M (1999) 'A cross-cultural race/class/ gender critique of contemporary population policy: The impact of globalization'. *Sociological Forum* **14**(3): 447–463

Lagos, M (1997) 'Latin America's smiling mask'. *Journal of Democracy* **8**(July): 125–138

Laut, J P (1990) 'Die alte Seidenstrasse im Licht neuerer Publikationen'. *Zeitschrift fur Religions- und Geisteswissenschaft* **42**(4): 367–370

Lavalette, M, and J Kennedy (1996) *Solidarity on the Waterfront: The Liverpool Lock Out of 1995–96*. Liver Press, Liverpool

Lave, C (1992) 'Cars and demographics'. *Access* **1**: 4–11, UC Berkeley, Transportation Center

Law, A (1999) 'Fuel Cells Become Clean Air Apparent For Auto Industry'. *Toronto Star*, 24 April

Law, R (1999) 'Beyond "women and transport": Towards new geographies of gender and daily mobility'. *Progress in Human Geography* **23**(4): 567–588

Lawless, P, R Martin and S Hardy (eds) (1998) *Unemployment and Social Exclusion: Landscapes of Labour Inequality*. Jessica Kingsley, London

Le Bris, E (ed) (1996) *Villes du Sud*. Orstom Editions, Paris

*Le Figaro* (1998) 'Enquête sur la Seine-Saint-Denis, le département le plus défavorisé'. *Le Figaro*, 25 April

Le Jalle, C (1999) *Water Supply and Sanitation in Peri-Urban Areas and Small Centres*. GRET, Programme Solidarite Eau, Paris

Lea, M J, R Welter and A Dübel (1997) *Study on Mortgage Credit in the European Economic Area*. European Commission, Directorate General XXIV and Empirica, Brussels

Leaf, M (1997) 'The many agendas of Habitat II'. *Cities* **14**(1): R5–R7

Leaf, M (2000) *A Tale of Two Villages: Globalization and Peri-Urban Change in China and Vietnam*. University of British Columbia, Vancouver

Leaf, M, and A Pamuk (1997) 'Habitat II and the globalization of ideas'. *Journal of Planning Education and Research* **17**(1): 71–78

Leckie, S (1994) *Towards an International Convention on Housing Rights: Options at Habitat II*. American Society of International Law, Washington, DC

Leckie, S (1999) 'Proposals for a comprehensive plan of action for the promotion and protection of housing and property rights in Kosovo'. A report prepared for UNCHS (Habitat), 30 August

Lederman, D, and N Loayza (1999) 'What causes crime and violence?' In C Moser and S Lister (eds) *Violence and Social Capital: Proceedings of the LCSES Seminar Series, 1997–1998. Urban Peace Program Series, Latin America and Caribbean Region Sustainable Development Working Paper No 5*. World Bank, Washington, DC

Lee, K, and R Dodgson (2000) 'Globalization and cholera: Implications for global governance'. *Global Governance* **6**: 213–236

Lee, L, E Petrova, M Shapiro and R Struyk (1998) 'Housing maintenance and management in Russia during the reforms'. *Housing Studies* **13**(5): 679–696

Lee, P, and A Murie (1999) 'Spatial and social divisions within British cities: Beyond residualisation'. *Housing Studies* **14**(5): 625–640

Lefèvre, C (1998a) 'Metropolitan government and governance in Western countries: A critical review'. *International Journal of Urban and Regional Research* **22**(1): 9–25

Lefèvre, C (1998b) 'Metropolitan areas: New actors on the political scene'. OECD Workshop on Urban Governance and Local Democracy, Athens, 13–15 September

Leitmann, J (1999) *Sustaining Cities: Environmental Planning and Management in Urban Design*. McGraw Hill, New York

Levitas, T (1999) *The Political Economy of Fiscal Decentralization and Local Government Finance Reform in Poland, 1989–1999*. Prepared for United States Agency for International Development, East European Regional Housing Sector Assistance Project

Lewin, A C (1981) *Housing Co-operatives in Developing Countries: A Manual for Self-help in Low-Cost Housing Schemes*. Intermediate Technology Publications and John Wiley & Sons, Chichester, England/New York

Lieberman, D (1999) 'America's digital divide'. *USA Today Tech Report*, 11 October

Lin, B (1999) 'Hydrogen fuel cell scooters for urban Asia'. Master's thesis, Center for Energy and Environmental Studies, Princeton University, Princeton, NJ. www.spinglass.net/scooters/

Link, B G, E Susser, J Phelan, M Bresnahan, A Stueve and R Moore (1994) 'Life-time and five-year prevalence of homelessness in the United States'. *American Journal of Public Health* **84**(12)

Lister, R (1995) 'Water poverty'. *Journal of the Royal Society of Health* **115**: 80–83

Litvack, J I, J Ahmad and R M Bird (1998) *Rethinking Decentralization in Developing Countries, Sector Studies Series*. World Bank, Washington, DC

Liu, H-J (1998) *The Silk Road: Overland Trade and Cultural Interactions in Eurasia*. American Historical Society, Washington, DC

Lobmayer, P, and R Wilkinson (2000) 'Income, inequality and mortality in 14 developed countries'. *Sociology of Health and Illness* **22**(4): 401–414

*Local Transport Today* (1999) 'Can transport policies help to re-integrate the socially excluded?' *Local Transport Today* **255**

Logan, J R, Y Bian and F Bian (1999) 'Housing inequality in urban China in the 1990s'. *International Journal of Urban and Regional Research* **23**(1): 7–25

London Pride Partnership (1995) *London Pride Prospectus*. London Pride Partnership, London

Londoño, J (1996) 'Violence, psyche and social capital'. Paper prepared for the 2nd annual World Bank Conference on Development in Latin American and the Caribbean. July, Bogotá

Londoño, L, and M Székely (1997) *Persistent Poverty and Excess Inequality: Latin America, 1970–95*, Working Paper Series 357, October. Inter-American Development Bank

Lora, E, and J L Londono (1998) 'Structural reforms and equity'. In; N Birdsall, C Graham, and R Sabot (eds) *Beyond Tradeoffs: Market Reform and Equitable Growth in Latin America*. Inter-American Development Bank/Brookings Institution Press, Washington, DC, pp 63–90

Losada, H, H Martinez, J Vieyra, R Pealing, R Zavala and J Cortes (1998) 'Urban agriculture in the metropolitan zone of Mexico City: Changes over time in urban, suburban and peri-urban areas'. *Environment and Urbanization* **10**(2): 37–54

Louw, A (1997) 'Surviving the transition: Trends and perceptions of crime in South Africa'. *Social Indicators Research* **41**: 137–168

Lynch, J, M Brown and L Baker (1999) 'Public–private partnerships in transitional land and housing markets: Case studies from Bulgaria and Russia'. In G Payne (ed) *Making Common Ground: Public–Private Partnerships in Land for Housing*. Intermediate Technology Publications, London

Lyon-Callo, V (1998) 'Constraining responses to homelessness: An ethnographic exploration of the impact of funding concerns on resistance'. *Human Organization* **57**(1): 1–7

McCarney, P L (ed) (1996) *The Changing Nature of Local Government in Developing Countries*. Centre for Urban and Community Studies, University of Toronto and the Federation of Canadian Municipalities International Office, Toronto

McCarthy, L (2000) 'European economic integration and urban inequalities in Western Europe'. *Environment and Planning A* **32**: 391–410

McCombie, S (1996) 'Treatment seeking for malaria: A review of recent research'. *Social Science and Medicine* **43**(6): 933–945

McCully, P (1996) *Silenced Rivers: The Ecology and Politics of Large Dams*. Zed Books, London

MacDonald, J, and D Simioni (1999) *Urban Consensus: Contributions from the Latin American and the Caribbean Regional Plan of Action on Human Settlements*. CEPAL/ECLAC, Santiago/Environment and Human Settlements Division, United Nations

MacDonald, J, F Otava, D Simioni and M Komorizono (1998) *Sustainable Development of Human Settlements: Achievements and Challenges in Housing and Urban Policy in Latin America and the Caribbean*. United Nations, ECLAC, Santiago

McDowell, L (1997) *Capital Culture*. Blackwell Publishers, Oxford

McGranahan ,G, and M Kjellen (1997) *Urban Water: Towards Health and Sustainability*. Stockholm Environment Institute, Stockholm

McGranahan, G, J Songsore and M Kjellén (1999) 'Sustainability, poverty and urban environmental transitions'. In: D Satterthwaite (ed) *The Earthscan Reader in Sustainable Cities*. Earthscan, London, pp 107–130

McGregor, A, and M McConnachie (1995) 'Social exclusion, urban regeneration and economic reintegration'. *Urban Studies* **32**(10): 1587–1600

McGregor, Jr, E B (1994) 'Economic development and public education: Strategies and standards'. *Educational Policy* **8**(3): 252–271

McIlwaine, C (1999) 'Geography and development: Violence and crime as development issues'. *Progress in Human Geography* **23**(3): 453–63

McKenzie, E (1994) *Privatopia: Homeowner Associations and the Rise of Residential Private Government*. Yale University Press, New Haven

MacKenzie, J (1997) *Climate Protection and the National Interest: The Links Among Climate Change, Air Pollution, and Energy Security*. World Resources Institute, Washington, DC

McKeown, T, R G Record and R D Turner (1975) 'An interpretation of the decline of mortality in England and Wales during the twentieth century'. *Population Studies* **29**(3): 391–422

McLarty, D G, N Unwin et al (1996) 'Diabetes mellitus as a cause of death in sub-Saharan Africa: Results of a community-based study in Tanzania. The Adult Morbidity and Mortality Project'. *Diabetic Medicine* **13**(11): 990–994

Maclennan, D, J Muellbauer and M Stephens (1998) 'Asymmetries in housing and financial market institutions and EMU'. *Oxford Review of Economic Policy* **13**(3): 54–80

McNeill, D (2000) 'McGuggenisation? National identity and globalisation in the Basque Country'. *Political Geography* **19**(4): 473–494

McSherry, J P (1999) 'The emergence of "guardian democracy"'. *NACLA Report on the Americas* **32**(November–December): 16–24

Macy, P (1999) *Urban Water Demand Management in Southern Africa: The Conservation Potential*. Publications on Water Resources no 13. SIDA, Swedish International Development Cooperation Agency, Stockholm

Madanipour, A, G Cars and J Allen (eds) (1998) *Social Exclusion in European Cities: Processes, Experiences and Responses*. Jessica Kingsley, London

Madon, S (1998) 'Information-based global economy and socioeconomic development: The case of Bangalore'. *The Information Society* **13**(3): 227–243

Mahalanabis, D, A S Faruque et al (1996) 'Maternal education and family income as determinants of

severe disease following acute diarrhoea in children: A case control study'. *Journal of Biosocial Science* **28**(2): 129–39

Manor, J (1999) *The Political Economy of Democratic Decentralization*. World Bank, Washington, DC

Mara, D, and M Schweiger (1996) 'Water meters and gastroenteritis'. *Water Quality International* pp 12–14.

Marcoux, A (1998) 'The feminization of poverty: Claims, facts, and data needs'. *Population and Environment Review* **24**(1)(March)

Marcuse, P (1985) 'Gentrification, abandonment, and displacement: Connections, causes, and policy responses in New York City'. *Journal of Urban and Contemporary Law* **28**: 195–240

Marcuse, P (1988) 'Stadt - Ort der Entwicklung'. *Demokratische Gemeinde* (November): 115–122

Marcuse, P (1991)'Housing markets and labour markets in the quartered city'. In J Allen and C Hamnett (eds) *Housing and Labour Markets: Building the Connections*. Unwin Hyman, London, pp 118–135

Marcuse, P (1992) 'Why conventional self help projects won't work'. In K Mathey (ed) *Beyond Self-Help Housing*. Mansell, London

Marcuse, P (1996) 'Space and race in the post-Fordist city: The outcast ghetto and advanced homelessness in the US today'. In E Mingione (ed) *Urban Poverty and the Underclass*. Blackwell, Oxford

Marino, M, and K E Kemper (1999) *Institutional Frameworks in Successful Water Markets: Brazil, Spain and Colorado, USA*. World Bank Technical Paper no 427, Washington, DC

Marquand, R (2000) 'India's moral dilemma over evicting poor'. *Christian Science Monitor* 15 August

Marris, P (1998) 'Planning and civil society in the twenty-first century: An introduction'. In: M Douglass and J Friedmann (eds) *Cities for Citizens: Planning and the Rise of Civil Society in a Global Age*. John Wiley, Chichester, UK, pp 9–18

Marsh, A, D Gordon, P Heslop et al (2000) 'Housing deprivation and health: A longitudinal analysis'. *Housing Studies* **15**(3): 411–428

Marsh, A, and D Mullins (1998) 'The social exclusion perspective and housing studies: Origins, applications and limitations'. *Housing Studies* **13**(6): 749–760

Marshall, T H (1950) *Citizenship and Social Class and Other Essays*. Cambridge University Press, Cambridge

Martin, F (1999) 'Financial reform'. In *Energy and Development Report 1999*. World Bank, Washington, DC, pp 6–18

Martinotti, G (1993) *La Metropoli di Seconda Generazione*. Il Mulino, Bologna

Massey, D S, and N A Denton (1993) *American Apartheid: Segregation and the Making of the Underclass*. Harvard University Press, Cambridge, Massachusetts

Matsumoto, C (2000) 'Plans for homeless raise questions and suspicions'. *Asahi Evening News* 15 December, Tokyo. Accessible at www.asahi.com/english/asahi/1215/asahi121501.html

Mattelart, A (1996) *The Invention of*

*Communication*. University of Minnesota Press, Minneapolis, Minnesota

Mattos, M (1999) 'Fuel cell buses for São Paulo, Brazil'. Report Presented at *1999 Environmental Vehicle Conference*, Ypsilanti, MI. http://evworld.com/reports2/

Matur, A, S Bali, M Balakrishnan, R Perumal and V Batra (1999) 'Demonstration of coal gas run molten carbonate fuel cell'. *International Journal of Energy Research* **23**: 1177–1185

Maxwell, S, and L Hammer (1999) 'For richer, for fairer: Poverty reduction and income distribution'. Overseas Development Institute web site, 1 March 2000. www.id21.org/insights31/art1.htm

May, N et al (1998) *La Ville Eclatée*. Editions de l'Aube, La Tour d'Aigues

Mayntz, R (1993) 'Governing failures and the problem of governability: Some comments on a theoretical paradigm'. In J Kooiman (ed) *Modern Governance*. Sage, London, pp 9–20

Mbizvo, M T, S Fawcus et al (1993) 'Maternal mortality in rural and urban Zimbabwe: Social and reproductive factors in an incident case-referent study'. *Social Science and Medicine* **36**(9): 1197–205

Mehta, M (1994) *Strategy: Down Marketing Housing Finance through Community Based Financial Systems*. Abt Associates, New Delhi

MELISSA Program (1998) '1997 Knowledge and Expertise Resource Network (KERN) Forum Proceedings, Dakar'. Managing the Environment Locally in Sub Saharan Africa (MELISSA), Pretoria

Melosi, M V (1994) 'Sanitary services and decision making in Houston, 1876–1945'. *Journal of Urban History* **20**: 356–406

Méndez, J E (1999) 'The problems of lawless violence: Introduction'. In J E Méndez, G O'Donnell and P S Pinheiro (eds) *The (Un)Rule of Law and the Underprivileged in Latin America*. University of Notre Dame Press, Notre Dame, pp 19–24

Méndez, J E, G O'Donnell and P S Pinheiro (1999) *The (Un)Rule of Law and the Underprivileged in Latin America*. University of Notre Dame Press, Notre Dame

Mexican Health Foundation (1999) 'Trends and empirical causes of violent crime in Mexico'. *Final Report World Bank Research Project on Crime in Latin American Countries*. World Bank, Washington, DC

Michaelis, L (1996) *Reforming Coal and Electricity Subsidies*. OECD Working Paper, Paris

Michel, S (2000) 'Place, power, and water pollution in the Californias: A geographical analysis of water quality politics in the Tijuana-San Diego Metropolitan Region'. Doctoral dissertation, University of Colorado, Boulder

Middleton J, and P Saunders (1997) 'Paying for water'. *Journal Of Public Health Medicine* **19**(1): 106–115

Milanovic, B (1999) 'Explaining the increase in inequality during the transition'. *Economics of Transition* **7**(2): 299–341

Miller, D E (1998) 'Something left to lose: Personal relations and survival among New York's homeless'. *Journal of Contemporary Ethnography*

**27**(3): 422–427

Ministry of Cooperation and Development (1998) *Eau Potable et Assainissement dans les Quartiers Péri-Urbains et les Petits Centres*. Coopération Française, Paris

Miraftab, F (2000) *Women's Empowerment Indicators: Synthesis of the Women and Habitat Indicators Project*. UNCHS (Habitat), Nairobi

Mirza, N M, L E Caulfield et al (1997) 'Risk factors for diarrheal duration'. *American Journal of Epidemiology* **146**(9): 776–85

Mitchell, J (1998) 'Early childhood diarrhea and primary school performance in the northern areas of Pakistan'. Doctoral dissertation, University of Colorado, Boulder

Mitlin, D (1997) 'Building with credit: Housing finance for low-income households'. *Third World Planning Review* **19**(1): 21–50

Mitlin, D (1999) *Civil Society and Urban Poverty, Urban Governance, Partnership and Poverty*. Working Paper 5. International Development Department, University of Birmingham, Birmingham

Mitlin, D, D Satterthwaite et al (1996) 'City inequality'. *Environment and Urbanisation* **8**(2): 3–7

Mitomo, H, and T Jitsuzumi (1999) 'The impact of telecommuting on mass transit congestion: The Tokyo case'. *Telecommunications Policy* **23**: 741–751

Mittelman, J (ed) (1996) *Globalization: Critical Reflections: International Political Economy Yearbook* vol 9. Lynne Rienner Publishers, Boulder

Mock, C N, F Abantanga et al (1999) 'Incidence and outcome of injury in Ghana: A community-based survey'. *Bulletin of the World Health Organization* **77**(12): 955–64

Mock, N B, T A Sellers et al (1993) 'Socioeconomic, environmental, demographic and behavioral factors associated with occurrence of diarrhea in young children in the Republic of Congo'. *Social Science and Medicine* **36**(6): 807–16

Mody, A, and World Bank (1996) *Infrastructure Delivery: Private Initiative and the Public Good*, EDI Development Studies. World Bank, Washington, DC

Moghadam, V (2000) 'Transnational feminist networks'. *International Sociology* **15**(1): 57–85

Mohan, D and G Tiwari (2000) 'Mobility, environment and safety in mega cities'. *IATSS Research* **24**(10): 39–46

Molbak, K, P Aaby et al (1992) 'Persistent and acute diarrhoea as the leading causes of child mortality in urban Guinea Bissau'. *Transactions of the Royal Society of Tropical Medicine and Hygiene* **86**(2): 216–20

Molbak, K, N Hojlyng et al (1993) 'Cryptosporidiosis in infancy and childhood mortality in Guinea Bissau, West Africa'. *BMJ* **307**(6901): 417–20

Mollenkopf, J H, and M Castells (eds) (1991) *Dual City: Restructuring New York*. Russell Sage Foundation, New York

Molotch, H (1993) 'The political economy of growth machines'. *Journal of Urban Affairs* **15**(1): 29–53

Molyneux, C S, V Mung'Ala-Odera et al (1999) 'Maternal responses to childhood fevers: A comparison of rural and urban residents in coastal Kenya'. *Tropical Medicine and International Health* **4**(12): 836–45

Monteiro, C A et al (2000) 'Shifting obesity trends in Brazil'. *European Journal of Clinical Nutrtition* **54**(4): 342–346

Moore, M, and J Putzel (1999) 'Politics and poverty: A background paper for the World Development Report 2000/1'. Institute of Development Studies, University of Sussex, Brighton

Moore, T (1997) 'Market potential high for fuel cells'. *EPRI Journal* **22**(3): 6–17

Morris, M, and B Western (1999) 'Inequality in earnings at the close of the twentieth century'. *Annual Review of Sociology* **25**: 623–657

Moser, C (1992) 'Women and self-help housing projects: A conceptual framework for analysis and policy making'. In K Mathey (ed) *Beyond Self-Help Housing*. Mansell, London

Moser, C (1996) *Confronting Crisis: A Comparative Study of Household Responses to Poverty and Vulnerability in Four Poor Urban Communities.* Environmentally Sustainable Studies and Monographs Series 8. World Bank, Washington, DC

Moser, C (1998) 'The asset vulnerability framework: Reassessing urban poverty reduction strategies'. *World Development* **26**(1): 1–19

Moser, C (2000) 'The gendered continuum of violence and conflict: An operational framework'. In C Moser and F Clark (eds) *Victims, Perpetrators or Actors? Gender, Armed Conflict and Political Violence.* Zed Publications, London

Moser, C and E Grant (forthcoming) 'Violence and security in urban areas: Relationships with governance, health and labour markets'. Working Paper for National Academy of Science Panel on Urban Population Dynamics

Moser, C and J Holland (1997) *Urban Poverty and Violence in Jamaica.* World Bank Latin American and Caribbean Studies. World Bank, Washington, DC

Moser, C and S Lister (eds) (1999) *Violence and Social Capital: Proceedings of the LCSES Seminar Series, 1997–1998.* Urban Peace Program Series, Latin America and Caribbean Region Sustainable Development Working Paper No 5. World Bank, Washington, DC

Moser, C and C McIlwaine (1999) 'Participatory urban appraisal and its application for research on violence'. *Environment and Urbanization* **11**(2): 203–226

Moser, C and C McIlwaine (2000a) *Urban Poor Perceptions of Violence and Exclusion in Colombia.* World Bank, Washington, DC

Moser, C and C McIlwaine (2000b) *Violence on a Post-Conflict Context: Urban Poor Perceptions from Guatemala.* World Bank, Washington, DC

Moser, C and E Shrader (1999) 'A conceptual framework for violence reduction'. Urban Peace Program Series, Latin America and Caribbean Region Sustainable Development Working Paper No. 2. World Bank, Washington, DC

Moser, C, and B Van Bronkhorst (1999) 'Youth violence in Latin America and the Caribbean: Costs, causes, and interventions'. *Urban Peace Program Series, Latin America and Caribbean Region Sustainable Development Working Paper No 3.* World Bank, Washington, DC

Moser, C, C McIlwaine, S Lister, E Shrader and A Tornqvist (2000) *Violence in Colombia: Building Sustainable Peace and Social Capital: A World Bank Country Study.* World Bank, Washington, DC

Mougeot, L (2000a) 'Brief 6 – The Hidden Significance of Urban Agriculture'. In J L Garrett and M T Ruel (eds) *2020 Focus 3: Achieving Urban Food and Nutrition Security in the Developing World.* August. International Food Policy Research Institute (IFPRI), Washington, DC

Mougeot, L (2000b) 'Urban agriculture: Definition, presence, potentials and risks'. In Nico Bakker et al (eds) *Growing Cities, Growing Food: Urban Agriculture on the Policy Agenda.* German Foundation for International Development (DSE), Feldafing, Germany

Muhuri, P and Menken, J (1997) 'Adverse effects of next birth, gender, and family composition on child survival in rural Bangladesh'. *Population Studies* **51**: 279–294

Muna, W F (1993) 'Cardiovascular disorders in Africa'. *World Health Statistics Quarterly* **46**(2): 125–33

Murdie, R A, and L E Borgegard (1998) 'Immigration,spatial segregation and housing segmentation of immigrants in metropolitan Stockholm, 1960–65'. *Urban Studies* **35**(10): 1869–1888

Murdock, G (1993) 'Communications and the constitution of modernity'. *Media, Culture, and Society* **15**: 521–539

Murillo, M V (1997) 'Union politics, market-oriented reforms, and the reshaping of Argentine Corporatism'. In: D Chalmers, C Vilas, K Hite, S Martin, K Piester and M Segarra (eds) *The new Politics of Inequality In Latin America: Rethinking Participation and Representation.* Oxford University Press, Oxford

Murota, Y and Y Yano (1993) 'Japan's policy on energy and the environment'. *Annual Review of Energy and the Environment* **18**: 89–135

Musterd, S, H Priemus et al (1999) 'Towards undivided cities: The potential of economic revitalisation and housing redifferentiation'. *Housing Studies* **14**(5): 573–584

Mutatkar, R K (1995) 'Public health problems of urbanization'. *Social Science and Medicine* **41**(7): 977–81

Mwaiselage, A (1997) 'Community and state infrastructure provision in Tanzania'. Workshop Proceedings *Training and Sustainable Infrastructure Development in the SADAC*, Moputo, 1–4 December 1997

NACLA (1996) 'Report on crime and impunity' *Report on the Americas* **30**(September/October): 17–43

Nagel, S S (2000) *Critical Issues in Cross-National Public Administration: Privatization, Democratization, Decentralization.* Quorum, Westport, CT

Naisbett, J (1994) *Global Paradox: The Bigger the World Economy, the More Powerful Its Smaller Players.* Allen and Unwin, Sydney

Najam, A (no date) *Community Level Sustainability Assessment-Dasudi, India.* A Case Study of

IUCN/International Development Research Council (IDRC) World Conservation Union

Narayan, D (1997) *Voices of the Poor: Poverty and Social Capital in Tanzania.* Environmentally Sustainable Studies and Monograph Series No 20. World Bank, Washington, DC

NCLC (1991) *Understanding Why Customers don't Pay: The Need for Flexible Collection Practices.* NCLC, Boston

Nee, V, and L Peng (1996) 'Market transition and societal transformation in reforming state socialism'. *Annual Review of Sociology* **22**: 401–435

Neil, K (1999) 'Bandwidth colonialism? The implications of Internet infrastructure on international e-commerce'. Mimeo

Neild, R (1999) 'From national security to citizen security: Civil society and the evolution of public order debates'. Mimeo

Newman, P and J Kenworthy (1999) *Sustainability and Cities: Overcoming Automobile Dependence.* Island Press, Washington, DC

Newman, P W G, J R Kenworthy and P Vintila (1995) 'Can we overcome automobile dependence? Physical planning in an age of urban cynicism'. *Cities* **12**(1): 53–65

Ngom, T (1989) 'Appropriate standards for infrastructure in Dakar'. In R E Stren and R R White (eds) *African Cities in Crisis.* Westview Press, Boulder, pp 176–202

Nickell, S (1997) 'Unemployment and labor market rigidities: Europe versus North America'. *Journal of Economic Perspectives* **11**(1): 55–74

Nientied, P (1998) 'The question of town and regional planning in Albania'. *Habitat International* **22**(1): 41–47

Nordstrom, H and S Vaughan (1999) *Trade and Environment.* World Trade Organization, Geneva

North, D (1990) *Institutions, Institutional Change, and Economic Performance.* Cambridge University Press, New York

Novello, A (1991) 'Violence is a greater killer of children than diseases'. *Public Health Reports* **106**(3): 6–11

Nozdrina, N, and G Sternik (1999) *Housing Markets And Migration In Cities Of Russia.* Executive Reports, No 6. Moscow Carnegie Center

NRC (1997) *Safe Water from Every Tap.* National Academy Press, Washington, DC

NTIA (1999) *Americans in the Information Age: Falling Through the Net.* NTIA, Washington, DC. www.ntia.doc.gov/ntiahome/digital-divide/

Ochwo, M T (1999) 'The Masese Women's association raises a community from a slum', *Women and Environments International* 46/47: 22–25

Odero, W (1995) 'Road traffic accidents in Kenya: An epidemiological appraisal'. *East African Medical Journal* **72**(5): 299–305

Odero, W, P Garner et al (1997) 'Road traffic injuries in developing countries: A comprehensive review of epidemiological studies'. *Tropical Medicine and International Health* **2**(5): 445–60

O'Donnell, G (1994) 'Delegative democracy'. *Journal of Democracy*

**5**(January): 56–69

O'Donnell, G, P Schmitter and L Whitehead (eds) (1986) *Transitions from Authoritarian Rule.* The Johns Hopkins University Press, Baltimore

OECD (1995) *Urban Energy Handbook: Good Local Practice.* OECD, Paris

OECD (1996) *Innovative Policies for Sustainable Urban Development: The Ecological City.* OECD, Paris

OECD (1997a) *Renewable Energy Policy in IEA Countries.* OECD/IEA, Paris

OECD (1997b) *Reforming Energy and Transport Subsidies: Environmental and Economic Implications.* OECD, Paris

OECD, Directorate for Financial, Fiscal and Enterprise Affairs (1999) *Fiscal Decentralization: Benchmarking the Policies of Fiscal Design.* OECD, Paris

OECD/The Local Economic and Employment Development Program (LEED) (1998) *Best Practices in Local Development.* OECD, Paris

OFWAT (1995) *Debt and Disconnection.* Note no 31. www.open.gov.uk/ofwat/

Ohmae, K (1990) *The Borderless World.* Fontana, London

OIT (Organización Internacional del Trabajo) (1993) *El Trabajo en el Mundo.* Organización Internacional del Trabajo, Geneva

OIT (1996) *La Situación Sociolaboral en las Zonas Francas y Empresas Maquiladoras del Istmo Centroamericano y República Dominicana.* Organización Internacional del Trabajo, Costa Rica

Okpala, D C I (1996) 'The Second United Nations Conference on Human Settlements (Habitat II): Viewpoint'. *Third World Planning Review* **18**(2): R3–R12

Olds, K (1998) 'Urban mega-events, evictions and housing rights: The Canadian case'. *Current Issues in Tourism* **1**(1): 2–46 (available at www.breadnotcircuses.org/kris_olds _toc.html)

Olson, M (1965) *The Logic of Collective Action; Public Goods and the Theory of Groups.* Schocken Books, New York

Olson, M (1982) *The Rise and Decline of Nations: Economic Growth, Stagflation, and Social Rigidities.* Yale University Press, New Haven, Connecticut

Olson, R S, with R Alvarez, B Baird, A Estrada, V T Gawronski and J P Sarmiento Preito (1999) *Disaster and Institutional Response: Hurricane Georges in the Dominican Republic and Hurricane Mitch in Honduras and Nicaragua, September-October, 1998.* Robert Olson Associates, Folsom, CA, pp 59–61

O'Meara, M (1999) *Reinventing Cities for People and the Planet.* Worldwatch Paper 147. Worldwatch Institute, Washington, DC

O'Meara, M (2000) 'Harnessing Information Technologies for the Environment'. In L R Brown/Worldwatch Institute (eds), *State of the World 2000.* Earthscan, London, pp 121–141

Orangi Pilot Project (1998) 76th Quarterly Report. OPP, Karachi

Oxhorn, P (1995) *Organizing Civil Society: The Popular Sectors and the Struggle for Democracy in Chile.* The Pennsylvania State University Press, University Park

Oxhorn, P (1997) 'Hacia un modelo alternativo de desarrollo para El Salvador: El papel de la sociedad civil'. In W Knut (ed) *Gobernabilidad y Desarrollo Humano Sostenible en El Salvador*. Fundación Centroamericana para el Desarrollo Humano Sustenible, San Salvador, pp 167–233

Oxhorn, P (1998) 'Is the century of corporatism over? Neoliberalism and the rise of neopluralism'. In P Oxhorn and G Ducatenzeiler (eds) *What Kind of Democracy? What Kind of Market? Latin America in the Age of Neoliberalism*. The Pennsylvania State University Press, University Park, pp 195–217

Oxhorn, P and G Ducatenzeiler (eds) (1998) *What Kind of Democracy? What Kind of Market? Latin America in the Age of Neoliberalism*. The Pennsylvania State University, University Park

Ozerdem, A (1999) 'Tiles, taps, and earthquake-proofing: Lessons for disaster management in Turkey'. *Environment and Urbanization* **11**(2): 177–179

PADCO (1991) 'India: Public–private partnerships in land development'. Washington, DC. Mimeo

Paes Manso, B (2000) 'Homicides'. Braudel Papers No 25. Fernand Braudel Institute of World Economics, São Paulo

Pahl, R E (1966) 'The rural–urban continuum'. *Sociologia Ruralis* **6**: 299–329

PAHO (Pan-American Health Organization) (1996). *Adolescent Programme Health Situation Analysis*. Technical Health Information System Mortality Database. PAHO, Washington, DC

PAHO (1998a). *Health in the Americas: 1998 Edition*. PAHO, Washington, DC

PAHO (1998b) *Juvenile Violence in the Americas: Innovative Studies in Research, Diagnosis and Prevention*. PAHO, Washington, DC

Pan American Development Foundation (2000) 'Programa Para el Desarrollo de la Capacitacion Inicial: Programa Municipal de Sistema de Alerta Temprana (PROMSAT)'. Conference proceedings, Tocoa, Honduras, 4–7 April

Parikh, J, M Panda and N Murthy (1997) 'Consumption patterns by income groups and carbon-dioxide implications for India: 1990–2010'. *International Journal of Global Energy Issues* **9**(4–6): 237–255

Parry, C (1995) 'Quantitative measurement of mental health problems in urban areas: Opportunities and constraints'. In T Harpham and I Blue (eds) *Urbanisation and Mental Health in Developing Countries*. Aldershot, Avebury, UK

Pastor, M Jr, Dreier, P et al (2000) *Regions that Work: How Cities and Suburbs can Grow together*. University of Minnesota Press, Minneapolis

Patel, S, J Bolnick and D Mitlin (2001) 'Squatting on the global highway'. In M Edwards and J Gaventa (eds) *Global Citizen Action*. Earthscan, London/Lynne Rienner Publishers, Boulder

Pathak, B (1999) 'Sanitation is the key to healthy cities: A profile of Sulabh International'. *Environment and Urbanization* **11**(1): 221–229

Pathak, P (1995) 'The impact of structural adjustment programme on women's employment in the informal sector'. In S Rguram, H Sievers and V Vyasulu (eds) *Structural adjust-*

*ment: Economy, environment and social concerns*. Macmillan, New Delhi

Payne, G (ed) (1999) *Making Common Ground: Public–Private Partnerships in Land for Housing*. Intermediate Technology Publications, London

Pearce, J (1998) 'From civil war to civil society: Has the end of the Cold War brought peace to Central America?' *International Affairs* **74**(3): 587–615

Pearson, P, and R Fouquet (1996) 'Energy efficiency, economic efficiency and future $CO_2$ emissions from the developing world'. *Energy Journal* **17**: 135–160

Pecaut, D (1997) 'Presente, pasado y futuro de la violencia en Colombia'. *Desarollo, Economico: Revista de Ciencias Sociales* **36**: 891–930

Pellow, D (2000) 'Environmental justice and the political process: Movements, corporations and the state', Department of Sociology, University of Colorado, Boulder

Peltonen, A (1999) 'Exchanging international experiences'. *Urban Age: The Global City Magazine* **7**(1): 4–7, 33

Peneiro, P (1993) 'Reflection on urban violence'. *Urban Age* **1**: 3–4

Peraldi, M and E Perrin (eds) (1996) *Reseaux Productifs et Territoires Urbains*. Presses Universitaires du Mirail, Toulouse

Perchard, T (1992) 'Water debt and disconnections'. *Consumer Policy Review* **1**, 1

Perez Montiel, R, and F Barten (1999) 'Urban governance and health development in Leon, Nicaragua'. *Environment and Urbanization* **11**(1): 11–26

Perrons, D (1999) 'Flexible working patterns and equal opportunities in the European Union'. *European Journal of Women's Studies* **6**: 391–418

Perumal, R (1998) 'Fuel cells: Why we should take them seriously'. *Tata Energy Research Institute (TERI) Newswire*, January

Petrella, R (1993) 'Vers un "techno-apartheid" global'. *Le Monde Diplomatique*, May, No 18

Pezzoli, K (1995) 'Mexico's urban housing environments: Economic and ecological challenges of the 1990s'. In B C Aldrich and R S Sandu (eds) *Housing and the Urban Poor: Policies and Practices in Developing Countries*. Zed, London

Picon, A (1998) *La Ville Territoire de Cyborgs*. L'Imprimeur, Paris

Piester, K (1997) 'Targeting the poor: The politics of social policy reform in Mexico'. In D Chalmers, C Vilas, K Hite, S Martin, K Piester and M Segarra (eds) *The New Politics of Inequality in Latin America: Rethinking Participation and Representation*. Oxford University Press, Oxford, pp 469–488

Pile, S, and M Keith (eds) (1997) *Geographies of Resistance*. Routledge, London

Pillon, T and A Querrien (eds) (1995) *Futur Anterieur* Special issue: *La Ville-Monde Aujourd'hui: Entre Virtualite et Ancrage* **30–32**. L'Harmattan, Paris

Pinheiro, P S (1999) 'The rule of law and the underprivileged in Latin America: Introduction'. In J E Méndez, G O'Donnell and P S Pinheiro (eds) *The (Un)Rule of Law and the Underprivileged in Latin America*. University of Notre Dame Press, Notre Dame, pp 1–15

Pirages, D, and P Runci (2000)

'Ecological interdependence and the spread of infectious disease'. In M K Cusimano (ed) *Beyond Sovereignty: Issues for a Global Agenda*. St Martin's Press, New York, pp 176–194

Plaza, B (1999) 'The Guggenheim-Bilbao Museum effect: A reply to Maria V Gomes' "Reflective images: The case of urban regeneration in Glasgow and Bilbao"'. *International Journal of Urban and Regional Research* **23**(3): 589–592

Polanyi, K (1957) *The Great Transformation*. Farrar and Rinehart, New York

Popkin B M (1999) 'Urbanization, lifestyle changes and the nutrition transition'. *World Development* **27**(11): 1905–1916

Portes, A (1994) 'By-passing the rules: The dialectics of labour standards and informalization in less developed countries'. In N Sensuberger and D Cambell (eds) *International Labor Standards and Economic Interdependence*. Institute for Labour Studies, Geneva, pp 159–176

Potts, D (1997) 'Urban lives: Adopting new strategies and adapting rural links'. In: C Radoki (ed) *The Urban Challenge in Africa: Growth and Management of its Large Cities*. United Nations University Press, Tokyo, pp 447–495

Pouliquen, L Y (1999) *Rural Infrastructure from a World Bank Perspective: A Knowledge Management Framework*. World Bank, Washington, DC

Power, A (1997) *Estates on the Edge: The Social Consequences of Mass Housing in Northern Europe*. Macmillan, London

Power, A (1999) 'High-rise estates in Europe: Is rescue possible?' *European Journal of Social Policy* **9**(2): 139–163

Preparatory Committee for the United Nations Conference on Human Settlements (1995) *From Vancouver to Istanbul: Persistent Problems, Common Goals and Shifting Approaches*. Report of the Secretary-General. Preparatory Committee for the United Nations Conference on Human Settlements, Second session, Nairobi

Prévôt-Schapira, M F (1996) 'Territoires urbains et politiques sociales en Amérique Latine: Réflexions à partir des cas Argentin et Mexicain'. In E Le Bris (ed) *Villes du Sud*. Orstom Editions, Paris

Prévôt-Schapira, M F (1999) 'La Ville Fragmentée'. *Esprit*, 128–144

Prud'homme, R (1994) *On the Dangers of Decentralization*. Transportation, Water, and Urban Development Department, World Bank, Washington, DC

Pryer, J (1993) 'The impact of adult ill-health on household income and nutrition in Khulna, Bangladesh'. *Environment and Urbanization* **5**(2)(October): 35–49

Pugh, C (1994a) 'Development of housing finance and the global strategy for shelter'. *Cities* **11**(6): 384–392

Pugh, C (1994b) 'The idea of enablement in housing sector development'. *Cities* **11**(6): 357–371

Pugh, C (1997a) 'Habitat II: Editor's introduction'. *Urban Studies* **34**(10): 1541–1546

Pugh, C (1997b) 'Poverty and progress? Reflections on housing and urban policies in developing countries, 1976–96'. *Urban Studies* **34**(10): 1547–1595

Pulido, L (1996) *Environmentalism and Economic Justice: Two Chicano Struggles in the Southwest*. University of Arizona Press, Tucson

Putnam, R D (1993) *Making Democracy Work: Civic Traditions in Modern Italy*. Princeton University Press, Princeton

Puzanov, A (1993) 'The quality of Moscow's housing and households' resources'. In: *Housing Market in Russia: Formation And Development Voprosy Ekonomiki* **7** [in Russian]

*Race, Poverty and Environment: A newsletter for social and environmental justice* (1992) Special issue on water. Earth Island Institute, San Francisco

Rakodi, C, R Gatabaki-Kamau and N Devas (2000) 'Poverty and political conflict in Mombasa'. *Environment and Urbanization* **12**(1): 153–171

Ramos-Schiffer, S R (1997) 'São Paulo: The challenge of globalization in an exclusionary urban structure'. Mimeo

Rapaport, R (1996) 'Bangalore'. *Wired*, February: 56–107

Ratcliffe, P (1998) '"Race", housing and social exclusion'. *Housing Studies* **13**(6): 807–818

Razavi, S (1999a) 'Gendered poverty and well-being'. *Development and Change* **30**(3): 409–433

Razavi, S (1999b) 'Seeing poverty through a gender lens'. *International Social Science Journal* **51**(4): 473–482

Razavi, S (2000) *Women in Contemporary Democratization* (Occasional Paper no 4). United Nations Research Institute for Social Develeopment, Geneva

Reddy, B (1997) 'Flow of energy in an urban society'. *Energy Sources* **19**: 271–294

Rees, J A (1998) 'Regulation and private participation in the water and sanitation sector'. *Natural Resources Forum* **22**(2): 95ff

Reich, R (1991) *The Work of Nations: Preparing Ourselves for 21st Century Capitalism*. Knopf, New York

Reisman, W M (1990) 'Sovereignty and human rights in contemporary international law'. *American Journal of International Law* **84**(4): 866–76

Reiss, A and J Roth (eds) (1993) *Understanding and Preventing Violence*. National Academy Press, Washington, DC

Renaud, B (1997) 'The 1985 to 1994 global real estate cycle: An overview'. *Journal of Real Estate Literature* **5**: 13–44

Renaud, B (1998) 'Restructuring Russia's housing sector: 1991–1997'. *Housing Studies* **13**(6): 852–854

*Report of the International Conference on Population and Development*, para 9.12

Revkin, A (1999) 'Sewage Plant Alchemy'. *New York Times*, 7 February, p 46

Rhodes, R A W (1996) 'The new governance: Governing without government'. *Political Studies* **44**: 652–67

Ridley, M A (1995) *World Bank Experiences with Mass Rapid Transit Projects*. The World Bank, Washington, DC

Riis, J (1891) *How the Other Half Lives: Studies Among the Poor*. Sampson Low, Marston, Searle, and Rivington, London

Robertson, R (1994) 'Globalisation or glocalisation?'. *The Journal of International Communication* **1**(1): 23–52

Rodriguez, A, and L Winchester (1996) 'Ville, démocratie et gouvernance en Amérique Latine'. *Revue Internationale des Sciences Sociales* **147**: 85–96

Rodriguez-Pose, A (1999) 'Convergence or divergence? Types of regional responses to socioeconomic change in Western Europe'. *Tijdschrift voor Economische en Sociale Geografie* **90**(4): 363–378

Roe, S, J Reisman, R Strait, M Doorn and S Thorneloe (1998) *Emerging Technologies for the Management and Utilization of Landfill Gas.* US Environmental Protection Agency, Washington, DC

Rogers, D (1999) 'Youth gangs and violence in Latin America and the Caribbean: A literature survey'. *Urban Peace Program Series, Latin America and Caribbean Region Sustainable Development Working Paper No 7.* World Bank, Washington, DC

Rogoff, K (1999) 'International institutions for reducing global financial instability'. *Journal of Economic Perspectives* **13**(4): 21–42

Rojas, E (2000) 'Making decentralization work: Supporting subnational development in Latin America and the Caribbean'. Internal Memo to the Inter American Development Bank, Sustainable Development Department, Social Programs Division

Rojas, E and M Greene (1995) 'Reaching the poor: Lessons from the Chilean housing experience'. *Environment and Urbanization* **7**(2): 31–50

Root, G (1997) 'Population density and spatial differentials in child mortality in Zimbabwe'. *Social Science and Medicine* **44**(3): 413–21

Roschelle, A R (1998) 'The unequal homeless: Men on the streets, women in their place'. *Journal of Contemporary Ethnography* **26**(4): 516–520

Rose, D (1984) 'Rethinking gentrification'. *Environment and Planning D: Society and Space* **2**: 47–74

Rosen, H, and A Keating (eds) (1991) *Water and the City; The Next Century.* Public Works Historical Society, Chicago

Rosenau, J (1992) *Governance Without Government.* Cambridge University Press, Cambridge

Rosenburg, M (1999) 'Violence as a public health problem'. In C Moser and S Lister (eds) *Violence and Social Capital: Proceedings of the LCSES Seminar Series, 1997–1998. Urban Peace Program Series, Latin America and Caribbean Region Sustainable Development Working Paper No 5.* World Bank, Washington, DC

Ross, A (1999) *The Celebration Chronicles: Life, Liberty and the Pursuit of Property Value in Disney's New Town.* Ballantine, New York

Rosser, J B R, MV Rosser and E Ahmed (2000) 'Income inequality and the informal economy in transition economies'. *Journal of Comparative Economics* **28**(1): 156–171

Rothstein, M (1998) 'Offices Plugged in and Ready to Go'. *New York Times,* 4 February

Rotzer, F (1995) *Die Telepolis: Urbanität im digitalen Zeitalter.* Bollmann, Mannheim

Roy, R, and M Mackintosh (1999) *Economic Decentralization and Public Management Reform, New Horizons in*

*Public Policy.* Edward Elgar, Cheltenham, UK

Rubio, M (1997) 'Perverse social capital: Some evidence from Colombia'. *Journal of Economic Issues* **31**(3): 805–16

Rumbold, G (1998) 'Two examples of the application of geographic information systems in drug research presented at the Second Symposium on GIS and Health'. *Second Symposium on GIS and Health, Developments in the Application of Geographic Information Systems Within the Health Sector.* Department of Geomatics, The University of Melbourne, Melbourne, Australia, 10 June. www.sli.unimelb.edu.au/HealthGIS98/presentations

Ruspini, E (1999) 'The contribution of longitudinal research to the study of women's poverty'. *Quality and Quantity* **33**: 323–338

Saito, S (1995) 'Fuel cell development by electric power industry'. *Japan 21st,* November: 21–23

Salamon, L M (1994) 'The rise of the nonprofit sector'. *Foreign Affairs* **73**: 109–122

Saleth, R M (1999) *Water Challenge and Institutional Response, Policy Research Working Papers; WPS/2045.* World Bank, Washington, DC

Sally, R (2000) 'Globalization and policy response: Three perspectives'. *Government and Opposition* **35**(2): 237–253

Salmi, J (1993) *Violence and Democratic Society: A New Approach to Human Rights.* Zed Books, London

Sancar, F (2000) 'Reflections on the 1999 earthquake in Turkey', unpublished paper, University of Colorado

Sandelin, S (1994) *Low-income Area Water Supply and Sanitation in Selected African Cities.* Tampere University of Technology, Institute of Water and Environmental Engineering, Tampere, Finland

D Sanderson (2000) 'Cities, disasters and livelihoods'. *Environment and Urbanization* **12**(2): 93–102

Sassen, S (1989) 'New trends in the sociospatial organization of the New York City economy'. In R A Beauregard (ed) *Economic Restructuring and Political Response.* Sage, Newbury Park, California

Sassen, S (1991) *The Global City.* Princeton University Press, Princeton

Sassen, S (1994) *Cities in a World Economy.* Pine Forge Press, Thousand Oaks, California

Sassen, S (1996) *Losing Control? Sovereignty in an Age of Globalization.* Columbia University Press, New York

Sassen, S (1998a) *Globalization and its Discontents.* New Press, New York

Sassen, S (1998b) 'Towards a feminist analytics of the global economy'. In Sassen, S (ed) *Globalization and Its Discontents: Essays on the New Mobility of People and Money.* New Press, New York, Chapter 5

Sassen, S (1999) 'Transnational economies and national migration policies'. In M J Castro (ed) *Free Markets, Open Societies, Closed Borders?* North-South Center Press, Miami

Sassen, S (2000a) *Cities in a World Economy,* 2nd edition. Pine Forge/Sage, Thousand Oaks, California

Sassen, S (ed) (2000b) *Cities and Their Cross-Border Networks.* Institute for Advanced Studies, United Nations University, Tokyo, Japan. To be published by the United Nations Press

Sassen, S (2000c) *The Global City: New York, London, Tokyo,* 2nd rev. edition. Princeton University Press, Princeton, New Jersey

Satterthwaite, D (1993) 'The impact on health of urban environments'. *Environment and Urbanisation* **5**(2): 87–111

Satterthwaite, D (1995a) 'The underestimation and misrepresentation of urban poverty'. *Environment and Urbanisation* **7**(1): 3–10

Satterthwaite, D (1995b) 'The underestimation of poverty and its health consequences'. *Third World Planning Review* **17**(4): iii-xii

Saunders, M, P Kimmel, M Sapde and N Brockway (1998) *Water Affordability Programs.* AWWARF, Denver

Savitch, H and J Thomas (1991) *Big City Politics in Transition.* Sage, Thousand Oaks

Schenker, J L (1999) 'A wider net new technology could help narrow the information gap between the developed and developing worlds'. *Time* **154**(15, October 11)

Schiller, D (1999) *Digital Capitalism: Networking the Global Market System.* MIT Press, Cambridge, Massachusetts

Schmitter, P (1995) 'The irony of modern democracy and the viability of efforts to reform its practice'. In E O Wright (ed) *Associations and Democracy: The Real Utopias Project,* Vol 1. Verso, London, pp 167–183

Schön, D, B Sanyal and W Mitchell (eds) *High Technology and Low Income Communities.* MIT Press, Cambridge, Massachusetts

Schuler, D (1996) *New Community Networks: Wired For Change.* Addison Wesley, New York

Schuurman, F J (2000) 'Paradigms lost, paradigms regained? Development studies in the twenty-first century'. *Third World Quarterly* **21**(1): 7–20

Schwab, J, with K C Topping, C C Eadie, R E Deyle and R A Smith (1998) *Planning for Post-Disaster Recovery and Reconstruction.* American Planning Association, Washington, DC, p 8

Schwemm, R (1990) *Housing Discrimination: Law and Litigation (with Annual Supplements).* Clark Boardman Callaghan, New York

Searle, G (1996) *Sydney as a Global City.* State of New South Wales, Sydney

Sen, A (1998) 'Nobody need starve'. *Urban Age* **5**(3): 14–17

Sen, A (1999a) *Development as Freedom.* Knopf, New York

Sen, A (1999b) 'Economics and health'. *The Lancet,* Special Supplement, 28 February 2000

Sendi, R (1999) 'Housing construction in the transition period: Slovenia's non-starter situation'. *Housing Studies* **14**(6): 803–819

Serageldin, I (1996) *Sustainability and the Wealth of Nations: First Steps in an Ongoing Journey.* Environmentally Sustainable Studies and Monograph Series No 5. World Bank, Washington, DC

Serageldin, I and A Steer (eds) (1994)

*Making Development Sustainable: From Concepts to Action.* World Bank, Washington, DC

SEWA Bank (1998) *Bridging the Market Gap: Housing Finance for Women in the Informal Sector.* Gujarat Mahila Housing and SEWA Trust, Ahmedabad

Shachar, A (1990) 'The global economy and world cities'. In A Shachar and S Öberg (eds) *The World Economy and the Spatial Organization of Power.* Avebury, Aldershot, UK/Brookfield, Vermont, pp 149–60

Shah, A (1997) *Balance, Accountability, and Responsiveness: Lessons about Decentralization.* World Bank, Washington, DC

Shahriani, H (no date) *Participatory Irrigation Management in Albania. Paper Prepared for the National Seminar on Participatory Irrigation Management. Triana, Albania.* World Bank. www.worldbank.org/wbi/pimelg/case3.htm

Shapiro, I, and R Greenstein (1999) *The Widening Income Gulf.* Center on Budget and Policy Priorities, Washington, DC

Shaw, M, and A Louw (1998) 'Environmental design for safer communities: Preventing crime in South Africa's cities and towns' *Monograph No. 24 Environmental Design for Safer Communities.* Johannesburg, South Africa

Shelton, D (1996) 'Glocalization: The precautionary principle and public participation, with special reference to the UN Framework Convention on Climate Change'. In D Freestone and E Hey (eds) *The Precautionary Principle and International Law: The Challenge of Implementation.* Kluwer/Boston, The Hague

Sheng, F (1997) *Public Environmental Expenditures: A Conceptual Framework.* Macroeconomics for Sustainable Development Program Office (MPO). WWF, Washington, DC

Short, J R and J Kim (1999) *Globalization and the City.* Prentice Hall, New Jersey/Longman, Harlow, UK

Skeates, R (1997) 'The infinite city'. *City* **8**: 6–20

Siembieda, W J and E Lopez Moreno (1999) 'From commercial banking systems to non-commercial banking systems in Mexico'. In K Datta and G Jones (eds) *Housing and Finance in Developing Countries.* Routledge, London

Siemens A G (1999) 'Shell and Siemens to develop emission-free fuel-cell power plant'. *Press Release,* 13 July. www.siemens.de/en/press_service/99071301e.html

Silver (1998) 'Cooperative housing'. In W van Vliet– (ed) *Encyclopedia of Housing.* Sage Publications, Thousand Oaks, California

Simmons, E (1999) *The Challenges of Globalization for U.S. Development Assistance* (National Policy Association Brief 294). National Policy Association, Washington, DC

Simpson-Hebert, M, et al (1998) *Ecological Sanitation.* SIDA, Swedish International Development Authority, Stockholm

Sinha, A, S Sazawal et al (1999) 'Typhoid fever in children aged less than five years'. *The Lancet* **354**(9180): 734–7

Smit, J, and J Nasr (1992) 'Urban agriculture for sustainable cities: Using wastes and idle land and water bodies as resources'. *Environment and Urbanization* **4**(2): 141–52

Smith, C (1999) 'Trek for African phones'. *Johannesburg Daily Mail and Guardian*, 18 March

Soares, K, I Blue, E Cano and J Mari (1998) 'Short report: Violent death in young people in the city of São Paulo, 1991–1993'. *Health and Place* **4**(2): 195–198

Soley, M (1996) 'Teaching about international conflict and peace'. *Social Education* **60**(7): 432–438

Solo, T M (1999) 'Small-scale entrepreneurs in the urban water and sanitation market'. *Environment and Urbanization* **11**(1): 117–131

Somerville, P (1998) 'Explanations of social exclusion: Where does housing fit in?' *Housing Studies*. **13**(6): 761–780

Souter, D (1999) 'The role of information and communication technologies in democratic development'. *Info* **1**(5): 405–417

South Africa Department of Health (1998) *South Africa Demographic and Health Survey 1998*. South Africa Department of Health, Pretoria

Souza, C (2000) 'Participatory budgeting in Brazilian cities: Limits and possibilities in building democratic institutions'. Urban governance, partnership and poverty working paper 28, University of Birmingham

SPARC, Mahila Milan and the National Slum Dwellers Federation In India (1998) *Citywatch: India* **6**(August). SPARC/Mahila Milan/National Slum Dwellers Federation in India, Mumbai

Speak, S, and S Graham (1999) 'Service not included: Marginalised neighbourhoods, private service disinvestment, and compound social exclusion'. *Environment and Planning A* **31**: 1985–2001

Spéder, Z (1998) 'Poverty dynamics in Hungary during the Transformation'. *Economic Transitions* **6**(1): 1–21

Springer, S (2000) 'Homelessness: A proposal for a global definition and classification'. *Habitat International* **24**(4): 475–484

Srinukoon C (1999) *Households waste minimisation in Bangkok Metropolis*. Policy paper / Centre for Developing Cities; no. 7

Stephens, C (1996) 'Healthy cities or unhealthy islands: The health and social implications of urban inequality'. *Environment and Urbanisation* **8**(2): 9–30

Stephens, C, I Timaeus et al (1994) *Environment and Health in Developing Countries: An Analysis of Intra-Urban Differentials Using Existing Data*. Monograph, London School of Tropical Medicine and Hygiene, London

Stephens, M (2000) 'Convergence in european mortgage systems before and after EMU'. *Journal of Housing and the Built Environment* **15**: 29–52.14

Steyn, K, J Fourie et al (1996) 'Hypertension in the black community of the Cape Peninsula, South Africa'. *East African Medical Journal* **73**(11): 758–63

Stiglitz, J E (1990) 'Peer monitoring in credit markets'. *World Bank Economic*

*Review* **IV**: 351–366

Stimson, R J (1995) 'Diverse multi-centered regions the future'. *Urban Net* **2**(2): 1–3

Stoel, T (1999) 'Reining in urban sprawl'. *Environment* **41**: 7–33

Stoker, G (1998) 'Governance as theory: Five propositions'. *International Social Science Journal* **155**: 17–28

Stolee, M K (1988) 'Homeless Children in the USSR 1917–1957'. *Soviet Studies* **40**(1): 64–83

Strassmann, W P (1997) 'Avoiding conflict and bold inquiry: A recapitulation of Habitat II'. *Urban Studies* **34**(10): 1729–1738

Stren, R (1996) 'The studies of cities: Popular perceptions, academic disciplines, and emerging agendas'. In M A Cohen, B A Ruble, J S Tulchin, and A M Garland (eds) *Preparing for the Urban Future. Global Pressures and Local Forces*. Woodrow Wilson Center Press, distributed by The Johns Hopkins University Press, Baltimore, pp 392–420

Struyk, R (ed) (1996) *Economic Restructuring Of The Former Soviet Bloc: The Case of Housing*. The Urban Institute, Washington, DC

Struyk, R (ed) (1997) *Restructuring Russia's Housing Sector: 1991–1997*. The Urban Institute, Washington, DC

Struyk, R J, A S Puzanov and L A Lee (1997) 'Monitoring Russia's experience with housing allowances'. *Urban Studies* **34**(11): 1789–1818

*Sunday Times* (2000) 'The dome's last chance'. *The Sunday Times*, London

Surjadi, C, L Padhmasutra, D Wahyuningsih, G McGranahan and M Kjellén (1994) *Household Environmental Problems in Jakarta*. Stockholm Environment Institute, Stockholm

Suro, R (1998) *Strangers Among Us: How Latino Immigration is Transforming America*. Alfred A. Knopf, New York

Sussman, G, and J Lent (1998) *Global Productions: Labor in the Making of the 'Information Society'*. Hampton Press, Cresskill, NJ

Swardson, A (1998) 'Win does little to elevate people of Saint-Denis', *The Washington Post*, 9 July

Swyngedouw, E (1992) 'Communication, mobility and the struggle for power over space'. In G Giannopoulos and A Gillespie (eds) (1993) *Transport and Communications in the New Europe*. Belhaven, London, pp 305–325

Swyngedouw, E A (1995) 'The contradictions of urban water provision: A study of Guayaquil, Ecuador'. *Third World Planning Review* **17**(4): 387–405

Swyngedouw, E (1995) 'Thirsty cities: Urban environments and water-supply in Latin America. Anton, D J'. Book review in *Third World Planning Review*. **17**(3): 362–364

Swyngedouw, E (1997) 'Neither global nor local: "Glocalization" and the politics of scale'. In K Cox (ed) *Spaces of Globalization*. Guilford, New York, pp137–66

Szelenyi, I (1983) *Inequalites under State Socialism*. Oxford University Press. Oxford

Szreter, S (1997) 'Economic growth, disruption, deprivation, disease and death: On the importance of the politics of pubic health for development'. *Population and Development*

*Review* **23**(4): 693–728

Tabak, F, and M A Chrichlow (eds) (2000) *Informalization: Process and Structure*. The Johns Hopkins University Press, Baltimore

Takoli, C (1998) 'Rural–urban interactions: A guide to the literature'. *Environment and Urbanisation* **10**(1): 147–166

Tanner, M, and T Harpham (1995) 'Features and determinants of urban health status'. In T Harpham and M Tanner (eds) *Urban Health in Developing Countries: Progress and Prospects*. Earthscan, London

Tanzi, V (2000) *Globalization and the Future of Social Protection*. IMF Working Paper WP/00/12

Tardanico, R, and R Menjivar (1997) *Global Restructuring, Employment, and Social Inequality in Urban Latin America*. University of Miami, North-South Center Press, Coral Gables, Florida

Tata Energy Research Institute (TERI) (1998) *Could Fuel Cell Vehicles be the Way Out?* TERI, New Delhi

Taylor, C E (1993) 'Learning from health care experiences in developing countries'. *American Journal of Public Health* **83**(11): 1531–32

Taylor, I and R Jamieson (1999) 'Sex trafficking and the mainstream of market culture: Challenges to organised crime analysis'. *Journal of Crime Law and Social Change* **32**(3)

Taylor, M (1998) 'Combating the social exclusion of housing estates'. *Housing Studies* **13**(6): 819–832

Taylor, P J (1995) 'World cities and territorial states: The rise and fall of their mutuality'. In P L Knox and P J Taylor (eds) *World Cities in a World-System*. Cambridge University Press, Cambridge, pp 48–62

Taylor, P (1999) 'Democratizing cities: Habitat's campaign on urban governance'. *Habitat Debate* **5**(4). Available at www.unchs/unchs/english/hdv5 n4/

Technology Transition Corporation (1995) *The Entry Market for Fuel Cells*. Fuel Cell Commercialization Group, Washington, DC. www.ttcorp.com/fccg/fcmabstr.htm

*Third World Planning Review* (1987) 'The United Nations International Year of Shelter For the Homeless'. *Third World Planning Review* **9**: 1–4

Thoits, P A (1995) 'Stress, coping, and social support processes: Where are we? What next?' *Journal of Health and Social Behavior* (Extra Issue): 53–79

Thompson, J (ed) (2000) *Drawers of Water II: Thirty Years of Change in Domestic Water Use and Environmental Health*. Brochure, IIED, London. www.iied.org/

Thompson, J, I Porras, E Wood, J Tumwine, M Mujwahuzi, M Katui-Katua and N Johnstone (2000) 'Waiting at the tap: Changes in urban water use in East Africa over three decades'. *Environment and Urbanization* **12**(2): 37–52

Thornley, A (2000) *Globalization, Urban Planning and Local Democracy*. London School of Economics, London

Thornton, R (1987) *American Indian Holocaust and Survival: A Population History Since 1492*. University of Oklahoma Press, Norman, pp 78–79

Timaeus, I, and A Lopez (1996)

'Introduction'. In I Timaeus, J Chackiel and L Ruzicka (eds) *Adult Mortality in Latin America*. Clarendo Press, Oxford, pp 5–13

Timaeus, M I, and L Lush (1995) 'Intra-urban differentials in child health'. *Health Transition Review* **5**: 163–190

Tinker, I, and G Summerfield (eds) (1999) *Women's Rights to House and Land: China, Laos, Vietnam*. Lynne Rienner Publishers, Boulder

Tjønneland, E N (1998) *The World Bank and Poverty in Sub-Saharan Africa: A Study of Operationalizing Policies for Poverty Reduction*. H Harboe, A M Jerve and N Kanji with contributions from W R Chilowa, N Jazdowska, A Madaris, A Mafeje, D Satterthwaite, N Simutanyi and E Øyen, Chr. Michelsen Institute in cooperation with the CROP

Todd, A (1996) 'Health inequalities in urban areas: A guide to the literature'. *Environment and Urbanisation* **8**(2): 141–152

Todd, D (1995) 'Development summit Battle lost in war on global poverty' *The Ottawa Citizen*, 9 March, p A6

Todd, G (1995) '"Going global" in the semi-periphery: World cities as political projects. The case of Toronto'. In P L Knox and P J Taylor (eds) *World Cities in a World-System*. Cambridge University Press, Cambridge, pp192–214

Töpfer, K (1999) 'The urban revolution'. United Nations Centre for Human Settlements (Habitat) web site. www.unchs.org/unchs/ english/feature/URBAN.html

Tokumoto, T (1995) 'Fuel cell development and commercialization in Japan'. In *The Strategic Value of Fossil Fuels: Challenges and Responses*. International Energy Agency, Houston, Texas, pp 235–241

Toll, S I (1969) *Zoned American*. Grossman, New York

Tomlinson, M (1999) 'Access to energy services: A brighter future?' In *Energy and Development Report 1999*. World Bank, Washington, DC, pp 79–80

Tosics, I (1997) 'Habitat II Conference on Human Settlements, Istanbul, June 1996'. *International Journal of Urban and Regional Research* **21**(2): 366–372

Townson, M (2000) *A Report Card on Women and Poverty*. Canadian Centre for Policy Alternatives. www.policyalternatives.ca

Trippel, C, W Stillinger, J Preston, J Trocciola and R Spiegel (2000) *Operating a Fuel Cell Using Landfill Gas*. Northeast Utilities Service Company, Groton, CN. www.nu.com/energy/fuelcell.htm

Tulla, S (1999) 'Securitisation and finance for social housing in Finland'. *Urban Studies* **36**(4): 647–656

Turnbull, S (1983) 'Cooperative land banking'. In Angel et al (eds) *Land for Housing the Poor*. Select Books, Singapore

United Nations (1997a) *The Earth Summit*. Briefing Papers series, www.un.org/geninfo/bp/enviro.html

United Nations (1997b) *The United Nations Energy Statistics Database*. Provided in the annual volumes published by the United Nations, entitled *Energy Statistics Yearbooks*, and supplemented by computerized files provided by the United Nations

Energy Statistics Unit, New York

United Nations (1997c) *World Summit for Children (1990)*. Briefing Papers series, www.un.org/geninfo/bp

United Nations Centre for Human Settlements (Habitat) (1990) *The Global Strategy for Shelter to the Year 2000* (HE/185/90 E). UNCHS, Nairobi

United Nations Centre for Human Settlements (Habitat) (1993) *Public–Private Partnerships in Enabling Shelter Strategies*, UNCHS, Nairobi

United Nations Centre for Human Settlements (Habitat) (1995a) *Training for Elected Leadership – 13 volumes*, UNCHS, Nairobi. This set is available in 13 languages. See http//www.unchs.org/llm/series/content.htm

United Nations Centre for Human Settlements (Habitat) (1995b) *Towards a Housing Rights Strategy: Practical Contributions by UNCHS (Habitat) on Promoting and Protecting the Full Realization of the Human Right to Adequate Housing.* UN doc. HS/C/15/INF.7

United Nations Centre for Human Settlements (Habitat) (1996a) *An Urbanizing World: Global Report on Human Settlements 1996.* Oxford University Press, Oxford

United Nations Centre for Human Settlements (Habitat) (1996b) *Managing Water Resources for Large Cities and Towns.* Report of the Beijing Water conference. UNCHS, Nairobi

United Nations Centre for Human Settlements (Habitat) (1996c) *The Human Settlements Conditions of the World's Urban Poor.* UNCHS, Nairobi, pp 17–21

United Nations Centre for Human Settlements (Habitat) (1997) *Partnership in the Water Sector for Cities in Africa.* Report of the Cape Town Consultations. UNCHS, Nairobi

United Nations Centre for Human Settlements (Habitat) (1998) *Global Urban Observatory Data Base.* UNCHS

United Nations Centre for Human Settlements (Habitat) (1999) *Practical Aspects in the Realisation of the Human Right to Adequate Housing: Guidelines for the Formulation of the Uniteed Nations Housing Rights Programme.* UNCHS, Nairobi

United Nations Centre for Human Settlements (Habitat) (2000) *The Urban Indicators Programme.* United Nations, New York. www.urbanob-servatory.org/indicators/uimain.html

United Nations Centre for Human Settlements (Habitat)/United Nations Environment Programme (1999) 'Managing water for African cities. Developing a strategy for urban water demand management'. Background paper no 1. Prepared for Expert Group Meeting, Cape Town, South Africa, 26–28 April 1999

United Nations Centre for Human Settlements (Habitat) *Community Infrastructure (Upgrading) Programme (CIP): Tanzania. Best Practices Database.* United Nations Centre for Human Settlements (Habitat). www.bestpractices.org

United Nations Centre for Human Settlements (Habitat) *Comprehensive Revitalization of Urban Settlements, Chengdu, China. Best Practices Database.* United Nations Centre for

Human Settlements (Habitat). www.bestpractices.org

United Nations Centre for Human Settlements (Habitat) *Democratization of Municipal Management for Equitable & Sustainable Development, Ecuador. Best Practices Database.* United Nations Centre for Human Settlements (Habitat). www.bestpractices.org

United Nations Centre for Human Settlements (Habitat) *Local Initiatives Program: Lublin, Poland. Best Practices Database.* United Nations Centre for Human Settlements (Habitat). www.bestpractices.org

United Nations Centre for Human Settlements (Habitat) *Luanda Sul Self-Financed Urban Infrastructure: Angola. Best Practices Database.* United Nations Centre for Human Settlements (Habitat). www.bestpractices.org

United Nations Centre for Human Settlements (Habitat) *Municipal Infrastructure Programme: South Africa. Best Practices Database.* United Nations Centre for Human Settlements (Habitat). www.bestpractices.org

United Nations Children's Fund (UNICEF) (2000) *The State of the World's Children 2000.* UNICEF, New York

United Nations Children's Fund (UNICEF)/Carol Bellamy (1999) *The State of the World's Children 1999.* UNICEF, New York

United Nations Department of Public Information (1997) *The World Conferences: Developing Priorities for the 21st Century.* UN DPI, New York

United Nations Development Programme (UNDP) (1996a) *Human Development Report 1996.* Oxford University Press, New York

United Nations Development Programme (UNDP) (1996b) *Urban Agriculture: Food, Jobs, and Sustainable Cities.* UNDP, New York

United Nations Development Programme UNDP (1997) *Governance for Sustainable Human Development.* UNDP, New York

United Nations Development Programme (UNDP) (1998) *Human Development Report 1998.* Oxford University Press, New York

United Nations Development Programme (UNDP) (1999) *Human Development Report 1999: Globalization with a Human Face.* Oxford University Press, New York, United Nations Development Programme. Available at www.undp.org/hdro/report.html

United Nations Development Programme (UNDP). *Draft Report on Global Workshop on UNDP/MIT Decentralized Governance Research Project. Amman, Jordan. 14–16 June 1998.* UNDP. www.undp.org

United Nations Economic Council for Latin America (UNECLA) (1998) *The Social Situation in Latin America.* UNECLA, Santiago

United Nations, Economic and Social Development (1999) *Agenda 21 Issues – Poverty.* www.un.org/esa/sustdev/poverty.htm

United Nations Environment Programme International Environmental Technology Centre (IETC) (1999) *International Symposium on Efficient Water Use in Urban Areas: Innovative Ways of Finding Water for Cities, 8–10 June

1999, Kobe, Japan.* UNEP International Environmental Technology Centre, Osaka/Shiga, Japan. www.unep.or.ip/ietc/News-Events/Issue-28.html

United Nations General Assembly, E A S C (2000) *Coordinated Implementation by the United Nations System of the Habitat Agenda: Report of the Secretary-General* (A/55/83-E/2000/62). United Nations, New York

United Nations High Commissioner for Human Rights (1995) *World Conference on Human Rights.* www.unhchr.ch/html/menu5/wchr.htm

United Nations High Commissioner for Human Rights (1998) *Human Rights Questions: Comprehensive Implementation of and Follow-up to the Vienna Declaration and Programme of Action*, para. 5

United Nations Interregional Crime and Justice Research Institute (UNICRI) (1995) *Criminal Victimization in the Developing World.* Publication No 55. United Nations, Rome

United Nations Interregional Crime and Justice Research Institute (UNICRI) (1998) *Victims of Crime in the Developing World.* Publication No 57. United Nations, Rome

United Nations Population Division, Department of Economic and Social Affairs (DESA) (1999) *World Population Prospects: The 1998 Revision*, Vol I: Comprehensive Tables, No E.99.XIII.9. Population Division, Department of Economic and Social Affairs (DESA), United Nations, New York

United Nations Population Division (2000) *World Urbanization Prospects: The 1999 Review – Data Tables and Highlights.* Population Division, Department of Economic and Social Affairs (DESA), United Nations Secretariat, ESA/P/WP/161, 27 March 2000

United Nations Research Institute for Social Development (UNRISD) (1995) *After the Summit: Implementing the Programme of Action.* UNRISD, Geneva

United States Agency for International Development. *Case Study: Improving the Management of Municipally-Controlled Infrastructure Systems in Brasov, Romania. Local Government Center, EUROPE & NIS-Innovative Practices in Addressing Urban Issues.* United States Agency for International Development. www.usaid.gov

United States Conference of Mayors (1999) *A Status Report on Hunger and Homelessness in America's Cities.* United States Conference of Mayors, Washington, DC

United States General Accounting Office (GAO) (1999) *Renewable Energy: DOE's Funding and Markets for Wind Energy and Solar Cell Technologies.* US GAO, Washington, DC

United States Geological Survey, US Army Corps of Engineers, and University of South Carolina (1999) *Evaluation of Housing and Infrastructure Reconstruction Following Hurricane Mitch, Honduras.* Washington, DC, January

Urban Redevelopment Authority (1991) *Living the Next Lap.* Urban Redevelopment Authority, Singapore

Urban Redevelopment Authority

(1998) *Towards a Tropical City of Excellence.* Urban Redevelopment Authority, Singapore

US Department of Agriculture. Rural Utilities Service. Water and environmental programs (1998a) www.usda.gov/rus

US Department of Agriculture. Rural Utilities Service. Water and environmental programs (1998b) National Drinking Water Clearinghouse. www.estd.wvu.edu/ndwc/NDWC_homepage.html

US Department of Energy (DOE) (1997) *Renewable Energy Technology Characterizations.* US DOE, Washington, DC

US Department of Housing and Urban Development. Office of Policy Development and Research (September 1999) *American Housing Survey for the United States 1997.* Current Housing Reports H150/97

US Energy Information Administration (EIA) (1997a) *Annual Energy Review 1996.* US Department of Energy, Washington, DC

US Energy Information Administration (EIA) (1997b) *The Effects of Title IV of the Clean Air Act Amendments of 1990 on Electric Utilities.* US Department of Energy, Washington, DC

US Energy Information Administration (EIA) (1997c) *Renewable Energy Annual 1996.* US Department of Energy, Washington, DC

US Energy Information Administration (EIA) (1998) *Renewable Energy Annual 1998 With Data for 1997.* US Department of Energy, Washington, DC. www.eia.doe.gov/cneaf/solar.renewables/rea_data/html/front-1.html#chapter1e

US Energy Information Administration (EIA) (1999) *International Energy Database.* US Department of Energy, Washington, DC. www.eia.doe.gov/emeu/iea/contents.html

US Environmental Protection Agency (EPA) (1997) *Public Health Effects of Ozone and Fine Particle Pollution.* US EPA, Washington, DC. www.epa.gov/unix0008/news/news9697/ofpo.html

US Environmental Protection Agency (EPA) (1998). *National Small Flows Clearinghouse.* www.estd.wvu.edu/nsfc

USAID (1996) *The Housing Indicators Program: Regional Housing Indicators Database in the Transitional Countries of Central and Eastern Europe*

Vakil, A C (1996) 'Understanding housing CBOs: Comparative case-studies from Zimbabwe'. *Third World Planning Review* **18**(3): 325–348

van Rie, A, N Beyers et al (1999) 'Childhood tuberculosis in an urban population in South Africa: Burden and risk factor'. *Archives of Disease in Childhood* **80**(5): 433–7

van Vliet–, W (1993) 'A house is not an elephant: Centering the marginal'. In E Arias (ed) *The Meaning and Use of Housing.* Avebury, Aldershot, UK, pp 555–564

van Vliet–, W (1997) 'Learning from experience: The ingredients and transferability of success'. In W van Vliet– (ed) *Affordable Housing and Urban Redevelopment in the United States.* Sage, Thousand Oaks, California, pp 246–276

van Vliet–, W (1998) *Encyclopedia of Housing.* Sage, Thousand Oaks, CA

van Vliet–, W, (2000) (review of *Homelessness in the United States,*

*Europe and Russia*, edited by Carl O Helvie and Wilfried Kunstmann (Bergin & Garvey, Westport, CT, 1999)) *Housing Studies* **15**(2): 321–323

van Wijk-Sijbesma, C A, M L Borba and I van Hooff (1996) Special issue: Low-income Urban Water Supply and Environmental Sanitation. Woman, Water, Sanitation. *Annual Abstract Journal* **6**

van Wijk-Sijbesma, C (1998) 'Gender in Water Resources Management, Water Supply and Sanitation: Roles and Realities Revisited'. TP 33-E. IRC, The Hague

Vance, D E (1995) 'A portrait of older homeless men: Identifying hopelessness and adaptation'. *Journal of Social Distress and the Homeless* **4**(1): 57–71

Vanderschueren, F (1996) 'From violence to justice and security in cities'. *Environment and Urbanization* **8**(1): 93–112

Vanderschueren, F, E Wegelin and K Wekwete (1996) 'Policy programme options for urban poverty reduction: A framework for action at the municipal level', UNDP/UNCHS/World Bank, Urban Management Programme, policy framework paper no 20

Varian, H R (1990) 'Monitoring agents with other agents'. *Journal of Institutional and Theoretical Economics* **CXLVI**: 153–174

Varley, A (1985) 'Ejido land development and regularisation in Mexico City'. PhD thesis, University College London, mimeo

Veiller, L (1910) *Housing Reform: A Handbook for Practical Use in American Cities*. Charities Publication Committee and Russell Sage Foundation, New York

Veltz, P (1996) *Mondialisation, Villes et Territoires: l'Économie d'Archipel*. Presses Universitaires de France, Paris

Venkateswaran, S (1996) *CommunitySanitation: Alternative Solid Waste Management Systems*. Communities in Action Series, National Institute of Urban Affairs, New Delhi

Verma, G D (2000) 'Indore's Habitat Improvement Project: Success or failure?' *Habitat International* **24**: 91–117

Vilas, C (1999) 'The decline of the steady job in Latin America'. *NACLA Report on the Americas* **32**(January–February): 15–20

Villar, M M A, and A O Lardizabal (1997) *Mobilizing Financial Resources: Lessons Learned from the Municipality of Bauan*. Proceedings of the Second International Expert Panel Meeting on Urban Infrastructure Development held in Bangkok, Thailand. United Nations Centre for Regional Development, Nagoya, Japan

*Villes en Developpment* (2000) Bulletin de la Cooperation Francaise pour le Developpement Urbain, l'Habitat et l'Amenagement Spatial, March

Vögele J (2000) 'Urbanization and the urban mortality change in Imperial Germany'. *Health and Place* **6**(1): 41–55

von Schirnding, Y, D Yach et al (1991) 'Environmental determinants of acute respiratory symptoms and diarrhoea in young coloured children living in urban and peri-urban areas of South Africa'. *South African Medical Journal* **79**:457–461

Vuchic, V R (1999) *Transportation for Livable Cities*. Center for Urban Policy Research, Rutgers University, New Brunswick, New Jersey

Wacker, C et al (1999) 'Partnerships for urban environmental management: The roles of urban authorities, researchers and civil society'. *Environment and Urbanization* **11**(2): 113–125

Waitzman, N J, and K R Smith (no date) 'Polarized communities, unhealthy lives: The effects of inequality and economic segregation on mortality in metropolitan America'. Unpublished paper. University of Utah

Wakeley, P (1996) 'Building on the Success of Habitat II'. *Third World Planning Review* **18**(3): iii–viii

Wald, M (1999) 'Energy to Count On'. *New York Times*, 17 August

Walker, A R (1995) 'Cancer outlook: An African perspective'. *Journal of the Royal Society of Medicine* **88**(1): 5–13

Walker, A R P (1999) 'Public health: the outlook for contrasting populations'. *The Lancet* **354**, Supplement 4, 18 December

Walker, A R, and P Sareli (1997) 'Coronary heart disease: Outlook for africa'. *Journal of the Royal Society of Medicine* **90**(1): 23–7

Walker, A R, and I Segal (1997) 'Health/ill-health transition in less privileged populations: What does the future hold?' *Journal of the Royal College of Physicians London* **31**(4): 392–5

Walzer, M (1999) 'Rescuing civil society'. *Dissent* (Winter): 62–67

Wang'ombe, J K (1995) 'Public health crises of cities in developing countries'. *Social Science and Medicine* **41**(6): 857–62

Wardhaugh, J (1999) 'The unaccommodated woman: Home, homelessness and identity'. *Sociological Review* **47**(1): 91–109

WASH (Water and Sanitation for Health Project) (1993) *Lessons Learned in Water, Sanitation, and Health: Thirteen Years of Experience in Developing Countries*. WASH, Alexandria, VA

Water Supply and Sanitation Collaborative Council (WSSCC) (1999) 'Water for people. Vision 21: a shared vision for hygiene, sanitation, and water supply and a framework for mobilisation of action'. WSSCC, New York

Waters, M C, and K Eschbach (1995) 'Immigration and ethnic and racial inequality in the United States'. *Annual Review of Sociology* **21**: 419–446

Watson, S with Austerberry, H (1986) *Housing and homelessness : a feminist perspective*. Routledge, London/Kegan Paul, Boston

Webber, M (1963) 'Order in diversity: Community without propinquity'. In Wingo, L (ed) *Cities and Space: the Future Use of Urban Land*. The Johns Hopkins University Press, Baltimore

Webber, M (1964) 'The urban place and the non-place urban realm'. In *Explorations in Urban Structures*. University of Pennsylvania Press, Philadelphia

Webber, M (1968) 'The post city age'. *Daedulus* **97**(4): 1093–1099

WEDC (1999) *Proceedings of the 25th WEDC Conference, Integrated Development for Water Supply and Sanitation*, Addis Ababa, Ethiopia

WEDO (1998) *Women Transform The Mainstream: 18 Case Studies of Women Activists. Challenging Industry, Demanding Clean Water and Calling for Gender Equality in Sustainable Development*. The Women's Environment and Development Organization (WEDO). www.un.org/esa/sustdev/wedo.htm

Weffort, F (1998) 'New democracies and economic crisis in Latin America'. In P Oxhorn and G Ducatenzeiler (eds) *What Kind of Democracy? What Kind of Market? Latin America in the Age of Neoliberalism*. The Pennsylvania State University Press, University Park, pp 219–226

Wegelin-Schuringa, M, and T Kodo (1997) 'Tenancy and sanitation provision in informal settlements in Nairobi: Revisiting the public latrine option'. *Environment and Urbanization* **9**(2): 181–90

Weinberg, C (1994) 'The restructuring of the electric utility: Technology forces, R&D and sustainability'. In N Steen (ed) *Sustainable Development and the Energy Industries*. Earthscan Publications, London

Wellman, B (ed) (1999) *Networks in the Global Village: Life in Contemporary Communities*. Westview Press, Boulder

Wenner, M D (1995) 'Group credit: A means to improve information transfer and loan repayment performance'. *The Journal of Development Studies* **32**(2): 263–281

Werna, E, T Harpham, I Blue and G Goldstein (1999) 'From healthy city projects to healthy cities'. *Environment and Urbanization* **11**(1): 27–40

Wescoat, J L, Jr (1995) 'Waterworks and culture in metropolitan Lahore'. *Asian Art and Culture* SpringSummer: 21–36

Wescoat, J L, Jr (1995) 'The right of thirst for animals in Islamic water law: A comparative perspective'. *Society and Space* **3**: 637–54

Wescoat, J L, Jr, and S Halvorson (2000) 'Ex post evaluation of dams and related water projects'. Report to the World Commission on Dams. Cape Town, South Africa

Wetzler, B (2000) 'Boomgalore'. *Wired*, March: 152–169

Wheeler, J E A (2000) *Cities in the Telecommunications Age: The Fracturing of Geographies*. Routledge, London

White, G F (1974) 'Domestic water supply: Right or good?' *Human Rights and Health. Ciba Foundation* **23**: 41–59

White, G F, D J Bradley and A U White (1972) *Drawers of Water:Domestic Water Use in East Africa*. University of Chicago Press, Chicago

White, A and Saegert, S (1997) 'Return from abandonment: The tenant interim lease program and the development of low income cooperatives in New York City's most neglected neighborhoods'. In van Vliet– (ed) *Affordable Housing and Urban Redevelopment in the United States*. Sage, Thousand Oaks, California

Wilkinson, R (1996) *Unhealthy Societies: The Afflictions of Inequality*. Routledge, London

Williamson, J (1990) *Latin American Adjustment: How Much Has Happened?* Institute for International Economics, Washington, DC

Willoughby, K (1994) 'The "local milieux" of knowledge-based industries'. In: J Brotchie, P Newton, P Hall, E Blakely, and M Battie (eds) *Cities in Competition*. Cheshire, Melbourne

Wilson, B (1998) 'Information networks: The global offshore labor force'. In G Sussman and J Lent (eds) *Global Productions: Labor in the Making of the 'Information Society'*. Hampton Press, Cresskill, NJ, pp 39–56

Wilson, B (1999) *Hunger Count 1999: A Growing Hunger for Change. Canada's Annual Survey of Emergency Food Programs*. The Canadian Association of Food Banks

Wilson, T D (1997a) 'Rape for profit: Trafficking of Nepali girls and women to India's brothels – Human Rights-Watch-Asia'. *International Migration Review* **31**(2)

Wilson, T D (1997b) 'Trafficking and prostitution: The growing exploitation of migrant women from Central and Eastern Europe – Migration-Information-Programme'. *International Migration Review* **31**(2)

Wilson, W J (1991) 'Studying inner-city social dislocations: The challenge of public agenda research'. *American Sociological Review* **56**(February): 6

Winger, A R (1997) 'Finally: A withering away of cities?' *Futures* **29**(3): 251–256

Wirth, D A (2000) 'Globalizing the Environment'. In M K Cusimano (ed) *Beyond Sovereignty: Issues for a Global Agenda*. St Martin's Press, New York, pp 198–216

*Wissenschaft Forum* (1995) Special Issue: Global City: Zitadellen der Internationalisierung **12**(2)

Withers, S D (1997) 'Demographic polarization of housing affordability in situ major United States metropolitan areas'. *Urban Geography* **18**(4): 296–323

Wolfensohn, J (2000) 'Listening to the Voices of Latin America's Poor', address to Western Hemisphere Finance Ministers Meeting in Cancun, 3 February

Wolff, E N (1995) *Top Heavy: A Study of the Increasing Inequality of Wealth in America*. Twentieth Century Fund Press, New York

Wood, D (2000) 'The international campaign against the Multilateral Agreement on Investment: A test case for the future of globalization?'. *Ethics, Place and Environment* **3**(1): 25–45

Woodbury, B, and T Thompson (1999) 'Broadband geared to metros'. Mimeo

World Bank (1995) *Monitoring Environmental Progress: A Report on Work in Progress*. World Bank, Washington, DC

World Bank (1999a) *World Development Report 1999/2000 – Entering the 21st Century: The Changing Development Landscape*. World Bank, Washington, DC

World Bank (1999b) *Fuel for Thought: A New Environmental Strategy for the Energy Sector*. World Bank, Washington, DC

World Bank (1999c) 'World Bank's total lending commitments to energy projects'. Internal report prepared in December, 1999. Emailed from Mirna Hussein, 20 April 2000. File available from author on request

World Bank (1999d) 'Serving the poor: How can partnerships increase access and improve efficiency?' Presented at 1999 Water Supply Sanitation Forum: Financing Sustainable Services. World Bank, Water and Sanitation Division, Washington, DC

World Bank (1999e) *Water and Sanitation Division. Benchmarking Water and Sanitation Utilities: A start-up kit.* Transportation, Water and Urban Development Department, Washington, DC

World Bank (2000) *Can Africa Claim the 21st Century?* World Bank, Washington, DC

World Bank *Decentralization and Infrastructure.* www1.worldbank.org/publicsector /decentralization/infra-structure.htm

World Energy Council (WEC) (1994) *New Renewable Energy Resources: A Guide to the Future.* Kogan Page, London

World Energy Council (WEC) (1995) *Survey of Energy Resources*, 17th edition. WEC, Paris

World Energy Council (WEC) (2000) *Energy For Tomorrow's World.* WEC, London. www.worldenergy.org

World Health Organization (1996) *Investing in Health Research and Development.* World Health Organization, Geneva

World Health Organization and UNICEF (1994) 'Water Supply and Sanitation Sector Monitoring Report 1994'. Water Supply and Sanitation Collaborative Council, WHO/UNICEF, Geneva

World Resources Institute (WRI) (1996) *World Resources 1996–97.* Oxford University Press, New York

Wright, I (1998) 'Mediating the global and the local: A natural crossroads for planning and planners?' *Plan Canada* **38**(6): 37–39

Wright, V, and S Cassese (1997) *La Recomposition de l'Etat en Europe.* La Découverte, Paris

Wu, F (1996) 'Changes in the structure of public housing provision in urban China'. *Urban Studies* **33**: 1601–1627

Xing Quan Zhang (2000) 'Privatization and the Chinese housing model'.

*International Planning Studies* **5**(2): 191–204

Yang, D (1999) 'Urban-biased policies and rising income inequality in China'. *American Economic Review* **89**(2): 306–310

Yao, S (1997) 'Industrialization and spatial income inequality in rural China, 1986–92'. *Economics of Transition* **5**(1): 41–45

Yao, S (1999) 'Economic growth, income inequality and poverty in China under economic reform'. *Journal of Development Studies* **35**(6): 104–130

Yates, J (1997) 'Changing directions in Australian housing policies: The end of muddling through?' *Housing Studies* **12**(2): 265–277

Yepes, G (1996) *Water and Wastewater Utilities: Indicators*, 2nd edition. World Bank, Washington, DC

Yinger, J (1995) *Closed Doors, Opportunities Lost.* Russell Sage Foundation, New York

Yomiuri (1999) 'MMC to Enter Technical Tie-Up to Make Fuel Cells'. *Daily Yomiuri*, 5 February

Zaidi, S A (1999) 'Is Poverty Now a Permanent Phenomenon in Pakistan?' *Economic and Social Weekly*, 9 October

Zapata, F (1998) 'Trade unions and the corporatist system in Mexico'. In P Oxhorn and G Ducatenzeiler (eds) *What Kind of Democracy? What Kind of Market? Latin America in the Age of Neoliberalism.* The Pennsylvania State University Press, University Park, pp 151–167

Zheng, B (1997) 'Aggregate poverty measures'. *Journal of Economic Surveys* **11**(2): 123–162

Zhou, M, and J R Logan (1996) 'Market transition and the commod-ification of housing in urban China'. *International Journal of Urban and Regional Research* **20**: 400–421

Zhou, X (2000) 'Economic transformation and income inequality in urban China: Evidence from panel data'. *American Journal of Sociology* **105**(4): 1135–1174

Zoraida, P (1998) *Latin America: No End on Poverty in Sight.* Inter Press Service, 5 January

# BACKGROUND PAPERS

Abiko, Alex K and Rubenio Simas (University of São Paulo, Brazil) '"Mutirão": Successful housing production by the state and organized communities'

Alam, Tariq (Village Internet Programme, Bangladesh) 'The village internet programme: Using ICTs to create jobs and stem urban migration'

Andersson, Cecilia (Safer Cities Programme) 'Crime in cities: New challenges for local policies'

Arrieta, Gerardo M Gonzales (Inter-American Housing Union, Lima, Peru) 'Access to housing and direct-demand subsidies: Lessons from Latin American experiences'

Ashton, Hazel and David Thorns (University of Canterbury, New Zealand) 'St Albans Web Community Development Project'

Baetens, Tency (Centre for Scientific Research, Auroville, India ) 'Integral options for a sustainable future'

Balbo, Marcello (Istituto Universitario di Architettura di Venezia, Italy) 'Fragmented cities'

Brkovic, Milica Bajic (University of Belgrade, Yugoslavia) 'The new information and communication technologies: A challenge for urban planning and management'

Camara, Paulo (Maunsell, UK/Brazil) 'Transport in the 21st century: The way forward'

Chant, Sylvia (London School of Economics and Political Science) 'Female-headed households in the South: Processes, patterns and prospects'

Chant, Sylvia (London School of Economics and Political Science) and Matthew Gutmann (Brown University, USA) '"Men-streaming" gender? Questions for gender and development policy in the twenty-first century'

Charles, Mou (Urban Management Programme, South Africa) 'Macro-economic policy implications for urban management in Africa: Critical issues in a globalizing world'

Chawla, Louise (Whitney Young College, Kentucky State University, USA) 'Insight, creativity, and thoughts on the environment: Integrating children and youth into human settlement development'

Chiu, Rebecca (University of Hong Kong) 'Housing in China and Hong Kong'

Clarke, Susan (University of Colorado, USA) 'Newly emerging forms of governance in an era of globalization'

Coit, Katherine (University of Rouen, France) 'Governments, sanitation, and environmental health'

Comerio, Mary C (University of California, Berkeley, USA) 'Natural hazards and human settlements: Issues and lessons from recent experience'

Davidson, Forbes (IHS, The Netherlands) 'The implications of globalization and polarization for capacity building'

Davis, Geoff (Center for International Development, Harvard University) 'Grameen poverty targeting and poverty measurement methodology in Mexico City'

DeSouza, Flávio (Universidade Federal de Alagoas, Brazil) 'Perceived security of housing land tenure'

Doig, Alan (Liverpool John Moore University, UK) 'Combating corruption in the context of globalization'

Emmel, Nick (The Nuffield Institute for Health, The University of Leeds, UK) 'Globalization, polarization and the poor'

Escobar, F, I Williamson (University of Melbourne) and J Green (Centre for Community Child Health, Royal Children's Hospital, Melbourne, Australia) ' The potential of GIS in improving urban health care delivery'

Ganapati, Sukumar (University of Southern Calfornia, USA) 'Scope of cooperatives for low-income housing'

Gilbert, Alan (University College of London, UK) 'Implications of globalization for urbanization and housing development in Latin America'

Graham, Stephen (University of Newcastle, UK) 'Bridging urban digital divides? Urban polarization and information and communication technologies'

Gu, Chaolin (Nanjing University, China) and Liu Haiyong (University of North Carolina, Chapel Hill, USA) 'New urban poverty and peasant enclaves in Beijing'

Harpham, Trudy (South Bank University, UK) and Sassy Molyneux (Kenya Medical Research Institute, Kenya) 'Urban health in the context of poverty, inequity and polarization trends in developing countries'

Hirayama, Yosuke (Kobe University, Japan) 'Issues in housing and urban development in the context of globalization in Japan'

Hodgson, Robert (University of Exeter, UK) 'Some observations on building for safety in Bangladesh'

Jafri, S S A (Gire Institute of Development Studies, India) 'India's rural habitat in need of rejuvenation'

Jenkins, R (University of London, UK) 'Reconceptualizing transparency: Grassroots movements for accountability to the poor'

Jones, Gareth A (London School of Economics, UK) 'Implications of globalization for land and housing developments in Latin America: Polarization, privatization and partnerships'

Kaganova, Olga (The Urban Institute, USA) 'Municipal governments as major property owners in countries in transition'

Kelly, Philip F (York University, Canada) 'Undermining 'balanced' development in Manila's mega-region'

Kendall, Stephen (Ball State University, USA) and Ulpu Tiuri (Helsinki University of Technology, Finland) 'Open building: An overview'

Kosareva, Nadezhda and Alexander Puzanov (Institute for Urban Economics, Russian Federation) 'The implications of globalization and privatization for the provision of and access to housing and urban development in the transition economies'

eaf, Michael (University of British Columbia, Canada) 'A tale of two villages: Globalization and peri-urban change in China and Vietnam'

eckie, Scott (COHRE, Switzerland) 'The implications of globalization for the human right to housing: Recent developments and actions for implementation'

ee, James and Yip Ngai Ming (City University of Hong Kong) 'Housing situations in Hong Kong'; 'Housing situations in Singapore'

efèvre, Christian (University of Paris 8, France) 'Urban governance in the context of globalization: A comparative analysis'

Marcuse, Peter (Columbia University, USA) 'Implications of globalization for cities'

Mathey, Kosta (Trialog, Germany) 'Current trends in slum upgrading strategies in the developing world'

Mitlin, Diana (People's Dialog, South Africa) 'The implications for globalization for the provision of and access to housing finance in developing countries'

Moser, Caroline (London School of Economics, UK) 'Implications of globalization for violence, crime and safety'

Muller, Brian and A Al-Gilani (University of Colorado, USA) 'GIS decision tools: Where will they lead us?'

Mullin, Patrick (Australian Housing and Urban Research Institute, Queensland, Australia) 'The communities of urban Australia'

Newman, Peter and Jeff Kenworthy (Murdoch University, Australia) 'Impacts of globalization on urban transportation'

Niemczynowicz, Janusz (University of Lund, Sweden) 'Community initiatives in water supply and sanitation'

Oxhorn, Philip (McGill University, Canada) 'Latin America's democratic challenge'

Payne, Geoffrey (London, UK) 'The role of partnerships in addressing the impacts of globalization on urban development and urbanization'

Perrons, Diane (London School of Economics, UK) 'Globalisation, feminisation and flexibility: Gender divisions and the work-life balance in the new economy'

Podobnik, Bruce (Lewis and Clark College, USA) 'Urban energy dilemmas in a globalizing world: Implications for economic growth, social justice and environmental sustainability'

Rakodi, Carole (Cardiff University, UK) 'Impacts of globalization on urbanization trends and housing sector development in Africa'

Rajabifard, A, M-E Feeney and I P Williamson (University of Melbourne, Australia) 'Spatial data infrastructures: An initiative to facilitate sustainable development'

Rao, P S N (School of Planning and Architecture, New Delhi, India) 'Private corporate real estate housing: The emerging scenario in India'

Ross, Robert J S (Clark University, USA) 'Immigrants and sweatshops in North America'

Sancar, Fahriye (University of Colorado, USA) 'Reflections on the 1999 earthquakes in Turkey'

Sandhu, R (Guru Nadak University, India) 'Poverty alleviation initiatives for sustainable cities in India'; 'Housing poverty in urban India'

Sassen, Saskia (University of Chicago, USA) 'Politics of the global city: Claiming rights to urban spaces'

Satterthwaite, David (IIED, UK) 'The role of donor and development agencies in combating poverty, inequity and polarization in a globalizing world'

Schlyter, Ann (The Nordic Africa Institute, Sweden) 'Fourth world conference on women'; 'Implications of globalization for social exclusion and housing of women'

Serageldin, Mona, Suzanne Kim and Sameh Wahba (Harvard University, USA) 'Decentralization of infrastructure management'

Siembieda, William and Bruce P Baird (California Polytechnic State University, USA and State of California, Governor's Office of Emergency Services, USA) 'Who governs reconstruction? Enhancing the classic post-disaster recovery model'

Simone, AbdouMaliq (New York University, USA) 'Toward the "Worlding" of African cities: Transurban approaches to economic development'

Stephens, Mark (University of Glasgow, UK) 'Implications of globalization for the provision of and access to housing finance in the advanced economies'

Thornley, Andrew (London School of Economics (UK) 'Globalization, urban planning and local democracy'

Trivedi, H R (Institute of Cultural and Urban Anthropology, Ahmedabad, India) 'Uneven patterns of human settlement in Asia'

Tucker, Robert S K and Mary Tomlinson (Banking Council of South Africa) 'The implications of globalisation on housing finance for low-income households in South Africa'

Waitzman, Norman J and Ken R Smith (University of Utah, USA) 'Polarized communities, unhealthy lives: The effects of inequality and economic segregation on mortality in metropolitan America'

Wegelin, Emiel A (IHS, The Netherlands) 'Urbanization, globalization and poverty reduction'

Werna, Edmundo (UNV, Brazil) 'Volunteer work in urban development and the role of UNV'

Wright, Talmadge (Loyola University, USA) 'Global homelessness and the poverty of neo-liberal strategies'

Yan, Xiaopei and Yang Fan (Zhongshan University, China) 'Urban housing conditions in China in the 1990s'

# STATISTICAL ANNEX

## ● General disclaimer

The designations employed and presentation of the data in this Statistical Annex do not imply the expression of any opinion whatsoever on the part of the Secretariat of the United Nations concerning the legal status of any country, city or area or of its authorities, or concerning the delimitation of its frontiers or boundaries.

PART · VII

# LIST OF TABLES

## Country Level Data

### Demographic indicators and household projections

A.1   Size and growth of total population, life expectancy at birth
A.2   Size and growth of urban and rural population, urbanization trends
A.3   Households: number and growth rate

### Housing and infrastructure indicators

A.4   Ownership of housing unit, selected countries
A.5   Living quarters by type, selected countries
A.6   Occupied housing units by water and toilet facilities
A.7   Access to improved water sources and improved sanitation
A.8   Energy and transport

### Spatial and economic and social indicators

A.9   Area, density and land use
A.10  Labour force and economic development indicators
A.11  Social indicators

## City Level Data

### Demographic indicators and household projections

B.1   Urban agglomerations: population size and growth rate
B.2   Households: number and size and population in specific age groups, selected cities

### Housing and infrastructure indicators

B.3   Ownership of housing units
B.4   Living quarters by type, selected cities
B.5   Occupied housing units by number of rooms and by number of occupants, selected cities
B.6   Housing units by water and toilet facilities, selected cities

### Economic and social indicators

B.7   Employment structure, selected cities
B.8   Social indicators, selected cities

# TECHNICAL NOTES

## Introductory Notes

The Statistical Annex comprises19 tables covering three broad categories: (i) demographic indicators and households data; (ii) housing and infrastructure indicators; and (iii) spatial and economic and social indicators. These tables contain data at the country as well as the city level. Tables A.1–A.11 are based on country level data and Tables B.1–B.8 are devoted to city level data, both levels covering the same three main categories. Data have been compiled from various primary and secondary sources from national statistical offices and from within the United Nations. The largest body of primary data stems from the Human Settlements Statistics Questionnaire 1999, jointly developed and processed by the United Nations Statistics Division and Statistics Programme of UNCHS (Habitat) with a view to collect most recent data from countries, at both national and city level. This questionnaire has captured the latest available data from 91 countries and 315 cities on various human settlements related topics. Household projections data are another important data set in the Annex since UNCHS (Habitat) is the unique producer of this kind of projection.

## Explanation of Symbols

The following symbols have been used in presenting data throughout the Annex.

| | |
|---|---|
| Category not applicable | .. |
| Data not available | ... |
| Magnitude zero | – |

## Country Groupings and Applied Growth Rate

*More developed regions* comprise all countries and areas of Europe and Northern America; and Australia, Japan and New Zealand.

*Less developed regions* comprise all countries and areas of Africa, Latin America, Asia (excluding Japan) and Oceania (excluding Australia and New Zealand).

*The annual growth rate*, calculated by UNCHS (Habitat), refers to the average annual percentage change of popula-tion during the indicated period for each country major regions and global totals. The formula used throughout the Annex is as follows:

$$r = [(1/t) \times ln(A2/A1)] \times 100$$

where:
$A1$ is a value at any given year
$A2$ is a value at any given year later than the year of $A1$
$t$ is the year interval between $A1$ and $A2$
$ln$ is the natural logarithm function

## Sources of Data

The tables in the Statistical Annex have been compiled by UNCHS (Habitat) from the Human Settlements Statistics Questionnaire 1999,[1] Habitat's Household Projections Project as well as the Human Settlements Statistics Database and UNCHS CitiBase. Various statistical publications from the United Nations and other organizations have been used as well. Notable among them are: United Nations, *World Population Prospects: The 1998 Revision*; United Nations, *World Urbanization Prospects: The 1999 Revision*; UNESCO, *Statistical Yearbook 1999*; UNDP, *Human Development Report 2000*; World Bank, *World Development Indicators 2000* (incl. CD-ROM Database); FAO, *Production Yearbook* (Vol. 39 and 51); WHO, *The International Drinking Water Supply and Sanitation Decade Review 1990 and 2000*; International Road Federation, *World Road Statistics*.

## Nomenclature and Order of Presentation

The countries or areas are presented in English alphabetical order within the macro regions of Africa, Asia, Europe, Latin America, Northern America and Oceania. Countries or area names are used from the United Nations commonly used list of names for statistical use. Due to space limitations, the short name in use for example for the United Kingdom of Great Britain and Northern Ireland is referred to as 'United Kingdom', the United States of America as 'United States'.

### Note

1 The questionnaire data are preliminary and subject to further revision.

# Table A.1

## Definitions

*Total population* data refer to the mid year population estimates for the world, region, countries or areas. The Population Division of the Department of Economic and Social Affairs updates, every two years, population estimates and projections by incorporating new data, new estimates and new analysis of data on population, fertility, mortality and international migration. Data from new population censuses and/or demographic surveys are used to verify and update old estimates of population or demographic indicators or to make new ones and to check the validity of the assumptions made in the projections.

Total population refers to the estimates and projections (medium variant) of the total population for each country region and major area.

*Life expectancy at birth* is the average number of years that a newborn infant is expected to live if the prevailing pattern of mortality for all people at the time of his or her birth were to stay the same throughout his or her lifetime.

## Notes

All population figures are presented in thousands. A figure of 0 means the population was below 500 persons.

1 Included Agalega, Rodrigues and St Brandon.
2 Including Ascension and Tristan da Cunha.
3 For statistical purposes, the data for China do not include Hong Kong Special Administrative Region (SAR) of China
4 As of 1 July 1997, Hong Kong became a Special Administrative Region (SAR) of China.
5 Refers to the Vatican City State.
6 The former Yugoslav Republic of Macedonia.
7 Including Christmas Island, Cocos (Keeling) Islands and Norfolk Island.

# Table A.2

## Definitions

*Level of urbanization* refers to the percentage of population residing in places classified as urban. Urban and rural settlements are defined in the national context and vary among countries (the definitions of urban are generally national definitions incorporated in the latest census).

*Urban and rural population* data refer to the mid year population.

## Notes

All population figures are presented in thousands. A figure of 0 means the population was below 500 persons.

1 Included Agalega, Rodrigues and St Brandon.
2 Including Ascension and Tristan da Cunha.
3 For statistical purposes, the data for China do not include Hong Kong Special Administrative Region (SAR) of China.
4 As of 1 July 1997, Hong Kong became a Special Administrative Region (SAR) of China.
5 Refers to the Vatican City State.
6 The former Yugoslav Republic of Macedonia.
7 Including Christmas Island, Cocos (Keeling) Islands and Norfolk Island.

# Table A.3

## Definitions

*Household*: The concept of household is based on the arrangements made by persons, individually or in groups, for providing themselves with food or other essentials for living. A household may be either:

(a) a one-person household, that is to say, a person who makes provision for his or her own food or other essentials for living without combining with any other person to form a part of a multi-person household or

(b) a multi-person household, that is to say a group of two or more persons living together who make common provision for food or other essentials for living. The persons in the group may pool their incomes and may, to a greater or lesser extent, have a common budget; they may be related or unrelated persons or constitute a combination of persons both related and unrelated. This concept of household is known as the 'housekeeping' concept. It does not assume that the number of households and housing units (see Table A.5) is equal. Although the concept of housing unit implies that it is a space occupied by one household, it may also be occupied by more than one household or by a part of a household (for example two nuclear households that share one housing unit for economic reasons or one household in polygamous society routinely occupying two or more housing units).

The household projections provided by UNCHS (Habitat) are unique in their completeness, as estimates for countries with insufficient data are provided. But they are not meant to compete with national projections and the results are reflecting trends and have to be treated with caution.

The household projections were based on different concepts and methods, in function of the data availability and reliability. The various types of projection approaches followed and the countries for which the respective approach has been applied are listed hereafter.

1 *Total headship rate based projection*
Algeria, Benin, Botswana, Burkina Faso, Cape Verde, Gambia, Kenya, Lesotho, Libyan Arab Jamahiriya, Madagascar, Malawi, Mali, Mauritius, Niger, Rwanda, South Africa, Sudan, Tunisia, United Rep. of Tanzania, Zambia and Zimbabwe.
Bangladesh, Brunei Darussalam, Cambodia, Cyprus, Georgia, India, Indonesia, Iraq, Japan, Kazakhstan, Kuwait, China Macau SAR, Malaysia, Maldives, Pakistan, Republic of Korea, Singapore, Sri Lanka, Thailand, Turkey, Viet Nam and Yemen.
Albania, Austria, Belarus, Bulgaria, Denmark, Estonia, Finland, France, Germany, Greece, Hungary, Ireland, Italy, Latvia, Lithuania, Luxembourg, Malta, The Netherlands, Poland, Portugal, Spain and Switzerland.

Bolivia, Brazil, Colombia, Dominican Republic, Ecuador, Guatemala, Haiti, Honduras, Jamaica, Mexico, Nicaragua, Paraguay, Peru and Venezuela. United States, Fiji, French Polynesia, New Caledonia, Solomon Islands.

2   *Headship size rate based projection*
Burundi, Central African Republic, Republic of Congo, Egypt, Liberia, Morocco and Réunion.
Armenia, Azerbaijan, Bahrain, China, China Hong Kong SAR, Iran (Islamic Republic of), Israel, Jordan, Kyrgyzstan, Nepal, Philippines, Syrian Arab Republic, Tajikistan, Turkmenistan and Uzbekistan.
Belgium, Norway, Republic of Moldova, Romania, Russian Federation, Sweden, Ukraine, United Kingdom and Yugoslavia.
Argentina, Bahamas, Barbados, Belize, Chile, Costa Rica, El Salvador, Guadeloupe, Guyana, Martinique, The Netherlands Antilles, Panama, Puerto Rico, Trinidad and Tobago and Uruguay.
Canada, Australia, Guam, New Zealand, Samoa and Vanuatu.

3   *Estimation on country level not possible*
Angola, Sierra Leone, Western Sahara, Afghanistan, Dem. People's Republic of Korea, East Timor, Gaza Strip, Lebanon, Bosnia and Herzegovina.

4   *Estimation on the basis of one data point*
Cameroon, Comoros, Cote d'Ivoire, Dem. Republic of the Congo, Eritrea, Ethiopia, Gabon, Ghana, Guinea, Guinea-Bissau, Mauritania, Mozambique, Namibia, Nigeria, Senegal, Togo and Uganda.
Mongolia, Myanmar, Oman, Qatar, United Arab Emirates, Croatia, Czech Republic, Iceland, Slovakia, Slovenia, TFYR Macedonia, Suriname and Papua New Guinea.

5   *Estimation with no data point*
Chad, Djibouti, Equatorial Guinea, Somalia, Swaziland, Bhutan, Lao People's Dem. Republic and Saudi Arabia.

The following countries are not included in the total number of households calculated for subregions, regions and other aggregates:

Bermuda, Greenland, Saint Pierre and Miquelon
Seychelles
Sao Tome and Principe
Saint Helena
Antigua and Barbuda, British Virgin Islands, Cayman Islands, Dominica, Grenada, Montserrat, Aruba, Saint Kitts and Nevis, Anguilla, Saint Lucia, Saint Vincent, Turks and Caicos Islands, US Virgin Islands
French Guiana, Falklands
Channel Islands, Faeroe Islands, Isle of Man
Andorra, San Marino, Gibraltar, Holy See
Liechtenstein, Monaco
Kiribati, Marshall Islands, Micronesia (Fed. States of), Nauru, Northern Mariana Islands, Palau
American Samoa, Cook Island, Niue, Pitcairn, Tokelau, Tonga, Tuvalu, Wallis and Futuna Islands

For the following countries the estimates are extremely rough and cannot be interpreted on their own. They have only been calculated for completeness reasons on the aggregate (subregional, regional and global) level. For further information refer to the technical report.

Democratic People's Republic of Korea
East Timor
Afghanistan
Gaza Strip and Lebanon
Angola
Western Sahara
Sierra Leone
Bosnia and Herzegovina

## Note

1   The first data point available for South Africa is 1992. A backward extrapolation further than to 1990 is not possible, therefore no data are available for 1985.

The growth rate has been calculated for the period 1990 to 2000, for the regional aggregate. An estimation has been used for the period 1985 to 2000.

For the aggregates, an estimation for the period of 1985 to 1990 has been used, as a retro projection was not possible.

# Table A.4

## Definitions

*Ownership of the housing unit*: This topic refers to whether the housing unit is owned by the household occupying it or by public or private entities.

*Owner household*: Living quarters are defined as owner-occupied if used wholly or partly for own occupation by the owner.

*Tenant household in publicly owned housing units*: This refers to a household residing in a housing unit it does not own, but is owned by a public institution (disregarding whether or not the institution is sponsored by central or local government). These institutions may be cooperatives, housing associations or government agencies.

*Tenant household in privately owned housing units*: This refers to a household residing in a housing unit it does not own, but is owned by a private sector. This includes persons renting a housing unit from individuals, such as landlords, or units owned by a private corporation, and so forth.

*Squatter household*: This category refers to a household that built a structure it occupies on land on which it does not have a title. Squatter settlements are usually built on fringes of large cities, without a predetermined plan and without any legal validation. Most of the structures of these settlements usually fall into the category of *marginal housing units* (see definitions for Table A.5 ) although they may also consist of more solid structures.

*Women-headed household*: In identifying the members of a household, it is traditional to identify first the household head or reference person and then remaining members of household according to their relationship to the head of reference person. The head of household is defined as that person in the household who is acknowledged as such by other members.

Thus, this category refers to households headed by women. It has been recognized that national practices in identifying household headship vary significantly on the basis of customs and cultural traditions.

## Notes

UN estimate.

Data for total country, tenant households in publicly owned housing units, includes all tenants disregarding the ownership of the unit. Data include data for privately owned housing units

Data refer to other households and households that have not been stated.

Data reported in percentages.

Data refer to those of rental accommodation.

Data refer to other housing units.

Data include tenant and subtenant housing units.

Data are that of number of free housing units.

Data are that of other and not stated housing units.

10 Data refer to dwellings.

11 Data include 611 dwellings owned by private employees and provided free of charge and 107 dwellings rented from private employees.

12 Data include 38 units rented from private employees and 185 units owned by private employees and provided free of charge.

13 Figures are greater than 0 and less than 5 are randomized to preserve confidentiality.

14 Data were reported in percentage except for Total Households.

15 Data were reported in percentages based on an integrated survey on a sample of 3600 households.

16 Data include 84,346 occupied housing units provided by employers (including all staff quarters) and are rent free units.

17 Data include households in premises not within a quarter (eg staircases, corridors and street sleeper's places).

18 Data include 14,322 occupied housing units provided by employers (including all staff quarters) and are rent free units.

19 Data include 2589 households in rent free units.

20 Data provided are for households in occupied conventional housing units.

21 Data under squatter households refer to free households.

22 Data for total do not add up due to exclusion of category others.

23 The table does not include households residing in Kibbutz community settlements.

24 Data are based on the prompt report of the basic findings.

25 Data were reported in percentages based on 6000 households (sampling survey).

26 Data are for Malaysia Peninsular.

27 Data refer to both publicly owned and privately owned housing units.

28 All data refer to Resident Private households.

29 Data for Squatter households refer to housing units where there is no payment.

30 Data are in thousands and in some cases has been rounded off.

31 Data are estimated from households budget survey.

32 Data refer to state subsidized (government rental housing).

33 Data refer to other rental housing.

34 Data refer to 2% sample.

35 Data for totals include households occupying housing units free of charge and non-respondents, hence owner households plus Central Office of Statistics, Lascaris, Valletta, MATLA do not add up to 119,479.

36 Data include 11,775 housing units with no information on Urban/Rural areas.

37 Data for tenant households in privately owned housing units are a combination of privately owned social landlords and other privately owned households.

38 The data are estimated due to the boycott of 1991 Population census from the side of the majority of Albanian population in Kosovo and Metohia.

39 Data refer to housing units occupied by dependency relationship.

40 Data refer to households that were ignored in the survey. The data includes owners of mobile households, households occupied through loans cessions or permission, de facto occupants and others.

41 Data on occupied housing units provided do not include collective houses.

42 Data for total country housing units include owner households but exclude collective housing units.

43 Data reported are only for those households headed by Tongans (including part-Togans).

44 Tenant households combines those publicly owned and private owners on rent or rent free basis. About 85.4% of data reported refer to those public plus private owned households on rented basis.

45 Data reported for tenant households are a combination of households publicly and privately owned on rent and rent free basis. About 79.7% of figure specified are households publicly or privately owned on rent-free basis.

# Table A.5

## Definitions

*Living quarters*: Living quarters are structurally separate and independent places of abode. They may (a) have been constructed, built, converted or arranged for human habitation, provided that they are not at the time of enumeration used wholly for other purposes and that, in the case of improvised housing units and collective living quarters, they are occupied at the time of the emuneration or (b) although not intended for habitation, actually be in use for such a purpose at the time of the enumeration.

Living quarters defined above are either housing units or collective living quarters. Housing units are intended for occupancy, or are occupied, by households. However, certain types of 'collective living quarters' are also of significance with respect to the housing conditions of households; these include hotels, rooming houses and other lodging houses and camps occupied by households.

*Housing unit*: A housing unit is a separate and independent place of abode intended for habitation by a single household, or one not intended for habitation but occupied as living quarters by a household at the time of the census. Thus it may be an occupied or vacant dwelling, an occupied mobile or improvised housing unit or any other place occupied as living quarters by a household at the time of the census. This category includes housing of various levels of permanency and acceptability and requires further classification in order to provide for a meaningful assessment of housing conditions.

Housing units, therefore, include conventional and basic dwellings, and temporary, mobile and marginal housing units. Definitions of these terms are listed below.

*Conventional dwelling*: A conventional dwelling is a room or suite of rooms and its accessories in a permanent building or structurally separated part thereof which, by the way it has been built, rebuilt or converted, is intended for habitation by one household and is not, at the time of the census, used wholly for other purposes. It should have a separate access to a street (direct or via a garden or grounds) or to a common space within the building (staircase, passage, gallery and so on). Examples of dwellings are houses, flats, suites of rooms, apartments and so forth.

It may be noted that the terms dwelling, dwelling unit, dwelling house, residential dwelling unit, family dwelling, house, lodgement, vivienda, unidad de vivienda and so forth have been used indiscriminately to refer to living quarters of any type. The reference of the term 'dwelling' is here limited to a housing unit located in a permanent building and designed for occupancy by one household. Although a conventional dwelling is a housing unit intended – that is to say, constructed or converted – for habitation by one household, it may, at the time of the census, be vacant or occupied by one or more households.

*Basic dwelling*: A basic dwelling is a housing unit that has some but not all of the essential facilities of a conventional dwelling. It is a permanent structure or a part of a permanent structure, hence it may be a room or a suite of rooms in a permanent building but it is without some of the conventional dwelling facilities such as kitchen, fixed bath or shower, piped water or toilet. In a number of countries or areas, a certain proportion of the housing inventory comprises such housing units which possess some but not all the characteristics of conventional dwellings.

With increased urbanization, the need for building low-cost housing units within the city limits has developed. This housing most frequently consists of buildings containing a number of separate rooms whose occupants share some or all facilities (bathing, toilet or cooking facilities). Those units do not meet all the criteria of a conventional dwelling, especially from the point of view of maintaining health standards and privacy. Such a unit is known as a *casa de palomar* in Latin America.

*Temporary housing unit*: The term 'temporary housing unit' refers to a structure that, by the way it has been built, is not expected to maintain its durability for as long a period of time, but has some of the facilities of a conventional dwelling.

For example, in some countries 'core' or 'nuclear' dwellings around which a dwelling will eventually be constructed are provided as part of the housing programmes. Under these programmes, the households move their impoverished shacks from the squatter area to a new location, the idea being that gradually, and generally with government assistance of one kind or another, the households with core or nuclear dwellings will keep adding to the nucleus until they can abandon their shacks entirely.

A core dwelling is sometimes only a sanitary unit containing bathing and toilet facilities, to which may be added, in subsequent phases, the other elements that will finally make up the completed dwelling. Such units do not fall within the definition of a conventional or basic dwelling as set out above. However, although the household obviously continues to occupy its original shelter (which would probably be classified as an 'improvized housing unit'), its housing situation is a vast improvement over that of households remaining in the squatter areas and the provision of the cores is a significant step towards the alleviation of housing shortages.

In still other countries and areas, the population has developed, over time, a traditional and typical type of housing unit that does not have all the characteristics of conventional or basic dwellings but is considered somewhat suitable from the point of view of climate and tradition. This is especially the case in many tropical and subtropical rural areas where housing units have been constructed or built with locally available raw materials such as bamboo, palm, straw or any similar materials. Such units often have mud walls, thatched roofs and so forth, and may be

expected to last only for a limited time (from a few months to 10 years), although occasionally they may last for longer periods. This category is intended to cover housing units that are typical and traditional in many tropical rural areas. Such units may be known, for example, as cabins, *ranchos* or *bohios* (Latin America), *barastis* (Bahrain), or *barong barong* (the Philippines).

*Mobile housing units*: A mobile housing unit is any type of living accommodation that has been produced to be transported (such as a tent) or is a moving unit (such as a ship, boat, barge, vessel, railroad car, caravan, trailer, yacht and so on) occupied as living quarters at the time of the census. Trailers and tents used as permanent living quarters are of special interest.

*Marginal housing units*: The term 'marginal housing unit' refers to those units that do not have many of the features of a conventional dwelling and are generally characterized as unfit for human habitation, but that are used for the purpose of habitation. Therefore, it is neither a permanent structure nor one equipped with any of the essential facilities.

Marginal housing units comprise three sub-groups, namely, 'improvised housing units', 'housing units in permanent buildings not intended for human habitation' and 'other premises not intended for human habitation'. These units are characterized by the fact that they are either makeshift shelters constructed of waste materials and generally considered unfit for habitation (squatters' huts, for example) or places that are not intended for human habitation although in use for that purpose (barns, warehouses, natural shelters and so on). Under almost all circumstances, such places of abode represent unacceptable housing. Each sub-group is defined below:

An *improvised housing unit* is an independent, makeshift shelter or structure, built of waste materials and without a predetermined plan for the purpose of habitation by one household, which is being used as living quarters. Included in this category are squatters' huts, *poblaciones callampas* (Chile), *hongos* (Peru), *favelas* (Brazil), *sarifas* (Iraq), *Jhuggis* (India and Pakistan), *gubuks* (Indonesia), *gacekondula* (Turkey) and any similar premises arranged and used as living quarters, though they may not comply with generally accepted standards for habitation, and do not have many of the characteristics of conventional dwellings. This type of housing unit is usually found in urban and suburban areas, particularly at the peripheries of the principal cities.

*Housing units in permanent buildings not intended for human habitation* are housing units (in permanent buildings) that have not been built, constructed, converted or arranged for human habitation but that are actually in use as living quarters at the time of the census. These include housing units in stables, barns, mills, garages, warehouses, offices, booths and so forth.

This category may also cover units and their occupants in buildings initially built for human habitation, but later abandoned with all services lacking because of deterioration. These dilapidated buildings can be found, especially in large cities, still standing, although marked for emolition. They should be included in this category of habited.

*Other premises not intended for human habitation* refer to ving quarters that are not intended for human habitation r located in permanent buildings but that are nevertheless eing used as living quarters at the time of the census. aves and other natural shelters fall within this category.

*Collective living quarters*: Collective living quarters nclude structurally separate and independent places of bode intended for habitation by large groups of individuals r several households and occupied at the time of the ensus. Such quarters usually have certain common facilies, such as cooking and toilet installations, baths, lounge ooms or dormitories, which are shared by the occupants. They may be further classified into hotels, rooming houses nd other lodging houses, institutions and camps.

## Notes

- Data refer to housing units.
- There is no concordance between the number of households and housing units.
- Data in percentages and are based on integrated survey on a sample of 3600 households.
- Data for marginal type of housing units temporary housing units.
- Data for temporary living quarters include 2291 domestic living quarters on board vessels.
- Data for collective living quarters in living quarters include 126 occupied marine vessels.
- Data for temporary housing units refer to both temporary housing units and floating units.
- Data for marginal type of housing units refer to other housing units.
- Data have been inferred.
- 0 Data refer to Malaysia Peninsular.
- 1 Data for marginal type of housing units include mobile housing units.
- 2 Households by type of living quarters are classified only in two groups namely: conventional and other. Other includes basic, temporary and marginal.
- 3 Data on conventional housing units are for residential buildings and other buildings with living quarters.
- 4 Data for temporary housing units are for permanently occupied accommodations.
- 5 Data for collective living quarters are for residential houses.
- 6 Data refer to 2% sample.
- 7 Data in Basic housing units include that of Temporary and Marginal housing units.
- 8 Data for not stated refer to diplomatic Portuguese population living abroad and population abroad.
- 9 Data refer only to the number of enumerated households due to the boycott of 1991 Population Census by the majority of Albanian population in Kosovo and Metohia.
- 20 Data include business offices, which have been settled in by necessity.
- 21 Data for conventional living quarters include type A apartments.
- 22 Data for basic living quarters include type B apartments.
- 23 Data for temporary living quarters include rented houses and hotels or boarding houses.
- 24 Data for marginal living quarters include huts and cabins.
- 25 Data for conventional households refer to adequate housing unit, ie a permanent unit equipped with both water supplies within the unit and sewage.
- 26 Data for basic households refer to inadequate housing unit, ie a permanent unit equipped without both water supply within the unit and sewage.
- 27 Data for marginal households refer to a particular improvized unit, ie a unit in a structure that is not conducive for habitation and also includes improvised housing units, huts, barracks and any other structure that is not conducive for habitation.
- 28 Data for conventional and basic households are based on 1992 estimates.
- 29 Data refer to households and not living quarters.

# Table A.6

## Definitions

*Water supply system*: This category refers to whether a housing unit has or does not have a piped water installation; in other words, whether or not water is provided to occupants from a community-wide system or an individual installation (a pressure tank, pump and so forth). With piped water inside the housing unit refers to the existence of water pipes within the walls that constitute a housing unit. Water can be piped from the community source, ie one that is subject to inspection and control by public authorities. Such systems are generally operated by a public body but in some cases they are generated by a cooperative or private enterprise. Water can be also piped into the unit from private source, such as a pressure tank, a pump or some other installation. The category piped water outside unit, but within 200 m refers to the unit where the piped water is not available to occupants within the unit they reside in, but is accessible within the range of 200 m, assuming that access to piped water within that distance allows occupants to provide water for household needs without being subjected to extreme efforts. Without piped water refers to units that do not have access to piped water at all, whose occupants satisfy their needs for water out of springs or wells, and to units whose occupants have access to piped water, but beyond 200 m.

*Toilet facilities*: A toilet may be defined as an installation for the disposal of human excreta. With toilet inside the housing unit refers to the unit where such an installation is located within the walls that constitute a unit. A flush toilet is an installation provided with piped water that permits humans to discharge their wastes and from which the wastes are flushed by water. A non-flush toilet is not equipped with piped water. With toilet outside unit refers to units where either a flush or a non-flush toilet is available to occupants, but is located outside the unit's walls. Without toilet refers to either when occupants of a housing unit discharge their wastes outdoors (in bushes and so forth) or when the toilet is not within a reasonable distance.

## Notes

1. Data include from community source and outside unit like a public tap.
2. Data include households without piped water inside the unit but with piped water inside the building.
3. Data refer to households without piped water.
4. Data include households with separate toilet and households with bathroom with toilet.
5. Data in percentages.
6. The given total is that of total piped water.
7. A toilet outside the housing unit is a pit latrine.
8. Data provided are not disaggregated by place of residence (rural or urban). In the same way data are also not available for Maseru.
9. Include private or shared well.
10. Data are for piped water outside unit and public fountain.
11. Data refer to tank wagon, well/river and other means of transporting water.
12. Data refer to wells and bore holes. It could also be piped water on site, public tap, water-carrier/tanker, borehole/rainwater/tank/well or dam/river/stream/spring.

13  Data refer to tap of neighbour, source or stream and others.

14  Data for households with non-flush toilet inside housing unit.

15  Data refer to public lavatory and 'field', sanitary and superficial pit, river or stream and system car.

16  Data refer to 14,254 households with access to treated piped water.

17  Data refer to 1917 households with access to standpipes with treated or untreated water.

18  Figures greater than 0 and less than 5 are randomized to preserve confidentiality.

19  Data include chemical toilet.

20  Data refer to pit latrine and bucket latrine.

21  Data represented in percentages and are based on integrated survey on a sample of 3600 households.

22  Data refer to households without flush toilet.

23  Data refer to population.

24  Data refer to number of housing units with toilet facilities.

25  Data with toilet inside the housing unit are for toilets used exclusively.

26  Data with toilet inside the housing unit are for toilets used jointly.

27  Data were reported in percentages and based on 6000 households (sampling survey).

28  Data refer to Malaysia Peninsular.

29  Data refer to private households. Data are in thousands and in some cases have been rounded.

30  Data refer to 2% sample and refer to conventional housing units.

31  Data include 11,775 households with no information on urban/rural areas.

32  Data refer to flush toilets from community source.

33  Data refer to local flush toilets from private source.

34  Data refer to urban, rural and England. Small discrepancies between cell counts and marginal totals may arise from rounding.

35  Data are estimated due to the boycott of 1991 Population Census by the majority of Albanian population in Kosovo and Metohia.

36  Data refer to households with latrines or a blind well.

37  Data refer to households that do not have any toilet facilities.

38  Data refer to units with hot and cold water in housing units.

39  Data include that of water, from community source, from private source and piped water outside unit, but within 200 m.

40  One household may have two or more sources of water supply available. For example, a household may have piped water as well as have its own water tank.

# Table A.7

The methodology approach of WHO/UNICEF has changed from an earlier self-assessment by governments to the present approach which collects data from thorough assessment questionnaires and household surveys. The definitions below have been taken from a WHO paper entitled 'Methodology for the Global Water Supply and Sanitation Assessment 2000'.

## Definitions

*Access to improved water sources*: The technology in actual use is decisive of whether or not one can speak of improved water sources. The following technologies were included in the assessment as representing improved water supply: Household connection, public standpipe, borehole, protected dug well, protected spring and rainwater collection.

The following technologies were not considered as improved: unprotected well, unprotected spring, vendor-provided water, bottled water,* tanker truck-provided water.

*Access to improved sanitation*: Similarly, the technology in actual use is decisive of whether or not improved sanitation is assessed. The following technologies are included in the assessment as representing improved sanitation:

connection to a public sewer, connection to septic system, pour-flush latrine, Simple pit latrine, ventilated improved pit latrine. The following technologies were not considered as improved: service or bucket latrines (where excreta are manually removed), public latrines, open latrines.

### Notes

\*  Considered as not improved because of concerns about the quantity of supplied water, not because of concerns over the water quality.

1  76% of global population represented.

2  89% of global population represented.

3  72% of regional population represented.

4  96% of regional population represented.

5  88% of regional population represented.

6  94% of regional population represented.

7  15% of regional population represented.

8  44% of regional population represented.

9  77% of regional population represented.

10  99% of regional population represented.

11  99.9% of regional population represented.

12  99.9% of regional population represented.

13  64% of regional population represented.

14  85% of regional population represented.

# Table A.8

## Definitions

*Commercial energy production* refers to commercial forms of primary energy – petroleum (crude oil, natural gas liquids and oil from non-conventional sources), natural gas and solid fuels (coal, lignite and other derived fuels) – and primary electricity, all converted into oil equivalents (measured in kilo tonnes of oil equivalent).

*Commercial energy use* refers to apparent consumption, which is equal to indigenous production plus imports and stock changes, minus exports and fuels supplied to ships and aircraft engaged in international transport (measured in kilogramme of oil equivalent per capita).

*Net energy imports* are calculated as energy use less production, both measured in oil equivalents. A negative value indicates that the country is a net exporter.

*Traditional fuels* include fuelwood, charcoal, bagasse, animal, vegetal and other wastes.

*Motor vehicles* refer to passenger cars and commercial vehicles. Special purpose vehicles such as two- or three-wheeled cycles and motorcycles, trams, trolley-buses, ambulances, hearses, military vehicles operated by police or other governmental security organisations are excluded.

# Table A.9

## Definitions

*Population density* is the total population divided by land area in hectares.

*Land area* is a country's total area, excluding area under inland water bodies, national claims to continental shelf and exclusive economic zones. In most cases the definition of inland water bodies includes major rivers and lakes.

*Arable land* includes land defined by FAO as land under temporary crops (double-cropped areas are counted once), temporary meadows for mowing or for pasture land under market or kitchen gardens and land temporarily fallow. Land abandoned as a result of shifting cultivation is excluded.

*Irrigated land* refers to areas purposely provided with water, including land irrigated by controlled flooding.

*Permanent cropland* is land cultivated with crops that occupy the land for long periods and need not be replanted after each harvest such as cocoa, coffee and rubber. This category includes land under flowering shrubs, fruit trees, nut trees and vines, but excludes land under trees grown for wood or timber.

*Other land* includes forest and woodland as well as logged-over areas to be forested in the near future. Also included are uncultivated land, grassland not used for pasture, wetlands, wastelands and built-up areas – residential, recreational and industrial lands and areas covered by roads and other fabricated infrastructure.

## Table A.10

### Definitions

*Labour force* comprises people who meet the ILO definition of the economically active population, which is: all people who supply labour for the production of goods and services during a specified period. It includes both the employed and the unemployed. While national practices vary in the treatment of such groups as the armed forces and seasonal or part-time workers, in general the labour force includes the armed forces, the unemployed and first-time-job seekers, but excludes homemakers and other unpaid caregivers and workers in the informal sector.

*Females as a percentage of the labour force* shows the extent to which women are active in the labour force.

*Unemployment* refers to the share of the labour force without work but available for and seeking employment. Definitions of labour force and unemployment differ by country.

*Gross domestic product (GDP)* is the total output of goods and services for final use produced by an economy by both residents and non-residents, regardless of the allocation to domestic and foreign claims. It does not include deductions for depreciation of physical capital or depletion and degradation of natural resources.

*GDP per capita* (PPP US$) is the GDP per capita of a country converted into US dollars on the basis of the purchasing power parity (PPP) exchange rate. At the PPP rate, one dollar has the same purchasing power over domestic GDP as the US dollar has over US GDP. PPP rates allow a standard comparison of real price levels between countries, just as conventional price indices allow comparison of real values over time. Normal exchange rates may over- or undervalue purchasing power.

*Capital expenditure* refers to the purchase of fixed assets (eg plant and equipment including such items as construction, improvement and land acquisitions), expenditure on trade investment (shares held by one company in another) or acquisitions of other businesses and expenditure on current assets (eg stocks).

## Table A.11

### Definitions

*Television sets* are the estimated number of television sets in use, per 1000 people.

*Personal computers* are the estimated number of self-contained computers designed to be used by a single individual, per 1000 people.

*Telephone mainlines* are telephone lines connecting a customer's equipment to the public switched telephone network. Data are represented for the entire country and for the largest city.

*Health expenditure* is the sum of public and private health expenditure. It covers the provision of health services (preventive and curative), family planning activities, nutrition activities and emergency aid designated for health but does not include provision of water and sanitation.

*Hospital beds* include inpatient beds available in public, private, general and specialized hospitals and rehabilitation centres. In most cases acute and chronic beds are included.

*Population below national poverty line (%)* is the percentage of the population living below the national poverty line. National estimates are based on population weighted subgroup estimates from household surveys.

*Illiteracy rate (adult)* is calculated as 100 minus the literacy rate (adult). The literacy rate (adult) is the percentage of people age 15 and above who can, with understanding, both read and write a short, simple statement on their everyday life.

The year in parenthesis at the upper right corner of a figure denotes the year of data other than that specified for the respective column.

## Table B.1

### Definitions

*Urban agglomeration* refers to the contours of contiguous territory without regard to administrative boundaries. It comprises the city or town proper and also suburban fringe lying outside of, but adjacent to, the city boundaries.

This table contains revised estimates and projections for all urban agglomerations comprising 750,000 or more inhabitants in 1995.

## Table B.2

### Definitions

Please note that *C* stands for city proper, *M* for metropolitan area and *A* for urban agglomeration.

*City proper* is an administrative city defined according to legal/political boundaries established in each country for each city.

*Metropolitan area* is a politically defined urban area

set up for planning or administrative purposes which may combine several jurisdictions (municipalities or cities).

*Urban agglomeration:* see definition for Table B.1.

*Population* in specific age groups (total, 0–19, > 65) for male and females have been compiled from the United Nations Human Settlements Statistics Questionnaire 1999.

The year in parenthesis at the upper right corner of a figure denotes the year of data other than that specified for the respective row.

# Table B.3

## Definitions

See Tables A.3 and A.4.

## Notes

1  Data for squatter households refer to other households and households not stated.
2  The figures of tenant households in publicly owned housing units include tenant households in privately owned.
3  The figures of tenant households in publicly owned housing units include tenant households in privately owned.
4  Data under squatter households refer to free households.
5  Data for tenant households in privately owned housing units refer to both publicly owned and privately owned housing unit.
6   Data for squatter households refer to not stated.
7  The head of the household is a member of the household and (in order of precedence) either the husband of the person, or the person, who:
   •  Owns the household accommodation
   •  Is legally responsible for the rent or
   •  Has the accommodation by virtue of some relationship to the owner in cases where the owner or tenant is not a household member.

   When two members of a different sex have equal claim, the male is taken as the household head. When two members of the same sex have equal claim, the elder is taken as the household head. By this definition, there are instances where the male is taken as the head even if this does not reflect 'who is acknowledged as such by other household members'.
8  Data are based on October 1999 census, which is the latest.
9  Data for tenant households in publicly owned housing units refer to housing units occupied by dependency relationship.
10  Data for owner households, tenant households in publicly owned housing units, tenant households in privately owned housing units and squatter households are based on owner households statistical estimates 1993.
11  Data for tenant households in privately owned housing units refer to both publicly owned and privately owned housing units.

# Table B.4

## Definitions

See Table A.4.

## Notes

1  Data for marginal type of housing units are for other housing units.
2  Data for marginal type of housing units include mobile housing units.
3  Data of household budget survey.
4  Data are for residential buildings and other buildings with living quarters.
5  Data are for permanently occupied accommodations.
6  Data are for residential houses.
7  Data include that of temporary and marginal housing units.
8  The data for total households are only for the number of censused households stated due to the boycott of 1991 Population Census by the majority of Albanian population in Kosovo and Metohia. The data include business offices, which have been settled in necessity.

# Table B.5

## Definitions

*Average persons per housing unit* refer to the ratio of total numbers of persons to the total number of housing units.

For more information and definitions of terms, see Table A.5.

## Note

1  Occupied housing units refer to dwellings.

# Table B.6

## Definitions

See Table A.6.

## Notes

1  The given total is that of total piped water.
2  Data refer to pit latrine.
3  Data are for toilet inside housing unit total is that on the main server.
4  Data refer to public tap.
5  Data refer to piped water inside housing unit.
6  Data refer to wells and bore holes.
7  Data refer to tap of neighbour, source or stream and others.
8  Data include:
   •  public tap
   •  water carrier/tanker
   •  borehole/rainwater/tank/well
   •  dam/river/steam/spring.
9  Data are for piped water outside and public fountain.
10  Data are for tank wagon, well/river.
11  Other refers to households without facilities for piped water.
12  Other refers to households without flush toilet.
13  Piped water outside the unit, without limit to distance.
14  Households in occupied housing units refer to dwellings.
15  Housing units are referred to as dwellings.
16  Data for total households with piped water inside the housing unit is 100%.
17  Data for households with piped water inside the housing unit from community source is 100%.
18  Data on households by toilet facilities does not distinguish between households with flush or non-flush toilets.

# Table B.7

## Definitions

*Economically active population*: The economically active population can be measured in many different ways, and the 1982 recommendations of ILO include, in particular, two useful ways of measuring the economically active population. One approach uses the usually active population, measured in relation to a long reference period such as a year, and the other uses the currently active population or, equivalently, the labour force, measured in relation to a short reference period such as one week or one day.

The unemployed comprise all persons above a specified age who during the reference period were: (a) without work, in other words, not in paid employment or self-employment, as defined above; (b) currently available for work, in other words, were available for paid employment or self-employment during the reference period; or (c) seeking work, in other words, took specific steps in a specified recent period to seek paid employment or self-employment. The specific steps may have included registration at a public or private employment exchange; application to employers; checking at work sites, farms, factory gates, markets or other places of assembly; placing or answering newspaper advertisements; seeking assistance of friends and relatives; looking for land, building, machinery or equipment to establish one's own enterprise; arranging for financial resources; applying for permits and licences; and so forth.

### Note

Dara for total unemployed refer to both unemployed and economically inactive population. They also include persons seeking job for the first time.

# Table B.8

### Definitions

See Table A.11.

The year in parenthesis at the upper right corner of a figure denotes the year of data other than that specified for the respective row.

### Notes

1   Data for number of motor vehicles, goods vehicles and for lorries.
2   Data for number of physicians include dentists and physicians working in hospitals.

## TABLE A.1

## Size and Growth of Total Population, Life Expectancy at Birth

| | Estimates and projections (thousands) | | | | Annual growth rate (%) | | | Life expectancy at birth (years) | | | | | |
|---|---|---|---|---|---|---|---|---|---|---|---|---|---|
| | 1985 | 2000 | 2015 | 2030 | 1985–2000 | 2000–2015 | 2015–2030 | 1995–2000 | | 2010–2015 | | 2025–2030 | |
| | | | | | | | | M | F | M | F | M | F |
| **WORLD** | **4837358** | **6055049** | **7154366** | **8111980** | **1.5** | **1.1** | **0.8** | **63.2** | **67.6** | **67.0** | **71.6** | **70.7** | **75.5** |
| More developed regions | 1114217 | 1187980 | 1214394 | 1209507 | 0.4 | 0.1 | 0.0 | 71.1 | 78.7 | 74.0 | 80.6 | 76.1 | 82.3 |
| Less developed regions | 3723141 | 4867069 | 5939972 | 6902473 | 1.8 | 1.3 | 1.0 | 61.8 | 65.0 | 65.7 | 69.6 | 69.8 | 74.1 |
| **AFRICA** | **536356** | **784445** | **1077795** | **1405925** | **2.5** | **2.1** | **1.8** | **50.0** | **52.8** | **54.8** | **57.3** | **62.5** | **65.7** |
| Algeria | 21887 | 31471 | 41199 | 49382 | 2.4 | 1.8 | 1.2 | 67.5 | 70.3 | 70.9 | 74.5 | 73.7 | 77.7 |
| Angola | 8005 | 12878 | 19702 | 27837 | 3.2 | 2.8 | 2.3 | 44.9 | 48.1 | 52.4 | 55.6 | 59.9 | 63.1 |
| Benin | 4019 | 6097 | 8940 | 12129 | 2.8 | 2.6 | 2.0 | 51.7 | 55.2 | 55.2 | 58.5 | 62.9 | 66.3 |
| Botswana | 1081 | 1622 | 1967 | 2361 | 2.7 | 1.3 | 1.2 | 46.2 | 48.4 | 48.5 | 49.2 | 59.7 | 61.0 |
| Burkina Faso | 7879 | 11937 | 18096 | 26049 | 2.8 | 2.8 | 2.4 | 43.6 | 45.2 | 52.3 | 54.2 | 59.9 | 62.0 |
| Burundi | 4741 | 6695 | 9492 | 12498 | 2.3 | 2.3 | 1.8 | 41.0 | 43.8 | 48.8 | 51.6 | 57.7 | 60.7 |
| Cameroon | 9970 | 15085 | 21503 | 28917 | 2.8 | 2.4 | 2.0 | 53.4 | 56.0 | 54.5 | 56.1 | 63.1 | 65.2 |
| Cape Verde | 310 | 428 | 579 | 717 | 2.2 | 2.0 | 1.4 | 65.5 | 71.3 | 69.7 | 75.2 | 72.9 | 78.2 |
| Central African Republic | 2607 | 3615 | 4764 | 6152 | 2.2 | 1.8 | 1.7 | 42.9 | 46.9 | 48.0 | 54.1 | 58.2 | 64.3 |
| Chad | 5116 | 7651 | 11185 | 15206 | 2.7 | 2.5 | 2.0 | 45.7 | 48.7 | 51.9 | 54.9 | 59.6 | 62.7 |
| Comoros | 456 | 694 | 998 | 1257 | 2.8 | 2.4 | 1.5 | 57.4 | 60.2 | 63.4 | 66.2 | 69.4 | 72.2 |
| Congo | 1922 | 2943 | 4415 | 6346 | 2.8 | 2.7 | 2.4 | 46.3 | 50.8 | 54.7 | 59.7 | 63.5 | 68.7 |
| Côte d'Ivoire | 9878 | 14786 | 20047 | 24777 | 2.7 | 2.0 | 1.4 | 46.2 | 47.3 | 53.9 | 55.8 | 62.9 | 65.6 |
| Dem. Republic of the Congo | 31669 | 51654 | 80261 | 117338 | 3.3 | 2.9 | 2.5 | 49.2 | 52.3 | 57.0 | 60.1 | 64.8 | 67.9 |
| Djibouti | 391 | 638 | 866 | 1099 | 3.3 | 2.0 | 1.6 | 48.7 | 52.0 | 54.7 | 58.0 | 61.2 | 64.5 |
| Egypt | 49748 | 68470 | 85224 | 100371 | 2.1 | 1.5 | 1.1 | 64.7 | 67.9 | 69.4 | 73.3 | 72.7 | 76.7 |
| Equatorial Guinea | 312 | 453 | 645 | 869 | 2.5 | 2.4 | 2.0 | 48.4 | 51.6 | 54.4 | 57.6 | 60.9 | 64.1 |
| Eritrea | 2701 | 3850 | 5498 | 7185 | 2.4 | 2.4 | 1.8 | 49.3 | 52.4 | 56.6 | 59.4 | 65.0 | 66.2 |
| Ethiopia | 41150 | 62565 | 90947 | 127816 | 2.8 | 2.5 | 2.3 | 42.4 | 44.3 | 51.2 | 53.4 | 59.7 | 62.4 |
| Gabon | 803 | 1226 | 1656 | 2139 | 2.8 | 2.0 | 1.7 | 51.1 | 53.8 | 52.9 | 55.0 | 62.0 | 64.9 |
| Gambia | 745 | 1305 | 1821 | 2303 | 3.7 | 2.2 | 1.6 | 45.4 | 48.6 | 51.4 | 54.7 | 57.3 | 60.7 |
| Ghana | 12933 | 20212 | 29820 | 40206 | 3.0 | 2.6 | 2.0 | 58.3 | 61.8 | 64.2 | 67.8 | 69.2 | 72.9 |
| Guinea | 4987 | 7430 | 10488 | 13381 | 2.7 | 2.3 | 1.6 | 46.0 | 47.0 | 52.0 | 53.0 | 58.5 | 59.5 |
| Guinea-Bissau | 877 | 1213 | 1622 | 2115 | 2.2 | 1.9 | 1.8 | 43.5 | 46.5 | 43.6 | 46.1 | 52.9 | 55.9 |
| Kenya | 19871 | 30080 | 37611 | 43916 | 2.8 | 1.5 | 1.0 | 51.1 | 53.0 | 50.5 | 51.5 | 59.9 | 62.3 |
| Lesotho | 1526 | 2153 | 2893 | 3793 | 2.3 | 2.0 | 1.8 | 54.7 | 57.3 | 58.3 | 60.0 | 65.8 | 68.4 |
| Liberia | 2193 | 3154 | 5131 | 7395 | 2.4 | 3.2 | 2.4 | 46.1 | 48.5 | 60.3 | 62.8 | 66.6 | 70.0 |
| Libyan Arab Jamahiriya | 3786 | 5605 | 7573 | 9200 | 2.6 | 2.0 | 1.3 | 68.3 | 72.2 | 71.9 | 76.3 | 74.5 | 79.1 |
| Madagascar | 10123 | 15942 | 23359 | 31592 | 3.0 | 2.5 | 2.0 | 56.0 | 59.0 | 62.0 | 65.0 | 67.5 | 71.0 |
| Malawi | 7243 | 10925 | 15770 | 22084 | 2.7 | 2.4 | 2.2 | 38.9 | 39.6 | 47.8 | 48.4 | 58.2 | 59.1 |
| Mali | 7915 | 11234 | 16657 | 23631 | 2.3 | 2.6 | 2.3 | 52.0 | 54.6 | 58.0 | 60.6 | 64.3 | 67.1 |
| Mauritania | 1766 | 2670 | 3885 | 5180 | 2.8 | 2.5 | 1.9 | 51.9 | 55.1 | 57.9 | 61.1 | 63.9 | 67.1 |
| Mauritius[1] | 1016 | 1158 | 1302 | 1407 | 0.9 | 0.8 | 0.5 | 67.9 | 75.1 | 71.3 | 78.1 | 73.9 | 80.5 |
| Morocco | 21647 | 28351 | 34784 | 40451 | 1.8 | 1.4 | 1.0 | 64.8 | 68.5 | 69.5 | 73.5 | 72.7 | 76.9 |
| Mozambique | 13535 | 19680 | 25212 | 33508 | 2.5 | 1.7 | 1.9 | 43.9 | 46.6 | 39.1 | 40.1 | 51.9 | 53.8 |
| Namibia | 1178 | 1726 | 2031 | 2495 | 2.5 | 1.1 | 1.4 | 51.8 | 53.0 | 41.6 | 41.3 | 54.9 | 56.2 |
| Niger | 6608 | 10730 | 16690 | 23915 | 3.2 | 2.9 | 2.4 | 46.9 | 50.1 | 52.9 | 56.2 | 59.3 | 62.8 |
| Nigeria | 75805 | 111506 | 153307 | 197134 | 2.6 | 2.1 | 1.7 | 48.7 | 51.5 | 52.4 | 54.9 | 60.5 | 63.4 |
| Réunion | 555 | 699 | 814 | 905 | 1.5 | 1.0 | 0.7 | 70.9 | 79.8 | 74.3 | 82.4 | 76.6 | 84.1 |
| Rwanda | 6054 | 7733 | 10537 | 13160 | 1.6 | 2.1 | 1.5 | 39.4 | 41.7 | 45.9 | 48.3 | 55.1 | 57.7 |
| Saint Helena[2] | 6 | 6 | 7 | 8 | – | 1.0 | 0.9 | .. | .. | .. | .. | .. | .. |
| Sao Tome and Principe | 106 | 147 | 190 | 231 | 2.2 | 1.7 | 1.3 | .. | .. | .. | .. | .. | .. |
| Senegal | 6375 | 9481 | 13665 | 18193 | 2.6 | 2.4 | 1.9 | 50.5 | 54.2 | 56.5 | 60.2 | 62.8 | 66.5 |
| Seychelles | 65 | 77 | 90 | 102 | 1.1 | 1.0 | 0.8 | .. | .. | .. | .. | .. | .. |
| Sierra Leone | 3583 | 4854 | 6677 | 8781 | 2.0 | 2.1 | 1.8 | 35.8 | 38.7 | 43.8 | 46.8 | 51.3 | 54.5 |
| Somalia | 6547 | 10097 | 16350 | 23684 | 2.9 | 3.2 | 2.5 | 45.4 | 48.6 | 51.4 | 54.6 | 57.4 | 60.6 |
| South Africa | 30718 | 40377 | 43387 | 47644 | 1.8 | 0.5 | 0.6 | 51.5 | 58.1 | 46.1 | 48.3 | 56.7 | 59.4 |
| Sudan | 21459 | 29490 | 39811 | 48960 | 2.1 | 2.0 | 1.4 | 53.6 | 56.4 | 59.6 | 62.4 | 65.6 | 68.7 |
| Swaziland | 649 | 1008 | 1470 | 1923 | 2.9 | 2.5 | 1.8 | 57.9 | 62.5 | 64.7 | 69.6 | 69.4 | 74.3 |
| Togo | 3026 | 4629 | 6749 | 9307 | 2.8 | 2.5 | 2.1 | 47.6 | 50.1 | 55.2 | 57.9 | 64.1 | 67.2 |
| Tunisia | 7334 | 9586 | 11607 | 13380 | 1.8 | 1.3 | 0.9 | 68.4 | 70.7 | 71.8 | 74.9 | 74.4 | 78.1 |
| Uganda | 14736 | 21778 | 34475 | 49221 | 2.6 | 3.1 | 2.4 | 38.9 | 40.4 | 50.1 | 52.4 | 58.2 | 60.9 |
| United Republic of Tanzania | 21775 | 33517 | 47221 | 63118 | 2.9 | 2.3 | 1.9 | 46.8 | 49.1 | 51.4 | 53.4 | 61.4 | 64.2 |
| Western Sahara | 171 | 293 | 417 | 498 | 3.6 | 2.4 | 1.2 | 59.8 | 63.1 | 66.6 | 69.9 | 70.5 | 74.6 |
| Zambia | 6410 | 9169 | 12817 | 16804 | 2.4 | 2.2 | 1.8 | 39.5 | 40.6 | 50.8 | 52.0 | 61.3 | 62.9 |
| Zimbabwe | 8388 | 11669 | 13572 | 15853 | 2.2 | 1.0 | 1.0 | 43.6 | 44.7 | 49.6 | 51.1 | 58.9 | 61.2 |
| **ASIA** | **2901221** | **3682550** | **4346894** | **4876580** | **1.6** | **1.1** | **0.8** | **64.8** | **67.9** | **68.9** | **72.8** | **72.1** | **76.5** |
| Afghanistan | 14519 | 22720 | 36781 | 48986 | 3.0 | 3.2 | 1.9 | 45.0 | 46.0 | 51.0 | 52.0 | 57.5 | 58.5 |
| Armenia | 3339 | 3520 | 3810 | 3988 | 0.4 | 0.5 | 0.3 | 67.2 | 73.6 | 70.2 | 76.4 | 72.6 | 78.8 |
| Azerbaijan | 6671 | 7734 | 8795 | 9602 | 1.0 | 0.9 | 0.6 | 65.5 | 74.1 | 69.5 | 76.7 | 72.3 | 78.8 |
| Bahrain | 413 | 617 | 762 | 896 | 2.7 | 1.4 | 1.1 | 71.1 | 75.3 | 73.8 | 78.3 | 76.0 | 80.7 |
| Bangladesh | 99373 | 129155 | 161540 | 187149 | 1.7 | 1.5 | 1.0 | 58.1 | 58.2 | 64.9 | 65.8 | 69.6 | 71.6 |
| Bhutan | 1486 | 2124 | 3113 | 4304 | 2.4 | 2.5 | 2.2 | 59.5 | 62.0 | 66.8 | 69.5 | 71.5 | 75.3 |
| Brunei Darussalam | 223 | 328 | 410 | 479 | 2.6 | 1.5 | 1.0 | 73.4 | 78.1 | 75.5 | 80.5 | 77.0 | 82.0 |
| Cambodia | 7385 | 11168 | 14403 | 17380 | 2.8 | 1.7 | 1.3 | 51.5 | 55.0 | 57.3 | 61.3 | 64.8 | 66.6 |
| China[3] | 1070175 | 1277558 | 1417720 | 1495944 | 1.2 | 0.7 | 0.4 | 67.9 | 72.0 | 71.3 | 75.9 | 74.1 | 78.7 |
| China, Hong Kong SAR[4] | 5456 | 6927 | 7689 | 7621 | 1.6 | 0.7 | -0.1 | 75.8 | 81.4 | 77.2 | 82.4 | 78.4 | 83.9 |
| China, Macau SAR | 306 | 473 | 512 | 531 | 2.9 | 0.5 | 0.2 | 75.1 | 80.1 | 76.6 | 81.6 | 78.0 | 83.0 |
| Cyprus | 647 | 786 | 866 | 909 | 1.3 | 0.6 | 0.3 | 75.5 | 80.0 | 77.0 | 81.5 | 78.3 | 82.9 |
| Dem. People's Rep. of Korea | 18945 | 24039 | 27370 | 30195 | 1.6 | 0.9 | 0.7 | 68.9 | 75.1 | 72.1 | 78.1 | 74.7 | 80.5 |
| East Timor | 659 | 885 | 1082 | 1229 | 2.0 | 1.3 | 0.8 | 46.7 | 48.4 | 54.2 | 55.9 | 61.7 | 63.4 |
| Gaza Strip | 527 | 1120 | 1987 | 3216 | 5.0 | 3.8 | 3.2 | 69.3 | 73.3 | 72.5 | 76.7 | 74.9 | 79.3 |
| Georgia | 5287 | 4968 | 5087 | 5206 | -0.4 | 0.2 | 0.2 | 68.5 | 76.8 | 71.3 | 78.6 | 73.7 | 80.1 |
| India | 767842 | 1013662 | 1211665 | 1382722 | 1.9 | 1.2 | 0.9 | 62.3 | 62.9 | 66.2 | 68.6 | 70.0 | 73.4 |
| Indonesia | 167332 | 212107 | 250383 | 283520 | 1.6 | 1.1 | 0.8 | 63.3 | 67.0 | 68.3 | 72.8 | 71.7 | 76.2 |

# TABLE A.1

**continued**

| | | | | | | | | | | | | |
|---|---|---|---|---|---|---|---|---|---|---|---|---|
| an (Islamic Republic of) | 47622 | 67702 | 83054 | 99186 | 2.3 | 1.4 | 1.2 | 68.5 | 70.0 | 71.9 | 74.7 | 74.5 | 77.9 |
| aq | 15317 | 23115 | 34062 | 43929 | 2.7 | 2.6 | 1.7 | 60.9 | 63.9 | 70.4 | 73.9 | 73.2 | 77.1 |
| rael | 4233 | 6217 | 7592 | 8577 | 2.6 | 1.3 | 0.8 | 75.7 | 79.7 | 77.2 | 81.5 | 78.5 | 82.9 |
| pan | 120837 | 126714 | 126070 | 118145 | 0.3 | 0.0 | −0.4 | 76.8 | 82.9 | 78.0 | 84.1 | 79.2 | 85.3 |
| rdan | 4123 | 6669 | 9909 | 13019 | 3.2 | 2.6 | 1.8 | 68.9 | 71.5 | 72.1 | 75.4 | 74.6 | 78.4 |
| azakhstan | 15827 | 16223 | 16919 | 17989 | 0.2 | 0.3 | 0.4 | 62.8 | 72.5 | 67.8 | 75.5 | 70.8 | 77.9 |
| uwait | 1720 | 1972 | 2622 | 3115 | 0.9 | 1.9 | 1.1 | 74.1 | 78.2 | 76.2 | 80.6 | 77.7 | 82.1 |
| yrgyzstan | 4014 | 4699 | 5461 | 6408 | 1.1 | 1.0 | 1.1 | 63.3 | 71.9 | 68.3 | 75.1 | 71.3 | 77.5 |
| ao People's Dem. Republic | 3594 | 5433 | 7844 | 10482 | 2.8 | 2.4 | 1.9 | 52.0 | 54.5 | 59.5 | 62.0 | 66.3 | 69.1 |
| ebanon | 2668 | 3282 | 3942 | 4606 | 1.4 | 1.2 | 1.0 | 68.1 | 71.7 | 70.9 | 74.9 | 73.5 | 77.7 |
| Malaysia | 15677 | 22244 | 27540 | 32549 | 2.3 | 1.4 | 1.1 | 69.9 | 74.3 | 73.1 | 77.5 | 75.5 | 80.1 |
| Maldives | 184 | 286 | 420 | 536 | 2.9 | 2.6 | 1.6 | 65.7 | 63.3 | 70.7 | 70.6 | 73.9 | 75.3 |
| Mongolia | 1909 | 2662 | 3307 | 3881 | 2.2 | 1.4 | 1.1 | 64.4 | 67.3 | 68.8 | 72.6 | 72.0 | 76.2 |
| Myanmar | 37544 | 45611 | 53533 | 60005 | 1.3 | 1.1 | 0.8 | 58.5 | 61.8 | 65.3 | 69.1 | 69.5 | 73.8 |
| Nepal | 16503 | 23930 | 32693 | 40344 | 2.5 | 2.1 | 1.4 | 57.6 | 57.1 | 64.7 | 64.6 | 69.4 | 71.6 |
| Oman | 1425 | 2542 | 4103 | 5996 | 3.9 | 3.2 | 2.5 | 68.9 | 73.3 | 72.1 | 76.7 | 74.7 | 79.3 |
| akistan | 101202 | 156483 | 222587 | 280245 | 2.9 | 2.3 | 1.5 | 62.9 | 65.1 | 68.4 | 71.7 | 71.8 | 75.6 |
| hilippines | 54668 | 75967 | 96732 | 114022 | 2.2 | 1.6 | 1.1 | 66.5 | 70.2 | 70.4 | 74.4 | 73.4 | 77.6 |
| Qatar | 358 | 599 | 732 | 793 | 3.4 | 1.3 | 0.5 | 70.0 | 75.4 | 73.0 | 78.4 | 75.4 | 80.5 |
| epublic of Korea | 40806 | 46844 | 51051 | 52898 | 0.9 | 0.6 | 0.2 | 68.8 | 76.0 | 72.0 | 78.8 | 74.6 | 80.9 |
| audi Arabia | 12648 | 21607 | 32623 | 42991 | 3.6 | 2.7 | 1.8 | 69.9 | 73.4 | 73.6 | 77.6 | 76.1 | 80.4 |
| ingapore | 2709 | 3567 | 3994 | 4205 | 1.8 | 0.8 | 0.3 | 74.9 | 79.3 | 77.5 | 81.9 | 78.9 | 83.6 |
| ri Lanka | 16046 | 18827 | 21883 | 24224 | 1.1 | 1.0 | 0.7 | 70.9 | 75.4 | 73.7 | 78.4 | 75.8 | 80.8 |
| yrian Arab Republic | 10397 | 16125 | 22646 | 28078 | 2.9 | 2.3 | 1.4 | 66.7 | 71.2 | 70.3 | 75.1 | 73.3 | 78.1 |
| ajikistan | 4567 | 6188 | 7756 | 9409 | 2.0 | 1.5 | 1.3 | 64.2 | 70.2 | 68.7 | 73.6 | 71.7 | 76.6 |
| hailand | 51146 | 61399 | 68872 | 74029 | 1.2 | 0.8 | 0.5 | 65.8 | 72.0 | 69.9 | 75.7 | 73.0 | 78.6 |
| urkey | 50345 | 66591 | 80284 | 91295 | 1.9 | 1.2 | 0.9 | 66.5 | 71.7 | 70.4 | 75.6 | 73.4 | 78.4 |
| urkmenistan | 3230 | 4459 | 5575 | 6641 | 2.1 | 1.5 | 1.2 | 61.9 | 68.9 | 66.9 | 72.8 | 71.1 | 76.0 |
| United Arab Emirates | 1552 | 2441 | 3026 | 3376 | 3.0 | 1.4 | 0.7 | 73.9 | 76.5 | 76.8 | 79.7 | 78.4 | 82.0 |
| zbekistan | 18174 | 24318 | 29883 | 35138 | 1.9 | 1.4 | 1.1 | 64.3 | 70.7 | 68.3 | 74.1 | 71.3 | 76.7 |
| iet Nam | 59898 | 79832 | 96610 | 112857 | 1.9 | 1.3 | 1.0 | 64.9 | 69.6 | 69.6 | 74.3 | 72.8 | 77.5 |
| emen | 9698 | 18112 | 29596 | 43734 | 4.2 | 3.3 | 2.6 | 57.4 | 58.4 | 64.7 | 65.9 | 69.4 | 71.7 |
| **EUROPE** | **706580** | **728887** | **719307** | **690976** | **0.2** | **−0.1** | **−0.3** | **69.2** | **77.4** | **72.4** | **79.5** | **74.9** | **81.4** |
| Albania | 2962 | 3113 | 3501 | 3957 | 0.3 | 0.8 | 0.8 | 69.9 | 75.9 | 72.5 | 78.3 | 74.9 | 80.7 |
| Andorra | 44 | 78 | 125 | 165 | 3.8 | 3.1 | 1.9 | .. | .. | .. | .. | .. | .. |
| Austria | 7558 | 8211 | 8329 | 8045 | 0.6 | 0.1 | −0.2 | 73.7 | 80.2 | 75.8 | 81.7 | 77.3 | 83.1 |
| Belarus | 9999 | 10236 | 9848 | 9307 | 0.2 | −0.3 | −0.4 | 62.2 | 73.9 | 66.1 | 76.4 | 69.8 | 78.8 |
| Belgium | 9857 | 10161 | 10085 | 9780 | 0.2 | −0.1 | −0.2 | 73.8 | 80.6 | 75.9 | 82.1 | 77.4 | 83.4 |
| Bosnia and Herzegovina | 4122 | 3972 | 4377 | 4250 | −0.2 | 0.6 | −0.2 | 70.5 | 75.9 | 72.9 | 78.0 | 74.4 | 79.5 |
| Bulgaria | 8960 | 8225 | 7526 | 6766 | −0.6 | −0.6 | −0.7 | 67.6 | 74.7 | 70.4 | 77.3 | 72.8 | 79.4 |
| Channel Islands | 135 | 153 | 166 | 176 | 0.8 | 0.5 | 0.4 | .. | .. | .. | .. | .. | .. |
| Croatia | 4471 | 4473 | 4350 | 4099 | − | −0.2 | −0.4 | 68.8 | 76.5 | 71.6 | 78.6 | 74.0 | 80.1 |
| Czech Republic | 10305 | 10244 | 9929 | 9229 | 0.0 | −0.2 | −0.5 | 70.3 | 77.4 | 73.7 | 80.6 | 76.2 | 82.7 |
| Denmark | 5114 | 5293 | 5309 | 5176 | 0.2 | 0.0 | −0.2 | 73.0 | 78.3 | 74.5 | 79.8 | 76.0 | 81.3 |
| Estonia | 1519 | 1396 | 1219 | 1092 | −0.6 | −0.9 | −0.7 | 63.0 | 74.5 | 68.0 | 77.1 | 71.0 | 79.2 |
| Faeroe Islands | 46 | 43 | 38 | 36 | −0.4 | −0.8 | −0.4 | .. | .. | .. | .. | .. | .. |
| Finland | 4902 | 5176 | 5255 | 5209 | 0.4 | 0.1 | −0.1 | 73.0 | 80.6 | 76.0 | 83.0 | 78.0 | 84.4 |
| France | 55170 | 59080 | 61108 | 61632 | 0.5 | 0.2 | 0.1 | 74.2 | 82.0 | 76.0 | 83.4 | 77.5 | 84.6 |
| Germany | 77668 | 82220 | 81574 | 79252 | 0.4 | −0.1 | −0.2 | 73.9 | 80.2 | 76.0 | 81.7 | 77.5 | 83.1 |
| Gibraltar | 28 | 25 | 23 | 21 | −0.8 | −0.6 | −0.6 | .. | .. | .. | .. | .. | .. |
| Greece | 9934 | 10645 | 10378 | 9571 | 0.5 | −0.2 | −0.5 | 75.6 | 80.7 | 77.1 | 82.2 | 78.4 | 83.5 |
| Holy See[5] | 1 | 1 | 1 | 1 | .. | .. | .. | .. | .. | .. | .. | .. | .. |
| Hungary | 10579 | 10036 | 9408 | 8627 | −0.4 | −0.4 | −0.6 | 66.8 | 74.9 | 70.3 | 77.5 | 72.9 | 78.9 |
| Iceland | 241 | 281 | 313 | 334 | 1.0 | 0.7 | 0.4 | 76.8 | 81.3 | 78.2 | 82.8 | 79.6 | 84.0 |
| Ireland | 3552 | 3730 | 4168 | 4484 | 0.3 | 0.7 | 0.5 | 73.6 | 79.2 | 76.4 | 81.8 | 78.4 | 83.5 |
| Isle of Man | 64 | 79 | 93 | 104 | 1.4 | 1.1 | 0.7 | .. | .. | .. | .. | .. | .. |
| Italy | 56771 | 57298 | 54448 | 49533 | 0.1 | −0.3 | −0.6 | 75.0 | 81.2 | 76.8 | 82.7 | 78.2 | 83.9 |
| Latvia | 2594 | 2357 | 2063 | 1874 | −0.6 | −0.9 | −0.6 | 62.5 | 74.4 | 67.0 | 76.5 | 70.0 | 78.3 |
| Liechtenstein | 27 | 33 | 38 | 42 | 1.3 | 0.9 | 0.7 | .. | .. | .. | .. | .. | .. |
| Lithuania | 3557 | 3670 | 3521 | 3326 | 0.2 | −0.3 | −0.4 | 64.3 | 75.6 | 68.8 | 78.0 | 71.6 | 79.8 |
| Luxembourg | 367 | 431 | 462 | 460 | 1.1 | 0.5 | − | 73.3 | 79.9 | 75.7 | 81.7 | 77.2 | 83.1 |
| Malta | 344 | 389 | 421 | 431 | 0.8 | 0.5 | 0.2 | 74.9 | 79.3 | 76.7 | 81.1 | 78.1 | 82.6 |
| Monaco | 28 | 34 | 38 | 41 | 1.3 | 0.7 | 0.5 | .. | .. | .. | .. | .. | .. |
| The Netherlands | 14492 | 15786 | 15937 | 15617 | 0.6 | 0.1 | −0.1 | 75.0 | 80.7 | 76.5 | 82.2 | 77.9 | 83.5 |
| Norway | 4153 | 4465 | 4716 | 4838 | 0.5 | 0.4 | 0.2 | 75.2 | 81.1 | 77.3 | 83.2 | 78.8 | 84.7 |
| Poland | 37203 | 38765 | 39350 | 38680 | 0.3 | 0.1 | −0.1 | 68.2 | 76.9 | 71.6 | 79.5 | 74.2 | 81.3 |
| Portugal | 9904 | 9875 | 9661 | 9163 | 0.0 | −0.1 | −0.4 | 71.8 | 78.8 | 74.4 | 80.9 | 76.2 | 82.4 |
| Republic of Moldova | 4215 | 4380 | 4474 | 4561 | 0.3 | 0.1 | 0.1 | 63.5 | 71.5 | 67.5 | 74.5 | 70.5 | 77.1 |
| Romania | 22725 | 22327 | 21067 | 19335 | −0.1 | −0.4 | −0.6 | 66.2 | 73.9 | 69.7 | 76.5 | 72.5 | 78.9 |
| Russian Federation | 143329 | 146934 | 142945 | 135207 | 0.2 | −0.2 | −0.4 | 60.6 | 72.6 | 65.3 | 75.2 | 69.5 | 77.6 |
| San Marino | 22 | 27 | 31 | 33 | 1.4 | 0.9 | 0.4 | .. | .. | .. | .. | .. | .. |
| Slovakia | 5140 | 5387 | 5466 | 5326 | 0.3 | 0.1 | −0.2 | 69.2 | 76.7 | 71.8 | 78.5 | 73.9 | 80.3 |
| Slovenia | 1881 | 1986 | 1916 | 1760 | 0.4 | −0.2 | −0.6 | 70.6 | 78.2 | 73.0 | 79.7 | 75.4 | 81.2 |
| Spain | 38474 | 39630 | 38465 | 35611 | 0.2 | −0.2 | −0.5 | 74.5 | 81.5 | 76.3 | 82.9 | 77.8 | 84.1 |
| Sweden | 8350 | 8910 | 9087 | 9047 | 0.4 | 0.1 | 0.0 | 76.3 | 80.8 | 78.4 | 82.9 | 79.8 | 84.3 |
| Switzerland | 6536 | 7386 | 7625 | 7503 | 0.8 | 0.2 | −0.1 | 75.4 | 81.8 | 76.9 | 83.2 | 78.3 | 84.4 |
| TFYR Macedonia[6] | 1828 | 2024 | 2189 | 2286 | 0.7 | 0.5 | 0.3 | 70.9 | 75.3 | 73.3 | 77.7 | 75.7 | 80.1 |
| Ukraine | 50941 | 50456 | 47880 | 44534 | −0.1 | −0.3 | −0.5 | 63.8 | 73.7 | 68.8 | 76.5 | 71.8 | 78.9 |
| United Kingdom | 56618 | 58830 | 59566 | 59619 | 0.3 | 0.1 | 0.0 | 74.5 | 79.8 | 76.3 | 81.6 | 77.8 | 83.0 |
| Yugoslavia | 9848 | 10640 | 10819 | 10833 | 0.5 | 0.1 | 0.0 | 70.2 | 75.5 | 72.6 | 77.9 | 75.0 | 80.3 |
| **LATIN AMERICA** | **400834** | **519143** | **631115** | **725536** | **1.7** | **1.3** | **0.9** | **66.1** | **72.6** | **69.4** | **75.7** | **72.0** | **78.1** |
| Anguilla | 7 | 8 | 10 | 11 | 0.9 | 1.5 | 0.6 | .. | .. | .. | .. | .. | .. |
| Antigua and Barbuda | 62 | 68 | 72 | 76 | 0.6 | 0.4 | 0.4 | .. | .. | .. | .. | .. | .. |
| Argentina | 30305 | 37032 | 43498 | 48896 | 1.3 | 1.1 | 0.8 | 69.7 | 76.8 | 72.4 | 79.5 | 74.7 | 81.8 |

# TABLE A.1

## continued

| | Estimates and projections (thousands) | | | | Annual growth rate (%) | | | Life expectancy at birth (years) | | | | | |
|---|---|---|---|---|---|---|---|---|---|---|---|---|---|
| | 1985 | 2000 | 2015 | 2030 | 1985–2000 | 2000–2015 | 2015–2030 | 1995–2000 | | 2010–2015 | | 2025–2030 | |
| | | | | | | | | M | F | M | F | M | F |
| Aruba | 63 | 103 | 185 | 281 | 3.3 | 3.9 | 2.8 | .. | .. | .. | .. | .. | .. |
| Bahamas | 232 | 307 | 375 | 433 | 1.9 | 1.3 | 1.0 | 70.5 | 77.1 | 73.3 | 79.9 | 75.7 | 82.0 |
| Barbados | 253 | 270 | 288 | 299 | 0.4 | 0.4 | 0.2 | 73.7 | 78.7 | 75.7 | 80.7 | 77.2 | 82.2 |
| Belize | 166 | 241 | 318 | 396 | 2.5 | 1.8 | 1.5 | 73.4 | 76.1 | 75.8 | 78.9 | 77.3 | 81.0 |
| Bolivia | 5895 | 8329 | 11219 | 14000 | 2.3 | 2.0 | 1.5 | 59.8 | 63.2 | 65.9 | 69.6 | 70.7 | 74.7 |
| Brazil | 135224 | 170115 | 200697 | 225161 | 1.5 | 1.1 | 0.8 | 63.1 | 71.0 | 66.8 | 74.6 | 69.7 | 77.4 |
| British Virgin Islands | 14 | 21 | 30 | 40 | 2.7 | 2.4 | 1.9 | .. | .. | .. | .. | .. | .. |
| Cayman Islands | 21 | 38 | 61 | 86 | 4.0 | 3.2 | 2.3 | .. | .. | .. | .. | .. | .. |
| Chile | 12047 | 15211 | 17912 | 20240 | 1.6 | 1.1 | 0.8 | 72.3 | 78.3 | 74.3 | 80.4 | 75.9 | 82.2 |
| Colombia | 31659 | 42321 | 53183 | 62695 | 1.9 | 1.5 | 1.1 | 67.3 | 74.3 | 71.0 | 77.1 | 73.2 | 79.6 |
| Costa Rica | 2642 | 4023 | 5232 | 6238 | 2.8 | 1.8 | 1.2 | 74.3 | 78.9 | 76.2 | 81.1 | 77.7 | 82.8 |
| Cuba | 10115 | 11201 | 11646 | 11791 | 0.7 | 0.3 | 0.1 | 74.2 | 78.0 | 75.9 | 80.0 | 77.2 | 81.7 |
| Dominica | 72 | 71 | 72 | 75 | -0.1 | 0.1 | 0.3 | .. | .. | .. | .. | .. | .. |
| Dominican Republic | 6376 | 8495 | 10251 | 11522 | 1.9 | 1.3 | 0.8 | 69.0 | 73.1 | 72.3 | 77.0 | 74.9 | 79.9 |
| Ecuador | 9099 | 12646 | 15936 | 18641 | 2.2 | 1.5 | 1.0 | 67.3 | 72.5 | 70.0 | 75.4 | 72.4 | 77.9 |
| El Salvador | 4769 | 6276 | 7977 | 9554 | 1.8 | 1.6 | 1.2 | 66.5 | 72.5 | 69.8 | 76.0 | 72.6 | 79.0 |
| Falkland Islands (Malvinas) | 2 | 2 | 2 | 3 | – | – | 2.7 | .. | .. | .. | .. | .. | .. |
| French Guiana | 91 | 181 | 312 | 466 | 4.6 | 3.6 | 2.7 | .. | .. | .. | .. | .. | .. |
| Grenada | 90 | 94 | 100 | 107 | 0.3 | 0.4 | 0.5 | .. | .. | .. | .. | .. | .. |
| Guadeloupe | 355 | 456 | 533 | 582 | 1.7 | 1.0 | 0.6 | 73.6 | 80.9 | 76.8 | 83.0 | 78.5 | 84.4 |
| Guatemala | 7738 | 11385 | 16385 | 21441 | 2.6 | 2.4 | 1.8 | 61.4 | 67.2 | 66.2 | 72.1 | 70.3 | 76.2 |
| Guyana | 793 | 861 | 961 | 1080 | 0.5 | 0.7 | 0.8 | 61.1 | 67.9 | 66.6 | 72.1 | 70.1 | 75.3 |
| Haiti | 6126 | 8222 | 10440 | 12730 | 2.0 | 1.6 | 1.3 | 51.4 | 56.2 | 56.9 | 61.7 | 64.4 | 68.2 |
| Honduras | 4186 | 6485 | 9044 | 11392 | 2.9 | 2.2 | 1.5 | 67.5 | 72.3 | 70.7 | 75.6 | 73.3 | 78.3 |
| Jamaica | 2297 | 2583 | 2945 | 3389 | 0.8 | 0.9 | 0.9 | 72.9 | 76.8 | 75.3 | 79.4 | 76.8 | 81.2 |
| Martinique | 341 | 395 | 432 | 456 | 1.0 | 0.6 | 0.4 | 75.5 | 82.0 | 77.0 | 83.3 | 78.3 | 84.5 |
| Mexico | 75465 | 98881 | 119178 | 134912 | 1.8 | 1.2 | 0.8 | 69.5 | 75.5 | 72.1 | 78.2 | 74.3 | 80.4 |
| Montserrat | 11 | 11 | 11 | 11 | – | – | – | .. | .. | .. | .. | .. | .. |
| Netherlands Antilles | 182 | 217 | 245 | 263 | 1.2 | 0.8 | 0.5 | 72.5 | 78.4 | 74.9 | 80.5 | 76.4 | 82.0 |
| Nicaragua | 3404 | 5074 | 7271 | 9353 | 2.7 | 2.4 | 1.7 | 65.8 | 70.6 | 69.8 | 74.7 | 72.4 | 77.9 |
| Panama | 2167 | 2856 | 3451 | 3918 | 1.8 | 1.3 | 0.8 | 71.8 | 76.4 | 73.9 | 78.8 | 75.4 | 80.5 |
| Paraguay | 3609 | 5496 | 7773 | 10104 | 2.8 | 2.3 | 1.7 | 67.5 | 72.0 | 70.7 | 75.2 | 73.3 | 78.0 |
| Peru | 19492 | 25662 | 31876 | 37201 | 1.8 | 1.4 | 1.0 | 65.9 | 70.9 | 69.9 | 75.3 | 72.9 | 78.5 |
| Puerto Rico | 3378 | 3869 | 4279 | 4560 | 0.9 | 0.7 | 0.4 | 69.4 | 78.5 | 71.8 | 80.2 | 74.2 | 81.7 |
| Saint Kitts and Nevis | 44 | 38 | 36 | 35 | -1.0 | -0.4 | -0.2 | .. | .. | .. | .. | .. | .. |
| Saint Lucia | 125 | 154 | 186 | 218 | 1.4 | 1.3 | 1.1 | .. | .. | .. | .. | .. | .. |
| Saint Vincent and the Grenadines | 102 | 114 | 125 | 133 | 0.7 | 0.6 | 0.4 | .. | .. | .. | .. | .. | .. |
| Suriname | 384 | 417 | 478 | 544 | 0.5 | 0.9 | 0.9 | 67.5 | 72.7 | 70.5 | 75.7 | 73.7 | 78.1 |
| Trinidad and Tobago | 1178 | 1295 | 1420 | 1518 | 0.6 | 0.6 | 0.4 | 71.5 | 76.2 | 74.3 | 79.0 | 76.1 | 81.1 |
| Turks and Caicos Islands | 9 | 17 | 27 | 37 | 4.2 | 3.1 | 2.1 | .. | .. | .. | .. | .. | .. |
| United States Virgin Islands | 99 | 93 | 85 | 83 | -0.4 | -0.6 | -0.2 | .. | .. | .. | .. | .. | .. |
| Uruguay | 3009 | 3337 | 3681 | 4016 | 0.7 | 0.7 | 0.6 | 70.5 | 78.0 | 73.6 | 80.6 | 76.0 | 82.7 |
| Venezuela | 17138 | 24170 | 30877 | 36548 | 2.3 | 1.6 | 1.1 | 70.0 | 75.7 | 72.7 | 78.5 | 74.9 | 80.7 |
| **NORTHERN AMERICA** | **267912** | **309631** | **343165** | **371775** | **1.0** | **0.7** | **0.5** | **73.6** | **80.2** | **75.9** | **81.7** | **77.4** | **83.1** |
| Bermuda | 57 | 65 | 72 | 77 | 0.9 | 0.7 | 0.4 | .. | .. | .. | .. | .. | .. |
| Canada | 25942 | 31147 | 35301 | 39011 | 1.2 | 0.8 | 0.7 | 76.1 | 81.8 | 78.0 | 83.6 | 78.8 | 84.4 |
| Greenland | 53 | 56 | 58 | 61 | 0.4 | 0.2 | 0.3 | .. | .. | .. | .. | .. | .. |
| Saint Pierre and Miquelon | 6 | 7 | 7 | 7 | 1.0 | – | – | .. | .. | .. | .. | .. | .. |
| United States | 241855 | 278357 | 307727 | 332619 | 0.9 | 0.7 | 0.5 | 73.4 | 80.1 | 75.8 | 81.6 | 77.3 | 83.0 |
| **OCEANIA** | **24455** | **30393** | **36089** | **41188** | **1.4** | **1.1** | **0.9** | **71.4** | **76.3** | **74.1** | **78.9** | **76.3** | **81.2** |
| American Samoa | 39 | 68 | 110 | 159 | 3.7 | 3.2 | 2.5 | .. | .. | .. | .. | .. | .. |
| Australia[7] | 15641 | 18886 | 21477 | 23777 | 1.3 | 0.9 | 0.7 | 75.5 | 81.1 | 77.0 | 82.6 | 78.4 | 83.8 |
| Cook Islands | 17 | 20 | 22 | 25 | 1.1 | 0.6 | 0.9 | .. | .. | .. | .. | .. | .. |
| Fiji | 699 | 817 | 994 | 1155 | 1.0 | 1.3 | 1.0 | 70.6 | 74.9 | 73.4 | 77.8 | 75.6 | 80.2 |
| French Polynesia | 174 | 235 | 290 | 340 | 2.0 | 1.4 | 1.1 | 69.3 | 74.6 | 73.2 | 78.5 | 75.7 | 81.0 |
| Guam | 119 | 168 | 205 | 238 | 2.3 | 1.3 | 1.0 | 73.0 | 77.4 | 74.5 | 78.9 | 76.0 | 80.4 |
| Kiribati | 67 | 83 | 103 | 127 | 1.4 | 1.4 | 1.4 | .. | .. | .. | .. | .. | .. |
| Marshall Islands | 40 | 64 | 99 | 141 | 3.1 | 2.9 | 2.4 | .. | .. | .. | .. | .. | .. |
| Micronesia (Fed. States of) | 95 | 119 | 158 | 205 | 1.5 | 1.9 | 1.7 | .. | .. | .. | .. | .. | .. |
| New Caledonia | 155 | 214 | 259 | 298 | 2.2 | 1.3 | 0.9 | 69.2 | 76.3 | 72.4 | 79.1 | 75.0 | 81.2 |
| New Zealand | 3247 | 3862 | 4376 | 4834 | 1.2 | 0.8 | 0.7 | 74.1 | 79.7 | 76.2 | 81.5 | 77.7 | 82.9 |
| Nauru | 8 | 12 | 15 | 19 | 2.7 | 1.5 | 1.6 | .. | .. | .. | .. | .. | .. |
| Niue | 3 | 2 | 2 | 1 | -2.7 | – | -4.6 | .. | .. | .. | .. | .. | .. |
| Northern Mariana Islands | 19 | 78 | 165 | 288 | 9.4 | 5.0 | 3.7 | .. | .. | .. | .. | .. | .. |
| Palau | 14 | 19 | 27 | 36 | 2.0 | 2.3 | 1.9 | .. | .. | .. | .. | .. | .. |
| Papua New Guinea | 3442 | 4807 | 6482 | 7880 | 2.2 | 2.0 | 1.3 | 57.2 | 58.7 | 63.2 | 64.7 | 68.2 | 70.7 |
| Samoa | 157 | 180 | 236 | 290 | 0.9 | 1.8 | 1.4 | 69.3 | 73.6 | 72.8 | 77.1 | 75.2 | 79.7 |
| Solomon Islands | 270 | 444 | 665 | 883 | 3.3 | 2.7 | 1.9 | 69.7 | 73.9 | 72.9 | 77.1 | 75.3 | 79.7 |
| Tokelau | 2 | 2 | 2 | 2 | – | – | – | .. | .. | .. | .. | .. | .. |
| Tonga | 94 | 99 | 103 | 106 | 0.3 | 0.3 | 0.2 | .. | .. | .. | .. | .. | .. |
| Tuvalu | 8 | 12 | 17 | 23 | 2.7 | 2.3 | 2.0 | .. | .. | .. | .. | .. | .. |
| Vanuatu | 132 | 190 | 266 | 342 | 2.4 | 2.2 | 1.7 | 65.5 | 69.5 | 69.8 | 74.2 | 72.9 | 77.4 |
| Wallis and Futuna Islands | 12 | 15 | 16 | 18 | 1.5 | 0.4 | 0.8 | .. | .. | .. | .. | .. | .. |

**Sources:** United Nations, World Population Prospects: The 1998 Revision and United Nations, World Urbanization Prospects: The 1999 Revision.
For footnotes, refer to technical notes.

# TABLE A.2

## Size and Growth of Urban and Rural Population, Urbanization Trends

| | Level of urbanization (%) | | | Urban population (thousands) | | | Annual growth (%) | | Rural population Estimates and Projections (thousands) | | | Annual growth rate (%) | |
|---|---|---|---|---|---|---|---|---|---|---|---|---|---|
| | 2000 | 2015 | 2030 | 2000 | 2015 | 2030 | 2000–2015 | 2015–2030 | 2000 | 2015 | 2030 | 2000–2015 | 2015–2030 |
| **WORLD** | **47.0** | **53.4** | **60.3** | **2845049** | **3817292** | **4889393** | **2.0** | **1.7** | **3210000** | **3337074** | **3222587** | **0.3** | **–0.2** |
| More developed regions | 76.0 | 79.7 | 83.5 | 902993 | 968223 | 1009808 | 0.5 | 0.3 | 284987 | 246171 | 199699 | –1.0 | –1.4 |
| Less developed regions | 39.9 | 48.0 | 56.2 | 1942056 | 2849069 | 3879585 | 2.6 | 2.1 | 2925013 | 3090903 | 3022888 | 0.4 | –0.2 |
| **AFRICA** | **37.9** | **46.5** | **54.5** | **297139** | **501015** | **765709** | **3.5** | **2.8** | **487306** | **576781** | **640216** | **1.1** | **0.7** |
| Algeria | 60.3 | 68.5 | 74.4 | 18969 | 28214 | 36721 | 2.7 | 1.8 | 12502 | 12985 | 12661 | 0.3 | –0.2 |
| Angola | 34.2 | 44.1 | 53.6 | 4404 | 8691 | 14911 | 4.5 | 3.6 | 8474 | 11011 | 12925 | 1.8 | 1.1 |
| Benin | 42.3 | 53.0 | 61.4 | 2577 | 4735 | 7449 | 4.1 | 3.0 | 3520 | 4206 | 4681 | 1.2 | 0.7 |
| Botswana | 50.3 | 58.4 | 66.0 | 815 | 1148 | 1558 | 2.3 | 2.0 | 807 | 819 | 803 | 0.1 | –0.1 |
| Burkina Faso | 18.5 | 27.4 | 37.0 | 2204 | 4953 | 9646 | 5.4 | 4.4 | 9733 | 13143 | 16403 | 2.0 | 1.5 |
| Burundi | 9.0 | 14.5 | 21.9 | 600 | 1378 | 2731 | 5.5 | 4.6 | 6095 | 8114 | 9767 | 1.9 | 1.2 |
| Cameroon | 48.9 | 58.9 | 66.4 | 7379 | 12657 | 19209 | 3.6 | 2.8 | 7706 | 8846 | 9708 | 0.9 | 0.6 |
| Cape Verde | 62.2 | 73.5 | 78.4 | 266 | 425 | 563 | 3.1 | 1.9 | 162 | 153 | 155 | –0.4 | 0.1 |
| Central African Republic | 41.2 | 49.7 | 58.6 | 1489 | 2368 | 3604 | 3.1 | 2.8 | 2126 | 2396 | 2548 | 0.8 | 0.4 |
| Chad | 23.8 | 30.9 | 40.8 | 1820 | 3459 | 6202 | 4.3 | 3.9 | 5831 | 7727 | 9005 | 1.9 | 1.0 |
| Comoros | 33.2 | 42.6 | 52.2 | 231 | 425 | 656 | 4.1 | 2.9 | 464 | 573 | 601 | 1.4 | 0.3 |
| Congo | 62.5 | 70.1 | 75.7 | 1841 | 3095 | 4803 | 3.5 | 2.9 | 1103 | 1320 | 1544 | 1.2 | 1.0 |
| Côte d'Ivoire | 46.4 | 55.5 | 63.6 | 6854 | 11125 | 15754 | 3.2 | 2.3 | 7932 | 8922 | 9023 | 0.8 | 0.1 |
| Dem. Republic of the Congo | 30.3 | 39.3 | 49.1 | 15641 | 31522 | 57562 | 4.7 | 4.0 | 36014 | 48739 | 59776 | 2.0 | 1.4 |
| Djibouti | 83.3 | 86.3 | 88.8 | 531 | 747 | 975 | 2.3 | 1.8 | 106 | 118 | 124 | 0.7 | 0.3 |
| Egypt | 45.2 | 51.2 | 59.9 | 30954 | 43641 | 60115 | 2.3 | 2.1 | 37515 | 41583 | 40256 | 0.7 | –0.2 |
| Equatorial Guinea | 48.2 | 61.4 | 68.6 | 218 | 396 | 596 | 4.0 | 2.7 | 234 | 249 | 273 | 0.4 | 0.6 |
| Eritrea | 18.7 | 26.2 | 35.7 | 722 | 1439 | 2568 | 4.6 | 3.9 | 3129 | 4058 | 4617 | 1.7 | 0.9 |
| Ethiopia | 17.6 | 25.8 | 35.3 | 11042 | 23441 | 45110 | 5.0 | 4.4 | 51523 | 67506 | 82706 | 1.8 | 1.4 |
| Gabon | 81.4 | 88.9 | 90.9 | 998 | 1472 | 1943 | 2.6 | 1.9 | 228 | 183 | 195 | –1.5 | 0.4 |
| Gambia | 32.5 | 42.5 | 52.1 | 424 | 774 | 1199 | 4.0 | 2.9 | 882 | 1047 | 1103 | 1.1 | 0.4 |
| Ghana | 38.4 | 47.8 | 56.9 | 7753 | 14247 | 22866 | 4.1 | 3.2 | 12460 | 15573 | 17340 | 1.5 | 0.7 |
| Guinea | 32.8 | 42.9 | 52.5 | 2435 | 4500 | 7019 | 4.1 | 3.0 | 4995 | 5989 | 6362 | 1.2 | 0.4 |
| Guinea-Bissau | 23.7 | 31.7 | 41.6 | 288 | 514 | 879 | 3.9 | 3.6 | 925 | 1108 | 1236 | 1.2 | 0.7 |
| Kenya | 33.1 | 44.5 | 54.0 | 9957 | 16752 | 23696 | 3.5 | 2.3 | 20123 | 20859 | 20220 | 0.2 | –0.2 |
| Lesotho | 28.0 | 38.9 | 48.7 | 602 | 1126 | 1848 | 4.2 | 3.3 | 1551 | 1767 | 1945 | 0.9 | 0.6 |
| Liberia | 44.9 | 53.9 | 62.2 | 1416 | 2767 | 4603 | 4.5 | 3.4 | 1738 | 2364 | 2792 | 2.1 | 1.1 |
| Libyan Arab Jamahiriya | 87.6 | 90.3 | 92.0 | 4911 | 6841 | 8465 | 2.2 | 1.4 | 693 | 732 | 735 | 0.4 | 0.0 |
| Madagascar | 29.6 | 39.7 | 49.5 | 4721 | 9277 | 15631 | 4.5 | 3.5 | 11221 | 14081 | 15961 | 1.5 | 0.8 |
| Malawi | 24.9 | 44.1 | 54.8 | 2723 | 6961 | 12097 | 6.3 | 3.7 | 8202 | 8809 | 9987 | 0.5 | 0.8 |
| Mali | 30.0 | 40.1 | 49.8 | 3375 | 6672 | 11768 | 4.5 | 3.8 | 7859 | 9985 | 11863 | 1.6 | 1.2 |
| Mauritania | 57.7 | 68.6 | 74.4 | 1541 | 2665 | 3856 | 3.7 | 2.5 | 1128 | 1221 | 1324 | 0.5 | 0.5 |
| Mauritius[1] | 41.3 | 48.6 | 57.6 | 478 | 632 | 810 | 1.9 | 1.7 | 680 | 670 | 597 | –0.1 | –0.8 |
| Morocco | 56.1 | 65.6 | 72.0 | 15902 | 22829 | 29139 | 2.4 | 1.6 | 12448 | 11955 | 11312 | –0.3 | –0.4 |
| Mozambique | 40.2 | 51.5 | 60.2 | 7917 | 12989 | 20160 | 3.3 | 2.9 | 11764 | 12222 | 13348 | 0.3 | 0.6 |
| Namibia | 30.9 | 39.4 | 49.2 | 533 | 801 | 1228 | 2.7 | 2.9 | 1193 | 1230 | 1267 | 0.2 | 0.2 |
| Niger | 20.6 | 29.1 | 38.9 | 2207 | 4865 | 9310 | 5.3 | 4.3 | 8523 | 11825 | 14605 | 2.2 | 1.4 |
| Nigeria | 44.0 | 55.4 | 63.5 | 49050 | 84875 | 125124 | 3.7 | 2.6 | 62456 | 68432 | 72010 | 0.6 | 0.3 |
| Réunion | 70.9 | 77.2 | 81.4 | 496 | 628 | 737 | 1.6 | 1.1 | 204 | 185 | 168 | –0.7 | –0.6 |
| Rwanda | 6.2 | 8.9 | 14.2 | 476 | 939 | 1864 | 4.5 | 4.6 | 7257 | 9599 | 11296 | 1.9 | 1.1 |
| Saint Helena[2] | 70.6 | 80.4 | 84.0 | 4 | 6 | 7 | 2.7 | 1.0 | 2 | 1 | 1 | –4.6 | – |
| Sao Tome and Principe | 46.7 | 56.2 | 64.2 | 69 | 107 | 148 | 2.9 | 2.2 | 78 | 83 | 83 | 0.4 | – |
| Senegal | 47.4 | 57.4 | 65.2 | 4498 | 7845 | 11863 | 3.7 | 2.8 | 4983 | 5820 | 6330 | 1.0 | 0.6 |
| Seychelles | 63.8 | 72.3 | 77.5 | 49 | 65 | 79 | 1.9 | 1.3 | 28 | 25 | 23 | –0.8 | –0.6 |
| Sierra Leone | 36.6 | 46.7 | 55.9 | 1779 | 3118 | 4909 | 3.7 | 3.0 | 3076 | 3559 | 3872 | 1.0 | 0.6 |
| Somalia | 27.5 | 35.9 | 45.8 | 2776 | 5869 | 10846 | 5.0 | 4.1 | 7321 | 10481 | 12838 | 2.4 | 1.4 |
| South Africa | 50.4 | 56.3 | 64.3 | 20330 | 24431 | 30624 | 1.2 | 1.5 | 20047 | 18955 | 17020 | –0.4 | –0.7 |
| Sudan | 36.1 | 48.7 | 57.7 | 10652 | 19381 | 28237 | 4.0 | 2.5 | 18838 | 20430 | 20723 | 0.5 | 0.1 |
| Swaziland | 26.4 | 32.7 | 42.3 | 266 | 481 | 813 | 4.0 | 3.5 | 742 | 989 | 1110 | 1.9 | 0.8 |
| Togo | 33.3 | 42.5 | 52.1 | 1540 | 2871 | 4851 | 4.2 | 3.5 | 3089 | 3878 | 4456 | 1.5 | 0.9 |
| Tunisia | 65.5 | 73.5 | 78.4 | 6281 | 8528 | 10491 | 2.0 | 1.4 | 3305 | 3079 | 2890 | –0.5 | –0.4 |
| Uganda | 14.2 | 20.7 | 29.5 | 3083 | 7132 | 14518 | 5.6 | 4.7 | 18695 | 27343 | 34703 | 2.5 | 1.6 |
| United Republic of Tanzania | 32.9 | 46.1 | 55.4 | 11021 | 21769 | 34948 | 4.5 | 3.2 | 22496 | 25452 | 28170 | 0.8 | 0.7 |
| Western Sahara | 95.4 | 97.9 | 98.2 | 280 | 408 | 490 | 2.5 | 1.2 | 14 | 9 | 9 | –3.0 | – |
| Zambia | 39.6 | 45.2 | 54.6 | 3632 | 5794 | 9169 | 3.1 | 3.1 | 5537 | 7023 | 7635 | 1.6 | 0.6 |
| Zimbabwe | 35.3 | 45.9 | 55.2 | 4121 | 6225 | 8745 | 2.8 | 2.3 | 7548 | 7346 | 7108 | –0.2 | –0.2 |
| **ASIA** | **36.7** | **44.7** | **53.4** | **1351806** | **1943245** | **2604757** | **2.4** | **2.0** | **2330744** | **2403649** | **2271823** | **0.2** | **–0.4** |
| Afghanistan | 21.9 | 30.1 | 39.9 | 4971 | 11066 | 19552 | 5.3 | 3.8 | 17749 | 25715 | 29433 | 2.5 | 0.9 |
| Armenia | 70.0 | 75.0 | 79.6 | 2462 | 2856 | 3175 | 1.0 | 0.7 | 1057 | 954 | 814 | –0.7 | –1.1 |
| Azerbaijan | 57.3 | 64.0 | 70.7 | 4429 | 5632 | 6791 | 1.6 | 1.3 | 3305 | 3163 | 2811 | –0.3 | –0.8 |
| Bahrain | 92.2 | 95.0 | 95.8 | 569 | 724 | 858 | 1.6 | 1.1 | 48 | 38 | 38 | –1.6 | – |
| Bangladesh | 24.5 | 33.9 | 43.8 | 31665 | 54758 | 81991 | 3.7 | 2.7 | 97490 | 106782 | 105157 | 0.6 | –0.1 |
| Bhutan | 7.1 | 11.6 | 17.9 | 152 | 360 | 771 | 5.8 | 5.1 | 1972 | 2753 | 3533 | 2.2 | 1.7 |
| Brunei Darussalam | 72.2 | 78.7 | 82.6 | 237 | 322 | 395 | 2.0 | 1.4 | 91 | 87 | 83 | –0.3 | –0.3 |
| Cambodia | 15.9 | 22.8 | 31.9 | 1778 | 3284 | 5539 | 4.1 | 3.5 | 9390 | 11119 | 11840 | 1.1 | 0.4 |
| China[3] | 32.1 | 40.7 | 50.3 | 409965 | 576634 | 752051 | 2.3 | 1.8 | 867593 | 841086 | 743892 | –0.2 | –0.8 |
| China, Hong Kong SAR[4] | 100.0 | 100.0 | 100.0 | 6927 | 7689 | 7621 | 0.7 | –0.1 | .. | .. | .. | – | – |
| China, Macau SAR | 98.8 | 99.0 | 99.2 | 468 | 507 | 527 | 0.5 | 0.3 | 5 | 5 | 4 | – | –1.5 |
| Cyprus | 56.8 | 64.6 | 71.2 | 446 | 559 | 647 | 1.5 | 1.0 | 340 | 307 | 262 | –0.7 | –1.1 |
| Dem. People's Rep. Of Korea | 60.2 | 65.6 | 72.0 | 14481 | 17950 | 21739 | 1.4 | 1.3 | 9558 | 9420 | 8456 | –0.1 | –0.7 |
| East Timor | 7.5 | 9.5 | 15.0 | 66 | 103 | 185 | 3.0 | 3.9 | 818 | 979 | 1044 | 1.2 | 0.4 |
| Gaza Strip | 94.6 | 95.5 | 96.2 | 1060 | 1897 | 3095 | 3.9 | 3.3 | 61 | 90 | 121 | 2.6 | 2.0 |
| Georgia | 60.7 | 67.7 | 73.7 | 3015 | 3445 | 3839 | 0.9 | 0.7 | 1952 | 1642 | 1367 | –1.2 | –1.2 |
| India | 28.4 | 35.9 | 45.8 | 288283 | 435113 | 633382 | 2.7 | 2.5 | 725379 | 776552 | 749340 | 0.5 | –0.2 |
| Indonesia | 40.9 | 54.8 | 63.5 | 86833 | 137177 | 179915 | 3.1 | 1.8 | 125275 | 113206 | 103605 | –0.7 | –0.6 |

# TABLE A.2

## continued

| | Level of urbanization (%) | | | Urban population (thousands) | | | Annual growth (%) | | Rural population Estimates and Projections (thousands) | | | Annual growth rate (%) | |
|---|---|---|---|---|---|---|---|---|---|---|---|---|---|
| | 2000 | 2015 | 2030 | 2000 | 2015 | 2030 | 2000–2015 | 2015–2030 | 2000 | 2015 | 2030 | 2000–2015 | 2015–2030 |
| Iran (Islamic Republic of) | 61.6 | 68.8 | 74.6 | 41709 | 57139 | 74011 | 2.1 | 1.7 | 25993 | 25915 | 25175 | 0.0 | −0.2 |
| Iraq | 76.8 | 81.6 | 85.0 | 17756 | 27804 | 37326 | 3.0 | 2.0 | 5359 | 6259 | 6603 | 1.0 | 0.4 |
| Israel | 91.2 | 92.6 | 93.8 | 5668 | 7026 | 8048 | 1.4 | 0.9 | 549 | 565 | 530 | 0.2 | −0.4 |
| Japan | 78.8 | 81.5 | 84.8 | 99788 | 102763 | 100157 | 0.2 | −0.2 | 26926 | 23306 | 17988 | −1.0 | −1.7 |
| Jordan | 74.2 | 79.8 | 83.5 | 4948 | 7906 | 10869 | 3.1 | 2.1 | 1721 | 2003 | 2150 | 1.0 | 0.5 |
| Kazakhstan | 56.4 | 60.6 | 67.9 | 9157 | 10258 | 12216 | 0.8 | 1.2 | 7066 | 6661 | 5773 | −0.4 | −1.0 |
| Kuwait | 97.6 | 98.2 | 98.5 | 1924 | 2574 | 3067 | 1.9 | 1.2 | 47 | 48 | 48 | 0.1 | – |
| Kyrgyzstan | 33.3 | 35.0 | 44.0 | 1563 | 1912 | 2817 | 1.3 | 2.6 | 3136 | 3549 | 3592 | 0.8 | 0.1 |
| Lao People's Dem. Republic | 23.5 | 32.7 | 42.6 | 1275 | 2566 | 4467 | 4.7 | 3.7 | 4158 | 5278 | 6015 | 1.6 | 0.9 |
| Lebanon | 89.7 | 92.6 | 93.9 | 2945 | 3651 | 4324 | 1.4 | 1.1 | 337 | 291 | 282 | −1.0 | −0.2 |
| Malaysia | 57.4 | 66.4 | 72.7 | 12772 | 18292 | 23656 | 2.4 | 1.7 | 9472 | 9248 | 8893 | −0.2 | −0.3 |
| Maldives | 26.1 | 31.5 | 41.3 | 75 | 132 | 222 | 3.8 | 3.5 | 211 | 288 | 315 | 2.1 | 0.6 |
| Mongolia | 63.5 | 70.5 | 76.0 | 1691 | 2330 | 2949 | 2.1 | 1.6 | 972 | 977 | 933 | 0.0 | −0.3 |
| Myanmar | 27.7 | 36.7 | 46.6 | 12628 | 19655 | 27959 | 3.0 | 2.4 | 32983 | 33878 | 32046 | 0.2 | −0.4 |
| Nepal | 11.9 | 18.1 | 26.4 | 2844 | 5912 | 10636 | 4.9 | 3.9 | 21087 | 26780 | 29708 | 1.6 | 0.7 |
| Oman | 84.0 | 92.8 | 94.0 | 2135 | 3805 | 5636 | 3.9 | 2.6 | 407 | 297 | 360 | −2.1 | 1.3 |
| Pakistan | 37.0 | 46.7 | 55.9 | 57968 | 103847 | 156567 | 3.9 | 2.7 | 98515 | 118741 | 123678 | 1.2 | 0.3 |
| Philippines | 58.6 | 67.8 | 73.8 | 44530 | 65542 | 84115 | 2.6 | 1.7 | 31437 | 31190 | 29907 | −0.1 | −0.3 |
| Qatar | 92.5 | 94.2 | 95.2 | 554 | 690 | 755 | 1.5 | 0.6 | 45 | 42 | 38 | −0.5 | −0.7 |
| Republic of Korea | 81.9 | 88.2 | 90.5 | 38354 | 45025 | 47893 | 1.1 | 0.4 | 8490 | 6025 | 5005 | −2.3 | −1.2 |
| Saudi Arabia | 85.7 | 89.7 | 91.5 | 18526 | 29259 | 39331 | 3.1 | 2.0 | 3081 | 3364 | 3660 | 0.6 | 0.6 |
| Singapore | 100.0 | 100.0 | 100.0 | 3567 | 3994 | 4205 | 0.8 | 0.3 | .. | .. | .. | – | – |
| Sri Lanka | 23.6 | 32.0 | 41.9 | 4435 | 7013 | 10159 | 3.1 | 2.5 | 14392 | 14870 | 14065 | 0.2 | −0.4 |
| Syrian Arab Republic | 54.5 | 62.1 | 69.1 | 8783 | 14063 | 19409 | 3.1 | 2.2 | 7342 | 8583 | 8669 | 1.0 | 0.1 |
| Tajikistan | 27.5 | 29.5 | 39.3 | 1704 | 2289 | 3699 | 2.0 | 3.2 | 4484 | 5467 | 5710 | 1.3 | 0.3 |
| Thailand | 21.6 | 29.3 | 39.1 | 13252 | 20194 | 28954 | 2.8 | 2.4 | 48147 | 48678 | 45075 | 0.1 | −0.5 |
| Turkey | 75.3 | 84.5 | 87.3 | 50164 | 67833 | 79681 | 2.0 | 1.1 | 16427 | 12451 | 11615 | −1.9 | −0.5 |
| Turkmenistan | 44.8 | 49.9 | 58.8 | 1997 | 2782 | 3902 | 2.2 | 2.3 | 2462 | 2792 | 2739 | 0.8 | −0.1 |
| United Arab Emirates | 85.9 | 88.8 | 90.8 | 2097 | 2688 | 3065 | 1.7 | 0.9 | 344 | 339 | 311 | −0.1 | −0.6 |
| Uzbekistan | 36.9 | 38.6 | 47.4 | 8968 | 11522 | 16658 | 1.7 | 2.5 | 15350 | 18361 | 18480 | 1.2 | 0.0 |
| Viet Nam | 19.7 | 24.3 | 33.7 | 15749 | 23484 | 37991 | 2.7 | 3.2 | 64083 | 73127 | 74866 | 0.9 | 0.2 |
| Yemen | 24.7 | 31.2 | 41.0 | 4476 | 9221 | 17943 | 4.8 | 4.4 | 13636 | 20374 | 25791 | 2.7 | 1.6 |
| **EUROPE** | **74.8** | **78.6** | **82.6** | **544848** | **565599** | **570612** | **0.3** | **0.1** | **184039** | **153709** | **120364** | **−1.2** | **−1.6** |
| Albania | 41.6 | 50.8 | 59.5 | 1294 | 1779 | 2356 | 2.1 | 1.9 | 1820 | 1722 | 1601 | −0.4 | −0.5 |
| Andorra | 93.0 | 93.0 | 94.2 | 73 | 116 | 156 | 3.1 | 2.0 | 5 | 9 | 10 | 3.9 | 0.7 |
| Austria | 64.7 | 68.5 | 74.4 | 5308 | 5706 | 5985 | 0.5 | 0.3 | 2902 | 2622 | 2061 | −0.7 | −1.6 |
| Belarus | 71.2 | 77.2 | 81.5 | 7283 | 7600 | 7582 | 0.3 | 0.0 | 2953 | 2248 | 1725 | −1.8 | −1.8 |
| Belgium | 97.3 | 98.0 | 98.3 | 9892 | 9882 | 9616 | 0.0 | −0.2 | 270 | 203 | 164 | −1.9 | −1.4 |
| Bosnia and Herzegovina | 43.0 | 50.8 | 59.5 | 1706 | 2223 | 2530 | 1.8 | 0.9 | 2266 | 2154 | 1720 | −0.3 | −1.5 |
| Bulgaria | 69.6 | 74.5 | 79.3 | 5722 | 5610 | 5363 | −0.1 | −0.3 | 2503 | 1916 | 1403 | −1.8 | −2.1 |
| Channel Islands | 29.9 | 36.9 | 46.8 | 46 | 61 | 82 | 1.9 | 2.0 | 107 | 105 | 93 | −0.1 | −0.8 |
| Croatia | 57.7 | 64.4 | 71.0 | 2582 | 2801 | 2912 | 0.5 | 0.3 | 1891 | 1548 | 1188 | −1.3 | −1.8 |
| Czech Republic | 74.7 | 77.4 | 81.6 | 7653 | 7683 | 7527 | 0.0 | −0.1 | 2591 | 2246 | 1702 | −1.0 | −1.9 |
| Denmark | 85.3 | 86.8 | 89.1 | 4516 | 4610 | 4611 | 0.1 | – | 777 | 699 | 566 | −0.7 | −1.4 |
| Estonia | 68.6 | 69.4 | 74.5 | 957 | 845 | 814 | −0.8 | −0.3 | 439 | 373 | 278 | −1.1 | −2.0 |
| Faeroe Islands | 38.2 | 47.0 | 56.2 | 16 | 18 | 20 | 0.8 | 0.7 | 26 | 20 | 16 | −1.8 | −1.5 |
| Finland | 67.3 | 74.2 | 79.0 | 3482 | 3897 | 4113 | 0.8 | 0.4 | 1694 | 1358 | 1096 | −1.5 | −1.4 |
| France | 75.6 | 79.4 | 83.2 | 44644 | 48544 | 51284 | 0.6 | 0.4 | 14436 | 12564 | 10348 | −0.9 | −1.3 |
| Germany | 87.5 | 89.9 | 91.7 | 71977 | 73340 | 72646 | 0.1 | −0.1 | 10244 | 8234 | 6606 | −1.5 | −1.5 |
| Gibraltar | 100.0 | 100.0 | 100.0 | 25 | 23 | 21 | −0.6 | −0.6 | .. | .. | .. | – | – |
| Greece | 60.1 | 65.1 | 71.6 | 6397 | 6755 | 6852 | 0.4 | 0.1 | 4248 | 3623 | 2719 | −1.1 | −1.9 |
| Holy See[5] | 100.0 | 100.0 | 100.0 | 1 | 1 | 1 | .. | −0.1 | .. | .. | .. | .. | .. |
| Hungary | 64.0 | 68.5 | 74.1 | 6422 | 6441 | 6396 | 0.0 | −0.1 | 3614 | 2968 | 2231 | −1.3 | −1.9 |
| Iceland | 92.5 | 94.4 | 95.4 | 260 | 296 | 319 | 0.9 | 0.5 | 21 | 18 | 15 | −1.0 | −1.2 |
| Ireland | 59.0 | 64.0 | 70.5 | 2201 | 2668 | 3159 | 1.3 | 1.1 | 1529 | 1501 | 1325 | −0.1 | −0.8 |
| Isle of Man | 76.6 | 80.7 | 84.2 | 61 | 75 | 87 | 1.4 | 1.0 | 19 | 18 | 16 | −0.4 | −0.8 |
| Italy | 67.0 | 70.7 | 76.2 | 38387 | 38500 | 37730 | 0.0 | −0.1 | 18911 | 15948 | 11804 | −1.1 | −2.0 |
| Latvia | 69.0 | 71.4 | 76.4 | 1626 | 1474 | 1432 | −0.7 | −0.2 | 731 | 589 | 442 | −1.4 | −1.9 |
| Liechtenstein | 22.6 | 31.0 | 40.9 | 7 | 12 | 17 | 3.6 | 2.3 | 25 | 26 | 25 | 0.3 | −0.3 |
| Lithuania | 68.4 | 71.4 | 76.5 | 2511 | 2515 | 2544 | 0.0 | 0.1 | 1159 | 1006 | 782 | −0.9 | −1.7 |
| Luxembourg | 91.5 | 94.9 | 95.9 | 394 | 439 | 442 | 0.7 | 0.1 | 37 | 23 | 19 | −3.2 | −1.3 |
| Malta | 90.5 | 92.6 | 93.9 | 352 | 390 | 404 | 0.7 | 0.2 | 37 | 31 | 26 | −1.2 | −1.2 |
| Monaco | 100.0 | 100.0 | 100.0 | 34 | 38 | 41 | 0.7 | 0.5 | .. | .. | .. | – | – |
| The Netherlands | 89.4 | 90.8 | 92.4 | 14108 | 14476 | 14433 | 0.2 | – | 1678 | 1461 | 1184 | −0.9 | −1.4 |
| Norway | 75.5 | 80.1 | 83.7 | 3369 | 3776 | 4051 | 0.8 | 0.5 | 1096 | 939 | 787 | −1.0 | −1.2 |
| Poland | 65.6 | 71.4 | 76.8 | 25415 | 28109 | 29690 | 0.7 | 0.4 | 13351 | 11240 | 8990 | −1.2 | −1.5 |
| Portugal | 64.4 | 77.5 | 81.6 | 6362 | 7486 | 7481 | 1.1 | – | 3512 | 2175 | 1682 | −3.2 | −1.7 |
| Republic of Moldova | 46.1 | 50.3 | 59.1 | 2022 | 2252 | 2697 | 0.7 | 1.2 | 2359 | 2222 | 1864 | −0.4 | −1.2 |
| Romania | 56.2 | 62.0 | 69.1 | 12539 | 13071 | 13357 | 0.3 | 0.1 | 9787 | 7996 | 5978 | −1.4 | −1.9 |
| Russian Federation | 77.7 | 82.0 | 85.2 | 114141 | 117155 | 115245 | 0.2 | −0.1 | 32793 | 25791 | 19962 | −1.6 | −1.7 |
| San Marino | 89.4 | 89.9 | 91.6 | 24 | 28 | 30 | 1.0 | 0.5 | 3 | 3 | 3 | – | – |
| Slovakia | 57.4 | 62.0 | 69.1 | 3094 | 3392 | 3679 | 0.6 | 0.5 | 2294 | 2075 | 1646 | −0.7 | −1.5 |
| Slovenia | 50.4 | 55.2 | 63.3 | 1000 | 1058 | 1115 | 0.4 | 0.4 | 986 | 858 | 645 | −0.9 | −1.9 |
| Spain | 77.6 | 81.3 | 84.7 | 30761 | 31271 | 30164 | 0.1 | −0.2 | 8868 | 7195 | 5447 | −1.4 | −1.9 |
| Sweden | 83.3 | 85.2 | 87.9 | 7424 | 7742 | 7948 | 0.3 | 0.2 | 1486 | 1345 | 1099 | −0.7 | −1.4 |
| Switzerland | 67.7 | 70.9 | 76.3 | 5003 | 5408 | 5729 | 0.5 | 0.4 | 2383 | 2217 | 1775 | −0.5 | −1.5 |
| TFYR Macedonia6 | 62.0 | 68.5 | 74.4 | 1255 | 1500 | 1701 | 1.2 | 0.8 | 769 | 688 | 585 | −0.7 | −1.1 |
| Ukraine | 68.0 | 71.5 | 76.6 | 34316 | 34222 | 34092 | 0.0 | 0.0 | 16140 | 13659 | 10441 | −1.1 | −1.8 |
| United Kingdom | 89.5 | 90.8 | 92.4 | 52639 | 54071 | 55071 | 0.2 | 0.1 | 6191 | 5496 | 4548 | −0.8 | −1.3 |
| Yugoslavia | 52.2 | 57.7 | 65.4 | 5551 | 6240 | 7089 | 0.8 | 0.9 | 5089 | 4579 | 3745 | −0.7 | −1.3 |

# TABLE A.2

## continued

| | | | | | | | | | | | | | |
|---|---|---|---|---|---|---|---|---|---|---|---|---|---|
| **LATIN AMERICA** | **75.3** | **79.9** | **83.2** | **390868** | **504184** | **604002** | **1.7** | **1.2** | **128275** | **126931** | **121534** | **-0.1** | **-0.3** |
| Anguilla | 12.0 | 18.1 | 26.3 | 1 | 2 | 3 | 4.6 | 2.7 | 7 | 8 | 8 | 0.9 | – |
| Antigua and Barbuda | 36.8 | 43.3 | 52.8 | 25 | 31 | 40 | 1.4 | 1.7 | 43 | 41 | 36 | -0.3 | -0.9 |
| Argentina | 89.9 | 92.6 | 93.9 | 33299 | 40281 | 45898 | 1.3 | 0.9 | 3733 | 3217 | 2998 | -1.0 | -0.5 |
| Aruba | ... | ... | ... | ... | ... | ... | ... | ... | ... | ... | ... | – | – |
| Bahamas | 88.5 | 91.5 | 92.9 | 271 | 343 | 402 | 1.6 | 1.1 | 35 | 32 | 31 | -0.6 | -0.2 |
| Barbados | 50.0 | 58.4 | 66.1 | 135 | 168 | 197 | 1.5 | 1.1 | 135 | 120 | 101 | -0.8 | -1.2 |
| Belize | 54.2 | 64.0 | 70.9 | 131 | 204 | 281 | 3.0 | 2.1 | 110 | 114 | 115 | 0.2 | 0.1 |
| Bolivia | 62.5 | 70.1 | 75.7 | 5203 | 7861 | 10591 | 2.8 | 2.0 | 3126 | 3358 | 3409 | 0.5 | 0.1 |
| Brazil | 81.3 | 86.5 | 88.9 | 138269 | 173564 | 200135 | 1.5 | 1.0 | 31846 | 27133 | 25026 | -1.1 | -0.5 |
| British Virgin Islands | 61.1 | 71.4 | 76.7 | 13 | 22 | 30 | 3.5 | 2.1 | 8 | 9 | 9 | 0.8 | – |
| Cayman Islands | 100.0 | 100.0 | 100.0 | 38 | 61 | 86 | 3.2 | 2.3 | .. | .. | .. | – | – |
| Chile | 85.7 | 88.7 | 90.7 | 13031 | 15887 | 18363 | 1.3 | 1.0 | 2181 | 2025 | 1877 | -0.5 | -0.5 |
| Colombia | 73.9 | 79.1 | 83.0 | 31274 | 42093 | 52021 | 2.0 | 1.4 | 11048 | 11090 | 10674 | 0.0 | -0.3 |
| Costa Rica | 47.8 | 53.4 | 61.4 | 1925 | 2794 | 3833 | 2.5 | 2.1 | 2099 | 2438 | 2405 | 1.0 | -0.1 |
| Cuba | 75.3 | 78.5 | 82.3 | 8436 | 9137 | 9702 | 0.5 | 0.4 | 2765 | 2509 | 2089 | -0.7 | -1.2 |
| Dominica | 71.0 | 76.0 | 80.5 | 50 | 54 | 60 | 0.5 | 0.7 | 20 | 17 | 15 | -1.1 | -0.8 |
| Dominican Republic | 65.0 | 72.6 | 77.7 | 5526 | 7447 | 8957 | 2.0 | 1.2 | 2969 | 2804 | 2565 | -0.4 | -0.6 |
| Ecuador | 65.3 | 75.8 | 80.6 | 8262 | 12074 | 15032 | 2.5 | 1.5 | 4384 | 3862 | 3609 | -0.9 | -0.5 |
| El Salvador | 46.6 | 53.6 | 62.0 | 2927 | 4278 | 5922 | 2.5 | 2.2 | 3349 | 3700 | 3632 | 0.7 | -0.1 |
| Falkland Islands (Malvinas) | 89.7 | 95.2 | 96.0 | 2 | 2 | 2 | – | – | .. | .. | .. | – | – |
| French Guiana | 78.1 | 82.3 | 85.5 | 142 | 257 | 398 | 4.0 | 2.9 | 40 | 55 | 68 | 2.1 | 1.4 |
| Grenada | 37.9 | 47.2 | 56.3 | 36 | 47 | 60 | 1.8 | 1.6 | 58 | 53 | 47 | -0.6 | -0.8 |
| Guadeloupe | 99.7 | 99.9 | 99.9 | 454 | 533 | 582 | 1.1 | 0.6 | 1 | 1 | 1 | – | – |
| Guatemala | 39.7 | 46.2 | 55.4 | 4515 | 7564 | 11884 | 3.4 | 3.0 | 6870 | 8821 | 9557 | 1.7 | 0.5 |
| Guyana | 38.2 | 48.0 | 57.1 | 329 | 461 | 617 | 2.3 | 1.9 | 532 | 500 | 464 | -0.4 | -0.5 |
| Haiti | 35.7 | 45.6 | 54.9 | 2935 | 4758 | 6994 | 3.2 | 2.6 | 5287 | 5682 | 5736 | 0.5 | 0.1 |
| Honduras | 52.7 | 64.3 | 71.0 | 3420 | 5817 | 8083 | 3.5 | 2.2 | 3065 | 3228 | 3309 | 0.4 | 0.2 |
| Jamaica | 56.1 | 63.5 | 70.3 | 1449 | 1870 | 2382 | 1.7 | 1.6 | 1134 | 1075 | 1007 | -0.4 | -0.4 |
| Martinique | 94.9 | 96.6 | 97.1 | 375 | 417 | 443 | 0.7 | 0.4 | 20 | 15 | 13 | -1.9 | -1.0 |
| Mexico | 74.4 | 77.9 | 81.9 | 73553 | 92887 | 110488 | 1.6 | 1.2 | 25328 | 26292 | 24424 | 0.3 | -0.5 |
| Montserrat | 18.4 | 26.7 | 36.3 | 2 | 3 | 4 | 2.7 | 1.9 | 9 | 8 | 7 | -0.8 | -0.9 |
| Netherlands Antilles | 70.4 | 75.6 | 80.1 | 153 | 185 | 210 | 1.3 | 0.9 | 64 | 60 | 52 | -0.4 | -1.0 |
| Nicaragua | 56.1 | 62.6 | 69.5 | 2848 | 4552 | 6504 | 3.1 | 2.4 | 2226 | 2720 | 2849 | 1.3 | 0.3 |
| Panama | 56.3 | 61.7 | 68.6 | 1606 | 2130 | 2687 | 1.9 | 1.6 | 1249 | 1321 | 1231 | 0.4 | -0.5 |
| Paraguay | 56.0 | 65.0 | 71.5 | 3077 | 5050 | 7223 | 3.3 | 2.4 | 2420 | 2723 | 2881 | 0.8 | 0.4 |
| Peru | 72.8 | 77.9 | 81.9 | 18674 | 24821 | 30485 | 1.9 | 1.4 | 6988 | 7055 | 6717 | 0.1 | -0.3 |
| Puerto Rico | 75.2 | 79.9 | 83.6 | 2910 | 3421 | 3813 | 1.1 | 0.7 | 959 | 858 | 747 | -0.7 | -0.9 |
| Saint Kitts and Nevis | 34.1 | 39.3 | 49.1 | 13 | 14 | 17 | 0.5 | 1.3 | 25 | 22 | 18 | -0.9 | -1.3 |
| Saint Lucia | 37.8 | 43.6 | 53.1 | 58 | 81 | 116 | 2.2 | 2.4 | 96 | 105 | 102 | 0.6 | -0.2 |
| Saint Vincent and the Grenadines | 54.8 | 68.0 | 73.9 | 62 | 85 | 99 | 2.1 | 1.0 | 52 | 40 | 35 | -1.8 | -0.9 |
| Suriname | 74.2 | 81.4 | 84.8 | 310 | 389 | 461 | 1.5 | 1.1 | 108 | 89 | 82 | -1.3 | -0.6 |
| Trinidad and Tobago | 74.1 | 79.3 | 83.1 | 959 | 1126 | 1262 | 1.1 | 0.8 | 336 | 294 | 257 | -0.9 | -0.9 |
| Turks and Caicos Islands | 45.2 | 53.0 | 61.4 | 8 | 14 | 23 | 3.7 | 3.3 | 9 | 12 | 14 | 1.9 | 1.0 |
| United States Virgin Islands | 46.4 | 53.9 | 62.2 | 43 | 46 | 52 | 0.5 | 0.8 | 50 | 39 | 31 | -1.7 | -1.5 |
| Uruguay | 91.3 | 93.6 | 94.8 | 3045 | 3445 | 3805 | 0.8 | 0.7 | 292 | 236 | 211 | -1.4 | -0.8 |
| Venezuela | 86.9 | 90.0 | 91.8 | 21010 | 27782 | 33547 | 1.9 | 1.3 | 3160 | 3096 | 3001 | -0.1 | -0.2 |
| **NORTHERN AMERICA** | **77.2** | **80.9** | **84.4** | **239049** | **277563** | **313663** | **1.0** | **0.8** | **70582** | **65602** | **58112** | **-0.5** | **-0.8** |
| Bermuda | 100.0 | 100.0 | 100.0 | 65 | 72 | 77 | 0.7 | 0.5 | .. | .. | .. | – | – |
| Canada | 77.1 | 79.9 | 83.6 | 24017 | 28197 | 32597 | 1.1 | 1.0 | 7129 | 7104 | 6414 | 0.0 | -0.7 |
| Greenland | 82.0 | 85.2 | 87.9 | 46 | 49 | 53 | 0.4 | 0.5 | 10 | 9 | 7 | -0.7 | -1.7 |
| Saint Pierre and Miquelon | 92.0 | 93.4 | 94.5 | 6 | 6 | 7 | – | 1.0 | 1 | .. | .. | – | – |
| United States | 77.2 | 81.0 | 84.5 | 214915 | 249239 | 280929 | 1.0 | 0.8 | 63442 | 58489 | 51690 | -0.5 | -0.8 |
| **OCEANIA** | **70.2** | **71.2** | **74.4** | **21338** | **25688** | **30650** | **1.2** | **1.2** | **9055** | **10401** | **10538** | **0.9** | **0.1** |
| American Samoa | 52.7 | 60.6 | 67.9 | 36 | 67 | 108 | 4.1 | 3.2 | 32 | 43 | 51 | 2.0 | 1.1 |
| Australia[7] | 84.7 | 86.0 | 88.5 | 15994 | 18462 | 21035 | 1.0 | 0.9 | 2892 | 3014 | 2742 | 0.3 | -0.6 |
| Cook Islands | 59.4 | 63.3 | 69.8 | 12 | 14 | 17 | 1.0 | 1.3 | 8 | 8 | 7 | – | -0.9 |
| Fiji | 49.4 | 59.9 | 67.5 | 404 | 596 | 780 | 2.6 | 1.8 | 413 | 398 | 375 | -0.3 | -0.4 |
| French Polynesia | 52.7 | 54.0 | 61.5 | 124 | 157 | 209 | 1.6 | 1.9 | 111 | 134 | 131 | 1.3 | -0.2 |
| Guam | 39.2 | 46.7 | 55.9 | 66 | 96 | 133 | 2.5 | 2.2 | 102 | 109 | 105 | 0.4 | -0.3 |
| Kiribati | 39.2 | 47.5 | 56.5 | 33 | 49 | 72 | 2.6 | 2.6 | 51 | 54 | 55 | 0.4 | 0.1 |
| Marshall Islands | 71.9 | 77.8 | 81.9 | 46 | 77 | 116 | 3.4 | 2.7 | 18 | 22 | 26 | 1.3 | 1.1 |
| Micronesia (Fed. States of) | 28.3 | 35.0 | 45.0 | 34 | 56 | 92 | 3.3 | 3.3 | 85 | 103 | 113 | 1.3 | 0.6 |
| Nauru | 100.0 | 100.0 | 100.0 | 12 | 15 | 19 | 1.5 | 1.6 | .. | .. | .. | – | – |
| New Caledonia | 76.9 | 87.6 | 90.3 | 165 | 227 | 269 | 2.1 | 1.1 | 49 | 32 | 29 | -2.8 | -0.7 |
| New Zealand | 85.8 | 87.7 | 89.8 | 3314 | 3837 | 4340 | 1.0 | 0.8 | 548 | 539 | 493 | -0.1 | -0.6 |
| Niue | 32.7 | 39.1 | 48.6 | 1 | 1 | 1 | – | – | 1 | 1 | 1 | – | – |
| Northern Mariana Islands | 52.7 | 56.2 | 63.7 | 41 | 93 | 183 | 5.5 | 4.5 | 37 | 72 | 104 | 4.4 | 2.5 |
| Palau | 72.4 | 76.8 | 81.1 | 14 | 21 | 29 | 2.7 | 2.2 | 5 | 6 | 7 | 1.2 | 1.0 |
| Papua New Guinea | 17.4 | 23.7 | 33.0 | 837 | 1538 | 2601 | 4.1 | 3.5 | 3970 | 4944 | 5280 | 1.5 | 0.4 |
| Pitcairn | .. | .. | .. | .. | .. | .. | .. | .. | .. | .. | .. | .. | .. |
| Samoa | 21.5 | 26.7 | 36.3 | 39 | 63 | 105 | 3.2 | 3.4 | 141 | 173 | 184 | 1.4 | 0.4 |
| Solomon Islands | 19.7 | 28.6 | 38.3 | 87 | 190 | 339 | 5.2 | 3.9 | 356 | 475 | 545 | 1.9 | 0.9 |
| Tokelau | .. | .. | .. | .. | .. | .. | .. | .. | 2 | 2 | 2 | – | – |
| Tonga | 38.0 | 47.1 | 56.3 | 37 | 48 | 60 | 1.7 | 1.5 | 61 | 54 | 46 | -0.8 | -1.1 |
| Tuvalu | 52.2 | 64.1 | 70.8 | 6 | 11 | 16 | 4.0 | 2.5 | 6 | 6 | 7 | – | 1.0 |
| Vanuatu | 20.0 | 27.0 | 36.7 | 38 | 72 | 126 | 4.3 | 3.7 | 152 | 194 | 217 | 1.6 | 0.8 |
| Wallis and Futuna Islands | .. | .. | .. | .. | .. | .. | | | 15 | 16 | 18 | 0.4 | 0.8 |

**Source:** United Nations, World Urbanization Prospects: The 1999 Revision.
For footnotes, refer to technical notes.

# TABLE A.3

## Households: Number and Growth Rate

| | Households: estimates and projections (thousands) | | | | Annual rate of changes (%) | | | 5-year increments (thousands) | | | | | |
|---|---|---|---|---|---|---|---|---|---|---|---|---|---|
| | 1985 | 2000 | 2015 | 2030 | 1985–2000 | 2000–2015 | 2015–2030 | 2000–2015 | 2005–2010 | 2010–2015 | 2015–2020 | 2020–2025 | 2025–2030 |
| **WORLD** | 1119111 | 1575277 | 2124072 | 2656033 | 2.3 | 2.2 | 2.1 | 175650 | 190376 | 182769 | 180552 | 177638 | 173771 |
| More Developed Regions | 381948 | 466938 | 541046 | 581851 | 1.3 | 1.0 | 0.5 | 27195 | 25962 | 20950 | 16868 | 13789 | 10148 |
| Less Developed Regions | 737164 | 1108339 | 1583026 | 2074182 | 2.7 | 2.4 | 1.8 | 148455 | 164414 | 161818 | 163684 | 163849 | 163623 |
| **AFRICA** | 109654 | 173413 | 268476 | 399055 | 3.1 | 3.1 | 3.1 | 28397 | 32368 | 34299 | 38977 | 43768 | 47834 |
| Algeria | 3064 | 4966 | 7167 | 9346 | 3.3 | 3.0 | 2.8 | 747 | 724 | 729 | 765 | 748 | 666 |
| Benin | 707 | 1054 | 1748 | 2747 | 2.7 | 3.1 | 3.4 | 205 | 235 | 254 | 287 | 333 | 379 |
| Botswana | 214 | 367 | 479 | 636 | 3.7 | 3.2 | 2.4 | 44 | 30 | 37 | 47 | 53 | 56 |
| Burkina Faso | 1275 | 1633 | 2180 | 3005 | 1.7 | 1.7 | 1.8 | 150 | 177 | 219 | 252 | 277 | 297 |
| Burundi | 967 | 1530 | 2476 | 3984 | 3.1 | 2.7 | 3.0 | 177 | 380 | 389 | 435 | 498 | 576 |
| Cameroon | 1877 | 3360 | 5795 | 9736 | 4.0 | 4.0 | 3.9 | 715 | 801 | 919 | 1095 | 1315 | 1531 |
| Cape Verde | 62 | 91 | 145 | 214 | 2.6 | 2.9 | 3.2 | 16 | 18 | 20 | 22 | 23 | 23 |
| Central African Republic | 495 | 751 | 1127 | 1738 | 2.8 | 2.8 | 2.8 | 108 | 125 | 143 | 172 | 205 | 235 |
| Chad | 885 | 1113 | 1560 | 2202 | 1.5 | 1.8 | 2.2 | 128 | 147 | 173 | 193 | 214 | 236 |
| Comoros | 59 | 98 | 160 | 238 | 3.4 | 3.6 | 3.5 | 20 | 20 | 22 | 24 | 27 | 28 |
| Congo | 376 | 703 | 1284 | 2386 | 4.3 | 4.1 | 4.0 | 149 | 188 | 244 | 306 | 366 | 431 |
| Côte d'Ivoire | 1618 | 2857 | 4332 | 6562 | 3.9 | 3.5 | 3.3 | 395 | 537 | 544 | 641 | 752 | 837 |
| Dem. Republic of the Congo | 5845 | 10797 | 18616 | 33750 | 4.2 | 3.9 | 3.9 | 1627 | 2682 | 3510 | 4289 | 4985 | 5860 |
| Djibouti | 57 | 134 | 191 | 282 | 5.8 | 3.9 | 2.8 | 9 | 23 | 25 | 27 | 30 | 34 |
| Egypt | 9187 | 13410 | 19828 | 25754 | 2.6 | 2.7 | 2.8 | 2063 | 2264 | 2091 | 2108 | 2020 | 1799 |
| Equatorial Guinea | 50 | 103 | 176 | 293 | 5.0 | 3.3 | 3.5 | 19 | 24 | 29 | 34 | 39 | 44 |
| Eritrea | 501 | 726 | 1268 | 2062 | 2.5 | 2.9 | 3.5 | 179 | 165 | 197 | 232 | 266 | 296 |
| Ethiopia | 7605 | 12303 | 19481 | 32603 | 3.3 | 3.2 | 3.1 | 1865 | 2339 | 2975 | 3664 | 4364 | 5093 |
| Gabon | 194 | 310 | 460 | 700 | 3.2 | 3.0 | 2.8 | 43 | 50 | 58 | 71 | 80 | 89 |
| Gambia | 87 | 164 | 268 | 396 | 4.3 | 4.6 | 3.9 | 35 | 33 | 36 | 40 | 43 | 45 |
| Ghana | 2415 | 4163 | 7138 | 11423 | 3.7 | 3.7 | 3.7 | 841 | 1000 | 1134 | 1258 | 1427 | 1599 |
| Guinea | 678 | 1115 | 1629 | 2445 | 3.4 | 3.1 | 3.3 | 85 | 213 | 215 | 242 | 275 | 300 |
| Guinea-Bissau | 106 | 139 | 196 | 279 | 1.8 | 2.1 | 2.3 | 18 | 19 | 21 | 23 | 27 | 33 |
| Kenya | 3679 | 7238 | 11769 | 17160 | 4.6 | 4.4 | 4.0 | 1485 | 1575 | 1470 | 1592 | 1794 | 2005 |
| Lesotho | 281 | 412 | 573 | 828 | 2.6 | 2.5 | 2.4 | 52 | 50 | 59 | 74 | 86 | 94 |
| Liberia | 352 | 307 | 810 | 1437 | -0.9 | 2.8 | 3.1 | 295 | 112 | 96 | 144 | 228 | 255 |
| Libyan Arab Jamahiriya | 538 | 789 | 1028 | 1300 | 2.6 | 2.3 | 2.2 | 99 | 87 | 53 | 59 | 87 | 126 |
| Madagascar | 2157 | 3280 | 5082 | 7600 | 2.8 | 2.7 | 2.6 | 454 | 553 | 795 | 814 | 832 | 872 |
| Malawi | 1794 | 1743 | 1611 | 2395 | -0.2 | -0.5 | -1.3 | -62 | -48 | -23 | 163 | 290 | 332 |
| Mali | 1268 | 1827 | 2836 | 4536 | 2.5 | 2.4 | 2.7 | 271 | 326 | 413 | 492 | 569 | 639 |
| Mauritania | 278 | 373 | 533 | 740 | 2.0 | 2.3 | 2.4 | 49 | 52 | 59 | 65 | 71 | 72 |
| Mauritius | 220 | 279 | 332 | 365 | 1.6 | 1.3 | 1.3 | 18 | 16 | 19 | 12 | 12 | 10 |
| Morocco | 3687 | 5390 | 7324 | 9344 | 2.6 | 2.5 | 2.4 | 663 | 667 | 603 | 710 | 684 | 626 |
| Mozambique | 2894 | 3228 | 3550 | 4651 | 0.7 | 0.9 | 1.3 | 176 | 69 | 77 | 266 | 384 | 451 |
| Namibia | 219 | 321 | 393 | 502 | 2.6 | 2.5 | 2.0 | 38 | 19 | 15 | 28 | 37 | 44 |
| Niger | 962 | 1307 | 1863 | 2595 | 2.1 | 2.1 | 2.2 | 153 | 180 | 223 | 233 | 243 | 255 |
| Nigeria | 12313 | 28009 | 49453 | 75707 | 5.6 | 4.9 | 4.4 | 6903 | 7494 | 7047 | 7619 | 8764 | 9870 |
| Réunion | 133 | 198 | 267 | 330 | 2.7 | 2.3 | 2.1 | 22 | 23 | 25 | 22 | 21 | 20 |
| Rwanda | 1328 | 1468 | 3007 | 4632 | 0.7 | 2.4 | 2.2 | 797 | 352 | 390 | 467 | 548 | 610 |
| Senegal | 605 | 928 | 1469 | 2270 | 2.9 | 2.9 | 3.0 | 148 | 179 | 213 | 240 | 268 | 294 |
| Somalia | 1002 | 1271 | 2204 | 3894 | 1.6 | 2.4 | 2.8 | 270 | 315 | 348 | 460 | 565 | 666 |
| South Africa[1] | 0 | 12228 | 20038 | 23325 | 0.3 | 8.7 | 5.6 | 3713 | 2969 | 1129 | 947 | 1134 | 1206 |
| Sudan | 3259 | 3315 | 4608 | 6423 | 0.1 | 0.5 | 1.4 | 258 | 519 | 516 | 559 | 606 | 650 |
| Swaziland | 63 | 212 | 419 | 640 | 8.5 | 6.9 | 5.7 | 65 | 75 | 66 | 69 | 74 | 77 |
| Togo | 583 | 957 | 1584 | 2654 | 3.4 | 3.3 | 3.3 | 166 | 203 | 258 | 303 | 356 | 411 |
| Tunisia | 1323 | 2023 | 2702 | 3229 | 2.9 | 2.6 | 2.4 | 246 | 235 | 198 | 177 | 177 | 173 |
| Uganda | 3102 | 3987 | 6273 | 10805 | 1.7 | 1.9 | 2.5 | 482 | 783 | 1019 | 1284 | 1537 | 1711 |
| United Republic of Tanzania | 4046 | 5977 | 7968 | 10785 | 2.6 | 2.4 | 2.1 | 554 | 669 | 768 | 858 | 943 | 1016 |
| Zambia | 1227 | 1665 | 2323 | 3404 | 2.1 | 2.2 | 2.2 | 192 | 196 | 270 | 324 | 366 | 390 |
| Zimbabwe | 1637 | 2940 | 4204 | 5923 | 4.0 | 3.4 | 2.6 | 418 | 403 | 443 | 520 | 596 | 603 |
| **ASIA** | 579696 | 854709 | 1188798 | 1501652 | 2.6 | 2.5 | 2.4 | 105831 | 116663 | 111595 | 108713 | 104157 | 99984 |
| Armenia | 671 | 680 | 703 | 693 | 0.1 | -0.1 | 0.1 | -2 | 18 | 8 | -8 | -4 | 1 |
| Azerbaijan | 1332 | 1561 | 1893 | 2067 | 1.1 | 0.9 | 1.2 | 83 | 128 | 121 | 61 | 54 | 59 |
| Bahrain | 68 | 100 | 128 | 140 | 2.7 | 2.0 | 1.7 | 9 | 9 | 10 | 7 | 3 | 2 |
| Bangladesh | 16541 | 24136 | 34608 | 43883 | 2.6 | 2.9 | 2.9 | 4062 | 3702 | 2708 | 3046 | 3224 | 3005 |
| Bhutan | 266 | 370 | 587 | 913 | 2.2 | 2.4 | 2.6 | 59 | 72 | 86 | 98 | 108 | 119 |
| Brunei Darussalam | 39 | 54 | 68 | 71 | 2.2 | 2.0 | 1.6 | 5 | 5 | 4 | 2 | 1 | – |
| Cambodia | 1442 | 2210 | 3479 | 4946 | 2.9 | 3.0 | 2.9 | 378 | 437 | 454 | 490 | 479 | 498 |
| China | 236260 | 360982 | 516781 | 667632 | 2.9 | 2.6 | 2.5 | 45770 | 56867 | 53162 | 51856 | 49594 | 49401 |
| China, Hong Kong SAR | 1445 | 1979 | 2675 | 2923 | 2.1 | 2.4 | 2.5 | 317 | 221 | 158 | 112 | 80 | 56 |
| China, Macau SAR | 75 | 154 | 234 | 279 | 4.9 | 4.4 | 3.5 | 32 | 25 | 23 | 19 | 15 | 12 |
| Cyprus | 176 | 200 | 230 | 234 | 0.9 | 1.1 | 1.2 | 13 | 10 | 7 | 3 | 1 | – |
| Georgia | 1274 | 1343 | 1340 | 1393 | 0.4 | -0.2 | -0.3 | -48 | 22 | 23 | 18 | 17 | 17 |
| India | 132023 | 185929 | 252432 | 308339 | 2.3 | 2.2 | 2.1 | 21655 | 22440 | 22407 | 20871 | 18996 | 16040 |
| Indonesia | 34864 | 52040 | 69127 | 83481 | 2.7 | 2.5 | 2.2 | 5871 | 5732 | 5484 | 5357 | 4742 | 4256 |
| Iran (Islamic Republic of) | 8885 | 15154 | 24070 | 31219 | 3.6 | 3.6 | 3.4 | 3115 | 2892 | 2909 | 2262 | 2375 | 2512 |
| Iraq | 2009 | 2722 | 3719 | 5654 | 2.1 | 2.0 | 1.9 | 295 | 340 | 363 | 583 | 663 | 688 |
| Israel | 1129 | 1661 | 2238 | 2637 | 2.6 | 2.9 | 2.8 | 216 | 187 | 173 | 153 | 136 | 111 |
| Japan | 37359 | 48520 | 54120 | 56049 | 1.8 | 1.5 | 1.1 | 2578 | 1824 | 1198 | 949 | 692 | 288 |
| Jordan | 327 | 652 | 1075 | 1659 | 4.7 | 3.7 | 4.3 | 123 | 143 | 158 | 180 | 198 | 206 |
| Kazakhstan | 4331 | 5710 | 6901 | 8271 | 1.9 | 1.5 | 1.2 | 314 | 439 | 439 | 442 | 449 | 479 |
| Kuwait | 234 | 260 | 399 | 458 | 0.7 | 0.5 | 0.2 | 57 | 50 | 32 | 24 | 19 | 16 |
| Kyrgyzstan | 814 | 936 | 1082 | 1251 | 0.9 | 0.6 | 0.7 | 25 | 58 | 63 | 62 | 57 | 51 |
| Lao People's Dem. Republic | 667 | 983 | 1581 | 2446 | 2.6 | 2.8 | 3.0 | 155 | 205 | 238 | 257 | 286 | 322 |
| Malaysia | 3008 | 4748 | 7003 | 9146 | 3.1 | 3.0 | 2.7 | 705 | 700 | 849 | 799 | 724 | 621 |

# TABLE A.3

continued

| | | | | | | | | | | | | | |
|---|---|---|---|---|---|---|---|---|---|---|---|---|---|
| Maldives | 27 | 40 | 66 | 99 | 2.6 | 3.2 | 3.5 | 8 | 9 | 9 | 10 | 11 | 12 |
| Mongolia | 360 | 532 | 746 | 879 | 2.6 | 2.6 | 2.6 | 70 | 82 | 61 | 49 | 43 | 42 |
| Myanmar | 6880 | 9893 | 12952 | 15430 | 2.5 | 2.5 | 2.2 | 1226 | 1003 | 832 | 856 | 831 | 790 |
| Nepal | 2849 | 4266 | 6688 | 9734 | 2.7 | 2.9 | 3.0 | 701 | 829 | 892 | 953 | 1021 | 1073 |
| Oman | 223 | 359 | 568 | 878 | 3.2 | 3.2 | 3.3 | 62 | 74 | 73 | 87 | 103 | 121 |
| Pakistan | 12294 | 15609 | 24982 | 37058 | 1.6 | 2.3 | 3.1 | 2601 | 3174 | 3599 | 3861 | 4032 | 4183 |
| Philippines | 9959 | 15661 | 23932 | 33320 | 3.1 | 3.0 | 3.1 | 2487 | 2804 | 2980 | 3199 | 3181 | 3008 |
| Qatar | 47 | 106 | 121 | 123 | 5.5 | 2.7 | 1.3 | 6 | 6 | 3 | 1 | – | – |
| Republic of Korea | 9618 | 14180 | 17662 | 20375 | 2.6 | 2.2 | 1.7 | 1329 | 1062 | 1091 | 997 | 919 | 798 |
| Saudi Arabia | 1645 | 2898 | 4328 | 6331 | 3.9 | 3.1 | 2.5 | 457 | 452 | 520 | 622 | 671 | 711 |
| Singapore | 578 | 728 | 768 | 722 | 1.6 | 1.0 | 0.5 | 17 | 11 | 12 | –4 | –16 | –26 |
| Sri Lanka | 3023 | 3867 | 4757 | 5418 | 1.7 | 1.7 | 1.6 | 360 | 289 | 242 | 230 | 218 | 213 |
| Syrian Arab Republic | 1580 | 2550 | 4067 | 5637 | 3.3 | 3.4 | 3.5 | 490 | 553 | 473 | 489 | 530 | 551 |
| Tajikistan | 838 | 1104 | 1414 | 1801 | 1.9 | 1.6 | 1.5 | 85 | 114 | 111 | 132 | 128 | 128 |
| Thailand | 10305 | 15840 | 19964 | 23006 | 2.9 | 2.4 | 1.9 | 1501 | 1476 | 1147 | 1070 | 1026 | 947 |
| Turkey | 9501 | 15779 | 22310 | 28529 | 3.4 | 3.1 | 2.8 | 2406 | 2001 | 2123 | 2195 | 2071 | 1953 |
| Turkmenistan | 508 | 605 | 721 | 951 | 1.2 | 1.1 | 1.1 | 33 | 44 | 40 | 78 | 78 | 74 |
| United Arab Emirates | 449 | 829 | 1018 | 1067 | 4.2 | 2.1 | 1.8 | 75 | 74 | 40 | 24 | 15 | 10 |
| Uzbekistan | 3213 | 4224 | 5531 | 6662 | 1.8 | 1.7 | 1.8 | 392 | 494 | 421 | 388 | 377 | 365 |
| VietNam | 11588 | 17678 | 25641 | 31834 | 2.9 | 2.8 | 2.7 | 2579 | 2650 | 2734 | 2217 | 2003 | 1973 |
| Yemen | 1292 | 3152 | 6448 | 12714 | 6.1 | 5.9 | 5.7 | 831 | 1074 | 1391 | 1788 | 2080 | 2397 |
| **EUROPE** | **243397** | **289735** | **326435** | **336943** | **1.2** | **1.1** | **1.0** | **14446** | **13442** | **8812** | **5875** | **3775** | **857** |
| Albania | 532 | 652 | 728 | 829 | 1.4 | 0.6 | 0.2 | –4 | 38 | 42 | 38 | 32 | 30 |
| Austria | 2864 | 3318 | 3770 | 3897 | 1.0 | 1.0 | 1.0 | 174 | 153 | 125 | 76 | 39 | 11 |
| Belarus | 2782 | 3134 | 3328 | 3265 | 0.8 | 0.7 | 0.7 | 99 | 86 | 9 | –37 | –21 | –5 |
| Belgium | 3781 | 4259 | 4702 | 4888 | 0.8 | 0.8 | 0.7 | 159 | 152 | 133 | 90 | 59 | 36 |
| Bulgaria | 3071 | 3285 | 3359 | 3236 | 0.5 | 0.2 | 0.3 | 40 | 41 | –7 | –38 | –39 | –47 |
| Croatia | 1485 | 1624 | 1708 | 1688 | 0.6 | 0.6 | 0.5 | 48 | 32 | 5 | –4 | –9 | –8 |
| Czech Republic | 3962 | 4375 | 4697 | 4639 | 0.7 | 0.8 | 0.7 | 130 | 114 | 78 | –3 | –17 | –38 |
| Denmark | 2168 | 2470 | 2672 | 2786 | 0.9 | 0.7 | 0.6 | 57 | 65 | 81 | 65 | 40 | 9 |
| Estonia | 479 | 582 | 610 | 607 | 1.3 | 0.9 | 0.5 | 13 | 18 | –3 | –2 | –4 | 3 |
| Finland | 1923 | 2247 | 2538 | 2680 | 1.1 | 0.9 | 0.9 | 108 | 94 | 88 | 62 | 45 | 36 |
| France | 20382 | 24176 | 27351 | 29331 | 1.1 | 1.1 | 0.9 | 1170 | 1086 | 920 | 763 | 647 | 570 |
| Germany | 32361 | 35888 | 38554 | 38815 | 0.7 | 0.7 | 0.6 | 962 | 1050 | 654 | 347 | 50 | –136 |
| Greece | 3094 | 3902 | 4358 | 4371 | 1.6 | 1.5 | 1.2 | 236 | 140 | 79 | 35 | 1 | –23 |
| Hungary | 3805 | 3978 | 4074 | 3946 | 0.3 | 0.3 | 0.3 | 36 | 33 | 27 | –22 | –46 | –61 |
| Iceland | 82 | 111 | 142 | 171 | 2.0 | 1.9 | 1.7 | 10 | 10 | 11 | 10 | 10 | 9 |
| Ireland | 955 | 1225 | 1538 | 1828 | 1.7 | 1.7 | 1.9 | 120 | 104 | 89 | 93 | 97 | 100 |
| Italy | 18916 | 22542 | 23825 | 23473 | 1.2 | 0.9 | 0.6 | 605 | 401 | 277 | 66 | –111 | –307 |
| Latvia | 788 | 871 | 868 | 839 | 0.7 | 0.3 | –0.1 | –6 | 11 | –8 | –18 | –10 | –2 |
| Lithuania | 1051 | 1305 | 1481 | 1528 | 1.5 | 1.2 | 0.9 | 63 | 68 | 44 | 19 | 13 | 15 |
| Luxembourg | 135 | 165 | 200 | 218 | 1.4 | 1.5 | 1.5 | 13 | 11 | 10 | 8 | 6 | 4 |
| Malta | 105 | 132 | 161 | 179 | 1.5 | 1.6 | 1.6 | 11 | 10 | 8 | 7 | 6 | 6 |
| Netherlands | 5465 | 6814 | 7815 | 8294 | 1.5 | 1.2 | 1.0 | 341 | 335 | 324 | 245 | 158 | 76 |
| Norway | 1639 | 1987 | 2348 | 2653 | 1.3 | 1.1 | 1.1 | 106 | 123 | 132 | 119 | 103 | 82 |
| Poland | 11833 | 13052 | 14324 | 14362 | 0.7 | 0.8 | 0.8 | 625 | 429 | 219 | 21 | 8 | 9 |
| Portugal | 3044 | 3649 | 3965 | 4072 | 1.2 | 1.0 | 0.7 | 144 | 88 | 85 | 56 | 36 | 16 |
| Republic of Moldova | 1131 | 1250 | 1428 | 1521 | 0.7 | 0.7 | 0.9 | 64 | 71 | 44 | 26 | 28 | 39 |
| Romania | 6908 | 7956 | 8496 | 8288 | 1.0 | 0.7 | 0.6 | 227 | 275 | 39 | –73 | –70 | –66 |
| Russian Federation | 49951 | 65782 | 79531 | 81907 | 1.9 | 1.8 | 1.6 | 5707 | 5305 | 2738 | 2025 | 1185 | –835 |
| Slovakia | 1744 | 2032 | 2321 | 2396 | 1.0 | 1.2 | 1.1 | 117 | 99 | 73 | 28 | 28 | 19 |
| Slovenia | 603 | 723 | 776 | 756 | 1.2 | 1.2 | 0.8 | 28 | 20 | 5 | –3 | –7 | –10 |
| Spain | 10439 | 12693 | 13124 | 12713 | 1.3 | 1.0 | 0.6 | 326 | 100 | 4 | –85 | –136 | –190 |
| Sweden | 3667 | 4285 | 4994 | 5362 | 1.0 | 1.0 | 1.0 | 201 | 253 | 255 | 164 | 112 | 92 |
| Switzerland | 2602 | 3303 | 3891 | 4171 | 1.6 | 1.4 | 1.2 | 207 | 199 | 182 | 137 | 92 | 51 |
| TFYR Macedonia | 457 | 547 | 643 | 724 | 1.2 | 1.3 | 1.2 | 36 | 32 | 28 | 27 | 28 | 26 |
| Ukraine | 14097 | 15855 | 17779 | 18603 | 0.8 | 0.9 | 0.8 | 704 | 749 | 471 | 294 | 260 | 271 |
| United Kingdom | 21125 | 24881 | 28961 | 32185 | 1.1 | 1.0 | 1.0 | 1274 | 1426 | 1381 | 1210 | 1053 | 961 |
| Yugoslavia | 2814 | 3411 | 3848 | 4153 | 1.3 | 1.3 | 1.1 | 174 | 146 | 117 | 97 | 98 | 111 |
| **LATIN AMERICA** | **84140** | **127264** | **177788** | **226703** | **2.8** | **2.7** | **2.5** | **16621** | **17002** | **16902** | **16706** | **16368** | **15841** |
| Argentina | 7900 | 10557 | 13863 | 17325 | 2.0 | 2.0 | 2.0 | 1075 | 1104 | 1127 | 1148 | 1163 | 1150 |
| Bahamas | 55 | 70 | 81 | 89 | 1.7 | 1.4 | 1.1 | 4 | 4 | 4 | 3 | 3 | 1 |
| Barbados | 72 | 85 | 100 | 111 | 1.2 | 1.2 | 1.1 | 5 | 5 | 5 | 4 | 3 | 3 |
| Belize | 31 | 48 | 76 | 109 | 3.1 | 3.1 | 3.1 | 8 | 9 | 11 | 11 | 11 | 10 |
| Bolivia | 1171 | 1616 | 2313 | 3165 | 2.2 | 2.4 | 2.4 | 205 | 230 | 261 | 284 | 287 | 282 |
| Brazil | 30093 | 45228 | 61712 | 75945 | 2.8 | 2.6 | 2.4 | 5841 | 5562 | 5082 | 4866 | 4760 | 4607 |
| Chile | 2718 | 4133 | 5915 | 7861 | 2.8 | 2.6 | 2.5 | 533 | 610 | 638 | 658 | 647 | 641 |
| Colombia | 5475 | 8776 | 13061 | 17660 | 3.2 | 2.9 | 2.8 | 1324 | 1411 | 1550 | 1555 | 1538 | 1507 |
| Costa Rica | 562 | 1026 | 1667 | 2329 | 4.1 | 3.9 | 3.8 | 210 | 219 | 212 | 214 | 222 | 227 |
| Cuba | 2777 | 4053 | 5069 | 5830 | 2.6 | 2.0 | 1.6 | 311 | 374 | 332 | 292 | 245 | 223 |
| Dominican Republic | 1300 | 2090 | 2980 | 3790 | 3.2 | 2.9 | 2.6 | 281 | 306 | 303 | 289 | 270 | 251 |
| Ecuador | 1800 | 3107 | 4810 | 6573 | 3.7 | 3.5 | 3.3 | 545 | 567 | 591 | 598 | 592 | 573 |
| El Salvador | 1086 | 1677 | 2609 | 3748 | 2.9 | 3.4 | 3.3 | 290 | 304 | 338 | 363 | 389 | 387 |
| Guadeloupe | 96 | 140 | 179 | 212 | 2.5 | 2.3 | 1.9 | 13 | 13 | 13 | 12 | 11 | 10 |
| Guatemala | 1287 | 1791 | 2692 | 3853 | 2.2 | 2.5 | 2.7 | 261 | 298 | 343 | 378 | 392 | 391 |
| Guyana | 158 | 182 | 208 | 229 | 0.9 | 0.7 | 0.8 | 9 | 8 | 9 | 8 | 6 | 6 |
| Haiti | 1139 | 1583 | 2323 | 3203 | 2.2 | 2.4 | 2.7 | 228 | 272 | 240 | 261 | 289 | 330 |
| Honduras | 689 | 1187 | 1997 | 2959 | 3.7 | 3.7 | 3.6 | 236 | 271 | 304 | 318 | 323 | 322 |
| Jamaica | 449 | 506 | 552 | 587 | 0.8 | 0.4 | 0.6 | 15 | 14 | 17 | 14 | 12 | 9 |
| Martinique | 97 | 127 | 154 | 176 | 1.8 | 1.6 | 1.4 | 9 | 10 | 9 | 8 | 7 | 7 |
| Mexico | 14340 | 22970 | 31880 | 39858 | 3.2 | 2.9 | 2.5 | 2945 | 2972 | 2993 | 2887 | 2672 | 2418 |
| Netherlands Antilles | 50 | 68 | 90 | 110 | 2.0 | 2.0 | 2.1 | 7 | 7 | 8 | 7 | 7 | 6 |
| Nicaragua | 502 | 833 | 1437 | 2263 | 3.4 | 3.6 | 3.7 | 176 | 193 | 235 | 263 | 279 | 284 |
| Panama | 446 | 707 | 1011 | 1297 | 3.1 | 2.8 | 2.6 | 97 | 103 | 104 | 101 | 96 | 89 |

# TABLE A.3

## continued

| | Households: estimates and projections (thousands) | | | | Annual rate of changes (%) | | | 5-year increments (thousands) | | | | | |
|---|---|---|---|---|---|---|---|---|---|---|---|---|---|
| | 1985 | 2000 | 2015 | 2030 | 1985–2000 | 2000–2015 | 2015–2030 | 2000–2015 | 2005–2010 | 2010–2015 | 2015–2020 | 2020–2025 | 2025–2030 |
| Paraguay | 677 | 1165 | 2016 | 3128 | 3.7 | 3.8 | 3.7 | 248 | 286 | 317 | 341 | 371 | 400 |
| Peru | 3805 | 5650 | 7922 | 9979 | 2.7 | 2.5 | 2.4 | 736 | 776 | 760 | 727 | 686 | 644 |
| Puerto Rico | 882 | 1177 | 1428 | 1681 | 2.0 | 1.7 | 1.5 | 86 | 79 | 85 | 86 | 86 | 81 |
| Suriname | 83 | 104 | 129 | 154 | 1.5 | 1.3 | 1.1 | 8 | 7 | 11 | 9 | 9 | 8 |
| Trinidad and Tobago | 256 | 296 | 355 | 381 | 1.0 | 1.1 | 1.4 | 25 | 21 | 13 | 8 | 8 | 11 |
| Uruguay | 861 | 1023 | 1215 | 1441 | 1.2 | 1.2 | 1.2 | 59 | 64 | 69 | 75 | 76 | 75 |
| Venezuela | 3284 | 5288 | 7942 | 10657 | 3.2 | 3.1 | 3.0 | 831 | 904 | 918 | 917 | 910 | 888 |
| **NORTHERN AMERICA** | **94964** | **119986** | **149271** | **175169** | **1.6** | **1.5** | **1.5** | **9362** | **9844** | **10078** | **9197** | **8506** | **8195** |
| Canada | 9150 | 12690 | 16880 | 20692 | 2.2 | 2.2 | 2.0 | 1360 | 1399 | 1430 | 1292 | 1255 | 1265 |
| United States | 85813 | 107296 | 132391 | 154477 | 1.5 | 1.4 | 1.4 | 8002 | 8445 | 8648 | 7905 | 7251 | 6930 |
| **OCEANIA** | **7261** | **10170** | **13304** | **16511** | **2.3** | **2.1** | **1.9** | **993** | **1057** | **1084** | **1084** | **1063** | **1060** |
| Australia | 5166 | 7269 | 9398 | 11471 | 2.3 | 2.1 | 1.8 | 688 | 714 | 727 | 709 | 684 | 679 |
| Fiji | 124 | 156 | 207 | 251 | 1.5 | 1.6 | 2.0 | 18 | 17 | 16 | 15 | 15 | 14 |
| French Polynesia | 35 | 54 | 73 | 91 | 2.8 | 2.3 | 2.1 | 6 | 7 | 7 | 6 | 6 | 5 |
| Guam | 28 | 37 | 46 | 54 | 2.0 | 1.6 | 1.3 | 2 | 3 | 4 | 3 | 2 | 2 |
| New Caledonia | 37 | 56 | 73 | 90 | 2.7 | 2.7 | 2.4 | 6 | 5 | 6 | 6 | 6 | 5 |
| New Zealand | 1062 | 1428 | 1821 | 2218 | 2.0 | 1.9 | 1.9 | 122 | 137 | 135 | 137 | 131 | 129 |
| Papua New Guinea | 709 | 1028 | 1467 | 2025 | 2.5 | 2.5 | 2.4 | 130 | 148 | 161 | 176 | 188 | 194 |
| Samoa | 30 | 36 | 51 | 72 | 1.1 | 1.4 | 1.9 | 4 | 5 | 6 | 7 | 7 | 8 |
| Solomon Islands | 43 | 73 | 118 | 175 | 3.6 | 3.6 | 3.5 | 13 | 15 | 17 | 18 | 19 | 20 |
| Vanuatu | 26 | 34 | 49 | 64 | 1.9 | 2.0 | 2.2 | 4 | 5 | 5 | 5 | 5 | 5 |

**Source:** United Nations, Centre for Human Settlements (Habitat), Statistics Programme, Household Projections Project.
For footnotes, refer to technical notes.

# TABLE A.4

## Ownership of Housing Unit, Selected Countries

| | | | Households in occupied housing units | | | | | | Women-headed households in occupied housing units | | | | |
|---|---|---|---|---|---|---|---|---|---|---|---|---|---|
| | | | | | Tenants in housing units | | | | | | Tenants in housing units | | |
| | | | Total | Owner (%) | Publicly owned (%) | Privately owned (%) | Squatters (%) | Women-headed households as % of total | Total | Owner (%) | Publicly owned (%) | Privately owned (%) | Squatters (%) |
| **AFRICA** | | | | | | | | | | | | | |
| Benin | 1994 | Total | [1]197600 | 60.1 | 23.7 | 13.0 | 3.2 | ... | ... | ... | ... | ... | ... |
| Benin | 1994 | Urban | [1]98900 | 40.1 | 27.9 | 28.1 | 3.8 | ... | ... | ... | ... | ... | ... |
| Benin | 1994 | Rural | [1]98700 | 71.8 | 21.2 | 4.2 | 2.8 | ... | ... | ... | ... | ... | ... |
| Burkina Faso | 1991 | Total | 1399149 | 89.0 | [2]3.8 | ... | 7.1 | 5.2 | 73148 | ... | ... | ... | ... |
| Burkina Faso | 1991 | Urban | 197871 | 65.6 | [2]22.0 | ... | 12.4 | 11.1 | 21945 | ... | ... | ... | ... |
| Burkina Faso | 1991 | Rural | 1201278 | 92.9 | [2]0.8 | ... | 6.3 | 4.3 | 51203 | ... | ... | ... | ... |
| Congo | 1984 | Total | 348998 | 63.5 | [2]24.9 | ... | 11.6 | ... | ... | ... | ... | ... | ... |
| Congo | 1984 | Urban | 176203 | 47.6 | [2]40.6 | ... | 11.8 | ... | ... | ... | ... | ... | ... |
| Congo | 1984 | Rural | 172795 | 79.6 | [2]8.9 | ... | 11.5 | ... | ... | ... | ... | ... | ... |
| Egypt | 1996 | Total | 12702600 | 69.3 | [2]30.7 | ... | ... | ... | ... | ... | ... | ... | ... |
| Egypt | 1996 | Urban | 5839877 | 49.1 | [2]50.9 | ... | ... | ... | ... | ... | ... | ... | ... |
| Egypt | 1996 | Rural | 6862723 | 86.6 | [2]13.4 | ... | ... | ... | ... | ... | ... | ... | ... |
| Gambia | 1993 | Total | 116001 | 61.3 | 8.5 | 27.4 | [3]2.8 | 15.9 | 18415 | 60.9 | 8.0 | 28.2 | [3]2.9 |
| Gambia | 1993 | Urban | 54042 | 34.9 | 10.5 | 52.0 | [3]2.6 | 19.4 | 10463 | 44.0 | 8.2 | 45.4 | [3]2.4 |
| Gambia | 1993 | Rural | 61959 | 84.3 | 6.8 | 5.9 | [3]3.0 | 12.8 | 7952 | 83.1 | 7.6 | 5.7 | [3]3.6 |
| Kenya | 1989 | Total | [4]100 | 73.0 | ... | [5]27.0 | ... | ... | 4100 | 82.1 | ... | 17.9 | ... |
| Kenya | 1989 | Urban | [4]100 | 20.2 | ... | [5]79.8 | ... | ... | ... | ... | ... | ... | ... |
| Kenya | 1989 | Rural | [4]100 | 88.0 | ... | [5]86.8 | ... | ... | ... | ... | ... | ... | ... |
| Lesotho | 1996 | Total | 370972 | 84.3 | ... | 11.6 | [6]4.1 | 29.4 | 108893 | ... | ... | ... | ... |
| Lesotho | 1996 | Urban | 79452 | ... | ... | ... | ... | 31.7 | 25198 | ... | ... | ... | ... |
| Lesotho | 1996 | Rural | 291520 | ... | ... | ... | ... | 28.7 | 83695 | ... | ... | ... | ... |
| Libyan Arab Jamahiriya | 1995 | Total | 711837 | 40.6 | 21.6 | 17.3 | 7.5 | ... | ... | ... | ... | ... | ... |
| Mauritius | 1990 | Total | 236725 | 75.9 | [7]15.2 | [8]8.8 | [9]0.1 | 17.6 | 41609 | ... | ... | ... | ... |
| Mauritius | 1990 | Urban | 97484 | 65.8 | [7]26.2 | [8]8.0 | [9]0.1 | ... | ... | ... | ... | ... | ... |
| Mauritius | 1990 | Rural | 139241 | 83.0 | [7]7.6 | [8]9.3 | [9]0.1 | ... | ... | ... | ... | ... | ... |
| Niger | 1998 | Total | 1129126 | 77.6 | 1.0 | 6.1 | 15.3 | ... | ... | ... | ... | ... | ... |
| Niger | 1998 | Urban | 182969 | 39.7 | 3.9 | 33.7 | 22.7 | ... | ... | ... | ... | ... | ... |
| Niger | 1998 | Rural | 946157 | 84.9 | 0.4 | 0.8 | 13.9 | ... | ... | ... | ... | ... | ... |
| Senegal | 1994 | Total | 777931 | 66.7 | [2]14.2 | ... | ... | 19.6 | 152197 | ... | ... | ... | ... |
| Senegal | 1994 | Urban | 330828 | 49.3 | ... | ... | ... | 27.1 | 89797 | ... | ... | ... | ... |
| Senegal | 1994 | Rural | 447103 | 79.7 | ... | ... | ... | 14.0 | 62450 | ... | ... | ... | ... |
| Seychelles | 1997 | Total | [10]17878 | 74.7 | 11.7 | [11]9.8 | ... | 47.9 | 8564 | 74.8 | ... | [12]7.5 | ... |
| South Africa[13] | 1996 | Total | 9059571 | 76.8 | [2]21.6 | ... | [6]1.7 | 37.8 | 3428796 | 80.1 | [2]18.2 | ... | [6]1.7 |
| South Africa[13] | 1996 | Urban | 5426873 | 74.3 | [2]24.0 | ... | [6]1.7 | 31.8 | 1726059 | 71.7 | [2]26.6 | ... | [6]1.7 |
| South Africa[13] | 1996 | Rural | 3632698 | 80.4 | [2]18.0 | ... | [6]1.6 | 46.9 | 1702737 | 88.7 | [2]9.7 | ... | [6]1.6 |
| St. Helena | 1998 | Total | 1577 | 78.8 | 7.4 | 13.9 | ... | ... | ... | ... | ... | ... | ... |
| St. Helena | 1998 | Urban | 280 | 61.4 | 10.4 | 28.2 | ... | ... | ... | ... | ... | ... | ... |
| St. Helena | 1998 | Rural | 1297 | 82.5 | 6.7 | 10.8 | ... | ... | ... | ... | ... | ... | ... |
| Zimbabwe | 1997 | Total | 2510410 | [14]58.7 | [14]3.8 | [14]16.3 | [14]1.5 | 32.8 | 822912 | ... | ... | ... | ... |
| Zimbabwe | 1997 | Urban | 926210 | [14]31.3 | [14]9.6 | [14]42.9 | [14]2.5 | ... | ... | ... | ... | ... | ... |
| Zimbabwe | 1997 | Rural | 1584200 | [14]74.8 | [14]0.5 | [14]0.8 | [14]0.9 | ... | ... | ... | ... | ... | ... |
| **ASIA** | | | | | | | | | | | | | |
| Armenia | 1998 | Total | [15]100 | 90.6 | 5.9 | 1.4 | [6]2.1 | ... | [15]100 | 91.3 | 6.3 | 1.0 | [6]1.4 |
| Armenia | 1998 | Urban | [15]100 | 89.4 | 7.2 | 2.0 | [6]1.4 | ... | [15]100 | 90.5 | 7.6 | 1.1 | [6]0.8 |
| Armenia | 1998 | Rural | [15]100 | 92.5 | 3.8 | 0.7 | [6]3.0 | ... | [15]100 | 93.1 | 3.6 | 1.0 | [6]2.3 |
| Azerbaijan | 1998 | Total | 1479504 | 76.1 | 23.9 | ... | ... | ... | ... | ... | ... | ... | ... |
| Azerbaijan | 1998 | Urban | 897283 | 62.2 | 37.8 | ... | ... | ... | ... | ... | ... | ... | ... |
| Azerbaijan | 1998 | Rural | 582221 | 97.5 | 2.5 | ... | ... | ... | ... | ... | ... | ... | ... |
| Cambodia | 1998 | Total | [4]100 | 95.3 | [15]2.6 | 1.6 | [6]0.6 | ... | ... | ... | ... | ... | ... |
| Cambodia | 1998 | Urban | [4]100 | 88.4 | [15]3.9 | 6.9 | [6]0.8 | ... | ... | ... | ... | ... | ... |
| Cambodia | 1998 | Rural | [4]100 | 96.5 | [15]2.3 | 0.7 | [6]0.5 | ... | ... | ... | ... | ... | ... |
| China, Hong Kong SAR | 1996 | Total | [16]1855553 | 43.6 | 36.4 | 13.9 | [17]1.5 | 27.2 | [18]504294 | 38.2 | 45.5 | 12.4 | [19]1.1 |
| China, Macau SAR | 1996 | Total | 119966 | 72.9 | 4.6 | [19]20.8 | 1.7 | 21.8 | 26170 | 70.0 | 2.0 | 25.9 | 2.1 |
| Cyprus[20] | 1992 | Total | 184161 | 69.3 | 10.6 | 13.0 | [21]6.8 | 13.9 | 25645 | 51.5 | 16.8 | 16.1 | [21]15.2 |
| Cyprus[20] | 1992 | Urban | 124673 | 64.7 | 12.1 | 17.4 | [21]5.5 | 14.1 | 17592 | 45.9 | 19.8 | 22.1 | [21]11.7 |
| Cyprus[20] | 1992 | Rural | 59488 | 78.9 | 7.5 | 3.8 | [21]9.4 | 13.5 | 8053 | 63.7 | 10.1 | 3.0 | [21]22.8 |
| Iran (Islamic Republic of) | 1996 | Total | [22]12280539 | 72.7 | 2.5 | 15.4 | 8.0 | ... | ... | ... | ... | ... | ... |
| Iran (Islamic Republic of) | 1996 | Urban | [22]7929830 | 66.7 | 2.6 | 20.9 | 8.4 | ... | ... | ... | ... | ... | ... |
| Iran (Islamic Republic of) | 1996 | Rural | [22]4350709 | 83.5 | 2.4 | 5.4 | 7.2 | ... | ... | ... | ... | ... | ... |
| Israel[23] | 1995 | Total | 1587000 | 62.5 | 5.5 | 14.1 | ... | 29.5 | 468940 | 54.8 | 8.0 | 18.0 | ... |
| Israel[23] | 1995 | Urban | 1490525 | 62.5 | 5.6 | 14.6 | ... | 30.0 | 447315 | 54.5 | 8.1 | 18.5 | ... |
| Israel[23] | 1995 | Rural | 96475 | 62.1 | 3.6 | 6.4 | ... | 22.4 | 21625 | 60.0 | 4.3 | 8.3 | ... |
| Japan | 1993 | Total | 40773300 | 59.8 | 7.1 | 26.4 | ... | [24]20.0 | 8170000 | 43.8 | 10.5 | 40.5 | ... |
| Japan | 1993 | Urban | 32941900 | 54.7 | 7.5 | 30.2 | ... | ... | ... | ... | ... | ... | ... |
| Japan | 1993 | Rural | 7831400 | 81.1 | 5.1 | 10.3 | ... | ... | ... | ... | ... | ... | ... |
| Kazakhstan | 1998 | Total | [25]100 | ... | 6.3 | 92.0 | 1.7 | ... | ... | ... | ... | ... | ... |
| Kazakhstan | 1998 | Urban | [25]100 | ... | 8.9 | 88.7 | 2.4 | ... | ... | ... | ... | ... | ... |
| Kazakhstan | 1998 | Rural | [25]100 | ... | 2.5 | 97.0 | 0.5 | ... | ... | ... | ... | ... | ... |
| Malaysia[26] | 1998 | Total | 3526675 | 84.9 | 7.3 | 5.5 | 2.2 | 18.5 | 652115 | 89.0 | 5.1 | 3.7 | 2.2 |
| Malaysia[26] | 1991 | Rural | 1572151 | 82.9 | 5.4 | 9.5 | 2.2 | 17.5 | 275649 | 88.5 | 3.7 | 5.7 | 2.2 |
| Malaysia[26] | 1991 | Urban | 1954524 | 86.6 | 8.9 | 2.4 | 2.2 | 19.3 | 376466 | 89.4 | 6.2 | 2.2 | 2.2 |
| Republic of Korea | 1995 | Total | 9204929 | 74.9 | ... | [27]25.1 | ... | ... | ... | ... | ... | ... | ... |
| Republic of Korea | 1995 | Urban | 6562695 | 70.5 | ... | [27]29.5 | ... | ... | ... | ... | ... | ... | ... |
| Republic of Korea | 1995 | Rural | 2642234 | 85.7 | ... | [27]14.3 | ... | ... | ... | ... | ... | ... | ... |
| Singapore[28] | 1995 | Total | 773722 | 90.2 | ... | 9.1 | [6]0.7 | ... | ... | ... | ... | ... | ... |
| Syrian Arab Republic | 1994 | Total | 2196084 | ... | ... | ... | ... | ... | ... | ... | ... | ... | ... |
| Syrian Arab Republic | 1994 | Urban | 1181158 | ... | ... | ... | ... | ... | ... | ... | ... | ... | ... |
| Syrian Arab Republic | 1994 | Rural | 1014926 | ... | ... | ... | ... | ... | ... | ... | ... | ... | ... |

# TABLE A.4

## continued

| | | | Households in occupied housing units | | | | | | Women-headed housolds in occupied housing units | | | | |
| | | | | Tenants in housing units | | | | | | | Tenants in housing units | | |
| | | | Total | Owner (%) | Publicly owned (%) | Privately owned (%) | Squatters (%) | Women-headed households as % of total | Total | Owner (%) | Publicly owned (%) | Privately owned (%) | Squatters (%) |
|---|---|---|---|---|---|---|---|---|---|---|---|---|---|
| Thailand | 1996 | Total | 15002591 | 82.8 | [2]13.3 | ... | 3.9 | ... | 4100 | 75.4 | 4.5 | 11.4 | 298.7 |
| Thailand | 1996 | Urban | 3046293 | 53.0 | [2]41.0 | ... | 6.0 | ... | ... | ... | ... | ... | ... |
| Thailand | 1996 | Rural | 11956299 | 90.4 | [2]6.3 | ... | 3.3 | ... | ... | ... | ... | ... | ... |
| **EUROPE** | | | | | | | | | | | | | |
| Austria | 1999 | Total | [30]3242400 | 56.5 | ... | 43.5 | – | 33.1 | [30]1072000 | 43.6 | ... | 56.4 | – |
| Austria | 1999 | Urban | [30]2559900 | 47.9 | ... | 52.1 | – | 36.1 | [30]924900 | 37.7 | ... | 62.3 | – |
| Austria | 1999 | Rural | [30]682500 | 88.8 | ... | 11.2 | – | 21.6 | [30]147100 | 80.6 | ... | 19.3 | – |
| Belgium | 1991 | Total | 3748164 | 64.5 | – | – | – | 26.2 | 981643 | – | – | – | – |
| Belgium | 1991 | Urban | 3740771 | 64.4 | – | – | – | 26.2 | 980241 | – | – | – | – |
| Belgium | 1991 | Rural | 7393 | 97.3 | – | – | – | 19.0 | 1402 | – | – | – | – |
| Bulgaria | 1992 | Total | 2950873 | 89.8 | 9.3 | 0.9 | ... | ... | ... | ... | ... | ... | ... |
| Bulgaria | 1992 | Urban | 1977184 | 86.3 | 12.5 | 1.2 | ... | ... | ... | ... | ... | ... | ... |
| Bulgaria | 1992 | Rural | 973689 | 96.9 | 2.8 | 0.2 | ... | ... | ... | ... | ... | ... | ... |
| Croatia | 1991 | Total | 1504702 | 66.5 | 26.1 | 7.4 | ... | ... | ... | ... | ... | ... | ... |
| Czech Republic | 1991 | Total | 4043250 | 38.4 | [2]61.6 | ... | ... | ... | ... | ... | ... | ... | ... |
| Czech Republic | 1991 | Urban | 3084245 | ... | ... | ... | ... | ... | ... | ... | ... | ... | ... |
| Czech Republic | 1991 | Rural | 959005 | ... | ... | ... | ... | ... | ... | ... | ... | ... | ... |
| Estonia[31] | 1998 | Total | 657000 | 76.1 | 7.7 | 11.1 | – | 54.2 | 356100 | 74.9 | 7.6 | 11.9 | – |
| Estonia[31] | 1998 | Urban | 524400 | 73.8 | 8.8 | 13.0 | – | 54.1 | 283700 | 72.1 | 8.6 | 14.0 | – |
| Estonia[31] | 1998 | Rural | 132600 | 85.1 | 3.4 | 3.8 | – | 54.6 | 72400 | 85.9 | 3.9 | 3.9 | – |
| Finland | 1998 | Total | 2247206 | 65.4 | [32]14.4 | [33]17.0 | ... | ... | ... | ... | ... | ... | ... |
| Finland | 1998 | Urban | 1422984 | 59.6 | [32]17.8 | [33]19.6 | ... | ... | ... | ... | ... | ... | ... |
| Finland | 1998 | Rural | 824222 | 75.3 | [32]8.6 | [33]12.4 | ... | ... | ... | ... | ... | ... | ... |
| France | 1990 | Total | 21542152 | 54.4 | 14.5 | 25.1 | 6.0 | ... | ... | ... | ... | ... | ... |
| France | 1990 | Urban | 16276780 | 47.8 | [2]46.6 | ... | 5.5 | ... | ... | ... | ... | ... | ... |
| France | 1990 | Rural | 5265372 | 74.8 | [2]17.9 | ... | 7.3 | ... | ... | ... | ... | ... | ... |
| Germany | 1998 | Total | 34865300 | 40.2 | 59.8 | ... | ... | 30.6 | 10675800 | 26.8 | 73.2 | ... | ... |
| Guernsey | 1996 | Total | 21862 | 69.5 | 9.8 | 20.7 | – | 27.1 | 5932 | 55.9 | 16.0 | 28.2 | ... |
| Hungary[34] | 1996 | Total | 3863502 | 89.1 | [2]9.9 | ... | ... | ... | ... | ... | ... | ... | ... |
| Hungary[34] | 1996 | Urban | 2490481 | 85.3 | [2]13.6 | ... | ... | ... | ... | ... | ... | ... | ... |
| Hungary[34] | 1996 | Rural | 1373021 | 96.2 | [2]3.2 | ... | ... | ... | ... | ... | ... | ... | ... |
| Ireland | 1991 | Total | 1019723 | 79.3 | 9.7 | 10.1 | [9]0.9 | 26.3 | 268420 | 69.9 | 13.5 | 15.5 | 1.1 |
| Ireland | 1991 | Urban | 593481 | 73.1 | 13.3 | 12.7 | [9]0.8 | 30.6 | 181537 | 63.2 | 16.9 | 18.9 | 1.0 |
| Ireland | 1991 | Rural | 426242 | 87.8 | 4.6 | 6.4 | [9]1.1 | 20.4 | 86883 | 84.0 | 6.3 | 6.3 | 1.4 |
| Lithuania[10] | 1999 | Total | 1306061 | 93.6 | 2.5 | 3.9 | ... | ... | ... | ... | ... | ... | ... |
| Lithuania[10] | 1999 | Urban | 890208 | 91.6 | 2.8 | 5.6 | ... | ... | ... | ... | ... | ... | ... |
| Lithuania[10] | 1999 | Rural | 415853 | 97.8 | 1.9 | 0.3 | ... | ... | ... | ... | ... | ... | ... |
| Malta | 1995 | Total | 119479 | [35]68.0 | [2]28.3 | ... | ... | 21.0 | [35]25051 | ... | ... | ... | ... |
| The Netherlands | 1998 | Total | 6641200 | 49.8 | 33.7 | 8.7 | 7.8 | 42.8 | 2843300 | 45.6 | 36.3 | 9.6 | 8.5 |
| The Netherlands | 1998 | Urban | 4406900 | 42.5 | 37.6 | 10.8 | 9.1 | 44.5 | 1960200 | 39.1 | 39.8 | 11.6 | 9.6 |
| The Netherlands | 1998 | Rural | 2234400 | 64.2 | 26.0 | 4.5 | 5.3 | 39.5 | 883200 | 60.2 | 28.5 | 5.1 | 6.2 |
| Norway | 1990 | Total | [36]1751363 | 78.2 | [2]21.8 | ... | ... | 34.3 | [36]600353 | 71.3 | [2]28.7 | ... | ... |
| Norway | 1990 | Urban | [36]1300372 | 78.2 | [2]21.8 | ... | ... | 35.7 | [36]463806 | 71.6 | [2]28.4 | ... | ... |
| Norway | 1990 | Rural | [36]439216 | 78.1 | [2]21.9 | ... | ... | 30.4 | [36]133442 | 70.5 | [2]29.5 | ... | ... |
| Poland | 1995 | Total | 12498473 | 50.3 | 21.9 | 27.8 | ... | 35.2 | 4396312 | ... | ... | ... | ... |
| Poland | 1995 | Urban | 8383622 | 38.7 | 24.9 | 36.4 | ... | 39.2 | 3282931 | ... | ... | ... | ... |
| Poland | 1995 | Rural | 4114851 | 73.8 | 15.9 | 10.3 | ... | 27.1 | 1113381 | ... | ... | ... | ... |
| Portugal | 1991 | Total | 3115122 | 64.6 | 3.6 | 30.8 | 1.1 | 19.8 | 617787 | 59.1 | 4.2 | 35.5 | 1.2 |
| Portugal | 1991 | Urban | 1539112 | 53.1 | 6.1 | 38.9 | 1.9 | 21.7 | 334665 | 44.0 | 6.8 | 47.3 | 1.9 |
| Portugal | 1991 | Rural | 1576010 | 75.7 | 1.1 | 22.8 | 0.3 | 18.0 | 283122 | 77.0 | 1.1 | 21.6 | 0.3 |
| Slovakia | 1991 | Total | 1832484 | ... | ... | ... | ... | 23.1 | 423327 | ... | ... | ... | ... |
| Slovakia | 1991 | Urban | 1051856 | ... | ... | ... | ... | ... | ... | ... | ... | ... | ... |
| Slovakia | 1991 | Rural | 780628 | ... | ... | ... | ... | ... | ... | ... | ... | ... | ... |
| Sweden | 1990 | Total | 3830035 | 3.9 | 38.7 | 20.9 | – | 37.0 | 1418595 | 25.3 | 48.5 | 25.4 | – |
| Sweden | 1990 | Urban | 32602955 | 3.3 | 4.5 | ... | ... | 3.9 | 1268749 | 20.3 | 53.8 | 25.2 | – |
| Sweden | 1990 | Rural | 569740 | 75.2 | 2.3 | ... | ... | 26.3 | 149846 | 67.8 | 3.4 | 27.0 | – |
| United Kingdom | 1998 | Total | 20423000 | 68.7 | 16.3 | 15.0 | ... | 25.3 | 5169000 | 50.8 | [37]27.5 | [37]21.6 | ... |
| United Kingdom | 1998 | Urban | 18911000 | 68.2 | 16.9 | 14.9 | ... | 25.9 | 4892000 | 50.3 | [37]28.1 | [37]21.6 | ... |
| United Kingdom | 1998 | Rural | 1512000 | 74.7 | 8.6 | 16.7 | ... | 18.3 | 277000 | 59.9 | [37]18.1 | [37]22.0 | ... |
| Yugoslavia[38] | 1991 | Total | 2648617 | ... | ... | ... | ... | 21.8 | 576361 | ... | ... | ... | ... |
| **LATIN AMERICA** | | | | | | | | | | | | | |
| Argentina | 1991 | Total | 8927289 | 61.5 | [39]3.6 | 12.3 | [40]22.6 | 22.4 | 1995907 | ... | ... | ... | ... |
| Argentina | 1991 | Urban | 7880607 | 63.9 | [39]1.7 | 13.3 | [40]21.1 | ... | ... | ... | ... | ... | ... |
| Argentina | 1991 | Rural | 1046682 | 42.9 | [39]18.2 | 5.1 | [40]33.8 | ... | ... | ... | ... | ... | ... |
| Bahamas | 1990 | Total | 61906 | 54.9 | – | 44.6 | ... | 35.8 | 22192 | ... | ... | ... | ... |
| Bahamas | 1990 | Urban | 50252 | 51.9 | – | ... | ... | 37.2 | 18678 | ... | ... | ... | ... |
| Bahamas | 1990 | Rural | 11654 | 67.7 | – | ... | ... | 30.2 | 3514 | ... | ... | ... | ... |
| Bolivia | 1997 | Total | 1822785 | 70.2 | ... | ... | ... | 18.1 | 329784 | 67.6 | ... | ... | ... |
| Bolivia | 1997 | Urban | 1094237 | 59.8 | ... | ... | ... | 20.9 | 228448 | 59.9 | ... | ... | ... |
| Bolivia | 1997 | Rural | 728548 | 85.8 | ... | ... | ... | 13.9 | 101336 | 85.0 | ... | ... | ... |
| Brazil | 1998 | Total | 41839703 | 74.0 | 11.8 | 13.7 | 0.6 | 23.1 | 9675173 | 74.6 | 9.5 | 15.3 | 0.6 |
| Brazil | 1998 | Urban | 33993829 | 7.5 | 8.9 | 16.3 | 0.5 | 25.3 | 8601559 | 73.6 | 9.0 | 16.9 | 0.5 |
| Brazil | 1998 | Rural | 7845874 | 73.2 | 24.0 | 2.2 | 0.6 | 13.7 | 1073614 | 82.8 | 13.7 | 2.4 | 1.1 |
| Colombia | 1993 | Total | 7159842 | 63.5 | ... | 27.7 | 8.8 | 24.4 | 1749420 | 65.6 | ... | 27.9 | 6.4 |
| Colombia | 1993 | Urban | 5348656 | 61.0 | ... | 34.1 | 5.5 | 27.1 | 1447461 | 62.7 | ... | 32.0 | 5.3 |
| Colombia | 1993 | Rural | 1775186 | 72.2 | ... | 9.1 | 18.6 | 17.0 | 301959 | 79.8 | ... | 8.6 | 11.6 |
| Costa Rica | 1997 | Total | [1]715264 | 67.5 | 15.9 | 15.9 | 0.7 | ... | ... | ... | ... | ... | ... |
| Costa Rica | 1997 | Urban | [1]341136 | 57.0 | 19.9 | ... | 1.0 | ... | ... | ... | ... | ... | ... |
| Costa Rica | 1997 | Rural | [1]722130 | 39.9 | 6.4 | ... | 0.2 | ... | ... | ... | ... | ... | ... |

# TABLE A.4

## continued

| | | | | | | | | | | | | | |
|---|---|---|---|---|---|---|---|---|---|---|---|---|---|
| Dominican Republic | 1993 | Total | 1629616 | 71.2 | ... | 22.4 | 6.5 | 32.8 | 534850 | ... | ... | ... | ... |
| Guatemala | 1994 | Total | ... | ... | ... | ... | ... | ... | 289040 | ... | ... | ... | ... |
| Guatemala | 1994 | Urban | ... | ... | ... | ... | ... | ... | 142287 | ... | ... | ... | ... |
| Guatemala | 1994 | Rural | ... | ... | ... | ... | ... | ... | 146753 | ... | ... | ... | ... |
| Mexico | 1996 | Total | 20199398 | 78.0 | ... | 21.8 | 0.2 | 16.3 | 3287122 | 75.6 | ... | 24.0 | 0.5 |
| Mexico | 1996 | Urban | 15318401 | 74.3 | ... | 25.5 | 0.2 | 17.9 | 2738112 | 72.6 | ... | 26.8 | 0.6 |
| Mexico | 1996 | Rural | 4880997 | 89.7 | ... | 10.3 | 0.0 | 11.2 | 549010 | 90.3 | ... | 9.7 | 0.0 |
| Nicaragua | 1998 | Total | 631326 | 54.8 | ... | 5.1 | 40.1 | 29.4 | 185352 | 57.4 | ... | 4.7 | 37.9 |
| Nicaragua | 1998 | Urban | 386047 | 54.1 | ... | 7.6 | 38.3 | 35.2 | 135970 | 57.0 | ... | 6.0 | 37.0 |
| Nicaragua | 1998 | Rural | 245279 | 56.0 | ... | 1.3 | 42.7 | 20.1 | 49382 | 58.6 | ... | 0.9 | 40.5 |
| Panama | 1990 | Total | 526456 | ... | ... | ... | ... | 22.3 | 117159 | ... | ... | ... | ... |
| Panama | 1990 | Urban | 296877 | ... | ... | ... | ... | 27.4 | 81486 | ... | ... | ... | ... |
| Panama | 1990 | Rural | 229579 | ... | ... | ... | ... | 15.5 | 35673 | ... | ... | ... | ... |
| Puerto Rico[41] | 1990 | Total | 1054924 | 72.1 | ... | ... | ... | 32.0 | 337338 | 55.8 | ... | ... | ... |
| Puerto Rico[41] | 1990 | Urban | 768650 | 68.7 | ... | ... | ... | 34.9 | 268271 | ... | ... | ... | ... |
| Puerto Rico[41] | 1990 | Rural | 286274 | 81.2 | ... | ... | ... | 24.1 | 69067 | ... | ... | ... | ... |
| Uruguay | 1996 | Total | [42]970037 | ... | ... | ... | ... | 29.2 | 283545 | ... | ... | ... | ... |
| Uruguay | 1996 | Urban | [42]884794 | ... | ... | ... | ... | 30.7 | 271595 | ... | ... | ... | ... |
| Uruguay | 1996 | Rural | [42]85243 | ... | ... | ... | ... | 14.0 | 11950 | ... | ... | ... | ... |
| **NORTHERN AMERICA** | | | | | | | | | | | | | |
| Bermuda | 1999 | Total | 22061 | 43.3 | ... | ... | ... | 34.4 | 7596 | 39.2 | ... | ... | ... |
| Bermuda | 1999 | Urban | 22061 | 43.3 | ... | ... | ... | 34.4 | 7596 | 39.2 | ... | ... | ... |
| Bermuda | 1999 | Rural | ... | ... | ... | ... | ... | ... | ... | ... | ... | ... | ... |
| Canada | 1998 | Total | 11690200 | 62.4 | 5.7 | 28.7 | ... | 46.6 | 5442600 | 59.1 | 7.5 | 30.3 | ... |
| Canada | 1998 | Urban | 9730000 | 58.6 | 5.8 | 32.4 | ... | 47.2 | 4593900 | 55.2 | 7.9 | 33.9 | ... |
| Canada | 1998 | Rural | 1960000 | 81.0 | 4.9 | 10.7 | ... | 43.3 | 848700 | 80.2 | 5.3 | 10.7 | ... |
| United States | 1997 | Total | 99487000 | 65.8 | 1.9 | 32.3 | ... | 29.0 | 28852000 | 51.2 | 4.6 | 44.3 | ... |
| United States | 1997 | Urban | 71317000 | 59.3 | 2.4 | 38.3 | ... | 32.0 | 22838000 | 45.7 | 5.2 | 49.0 | ... |
| United States | 1997 | Rural | 28170000 | 82.4 | 0.6 | 17.0 | ... | 21.3 | 6013000 | 71.7 | 2.1 | 26.1 | ... |
| **OCEANIA** | | | | | | | | | | | | | |
| Australia | 1966 | Total | ... | ... | ... | ... | ... | ... | 1276064 | 60.5 | 1.3 | 36.0 | 2.2 |
| Guam | 1990 | Total | 31373 | 45.6 | 54.4 | ... | ... | ... | ... | ... | ... | ... | ... |
| Guam | 1990 | Urban | 12351 | 35.5 | 64.5 | ... | ... | ... | ... | ... | ... | ... | ... |
| Guam | 1990 | Rural | 19022 | 52.1 | 47.9 | ... | ... | ... | ... | ... | ... | ... | ... |
| Pitcairn | 1999 | Rural | 15 | 86.7 | 6.7 | 6.7 | ... | 33.3 | 5 | 80.0 | 20.0 | ... | ... |
| Tonga[43] | 1996 | Total | 15670 | 83.3 | [44]14.9 | ... | [9]1.8 | ... | 3003 | 86.0 | [45]12.6 | [9]1.3 | |

**Source:** United Nations, Human Settlement Statistics Questionnaire 1999.
For footnotes, refer to technical notes.

## TABLE A.5

### Living Quarters by Type, Selected Countries

| | | | | Living quarters | | | | | |
|---|---|---|---|---|---|---|---|---|---|
| | | | | Type of housing unit | | | | | |
| | | | Total | Conventional | Basic | Temporary | Marginal | Collective | Not stated |
| **AFRICA** | | | | | | | | | |
| Benin[29] | 1994 | Total | 832526 | ... | ... | ... | ... | ... | ... |
| Benin[29] | 1994 | Urban | 306780 | ... | ... | ... | ... | ... | ... |
| Benin[29] | 1994 | Rural | 525746 | ... | ... | ... | ... | ... | ... |
| Botswana[29] | 1996 | Total | 276209 | ... | ... | ... | ... | ... | ... |
| Burkina Faso[29] | 1991 | Total | 1399149 | ... | ... | ... | ... | ... | ... |
| Burkina Faso[29] | 1991 | Urban | 197871 | ... | ... | ... | ... | ... | ... |
| Burkina Faso[29] | 1991 | Rural | 1201278 | ... | ... | ... | ... | ... | ... |
| Congo[29] | 1984 | Total | 363140 | – | – | – | – | – | – |
| Congo[29] | 1984 | Urban | 181331 | – | – | – | – | – | – |
| Congo[29] | 1984 | Rural | 181809 | – | – | – | – | – | – |
| Egypt | 1996 | Total | 18691143 | 703213 | 15507092 | ... | 2461191 | ... | 19647 |
| Egypt | 1996 | Urban | 10122361 | 533536 | 7920158 | ... | 1657490 | ... | 11177 |
| Egypt | 1996 | Rural | 8568782 | 169677 | 7586934 | ... | 803701 | ... | 8470 |
| Gambia[29] | 1993 | Total | 116001 | ... | ... | ... | ... | ... | ... |
| Gambia[29] | 1993 | Urban | 54042 | ... | ... | ... | ... | ... | ... |
| Gambia[29] | 1993 | Rural | 61959 | ... | ... | ... | ... | ... | ... |
| Kenya[29] | 1989 | Total | 4352751 | | | | | | |
| Lesotho | 1996 | Total | 370972 | ... | ... | ... | ... | ... | ... |
| Lesotho | 1996 | Urban | 79452 | ... | ... | ... | ... | ... | ... |
| Lesotho | 1996 | Rural | 291520 | ... | ... | ... | ... | ... | ... |
| Libyan Arab Jamahiriya | 1995 | Total | 730757 | 79619 | 114334 | 494429 | 18920 | ... | 23455 |
| Libyan Arab Jamahiriya[29] | 1995 | Urban | 545998 | 84461 | 102490 | 336444 | 9539 | 532934 | 13064 |
| Libyan Arab Jamahiriya[29] | 1995 | Rural | 88921 | 5261 | 2236 | 71931 | 2510 | 882938 | 6983 |
| Mauritius | 1990 | Total | [1]223821 | ... | ... | ... | ... | ... | ... |
| Mauritius | 1990 | Urban | [1]92772 | ... | ... | ... | ... | ... | ... |
| Mauritius[29] | 1990 | Rural | [1]139194 | ... | ... | ... | ... | ... | ... |
| Niger | 1998 | Total | 1129126 | 12420 | 1088479 | 14679 | ... | ... | 13550 |
| Niger | 1998 | Urban | 182969 | 10612 | 165953 | 2379 | ... | ... | 4025 |
| Niger | 1998 | Rural | 946157 | 946 | 922503 | 13246 | ... | ... | 9462 |
| Senegal[2] | 1994 | Total | 777931 | ... | ... | ... | ... | ... | ... |
| Senegal[2] | 1994 | Urban | 330828 | ... | ... | ... | ... | ... | ... |
| Senegal[2] | 1994 | Rural | 447103 | ... | ... | ... | ... | ... | ... |
| Seychelles[29] | 1997 | Total | 17878 | 12905 | ... | 3403 | 993 | ... | 577 |
| South Africa[29] | 1996 | Total | 9059573 | 5211728 | 2127848 | 1592648 | ... | 17126 | 110223 |
| South Africa[29] | 1996 | Urban | 5426875 | 3563620 | 475313 | 1312797 | ... | 80405 | 66740 |
| South Africa[29] | 1996 | Rural | 3632698 | 1648108 | 1652535 | 279851 | ... | 8721 | 43483 |
| St. Helena | 1998 | Urban | 288 | ... | ... | ... | ... | ... | ... |
| St. Helena | 1998 | Rural | 1322 | 1322 | ... | ... | ... | ... | ... |
| Zimbabwe[29] | 1997 | Total | 2510410 | ... | ... | ... | ... | ... | ... |
| Zimbabwe[29] | 1997 | Urban | 926210 | ... | ... | ... | ... | ... | ... |
| Zimbabwe[29] | 1997 | Rural | 1584200 | ... | ... | ... | ... | ... | ... |
| **ASIA** | | | | | | | | | |
| Armenia | 1998 | Total | [3]100 | 28 | 68 | ... | [4]3 | 1 | ... |
| Armenia | 1998 | Urban | [3]100 | 48 | 48 | ... | [4]3 | 2 | ... |
| Armenia | 1998 | Rural | [3]100 | 8.9 | 88 | ... | [4]3 | ... | ... |
| China, Hong Kong SAR | 1996 | Total | 1781835 | 1732248 | ... | [5]43355 | ... | [6]6232 | ... |
| China, Macau SAR | 1996 | Total | 115487 | 112004 | ... | [7]2188 | 110 | 1185 | ... |
| Cyprus | 1992 | Total | 233210 | 231930 | ... | ... | [8]1065 | 215 | ... |
| Cyprus | 1992 | Urban | 83847 | 83363 | ... | ... | [8]426 | 58 | ... |
| Cyprus | 1992 | Rural | 83847 | 83363 | ... | ... | [8]426 | 58 | ... |
| Georgia[29] | 1998 | Total | 1412939 | ... | ... | ... | ... | ... | ... |
| Georgia | 1998 | Urban | 5096 | ... | ... | ... | ... | ... | ... |
| Georgia[29] | 1998 | Rural | 660265 | ... | ... | ... | ... | ... | ... |
| Iran (Islamic Republic of)[29] | 1996 | Total | 12398235 | ... | ... | ... | ... | ... | ... |
| Iran (Islamic Republic of)[29] | 1996 | Urban | 7948925 | ... | ... | ... | ... | ... | ... |
| Iran (Islamic Republic of)[29] | 1996 | Rural | 4449310 | ... | ... | ... | ... | ... | ... |
| Israel[29] | 1995 | Total | 1773624 | ... | ... | ... | ... | 150945 | 1622679 |
| Israel[29] | 1995 | Urban | 1596289 | ... | ... | ... | ... | 121360 | 1474929 |
| Israel[29] | 1995 | Rural | 177335 | ... | ... | ... | ... | 29585 | 147750 |
| Japan | 1993 | Total | 45878800 | ... | ... | ... | ... | 159300 | ... |
| Japan | 1993 | Urban | 37161200 | ... | ... | ... | ... | 117100 | ... |
| Japan | 1993 | Rural | [9]8717600 | ... | ... | ... | ... | ... | ... |
| Kazakhstan[29] | 1998 | Total | [3]100 | 54.1 | 42.5 | ... | ... | 3.3 | 0.1 |
| Kazakhstan[29] | 1998 | Urban | [3]100 | 77.3 | 17.6 | ... | ... | 5.0 | 0.1 |
| Kazakhstan[29] | 1998 | Rural | [3]100 | 18.9 | 80.5 | ... | ... | 0.5 | 0.1 |
| Malaysia[10] | 1991 | Total | 3482969 | 3448430 | 12066 | 22473 | ... | ... | ... |
| Malaysia[10] | 1991 | Urban | 1908771 | 1892645 | 4450 | 11676 | ... | ... | ... |
| Malaysia[10] | 1991 | Rural | 1574198 | 1555785 | 7616 | 10797 | ... | ... | ... |
| Pakistan[29] | 1998 | Total | 19344232 | ... | ... | ... | ... | ... | ... |
| Pakistan[29] | 1998 | Urban | 6240469 | ... | ... | ... | ... | ... | ... |
| Pakistan[29] | 1998 | Rural | 13103763 | ... | ... | ... | ... | ... | ... |
| Republic of Korea | 1995 | Total | 9253367 | 9204929 | 8956 | ... | 33532 | 5950 | ... |
| Republic of Korea | 1995 | Urban | 6599744 | 6562695 | 8482 | ... | 24851 | 3716 | ... |
| Republic of Korea | 1995 | Rural | 2653623 | 2642234 | 474 | ... | 8681 | 2234 | ... |
| Syrian Arab Republic[29] | 1994 | Total | 2196084 | ... | ... | ... | ... | ... | ... |
| Syria Arab Republic[29] | 1994 | Urban | 1181158 | ... | ... | ... | ... | ... | ... |
| Syria Arab Republic[29] | 1994 | Rural | 1014926 | ... | ... | ... | ... | ... | ... |
| Thailand[29] | 1996 | Total | 15002591 | ... | ... | ... | ... | ... | ... |
| Thailand[29] | 1996 | Urban | 3046293 | ... | ... | ... | ... | ... | ... |
| Thailand[29] | 1996 | Rural | 11956299 | ... | ... | ... | ... | ... | ... |
| Singapore[29] | 1995 | Total | 733722 | 729996 | ... | ... | ... | ... | 3726 |

# TABLE A.5

*continued*

| | | | Total | | | | | | |
|---|---|---|---|---|---|---|---|---|---|
| **EUROPE** | | | | | | | | | |
| Austria | 1991 | Total | 8162 | .. | .. | .. | .. | 8162 | .. |
| Austria | 1991 | Urban | 5772 | .. | .. | .. | .. | 5772 | .. |
| Austria | 1991 | Rural | 2390 | 2390 | .. | .. | .. | 2390 | .. |
| Belgium | 1991 | Total | 3748164 | ... | .. | .. | .. | 5227 | ... |
| Belgium | 1991 | Urban | 3740771 | 2145326 | 1036537 | 529662 | 29246 | 5213 | ... |
| Belgium | 1991 | Rural | 7393 | 2468 | 2775 | 2052 | 98 | 14 | ... |
| Croatia | 1991 | Total | ... | 1457370 | ... | ... | [11]9046 | ... | ... |
| Croatia | 1991 | Urban | ... | 826845 | ... | ... | [11]6748 | ... | ... |
| Croatia | 1991 | Rural | ... | 630525 | ... | ... | [11]2298 | ... | ... |
| Czech Republic | 1991 | Total | 3705681 | ... | ... | ... | ... | ... | ... |
| Czech Republic | 1991 | Urban | 2846718 | ... | ... | ... | ... | ... | ... |
| Czech Republic | 1991 | Rural | [12]858963 | ... | ... | ... | ... | ... | ... |
| Estonia[29] | 1998 | Total | 657000 | ... | ... | ... | ... | ... | ... |
| Estonia[29] | 1998 | Urban | 524800 | ... | ... | ... | ... | ... | ... |
| Estonia[29] | 1998 | Rural | 132200 | ... | ... | ... | ... | ... | ... |
| Finland[29] | 1998 | Total | 2247000 | 2247000 | ... | ... | ... | ... | ... |
| Finland[29] | 1998 | Urban | 1423000 | 1423000 | ... | ... | ... | ... | ... |
| Finland[29] | 1998 | Rural | 824000 | 824000 | ... | ... | ... | ... | ... |
| France[1] | 1999 | Total | 28696156 | ... | ... | ... | ... | ... | ... |
| France[1] | 1999 | Urban | 20797343 | ... | ... | ... | ... | ... | ... |
| France[1] | 1999 | Rural | 7898813 | ... | ... | ... | ... | ... | ... |
| Germany | 1998 | Total | 34541200 | [13]34283400 | ... | 1414000 | ... | 15243800 | ... |
| Guernsey[29] | 1996 | Total | 22216 | 21862 | ... | ... | ... | 354 | ... |
| Hungary[16] | 1996 | Total | 3997023 | 3991590 | [17]5439 | ... | ... | ... | ... |
| Hungary[16] | 1996 | Urban | 2557109 | 2554218 | [17]2891 | ... | ... | ... | ... |
| Hungary[16] | 1996 | Rural | 1439920 | 1437372 | [17]2548 | ... | ... | ... | ... |
| Ireland[29] | 1996 | Total | 1127318 | 1033191 | 81783 | 8264 | ... | 4080 | ... |
| Ireland[29] | 1996 | Urban | 672170 | 590055 | 77374 | 1993 | ... | 2748 | ... |
| Ireland[29] | 1996 | Rural | 455148 | 443136 | 4409 | 6271 | ... | 1332 | ... |
| Isle of Man[29] | 1996 | Total | 29377 | 29373 | ... | 4 | ... | ... | ... |
| Isle of Man[29] | 1996 | Urban | 21623 | 21623 | ... | ... | ... | ... | ... |
| Isle of Man[29] | 1996 | Rural | 7754 | 7750 | ... | 4 | ... | ... | ... |
| Lithuania[29] | 1999 | Total | 1400000 | ... | ... | ... | ... | ... | ... |
| The Netherlands | 1998 | Total | 6606000 | 6598900 | 700 | 4800 | 1600 | ... | ... |
| The Netherlands | 1998 | Urban | 4383700 | 4381700 | 700 | 1000 | 300 | ... | ... |
| The Netherlands | 1998 | Rural | 2222300 | 2217200 | .. | 3800 | 1300 | ... | ... |
| Norway[29] | 1990 | Total | 1751363 | 1751363 | ... | ... | ... | ... | ... |
| Norway[29] | 1990 | Urban | 1300372 | 1288597 | ... | ... | ... | ... | ... |
| Norway[29] | 1990 | Rural | 439216 | 427441 | ... | ... | ... | ... | ... |
| Malta[29] | 1995 | Total | 119479 | ... | ... | ... | ... | ... | ... |
| Poland[29] | 1995 | Total | 12500802 | ... | ... | ... | ... | ... | ... |
| Poland[29] | 1995 | Urban | 8384496 | ... | ... | ... | ... | ... | ... |
| Poland[29] | 1995 | Rural | 4116306 | ... | ... | ... | ... | ... | ... |
| Portugal | 1991 | Total | 3376733 | 3055504 | 26334 | 281564 | 1308 | 11306 | [18]717 |
| Portugal | 1991 | Urban | 1608701 | 1501870 | 16884 | 82044 | 632 | 6875 | [18]396 |
| Portugal | 1991 | Rural | 1768032 | 1553634 | 9450 | 199520 | 676 | 4431 | [18]321 |
| Slovakia[29] | 1991 | Total | 1832484 | ... | ... | ... | ... | ... | ... |
| Slovakia[29] | 1991 | Urban | 1051856 | ... | ... | ... | ... | ... | ... |
| Slovakia[29] | 1991 | Rural | 780628 | ... | ... | ... | ... | ... | ... |
| Spain | 1996 | Total | 17245314 | 17220399 | ... | ... | ... | 24915 | ... |
| Spain | 1996 | Urban | 13056997 | 13037359 | ... | ... | ... | 19638 | ... |
| Spain | 1996 | Rural | 4188317 | 4183040 | ... | ... | ... | 5277 | ... |
| Sweden | 1990 | Total | 3830035 | 3782801 | 18566 | ... | ... | ... | 28668 |
| Sweden | 1990 | Urban | 3260295 | 3222090 | 15638 | ... | ... | ... | 22567 |
| Sweden | 1990 | Rural | 569740 | 560711 | 2928 | ... | ... | ... | 6101 |
| United Kingdom[29] | 1989 | Total | 20423000 | 20423000 | ... | ... | ... | ... | ... |
| United Kingdom[29] | 1989 | Urban | 18911000 | 18911000 | ... | ... | ... | ... | ... |
| United Kingdom[29] | 1989 | Rural | 1512000 | 1512000 | ... | ... | ... | ... | ... |
| Yugoslavia[19] | 1991 | Total | 2899961 | 2686347 | ... | 199995 | ... | ... | [20]13619 |
| Yugoslavia[19] | 1991 | Urban | 1541982 | 1495332 | ... | 36051 | ... | ... | [20]10599 |
| Yugoslavia[19] | 1991 | Rural | 1357979 | 1191015 | ... | 163944 | ... | ... | [20]3020 |
| Switzerland[29] | 1991 | Total | 2841850 | ... | ... | ... | ... | ... | ... |
| Switzerland[29] | 1991 | Urban | 2058770 | ... | ... | ... | ... | ... | ... |
| Switzerland[29] | 1991 | Rural | 783080 | ... | ... | ... | ... | ... | ... |
| **LATIN AMERICA** | | | | | | | | | |
| Argentina | 1991 | Total | 8532916 | [21]6282798 | [22]1408070 | [23]85080 | [24]589374 | 17475 | 150119 |
| Argentina | 1991 | Urban | 7520603 | [21]5918795 | [22]992262 | [23]73011 | [24]391683 | 15015 | 129867 |
| Argentina | 1991 | Rural | 1012313 | [21]364003 | [22]415838 | [23]12069 | [24]197691 | 2460 | 20252 |
| Bahamas[29] | 1990 | Total | 66962 | 61906 | ... | ... | ... | ... | 88 |
| Bolivia[29] | 1997 | Total | 1822785 | 289453 | 1201117 | 325301 | 6914 | ... | ... |
| Bolivia[29] | 1997 | Urban | 1094237 | 282374 | 793269 | 12228 | 6366 | ... | ... |
| Bolivia[29] | 1997 | Rural | 728548 | 7079 | 407848 | 313073 | 548 | ... | ... |
| Brazil | 1998 | Total | 41929992 | [25]34847556 | [26]6992147 | ... | [27]39583 | 50706 | ... |
| Brazil | 1998 | Urban | 34057349 | [25]31165998 | [26]2827831 | ... | [27]24185 | 39335 | ... |
| Colombia | 1993 | Total | 6923945 | [25]6551734 | [26]337137 | ... | [27]35074 | ... | ... |
| Colombia | 1993 | Urban | 4819944 | 4517160 | 277242 | ... | 25542 | ... | ... |
| Colombia | 1993 | Rural | 2104001 | 2034574 | 59895 | ... | 9532 | ... | ... |
| Costa Rica | 1997 | Total | ... | 784128 | 776821 | 1997 | 5310 | ... | ... |
| Costa Rica | 1997 | Urban | ... | 356259 | 351771 | 1505 | 2983 | ... | ... |
| Costa Rica | 1997 | Rural | ... | 427869 | 425050 | 492 | 2327 | ... | ... |
| Dominican Republic | 1993 | Total | 1629616 | [28]1513078 | [28]113258 | ... | ... | ... | 3280 |
| Jamaica | 1991 | Total | 568569 | 563307 | ... | ... | 3029 | ... | 2233 |

# TABLE A.5

## continued

| | | | | Living quarters | | | | | |
| | | | | Type of housing unit | | | | | |
| | | | Total | Conventional | Basic | Temporary | Marginal | Collective | Not stated |
|---|---|---|---|---|---|---|---|---|---|
| Guatemala | 1994 | Total | 1805732 | 1494786 | 51031 | 227256 | 32659 | .. | .. |
| Guatemala | 1994 | Urban | 645053 | 572650 | 49555 | 8698 | 14150 | .. | .. |
| Guatemala | 1994 | Rural | 1160679 | 922136 | 1476 | 218558 | 18509 | .. | .. |
| Mexico | 1995 | Total | 19412123 | 19403409 | .. | .. | .. | 8714 | .. |
| Mexico | 1995 | Urban | 14743341 | 14736257 | .. | .. | .. | 7084 | .. |
| Mexico | 1995 | Rural | 4668782 | 4667152 | .. | .. | .. | 1630 | .. |
| Nicaragua | 1995 | Total | 721205 | 149892 | 520839 | 31523 | 18951 | .. | .. |
| Nicaragua | 1995 | Urban | 408614 | 144559 | 247159 | 4691 | 12205 | .. | .. |
| Nicaragua | 1995 | Rural | 312590 | 5332 | 273680 | 26832 | 6746 | .. | .. |
| Panama | 1990 | Total | 524284 | 460630 | 35685 | 91645 | 12839 | 725 | ... |
| Panama | 1990 | Urban | 295105 | 251811 | 29104 | 10261 | 3929 | 421 | ... |
| Panama[29] | 1990 | Rural | 229179 | 153877 | 3224 | 66310 | 5768 | 304 | |
| Puerto Rico | 1990 | Total | 1188985 | 1125318 | 63667 | .. | .. | .. | .. |
| Puerto Rico | 1990 | Urban | 851037 | 822273 | 28764 | .. | .. | .. | .. |
| Puerto Rico | 1990 | Rural | 337948 | 303045 | 34903 | .. | .. | .. | .. |
| Uruguay | 1996 | Total | 1126502 | ... | ... | ... | ... | 6459 | ... |
| Uruguay | 1996 | Urban | 1020046 | ... | ... | ... | ... | 3200 | ... |
| Uruguay | 1996 | Rural | 106456 | ... | ... | ... | ... | 3259 | ... |
| **NORTHERN AMERICA** | | | | | | | | | |
| Bermuda | 1991 | Total | 22430 | 21950 | 83 | .. | .. | 369 | 28 |
| Bermuda | 1991 | Urban | 22430 | 21950 | 83 | .. | .. | 369 | 28 |
| Canada[29] | 1998 | Total | 11690000 | ... | ... | ... | ... | ... | ... |
| Canada[29] | 1998 | Urban | 9730000 | ... | ... | ... | ... | ... | ... |
| Canada[29] | 1998 | Rural | 1960000 | ... | ... | ... | ... | ... | ... |
| Greenland[29] | 1999 | Total | 20350 | ... | ... | ... | ... | ... | ... |
| Greenland[29] | 1999 | Urban | 17467 | ... | ... | ... | ... | ... | ... |
| Greenland[29] | 1999 | Rural | 2883 | ... | ... | ... | ... | ... | ... |
| United States | 1997 | Total | 112357000 | 104865000 | 7492000 | .. | .. | .. | .. |
| United States | 1997 | Urban | 78636000 | 73251000 | 5385000 | .. | .. | .. | .. |
| United States | 1997 | Rural | 33721000 | 31614000 | 2107000 | .. | .. | .. | .. |
| **OCEANIA** | | | | | | | | | |
| Australia | 1996 | Total | 7195170 | 6906009 | ... | 113224 | ... | ... | 175937 |
| Tonga[29] | 1990 | Total | 16194 | ... | ... | ... | ... | ... | ... |
| Tonga[29] | 1990 | Urban | 3665 | ... | ... | ... | ... | ... | ... |
| Tonga[29] | 1990 | Rural | 12529 | ... | ... | ... | ... | ... | ... |
| Guam | 1990 | Total | 35223 | ... | ... | ... | ... | ... | ... |
| Guam | 1990 | Urban | 13805 | ... | ... | ... | ... | ... | ... |
| Guam | 1990 | Rural | 21418 | ... | ... | ... | ... | ... | ... |

**Source:** United Nations, Human Settlements Statistics Questionnaire 1999.

For footnotes, refer to technical notes.

# TABLE A.6

## Occupied Housing Units by Water and Toilet Facilities

| | | | | Water supply system in housing unit | | | | Toilet installation | | | | | |
| | | | | Piped water | | | | Toilet inside | | | | | |
| | | | Number of housing units | Total inside (%) | Outside but within 200 metres (%) | Without piped water (%) | Not stated (%) | Total (%) | Flush toilet (%) | Non-flush toilet (%) | Toilet outside unit (%) | Other (%) | Not stated (%) |
|---|---|---|---|---|---|---|---|---|---|---|---|---|---|
| **AFRICA** | | | | | | | | | | | | | |
| Benin | 1994 | Total | ... | ... | ... | ... | ... | 17.6 | 1.5 | 16.1 | 16.1 | 66.0 | 0.3 |
| Botswana | 1996 | Total | 276209 | 77.0 | .. | 23.0 | – | ... | 14.0 | ... | 41.0 | – | – |
| Botswana | 1996 | Urban | 140883 | 100.0 | .. | – | – | ... | 23.6 | ... | 57.7 | – | – |
| Botswana | 1996 | Rural | 135326 | 53.1 | .. | 46.9 | – | ... | 3.3 | ... | 21.6 | – | – |
| Burkina Faso | 1991 | Total | 1407164 | 4.7 | .. | 95.3 | .. | 13.4 | 0.5 | 13.0 | ... | 86.6 | ... |
| Burkina Faso | 1991 | Urban | 198310 | 32.2 | .. | 67.8 | .. | 48.2 | 3.4 | 44.8 | ... | 51.8 | ... |
| Burkina Faso | 1991 | Rural | 1208854 | 0.1 | .. | 99.9 | .. | 7.7 | 0.0 | 7.7 | ... | 92.3 | ... |
| Congo | 1984 | Total | 183727 | 33.6 | 44.3 | 22.2 | – | 6.5 | – | – | 24.8 | 59.9 | 8.8 |
| Congo | 1984 | Urban | 167715 | 34.6 | 41.1 | 24.3 | – | 9.6 | – | – | 5.1 | 78.3 | 6.9 |
| Congo | 1984 | Rural | 67077 | 5.5 | 18.4 | 76.1 | – | 0.0 | – | – | 44.4 | 41.5 | 10.8 |
| Egypt | 1996 | Total | 12702600 | [1]82.6 | [2]19.4 | [3]17.4 | – | [4]85.3 | – | – | 9.3 | 105.3 | – |
| Egypt | 1996 | Urban | 5839877 | [1]96.5 | [2]10.2 | [3]3.5 | – | [4]94.6 | – | – | 8.3 | 97.1 | – |
| Egypt | 1996 | Rural | 6862723 | [1]70.7 | [2]27.1 | [3]29.3 | – | [4]77.5 | – | – | 10.2 | 112.3 | – |
| Gambia | 1993 | Total | 116001 | 15.7 | 17.7 | 64.0 | 2.6 | 71.2 | 7.9 | 63.3 | 14.5 | 9.8 | 4.6 |
| Gambia | 1993 | Urban | 54042 | 32.0 | 29.3 | 36.3 | 2.5 | 79.3 | 15.8 | 63.6 | 14.4 | 2.6 | 3.7 |
| Gambia | 1993 | Rural | 61959 | 1.5 | 7.6 | 88.2 | 2.8 | 64.1 | 1.1 | 63.1 | 14.5 | 16.0 | 5.3 |
| Kenya | 1989 | Total | [5]100 | [6]31.9 | ... | 68.1 | ... | 6.7 | .. | .. | [7]68.5 | 24.8 | .. |
| Kenya | 1989 | Urban | [5]100 | [6]84.8 | ... | 15.2 | ... | 28.7 | .. | .. | [7]57.0 | 14.3 | .. |
| Kenya | 1989 | Rural | [5]100 | [6]16.6 | ... | 83.4 | ... | 0.4 | .. | .. | [7]71.8 | 27.8 | .. |
| Lesotho[8] | 1996 | Total | 370972 | 47.8 | 51.9 | 0.3 | ... | ... | ... | ... | ... | ... | ... |
| Libyan Arab Jamahiriya | 1995 | Total | 589427 | 89.0 | – | [9]10.5 | 0.5 | 93.4 | 93.4 | .. | 3.4 | .. | 3.2 |
| Libyan Arab Jamahiriya | 1995 | Urban | 498465 | 91.1 | – | [9]8.4 | 0.5 | – | ... | ... | – | ... | ... |
| Libyan Arab Jamahiriya | 1995 | Rural | 90962 | 77.3 | – | [9]22.4 | 0.3 | – | ... | ... | – | ... | ... |
| Mauritius | 1990 | Total | 236635 | 56.0 | [10]39.2 | [11]4.8 | – | 99.3 | 62.8 | 36.5 | ... | 0.7 | – |
| Mauritius | 1990 | Urban | 97441 | 72.4 | [10]26.1 | [11]1.5 | – | 99.7 | 83.6 | 16.1 | – | 0.3 | – |
| Mauritius | 1990 | Rural | 139194 | 44.6 | [10]48.4 | [11]7.0 | – | 98.9 | 48.2 | 50.7 | – | 1.1 | – |
| Niger | 1998 | Total | 1129126 | 15.0 | 10.8 | 74.2 | ... | 1.2 | .. | .. | 13.6 | 84.8 | 0.4 |
| Niger | 1998 | Urban | 182969 | 81.1 | 3.6 | 15.3 | ... | 6.0 | ... | ... | 63.2 | 29.5 | 1.3 |
| Niger | 1998 | Rural | 946157 | 2.2 | 12.2 | 85.6 | ... | 0.3 | .. | .. | 4.0 | 95.5 | 0.2 |
| Senegal | 1994 | Total | 777931 | [1]47.6 | [12]44.2 | [13]8.1 | – | 42.4 | 6.7 | [14]35.7 | 30.5 | [15]27.2 | – |
| Senegal | 1994 | Urban | 330828 | [1]80.0 | [12]13.7 | [13]6.3 | – | 77.4 | 15.4 | [14]62.0 | 4.3 | [15]18.3 | – |
| Senegal | 1994 | Rural | 447103 | [1]23.2 | [12]66.8 | [13]10.1 | – | 16.4 | 0.3 | [14]16.2 | 49.8 | [15]33.7 | – |
| Seychelles | 1997 | Total | 17878 | [16]85.0 | [17]12.2 | ... | 2.8 | 86.3 | 86.3 | – | 9.0 | 1.4 | 3.3 |
| Seychelles | 1997 | Urban | ... | ... | ... | ... | ... | ... | ... | ... | ... | ... | ... |
| Seychelles | 1997 | Rural | 12063 | [16]80.9 | [17]16.0 | – | 3.0 | 83.4 | 83.4 | – | 11.5 | 1.5 | 3.6 |
| South Africa[18] | 1996 | Total | 9059571 | 43.9 | [12]54.4 | 1.1 | 0.6 | – | [19]50.3 | [20]36.9 | – | 12.3 | 0.5 |
| South Africa[18] | 1996 | Urban | 5426873 | 66.0 | [12]32.7 | 0.9 | 0.5 | 0.0 | [19]78.1 | [20]17.8 | – | 3.7 | 0.5 |
| South Africa[18] | 1996 | Rural | 3632698 | 10.9 | [12]86.8 | 1.6 | 0.7 | 0.0 | [19]8.6 | [20]65.4 | – | 25.3 | 0.7 |
| St. Helena | 1998 | Total | 1577 | 95.2 | 3.0 | 1.8 | ... | 99.7 | 95.2 | 4.6 | – | 0.3 | ... |
| St. Helena | 1998 | Urban | 280 | 99.6 | 0.4 | – | ... | 100.0 | 99.3 | 0.7 | – | – | ... |
| St. Helena | 1998 | Rural | 1297 | 94.2 | 3.6 | 2.2 | ... | 99.7 | 94.3 | 5.4 | – | 0.3 | ... |
| Zimbabwe | 1997 | Total | 2510410 | ... | ... | ... | ... | ... | ... | ... | ... | ... | ... |
| Zimbabwe | 1997 | Urban | 926210 | ... | ... | ... | ... | ... | ... | ... | ... | ... | ... |
| Zimbabwe | 1997 | Rural | 1584200 | ... | ... | ... | ... | ... | ... | ... | ... | ... | ... |
| **ASIA** | | | | | | | | | | | | | |
| Armenia | 1998 | Total | [21]100 | 66.7 | 19.1 | 5.9 | 8.3 | 61.4 | 61.4 | – | 38.8 | – | – |
| Armenia | 1998 | Urban | [21]100 | 21.7 | 4.9 | 1.2 | 2.2 | 90.1 | 90.1 | – | 9.9 | – | – |
| Armenia | 1998 | Rural | [21]100 | 28.1 | 41.1 | 13.0 | 17.8 | 17.4 | 17.4 | – | 82.6 | – | – |
| Azerbaijan | 1998 | Total | 880161 | ... | ... | ... | ... | 69.1 | ... | ... | ... | ... | ... |
| Azerbaijan | 1998 | Urban | 774877 | ... | ... | ... | ... | 76.5 | ... | ... | ... | ... | ... |
| Azerbaijan | 1998 | Rural | 105284 | ... | ... | ... | ... | 14.8 | ... | ... | ... | ... | ... |
| China, Macau SAR | 1996 | Total | 113794 | ... | ... | 0.4 | ... | 99.5 | 98.3 | 1.2 | 0.4 | 0.1 | – |
| Cyprus | 1992 | Total | 185235 | 95.3 | 3.7 | [3]0.8 | 0.2 | 91.0 | 91.0 | – | 6.5 | [22]2.3 | 0.2 |
| Cyprus | 1992 | Urban | 125320 | 98.1 | 1.2 | [3]0.5 | 0.3 | 96.2 | 96.2 | – | 2.8 | [22]0.8 | 0.2 |
| Cyprus | 1992 | Rural | 59915 | 89.4 | 9.1 | [3]1.4 | 0.1 | 80.2 | 80.2 | – | 14.2 | [22]5.5 | 0.1 |
| Georgia | 1989 | Total | [23]5165723 | 59.1 | ... | ... | ... | ... | ... | ... | ... | ... | ... |
| Georgia | 1989 | Urban | [23]2821491 | 90.1 | ... | ... | ... | ... | ... | ... | ... | ... | ... |
| Georgia | 1989 | Rural | [23]2344232 | 21.9 | ... | ... | ... | ... | ... | ... | ... | ... | ... |
| Iran (Islamic Republic of) | 1996 | Total | 12280539 | 87.2 | ... | ... | ... | 98.4 | – | – | 1.6 | – | – |
| Iran (Islamic Republic of) | 1996 | Urban | 7929830 | 96.3 | ... | ... | ... | 99.6 | – | – | 0.4 | – | – |
| Iran (Islamic Republic of) | 1996 | Rural | 4350709 | 70.8 | ... | ... | ... | 96.2 | – | – | 3.8 | – | – |
| Japan | 1993 | Total | [24]40773300 | ... | ... | ... | ... | 97.2 | 74.7 | 22.5 | 1.0 | 1.7 | ... |
| Japan | 1993 | Urban | [24]32941900 | ... | ... | ... | ... | 96.7 | 81.0 | 15.8 | 1.2 | 2.1 | 0.0 |
| Japan | 1993 | Rural | [24]7831400 | ... | ... | ... | ... | [25]99.3 | 48.5 | [26]50.8 | 0.5 | – | 0.0 |
| Kazakhstan | 1998 | Total | [27]100 | 61.4 | 34.9 | 3.7 | ... | ... | ... | ... | ... | ... | ... |
| Kazakhstan | 1998 | Urban | [27]100 | 87.6 | 12.3 | 0.1 | ... | ... | ... | ... | ... | ... | ... |
| Kazakhstan | 1998 | Rural | [27]100 | 21.5 | 69.3 | 9.2 | ... | ... | ... | ... | ... | ... | ... |
| Malaysia[28] | 1991 | Total | 3526675 | 77.5 | 8.3 | 14.2 | ... | 87.6 | 46.6 | 41.0 | 7.6 | ... | 4.8 |
| Malaysia[28] | 1991 | Urban | 1954524 | 90.3 | 5.1 | 4.5 | ... | 94.1 | 68.9 | 25.2 | 4.8 | ... | 1.1 |
| Malaysia[28] | 1991 | Rural | 1572151 | 61.4 | 12.3 | 26.2 | ... | 79.5 | 18.9 | 60.6 | 11.2 | ... | 9.3 |
| Pakistan | 1998 | Total | 19344232 | 27.4 | 3.9 | 68.7 | ... | 33.0 | 31.7 | 1.3 | ... | ... | ... |
| Pakistan | 1998 | Urban | 6240469 | 58.3 | 4.7 | 36.9 | – | 35.7 | 34.7 | 1.0 | ... | ... | ... |
| Pakistan | 1998 | Rural | 13103763 | 12.7 | 3.5 | 83.8 | – | 26.3 | 24.5 | 1.9 | ... | ... | ... |
| Republic of Korea | 1995 | Total | 11354540 | 97.3 | ... | 1.5 | 1.2 | 99.4 | 75.1 | 24.4 | 0.6 | – | – |
| Republic of Korea | 1995 | Urban | 8462417 | 98.1 | ... | 0.4 | 1.5 | 99.4 | 84.2 | 15.2 | 0.6 | – | – |
| Republic of Korea | 1995 | Rural | 2892123 | 95.0 | ... | 4.6 | 0.4 | 99.6 | 43.8 | 55.8 | 0.4 | – | – |

# TABLE A.6

## continued

| | | | | Water supply system in housing unit | | | | Toilet installation | | | | | |
| | | | | Piped water | | | | Toilet inside | | | | | |
| | | | Number of housing units | Total inside (%) | Outside but within 200 metres (%) | Without piped water (%) | Not stated (%) | Total (%) | Flush toilet (%) | Non-flush toilet (%) | Toilet outside unit (%) | Other (%) | Not stated (%) |
|---|---|---|---|---|---|---|---|---|---|---|---|---|---|
| Syrian Arab Republic | 1994 | Total | 2185757 | 88.5 | 1.9 | 12.8 | – | ... | ... | ... | ... | ... | ... |
| Syrian Arab Republic | 1994 | Urban | 1178106 | 97.5 | 0.4 | 2.1 | – | ... | ... | ... | ... | ... | ... |
| Syrian Arab Republic | 1994 | Rural | 1007651 | 78.0 | 3.8 | 18.2 | – | ... | ... | ... | ... | ... | ... |
| Thailand | 1994 | Total | 15002591 | 18.7 | 2.3 | 78.9 | – | 90.6 | 6.8 | 83.7 | 6.2 | 0.6 | 2.6 |
| Thailand | 1994 | Urban | 3046293 | 48.1 | 6.2 | 45.6 | 0.1 | 84.9 | 17.3 | 67.6 | 14.7 | 0.1 | 0.3 |
| Thailand | 1994 | Rural | 11956299 | 11.2 | 1.3 | 87.4 | – | 92.0 | 4.2 | 87.8 | 4.1 | 0.7 | 3.2 |
| Turkey | 1994 | Total | 13382841 | 85.6 | ... | 14.4 | ... | ... | ... | ... | ... | ... | ... |
| Turkey | 1994 | Urban | 7515762 | 96.7 | ... | 3.3 | ... | ... | ... | ... | ... | ... | ... |
| Turkey | 1994 | Rural | 5867079 | 71.4 | ... | 28.6 | ... | ... | ... | ... | ... | ... | ... |
| **EUROPE** | | | | | | | | | | | | | |
| Austria | 1999 | Total | [29]3242400 | 99.7 | 0.3 | – | – | 96.0 | – | – | 4.0 | – | – |
| Austria | 1999 | Urban | [29]2559900 | 99.7 | 0.3 | – | – | 95.4 | – | – | 4.6 | – | – |
| Austria | 1999 | Rural | [29]682500 | 99.8 | 0.2 | – | – | 98.4 | – | – | 1.6 | – | – |
| Belgium | 1991 | Total | 3748164 | 99.6 | – | – | – | 95.7 | 91.9 | 3.8 | 3.8 | – | – |
| Belgium | 1991 | Urban | 3740771 | 99.6 | – | ... | – | 91.9 | 91.9 | 0.0 | 0.0 | – | – |
| Belgium | 1991 | Rural | 7393 | 98.9 | – | ... | – | 82.3 | 82.3 | 0.0 | 0.0 | – | – |
| Bulgaria | 1992 | Total | 2950873 | 89.4 | 9.0 | 1.6 | ... | 59.0 | – | – | 41.0 | – | – |
| Bulgaria | 1992 | Urban | 1977184 | 96.4 | 3.3 | 0.3 | ... | 82.4 | – | – | 17.6 | – | – |
| Bulgaria | 1992 | Rural | 973689 | 75.2 | 20.7 | 4.1 | ... | 11.4 | – | – | 88.6 | – | – |
| Croatia | 1991 | Total | 1544250 | 83.9 | – | 16.1 | – | 81.8 | ... | ... | ... | ... | ... |
| Croatia | 1991 | Urban | 878282 | 96.3 | – | 3.7 | – | ... | ... | ... | ... | ... | ... |
| Croatia | 1991 | Rural | 665968 | 67.6 | – | 32.4 | – | ... | ... | ... | ... | ... | ... |
| Czech Republic | 1991 | Total | 4043250 | 97.0 | 1.1 | 1.9 | 0.0 | 94.7 | 88.6 | 6.1 | 5.2 | ... | 0.1 |
| Czech Republic | 1991 | Urban | 3084245 | ... | ... | ... | ... | ... | ... | ... | ... | ... | ... |
| Czech Republic | 1991 | Rural | 959005 | ... | ... | ... | ... | ... | ... | ... | ... | ... | ... |
| Finland | 1998 | Total | 2449115 | 96.8 | ... | ... | ... | 95.0 | ... | ... | ... | ... | ... |
| Finland | 1998 | Urban | 1541437 | 98.7 | ... | ... | ... | 97.7 | ... | ... | ... | ... | ... |
| Finland | 1998 | Rural | 907678 | 93.5 | ... | ... | ... | 90.2 | ... | ... | ... | ... | ... |
| France | 1990 | Total | [24]21542152 | ... | ... | ... | ... | 93.5 | – | – | 6.5 | – | – |
| France | 1990 | Urban | [24]16276780 | ... | ... | ... | ... | 94.5 | – | – | 5.5 | – | – |
| France | 1990 | Rural | [24]5265372 | ... | ... | ... | ... | 90.6 | – | – | 9.4 | – | – |
| Germany | 1998 | Total | 34865300 | 100.0 | .. | .. | .. | ... | ... | ... | ... | ... | ... |
| Hungary[30] | 1996 | Total | 3991590 | 87.6 | ... | ... | ... | 80.6 | 80.6 | ... | ... | ... | ... |
| Hungary[30] | 1996 | Urban | 2554218 | 93.7 | ... | ... | ... | 88.6 | 88.6 | ... | ... | ... | ... |
| Hungary[30] | 1996 | Rural | 1437372 | 76.8 | ... | ... | ... | 66.4 | 66.4 | ... | ... | ... | ... |
| Ireland | 1991 | Total | 2026139 | 98.6 | ... | 1.2 | 0.2 | 97.2 | 96.4 | 0.8 | – | 2.0 | 0.8 |
| Ireland | 1991 | Urban | 1174176 | 99.9 | ... | 0.0 | 0.1 | 99.2 | 99.1 | 0.1 | – | – | 0.8 |
| Ireland | 1991 | Rural | 852053 | 96.8 | ... | 2.9 | 0.3 | 94.5 | 92.8 | 1.7 | – | 4.6 | 0.9 |
| Latvia | 1998 | Total | 279810 | ... | ... | ... | ... | ... | ... | ... | ... | ... | ... |
| Lithuania | 1999 | Total | 1306061 | 74.5 | ... | ... | ... | 72.9 | ... | ... | ... | ... | ... |
| Lithuania | 1999 | Urban | 890208 | 89.7 | ... | ... | ... | 89.5 | ... | ... | ... | ... | ... |
| Lithuania | 1999 | Rural | 415853 | 41.9 | ... | ... | ... | 37.6 | ... | ... | ... | ... | ... |
| Malta | 1995 | Total | ... | ... | ... | ... | 98.2 | 95.7 | 2.4 | 1.8 | ... | ... | |
| The Netherlands | 1993 | Total | 6676700 | 100.0 | .. | .. | .. | 100.0 | 100.0 | ... | ... | ... | ... |
| The Netherlands | 1993 | Urban | 4430200 | 100.0 | .. | .. | .. | 100.0 | 100.0 | ... | ... | ... | ... |
| The Netherlands | 1993 | Rural | 2246500 | 100.0 | .. | .. | .. | 100.0 | 100.0 | ... | ... | ... | ... |
| Norway | 1990 | Total | [24]1751363 | ... | ... | ... | ... | [31]100.0 | 96.1 | 3.9 | – | – | – |
| Norway | 1990 | Urban | [24]1300372 | ... | ... | ... | ... | [31]100.0 | 97.2 | 2.8 | – | – | – |
| Norway | 1990 | Rural | [24]439216 | ... | ... | ... | ... | [31]100.0 | 92.9 | 7.1 | – | – | – |
| Poland | 1995 | Total | 12498473 | 90.2 | ... | ... | ... | 79.0 | [32]52.9 | [33]26.2 | ... | ... | ... |
| Poland | 1995 | Urban | 8383622 | 97.1 | ... | ... | ... | 89.6 | [32]76.3 | [33]13.3 | ... | ... | ... |
| Poland | 1995 | Rural | 4114851 | 76.0 | ... | ... | ... | 57.5 | [32]5.1 | [33]52.4 | ... | ... | ... |
| Portugal | 1991 | Total | 3143272 | 86.9 | 1.8 | – | 11.3 | 88.6 | 8.1 | 7.3 | 3.3 | – | 8.1 |
| Portugal | 1991 | Urban | 1557120 | 96.0 | 0.7 | – | 3.3 | 95.3 | 91.3 | 4.0 | 2.5 | – | 2.2 |
| Portugal | 1991 | Rural | 1586152 | 77.9 | 2.9 | – | 19.2 | 82.0 | 71.5 | 10.5 | 4.1 | – | 13.9 |
| Slovakia | 1991 | Total | 1617828 | 92.7 | ... | ... | ... | 81.9 | 81.9 | – | ... | ... | ... |
| Slovakia | 1991 | Urban | 967595 | 98.4 | ... | ... | ... | 95.9 | 95.9 | – | ... | ... | ... |
| Slovakia | 1991 | Rural | 650233 | 84.3 | ... | ... | ... | 60.9 | 60.9 | – | ... | ... | ... |
| United Kingdom[34] | 1998 | Total | 48705000 | 99.1 | ... | 0.9 | ... | ... | ... | ... | ... | ... | ... |
| United Kingdom[34] | 1998 | Urban | 44992000 | 99.2 | ... | 0.8 | ... | 99.0 | 99.0 | – | – | 1.0 | ... |
| United Kingdom[34] | 1998 | Rural | 3712000 | 98.1 | ... | 1.9 | ... | 99.8 | 99.8 | – | – | 0.2 | – |
| Yugoslavia[35] | 1991 | Total | 2648617 | 85.0 | ... | 15.0 | ... | ... | ... | ... | ... | ... | ... |
| **LATIN AMERICA** | | | | | | | | | | | | | |
| Argentina | 1991 | Total | 8515441 | 77.4 | 14.9 | 5.3 | 2.4 | 98.9 | 84.4 | 14.5 | – | – | 1.1 |
| Argentina | 1991 | Urban | 7505862 | 82.4 | 12.0 | 3.5 | 2.2 | 99.0 | 88.9 | 10.1 | – | – | 1.0 |
| Argentina | 1991 | Rural | 1009579 | 39.9 | 37.1 | 18.5 | 4.5 | 97.8 | 51.1 | 46.7 | – | – | 2.2 |
| Bahamas | 1990 | Total | 61906 | 76.9 | 3.3 | 19.5 | 0.3 | 77.0 | 77.0 | – | 16.1 | 6.6 | 0.3 |
| Bahamas | 1990 | Urban | 50252 | ... | ... | ... | ... | 81.0 | 81.0 | – | 12.9 | 6.0 | 0.0 |
| Bahamas | 1990 | Rural | 11654 | ... | ... | ... | ... | 60.0 | 60.0 | – | 29.5 | 9.1 | 0.0 |
| Bolivia | 1997 | Total | 1822785 | 64.9 | 6.2 | 27.6 | 1.3 | 59.1 | 25.4 | 33.8 | ... | 40.9 | ... |
| Bolivia | 1997 | Urban | 1094237 | 88.8 | 4.9 | 5.4 | 0.9 | 78.1 | 40.7 | 37.4 | ... | 21.9 | ... |
| Bolivia | 1997 | Rural | 728548 | 29.1 | 8.1 | 61.0 | 1.8 | 30.8 | 2.4 | 28.3 | ... | 69.2 | ... |
| Brazil | 1998 | Total | 41839703 | 84.7 | 3.6 | 11.6 | ... | 91.0 | ... | ... | 9.0 | – | – |
| Brazil | 1998 | Urban | 33993829 | 92.8 | 3.3 | 3.9 | ... | 96.9 | ... | ... | 3.1 | – | – |
| Brazil | 1998 | Rural | 7845874 | 49.7 | 5.1 | 45.2 | ... | 65.5 | ... | ... | 34.5 | – | – |
| Colombia | 1993 | Total | 6885748 | 79.7 | 8.0 | 12.3 | ... | 84.9 | 75.6 | 9.3 | – | – | 15.1 |
| Colombia | 1993 | Urban | 5173367 | 93.5 | 2.3 | 4.2 | ... | 95.1 | 88.5 | 6.6 | – | – | 4.9 |
| Colombia | 1993 | Rural | 1712381 | 38.0 | 25.1 | 36.9 | ... | 54.0 | 36.6 | 17.3 | – | – | 46.0 |

# TABLE A.6

**continued**

| | Year | | | | | | | | | | | | |
|---|---|---|---|---|---|---|---|---|---|---|---|---|---|
| Costa Rica | 1997 | Total | 784128 | 97.8 | 1.9 | 0.3 | 2.2 | 89.5 | 60.5 | 29.0 | 9.3 | 0.4 | 0.8 |
| Costa Rica | 1997 | Urban | 356259 | 99.9 | 0.7 | 0.2 | 0.1 | 98.0 | 45.0 | 53.0 | 0.9 | 0.7 | 0.4 |
| Costa Rica | 1997 | Rural | 427869 | 96.1 | 2.9 | 0.4 | 3.9 | 164.0 | 73.4 | 90.6 | 16.2 | 0.2 | 1.1 |
| Dominican Republic | 1993 | Total | 1629616 | 67.2 | ... | 32.8 | ... | ... | ... | ... | ... | ... | ... |
| Guatemala | 1994 | Total | 1591823 | 62.7 | 5.7 | [11]31.6 | – | 35.2 | 29.5 | [36]5.7 | 51.8 | [37]13.0 | – |
| Guatemala | 1994 | Urban | 604029 | 87.8 | 4.3 | [11]7.9 | – | 78.3 | 64.5 | [36]8.9 | 24.1 | [37]2.6 | – |
| Guatemala | 1994 | Rural | 987794 | 47.4 | 6.6 | [11]46.0 | – | 11.9 | 8.1 | [36]3.8 | 68.7 | [37]19.4 | – |
| Jamaica | 1991 | Total | 588340 | 39.1 | 40.7 | 19.4 | 0.7 | 42.0 | 42.0 | – | 50.8 | [37]2.6 | 4.6 |
| Jamaica | 1991 | Urban | 353195 | 53.8 | 39.8 | 5.8 | 0.7 | 60.4 | 60.4 | – | 33.2 | [37]1.9 | 4.4 |
| Jamaica | 1991 | Rural | 235145 | 17.1 | 42.2 | 39.9 | 0.8 | 14.3 | 14.3 | – | 77.2 | [37]3.6 | 4.8 |
| Mexico | 1996 | Total | 20199398 | 57.3 | 28.4 | [11]4.3 | ... | 71.1 | 53.6 | 17.5 | 17.3 | 11.5 | ... |
| Mexico | 1996 | Urban | 15318401 | 69.9 | 23.5 | [11]6.6 | ... | 84.5 | 66.4 | 18.1 | 11.1 | 4.4 | ... |
| Mexico | 1996 | Rural | 4880997 | 17.6 | 43.9 | [11]38.4 | ... | 29.2 | 13.6 | 15.6 | 36.7 | 34.1 | ... |
| Nicaragua | 1998 | Total | 473434 | 44.5 | 54.5 | 0.9 | ... | 25.0 | 25.0 | ... | 14.5 | 60.5 | ... |
| Nicaragua | 1998 | Urban | 369890 | 51.0 | 48.9 | 0.1 | ... | 210.8 | 26.0 | ... | 15.4 | 58.7 | ... |
| Nicaragua | 1998 | Rural | 103544 | 21.4 | 74.8 | 3.8 | ... | 32.8 | 1.0 | ... | 0.4 | 98.7 | ... |
| Panama | 1990 | Total | 524284 | 80.7 | ... | 19.3 | ... | 50.2 | 50.2 | ... | [7]49.8 | ... | ... |
| Panama | 1990 | Urban | 295105 | 97.4 | ... | 2.6 | ... | 70.4 | 70.4 | ... | [7]29.6 | ... | ... |
| Panama | 1990 | Rural | 229179 | 59.2 | ... | 40.8 | ... | 15.9 | 15.9 | ... | [7]84.1 | ... | ... |
| Puerto Rico | 1990 | Total | 1054924 | 95.9 | ... | 1.4 | ... | 95.9 | ... | ... | ... | 4.1 | ... |
| Uruguay | 1996 | Total | 970037 | 76.8 | 8.0 | 14.6 | 0.6 | 95.6 | 81.5 | 14.1 | 4.4 | – | – |
| Uruguay | 1996 | Urban | 884794 | 83.3 | 8.5 | 7.6 | ... | 96.4 | 84.6 | 11.9 | 3.6 | – | – |
| Uruguay | 1996 | Rural | 85243 | 9.0 | 2.6 | 87.0 | 1.4 | 87.5 | 50.1 | 37.4 | 12.5 | – | – |
| **NORTHERN AMERICA** | | | | | | | | | | | | | |
| Bermuda | 1991 | Total | 22061 | 98.0 | 0.9 | 0.7 | 0.3 | ... | ... | ... | ... | ... | ... |
| Bermuda | 1991 | Urban | 22061 | 98.0 | 0.9 | 0.7 | 0.3 | ... | ... | ... | ... | ... | ... |
| Bermuda | 1991 | Rural | ... | ... | ... | ... | ... | ... | ... | ... | ... | ... | ... |
| Canada | 1997 | Total | 11580000 | 99.8 | 0.1 | ... | ... | 99.8 | ... | ... | ... | ... | ... |
| Canada | 1997 | Urban | ... | ... | ... | ... | ... | 99.8 | ... | ... | ... | ... | ... |
| Canada | 1997 | Rural | ... | ... | ... | ... | ... | 99.5 | ... | ... | ... | ... | ... |
| United States | 1997 | Total | 99487000 | [38]99.6 | ... | ... | ... | 99.7 | 99.7 | – | ... | ... | ... |
| United States | 1997 | Urban | 71317000 | [38]99.7 | ... | ... | ... | 99.7 | 99.7 | – | ... | ... | ... |
| United States | 1997 | Rural | 28170000 | [38]99.4 | ... | ... | ... | 99.7 | 99.7 | – | ... | ... | ... |
| **OCEANIA** | | | | | | | | | | | | | |
| Australia | 1998 | Total | 6999700 | 92.8 | ... | ... | ... | 63.2 | ... | ... | 11.3 | ... | ... |
| Australia | 1998 | Urban | 4293000 | 98.2 | ... | ... | ... | 63.3 | ... | ... | 10.2 | ... | ... |
| Australia | 1998 | Rural | 2706700 | 84.3 | ... | ... | ... | 63.0 | ... | ... | 13.1 | ... | ... |
| Guam | 1990 | Total | 31373 | 99.5 | 0.2 | 0.3 | – | 95.5 | 95.5 | – | 1.1 | 3.4 | – |
| Guam | 1990 | Urban | 12351 | 99.7 | 0.1 | 0.2 | – | 97.5 | 97.5 | – | 0.4 | 2.2 | – |
| Guam | 1990 | Rural | 19022 | 99.3 | 0.3 | 0.4 | – | 94.2 | 94.2 | – | 1.7 | 4.1 | – |
| Tonga | 1996 | Total | 16194 | [38]84.6 | ... | [40]61.8 | ... | ... | ... | ... | ... | ... | ... |

**Source:** United Nations, Human Settlements Statistics Questionnaire 1999.

For sources and footnotes, refer to technical notes.

## TABLE A.7

## Access to Improved Water Sources and Improved Sanitation

| | Access to improved water sources (percentage) | | | | | | Access to improved sanitation (percentage) | | | | | |
|---|---|---|---|---|---|---|---|---|---|---|---|---|
| | Total | | Urban | | Rural | | Total | | Urban | | Rural | |
| | 1990 | 2000 | 1990 | 2000 | 1990 | 2000 | 1990 | 2000 | 1990 | 2000 | 1990 | 2000 |
| **WORLD** | [1]79 | [2]82 | [1]95 | [2]94 | [1]66 | [2]71 | [1]55 | [2]60 | [1]82 | [2]86 | [1]35 | [2]38 |
| **AFRICA** | [3]57 | [4]62 | [3]84 | [4]85 | [3]44 | [4]47 | [3]61 | [4]60 | [3]85 | [4]84 | [3]49 | [4]45 |
| Algeria | ... | 94 | ... | 98 | ... | 88 | ... | 73 | ... | 90 | ... | 47 |
| Angola | ... | 38 | ... | 34 | ... | 40 | ... | 44 | ... | 70 | ... | 30 |
| Benin | ... | 63 | ... | 74 | ... | 55 | 20 | 23 | 46 | 46 | 6 | 6 |
| Botswana | 95 | ... | 100 | 100 | 91 | ... | 61 | ... | 84 | ... | 44 | ... |
| Burkina Faso | 53 | ... | 74 | 84 | 50 | ... | 24 | 29 | 88 | 88 | 14 | 16 |
| Burundi | 65 | ... | 94 | 96 | 63 | ... | 89 | ... | 67 | 79 | 90 | ... |
| Cameroon | 52 | 62 | 76 | 82 | 36 | 42 | 87 | 92 | 99 | 99 | 79 | 85 |
| Cape Verde | ... | 74 | ... | 64 | ... | 89 | ... | 71 | ... | 95 | ... | 32 |
| Central African Republic | 59 | 60 | 80 | 80 | 46 | 46 | 30 | 31 | 43 | 43 | 23 | 23 |
| Chad | ... | 27 | ... | 31 | ... | 26 | 18 | 29 | 70 | 81 | 4 | 13 |
| Comoros | 88 | 96 | 97 | 98 | 84 | 95 | 98 | 98 | 98 | 98 | 98 | 98 |
| Congo | ... | 51 | ... | 71 | ... | 17 | ... | ... | ... | 14 | ... | ... |
| Côte d'Ivoire | 65 | 77 | 89 | 90 | 49 | 65 | 49 | ... | 78 | ... | 30 | ... |
| Dem. Republic of the Congo | ... | 45 | ... | 89 | ... | 26 | ... | 20 | ... | 53 | ... | 6 |
| Djibouti | ... | 100 | ... | 100 | ... | 100 | ... | 91 | ... | 99 | ... | 50 |
| Egypt | 94 | 95 | 97 | 96 | 91 | 94 | 87 | 94 | 96 | 98 | 80 | 91 |
| Equatorial Guinea | ... | 43 | ... | 45 | ... | 42 | ... | 53 | ... | 60 | ... | 46 |
| Eritrea | ... | 46 | ... | 63 | ... | 42 | ... | 13 | ... | 66 | ... | 1 |
| Ethiopia | 22 | 24 | 77 | 77 | 13 | 13 | 13 | 15 | 58 | 58 | 6 | 6 |
| Gabon | ... | 70 | ... | 73 | ... | 55 | ... | 21 | ... | 25 | ... | 4 |
| Gambia | ... | 62 | ... | 80 | ... | 53 | ... | 37 | ... | 41 | ... | 35 |
| Ghana | 56 | 64 | 83 | 87 | 43 | 49 | 60 | 63 | 59 | 62 | 61 | 64 |
| Guinea | 45 | 48 | 72 | 72 | 36 | 36 | 55 | 58 | 94 | 94 | 41 | 41 |
| Guinea-Bissau | ... | 49 | ... | 29 | ... | 55 | ... | 47 | ... | 88 | ... | 34 |
| Kenya | 40 | 49 | 89 | 87 | 25 | 31 | 84 | 86 | 94 | 96 | 81 | 81 |
| Lesotho | ... | 91 | ... | 98 | ... | 88 | ... | 92 | ... | 93 | ... | 92 |
| Libyan Arab Jamahiriya | 71 | 72 | 72 | 72 | 68 | 68 | 97 | 97 | 97 | 97 | 96 | 96 |
| Madagascar | 44 | 47 | 85 | 85 | 31 | 31 | 36 | 42 | 70 | 70 | 25 | 30 |
| Malawi | 49 | 57 | 90 | 95 | 43 | 44 | 73 | 77 | 96 | 96 | 70 | 70 |
| Mali | 55 | 65 | 65 | 74 | 52 | 61 | 70 | 69 | 95 | 93 | 62 | 58 |
| Mauritania | 37 | 37 | 34 | 34 | 40 | 40 | 30 | 33 | 44 | 44 | 19 | 19 |
| Mauritius | 100 | 100 | 100 | 100 | 100 | 100 | 100 | 99 | 100 | 100 | 100 | 99 |
| Morocco | 75 | 82 | 94 | 100 | 58 | 58 | 62 | 75 | 95 | 100 | 31 | 42 |
| Mozambique | ... | 60 | ... | 86 | ... | 43 | ... | 43 | ... | 69 | ... | 26 |
| Namibia | 72 | 77 | 98 | 100 | 63 | 67 | 33 | 41 | 84 | 96 | 14 | 17 |
| Niger | 53 | 59 | 65 | 70 | 51 | 56 | 15 | 20 | 71 | 79 | 4 | 5 |
| Nigeria | 49 | 57 | 78 | 81 | 33 | 39 | 60 | 63 | 77 | 85 | 51 | 45 |
| Rwanda | ... | 41 | ... | 60 | ... | 40 | ... | 8 | ... | 12 | ... | 8 |
| Senegal | 72 | 78 | 90 | 92 | 60 | 65 | 57 | 70 | 86 | 94 | 38 | 48 |
| Sierra Leone | ... | 28 | ... | 23 | ... | 31 | ... | 28 | ... | 23 | ... | 31 |
| South Africa | ... | 86 | ... | 92 | ... | 80 | ... | 86 | ... | 99 | ... | 73 |
| Sudan | 67 | 75 | 86 | 86 | 60 | 69 | 58 | 62 | 87 | 87 | 48 | 48 |
| Togo | 51 | 54 | 82 | 85 | 38 | 38 | 37 | 34 | 71 | 69 | 24 | 17 |
| Tunisia | 80 | ... | 94 | ... | 61 | ... | 76 | ... | 97 | ... | 48 | ... |
| Uganda | 44 | 50 | 80 | 72 | 40 | 46 | 84 | 75 | 96 | 96 | 82 | 72 |
| United Republic of Tanzania | 50 | 54 | 80 | 80 | 42 | 42 | 88 | 90 | 97 | 98 | 86 | 86 |
| Western Sahara | ... | ... | 89 | ... | ... | ... | ... | ... | ... | ... | ... | ... |
| Zambia | 52 | 64 | 88 | 88 | 28 | 48 | 63 | 78 | 86 | 99 | 48 | 64 |
| Zimbabwe | 77 | 85 | 99 | 100 | 68 | 77 | 64 | 68 | 98 | 99 | 51 | 51 |
| **ASIA** | [5]76 | [6]81 | [5]94 | [6]93 | [5]67 | [6]75 | [5]37 | [6]48 | [5]67 | [6]78 | [5]23 | [6]31 |
| Afghanistan | ... | 13 | ... | 19 | ... | 11 | ... | 12 | ... | 25 | ... | 8 |
| Bangladesh | 91 | 97 | 98 | 99 | 89 | 97 | 37 | 53 | 78 | 82 | 27 | 44 |
| Bhutan | ... | 62 | ... | 86 | ... | 60 | ... | 69 | ... | 65 | ... | 70 |
| Cambodia | ... | 30 | ... | 53 | ... | 25 | ... | 18 | ... | 58 | ... | 10 |
| China | 71 | 75 | 99 | 94 | 60 | 66 | 29 | 38 | 57 | ... | 18 | 24 |
| Cyprus | 100 | 100 | 100 | 100 | 100 | 100 | 100 | 100 | 100 | 100 | 100 | 100 |
| Dem. People's Rep. of Korea | ... | 100 | ... | 100 | ... | 100 | ... | 99 | ... | 99 | ... | 100 |
| India | 78 | 88 | 92 | 92 | 73 | 86 | 21 | ... | 58 | 73 | 8 | 14 |
| Indonesia | 69 | 76 | 90 | 91 | 60 | 65 | 54 | 66 | 76 | 87 | 44 | 52 |
| Iran (Islamic Republic of) | 86 | 95 | 95 | 99 | 75 | 89 | 81 | 81 | 86 | 86 | 74 | 74 |
| Iraq | ... | 85 | ... | 96 | ... | 48 | ... | 79 | ... | 93 | ... | 31 |
| Jordan | 97 | 96 | 99 | 100 | 92 | 84 | 98 | 99 | 100 | 100 | 95 | 98 |
| Kazakhstan | ... | 91 | ... | 98 | ... | 82 | ... | 99 | ... | 100 | ... | 98 |
| Kyrgyzstan | ... | 77 | ... | 98 | ... | 66 | ... | 100 | ... | 100 | ... | 100 |
| Lao, People's Dem. Republic | ... | 90 | ... | 59 | ... | 100 | ... | 46 | ... | 84 | ... | 34 |
| Lebanon | ... | 100 | ... | 100 | ... | 100 | ... | 99 | ... | 100 | ... | 87 |
| Malaysia | ... | ... | ... | ... | ... | 94 | ... | ... | ... | ... | ... | 98 |
| Maldives | ... | 100 | ... | 100 | ... | 100 | ... | 56 | ... | 100 | ... | 41 |
| Mongolia | ... | 60 | ... | 77 | ... | 30 | ... | 30 | ... | 46 | ... | 2 |
| Myanmar | 64 | 68 | 88 | 88 | 56 | 60 | 45 | 46 | 65 | 65 | 38 | 39 |
| Nepal | 66 | 81 | 96 | 85 | 63 | 80 | 21 | 27 | 68 | 75 | 16 | 20 |
| Oman | 37 | 39 | 41 | 41 | 30 | 30 | 84 | 92 | 98 | 98 | 61 | 61 |
| Pakistan | 84 | 88 | 96 | 96 | 79 | 84 | 34 | 61 | 78 | 94 | 13 | 42 |
| Philippines | 87 | 87 | 94 | 92 | 81 | 80 | 74 | 83 | 85 | 92 | 64 | 71 |
| Republic of Korea | ... | 92 | ... | 97 | ... | 71 | ... | 63 | ... | 76 | ... | 4 |
| Saudi Arabia | ... | 95 | ... | 100 | ... | 64 | ... | 100 | ... | 100 | ... | 100 |
| Singapore | 100 | 100 | 100 | 100 | ... | ... | 100 | 100 | 100 | 100 | ... | ... |
| Sri Lanka | 66 | 83 | 90 | 91 | 59 | 80 | 82 | 83 | 93 | 91 | 79 | 80 |
| Syrian Arab Republic | ... | 80 | ... | 94 | ... | 64 | ... | 90 | ... | 98 | ... | 81 |
| Thailand | 71 | 80 | 83 | 89 | 68 | 77 | 86 | 96 | 97 | 97 | 83 | 96 |

# TABLE A.7

## continued

| | | | | | | | | | | | | |
|---|---|---|---|---|---|---|---|---|---|---|---|---|
| Turkey | 80 | 83 | 82 | 82 | 76 | 84 | 87 | 91 | 98 | 98 | 70 | 70 |
| Uzbekistan | ... | 85 | ... | 96 | ... | 78 | ... | 100 | ... | 100 | ... | 100 |
| Viet Nam | 48 | 56 | 81 | 81 | 40 | 50 | 73 | 73 | 86 | 86 | 70 | 70 |
| Yemen | 66 | 69 | 85 | 85 | 60 | 64 | 39 | 45 | 80 | 87 | 27 | 31 |
| **EUROPE** | [7]100 | [8]96 | [7]100 | [8]100 | [7]100 | [8]87 | [7]100 | [8]92 | [7]100 | [8]99 | [7]100 | [8]74 |
| Andorra | ... | 100 | ... | 100 | ... | 100 | ... | 100 | ... | 100 | ... | 100 |
| Austria | 100 | 100 | 100 | 100 | 100 | 100 | 100 | 100 | 100 | 100 | 100 | 100 |
| Belarus | ... | 100 | ... | 100 | ... | ... | ... | ... | ... | ... | ... | ... |
| Bulgaria | ... | 100 | ... | 100 | ... | 100 | ... | 100 | ... | 100 | ... | 100 |
| Denmark | ... | 100 | ... | 100 | ... | 100 | ... | ... | ... | ... | ... | ... |
| Estonia | ... | ... | ... | ... | ... | ... | ... | ... | ... | 93 | ... | ... |
| Finland | 100 | 100 | 100 | 100 | 100 | 100 | 100 | 100 | 100 | 100 | 100 | 100 |
| Hungary | 99 | 99 | 100 | 100 | 98 | 98 | 99 | 99 | 100 | 100 | 98 | 98 |
| Malta | 100 | 100 | 100 | 100 | 100 | 100 | 100 | 100 | 100 | 100 | 100 | 100 |
| Monaco | ... | 100 | ... | 100 | ... | 100 | ... | 100 | ... | 100 | ... | 100 |
| The Netherlands | 100 | 100 | 100 | 100 | 100 | 100 | 100 | 100 | 100 | 100 | 100 | 100 |
| Norway | 100 | 100 | 100 | 100 | 100 | 100 | ... | ... | 100 | ... | ... | 100 |
| Republic of Moldova | ... | 100 | ... | 100 | ... | 100 | ... | 100 | ... | 100 | ... | 100 |
| Romania | ... | 58 | ... | 91 | ... | 16 | ... | 53 | ... | 86 | ... | 10 |
| Russian Federation | ... | 99 | ... | 100 | ... | 96 | ... | ... | ... | ... | ... | ... |
| Slovakia | ... | 100 | ... | 100 | ... | 100 | ... | 100 | ... | 100 | ... | 100 |
| Slovenia | 100 | 100 | 100 | 100 | 100 | 100 | ... | ... | 100 | ... | ... | ... |
| Sweden | 100 | 100 | 100 | 100 | 100 | 100 | 100 | 100 | 100 | 100 | 100 | 100 |
| Switzerland | 100 | 100 | 100 | 100 | 100 | 100 | 100 | 100 | 100 | 100 | 100 | 100 |
| United Kingdom | 100 | 100 | 100 | 100 | 100 | 100 | 100 | 100 | 100 | 100 | 100 | 100 |
| **LATIN AMERICA** | [9]82 | [10]85 | [9]92 | [10]93 | [9]56 | [10]62 | [9]72 | [10]78 | [9]85 | [10]87 | [9]39 | [10]49 |
| Anguilla | ... | 60 | ... | 60 | ... | 60 | ... | 99 | ... | 99 | ... | 99 |
| Antigua and Barbuda | ... | 91 | ... | 95 | ... | 88 | ... | 96 | ... | 98 | ... | 94 |
| Argentina | ... | 79 | ... | 85 | ... | 30 | ... | 85 | ... | 89 | ... | 48 |
| Aruba | ... | 100 | ... | ... | ... | ... | ... | ... | ... | ... | ... | ... |
| Bahamas | ... | 96 | ... | 98 | ... | 86 | ... | 93 | ... | 93 | ... | 94 |
| Barbados | 100 | 100 | 100 | 100 | 100 | 100 | 100 | 100 | 100 | 100 | 100 | 100 |
| Belize | ... | 76 | ... | 83 | ... | 69 | ... | 42 | ... | 59 | ... | 21 |
| Bolivia | 74 | 79 | 92 | 93 | 52 | 55 | 55 | 66 | 77 | 82 | 28 | 38 |
| Brazil | 82 | 87 | 93 | 95 | 50 | 54 | 72 | 77 | 84 | 85 | 37 | 40 |
| British Virgin Islands | ... | 98 | ... | 98 | ... | 98 | ... | 100 | ... | 100 | ... | 100 |
| Chile | 90 | 94 | 98 | 99 | 48 | 66 | 97 | 97 | 98 | 98 | 93 | 93 |
| Colombia | 87 | 91 | 95 | 98 | 68 | 73 | 82 | 85 | 95 | 97 | 53 | 51 |
| Costa Rica | ... | 98 | ... | 98 | ... | 98 | ... | 96 | ... | 98 | ... | 95 |
| Cuba | ... | 95 | ... | 99 | ... | 82 | ... | 95 | ... | 96 | ... | 91 |
| Dominica | ... | 97 | ... | 100 | ... | 90 | ... | ... | ... | ... | ... | ... |
| Dominican Republic | 78 | 79 | 83 | 83 | 70 | 70 | 60 | 71 | 66 | 75 | 52 | 64 |
| Ecuador | ... | 71 | ... | 81 | ... | 51 | ... | 59 | ... | 70 | ... | 37 |
| El Salvador | ... | 74 | ... | 88 | 47 | 61 | ... | 83 | ... | 88 | ... | 78 |
| French Guiana | ... | 84 | ... | 88 | ... | 71 | ... | 79 | ... | 85 | ... | 57 |
| Grenada | ... | 94 | ... | 97 | ... | 93 | ... | 97 | ... | 96 | ... | 97 |
| Guadeloupe | ... | 94 | ... | 94 | ... | 94 | ... | 61 | ... | 61 | ... | 61 |
| Guatemala | 78 | 92 | 88 | 97 | 72 | 88 | 77 | 85 | 94 | 98 | 66 | 76 |
| Guyana | ... | 94 | ... | 98 | ... | 91 | ... | 87 | ... | 97 | ... | 81 |
| Haiti | 46 | 46 | 55 | 49 | 42 | 45 | 25 | 28 | 48 | 50 | 15 | 16 |
| Honduras | 84 | 90 | 90 | 97 | 79 | 82 | ... | 77 | 85 | 94 | ... | 57 |
| Jamaica | ... | 71 | ... | 81 | ... | 59 | ... | 84 | ... | 98 | 28 | 66 |
| Mexico | 83 | 86 | 92 | 94 | 61 | 63 | 69 | 73 | 85 | 87 | 28 | 32 |
| Montserrat | 100 | 100 | 100 | 100 | 100 | 100 | 100 | 100 | 100 | 100 | 100 | 100 |
| Nicaragua | 70 | 79 | 93 | 95 | 44 | 59 | 76 | 84 | 97 | 96 | 53 | 68 |
| Panama | ... | 87 | ... | 88 | ... | 86 | ... | 94 | ... | 99 | ... | 87 |
| Paraguay | 63 | 79 | 80 | 95 | 47 | 58 | 89 | 95 | 92 | 95 | 87 | 95 |
| Peru | 72 | 77 | 84 | 87 | 47 | 51 | 64 | 76 | 81 | 90 | 26 | 40 |
| Saint Kitts and Nevis | ... | 98 | ... | ... | ... | ... | ... | 96 | ... | ... | ... | ... |
| Saint Lucia | ... | 98 | ... | ... | ... | ... | ... | ... | ... | ... | ... | ... |
| Saint Vincent and the Grenadines | ... | 93 | ... | ... | ... | ... | ... | 96 | ... | ... | ... | ... |
| Suriname | ... | 95 | ... | 94 | ... | 96 | ... | 83 | ... | 100 | ... | 34 |
| Trinidad and Tobago | ... | 86 | ... | ... | ... | ... | ... | 88 | ... | 98 | ... | 94 |
| Turks and Caicos Islands | ... | 100 | ... | 100 | ... | 100 | ... | 96 | ... | 96 | ... | 89 |
| Uruguay | ... | 98 | ... | 98 | ... | 93 | ... | 95 | ... | 75 | ... | 69 |
| Venezuela | ... | 84 | ... | 88 | ... | 58 | ... | 74 | ... | ... | ... | ... |
| **NORTHERN AMERICA** | [11]100 | [12]100 | [11]100 | [12]100 | [11]100 | [12]100 | [11]100 | [12]100 | [11]100 | [12]100 | [11]100 | [12]100 |
| Canada | 100 | 100 | 100 | 100 | 99 | 99 | 100 | 100 | 100 | 100 | 99 | 99 |
| United States of America | 100 | 100 | 100 | 100 | 100 | 100 | 100 | 100 | 100 | 100 | 100 | 100 |
| **OCEANIA** | [13]88 | [14]88 | [13]100 | [14]98 | [13]62 | [14]63 | [13]96 | [14]93 | [13]99 | [14]99 | [13]89 | [14]81 |
| American Samoa | 100 | 100 | 100 | 100 | 100 | 100 | ... | ... | ... | ... | ... | ... |
| Australia | 100 | 100 | 100 | 100 | 100 | 100 | 100 | 100 | 100 | 100 | 100 | 100 |
| Cook Islands | 100 | 100 | 100 | 100 | 100 | 100 | 100 | 100 | 100 | 100 | 100 | 100 |
| Fiji | ... | 47 | ... | 43 | ... | 51 | ... | 43 | ... | 75 | ... | 12 |
| French Polynesia | ... | 100 | ... | 100 | ... | 100 | ... | 98 | 100 | 99 | ... | 97 |
| Kiribati | ... | 47 | ... | 82 | ... | 25 | ... | 48 | ... | 54 | ... | 44 |
| New Zealand | ... | ... | 100 | 100 | ... | ... | ... | ... | ... | ... | ... | ... |
| Niue | 100 | 100 | 100 | 100 | 100 | 100 | 100 | 100 | 100 | 100 | 100 | 92 |
| Northern Mariana Islands | ... | ... | ... | ... | ... | ... | ... | ... | ... | ... | ... | ... |
| Palau | ... | 79 | ... | 100 | ... | 20 | ... | 100 | ... | 100 | ... | 100 |
| Papua New Guinea | 42 | 42 | 88 | 88 | 32 | 32 | 82 | 82 | 92 | 92 | 80 | 80 |
| Samoa | ... | 99 | ... | 95 | ... | 100 | ... | 99 | ... | 95 | ... | 100 |
| Solomon Islands | ... | 71 | ... | 94 | ... | 65 | ... | 34 | ... | 98 | ... | 18 |
| Tokelau | ... | 48 | ... | 97 | ... | 48 | ... | ... | ... | ... | ... | ... |
| Tonga | ... | 100 | ... | 100 | ... | 100 | ... | ... | ... | ... | ... | ... |
| Tuvalu | ... | 100 | ... | 100 | ... | 100 | ... | 100 | ... | 100 | ... | 100 |
| Vanuatu | ... | 88 | ... | 63 | ... | 94 | ... | 100 | ... | 100 | ... | 100 |
| Wallis and Futuna Islands | ... | 100 | ... | ... | ... | ... | ... | 80 | ... | ... | ... | ... |

**Source:** WHO/UNICEF, Global Water Supply and Sanitation Assessment 2000 Report.
For footnotes, refer to technical notes.

## TABLE A.8

### Energy and Transport

| | Motor vehicles (per 1000 people) | | | Motor vehicles (per km of road) | | | Commercial energy production (kt of oil equivalent) | | | Commercial energy use (kg of oil equivalent per capita) | | |
|---|---|---|---|---|---|---|---|---|---|---|---|---|
| | 1990 | 1995 | 1998 | 1990 | 1995 | 1998 | 1990 | 1995 | 1998 | 1990 | 1995 | 1998 |
| **AFRICA** | | | | | | | | | | | | |
| Algeria | ... | 53 | ... | ... | 15 | ... | 83329 | 103520 | 109631 | 885.8 | 958.0 | 866.1 |
| Angola | 19 | 20 | ... | ... | 3 | ... | 15766 | 28873 | 31354 | 615.1 | 608.6 | 558.1 |
| Benin | 3 | 7 | ... | 2 | 5 | ... | 1704 | 1774 | 1852 | 386.6 | 354.2 | 341.4 |
| Botswana | 19 | 41 | ... | 3 | 3 | ... | ... | ... | ... | ... | ... | ... |
| Burkina Faso | 4 | 5 | ... | 3 | 4 | ... | ... | ... | ... | ... | ... | ... |
| Cameroon | 10 | 12 | ... | 3 | 5 | ... | 12110 | 12596 | 10654 | 453.8 | 440.9 | 415.6 |
| Cape Verde | 8 | 9 | ... | 3 | 3 | ... | ... | ... | ... | ... | ... | ... |
| Central African Republic | ... | 1 | ... | ... | 1 | ... | ... | ... | ... | ... | ... | ... |
| Chad | 5 | 8 | ... | ... | 1 | ... | ... | ... | ... | ... | ... | ... |
| Comoros | 10 | 18 | ... | 7 | 14 | ... | ... | ... | ... | ... | ... | ... |
| Côte d'Ivoire | 23 | 28 | ... | 6 | 8 | ... | 3801 | 3402 | 4201 | 385.8 | 395.0 | 379.1 |
| Congo | 18 | 20 | ... | 3 | 4 | ... | 6762 | 9008 | 10371 | 518.2 | 503.2 | 467.0 |
| Dem. Republic of the Congo | ... | ... | ... | ... | ... | ... | 10660 | 11978 | 13673 | 318.4 | 317.4 | 314.3 |
| Djibouti | 16 | 20 | ... | 2 | 4 | ... | ... | ... | ... | ... | ... | ... |
| Egypt | 26 | 28 | ... | 33 | 29 | ... | 50962 | 54869 | 59923 | 547.2 | 608.2 | 607.1 |
| Equatorial Guinea | 3 | 4 | ... | 1 | 1 | ... | ... | ... | ... | ... | ... | ... |
| Eritrea | 1 | 2 | ... | 1 | 1 | ... | ... | ... | ... | ... | ... | ... |
| Ethiopia | 1 | 1 | 2 | 2 | 3 | 4 | 12103 | 14215 | 15525 | 293.4 | 297.1 | 295.0 |
| Gabon | 26 | 29 | ... | 4 | 5 | ... | 9433 | 14464 | 19422 | 1845.4 | 1320.8 | 1364.3 |
| Gambia | 14 | 16 | ... | 5 | 6 | ... | ... | ... | ... | ... | ... | ... |
| Ghana | ... | 7 | ... | ... | 4 | ... | 3567 | 4392 | 5563 | 343.0 | 351.9 | 392.3 |
| Guinea | 4 | 5 | ... | 1 | 1 | ... | ... | ... | ... | ... | ... | ... |
| Guinea-Bissau | 7 | 10 | ... | 2 | 3 | ... | ... | ... | ... | ... | ... | ... |
| Kenya | 13 | 14 | ... | 5 | 6 | ... | 9024 | 10272 | 11145 | 546.7 | 529.8 | 484.4 |
| Lesotho | 11 | 16 | ... | 4 | 7 | ... | ... | ... | ... | ... | ... | ... |
| Liberia | 15 | 12 | ... | 4 | 4 | ... | ... | ... | ... | ... | ... | ... |
| Libya | ... | 259 | ... | ... | 47 | ... | 57335 | 73268 | 77950 | 2772.3 | 2659.6 | 3202.3 |
| Madagascar | 6 | 5 | ... | 2 | 2 | ... | ... | ... | ... | ... | ... | ... |
| Malawi | 4 | 5 | ... | 2 | 2 | ... | ... | ... | ... | ... | ... | ... |
| Mali | 4 | 5 | ... | 2 | 3 | ... | ... | ... | ... | ... | ... | ... |
| Mauritania | 9 | 11 | ... | 3 | 4 | ... | ... | ... | ... | ... | ... | ... |
| Mauritius | 60 | 79 | 92 | 35 | 47 | 57 | ... | ... | ... | ... | ... | ... |
| Morocco | 37 | 48 | ... | 15 | 21 | ... | 874 | 773 | 838 | 250.3 | 280.5 | 313.7 |
| Mozambique | 4 | 2 | ... | 2 | 1 | ... | 7236 | 6847 | 6981 | 569.5 | 517.1 | 473.6 |
| Namibia | 71 | 81 | ... | 2 | ... | ... | ... | ... | ... | ... | ... | ... |
| Niger | 6 | 6 | ... | 4 | 5 | ... | ... | ... | ... | ... | ... | ... |
| Nigeria | ... | 28 | ... | ... | 14 | ... | 128447 | 150453 | 169260 | 743.8 | 737.0 | 747.5 |
| Rwanda | 2 | 3 | ... | 1 | 2 | ... | ... | ... | ... | ... | ... | ... |
| Sao Tome and Principe | 35 | 41 | ... | 15 | 17 | ... | ... | ... | ... | ... | ... | ... |
| Senegal | 11 | 13 | ... | 6 | 8 | ... | 1185 | 1362 | 1569 | 309.2 | 302.0 | 300.2 |
| Seychelles | 102 | 116 | ... | 29 | 32 | ... | ... | ... | ... | ... | ... | ... |
| Sierra Leone | 10 | 9 | ... | 4 | 4 | ... | ... | ... | ... | ... | ... | ... |
| Somalia | 2 | 1 | ... | 1 | ... | ... | ... | ... | ... | ... | ... | ... |
| South Africa | 160 | 132 | ... | 26 | 17 | ... | 109526 | 114534 | 133663 | 2770.6 | 2591.7 | 2663.6 |
| Sudan | 9 | 10 | ... | 22 | 27 | ... | 8033 | 8775 | 9373 | 442.8 | 441.9 | 411.6 |
| Swaziland | 72 | 66 | ... | 18 | 16 | ... | ... | ... | ... | ... | ... | ... |
| Togo | 24 | 27 | ... | 11 | 14 | ... | ... | ... | ... | ... | ... | ... |
| Tunisia | 48 | 60 | ... | 19 | 24 | ... | 6910 | 6080 | 5757 | 643.2 | 696.8 | 723.4 |
| Uganda | 2 | 4 | ... | ... | ... | ... | ... | ... | ... | ... | ... | ... |
| United Republic of Tanzania | 5 | 5 | ... | 2 | 2 | ... | 10579 | 11785 | 13055 | 517.2 | 491.9 | 464.8 |
| Zambia | 15 | 22 | ... | 3 | 6 | ... | 4834 | 4816 | 5360 | 771.0 | 670.6 | 643.7 |
| Zimbabwe | ... | 31 | ... | ... | 19 | ... | 6344 | 8102 | 8244 | 892.9 | 916.6 | 892.5 |
| **ASIA** | | | | | | | | | | | | |
| Afghanistan | ... | 3 | ... | ... | 3 | ... | ... | ... | ... | ... | ... | ... |
| Armenia | 5 | 2 | ... | 2 | 1 | ... | 1512 | 137 | 245 | 1478.9 | 2240.1 | 444.4 |
| Azerbaijan | 52 | 48 | 47 | 7 | 15 | 15 | 24697 | 20363 | 14725 | 4927.1 | 3190.5 | 1691.5 |
| Bahrain | 265 | 304 | 305 | 49 | 61 | 62 | 6180 | 7195 | 7473 | 10969.4 | 10982.1 | 10173.3 |
| Bangladesh | 1 | 1 | ... | 1 | 1 | ... | 15744 | 18778 | 21495 | 176.8 | 189.7 | 198.8 |
| Bhutan | ... | 2 | ... | ... | 3 | ... | ... | ... | ... | ... | ... | ... |
| Brunei | 463 | ... | ... | 119 | ... | ... | 16008 | 15477 | 18213 | 6524.7 | 5743.2 | 6717.7 |
| Cambodia | 1 | 5 | ... | ... | 1 | ... | ... | ... | ... | ... | ... | ... |
| China | 5 | 8 | ... | 5 | 6 | ... | 761906 | 894086 | 1072980 | 678.5 | 763.5 | 891.2 |
| China, Hong Kong SAR | 33 | 77 | 77 | 253 | 280 | 279 | 42 | 43 | 47 | 1396.1 | 1832.8 | 2243.2 |
| China, Macau SAR | ... | 97 | 122 | ... | ... | ... | ... | ... | ... | ... | ... | ... |
| Cyprus | 441 | 501 | 544 | 28 | 32 | 34 | 7 | 6 | 15 | 1659.0 | 2255.5 | 2701.2 |
| Georgia | 108 | 92 | ... | 27 | 23 | ... | 1903 | 1330 | 566 | 1157.7 | 1939.5 | 271.2 |
| India | 4 | 7 | ... | 2 | 3 | ... | 278285 | 333567 | 386180 | 382.0 | 423.6 | 469.9 |
| Indonesia | 16 | 20 | ... | 10 | 11 | ... | 135281 | 167501 | 208281 | 449.3 | 554.6 | 644.0 |
| Iran (Islamic Republic of) | 29 | 35 | ... | 14 | 15 | ... | 127722 | 181329 | 221122 | 1148.6 | 1329.8 | 1661.3 |
| Iraq | ... | 56 | ... | 6 | 24 | ... | 74960 | 106715 | 31126 | 1180.5 | 1152.8 | 1207.3 |
| Israel | 203 | 248 | 264 | 74 | 95 | 100 | 282 | 433 | 565 | 1939.1 | 2558.6 | 3083.3 |
| Japan | 469 | 537 | 560 | 52 | 59 | ... | 67655 | 75589 | 99059 | 3039.5 | 3551.9 | 3962.3 |
| Jordan | 55 | 62 | ... | 26 | 39 | ... | 1 | 104 | 194 | 1068.1 | 1086.8 | 1029.8 |
| Kazakhstan | 74 | 92 | 82 | 8 | 10 | 11 | 85939 | 89613 | 62773 | 6234.3 | 6485.7 | 3424.0 |
| Kuwait | ... | 462 | ... | ... | 159 | ... | 58887 | 66862 | 112394 | 7774.5 | 6179.8 | 9885.2 |
| Kyrgyzstan | 45 | 36 | ... | 10 | 9 | ... | 2321 | 2378 | 1383 | 476.0 | 426.6 | 587.5 |
| Lao People's Dem. Republic | 9 | 5 | ... | 3 | 1 | ... | ... | ... | ... | ... | ... | ... |
| Lebanon | 788 | 786 | ... | 183 | 202 | ... | 155 | 143 | 186 | 850.4 | 631.9 | 1149.6 |
| Malaysia | 127 | 155 | ... | 26 | 33 | ... | 34141 | 49020 | 64742 | 1087.3 | 1317.1 | 1692.0 |

# TABLE A.8

**continued**

| | | | | | | | | | | | | |
|---|---|---|---|---|---|---|---|---|---|---|---|---|
| Maldives | 7 | 8 | ... | ... | ... | ... | ... | ... | ... | ... | ... | ... |
| Mongolia | 20 | 24 | 30 | 1 | 1 | 2 | ... | ... | ... | ... | ... | ... |
| Myanmar | ... | 2 | ... | ... | 3 | ... | 10670 | 10936 | 11803 | 281.6 | 266.2 | 285.4 |
| Nepal | ... | ... | ... | ... | ... | ... | 5002 | 5636 | 6355 | 315.8 | 310.8 | 327.4 |
| Oman | 105 | 146 | ... | 9 | 10 | ... | 26750 | 38060 | 48402 | 1770.9 | 2669.3 | 2937.2 |
| Pakistan | 6 | 7 | 8 | 4 | 4 | 4 | 26111 | 34343 | 40128 | 346.4 | 400.4 | 432.8 |
| Philippines | 10 | 27 | 31 | 4 | 11 | 11 | 14947 | 15903 | 16772 | 418.6 | 452.0 | 499.9 |
| Qatar | ... | 336 | ... | ... | 157 | ... | 20492 | 26113 | 32301 | 14343.6 | 11831.3 | 17963.4 |
| Republic of Korea | 79 | 188 | 226 | 60 | 114 | 120 | 15048 | 22252 | 21151 | 1307.4 | 2132.1 | 3293.5 |
| Saudi Arabia | 166 | 167 | ... | 19 | 18 | ... | 200790 | 368753 | 470729 | 4217.8 | 4004.0 | 4408.1 |
| Singapore | 147 | 163 | ... | 142 | 163 | ... | ... | ... | ... | 3147.8 | 4937.7 | 7179.3 |
| Sri Lanka | 20 | 28 | 34 | 4 | 5 | 7 | 3775 | 4191 | 4022 | 313.1 | 322.3 | 337.2 |
| Syrian Arab Republic | 24 | 26 | ... | 10 | 11 | ... | 9661 | 22570 | 34292 | 856.8 | 984.5 | 1001.0 |
| Tajikistan | 3 | 2 | ... | 1 | 1 | ... | 2047 | 1868 | 1325 | 651.7 | 616.3 | 562.6 |
| Thailand | 46 | 93 | ... | 36 | 90 | ... | 17698 | 26541 | 38973 | 519.4 | 786.1 | 1191.7 |
| Turkey | 49 | 65 | 81 | 8 | 11 | 10 | 21672 | 25682 | 26139 | 773.1 | 935.4 | 1026.2 |
| Turkmenistan | ... | ... | ... | ... | ... | ... | 73395 | 74456 | 33517 | 5470.0 | 5158.9 | 3231.8 |
| United Arab Emirates | 14 | 14 | ... | 52 | 52 | ... | 73621 | 123986 | 141675 | 11865.1 | 11660.5 | 11728.7 |
| Uzbekistan | ... | ... | ... | ... | ... | ... | 32303 | 38657 | 47220 | 2105.0 | 2130.0 | 1803.8 |
| Viet Nam | ... | ... | ... | ... | ... | ... | 19755 | 24677 | 34364 | 363.2 | 369.4 | 397.4 |
| Yemen | 31 | 31 | ... | 8 | 8 | ... | 69 | 9792 | 18021 | 228.0 | 224.4 | 207.0 |
| **EUROPE** | | | | | | | | | | | | |
| Albania | 12 | 28 | 40 | ... | 5 | 8 | 2879 | 2355 | 1000 | 938.1 | 782.1 | 338.0 |
| Austria | 422 | 484 | 521 | 30 | 30 | 13 | 7474 | 8379 | 8537 | 3071.9 | 3326.4 | 3267.7 |
| Belarus | 60 | 92 | ... | 13 | 19 | ... | 4800 | 3705 | 3316 | 3897.4 | 4195.9 | 2389.0 |
| Belgium | 424 | 463 | 485 | 30 | 33 | ... | 13955 | 12801 | 11665 | 4532.7 | 4858.4 | 5169.1 |
| Bosnia and Herzegovina | 113 | 17 | ... | 24 | 3 | ... | ... | 263 | 626 | 106.1 | 169.2 | 512.4 |
| Bulgaria | 158 | 226 | 252 | 39 | 51 | 56 | 9530 | 9796 | 10029 | 3463.1 | 3111.5 | 2726.7 |
| Croatia | ... | ... | ... | ... | ... | ... | 1674 | 1951 | 4184 | 546.1 | 611.1 | 1524.7 |
| Czech Republic | 246 | 322 | 402 | 46 | 59 | 32 | 44309 | 38961 | 31819 | 4725.3 | 4344.3 | 3842.2 |
| Denmark | 368 | 388 | 413 | 27 | 3 | 3 | 4879 | 9983 | 15497 | 3895.0 | 3556.8 | 3881.2 |
| Estonia | 207 | 309 | 372 | 22 | 30 | 11 | 6207 | 5415 | 3263 | 3709.6 | 6469.1 | 3481.1 |
| Finland | 440 | 426 | 448 | 29 | 28 | 30 | 10376 | 11723 | 12926 | 5406.8 | 5778.8 | 5729.1 |
| France | 495 | 519 | ... | 32 | 34 | ... | 85951 | 110750 | 126927 | 3628.2 | 4011.6 | 4152.0 |
| Germany | 499 | 522 | ... | 53 | 67 | ... | 209579 | 185686 | 142489 | 4649.4 | 4478.4 | 4162.9 |
| Greece | 248 | 295 | ... | 22 | 27 | ... | 6954 | 8802 | 9024 | 1868.9 | 2170.7 | 2263.4 |
| Hungary | 212 | 284 | 268 | 21 | 18 | 16 | 16880 | 14200 | 13045 | 2873.4 | 2746.1 | 2472.0 |
| Iceland | 524 | 505 | 576 | 12 | 11 | 13 | 1158 | 1325 | 1379 | 7249.0 | 8230.0 | 7996.3 |
| Ireland | 268 | 307 | ... | 10 | 12 | ... | 2845 | 3359 | 4258 | 2502.8 | 2984.5 | 3152.4 |
| Italy | 529 | 567 | ... | 99 | 104 | ... | 22286 | 24763 | 28498 | 2394.4 | 2703.1 | 2823.1 |
| Latvia | 136 | 167 | 237 | 6 | 7 | 10 | 352 | 387 | 724 | 281.6 | 1225.9 | 1581.1 |
| Lithuania | 158 | 226 | 293 | 12 | 14 | 15 | 2969 | 4837 | 3554 | 4531.2 | 4627.6 | 2361.8 |
| Luxembourg | 517 | 603 | 619 | 38 | 48 | 51 | 31 | 31 | 47 | 8586.6 | 9350.6 | 8244.2 |
| Malta | ... | 485 | 578 | ... | 86 | 104 | ... | ... | ... | 1151.2 | 2185.2 | 2261.5 |
| Moldova | 53 | 65 | ... | 17 | 19 | ... | 27 | 22 | 48 | 2141.5 | 2283.1 | 1015.2 |
| Monaco | 787 | 781 | ... | 534 | 545 | ... | ... | ... | ... | ... | ... | ... |
| The Netherlands | 403 | 400 | 421 | 58 | 54 | 57 | 66345 | 59985 | 65703 | 4251.9 | 4453.8 | 4745.0 |
| Norway | 457 | 473 | 498 | 22 | 23 | 24 | 72876 | 120119 | 182370 | 4894.3 | 5058.6 | 5396.8 |
| Poland | 168 | 233 | 273 | 18 | 24 | 28 | 124551 | 99605 | 99509 | 3355.0 | 2626.4 | 2573.8 |
| Portugal | 221 | 340 | ... | 34 | 50 | ... | 1943 | 2066 | 1873 | 1140.0 | 1659.2 | 1938.8 |
| Romania | 72 | 114 | ... | 11 | 17 | ... | 54317 | 39719 | 31741 | 2844.3 | 2633.6 | 2013.5 |
| Russian Federation | ... | 121 | ... | ... | 37 | ... | 1122720 | 1264890 | 950978 | 6317.0 | 6112.5 | 4215.0 |
| Slovakia | 194 | 219 | 253 | 57 | 66 | 77 | 4817 | 5280 | 4927 | 4170.2 | 4043.7 | 3253.6 |
| Slovenia | 306 | 381 | 440 | 42 | 51 | 44 | 2793 | 2665 | 2811 | 2631.3 | 2627.5 | 2954.8 |
| Spain | 351 | 425 | ... | 43 | 50 | ... | 26487 | 34061 | 31419 | 1868.5 | 2331.7 | 2630.1 |
| Sweden | 462 | 447 | 468 | 29 | 19 | 20 | 26863 | 29751 | 31914 | 5700.1 | 5578.6 | 5775.7 |
| Switzerland | 497 | 496 | 516 | 46 | 49 | 51 | 9413 | 9723 | 10963 | 3561.4 | 3724.4 | 3577.3 |
| Ukraine | 68 | 88 | ... | 20 | 26 | ... | 148364 | 135424 | 82987 | 4883.9 | 4868.4 | 3211.5 |
| United Kingdom | 412 | 406 | 439 | 64 | 63 | 67 | 238152 | 208940 | 258301 | 3595.4 | 3702.0 | 3831.3 |
| TFYR Macedonia | 124 | 163 | ... | 30 | 37 | ... | ... | ... | ... | ... | ... | ... |
| Yugoslavia | 137 | 165 | 188 | 31 | 35 | 42 | ... | ... | ... | ... | ... | ... |
| **LATIN AMERICA** | | | | | | | | | | | | |
| Argentina | ... | 170 | ... | 27 | 33 | ... | 42555 | 47039 | 69184 | 1364.4 | 1331.6 | 1613.1 |
| Bahamas | ... | 207 | ... | ... | 24 | ... | ... | ... | ... | ... | ... | ... |
| Barbados | ... | 173 | ... | ... | 27 | ... | ... | ... | ... | ... | ... | ... |
| Belize | 64 | 85 | 91 | ... | ... | 8 | ... | ... | ... | ... | ... | ... |
| Bolivia | 44 | 51 | ... | 6 | 7 | ... | 4792 | 4881 | 5364 | 468.0 | 440.6 | 489.2 |
| Brazil | 88 | 84 | ... | 8 | 7 | ... | 95227 | 99086 | 106420 | 893.4 | 920.2 | 981.3 |
| Chile | 81 | 103 | ... | 13 | 18 | ... | 6649 | 7465 | 7912 | 796.1 | 1059.3 | 1314.6 |
| Colombia | ... | 40 | ... | ... | 13 | ... | 25418 | 48103 | 61187 | 699.3 | 765.3 | 798.8 |
| Costa Rica | 87 | 121 | ... | 7 | 11 | ... | 1003 | 1032 | 1075 | 631.7 | 676.4 | 788.2 |
| Cuba | ... | ... | ... | ... | ... | ... | 4587 | 6125 | 6922 | 1406.2 | 1548.8 | 1159.6 |
| Dominican Republic | 72 | 43 | ... | 48 | 29 | ... | 1362 | 1051 | 1449 | 575.9 | 558.8 | 654.7 |
| Ecuador | 35 | 44 | ... | 9 | 12 | ... | 15946 | 16400 | 21837 | 648.4 | 638.9 | 669.5 |
| El Salvador | 34 | 56 | ... | 14 | 31 | ... | 2199 | 1883 | 2521 | 598.0 | 527.4 | 729.8 |
| Guatemala | ... | 18 | ... | ... | 16 | ... | 2791 | 3305 | 3622 | 494.8 | 500.3 | 518.5 |
| Haiti | ... | 7 | ... | ... | 13 | ... | 1632 | 1253 | 1392 | 323.7 | 244.9 | 239.4 |
| Honduras | 23 | 35 | ... | 10 | 12 | ... | 1469 | 1695 | 1728 | 486.1 | 500.5 | 511.9 |
| Jamaica | ... | 49 | ... | ... | 7 | ... | 252 | 459 | 500 | 803.5 | 1263.6 | 1384.6 |
| Mexico | 122 | 137 | 144 | 41 | 41 | ... | 194109 | 194613 | 202322 | 1476.4 | 1492.2 | 1456.1 |
| Netherlands Antilles | ... | ... | ... | ... | ... | ... | ... | ... | ... | 10060.6 | 10870.7 | 13219.5 |
| Nicaragua | 20 | 34 | ... | 5 | 8 | ... | 1308 | 1495 | 1495 | 582.8 | 568.1 | 521.7 |
| Panama | 74 | 94 | ... | 18 | 23 | ... | 602 | 595 | 720 | 702.4 | 640.1 | 775.4 |
| Paraguay | ... | 25 | ... | ... | 4 | ... | 2035 | 4579 | 6026 | 645.1 | 734.1 | 820.8 |

# TABLE A.8

## *continued*

| | Motor vehicles (per 1000 people) | | | Motor vehicles (per km of road) | | | Commercial energy production (kt of oil equivalent) | | | Commercial energy use (kg of oil equivalent per capita) | | |
|---|---|---|---|---|---|---|---|---|---|---|---|---|
| | 1990 | 1995 | 1998 | 1990 | 1995 | 1998 | 1990 | 1995 | 1998 | 1990 | 1995 | 1998 |
| Peru | ... | 36 | 42 | ... | 12 | 13 | 15450 | 12221 | 12307 | 591.5 | 535.4 | 586.4 |
| Puerto Rico | ... | 286 | ... | ... | 76 | ... | ... | ... | ... | ... | ... | ... |
| St. Lucia | 887 | 926 | ... | 8 | 12 | ... | ... | ... | ... | ... | ... | ... |
| Suriname | 125 | 163 | ... | 12 | 15 | ... | ... | ... | ... | ... | ... | ... |
| Trinidad and Tobago | ... | 110 | ... | ... | 18 | ... | 12412 | 12256 | 13017 | 4022.1 | 4680.7 | 5507.1 |
| Uruguay | 137 | 162 | ... | 45 | 59 | ... | 1137 | 1171 | 1038 | 671.3 | 718.9 | 798.0 |
| Venezuela | ... | 91 | ... | ... | 24 | ... | 111694 | 130978 | 187052 | 2176.2 | 2094.7 | 2191.6 |
| **NORTHERN AMERICA** | | | | | | | | | | | | |
| Canada | 644 | 578 | ... | 20 | 19 | ... | 241234 | 274145 | 349084 | 7453.7 | 7546.0 | 7901.5 |
| United States | 753 | 759 | ... | 30 | 32 | ... | 1570200 | 1648760 | 1663560 | 7488.6 | 7720.0 | 7952.8 |
| **OCEANIA** | | | | | | | | | | | | |
| Australia | 530 | 592 | ... | 11 | 12 | ... | 125290 | 157156 | 186690 | 4690.4 | 5107.2 | 5232.7 |
| Fiji | ... | 75 | ... | ... | 18 | ... | ... | ... | ... | ... | ... | ... |
| New Zealand | 528 | 567 | ... | 19 | 22 | ... | 8990 | 12184 | 12471 | 3507.6 | 4120.0 | 4223.2 |
| Papua New Guinea | ... | 27 | ... | ... | 6 | ... | ... | ... | ... | ... | ... | ... |
| Tonga | ... | 19 | ... | ... | 3 | ... | ... | ... | ... | ... | ... | ... |
| Honduras | 23 | 35 | ... | 10 | 12 | ... | 1469 | 1695 | 1728 | 486.1 | 500.5 | 511.9 |
| Vanuatu | ... | 35 | ... | ... | 6 | ... | ... | ... | ... | ... | ... | ... |

**Sources:** International Road Federation: World Road Statistics, World Bank: World Development Indicators 2000 on CD-ROM.
For footnotes, refer to technical notes.

# TABLE A.9

## Area, Density and Land Use

| | Population density (persons per 1000 ha) | | | Land area (000 ha) | Arable land (hectares per person) | | Land use by type | | | | | | | |
|---|---|---|---|---|---|---|---|---|---|---|---|---|---|---|
| | | | | | | | Arable land (% of land area) | Irrigated land (% of cropland) | | Permanent cropland (% of land area) | | Other (% of land area) | |
| | 1985 | 2000 | 2015 | 1997 | 1985 | 1997 | 1997 | 1985 | 1997 | 1985 | 1997 | 1985 | 1997 |
| **AFRICA** | | | | | | | | | | | | | |
| Algeria | 92 | 132 | 173 | 238174 | 0.32 | 0.26 | 3.16 | 4.50 | 6.97 | 0.25 | 0.22 | 96.85 | 96.62 |
| Angola | 64 | 103 | 158 | 124670 | 0.36 | 0.26 | 2.41 | 2.21 | 2.14 | 0.40 | 0.40 | 97.27 | 97.19 |
| Benin | 363 | 551 | 808 | 11062 | 0.34 | 0.25 | 13.06 | 0.40 | 1.25 | 0.90 | 1.36 | 86.53 | 85.58 |
| Botswana | 19 | 29 | 35 | 56673 | 0.38 | 0.22 | 0.61 | 0.49 | 0.29 | 0.00 | 0.01 | 99.28 | 99.39 |
| Burkina Faso | 288 | 436 | 661 | 27360 | 0.37 | 0.32 | 12.39 | 0.40 | 0.73 | 0.29 | 0.18 | 88.91 | 87.43 |
| Burundi | 1846 | 2607 | 3696 | 2568 | 0.19 | 0.12 | 29.98 | 1.19 | 1.27 | 11.29 | 12.85 | 54.05 | 57.17 |
| Cameroon | 214 | 324 | 462 | 46540 | 0.59 | 0.43 | 12.81 | 0.29 | 0.29 | 2.69 | 2.58 | 84.62 | 84.62 |
| Cape Verde | 769 | 1062 | 1437 | 403 | 0.12 | 0.1 | 9.68 | 5.00 | 7.32 | 0.50 | 0.50 | 90.07 | 89.83 |
| Central African Republic | 42 | 58 | 76 | 62298 | 0.73 | 0.56 | 3.1 | ... | ... | 0.13 | 0.14 | 96.82 | 96.76 |
| Chad | 41 | 61 | 89 | 125920 | 0.61 | 0.46 | 2.56 | 0.32 | 0.61 | 0.02 | 0.02 | 97.49 | 97.41 |
| Comoros | 2045 | 3112 | 4475 | 223 | 0.2 | 0.15 | 34.98 | ... | ... | 13.45 | 17.94 | 52.47 | 47.09 |
| Congo | 56 | 86 | 129 | 34150 | 0.07 | 0.05 | 0.41 | 0.57 | 0.54 | 0.12 | 0.13 | 99.48 | 99.46 |
| Côte d'Ivoire | 311 | 465 | 630 | 31800 | 0.24 | 0.21 | 9.28 | 1.04 | 0.99 | 8.81 | 13.84 | 83.71 | 76.89 |
| Dem. Republic of the Congo | 140 | 228 | 354 | 226705 | 0.21 | 0.14 | 2.96 | 0.12 | 0.14 | 0.49 | 0.52 | 96.56 | 96.52 |
| Djibouti | 169 | 275 | 374 | 2318 | .. | .. | ... | ... | ... | ... | ... | ... | ... |
| Egypt | 500 | 688 | 856 | 99545 | 0.05 | 0.05 | 2.85 | ... | ... | 0.19 | 0.47 | 97.49 | 96.68 |
| Equatorial Guinea | 111 | 162 | 230 | 2805 | 0.42 | 0.31 | 4.63 | ... | ... | 3.57 | 3.57 | 91.80 | 91.80 |
| Eritrea | ... | 381 | 544 | 10100 | .. | 0.1 | 3.87 | ... | 7.12 | ... | 0.02 | ... | 96.11 |
| Ethiopia | .... | 626 | 909 | 100000 | .. | 0.16 | 9.85 | ... | 1.81 | ... | 0.65 | ... | 89.50 |
| Gabon | 31 | 48 | 64 | 25767 | 0.36 | 0.28 | 1.26 | 0.88 | 1.41 | 0.63 | 0.66 | 98.25 | 98.08 |
| Gambia | 745 | 1305 | 1821 | 1000 | 0.22 | 0.17 | 19.5 | 0.59 | 1.00 | 0.40 | 0.50 | 83.10 | 80.00 |
| Ghana | 568 | 888 | 1311 | 22754 | 0.19 | 0.16 | 12.53 | 0.17 | 0.24 | 7.03 | 7.47 | 82.42 | 80.00 |
| Guinea | 203 | 302 | 427 | 24572 | 0.15 | 0.13 | 3.6 | 7.53 | 6.40 | 1.91 | 2.44 | 95.14 | 93.96 |
| Guinea-Bissau | 312 | 431 | 577 | 2812 | 0.33 | 0.26 | 10.67 | 5.31 | 4.86 | 1.07 | 1.78 | 88.62 | 87.55 |
| Kenya | 349 | 529 | 661 | 56914 | 0.2 | 0.14 | 7.03 | 0.94 | 1.48 | 0.86 | 0.91 | 92.11 | 92.06 |
| Lesotho | 503 | 709 | 953 | 3035 | 0.2 | 0.16 | 10.71 | ... | ... | ... | ... | ... | ... |
| Liberia | 228 | 328 | 533 | 9632 | 0.06 | 0.04 | 1.32 | 0.54 | 0.61 | 2.54 | 2.08 | 96.15 | 96.61 |
| Libyan Arab Jamahiriya | 22 | 32 | 43 | 175954 | 0.47 | 0.35 | 1.03 | 14.10 | 22.22 | 0.19 | 0.17 | 98.79 | 98.80 |
| Madagascar | 174 | 274 | 402 | 58154 | 0.25 | 0.18 | 4.41 | 27.17 | 35.07 | 0.94 | 0.93 | 94.77 | 94.66 |
| Malawi | 770 | 1161 | 1676 | 9408 | 0.19 | 0.15 | 16.85 | 1.22 | 1.64 | 1.01 | 1.33 | 84.38 | 81.82 |
| Mali | 65 | 92 | 137 | 122019 | 0.28 | 0.45 | 3.77 | 2.89 | 1.85 | 0.03 | 0.04 | 98.30 | 96.19 |
| Mauritania | 17 | 26 | 38 | 102522 | 0.17 | 0.2 | 0.48 | 16.07 | 9.76 | 0.00 | 0.01 | 99.70 | 99.51 |
| Mauritius | 5005 | 5704 | 6414 | 203 | 0.1 | 0.09 | 49.26 | 15.89 | 16.98 | 3.45 | 2.96 | 47.29 | 47.78 |
| Morocco | 485 | 635 | 779 | 44630 | 0.36 | 0.32 | 19.6 | 14.98 | 13.04 | 1.39 | 1.90 | 81.38 | 78.50 |
| Mozambique | 173 | 251 | 322 | 78409 | 0.21 | 0.18 | 3.76 | 3.01 | 3.36 | 0.29 | 0.29 | 96.06 | 95.94 |
| Namibia | 14 | 21 | 25 | 82329 | 0.56 | 0.5 | 0.99 | 0.60 | 0.85 | 0.00 | 0.00 | 99.20 | 99.00 |
| Niger | 52 | 85 | 132 | 126670 | 0.53 | 0.51 | 3.94 | 0.85 | 1.32 | 0.00 | 0.00 | 97.21 | 96.05 |
| Nigeria | 832 | 1224 | 1683 | 91077 | 0.34 | 0.24 | 30.96 | 0.64 | 0.76 | 2.78 | 2.79 | 65.92 | 66.25 |
| Rwanda | 2454 | 3135 | 4271 | 2467 | 0.14 | 0.11 | 34.45 | 0.36 | 0.35 | 11.84 | 12.16 | 54.64 | 53.38 |
| Sao Tome and Principe | 1104 | 1531 | 1979 | 96 | 0.02 | 0.01 | 2.08 | 27.03 | 24.39 | 36.46 | 40.63 | 61.46 | 57.29 |
| Senegal | 331 | 492 | 710 | 19253 | 0.37 | 0.25 | 11.58 | 3.83 | 3.13 | 0.07 | 0.19 | 87.79 | 88.23 |
| Seychelles | 1444 | 1711 | 2000 | 45 | 0.01 | 0.01 | 2.22 | ... | ... | 11.11 | 13.33 | 86.67 | 84.44 |
| Sierra Leone | 500 | 678 | 932 | 7162 | 0.13 | 0.1 | 6.79 | 5.30 | 5.31 | 0.74 | 0.84 | 92.63 | 92.38 |
| Somalia | 104 | 161 | 261 | 62734 | 0.15 | 0.12 | 1.66 | 17.56 | 18.85 | 0.03 | 0.04 | 98.37 | 98.31 |
| South Africa | 252 | 331 | 355 | 122104 | 0.39 | 0.38 | 12.58 | 8.57 | 7.79 | 0.67 | 0.77 | 89.21 | 86.65 |
| Sudan | 90 | 124 | 168 | 237600 | 0.59 | 0.6 | 7.03 | 15.22 | 11.54 | 0.08 | 0.08 | 94.62 | 92.89 |
| Swaziland | 377 | 586 | 855 | 1720 | 0.23 | 0.18 | 9.77 | 37.80 | 38.33 | 0.81 | 0.70 | 90.47 | 89.53 |
| Togo | 556 | 851 | 1241 | 5439 | 0.66 | 0.48 | 38.06 | 0.30 | 0.29 | 6.62 | 6.62 | 56.61 | 55.32 |
| Tunisia | 472 | 617 | 747 | 15536 | 0.42 | 0.31 | 18.67 | 6.08 | 7.76 | 12.02 | 12.87 | 68.22 | 68.46 |
| Uganda | 738 | 1091 | 1727 | 19965 | 0.35 | 0.25 | 25.34 | 0.14 | 0.13 | 8.51 | 8.77 | 66.94 | 65.89 |
| United Republic of Tanzania | 246 | 379 | 534 | 88359 | 0.1 | 0.1 | 3.51 | 4.19 | 3.88 | 0.85 | 1.02 | 96.57 | 95.47 |
| Zambia | 86 | 123 | 172 | 74339 | 0.77 | 0.56 | 7.06 | 0.54 | 0.87 | 0.02 | 0.03 | 93.02 | 92.92 |
| Zimbabwe | 217 | 302 | 351 | 38685 | 0.32 | 0.27 | 7.96 | 3.20 | 4.67 | 0.28 | 0.34 | 92.74 | 91.70 |
| **ASIA** | | | | | | | | | | | | | |
| Afghanistan | 223 | 348 | 564 | 65209 | 0.5 | 0.33 | 12.13 | 32.11 | 34.77 | 0.22 | 0.22 | 87.65 | 87.65 |
| Armenia | .... | 1248 | 1351 | 2820 | .. | 0.13 | 17.52 | ... | 51.88 | ... | 2.30 | ... | 80.18 |
| Azerbaijan | .... | 893 | 1016 | 8660 | .. | 0.21 | 19.31 | ... | 75.19 | ... | 3.04 | ... | 77.66 |
| Bahrain | 5986 | 8942 | 11043 | 69 | 0 | 0 | 2.9 | 25.00 | 100.00 | 2.90 | 4.35 | 94.20 | 92.75 |
| Bangladesh | 7634 | 9922 | 12410 | 13017 | 0.09 | 0.06 | 60.81 | 22.69 | 44.81 | 2.11 | 2.50 | 29.82 | 36.69 |
| Bhutan | 316 | 452 | 662 | 4700 | 0.2 | 0.19 | 2.98 | 23.26 | 25.00 | 0.40 | 0.43 | 97.26 | 96.60 |
| Brunei Darussalam | 423 | 622 | 778 | 527 | 0.01 | 0.01 | 0.57 | 14.29 | 14.29 | 0.76 | 0.76 | 98.67 | 98.67 |
| Cambodia | 418 | 633 | 816 | 17652 | 0.29 | 0.33 | 20.96 | 7.59 | 7.09 | 0.40 | 0.61 | 86.57 | 78.43 |
| China | 1148 | 1370 | 1520 | 932641 | 0.11 | 0.1 | 13.31 | 35.41 | 38.28 | 0.55 | 1.20 | 86.50 | 85.49 |
| China, Hong Kong SAR | 55111 | 69970 | 77667 | 99 | 0 | 0 | 5.05 | 37.50 | 33.33 | 1.01 | 1.01 | 91.92 | 93.94 |
| China, Macau SAR | 153000 | ... | 256000 | 2 | .. | .. | ... | ... | ... | ... | ... | ... | ... |
| Cyprus | 700 | 851 | 937 | 924 | 0.16 | 0.13 | 10.5 | 18.99 | 27.59 | 5.95 | 5.19 | 82.90 | 84.31 |
| Dem. People's Rep. of Korea | 1573 | 1996 | 2273 | 12041 | 0.09 | 0.07 | 14.12 | 64.96 | 73.00 | 2.45 | 2.49 | 83.76 | 83.39 |
| Georgia | .... | 713 | 730 | 6970 | .. | 0.14 | 11.21 | ... | 44.09 | ... | 4.09 | ... | 84.71 |
| India | 2583 | 3409 | 4075 | 297319 | 0.21 | 0.17 | 54.47 | 24.72 | 33.56 | 1.95 | 2.66 | 43.15 | 42.87 |
| Indonesia | 924 | 1171 | 1382 | 181157 | 0.12 | 0.09 | 9.9 | 15.64 | 15.54 | 4.42 | 7.20 | 84.82 | 82.89 |
| Iran (Islamic Republic of) | 294 | 417 | 512 | 162200 | 0.32 | 0.29 | 10.94 | 42.85 | 37.45 | 0.60 | 1.02 | 90.22 | 88.04 |
| Iraq | 350 | 529 | 779 | 43737 | 0.34 | 0.24 | 11.89 | 31.76 | 63.63 | 0.59 | 0.78 | 87.40 | 87.33 |
| Israel | 2053 | 3015 | 3682 | 2062 | 0.08 | 0.06 | 17.02 | 55.48 | 45.54 | 4.51 | 4.17 | 79.63 | 78.81 |
| Japan | 3209 | 3365 | 3348 | 37652 | 0.03 | 0.03 | 10.4 | 62.04 | 62.89 | 1.46 | 1.01 | 87.36 | 88.59 |
| Jordan | 464 | 750 | 1114 | 8893 | 0.11 | 0.06 | 2.87 | 13.56 | 19.23 | 0.56 | 1.52 | 96.02 | 95.61 |
| Kazakhstan | .... | 61 | 63 | 267073 | .. | 1.9 | 11.23 | ... | 7.13 | ... | 0.05 | ... | 88.72 |
| Kuwait | 965 | 1107 | 1471 | 1782 | 0 | 0 | 0.34 | ... | 71.43 | ... | 0.06 | ... | 99.61 |
| Kyrgyzstan | .... | 245 | 285 | 19180 | .. | 0.29 | 7.04 | ... | 75.37 | ... | 0.39 | ... | 92.57 |

# TABLE A.9

## continued

| | Population density (persons per 1000 ha) | | | Land area (000 ha) | Arable land (hectares per person) | | Land use by type | | | | | | |
|---|---|---|---|---|---|---|---|---|---|---|---|---|---|
| | | | | | | | Arable land (% of land area) | Irrigated land (% of cropland) | | Permanent cropland (% of land area) | | Other (% of land area) | |
| | 1985 | 2000 | 2015 | 1997 | 1985 | 1997 | 1997 | 1985 | 1997 | 1985 | 1997 | 1985 | 1997 |
| Lao People's Dem. Republic | 156 | 235 | 340 | 23080 | 0.23 | 0.16 | 3.47 | 13.68 | 19.25 | 0.15 | 0.23 | 96.23 | 96.31 |
| Lebanon | 2608 | 3208 | 3853 | 1023 | 0.06 | 0.04 | 17.6 | 28.76 | 37.99 | 9.29 | 12.51 | 70.77 | 69.89 |
| Malaysia | 477 | 677 | 838 | 32855 | 0.08 | 0.08 | 5.54 | 6.04 | 4.47 | 12.94 | 17.61 | 83.17 | 76.85 |
| Maldives | 6133 | 9533 | 14000 | 30 | 0.01 | 0 | 3.33 | ... | ... | 6.67 | 6.67 | 90.00 | 90.00 |
| Mongolia | 12 | 17 | 21 | 156650 | 0.71 | 0.52 | 0.84 | 4.43 | 6.36 | 0.00 | 0.00 | 99.14 | 99.16 |
| Myanmar | 571 | 694 | 814 | 65755 | 0.26 | 0.22 | 14.53 | 10.78 | 15.33 | 0.72 | 0.90 | 84.69 | 84.56 |
| Nepal | 1154 | 1673 | 2286 | 14300 | 0.14 | 0.13 | 20.27 | 32.63 | 38.24 | 0.38 | 0.49 | 83.71 | 79.24 |
| Oman | 67 | 120 | 193 | 21246 | 0.01 | 0.01 | 0.08 | 87.23 | 98.41 | 0.15 | 0.22 | 99.78 | 99.70 |
| Pakistan | 1313 | 2030 | 2887 | 77088 | 0.21 | 0.16 | 27.29 | 76.47 | 81.39 | 0.53 | 0.73 | 73.26 | 71.98 |
| Philippines | 1834 | 2548 | 3244 | 29817 | 0.08 | 0.07 | 17.17 | 16.09 | 16.28 | 14.76 | 14.76 | 69.98 | 68.07 |
| Qatar | 326 | 545 | 665 | 1100 | 0.02 | 0.02 | 1.27 | 55.56 | 76.47 | 0.09 | 0.27 | 99.18 | 98.45 |
| Republic of Korea | 4133 | 4745 | 5171 | 9873 | 0.05 | 0.04 | 17.46 | 61.80 | 60.45 | 1.37 | 2.03 | 78.28 | 80.51 |
| Saudi Arabia | 59 | 101 | 152 | 214969 | 0.21 | 0.18 | 1.72 | 43.81 | 42.30 | 0.03 | 0.06 | 98.78 | 98.22 |
| Singapore | 44410 | 58475 | 65475 | 61 | 0 | 0 | 1.64 | ... | ... | 4.92 | ... | 91.80 | ... |
| Sri Lanka | 2483 | 2913 | 3386 | 6463 | 0.05 | 0.05 | 13.43 | 31.08 | 31.78 | 15.94 | 15.78 | 70.97 | 70.79 |
| Syrian Arab Republic | 566 | 877 | 1232 | 18378 | 0.48 | 0.32 | 25.96 | 11.60 | 21.16 | 3.18 | 4.08 | 69.40 | 69.96 |
| Tajikistan | ... | 440 | 552 | 14060 | .. | 0.13 | 5.41 | | 80.90 | | 0.92 | | 93.67 |
| Thailand | 1001 | 1202 | 1348 | 51089 | 0.35 | 0.28 | 33.44 | 19.26 | 24.50 | 4.22 | 6.58 | 61.15 | 59.98 |
| Turkey | 654 | 865 | 1043 | 76963 | 0.49 | 0.43 | 34.53 | 11.62 | 14.40 | 3.81 | 3.36 | 64.23 | 62.11 |
| Turkmenistan | ... | 95 | 119 | 46993 | .. | 0.35 | 3.47 | | | ... | 0.14 | | 96.39 |
| United Arab Emirates | 186 | 292 | 362 | 8360 | 0.02 | 0.02 | 0.48 | ... | ... | 0.11 | 0.49 | 99.58 | 99.03 |
| Uzbekistan | ... | 587 | 721 | 41424 | .. | 0.19 | 10.8 | | 88.27 | | 0.91 | | 88.29 |
| Viet Nam | 1840 | 2453 | 2968 | 32549 | 0.1 | 0.08 | 17.41 | 27.57 | 31.94 | 2.47 | 4.71 | 80.27 | 77.87 |
| Yemen Republic | 184 | 343 | 561 | 52797 | 0.14 | 0.09 | 2.73 | 20.54 | 31.19 | 0.19 | 0.21 | 97.22 | 97.05 |
| **EUROPE** | | | | | | | | | | | | | |
| Albania | 1081 | 1136 | 1278 | 2740 | 0.2 | 0.17 | 21.06 | 55.96 | 48.43 | 4.53 | 4.56 | 73.98 | 74.38 |
| Andorra | 978 | 1733 | 2778 | 45 | .. | .. | 2.22 | ... | ... | ... | ... | ... | ... |
| Aruba | 0 | 0 | 0 | 19 | .. | .. | 10.53 | ... | ... | ... | ... | ... | ... |
| Austria | 914 | 993 | 1007 | 8273 | 0.19 | 0.17 | 16.89 | 0.26 | 0.27 | 0.93 | 0.99 | 81.57 | 82.12 |
| Belarus | ... | 493 | 475 | 20748 | .. | 0.6 | 29.76 | | 1.82 | | 0.69 | | 69.54 |
| Belgium | 3003 | 3096 | 3073 | 3282 | .. | .. | 23.4 | 2.19 | 4.46 | 0.40 | 0.52 | 76.33 | 76.08 |
| Bosnia and Herzegovina | ... | 779 | 858 | 5100 | .. | 0.14 | 9.8 | | 0.31 | | 2.94 | | 87.25 |
| Bulgaria | 811 | 744 | 681 | 11055 | 0.43 | 0.52 | 39 | 29.73 | 17.73 | 2.93 | 1.80 | 62.61 | 59.19 |
| Croatia | ... | 800 | 778 | 5592 | .. | 0.29 | 23.55 | | 0.21 | | 2.24 | | 74.21 |
| Czech Republic | ... | 1326 | 1285 | 7728 | .. | 0.3 | 40.05 | | 0.72 | | 3.05 | | 56.90 |
| Denmark | 1207 | 1248 | 1251 | 4243 | 0.51 | 0.45 | 55.74 | 15.68 | 20.06 | 0.31 | 0.19 | 38.32 | 44.07 |
| Estonia | ... | 330 | 288 | 4227 | .. | 0.77 | 26.69 | | 0.35 | | 0.35 | | 72.96 |
| Faeroe Islands | 329 | 307 | 271 | 140 | .. | .. | 2.14 | ... | ... | ... | ... | ... | ... |
| Finland | 161 | 170 | 173 | 30459 | 0.46 | 0.41 | 6.98 | | 3.01 | | 0.01 | | 93.01 |
| France | 1003 | 1074 | 1111 | 55010 | 0.32 | 0.31 | 33.28 | 5.46 | 8.58 | 2.40 | 2.11 | 65.02 | 64.61 |
| Germany | 2224 | 2354 | 2336 | 34927 | 0.15 | 0.14 | 33.88 | 3.78 | 3.94 | 1.34 | 0.65 | 64.42 | 65.47 |
| Greece | 771 | 826 | 805 | 12890 | 0.29 | 0.27 | 21.9 | 27.89 | 35.38 | 8.07 | 8.47 | 69.43 | 69.63 |
| Hungary | 1146 | 1087 | 1019 | 9234 | 0.48 | 0.47 | 52.2 | 2.61 | 4.16 | 2.78 | 2.46 | 42.68 | 45.34 |
| Iceland | 24 | 28 | 31 | 10025 | 0.03 | 0.02 | 0.06 | ... | ... | ... | ... | ... | ... |
| Ireland | 516 | 541 | 605 | 6889 | 0.29 | 0.37 | 19.49 | ... | ... | 0.04 | 0.04 | 85.02 | 80.46 |
| Italy | 1931 | 1949 | 1852 | 29406 | 0.16 | 0.14 | 28.17 | 20.02 | 24.69 | 10.42 | 8.99 | 58.80 | 62.84 |
| Latvia | ... | 380 | 332 | 6205 | .. | 0.73 | 29.01 | | 1.09 | | 0.48 | | 70.51 |
| Liechtenstein | 1688 | 2063 | 2375 | 16 | .. | .. | 25 | ... | ... | ... | ... | ... | ... |
| Lithuania | ... | 566 | 543 | 6480 | .. | 0.8 | 45.46 | | 0.30 | | 0.93 | | 53.61 |
| Malta | 10750 | 12156 | 13156 | 32 | 0.03 | 0.03 | 31.25 | 7.69 | 18.18 | 3.13 | 3.13 | 59.38 | 65.63 |
| The Netherlands | 4272 | 4654 | 4698 | 3392 | 0.06 | 0.06 | 26.53 | 61.99 | 60.43 | 0.85 | 1.03 | 74.79 | 72.44 |
| Norway | 135 | 146 | 154 | 30683 | 0.21 | 0.2 | 2.94 | ... | ... | ... | ... | ... | ... |
| Poland | 1222 | 1273 | 1293 | 30442 | 0.39 | 0.36 | 46.18 | 0.67 | 0.69 | 1.10 | 1.20 | 51.25 | 52.62 |
| Portugal | 1082 | 1079 | 1056 | 9150 | 0.24 | 0.22 | 23.53 | 19.96 | 21.79 | 8.28 | 8.16 | 65.51 | 68.31 |
| Republic of Moldova | ... | 1329 | 1357 | 3297 | .. | 0.41 | 54.11 | | 14.15 | | 12.10 | | 33.79 |
| Romania | 987 | 969 | 915 | 23034 | 0.44 | 0.41 | 40.38 | 27.83 | 31.20 | 2.77 | 2.60 | 53.89 | 57.02 |
| Russian Federation | ... | 87 | 85 | 1688850 | .. | 0.86 | 7.46 | | 3.90 | | 0.11 | | 92.42 |
| Slovakia | ... | 1120 | 1137 | 4808 | .. | 0.27 | 30.74 | | 11.84 | | 2.64 | | 66.62 |
| Slovenia | ... | 987 | 952 | 2012 | .. | 0.12 | 11.48 | | 0.70 | | 2.68 | | 85.83 |
| Spain | 770 | 794 | 770 | 49944 | 0.41 | 0.36 | 28.72 | 15.76 | 18.80 | 9.71 | 9.65 | 59.12 | 61.63 |
| Sweden | 203 | 217 | 221 | 41162 | 0.35 | 0.32 | 6.8 | ... | ... | ... | ... | ... | ... |
| Switzerland | 1653 | 1868 | 1928 | 3955 | 0.06 | 0.06 | 10.62 | 6.07 | 5.63 | 0.53 | 0.61 | 89.58 | 88.77 |
| TFYR Macedonia | ... | 796 | 861 | 2543 | .. | 0.3 | 23.95 | | 8.36 | | 1.93 | | 74.13 |
| Ukraine | ... | 871 | 826 | 57935 | .. | 0.65 | 57.1 | | 7.24 | | 1.73 | | 41.17 |
| United Kingdom | 2343 | 2435 | 2465 | 24160 | 0.12 | 0.11 | 26.41 | 2.15 | 1.68 | 0.23 | 0.19 | 70.78 | 73.73 |
| Yugoslavia | ... | 1043 | 1061 | 10200 | .. | 0.35 | 36.34 | | 1.60 | | 3.44 | | 60.22 |
| **LATIN AMERICA** | | | | | | | | | | | | | |
| Antigua and Barbuda | 1409 | 1546 | 1636 | 44 | 0.13 | 0.12 | 18.18 | | | | | | |
| Argentina | 111 | 135 | 159 | 273669 | 0.82 | 0.7 | 9.14 | 5.96 | 6.25 | 0.80 | 0.80 | 90.06 | 90.06 |
| Bahamas | 232 | 307 | 375 | 1001 | 0.03 | 0.02 | 0.6 | ... | ... | 0.20 | 0.40 | 99.00 | 99.00 |
| Barbados | 5884 | 6279 | 6698 | 43 | 0.06 | 0.06 | 37.21 | 5.88 | 5.88 | 2.33 | 2.33 | 60.47 | 60.47 |
| Belize | 73 | 106 | 139 | 2280 | 0.26 | 0.28 | 2.81 | 3.77 | 3.37 | 0.44 | 1.10 | 97.68 | 96.10 |
| Bolivia | 54 | 77 | 103 | 108438 | 0.34 | 0.24 | 1.73 | 5.69 | 4.19 | 0.18 | 0.21 | 97.97 | 98.06 |
| Brazil | 160 | 201 | 237 | 845651 | 0.31 | 0.33 | 6.3 | 4.02 | 4.85 | 1.17 | 1.42 | 93.82 | 92.28 |
| Cayman Islands | 808 | 1462 | 2346 | 26 | .. | .. | ... | ... | ... | ... | ... | ... | ... |
| Chile | 161 | 203 | 239 | 74880 | 0.29 | 0.14 | 2.65 | 34.23 | 55.29 | 0.30 | 0.42 | 95.10 | 96.93 |
| Colombia | 305 | 407 | 512 | 103870 | 0.12 | 0.05 | 1.86 | 8.81 | 23.95 | 1.43 | 2.41 | 94.92 | 95.74 |
| Costa Rica | 517 | 788 | 1025 | 5106 | 0.11 | 0.06 | 4.41 | 21.03 | 24.95 | 4.66 | 5.48 | 89.76 | 90.11 |
| Cuba | 921 | 1020 | 1060 | 10982 | 0.28 | 0.33 | 33.69 | 24.13 | 20.45 | 6.54 | 6.83 | 67.51 | 59.48 |

## TABLE A.9

**continued**

| | | | | | | | | | | | | | |
|---|---|---|---|---|---|---|---|---|---|---|---|---|---|
| Dominica | 960 | 947 | 960 | 75 | 0.08 | 0.04 | 4 | ... | ... | 14.67 | 16.00 | 77.33 | 80.00 |
| Dominican Republic | 1318 | 1756 | 2119 | 4838 | 0.17 | 0.13 | 21.08 | 13.85 | 17.27 | 7.34 | 9.92 | 70.44 | 69.00 |
| Ecuador | 329 | 457 | 576 | 27684 | 0.17 | 0.13 | 5.69 | 11.86 | 8.33 | 3.40 | 5.15 | 90.86 | 89.16 |
| El Salvador | 2302 | 3029 | 3850 | 2072 | 0.1 | 0.1 | 27.27 | 14.53 | 14.71 | 12.40 | 12.11 | 63.47 | 60.62 |
| Grenada | 2647 | 2765 | 2941 | 34 | 0.03 | 0.02 | 5.88 | ... | ... | 29.41 | 26.47 | 61.76 | 67.65 |
| Guatemala | 714 | 1050 | 1511 | 10843 | 0.17 | 0.13 | 12.54 | 5.71 | 6.56 | 4.47 | 5.03 | 83.54 | 82.43 |
| Guyana | 40 | 44 | 49 | 19685 | 0.61 | 0.57 | 2.44 | 25.66 | 26.21 | 0.08 | 0.08 | 97.49 | 97.48 |
| Haiti | 2223 | 2983 | 3788 | 2756 | 0.09 | 0.07 | 20.32 | 7.75 | 9.89 | 12.70 | 12.70 | 67.24 | 66.98 |
| Honduras | 374 | 580 | 808 | 11189 | 0.38 | 0.28 | 15.15 | 4.05 | 3.62 | 1.81 | 3.13 | 84.11 | 81.72 |
| Jamaica | 2121 | 2385 | 2719 | 1083 | 0.05 | 0.07 | 16.07 | 15.00 | 12.04 | 9.70 | 9.23 | 79.69 | 74.70 |
| Mexico | 395 | 518 | 624 | 190869 | 0.31 | 0.27 | 13.2 | 21.14 | 23.81 | 0.89 | 1.10 | 86.90 | 85.70 |
| Netherlands Antilles | 2275 | 2713 | 3063 | 80 | 0.04 | 0.04 | 10 | ... | ... | ... | ... | ... | ... |
| Nicaragua | 280 | 418 | 599 | 12140 | 0.46 | 0.53 | 20.24 | 4.68 | 3.20 | 1.78 | 2.38 | 85.40 | 77.38 |
| Panama | 291 | 384 | 464 | 7443 | 0.21 | 0.18 | 6.72 | 5.04 | 4.89 | 1.75 | 2.08 | 92.01 | 91.20 |
| Paraguay | 91 | 138 | 196 | 39730 | 0.53 | 0.43 | 5.54 | 3.24 | 2.93 | 0.26 | 0.21 | 94.96 | 94.25 |
| Peru | 152 | 201 | 249 | 128000 | 0.17 | 0.15 | 2.89 | 32.39 | 41.90 | 0.28 | 0.39 | 97.08 | 96.72 |
| Puerto Rico | 3808 | 4362 | 4824 | 887 | 0.01 | 0.01 | 3.72 | 39.00 | 51.28 | 5.64 | 5.07 | 88.73 | 91.21 |
| Saint Kitts and Nevis | 1222 | 1056 | 1000 | 36 | 0.19 | 0.15 | 16.67 | ... | ... | 11.11 | 2.78 | 66.67 | 80.56 |
| Saint Lucia | 2049 | 2525 | 3049 | 61 | 0.04 | 0.02 | 4.92 | 5.88 | 17.65 | 19.67 | 22.95 | 72.13 | 72.13 |
| Saint Vincent & the Grenadines | 2615 | 2923 | 3205 | 39 | 0.04 | 0.04 | 10.26 | 10.00 | 9.09 | 15.38 | 17.95 | 74.36 | 71.79 |
| Suriname | 25 | 27 | 31 | 15600 | 0.14 | 0.14 | 0.37 | 88.71 | 89.55 | 0.06 | 0.06 | 99.60 | 99.57 |
| Trinidad and Tobago | 2296 | 2524 | 2768 | 513 | 0.06 | 0.06 | 14.62 | 18.64 | 18.03 | 8.97 | 9.16 | 77.00 | 76.22 |
| United States Virgin Islands | 412 | 618 | 2500 | 34 | 0.05 | 0.04 | 14.71 | ... | ... | 5.88 | 5.88 | 79.41 | 79.41 |
| Uruguay | 172 | 191 | 211 | 17481 | 0.43 | 0.39 | 7.21 | 7.32 | 10.71 | 0.26 | 0.27 | 92.41 | 92.52 |
| Venezuela | 194 | 274 | 350 | 88205 | 0.17 | 0.12 | 2.99 | 4.51 | 5.87 | 1.01 | 0.96 | 95.70 | 96.04 |
| **NORTHERN AMERICA** | | | | | | | | | | | | | |
| Bermuda | 11400 | 13000 | 14400 | 5 | .. | .. | ... | ... | ... | ... | ... | ... | ... |
| Canada | 28 | 34 | 38 | 922097 | 1.77 | 1.52 | 4.94 | 1.63 | 1.58 | 0.01 | 0.02 | 95.01 | 95.04 |
| Greenland | 2 | 2 | 2 | 34170 | .. | .. | ... | ... | ... | ... | ... | ... | ... |
| United States | 264 | 304 | 336 | 915912 | 0.79 | 0.66 | 19.32 | 10.45 | 11.96 | 0.22 | 0.22 | 79.28 | 80.46 |
| **OCEANIA** | | | | | | | | | | | | | |
| American Samoa | 1950 | 3400 | 5500 | 20 | 0.05 | 0.02 | 5 | ... | ... | 10.00 | 10.00 | 80.00 | 85.00 |
| Australia | 20 | 25 | 28 | 768230 | 2.99 | 2.85 | 6.88 | 3.59 | 5.08 | 0.02 | 0.03 | 93.84 | 93.09 |
| Fiji | 383 | 447 | 544 | 1827 | 0.17 | 0.26 | 10.95 | 0.50 | 1.05 | 4.38 | 4.65 | 89.05 | 84.40 |
| French Polynesia | 475 | 642 | 792 | 366 | 0.03 | 0.03 | 1.64 | ... | ... | 6.01 | 6.01 | 92.62 | 92.35 |
| Guam | 2164 | 3055 | 3727 | 55 | 0.05 | 0.04 | 10.91 | ... | ... | 10.91 | 10.91 | 78.18 | 78.18 |
| Kiribati | 918 | 1137 | 1411 | 73 | .. | .. | ... | ... | ... | 50.68 | 50.68 | ... | ... |
| New Caledonia | 85 | 117 | 142 | 1828 | 0.07 | 0.03 | 0.38 | ... | ... | 0.44 | 0.33 | 99.02 | 99.29 |
| New Zealand | 121 | 144 | 163 | 26799 | 0.76 | 0.41 | 5.8 | 7.31 | 8.69 | 3.73 | 6.44 | 86.94 | 87.76 |
| Palau | .... | 413 | 587 | 46 | .. | 0.55 | 21.74 | ... | ... | ... | ... | ... | ... |
| Papua New Guinea | 76 | 106 | 143 | 45286 | 0.01 | 0.01 | 0.13 | ... | ... | 1.15 | 1.35 | 98.79 | 98.52 |
| Samoa | 555 | 636 | 834 | 283 | 0.35 | 0.33 | 19.43 | ... | ... | 23.67 | 23.67 | 56.89 | 56.89 |
| Solomon Islands | 97 | 159 | 238 | 2799 | 0.15 | 0.1 | 1.5 | ... | ... | 0.54 | 0.64 | 98.04 | 97.86 |
| Tonga | 1306 | 1375 | 1431 | 72 | 0.18 | 0.17 | 23.61 | ... | ... | 43.06 | 43.06 | 33.33 | 33.33 |
| Vanuatu | 108 | 156 | 218 | 1219 | 0.15 | 0.17 | 2.46 | ... | ... | 7.38 | 7.38 | 90.98 | 90.16 |

**Sources:** United Nations, World Urbanization Prospects: The 1999 Revision, Food and Agriculture Organization: Production Yearbook , World Bank: World Development Indicators 2000 on CD-ROM.

For footnotes, refer to technical notes.

## TABLE A.10

### Labour Force and Economic Development Indicators

| | Labour force | | | | GDP per capita (PPP US$) | | | | Capital expenditure (% of total expenditure) | | | | Unemployment Total (% of labour force) | |
|---|---|---|---|---|---|---|---|---|---|---|---|---|---|---|
| | Total (000s) | Women (%) | Total (000s) | Women (%) | | | | | | | | | | |
| | 1985 | 1985 | 1998 | 1998 | 1985 | 1990 | 1995 | 1998 | 1985 | 1990 | 1995 | 1998 | 1990 | 1995 |
| **AFRICA** | | | | | | | | | | | | | | |
| Algeria | 5907 | 21.3 | 9874 | 26.4 | 4082 | 4546 | 4697 | 4792 | ... | ... | 29.0 | ... | 19.7 | 28.1 |
| Angola | 3842 | 46.8 | 5521 | 46.3 | 1396 | 1890 | 2590 | 1821 | ... | ... | ... | ... | ... | ... |
| Benin | 1860 | 47.7 | 2677 | 48.3 | 600 | 675 | 828 | 867 | ... | ... | ... | ... | ... | ... |
| Botswana | 476 | 48.5 | 687 | 45.5 | 2730 | 4773 | 5764 | 6103 | 22.6 | 21.5 | 16.3 | ... | ... | 21.5 |
| Burkina Faso | 4177 | 47.2 | 5365 | 46.6 | 530 | 675 | 813 | 870 | 9.9 | 22.8 | ... | ... | ... | ... |
| Burundi | 2560 | 49.7 | 3536 | 48.9 | 539 | 711 | 645 | 570 | ... | ... | 41.7 | ... | ... | ... |
| Cameroon | 4088 | 36.9 | 5864 | 37.8 | 1597 | 1556 | 1415 | 1474 | 42.7 | 26.0 | 8.4 | ... | ... | ... |
| Cape Verde | 109 | 36.5 | 166 | 39.0 | ... | 2382 | 3157 | 3233 | ... | ... | ... | ... | ... | ... |
| Central African Republic | ... | ... | ... | ... | 946 | 1059 | 1147 | 1118 | ... | ... | ... | ... | ... | ... |
| Chad | 2507 | 43.7 | 3496 | 44.6 | 613 | 751 | 817 | 856 | ... | 56.3 | ... | ... | ... | ... |
| Comoros | 171 | 43.0 | 239 | 42.3 | 1330 | 1596 | 1552 | 1398 | 37.6 | ... | ... | ... | ... | ... |
| Congo | 807 | 42.8 | 1141 | 43.4 | 925 | 1007 | 1027 | 995 | ... | ... | 9.1 | ... | ... | ... |
| Côte d'Ivoire | 3852 | 32.3 | 5797 | 33.1 | 1187 | 1402 | 1475 | 1598 | 0.0 | 0.0 | 21.2 | 29.3 | ... | ... |
| Dem. Republic of the Congo | 13618 | 44.2 | 20251 | 43.5 | 1343 | 1421 | 947 | 822 | 28.6 | 16.4 | 3.2 | ... | ... | ... |
| Djibouti | ... | ... | ... | ... | ... | ... | ... | ... | 10.6 | ... | ... | ... | ... | ... |
| Egypt | 16279 | 26.8 | 22718 | 29.7 | 1602 | 2343 | 2870 | 3041 | 13.7 | 17.3 | 19.2 | ... | 8.6 | 11.3 |
| Equatorial Guinea | 134 | 35.3 | 181 | 35.5 | ... | ... | ... | ... | ... | ... | ... | ... | ... | ... |
| Eritrea | 1378 | 47.5 | 1940 | 47.4 | ... | ... | 782 | 833 | ... | ... | ... | ... | ... | ... |
| Ethiopia | 19508 | 41.6 | 26344 | 40.9 | 336 | 468 | 549 | 574 | 20.0 | 16.3 | ... | ... | ... | ... |
| Gabon | 416 | 44.6 | 543 | 44.5 | 4751 | 5347 | 6320 | 6353 | 53.0 | 31.9 | ... | ... | ... | ... |
| Gambia | 380 | 44.7 | 620 | 45.0 | 1100 | 1378 | 1452 | 1453 | ... | 34.2 | ... | ... | ... | ... |
| Ghana | 5931 | 51.0 | 8676 | 50.6 | 1026 | 1394 | 1685 | 1735 | 16.0 | 19.0 | ... | ... | ... | ... |
| Guinea | 2494 | 47.3 | 3400 | 47.2 | ... | 1415 | 1717 | 1782 | ... | 52.7 | ... | 33.3 | ... | ... |
| Guinea-Bissau | 430 | 40.0 | 546 | 40.4 | 465 | 702 | 852 | 616 | 64.8 | ... | ... | ... | ... | ... |
| Kenya | 9339 | 46.0 | 14940 | 46.1 | 662 | 930 | 997 | 980 | 16.2 | 19.9 | 11.1 | ... | ... | ... |
| Lesotho | 626 | 37.2 | 844 | 36.8 | 703 | 1097 | 1430 | 1626 | ... | 44.6 | 33.3 | 19.3 | ... | ... |
| Liberia | 899 | 38.8 | 1214 | 39.5 | ... | ... | ... | ... | 16.1 | ... | ... | ... | ... | ... |
| Libya | 1136 | 18.4 | 1538 | 22.1 | ... | ... | ... | ... | ... | ... | ... | ... | ... | ... |
| Madagascar | 4859 | 45.1 | 6858 | 44.7 | 620 | 784 | 777 | 756 | ... | 43.2 | 34.5 | ... | ... | ... |
| Malawi | 3594 | 50.0 | 5056 | 48.8 | 391 | 469 | 489 | 523 | 30.6 | 24.0 | ... | ... | ... | ... |
| Mali | 3768 | 46.7 | 5192 | 46.3 | 489 | 567 | 666 | 681 | 2.5 | ... | ... | ... | ... | ... |
| Mauritania | 830 | 44.7 | 1163 | 43.8 | 1179 | 1273 | 1534 | 1563 | ... | ... | ... | ... | ... | ... |
| Mauritius | 386 | 28.0 | 499 | 32.2 | 3131 | 5422 | 7480 | 8312 | 14.3 | 16.8 | 16.8 | 12.2 | ... | 9.8 |
| Morocco | 8010 | 34.0 | 10832 | 34.7 | 1968 | 2780 | 3053 | 3305 | 19.3 | 27.9 | 21.6 | ... | 15.4 | 22.3 |
| Mozambique | 7312 | 48.7 | 8812 | 48.4 | 337 | 532 | 644 | 782 | ... | ... | ... | ... | ... | ... |
| Namibia | 495 | 40.3 | 682 | 40.8 | 3315 | 4214 | 5307 | 5176 | ... | 15.2 | ... | ... | ... | ... |
| Niger | 3238 | 44.3 | 4767 | 44.3 | 587 | 719 | 726 | 739 | ... | ... | ... | ... | ... | ... |
| Nigeria | 34110 | 35.8 | 48327 | 36.3 | 496 | 701 | 832 | 795 | 43.1 | ... | ... | ... | ... | ... |
| Rwanda | 3149 | 49.0 | 4377 | 48.9 | ... | ... | ... | ... | ... | 33.1 | ... | ... | ... | ... |
| Sao Tome and Principe | ... | ... | ... | ... | ... | 1399 | 1545 | 1469 | ... | ... | ... | ... | ... | ... |
| Senegal | 2869 | 42.3 | 4067 | 42.6 | 892 | 1145 | 1246 | 1307 | ... | ... | ... | ... | ... | ... |
| Seychelles | ... | ... | ... | ... | 5224 | 8390 | 10350 | 10600 | 22.2 | ... | 11.8 | 21.5 | ... | ... |
| Sierra Leone | 1362 | 35.5 | 1796 | 36.6 | 599 | 757 | 600 | 458 | 27.5 | 8.1 | 23.7 | ... | ... | ... |
| Somalia | 2946 | 43.3 | 3903 | 43.4 | ... | ... | ... | ... | ... | ... | ... | ... | ... | ... |
| South Africa | 11897 | 36.0 | 16147 | 37.6 | 6444 | 7934 | 8582 | 8488 | 10.8 | 10.4 | 4.6 | 4.0 | ... | 4.5 |
| Sudan | 7940 | 27.0 | 11055 | 29.0 | 721 | 900 | 1331 | 1394 | ... | ... | ... | ... | ... | ... |
| Swaziland | 231 | 35.3 | 356 | 37.6 | 2009 | 3543 | 3948 | 3816 | 33.9 | 24.0 | ... | ... | ... | ... |
| Togo | 1301 | 39.5 | 1828 | 40.0 | 1120 | 1377 | 1352 | 1372 | 27.3 | ... | ... | ... | ... | ... |
| Tunisia | 2542 | 29.0 | 3641 | 31.2 | 2944 | 3840 | 4870 | 5404 | 30.4 | 21.9 | 19.8 | ... | ... | ... |
| Uganda | 7208 | 47.8 | 10240 | 47.6 | 511 | 719 | 992 | 1074 | 15.4 | ... | ... | ... | ... | ... |
| United Republic of Tanzania | 11105 | 49.7 | 16386 | 49.2 | ... | 437 | 461 | 480 | 20.1 | ... | ... | ... | ... | ... |
| Zambia | 2747 | 45.5 | 4060 | 45.0 | 623 | 735 | 733 | 719 | 25.7 | ... | ... | ... | ... | ... |
| Zimbabwe | 3827 | 44.3 | 5377 | 44.5 | 1774 | 2385 | 2512 | 2669 | 7.8 | 10.2 | 10.1 | ... | ... | ... |
| **ASIA** | | | | | | | | | | | | | | |
| Afghanistan | 6632 | 34.4 | 10521 | 35.2 | ... | ... | ... | ... | ... | ... | ... | ... | ... | ... |
| Armenia | 1569 | 47.8 | 1860 | 48.4 | ... | 3287 | 1896 | 2072 | ... | ... | 6.2 | 21.2 | ... | ... |
| Azerbaijan | 2868 | 45.4 | 3480 | 44.2 | ... | 4791 | 1947 | 2175 | 32.3 | 25.5 | 17.2 | 18.1 | ... | 1.0 |
| Bahrain | 179 | 13.9 | 289 | 20.1 | 8776 | 10800 | 13803 | 13111 | ... | ... | ... | ... | ... | ... |
| Bangladesh | 46073 | 41.9 | 64071 | 42.3 | 700 | 953 | 1254 | 1361 | 15.3 | ... | ... | ... | 1.9 | ... |
| Bhutan | 275 | 39.5 | 364 | 39.8 | 722 | 1167 | 1571 | 1536 | 59.8 | 39.8 | 47.8 | 55.3 | ... | ... |
| Brunei | 87 | 27.5 | 139 | 34.9 | ... | 15688 | 16917 | 16765 | ... | ... | ... | ... | ... | ... |
| Cambodia | 4136 | 54.5 | 5979 | 51.9 | ... | 963 | 1285 | 1257 | ... | ... | ... | ... | ... | ... |
| China | 599077 | 44.0 | 743160 | 45.2 | 782 | 1338 | 2561 | 3105 | ... | ... | ... | ... | 2.5 | 2.9 |
| China, Hong Kong SAR | 2728 | 35.5 | 3477 | 36.9 | 9218 | 16018 | 22166 | 20763 | ... | ... | ... | ... | 1.3 | 3.2 |
| China, Macau SAR | 156 | 38.7 | 234 | 41.9 | ... | ... | ... | ... | ... | ... | ... | ... | 3.2 | 3.6 |
| Cyprus | 305 | 36.2 | 362 | 38.6 | 7490 | 12605 | 16792 | 17482 | 12.4 | 11.3 | 11.7 | ... | 1.8 | 2.6 |
| Dem. People's Rep. of Korea | 8904 | 44.3 | 12281 | 43.4 | ... | ... | ... | ... | ... | ... | ... | ... | ... | ... |
| Georgia | 2644 | 47.7 | 2667 | 46.6 | 8736 | 8304 | 2705 | 3353 | ... | ... | ... | 4.4 | ... | ... |
| India | 329013 | 32.5 | 431056 | 32.1 | 893 | 1382 | 1877 | 2077 | 13.9 | 11.2 | 11.2 | 11.2 | ... | ... |
| Indonesia | 68475 | 36.8 | 97766 | 40.4 | 1131 | 1858 | 2870 | 2651 | 45.0 | 43.5 | 46.0 | 32.0 | ... | ... |
| Iran (Islamic Republic of) | 13659 | 20.8 | 18584 | 25.9 | 3435 | 3798 | 4968 | 5121 | 20.6 | 24.8 | 32.6 | 33.2 | ... | ... |
| Iraq | 3982 | 16.8 | 6028 | 19.0 | ... | ... | ... | ... | ... | ... | ... | ... | ... | ... |
| Israel | 1609 | 35.8 | 2564 | 40.6 | 9257 | 13131 | 17395 | 17301 | 3.0 | 5.9 | 8.7 | 6.2 | 9.6 | 6.9 |
| Japan | 60377 | 38.8 | 68261 | 41.2 | 12300 | 19062 | 23212 | 23257 | 14.2 | 12.5 | ... | ... | 2.1 | 3.2 |
| Jordan | 661 | 16.2 | 1323 | 23.3 | 2307 | 2273 | 2844 | 3347 | 22.2 | 16.2 | 19.3 | ... | ... | ... |
| Kazakhstan | 7343 | 46.9 | 7485 | 46.8 | ... | 6278 | 4336 | 4378 | ... | ... | ... | ... | ... | 2.1 |
| Kuwait | 668 | 17.9 | 728 | 31.2 | ... | ... | ... | ... | 29.9 | 18.4 | 14.2 | 13.0 | ... | ... |
| Kyrgyzstan | 1678 | 46.8 | 2021 | 47.0 | ... | 3558 | 2022 | 2317 | ... | ... | ... | ... | ... | ... |

# TABLE A.10

## continued

| | | | | | | | | | | | | | | |
|---|---|---|---|---|---|---|---|---|---|---|---|---|---|---|
| Lao People's Dem. Republic | ... | ... | ... | ... | ... | 1141 | 1574 | 1734 | ... | ... | ... | ... | ... | ... |
| Lebanon | 982 | 24.6 | 1432 | 29.0 | ... | 2007 | 3964 | 4326 | ... | ... | 26.8 | 18.9 | ... | ... |
| Malaysia | 6114 | 34.7 | 9094 | 37.5 | 3506 | 5328 | 8146 | 8137 | 10.4 | 24.2 | 22.7 | ... | 5.1 | 2.8 |
| Maldives | 81 | 39.7 | 108 | 43.1 | 1501 | 2676 | 3744 | 4083 | 39.8 | 51.3 | 48.9 | 40.1 | ... | ... |
| Mongolia | 878 | 46.0 | 1266 | 46.9 | 1291 | 1699 | 1446 | 1541 | ... | ... | 22.1 | 13.8 | ... | ... |
| Myanmar | 19147 | 43.7 | 23566 | 43.4 | ... | ... | ... | ... | 27.3 | 28.9 | 49.1 | ... | ... | ... |
| Nepal | 7756 | 39.6 | 10512 | 40.5 | 619 | 861 | 1126 | 1157 | ... | ... | ... | ... | ... | ... |
| Oman | 405 | 8.4 | 622 | 15.7 | ... | ... | ... | ... | 25.3 | 10.6 | 15.1 | 13.6 | ... | ... |
| Pakistan | 34126 | 23.4 | 48685 | 27.7 | 848 | 1313 | 1734 | 1715 | 11.9 | 11.6 | 16.1 | 11.9 | 3.1 | 5.4 |
| Philippines | 21867 | 35.8 | 31573 | 37.6 | 2215 | 3083 | 3519 | 3555 | 13.7 | 15.7 | 15.4 | ... | 8.1 | 8.4 |
| Qatar | 183 | 9.0 | 408 | 14.1 | ... | ... | ... | ... | ... | ... | ... | ... | ... | ... |
| Republic of Korea | 17547 | 39.0 | 23215 | 41.0 | 4453 | 8596 | 13503 | 13478 | 13.6 | 15.0 | 20.0 | ... | 2.4 | 2.0 |
| Republic of Yemen | 3023 | 31.1 | 5312 | 28.0 | ... | 664 | 704 | 719 | ... | 33.4 | 11.2 | 17.9 | ... | ... |
| Saudi Arabia | 3961 | 8.6 | 6844 | 14.8 | 8169 | 10045 | 10766 | 10158 | ... | ... | ... | ... | ... | ... |
| Singapore | 1217 | 36.7 | 1582 | 39.0 | 8088 | 13768 | 22271 | 24210 | 30.9 | 23.6 | 22.8 | ... | 1.7 | 2.7 |
| Sri Lanka | 6018 | 30.6 | 8075 | 36.2 | 1418 | 2011 | 2741 | 2979 | 39.7 | 21.4 | 21.3 | 21.3 | 14.4 | 12.5 |
| Syrian Arab Republic | 2911 | 24.0 | 4736 | 26.5 | 2048 | 2389 | 3212 | 2892 | ... | 26.5 | 38.1 | ... | ... | ... |
| Tajikistan | 1695 | 44.5 | 2324 | 44.3 | ... | 2495 | 1006 | 1041 | ... | ... | ... | ... | ... | 2.0 |
| Thailand | 28130 | 47.0 | 36721 | 46.3 | 2012 | 3821 | 6217 | 5456 | 19.2 | 18.2 | 34.5 | 36.4 | 2.2 | 1.1 |
| Turkey | 21623 | 35.0 | 29822 | 37.0 | 3108 | 4663 | 5804 | 6422 | 18.4 | 13.3 | 8.5 | ... | 8.0 | 6.9 |
| Turkmenistan | 1324 | 45.8 | 2029 | 45.7 | ... | 5848 | 2009 | ... | ... | ... | ... | ... | ... | ... |
| United Arab Emirates | 717 | 8.4 | 1362 | 14.1 | 18705 | 19880 | 19935 | 17719 | 3.4 | 1.3 | ... | 5.1 | ... | 0.4 |
| Uzbekistan | 7245 | 46.8 | 10101 | 46.6 | ... | ... | 2043 | 2053 | ... | ... | ... | ... | ... | ... |
| Viet Nam | 28845 | 48.9 | 39025 | 49.1 | ... | ... | 1479 | 1689 | ... | ... | 22.1 | 28.9 | ... | ... |
| **EUROPE** | | | | | | | | | | | | | | |
| Albania | 1360 | 39.5 | 1636 | 41.1 | ... | 2648 | 2717 | 2804 | ... | ... | 17.8 | 15.8 | 9.5 | ... |
| Austria | 3475 | 40.5 | 3797 | 40.3 | 12600 | 18227 | 22090 | 23166 | 8.6 | 8.7 | 7.3 | ... | 3.2 | 4.3 |
| Belarus | 5187 | 49.3 | 5324 | 48.8 | ... | 6714 | 5109 | 6319 | ... | ... | 13.5 | 14.7 | ... | 2.7 |
| Belgium | 3943 | 36.7 | 4184 | 40.6 | 12745 | 18501 | 22333 | 23223 | 6.4 | 4.8 | 4.9 | ... | 7.2 | 9.3 |
| Bosnia and Herzegovina | 1813 | 35.2 | 1733 | 38.1 | ... | ... | ... | ... | ... | ... | ... | ... | ... | ... |
| Bulgaria | 4560 | 46.7 | 4211 | 48.2 | 3824 | 5344 | 5609 | 4809 | ... | 2.9 | 3.8 | 9.0 | 1.7 | 16.5 |
| Croatia | 2209 | 41.5 | 2115 | 43.9 | ... | 6781 | 5777 | 6749 | ... | ... | 8.0 | 10.5 | 8.2 | ... |
| Czech Republic | 5374 | 47.3 | 5765 | 47.4 | 9066 | 12368 | 12426 | 12362 | ... | ... | 12.1 | 8.6 | ... | 4.1 |
| Denmark | 2813 | 45.0 | 2969 | 46.4 | 13370 | 17942 | 22947 | 24218 | 4.5 | 3.3 | 3.5 | ... | 8.3 | 7.0 |
| Estonia | 845 | 50.0 | 797 | 49.0 | ... | 7775 | 6435 | 7682 | ... | ... | 6.6 | 8.6 | 0.8 | 9.7 |
| Finland | 2500 | 46.8 | 2628 | 47.9 | 11697 | 17172 | 18764 | 20847 | 8.2 | 6.8 | 4.8 | ... | 3.4 | 17.0 |
| France | 24275 | 41.8 | 26481 | 44.8 | 12005 | 17278 | 20492 | 21175 | 4.1 | 6.0 | 4.6 | ... | 9.2 | 11.6 |
| Germany | 38072 | 41.0 | 41024 | 42.1 | ... | ... | 21479 | 22169 | 5.5 | 4.5 | 4.9 | 4.3 | ... | 8.1 |
| Greece | 3974 | 31.6 | 4521 | 37.4 | 8145 | 11049 | 13147 | 13943 | 12.8 | 7.8 | 13.4 | ... | 7.0 | 9.1 |
| Hungary | 4972 | 43.7 | 4855 | 44.6 | 6802 | 9009 | 9315 | 10232 | 10.6 | 3.7 | 8.6 | 9.3 | 1.7 | 10.2 |
| Iceland | 130 | 43.2 | 153 | 45.3 | 14393 | 20112 | 22750 | 25110 | 14.6 | 11.7 | 7.9 | ... | 1.8 | 4.8 |
| Ireland | 1310 | 29.9 | 1519 | 33.9 | 7066 | 11364 | 17264 | 21482 | 6.6 | 7.0 | 9.9 | ... | 13.0 | 12.2 |
| Isle of Man | ... | ... | ... | ... | ... | ... | ... | ... | ... | ... | ... | ... | 2.1 | 4.4 |
| Italy | 23203 | 34.8 | 25339 | 38.2 | 11641 | 16997 | 20513 | 20585 | ... | 8.4 | 5.2 | 5.5 | 11.4 | 12.3 |
| Latvia | 1442 | 50.2 | 1322 | 50.3 | 5572 | 8122 | 4919 | 5728 | ... | ... | 3.9 | 7.5 | ... | 18.9 |
| Lithuania | 1843 | 48.8 | 1926 | 48.0 | ... | ... | 5569 | 6436 | ... | ... | 9.7 | 10.3 | ... | 7.3 |
| Luxembourg | 158 | 34.3 | 183 | 36.6 | 13637 | 22756 | 31807 | 33505 | 12.0 | 11.4 | 11.1 | ... | 1.6 | 2.9 |
| Malta | 124 | 23.0 | 143 | 27.3 | 4567 | 7592 | 11000 | 23306 | 20.1 | 31.5 | 14.1 | ... | 3.8 | 3.6 |
| Moldova | 2096 | 49.5 | 2149 | 48.6 | ... | ... | 2320 | 1947 | ... | ... | ... | ... | ... | 1.0 |
| The Netherlands | 6232 | 35.2 | 7378 | 40.2 | 11796 | 16848 | 20812 | 22176 | 8.2 | 5.8 | 4.9 | ... | 7.4 | 7.0 |
| Norway | 2035 | 42.7 | 2305 | 46.1 | 13648 | 18389 | 24694 | 26342 | 4.7 | 5.2 | 5.0 | ... | 5.1 | 5.0 |
| Poland | 18974 | 45.4 | 19720 | 46.2 | 3955 | 5538 | 6606 | 7619 | 6.9 | ... | 3.6 | 5.4 | ... | 13.3 |
| Portugal | 4805 | 40.7 | 4984 | 43.8 | 6528 | 10880 | 13613 | 14701 | 9.4 | 11.6 | 12.1 | ... | 4.8 | 7.4 |
| Romania | 10908 | 45.0 | 10576 | 44.5 | 5733 | 6090 | 6431 | 5648 | 36.6 | 17.3 | 12.6 | ... | ... | 8.0 |
| Russian Federation | 76245 | 48.9 | 77862 | 48.9 | ... | 9875 | 7093 | 6460 | ... | ... | ... | ... | ... | 8.8 |
| Slovakia | 2596 | 46.5 | 2911 | 47.8 | 6490 | 8646 | 8487 | 9699 | ... | ... | ... | ... | ... | 13.1 |
| Slovenia | 987 | 46.0 | 991 | 46.5 | ... | ... | 12978 | 14293 | ... | ... | ... | ... | 4.7 | 7.4 |
| Spain | 14979 | 31.5 | 17323 | 36.7 | 7992 | 12444 | 15163 | 16212 | 10.9 | 9.4 | 5.2 | ... | 16.0 | 22.7 |
| Sweden | 4342 | 45.8 | 4780 | 47.9 | 12702 | 17537 | 20031 | 20659 | 3.1 | 2.5 | 2.8 | 2.5 | 1.6 | 7.6 |
| Switzerland | 3300 | 38.0 | 3837 | 40.2 | 16667 | 23257 | 25475 | 25512 | ... | ... | 4.2 | ... | 0.5 | 3.3 |
| TFYR Macedonia | 866 | 38.0 | 925 | 41.3 | ... | 4181 | 4254 | ... | ... | ... | ... | ... | 23.6 | 35.6 |
| Ukraine | 25968 | 49.5 | 25148 | 48.7 | ... | 6372 | 3734 | 3194 | ... | ... | ... | ... | ... | 5.6 |
| United Kingdom | 27776 | 40.7 | 29528 | 43.7 | 11007 | 16144 | 19465 | 20336 | 5.2 | 10.0 | 6.1 | 4.0 | 6.8 | 8.6 |
| Yugoslavia | 4697 | 40.2 | 5096 | 42.7 | ... | ... | ... | ... | ... | ... | ... | ... | ... | ... |
| **LATIN AMERICA** | | | | | | | | | | | | | | |
| Antigua and Barbuda | ... | ... | ... | ... | 3943 | 6741 | 8425 | 9277 | ... | ... | ... | ... | ... | ... |
| Argentina | 11516 | 28.0 | 14450 | 32.3 | 6535 | 7448 | 10736 | 12013 | 8.5 | 4.6 | 7.3 | ... | 9.2 | 15.9 |
| Bahamas | 107 | 44.9 | 159 | 47.0 | 10938 | 14226 | 14639 | 14614 | 9.8 | 11.6 | 10.7 | 10.2 | ... | 11.1 |
| Barbados | 119 | 45.2 | 141 | 46.3 | ... | ... | ... | ... | ... | ... | 15.0 | 19.7 | ... | ... |
| Belize | 50 | 20.8 | 81 | 23.6 | 2159 | 3792 | 4693 | 4566 | 12.1 | ... | ... | ... | ... | 12.5 |
| Bolivia | 2299 | 35.1 | 3180 | 37.6 | ... | 1751 | 2186 | 2269 | ... | 15.1 | 19.2 | 15.6 | 7.3 | 3.6 |
| Brazil | 56794 | 31.6 | 76302 | 35.4 | 4444 | 5346 | 6572 | 6625 | 3.8 | 2.0 | ... | ... | 3.7 | ... |
| Cayman Islands | ... | ... | ... | ... | ... | ... | ... | ... | 14.3 | 14.9 | ... | ... | ... | ... |
| Chile | 4337 | 28.1 | 5929 | 32.9 | 3023 | 4813 | 7545 | 8787 | 10.0 | 11.2 | 15.7 | 16.5 | 5.7 | 4.7 |
| Colombia | 11714 | 31.0 | 17546 | 38.2 | 3938 | 5629 | 6151 | 6006 | 18.3 | 22.2 | 24.9 | 20.3 | 10.2 | 8.7 |
| Costa Rica | 951 | 24.5 | 1410 | 30.5 | 3283 | 4606 | 5940 | 5987 | 15.9 | 11.5 | 8.5 | ... | 4.6 | 5.2 |
| Cuba | 4248 | 33.7 | 5441 | 38.9 | ... | ... | ... | ... | ... | ... | ... | ... | ... | ... |
| Dominica | ... | ... | ... | ... | 2327 | 3930 | 4821 | 5102 | ... | ... | ... | ... | ... | ... |
| Dominican Republic | 2487 | 25.9 | 3549 | 30.1 | 2386 | 3122 | 3998 | 4598 | 25.5 | 43.5 | 42.1 | ... | ... | 15.9 |
| Ecuador | 3094 | 22.5 | 4627 | 27.4 | 2105 | 2624 | 3163 | 3003 | ... | 18.2 | ... | ... | 6.1 | ... |
| El Salvador | 1717 | 29.0 | 2544 | 35.5 | 2212 | 2886 | 4041 | 4036 | ... | ... | ... | ... | 10.0 | 7.7 |
| Grenada | ... | ... | ... | ... | 2594 | 4380 | 5223 | 5838 | ... | ... | 24.5 | ... | ... | ... |
| Guatemala | 2631 | 22.9 | 3888 | 27.8 | 2144 | 2770 | 3444 | 3505 | ... | ... | ... | ... | ... | ... |

# TABLE A.10

## continued

| | Labour force | | | | GDP per capita (PPP US$) | | | | Capital expenditure (% of total expenditure) | | | | Unemployment Total (% of labour force) | |
|---|---|---|---|---|---|---|---|---|---|---|---|---|---|---|
| | Total (000s) | Women (%) | Total (000s) | Women (%) | | | | | | | | | | |
| | 1985 | 1985 | 1998 | 1998 | 1985 | 1990 | 1995 | 1998 | 1985 | 1990 | 1995 | 1998 | 1990 | 1995 |
| Guyana | 285 | 28.3 | 365 | 33.6 | 1820 | 2037 | 3163 | 3403 | 24.0 | ... | ... | ... | ... | ... |
| Haiti | 2696 | 43.9 | 3365 | 43.0 | 1389 | 1603 | 1410 | 1383 | 0.6 | ... | ... | ... | ... | ... |
| Honduras | 1423 | 26.5 | 2278 | 31.0 | 1588 | 2057 | 2423 | 2433 | ... | ... | ... | ... | 4.8 | 3.2 |
| Jamaica | 1086 | 46.3 | 1340 | 46.2 | 2052 | 3167 | 3619 | 3389 | 14.7 | ... | ... | ... | 15.7 | 16.2 |
| Mexico | 26413 | 28.5 | 38338 | 32.6 | 4990 | 6225 | 7061 | 7704 | 15.9 | 14.0 | 11.6 | ... | ... | 5.7 |
| Netherlands Antilles | 78 | 42.5 | 96 | 43.0 | ... | ... | ... | ... | 13.7 | 16.5 | 18.9 | ... | 17.0 | 12.8 |
| Nicaragua | 1191 | 29.6 | 1918 | 35.1 | 1634 | 1605 | 2073 | 2142 | 11.6 | 4.4 | 32.9 | ... | 11.1 | ... |
| Panama | 802 | 31.1 | 1161 | 34.7 | 3348 | 3698 | 5067 | 5249 | 7.3 | 1.9 | 11.4 | ... | ... | 14.0 |
| Paraguay | 1335 | 27.4 | 1931 | 29.6 | 2987 | 3876 | 4599 | 4288 | 16.2 | 16.8 | ... | ... | 6.6 | ... |
| Peru | 6432 | 25.7 | 9176 | 30.6 | 2838 | 2814 | 4330 | 4282 | 15.4 | 8.2 | 17.2 | 16.0 | ... | ... |
| Puerto Rico | 1114 | 32.9 | 1428 | 36.6 | ... | ... | ... | ... | ... | ... | ... | ... | 14.1 | 13.7 |
| Saint Kitts and Nevis | ... | ... | ... | ... | 3583 | 6342 | 9238 | 10672 | 21.1 | 11.5 | ... | ... | ... | ... |
| Saint Lucia | ... | ... | ... | ... | 2304 | 4204 | 5247 | 5183 | 16.2 | 22.4 | ... | ... | ... | 15.9 |
| Saint Vincent and the Grenadines | ... | ... | ... | ... | 2069 | 3440 | 4342 | 4692 | 6.8 | 31.1 | 9.7 | 28.6 | ... | ... |
| Suriname | 119 | 28.4 | 152 | 33.0 | ... | ... | ... | ... | 6.1 | ... | ... | ... | 15.8 | 8.4 |
| Trinidad and Tobago | 459 | 31.3 | 565 | 33.7 | 5358 | 5887 | 6979 | 7485 | ... | ... | 10.1 | ... | 20.0 | 17.2 |
| United States Virgin Islands | ... | ... | ... | ... | ... | ... | ... | ... | ... | ... | ... | ... | 2.8 | 5.7 |
| Uruguay | 1264 | 35.0 | 1480 | 41.3 | 4104 | 5905 | 7832 | 8623 | 6.2 | 7.3 | 6.5 | 5.1 | 8.5 | 10.2 |
| Venezuela | 6170 | 29.0 | 9297 | 34.1 | 3879 | 5019 | 5980 | 5808 | 17.3 | 16.1 | 15.5 | 19.2 | 10.4 | 10.3 |
| **NORTHERN AMERICA** | | | | | | | | | | | | | | |
| Bermuda | ... | ... | ... | ... | 13935 | 19017 | 22388 | ... | ... | ... | ... | ... | ... | ... |
| Canada | 13230 | 41.8 | 16363 | 45.4 | 14496 | 19672 | 23085 | 23582 | 1.8 | 1.9 | 1.9 | ... | 8.1 | 9.5 |
| Greenland | ... | ... | ... | ... | ... | ... | ... | ... | ... | ... | ... | ... | ... | ... |
| United States | 116583 | 42.7 | 137852 | 45.7 | 16304 | 22537 | 27395 | 29605 | 4.6 | 7.6 | 3.4 | 3.0 | 5.6 | 5.6 |
| **OCEANIA** | | | | | | | | | | | | | | |
| Australia | 7564 | 39.0 | 9563 | 43.3 | 12355 | 16484 | 21268 | 22452 | 10.1 | 8.8 | 6.2 | 5.2 | 7.0 | 8.1 |
| Fiji | 230 | 20.4 | 308 | 29.2 | 2620 | 3761 | 4609 | 4231 | 14.3 | 17.3 | 9.7 | ... | 6.4 | 5.4 |
| French Polynesia | ... | ... | ... | ... | 11645 | 16277 | 19607 | ... | ... | ... | ... | ... | ... | ... |
| Guam | ... | ... | ... | ... | ... | ... | ... | ... | ... | ... | ... | ... | 2.8 | ... |
| Kiribati | ... | ... | ... | ... | 1233 | 1486 | 1859 | 1891 | ... | ... | ... | ... | ... | ... |
| New Zealand | 1472 | 38.7 | 1896 | 44.6 | 11464 | 14088 | 17706 | 17288 | 6.2 | 2.0 | 2.0 | 2.7 | 7.8 | 6.3 |
| Papua New Guinea | 1687 | 41.5 | 2255 | 42.0 | 1434 | 1726 | 2606 | 2359 | 7.5 | 10.6 | ... | ... | ... | ... |
| Samoa | ... | ... | ... | ... | 2478 | 3039 | 2905 | 3832 | ... | ... | ... | ... | ... | ... |
| Solomon Islands | 138 | 47.3 | 212 | 46.6 | 1206 | 1797 | 2282 | 1940 | 18.7 | 12.5 | ... | ... | ... | ... |
| Tonga | ... | ... | ... | ... | 2642 | 3364 | 4678 | 4101 | 48.9 | 46.0 | ... | ... | ... | ... |
| Vanuatu | ... | ... | ... | ... | 2627 | 3162 | 3205 | 3120 | 23.0 | 42.5 | ... | ... | ... | ... |

**Sources:** International Labour Organization Database, Estimates and Projections of the Economically Active Population, 1950–2010, International Labour Organization Database Key Indicators of the Labour Market 1999 (issue), World Bank: World Development Indicators 2000 on CD-ROM.
For footnotes, refer to technical notes.

# TABLE A.11

## Social Indicators

| | Personal computers (per 1000 people) | | Telephone mainlines (per 1000 people) | | Television sets (per 1000 people) | | Hospital beds (per 1000 people) | | Health expenditure (% of GDP) | | | Population below national poverty line (%) | Illiteracy rate Population aged 15 years and over (%) | | |
|---|---|---|---|---|---|---|---|---|---|---|---|---|---|---|---|
| | 1990 | 1998 | 1990 | 1998 | 1985 | 1995 | 1990 | 1995 | 1990 | 1995 | 1998 | 1987–1997 | Total 2000 | M 2000 | F 2000 |
| **AFRICA** | | | | | | | | | | | | | | | |
| Algeria | 1 | ... | 32 | 53 | 69 | 88 | 2.5 | ... | 4.2 | 4.6 | ... | 22.6 | 36.7 | 24.9 | 48.7 |
| Angola | ... | 1 | 8 | 6 | 5 | 14[1998] | 1.3 | ... | ... | ... | ... | ... | ... | ... | ... |
| Benin | ... | ... | 3 | 7 | 4 | 6 | 0.8 | ... | 2.0 | 2.0 | 2.0 | 33.0 | 62.5 | 47.8 | 76.4 |
| Botswana | ... | 25 | 21 | 65 | 16[1990] | 19 | 1.6 | ... | 3.0 | 3.7 | 4.3 | ... | 22.8 | 25.6 | 20.2 |
| Burkina Faso | – | ... | 2 | 4 | 5 | 6 | 0.3 | 1.3 | 4.1 | 3.9 | 3.9 | ... | 77.0 | 66.8 | 86.9 |
| Burundi | ... | ... | 2 | 3 | – | 2 | ... | ... | 3.6 | 4.4 | 3.6 | 36.2 | 51.9 | 43.7 | 59.5 |
| Cameroon | 1 | ... | 3 | ... | 23[1990] | 24 | 2.6 | ... | 1.7 | 3.9 | ... | ... | 24.6 | 18.2 | 30.8 |
| Cape Verde | ... | ... | 24 | 98 | 3[1990] | 3 | ... | ... | ... | ... | ... | ... | 26.5 | 15.7 | 34.7 |
| Central African Republic | ... | ... | 2 | 3 | 2 | 5 | 0.9 | ... | ... | 2.7 | ... | ... | 53.5 | 40.4 | 65.5 |
| Chad | ... | ... | 1 | 1 | 1[1990] | 1 | ... | ... | ... | 3.0 | ... | ... | 46.4 | 33.1 | 59.2 |
| Comoros | – | ... | 8 | 9 | 2[1990] | 4 | 2.8 | ... | ... | ... | ... | ... | 43.8 | 36.5 | 50.9 |
| Congo | ... | ... | 7 | 8 | 3 | 8 | 3.4 | ... | 2.6 | 5.3 | ... | ... | 19.3 | 12.5 | 25.6 |
| Côte d'Ivoire | ... | ... | 6 | 12 | 50 | 70[1998] | 0.8 | ... | 3.2 | 3.4 | ... | ... | 53.2 | 45.4 | 61.5 |
| Dem. Republic of the Congo | ... | ... | 1 | ... | 1[1990] | 40 | 1.4 | ... | ... | ... | ... | ... | ... | ... | ... |
| Djibouti | 2 | ... | 11 | 13 | 31 | 45 | 2.5 | ... | ... | ... | ... | ... | 48.6 | 35.0 | 61.6 |
| Egypt | ... | 9 | 30 | 60 | 80 | 117 | 2.1 | ... | 4.3 | 3.7 | ... | ... | 44.7 | 33.4 | 56.3 |
| Equatorial Guinea | ... | 2 | 4 | 13 | 7 | 162[1998] | ... | ... | 6.3 | 4.4 | ... | ... | 16.8 | 7.5 | 25.5 |
| Eritrea | ... | ... | ... | 7 | ... | 14[1998] | ... | ... | ... | ... | ... | ... | ... | ... | ... |
| Ethiopia | ... | ... | 3 | 3 | 2 | 4 | 0.2 | ... | 2.4 | 3.8 | 4.1 | ... | 61.3 | 56.1 | 66.6 |
| Gabon | ... | 9 | 22 | ... | 25 | 47 | 3.2 | ... | ... | ... | ... | ... | 29.2 | 20.2 | 37.8 |
| Gambia | ... | ... | 7 | 21 | – | 4 | 0.6 | ... | ... | ... | ... | 64.0 | 63.5 | 56.2 | 70.4 |
| Ghana | – | ... | 3 | 8 | 12 | 99[1998] | 1.5 | ... | 4.1 | 3.9 | 4.7 | 31.4 | 29.8 | 20.5 | 38.8 |
| Guinea | ... | ... | 2 | 5 | 2 | 27 | 0.6 | ... | ... | ... | ... | ... | 58.9 | 44.9 | 73.0 |
| Guinea-Bissau | ... | ... | 6 | 7 | – | ... | 1.5 | ... | ... | ... | ... | 48.8 | 63.2 | 47.0 | 78.6 |
| Kenya | – | ... | 8 | ... | 7 | 18 | 1.6 | ... | ... | ... | ... | 42.0 | 17.5 | 11.0 | 24.0 |
| Lesotho | ... | ... | 7 | 10 | – | 12 | ... | ... | ... | ... | ... | 49.2 | 16.1 | 26.4 | 6.4 |
| Liberia | ... | ... | 4 | ... | 16 | 20 | ... | ... | ... | ... | ... | ... | 46.6 | 30.1 | 63.2 |
| Libya | ... | ... | 48 | 84 | 62 | 102 | 4.2 | ... | ... | ... | ... | ... | 20.2 | 9.1 | 32.4 |
| Madagascar | ... | ... | 2 | 3 | 5 | 20 | 0.9 | ... | ... | ... | ... | ... | ... | ... | ... |
| Malawi | ... | ... | 3 | 3 | – | 2 | 1.6 | ... | ... | ... | 3.3 | 54.0 | 39.7 | 25.5 | 53.3 |
| Mali | ... | ... | 1 | 3 | 6 | 10 | ... | ... | 3.0 | ... | 3.8 | ... | 59.7 | 52.1 | 66.8 |
| Mauritania | ... | ... | 3 | 6 | – | 91[1998] | 0.7 | ... | ... | ... | ... | 57.0 | 60.1 | 49.4 | 70.5 |
| Mauritius | 4 | 87 | 52 | 214 | 128 | 221 | ... | ... | ... | ... | 3.5 | 10.6 | 15.7 | 12.3 | 19.0 |
| Morocco | ... | ... | 16 | 54 | 63 | 158 | 1.3 | ... | 2.5 | ... | ... | 26.0 | 51.1 | 38.1 | 64.0 |
| Mozambique | ... | ... | 3 | 4 | – | 3 | 0.9 | ... | ... | ... | ... | ... | 56.2 | 40.1 | 71.6 |
| Namibia | ... | ... | 39 | 69 | 14 | 30 | ... | ... | ... | ... | ... | ... | 17.9 | 17.1 | 18.8 |
| Niger | ... | ... | 1 | 2 | 2 | 24 | ... | 0.1 | ... | ... | ... | 63.0 | 84.3 | 76.5 | 91.7 |
| Nigeria | ... | ... | 3 | 4 | 7 | 59 | 1.7 | ... | ... | ... | ... | 43.0 | 35.9 | 27.7 | 43.8 |
| Reunion | ... | ... | ... | ... | ... | ... | ... | ... | ... | ... | ... | ... | 12.9 | 15.2 | 10.8 |
| Rwanda | ... | ... | 2 | 2 | – | – | 1.7 | ... | ... | ... | ... | 51.2 | 33.0 | 26.3 | 39.4 |
| Senegal | 2 | ... | 6 | 16 | 31 | 38 | 0.7 | ... | ... | ... | ... | 33.4 | 62.7 | 52.8 | 72.4 |
| Seychelles | ... | ... | 124 | 244 | 31 | 133 | ... | ... | ... | ... | ... | ... | ... | ... | ... |
| Sierra Leone | ... | ... | 3 | 4 | 8 | 13[1998] | ... | ... | ... | ... | ... | 68.0 | 63.7 | 49.3 | 77.4 |
| Somalia | ... | ... | 2 | 1 | – | 14 | 0.8 | ... | ... | ... | ... | 35.3 | ... | ... | ... |
| South Africa | 7 | 47 | 87 | 115 | 89 | 127 | ... | ... | ... | ... | ... | ... | 14.9 | 14.2 | 15.5 |
| Sudan | ... | 2 | 3 | 6 | 51 | 87[1998] | 1.1 | ... | ... | ... | ... | ... | 42.9 | 31.7 | 54.0 |
| Swaziland | ... | ... | 17 | 30 | 11 | 99 | ... | ... | ... | ... | ... | ... | 20.2 | 19.1 | 21.3 |
| Togo | ... | 7 | 3 | 7 | 5 | 18[1998] | 1.5 | ... | ... | ... | ... | 32.3 | 42.9 | 27.8 | 57.4 |
| Tunisia | 3 | 15 | 38 | 81 | 56 | 198[1998] | 1.9 | ... | 5.6 | 5.9 | ... | 19.9 | 29.2 | 18.6 | 39.9 |
| Uganda | ... | ... | 2 | 3 | 6 | 26 | ... | ... | ... | ... | ... | 55.0 | 32.7 | 22.3 | 42.9 |
| United Republic of Tanzania | ... | ... | 3 | 4 | 2[1990] | 17 | 1.0 | ... | ... | ... | ... | 51.1 | 24.8 | 15.9 | 33.4 |
| Zambia | ... | ... | 9 | 9 | 13 | 137[1998] | ... | ... | 3.3 | ... | 4.1 | 86.0 | 22.0 | 14.8 | 28.8 |
| Zimbabwe | – | ... | 12 | ... | 21 | 29 | 0.5 | ... | ... | ... | 6.4 | 25.5 | 7.3 | 4.5 | 10.1 |
| **ASIA** | | | | | | | | | | | | | | | |
| Afghanistan | ... | ... | 2 | 1 | 7 | 10 | 0.2 | ... | ... | ... | ... | ... | 63.7 | 49.0 | 79.2 |
| Armenia | ... | 4 | 157 | 157 | 196 | 216 | 8.6 | 7.6 | ... | 7.8 | ... | ... | ... | ... | ... |
| Azerbaijan | ... | ... | 86 | 89 | 180 | 254[1998] | 9.9 | 9.9 | 8.8 | 7.5 | ... | ... | ... | ... | ... |
| Bahrain | ... | 93 | 192 | 245 | 411 | 439 | ... | ... | 7.0 | 5.1 | 4.3 | ... | 12.4 | 9.0 | 17.3 |
| Bangladesh | ... | ... | 2 | 3 | 3 | 7 | 0.3 | ... | 2.8 | 3.3 | 3.5 | 35.6 | 59.2 | 48.3 | 70.5 |
| Bhutan | ... | 4 | 4 | 16 | ... | 17 | 0.8 | ... | 4.7 | 5.6 | 6.9 | ... | 52.7 | 38.9 | 66.4 |
| Brunei Darussalam | ... | ... | 136 | 247 | 199 | 387 | ... | ... | ... | ... | ... | ... | 8.4 | 5.3 | 11.8 |
| Cambodia | ... | ... | – | 2 | 7 | 60 | 2.1 | ... | ... | 6.5 | 6.9 | ... | ... | ... | ... |
| China | – | 9 | 6 | 70 | 38 | 243 | 2.3 | 2.8 | 3.5 | 3.9 | ... | 6.00 | 15.0 | 7.7 | 22.6 |
| China, Hong Kong SAR | 47 | 254 | 450 | 558 | 234 | 431[1998] | ... | ... | 3.7 | 5.0 | ... | ... | 6.6 | 3.5 | 10.0 |
| China, Macau SAR | ... | ... | 255 | 409 | 286[1990] | 290 | ... | ... | ... | ... | ... | ... | 6.8 | 3.4 | 9.9 |
| Cyprus | 9 | ... | 428 | 585 | 138 | 163 | ... | ... | ... | ... | ... | ... | 3.1 | 1.3 | 5.0 |
| Dem. People's Rep. of Korea | ... | ... | 38 | 47 | 10 | 48 | ... | ... | ... | ... | ... | ... | ... | ... | ... |
| Gaza Strip | ... | ... | ... | ... | ... | ... | ... | ... | ... | 6.2 | ... | ... | ... | ... | ... |
| Georgia | ... | ... | 99 | 115 | 190 | 470 | 9.7 | 6.6 | ... | ... | ... | ... | ... | ... | ... |
| India | – | 3 | 6 | 22 | 5 | 61 | ... | ... | 5.6 | ... | ... | 35.0 | 44.2 | 31.4 | 57.9 |
| Indonesia | 1 | 8 | 6 | 27 | 39 | 136[1998] | 0.7 | ... | 1.2 | 1.2 | 1.3 | 15.1 | 13.0 | 8.1 | 17.9 |
| Iran (Islamic Republic) | ... | ... | 40 | 112 | 51 | 157[1998] | 1.4 | ... | 4.8 | ... | ... | ... | 23.1 | 16.3 | 30.0 |
| Iraq | ... | ... | 37 | 31 | 59 | 80 | 1.7 | ... | ... | ... | ... | ... | ... | ... | ... |
| Israel | 63 | 217 | 343 | 471 | 260 | 318[1998] | 6.2 | 6.0 | 9.9 | 10.3 | 10.4 | ... | 3.9 | 2.6 | 7.0 |
| Japan | 60 | 237 | 441 | 503 | 580 | 681 | 16.0 | 16.2 | 6.1 | 7.2 | ... | ... | ... | ... | ... |
| Jordan | ... | ... | 58 | 86 | 91 | 52[1998] | 1.8 | ... | 6.9 | 7.9 | ... | 15.0 | 10.2 | 5.1 | 15.6 |
| Kazakhstan | ... | ... | 80 | 104 | 266 | 277 | 13.6 | 11.6 | ... | 4.2 | ... | ... | ... | ... | ... |
| Kuwait | 7 | 105 | 247 | 236 | 262 | 373 | ... | ... | ... | ... | ... | ... | 17.7 | 15.7 | 20.1 |

# TABLE A.11

## continued

| | Personal computers (per 1000 people) | | Telephone mainlines (per 1000 people) | | Television sets (per 1000 people) | | Hospital beds (per 1000 people) | | Health expenditure (% of GDP) | | | Population below national poverty line (%) | Illiteracy rate Population aged 15 years and over (%) | | |
|---|---|---|---|---|---|---|---|---|---|---|---|---|---|---|---|
| | 1990 | 1998 | 1990 | 1998 | 1985 | 1995 | 1990 | 1995 | 1990 | 1995 | 1998 | 1987–1997 | Total 2000 | M 2000 | F 2000 |
| Kyrgyzstan | ... | ... | 72 | 76 | 226 | ... | 12.0 | 9.0 | 4.4 | 4.3 | 3.1 | ... | ... | ... | ... |
| Lao People's Dem. Republic | ... | ... | 2 | 6 | – | 10 | 2.6 | ... | ... | 3.1 | 2.6 | ... | 38.2 | 26.4 | 49.5 |
| Lebanon | ... | 39 | 118 | 194 | 260 | 357 | 1.7 | ... | ... | ... | ... | ... | 13.9 | 7.7 | 19.6 |
| Malaysia | 8 | 59 | 89 | 198 | 115 | 169 | 2.1 | 2.0 | 2.5 | 2.3 | 2.4 | 15.5 | 15.5 | 10.5 | 20.6 |
| Maldives | ... | ... | 29 | 71 | 17 | 40 | 0.8 | ... | 8.0 | 10.0 | 10.7 | ... | 3.7 | 3.7 | 3.6 |
| Mongolia | ... | ... | 32 | ... | 24 | 62 | ... | ... | 6.7 | ... | ... | ... | 0.7 | 0.8 | 0.7 |
| Myanmar | ... | ... | 2 | 5 | 1 | 7 | 0.6 | ... | 1.9 | 1.4 | 1.1 | ... | 15.3 | 11.0 | 19.4 |
| Nepal | ... | ... | 3 | 8 | 1 | 3 | 0.2 | 0.2 | 4.5 | 4.5 | 5.5 | 42.0 | 58.6 | 40.9 | 76.2 |
| Oman | 2 | 21 | 60 | 92 | 644 | 603 | 2.1 | ... | ... | ... | ... | ... | 28.1 | 19.6 | 38.3 |
| Pakistan | 1 | 4 | 8 | 19 | 13 | 88(1998) | 0.6 | ... | 4.4 | 4.1 | 3.9 | 34.0 | 56.7 | 42.4 | 72.2 |
| Philippines | 3 | 15 | 10 | 37 | 27 | 105 | 1.4 | ... | 2.9 | 3.2 | 3.7 | 37.5 | 4.6 | 4.5 | 4.8 |
| Qatar | ... | 121 | 190 | 260 | 335 | 457 | ... | ... | ... | ... | 3.50 | ... | 18.7 | 19.5 | 16.8 |
| Republic of Korea | 37 | 157 | 310 | 433 | 189 | 346(1998) | 3.1 | 4.4 | 5.18 | 5.08 | ... | ... | 2.2 | 0.8 | 3.6 |
| Saudi Arabia | 24 | 50 | 77 | 143 | 245 | 258 | 2.5 | ... | ... | ... | ... | ... | 23.0 | 15.9 | 32.8 |
| Singapore | 74 | 458 | 390 | 562 | 342 | 348(1998) | 3.6 | ... | 3.28 | 3.31 | 3.15 | ... | 7.6 | 3.6 | 11.5 |
| Sri Lanka | – | ... | 7 | 28 | 28 | 78 | 2.7 | ... | 2.77 | 3.02 | 2.57 | 35.3 | 8.4 | 5.5 | 11.1 |
| Syrian Arab Republic | ... | ... | 40 | 95 | 58 | 92 | 1.1 | ... | ... | ... | ... | ... | 25.6 | 11.7 | 39.6 |
| Tajikistan | ... | ... | 45 | 37 | 176 | 257 | 10.7 | ... | ... | ... | ... | ... | 0.8 | 0.4 | 1.1 |
| Thailand | 4 | 22 | 24 | 84 | 98 | 185 | 1.6 | 2.0 | 5.4 | 5.0 | 6.2 | 13.1 | 4.4 | 2.8 | 6.0 |
| Turkey | 5 | 23 | 121 | 254 | 158 | 240 | 2.1 | 2.5 | 4.4 | 4.7 | ... | ... | 14.8 | 6.4 | 23.3 |
| Turkmenistan | ... | ... | 60 | 82 | 186 | 201(1998) | 11.5 | ... | ... | ... | ... | ... | ... | ... | ... |
| United Arab Emirates | ... | 106 | 206 | 389 | 94 | 281 | 2.6 | ... | ... | ... | ... | ... | 23.5 | 24.8 | 20.5 |
| Uzbekistan | ... | ... | 69 | 65 | 177 | 194 | 12.4 | 8.3 | ... | ... | ... | 31.3 | ... | ... | ... |
| Viet Nam | ... | 6 | 1 | 26 | 33 | 163 | 3.8 | ... | 2.9 | ... | ... | 50.9 | 6.7 | 4.3 | 9.0 |
| Yemen | ... | ... | 11 | ... | 245 | 273 | 0.8 | ... | 2.5 | ... | ... | 19.1 | 53.8 | 32.6 | 75.0 |
| **EUROPE** | | | | | | | | | | | | | | | |
| Albania | ... | ... | 12 | 31 | 78 | 97 | 4.0 | 3.2 | ... | ... | ... | ... | ... | ... | ... |
| Andorra | ... | ... | 414 | 441 | 136 | 400(1998) | ... | ... | ... | ... | ... | ... | ... | ... | ... |
| Austria | 65 | 233 | 418 | 491 | 431 | 516(1998) | 10.2 | 9.3 | 7.2 | 8.0 | ... | ... | ... | ... | ... |
| Belarus | ... | ... | 153 | 241 | 251 | 292 | 13.2 | 12.3 | ... | 6.2 | 6.0 | ... | 0.6 | 0.3 | 0.8 |
| Belgium | 88 | 286 | 393 | 500 | 401 | 464 | 8.0 | 7.3 | 7.5 | 7.9 | ... | ... | ... | ... | ... |
| Bosnia and Herzegovina | ... | ... | ... | 91 | ... | 4 | 4.5 | 1.8 | ... | ... | ... | ... | ... | ... | ... |
| Bulgaria | ... | ... | 242 | 329 | 248 | 358 | 10.1 | 10.6 | 4.1 | 4.0 | 4.0 | ... | 1.5 | 0.9 | 2.0 |
| Croatia | ... | 112 | 172 | 348 | 215(1990) | 264 | 7.4 | ... | 11.7 | 10.1 | ... | ... | 2.6 | 0.9 | 4.0 |
| Czech Republic | 12 | 97 | 158 | 364 | ... | 406 | 11.3 | 9.5 | 5.0 | 7.3 | 7.0 | ... | ... | ... | ... |
| Denmark | 115 | 377 | 567 | 660 | 523 | 585(1998) | 5.6 | 4.9 | 8.3 | 8.1 | ... | ... | ... | ... | ... |
| Estonia | ... | 34 | 204 | 343 | 319 | 411 | 11.6 | 8.1 | ... | 7.2 | 6.4 | ... | ... | ... | ... |
| Faeroe Islands | ... | ... | 481 | 544 | 197 | ... | ... | ... | ... | ... | ... | ... | ... | ... | ... |
| Finland | 100 | 349 | 534 | 554 | 469 | 640(1998) | 12.5 | 9.3 | 8.0 | 7.7 | ... | ... | ... | ... | ... |
| France | 71 | 208 | 495 | 570 | 434 | 597 | 9.7 | 8.9 | 8.9 | 8.0 | ... | ... | ... | ... | ... |
| Germany | 91 | 305 | 441 | 567 | 483 | 580(1998) | 8.3 | 9.7 | ... | 10.4 | ... | ... | ... | ... | ... |
| Greece | 17 | 52 | 389 | 522 | 191 | 443 | 5.1 | 5.0 | 6.3 | 7.8 | ... | ... | 2.8 | 1.4 | 4.0 |
| Hungary | 10 | 59 | 96 | 336 | 402 | 427 | 10.1 | 9.1 | ... | 6.9 | ... | ... | 0.6 | 0.5 | 0.7 |
| Iceland | 39 | 326 | 510 | 646 | 311 | 447 | 16.7 | 15.0 | 8.0 | 8.2 | ... | ... | ... | ... | ... |
| Ireland | 86 | 272 | 281 | 435 | 257 | 380 | 3.9 | 3.8 | 6.7 | 7.0 | ... | ... | ... | ... | ... |
| Isle of Man | ... | ... | ... | ... | ... | ... | ... | ... | ... | ... | ... | ... | ... | ... | ... |
| Italy | 36 | 173 | 388 | 451 | 413 | 486(1998) | 7.2 | 6.2 | 8.1 | 7.7 | ... | ... | 1.5 | 1.1 | 1.9 |
| Latvia | ... | ... | 234 | 302 | 329 | ... | 14.0 | 11.1 | 4.3 | 6.5 | 6.4 | ... | 0.3 | 0.2 | 0.4 |
| Liechtenstein | ... | ... | 572 | ... | 322 | 442 | ... | ... | ... | ... | ... | ... | ... | ... | ... |
| Lithuania | ... | 54 | 212 | 300 | 223 | 364 | 12.4 | 10.8 | 7.2 | 5.2 | 8.3 | ... | 0.5 | 0.3 | 0.6 |
| Luxembourg | ... | 732 | 481 | 692 | 332 | 593 | 11.7 | 8.3 | 6.31 | 6.54 | ... | ... | ... | ... | ... |
| Malta | 14 | 260 | 360 | 499 | 683 | 447 | ... | 5.4 | ... | ... | ... | ... | 7.9 | 8.6 | 7.2 |
| The Netherlands | 94 | 318 | 464 | 593 | 462 | 494 | 11.5 | 11.3 | 8.33 | 8.76 | ... | ... | ... | ... | ... |
| Norway | ... | 373 | 503 | 660 | 395 | 562 | ... | 15.1 | 7.79 | 8.00 | ... | ... | ... | ... | ... |
| Poland | 8 | 44 | 86 | 228 | 280 | 413(1998) | 5.7 | 5.5 | ... | 5.86 | 5.90 | ... | 0.2 | 0.2 | 0.2 |
| Portugal | 27 | 81 | 243 | 413 | 183 | 542(1998) | 4.6 | 4.1 | 6.39 | 7.84 | ... | ... | 7.8 | 5.2 | 10.0 |
| Republic of Moldova | ... | 6 | 106 | 150 | 190 | 297(1998) | 13.1 | 12.2 | 5.2 | 6.5 | ... | ... | 1.1 | 0.4 | 1.7 |
| Romania | – | 10 | 102 | 162 | 195 | 203 | 8.9 | 7.6 | 5.1 | 4.6 | ... | ... | 1.8 | 0.9 | 2.7 |
| Russian Federation | 3 | 41 | 140 | 197 | 365(1990) | 420(1998) | 13.0 | 11.7 | ... | 5.7 | ... | ... | 0.6 | 0.2 | 0.8 |
| Slovakia | ... | 65 | 135 | 286 | ... | 380 | 7.4 | 7.6 | 5.9 | 6.8 | 6.8 | ... | ... | ... | ... |
| Slovenia | ... | 251 | 211 | 375 | 275(1990) | 356(1998) | 6.0 | 5.7 | ... | 8.7 | 7.8 | ... | 0.3 | 0.3 | 0.4 |
| Spain | 28 | 145 | 316 | 414 | 270 | 490 | 4.3 | 3.9 | 6.9 | 7.3 | ... | ... | 2.3 | 1.4 | 3.2 |
| Sweden | 105 | 361 | 681 | 674 | 464 | 476 | 12.4 | 6.1 | 8.8 | 8.5 | ... | ... | ... | ... | ... |
| Switzerland | 87 | 422 | 574 | 675 | 390 | 459 | ... | ... | 8.3 | 9.6 | ... | ... | ... | ... | ... |
| TFYR Macedonia | ... | ... | 148 | ... | 173(1990) | 250(1998) | 6.3 | 5.4 | ... | 7.5 | ... | ... | ... | ... | ... |
| Ukraine | ... | 14 | 136 | 191 | 298 | 339 | 12.9 | 11.8 | ... | 5.8 | ... | ... | ... | ... | ... |
| United Kingdom | 108 | 263 | 441 | 557 | 433 | 645(1998) | 5.9 | 4.7 | 6.0 | 7.0 | ... | ... | ... | ... | ... |
| Yugoslavia | ... | 19 | 166 | 218 | 457 | 185 | 5.9 | 5.3 | ... | ... | ... | ... | ... | ... | ... |
| **LATIN AMERICA** | | | | | | | | | | | | | | | |
| Antigua and Barbuda | ... | ... | 253 | 468 | 306 | 405 | 6.6 | ... | 4.5 | 5.4 | 1.9 | ... | ... | ... | ... |
| Argentina | 7 | 44 | 95 | 203 | 215 | 276 | 4.6 | ... | 10.5 | 10.8 | 9.6 | 25.5 | 3.1 | 3.1 | 3.1 |
| Aruba | ... | ... | 282 | ... | ... | 405 | ... | ... | ... | ... | ... | ... | ... | ... | ... |
| Bahamas | ... | ... | 274 | 352 | 218 | 233 | 4.0 | ... | 5.0 | 3.9 | 4.3 | ... | 3.9 | 4.6 | 3.2 |
| Barbados | ... | 75 | 281 | 424 | 237 | 287 | 8.4 | ... | 7.2 | 7.0 | 7.0 | ... | ... | ... | ... |
| Belize | ... | 130 | 92 | 138 | 164(1990) | 181 | 2.7 | ... | 2.7 | 3.2 | 2.70 | ... | ... | ... | ... |
| Bolivia | ... | 8 | 28 | ... | 71 | 202 | 1.3 | ... | 3.4 | 3.0 | 2.6 | ... | 14.4 | 7.9 | 20.6 |
| Brazil | 3 | 30 | 65 | 121 | 185 | 250 | 3.3 | ... | 7.0 | 6.2 | ... | 17.4 | 14.9 | 14.9 | 14.6 |
| Cayman Islands | ... | ... | 470 | 654 | 190 | 194 | ... | ... | 4.2 | ... | ... | ... | ... | ... | ... |

# TABLE A.11

## continued

| | | | | | | | | | | | | | | | |
|---|---|---|---|---|---|---|---|---|---|---|---|---|---|---|---|
| Chile | 11 | 48 | 66 | 205 | 145 | 224 | 3.2 | ... | 4.6 | 4.3 | 3.9 | 20.5 | 4.3 | 4.1 | 4.5 |
| Colombia | ... | 28 | 75 | 173 | 92 | 208 | 1.4 | ... | 4.8 | 6.8 | ... | 17.7 | 8.2 | 8.2 | 8.2 |
| Costa Rica | ... | 39 | 101 | 172 | 76 | 225 | 2.5 | ... | 8.3 | 8.2 | 9.0 | ... | 4.4 | 4.5 | 4.3 |
| Cuba | ... | ... | 31 | 35 | 192 | 239(1998) | 5.4 | ... | ... | ... | ... | ... | 3.6 | 3.5 | 3.6 |
| Dominica | ... | ... | 164 | ... | 70(1990) | 136 | 3.0 | ... | 6.1 | 6.1 | 6.1 | ... | ... | ... | ... |
| Dominican Republic | ... | ... | 48 | 93 | 78 | 86 | 1.9 | ... | 6.7 | 5.4 | ... | 20.6 | 16.2 | 16.0 | 16.3 |
| Ecuador | ... | 18 | 48 | 78 | 66 | 148 | 1.6 | ... | 4.3 | 4.4 | 4.9 | 35.0 | 8.1 | 6.4 | 9.8 |
| El Salvador | ... | ... | 24 | 80 | 74 | 230 | 1.5 | ... | 4.8 | 6.8 | 7.0 | 48.3 | 21.3 | 18.4 | 23.9 |
| Grenada | ... | 96 | 177 | 263 | 11 | 334 | 8.0 | ... | 5.9 | 5.4 | 5.4 | ... | ... | ... | ... |
| Guatemala | ... | 8 | 21 | ... | 26 | 130 | 1.1 | ... | 1.8 | 2.1 | 2.4 | ... | 31.3 | 23.8 | 38.9 |
| Guyana | ... | 24 | 16 | 70 | 35(1990) | 42 | ... | ... | 3.8 | 5.2 | 5.4 | ... | 1.5 | 1.0 | 1.9 |
| Haiti | ... | ... | 7 | ... | 3 | 5 | 0.8 | ... | 4.0 | 3.5 | 3.4 | 65.0 | 51.4 | 49.0 | 53.5 |
| Honduras | ... | 8 | 17 | 38 | 67 | 76 | 1.0 | ... | 8.4 | 8.1 | 8.3 | 50.0 | 27.8 | 27.5 | 28.0 |
| Jamaica | ... | 39 | 45 | ... | 93 | 309 | 2.2 | ... | 4.7 | 4.6 | 4.7 | 34.2 | 13.3 | 17.5 | 9.3 |
| Martinique | ... | ... | ... | ... | ... | ... | ... | ... | ... | ... | ... | ... | 2.6 | 3.0 | 2.1 |
| Mexico | 8 | 47 | 65 | 104 | 114 | 261(1998) | 0.7 | 1.2 | 3.6 | 4.9 | ... | 10.1 | 9.0 | 6.9 | 10.9 |
| Netherlands Antilles | ... | ... | 247 | ... | 319 | 314 | ... | ... | 4.1 | ... | ... | ... | 3.4 | 3.4 | 3.4 |
| Nicaragua | ... | 8 | 13 | 31 | 59 | 161 | 1.8 | ... | 1.5 | 11.3 | 9.7 | 50.3 | 35.7 | 35.8 | 35.6 |
| Panama | ... | 27 | 93 | 151 | 162 | 232 | 2.5 | ... | 7.7 | 7.8 | 7.7 | ... | 8.1 | 7.4 | 8.7 |
| Paraguay | ... | 10 | 27 | 55 | 23 | 147 | 0.9 | ... | 4.3 | 5.7 | 7.4 | 21.8 | 6.7 | 5.6 | 7.8 |
| Peru | ... | 18 | 26 | 67 | 77 | 140 | 1.4 | ... | 6.6 | 5.1 | 5.6 | 49.0 | 10.1 | 5.3 | 14.6 |
| Puerto Rico | ... | ... | 279 | ... | 253 | 312 | ... | ... | ... | ... | ... | ... | 6.2 | 6.3 | 6.0 |
| Saint Kitts and Nevis | ... | 122 | 237 | ... | 118 | 244 | 9.2 | ... | 4.9 | 5.2 | 5.7 | ... | ... | ... | ... |
| Saint Lucia | ... | 136 | 127 | 268 | 18 | 344 | 4.0 | ... | 3.5 | 3.8 | 3.8 | ... | ... | ... | ... |
| Saint Vincent and the Grenadines | ... | 89 | 124 | 188 | 59 | 235 | 4.7 | ... | 6.3 | 5.7 | 6.3 | ... | ... | ... | ... |
| Suriname | ... | ... | 92 | 152 | 117 | 195 | 5.7 | ... | 5.9 | ... | ... | ... | 5.8 | 4.1 | 7.4 |
| Trinidad and Tobago | ... | 47 | 141 | 206 | 276 | 333 | 4.0 | ... | 4.3 | 4.2 | 4.3 | 21.0 | 1.8 | 1.0 | 2.5 |
| United States Virgin Islands | ... | ... | 463 | 600 | 596 | 648 | 4.8 | ... | ... | ... | ... | ... | ... | ... | ... |
| Uruguay | ... | 91 | 134 | 250 | 233 | 304 | 4.5 | ... | 5.6 | 8.7 | 8.4 | ... | 2.2 | 2.6 | 1.8 |
| Venezuela | 11 | 43 | 82 | 117 | 131 | 185(1998) | 2.7 | ... | 6.9 | ... | ... | 31.3 | 7.0 | 6.7 | 7.3 |
| **NORTHERN AMERICA** | | | | | | | | | | | | | | | |
| Bermuda | ... | ... | 617 | 840 | 804 | 1048 | ... | ... | 3.5 | ... | ... | ... | ... | ... | ... |
| Canada | 107 | 330 | 565 | 634 | 541 | 703 | 6.2 | 4.8 | 9.2 | 9.4 | ... | ... | ... | ... | ... |
| Greenland | ... | ... | 299 | 444 | 125 | 358 | ... | ... | ... | ... | ... | ... | ... | ... | ... |
| United States | 217 | 459 | 545 | 661 | 650 | 825 | 4.9 | 4.1 | 12.6 | 14.1 | ... | ... | ... | ... | ... |
| **OCEANIA** | | | | | | | | | | | | | | | |
| American Samoa | ... | ... | 118 | 214 | 179 | 231 | ... | ... | ... | ... | ... | ... | ... | ... | ... |
| Australia | 150 | 412 | 456 | 512 | 443 | 697 | ... | 8.8 | 8.2 | 8.4 | ... | ... | ... | ... | ... |
| Fiji | ... | ... | 57 | 97 | 15(1990) | 91 | ... | ... | ... | 3.9 | 4.3 | ... | 7.1 | 5.0 | 9.1 |
| French Polynesia | ... | ... | 194 | 230 | 155 | 177 | ... | ... | ... | ... | ... | ... | ... | ... | ... |
| Guam | ... | ... | 293 | ... | 681 | 667 | ... | ... | ... | ... | ... | ... | ... | ... | ... |
| Kiribati | ... | 7 | 17 | 35 | – | 22(1998) | 4.3 | ... | ... | ... | ... | ... | ... | ... | ... |
| Marshall Islands | – | ... | 11 | 62 | ... | ... | 2.3 | ... | ... | ... | ... | ... | ... | ... | ... |
| Mayotte | ... | ... | 31 | 114 | ... | ... | ... | ... | ... | ... | ... | ... | ... | ... | ... |
| Micronesia (Fed. States of) | ... | ... | 25 | 80 | 4 | 21 | ... | ... | ... | ... | ... | ... | ... | ... | ... |
| New Caledonia | ... | ... | 169 | 239 | 258 | 409 | ... | ... | ... | ... | ... | ... | ... | ... | ... |
| New Zealand | ... | 282 | 434 | 479 | 356 | 501 | 8.5 | 6.2 | 7.0 | 7.3 | ... | ... | ... | ... | ... |
| Northern Mariana Islands | ... | ... | ... | ... | ... | ... | ... | ... | ... | ... | ... | ... | 24.0 | 16.3 | 32.3 |
| Papua New Guinea | ... | ... | 8 | ... | 2(1990) | 4 | 4.0 | ... | ... | ... | ... | ... | ... | ... | ... |
| Samoa | ... | 5 | 26 | 49 | 32 | 69(1998) | ... | ... | ... | ... | ... | ... | ... | ... | ... |
| Sao Tome and Principe | ... | ... | 19 | 22 | – | 227(1998) | ... | ... | ... | ... | ... | ... | ... | ... | ... |
| Solomon Islands | ... | ... | 14 | 19 | ... | 14(1998) | 0.8 | ... | ... | ... | ... | ... | ... | ... | ... |
| Tonga | ... | ... | 46 | ... | – | 41 | ... | ... | ... | ... | ... | ... | ... | ... | ... |
| Vanuatu | ... | ... | 18 | 28 | – | 12 | ... | ... | ... | ... | ... | ... | ... | ... | ... |

**Source:** International Telecommunications Union World Telecommunication Development Report 1999, World Health Organization: World Health Report 2000, UNDP: Human Development Report 2000, UNESCO Statistical Yearbook, 1999, World Bank: World Development Indicators 2000 on CD-ROM.
For footnotes, refer to technical notes.

# TABLE B.1

## Urban Agglomerations: Population Size and Growth Rate

| | | Estimates and projections (thousands) | | | | | | | Annual growth rate (%) | | | Share in country's urban population (%) | | |
|---|---|---|---|---|---|---|---|---|---|---|---|---|---|---|
| | | 1985 | 1990 | 1995 | 2000 | 2005 | 2010 | 2015 | 1985–1995 | 1995–2005 | 2005–2015 | 1985 | 2000 | 2015 |
| **AFRICA** | | | | | | | | | | | | | | |
| Algeria | Algiers | 1480 | 1561 | 1687 | 1885 | 2142 | 2407 | 2622 | 1.3 | 2.4 | 2.0 | 14.1 | 9.9 | 9.3 |
| Algeria | Oran | 604 | 679 | 774 | 895 | 1034 | 1171 | 1282 | 2.5 | 2.9 | 2.2 | 5.8 | 4.7 | 4.5 |
| Angola | Luanda | 1227 | 1606 | 2105 | 2677 | 3353 | 4093 | 4936 | 5.4 | 4.7 | 3.9 | 63.4 | 60.8 | 56.8 |
| Burkina Faso | Ouagadougou | 423 | 594 | 824 | 1130 | 1518 | 1990 | 2546 | 6.7 | 6.1 | 5.2 | 47.1 | 51.3 | 51.4 |
| Cameroon | Douala | 723 | 1001 | 1320 | 1670 | 2041 | 2414 | 2776 | 6.0 | 4.4 | 3.1 | 20.3 | 22.6 | 21.9 |
| Cameroon | Yaoundé | 571 | 823 | 1119 | 1444 | 1780 | 2110 | 2429 | 6.7 | 4.6 | 3.1 | 16.0 | 19.6 | 19.2 |
| Chad | Ndjamena | 455 | 613 | 826 | 1043 | 1289 | 1581 | 1935 | 6.0 | 4.5 | 4.1 | 44.6 | 57.3 | 56.0 |
| Congo | Brazzaville | 617 | 798 | 1005 | 1234 | 1473 | 1715 | 1988 | 4.9 | 3.8 | 3.0 | 67.6 | 67.1 | 64.2 |
| Côte d'Ivoire | Abidjan | 1663 | 2189 | 2777 | 3305 | 3871 | 4464 | 5068 | 5.1 | 3.3 | 2.7 | 44.9 | 48.2 | 45.6 |
| Dem. Republic of the Congo | Kinshasa | 2782 | 3444 | 4240 | 5064 | 6153 | 7630 | 9366 | 4.2 | 3.7 | 4.2 | 31.4 | 32.4 | 29.7 |
| Dem. Republic of the Congo | Lubumbashi | 564 | 671 | 810 | 967 | 1186 | 1488 | 1848 | 3.6 | 3.8 | 4.4 | 6.4 | 6.2 | 5.9 |
| Egypt | Alexandria | 2835 | 3212 | 3648 | 4113 | 4586 | 5051 | 5525 | 2.5 | 2.3 | 1.9 | 13.0 | 13.3 | 12.7 |
| Egypt | Cairo | 7691 | 8572 | 9533 | 10552 | 11605 | 12664 | 13751 | 2.2 | 2.0 | 1.7 | 35.2 | 34.1 | 31.5 |
| Egypt | Shubra El-Khemia | 661 | 789 | 906 | 1033 | 1163 | 1294 | 1430 | 3.2 | 2.5 | 2.1 | 3.0 | 3.3 | 3.3 |
| Ethiopia | Addis Ababa | 1486 | 1793 | 2165 | 2639 | 3258 | 4070 | 5095 | 3.8 | 4.1 | 4.5 | 30.9 | 23.9 | 21.7 |
| Ghana | Accra | 1180 | 1385 | 1649 | 1976 | 2383 | 2873 | 3410 | 3.4 | 3.7 | 3.6 | 28.3 | 25.5 | 23.9 |
| Guinea | Conakry | 825 | 1123 | 1541 | 1824 | 2220 | 2671 | 3153 | 6.3 | 3.7 | 3.5 | 74.3 | 74.9 | 70.1 |
| Kenya | Nairobi | 1100 | 1403 | 1810 | 2310 | 2841 | 3346 | 3773 | 5.0 | 4.5 | 2.8 | 28.0 | 23.2 | 22.5 |
| Libyan Arab Jamahiriya | Benghazi | 508 | 634 | 752 | 871 | 987 | 1087 | 1171 | 3.9 | 2.7 | 1.7 | 17.5 | 17.7 | 17.1 |
| Libyan Arab Jamahiriya | Tripoli | 1040 | 1318 | 1573 | 1822 | 2056 | 2253 | 2413 | 4.1 | 2.7 | 1.6 | 35.9 | 37.1 | 35.3 |
| Madagascar | Antananarivo | 690 | 896 | 1164 | 1507 | 1921 | 2395 | 2915 | 5.2 | 5.0 | 4.2 | 32.8 | 31.9 | 31.4 |
| Mali | Bamako | 599 | 738 | 912 | 1131 | 1404 | 1738 | 2130 | 4.2 | 4.3 | 4.2 | 36.0 | 33.5 | 31.9 |
| Morocco | Casablanca | 2387 | 2721 | 3101 | 3541 | 4019 | 4477 | 4862 | 2.6 | 2.6 | 1.9 | 24.7 | 22.3 | 21.3 |
| Morocco | Rabat | 967 | 1118 | 1293 | 1496 | 1716 | 1926 | 2105 | 2.9 | 2.8 | 2.0 | 10.0 | 9.4 | 9.2 |
| Mozambique | Maputo | 1067 | 1516 | 2218 | 3025 | 3713 | 4186 | 4743 | 7.3 | 5.2 | 2.5 | 40.6 | 38.2 | 36.5 |
| Nigeria | Ibadan | 1121 | 1290 | 1484 | 1731 | 2044 | 2410 | 2791 | 2.8 | 3.2 | 3.1 | 4.8 | 3.5 | 3.3 |
| Nigeria | Lagos | 5827 | 7742 | 10287 | 13427 | 16864 | 20192 | 23173 | 5.7 | 4.9 | 3.2 | 25.0 | 27.4 | 27.3 |
| Senegal | Dakar | 1150 | 1401 | 1708 | 2079 | 2514 | 2995 | 3495 | 4.0 | 3.9 | 3.3 | 48.1 | 46.2 | 44.6 |
| Somalia | Mogadishu | 548 | 779 | 965 | 1219 | 1552 | 1955 | 2443 | 5.7 | 4.8 | 4.5 | 36.1 | 43.9 | 41.6 |
| South Africa | Cape Town | 1933 | 2296 | 2727 | 2993 | 3164 | 3296 | 3437 | 3.4 | 1.5 | 0.8 | 13.0 | 14.7 | 14.1 |
| South Africa | Durban | 990 | 1119 | 1264 | 1335 | 1382 | 1433 | 1500 | 2.4 | 0.9 | 0.8 | 6.7 | 6.6 | 6.1 |
| South Africa | East Rand | 1054 | 1335 | 1691 | 1956 | 2135 | 2258 | 2366 | 4.7 | 2.3 | 1.0 | 7.1 | 9.6 | 9.7 |
| South Africa | Johannesburg | 1625 | 1879 | 2172 | 2335 | 2438 | 2531 | 2641 | 2.9 | 1.2 | 0.8 | 10.9 | 11.5 | 10.8 |
| South Africa | Port Elizabeth | 662 | 828 | 1035 | 1186 | 1290 | 1365 | 1435 | 4.5 | 2.2 | 1.1 | 4.5 | 5.8 | 5.9 |
| South Africa | Pretoria | 835 | 1047 | 1314 | 1508 | 1640 | 1734 | 1820 | 4.5 | 2.2 | 1.0 | 5.6 | 7.4 | 7.5 |
| South Africa | Sasolburg | 551 | 743 | 1002 | 1219 | 1374 | 1475 | 1554 | 6.0 | 3.2 | 1.2 | 3.7 | 6.0 | 6.4 |
| South Africa | West Rand | 658 | 841 | 1076 | 1255 | 1380 | 1465 | 1541 | 4.9 | 2.5 | 1.1 | 4.4 | 6.2 | 6.3 |
| Sudan | Khartoum | 1485 | 1828 | 2249 | 2731 | 3299 | 3950 | 4615 | 4.2 | 3.8 | 3.4 | 30.9 | 25.6 | 23.8 |
| Tunisia | Tunis | 1428 | 1568 | 1722 | 1897 | 2087 | 2279 | 2454 | 1.9 | 1.9 | 1.6 | 36.2 | 30.2 | 28.8 |
| Uganda | Kampala | 597 | 755 | 955 | 1212 | 1557 | 2016 | 2599 | 4.7 | 4.9 | 5.1 | 40.9 | 39.3 | 36.4 |
| United Republic of Tanzania | Dar es Salaam | 1096 | 1436 | 1873 | 2347 | 2936 | 3616 | 4251 | 5.4 | 4.5 | 3.7 | 28.6 | 21.3 | 19.5 |
| United Republic of Tanzania | Mwanza | 252 | 460 | 783 | 1155 | 1547 | 1938 | 2288 | 11.3 | 6.8 | 3.9 | 6.6 | 10.5 | 10.5 |
| United Republic of Tanzania | Tabora | 214 | 498 | 1029 | 1703 | 2385 | 3007 | 3540 | 15.7 | 8.4 | 4.0 | 5.6 | 15.5 | 16.3 |
| Zambia | Lusaka | 721 | 974 | 1317 | 1640 | 1958 | 2291 | 2672 | 6.0 | 4.0 | 3.1 | 28.4 | 45.2 | 46.1 |
| Zimbabwe | Harare | 778 | 1048 | 1410 | 1752 | 2061 | 2360 | 2650 | 6.0 | 3.8 | 2.5 | 36.8 | 42.5 | 42.6 |
| **ASIA** | | | | | | | | | | | | | | |
| Afghanistan | Kabul | 1237 | 1565 | 2029 | 2590 | 3468 | 4355 | 5299 | 5.0 | 5.4 | 4.2 | 50.4 | 52.1 | 47.9 |
| Armenia | Yerevan | 1123 | 1210 | 1265 | 1284 | 1309 | 1358 | 1410 | 1.2 | 0.3 | 0.7 | 50.5 | 52.2 | 49.4 |
| Azerbaijan | Baku | 1660 | 1751 | 1849 | 1936 | 2036 | 2164 | 2310 | 1.1 | 1.0 | 1.3 | 46.4 | 43.7 | 41.0 |
| Bangladesh | Chittagong | 1744 | 2265 | 2941 | 3581 | 4295 | 5087 | 5875 | 5.2 | 3.8 | 3.1 | 10.3 | 11.3 | 10.7 |
| Bangladesh | Dhaka | 4652 | 6619 | 9416 | 12317 | 15366 | 18387 | 21119 | 7.1 | 4.9 | 3.2 | 27.6 | 38.9 | 38.6 |
| Bangladesh | Khulna | 781 | 972 | 1209 | 1426 | 1681 | 1986 | 2305 | 4.4 | 3.3 | 3.2 | 4.6 | 4.5 | 4.2 |
| Bangladesh | Rajshahi | 353 | 517 | 756 | 1016 | 1297 | 1584 | 1852 | 7.6 | 5.4 | 3.6 | 2.1 | 3.2 | 3.4 |
| Cambodia | Phnom Penh | 461 | 594 | 765 | 984 | 1229 | 1510 | 1833 | 5.1 | 4.7 | 4.0 | 49.6 | 55.4 | 55.8 |
| China | Anshan | 1295 | 1442 | 1448 | 1453 | 1487 | 1568 | 1693 | 1.1 | 0.3 | 1.3 | 0.5 | 0.4 | 0.3 |
| China | Baotou | 1127 | 1229 | 1273 | 1319 | 1385 | 1483 | 1612 | 1.2 | 0.8 | 1.5 | 0.5 | 0.3 | 0.3 |
| China | Beijing | 9797 | 10819 | 10829 | 10839 | 11035 | 11529 | 12299 | 1.0 | 0.2 | 1.1 | 4.0 | 2.6 | 2.1 |
| China | Benxi | 844 | 938 | 947 | 957 | 985 | 1043 | 1130 | 1.2 | 0.4 | 1.4 | 0.3 | 0.2 | 0.2 |
| China | Changchun | 1909 | 2192 | 2604 | 3093 | 3617 | 4120 | 4570 | 3.1 | 3.3 | 2.3 | 0.8 | 0.8 | 0.8 |
| China | Changde | 992 | 1180 | 1273 | 1374 | 1490 | 1626 | 1780 | 2.5 | 1.6 | 1.8 | 0.4 | 0.3 | 0.3 |
| China | Changsha | 1165 | 1329 | 1536 | 1775 | 2032 | 2289 | 2535 | 2.8 | 2.8 | 2.2 | 0.5 | 0.4 | 0.4 |
| China | Changzhou | 577 | 730 | 804 | 886 | 978 | 1079 | 1189 | 3.3 | 2.0 | 2.0 | 0.2 | 0.2 | 0.2 |
| China | Chengdu | 2639 | 2955 | 3120 | 3294 | 3506 | 3774 | 4095 | 1.7 | 1.2 | 1.6 | 1.1 | 0.8 | 0.7 |
| China | Chifeng | 601 | 987 | 1036 | 1087 | 1153 | 1242 | 1355 | 5.5 | 1.1 | 1.6 | 0.2 | 0.3 | 0.2 |
| China | Chongqing | 2808 | 3123 | 4073 | 5312 | 6691 | 7954 | 8949 | 3.7 | 5.0 | 2.9 | 1.1 | 1.3 | 1.6 |
| China | Dalian | 1793 | 2472 | 2549 | 2628 | 2745 | 2924 | 3162 | 3.5 | 0.7 | 1.4 | 0.7 | 0.6 | 0.6 |
| China | Daqing | 844 | 997 | 1035 | 1076 | 1132 | 1214 | 1322 | 2.0 | 0.9 | 1.6 | 0.3 | 0.3 | 0.2 |
| China | Datong | 1074 | 1277 | 1220 | 1165 | 1189 | 1252 | 1353 | 1.3 | –0.3 | 1.3 | 0.4 | 0.3 | 0.2 |
| China | Dongguan | 1344 | 1737 | 1514 | 1319 | 1346 | 1417 | 1530 | 1.2 | –1.2 | 1.3 | 0.6 | 0.3 | 0.3 |
| China | Fushun | 1263 | 1388 | 1400 | 1413 | 1451 | 1534 | 1658 | 1.0 | 0.4 | 1.3 | 0.5 | 0.3 | 0.3 |
| China | Fuxin | 680 | 743 | 764 | 785 | 819 | 875 | 953 | 1.2 | 0.7 | 1.5 | 0.3 | 0.2 | 0.2 |
| China | Fuyu | 907 | 945 | 984 | 1025 | 1081 | 1161 | 1265 | 0.8 | 0.9 | 1.6 | 0.4 | 0.3 | 0.2 |
| China | Fuzhou | 1223 | 1396 | 1396 | 1397 | 1426 | 1501 | 1620 | 1.3 | 0.2 | 1.3 | 0.5 | 0.3 | 0.3 |
| China | Guangzhou | 3418 | 3918 | 3906 | 3893 | 3966 | 4158 | 4461 | 1.3 | 0.2 | 1.2 | 1.4 | 1.0 | 0.8 |
| China | Guiyang | 1440 | 1665 | 2054 | 2533 | 3054 | 3545 | 3965 | 3.6 | 4.0 | 2.6 | 0.6 | 0.6 | 0.7 |
| China | Handan | 1190 | 1769 | 1879 | 1996 | 2136 | 2310 | 2516 | 4.6 | 1.3 | 1.6 | 0.5 | 0.5 | 0.4 |
| China | Hangzhou | 1291 | 1476 | 1621 | 1780 | 1957 | 2151 | 2360 | 2.3 | 1.9 | 1.9 | 0.5 | 0.4 | 0.4 |
| China | Harbin | 2702 | 2991 | 2959 | 2928 | 2985 | 3132 | 3366 | 0.9 | 0.1 | 1.2 | 1.1 | 0.7 | 0.6 |

## TABLE B.1

*continued*

| | | | | | | | | | | | | | |
|---|---|---|---|---|---|---|---|---|---|---|---|---|---|
| China | Hefei | 917 | 1100 | 1169 | 1242 | 1331 | 1442 | 1575 | 2.4 | 1.3 | 1.7 | 0.4 | 0.3 | 0.3 |
| China | Heze | 1040 | 1201 | 1386 | 1600 | 1830 | 2062 | 2284 | 2.9 | 2.8 | 2.2 | 0.4 | 0.4 | 0.4 |
| China | Huaian | 1057 | 1113 | 1171 | 1232 | 1310 | 1413 | 1541 | 1.0 | 1.1 | 1.6 | 0.4 | 0.3 | 0.3 |
| China | Huainan | 1097 | 1228 | 1289 | 1354 | 1436 | 1547 | 1686 | 1.6 | 1.1 | 1.6 | 0.5 | 0.3 | 0.3 |
| China | Huhehaote | 810 | 938 | 958 | 978 | 1014 | 1079 | 1172 | 1.7 | 0.6 | 1.5 | 0.3 | 0.2 | 0.2 |
| China | Huzhou | 976 | 1028 | 1052 | 1077 | 1120 | 1193 | 1295 | 0.8 | 0.6 | 1.5 | 0.4 | 0.3 | 0.2 |
| China | Jiamusi | 575 | 660 | 759 | 874 | 999 | 1126 | 1251 | 2.8 | 2.8 | 2.3 | 0.2 | 0.2 | 0.2 |
| China | Jiaxing | 696 | 741 | 766 | 791 | 829 | 888 | 967 | 1.0 | 0.8 | 1.5 | 0.3 | 0.2 | 0.2 |
| China | Jilin | 1164 | 1320 | 1376 | 1435 | 1513 | 1624 | 1767 | 1.7 | 1.0 | 1.6 | 0.5 | 0.4 | 0.3 |
| China | Jinan | 1667 | 2404 | 2484 | 2568 | 2687 | 2866 | 3102 | 4.0 | 0.8 | 1.4 | 0.7 | 0.6 | 0.5 |
| China | Jining | 633 | 871 | 942 | 1019 | 1107 | 1211 | 1328 | 4.0 | 1.6 | 1.8 | 0.3 | 0.3 | 0.2 |
| China | Jingmen | 918 | 1017 | 1083 | 1153 | 1237 | 1343 | 1468 | 1.7 | 1.3 | 1.7 | 0.4 | 0.3 | 0.3 |
| China | Jinxi | 943 | 1350 | 1934 | 2771 | 3765 | 4692 | 5393 | 7.2 | 6.7 | 3.6 | 0.4 | 0.7 | 0.9 |
| China | Jinzhou | 631 | 736 | 784 | 834 | 896 | 973 | 1066 | 2.2 | 1.3 | 1.7 | 0.3 | 0.2 | 0.2 |
| China | Jixi | 792 | 836 | 890 | 949 | 1020 | 1108 | 1213 | 1.2 | 1.4 | 1.7 | 0.3 | 0.2 | 0.2 |
| China | Kaohsiung | 1290 | 1380 | 1421 | 1463 | 1528 | 1630 | 1768 | 1.0 | 0.7 | 1.5 | 0.5 | 0.4 | 0.3 |
| China | Kunming | 1493 | 1612 | 1656 | 1701 | 1773 | 1889 | 2046 | 1.0 | 0.7 | 1.4 | 0.6 | 0.4 | 0.4 |
| China | Lanzhou | 1489 | 1618 | 1673 | 1730 | 1812 | 1936 | 2100 | 1.2 | 0.8 | 1.5 | 0.6 | 0.4 | 0.4 |
| China | Leshan | 996 | 1070 | 1103 | 1137 | 1189 | 1270 | 1381 | 1.0 | 0.8 | 1.5 | 0.4 | 0.3 | 0.2 |
| China | Linqing | 614 | 696 | 787 | 891 | 1005 | 1124 | 1245 | 2.5 | 2.5 | 2.1 | 0.3 | 0.2 | 0.2 |
| China | Linyi | 1453 | 1741 | 2085 | 2498 | 2942 | 3367 | 3746 | 3.6 | 3.4 | 2.4 | 0.6 | 0.6 | 0.7 |
| China | Liuan | 1336 | 1481 | 1641 | 1818 | 2014 | 2223 | 2442 | 2.1 | 2.1 | 1.9 | 0.5 | 0.4 | 0.4 |
| China | Liupanshui | 1761 | 1845 | 1932 | 2023 | 2140 | 2299 | 2498 | 0.9 | 1.0 | 1.6 | 0.7 | 0.5 | 0.4 |
| China | Liuzhou | 643 | 751 | 835 | 928 | 1030 | 1142 | 1260 | 2.6 | 2.1 | 2.0 | 0.3 | 0.2 | 0.2 |
| China | Luoyang | 1055 | 1202 | 1321 | 1451 | 1596 | 1757 | 1929 | 2.3 | 1.9 | 1.9 | 0.4 | 0.4 | 0.3 |
| China | Mianyang | 812 | 876 | 965 | 1065 | 1175 | 1297 | 1428 | 1.7 | 2.0 | 2.0 | 0.3 | 0.3 | 0.3 |
| China | Mudanjiang | 640 | 751 | 775 | 801 | 839 | 899 | 979 | 1.9 | 0.8 | 1.5 | 0.3 | 0.2 | 0.2 |
| China | Nanchang | 1133 | 1262 | 1474 | 1722 | 1990 | 2253 | 2501 | 2.6 | 3.0 | 2.3 | 0.5 | 0.4 | 0.4 |
| China | Nanchong | ... | 619 | 860 | 1197 | 1591 | 1961 | 2252 | ... | 6.2 | 3.5 | ... | 0.3 | 0.4 |
| China | Nanjing | 2302 | 2611 | 2674 | 2740 | 2847 | 3023 | 3265 | 1.5 | 0.6 | 1.4 | 0.9 | 0.7 | 0.6 |
| China | Nanning | 964 | 1159 | 1233 | 1311 | 1406 | 1524 | 1664 | 2.5 | 1.3 | 1.7 | 0.4 | 0.3 | 0.3 |
| China | Neijiang | ... | 1289 | 1340 | 1393 | 1467 | 1572 | 1710 | ... | 0.9 | 1.5 | ... | 0.3 | 0.3 |
| China | Ningbo | 1023 | 1142 | 1157 | 1173 | 1209 | 1282 | 1388 | 1.2 | 0.4 | 1.4 | 0.4 | 0.3 | 0.2 |
| China | Pingdingshan | 628 | 997 | 849 | 723 | 739 | 779 | 844 | 3.0 | -1.4 | 1.3 | 0.3 | 0.2 | 0.2 |
| China | Pingxiang | 1284 | 1388 | 1444 | 1502 | 1582 | 1695 | 1843 | 1.2 | 0.9 | 1.5 | 0.5 | 0.4 | 0.3 |
| China | Qingdao | 1461 | 2102 | 2206 | 2316 | 2455 | 2639 | 2865 | 4.1 | 1.1 | 1.5 | 0.6 | 0.6 | 0.5 |
| China | Qiqihar | 1288 | 1401 | 1418 | 1435 | 1478 | 1564 | 1692 | 1.0 | 0.4 | 1.4 | 0.5 | 0.4 | 0.3 |
| China | Shanghai | 12396 | 13342 | 13112 | 12887 | 13106 | 13678 | 14575 | 0.6 | 0.0 | 1.1 | 5.0 | 3.1 | 2.5 |
| China | Shantou | 780 | 885 | 1020 | 1176 | 1345 | 1516 | 1682 | 2.7 | 2.8 | 2.2 | 0.3 | 0.3 | 0.3 |
| China | Shenyang | 4237 | 4655 | 4741 | 4828 | 4989 | 5271 | 5668 | 1.1 | 0.5 | 1.3 | 1.7 | 1.2 | 1.0 |
| China | Shenzhen | 495 | 875 | 995 | 1131 | 1279 | 1432 | 1585 | 7.0 | 2.5 | 2.2 | 0.2 | 0.3 | 0.3 |
| China | Shijiazhuang | 1172 | 1372 | 1483 | 1603 | 1741 | 1900 | 2079 | 2.4 | 1.6 | 1.8 | 0.5 | 0.4 | 0.4 |
| China | Suining | 1183 | 1260 | 1341 | 1428 | 1532 | 1661 | 1814 | 1.3 | 1.3 | 1.7 | 0.5 | 0.4 | 0.3 |
| China | Suqian | 970 | 1061 | 1123 | 1189 | 1269 | 1373 | 1499 | 1.5 | 1.2 | 1.7 | 0.4 | 0.3 | 0.3 |
| China | Suzhou | 743 | 875 | 1017 | 1183 | 1362 | 1542 | 1713 | 3.1 | 2.9 | 2.3 | 0.3 | 0.3 | 0.3 |
| China | Taian | 1322 | 1413 | 1457 | 1503 | 1571 | 1677 | 1820 | 1.0 | 0.8 | 1.5 | 0.5 | 0.4 | 0.3 |
| China | Taichung | 664 | 754 | 847 | 950 | 1064 | 1185 | 1309 | 2.4 | 2.3 | 2.1 | 0.3 | 0.2 | 0.2 |
| China | Taipei | 2446 | 2711 | 2629 | 2550 | 2600 | 2730 | 2936 | 0.7 | -0.1 | 1.2 | 1.0 | 0.6 | 0.5 |
| China | Taiyuan | 1932 | 2225 | 2318 | 2415 | 2544 | 2725 | 2954 | 1.8 | 0.9 | 1.5 | 0.8 | 0.6 | 0.5 |
| China | Tangshan | 1391 | 1485 | 1575 | 1671 | 1787 | 1933 | 2108 | 1.2 | 1.3 | 1.7 | 0.6 | 0.4 | 0.4 |
| China | Tianjin | 8133 | 8785 | 8969 | 9156 | 9471 | 9995 | 10713 | 1.0 | 0.5 | 1.2 | 3.3 | 2.2 | 1.9 |
| China | Tianmen | 1356 | 1484 | 1625 | 1779 | 1951 | 2142 | 2348 | 1.8 | 1.8 | 1.9 | 0.6 | 0.4 | 0.4 |
| China | Tianshui | 826 | 1040 | 1111 | 1187 | 1278 | 1389 | 1519 | 3.0 | 1.4 | 1.7 | 0.3 | 0.3 | 0.3 |
| China | Wanxian | 1267 | 1414 | 1577 | 1759 | 1959 | 2170 | 2387 | 2.2 | 2.2 | 2.0 | 0.5 | 0.4 | 0.4 |
| China | Weifang | 779 | 1152 | 1217 | 1287 | 1373 | 1484 | 1619 | 4.5 | 1.2 | 1.7 | 0.3 | 0.3 | 0.3 |
| China | Wenzhou | 543 | 604 | 987 | 1611 | 2432 | 3232 | 3818 | 6.0 | 9.0 | 4.5 | 0.2 | 0.4 | 0.7 |
| China | Wuhan | 3458 | 3833 | 4451 | 5169 | 5933 | 6673 | 7350 | 2.5 | 2.9 | 2.1 | 1.4 | 1.3 | 1.3 |
| China | Wulumuqi | 1029 | 1161 | 1282 | 1415 | 1563 | 1724 | 1895 | 2.2 | 2.0 | 1.9 | 0.4 | 0.4 | 0.3 |
| China | Wuxi | 881 | 1009 | 1066 | 1127 | 1203 | 1301 | 1421 | 1.9 | 1.2 | 1.7 | 0.4 | 0.3 | 0.3 |
| China | Xian | 2429 | 2873 | 2995 | 3123 | 3291 | 3523 | 3814 | 2.1 | 0.9 | 1.5 | 1.0 | 0.8 | 0.7 |
| China | Xiangxiang | 827 | 853 | 880 | 908 | 950 | 1017 | 1106 | 0.6 | 0.8 | 1.5 | 0.3 | 0.2 | 0.2 |
| China | Xiantao | 1250 | 1361 | 1482 | 1614 | 1763 | 1931 | 2116 | 1.7 | 1.7 | 1.8 | 0.5 | 0.4 | 0.4 |
| China | Xianyang | ... | 737 | 813 | 896 | 989 | 1092 | 1204 | ... | 2.0 | 2.0 | ... | 0.2 | 0.2 |
| China | Xiaogan | ... | 1255 | 914 | 665 | 679 | 717 | 777 | ... | -3.0 | 1.4 | ... | 0.2 | 0.1 |
| China | Xiaoshan | 1108 | 1113 | 1119 | 1124 | 1152 | 1216 | 1316 | 0.1 | 0.3 | 1.3 | 0.5 | 0.3 | 0.2 |
| China | Xinghua | 1468 | 1497 | 1526 | 1556 | 1613 | 1712 | 1854 | 0.4 | 0.6 | 1.4 | 0.6 | 0.4 | 0.3 |
| China | Xintai | 1298 | 1306 | 1315 | 1325 | 1359 | 1435 | 1551 | 0.1 | 0.3 | 1.3 | 0.5 | 0.3 | 0.3 |
| China | Xinyi | 842 | 884 | 927 | 973 | 1033 | 1114 | 1216 | 1.0 | 1.1 | 1.6 | 0.3 | 0.2 | 0.2 |
| China | Xuanzhou | 743 | 769 | 796 | 823 | 863 | 925 | 1008 | 0.7 | 0.8 | 1.6 | 0.3 | 0.2 | 0.2 |
| China | Xuzhou | 837 | 944 | 1329 | 1873 | 2512 | 3111 | 3572 | 4.6 | 6.4 | 3.5 | 0.3 | 0.5 | 0.6 |
| China | Yancheng | 1258 | 1352 | 1453 | 1562 | 1688 | 1837 | 2009 | 1.4 | 1.5 | 1.7 | 0.5 | 0.4 | 0.4 |
| China | Yantai | 515 | 838 | 1320 | 2080 | 3050 | 3982 | 4665 | 9.4 | 8.4 | 4.3 | 0.2 | 0.5 | 0.8 |
| China | Yichun (Heilongjiang) | 832 | 882 | 893 | 904 | 932 | 989 | 1072 | 0.7 | 0.4 | 1.4 | 0.3 | 0.2 | 0.2 |
| China | Yichun (Jiangxi) | 816 | 836 | 854 | 871 | 905 | 963 | 1046 | 0.5 | 0.6 | 1.5 | 0.3 | 0.2 | 0.2 |
| China | Yixing | 1044 | 1065 | 1086 | 1108 | 1148 | 1221 | 1324 | 0.4 | 0.6 | 1.4 | 0.4 | 0.3 | 0.2 |
| China | Yiyang | 939 | 1062 | 1194 | 1343 | 1505 | 1675 | 1849 | 2.4 | 2.3 | 2.1 | 0.4 | 0.3 | 0.3 |
| China | Yongzhou | 878 | 946 | 1019 | 1097 | 1189 | 1297 | 1422 | 1.5 | 1.5 | 1.8 | 0.4 | 0.3 | 0.3 |
| China | Yueyang | 1016 | 1078 | 1143 | 1213 | 1297 | 1405 | 1534 | 1.2 | 1.3 | 1.7 | 0.4 | 0.3 | 0.3 |
| China | Yulin | 1220 | 1323 | 1436 | 1558 | 1697 | 1856 | 2033 | 1.6 | 1.7 | 1.8 | 0.5 | 0.4 | 0.4 |
| China | Yuyao | 769 | 794 | 821 | 848 | 889 | 952 | 1037 | 0.7 | 0.8 | 1.5 | 0.3 | 0.2 | 0.2 |
| China | Yuzhou | 1026 | 1073 | 1122 | 1173 | 1241 | 1334 | 1454 | 0.9 | 1.0 | 1.6 | 0.4 | 0.3 | 0.3 |
| China | Zaoyang | 892 | 962 | 1039 | 1121 | 1216 | 1329 | 1457 | 1.5 | 1.6 | 1.8 | 0.4 | 0.3 | 0.3 |
| China | Zaozhuang | 1423 | 1793 | 1916 | 2048 | 2202 | 2389 | 2605 | 3.0 | 1.4 | 1.7 | 0.6 | 0.5 | 0.5 |
| China | Zhangjiakou | 646 | 720 | 796 | 880 | 974 | 1077 | 1188 | 2.1 | 2.0 | 2.0 | 0.3 | 0.2 | 0.2 |

# TABLE B.1

**continued**

| | | Estimates and projections (thousands) | | | | | | | Annual growth rate (%) | | | Share in country's urban population (%) | | |
|---|---|---|---|---|---|---|---|---|---|---|---|---|---|---|
| | | 1985 | 1990 | 1995 | 2000 | 2005 | 2010 | 2015 | 1985–1995 | 1995–2005 | 2005–2015 | 1985 | 2000 | 2015 |
| China | Zhangjiangang | 750 | 793 | 838 | 886 | 945 | 1023 | 1119 | 1.1 | 1.2 | 1.7 | 0.3 | 0.2 | 0.2 |
| China | Zhanjiang | 931 | 1049 | 1198 | 1368 | 1552 | 1740 | 1925 | 2.5 | 2.6 | 2.2 | 0.4 | 0.3 | 0.3 |
| China | Zhaodong | 772 | 797 | 824 | 851 | 892 | 955 | 1040 | 0.7 | 0.8 | 1.5 | 0.3 | 0.2 | 0.2 |
| China | Zhengzhou | 1542 | 1752 | 1905 | 2070 | 2256 | 2467 | 2698 | 2.1 | 1.7 | 1.8 | 0.6 | 0.5 | 0.5 |
| China | Zibo | 2323 | 2484 | 2578 | 2675 | 2808 | 3000 | 3248 | 1.0 | 0.9 | 1.5 | 0.9 | 0.7 | 0.6 |
| China | Zigong | 912 | 977 | 1023 | 1072 | 1135 | 1223 | 1333 | 1.2 | 1.0 | 1.6 | 0.4 | 0.3 | 0.2 |
| China, Hong Kong SAR | Hong Kong | 5070 | 5701 | 6224 | 6927 | 7321 | 7552 | 7689 | 2.1 | 1.6 | 0.5 | ... | ... | ... |
| Dem. People's Rep. of Korea | Nampo | 417 | 580 | 808 | 1046 | 1241 | 1371 | 1455 | 6.6 | 4.3 | 1.6 | 3.8 | 7.2 | 8.1 |
| Dem. People's Rep. of Korea | Pyongyang | 2134 | 2473 | 2865 | 3197 | 3457 | 3662 | 3834 | 3.0 | 1.9 | 1.0 | 19.5 | 22.1 | 21.4 |
| Gaza Strip | Gaza Strip (Urban) | 486 | 601 | 853 | 1060 | 1299 | 1575 | 1897 | 5.6 | 4.2 | 3.8 | ... | ... | ... |
| Georgia | Tbilisi | 1180 | 1277 | 1310 | 1310 | 1328 | 1363 | 1408 | 1.1 | 0.1 | 0.6 | 41.5 | 43.4 | 40.9 |
| India | Agra | 829 | 933 | 1051 | 1169 | 1309 | 1472 | 1657 | 2.4 | 2.2 | 2.4 | 0.4 | 0.4 | 0.4 |
| India | Ahmedabad | 2855 | 3255 | 3711 | 4160 | 4664 | 5218 | 5824 | 2.6 | 2.3 | 2.2 | 1.5 | 1.4 | 1.3 |
| India | Allahabad | 728 | 830 | 946 | 1062 | 1197 | 1350 | 1521 | 2.6 | 2.4 | 2.4 | 0.4 | 0.4 | 0.4 |
| India | Amritsar | 642 | 701 | 765 | 830 | 917 | 1027 | 1157 | 1.8 | 1.8 | 2.3 | 0.3 | 0.3 | 0.3 |
| India | Asansol | 504 | 728 | 1051 | 1425 | 1797 | 2116 | 2398 | 7.4 | 5.4 | 2.9 | 0.3 | 0.5 | 0.6 |
| India | Aurangabad | 415 | 569 | 778 | 1012 | 1245 | 1454 | 1649 | 6.3 | 4.7 | 2.8 | 0.2 | 0.4 | 0.4 |
| India | Bangalore | 3395 | 4036 | 4799 | 5561 | 6354 | 7155 | 7981 | 3.5 | 2.8 | 2.3 | 1.8 | 1.9 | 1.8 |
| India | Bhopal | 819 | 1031 | 1297 | 1576 | 1860 | 2132 | 2404 | 4.6 | 3.6 | 2.6 | 0.4 | 0.6 | 0.6 |
| India | Mumbai | 9907 | 12246 | 15138 | 18066 | 20940 | 23593 | 26138 | 4.2 | 3.2 | 2.2 | 5.3 | 6.3 | 6.0 |
| India | Calcutta | 9946 | 10890 | 11923 | 12918 | 14142 | 15601 | 17252 | 1.8 | 1.7 | 2.0 | 5.3 | 4.5 | 4.0 |
| India | Coimbatore | 995 | 1088 | 1190 | 1292 | 1426 | 1594 | 1790 | 1.8 | 1.8 | 2.3 | 0.5 | 0.5 | 0.4 |
| India | Delhi | 6770 | 8207 | 9948 | 11695 | 13451 | 15137 | 16808 | 3.9 | 3.0 | 2.2 | 3.6 | 4.1 | 3.9 |
| India | Dhanbad | 734 | 805 | 883 | 961 | 1063 | 1191 | 1340 | 1.9 | 1.9 | 2.3 | 0.4 | 0.3 | 0.3 |
| India | Durg-Bhilainagar | 568 | 673 | 798 | 925 | 1062 | 1208 | 1364 | 3.4 | 2.9 | 2.5 | 0.3 | 0.3 | 0.3 |
| India | Faridabad | 434 | 593 | 810 | 1051 | 1292 | 1509 | 1710 | 6.2 | 4.7 | 2.8 | 0.2 | 0.4 | 0.4 |
| India | Gwalior | 621 | 706 | 802 | 898 | 1011 | 1141 | 1287 | 2.6 | 2.3 | 2.4 | 0.3 | 0.3 | 0.3 |
| India | Hyderabad | 3210 | 4193 | 5477 | 6842 | 8173 | 9359 | 10457 | 5.3 | 4.0 | 2.5 | 1.7 | 2.4 | 2.4 |
| India | Indore | 941 | 1088 | 1258 | 1428 | 1619 | 1828 | 2056 | 2.9 | 2.5 | 2.4 | 0.5 | 0.5 | 0.5 |
| India | Jabalpur | 812 | 880 | 953 | 1027 | 1130 | 1262 | 1420 | 1.6 | 1.7 | 2.3 | 0.4 | 0.4 | 0.3 |
| India | Jaipur | 1209 | 1478 | 1808 | 2145 | 2494 | 2839 | 3190 | 4.0 | 3.2 | 2.5 | 0.7 | 0.7 | 0.7 |
| India | Jamshedpur | 735 | 817 | 910 | 1002 | 1116 | 1254 | 1412 | 2.1 | 2.0 | 2.4 | 0.4 | 0.4 | 0.3 |
| India | Jodhpur | 570 | 654 | 750 | 847 | 958 | 1084 | 1223 | 2.7 | 2.5 | 2.4 | 0.3 | 0.3 | 0.3 |
| India | Kanpur | 1798 | 2001 | 2227 | 2450 | 2721 | 3040 | 3402 | 2.1 | 2.0 | 2.2 | 1.0 | 0.9 | 0.8 |
| India | Kochi (Cochin) | 855 | 1103 | 1422 | 1762 | 2102 | 2420 | 2728 | 5.1 | 3.9 | 2.6 | 0.5 | 0.6 | 0.6 |
| India | Kozhikode (Calicut) | 645 | 781 | 946 | 1115 | 1294 | 1476 | 1665 | 3.8 | 3.1 | 2.5 | 0.4 | 0.4 | 0.4 |
| India | Lucknow | 1254 | 1614 | 2078 | 2568 | 3057 | 3511 | 3947 | 5.1 | 3.9 | 2.6 | 0.7 | 0.9 | 0.9 |
| India | Ludhiana | 768 | 1006 | 1318 | 1655 | 1990 | 2299 | 2594 | 5.4 | 4.1 | 2.7 | 0.4 | 0.6 | 0.6 |
| India | Madras | 4748 | 5338 | 6002 | 6648 | 7390 | 8225 | 9145 | 2.3 | 2.1 | 2.1 | 2.5 | 2.3 | 2.1 |
| India | Madurai | 981 | 1073 | 1174 | 1275 | 1407 | 1573 | 1767 | 1.8 | 1.8 | 2.3 | 0.5 | 0.4 | 0.4 |
| India | Meerut | 655 | 824 | 1037 | 1261 | 1488 | 1709 | 1929 | 4.6 | 3.6 | 2.6 | 0.4 | 0.4 | 0.4 |
| India | Nagpur | 1448 | 1637 | 1851 | 2062 | 2309 | 2590 | 2903 | 2.5 | 2.2 | 2.3 | 0.8 | 0.7 | 0.7 |
| India | Nashik | 539 | 700 | 911 | 1136 | 1364 | 1576 | 1783 | 5.3 | 4.0 | 2.7 | 0.3 | 0.4 | 0.4 |
| India | Patna | 993 | 1087 | 1189 | 1291 | 1425 | 1593 | 1790 | 1.8 | 1.8 | 2.3 | 0.5 | 0.5 | 0.4 |
| India | Pune (Poona) | 1998 | 2430 | 2955 | 3489 | 4038 | 4579 | 5128 | 3.9 | 3.1 | 2.4 | 1.1 | 1.2 | 1.2 |
| India | Rajkot | 526 | 638 | 774 | 913 | 1060 | 1211 | 1369 | 3.9 | 3.1 | 2.6 | 0.3 | 0.3 | 0.3 |
| India | Surat | 1139 | 1469 | 1893 | 2344 | 2794 | 3211 | 3612 | 5.1 | 3.9 | 2.6 | 0.6 | 0.8 | 0.8 |
| India | Thane | 533 | 766 | 1099 | 1484 | 1866 | 2195 | 2486 | 7.2 | 5.3 | 2.9 | 0.3 | 0.5 | 0.6 |
| India | Thiruvananthapuram | 636 | 801 | 1010 | 1229 | 1452 | 1668 | 1884 | 4.6 | 3.6 | 2.6 | 0.3 | 0.4 | 0.4 |
| India | Tiruchchirapalli | 652 | 705 | 761 | 820 | 901 | 1007 | 1135 | 1.6 | 1.7 | 2.3 | 0.4 | 0.3 | 0.3 |
| India | Ulhasnagar | 805 | 1031 | 1322 | 1630 | 1940 | 2232 | 2517 | 5.0 | 3.8 | 2.6 | 0.4 | 0.6 | 0.6 |
| India | Vadodara | 891 | 1096 | 1348 | 1608 | 1877 | 2142 | 2412 | 4.1 | 3.3 | 2.5 | 0.5 | 0.6 | 0.6 |
| India | Vijayawada | 658 | 821 | 1025 | 1237 | 1455 | 1668 | 1883 | 4.4 | 3.5 | 2.6 | 0.4 | 0.4 | 0.4 |
| India | Varanasi (Benares) | 891 | 1013 | 1152 | 1291 | 1452 | 1635 | 1839 | 2.6 | 2.3 | 2.4 | 0.5 | 0.5 | 0.4 |
| India | Visakhapatnam | 770 | 1018 | 1348 | 1705 | 2060 | 2383 | 2690 | 5.6 | 4.2 | 2.7 | 0.4 | 0.6 | 0.6 |
| Indonesia | Bandung | 2090 | 2460 | 2896 | 3409 | 4007 | 4645 | 5241 | 3.3 | 3.3 | 2.7 | 4.8 | 3.9 | 3.8 |
| Indonesia | Jakarta | 6788 | 7650 | 9161 | 11018 | 13153 | 15336 | 17256 | 3.0 | 3.6 | 2.7 | 15.5 | 12.7 | 12.6 |
| Indonesia | Medan | 1390 | 1537 | 1699 | 1879 | 2102 | 2370 | 2653 | 2.0 | 2.1 | 2.3 | 3.2 | 2.2 | 1.9 |
| Indonesia | Palembang | 880 | 1033 | 1212 | 1422 | 1670 | 1940 | 2199 | 3.2 | 3.2 | 2.8 | 2.0 | 1.6 | 1.6 |
| Indonesia | Semarang | 812 | 804 | 795 | 787 | 814 | 877 | 968 | –0.2 | 0.2 | 1.7 | 1.9 | 0.9 | 0.7 |
| Indonesia | Surabaja | 1887 | 2062 | 2253 | 2461 | 2727 | 3054 | 3405 | 1.8 | 1.9 | 2.2 | 4.3 | 2.8 | 2.5 |
| Indonesia | Ujung Pandang | 719 | 816 | 926 | 1051 | 1201 | 1375 | 1551 | 2.5 | 2.6 | 2.6 | 1.6 | 1.2 | 1.1 |
| Iran (Islamic Republic of) | Ahvaz | 548 | 688 | 845 | 997 | 1115 | 1238 | 1363 | 4.3 | 2.8 | 2.0 | 2.2 | 2.4 | 2.4 |
| Iran (Islamic Republic of) | Esfahan | 980 | 1326 | 1924 | 2589 | 3126 | 3564 | 3921 | 6.8 | 4.9 | 2.3 | 3.9 | 6.2 | 6.9 |
| Iran (Islamic Republic of) | Kermanshah | 453 | 585 | 756 | 929 | 1065 | 1195 | 1319 | 5.1 | 3.4 | 2.1 | 1.8 | 2.2 | 2.3 |
| Iran (Islamic Republic of) | Mashhad | 1347 | 1681 | 2016 | 2328 | 2566 | 2823 | 3088 | 4.0 | 2.4 | 1.9 | 5.3 | 5.6 | 5.4 |
| Iran (Islamic Republic of) | Shiraz | 819 | 946 | 1023 | 1090 | 1146 | 1242 | 1361 | 2.2 | 1.1 | 1.7 | 3.2 | 2.6 | 2.4 |
| Iran (Islamic Republic of) | Tabriz | 1117 | 1296 | 1452 | 1590 | 1698 | 1849 | 2023 | 2.6 | 1.6 | 1.8 | 4.4 | 3.8 | 3.5 |
| Iran (Islamic Republic of) | Teheran | 5822 | 6360 | 6836 | 7225 | 7523 | 8054 | 8709 | 1.6 | 1.0 | 1.5 | 22.9 | 17.3 | 15.2 |
| Iraq | Arbil | 691 | 1157 | 1743 | 2369 | 2925 | 3380 | 3768 | 9.3 | 5.2 | 2.5 | 6.6 | 13.3 | 13.6 |
| Iraq | Baghdad | 3681 | 4039 | 4336 | 4797 | 5438 | 6155 | 6833 | 1.6 | 2.3 | 2.3 | 35.0 | 27.0 | 24.6 |
| Iraq | Mosul | 603 | 744 | 879 | 1034 | 1210 | 1390 | 1560 | 3.8 | 3.2 | 2.5 | 5.7 | 5.8 | 5.6 |
| Israel | Tel-Aviv–Yafo | 1621 | 1790 | 1976 | 2181 | 2370 | 2524 | 2631 | 2.0 | 1.8 | 1.0 | 42.7 | 38.5 | 37.5 |
| Japan | Hiroshima | 797 | 842 | 1094 | 1437 | 1640 | 1710 | 1718 | 3.2 | 4.1 | 0.5 | 0.9 | 1.4 | 1.7 |
| Japan | Kitakyushu | 2217 | 2487 | 2619 | 2750 | 2750 | 2750 | 2750 | 1.7 | 0.5 | 0.0 | 2.4 | 2.8 | 2.7 |
| Japan | Kyoto | 1714 | 1760 | 1804 | 1849 | 1849 | 1849 | 1849 | 0.5 | 0.3 | 0.0 | 1.9 | 1.9 | 1.8 |
| Japan | Nagoya | 2708 | 2948 | 3055 | 3157 | 3157 | 3157 | 3157 | 1.2 | 0.3 | 0.0 | 2.9 | 3.2 | 3.1 |
| Japan | Osaka | 10351 | 11035 | 11043 | 11013 | 11013 | 11013 | 11013 | 0.7 | 0.0 | 0.0 | 11.2 | 11.0 | 10.7 |
| Japan | Sapporo | 1379 | 1538 | 1746 | 1984 | 2016 | 2016 | 2016 | 2.4 | 1.4 | 0.0 | 1.5 | 2.0 | 2.0 |
| Japan | Sendai | 722 | 760 | 960 | 1223 | 1362 | 1400 | 1400 | 2.9 | 3.5 | 0.3 | 0.8 | 1.2 | 1.4 |
| Japan | Tokyo | 23322 | 25081 | 25785 | 26444 | 26444 | 26444 | 26444 | 1.0 | 0.3 | 0.0 | 25.2 | 26.5 | 25.7 |

# TABLE B.I

**continued**

| | | | | | | | | | | | | | | |
|---|---|---|---|---|---|---|---|---|---|---|---|---|---|---|
| rdan | Amman | 782 | 955 | 1179 | 1430 | 1700 | 1965 | 2212 | 4.1 | 3.7 | 2.6 | 29.6 | 28.9 | 28.0 |
| azakhstan | Alma-Ata | 1043 | 1150 | 1248 | 1248 | 1248 | 1248 | 1292 | 1.8 | 0.0 | 0.4 | 11.8 | 13.6 | 12.6 |
| uwait | Kuwait City | 942 | 1090 | 1090 | 1190 | 1313 | 1418 | 1513 | 1.5 | 1.9 | 1.4 | 58.4 | 61.8 | 58.8 |
| ebanon | Beirut | 1385 | 1582 | 1826 | 2055 | 2238 | 2366 | 2468 | 2.8 | 2.0 | 1.0 | 65.4 | 69.8 | 67.6 |
| alaysia | Kuala Lumpur | 1016 | 1120 | 1236 | 1378 | 1539 | 1703 | 1857 | 2.0 | 2.2 | 1.9 | 14.1 | 10.8 | 10.2 |
| yanmar | Yangon | 2788 | 3299 | 3742 | 4196 | 4721 | 5375 | 6049 | 2.9 | 2.3 | 2.5 | 30.9 | 33.2 | 30.8 |
| akistan | Faisalabad | 1284 | 1540 | 1845 | 2232 | 2687 | 3208 | 3758 | 3.6 | 3.8 | 3.4 | 4.3 | 3.9 | 3.6 |
| akistan | Gujranwala | 898 | 1248 | 1635 | 2051 | 2488 | 2973 | 3484 | 6.0 | 4.2 | 3.4 | 3.0 | 3.5 | 3.4 |
| akistan | Hyderabad | 824 | 937 | 1088 | 1304 | 1571 | 1883 | 2214 | 2.8 | 3.7 | 3.4 | 2.7 | 2.3 | 2.1 |
| akistan | Islamabad | 336 | 557 | 813 | 1068 | 1312 | 1575 | 1854 | 8.8 | 4.8 | 3.5 | 1.1 | 1.8 | 1.8 |
| akistan | Karachi | 6336 | 7945 | 9731 | 11794 | 14067 | 16595 | 19211 | 4.3 | 3.7 | 3.1 | 21.0 | 20.4 | 18.5 |
| akistan | Lahore | 3462 | 4179 | 5012 | 6040 | 7224 | 8563 | 9961 | 3.7 | 3.7 | 3.2 | 11.5 | 10.4 | 9.6 |
| akistan | Multan | 854 | 1028 | 1236 | 1500 | 1811 | 2169 | 2547 | 3.7 | 3.8 | 3.4 | 2.8 | 2.6 | 2.5 |
| akistan | Peshawar | 823 | 1214 | 1648 | 2098 | 2552 | 3047 | 3571 | 6.9 | 4.4 | 3.4 | 2.7 | 3.6 | 3.4 |
| akistan | Rawalpindi | 906 | 1068 | 1268 | 1531 | 1847 | 2211 | 2596 | 3.4 | 3.8 | 3.4 | 3.0 | 2.6 | 2.5 |
| hilippines | Davao | 723 | 851 | 1011 | 1202 | 1402 | 1582 | 1719 | 3.4 | 3.3 | 2.0 | 3.1 | 2.7 | 2.6 |
| hilippines | Metro Manila | 6888 | 7968 | 9303 | 10870 | 12475 | 13857 | 14825 | 3.0 | 2.9 | 1.7 | 29.3 | 24.4 | 22.6 |
| epublic of Korea | Inch'on | 1365 | 1785 | 2272 | 2884 | 3147 | 3233 | 3295 | 5.1 | 3.3 | 0.5 | 5.2 | 7.5 | 7.3 |
| epublic of Korea | Kwangju | 893 | 1122 | 1249 | 1379 | 1379 | 1379 | 1396 | 3.4 | 1.0 | 0.1 | 3.4 | 3.6 | 3.1 |
| epublic of Korea | Puch'on | 435 | 651 | 771 | 900 | 919 | 919 | 932 | 5.7 | 1.8 | 0.1 | 1.6 | 2.4 | 2.1 |
| epublic of Korea | Pusan | 3490 | 3778 | 3813 | 3830 | 3830 | 3830 | 3859 | 0.9 | 0.0 | 0.1 | 13.2 | 10.0 | 8.6 |
| epublic of Korea | Seoul | 9549 | 10544 | 10256 | 9888 | 9888 | 9888 | 9923 | 0.7 | -0.4 | 0.0 | 36.1 | 25.8 | 22.0 |
| epublic of Korea | Songnam | 443 | 534 | 842 | 1353 | 1785 | 2058 | 2201 | 6.4 | 7.5 | 2.1 | 1.7 | 3.5 | 4.9 |
| epublic of Korea | Taegu | 1999 | 2215 | 2434 | 2675 | 2675 | 2675 | 2699 | 2.0 | 0.9 | 0.1 | 7.6 | 7.0 | 6.0 |
| epublic of Korea | Taejon | 850 | 1036 | 1256 | 1522 | 1602 | 1613 | 1636 | 3.9 | 2.4 | 0.2 | 3.2 | 4.0 | 3.6 |
| epublic of Korea | Ulsan | 541 | 673 | 945 | 1340 | 1599 | 1736 | 1814 | 5.6 | 5.3 | 1.3 | 2.0 | 3.5 | 4.0 |
| audi Arabia | Jeddah | 952 | 1216 | 1492 | 1810 | 2139 | 2460 | 2753 | 4.5 | 3.6 | 2.5 | 10.4 | 9.8 | 9.4 |
| audi Arabia | Mecca | 550 | 663 | 777 | 919 | 1079 | 1244 | 1399 | 3.5 | 3.3 | 2.6 | 6.0 | 5.0 | 4.8 |
| audi Arabia | Riyadh | 1401 | 1975 | 2619 | 3324 | 3990 | 4587 | 5111 | 6.3 | 4.2 | 2.5 | 15.2 | 17.9 | 17.5 |
| ingapore | Singapore | 2709 | 3016 | 3321 | 3567 | 3754 | 3885 | 3994 | 2.0 | 1.2 | 0.6 | 100.0 | 100.0 | 100.0 |
| yrian Arab Republic | Aleppo | 1288 | 1543 | 1840 | 2173 | 2536 | 2923 | 3305 | 3.6 | 3.2 | 2.7 | 25.6 | 24.7 | 23.5 |
| yrian Arab Republic | Damascus | 1585 | 1790 | 2036 | 2335 | 2694 | 3096 | 3500 | 2.5 | 2.8 | 2.6 | 31.5 | 26.6 | 24.9 |
| Thailand | Bangkok | 5279 | 5901 | 6567 | 7281 | 8081 | 9030 | 10143 | 2.2 | 2.1 | 2.3 | 57.8 | 54.9 | 50.2 |
| Turkey | Adana | 751 | 906 | 1087 | 1294 | 1485 | 1643 | 1757 | 3.7 | 3.1 | 1.7 | 2.8 | 2.6 | 2.6 |
| Turkey | Ankara | 2261 | 2542 | 2846 | 3203 | 3544 | 3849 | 4082 | 2.3 | 2.2 | 1.4 | 8.6 | 6.4 | 6.0 |
| Turkey | Bursa | 645 | 822 | 1045 | 1304 | 1539 | 1721 | 1845 | 4.8 | 3.9 | 1.8 | 2.4 | 2.6 | 2.7 |
| Turkey | Gaziantep | 472 | 595 | 750 | 930 | 1094 | 1224 | 1315 | 4.6 | 3.8 | 1.8 | 1.8 | 1.9 | 1.9 |
| Turkey | Istanbul | 5408 | 6544 | 7911 | 9451 | 10807 | 11837 | 12492 | 3.8 | 3.1 | 1.5 | 20.5 | 18.8 | 18.4 |
| Turkey | Izmir | 1472 | 1740 | 2052 | 2409 | 2736 | 3007 | 3200 | 3.3 | 2.9 | 1.6 | 5.6 | 4.8 | 4.7 |
| Jnited Arab Emirates | Abu Dhabi | 415 | 624 | 799 | 927 | 1022 | 1093 | 1153 | 6.6 | 2.5 | 1.2 | 34.8 | 44.2 | 42.9 |
| Jzbekistan | Tashkent | 1958 | 2074 | 2111 | 2148 | 2205 | 2292 | 2434 | 0.8 | 0.4 | 1.0 | 26.5 | 24.0 | 21.1 |
| viet Nam | Haiphong | 1379 | 1471 | 1570 | 1679 | 1814 | 2003 | 2282 | 1.3 | 1.3 | 2.3 | 11.8 | 10.7 | 9.7 |
| viet Nam | Hanoi | 2855 | 3127 | 3424 | 3734 | 4071 | 4498 | 5102 | 1.8 | 1.8 | 2.3 | 24.4 | 23.7 | 21.7 |
| viet Nam | Ho Chi Minh City | 3717 | 3996 | 4296 | 4615 | 4982 | 5478 | 6201 | 1.5 | 1.4 | 2.2 | 31.7 | 29.3 | 26.4 |
| yemen | Sana'a | 402 | 678 | 965 | 1303 | 1697 | 2157 | 2709 | 8.8 | 6.5 | 4.7 | 18.8 | 29.1 | 29.4 |
| **EUROPE** | | | | | | | | | | | | | | |
| Austria | Vienna | 2049 | 2055 | 2060 | 2070 | 2081 | 2090 | 2099 | 0.1 | 0.1 | 0.1 | 41.9 | 39.0 | 36.8 |
| Belarus | Minsk | 1474 | 1617 | 1692 | 1772 | 1812 | 1835 | 1845 | 1.4 | 0.7 | 0.2 | 23.8 | 24.3 | 24.3 |
| Belgium | Brussels | 1175 | 1148 | 1122 | 1122 | 1122 | 1122 | 1122 | -0.5 | 0.0 | 0.0 | 12.4 | 11.3 | 11.4 |
| Bulgaria | Sofia | 1182 | 1191 | 1192 | 1192 | 1192 | 1192 | 1192 | 0.1 | 0.0 | 0.0 | 20.5 | 20.8 | 21.3 |
| Croatia | Zagreb | 735 | 849 | 981 | 1060 | 1106 | 1134 | 1149 | 2.9 | 1.2 | 0.4 | 31.4 | 41.1 | 41.0 |
| Czech Republic | Prague | 1194 | 1207 | 1220 | 1226 | 1228 | 1229 | 1230 | 0.2 | 0.1 | 0.0 | 15.5 | 16.0 | 16.0 |
| Denmark | Copenhagen | 1364 | 1345 | 1359 | 1388 | 1405 | 1412 | 1415 | 0.0 | 0.3 | 0.1 | 31.6 | 30.7 | 30.7 |
| Finland | Helsinki | 722 | 872 | 1057 | 1167 | 1230 | 1269 | 1293 | 3.8 | 1.5 | 0.5 | 24.6 | 33.5 | 33.2 |
| France | Lille | 945 | 960 | 975 | 991 | 1006 | 1020 | 1033 | 0.3 | 0.3 | 0.3 | 2.3 | 2.2 | 2.1 |
| France | Lyon | 1208 | 1266 | 1318 | 1358 | 1384 | 1403 | 1417 | 0.9 | 0.5 | 0.2 | 3.0 | 3.0 | 2.9 |
| France | Marseilles | 1243 | 1230 | 1233 | 1241 | 1255 | 1270 | 1284 | -0.1 | 0.2 | 0.2 | 3.1 | 2.8 | 2.7 |
| France | Paris | 9105 | 9334 | 9514 | 9624 | 9668 | 9677 | 9677 | 0.4 | 0.2 | 0.0 | 22.4 | 21.6 | 19.9 |
| Germany | Aachen | 960 | 1001 | 1040 | 1063 | 1072 | 1074 | 1074 | 0.8 | 0.3 | 0.0 | 1.5 | 1.5 | 1.5 |
| Germany | Berlin | 3268 | 3288 | 3317 | 3324 | 3327 | 3327 | 3327 | 0.2 | 0.0 | 0.0 | 5.0 | 4.6 | 4.5 |
| Germany | Bielefeld | 1137 | 1201 | 1262 | 1297 | 1311 | 1314 | 1314 | 1.0 | 0.4 | 0.0 | 1.7 | 1.8 | 1.8 |
| Germany | Bremen | 815 | 840 | 867 | 882 | 888 | 889 | 889 | 0.6 | 0.2 | 0.0 | 1.3 | 1.2 | 1.2 |
| Germany | Cologne | 2714 | 2855 | 2984 | 3054 | 3083 | 3089 | 3089 | 1.0 | 0.3 | 0.0 | 4.2 | 4.2 | 4.2 |
| Germany | Düsseldorf | 2349 | 2700 | 3031 | 3238 | 3324 | 3342 | 3342 | 2.6 | 0.9 | 0.1 | 3.6 | 4.5 | 4.6 |
| Germany | Essen | 6217 | 6353 | 6483 | 6541 | 6564 | 6569 | 6569 | 0.4 | 0.1 | 0.0 | 9.5 | 9.1 | 9.0 |
| Germany | Frankfurt | 3293 | 3456 | 3606 | 3687 | 3720 | 3726 | 3726 | 0.9 | 0.3 | 0.0 | 5.1 | 5.1 | 5.1 |
| Germany | Hamburg | 2451 | 2540 | 2625 | 2668 | 2685 | 2689 | 2689 | 0.7 | 0.2 | 0.0 | 3.8 | 3.7 | 3.7 |
| Germany | Hanover | 1194 | 1230 | 1267 | 1287 | 1295 | 1296 | 1296 | 0.6 | 0.2 | 0.0 | 1.8 | 1.8 | 1.8 |
| Germany | Karlsruhe | 869 | 912 | 954 | 979 | 989 | 991 | 991 | 0.9 | 0.4 | 0.0 | 1.3 | 1.4 | 1.4 |
| Germany | Mannheim | 1432 | 1503 | 1571 | 1608 | 1623 | 1626 | 1626 | 0.9 | 0.3 | 0.0 | 2.2 | 2.2 | 2.2 |
| Germany | Munich | 2023 | 2134 | 2237 | 2294 | 2317 | 2322 | 2322 | 1.0 | 0.4 | 0.0 | 3.1 | 3.2 | 3.2 |
| Germany | Nuremberg | 1048 | 1106 | 1160 | 1192 | 1205 | 1208 | 1208 | 1.0 | 0.4 | 0.0 | 1.6 | 1.7 | 1.7 |
| Germany | Saarland | 872 | 878 | 888 | 893 | 895 | 895 | 895 | 0.2 | 0.1 | 0.0 | 1.3 | 1.2 | 1.2 |
| Germany | Stuttgart | 2351 | 2485 | 2608 | 2676 | 2704 | 2709 | 2709 | 1.0 | 0.4 | 0.0 | 3.6 | 3.7 | 3.7 |
| Greece | Athens | 3047 | 3070 | 3093 | 3116 | 3130 | 3135 | 3136 | 0.2 | 0.1 | 0.0 | 52.5 | 48.7 | 46.4 |
| Greece | Thessaloniki | 724 | 746 | 768 | 789 | 805 | 815 | 818 | 0.6 | 0.5 | 0.2 | 12.5 | 12.3 | 12.1 |
| Hungary | Budapest | 2037 | 2009 | 1915 | 1825 | 1825 | 1825 | 1825 | -0.6 | -0.5 | 0.0 | 32.3 | 28.4 | 28.3 |
| Ireland | Dublin | 920 | 916 | 947 | 985 | 1026 | 1073 | 1127 | 0.3 | 0.8 | 0.9 | 46.0 | 44.7 | 42.3 |
| Italy | Florence | 865 | 820 | 778 | 778 | 778 | 778 | 778 | -1.1 | 0.0 | 0.0 | 2.3 | 2.0 | 2.0 |
| Italy | Genoa | 1000 | 943 | 890 | 890 | 890 | 890 | 890 | -1.2 | 0.0 | 0.0 | 2.6 | 2.3 | 2.3 |
| Italy | Milan | 4984 | 4603 | 4251 | 4251 | 4251 | 4251 | 4251 | -1.6 | 0.0 | 0.0 | 13.1 | 11.1 | 11.0 |
| Italy | Naples | 3421 | 3210 | 3012 | 3012 | 3012 | 3012 | 3012 | -1.3 | 0.0 | 0.0 | 9.0 | 7.9 | 7.8 |
| Italy | Rome | 2930 | 2807 | 2688 | 2688 | 2688 | 2688 | 2688 | -0.9 | 0.0 | 0.0 | 7.7 | 7.0 | 7.0 |
| Italy | Turin | 1502 | 1394 | 1294 | 1294 | 1294 | 1294 | 1294 | -1.5 | 0.0 | 0.0 | 4.0 | 3.4 | 3.4 |

# TABLE B.1

**continued**

| | | Estimates and projections (thousands) | | | | | | | Annual growth rate (%) | | | Share in country's urban population (%) | | |
|---|---|---|---|---|---|---|---|---|---|---|---|---|---|---|
| | | 1985 | 1990 | 1995 | 2000 | 2005 | 2010 | 2015 | 1985–1995 | 1995–2005 | 2005–2015 | 1985 | 2000 | 2015 |
| Latvia | Riga | 882 | 892 | 833 | 775 | 775 | 775 | 775 | -0.6 | -0.7 | 0.0 | 48.8 | 47.7 | 52.6 |
| The Netherlands | Amsterdam | 995 | 1053 | 1102 | 1144 | 1168 | 1178 | 1180 | 1.0 | 0.6 | 0.1 | 7.8 | 8.1 | 8.2 |
| The Netherlands | Rotterdam | 1035 | 1047 | 1078 | 1105 | 1120 | 1126 | 1127 | 0.4 | 0.4 | 0.1 | 8.1 | 7.8 | 7.8 |
| Norway | Oslo | 661 | 681 | 858 | 978 | 1045 | 1084 | 1108 | 2.6 | 2.0 | 0.6 | 22.3 | 29.0 | 29.3 |
| Poland | Crakow | 781 | 806 | 832 | 857 | 879 | 900 | 918 | 0.6 | 0.6 | 0.4 | 3.5 | 3.4 | 3.3 |
| Poland | Gdansk | 840 | 857 | 875 | 893 | 911 | 931 | 948 | 0.4 | 0.4 | 0.4 | 3.8 | 3.5 | 3.4 |
| Poland | Katowice | 3291 | 3357 | 3425 | 3487 | 3541 | 3588 | 3622 | 0.4 | 0.3 | 0.2 | 14.8 | 13.7 | 12.9 |
| Poland | Lodz | 1019 | 1030 | 1041 | 1055 | 1071 | 1091 | 1110 | 0.2 | 0.3 | 0.4 | 4.6 | 4.2 | 4.0 |
| Poland | Warsaw | 2112 | 2165 | 2219 | 2269 | 2313 | 2352 | 2381 | 0.5 | 0.4 | 0.3 | 9.5 | 8.9 | 8.5 |
| Portugal | Lisbon | 1762 | 2434 | 3363 | 3826 | 4155 | 4359 | 4401 | 6.5 | 2.1 | 0.6 | 47.9 | 60.1 | 58.8 |
| Portugal | Porto | 758 | 1107 | 1615 | 1922 | 2149 | 2287 | 2324 | 7.6 | 2.9 | 0.8 | 20.6 | 30.2 | 31.0 |
| Romania | Bucharest | 2008 | 2054 | 2054 | 2054 | 2054 | 2054 | 2054 | 0.2 | 0.0 | 0.0 | 17.2 | 16.4 | 15.7 |
| Russian Federation | Chelyabinsk | 1098 | 1153 | 1178 | 1185 | 1188 | 1189 | 1189 | 0.7 | 0.1 | 0.0 | 1.1 | 1.0 | 1.0 |
| Russian Federation | Ekaterinburg | 1303 | 1379 | 1417 | 1431 | 1437 | 1438 | 1438 | 0.8 | 0.1 | 0.0 | 1.3 | 1.3 | 1.2 |
| Russian Federation | Kazan | 1056 | 1108 | 1131 | 1137 | 1140 | 1140 | 1140 | 0.7 | 0.1 | 0.0 | 1.0 | 1.0 | 1.0 |
| Russian Federation | Krasnoyarsk | 868 | 928 | 962 | 977 | 983 | 984 | 984 | 1.0 | 0.2 | 0.0 | 0.8 | 0.9 | 0.8 |
| Russian Federation | Moscow | 8580 | 9048 | 9256 | 9321 | 9348 | 9353 | 9353 | 0.8 | 0.1 | 0.0 | 8.3 | 8.2 | 8.0 |
| Russian Federation | Nizhni Novgorod | 1401 | 1447 | 1458 | 1458 | 1458 | 1458 | 1458 | 0.4 | 0.0 | 0.0 | 1.4 | 1.3 | 1.2 |
| Russian Federation | Novosibirsk | 1387 | 1449 | 1473 | 1478 | 1479 | 1480 | 1480 | 0.6 | 0.0 | 0.0 | 1.4 | 1.3 | 1.3 |
| Russian Federation | Omsk | 1097 | 1166 | 1202 | 1216 | 1222 | 1223 | 1223 | 0.9 | 0.2 | 0.0 | 1.1 | 1.1 | 1.0 |
| Russian Federation | Perm | 1054 | 1098 | 1115 | 1118 | 1119 | 1119 | 1119 | 0.6 | 0.0 | 0.0 | 1.0 | 1.0 | 1.0 |
| Russian Federation | Rostov-on-Don | 986 | 1029 | 1046 | 1049 | 1051 | 1051 | 1051 | 0.6 | 0.1 | 0.0 | 1.0 | 0.9 | 0.9 |
| Russian Federation | Samara | 1241 | 1260 | 1260 | 1260 | 1260 | 1260 | 1260 | 0.2 | 0.0 | 0.0 | 1.2 | 1.1 | 1.1 |
| Russian Federation | Saratov | 887 | 911 | 915 | 915 | 915 | 915 | 915 | 0.3 | 0.0 | 0.0 | 0.9 | 0.8 | 0.8 |
| Russian Federation | Saint Petersburg | 4844 | 5053 | 5124 | 5133 | 5136 | 5137 | 5137 | 0.6 | 0.0 | 0.0 | 4.7 | 4.5 | 4.4 |
| Russian Federation | Ufa | 1041 | 1100 | 1129 | 1139 | 1144 | 1145 | 1145 | 0.8 | 0.1 | 0.0 | 1.0 | 1.0 | 1.0 |
| Russian Federation | Volgograd | 973 | 1008 | 1019 | 1020 | 1020 | 1020 | 1020 | 0.5 | 0.0 | 0.0 | 0.9 | 0.9 | 0.9 |
| Russian Federation | Voronezh | 847 | 900 | 929 | 940 | 945 | 946 | 946 | 0.9 | 0.2 | 0.0 | 0.8 | 0.8 | 0.8 |
| Spain | Barcelona | 3010 | 2913 | 2819 | 2819 | 2819 | 2819 | 2819 | -0.7 | 0.0 | 0.0 | 10.5 | 9.2 | 9.0 |
| Spain | Madrid | 4273 | 4172 | 4072 | 4072 | 4072 | 4072 | 4072 | -0.5 | 0.0 | 0.0 | 15.0 | 13.2 | 13.0 |
| Spain | Valencia | 747 | 749 | 751 | 754 | 755 | 756 | 756 | 0.1 | 0.1 | 0.0 | 2.6 | 2.5 | 2.4 |
| Sweden | Göteborg | 703 | 729 | 753 | 766 | 774 | 777 | 780 | 0.7 | 0.3 | 0.1 | 10.1 | 10.3 | 10.1 |
| Sweden | Stockholm | 1432 | 1487 | 1548 | 1583 | 1604 | 1612 | 1613 | 0.8 | 0.4 | 0.1 | 20.6 | 21.3 | 20.8 |
| Switzerland | Zurich | 765 | 834 | 926 | 983 | 1018 | 1038 | 1051 | 1.9 | 1.0 | 0.3 | 20.1 | 19.7 | 19.4 |
| Ukraine | Dnepropetrovsk | 1136 | 1169 | 1149 | 1129 | 1129 | 1129 | 1129 | 0.1 | -0.2 | 0.0 | 3.5 | 3.3 | 3.3 |
| Ukraine | Donetsk | 1076 | 1104 | 1089 | 1075 | 1075 | 1075 | 1075 | 0.1 | -0.1 | 0.0 | 3.3 | 3.1 | 3.1 |
| Ukraine | Kharkov | 1544 | 1591 | 1558 | 1526 | 1526 | 1526 | 1526 | 0.1 | -0.2 | 0.0 | 4.7 | 4.5 | 4.5 |
| Ukraine | Kiev | 2410 | 2582 | 2626 | 2670 | 2678 | 2678 | 2678 | 0.9 | 0.2 | 0.0 | 7.3 | 7.8 | 7.8 |
| Ukraine | Lvov | 741 | 789 | 801 | 813 | 815 | 815 | 815 | 0.8 | 0.2 | 0.0 | 2.3 | 2.4 | 2.4 |
| Ukraine | Odessa | 1081 | 1089 | 1050 | 1012 | 1012 | 1012 | 1012 | -0.3 | -0.4 | 0.0 | 3.3 | 3.0 | 3.0 |
| Ukraine | Zaporozhye | 844 | 880 | 879 | 878 | 878 | 878 | 878 | 0.4 | 0.0 | 0.0 | 2.6 | 2.6 | 2.6 |
| United Kingdom | Birmingham | 2330 | 2301 | 2272 | 2272 | 2272 | 2272 | 2272 | -0.3 | 0.0 | 0.0 | 4.6 | 4.3 | 4.2 |
| United Kingdom | Leeds | 1465 | 1449 | 1433 | 1433 | 1433 | 1433 | 1433 | -0.2 | 0.0 | 0.0 | 2.9 | 2.7 | 2.7 |
| United Kingdom | Liverpool | 788 | 831 | 876 | 914 | 937 | 946 | 948 | 1.1 | 0.7 | 0.1 | 1.6 | 1.7 | 1.8 |
| United Kingdom | London | 7666 | 7653 | 7640 | 7640 | 7640 | 7640 | 7640 | 0.0 | 0.0 | 0.0 | 15.2 | 14.5 | 14.1 |
| United Kingdom | Manchester | 2313 | 2282 | 2252 | 2252 | 2252 | 2252 | 2252 | -0.3 | 0.0 | 0.0 | 4.6 | 4.3 | 4.2 |
| United Kingdom | Tyneside (Newcastle) | 825 | 877 | 933 | 980 | 1009 | 1021 | 1023 | 1.2 | 0.8 | 0.1 | 1.6 | 1.9 | 1.9 |
| Yugoslavia | Belgrade | 1188 | 1318 | 1462 | 1482 | 1493 | 1519 | 1561 | 2.1 | 0.2 | 0.5 | 24.8 | 26.7 | 25.0 |
| **LATIN AMERICA** | | | | | | | | | | | | | | |
| Argentina | Buenos Aires | 10539 | 11182 | 11864 | 12560 | 13208 | 13727 | 14076 | 1.2 | 1.1 | 0.6 | 41.0 | 37.7 | 34.9 |
| Argentina | Córdoba | 1078 | 1188 | 1310 | 1434 | 1548 | 1642 | 1711 | 2.0 | 1.7 | 1.0 | 4.2 | 4.3 | 4.3 |
| Argentina | Mendoza | 675 | 758 | 851 | 946 | 1032 | 1100 | 1151 | 2.3 | 1.9 | 1.1 | 2.6 | 2.8 | 2.9 |
| Argentina | Rosario | 1026 | 1105 | 1189 | 1278 | 1365 | 1442 | 1503 | 1.5 | 1.4 | 1.0 | 4.0 | 3.8 | 3.7 |
| Bolivia | La Paz | 871 | 1044 | 1271 | 1480 | 1695 | 1921 | 2145 | 3.8 | 2.9 | 2.4 | 29.3 | 28.5 | 27.3 |
| Bolivia | Santa Cruz | 447 | 616 | 837 | 1065 | 1287 | 1492 | 1676 | 6.3 | 4.3 | 2.6 | 15.0 | 20.5 | 21.3 |
| Brazil | Belém | 1134 | 1293 | 1473 | 1638 | 1786 | 1913 | 2012 | 2.6 | 1.9 | 1.2 | 1.2 | 1.2 | 1.2 |
| Brazil | Belo Horizonte | 2943 | 3333 | 3775 | 4170 | 4516 | 4805 | 5020 | 2.5 | 1.8 | 1.1 | 3.1 | 3.0 | 2.9 |
| Brazil | Brasilia | 1346 | 1547 | 1778 | 1990 | 2176 | 2331 | 2450 | 2.8 | 2.0 | 1.2 | 1.4 | 1.4 | 1.4 |
| Brazil | Campinas | 1116 | 1339 | 1607 | 1862 | 2079 | 2247 | 2366 | 3.7 | 2.6 | 1.3 | 1.2 | 1.4 | 1.4 |
| Brazil | Curitiba | 1664 | 1930 | 2240 | 2525 | 2772 | 2972 | 3118 | 3.0 | 2.1 | 1.2 | 1.7 | 1.8 | 1.8 |
| Brazil | Fortaleza | 1865 | 2213 | 2627 | 3014 | 3342 | 3595 | 3771 | 3.4 | 2.4 | 1.2 | 2.0 | 2.2 | 2.2 |
| Brazil | Goiânia | 799 | 896 | 1006 | 1106 | 1198 | 1282 | 1352 | 2.3 | 1.8 | 1.2 | 0.8 | 0.8 | 0.8 |
| Brazil | Manaus | 767 | 959 | 1199 | 1436 | 1637 | 1785 | 1886 | 4.5 | 3.1 | 1.4 | 0.8 | 1.0 | 1.1 |
| Brazil | Porto Alegre | 2590 | 2944 | 3346 | 3708 | 4024 | 4287 | 4484 | 2.6 | 1.9 | 1.1 | 2.7 | 2.7 | 2.6 |
| Brazil | Recife | 2564 | 2810 | 3080 | 3315 | 3536 | 3744 | 3914 | 1.8 | 1.4 | 1.0 | 2.7 | 2.4 | 2.3 |
| Brazil | Rio de Janeiro | 9208 | 9682 | 10181 | 10582 | 11017 | 11496 | 11905 | 1.0 | 0.8 | 0.8 | 9.6 | 7.7 | 6.9 |
| Brazil | Salvador | 2055 | 2404 | 2811 | 3187 | 3509 | 3762 | 3942 | 3.1 | 2.2 | 1.2 | 2.2 | 2.3 | 2.3 |
| Brazil | Santos | 985 | 1075 | 1173 | 1260 | 1346 | 1432 | 1507 | 1.8 | 1.4 | 1.1 | 1.0 | 0.9 | 0.9 |
| Brazil | São José dos Campos | 502 | 631 | 792 | 952 | 1089 | 1192 | 1262 | 4.6 | 3.2 | 1.5 | 0.5 | 0.7 | 0.7 |
| Brazil | São Luis | 544 | 664 | 809 | 950 | 1072 | 1167 | 1235 | 4.0 | 2.8 | 1.4 | 0.6 | 0.7 | 0.7 |
| Brazil | São Paulo | 13758 | 15082 | 16533 | 17755 | 18823 | 19738 | 20397 | 1.8 | 1.3 | 0.8 | 14.4 | 12.8 | 11.8 |
| Chile | Santiago | 4149 | 4568 | 5029 | 5538 | 5966 | 6327 | 6613 | 1.9 | 1.7 | 1.0 | 41.7 | 42.5 | 41.6 |
| Colombia | Barranquilla | 921 | 1145 | 1433 | 1736 | 2015 | 2244 | 2421 | 4.4 | 3.4 | 1.8 | 4.3 | 5.6 | 5.8 |
| Colombia | Bogotá | 4372 | 4970 | 5631 | 6288 | 6925 | 7510 | 8006 | 2.5 | 2.1 | 1.5 | 20.6 | 20.1 | 19.0 |
| Colombia | Cali | 1416 | 1773 | 2230 | 2710 | 3147 | 3498 | 3764 | 4.5 | 3.4 | 1.8 | 6.7 | 8.7 | 8.9 |
| Colombia | Medellín | 2091 | 2367 | 2659 | 2951 | 3246 | 3530 | 3782 | 2.4 | 2.0 | 1.5 | 9.9 | 9.4 | 9.0 |
| Costa Rica | San José | 686 | 775 | 875 | 988 | 1114 | 1251 | 1393 | 2.4 | 2.4 | 2.2 | 58.1 | 51.3 | 49.9 |
| Cuba | Havana | 2005 | 2108 | 2183 | 2256 | 2306 | 2342 | 2366 | 0.9 | 0.6 | 0.3 | 27.9 | 26.7 | 25.9 |
| Dominican Republic | Santiago de los | 672 | 931 | 1289 | 1539 | 1767 | 1960 | 2109 | 6.5 | 3.2 | 1.8 | 19.3 | 27.9 | 28.3 |
| Dominican Republic | Santo Domingo | 1861 | 2427 | 3166 | 3599 | 4000 | 4365 | 4660 | 5.3 | 2.3 | 1.5 | 53.4 | 65.1 | 62.6 |

# TABLE B.1

## continued

| | | | | | | | | | | | | | | |
|---|---|---|---|---|---|---|---|---|---|---|---|---|---|
| cuador | Guayaquil | 1292 | 1491 | 1843 | 2293 | 2667 | 2999 | 3298 | 3.6 | 3.7 | 2.1 | 27.7 | 27.8 | 27.3 |
| cuador | Quito | 936 | 1088 | 1376 | 1754 | 2082 | 2371 | 2623 | 3.9 | 4.1 | 2.3 | 20.1 | 21.2 | 21.7 |
| Salvador | San Salvador | 883 | 1035 | 1214 | 1408 | 1613 | 1818 | 2021 | 3.2 | 2.8 | 2.3 | 43.3 | 48.1 | 47.2 |
| uatemala | Guatemala City | 1090 | 1676 | 2577 | 3242 | 3869 | 4542 | 5282 | 8.6 | 4.1 | 3.1 | 37.3 | 71.8 | 69.8 |
| aiti | Port-au-Prince | 881 | 1134 | 1427 | 1769 | 2121 | 2499 | 2887 | 4.8 | 4.0 | 3.1 | 54.7 | 60.3 | 60.7 |
| onduras | Tegucigalpa | 560 | 711 | 814 | 950 | 1126 | 1328 | 1524 | 3.7 | 3.2 | 3.0 | 35.5 | 27.8 | 26.2 |
| lexico | Ciudad Juárez | 660 | 799 | 966 | 1168 | 1292 | 1386 | 1473 | 3.8 | 2.9 | 1.3 | 1.3 | 1.6 | 1.6 |
| lexico | Guadalajara | 2604 | 3011 | 3430 | 3908 | 4115 | 4271 | 4457 | 2.8 | 1.8 | 0.8 | 5.0 | 5.3 | 4.8 |
| lexico | León | 720 | 817 | 926 | 1050 | 1104 | 1149 | 1207 | 2.5 | 1.8 | 0.9 | 1.4 | 1.4 | 1.3 |
| lexico | Mexico City | 14474 | 15130 | 16562 | 18131 | 18452 | 18682 | 19180 | 1.4 | 1.1 | 0.4 | 27.6 | 24.7 | 20.7 |
| lexico | Monterrey | 2287 | 2624 | 2994 | 3416 | 3603 | 3744 | 3911 | 2.7 | 1.9 | 0.8 | 4.4 | 4.6 | 4.2 |
| lexico | Puebla | 1289 | 1507 | 1722 | 1968 | 2079 | 2167 | 2271 | 2.9 | 1.9 | 0.9 | 2.5 | 2.7 | 2.5 |
| lexico | San Luis Potosí | 506 | 620 | 760 | 931 | 1042 | 1126 | 1201 | 4.1 | 3.2 | 1.4 | 1.0 | 1.3 | 1.3 |
| lexico | Tijuana | 553 | 709 | 910 | 1167 | 1353 | 1493 | 1604 | 5.0 | 4.0 | 1.7 | 1.1 | 1.6 | 1.7 |
| lexico | Toluca | 369 | 544 | 803 | 1184 | 1536 | 1812 | 1997 | 7.8 | 6.5 | 2.6 | 0.7 | 1.6 | 2.2 |
| lexico | Torreón | 594 | 696 | 814 | 953 | 1028 | 1086 | 1148 | 3.2 | 2.3 | 1.1 | 1.1 | 1.3 | 1.2 |
| icaragua | Managua | 611 | 710 | 825 | 959 | 1117 | 1291 | 1475 | 3.0 | 3.0 | 2.8 | 34.7 | 33.7 | 32.4 |
| anama | Panama City | 721 | 848 | 998 | 1173 | 1299 | 1424 | 1543 | 3.3 | 2.6 | 1.7 | 63.9 | 73.0 | 72.4 |
| araguay | Asunción | 796 | 928 | 1081 | 1262 | 1472 | 1711 | 1959 | 3.1 | 3.1 | 2.9 | 49.1 | 41.0 | 38.8 |
| eru | Lima | 5090 | 5826 | 6667 | 7443 | 8185 | 8843 | 9388 | 2.7 | 2.1 | 1.4 | 39.1 | 39.9 | 37.8 |
| uerto Rico | San Juan | 1153 | 1226 | 1304 | 1381 | 1452 | 1511 | 1556 | 1.2 | 1.1 | 0.7 | 49.4 | 47.5 | 45.5 |
| Jruguay | Montevideo | 1249 | 1247 | 1242 | 1236 | 1244 | 1260 | 1284 | −0.1 | 0.0 | 0.3 | 47.6 | 40.6 | 37.3 |
| enezuela | Barquisimeto | 666 | 743 | 828 | 923 | 1005 | 1085 | 1164 | 2.2 | 1.9 | 1.5 | 4.7 | 4.4 | 4.2 |
| enezuela | Caracas | 2734 | 2867 | 3007 | 3153 | 3261 | 3403 | 3587 | 1.0 | 0.8 | 1.0 | 19.5 | 15.0 | 12.9 |
| enezuela | Maracaibo | 1139 | 1351 | 1603 | 1901 | 2172 | 2408 | 2604 | 3.4 | 3.0 | 1.8 | 8.1 | 9.1 | 9.4 |
| enezuela | Maracay | 676 | 795 | 935 | 1100 | 1249 | 1383 | 1498 | 3.2 | 2.9 | 1.8 | 4.8 | 5.2 | 5.4 |
| enezuela | Valencia | 872 | 1129 | 1462 | 1893 | 2320 | 2682 | 2948 | 5.2 | 4.6 | 2.4 | 6.2 | 9.0 | 10.6 |
| **NORTHERN AMERICA** | | | | | | | | | | | | | | |
| Canada | Calgary | 656 | 738 | 833 | 899 | 956 | 1004 | 1047 | 2.4 | 1.4 | 0.9 | 3.3 | 3.7 | 3.7 |
| Canada | Edmonton | 756 | 830 | 882 | 908 | 939 | 974 | 1014 | 1.5 | 0.6 | 0.8 | 3.8 | 3.8 | 3.6 |
| Canada | Montreal | 2904 | 3088 | 3324 | 3448 | 3567 | 3682 | 3798 | 1.4 | 0.7 | 0.6 | 14.7 | 14.4 | 13.5 |
| Canada | Ottawa | 803 | 901 | 1025 | 1112 | 1187 | 1246 | 1297 | 2.4 | 1.5 | 0.9 | 4.1 | 4.6 | 4.6 |
| Canada | Toronto | 3356 | 3802 | 4306 | 4651 | 4925 | 5124 | 5283 | 2.5 | 1.3 | 0.7 | 16.9 | 19.4 | 18.7 |
| Canada | Vancouver | 1359 | 1559 | 1828 | 2033 | 2195 | 2310 | 2399 | 3.0 | 1.8 | 0.9 | 6.9 | 8.5 | 8.5 |
| United States | Atlanta | 1879 | 2174 | 2462 | 2691 | 2838 | 2932 | 3012 | 2.7 | 1.4 | 0.6 | 1.0 | 1.3 | 1.2 |
| United States | Baltimore | 1825 | 1893 | 1967 | 2042 | 2112 | 2177 | 2242 | 0.8 | 0.7 | 0.6 | 1.0 | 1.0 | 0.9 |
| United States | Boston | 2729 | 2778 | 2840 | 2918 | 3001 | 3083 | 3166 | 0.4 | 0.6 | 0.5 | 1.5 | 1.4 | 1.3 |
| United States | Buffalo | 977 | 953 | 962 | 984 | 1015 | 1050 | 1087 | −0.2 | 0.5 | 0.7 | 0.5 | 0.5 | 0.4 |
| United States | Chicago | 6786 | 6792 | 6844 | 6951 | 7089 | 7236 | 7386 | 0.1 | 0.4 | 0.4 | 3.8 | 3.2 | 3.0 |
| United States | Cincinnati | 1169 | 1215 | 1264 | 1316 | 1365 | 1411 | 1457 | 0.8 | 0.8 | 0.7 | 0.7 | 0.6 | 0.6 |
| United States | Cleveland | 1713 | 1676 | 1690 | 1725 | 1774 | 1828 | 1884 | −0.1 | 0.5 | 0.6 | 1.0 | 0.8 | 0.8 |
| United States | Columbus | 890 | 948 | 1007 | 1061 | 1107 | 1148 | 1187 | 1.2 | 1.0 | 0.7 | 0.5 | 0.5 | 0.5 |
| United States | Dallas | 2819 | 3220 | 3609 | 3915 | 4110 | 4233 | 4337 | 2.5 | 1.3 | 0.5 | 1.6 | 1.8 | 1.7 |
| United States | Denver | 1437 | 1522 | 1609 | 1688 | 1756 | 1813 | 1870 | 1.1 | 0.9 | 0.6 | 0.8 | 0.8 | 0.8 |
| United States | Detroit | 3750 | 3695 | 3723 | 3788 | 3877 | 3974 | 4074 | −0.1 | 0.4 | 0.5 | 2.1 | 1.8 | 1.6 |
| United States | Fort Lauderdale | 1123 | 1245 | 1363 | 1463 | 1536 | 1590 | 1641 | 1.9 | 1.2 | 0.7 | 0.6 | 0.7 | 0.7 |
| United States | Houston | 2658 | 2915 | 3164 | 3367 | 3511 | 3614 | 3707 | 1.7 | 1.0 | 0.5 | 1.5 | 1.6 | 1.5 |
| United States | Indianapolis | 877 | 917 | 959 | 1003 | 1043 | 1081 | 1118 | 0.9 | 0.8 | 0.7 | 0.5 | 0.5 | 0.5 |
| United States | Jacksonville | 668 | 742 | 816 | 878 | 925 | 962 | 996 | 2.0 | 1.3 | 0.7 | 0.4 | 0.4 | 0.4 |
| United States | Kansas City | 1188 | 1280 | 1372 | 1452 | 1516 | 1569 | 1619 | 1.4 | 1.0 | 0.7 | 0.7 | 0.7 | 0.7 |
| United States | Las Vegas | 556 | 706 | 863 | 990 | 1069 | 1116 | 1154 | 4.4 | 2.1 | 0.8 | 0.3 | 0.5 | 0.5 |
| United States | Los Angeles | 10445 | 11456 | 12409 | 13140 | 13591 | 13859 | 14080 | 1.7 | 0.9 | 0.4 | 5.8 | 6.1 | 5.7 |
| United States | Louisville | 758 | 755 | 762 | 780 | 806 | 835 | 866 | 0.1 | 0.6 | 0.7 | 0.4 | 0.4 | 0.4 |
| United States | Memphis | 801 | 827 | 856 | 889 | 923 | 957 | 991 | 0.7 | 0.8 | 0.7 | 0.4 | 0.4 | 0.4 |
| United States | Miami | 1762 | 1923 | 2080 | 2212 | 2309 | 2383 | 2452 | 1.7 | 1.0 | 0.6 | 1.0 | 1.0 | 1.0 |
| United States | Milwaukee | 1217 | 1227 | 1246 | 1278 | 1318 | 1362 | 1407 | 0.2 | 0.6 | 0.7 | 0.7 | 0.6 | 0.6 |
| United States | Minneapolis | 1935 | 2088 | 2237 | 2365 | 2462 | 2539 | 2611 | 1.5 | 1.0 | 0.6 | 1.1 | 1.1 | 1.1 |
| United States | New Orleans | 1058 | 1039 | 1049 | 1073 | 1106 | 1143 | 1183 | −0.1 | 0.5 | 0.7 | 0.6 | 0.5 | 0.5 |
| United States | New York | 15827 | 16056 | 16331 | 16640 | 16929 | 17186 | 17432 | 0.3 | 0.4 | 0.3 | 8.8 | 7.7 | 7.0 |
| United States | Norfolk | 1024 | 1341 | 1680 | 1952 | 2113 | 2198 | 2263 | 5.0 | 2.3 | 0.7 | 0.6 | 0.9 | 0.9 |
| United States | Oklahoma City | 730 | 787 | 845 | 896 | 939 | 975 | 1009 | 1.5 | 1.1 | 0.7 | 0.4 | 0.4 | 0.4 |
| United States | Orlando | 723 | 897 | 1075 | 1219 | 1309 | 1363 | 1408 | 4.0 | 2.0 | 0.7 | 0.4 | 0.6 | 0.6 |
| United States | Philadelphia | 4170 | 4225 | 4302 | 4402 | 4512 | 4623 | 4734 | 0.3 | 0.5 | 0.5 | 2.3 | 2.1 | 1.9 |
| United States | Phoenix | 1696 | 2024 | 2351 | 2609 | 2768 | 2864 | 2943 | 3.3 | 1.6 | 0.6 | 0.9 | 1.2 | 1.2 |
| United States | Pittsburgh | 1740 | 1676 | 1690 | 1725 | 1773 | 1828 | 1884 | −0.3 | 0.5 | 0.6 | 1.0 | 0.8 | 0.8 |
| United States | Portland | 1100 | 1176 | 1252 | 1321 | 1377 | 1426 | 1472 | 1.3 | 1.0 | 0.7 | 0.6 | 0.6 | 0.6 |
| United States | Providence | 822 | 848 | 877 | 910 | 945 | 979 | 1014 | 0.7 | 0.8 | 0.7 | 0.5 | 0.4 | 0.4 |
| United States | Riverside-San Bernardino | 920 | 1185 | 1465 | 1689 | 1824 | 1898 | 1956 | 4.7 | 2.2 | 0.7 | 0.5 | 0.8 | 0.8 |
| United States | Sacramento | 942 | 1106 | 1269 | 1400 | 1486 | 1543 | 1593 | 3.0 | 1.6 | 0.7 | 0.5 | 0.7 | 0.6 |
| United States | Salt Lake City | 732 | 793 | 853 | 906 | 949 | 986 | 1021 | 1.5 | 1.1 | 0.7 | 0.4 | 0.4 | 0.4 |
| United States | San Antonio | 1038 | 1134 | 1229 | 1311 | 1373 | 1423 | 1469 | 1.7 | 1.1 | 0.7 | 0.6 | 0.6 | 0.6 |
| United States | San Diego | 2017 | 2367 | 2714 | 2986 | 3156 | 3260 | 3346 | 3.0 | 1.5 | 0.6 | 1.1 | 1.4 | 1.3 |
| United States | San Francisco | 3414 | 3641 | 3863 | 4054 | 4199 | 4313 | 4418 | 1.2 | 0.8 | 0.5 | 1.9 | 1.9 | 1.8 |
| United States | San Jose | 1341 | 1440 | 1539 | 1626 | 1695 | 1752 | 1807 | 1.4 | 1.0 | 0.6 | 0.7 | 0.8 | 0.7 |
| United States | Seattle | 1567 | 1754 | 1937 | 2086 | 2189 | 2262 | 2329 | 2.1 | 1.2 | 0.6 | 0.9 | 1.0 | 0.9 |
| United States | Saint Louis | 1899 | 1949 | 2007 | 2072 | 2139 | 2204 | 2268 | 0.6 | 0.6 | 0.6 | 1.1 | 1.0 | 0.9 |
| United States | Tampa | 1530 | 1719 | 1903 | 2053 | 2156 | 2229 | 2294 | 2.2 | 1.3 | 0.6 | 0.9 | 1.0 | 0.9 |
| United States | Washington, DC | 3063 | 3380 | 3685 | 3931 | 4099 | 4215 | 4319 | 1.9 | 1.1 | 0.5 | 1.7 | 1.8 | 1.7 |
| United States | West Palm Beach | 630 | 805 | 989 | 1137 | 1229 | 1282 | 1324 | 4.5 | 2.2 | 0.7 | 0.4 | 0.5 | 0.5 |
| **OCEANIA** | | | | | | | | | | | | | | |
| Australia | Adelaide | 994 | 1019 | 1039 | 1063 | 1092 | 1125 | 1163 | 0.4 | 0.5 | 0.6 | 7.4 | 6.7 | 6.3 |
| Australia | Brisbane | 1175 | 1303 | 1450 | 1591 | 1702 | 1779 | 1840 | 2.1 | 1.6 | 0.8 | 8.8 | 10.0 | 10.0 |
| Australia | Melbourne | 2906 | 3003 | 3094 | 3187 | 3276 | 3362 | 3451 | 0.6 | 0.6 | 0.5 | 21.7 | 19.9 | 18.7 |
| Australia | Perth | 1023 | 1123 | 1220 | 1313 | 1389 | 1448 | 1498 | 1.8 | 1.3 | 0.8 | 7.7 | 8.2 | 8.1 |

## TABLE B.1

**continued**

| | | Estimates and projections (thousands) | | | | | | | Annual growth rate (%) | | | Share in country's urban population (%) | | |
|---|---|---|---|---|---|---|---|---|---|---|---|---|---|---|
| | | 1985 | 1990 | 1995 | 2000 | 2005 | 2010 | 2015 | 1985–1995 | 1995–2005 | 2005–2015 | 1985 | 2000 | 2015 |
| Australia | Sydney | 3433 | 3524 | 3590 | 3664 | 3744 | 3832 | 3928 | 0.5 | 0.4 | 0.5 | 25.7 | 22.9 | 21.3 |
| New Zealand | Auckland | 812 | 870 | 976 | 1102 | 1202 | 1280 | 1338 | 1.8 | 2.1 | 1.1 | 29.9 | 33.2 | 34.9 |

**Source:** Population Division of the Department of Economic and Social Affairs of the United Nations Secretariat, World Urbanization Prospects: The 1999 Revision.
For sources and footnotes, refer to technical notes.

# TABLE B.2

## Households: Number and Size and Population in Specific Age Groups, Selected Cities

| | | | Total number | | | | | | | Average | Women-headed households | Population in specific age groups | | | | | |
|---|---|---|---|---|---|---|---|---|---|---|---|---|---|---|---|---|---|
| | | | | | | | | | | | | | Male | | | Female | |
| | | | Total | 1 | 2 | 3 | 4 | 5 | 6 | Average | (% of total) | Total | 0–19 | >65 | Total | 0–19 | >65 |
| **AFRICA** | | | | | | | | | | | | | | | | | |
| Benin | Abomey | 1994 | ... | ... | ... | ... | ... | ... | ... | ... | ... | 31046 | 59.4 | 3.8 | 35549 | 49.1 | 4.6 |
| Benin | Cotonou | 1994 | ... | ... | ... | ... | ... | ... | ... | ... | ... | 262812 | 50.4 | 1.1 | 274015 | 54.0 | 1.5 |
| Benin | Parakou | 1994 | ... | ... | ... | ... | ... | ... | ... | ... | ... | 52996 | 55.8 | 1.6 | 50581 | 57.3 | 1.4 |
| Benin | Porto-Novo | 1994 | ... | ... | ... | ... | ... | ... | ... | ... | ... | 86491 | 57.5 | 1.9 | 92647 | 54.1 | 5.5 |
| Botswana | Francistown | 1996 | ... | ... | ... | ... | ... | ... | ... | ... | ... | 31665 | 43.0 | 2.0 | 33579 | 48.4 | 1.9 |
| Botswana | Gaberone | 1996 | ... | ... | ... | ... | ... | ... | ... | ... | ... | 68248 | 35.5 | 0.9 | 65220 | 43.0 | 2.3 |
| Burkina Faso | Bobo Dioulasso | 1991 | ... | ... | ... | ... | ... | ... | ... | ... | ... | 133843 | 57.8 | 2.7 | 135517 | 57.7 | 2.1 |
| Burkina Faso | Koudougou | 1991 | ... | ... | ... | ... | ... | ... | ... | ... | ... | 28722 | 62.2 | 2.2 | 30116 | 57.5 | 1.9 |
| Burkina Faso | Ouagadougou | 1991 | ... | ... | ... | ... | ... | ... | ... | ... | ... | 322125 | 55.5 | 1.7 | 312354 | 56.6 | 3.5 |
| Burkina Faso | Ouahigouya | 1991 | ... | ... | ... | ... | ... | ... | ... | ... | ... | 25979 | 59.3 | 6.5 | 29154 | 59.4 | 4.5 |
| Chad | Ndjamena | 1993 C | 105020 | 14.9 | 14.7 | 13.5 | 12.0 | 45.0 | ... | 5.0 | 20.8 | ... | ... | ... | ... | ... | ... |
| Egypt | Alexandria | 1996 | ... | ... | ... | ... | ... | ... | ... | ... | ... | 1707477 | 42.5 | 4.2 | 1631599 | 42.3 | 3.2 |
| Egypt | Cairo | 1996 | ... | ... | ... | ... | ... | ... | ... | ... | ... | 3486260 | 42.1 | 4.2 | 3314732 | 42.0 | 8.4 |
| Egypt | Giza | 1996 | ... | ... | ... | ... | ... | ... | ... | ... | ... | 1139665 | 44.4 | 3.3 | 1082152 | 44.2 | 2.6 |
| Egypt | Shubra-El-Khema | 1996 | ... | ... | ... | ... | ... | ... | ... | ... | ... | 449271 | 48.0 | 2.3 | 421505 | 48.9 | 1.7 |
| Gambia | Kanifing | 1993 | ... | ... | ... | ... | ... | ... | ... | ... | ... | 118257 | 45.7 | 1.9 | 109957 | 53.2 | 2.3 |
| Gambia | Ban Jul | 1993 C | 802[(1983)] | ... | ... | ... | ... | ... | ... | 5.3 | ... | 22268 | 40.0 | 6.0 | 20058 | 49.3 | 16.0 |
| Kenya | Kisumu | 1989 C | 47690 | ... | ... | ... | ... | ... | ... | 4.0 | ... | 99879 | 53.3 | 1.2 | 92854 | 62.4 | 1.3 |
| Kenya | Mombasa | 1989 C | 124468 | ... | ... | ... | ... | ... | ... | 3.7 | ... | 256674 | 43.0 | 1.4 | 205079 | 54.4 | 1.6 |
| Kenya | Nairobi | 1989 C | 382863 | ... | ... | ... | ... | ... | ... | 3.5 | ... | 752597 | 34.5 | 0.9 | 571973 | 49.6 | 2.0 |
| Kenya | Nakuru | 1989 C | 46800 | ... | ... | ... | ... | ... | ... | 3.5 | ... | 88042 | 48.3 | 0.8 | 75885 | 59.3 | 1.0 |
| Lesotho | Maseru | 1996 | ... | ... | ... | ... | ... | ... | ... | ... | ... | 64315 | 82.3 | ... | 73522 | 83.6 | 0.0 |
| Libyan Arab Jamahiriya | Bengazi | 1995 | ... | ... | ... | ... | ... | ... | ... | ... | ... | 350149 | 36.2 | 2.6 | 316550 | 38.4 | 2.8 |
| Libyan Arab Jamahiriya | Misurata | 1995 | ... | ... | ... | ... | ... | ... | ... | ... | ... | 250619 | 40.7 | 4.0 | 237948 | 41.3 | 4.4 |
| Libyan Arab Jamahiriya | Tripoli | 1995 | ... | ... | ... | ... | ... | ... | ... | ... | ... | 684923 | 35.3 | 3.6 | 626828 | 37.4 | 9.6 |
| Libyan Arab Jamahiriya | Zawia | 1995 | ... | ... | ... | ... | ... | ... | ... | ... | ... | 271164 | 35.3 | 4.4 | 245720 | 37.5 | 4.3 |
| Mali | Bamako | 1987 | 105394 | 11.5 | 9.2 | 11.4 | 11.0 | 10.1 | 46.8 | 6.2 | 14.2 | ... | ... | ... | ... | ... | ... |
| Senegal | Dakar | 1991 C | 198893[(1988)] | ... | ... | ... | ... | ... | ... | 7.8 | 22.7 | 649735 | 53.0 | 1.3 | 650956 | 56.1 | 3.5 |
| Seychelles | Port Victoria | 1997 C | ... | ... | ... | ... | ... | ... | ... | ... | ... | 12170 | 38.2 | 6.9 | 12531 | 36.2 | 29.7 |
| South Africa | Cape Town | 1996 C | 483121[(1985)] | ... | ... | ... | ... | ... | ... | ... | ... | 83359 | 28.0 | 7.7 | 92814 | 25.0 | 11.6 |
| South Africa | Durban | 1996 C | 164476[(1991)] | 10.3 | 17.0 | 15.7 | 20.6 | 17.2 | 19.2 | 4.5 | 10.9 | 273538 | 29.7 | 5.9 | 284388 | 28.8 | 8.6 |
| South Africa | Johannesburg | 1996 | ... | ... | ... | ... | ... | ... | ... | ... | ... | 379075 | 26.7 | 4.8 | 366503 | 27.6 | 7.0 |
| South Africa | Pretoria | 1996 | ... | ... | ... | ... | ... | ... | ... | ... | ... | 334219 | 29.9 | 5.0 | 345895 | 28.7 | 26.7 |
| Togo | Lome | 1981 C | 74758 | 16.1 | 13.1 | 13.7 | 12.5 | 10.3 | 34.2 | 5.0 | 25.6 | ... | ... | ... | ... | ... | ... |
| Togo | Lome | 1981 M | 87375 | 15.5 | 12.7 | 13.7 | 12.5 | 10.3 | 35.2 | ... | 24.6 | ... | ... | ... | ... | ... | ... |
| Zimbabwe | Bulawayo | 1997 | ... | ... | ... | ... | ... | ... | ... | ... | ... | 367558 | 47.5 | 2.7 | 37456 | ... | 20.8 |
| Zimbabwe | Harare | 1997 | ... | ... | ... | ... | ... | ... | ... | ... | ... | 909887 | 45.1 | 2.0 | 857160 | 49.3 | 3.1 |
| **ASIA** | | | | | | | | | | | | | | | | | |
| Armenia | Kirovakan | 1994 C | 51344 | 8.3 | 25.0 | 22.3 | 28.9 | 6.9 | 8.4 | 3.1 | 12.7 | ... | ... | ... | ... | ... | ... |
| Armenia | Yerevan | 1998 C | 253037[(1989)] | 6.6 | 12.5 | 14.2 | 27.3 | 17.3 | 22.2 | 4.6 | ... | 601456 | 31.5 | 7.6 | 647220 | 27.7 | 35.7 |
| Armenia | Yerevan | 1989 M | 256092 | 6.6 | 12.5 | 14.2 | 27.2 | 17.3 | 22.3 | 4.6 | ... | 876400 | 39.4 | 3.8 | 918500 | 33.7 | 24.0 |
| Bahrain | Manama | 1991 C | 25350 | 16.1 | 13.9 | 14.9 | 16.9 | 11.4 | 26.9 | 4.0 | ... | ... | ... | ... | ... | ... | ... |
| Cambodia | Bat Dambang | 1998 | ... | ... | ... | ... | ... | ... | ... | ... | ... | 388599 | 58.2 | 2.6 | 404530 | 53.5 | 3.7 |
| Cambodia | Kampong Cham | 1998 | ... | ... | ... | ... | ... | ... | ... | ... | ... | 775796 | 56.8 | 3.8 | 833118 | 50.9 | 4.6 |
| Cambodia | Phnom Penh | 1998 | ... | ... | ... | ... | ... | ... | ... | ... | ... | 481911 | 48.7 | 2.2 | 517893 | 46.5 | 7.4 |
| Cambodia | Siem Riab | 1998 | ... | ... | ... | ... | ... | ... | ... | ... | ... | 336685 | 59.8 | 2.1 | 359479 | 54.4 | 2.9 |
| Cyprus | Larnaca | 1992 C | 13184[(1982)] | ... | ... | ... | ... | ... | ... | ... | ... | 29883 | 34.2 | 9.5 | 30674 | 31.5 | 11.9 |
| Cyprus | Limassol | 1992 C | 29880[(1982)] | ... | ... | ... | ... | ... | ... | ... | ... | 67767 | 33.3 | 8.0 | 68974 | 31.1 | 9.7 |
| Cyprus | Nicosia | 1992 M | 55059 | 13.0 | 23.0 | 18.5 | 28.4 | 12.5 | 4.4 | 3.4 | 15.0 | 87562 | 31.9 | 9.1 | 89889 | 29.5 | 37.4 |
| Cyprus | Patos | 1992 | ... | ... | ... | ... | ... | ... | ... | ... | ... | 16599 | 35.5 | 7.6 | 15976 | 34.1 | 8.7 |
| China, Hong Kong SAR | Hong Kong | 1996 A | 1580072[(1991)] | ... | ... | ... | ... | ... | ... | 3.5 | ... | 3108107 | 26.1 | 9.1 | 3109449 | 24.3 | 45.8 |
| China, Macau SAR | Macau | 1996 A | 98961[(1991)] | ... | ... | ... | ... | ... | ... | 3.6 | ... | 199257 | 33.6 | 5.7 | 214871 | 29.6 | 26.9 |
| China, Macau SAR | Macau | 1991 C | 97503 | 14.0 | 17.8 | 20.0 | 22.5 | 13.9 | 11.8 | 3.5 | 20.6 | ... | ... | ... | ... | ... | ... |
| India | Abohar | 1991 C | 18057 | ... | ... | ... | ... | ... | ... | 5.9 | ... | ... | ... | ... | ... | ... | ... |
| India | Ambala | 1993 C | 21972 | 5.0 | 8.0 | 20.0 | 25.0 | 25.0 | 17.0 | 5.0 | 70.0 | ... | ... | ... | ... | ... | ... |
| India | Bhiwani | 1991 C | 19142 | 1.0 | 3.4 | 7.1 | 13.1 | 22.7 | 52.6 | 6.0 | 4.5 | ... | ... | ... | ... | ... | ... |
| India | Dindigul | 1994 C | 29814 | ... | 0.4 | 15.1 | 41.1 | 20.5 | 23.0 | 6.0 | 18.2 | ... | ... | ... | ... | ... | ... |
| India | Faridabad | 1991 C | 133180 | 2.0 | 5.0 | 2.5 | 25.0 | 40.0 | 25.5 | 5.0 | 0.5 | ... | ... | ... | ... | ... | ... |
| India | Gurgaon | 1993 C | 33542 | ... | 3.0 | 16.0 | 21.0 | 36.0 | 24.0 | 4.0 | 3.3 | ... | ... | ... | ... | ... | ... |
| India | Madurai | 1995 C | 299986 | 0.5 | 9.7 | 17.0 | 16.2 | 19.2 | 37.5 | 5.0 | 19.0 | ... | ... | ... | ... | ... | ... |
| India | Panipat | 1991 C | 34569 | 0.6 | 2.7 | 13.0 | 52.9 | 18.0 | 12.8 | 6.0 | 0.5 | ... | ... | ... | ... | ... | ... |
| India | Rohtak | 1994 C | 36475 | 5.0 | 6.0 | 9.0 | 25.0 | 30.0 | 25.0 | 4.7 | 9.9 | ... | ... | ... | ... | ... | ... |
| India | Shillong | 1993 C | 24600 | 12.2 | 12.6 | 11.0 | 11.8 | 24.4 | 28.0 | 4.4 | 23.2 | ... | ... | ... | ... | ... | ... |
| India | Shillong | 1993 M | 40200 | 21.6 | 9.5 | 7.0 | 12.4 | 22.4 | 27.1 | 4.1 | 20.1 | ... | ... | ... | ... | ... | ... |
| India | Sirsa | 1991 C | 20325 | 1.6 | 9.8 | 12.2 | 13.8 | 18.5 | 44.1 | 5.0 | ... | ... | ... | ... | ... | ... | ... |
| India | Sonipat | 1991 C | 25722 | 0.4 | 0.9 | 4.0 | 72.7 | 12.8 | 9.1 | 6.0 | 0.5 | ... | ... | ... | ... | ... | ... |
| India | Yamunanagar | 1991 C | 25570 | 0.3 | 0.4 | 4.8 | 23.2 | 35.3 | 36.0 | 6.0 | 3.0 | ... | ... | ... | ... | ... | ... |
| Indonesia | Cuddalore | 1995 C | 30590 | 0.3 | 0.7 | 1.2 | 22.3 | 47.2 | 28.4 | 5.0 | 4.9 | ... | ... | ... | ... | ... | ... |
| Israel | Jerusalem | 1991 C | 105800 | 20.3 | 26.3 | 18.1 | 19.8 | 15.4 | ... | 3.6 | ... | 305569 | 46.8 | 6.8 | 311473 | 43.1 | 20.0 |
| Israel | Jerusalem | 1992 C | 138400 | 15.5 | 20.1 | 13.9 | 15.2 | 12.1 | 23.3 | 4.0 | ... | ... | ... | ... | ... | ... | ... |
| Israel | Tel-Aviv–Yafo | 1992 C | ... | 31.7 | 27.7 | 11.9 | 14.9 | 8.9 | 5.0 | 2.6 | ... | 123236 | 30.7 | 15.6 | 132678 | 25.9 | 19.6 |
| Japan | Higashikurume | 1994 C | 38569 | 21.4 | 19.6 | 20.7 | 27.8 | 7.9 | 2.6 | 2.9 | ... | ... | ... | ... | ... | ... | ... |
| Japan | Ichihara | 1992 C | 81339 | 20.4 | 16.5 | 18.9 | 27.1 | 10.2 | 6.9 | 3.1 | ... | ... | ... | ... | ... | ... | ... |
| Japan | Kakamigahara | 1994 C | 38188 | 15.0 | 17.6 | 18.8 | 27.1 | 12.0 | 9.6 | 3.4 | 4.3 | ... | ... | ... | ... | ... | ... |
| Japan | Kawasaki | 1992 C | 462553 | 35.5 | 18.7 | 16.7 | 20.2 | 6.3 | 2.6 | 2.5 | ... | ... | ... | ... | ... | ... | ... |
| Japan | Kodaira | 1994 C | 66870 | 35.3 | 20.3 | 17.7 | 19.0 | 6.1 | 1.6 | 2.5 | ... | ... | ... | ... | ... | ... | ... |
| Japan | Osaka | 1995 C | 967250[(1988)] | ... | ... | ... | ... | ... | ... | ... | ... | 1278212 | 20.3 | 11.6 | 1324209 | 18.7 | 16.5 |
| Japan | Sapporo | 1995 C | 575950[(1988)] | ... | ... | ... | ... | ... | ... | ... | ... | 843170 | 24.5 | 10.1 | 912093 | 21.6 | 12.9 |
| Japan | Tokyo | 1995 C | 3137010[(1988)] | ... | ... | ... | ... | ... | ... | ... | ... | 3959416 | 18.3 | 11.4 | 4008198 | 17.3 | 92.4 |
| Japan | Yokohama | 1995 C | 1009020[(1988)] | ... | ... | ... | ... | ... | ... | ... | ... | 1685332 | 21.5 | 9.5 | 1621804 | 21.1 | 12.6 |

# TABLE B.2

## continued

| | | | Total number | | | | | | | Average | Women-headed households | Population in specific age groups | | | | | |
|---|---|---|---|---|---|---|---|---|---|---|---|---|---|---|---|---|---|
| | | | | | Distribution of households by size | | | | | | | | Male | | | Female | |
| | | | Total | 1 | 2 | 3 | 4 | 5 | 6 | Average | (% of total) | Total | 0–19 | >65 | Total | 0–19 | >65 |
| Kazakhstan | Aktau | 1998 C | ... | ... | ... | ... | ... | ... | ... | 3.7 | ... | 8878 | 44.4 | 2.2 | 10196 | 32.2 | 15.1 |
| Kazakhstan | Semipalatinsk | 1995 C | 83090[(1989)] | ... | 25.9 | 27.7 | 28.5 | 10.6 | 7.3 | 3.5 | ... | 1898054 | 33.0 | 3.1 | 1911564 | 29.9 | 5.9 |
| Malaysia | George Town | 1999 | ... | ... | ... | ... | ... | ... | ... | ... | ... | 123000 | 31.5 | 5.4 | 126100 | 29.3 | 7.3 |
| Malaysia | Majlis Perbandaran Johor Bharu | 1999 | ... | ... | ... | ... | ... | ... | ... | ... | ... | 236600 | 38.9 | 2.2 | 209500 | 40.7 | 3.2 |
| Malaysia | W.P Kuala Lumpur | 1999 | ... | ... | ... | ... | ... | ... | ... | ... | ... | 717800 | 37.2 | 2.9 | 689400 | 36.0 | 11.0 |
| Malaysia | Keningau | 1999 | ... | ... | ... | ... | ... | ... | ... | ... | ... | 5800 | 41.4 | 1.7 | 4900 | 46.9 | 0.0 |
| Malaysia | Kota Kinabalu | 1999 | ... | ... | ... | ... | ... | ... | ... | ... | ... | 70200 | 40.6 | 1.7 | 65100 | 41.9 | 5.5 |
| Malaysia | Sandakan | 1999 | ... | ... | ... | ... | ... | ... | ... | ... | ... | 116100 | 43.5 | 2.2 | 107500 | 45.8 | 2.2 |
| Malaysia | Tawau | 1999 | ... | ... | ... | ... | ... | ... | ... | ... | ... | 84300 | 41.5 | 1.3 | 71500 | 45.9 | 1.8 |
| Malaysia | Bandaraya Kuching City | 1999 | ... | ... | ... | ... | ... | ... | ... | ... | ... | 92600 | 42.9 | 2.7 | 95600 | 40.4 | 10.1 |
| Malaysia | Miri | 1999 | ... | ... | ... | ... | ... | ... | ... | ... | ... | 82300 | 41.3 | 2.3 | 78100 | 41.9 | 3.2 |
| Malaysia | Sibu | 1999 | ... | ... | ... | ... | ... | ... | ... | ... | ... | 76300 | 45.5 | 2.9 | 81100 | 40.9 | 4.7 |
| Philippines | Calbayog | 1993 C | 21888 | 2.6 | 8.7 | 13.6 | 16.3 | 16.0 | 42.7 | 5.3 | 9.0 | ... | ... | ... | ... | ... | ... |
| Republic of Korea | Taegu | 1995 C | 597150[(1990)] | 10.0 | 13.3 | 19.7 | 30.7 | 17.4 | 8.8 | 3.7 | ... | 1231609 | 34.2 | 3.1 | 1213679 | 29.9 | 6.0 |
| Republic of Korea | Suweon | 1995 | ... | ... | ... | ... | ... | ... | ... | ... | ... | 379435 | 34.9 | 2.5 | 375235 | 33.1 | 4.7 |
| Singapore | Singapore | 1999 C | 661730[(1990)] | 5.2 | 12.2 | 16.3 | 25.0 | 20.6 | 20.7 | 4.2 | 16.7 | 1613600 | 29.7 | 6.6 | 1603900 | 27.9 | 28.9 |
| Sri Lanka | Colombo | 1994 | ... | ... | ... | ... | ... | ... | ... | ... | ... | 1010707 | 33.4 | 5.6 | 1046647 | 32.6 | 19.7 |
| Sri Lanka | Gampaha | 1994 | ... | ... | ... | ... | ... | ... | ... | ... | ... | 838175 | 35.7 | 6.5 | 869513 | 34.3 | 6.6 |
| Sri Lanka | Kalutara | 1994 | ... | ... | ... | ... | ... | ... | ... | ... | ... | 464592 | 38.2 | 6.9 | 473754 | 35.9 | 7.1 |
| Sri Lanka | Kandy | 1994 | ... | ... | ... | ... | ... | ... | ... | ... | ... | 593760 | 40.4 | 5.5 | 627259 | 38.0 | 4.9 |
| Thailand | Bangkok | 1998 C | 1319000[(1990)] | ... | ... | ... | ... | ... | ... | 4.5 | ... | 2762252 | 28.9 | 3.9 | 2885547 | 26.4 | 20.4 |
| Thailand | Chon Buri | 1998 C | 202000[(1990)] | ... | ... | ... | ... | ... | ... | 4.2 | ... | 533435 | 29.8 | 4.3 | 519998 | 29.1 | 5.3 |
| Thailand | Nakhon Si Thammarat | 1998 C | 293000[(1990)] | ... | ... | ... | ... | ... | ... | 4.8 | ... | 758067 | 35.6 | 5.5 | 762990 | 33.4 | 6.9 |
| Thailand | Songkhla | 1998 C | 244000[(1990)] | ... | ... | ... | ... | ... | ... | 4.5 | ... | 598968 | 36.0 | 5.3 | 611953 | 33.4 | 6.4 |
| **EUROPE** | | | | | | | | | | | | | | | | | |
| Austria | Innsbruck | 1991 C | 50745 | 36.8 | 27.9 | 16.2 | 11.8 | 4.0 | 3.3 | 2.3 | ... | ... | ... | ... | ... | ... | ... |
| Austria | Salzburg | 1991 C | 65354 | 40.1 | 28.2 | 15.6 | 10.8 | 3.6 | 1.8 | 2.1 | ... | ... | ... | ... | ... | ... | ... |
| Austria | Vienna | 1991 C | 746760 | 41.6 | 31.2 | 15.0 | 8.7 | 2.4 | 1.1 | 2.0 | ... | ... | ... | ... | ... | ... | ... |
| Belgium | Bruxelles | 1999 | ... | ... | ... | ... | ... | ... | ... | ... | ... | 449550 | 25.0 | 13.3 | 504495 | 21.4 | 99.0 |
| Belgium | Antwerp | 1999 C | 226258[(1993)] | 45.4 | 28.7 | 12.5 | 8.1 | 3.0 | 2.3 | 2.1 | ... | 2925 | ... | ... | 252851 | 24.5 | 21.5 |
| Belgium | Charleroi | 1999 C | 89842[(1991)] | 35.9 | 29.2 | 17.2 | 11.1 | 4.2 | 2.4 | 2.3 | 31.1 | 98305 | 25.8 | 12.6 | 107909 | 22.5 | 20.3 |
| Belgium | Charleroi | 1999 M | 175369[(1991)] | 31.1 | 29.4 | 19.0 | 12.9 | 4.9 | 2.6 | 2.4 | 28.5 | 110959 | 22.8 | 14.0 | 119189 | 20.3 | 20.8 |
| Belgium | Gent | 1993 C | 106814 | 40.0 | 30.5 | 14.2 | 9.8 | 3.6 | 2.0 | 2.1 | 31.6 | ... | ... | ... | ... | ... | ... |
| Bulgaria | Bourgas | 1998 | ... | ... | ... | ... | ... | ... | ... | ... | ... | 95209 | 24.8 | 9.0 | 100046 | 22.9 | 11.4 |
| Bulgaria | Plovdiv | 1998 | ... | ... | ... | ... | ... | ... | ... | ... | ... | 163281 | 24.8 | 10.8 | 179303 | 21.5 | 13.1 |
| Bulgaria | Sofia | 1998 | ... | ... | ... | ... | ... | ... | ... | ... | ... | 532449 | 22.5 | 12.6 | 589853 | 19.5 | 81.7 |
| Bulgaria | Varna | 1998 | ... | ... | ... | ... | ... | ... | ... | ... | ... | 146201 | 24.1 | 9.9 | 153600 | 21.7 | 12.2 |
| Croatia | Split | 1998 | ... | ... | ... | ... | ... | ... | ... | ... | ... | 116301 | 30.0 | 7.1 | 125640 | 26.3 | 10.3 |
| Croatia | Zagreb | 1998 | ... | ... | ... | ... | ... | ... | ... | ... | ... | 211335 | 26.7 | 9.9 | 238212 | 22.7 | 61.8 |
| Czech Republic | Brno | 1998 C | 165880[(1991)] | 31.1 | 29.6 | 18.7 | 17.0 | 3.1 | 0.6 | 2.3 | 30.9 | 155886 | 25.4 | 9.4 | 166225 | 22.8 | 15.3 |
| Czech Republic | Brno | 1991 M | 58729 | 23.3 | 28.4 | 19.2 | 21.4 | 6.4 | 1.3 | 2.6 | 22.6 | ... | ... | ... | ... | ... | ... |
| Czech Republic | Gottwaldov | 1991 M | 33497 | 25.0 | 29.1 | 19.3 | 22.1 | 4.0 | 0.5 | 2.5 | ... | ... | ... | ... | ... | ... | ... |
| Czech Republic | Ostrava | 1998 C | 131071[(1991)] | 29.6 | 27.2 | 19.1 | 19.6 | 3.6 | 0.9 | 2.4 | 10.0 | 81018 | 23.1 | 12.0 | 87404 | 20.6 | 16.9 |
| Czech Republic | Plzen | 1991 C | 72833 | 29.8 | 29.2 | 19.3 | 18.5 | 2.8 | 0.5 | 2.4 | ... | ... | ... | ... | ... | ... | ... |
| Czech Republic | Praha | 1998 C | 538331[(1991)] | 33.0 | 30.3 | 18.8 | 14.9 | 2.5 | 0.5 | 2.3 | ... | 564396 | 22.4 | 13.1 | 628874 | 19.1 | 100.0 |
| Denmark | Arhus | 1994 C | 126343 | 38.4 | 31.6 | 14.0 | 11.1 | 4.9 | ... | 2.2 | ... | ... | ... | ... | ... | ... | ... |
| Denmark | Arhus | 1994 M | 270928 | 34.4 | 32.4 | 14.7 | 13.0 | 5.4 | ... | ... | ... | ... | ... | ... | ... | ... | ... |
| Denmark | Kobenhavn | 1994 C | 263869 | 54.6 | 28.8 | 9.3 | 5.0 | 1.4 | 0.9 | 1.7 | 36.3 | ... | ... | ... | ... | ... | ... |
| Denmark | Kobenhavn | 1994 M | 828875 | 40.3 | 32.1 | 13.7 | 10.2 | 2.5 | 1.2 | 2.1 | 27.6 | ... | ... | ... | ... | ... | ... |
| Denmark | Odense | 1994 C | 103852 | 53.6 | 28.7 | 8.9 | 7.0 | 1.5 | 0.3 | 1.8 | ... | ... | ... | ... | ... | ... | ... |
| Estonia | Kohtla-Järve | 1999 | ... | ... | ... | ... | ... | ... | ... | ... | ... | 30197 | 27.0 | 11.2 | 36345 | 21.8 | 19.3 |
| Estonia | Narva | 1999 | ... | ... | ... | ... | ... | ... | ... | ... | ... | 33048 | 28.2 | 9.2 | 40783 | 22.1 | 16.1 |
| Estonia | Tallinn | 1999 | ... | ... | ... | ... | ... | ... | ... | ... | ... | 188565 | 26.0 | 9.9 | 223029 | 21.0 | 83.1 |
| Estonia | Tartu | 1999 | ... | ... | ... | ... | ... | ... | ... | ... | ... | 45888 | 28.5 | 10.5 | 54689 | 23.1 | 18.0 |
| Finland | Espoo | 1989 C | 66493[(1989)] | ... | ... | ... | ... | ... | ... | 2.6 | ... | 99993 | 28.7 | 6.8 | 104969 | 26.5 | 9.9 |
| Finland | Helsinki | 1994 A | 485279[(1994)] | 37.8 | 30.1 | 14.7 | 12.1 | 3.9 | 1.4 | 2.2 | ... | 252366 | 28.9 | 9.7 | 293951 | 25.4 | 66.0 |
| Finland | Helsinki | 1994 C | 252563 | 45.7 | 29.9 | 12.2 | 8.6 | 2.6 | 1.0 | 2.0 | 46.8 | ... | ... | ... | ... | ... | ... |
| Finland | Helsinki | 1994 M | 396054 | 40.0 | 30.3 | 14.0 | 11.1 | 3.4 | 1.2 | 2.1 | ... | ... | ... | ... | ... | ... | ... |
| Finland | Oulu | 1994 C | 45056 | 35.6 | 29.3 | 15.4 | 12.9 | 4.6 | 2.1 | 2.3 | ... | ... | ... | ... | ... | ... | ... |
| Finland | Tampere | 1999 C | 78253[(1989)] | ... | ... | ... | ... | ... | ... | 2.2 | ... | 90480 | 22.9 | 10.6 | 100774 | 20.3 | 18.3 |
| Finland | Turku | 1999 C | 75033[(1989)] | ... | ... | ... | ... | ... | ... | 2.1 | ... | 79617 | 22.0 | 12.1 | 91314 | 18.8 | 20.2 |
| Finland | Vantaa | 1993 C | 67720 | 30.8 | 31.1 | 17.5 | 14.8 | 4.3 | 1.4 | 2.4 | ... | ... | ... | ... | ... | ... | ... |
| Germany | Berlin (West) | 1998 C | 1111010[(1987)] | ... | ... | ... | ... | ... | ... | 1.8 | ... | 1648500 | 21.7 | 9.6 | 1750300 | 19.4 | 91.6 |
| Germany | Cottbus | 1994 C | 54200 | 30.4 | 33.2 | 20.5 | 15.9 | ... | ... | 2.3 | ... | ... | ... | ... | ... | ... | ... |
| Germany | Dresden | 1993 C | 220600 | 35.1 | 33.0 | 16.9 | 12.5 | 2.6 | ... | ... | 22.8 | ... | ... | ... | ... | ... | ... |
| Germany | Halle | 1995 C | 130600 | 31.6 | 34.2 | 19.4 | 11.6 | 3.2 | ... | 2.2 | 20.2 | ... | ... | ... | ... | ... | ... |
| Germany | Hamburg | 1998 C | 841173[(1987)] | ... | ... | ... | ... | ... | ... | 1.9 | ... | 821500 | 20.3 | 12.4 | 878600 | 17.9 | 20.7 |
| Germany | Koln | 1998 C | 476165[(1987)] | 45.6 | 54.4 | ... | ... | ... | ... | ... | ... | 466100 | 20.7 | 11.9 | 496500 | 18.6 | 18.7 |
| Germany | Leipzig | 1995 C | 231700 | 37.2 | 32.1 | 17.7 | 10.6 | 2.4 | ... | ... | 23.2 | ... | ... | ... | ... | ... | ... |
| Germany | Magdeburg | 1995 C | 127000 | 36.2 | 34.2 | 17.1 | 10.9 | 1.6 | ... | ... | ... | ... | ... | ... | ... | ... | ... |
| Germany | Potsdam | 1994 C | 61700 | 31.0 | 32.9 | 16.2 | 17.2 | 2.8 | ... | 2.3 | ... | ... | ... | ... | ... | ... | ... |
| Greece | Athens | 1991 C | 285057 | 28.6 | 28.6 | 19.6 | 18.1 | 4.1 | 1.1 | 2.4 | 33.9 | ... | ... | ... | ... | ... | ... |
| Greece | Larissa | 1991 C | 33659 | 13.0 | 22.0 | 21.3 | 30.7 | 9.5 | 3.5 | 3.1 | 16.4 | ... | ... | ... | ... | ... | ... |
| Iceland | Reykjavik | 1992 C | 56912 | 57.8 | 21.6 | 9.9 | 7.4 | 2.8 | 0.5 | 1.8 | ... | ... | ... | ... | ... | ... | ... |
| Ireland | Dublin | 1991 C | 159163 | 28.2 | 23.7 | 15.2 | 13.6 | 9.5 | 9.7 | 3.1 | 37.8 | ... | ... | ... | ... | ... | ... |
| Isle of Man | Douglas | 1996 | ... | ... | ... | ... | ... | ... | ... | ... | ... | 11430 | 25.2 | 12.5 | 12057 | 22.8 | 81.9 |

# TABLE B.2

*continued*

| Country | City | Year | | | | | | | | | | | | | | | |
|---|---|---|---|---|---|---|---|---|---|---|---|---|---|---|---|---|---|
| Italy | Allessandria | 1991 C | 36805 | 25.7 | 29.9 | 25.8 | 14.5 | 3.2 | 0.9 | 2.4 | ... | ... | ... | ... | ... | ... | ... |
| Italy | Ancona | 1991 C | 37220 | 20.8 | 27.0 | 23.4 | 21.3 | 5.6 | 1.8 | 2.7 | ... | ... | ... | ... | ... | ... | ... |
| Italy | Bari | 1991 C | 108287 | 15.9 | 21.2 | 20.3 | 26.5 | 11.2 | 5.0 | 3.1 | ... | ... | ... | ... | ... | ... | ... |
| Italy | Bergamo | 1991 C | 44933 | 28.4 | 26.5 | 21.2 | 17.7 | 4.9 | 1.3 | 2.5 | ... | ... | ... | ... | ... | ... | ... |
| Italy | Bologna | 1991 C | 171233 | 28.9 | 30.7 | 23.6 | 12.8 | 3.0 | 0.8 | 2.3 | 19.6 | ... | ... | ... | ... | ... | ... |
| Italy | Bolzano | 1991 C | 38241 | 26.5 | 26.4 | 22.9 | 18.1 | 4.8 | 1.4 | 2.5 | ... | ... | ... | ... | ... | ... | ... |
| Italy | Brescia | 1991 C | 76312 | 26.9 | 26.8 | 22.8 | 17.6 | 4.6 | 1.3 | 2.5 | ... | ... | ... | ... | ... | ... | ... |
| Italy | Cagliari | 1991 C | 64914 | 18.9 | 19.9 | 19.9 | 24.1 | 11.1 | 6.2 | 3.1 | ... | ... | ... | ... | ... | ... | ... |
| Italy | Catania | 1991 C | 109337 | 18.5 | 23.0 | 19.7 | 22.9 | 10.5 | 5.4 | 3.0 | ... | ... | ... | ... | ... | ... | ... |
| Italy | Catanzaro | 1991 C | 29997 | 16.0 | 19.7 | 19.3 | 26.9 | 12.5 | 5.6 | 3.2 | ... | ... | ... | ... | ... | ... | ... |
| Italy | Como | 1994 C | 33765 | 29.0 | 26.5 | 21.6 | 17.3 | 4.4 | 1.3 | 2.5 | 19.6 | ... | ... | ... | ... | ... | ... |
| Italy | Cosenza | 1991 C | 28853 | 22.4 | 20.4 | 18.9 | 22.6 | 10.1 | 5.6 | 3.0 | 0.0 | ... | ... | ... | ... | ... | ... |
| Italy | Ferrara | 1991 C | 38096 | 25.1 | 30.5 | 25.9 | 14.3 | 3.3 | 0.8 | 2.4 | 29.6 | ... | ... | ... | ... | ... | ... |
| Italy | Ferrara | 1991 C | 53980 | 22.3 | 30.0 | 26.9 | 15.3 | 4.1 | 1.4 | 2.5 | 26.4 | ... | ... | ... | ... | ... | ... |
| Italy | Firenze | 1991 C | 162422 | 29.7 | 27.3 | 21.4 | 15.4 | 4.6 | 1.6 | 2.5 | ... | ... | ... | ... | ... | ... | ... |
| Italy | Foggia | 1991 C | 46432 | 13.4 | 20.0 | 18.6 | 26.5 | 14.6 | 6.9 | 3.3 | ... | ... | ... | ... | ... | ... | ... |
| Italy | Forli | 1991 C | 41133 | 21.1 | 28.0 | 26.0 | 18.2 | 4.8 | 1.9 | 2.7 | ... | ... | ... | ... | ... | ... | ... |
| Italy | Genoa | 1991 C | 276531 | 26.5 | 29.7 | 24.2 | 15.3 | 3.5 | 0.9 | 2.4 | ... | ... | ... | ... | ... | ... | ... |
| Italy | La Spezia | 1991 C | 40914 | 24.7 | 30.2 | 24.8 | 15.7 | 3.7 | 0.9 | 2.5 | ... | ... | ... | ... | ... | ... | ... |
| Italy | Lecce | 1991 C | 35111 | 23.2 | 21.5 | 19.6 | 23.7 | 8.9 | 3.0 | 2.8 | ... | ... | ... | ... | ... | ... | ... |
| Italy | Livorno | 1991 C | 59622 | 19.2 | 26.7 | 24.6 | 20.8 | 6.2 | 2.5 | 2.8 | ... | ... | ... | ... | ... | ... | ... |
| Italy | Massa | 1991 C | 23054 | 16.9 | 24.9 | 25.9 | 22.7 | 6.8 | 2.9 | 2.9 | ... | ... | ... | ... | ... | ... | ... |
| Italy | Messina | 1991 C | 75552 | 17.2 | 23.3 | 20.2 | 23.9 | 10.5 | 4.9 | 3.0 | ... | ... | ... | ... | ... | ... | ... |
| Italy | Modena | 1991 C | 69703 | 24.1 | 29.0 | 25.4 | 16.1 | 4.1 | 1.3 | 2.5 | ... | ... | ... | ... | ... | ... | ... |
| Italy | Monza | 1991 C | 44645 | 21.3 | 25.8 | 24.8 | 21.7 | 5.2 | 1.2 | 2.6 | ... | ... | ... | ... | ... | ... | ... |
| Italy | Novara | 1991 C | 39585 | 24.7 | 28.5 | 24.8 | 17.7 | 3.4 | 0.8 | 2.5 | ... | ... | ... | ... | ... | ... | ... |
| Italy | Padova | 1991 C | 81043 | 24.6 | 26.3 | 23.0 | 18.9 | 5.4 | 1.7 | 2.6 | ... | ... | ... | ... | ... | ... | ... |
| Italy | Palermo | 1991 C | 219434 | 16.3 | 20.8 | 19.9 | 25.0 | 12.1 | 5.9 | 3.2 | ... | ... | ... | ... | ... | ... | ... |
| Italy | Parma | 1991 C | 68151 | 25.2 | 28.8 | 25.5 | 15.7 | 3.6 | 1.1 | 2.5 | ... | ... | ... | ... | ... | ... | ... |
| Italy | Perugia | 1991 C | 49318 | 18.4 | 24.6 | 23.1 | 21.4 | 8.3 | 4.2 | 2.9 | ... | ... | ... | ... | ... | ... | ... |
| Italy | Pescara | 1991 C | 40793 | 15.8 | 24.6 | 22.3 | 25.1 | 8.7 | 3.4 | 3.0 | ... | ... | ... | ... | ... | ... | ... |
| Italy | Piacenza | 1991 C | 41200 | 25.7 | 28.5 | 25.7 | 16.0 | 3.3 | 0.7 | 2.5 | ... | ... | ... | ... | ... | ... | ... |
| Italy | Pisa | 1991 C | 38124 | 25.6 | 27.0 | 23.3 | 17.3 | 5.1 | 1.7 | 2.5 | ... | ... | ... | ... | ... | ... | ... |
| Italy | Prato | 1991 C | 55098 | 14.1 | 24.7 | 26.7 | 22.6 | 8.2 | 3.8 | 3.0 | ... | ... | ... | ... | ... | ... | ... |
| Italy | Ravenna | 1991 C | 51584 | 21.7 | 27.9 | 26.3 | 18.0 | 4.6 | 1.5 | 2.6 | ... | ... | ... | ... | ... | ... | ... |
| Italy | Reggio Di Calabria | 1991 C | 56229 | 15.9 | 22.4 | 19.3 | 25.2 | 12.0 | 5.3 | 3.1 | ... | ... | ... | ... | ... | ... | ... |
| Italy | Reggio Nell' Emilia | 1991 C | 51697 | 24.8 | 28.5 | 24.8 | 15.9 | 4.4 | 1.5 | 2.5 | ... | ... | ... | ... | ... | ... | ... |
| Italy | Rimini | 1991 C | 46166 | 20.2 | 25.8 | 24.3 | 21.9 | 6.0 | 1.9 | 3.6 | ... | ... | ... | ... | ... | ... | ... |
| Italy | Sassari | 1991 C | 37879 | 16.3 | 19.9 | 20.2 | 25.7 | 11.6 | 6.2 | 3.2 | ... | ... | ... | ... | ... | ... | ... |
| Italy | Savona | 1991 C | 28270 | 27.8 | 31.0 | 24.3 | 13.5 | 2.7 | 0.8 | 2.4 | ... | ... | ... | ... | ... | ... | ... |
| Italy | Siracusa | 1991 C | 41667 | 19.1 | 21.2 | 19.9 | 25.8 | 10.1 | 3.9 | 3.0 | ... | ... | ... | ... | ... | ... | ... |
| Italy | Taranto | 1991 M | 72129 | 13.3 | 21.6 | 20.9 | 27.2 | 11.7 | 5.2 | 3.2 | 7.5 | ... | ... | ... | ... | ... | ... |
| Italy | Taranto | 1991 C | 110891 | 13.4 | 21.6 | 19.6 | 27.1 | 13.4 | 4.7 | 3.24 | ... | ... | ... | ... | ... | ... | ... |
| Italy | Terni | 1991 C | 38975 | 17.8 | 27.8 | 25.1 | 21.4 | 5.8 | 2.1 | 0.0 | ... | ... | ... | ... | ... | ... | ... |
| Italy | Torino | 1991 C | 405852 | 30.8 | 28.1 | 21.9 | 15.3 | 3.1 | 0.8 | 2.3 | ... | ... | ... | ... | ... | ... | ... |
| Italy | Torre Del Greco | 1991 C | 27888 | 10.7 | 15.6 | 18.8 | 27.4 | 17.1 | 10.4 | 3.6 | ... | ... | ... | ... | ... | ... | ... |
| Italy | Trento | 1991 C | 38420 | 24.1 | 26.4 | 23.2 | 19.9 | 5.0 | 1.4 | 2.6 | ... | ... | ... | ... | ... | ... | ... |
| Italy | Trieste | 1991 C | 104858 | 34.5 | 31.4 | 20.2 | 11.3 | 2.2 | 0.5 | 2.2 | ... | ... | ... | ... | ... | ... | ... |
| Italy | Udine | 1991 C | 41577 | 30.9 | 28.0 | 22.0 | 15.0 | 3.2 | 0.8 | 2.3 | ... | ... | ... | ... | ... | ... | ... |
| Italy | Verona | 1991 C | 98447 | 25.1 | 27.5 | 23.1 | 18.1 | 4.8 | 1.4 | 2.5 | ... | ... | ... | ... | ... | ... | ... |
| Italy | Vicenza | 1991 C | 40788 | 24.9 | 27.2 | 22.8 | 18.4 | 5.0 | 1.6 | 2.6 | ... | ... | ... | ... | ... | ... | ... |
| Latvia | Daugavpils | 1991 C | 51400 | ... | ... | ... | ... | ... | ... | 2.4 | ... | 53266 | 26.0 | 9.6 | 62184 | 22.1 | 16.6 |
| Latvia | Júrmala | 1999 | ... | ... | ... | ... | ... | ... | ... | ... | ... | 26264 | 26.9 | 10.9 | 32601 | 21.3 | 18.8 |
| Latvia | Liepaya | 1991 C | 49092 | ... | ... | ... | ... | ... | ... | 2.3 | ... | 44092 | 27.7 | 9.3 | 51335 | 22.7 | 16.5 |
| Latvia | Riga | 1991 C | 383927 | ... | ... | ... | ... | ... | ... | 2.4 | ... | 360250 | 25.5 | 10.6 | 436482 | 20.2 | 92.4 |
| Lithuania | Kaunas | 1993 C | 141921 | 21.2 | 24.6 | 24.0 | 20.7 | 6.2 | 3.3 | 2.8 | ... | 190277 | 28.3 | 8.9 | 223897 | 23.2 | 14.8 |
| Lithuania | Klaipeda | 1999 | ... | ... | ... | ... | ... | ... | ... | ... | ... | 96408 | 28.7 | 7.7 | 106120 | 24.7 | 12.6 |
| Lithuania | Shaulyai | 1993 C | 49499 | 20.3 | 24.6 | 25.3 | 22.0 | 5.4 | 2.5 | 2.8 | ... | 67984 | 30.4 | 7.6 | 78816 | 25.4 | 12.9 |
| Lithuania | Vilnius | 1993 C | 198528 | 24.6 | 22.6 | 24.2 | 20.8 | 5.3 | 2.5 | 2.7 | | | | | | | |
| Malta | Valletta | 1995 | ... | ... | ... | ... | ... | ... | ... | ... | 3482 | 24.0 | 18.1 | 3780 | 20.8 | 116.0 |
| The Netherlands | Arnhem | 1993 C | 76825 | 59.4 | 20.2 | 9.4 | 8.1 | 2.2 | 0.7 | 1.8 | 38.0 | ... | ... | ... | ... | ... | ... |
| The Netherlands | Dordrecht | 1993 C | 46272 | 31.3 | 35.1 | 14.7 | 13.7 | 3.8 | 1.4 | 2.2 | ... | ... | ... | ... | ... | ... | ... |
| The Netherlands | Eindhoven | 1993 C | 82748 | 31.1 | 34.7 | 14.8 | 13.5 | 4.0 | 2.0 | 2.3 | ... | ... | ... | ... | ... | ... | ... |
| The Netherlands | Enschede | 1993 C | 76614 | 53.1 | 21.5 | 10.6 | 10.7 | 3.0 | 1.0 | 1.9 | ... | ... | ... | ... | ... | ... | ... |
| The Netherlands | Groningen | 1994 C | 75890 | 40.2 | 32.1 | 12.8 | 10.1 | 4.8 | ... | 2.1 | 37.4 | ... | ... | ... | ... | ... | ... |
| The Netherlands | Maastricht | 1993 C | 29881 | ... | 47.7 | 26.0 | 20.6 | 4.7 | 1.0 | 2.9 | 10.6 | ... | ... | ... | ... | ... | ... |
| The Netherlands | Rotterdam | 1993 C | 264008 | 37.0 | 32.5 | 14.1 | 10.0 | 3.5 | 2.9 | 2.3 | 34.7 | ... | ... | ... | ... | ... | ... |
| The Netherlands | Tilburg | 1994 C | 65523 | 28.4 | 32.9 | 16.1 | 15.6 | 4.7 | 2.3 | 2.5 | 38.6 | ... | ... | ... | ... | ... | ... |
| The Netherlands | Zaanstad | 1994 C | 53142 | 25.8 | 34.4 | 16.2 | 17.3 | 4.6 | 1.8 | 2.5 | 7.2 | ... | ... | ... | ... | ... | ... |
| The Netherlands | Zoetermeer | 1993 C | 39416 | 22.9 | 31.3 | 16.8 | 20.9 | 6.1 | 2.0 | 2.6 | ... | ... | ... | ... | ... | ... | ... |
| The Netherlands | 'S-Hertogenbosch | 1993 C | 40217 | 30.6 | 33.3 | 15.7 | 14.3 | 4.2 | 1.8 | 2.4 | ... | ... | ... | ... | ... | ... | ... |
| Portugal | Amandora | 1991 | ... | ... | ... | ... | ... | ... | ... | ... | ... | 59772 | 27.4 | 8.2 | 65089 | 24.7 | 11.4 |
| Portugal | Porto | 1991 | ... | ... | ... | ... | ... | ... | ... | ... | ... | 137912 | 28.1 | 11.6 | 164555 | 22.9 | 17.5 |
| Portugal | Lisboa | 1991 C | 245070 | 23.9 | 28.4 | 21.4 | 16.3 | 6.1 | 4.0 | 2.7 | ... | 302822 | 24.1 | 15.1 | 360493 | 19.7 | 111.2 |
| Portugal | Setúbal | 1991 | ... | ... | ... | ... | ... | ... | ... | ... | ... | 40212 | 30.0 | 10.3 | 43008 | 27.4 | 13.6 |
| Republic of Moldova | Balti | 1998 | ... | ... | ... | ... | ... | ... | ... | ... | ... | 74103 | 30.1 | 5.7 | 76787 | 28.5 | 9.8 |
| Republic of Moldova | Bender | 1998 | ... | ... | ... | ... | ... | ... | ... | ... | ... | 61851 | 29.5 | 5.6 | 63418 | 28.1 | 9.8 |
| Republic of Moldova | Chisinau | 1998 | ... | ... | ... | ... | ... | ... | ... | ... | ... | 318057 | 30.8 | 4.8 | 339563 | 27.6 | 29.6 |
| Republic of Moldova | Tiraspol | 1998 | ... | ... | ... | ... | ... | ... | ... | ... | ... | 80895 | 32.6 | 6.3 | 95231 | 27.3 | 10.3 |
| Republic of Moldova | Beltsy | 1994 C | 50800 | 15.7 | 25.0 | 30.7 | 20.9 | 6.1 | 1.6 | 3.2 | 19.8 | ... | ... | ... | ... | ... | ... |
| Romania | Arad | 1992 C | 68034 | 21.7 | 26.9 | 25.0 | 16.8 | 5.9 | 3.7 | 2.7 | 26.9 | ... | ... | ... | ... | ... | ... |
| Romania | Baia Mare | 1992 C | 47841 | 15.8 | 22.3 | 25.5 | 24.5 | 7.7 | 4.1 | 3.0 | 20.9 | ... | ... | ... | ... | ... | ... |
| Romania | Braila | 1992 C | 74340 | 13.7 | 23.9 | 25.3 | 22.7 | 8.6 | 5.8 | 3.1 | 20.4 | ... | ... | ... | ... | ... | ... |

# TABLE B.2

## *continued*

| | | | Total number | Distribution of households by size | | | | | | Average | Women-headed households | Population in specific age groups | | | | | |
|---|---|---|---|---|---|---|---|---|---|---|---|---|---|---|---|---|---|
| | | | | | | | | | | | | Male | | | Female | | |
| | | | Total | 1 | 2 | 3 | 4 | 5 | 6 | Average | (% of total) | Total | 0–19 | >65 | Total | 0–19 | >65 |
| Romania | Iasi | 1992 C | 102860 | 15.6 | 22.7 | 23.5 | 24.5 | 8.4 | 5.4 | 3.0 | 23.0 | ... | ... | ... | ... | ... | ... |
| Romania | Piatra Neamt | 1992 C | 40294 | 14.2 | 23.7 | 27.6 | 24.3 | 6.7 | 3.5 | 3.0 | 20.2 | ... | ... | ... | ... | ... | ... |
| Romania | Pitesti | 1992 C | 57336 | 13.9 | 21.4 | 25.8 | 27.9 | 7.2 | 3.8 | 3.1 | 20.3 | ... | ... | ... | ... | ... | ... |
| Romania | Resita | 1992 C | 30661 | 16.5 | 24.8 | 26.2 | 21.5 | 11.1 | ... | ... | 23.0 | ... | ... | ... | ... | ... | ... |
| Romania | Satu-Mare | 1992 C | 42426 | 14.9 | 22.5 | 26.2 | 24.3 | 7.8 | 4.2 | 3.1 | 21.8 | ... | ... | ... | ... | ... | ... |
| Romania | Sibiu | 1992 C | 54622 | 16.8 | 23.2 | 23.4 | 23.9 | 8.1 | 4.6 | 3.0 | 23.8 | ... | ... | ... | ... | ... | ... |
| Romania | Tirgus-Mures | 1992 C | 55665 | 17.9 | 24.3 | 25.3 | 23.8 | 6.1 | 2.7 | 2.9 | 22.9 | ... | ... | ... | ... | ... | ... |
| Russian Federation | Dzhezhinsk/Gorkovskaya | 1993 C | 117500 | 10.7 | 13.3 | 21.0 | 42.0 | 10.0 | 3.0 | 3.2 | ... | ... | ... | ... | ... | ... | ... |
| Russian Federation | Ufa | 1993 C | 278883 | ... | 27.8 | 28.8 | 28.6 | 9.8 | 5.0 | 3.4 | ... | ... | ... | ... | ... | ... | ... |
| Slovakia | Bratislava | 1991 | ... | ... | ... | | | | | | | 331545 | 26.6 | 8.7 | 375225 | 22.4 | 62.5 |
| Slovakia | Bratislava | 1998 C | 174966[(1991)] | 28.4 | 25.2 | 19.3 | 21.4 | 4.7 | 1.1 | 2.5 | ... | 128121 | 33.9 | 17.5 | 202606 | 20.6 | 18.2 |
| Slovakia | Košice | 1991 C | 85420 | 24.3 | 23.0 | 19.3 | 24.2 | 6.8 | 2.4 | 2.8 | 12.1 | | | | | | |
| Spain | Alicante | 1994 C | 95031 | 23.6 | 22.4 | 18.6 | 21.5 | 9.4 | 4.5 | 2.9 | 28.6 | ... | ... | ... | ... | ... | ... |
| Spain | Alicante | 1994 M | 1234 | 18.5 | 26.4 | 16.5 | 18.3 | 11.5 | 8.8 | 3.1 | 17.0 | ... | ... | ... | ... | ... | ... |
| Spain | Badalona | 1991 M | 65808 | 10.7 | 22.5 | 22.6 | 27.0 | 11.9 | 5.2 | 3.3 | ... | | | | | | |
| Spain | Barcelona | 1991 C | 596186 | ... | ... | ... | ... | ... | ... | ... | ... | 703231 | 19.0 | 16.3 | 802350 | 15.9 | 21.6 |
| Spain | Las Palmas | 1991 C | 97273 | 12.1 | 18.3 | 18.8 | 22.1 | 14.0 | 14.7 | 3.7 | ... | | | | | | |
| Spain | Madrid | 1991 C | 1004786 | ... | ... | ... | ... | ... | ... | ... | ... | 1346167 | 20.2 | 14.5 | 1535337 | 16.9 | 112.6 |
| Spain | Sabadell | 1994 C | 60998 | 14.3 | 23.9 | 22.4 | 24.8 | 9.9 | 4.7 | 3.1 | ... | | | | | | |
| Spain | Sevilla | 1991 C | 205263 | ... | ... | ... | ... | ... | ... | ... | ... | 3351211 | 2.6 | 1.1 | 388201 | 20.9 | 15.8 |
| Spain | Sevilla | 1993 C | 214516 | 17.1 | 19.5 | 18.0 | 23.1 | 13.0 | 9.2 | 3.3 | ... | | | | | | |
| Spain | Valencia | 1991 C | 261218 | ... | ... | ... | ... | ... | ... | ... | ... | 351211 | 22.0 | 13.8 | 388201 | 18.9 | 19.5 |
| Spain | Valladolid | 1991 C | 97897 | 11.7 | 21.0 | 20.9 | 26.5 | 12.4 | 7.6 | 3.3 | ... | ... | ... | ... | ... | ... | ... |
| Ukraine | Mariupol | 1993 A | 184134 | 18.6 | 27.1 | 23.5 | 19.9 | 6.9 | 4.0 | 3.0 | ... | ... | ... | ... | ... | ... | ... |
| Ukraine | Mariupol | 1993 C | 178390 | 18.6 | 27.1 | 23.5 | 19.9 | 6.9 | 4.0 | 3.0 | ... | ... | ... | ... | ... | ... | ... |
| United Kingdom | Amber Valley | 1991 C | 44603 | 23.7 | 35.2 | 17.6 | 17.0 | 4.9 | 1.5 | 2.5 | 25.7 | ... | ... | ... | ... | ... | ... |
| United Kingdom | Barnsley | 1991 C | 87095 | 24.0 | 33.9 | 18.7 | 16.4 | 5.2 | 1.8 | 0.0 | 27.9 | ... | ... | ... | ... | ... | ... |
| United Kingdom | Blackpool | 1991 C | 61518 | 31.6 | 35.5 | 15.2 | 12.0 | 4.1 | 1.6 | 2.3 | 34.9 | ... | ... | ... | ... | ... | ... |
| United Kingdom | Bolton | 1991 M | 101713 | 31.9 | 51.4 | 11.9 | 4.7 | ... | ... | 2.5 | 57.0 | ... | ... | ... | ... | ... | ... |
| United Kingdom | Bournemouth | 1991 C | 65532 | 33.6 | 36.7 | 13.2 | 16.5 | ... | ... | ... | ... | ... | ... | ... | ... | ... | ... |
| United Kingdom | Bracknell Forest | 1991 A | 36510 | 22.2 | 33.9 | 16.9 | 18.7 | 6.0 | 1.6 | 2.6 | ... | ... | ... | ... | ... | ... | ... |
| United Kingdom | Bradford | 1991 M | 174087 | 27.3 | 31.4 | 15.8 | 15.2 | 5.7 | 4.6 | 2.6 | 32.2 | ... | ... | ... | ... | ... | ... |
| United Kingdom | Carlisle | 1991 C | 40883 | 27.3 | 33.6 | 16.9 | 22.1 | ... | ... | ... | ... | ... | ... | ... | ... | ... | ... |
| United Kingdom | Chelmsford | 1991 C | 58847 | 22.5 | 34.4 | 16.5 | 19.2 | 5.8 | 1.7 | 2.6 | 24.6 | ... | ... | ... | ... | ... | ... |
| United Kingdom | Dundee | 1991 C | 72200 | 33.4 | 32.6 | 16.0 | 12.6 | 4.0 | 1.4 | 2.0 | ... | ... | ... | ... | ... | ... | ... |
| United Kingdom | Edinburgh | 1991 C | 185664 | 34.8 | 33.3 | 14.6 | 12.1 | 3.9 | 1.3 | 2.2 | ... | ... | ... | ... | ... | ... | ... |
| United Kingdom | Glasgow | 1991 C | 289855 | 35.9 | 30.7 | 15.2 | 11.4 | 4.5 | 2.2 | 2.3 | ... | ... | ... | ... | ... | ... | ... |
| United Kingdom | Ipswich | 1991 C | 47748 | 28.1 | 34.2 | 15.1 | 15.0 | 5.4 | 2.1 | 2.4 | 31.0 | ... | ... | ... | ... | ... | ... |
| United Kingdom | Kingston Upon Hull | 1991 C | 103246 | 29.5 | 32.0 | 15.9 | 14.6 | 5.7 | 2.4 | 2.4 | 33.8 | ... | ... | ... | ... | ... | ... |
| United Kingdom | Luton | 1991 C | 65475 | 24.0 | 32.5 | 16.2 | 26.0 | ... | ... | 2.6 | ... | ... | ... | ... | ... | ... | ... |
| United Kingdom | Milton Keynes | 1991 C | 54725 | 24.1 | 32.1 | 16.7 | 17.7 | 9.4 | ... | 2.6 | 29.0 | ... | ... | ... | ... | ... | ... |
| United Kingdom | Milton Keynes | 1991 M | 67205 | 23.5 | 32.4 | 16.7 | 18.2 | 6.7 | 2.5 | 2.6 | 27.8 | ... | ... | ... | ... | ... | ... |
| United Kingdom | North Tyneside | 1991 C | 80481 | 29.2 | 33.5 | 16.6 | 14.9 | 4.5 | 1.4 | 2.4 | 32.8 | ... | ... | ... | ... | ... | ... |
| United Kingdom | North Tyneside | 1991 M | 452908 | 29.4 | 32.3 | 17.1 | 14.8 | 4.8 | 1.7 | 2.4 | 33.8 | ... | ... | ... | ... | ... | ... |
| United Kingdom | Norwich | 1991 C | 52733 | 32.9 | 34.7 | 14.5 | 12.1 | 4.3 | 1.6 | 2.3 | 36.4 | ... | ... | ... | ... | ... | ... |
| United Kingdom | Nottingham | 1991 C | 109356 | 31.0 | 33.3 | 15.6 | 12.3 | 5.0 | 2.8 | 2.4 | 36.4 | ... | ... | ... | ... | ... | ... |
| United Kingdom | Oxford | 1991 C | 43887 | 30.6 | 32.3 | 15.3 | 13.2 | 5.7 | 2.9 | 2.4 | 37.3 | ... | ... | ... | ... | ... | ... |
| United Kingdom | Perth & Kinross | 1991 C | 17404 | 30.3 | 33.5 | 16.0 | 14.3 | 4.4 | 1.5 | 2.3 | 35.8 | ... | ... | ... | ... | ... | ... |
| United Kingdom | Poole | 1991 C | 54200 | 25.8 | 37.2 | 15.6 | 14.9 | 4.8 | 1.6 | 2.4 | ... | ... | ... | ... | ... | ... | ... |
| United Kingdom | Portsmouth | 1991 C | 72590 | 30.3 | 34.6 | 15.5 | 13.3 | 4.6 | 1.9 | 2.3 | 20.9 | ... | ... | ... | ... | ... | ... |
| United Kingdom | Preston | 1991 M | 49313 | 29.2 | 30.9 | 16.0 | 14.6 | 5.7 | 3.6 | 2.6 | ... | ... | ... | ... | ... | ... | ... |
| United Kingdom | Reading | 1991 C | 52172 | 4.2 | 4.7 | 8.3 | 17.8 | 28.6 | 36.5 | ... | ... | ... | ... | ... | ... | ... | ... |
| United Kingdom | Rochdale | 1991 C | 36415 | 27.6 | 31.4 | 16.7 | 14.4 | 5.4 | 4.6 | 2.6 | 33.1 | ... | ... | ... | ... | ... | ... |
| United Kingdom | Sefton | 1991 C | 112375 | 26.9 | 31.6 | 16.8 | 16.0 | 6.3 | 2.4 | 2.5 | 33.0 | ... | ... | ... | ... | ... | ... |
| United Kingdom | Sheffield | 1991 C | 210973 | 30.1 | 33.5 | 16.1 | 14.3 | 4.2 | 1.7 | 2.4 | 32.9 | ... | ... | ... | ... | ... | ... |
| United Kingdom | South Tyneside | 1991 M | 64023 | 29.3 | 32.1 | 17.4 | 14.8 | 4.8 | 1.5 | 2.4 | 33.8 | ... | ... | ... | ... | ... | ... |
| United Kingdom | Southampton | 1991 C | 81140 | 29.8 | 33.7 | 15.3 | 21.2 | ... | ... | 2.4 | ... | ... | ... | ... | ... | ... | ... |
| United Kingdom | Southwark | 1991 C | 96633 | 36.7 | 30.8 | 15.2 | 10.4 | 4.4 | 2.5 | 2.3 | 43.6 | ... | ... | ... | ... | ... | ... |
| United Kingdom | Stockton-On-Tees | 1991 C | 67689 | 24.7 | 31.9 | 17.9 | 17.6 | 5.7 | 2.0 | 2.6 | 29.2 | ... | ... | ... | ... | ... | ... |
| United Kingdom | Stockton-On-Tees | 1991 M | 214633 | 25.6 | 31.7 | 17.8 | 16.7 | 5.9 | 2.3 | 2.6 | 30.9 | ... | ... | ... | ... | ... | ... |
| United Kingdom | Stoke On Trent | 1991 C | 97724 | 25.6 | 33.5 | 18.7 | 14.9 | 5.0 | 2.2 | 2.5 | 30.3 | ... | ... | ... | ... | ... | ... |
| United Kingdom | Stoke On Trent | 1991 M | 158250 | 24.8 | 33.6 | 18.7 | 15.8 | 5.2 | 2.0 | 2.5 | 28.8 | ... | ... | ... | ... | ... | ... |
| United Kingdom | Swansea | 1991 C | 72655 | 27.2 | 32.8 | 16.9 | 15.5 | 5.6 | 2.1 | 2.5 | ... | ... | ... | ... | ... | ... | ... |
| United Kingdom | Thamesdown | 1991 C | 57719 | 23.7 | 35.5 | 16.9 | 23.9 | ... | ... | 2.5 | ... | ... | ... | ... | ... | ... | ... |
| United Kingdom | Wigan | 1991 M | 118726 | 24.1 | 30.9 | 19.2 | 17.9 | 5.9 | 1.9 | 2.6 | 28.1 | ... | ... | ... | ... | ... | ... |
| United Kingdom | Windsor and Maidenhead | 1991 C | 51827 | 24.4 | 35.1 | 15.9 | 17.1 | 5.5 | 2.0 | 2.5 | 27.2 | ... | ... | ... | ... | ... | ... |
| Yugoslavia | Kragujewac | 1991 C | 45666 | 13.6 | 19.4 | 21.9 | 31.5 | 8.4 | 5.1 | 3.2 | 7.4 | 88212 | 29.0 | 7.5 | 91827 | 27.0 | 10.3 |
| Yugoslavia | Nis | 1991 C | 56951 | 12.9 | 23.6 | 23.1 | 29.6 | 6.8 | 4.0 | 3.1 | ... | 121441 | 27.0 | 8.7 | 124743 | 25.0 | 10.7 |
| Yugoslavia | Nis | 1991 M | 58288 | 12.9 | 23.6 | 23.1 | 29.5 | 6.8 | 4.1 | 3.1 | ... | ... | ... | ... | ... | ... | ... |
| Yugoslavia | Novi Sad | 1993 C | 65087 | 20.2 | 25.6 | 23.0 | 24.1 | 5.1 | 2.0 | 2.9 | ... | 84626 | 26.8 | 8.6 | 95000 | 23.0 | 11.9 |
| Yugoslavia | Podgorica | 1991 C | 32210 | 12.2 | 14.5 | 16.3 | 28.4 | 17.6 | 11.1 | 3.7 | ... | ... | ... | ... | ... | ... | ... |
| Yugoslavia | Podgorica | 1991 C | 32747 | 12.1 | 14.4 | 16.1 | 28.2 | 17.6 | 11.5 | 3.7 | ... | ... | ... | ... | ... | ... | ... |
| Yugoslavia | Subotica | 1991 M | 37943 | 23.2 | 27.5 | 21.5 | 21.7 | 4.4 | 1.7 | 2.6 | ... | ... | ... | ... | ... | ... | ... |
| Yugoslavia | Subotica | 1991 C | 28608 | 32.4 | 38.9 | 30.7 | 31.1 | 6.3 | 2.5 | 2.7 | ... | ... | ... | ... | ... | ... | ... |
| Yugoslavia | Zrenjanin | 1991 C | 28608 | 18.3 | 26.0 | 22.2 | 25.6 | 5.3 | 2.6 | 2.8 | ... | ... | ... | ... | ... | ... | ... |
| Yugoslavia | Beograd | 1991 C | 390065 | 17.8 | 22.6 | 22.9 | 24.7 | 7.2 | 4.8 | 3.0 | ... | ... | ... | ... | ... | ... | ... |
| Yugoslavia | Beograd | 1991 M | 434778 | 17.3 | 22.3 | 22.6 | 25.2 | 7.4 | 5.2 | 3.0 | ... | ... | ... | ... | ... | ... | ... |

# TABLE B.2

*continued*

**LATIN AMERICA**

| Country | City | Year | | | | | | | | | | | | | | | |
|---|---|---|---|---|---|---|---|---|---|---|---|---|---|---|---|---|---|
| Argentina | Avellaneda | 1991 C | 104470 | 14.4 | 23.7 | 20.2 | 20.4 | 11.8 | 9.6 | 3.3 | 23.7 | ... | ... | ... | ... | ... | ... |
| Argentina | Buenos Aires | 1991 C | 1023464 | 21.9 | 28.8 | 19.0 | 16.3 | 8.4 | 5.6 | 2.8 | 31.6 | 5410716 | 37.1 | 8.5 | 5884839 | 33.7 | 35.1 |
| Argentina | Cordoba | 1991 | | | | | | | 578229 | 39.8 | 6.4 | 630484 | 36.3 | 9.2 | | | |
| Argentina | Godoy Cruz | 1991 C | 46181 | 8.7 | 91.3 | ... | ... | ... | ... | 3.9 | 21.3 | | | | | | |
| Argentina | La Plata | 1991 | ... | ... | ... | ... | ... | ... | ... | ... | ... | 548999 | 63.4 | 5.1 | 331980 | 32.6 | 13.1 |
| Argentina | Resistencia | 1991 M | 73089 | 9.9 | 15.3 | 17.2 | 19.6 | 16.3 | 21.8 | 4.1 | 21.8 | 20060 | ... | ... | 20838 | ... | ... |
| Argentina | Rio Cuarto | 1991 M | 63825 | 13.4 | 22.4 | 20.0 | 20.0 | 13.5 | 10.7 | 3.4 | 22.7 | 270601 | 43.6 | 6.2 | 289683 | 38.0 | 7.5 |
| Argentina | Rio Cuarto | 1991 C | 43894 | ... | ... | ... | ... | ... | ... | ... | 22.7 | 83515 | 39.3 | 3.0 | 88681 | 36.8 | 12.3 |
| Argentina | Rosario | 1991 | | | | | | | | | | 535046 | 38.3 | 8.8 | 583938 | 34.9 | 12.5 |
| Argentina | Salta | 1991 C | 82427 | 9.6 | 14.0 | 15.9 | 18.1 | 16.6 | 25.9 | 5.0 | 26.2 | 359107 | 45.3 | 5.0 | 399034 | 42.0 | 11.8 |
| Argentina | San Juan | 1991 C | 114738 | 6.3 | 13.2 | 15.5 | 18.7 | 17.1 | 29.2 | 4.0 | ... | 99815 | 45.2 | 5.0 | 102733 | 46.7 | 4.4 |
| Argentina | San Nicolas | 1991 C | 35858 | 10.4 | 19.3 | 19.3 | 20.8 | 15.7 | 14.4 | 3.6 | 16.9 | 444420 | 57.8 | 3.2 | 470375 | 49.9 | 2.9 |
| Argentina | San Salvador De Jujuy | 1991 M | 43354 | 10.2 | 13.6 | 16.5 | 18.3 | 15.8 | 25.6 | 4.3 | 27.4 | ... | ... | ... | ... | ... | ... |
| Bolivia | La Paz | 1992 C | 170497 | 5.6 | 10.6 | 15.1 | 21.6 | 21.6 | 24.0 | 4.2 | 26.4 | ... | ... | ... | ... | ... | ... |
| Bolivia | La Paz | 1992 M | 243300 | 5.5 | 10.1 | 15.2 | 21.0 | 21.3 | 26.5 | 4.5 | 26.6 | ... | ... | ... | ... | ... | ... |
| Brazil | Araraguara | 1991 C | 43847 | 6.6 | 17.3 | 21.8 | 25.1 | 16.7 | 12.6 | 3.8 | ... | ... | ... | ... | ... | ... | ... |
| Brazil | Belo Horizonte | 1991 C | 503311 | ... | ... | ... | ... | ... | ... | 4.0 | ... | 1911629 | 40.1 | 3.9 | 2068223 | 38.5 | 5.3 |
| Brazil | Brasilia, Df | 1998 | ... | ... | ... | ... | ... | ... | ... | ... | 916732 | 41.2 | 2.8 | 1017708 | 39.3 | 8.6 |
| Brazil | Juazeiro Do Norte | 1994 C | 37000 | 5.4 | 5.4 | 27.0 | 13.5 | 40.5 | 8.1 | 6.0 | 8.6 | ... | ... | ... | ... | ... | ... |
| Brazil | Maraba | 1994 C | 28000 | 0.5 | 0.6 | 1.3 | 15.9 | 71.8 | 10.0 | 5.0 | ... | ... | ... | ... | ... | ... | ... |
| Brazil | Sao Jose | 1991 M | 36593 | 8.5 | 14.3 | 22.4 | 24.5 | 16.3 | 14.0 | 3.9 | 0.0 | ... | ... | ... | ... | ... | ... |
| Brazil | Sao Jose Dos Campos | 1992 C | 109280 | 3.3 | 11.4 | 19.7 | 27.7 | 19.7 | 18.1 | 4.2 | 0.0 | ... | ... | ... | ... | ... | ... |
| Brazil | Sao Paulo | 1991 M | 4587159 | 7.6 | 16.9 | 20.2 | 24.7 | 17.2 | 13.4 | 3.8 | 0.0 | 8271731 | 38.1 | 4.7 | 8876315 | 34.5 | 6.9 |
| Brazil | Sapucaia Do Sul | 1993 C | 30650 | 4.0 | 10.0 | 35.0 | 41.0 | 7.0 | 3.0 | 5.0 | 21.6 | ... | ... | ... | ... | ... | ... |
| Chile | Antofagasta | 1994 C | 27399 | 9.5 | 16.1 | 23.2 | 22.7 | 15.4 | 13.1 | 4.5 | 27.3 | ... | ... | ... | ... | ... | ... |
| Chile | Arica | 1992 C | 41163 | 8.2 | 12.8 | 23.5 | 22.3 | 15.6 | 17.6 | 4.1 | 25.9 | ... | ... | ... | ... | ... | ... |
| Chile | Chillan | 1992 C | 34714 | 6.0 | 12.6 | 19.0 | 23.0 | 18.8 | 20.6 | 4.2 | 29.5 | ... | ... | ... | ... | ... | ... |
| Chile | Concepcion | 1992 C | 78245 | 7.0 | 13.4 | 19.3 | 23.2 | 17.9 | 19.2 | 4.0 | 25.7 | 182394 | ... | ... | ... | ... | ... |
| Chile | Concepcion | 1992 M | 79136 | 7.0 | 13.1 | 19.3 | 23.2 | 17.8 | 19.3 | 4.1 | 25.6 | ... | ... | ... | ... | ... | ... |
| Chile | La Florida | 1992 C | 82335 | 5.6 | 12.9 | 20.0 | 27.0 | 19.0 | 15.5 | 4.0 | 24.3 | ... | ... | ... | ... | ... | ... |
| Chile | La Pintana | 1992 M | 39794 | 4.7 | 10.0 | 18.9 | 26.5 | 19.5 | 20.4 | 4.5 | ... | ... | ... | ... | ... | ... | ... |
| Chile | Lo Prado Arriba | 1992 C | 28132 | 7.5 | 14.3 | 21.6 | 23.2 | 16.5 | 16.9 | 3.9 | 28.6 | ... | ... | ... | ... | ... | ... |
| Chile | Los Angeles | 1992 C | 33070 | 6.6 | 12.0 | 19.2 | 22.4 | 18.0 | 21.7 | 4.0 | 22.7 | ... | ... | ... | ... | ... | ... |
| Chile | San Joaquin | 1992 C | 29127 | 7.9 | 15.3 | 21.3 | 22.4 | 17.2 | 15.9 | 3.9 | 31.5 | ... | ... | ... | ... | ... | ... |
| Chile | Temuco | 1992 C | 58313 | 6.9 | 13.4 | 19.7 | 22.5 | 17.5 | 9.4 | 4.2 | 26.1 | ... | ... | ... | ... | ... | ... |
| Chile | Temuco | 1992 M | 50985 | 6.8 | 13.6 | 20.1 | 23.1 | 17.6 | 18.8 | 4.1 | ... | ... | ... | ... | ... | ... | ... |
| Chile | Vina Del Mar | 1992 C | 81571 | 9.8 | 18.3 | 20.9 | 22.3 | 14.8 | 13.9 | 3.5 | 29.1 | 161661 | ... | ... | ... | ... | ... |
| Colombia | Barranquilla | 1993 | ... | ... | ... | ... | ... | ... | ... | ... | ... | 470637 | 43.1 | 4.4 | 523122 | 40.0 | 5.3 |
| Colombia | Bogota | 1991 C | 1197637 | 5.3 | 11.9 | 18.6 | 24.7 | 18.8 | 20.7 | 4.0 | ... | 2341775 | 40.6 | 3.4 | 2603673 | 37.7 | 11.4 |
| Colombia | Cali | 1993 | ... | ... | ... | ... | ... | ... | ... | ... | ... | 787905 | 39.6 | 4.4 | 878563 | 37.1 | 5.0 |
| Colombia | Medellin | 1993 | ... | ... | ... | ... | ... | ... | ... | ... | ... | 753220 | 39.9 | 4.7 | 876789 | 35.2 | 5.9 |
| Costa Rica | San Jose | 1997 | ... | ... | ... | ... | ... | ... | ... | ... | ... | 1688946 | 44.0 | 3.4 | 1723667 | 41.9 | 8.8 |
| Dominican Republic | La Romana | 1993 | ... | ... | ... | ... | ... | ... | ... | ... | ... | 80116 | 47.2 | 3.8 | 86434 | 44.4 | 4.2 |
| Dominican Republic | San Pedro De Macoris | 1993 | | | | | | | | | | 104341 | 47.1 | 3.9 | 108027 | 45.5 | 3.9 |
| Dominican Republic | Santiago De Los Caballeros | 1993 | ... | ... | ... | ... | ... | ... | ... | ... | ... | 344135 | 45.5 | 4.7 | 366668 | 44.1 | 5.1 |
| Dominican Republic | Santo Domingo | 1993 | ... | ... | ... | ... | ... | ... | ... | ... | ... | 1015462 | 45.6 | 3.2 | 1177584 | 57.6 | 6.7 |
| Mexico | Guadalajara | 1995 | ... | ... | ... | ... | ... | ... | ... | ... | ... | 1683721 | 47.0 | 3.7 | 1766585 | 43.8 | 4.6 |
| Mexico | Monterrey | 1995 | ... | ... | ... | ... | ... | ... | ... | ... | ... | 1487357 | 42.3 | 3.6 | 1500724 | 40.9 | 4.3 |
| Mexico | Puebla | 1995 | ... | ... | ... | ... | ... | ... | ... | ... | ... | 1027064 | 46.3 | 4.0 | 1092065 | 43.3 | 4.6 |
| Nicaragua | Jinotepe | 1995 | ... | ... | ... | ... | ... | ... | ... | ... | ... | 11804 | 52.2 | 4.3 | 13328 | 46.9 | 5.9 |
| Nicaragua | Leon | 1995 | ... | ... | ... | ... | ... | ... | ... | ... | ... | 58119 | 54.2 | 3.4 | 65746 | 47.2 | 5.4 |
| Nicaragua | Managua | 1995 | ... | ... | ... | ... | ... | ... | ... | ... | ... | 409308 | 53.1 | 3.0 | 454893 | 48.2 | 8.2 |
| Nicaragua | Matagalpa | 1995 | ... | ... | ... | ... | ... | ... | ... | ... | ... | 27422 | 56.1 | 2.9 | 31975 | 50.7 | 3.8 |
| Paraguay | Asuncion | 1992 C | 109975 | 8.7 | 14.0 | 15.9 | 17.6 | 15.4 | 28.5 | 4.4 | 28.2 | ... | ... | ... | ... | ... | ... |
| Peru | Ayacucho | 1991 M | 25260 | 5.0 | 3.0 | 10.0 | 14.0 | 48.0 | 20.0 | 6.0 | 18.0 | ... | ... | ... | ... | ... | ... |
| Uruguay | Montevideo | 1996 | ... | ... | ... | ... | ... | ... | ... | ... | ... | 605658 | 32.5 | 11.5 | 697524 | 27.5 | 62.4 |
| Uruguay | Paysandu | 1996 | ... | ... | ... | ... | ... | ... | ... | ... | ... | 35438 | 37.4 | 11.4 | 39130 | 34.2 | 14.0 |
| Uruguay | Rivera | 1996 | ... | ... | ... | ... | ... | ... | ... | ... | ... | 29481 | 40.7 | 9.1 | 33378 | 35.2 | 12.3 |
| Uruguay | Salto | 1996 | ... | ... | ... | ... | ... | ... | ... | ... | ... | 44366 | 41.9 | 8.9 | 48751 | 37.9 | 11.9 |
| Venezuela | Ciudad Guayana | 1992 C | 96985 | 4.1 | 6.8 | 12.5 | 18.2 | 19.1 | 39.4 | 5.3 | ... | ... | ... | ... | ... | ... | ... |

**NORTHERN AMERICA**

| Country | City | Year | | | | | | | | | | | | | | | |
|---|---|---|---|---|---|---|---|---|---|---|---|---|---|---|---|---|---|
| Bermuda | Hamilton | 1991 | ... | ... | ... | ... | ... | ... | ... | ... | ... | 585 | 21.7 | 8.4 | 515 | 25.4 | 50.4 |
| Canada | Burlington | 1991 C | 46246 | 17.4 | 33.0 | 18.5 | 20.8 | 10.2 | ... | 2.8 | 26.4 | ... | ... | ... | ... | ... | ... |
| Canada | Calgary | 1998 | ... | ... | ... | ... | ... | ... | ... | ... | ... | 2876 | 34.7 | 4.3 | 2509 | 37.9 | 5.5 |
| Canada | Chicoutimi-Jonquiere | 1991 C | 22615 | 20.9 | 29.3 | 20.4 | 27.5 | ... | 1.9 | 2.8 | ... | ... | ... | ... | ... | ... | ... |
| Canada | Edmonton | 1991 C | 236120 | 26.5 | 31.4 | 16.7 | 22.1 | ... | 3.3 | 2.6 | ... | ... | ... | ... | ... | ... | ... |
| Canada | Edmonton | 1991 M | 306180 | 23.1 | 30.4 | 17.2 | 25.7 | ... | 3.6 | ... | ... | ... | ... | ... | ... | ... | ... |
| Canada | Etobicoke | 1991 C | 115230 | 22.4 | 33.0 | 17.9 | 22.9 | ... | 3.8 | 2.7 | 9.3 | ... | ... | ... | ... | ... | ... |
| Canada | Etobicoke | 1991 M | 864545 | 27.4 | 30.2 | 16.6 | 21.6 | ... | 4.2 | ... | 9.3 | ... | ... | ... | ... | ... | ... |
| Canada | Gloucester | 1991 C | 32595 | 11.9 | 28.1 | 21.8 | 34.9 | ... | 3.2 | 3.0 | 9.0 | ... | ... | ... | ... | ... | ... |
| Canada | Halifax | 1991 C | 48425 | 31.5 | 35.1 | 16.0 | 15.6 | ... | 1.7 | 2.3 | ... | ... | ... | ... | ... | ... | ... |
| Canada | Halifax | 1991 M | 118320 | 21.5 | 32.0 | 19.4 | 24.8 | ... | 2.4 | ... | ... | ... | ... | ... | ... | ... | ... |
| Canada | Markham | 1991 C | 43660 | 8.8 | 20.8 | 18.2 | 44.1 | ... | 8.1 | 3.5 | ... | ... | ... | ... | ... | ... | ... |
| Canada | Montreal | 1991 C | 160175 | 110.5 | 91.9 | 41.5 | 27.9 | 10.3 | 5.2 | 2.1 | 89.5 | 7277 | 29.3 | 2.6 | 6289 | 31.8 | 11.0 |
| Canada | Montreal | 1991 M | 1235720 | 27.2 | 31.5 | 17.9 | 15.6 | ... | 5.7 | 2.1 | 24.6 | ... | ... | ... | ... | ... | ... |
| Canada | Oakville | 1991 C | 37910 | 14.1 | 29.5 | 19.1 | 33.6 | ... | 3.8 | 3.2 | 5.6 | ... | ... | ... | ... | ... | ... |
| Canada | Oshawa | 1991 C | 46945 | 19.7 | 31.6 | 19.5 | 26.5 | ... | 2.7 | 2.7 | ... | ... | ... | ... | ... | ... | ... |
| Canada | Ottawa | 1992 C | 349805 | ... | ... | ... | ... | ... | ... | 2.6 | ... | 2416 | 31.5 | 4.7 | 2213 | 35.0 | 5.9 |

# TABLE B.2

## continued

| | | | Total number | Distribution of households by size | | | | | | Average | Women-headed households | Population in specific age groups | | | | | |
|---|---|---|---|---|---|---|---|---|---|---|---|---|---|---|---|---|---|
| | | | | | | | | | | | | | Male | | | Female | |
| | | | Total | 1 | 2 | 3 | 4 | 5 | 6 | Average | (% of total) | Total | 0–19 | >65 | Total | 0–19 | >65 |
| Canada | Quebec | 1991 C | 78440 | 39.7 | 32.1 | 14.6 | 12.8 | … | 0.9 | 2.2 | … | … | … | … | … | … | … |
| Canada | Quebec | 1991 M | 253350 | 26.6 | 31.3 | 18.4 | 22.3 | … | 1.4 | … | … | … | … | … | … | … | … |
| Canada | Richmond | 1991 C | 44455 | 19.3 | 31.4 | 17.6 | 27.2 | … | 4.6 | 3.1 | … | … | … | … | … | … | … |
| Canada | Scarborough | 1991 C | 174910 | 17.5 | 28.1 | 19.6 | 29.0 | … | 5.8 | 3.0 | 11.4 | … | … | … | … | … | … |
| Canada | Scarborough | 1991 M | 864555 | 27.4 | 30.2 | 16.6 | 21.6 | … | 4.2 | … | 9.3 | … | … | … | … | … | … |
| Canada | Sherbrooke | 1991 C | 33470 | 35.4 | 33.7 | 15.1 | 14.7 | … | 1.0 | 2.2 | … | … | … | … | … | … | … |
| Canada | Surrey | 1991 C | 82155 | 15.6 | 32.2 | 17.7 | 29.1 | … | 5.4 | 3.0 | … | … | … | … | … | … | … |
| Canada | Toronto | 1991 C | 270660 | 37.8 | 29.8 | 13.4 | 15.6 | … | 3.4 | 2.3 | … | 2303164 | 26.9 | 9.7 | 2377086 | 24.6 | 12.6 |
| Canada | Toronto | 1991 M | 593895 | 22.6 | 30.4 | 18.1 | 24.3 | … | 4.6 | … | … | … | … | … | … | … | … |
| Canada | Vancouver | 1991 C | 199535 | 38.4 | 29.6 | 12.1 | 15.8 | … | 4.2 | 2.3 | 7.1 | … | … | … | … | … | … |
| Canada | Vancouver | 1992 C | 610305 | … | … | … | … | … | … | 2.6 | … | 809048 | 30.8 | 6.6 | 821505 | 28.9 | 39.7 |
| Greenland | Ilulisat | 1999 | … | … | … | … | … | … | … | … | … | 1750055 | 32.2 | 8.0 | 1735343 | 27.3 | 11.9 |
| Greenland | Nuuk | 1999 | … | … | … | … | … | … | … | … | … | 3437687 | 27.9 | 10.4 | 3884877 | 23.9 | 15.3 |
| Greenland | Sisimiut | 1999 | … | … | … | … | … | … | … | … | … | 282970 | 24.8 | 10.1 | 323930 | 21.6 | 70.6 |
| **OCEANIA** | | | | | | | | | | | | | | | | | |
| Australia | Adelaide | 1991 M | 371244 | 23.7 | 33.2 | 17.0 | 17.1 | 6.6 | 2.4 | 2.6 | … | 16250 | 41.4 | 4.5 | 15478 | 41.9 | 10.3 |
| Australia | Fairfield | 1991 C | 49222 | 11.4 | 22.2 | 19.1 | 23.2 | 13.4 | 10.8 | 2.8 | … | … | … | … | … | … | … |
| Australia | Goesford | 1991 C | 46166 | 21.1 | 34.6 | 15.6 | 17.5 | 8.3 | 3.0 | 2.8 | … | … | … | … | … | … | … |
| Australia | Melbourne | 1991 C | 830 | … | … | … | … | … | … | 1.9 | … | 9409 | 25.8 | 4.1 | 7264 | 32.4 | 4.4 |
| Australia | Sydney | 1991 C | 2750 | 42.6 | 35.2 | 13.3 | 5.6 | 2.1 | 1.2 | 1.9 | … | 23 | 30.4 | 17.4 | 21 | 14.3 | 200.0 |
| New Zealand | Auckland | 1991 M | 109272 | 24.9 | 32.2 | 16.7 | 14.0 | 6.7 | 4.7 | 2.6 | … | … | … | … | … | … | … |
| New Zealand | Dunedin | 1991 C | 40926 | 23.3 | 32.4 | 16.6 | 16.6 | 8.0 | 3.2 | 2.7 | … | … | … | … | … | … | … |
| New Zealand | Dunedin | 1991 M | 38583 | 23.5 | 32.3 | 16.7 | 16.5 | 7.9 | 3.2 | 2.7 | … | … | … | … | … | … | … |
| New Zealand | Hamilton | 1991 C | 34497 | 19.6 | 32.5 | 18.6 | 17.1 | 8.0 | 4.3 | 2.8 | … | … | … | … | … | … | … |
| New Zealand | Hamilton | 1991 M | 40941 | 18.3 | 31.9 | 18.6 | 17.6 | 8.7 | 4.9 | 2.9 | … | … | … | … | … | … | … |
| New Zealand | Manukau | 1991 M | 77904 | 13.8 | 27.5 | 18.5 | 19.8 | 10.8 | 9.7 | 3.3 | … | … | … | … | … | … | … |
| New Zealand | Napier | 1991 C | 18723 | 22.2 | 34.5 | 16.5 | 15.6 | 7.4 | 3.4 | 3.0 | … | … | … | … | … | … | … |
| New Zealand | Northshore | 1991 C | 54168 | 18.9 | 33.6 | 18.0 | 18.7 | 7.8 | 3.0 | 2.8 | … | … | … | … | … | … | … |
| New Zealand | Northshore | 1991 M | 63111 | 19.0 | 34.7 | 17.6 | 18.2 | 7.6 | 2.9 | 2.7 | … | … | … | … | … | … | … |
| New Zealand | Waitarere | 1991 C | 44829 | 14.8 | 30.6 | 19.4 | 19.7 | 9.5 | 5.7 | 3.0 | … | … | … | … | … | … | … |
| New Zealand | Waitarere | 1991 M | 45996 | 14.6 | 30.6 | 19.4 | 19.8 | 9.6 | 5.7 | 3.0 | … | … | … | … | … | … | … |
| New Zealand | Wellington | 1991 M | 55251 | 23.9 | 32.6 | 17.4 | 15.0 | 7.0 | 3.4 | 2.6 | … | … | … | … | … | … | … |

**Sources:** UNCHS (Habitat), Citybase Database; United Nations, Human Settlements Questionnaire 1999.
For footnotes refer to technical notes.

# TABLE B.3

## Ownership of Housing Units

| | | | Households in occupied housing units | | | | | Women-headed households | | | | |
|---|---|---|---|---|---|---|---|---|---|---|---|---|
| | | | | Tenants in housing unit | | | | | Tenants in housing unit | | | |
| | | | Total | Owner (%) | Publicly owned (%) | Privately owned (%) | Squatters (%) | Total (%) | Owner (%) | Publicly owned (%) | Privately owned (%) | Squatters (%) |
| **AFRICA** | | | | | | | | | | | | |
| Benin | Cotonou | 1993 | ... | 25.7 | 25.1 | 45.1 | 4.0 | | ... | ... | ... | ... |
| Benin | Parakou | 1993 | ... | 39.2 | 15.6 | 42.3 | 2.9 | | ... | ... | ... | ... |
| Benin | Porto-Novo | 1993 | ... | 28.2 | 43.4 | 23.2 | 5.2 | | ... | ... | ... | ... |
| Burkina Faso | Bobo Dioulasso | 1991 | 42279 | 48.8 | 32.1 | ... | 19.1 | | ... | ... | ... | ... |
| Burkina Faso | Koudougou | 1991 | 7572 | 58.6 | 28.6 | ... | 12.8 | | ... | ... | ... | ... |
| Burkina Faso | Ouagadougou | 1991 | ... | 70.7 | 18.4 | ... | 10.9 | | ... | ... | ... | ... |
| Burkina Faso | Ouahigouya | 1991 | 7543 | 85.3 | 8.0 | ... | 6.7 | | ... | ... | ... | ... |
| Egypt | Alexandria | 1996 | 799755 | 37.8 | [5]62.2 | ... | ... | | ... | ... | ... | ... |
| Egypt | Cairo | 1996 | 1657081 | 37.1 | [5]62.9 | ... | ... | | ... | ... | ... | ... |
| Egypt | Giza | 1996 | 534180 | 40.1 | [5]59.9 | ... | ... | | ... | ... | ... | ... |
| Egypt | Shubra-El-Khema | 1996 | 192448 | 33.6 | [5]66.4 | ... | ... | | ... | ... | ... | ... |
| Gambia | Banjul | 1993 | 7032 | 22.9 | 10.7 | 65.5 | [8]0.9 | 1766 | 40.8 | 7.0 | 51.4 | 0.8 |
| Gambia | Kanifing | 1993 | 31426 | 33.2 | 10.7 | 53.4 | [8]2.7 | 5653 | 40.9 | 8.2 | 48.5 | 2.4 |
| Kenya | Mombasa | 1989 | ... | 23.1 | ... | [10]76.9 | ... | | 27.2 | ... | 72.8 | ... |
| Kenya | Nairobi | 1989 | | 13.4 | ... | [10]86.6 | ... | | 16.8 | ... | 83.2 | ... |
| Libyan Arab Jamahiriya | Bengazi | 1995 | 101694 | 32.3 | 34.9 | 24.0 | 8.7 | | ... | ... | ... | ... |
| Libyan Arab Jamahiriya | Misurata | 1995 | 66908 | 64.0 | 13.9 | 13.4 | 8.7 | | ... | ... | ... | ... |
| Libyan Arab Jamahiriya | Tripoli | 1995 | 206292 | 60.3 | 22.6 | 10.7 | 6.5 | | ... | ... | ... | ... |
| Libyan Arab Jamahiriya | Zawia | 1995 | 78594 | 59.3 | 8.5 | 22.3 | 9.8 | | ... | ... | ... | ... |
| Mauritius | Port-Louis | 1990 | 30786 | 59.6 | 31.0 | 9.3 | 0.1 | 30633 | ... | ... | ... | ... |
| Senegal | Dakar | 1994 | 183349 | ... | ... | ... | ... | | ... | ... | ... | ... |
| South Africa | Cape Town | 1996 | 60269 | 54.8 | [5]44.2 | ... | 1.0 | 21089 | 45.1 | 53.9 | ... | 1.0 |
| South Africa | Durban | 1996 | 164740 | 61.6 | [5]37.2 | ... | 1.2 | 53402 | 54.3 | 44.4 | ... | 1.2 |
| South Africa | Johannesburg | 1996 | 228137 | 54.2 | [5]42.4 | ... | 3.4 | 73089 | 45.0 | 51.2 | ... | 3.8 |
| South Africa | Pretoria | 1996 | 214633 | 63.0 | [5]34.6 | ... | 2.4 | 63783 | 50.4 | 47.4 | ... | 2.2 |
| **ASIA** | | | | | | | | | | | | |
| Azerbaijan | Baku | 1998 | 467432 | 58.4 | 41.6 | ... | ... | | ... | ... | ... | ... |
| Azerbaijan | Giandja | 1998 | 62441 | 67.2 | 32.8 | ... | ... | | ... | ... | ... | ... |
| Azerbaijan | Sumgait | 1998 | 76568 | 35.2 | 64.8 | ... | ... | | ... | ... | ... | ... |
| Azerbaijan | Mingecheviz | 1998 | 19894 | 60.5 | 39.5 | ... | ... | | ... | ... | ... | ... |
| Cambodia | Bat Dambang | 1998 | 100.00 | 90.9 | 4.5 | 3.9 | 0.72 | | ... | ... | ... | ... |
| Cambodia | Kampong Cham | 1998 | 100.00 | 93.0 | 5.3 | 0.5 | 1.13 | | ... | ... | ... | ... |
| Cambodia | Phnom Penh | 1998 | 100.00 | 83.8 | 3.8 | 11.5 | 0.91 | | ... | ... | ... | ... |
| Cambodia | Siem Riab | 1998 | 100.00 | 97.6 | 1.5 | 0.6 | 0.38 | | ... | ... | ... | ... |
| Cyprus | Larnaka | 1992 | 18300 | 59.7 | 22.8 | 12.3 | [4]5.2 | 2825 | 35.8 | 37.7 | 14.8 | 11.7 |
| Cyprus | Limassol | 1992 | 41792 | 66.4 | 9.1 | 19.3 | [4]5.2 | 5575 | 48.1 | 15.1 | 25.3 | 11.5 |
| Cyprus | Nicosia | 1992 | 54786 | 64.9 | 11.7 | 17.4 | [4]5.6 | 8149 | 46.7 | 18.1 | 22.3 | 12.8 |
| Cyprus | Patos | 1992 | 9795 | 69.2 | 7.2 | 19.1 | [4]4.5 | 1043 | 55.5 | 10.0 | 22.0 | 12.6 |
| Israel | Haifa | 1993 | 92435 | 72.6 | 5.3 | 22.1 | ... | 63210 | 44.1 | 4.5 | 29.6 | 21.8 |
| Israel | Jerusalem | 1993 | 158055 | 68.8 | 4.1 | 27.2 | ... | 47045 | 43.2 | 4.3 | 22.3 | 30.1 |
| Israel | Rishon L'zion | 1993 | 47820 | 81.1 | 2.4 | 16.5 | ... | 12620 | 63.3 | 3.4 | 18.9 | 14.4 |
| Israel | Tel Aviv–Jaffa | 1993 | 149185 | 60.9 | 4.9 | 34.2 | ... | 32430 | 58.1 | 5.6 | 21.8 | 14.6 |
| Japan | Osaka | 1993 | 1038200 | 39.4 | 13.6 | 47.1 | ... | | ... | ... | ... | ... |
| Japan | Sapporo | 1993 | 660800 | 48.0 | 5.8 | 46.2 | ... | | ... | ... | ... | ... |
| Japan | Tokyo | 1993 | 3300100 | 44.2 | 9.2 | 46.6 | ... | | ... | ... | ... | ... |
| Japan | Yokohama | 1993 | 1111600 | 56.6 | 7.8 | 35.6 | ... | | ... | ... | ... | ... |
| Malaysia | Bandaraya Kuching City | 1991 | 68344 | 88.2 | 6.9 | 3.6 | 1.3 | 12003 | 92.2 | 4.1 | 2.3 | 1.5 |
| Malaysia | George Town | 1991 | 43152 | 82.7 | 9.7 | 4.3 | 3.3 | 10765 | 86.5 | 6.5 | 3.6 | 3.4 |
| Malaysia | Keningau | 1991 | 17486 | 69.5 | 6.8 | 11.7 | 12.0 | 3343 | 72.9 | 5.4 | 7.7 | 14.0 |
| Malaysia | Kota Kinabalu | 1991 | 38740 | 78.5 | 11.2 | 5.9 | 4.4 | 6740 | 81.9 | 10.1 | 4.5 | 3.5 |
| Malaysia | Majlis Perbandaran Ipoh | 1991 | 84762 | 89.9 | 6.4 | 1.5 | 2.1 | 18250 | 90.3 | 4.6 | 3.1 | 2.1 |
| Malaysia | Majlis Perbandaran Johor Bharu | 1991 | 69612 | 82.2 | 13.4 | 1.7 | 2.7 | 11112 | 83.8 | 10.0 | 3.0 | 3.1 |
| Malaysia | Miri | 1991 | 33284 | 76.1 | 11.8 | 10.3 | 1.8 | 6361 | 83.4 | 9.8 | 5.4 | 1.3 |
| Malaysia | Sandakan | 1991 | 40367 | 73.5 | 8.4 | 14.1 | 4.0 | 8298 | 83.3 | 4.8 | 7.8 | 4.1 |
| Malaysia | Sibu | 1991 | 34658 | 81.9 | 7.7 | 9.4 | 1.0 | 9624 | 87.6 | 5.3 | 6.1 | 1.0 |
| Malaysia | Tawau | 1991 | 48051 | 55.7 | 9.0 | 31.5 | 3.8 | 8167 | 67.1 | 7.4 | 21.7 | 3.9 |
| Malaysia | W.P Kuala Lumpur | 1991 | 242380 | 78.4 | 16.7 | 2.5 | 2.4 | 50704 | 81.2 | 14.2 | 2.3 | 2.3 |
| Republic of Korea | Pusan | 1995 | 659924 | 72.2 | ... | [11]27.8 | ... | | ... | ... | ... | ... |
| Republic of Korea | Seoul | 1995 | 1688111 | 69.6 | ... | [11]30.4 | ... | | ... | ... | ... | ... |
| Republic of Korea | Suweon | 1995 | 130275 | 71.9 | ... | [11]28.1 | ... | | ... | ... | ... | ... |
| Republic of Korea | Taegu | 1995 | 425930 | 72.5 | ... | [11]27.5 | ... | | ... | ... | ... | ... |
| Syrian Arab Republic | Aleppo | 1994 | 308551 | ... | ... | ... | ... | | ... | ... | ... | ... |
| Syrian Arab Republic | Damascus | 1994 | 271378 | ... | ... | ... | ... | | ... | ... | ... | ... |
| Syrian Arab Republic | Homs | 1994 | 110149 | ... | ... | ... | ... | | ... | ... | ... | ... |
| Syrian Arab Republic | Lattakia | 1994 | 132778 | ... | ... | ... | ... | | ... | ... | ... | ... |
| Turkey | Adana | 1994 | 229680 | 58.2 | 0.3 | 25.8 | 15.8 | 27840 | 71.3 | ... | 16.3 | 12.5 |
| Turkey | Ankara | 1994 | 643500 | 40.2 | 3.5 | 22.1 | 34.2 | 57525 | 62.7 | ... | 13.6 | 23.7 |
| Turkey | Istanbul | 1994 | 1779870 | 57.5 | 0.4 | 31.6 | 10.5 | 117156 | 63.5 | ... | 23.1 | 13.5 |
| Turkey | Izmir | 1994 | 496980 | 53.0 | 0.3 | 28.6 | 18.0 | 48945 | 56.9 | ... | 16.9 | 26.2 |
| Thailand | Bangkok | 1994 | ... | 41.5 | 10.1 | [11]35.3 | 13 | 100 | 41.0 | 10.0 | 35.0 | 13 |
| **EUROPE** | | | | | | | | | | | | |
| Belgium | Antwerpen | 1991 | 207730 | ... | ... | ... | ... | 68479 | ... | ... | ... | ... |
| Belgium | Bruxelles | 1991 | 394468 | ... | ... | ... | ... | 171370 | ... | ... | ... | ... |
| Belgium | Charleroi | 1991 | 81044 | ... | ... | ... | ... | 27904 | ... | ... | ... | ... |
| Belgium | Gent | 1991 | 96526 | ... | ... | ... | ... | 30779 | ... | ... | ... | ... |

## TABLE B.3

### continued

| | | | Households in occupied housing units | | | | | Women-headed households | | | | |
|---|---|---|---|---|---|---|---|---|---|---|---|---|
| | | | | | Tenants in housing unit | | | | | Tenants in housing unit | | |
| | | | Total | Owner (%) | Publicly owned (%) | Privately owned (%) | Squatters (%) | Total (%) | Owner (%) | Publicly owned (%) | Privately owned (%) | Squatters (%) |
| Czech Republic | Brno | 1991 | 165622 | ... | ... | ... | ... | | ... | ... | ... | ... |
| Czech Republic | Ostrava | 1991 | 133434 | ... | ... | ... | ... | | ... | ... | ... | ... |
| Czech Republic | Plzen | 1991 | 72675 | ... | ... | ... | ... | | ... | ... | ... | ... |
| Czech Republic | Praha | 1991 | 545781 | 11.4 | [5]88.6 | ... | ... | ... | ... | ... | ... | ... |
| Estonia[7] | Tallinn | 1998 | 186100 | 68.9 | 10.8 | 20.3 | ... | 101100 | 64.0 | 9.8 | 20.4 | 5.8 |
| Finland | Espoo | 1998 | 84386 | 20.6 | 74.2 | 5.2 | ... | ... | ... | ... | ... | ... |
| Finland | Helsinki | 1998 | 271794 | 50.8 | 21.9 | 27.2 | ... | ... | ... | ... | ... | ... |
| Finland | Tampere | 1998 | 92105 | 60.5 | 19.3 | 20.2 | ... | ... | ... | ... | ... | ... |
| Finland | Turku | 1998 | 86579 | 59.1 | 16.4 | 24.5 | ... | ... | ... | ... | ... | ... |
| France | Lyon | 1990 | 493008 | 41.8 | 19.3 | 34.5 | 4.4 | | ... | ... | ... | ... |
| France | Marseille | 1990 | 481172 | 46.9 | 14.8 | 32.2 | 6.1 | | ... | ... | ... | ... |
| France | Paris | 1990 | 3773848 | 40.2 | 21.3 | 32.7 | 5.8 | | ... | ... | ... | ... |
| France | Toulouse | 1990 | 264076 | 47.0 | 13.2 | 34.6 | 5.3 | | ... | ... | ... | ... |
| Germany | Berlin | 1998 | 1718900 | 10.7 | ... | ... | ... | 716400 | 8.5 | 91.5 | ... | ... |
| Germany | Hamburg | 1998 | 835900 | 19.5 | ... | ... | ... | 332400 | 13.9 | 86.2 | ... | ... |
| Hungary | Budapest | 1996 | 796565 | 79.4 | [5]20.6 | ... | ... | | ... | ... | ... | ... |
| Ireland | Cork | 1991 | 38100 | 66.7 | 18.1 | 14.8 | [9]0.5 | 12316 | 58.0 | 19.7 | 21.6 | 0.6 |
| Ireland | Dublin | 1991 | 158916 | 62.7 | 17.0 | 18.9 | [9]1.4 | 60104 | 53.8 | 19.7 | 25.0 | 1.5 |
| Ireland | Galway | 1991 | 14411 | 69.1 | 8.9 | 21.7 | [9]0.3 | 4900 | 57.6 | 11.2 | 30.8 | 0.3 |
| Ireland | Limerick | 1991 | 15604 | 67.4 | 19.1 | 12.9 | [9]0.6 | 4811 | 56.7 | 23.3 | 19.2 | 0.9 |
| Lithuania | Kaunas | 1999 | 174147 | 92.0 | 4.1 | 3.9 | ... | | ... | ... | ... | ... |
| Lithuania | Klaipeda | 1999 | 71130 | 95.8 | 2.6 | 1.6 | ... | | ... | ... | ... | ... |
| Lithuania | Siauliai | 1999 | 52224 | 94.5 | 1.1 | 4.4 | ... | | ... | ... | ... | ... |
| Lithuania | Vilnius | 1999 | 192566 | 86.6 | 2.2 | 11.3 | ... | | ... | ... | ... | ... |
| Malta | Valletta | 1995 | 2750 | 13.4 | 86.6 | ... | ... | 1001 | ... | ... | ... | ... |
| The Netherlands | Amsterdam | 1998 | 395300 | 15.6 | 47.0 | 27.3 | 10.2 | | 63.2 | 20.3 | 12.0 | 4.4 |
| The Netherlands | Rotterdam | 1998 | 280800 | 26.0 | 41.6 | 7.4 | 25.0 | 129600 | 23.8 | 43.4 | 6.9 | 25.8 |
| The Netherlands | 'S Gravenhage | 1998 | 221100 | 32.0 | 37.0 | 23.4 | 7.6 | 105900 | 29.6 | 38.1 | 24.5 | 7.8 |
| The Netherlands | Utrecht | 1998 | 117600 | 35.2 | 37.8 | 18.4 | 8.7 | 59100 | 36.0 | 40.3 | 15.2 | 8.5 |
| Norway | Bergen | 1990 | 93949 | 76.3 | 23.7 | ... | ... | 34895 | 69.2 | 30.8 | ... | ... |
| Norway | Oslo | 1990 | 244434 | 76.0 | 24.0 | ... | ... | 105447 | 72.5 | 27.5 | ... | ... |
| Norway | Stavanger | 1990 | 42680 | 77.7 | 22.3 | ... | ... | 15081 | 71.1 | 28.9 | ... | ... |
| Norway | Trondheim | 1990 | 60407 | 77.1 | 22.9 | ... | ... | 22069 | 72.0 | 28.0 | ... | ... |
| Poland | Krakow | 1995 | 269640 | ... | ... | ... | ... | | ... | ... | ... | ... |
| Poland | Lodz | 1995 | 346840 | ... | ... | ... | ... | | ... | ... | ... | ... |
| Poland | Warszawa | 1995 | 652311 | ... | ... | ... | ... | | ... | ... | ... | ... |
| Poland | Wroclaw | 1995 | 234866 | ... | ... | ... | ... | | ... | ... | ... | ... |
| Portugal | Amandora | 1991 | 42081 | 62.7 | 0.7 | 36.4 | 0.2 | 8959 | 55.6 | 0.9 | 43.2 | 0.3 |
| Portugal | Lisboa | 1991 | 236580 | 33.4 | 12.7 | 50.0 | 3.8 | 75625 | 28.8 | 10.7 | 57.0 | 3.5 |
| Portugal | Porto | 1991 | 98121 | 36.2 | 14.8 | 47.1 | 2.0 | 27804 | 31.3 | 14.9 | 52.2 | 1.6 |
| Portugal | Setúbal | 1991 | 27767 | 54.9 | 8.9 | 31.5 | 4.7 | 5423 | 46.5 | 8.7 | 41.2 | 3.6 |
| Slovakia | Bratislava | 1991 | 177966 | ... | ... | ... | ... | | ... | ... | ... | ... |
| Slovakia | Košice | 1991 | 85420 | ... | ... | ... | ... | | ... | ... | ... | ... |
| Sweden | Goteborg | 1990 | 209779 | 18.3 | 51.7 | 30.0 | ... | 89412 | 10.8 | 55.1 | 33.6 | 0.5 |
| Sweden | Malmo | 1990 | 120464 | 15.1 | 49.2 | 35.8 | ... | 52852 | 8.7 | 51.3 | 39.7 | 0.4 |
| Sweden | Stockholm | 1990 | 351314 | 10.2 | 53.7 | 36.1 | ... | 168768 | 5.9 | 54.6 | 38.7 | 0.8 |
| Sweden | Uppsala | 1990 | 72504 | 27.5 | 63.1 | 9.4 | ... | 29001 | 16.3 | 73.8 | 9.5 | 0.3 |
| United Kingdom[12] | London | 1991 | 2954000 | 57.8 | 19.9 | 22.3 | ... | 916000 | 40.5 | 30.3 | 29.1 | ... |
| Yugoslavia | Beograd | 1991 | 390065 | ... | ... | ... | ... | | ... | ... | ... | ... |
| Yugoslavia | Kragujevac | 1991 | 45666 | ... | ... | ... | ... | | ... | ... | ... | ... |
| Yugoslavia | Nis | 1991 | 56951 | ... | ... | ... | ... | | ... | ... | ... | ... |
| Yugoslavia | Novi Sad | 1991 | 65087 | ... | ... | ... | ... | | ... | ... | ... | ... |
| **LATIN AMERICA** | | | | | | | | | | | | |
| Argentina | Buenos Aires | 1991 | [3]3569557 | [1]73.8 | [2]15.5 | 10.7 | ... | 967823 | ... | ... | ... | ... |
| Argentina | Cordoba | 1991 | 377980 | [1]61.4 | [2]25.9 | 12.7 | ... | 116971 | ... | ... | ... | ... |
| Argentina | La Plata | 1991 | 210890 | 70.3 | 17.3 | 12.4 | ... | 60801 | ... | ... | ... | ... |
| Argentina | Rosario | 1991 | 385577 | [1]69.5 | [2]13.6 | 16.8 | ... | 109565 | ... | ... | ... | ... |
| Bahamas | Gr. Bahama | 1990 | 10388 | 47.7 | ... | 52.3 | ... | 3491 | ... | ... | ... | ... |
| Bahamas | Nassau | 1990 | 39864 | 53.3 | ... | 46.7 | ... | 15187 | ... | ... | ... | ... |
| Bolivia | Cochabamba | 1997 | 127761 | ... | ... | ... | ... | 30291 | 67.6 | ... | ... | 32.4 |
| Bolivia | La Paz | 1997 | 179460 | ... | ... | ... | ... | 35591 | 55.8 | ... | ... | 44.2 |
| Bolivia | Oruro | 1997 | 51626 | ... | ... | ... | ... | 9489 | 51.7 | ... | ... | 48.3 |
| Bolivia | Santa Cruz De La Sierra | 1997 | 192990 | ... | ... | ... | ... | 38636 | 50.1 | ... | ... | 49.9 |
| Colombia | Barranquilla | 1993 | 332700 | 69.0 | ... | 25.1 | 5.9 | 53700 | 71.3 | ... | 23.1 | 5.6 |
| Colombia | Bogota | 1993 | 1255108 | 54.0 | ... | 41.6 | 4.4 | 329919 | 53.7 | ... | 41.6 | 4.7 |
| Colombia | Cali | 1993 | 1450300 | 57.4 | ... | 35.0 | 7.5 | 113648 | 60.6 | ... | 32.6 | 6.9 |
| Colombia | Medellin | 1993 | 1656600 | 61.8 | ... | 34.0 | 4.2 | 117931 | 63.3 | ... | 32.5 | 4.2 |
| Dominican Republic | La Romana | 1993 | 37781 | [6]54.5 | ... | 33.9 | 11.6 | 14158 | ... | ... | ... | ... |
| Dominican Republic | San Pedro De Macoris | 1993 | 48017 | [6]59.2 | ... | 23.3 | 17.5 | 20769 | ... | ... | ... | ... |
| Dominican Republic | Santiago De Los Caballeros | 1993 | 161654 | [6]73.7 | ... | 20.5 | 5.7 | 50706 | ... | ... | ... | ... |
| Dominican Republic | Santo Domingo | 1993 | 512701 | [6]58.1 | ... | 37.5 | 4.3 | 180996 | ... | ... | ... | ... |
| Nicaragua | Jinotepe | 1998 | 3229 | 66.0 | ... | 15.5 | 18.5 | 1132 | 58.8 | ... | 8.5 | 32.7 |
| Nicaragua | Leon | 1998 | 18423 | 64.2 | ... | 11.8 | 24.0 | 8378 | 67.1 | ... | 6.6 | 26.3 |
| Nicaragua | Managua | 1998 | 152920 | 44.6 | ... | 6.6 | 48.9 | 66078 | 37.5 | 15.1 | 3.4 | 44.0 |
| Nicaragua | Matagalpa | 1998 | 9584 | 79.5 | ... | 4.2 | 16.2 | 3521 | 83.1 | ... | 5.7 | 11.2 |

# TABLE B.3

## ontinued

| | | | | | | | | | | | | |
|---|---|---|---|---|---|---|---|---|---|---|---|---|
| anama | Colon | 1990 | 15520 | ... | ... | ... | ... | 5380 | ... | ... | ... | ... |
| anama | David | 1990 | 23768 | ... | ... | ... | ... | 6584 | ... | ... | ... | ... |
| anama | Panama | 1990 | 106887 | ... | ... | ... | ... | 32882 | ... | ... | ... | ... |
| anama | San Miguelito | 1990 | 51667 | ... | ... | ... | ... | 12808 | ... | ... | ... | ... |
| uerto Rico | Bayamon | 1990 | 56785 | ... | ... | ... | ... | 20328 | 56.1 | ... | ... | ... |
| uerto Rico | Carolina | 1990 | 54466 | ... | ... | ... | ... | 18861 | 54.8 | ... | ... | ... |
| uerto Rico | Ponce | 1990 | 54191 | ... | ... | ... | ... | 18874 | 37.0 | ... | ... | ... |
| uerto Rico | San Juan | 1990 | 150592 | ... | ... | ... | ... | 65649 | 41.0 | ... | ... | ... |
| ruguay | Montevideo | 1996 | 413998 | ... | ... | ... | ... | 137965 | ... | ... | ... | ... |
| ruguay | Paysandu | 1996 | 21451 | ... | ... | ... | ... | 5930 | ... | ... | ... | ... |
| ruguay | Rivera | 1996 | 18437 | ... | ... | ... | ... | 5797 | ... | ... | ... | ... |
| ruguay | Salto | 1996 | 24587 | ... | ... | ... | ... | 6809 | ... | ... | ... | ... |
| **NORTHERN AMERICA** | | | | | | | | | | | | |
| ermuda | Hamilton | 1999 | 388 | ... | ... | ... | ... | 161 | 17.4 | ... | ... | 82.6 |
| anada | Calgary | 1998 | 332700 | 68.2 | 6.8 | 25.0 | ... | 171600 | 63.1 | ... | 23.1 | 13.9 |
| anada | Montreal | 1998 | 1450300 | 46.6 | 3.6 | 49.8 | ... | 580300 | 33.8 | ... | 57.9 | 8.3 |
| anada | Ottawa | 1998 | 313200 | 67.5 | ... | 32.5 | ... | 179100 | 61.9 | ... | 30.5 | 7.6 |
| anada | Toronto | 1998 | 1656600 | 57.9 | 7.2 | 34.9 | ... | 747400 | 54.0 | 9.8 | 33.8 | 2.4 |
| United States | Houston | 1998 | 1264200 | 56.9 | 3.7 | 39.4 | ... | 326000 | 42.5 | 6.0 | 51.4 | ... |
| United States | Los Angeles | 1998 | 2947500 | 46.7 | 1.2 | 52.1 | ... | 884700 | 36.6 | | 63.4 | |
| United States | New York | 1998 | 4156100 | 44.8 | 5.8 | 49.4 | ... | 1482000 | 30.0 | 11.3 | 58.6 | ... |
| United States | Washington, DC | 1998 | 1519200 | 61.8 | 2.2 | 36.0 | ... | 465200 | 45.9 | 5.2 | 48.9 | ... |
| **OCEANIA** | | | | | | | | | | | | |
| Australia | Adelaide | 1996 | ... | ... | ... | ... | 79683 | 62.5 | 1.9 | 35.6 | ... | |
| Australia | Brisbane | 1996 | ... | ... | ... | ... | 110422 | 59.4 | 1.8 | 38.6 | 0.2 | |
| Australia | Melbourne | 1996 | ... | ... | ... | ... | 233720 | 64.0 | 1.0 | 28.3 | 6.7 | |
| Australia | Sydney | 1996 | ... | ... | ... | ... | 267210 | 59.2 | 1.1 | 37.4 | 2.3 | |
| Guam | Dededo | 1990 | 6963 | 58.9 | 41.1 | ... | ... | | | ... | ... | ... |
| Guam | Santa Rita | 1990 | 2287 | 25.1 | 74.9 | ... | ... | | | ... | ... | ... |
| Guam | Tamuning | 1990 | 4982 | 24.3 | 75.7 | ... | ... | | | ... | ... | ... |
| Guam | Yigo | 1990 | 3370 | 36.1 | 63.9 | ... | ... | | | ... | ... | ... |

**Source:** United Nations, Human Settlements Statistics Questionnaire 1999.
For sources and footnotes, refer to technical notes.

# TABLE B.4

## Living Quarters by Type, Selected Cities

| | | | | Living quarters | | | | | |
| | | | | Total | Type of housing units | | | | |
| | | | Total households | Total | Conventional | Basic | Temporary | Marginal | Collective | Not stated |
|---|---|---|---|---|---|---|---|---|---|---|
| **AFRICA** | | | | | | | | | | |
| Botswana | Francistown | 1996 | 16789 | ... | ... | ... | ... | ... | ... | ... |
| Botswana | Gaberone | 1996 | 36639 | ... | ... | ... | ... | ... | ... | ... |
| Burkina Faso | Bobo Dioulasso | 1991 | 42279 | ... | ... | ... | ... | ... | ... | ... |
| Burkina Faso | Koudougou | 1991 | 7572 | ... | ... | ... | ... | ... | ... | ... |
| Burkina Faso | Ouagadougou | 1991 | 98033 | ... | ... | ... | ... | ... | ... | ... |
| Burkina Faso | Ouahigouya | 1991 | 7543 | ... | ... | ... | ... | ... | ... | ... |
| Congo | Brazzaville | 1984 | 103263 | ... | ... | ... | ... | ... | ... | ... |
| Congo | Doligie | 1984 | 9048 | ... | ... | ... | ... | ... | ... | ... |
| Congo | Nkayi | 1984 | 7242 | ... | ... | ... | ... | ... | ... | ... |
| Congo | Pointe-Noire | 1984 | 56523 | ... | ... | ... | ... | ... | ... | ... |
| Egypt | Alexandria | 1996 | 799755 | ... | ... | ... | ... | ... | ... | ... |
| Egypt | Cairo | 1996 | 1657081 | 2810584 | 236644 | 2142902 | – | 427082 | | 3956 |
| Egypt | Giza | 1996 | 534180 | ... | ... | ... | ... | ... | ... | ... |
| Egypt | Shubra-El-Khema | 1996 | 192448 | ... | ... | ... | ... | ... | ... | ... |
| Gambia | Banjul | 1993 | 7032 | ... | ... | ... | ... | ... | ... | ... |
| Gambia | Kanifing | 1993 | 31426 | ... | ... | ... | ... | ... | ... | ... |
| Kenya | Kisumu | 1997 | 47690 | ... | ... | ... | ... | ... | ... | ... |
| Kenya | Mombasa | 1997 | 124468 | ... | ... | ... | ... | ... | ... | ... |
| Kenya | Nairobi | 1997 | 382863 | ... | ... | ... | ... | ... | ... | ... |
| Kenya | Nakuru | 1997 | 46800 | ... | ... | ... | ... | ... | ... | ... |
| Lesotho | Maseru | 1997 | 83961 | 83961 | ... | ... | ... | ... | ... | ... |
| Libyan Arab Jamahiriya | Tripoli | 1995 | ... | 207948 | 27164 | 45909 | 125742 | 1656 | 200471 | 7477 |
| Mauritius | Port-Louis | 1990 | 30780 | 29456 | ... | ... | ... | ... | ... | ... |
| South Africa | Cape Town | 1996 | 60267 | ... | ... | ... | ... | ... | ... | ... |
| South Africa | Durban | 1996 | 164738 | ... | ... | ... | ... | ... | ... | ... |
| South Africa | Johannesburg | 1996 | 228135 | ... | ... | ... | ... | ... | ... | ... |
| South Africa | Pretoria | 1996 | 214633 | ... | ... | ... | ... | ... | ... | ... |
| Zimbabwe | Bulawayo | 1997 | 146062 | ... | ... | ... | ... | ... | ... | ... |
| Zimbabwe | Chitungwiza | 1997 | 62788 | ... | ... | ... | ... | ... | ... | ... |
| Zimbabwe | Harare | 1997 | 301506 | ... | ... | ... | ... | ... | ... | ... |
| **ASIA** | | | | | | | | | | |
| Cyprus | Larnaka | 1992 | 18485 | ... | ... | ... | ... | ... | ... | ... |
| Cyprus | Limassol | 1992 | 42031 | ... | ... | ... | ... | ... | ... | ... |
| Cyprus | Nicosia | 1992 | 55059 | 60855 | 60582 | ... | ... | 1220 | 53 | ... |
| Cyprus | Patos | 1992 | 9910 | ... | ... | ... | ... | ... | ... | ... |
| Georgia | Batumi | 1998 | 38483 | ... | ... | ... | ... | ... | ... | ... |
| Georgia | Kutaisi | 1998 | 56544 | ... | ... | ... | ... | ... | ... | ... |
| Georgia | Rustavi | 1998 | 43619 | ... | ... | ... | ... | ... | ... | ... |
| Georgia | Tbilisi | 1998 | 344919 | 2585 | ... | ... | ... | ... | ... | ... |
| Iran (Islamic Republic of) | Esfahan | 1996 | 297546 | ... | ... | ... | ... | ... | ... | ... |
| Iran (Islamic Republic of) | Mashhad | 1996 | 408302 | ... | ... | ... | ... | ... | ... | ... |
| Iran (Islamic Republic of) | Tabriz City | 1996 | 268915 | ... | ... | ... | ... | ... | ... | ... |
| Iran (Islamic Republic of) | Teheran | 1996 | 1660517 | ... | ... | ... | ... | ... | ... | ... |
| Israel | Haifa | 1995 | 101571 | ... | ... | ... | ... | ... | ... | ... |
| Israel | Jerusalem | 1995 | 185817 | ... | ... | ... | ... | ... | ... | ... |
| Israel | Rishon L'zion | 1995 | 49396 | ... | ... | ... | ... | ... | ... | ... |
| Israel | Tel Aviv–Jaffa | 1995 | 153091 | ... | ... | ... | ... | ... | ... | ... |
| Japan | Osaka | 1993 | 1041600 | ... | ... | ... | ... | ... | ... | ... |
| Japan | Sapporo | 1993 | 665300 | ... | ... | ... | ... | ... | ... | ... |
| Japan | Tokyo | 1993 | 3330500 | 3787600 | ... | ... | ... | ... | 9800 | ... |
| Japan | Yokohama | 1993 | 1118700 | ... | ... | ... | ... | ... | ... | ... |
| Malaysia | Bandaraya Kuching City | 1991 | 68344 | 66643 | 66233 | 35 | 375 | ... | ... | ... |
| Malaysia | George Town | 1991 | 43152 | ... | ... | ... | ... | ... | ... | ... |
| Malaysia | Keningau | 1991 | 17486 | ... | ... | ... | ... | ... | ... | ... |
| Malaysia | Kota Kinabalu | 1991 | 38740 | 35153 | 34064 | 50 | 1039 | ... | ... | ... |
| Malaysia | Majlis Perbandaran Ipoh | 1991 | 84762 | ... | ... | ... | ... | ... | ... | ... |
| Malaysia | Majlis Perbandaran Johor Bharu | 1991 | 69612 | ... | ... | ... | ... | ... | ... | ... |
| Malaysia | Miri | 1991 | 33284 | ... | ... | ... | ... | ... | ... | ... |
| Malaysia | Sandakan | 1991 | 40367 | ... | ... | ... | ... | ... | ... | ... |
| Malaysia | Sibu | 1991 | 34658 | ... | ... | ... | ... | ... | ... | ... |
| Malaysia | Tawau | 1991 | 48051 | ... | ... | ... | ... | ... | ... | ... |
| Malaysia | W.P Kuala Lumpur | 1991 | 242380 | 237189 | 233804 | 1443 | 1942 | ... | ... | ... |
| Pakistan | Faisalabad | 1998 | 278924 | ... | ... | ... | ... | ... | ... | ... |
| Pakistan | Islamabad | 1998 | 86575 | 86575 | ... | ... | ... | ... | ... | ... |
| Pakistan | Karachi | 1998 | 1436373 | ... | ... | ... | ... | ... | ... | ... |
| Pakistan | Lahore | 1998 | 740638 | ... | ... | ... | ... | ... | ... | ... |
| Republic of Korea | Pusan | 1995 | 1080205 | ... | ... | ... | ... | ... | ... | ... |
| Republic of Korea | Seoul | 1995 | 2968615 | 1701587 | 1688111 | 3889 | ... | 8983 | 604 | ... |
| Republic of Korea | Suweon | 1995 | 216765 | ... | ... | ... | ... | ... | ... | ... |
| Republic of Korea | Taegu | 1995 | 704312 | ... | ... | ... | ... | ... | ... | ... |
| Syrian Arab Republic | Aleppo | 1994 | 308551 | ... | ... | ... | ... | ... | ... | ... |
| Syrian Arab Republic | Damascus | 1994 | 271378 | ... | ... | ... | ... | ... | ... | ... |
| Syrian Arab Republic | Homs | 1994 | 110149 | ... | ... | ... | ... | ... | ... | ... |
| Syrian Arab Republic | Lattakia | 1994 | 132778 | ... | ... | ... | ... | ... | ... | ... |
| **EUROPE** | | | | | | | | | | |
| Austria | Wien | 1991 | 746760 | 893 | ... | ... | ... | ... | 893 | ... |
| Austria | Graz | 1991 | 105563 | ... | ... | ... | ... | ... | ... | ... |
| Austria | Linz | 1991 | 89599 | ... | ... | ... | ... | ... | ... | ... |
| Austria | Salzburg | 1991 | 65137 | ... | ... | ... | ... | ... | ... | ... |

# TABLE B.4

**continued**

| | | | | | | | | | |
|---|---|---|---|---|---|---|---|---|---|
| Belgium | Bruxelles | 1991 | 460091 | 394468 | 256559 | 70758 | 60946 | 6205 | 555 | ... |
| Belgium | Antwerpen | 1991 | 220150 | ... | ... | ... | ... | ... | ... | ... |
| Belgium | Gent | 1991 | 102916 | ... | ... | ... | ... | ... | ... | ... |
| Belgium | Charleroi | 1991 | 89842 | ... | ... | ... | ... | ... | ... | ... |
| Croatia | Zagreb | 1991 | 252874 | ... | 333660 | ... | ... | [2]2333 | ... | ... |
| Croatia | Split | 1991 | 58763 | ... | ... | ... | ... | ... | ... | ... |
| Croatia | Rijeka | 1991 | 60196 | ... | ... | ... | ... | ... | ... | ... |
| Croatia | Osijek | 1991 | 38362 | ... | ... | ... | ... | ... | ... | ... |
| Czech Republic | Praha | 1991 | 547290 | 495804 | ... | ... | ... | ... | ... | ... |
| Czech Republic | Brno | 1991 | 165880 | ... | ... | ... | ... | ... | ... | ... |
| Czech Republic | Ostrava | 1991 | 134149 | ... | ... | ... | ... | ... | ... | ... |
| Czech Republic | Plzen | 1991 | 72833 | ... | ... | ... | ... | ... | ... | ... |
| Estonia[3] | Tallinn | 1998 | 190000 | ... | ... | ... | ... | ... | ... | ... |
| Finland | Helsinki | 1998 | 272000 | ... | ... | ... | ... | ... | ... | ... |
| Finland | Tampere | 1998 | 92000 | ... | ... | ... | ... | ... | ... | ... |
| Finland | Espoo | 1998 | 84000 | ... | ... | ... | ... | ... | ... | ... |
| Finland | Turku | 1998 | 87000 | ... | ... | ... | ... | ... | ... | ... |
| France | Paris | 1999 | 3981495 | 7898813 | ... | ... | ... | ... | ... | ... |
| France | Marseille | 1999 | 528144 | ... | ... | ... | ... | ... | ... | ... |
| France | Lyon | 1999 | 546082 | ... | ... | ... | ... | ... | ... | ... |
| France | Toulouse | 1998 | 327931 | ... | ... | ... | ... | ... | ... | ... |
| Germany | Berlin | 1998 | 1718900 | 1692100 | [4]1669300 | ... | [5]700 | ... | [6]22200 | ... |
| Germany | Hamburg | 1998 | 835900 | ... | ... | ... | ... | ... | ... | ... |
| Hungary | Budapest | 1996 | 797545 | 816518 | 815489 | [7]1029 | ... | ... | ... | ... |
| Ireland | Dublin | 1996 | 173085 | ... | ... | ... | ... | ... | ... | ... |
| Ireland | Cork | 1996 | 41452 | ... | ... | ... | ... | ... | ... | ... |
| Ireland | Limerick | 1996 | 17054 | ... | ... | ... | ... | ... | ... | ... |
| Ireland | Galway | 1996 | 17334 | ... | ... | ... | ... | ... | ... | ... |
| Malta | Valletta | 1995 | 2750 | ... | ... | ... | ... | ... | ... | ... |
| The Netherlands | Amsterdam | 1998 | ... | 392200 | 392200 | ... | ... | ... | ... | ... |
| Norway | Oslo | 1990 | 244434 | ... | ... | ... | ... | ... | ... | ... |
| Norway | Bergen | 1990 | 93949 | ... | ... | ... | ... | ... | ... | ... |
| Norway | Trondheim | 1990 | 60407 | ... | ... | ... | ... | ... | ... | ... |
| Norway | Stavanger | 1990 | 42680 | ... | ... | ... | ... | ... | ... | ... |
| Poland | Warszawa | 1995 | 652432 | ... | ... | ... | ... | ... | ... | ... |
| Poland | Lodz | 1995 | 346898 | ... | ... | ... | ... | ... | ... | ... |
| Poland | Krakow | 1995 | 269720 | ... | ... | ... | ... | ... | ... | ... |
| Poland | Wroclaw | 1995 | 234909 | ... | ... | ... | ... | ... | ... | ... |
| Portugal | Lisboa | 1991 | 244634 | 241556 | 227580 | 7090 | 5506 | 108 | 1201 | 71 |
| Portugal | Porto | 1991 | 99324 | ... | ... | ... | ... | ... | ... | ... |
| Portugal | Amandora | 1991 | 43710 | ... | ... | ... | ... | ... | ... | ... |
| Portugal | Setúbal | 1991 | 28084 | ... | ... | ... | ... | ... | ... | ... |
| Slovakia | Bratislava | 1991 | 177966 | ... | ... | ... | ... | ... | ... | ... |
| Slovakia | Košice | 1991 | 85420 | ... | ... | ... | ... | ... | ... | ... |
| Spain | Madrid | 1991 | 963909 | 1173619 | 1171675 | ... | ... | ... | 1944 | ... |
| Spain | Barcelona | 1991 | 572224 | ... | ... | ... | ... | ... | ... | ... |
| Spain | Valencia | 1991 | 252162 | ... | ... | ... | ... | ... | ... | ... |
| Spain | Sevilla | 1991 | 197009 | ... | ... | ... | ... | ... | ... | ... |
| Sweden | Stockholm | 1990 | 351314 | 351314 | 345528 | 3002 | ... | ... | ... | 2784 |
| Sweden | Goteborg | 1990 | 209779 | ... | ... | ... | ... | ... | ... | ... |
| Sweden | Malmo | 1990 | 120464 | ... | ... | ... | ... | ... | ... | ... |
| Sweden | Uppsala | 1990 | 72504 | ... | ... | ... | ... | ... | ... | ... |
| Switzerland | Berne | 1990 | 69182 | ... | ... | ... | ... | ... | ... | ... |
| Switzerland | Zurich | 1990 | 189296 | ... | ... | ... | ... | ... | ... | ... |
| Switzerland | Geneva | 1990 | 90999 | ... | ... | ... | ... | ... | ... | ... |
| Switzerland | Bale | 1990 | 85702 | ... | ... | ... | ... | ... | ... | ... |
| United kingdom | London | | 2954000 | ... | ... | ... | ... | ... | ... | ... |
| Yugoslavia | Beograd | 1991 | [8]390065 | 535809 | 503077 | ... | 27073 | ... | ... | 5659 |
| Yugoslavia | Novi Sad | 1991 | [8]65087 | ... | ... | ... | ... | ... | ... | ... |
| Yugoslavia | Nis | 1991 | [8]56951 | ... | ... | ... | ... | ... | ... | ... |
| Yugoslavia | Kragujevac | 1991 | [8]45666 | ... | ... | ... | ... | ... | ... | ... |
| **LATIN AMERICA** | | | | | | | | | | |
| Argentina | Buenos Aires | 1991 | 3287811 | 3155743 | 2539643 | 333556 | 27301 | 202021 | 5585 | 47637 |
| Argentina | Cordoba | 1991 | 326235 | ... | ... | ... | ... | ... | ... | ... |
| Argentina | Rosario | 1991 | 327314 | ... | ... | ... | ... | ... | ... | ... |
| Bolivia | Cochabamba | 1997 | 127761 | ... | ... | ... | ... | ... | ... | ... |
| Bolivia | La Paz | 1997 | 179460 | ... | ... | ... | ... | ... | ... | ... |
| Bolivia | Oruro | 1997 | 51626 | ... | ... | ... | ... | ... | ... | ... |
| Bolivia | Santa Cruz De La Sierra | 1997 | 192990 | ... | ... | ... | ... | ... | ... | ... |
| Brazil | Brasilia, Df | 1998 | 508425 | ... | ... | ... | ... | ... | ... | ... |
| Colombia | Bogota | 1993 | 1255108 | 944088 | 889888 | 46366 | ... | 7834 | ... | ... |
| Dominican Republic | La Romana | 1993 | 40393 | ... | ... | ... | ... | ... | ... | ... |
| Dominican Republic | San Pedro De Macoris | 1993 | 53964 | ... | ... | ... | ... | ... | ... | ... |
| Dominican Republic | Santiago De Los Caballeros | 1993 | 164843 | ... | ... | ... | ... | ... | ... | ... |
| Dominican Republic | Santo Domingo | 1993 | 519445 | 512701 | 455560 | 55991 | ... | ... | ... | 1150 |
| Guatemala | Guatemala City | 1994 | 182171 | 183618 | 155524 | 22596 | 269 | 5229 | ... | ... |
| Guatemala | Mazatenango | 1994 | 6574 | ... | ... | ... | ... | ... | ... | ... |
| Guatemala | Puerto Barrios | 1994 | 6743 | ... | ... | ... | ... | ... | ... | ... |
| Guatemala | Quezaltenango | 1994 | 18019 | ... | ... | ... | ... | ... | ... | ... |
| Jamaica | Kingston | 1991 | 147279 | 141766 | 140334 | ... | ... | 880 | ... | 552 |
| Jamaica | Montego Bay | 1991 | 21316 | ... | ... | ... | ... | ... | ... | ... |
| Jamaica | Portmore | 1991 | 22030 | ... | ... | ... | ... | ... | ... | ... |
| Jamaica | Spanish Town | 1991 | 26666 | ... | ... | ... | ... | ... | ... | ... |
| Nicaragua | Jinotepe | 1995 | 4325 | ... | ... | ... | ... | ... | ... | ... |
| Nicaragua | Leon | 1995 | 22283 | ... | ... | ... | ... | ... | ... | ... |

# TABLE B.4

## continued

| | | | | Living quarters | | | | | | |
| | | | | Type of housing units | | | | | | |
| | | | Total households | Total | Conventional | Basic | Temporary | Marginal | Collective | Not stated |
|---|---|---|---|---|---|---|---|---|---|---|
| Nicaragua | Managua | 1995 | 157202 | 146652 | 81475 | 58556 | 741 | 5880 | ... | ... |
| Nicaragua | Matagalpa | 1995 | 9770 | ... | ... | ... | ... | ... | ... | ... |
| Panama | Colon | 1990 | 15520 | ... | ... | ... | ... | ... | ... | ... |
| Panama | David | 1990 | 23768 | ... | ... | ... | ... | ... | ... | ... |
| Panama | Panama | 1990 | 106887 | 105409 | 87968 | 15277 | 1630 | 534 | 178 | ... |
| Panama | San Miguelito | 1990 | 51667 | ... | ... | ... | ... | ... | ... | ... |
| Puerto Rico | Bayamon | 1990 | 65785 | ... | ... | ... | ... | ... | ... | ... |
| Puerto Rico | Ponce | 1990 | 54191 | ... | ... | ... | ... | ... | ... | ... |
| Puerto Rico | San Juan | 1990 | 150592 | 167979 | 164832 | 3147 | ... | ... | ... | ... |
| Uruguay | Montevideo | 1996 | 415038 | 441809 | ... | ... | ... | ... | 1209 | ... |
| Uruguay | Paysandu | 1996 | 21505 | ... | ... | ... | ... | ... | ... | ... |
| Uruguay | Rivera | 1996 | 18460 | ... | ... | ... | ... | ... | ... | ... |
| Uruguay | Salto | 1996 | 24651 | ... | ... | ... | ... | ... | ... | ... |
| **NORTHERN AMERICA** | | | | | | | | | | |
| Canada | Calgary | 1998 | 332700 | ... | ... | ... | ... | ... | ... | ... |
| Canada | Montreal | 1998 | 1450300 | ... | ... | ... | ... | ... | ... | ... |
| Canada | Ottawa | 1998 | 313200 | ... | ... | ... | ... | ... | ... | ... |
| Canada | Toronto | 1998 | 1656600 | ... | ... | ... | ... | ... | ... | ... |
| Greenland | Ilulisat | 1999 | 1677 | ... | ... | ... | ... | ... | ... | ... |
| Greenland | Nuuk | 1999 | 5563 | ... | ... | ... | ... | ... | ... | ... |
| Greenland | Qaqortoq | 1999 | 1417 | ... | ... | ... | ... | ... | ... | ... |
| Greenland | Sisimiut | 1999 | 1886 | ... | ... | ... | ... | ... | ... | ... |
| United States | Houston | 1991 | 1264200 | ... | ... | ... | ... | ... | ... | ... |
| United States | Los Angeles | 1995 | 2947500 | ... | ... | ... | ... | ... | ... | ... |
| United States | New York | 1991 | 4156100 | ... | ... | ... | ... | ... | ... | ... |
| United States | Washington, DC | 1993 | 1519200 | 1642400 | 1611100 | 31300 | ... | ... | ... | ... |
| **OCEANIA** | | | | | | | | | | |
| Australia | Adelaide | 1996 | 440271 | ... | ... | ... | ... | ... | ... | ... |
| Australia | Sydney | 1996 | ... | 1428888 | 1381804 | ... | 6515 | ... | ... | 40569 |
| Guam | Dededo | 1990 | 6963 | 7541 | ... | ... | ... | ... | ... | ... |
| Guam | Santa Rita | 1990 | 2287 | ... | ... | ... | ... | ... | ... | ... |
| Guam | Tamuning | 1990 | 4982 | ... | ... | ... | ... | ... | ... | ... |
| Guam | Yigo | 1990 | 3370 | ... | ... | ... | ... | ... | ... | ... |

**Source:** United Nations, Human Settlements Statistics Questionnaire 1999.
For sources and footnotes, refer to technical notes.

## TABLE B.5

## Occupied Housing Units by Number of Rooms and by Number of Occupants, Selected Cities

| | | | | Distribution of housing units by number of rooms | | | | | Distribution of occupants by size of housing units | | | | | |
|---|---|---|---|---|---|---|---|---|---|---|---|---|---|---|---|
| | | | Total occupied housing units | 1 room (%) | 2 room (%) | 3 room (%) | 4 room (%) | 5+ room (%) | Total number of occupants | 1 room (%) | 2 room (%) | 3 room (%) | 4 room (%) | 5+ room (%) | Average persons |
| **AFRICA** | | | | | | | | | | | | | | | |
| Burkina Faso | Bobo Dioulasso | 1991 | 4230 | ... | ... | ... | ... | ... | 268926 | ... | ... | ... | ... | ... | 6.4 |
| Burkina Faso | Koudougou | 1991 | 7664 | ... | ... | ... | ... | ... | 58838 | ... | ... | ... | ... | ... | 7.7 |
| Burkina Faso | Ouagadougou | 1991 | 101714 | ... | ... | ... | ... | ... | 634479 | ... | ... | ... | ... | ... | 6.2 |
| Burkina Faso | Ouahigouya | 1991 | 6963 | ... | ... | ... | ... | ... | 55133 | ... | ... | ... | ... | ... | 7.9 |
| Central African Republic | Bangui | | ... | ... | ... | ... | ... | ... | 6554 | ... | ... | ... | ... | ... | |
| Egypt | Alexandria | 1996 | 799755 | 6.8 | 12.6 | 38.2 | 30.8 | 11.6 | 3321844 | 5.7 | 12.4 | 38.5 | 31.4 | 12.0 | 4.2 |
| Egypt | Cairo | 1996 | 1657081 | 8.2 | 11.4 | 36.8 | 32.8 | 10.8 | 6735172 | 7.0 | 11.5 | 37.3 | 33.4 | 10.8 | 4.1 |
| Egypt | Giza | 1996 | 534180 | 5.4 | 9.0 | 39.0 | 36.7 | 9.8 | 2203688 | 4.7 | 9.0 | 39.5 | 37.1 | 9.7 | 4.1 |
| Egypt | Shubra-El-Khema | 1996 | 192448 | 6.8 | 10.4 | 44.3 | 34.6 | 3.9 | 869853 | 5.6 | 10.1 | 44.8 | 35.0 | 4.5 | 4.5 |
| Gambia | Banjul | 1993 | 7032 | 16.2 | 12.4 | 11.3 | 10.0 | 50.1 | 40550 | 2.8 | 4.3 | 5.9 | 7.0 | 80.1 | 5.8 |
| Gambia | Kanifing | 1993 | 31426 | 10.0 | 9.6 | 9.5 | 9.6 | 31.3 | 225281 | 1.4 | 2.7 | 4.0 | 5.4 | 27.7 | 7.2 |
| Lesotho | Maseru | 1996 | 83961 | ... | ... | ... | ... | ... | ... | ... | ... | ... | ... | ... | ... |
| Libyan Arab Jamahiriya | Bengazi | 1995 | 101694 | 3.0 | 8.8 | 34.3 | 34.8 | 17.0 | 116282 | 1.9 | 6.0 | 7.3 | 10.7 | 58.1 | 1.1 |
| Libyan Arab Jamahiriya | Misurata | 1995 | 66908 | 1.3 | 6.1 | 24.8 | 52.2 | 13.3 | 92157 | 2.6 | 4.6 | 4.5 | 5.4 | 50.8 | 1.4 |
| Libyan Arab Jamahiriya | Tripoli | 1995 | 150578 | 2.6 | 9.9 | 4.1 | 55.0 | 23.4 | 258874 | 5.8 | 5.3 | 6.2 | 7.6 | 49.9 | 1.7 |
| Libyan Arab Jamahiriya | Zawia | 1995 | 78599 | 2.2 | 7.3 | 24.9 | 47.3 | 12.8 | 101060 | 6.0 | 6.0 | 6.0 | 6.5 | 47.9 | 1.3 |
| Mauritius | Port-Louis | 1990 | 28743 | 9.3 | 22.5 | 20.9 | 24.4 | 22.9 | 132229 | 5.6 | 18.7 | 20.4 | 25.8 | 29.5 | 4.6 |
| South Africa | Cape Town | 1996 | 184703 | 4.0 | 5.7 | 10.1 | 24.3 | 55.0 | ... | ... | ... | ... | ... | ... | ... |
| South Africa | Durban | 1996 | 566120 | 8.4 | 7.8 | 10.5 | 20.9 | 51.4 | ... | ... | ... | ... | ... | ... | ... |
| South Africa | Johannesburg | 1996 | 2203960 | 9.4 | 7.2 | 8.9 | 18.7 | 53.7 | ... | ... | ... | ... | ... | ... | ... |
| South Africa | Pretoria | 1996 | 692348 | 8.0 | 5.6 | 6.7 | 17.8 | 59.3 | ... | ... | ... | ... | ... | ... | ... |
| **ASIA** | | | | | | | | | | | | | | | |
| Azerbaijan | Baku | 1998 | 467432 | 16.6 | 42.6 | 32.7 | 8.0 | ... | 1721372 | 9.5 | 36.5 | 41.2 | 12.8 | ... | 3.7 |
| Azerbaijan | Giandja | 1998 | 62441 | 28.4 | 38.0 | 23.9 | 9.7 | ... | 279043 | 18.9 | 35.4 | 30.5 | 15.2 | ... | 4.5 |
| Azerbaijan | Mingecheviz | 1998 | 19894 | 13.4 | 38.1 | 34.0 | 14.6 | ... | 86294 | 6.5 | 30.2 | 37.2 | 26.1 | ... | 4.3 |
| Azerbaijan | Sumgait | 1998 | 76568 | 23.9 | 38.3 | 33.2 | 3.3 | 1.3 | 320731 | 15.1 | 39.1 | 40.8 | 5.0 | ... | 4.2 |
| Cambodia | Bat Dambang | 1998 | 134828 | 74.1 | 21.9 | 2.9 | 0.7 | 0.3 | 144833 | ... | ... | ... | ... | ... | 1.1 |
| Cambodia | Kampong Cham | 1998 | 287254 | 87.7 | 10.3 | 1.5 | 0.3 | 0.1 | 305622 | ... | ... | ... | ... | ... | 1.1 |
| Cambodia | Phnom Penh | 1998 | 116418 | 63.7 | 21.6 | 8.9 | 3.1 | 2.7 | 163540 | ... | ... | ... | ... | ... | 1.4 |
| Cambodia | Siem Riab | 1998 | 119468 | 73.1 | 23.9 | 2.0 | 0.5 | 0.4 | 123809 | ... | ... | ... | ... | ... | 1.0 |
| Cyprus | Larnaka | 1992 | 18260 | 0.5 | 3.8 | 5.9 | 21.2 | 68.5 | 59832 | 0.2 | 1.6 | 3.2 | 17.1 | 77.6 | 3.3 |
| Cyprus | Limassol | 1992 | 41614 | 0.5 | 3.0 | 8.6 | 17.2 | 70.8 | 135469 | 0.2 | 1.4 | 5.2 | 14.5 | 78.6 | 3.3 |
| Cyprus | Nicosia | 1992 | 54668 | 0.4 | 2.6 | 6.0 | 14.7 | 76.3 | 175310 | 0.1 | 1.2 | 3.1 | 11.9 | 83.6 | 3.2 |
| Cyprus | Patos | 1992 | 9770 | 1.1 | 4.7 | 8.7 | 16.8 | 68.7 | 32251 | 0.4 | 2.4 | 5.5 | 14.2 | 77.4 | 3.3 |
| Israel | Haifa | 1995 | 149185 | 7.9 | 26.9 | 39.6 | 17.8 | 7.9 | ... | ... | ... | ... | ... | ... | ... |
| Israel | Jerusalem | 1995 | 158055 | 8.8 | 21.7 | 36.1 | 23.9 | 9.5 | ... | ... | ... | ... | ... | ... | ... |
| Israel | Rishon L'zion | 1995 | 47820 | 1.5 | 8.6 | 33.4 | 36.9 | 19.6 | ... | ... | ... | ... | ... | ... | ... |
| Israel | Tel Aviv–Jaffa | 1995 | 92435 | 3.9 | 19.5 | 41.2 | 23.8 | 11.6 | ... | ... | ... | ... | ... | ... | ... |
| Japan | Osaka | 1993 | 1038200 | 12.3 | 17.2 | 20.0 | 24.2 | 24.3 | ... | ... | ... | ... | ... | ... | ... |
| Japan | Sapporo | 1993 | 660800 | 7.5 | 12.6 | 20.8 | 17.7 | 37.7 | ... | ... | ... | ... | ... | ... | ... |
| Japan | Tokyo | 1993 | 3300100 | 15.9 | 17.7 | 20.4 | 18.1 | 21.1 | ... | ... | ... | ... | ... | ... | ... |
| Japan | Yokohama | 1993 | 1111600 | 8.4 | 12.0 | 19.1 | 25.9 | 33.2 | ... | ... | ... | ... | ... | ... | ... |
| Republic of Korea | Pusan | 1995 | 659924 | 1.1 | 5.7 | 21.9 | 35.3 | 36.0 | 3712976 | ... | ... | ... | ... | ... | 5.6 |
| Republic of Korea | Seoul | 1995 | 1688111 | 0.7 | 4.3 | 24.1 | 35.0 | 35.8 | 9973958 | ... | ... | ... | ... | ... | 5.9 |
| Republic of Korea | Suweon | 1995 | 130275 | 0.5 | 2.0 | 26.8 | 41.4 | 29.4 | 128420 | ... | ... | ... | ... | ... | 1.0 |
| Republic of Korea | Taegu | 1995 | 425930 | 0.8 | 4.0 | 19.6 | 30.2 | 45.4 | 2384635 | ... | ... | ... | ... | ... | 5.6 |
| Malaysia | Bandaraya Kuching City | 1991 | 66643 | ... | ... | ... | ... | ... | 367914 | ... | ... | ... | ... | ... | 5.5 |
| Malaysia | George Town | 1991 | 37945 | ... | ... | ... | ... | ... | 290362 | ... | ... | ... | ... | ... | 7.7 |
| Malaysia | Keningau | 1991 | 16912 | ... | ... | ... | ... | ... | 88285 | ... | ... | ... | ... | ... | 5.2 |
| Malaysia | Kota Kinabalu | 1991 | 35153 | ... | ... | ... | ... | ... | 207442 | ... | ... | ... | ... | ... | 5.9 |
| Malaysia | Majlis Perbandaran Ipoh | 1991 | 82061 | ... | ... | ... | ... | ... | 495175 | ... | ... | ... | ... | ... | 6.0 |
| Malaysia | Majlis Perbandaran Johor Bharu | 1991 | 66227 | ... | ... | ... | ... | ... | 317909 | ... | ... | ... | ... | ... | 4.8 |
| Malaysia | Miri | 1991 | 32671 | ... | ... | ... | ... | ... | 160133 | ... | ... | ... | ... | ... | 4.9 |
| Malaysia | Sandakan | 1991 | 38164 | ... | ... | ... | ... | ... | 222402 | ... | ... | ... | ... | ... | 5.8 |
| Malaysia | Sibu | 1991 | 31982 | ... | ... | ... | ... | ... | 169246 | ... | ... | ... | ... | ... | 5.3 |
| Malaysia | Tawau | 1991 | 44553 | ... | ... | ... | ... | ... | 243332 | ... | ... | ... | ... | ... | 5.5 |
| Malaysia | W.P Kuala Lumpur | 1991 | 237189 | ... | ... | ... | ... | ... | 1100945 | ... | ... | ... | ... | ... | 4.6 |
| Pakistan | Islamabad | 1998 | 86575 | 16.1 | 29.2 | 25.0 | 12.7 | 17.1 | 524359 | 11.7 | 28.6 | 25.4 | 13.9 | 20.2 | 6.1 |
| Syrian Arab Republic | Aleppo | 1994 | 458237 | 7.7 | 27.1 | 32.2 | 19.1 | 13.6 | 259053 | 5.2 | 18.2 | 37.3 | 21.3 | 18.0 | 0.6 |
| Syrian Arab Republic | Damascus | 1994 | 233859 | 5.6 | 19.3 | 28.4 | 23.6 | 22.4 | 1384017 | 3.8 | 16.4 | 27.2 | 24.2 | 27.7 | 5.9 |
| Syrian Arab Republic | Homs | 1994 | 179387 | 5.1 | 21.3 | 30.2 | 24.9 | 18.3 | 1205785 | 3.3 | 18.7 | 29.5 | 26.1 | 22.2 | 6.7 |
| Syrian Arab Republic | Lattakia | 1994 | 129784 | 7.2 | 20.8 | 31.7 | 24.5 | 15.7 | 741372 | 4.9 | 18.4 | 31.4 | 26.4 | 18.6 | 5.7 |
| Turkey | Adana | 1994 | 229680 | 1.8 | 12.6 | 53.9 | 28.5 | 3.0 | 1018248 | 1.4 | 12.3 | 54.0 | 28.4 | 0.4 | 4.4 |
| Turkey | Ankara | 1994 | 643500 | 0.3 | 8.2 | 35.6 | 52.1 | 3.8 | 2669550 | 0.4 | 7.2 | 35.2 | 53.0 | 4.2 | 4.1 |
| Turkey | Istanbul | 1994 | 1779870 | 0.6 | 9.5 | 47.2 | 36.5 | 5.8 | 7362804 | 0.6 | 9.1 | 45.7 | 37.1 | 3.0 | 4.1 |
| Turkey | Izmir | 1994 | 496980 | 0.8 | 11.4 | 42.3 | 40.9 | 3.3 | 1902831 | 0.7 | 12.1 | 41.6 | 39.7 | 2.0 | 3.8 |
| **EUROPE** | | | | | | | | | | | | | | | |
| Belgium | Antwerpen | 1991 | 96526 | 1.3 | 13.9 | 24.5 | 25.2 | 35.0 | 217112 | ... | ... | ... | ... | ... | 2.2 |
| Belgium | Bruxelles | 1991 | 394468 | 2.6 | 26.9 | 30.9 | 17.6 | 22.0 | 835465 | ... | ... | ... | ... | ... | 2.1 |
| Belgium | Charleroi | 1991 | 81044 | 2.1 | 11.3 | 25.7 | 30.7 | 30.2 | 188924 | ... | ... | ... | ... | ... | 2.3 |
| Belgium | Gent | 1991 | 207730 | 1.3 | 20.8 | 33.0 | 22.4 | 22.5 | 443479 | ... | ... | ... | ... | ... | 2.1 |
| Croatia | Osijek | 1991 | 36241 | ... | ... | ... | ... | ... | 103337 | 165.7 | 36.7 | 26.3 | 11.3 | 9.1 | |
| Croatia | Rijeka | 1991 | 55570 | ... | ... | ... | ... | ... | 164781 | 11.8 | 35.3 | 36.1 | 13.1 | 3.6 | |
| Croatia | Split | 1991 | 54215 | ... | ... | ... | ... | ... | 185493 | 10.7 | 39.9 | 37.3 | 9.7 | 2.7 | |
| Croatia | Zagreb | 1991 | 238542 | ... | ... | ... | ... | ... | 694889 | 16.4 | 41.5 | 26.1 | 9.7 | 6.3 | |
| Czech Republic | Praha | 1991 | 495804 | 28.9 | 31.2 | 30.8 | 6.7 | 2.4 | 1209206 | 18.6 | 29.1 | 39.1 | 9.5 | 3.6 | |
| Finland | Espoo | 1998 | 84386 | 10.5 | 27.8 | 26.3 | 20.6 | 13.7 | 201335 | 5.3 | 19.2 | 28.4 | 26.8 | 19.4 | |
| Finland | Helsinki | 1998 | 271794 | 23.4 | 36.7 | 21.9 | 11.6 | 5.8 | 523443 | 14.5 | 30.2 | 27.6 | 17.9 | 9.2 | |

# TABLE B.5

## continued

| | | | Total occupied housing units | Distribution of housing units by number of rooms | | | | | Total number of occupants | Distribution of occupants by size of housing units | | | | | Average persons |
|---|---|---|---|---|---|---|---|---|---|---|---|---|---|---|---|
| | | | | 1 room (%) | 2 room (%) | 3 room (%) | 4 room (%) | 5+ room (%) | | 1 room (%) | 2 room (%) | 3 room (%) | 4 room (%) | 5+ room (%) | |
| Finland | Tampere | 1998 | 92105 | 18.4 | 37.0 | 23.2 | 13.8 | 6.6 | 185796 | 10.9 | 29.5 | 27.9 | 20.2 | 10.6 | |
| Finland | Turku | 1998 | 86579 | 19.7 | 36.1 | 24.5 | 12.4 | 6.0 | 165042 | 12.3 | 29.4 | 25.8 | 18.3 | 9.3 | |
| France | Lyon | 1990 | 493008 | 7.9 | 17.2 | 27.1 | 27.6 | 20.2 | 1226368 | 3.8 | 10.3 | 23.1 | 32.9 | 30.0 | |
| France | Marseille | 1990 | 481172 | 7.6 | 16.1 | 33.0 | 28.6 | 14.8 | 1198376 | 3.8 | 10.0 | 29.6 | 34.5 | 22.0 | |
| France | Paris | 1990 | 3773848 | 13.0 | 22.4 | 28.4 | 21.3 | 14.9 | 9109496 | 7.1 | 15.5 | 27.8 | 27.1 | 22.5 | |
| France | Toulouse | 1990 | 264076 | 10.2 | 14.1 | 21.2 | 29.7 | 24.7 | 632484 | 4.9 | 8.5 | 17.5 | 34.0 | 35.1 | |
| Germany | Berlin | 1998 | 1692100 | ... | ... | ... | ... | ... | ... | ... | ... | ... | ... | ... | |
| Germany | Hamburg | 1998 | 819300 | ... | ... | ... | ... | ... | ... | ... | ... | ... | ... | ... | |
| Hungary | Budapest | 1990 | 775523 | 4.6 | 24.5 | 35.8 | 25.7 | 9.3 | 1951835 | 2.8 | 18.0 | 34.1 | 31.6 | 13.5 | |
| Hungary | Debrecen | 1990 | 73850 | 3.1 | 18.0 | 39.7 | 29.0 | 10.2 | 202003 | 1.8 | 13.2 | 37.3 | 34.1 | 13.7 | |
| Hungary | Miskolc | 1990 | 69463 | 3.7 | 18.2 | 43.0 | 28.3 | 6.8 | 188114 | 2.3 | 13.9 | 40.9 | 33.8 | 9.2 | |
| Hungary | Szeged | 1990 | 64734 | 2.1 | 13.4 | 45.1 | 28.4 | 11.1 | 167627 | 1.3 | 9.1 | 40.4 | 33.7 | 15.6 | |
| Lithuania | Kaunas | 1998 | 174147 | 17.9 | 42.8 | 25.7 | 9.9 | 3.7 | ... | ... | ... | ... | ... | ... | |
| Lithuania | Klaipeda | 1998 | 71130 | 23.2 | 40.7 | 29.7 | 5.4 | 0.9 | ... | ... | ... | ... | ... | ... | |
| Lithuania | Siauliai | 1998 | 52224 | 23.2 | 44.0 | 23.3 | 7.0 | 2.5 | ... | ... | ... | ... | ... | ... | |
| Lithuania | Vilnius | 1998 | 192566 | 23.0 | 37.7 | 31.6 | 5.5 | 2.3 | ... | ... | ... | ... | ... | ... | |
| The Netherlands | Amsterdam | 1998 | 398000 | 7.0 | 22.8 | 37.8 | 23.0 | 9.5 | 706100 | 4.0 | 16.2 | 35.0 | 29.7 | 15.1 | |
| The Netherlands | Rotterdam | 1998 | ... | ... | ... | ... | ... | ... | 555600 | 1.8 | 9.4 | 31.7 | 32.9 | 24.3 | |
| The Netherlands | 'S Gravenhage | 1998 | | ... | ... | ... | ... | ... | 437200 | 1.9 | 10.7 | 26.5 | 33.8 | 27.1 | |
| The Netherlands | Utrecht | 1998 | | ... | ... | ... | ... | ... | 218700 | 6.1 | 9.0 | 22.6 | 33.7 | 28.6 | |
| Norway | Bergen | 1990 | 93949 | 5.7 | 18.7 | 27.4 | 24.7 | 23.4 | 210227 | 3.3 | 12.1 | 28.2 | 33.7 | | |
| Norway | Oslo | 1990 | 244434 | 12.4 | 25.0 | 29.9 | 17.2 | 15.5 | 453243 | 7.5 | 18.4 | 28.3 | 21.6 | 24.2 | |
| Norway | Stavanger | 1990 | 42680 | 5.4 | 18.5 | 22.2 | 24.2 | 29.7 | 97393 | 3.2 | 11.5 | ... | 25.4 | 42.0 | |
| Norway | Trondheim | 1990 | 60407 | 6.7 | 19.5 | 24.8 | 24.7 | 24.4 | 136380 | 3.6 | 12.3 | ... | 28.2 | 34.7 | |
| Poland | Krakow | 1995 | 238760 | ... | 25.8 | 34.4 | 30.3 | 9.4 | 719520 | ... | 18.1 | 32.6 | 36.2 | 13.1 | |
| Poland | Lodz | 1995 | 314766 | ... | 31.5 | 43.2 | 20.0 | 5.3 | 811652 | ... | 24.9 | 42.6 | 24.2 | 8.3 | |
| Poland | Warszawa | 1995 | 594473 | ... | 25.6 | 35.8 | 30.2 | 8.4 | 1635557 | ... | 19.1 | 33.7 | 35.5 | 11.7 | |
| Poland | Wroclaw | 1995 | 204893 | ... | 22.5 | 31.6 | 27.9 | 17.7 | 618469 | ... | 16.4 | 28.7 | 31.4 | 23.5 | |
| Portugal | Amandora | 1991 | 41047 | 1.7 | 11.9 | 21.1 | 42.7 | 22.7 | 118470 | 1.2 | 10.1 | 19.7 | 43.2 | 25.8 | |
| Portugal | Lisboa | 1991 | 227580 | 2.1 | 10.0 | 19.0 | 27.9 | 40.9 | 629772 | 1.7 | 8.2 | 17.3 | 27.5 | 45.3 | |
| Portugal | Porto | 1991 | 94569 | 3.6 | 12.7 | 19.2 | 24.3 | 40.2 | 295288 | 2.7 | 10.1 | 17.6 | 24.3 | 45.3 | |
| Portugal | Setúbal | 1991 | 27105 | 1.2 | 8.9 | 21.1 | 33.5 | 35.1 | 81819 | 0.8 | 7.2 | 20.1 | 33.4 | 38.5 | |
| Slovakia | Bratislava | 1991 | 161494 | 17.5 | 25.5 | 40.6 | 14.1 | 2.3 | 442197 | ... | ... | ... | ... | ... | |
| Slovakia | Košice | 1991 | 79255 | 14.6 | 25.3 | 47.0 | 10.1 | 3.0 | 235160 | ... | ... | ... | ... | ... | |
| Sweden | Goteborg | 1990 | 209779 | 2.5 | 10.2 | 31.1 | 27.1 | 27.7 | 401370 | 1.4 | 5.9 | 21.6 | 28.5 | 38.9 | |
| Sweden | Malmo | 1990 | 120464 | 2.7 | 8.4 | 30.1 | 30.1 | 26.6 | 221673 | 1.6 | 5.0 | 21.3 | 31.6 | 37.5 | |
| Sweden | Stockholm | 1990 | 351314 | 6.5 | 16.9 | 29.3 | 25.1 | 21.5 | 614968 | 4.1 | 11.0 | 22.7 | 28.3 | 33.2 | |
| Sweden | Uppsala | 1990 | 72504 | 2.4 | 8.0 | 23.7 | 25.9 | 39.2 | 156824 | 1.2 | 4.2 | 14.9 | 24.1 | 50.4 | |
| United Kingdom | London | 1998 | 2954000 | 1.3 | 4.9 | 15.1 | 23.0 | 55.7 | 7050000 | 0.6 | 2.5 | 9.5 | 20.1 | 67.3 | |
| Yugoslavia | Kragujevac | 1991 | 57617 | 19.1 | 43.7 | 23.2 | 8.0 | 5.7 | 1786677 | ... | ... | ... | ... | ... | |
| Yugoslavia | Beograd | 1991 | 503077 | 23.2 | 41.4 | 22.6 | 7.3 | 5.2 | 1574822 | ... | ... | ... | ... | ... | |
| Yugoslavia | Nis | 1991 | 76706 | 9.5 | 38.8 | 35.9 | 9.9 | 5.9 | 247447 | ... | ... | ... | ... | ... | |
| Yugoslavia | Novi Sad | 1991 | 91475 | 20.0 | 39.8 | 25.1 | 8.3 | 6.5 | 264087 | ... | ... | ... | ... | ... | |
| **LATIN AMERICA** | | | | | | | | | | | | | | | |
| Argentina | Buenos Aires | 1991 | 3269316 | ... | ... | ... | ... | ... | 11298030 | ... | ... | ... | ... | ... | |
| Argentina | Cordoba | 1991 | 316195 | ... | ... | ... | ... | ... | 1208554 | ... | ... | ... | ... | ... | |
| Argentina | La Plata | 1991 | 190358 | ... | ... | ... | ... | ... | 642979 | ... | ... | ... | ... | ... | |
| Argentina | Rosario | 1991 | 326673 | ... | ... | ... | ... | ... | 1118905 | ... | ... | ... | ... | ... | |
| Bahamas | Gr Bahama | 1990 | 10388 | 7.7 | 20.7 | 21.8 | 19.7 | 21.4 | 40898 | 5.0 | 12.6 | 18.7 | ... | 25.4 | |
| Bahamas | Nassau | 1990 | 39864 | 6.8 | 13.2 | 27.0 | 22.6 | 21.9 | 172196 | 2.8 | 7.7 | 22.2 | 22.7 | 23.8 | |
| Brazil | Belo Horizonte | 1998 | 1045310 | 0.9 | 3.3 | 8.4 | 15.2 | 72.1 | 3978856 | 0.6 | 2.6 | 7.2 | 14.0 | 75.7 | |
| Brazil | Brasilia, Df | 1998 | 506538 | 2.4 | 5.6 | 7.7 | 14.4 | 69.9 | 1927737 | 1.4 | 4.5 | 6.7 | 12.4 | 75.0 | |
| Brazil | Rio De Janeiro | 1998 | 3167596 | 0.9 | 2.8 | 7.4 | 20.8 | 67.9 | 10382082 | 0.7 | 2.0 | 6.7 | 18.5 | 72.0 | |
| Brazil | Sao Paolo | 1998 | 4653683 | 0.8 | 5.0 | 16.2 | 19.4 | 58.5 | 17119420 | 0.6 | 4.3 | 14.5 | 18.9 | 61.6 | |
| Colombia | Barranquilla | 1993 | 201394 | 10.4 | 16.5 | 19.0 | 21.0 | 16.3 | ... | ... | ... | ... | ... | ... | ... |
| Colombia | Bogota | 1993 | 1255108 | 17.8 | 21.7 | 17.0 | 19.3 | 23.7 | 4934591 | 13.6 | 20.8 | 17.2 | 20.2 | 28.1 | |
| Colombia | Cali | 1993 | 404805 | 15.4 | 16.3 | 16.3 | 20.7 | 15.4 | ... | ... | ... | ... | ... | ... | |
| Colombia | Medellin | 1993 | 388688 | 9.0 | 14.5 | 17.3 | 20.3 | 21.3 | ... | ... | ... | ... | ... | ... | |
| Costa Rica | San Jose | 1997 | | ... | ... | ... | ... | ... | ... | ... | ... | ... | ... | ... | |
| Guatemala | Guatemala City | 1994 | 169915 | ... | ... | ... | ... | ... | ... | ... | ... | ... | ... | ... | |
| Guatemala | Mazatenango | 1994 | 6532 | ... | ... | ... | ... | ... | ... | ... | ... | ... | ... | ... | |
| Guatemala | Puerto Barrios | 1994 | 6710 | ... | ... | ... | ... | ... | ... | ... | ... | ... | ... | ... | |
| Guatemala | Quezaltenango | 1994 | 17293 | ... | ... | ... | ... | ... | ... | ... | ... | ... | ... | ... | |
| Mexico | Cuidad De Mexico | 1995 | 3136788 | 7.5 | 18.0 | 21.1 | 20.1 | 33.0 | 16784109 | ... | ... | ... | ... | 0.9 | |
| Mexico | Guadalajara | 1995 | 577019 | 3.3 | 12.5 | 24.1 | 24.7 | 35.4 | 3450306 | ... | ... | ... | ... | 0.7 | |
| Mexico | Monterrey | 1995 | 528651 | 6.6 | 12.8 | 17.7 | 21.9 | 41.0 | 2988081 | ... | ... | ... | ... | 0.9 | 5.7 |
| Mexico | Puebla | 1995 | 354210 | 8.1 | 18.8 | 21.1 | 19.0 | 32.7 | 2119129 | ... | ... | ... | ... | 0.7 | 6.0 |
| Nicaragua | Jinotepe | 1995 | 4395 | 12.2 | 30.6 | 24.7 | 16.0 | 16.5 | 25034 | 10.3 | 28.2 | 26.1 | 16.6 | 18.7 | 5.7 |
| Nicaragua | Leon | 1995 | 21906 | 29.7 | 31.3 | 20.9 | 10.5 | 7.6 | 123687 | 26.1 | 30.1 | 22.4 | 12.0 | 9.4 | 5.6 |
| Nicaragua | Managua | 1995 | 160811 | 29.7 | 28.9 | 21.6 | 12.0 | 8.0 | 862240 | 25.5 | 28.2 | 23.2 | 13.4 | 9.6 | 5.4 |
| Nicaragua | Matagalpa | 1995 | 10703 | 20.2 | 30.6 | 24.4 | 13.8 | 10.9 | 59349 | 17.6 | 28.8 | 25.2 | 15.6 | 12.8 | 5.5 |
| Panama | Colon | 1990 | 15471 | 55.8 | 25.5 | 12.1 | 3.8 | 2.8 | 53638 | ... | ... | ... | ... | ... | 3.5 |
| Panama | David | 1990 | 23741 | 12.7 | 17.0 | 26.4 | 24.6 | 19.3 | 101246 | ... | ... | ... | ... | ... | 4.3 |
| Panama | Panama | 1990 | 105409 | 21.4 | 20.2 | 21.0 | 20.3 | 17.1 | 402530 | ... | ... | ... | ... | ... | 3.8 |
| Panama | San Miguelito | 1990 | 15645 | 30.0 | 22.0 | 29.9 | 30.2 | 23.9 | 242850 | ... | ... | ... | ... | ... | 3.5 |
| Puerto Rico | Bayamon | 1990 | 65785 | 1.0 | 2.5 | 7.3 | 13.0 | 76.2 | 216438 | 0.5 | 1.5 | 6.0 | 11.5 | 80.4 | 3.3 |
| Puerto Rico | Carolina | 1990 | 54466 | 2.0 | 2.8 | 8.2 | 14.5 | 72.6 | 176099 | 1.0 | 1.9 | 6.4 | 12.8 | 77.9 | 3.2 |
| Puerto Rico | Ponce | 1990 | 54191 | 1.3 | 3.2 | 10.2 | 18.2 | 67.0 | 185217 | 0.7 | 2.1 | 8.0 | 16.7 | 72.5 | 3.4 |
| Puerto Rico | San Juan | 1990 | 150592 | 2.6 | 4.9 | 12.2 | 18.6 | 61.7 | 429112 | 1.3 | 3.2 | 9.0 | 17.1 | 69.3 | 2.8 |
| Uruguay | Montevideo | 1996 | 397689 | 8.9 | 20.9 | 34.0 | 21.0 | 15.2 | 1282277 | 7.3 | 17.6 | 32.7 | 23.0 | 19.4 | 3.2 |
| Uruguay | Paysandu | 1996 | 20561 | 10.7 | 17.0 | 30.7 | 23.6 | 17.9 | 73737 | 9.3 | 15.6 | 30.1 | 24.7 | 20.4 | 3.6 |

# TABLE B.5

## continued

| | | | | | | | | | | | | | | | |
|---|---|---|---|---|---|---|---|---|---|---|---|---|---|---|---|
| Uruguay | Rivera | 1996 | 18010 | 9.6 | 17.6 | 31.2 | 24.1 | 17.5 | 62391 | 7.7 | 15.7 | 30.9 | 25.7 | 20.0 | 3.5 |
| Uruguay | Salto | 1996 | 23411 | 8.9 | 15.0 | 32.7 | 26.1 | 17.3 | 92030 | 8.0 | 14.2 | 30.9 | 27.6 | 19.3 | 3.9 |
| **NORTHERN AMERICA** | | | | | | | | | | | | | | | |
| Bermuda | Hamilton | 1991 | 387 | 5.7 | 13.4 | 21.2 | 26.9 | 32.8 | 964 | 3.6 | 7.2 | 17.7 | 28.8 | 42.6 | 2.5 |
| Canada | Ottawa | 1996 | 385140 | 1.0 | 2.6 | 9.4 | 13.0 | 73.9 | 994110 | 0.5 | 1.4 | 5.3 | 9.6 | 83.0 | 2.6 |
| Greenland | Ilulisat | 1999 | 1413 | 9.4 | 21.0 | 23.4 | 22.9 | 4.5 | ... | ... | ... | ... | ... | ... | ... |
| Greenland | Nuuk | 1999 | 4871 | 11.2 | 22.2 | 23.4 | 20.8 | 9.1 | ... | ... | ... | ... | ... | ... | ... |
| Greenland | Qaqortoq | 1999 | 1208 | 13.2 | 20.9 | 17.4 | 16.5 | 6.1 | ... | ... | ... | ... | ... | ... | ... |
| Greenland | Sisimiut | 1999 | 1715 | 9.3 | 19.2 | 19.4 | 22.9 | 4.7 | ... | ... | ... | ... | ... | ... | ... |
| United States of America | Houston | 1991 | 1264200 | 0.2 | 0.4 | 10.9 | 18.5 | 70.1 | 3416800 | ... | ... | ... | ... | ... | 2.7 |
| United States of America | Los Angeles | 1995 | 2947500 | 1.4 | 3.2 | 14.6 | 22.6 | 58.2 | 8629600 | ... | ... | ... | ... | ... | 2.9 |
| United States of America | New York | 1991 | 4156100 | 1.8 | 4.4 | 19.7 | 22.1 | 52.1 | 10883900 | ... | ... | ... | ... | ... | 2.6 |
| United States of America | Washington, DC | 1993 | 1519200 | 0.8 | 1.4 | 8.8 | 13.8 | 75.2 | 3928100 | ... | ... | ... | ... | ... | 2.6 |
| **OCEANIA** | | | | | | | | | | | | | | | |
| Guam | Yigo | 1990 | 3370 | 1.1 | 2.0 | 4.9 | 11.7 | 80.3 | 13081 | ... | ... | ... | ... | ... | 3.9 |
| Guam | Dededo | 1990 | 6963 | 1.0 | 2.7 | 6.9 | 16.0 | 73.4 | 30933 | ... | ... | ... | ... | ... | 4.4 |
| Guam | Tamuning | 1990 | 4982 | 2.2 | 5.3 | 14.8 | 30.4 | 47.4 | 15076 | ... | ... | ... | ... | ... | 3.0 |
| Tonga | Nuku'alofa | 1996 | 3665 | ... | ... | ... | ... | 0.0 | 22400 | ... | ... | ... | ... | ... | 6.1 |

**Source:** United Nations, Human Settlements Statistics Questionnaire 1999.
For sources and footnotes, refer to technical notes.

# TABLE B.6

## Housing Units by Water and Toilet Facilities, Selected Cities

| | | | Water supply system in housing unit | | | | | | | Toilet installation | | | | | | |
|---|---|---|---|---|---|---|---|---|---|---|---|---|---|---|---|---|
| | | | Piped water inside | | | | | Other | Not stated | | Toilet inside | | | With toilet ouside | Other | Not stated |
| | | | Number of housing units | Total (%) | From community source (%) | From private source (%) | Outside but within 200 metres (%) | (%) | (%) | Number of housing units | Total (%) | Flush toilet (%) | Non-flush toilet (%) | (%) | (%) | (%) |
| **AFRICA** | | | | | | | | | | | | | | | | |
| Botswana | Francistown | 1996 | 16789 | 100.0 | 71.7 | 28.3 | ... | ... | ... | 16789 | ... | 21.0 | ... | 54.0 | ... | ... |
| Botswana | Gaberone | 1996 | 36639 | 100.0 | 56.5 | 43.5 | ... | ... | ... | 36639 | ... | 33.5 | ... | 63.5 | ... | ... |
| Burkina Faso | Bobo Dioulasso | 1991 | 42205 | 47.6 | ... | ... | ... | 52.4 | ... | 42205 | 28.1 | 4.7 | 23.4 | ... | 71.9 | ... |
| Burkina Faso | Koudougou | 1991 | 7622 | 38.4 | ... | ... | ... | 61.6 | ... | 7622 | 61.7 | 3.0 | 58.8 | ... | 38.3 | ... |
| Burkina Faso | Ouagadougou | 1991 | 98206 | 32.7 | ... | ... | ... | 67.3 | ... | 98206 | 58.8 | 3.4 | 55.5 | ... | 41.2 | ... |
| Burkina Faso | Ouahigouya | 1991 | 7585 | 11.5 | ... | ... | ... | 88.5 | ... | 7585 | 50.6 | 1.0 | 49.6 | ... | 49.4 | ... |
| Egypt | Alexandria | 1996 | 799755 | 99.9 | 92.7 | ... | 7.2 | 0.1 | ... | 799755 | 92.4 | ... | ... | 10.2 | 97.5 | ... |
| Egypt | Cairo | 1996 | 1657081 | 97.2 | 87.3 | ... | 9.9 | 2.8 | ... | 1657081 | 94.7 | ... | ... | 9.8 | 95.5 | ... |
| Egypt | Giza | 1996 | 534180 | 93.5 | 85.4 | ... | 8.2 | 6.5 | ... | 534180 | 95.8 | ... | ... | 6.7 | 97.5 | ... |
| Egypt | Shubra-El-Khema | 1996 | 192448 | 91.1 | 82.2 | ... | 8.8 | 8.9 | ... | 192448 | 92.1 | ... | ... | 9.0 | 98.9 | ... |
| Gambia | Banjul | 1990 | 10577 | 50.4 | ... | ... | 48.1 | 0.7 | 0.8 | 7032 | 90.4 | 33.9 | 56.5 | 7.4 | 0.9 | 1.3 |
| Gambia | Kanifing | 1990 | 31426 | 37.4 | ... | ... | 18.4 | 41.6 | 2.6 | 31426 | 80.1 | 17.4 | 62.7 | 13.9 | 2.1 | 3.9 |
| Kenya[17] | Mombasa | 1989 | ... | [4]92.3 | ... | ... | ... | 7.7 | ... | ... | 10.0 | ... | ... | [18]68.6 | 21.4 | ... |
| Kenya[17] | Nairobi | 1989 | ... | [4]96.3 | ... | ... | ... | 3.7 | ... | ... | 50.3 | ... | ... | [18]39.4 | 10.3 | ... |
| Libyan Arab Jamahiriya | Bengazi | 1995 | 64671 | 95.4 | 91.0 | 4.4 | ... | 3.4 | 1.1 | 101694 | 96.8 | 96.8 | ... | 1.3 | ... | 2.0 |
| Libyan Arab Jamahiriya | Misurata | 1995 | 58224 | 38.7 | 80.7 | 9.6 | ... | 9.7 | 0.0 | 66908 | 94.2 | 94.2 | ... | 3.7 | ... | 2.2 |
| Libyan Arab Jamahiriya | Tripoli | 1995 | 162084 | 97.6 | 75.4 | 22.1 | ... | 1.7 | 0.7 | 206292 | 95.1 | 95.1 | ... | 1.2 | ... | 3.6 |
| Libyan Arab Jamahiriya | Zawia | 1995 | 72414 | 84.4 | 57.4 | 27.0 | ... | 14.7 | 0.9 | 78594 | 91.0 | 91.0 | ... | 3.5 | ... | 5.4 |
| Mauritius | Port-Louis | 1990 | 30780 | 52.1 | 52.1 | ... | [10]45.6 | [11]2.3 | 0.0 | 30780 | 99.4 | 84.5 | 15.5 | ... | 0.6 | 1.0 |
| Senegal | Dakar | 1994 | 183533 | 83.4 | [12]22.6 | [13]60.8 | [14]9.2 | [15]7.4 | ... | 183533 | 90.0 | 16.8 | 73.2 | 2.3 | 7.7 | ... |
| Seychelles | Port Victoria | 1997 | 5815 | 93.5 | ... | ... | 4.2 | 2.2 | | 5815 | 92.3 | 92.3 | – | 3.6 | 1.3 | 2.8 |
| South Africa | Cape Town | 1996 | 60271 | 95.0 | ... | ... | [16]4.6 | 0.1 | 0.3 | 60268 | 96.3 | 96.3 | 2.1 | ... | 1.2 | 0.3 |
| South Africa | Durban | 1996 | 164740 | 85.7 | ... | ... | [16]12.9 | 1.1 | 0.3 | 164740 | 85.9 | 85.9 | 11.9 | ... | 2.0 | 0.3 |
| South Africa | Johannesburg | 1996 | 228135 | 86.0 | ... | ... | [16]12.8 | 0.2 | 1.0 | 228140 | 92.2 | 92.2 | 5.9 | ... | 1.0 | 0.9 |
| South Africa | Pretoria | 1996 | 214633 | 86.8 | ... | ... | [16]12.5 | 0.2 | 0.5 | 214634 | 92.3 | 92.3 | 6.0 | ... | 1.2 | 0.5 |
| Zimbabwe | Bulawayo | 1997 | 162281 | ... | ... | ... | ... | ... | ... | 162281 | ... | ... | ... | ... | ... | ... |
| Zimbabwe | Harare | 1997 | 453037 | ... | ... | ... | ... | ... | ... | 453037 | ... | ... | ... | ... | ... | ... |
| **ASIA** | | | | | | | | | | | | | | | | |
| Azerbaijan | Baku | 1998 | 463713 | ... | ... | ... | ... | ... | ... | 324417 | 100.0 | ... | ... | ... | ... | ... |
| Azerbaijan | Giandja | 1998 | 61257 | ... | ... | ... | ... | ... | ... | 60804 | 100.0 | ... | ... | ... | ... | ... |
| Azerbaijan | Mingecheviz | 1998 | 19894 | ... | ... | ... | ... | ... | ... | 10894 | 100.0 | ... | ... | ... | ... | ... |
| Azerbaijan | Sumgait | 1998 | 76543 | ... | ... | ... | ... | ... | ... | 75546 | 100.0 | ... | ... | ... | ... | ... |
| Cyprus | Larnaka | 1992 | 18467 | 96.6 | 96.6 | – | 1.9 | [1]0.5 | 1.0 | 18467 | 94.8 | 94.8 | – | 3.6 | [9]0.6 | 1.0 |
| Cyprus | Limassol | 1992 | 41973 | 98.1 | 98.1 | – | 1.3 | [1]0.6 | 0.1 | 41973 | 95.3 | 95.3 | – | 3.4 | [9]1.2 | 0.1 |
| Cyprus | Nicosia | 1992 | 55006 | 99.1 | 99.1 | – | 0.5 | [1]0.3 | 0.2 | 55006 | 98.0 | 98.0 | – | 1.5 | [9]0.4 | 0.1 |
| Cyprus | Patos | 1992 | 9874 | 95.3 | 95.3 | – | 3.7 | [1]0.8 | 0.2 | 9874 | 92.7 | 92.7 | – | 5.9 | [9]1.3 | 0.2 |
| Georgia | Tbilisi | 1989 | 1182012 | 98.0 | ... | ... | ... | ... | ... | ... | ... | ... | ... | ... | ... | ... |
| Japan | Osaka | 1993 | ... | ... | ... | ... | ... | ... | ... | 1038200 | 94.4 | 94.3 | 0.0 | 3.6 | 2.0 | ... |
| Japan | Sapporo | 1993 | ... | ... | ... | ... | ... | ... | ... | 660800 | 95.1 | 94.1 | 1.1 | 1.2 | 3.6 | ... |
| Japan | Tokyo | 1993 | ... | ... | ... | ... | ... | ... | ... | 3300100 | 90.3 | 89.7 | 0.6 | 3.0 | 6.7 | ... |
| Japan | Yokohama | 1993 | ... | ... | ... | ... | ... | ... | ... | 1111600 | 97.9 | 96.1 | 1.7 | 0.7 | 1.4 | ... |
| Malaysia | Bandaraya Kuching City | 1991 | 68344 | 81.7 | 81.7 | ... | 10.5 | 7.8 | ... | 68344 | 87.7 | 60.7 | 27.0 | 9.6 | ... | 2.6 |
| Malaysia | George Town | 1991 | 43152 | 98.4 | 98.4 | ... | 1.3 | 0.4 | ... | 43152 | 96.0 | 74.5 | 21.5 | 3.7 | ... | 0.3 |
| Malaysia | Keningau | 1991 | 17486 | 34.6 | 34.6 | ... | 30.8 | 34.5 | ... | 17486 | 42.0 | 19.4 | 22.6 | 48.7 | ... | 9.3 |
| Malaysia | Kota Kinabalu | 1991 | 38740 | 73.4 | 73.4 | ... | 17.2 | 9.4 | ... | 38740 | 69.2 | 58.8 | 10.4 | 27.7 | ... | 3.1 |
| Malaysia | Majlis Perbandaran Ipoh | 1991 | 84762 | 93.7 | 93.7 | ... | 3.0 | 3.3 | ... | 84762 | 95.1 | 82.5 | 12.6 | 4.6 | ... | 0.3 |
| Malaysia | Majlis Perbandaran Johor Bharu | 1991 | 69612 | 91.5 | 91.5 | ... | 4.9 | 3.6 | ... | 69612 | 98.2 | 68.7 | 29.6 | 1.6 | ... | 0.2 |
| Malaysia | Miri | 1991 | 33284 | 66.6 | 66.6 | ... | 9.6 | 23.8 | | 33284 | 72.8 | 50.5 | 22.4 | 23.6 | ... | 3.6 |
| Malaysia | Sandakan | 1991 | 40367 | 50.1 | 50.1 | ... | 25.1 | 24.8 | ... | 40367 | 42.8 | 35.4 | 7.4 | 52.2 | ... | 5.0 |
| Malaysia | Sibu | 1991 | 34658 | 74.0 | 74.0 | ... | 10.2 | 15.8 | ... | 34658 | 80.1 | 64.8 | 15.3 | 15.1 | ... | 4.8 |
| Malaysia | Tawau | 1991 | 48051 | 51.0 | 51.0 | ... | 13.3 | 35.7 | ... | 48051 | 51.2 | 35.9 | 15.2 | 35.6 | ... | 13.2 |
| Malaysia | W.P Kuala Lumpur | 1991 | 242380 | 94.4 | 94.4 | ... | 4.3 | 1.3 | ... | 242380 | 97.8 | 81.7 | 16.2 | 1.9 | ... | 0.3 |
| Pakistan | Islamabad | 1998 | 86575 | 75.2 | 75.2 | – | 6.8 | 18.0 | ... | ... | ... | ... | ... | ... | ... | ... |
| Republic of Korea | Pusan | 1995 | 993375 | 97.3 | 91.7 | 5.6 | ... | 0.7 | 2.0 | 1079417 | 98.9 | 78.9 | 20.0 | 1.1 | ... | ... |
| Republic of Korea | Seoul | 1995 | 2814845 | 98.0 | 95.6 | 2.4 | ... | 0.1 | 1.9 | 2965794 | 99.1 | 91.0 | 8.1 | 0.9 | ... | ... |
| Republic of Korea | Suweon | 1995 | 171605 | 99.1 | 84.6 | 14.5 | ... | 0.1 | 0.8 | 216432 | 99.8 | 84.6 | 15.2 | 0.2 | ... | ... |
| Republic of Korea | Taegu | 1995 | 597150 | 99.0 | 95.7 | 3.3 | ... | 0.3 | 0.7 | 703464 | 99.6 | 74.5 | 25.2 | 0.4 | ... | ... |
| Syrian Arab Republic | Aleppo | 1994 | 458237 | 89.2 | 71.0 | 18.2 | 1.3 | 9.5 | 0.0 | ... | ... | ... | ... | ... | ... | ... |
| Syrian Arab Republic | Damascus | 1994 | 233859 | 98.4 | 94.8 | 3.6 | 0.1 | 1.5 | 0.0 | ... | ... | ... | ... | ... | ... | ... |
| Syrian Arab Republic | Homs | 1994 | 179387 | 95.0 | 75.8 | 19.1 | 1.2 | 3.9 | 0.0 | ... | ... | ... | ... | ... | ... | ... |
| Syrian Arab Republic | Lattakia | 1994 | 129784 | 84.5 | 68.7 | 15.8 | 4.2 | 11.3 | 0.0 | ... | ... | ... | ... | ... | ... | ... |
| Turkey | Adana | 1994 | 229680 | 99.7 | ... | ... | ... | 0.3 | ... | 231420 | 72.5 | ... | ... | 27.4 | 0.2 | ... |
| Turkey | Ankara | 1994 | 643500 | 97.0 | ... | ... | ... | 3.0 | | 650325 | 92.2 | ... | ... | 7.8 | – | ... |
| Turkey | Istanbul | 1994 | 1779870 | 96.6 | ... | ... | ... | 3.4 | | 1779870 | 99.9 | ... | ... | 0.1 | – | ... |
| Turkey | Izmir | 1994 | 496980 | 98.0 | ... | ... | ... | 2.0 | | 502251 | 87.3 | ... | ... | 12.7 | – | ... |
| **EUROPE** | | | | | | | | | | | | | | | | |
| Belgium | Antwerpen | 1991 | 207730 | 100.0 | 100.0 | ... | ... | ... | ... | 207730 | 98.2 | 98.2 | ... | ... | ... | ... |
| Belgium | Bruxelles | 1991 | 394468 | 99.8 | 99.8 | ... | ... | ... | ... | 394468 | 94.0 | 94.0 | ... | ... | ... | ... |
| Belgium | Charleroi | 1991 | 81044 | 99.8 | 99.8 | ... | ... | ... | ... | 81044 | 92.1 | 92.1 | ... | ... | ... | ... |
| Belgium | Gent | 1991 | 96526 | 99.7 | 99.7 | ... | ... | ... | ... | 96526 | 90.8 | 90.8 | ... | ... | ... | ... |
| Czech Republic | Brno | 1991 | 165622 | 99.5 | ... | ... | [2]0.2 | 0.2 | 0.0 | 165622 | 95.7 | 94.6 | 1.1 | 4.3 | ... | 0.0 |
| Czech Republic | Ostrava | 1991 | 133434 | 99.8 | ... | ... | [2]0.1 | 0.0 | 0.1 | 133434 | 97.2 | 96.4 | 0.8 | 2.7 | ... | 0.1 |
| Czech Republic | Plzen | 1991 | 72675 | 98.1 | ... | ... | [2]1.6 | 0.3 | 0.0 | 72675 | 94.2 | 92.9 | 1.2 | 5.7 | ... | 0.1 |
| Czech Republic | Praha | 1991 | 545781 | 99.1 | ... | ... | [2]0.6 | 0.2 | 0.0 | 545781 | 94.3 | 93.7 | 0.6 | 5.6 | ... | 0.1 |

# TABLE B.6

## continued

| Country | City | Year | | | | | | | | | | | | | | |
|---|---|---|---|---|---|---|---|---|---|---|---|---|---|---|---|---|
| Finland | Espoo | 1998 | ³88640 | 98.7 | ... | ... | ... | ... | ... | 88640 | 97.6 | ... | ... | ... | ... | ... |
| Finland | Helsinki | 1998 | ³290128 | 99.8 | ... | ... | ... | ... | ... | 290128 | 98.9 | ... | ... | ... | ... | ... |
| Finland | Tampere | 1998 | ³100730 | 99.4 | ... | ... | ... | ... | ... | 100119 | 99.0 | ... | ... | ... | ... | ... |
| Finland | Turku | 1998 | ³96542 | 98.8 | ... | ... | ... | ... | ... | 96542 | 97.5 | ... | ... | ... | ... | ... |
| France | Lyon | 1990 | ... | ... | ... | ... | ... | ... | ... | 493008 | 96.4 | ... | ... | ... | ... | ... |
| France | Marseille | 1990 | ... | ... | ... | ... | ... | ... | ... | 481172 | 94.9 | ... | ... | ... | ... | ... |
| France | Paris | 1990 | ... | ... | ... | ... | ... | ... | ... | 3773848 | 93.2 | ... | ... | 6.8 | ... | ... |
| France | Toulouse | 1990 | ... | ... | ... | ... | ... | ... | ... | 264076 | 96.1 | ... | ... | ... | ... | ... |
| Germany | Berlin | 1998 | 1718900 | 100.0 | ... | ... | ... | ... | ... | ... | ... | ... | ... | ... | ... | ... |
| Germany | Hamburg | 1998 | 835900 | 100.0 | ... | ... | ... | ... | ... | ... | ... | ... | ... | ... | ... | ... |
| Hungary | Budapest | 1996 | 815489 | 99.0 | 99.8 | 0.2 | ... | ... | ... | 815489 | ... | 100.0 | ... | ... | ... | |
| Ireland | Cork | 1991 | 75142 | 100.0 | 100.0 | – | – | – | – | 75158 | 99.9 | 99.9 | 0.0 | ... | 0.0 | 0.0 |
| Ireland | Dublin | 1991 | 1658598 | 100.0 | 100.0 | – | – | – | – | 309422 | 98.5 | 98.5 | 0.0 | ... | 0.0 | 1.5 |
| Ireland | Galway | 1991 | 28540 | 99.9 | 99.9 | – | – | – | 0.1 | 28515 | 99.2 | 99.2 | 0.0 | ... | 0.1 | 0.6 |
| Ireland | Limerick | 1991 | 30890 | 99.9 | 99.9 | – | – | – | 0.1 | 30910 | 99.1 | 99.1 | 0.0 | ... | 0.0 | 0.8 |
| Latvia | Daugavpils | 1998 | 17941 | ... | ... | ... | ... | ... | ... | ... | ... | ... | ... | ... | ... | ... |
| Latvia | Júrmala | 1998 | 5255 | ... | ... | ... | ... | ... | ... | ... | ... | ... | ... | ... | ... | ... |
| Latvia | Liepája | 1998 | 12607 | ... | ... | ... | ... | ... | ... | ... | ... | ... | ... | ... | ... | ... |
| Latvia | Ríga | 1998 | 101287 | ... | ... | ... | ... | ... | ... | ... | ... | ... | ... | ... | ... | ... |
| Lithuania | Kaunas | 1999 | ⁵174147 | 96.3 | ... | ... | ... | ... | ... | 174147 | 95.9 | ... | ... | ... | ... | ... |
| Lithuania | Klaipeda | 1999 | ⁵71130 | 98.0 | ... | ... | ... | ... | ... | 71130 | 97.8 | ... | ... | ... | ... | ... |
| Lithuania | Siauliai | 1999 | ⁵52224 | 91.6 | ... | ... | ... | ... | ... | 52224 | 91.5 | ... | ... | ... | ... | ... |
| Lithuania | Vilnius | 1999 | ⁵192566 | 94.9 | ... | ... | ... | ... | ... | 192566 | 94.8 | ... | ... | ... | ... | ... |
| Malta | Valletta | 1995 | ... | ... | ... | ... | ... | ... | ... | 2746 | 94.6 | 89.6 | 5.0 | 5.4 | ... | ... |
| The Netherlands[6,7] | Amsterdam | 1993 | 401500 | 100.0 | 100.0 | ... | ... | ... | ... | 401500 | 100.0 | 100.0 | ... | ... | ... | ... |
| The Netherlands[6,7] | Rotterdam | 1993 | 285700 | 100.0 | 100.0 | ... | ... | ... | ... | 285700 | 100.0 | 100.0 | ... | ... | ... | ... |
| The Netherlands[6,7] | 'S Gravenhage | 1993 | 226400 | 100.0 | 100.0 | ... | ... | ... | ... | 226400 | 100.0 | 100.0 | ... | ... | ... | ... |
| The Netherlands[6,7] | Utrecht | 1993 | 122100 | 100.0 | 100.0 | ... | ... | ... | ... | 122100 | 100.0 | 100.0 | ... | ... | ... | ... |
| Norway | Bergen | 1990 | ... | ... | ... | ... | ... | ... | ... | 93949 | 100.0 | 97.1 | 2.9 | ... | ... | ... |
| Norway | Oslo | 1990 | ... | ... | ... | ... | ... | ... | ... | 244440 | 100.0 | 96.3 | 3.7 | ... | ... | ... |
| Norway | Stavanger | 1990 | ... | ... | ... | ... | ... | ... | ... | 42680 | 100.0 | 98.8 | 1.2 | ... | ... | ... |
| Norway | Trondheim | 1990 | ... | ... | ... | ... | ... | ... | ... | 60407 | 100.0 | 97.0 | 3.0 | ... | ... | ... |
| Poland | Krakow | 1995 | 238760 | 97.7 | 92.4 | 5.3 | ... | ... | ... | 238760 | 95.6 | 90.3 | 5.2 | ... | ... | ... |
| Poland | Lodz | 1995 | 314766 | 95.9 | 93.8 | 2.1 | ... | ... | ... | 314766 | 83.0 | 78.5 | 4.5 | ... | ... | ... |
| Poland | Warszawa | 1995 | 594473 | 98.8 | 94.7 | 4.1 | ... | ... | ... | 594473 | 97.1 | 90.8 | 6.3 | ... | ... | ... |
| Poland | Wroclaw | 1995 | 240293 | 84.1 | 83.1 | 0.9 | ... | ... | ... | 204293 | 92.0 | 85.0 | 7.0 | ... | ... | ... |
| Portugal | Amandora | 1991 | 46694 | 97.3 | 96.6 | 0.7 | 0.5 | ... | 2.0 | 43694 | 98.5 | 96.1 | 2.3 | 0.9 | ... | 0.6 |
| Portugal | Lisboa | 1991 | 244013 | 96.7 | 94.7 | 2.0 | 0.3 | ... | 3.1 | 244013 | 97.2 | 91.9 | 5.3 | 1.2 | ... | 1.6 |
| Portugal | Porto | 1991 | 98895 | 95.8 | 93.7 | 3.0 | 1.1 | ... | 2.2 | 98895 | 92.1 | 90.2 | 1.9 | 5.4 | ... | 2.5 |
| Portugal | Setúbal | 1991 | 28073 | 98.1 | 97.1 | 0.9 | 0.6 | ... | 1.3 | 28073 | 96.2 | 94.2 | 2.0 | 1.1 | ... | 2.8 |
| Slovakia | Bratislava | 1991 | 161494 | 99.8 | ... | ... | ... | ... | ... | 161494 | 99.2 | 99.2 | ... | ... | ... | ... |
| Slovakia | Košice | 1991 | 79255 | 99.3 | ... | ... | ... | ... | ... | 79255 | 98.3 | 98.3 | ... | ... | ... | ... |
| Yugoslavia | Beograd | 1991 | 390065 | 98.1 | 97.4 | 0.7 | ... | 1.9 | ... | 390065 | ... | ... | ... | ... | ... | ... |
| Yugoslavia | Kragujevac | 1991 | 45666 | 92.4 | 87.7 | 4.6 | ... | 7.6 | ... | 45666 | ... | ... | ... | ... | ... | ... |
| Yugoslavia | Nis | 1991 | 56951 | 97.9 | 96.9 | 1.0 | ... | 2.1 | ... | 56951 | ... | ... | ... | ... | ... | ... |
| Yugoslavia | Novi Sad | 1991 | 65087 | 97.5 | 96.8 | 0.7 | ... | 2.5 | ... | 65087 | ... | ... | ... | ... | ... | ... |
| **LATIN AMERICA** | | | | | | | | | | | | | | | | |
| Argentina | Buenos Aires | 1991 | 3150158 | ... | ... | ... | ... | ... | ... | 3150158 | ... | ... | ... | ... | ... | ... |
| Argentina | Cordoba | 1991 | 304002 | ... | ... | ... | ... | ... | ... | 304002 | ... | ... | ... | ... | ... | ... |
| Argentina | La Plata | 1991 | 183593 | ... | ... | ... | ... | ... | ... | 183593 | ... | ... | ... | ... | ... | ... |
| Argentina | Rosario | 1991 | 315250 | ... | ... | ... | ... | ... | ... | 315250 | ... | ... | ... | ... | ... | ... |
| Bahamas | Gr. Bahama | 1990 | 10388 | 84.8 | 77.3 | 7.5 | 3.2 | 11.8 | 24 | 10388 | 84.1 | 84.1 | ... | 14.2 | 1.5 | 0.2 |
| Bahamas | Nassau | 1990 | 39864 | 79.6 | 51.5 | 28.1 | 2.1 | 18.3 | 0.0 | 39864 | 80.2 | 80.2 | ... | 12.6 | 7.2 | ... |
| Bolivia | Cochabamba | 1997 | 127761 | 80.7 | ... | ... | 1.4 | 17.4 | 0.5 | 127761 | 94.3 | 47.3 | 47.0 | ... | 5.7 | ... |
| Bolivia | La Paz | 1997 | 179460 | 89.6 | ... | ... | 8.3 | 1.2 | 0.9 | 179460 | 79.8 | 48.6 | 31.2 | ... | 20.2 | ... |
| Bolivia | Oruro | 1997 | 51626 | 95.1 | ... | ... | 2.4 | 0.0 | 2.5 | 51626 | 55.1 | 25.8 | 29.3 | ... | 44.9 | ... |
| Bolivia | Santa Cruz De La Sierra | 1997 | 192990 | 97.6 | ... | ... | 0.9 | 1.2 | 0.3 | 192990 | 96.2 | 64.6 | 31.6 | ... | 3.8 | ... |
| Colombia[8] | Barranquilla | 1993 | 193191 | 93.4 | 93.4 | ... | 0.8 | 5.8 | ... | 210394 | 87.4 | 74.6 | 14.2 | ... | ... | 6.9 |
| Colombia | Bogota | 1993 | 1206384 | 97.8 | 97.8 | ... | 0.6 | 1.6 | ... | 1255108 | 98.9 | 96.7 | 2.2 | ... | ... | 1.1 |
| Colombia[8] | Cali | 1993 | 379382 | 97.1 | 97.1 | ... | 1.1 | 1.8 | ... | 404805 | 98.5 | 95.0 | 3.5 | ... | ... | 1.5 |
| Colombia[8] | Medellin | 1993 | 382108 | 97.8 | 97.8 | ... | 0.4 | 1.8 | ... | 388688 | 98.9 | 97.0 | 1.9 | ... | ... | 1.1 |
| Dominican Republic | La Romana | 1993 | 37781 | 80.5 | 80.5 | ... | ... | 19.5 | ... | 40393 | 42.3 | 42.3 | ... | 42.6 | ... | ... |
| Dominican Republic | Santiago De Los Caballeros | 1993 | 161654 | 65.5 | 65.5 | ... | ... | 34.5 | ... | 164843 | 48.3 | 48.3 | ... | 48.6 | ... | ... |
| Dominican Republic | Santo Domingo | 1993 | 512701 | 86.8 | 86.8 | ... | ... | 13.2 | ... | 519445 | 73.0 | 73.0 | ... | 22.5 | 6.3 | ... |
| Dominican Republic | San Pedro De Macoris | 1993 | 48017 | 73.7 | 73.7 | ... | ... | 26.3 | ... | 53964 | 37.7 | 37.7 | ... | 45.9 | ... | ... |
| Nicaragua | Jinotepe | 1998 | 4211 | 85.0 | 85.0 | ... | 15.0 | ... | ... | 4326 | 68.5 | 68.5 | ... | 10.6 | 30.5 | ... |
| Nicaragua | Leon | 1998 | 21008 | 71.5 | 71.5 | ... | 28.5 | ... | ... | 22291 | 30.2 | 30.2 | ... | 17.5 | 52.2 | ... |
| Nicaragua | Managua | 1998 | 160149 | 58.4 | 58.4 | ... | 41.6 | ... | ... | 162925 | 36.6 | 36.6 | ... | 21.8 | 114.4 | ... |
| Nicaragua | Matagalpa | 1998 | 9377 | 48.2 | 48.2 | ... | 49.8 | 2.0 | ... | 9962 | 46.8 | 46.8 | ... | 13.9 | 84.1 | ... |
| Panama | Colon | 1990 | 37118 | 58.7 | 58.7 | 0.3 | 41.0 | 0.3 | ... | 15471 | 51.2 | 51.2 | ... | 46.3 | ... | 2.5 |
| Panama | David | 1990 | 23741 | 59.9 | 59.9 | 0.7 | 28.0 | 12.1 | ... | 23741 | 46.8 | 46.8 | ... | 49.9 | ... | 3.3 |
| Panama | Panama | 1990 | 105409 | 81.7 | 81.7 | ... | 17.8 | 0.5 | ... | 105409 | 75.9 | 75.9 | ... | 23.2 | ... | 0.9 |
| Panama | San Miguelito | 1990 | 51645 | 71.6 | 71.6 | 0.3 | 28.1 | 0.4 | ... | 51645 | 54.9 | 54.9 | ... | 43.2 | ... | 1.9 |
| Puerto Rico | Carolina | 1990 | 54466 | 99.6 | 0.1 | 0.2 | ... | 0.2 | ... | 54466 | 99.4 | ... | ... | ... | 0.6 | ... |
| Puerto Rico | Ponce | 1990 | 54191 | 95.7 | 1.3 | 1.5 | ... | 1.5 | ... | 54191 | 96.9 | ... | ... | ... | 3.1 | ... |
| Puerto Rico | San Juan | 1990 | 150592 | 99.7 | 0.0 | 0.2 | ... | 0.1 | ... | 150592 | 99.2 | ... | ... | ... | 0.8 | ... |
| Uruguay | Montevideo | 1996 | 413998 | ... | ... | ... | ... | ... | ... | 413998 | ... | ... | ... | ... | ... | ... |
| Uruguay | Paysandu | 1996 | 21451 | ... | ... | ... | ... | ... | ... | 21451 | ... | ... | ... | ... | ... | ... |
| Uruguay | Rivera | 1996 | 18437 | ... | ... | ... | ... | ... | ... | 18437 | ... | ... | ... | ... | ... | ... |
| Uruguay | Salto | 1996 | 24587 | ... | ... | ... | ... | ... | ... | 24587 | ... | ... | ... | ... | ... | ... |

# TABLE B.6

## *continued*

| | | | Water supply system in housing unit | | | | | | | Toilet installation | | | | | | |
| | | | Piped water inside | | | | | | | Toilet inside | | | | | | |
| | | | Number of housing units | Total (%) | From community source (%) | From private source (%) | Outside but within 200 metres (%) | Other (%) | Not stated (%) | Number of housing units | Total (%) | Flush toilet (%) | Non-flush toilet (%) | With toilet ouside (%) | Other (%) | Not stated (%) |
|---|---|---|---|---|---|---|---|---|---|---|---|---|---|---|---|---|
| **NORTHERN AMERICA** | | | | | | | | | | | | | | | | |
| Bermuda | Hamilton | 1991 | 388 | 99.2 | 90.2 | ... | ... | ... | 0.8 | ... | ... | ... | ... | ... | ... | ... |
| United States | Houston | 1991 | 1263800 | 100.0 | 92.1 | 7.9 | ... | ... | ... | 1264200 | 100.0 | 100.0 | ... | ... | ... | ... |
| United States | Los Angeles | 1993 | 2983500 | 100.0 | 99.3 | 0.7 | ... | ... | ... | 2947500 | 99.9 | 99.9 | ... | ... | ... | ... |
| United States | New York | 1991 | 4155300 | 100.0 | 97.6 | 2.4 | ... | ... | ... | 4156100 | 99.4 | 99.4 | ... | ... | ... | ... |
| United States | Washington, DC | 1995 | 1518900 | 100.0 | 93.5 | 6.5 | ... | ... | ... | 1519200 | 99.9 | 99.9 | ... | ... | ... | ... |
| **OCEANIA** | | | | | | | | | | | | | | | | |
| Guam | Dededo | 1990 | 6963 | 99.5 | 94.4 | 0.2 | 0.2 | 0.3 | | 6963 | 95.2 | 95.2 | ... | 90 | 3.6 | ... |
| Guam | Santa Rita | 1990 | 2287 | 99.7 | 99.7 | 0.1 | – | 0.3 | ... | 2287 | 98.7 | 98.7 | ... | 10 | 20 | ... |
| Guam | Tamuning | 1990 | 4982 | 99.9 | 99.8 | 0.0 | 0.1 | 0.0 | | 4982 | 99.1 | 99.1 | ... | 16 | 29 | ... |
| Guam | Yigo | 1990 | 3370 | 99.0 | 99.0 | 0.0 | 0.4 | 0.6 | | 3370 | 94.0 | 94.0 | ... | 24 | 5.6 | ... |

**Source:** United Nations, Human Settlements Statistics Questionnaire 1999.
For sources and footnotes, refer to technical notes.

# TABLE B.7

## Employment Structure, Selected Cities

| | City | Year | Total employment | Manufact-uring (%) | Const-ruction (%) | Electricity (%) | Wholesale trade (%) | Hotel (%) | Transport (%) | Financial (%) | Public administration (%) | Education (%) | Health comm and other social (%) | Unempl-oyed[1] | Unempl-oyed (%) |
|---|---|---|---|---|---|---|---|---|---|---|---|---|---|---|---|
| **AFRICA** | | | | | | | | | | | | | | | |
| Botswana | Francistown | 1991 | 24888 | ... | ... | ... | ... | ... | ... | ... | ... | ... | ... | ... | ... |
| Botswana | Gaberone | 1991 | 65725 | ... | ... | ... | ... | ... | ... | ... | ... | ... | ... | ... | ... |
| Burkina Faso | Bobo Dioulasso | 1991 | 66686 | ... | ... | ... | ... | ... | ... | ... | ... | ... | ... | 7424 | 10.0 |
| Burkina Faso | Koudougou | 1991 | 19930 | ... | ... | ... | ... | ... | ... | ... | ... | ... | ... | 1136 | 5.4 |
| Burkina Faso | Ouagadougou | 1991 | 196295 | ... | ... | ... | ... | ... | ... | ... | ... | ... | ... | ... | 12.8 |
| Burkina Faso | Ouahigouya | 1991 | 23748 | ... | ... | ... | ... | ... | ... | ... | ... | ... | ... | 684 | 2.8 |
| Egypt | Alexandria | 1996 | 974530 | 25.6 | 12.5 | 1.7 | 15.1 | 2.0 | 9.5 | 5.4 | 7.5 | 8.3 | 5.8 | 76401 | 7.3 |
| Egypt | Cairo | 1996 | 1977590 | 22.0 | 12.5 | 1.2 | 16.1 | 2.4 | 8.8 | 7.7 | 10.5 | 8.9 | 7.4 | 155780 | 7.3 |
| Egypt | Giza | 1996 | 639776 | 17.8 | 12.8 | 0.9 | 16.9 | 3.5 | 8.1 | 9.6 | 11.0 | 9.2 | 8.5 | 40382 | 5.9 |
| Egypt | Shubra-El-Khema | 1996 | 236330 | 34.4 | 13.4 | 1.3 | 14.4 | 2.1 | 9.4 | 4.9 | 7.1 | 6.3 | 4.3 | 16652 | 6.6 |
| Gambia | Banjul | 1997 | 14491 | 10.7 | 1.9 | 1.0 | 35.0 | 3.9 | 9.7 | 3.3 | 29.4 | ... | ... | 1458 | 9.1 |
| Gambia | Kanifing | 1997 | 64634 | 12.5 | 7.0 | 1.4 | 27.9 | 6.0 | 9.3 | 1.9 | 27.9 | ... | ... | 5035 | 7.2 |
| Libyan Arab Jamahiriya | Bengazi | 1995 | 157911 | 10.6 | 8.5 | 3.3 | 13.5 | 1.5 | 8.0 | 1.9 | 17.8 | 11.6 | 12.4 | 19000 | 10.7 |
| Libyan Arab Jamahiriya | Misurata | 1995 | 93532 | 14.9 | 6.2 | 3.2 | 8.3 | 0.6 | 8.1 | 0.9 | 15.8 | 16.0 | 65.4 | 8559 | 8.4 |
| Libyan Arab Jamahiriya | Tripoli | 1995 | 316033 | 9.8 | 6.9 | 2.5 | 10.1 | 1.2 | 7.2 | 2.7 | 20.2 | 17.6 | 9.8 | 37741 | 10.7 |
| Libyan Arab Jamahiriya | Zawia | 1995 | 140628 | 8.1 | 7.4 | 2.2 | 6.6 | 0.5 | 3.2 | 1.4 | 21.0 | 23.3 | 6.6 | 10964 | 7.2 |
| Seychelles | Port Victoria | 1997 | 10959 | ... | ... | ... | ... | ... | ... | ... | ... | ... | ... | 1227 | 10.1 |
| South Africa | Cape Town | 1996 | 79763 | 16.3 | 4.0 | 1.0 | 18.3 | ... | 5.8 | 18.1 | ... | ... | ... | 7686 | 8.8 |
| South Africa | Durban | 1996 | 217742 | 17.7 | 5.5 | 0.9 | 13.6 | ... | 6.8 | 11.7 | ... | ... | ... | 55740 | 20.4 |
| South Africa | Johannesburg | 1996 | 324537 | 10.2 | 5.3 | 1.4 | 16.5 | ... | 5.2 | 18.1 | ... | ... | ... | 69438 | 17.6 |
| South Africa | Pretoria | 1996 | 299835 | 7.7 | 4.6 | 1.0 | 11.4 | ... | 5.3 | 18.4 | ... | ... | ... | 41031 | 12.0 |
| **ASIA** | | | | | | | | | | | | | | | |
| Armenia | Yerevan | 1998 | 394100 | 24.8 | 6.8 | 3.6 | 14.5 | 1.5 | 8.3 | 0.7 | 4.3 | 13.2 | 10.3 | 34600 | 8.1 |
| Cambodia | Bat Dambang | 1996 | 46977 | ... | ... | ... | ... | ... | ... | ... | ... | ... | ... | 5262 | 10.1 |
| Cambodia | Kampong Cham | 1996 | 688165 | ... | ... | ... | ... | ... | ... | ... | ... | ... | ... | 25135 | 3.5 |
| Cambodia | Phnom Penh | 1996 | 368221 | ... | ... | ... | ... | ... | ... | ... | ... | ... | ... | 39100 | 9.6 |
| Cambodia | Siem Riab | 1996 | 298704 | ... | ... | ... | ... | ... | ... | ... | ... | ... | ... | 10232 | 3.3 |
| Cyprus | Larnaka | 1992 | 25242 | 18.4 | 10.9 | 1.3 | 17.9 | 8.8 | 8.3 | 3.6 | 5.9 | 5.1 | 6.7 | 539 | 2.1 |
| Cyprus | Limassol | 1992 | 59202 | 19.8 | 9.9 | 0.8 | 18.4 | 8.9 | 8.1 | 3.6 | 5.4 | 5.3 | 6.6 | 1703 | 2.8 |
| Cyprus | Nicosia | 1992 | 82827 | 18.4 | 7.9 | 0.8 | 17.4 | 3.3 | 5.9 | 6.1 | 11.7 | 6.5 | 9.3 | 1637 | 1.9 |
| Cyprus | Patos | 1992 | 14359 | 8.8 | 12.3 | 0.5 | 14.4 | 22.5 | 5.0 | 3.5 | 7.8 | 5.9 | 7.4 | 209 | 1.4 |
| Georgia | Tbilisi | 1998 | 323400 | ... | ... | ... | ... | ... | ... | ... | ... | ... | ... | 146200 | 31.1 |
| Israel | Haifa | 1995 | 109190 | 14.9 | 3.6 | 2.3 | 11.7 | 3.2 | 6.2 | 3.1 | 4.2 | 13.0 | 13.4 | 5420 | 4.7 |
| Israel | Jerusalem | 1995 | 200860 | 7.7 | 4.8 | 0.4 | 8.7 | 4.3 | 4.7 | 2.2 | 7.8 | 11.2 | 12.7 | 8930 | 4.3 |
| Israel | Rishon L'zion | 1995 | 75350 | 18.0 | 4.2 | 0.9 | 14.4 | 2.9 | 6.0 | 5.1 | 5.5 | 8.1 | 10.3 | 2805 | 3.6 |
| Israel | Tel Aviv–Jaffa | 1995 | 168705 | 12.0 | 3.0 | 0.6 | 12.0 | 4.3 | 6.0 | 4.9 | 3.2 | 7.0 | 12.8 | 5210 | 3.0 |
| Japan | Osaka | 1995 | 1336176 | 21.8 | 10.4 | 0.4 | 29.3 | 24.4 | 6.7 | 2.6 | 1.3 | ... | ... | 114138 | 7.9 |
| Japan | Sapporo | 1995 | 845813 | 7.3 | 12.9 | 0.6 | 29.1 | 30.8 | 7.5 | 3.8 | 4.2 | ... | ... | 47723 | 5.3 |
| Japan | Tokyo | 1995 | 4371922 | 16.6 | 8.4 | 0.4 | 27.5 | 29.1 | 6.4 | 4.3 | 2.4 | ... | ... | 225656 | 4.9 |
| Japan | Yokohama | 1995 | 1700629 | 18.7 | 10.5 | 0.6 | 23.6 | 28.3 | 7.8 | 1.2 | 2.6 | ... | ... | 79438 | 4.5 |
| Kazakhstan | Almaty | 1998 | 546900 | 7.4 | 3.6 | 1.9 | 3.6 | ... | ... | ... | 3.7 | 14.4 | ... | 88200 | 13.9 |
| Kazakhstan | Astana | 1998 | 142800 | 6.2 | 8.5 | 3.6 | 3.6 | ... | ... | ... | 9.0 | 13.7 | ... | 21400 | 13.0 |
| Malaysia | Bandaraya Kuching City | 1991 | 125515 | 12.9 | 9.6 | 1.3 | 19.9 | ... | 5.2 | 5.4 | 32.7 | ... | ... | 684 | 0.5 |
| Malaysia | George Town | 1991 | 89434 | 29.8 | 6.9 | 0.6 | 28.3 | ... | 4.6 | 5.8 | 21.7 | ... | ... | 95 | 0.1 |
| Malaysia | Keningau | 1991 | 28644 | 21.9 | 4.4 | 0.4 | 9.4 | ... | 2.7 | 0.9 | 18.0 | ... | ... | 120 | 0.4 |
| Malaysia | Kota Kinabalu | 1991 | 74672 | 7.7 | 11.1 | 0.8 | 24.4 | ... | 6.8 | 6.6 | 32.4 | ... | ... | 253 | 0.3 |
| Malaysia | Majlis Perbandaran Ipoh | 1991 | 139011 | 23.4 | 8.4 | 0.9 | 17.8 | ... | 4.3 | 4.6 | 28.3 | ... | ... | 178 | 0.1 |
| Malaysia | Majlis Perbandaran Johor | 1991 | 134097 | 31.1 | 9.9 | 0.6 | 0.0 | ... | 6.1 | 7.0 | 23.1 | ... | ... | 42 | ... |
| Malaysia | Miri | 1991 | 60163 | 12.0 | 10.4 | 0.6 | 14.5 | ... | 4.5 | 2.7 | 19.1 | ... | ... | 239 | 0.4 |
| Malaysia | Sandakan | 1991 | 69824 | 12.9 | 7.2 | 0.6 | 17.7 | ... | 6.0 | 3.1 | 21.6 | ... | ... | 409 | 0.6 |
| Malaysia | Sibu | 1991 | 59042 | 20.9 | 9.1 | 0.9 | 18.2 | ... | 5.2 | 4.2 | 22.0 | ... | ... | 376 | 0.6 |
| Malaysia | Tawau | 1991 | 84439 | 9.0 | 5.5 | 0.4 | 14.4 | ... | 5.0 | 2.1 | 15.5 | ... | ... | 552 | 0.6 |
| Malaysia | W.P Kuala Lumpur | 1991 | 477365 | 15.4 | 6.5 | 0.5 | 19.0 | ... | 5.1 | 10.4 | 27.3 | ... | ... | 599 | 0.1 |
| Pakistan | Islamabad | 1996 | 114987 | 0.0 | 0.0 | ... | ... | ... | ... | ... | ... | ... | ... | 12562 | 9.8 |
| Republic of Korea | Pusan | 1995 | 1432836 | 28.1 | 9.2 | 0.4 | 20.4 | 7.6 | 8.9 | 3.6 | 3.1 | 5.7 | 6.1 | [1]476815 | 50.8 |
| Republic of Korea | Seoul | 1995 | 4037210 | 23.8 | 10.0 | 0.5 | 22.0 | 7.1 | 6.0 | 5.2 | 3.6 | 5.8 | 7.4 | [1]3853030 | 48.8 |
| Republic of Korea | Taegu | 1995 | 915009 | 30.4 | 10.2 | 0.4 | 20.4 | 6.5 | 5.0 | 3.7 | 3.7 | 6.1 | 5.8 | [1]932079 | 50.5 |
| Syrian Arab Republic | Aleppo | 1994 | 64758 | ... | ... | ... | ... | ... | ... | ... | ... | ... | ... | 2927 | 4.3 |
| Syrian Arab Republic | Damascus | 1994 | 32693 | ... | ... | ... | ... | ... | ... | ... | ... | ... | ... | 32693 | 50.0 |
| Syrian Arab Republic | Homs | 1994 | 27852 | ... | ... | ... | ... | ... | ... | ... | ... | ... | ... | 2372 | 7.8 |
| Syrian Arab Republic | Lattakia | 1994 | 21386 | ... | ... | ... | ... | ... | ... | ... | ... | ... | ... | 1883 | 8.1 |
| Thailand | Bangkok | 1999 | 3905818 | 25.1 | 3.7 | 1.4 | 29.5 | 29.4 | 9.4 | ... | ... | ... | ... | 155098 | 3.8 |
| Thailand | Chon Buri | 1999 | 537316 | 28.6 | 6.0 | 0.3 | 20.1 | 20.9 | 7.0 | ... | ... | ... | ... | 10010 | 1.8 |
| Thailand | Nakhon Si Thammarat | 1999 | 766276 | 7.3 | 3.0 | ... | 19.7 | 13.2 | 2.3 | ... | ... | ... | ... | 22235 | 2.8 |
| Thailand | Songkhia | 1999 | 645235 | 18.1 | 3.8 | 0.1 | 20.8 | 19.0 | 2.7 | ... | ... | ... | ... | 27104 | 4.0 |
| Turkey | Adana | 1990 | 642195 | 15.0 | 5.6 | 0.4 | 9.9 | ... | 4.2 | ... | 15.1 | ... | ... | 74170 | 10.4 |
| Turkey | Ankara | 1990 | 1078180 | 13.3 | 7.4 | 0.9 | 12.3 | ... | 5.7 | ... | 35.4 | ... | ... | 86019 | 7.4 |
| Turkey | Istanbul | 1990 | 2460408 | 33.9 | 9.1 | 0.4 | 19.8 | ... | 6.8 | ... | 18.9 | ... | ... | 156666 | 6.0 |
| Turkey | Izmir | 1990 | 1037544 | 20.5 | 6.6 | 0.4 | 13.0 | ... | 4.5 | ... | 20.0 | ... | ... | 60381 | 5.5 |
| **EUROPE** | | | | | | | | | | | | | | | |
| Austria | Graz | 1998 | 102196 | 19.1 | 5.5 | 1.3 | 19.3 | 4.9 | 7.0 | 4.6 | 11.4 | 9.8 | 15.2 | 7632 | 6.9 |
| Austria | Linz | 1998 | 94600 | 26.5 | 7.1 | 1.3 | 18.2 | 4.7 | 7.8 | 4.2 | 10.2 | 6.2 | 12.9 | 7951 | 7.8 |
| Austria | Salzburg | 1998 | 69197 | 16.4 | 6.1 | 1.3 | 21.0 | 7.4 | 8.0 | 4.7 | 9.3 | 7.0 | 14.8 | 3671 | 5.0 |
| Austria | Wien | 1998 | 702547 | 20.7 | 7.2 | 1.1 | 20.7 | 5.6 | 8.5 | 5.5 | 8.3 | 5.5 | 15.3 | 71923 | 9.3 |
| Belgium | Antwerpen | 1999 | 165205 | 16.5 | 2.8 | 1.0 | 24.8 | 15.4 | 9.4 | 22.2 | ... | ... | ... | 24124 | 14.3 |
| Belgium | Bruxelles | 1999 | 305077 | 9.1 | 3.3 | 0.7 | 30.5 | 17.5 | 4.7 | 20.8 | ... | ... | ... | 58622 | 11.4 |
| Belgium | Charleroi | 1999 | 59425 | 18.7 | 5.7 | 1.1 | 34.5 | 16.2 | 6.6 | 11.5 | ... | ... | ... | 17720 | 23.0 |
| Belgium | Gent | 1999 | 86580 | 18.7 | 4.1 | 1.1 | 36.2 | 16.9 | 7.4 | 6.6 | ... | ... | ... | 11734 | 11.9 |

# TABLE B.7

## continued

| | | | Total employment | Manufact-uring | Const-ruction | Electricity | Wholesale trade | Hotel | Transport | Financial | Public administration | Education | Health comm and other social | Unempl-oyed[1] | Unempl-oyed |
|---|---|---|---|---|---|---|---|---|---|---|---|---|---|---|---|
| | | | | (%) | (%) | (%) | (%) | (%) | (%) | (%) | (%) | (%) | (%) | | (%) |
| Bulgaria | Bourgas | 1999 | 85051 | ... | ... | ... | ... | ... | ... | ... | ... | ... | ... | 6290 | 3.1 |
| Bulgaria | Plovdiv | 1999 | 144791 | ... | ... | ... | ... | ... | ... | ... | ... | ... | ... | 12451 | 12.8 |
| Bulgaria | Sofia | 1999 | 456202 | ... | ... | ... | ... | ... | ... | ... | ... | ... | ... | 19878 | 13.4 |
| Bulgaria | Varna | 1999 | 128623 | ... | ... | ... | ... | ... | ... | ... | ... | ... | ... | 17915 | 2.8 |
| Czech Republic | Brno | 1991 | 197473 | ... | 10.6 | ... | ... | ... | 6.9 | ... | ... | ... | ... | 2215 | 2.4 |
| Czech Republic | Ostrava | 1991 | 166526 | ... | 8.4 | ... | ... | ... | 8.0 | ... | ... | ... | 6.4 | 21200 | 9.4 |
| Czech Republic | Plzen | 1991 | 91008 | ... | 7.3 | ... | ... | ... | 9.4 | ... | ... | ... | 6.5 | 3200 | 6.9 |
| Czech Republic | Praha | 1991 | 631078 | ... | 10.7 | ... | ... | ... | 8.4 | ... | ... | ... | ... | 5742 | 3.3 |
| Estonia | Narva | 1998 | 31700 | 32.8 | 14.5 | ... | 12.0 | ... | 7.6 | ... | ... | 7.9 | 6.1 | 17105 | 18.4 |
| Estonia | Tallinn | 1998 | 204800 | 18.7 | 0.0 | 8.5 | 16.4 | 2.9 | 12.6 | 2.1 | 6.6 | 7.2 | 6.0 | 5200 | 14.1 |
| Estonia | Tartu | 1998 | 42900 | 18.6 | 0.0 | 6.5 | 15.9 | ... | 6.3 | ... | ... | 13.1 | 19.6 | 38159 | 13.6 |
| Finland | Espoo | 1998 | 95899 | 17.7 | 3.6 | 0.6 | 18.4 | 2.5 | 6.7 | 4.5 | 6.4 | 7.0 | 16.5 | 423784 | 9.3 |
| Finland | Helsinki | 1998 | 241852 | 32.2 | 3.2 | 0.8 | 14.3 | 4.3 | 9.4 | 4.1 | 7.9 | 7.3 | 18.4 | 9805 | 17.3 |
| Finland | Tampere | 1998 | 75615 | 34.5 | 4.9 | 0.9 | 12.5 | 3.4 | 7.1 | 1.8 | 1.4 | 7.9 | 19.2 | 14033 | 9.0 |
| Finland | Turku | 1998 | 67230 | 19.4 | 5.5 | 0.6 | 11.3 | 2.8 | 8.6 | 2.2 | 5.6 | 8.7 | 20.5 | 90176 | 17.3 |
| France | Lyon | 1990 | 534337 | 20.6 | 6.6 | 1.0 | 14.1 | 2.9 | 7.1 | 3.4 | 7.4 | 7.6 | 17.9 | 279 | 15.9 |
| France | Marseille | 1990 | 432158 | 11.7 | 6.7 | 1.2 | 15.5 | 2.7 | 9.5 | 3.5 | 11.3 | 7.7 | 16.1 | 35288 | 11.6 |
| France | Paris | 1990 | 4303931 | 15.7 | 5.9 | 1.0 | 13.2 | 3.8 | 7.8 | 5.6 | 9.1 | 6.2 | 10.9 | 56130 | 9.5 |
| France | Toulouse | 1990 | 268366 | 15.6 | 6.6 | 1.0 | 13.8 | 2.6 | 6.9 | 2.9 | 9.8 | 9.5 | 18.8 | 80 | 9.2 |
| Germany | Berlin | 1998 | 1477 | 12.2 | 9.3 | 1.0 | 12.4 | 4.1 | 6.5 | 3.1 | 11.2 | 7.5 | 11.3 | ... | ... |
| Germany | Hamburg | 1998 | 787 | 15.0 | 6.4 | 0.9 | 17.3 | 4.1 | 8.0 | 5.2 | 6.9 | 5.0 | 11.6 | ... | ... |
| Germany | Kôln | 1998 | 17168 | ... | ... | ... | ... | ... | ... | ... | ... | ... | 6.9 | | 14.1 |
| Germany | Munchen | 1998 | 41169 | ... | ... | ... | ... | ... | ... | ... | ... | ... | 263.0 | | |
| Hungary | Budapest | 1999 | 21563 | 55.8 | 23.9 | 46.8 | 61.9 | 14.7 | 32.5 | 14.1 | 26.7 | 31.2 | 29.4 | 38700 | 12.3 |
| Latvia | Riga | 1999 | 343700 | 18.6 | 6.6 | 2.0 | 20.0 | 3.1 | 11.1 | 1.8 | 7.4 | 8.0 | 10.3 | 23300 | 11.1 |
| Lithuania | Kaunas | 1998 | 186100 | 27.8 | 8.0 | 2.3 | 24.8 | 2.8 | 7.6 | 0.8 | 4.2 | 11.1 | 15.1 | 12900 | 18.1 |
| Lithuania | Klaipeda | 1998 | 97100 | 31.1 | 8.4 | 2.0 | 20.3 | 0.9 | 15.7 | 0.4 | 3.7 | 12.6 | 7.6 | 57208 | 15.8 |
| Lithuania | Siauliai | 1998 | 58400 | 32.5 | 7.2 | 5.3 | 22.1 | 1.2 | 9.1 | 2.4 | 8.2 | 10.6 | 7.5 | 24012 | 12.7 |
| Lithuania | Vilnius | 1998 | 276200 | 23.3 | 8.9 | 2.2 | 19.8 | 3.2 | 11.3 | 3.2 | 6.8 | 10.1 | 10.3 | 14000 | 12.6 |
| The Netherlands | Amsterdam | 1998 | 337000 | 6.5 | 3.0 | ... | 12.5 | 5.3 | 6.8 | 5.6 | 5.9 | 8.3 | 23.1 | 25000 | 6.9 |
| The Netherlands | Rotterdam | 1998 | 242000 | 9.1 | 5.8 | ... | 12.8 | 3.7 | 10.7 | 3.7 | 7.4 | 5.8 | 9.1 | 25000 | 9.4 |
| The Netherlands | S Gravenhage | 1998 | 205000 | 6.3 | 3.4 | ... | 12.7 | 3.9 | 6.8 | 4.9 | 11.7 | 6.3 | 17.6 | 11000 | 5.1 |
| The Netherlands | Utrecht | 1998 | 119000 | 6.7 | 0.0 | ... | 10.1 | 5.0 | 6.7 | 5.0 | 8.4 | 12.6 | 13.4 | 5000 | 4.0 |
| Norway | Bergen | 1990 | 94837 | 11.8 | 6.8 | 0.7 | 16.2 | 3.0 | 8.5 | 4.4 | 7.5 | 9.6 | 22.5 | 4951 | 5.0 |
| Norway | Oslo | 1990 | 210873 | 10.7 | 4.4 | 0.7 | 17.4 | 2.9 | 8.5 | 6.0 | 7.9 | 6.1 | 24.8 | 8382 | 3.8 |
| Norway | Stavanger | 1990 | 43190 | 14.4 | 6.6 | 0.5 | 14.0 | 2.7 | 7.0 | 3.3 | 6.0 | 7.8 | 19.2 | 1835 | 4.1 |
| Norway | Trondheim | 1990 | 61805 | 12.0 | 5.6 | 1.2 | 17.0 | 3.0 | 8.4 | 4.0 | 5.9 | 11.8 | 23.3 | 3049 | 4.7 |
| Poland | Warszawa | 1995 | 688000 | ... | ... | ... | ... | ... | ... | ... | ... | ... | ... | 47000 | 6.4 |
| Portugal | Amandora | 1991 | 59057 | 18.2 | 7.9 | 0.9 | 20.0 | 5.9 | 7.4 | 5.3 | 11.6 | 5.2 | 8.6 | 4493 | 7.1 |
| Portugal | Lisboa | 1991 | 280725 | 12.9 | 6.5 | 0.7 | 18.1 | 5.8 | 7.6 | 4.7 | 12.6 | 6.8 | 10.8 | 21808 | 7.2 |
| Portugal | Porto | 1991 | 133224 | 24.1 | 4.4 | 0.6 | 20.9 | 4.9 | 5.3 | 4.4 | 6.8 | 7.9 | 9.7 | 9803 | 6.9 |
| Portugal | Setúbal | 1991 | 33120 | 23.2 | 7.8 | 1.4 | 17.9 | 6.0 | 5.6 | 2.2 | 11.6 | 7.3 | 8.1 | 4722 | 12.5 |
| Slovakia | Bratislava | 1991 | 225846 | 18.6 | 9.4 | ... | 12.2 | ... | 7.9 | ... | ... | 5.4 | 38.3 | 9836 | 4.2 |
| Slovakia | Košice | 1991 | 116340 | 31.6 | 10.9 | ... | 9.3 | ... | 9.0 | ... | ... | 2.1 | 31.3 | 6246 | 5.1 |
| Spain | Barcelona | 1998 | 110920 | 9.6 | 11.9 | 1.1 | 20.2 | 14.6 | 11.5 | 3.3 | 7.9 | 3.4 | 13.0 | 16136 | 12.7 |
| Spain | Madrid | 1998 | 976179 | 15.2 | 7.1 | 0.7 | 14.7 | 5.4 | 10.1 | 6.7 | 10.1 | 7.8 | 11.9 | 191434 | 16.4 |
| Spain | Sevilla | 1998 | 194488 | 12.3 | 8.1 | 0.3 | 25.8 | 7.3 | 7.9 | 3.4 | 8.7 | 11.2 | 16.5 | 80671 | 29.3 |
| Spain | Valencia | 1998 | 241980 | 20.2 | 7.5 | 1.1 | 23.4 | 4.3 | 7.8 | 3.4 | 8.4 | 7.4 | 12.4 | 60571 | 20.0 |
| Yugoslavia | Beograd | 1998 | 465566 | 17.2 | 7.6 | ... | 15.6 | ... | 8.6 | 6.1 | 5.8 | 10.4 | 9.0 | 50880 | 9.9 |
| Yugoslavia | Kragujevac | 1998 | 60910 | 44.1 | 3.4 | ... | 13.8 | ... | 4.1 | 5.6 | 2.6 | 6.4 | 7.4 | 7508 | 11.0 |
| Yugoslavia | Nis | 1998 | 66702 | 44.3 | 5.8 | ... | 20.5 | ... | 10.9 | 4.2 | 3.4 | 9.5 | 10.9 | 12322 | 15.6 |
| Yugoslavia | Novi Sad | 1998 | 74425 | 28.2 | 9.8 | ... | 18.6 | ... | 8.7 | 9.6 | 6.3 | 16.8 | 15.7 | 7294 | 8.9 |
| **LATIN AMERICA** | | | | | | | | | | | | | | | |
| Argentina | Buenos Aires | 1991 | 4680358 | 16.9 | 7.2 | 0.5 | 18.4 | 3.2 | 9.7 | 12.1 | 5.2 | 6.90 | 11.5 | 790391 | 14.4 |
| Argentina | Cordoba | 1991 | 462003 | 13.7 | 10.0 | 0.6 | 20.4 | 3.3 | 7.7 | 8.3 | 6.3 | 8.1 | 11.7 | 76673 | 14.2 |
| Argentina | La Plata | 1991 | 259999 | 8.0 | 7.7 | 1.1 | 15.5 | 3.2 | 6.1 | 8.6 | 18.3 | 7.6 | 13.5 | 36614 | 12.3 |
| Argentina | Rosario | 1991 | 431416 | 18.0 | 8.0 | 0.7 | 2.5 | 2.8 | 7.0 | 7.9 | 6.0 | 7.3 | 10.9 | 75810 | 14.9 |
| Bahamas | Nassau | 1990 | 103270 | 2.8 | 6.1 | 1.0 | 9.4 | 11.8 | 5.3 | 6.9 | ... | 24.9 | ... | 8100 | 7.3 |
| Bahamas | Gr. Bahama | 1990 | 20090 | 5.2 | 7.0 | 0.7 | 12.3 | 20.7 | 8.1 | ... | ... | ... | ... | 2110 | 9.5 |
| Bolivia | Cochabamba | 1997 | 220969 | 15.4 | 8.9 | 0.5 | 22.9 | 5.4 | 9.5 | 1.1 | 4.5 | 8.9 | 8.1 | 9613 | 4.2 |
| Bolivia | La Paz | 1997 | 299867 | 19.0 | 6.1 | 1.0 | 22.4 | 5.0 | 9.8 | 1.9 | 5.3 | 7.0 | 8.5 | 17129 | 5.4 |
| Bolivia | Oruro | 1997 | 73469 | 15.7 | 7.9 | 0.7 | 28.2 | 4.7 | 11.4 | 1.8 | 4.2 | 10.0 | 6.5 | 2594 | 3.4 |
| Bolivia | Santa Cruz De La Sierra | 1997 | 343964 | 23.1 | 8.5 | 0.7 | 23.3 | 5.6 | 8.7 | 1.8 | 3.2 | 5.6 | 6.8 | 11160 | 3.1 |
| Colombia | Barranquilla | 1993 | 329969 | 11.9 | 4.7 | 0.5 | 24.2 | 2.0 | 4.2 | 1.3 | 1.7 | 3.8 | 4.9 | 26717 | 7.5 |
| Colombia | Bogota | 1993 | 2030856 | 15.5 | 5.6 | 0.3 | 20.2 | 2.5 | 4.6 | 2.3 | 2.7 | 3.8 | 5.7 | 83337 | 3.9 |
| Colombia | Cali | 1993 | 663385 | 13.4 | 7.3 | 0.2 | 20.9 | 2.0 | 4.8 | 1.4 | 1.7 | 3.0 | 4.7 | 36909 | 5.3 |
| Colombia | Medellin | 1993 | 600591 | 16.5 | 6.6 | 0.3 | 20.8 | 2.0 | 4.3 | 1.6 | 1.8 | 3.5 | 5.1 | 32181 | 5.1 |
| Dominican Republic | La Romana | 1993 | 59001 | 30.3 | 6.0 | 0.2 | ... | 26.7 | 4.9 | 2.4 | ... | ... | 14.7 | 6946 | 10.5 |
| Dominican Republic | San Pedro De Macoris | 1993 | 66741 | 39.0 | 4.3 | 0.5 | ... | 12.7 | 4.2 | 2.1 | ... | ... | 16.3 | 12794 | 16.1 |
| Dominican Republic | Santiago De Los Caballeros | 1993 | 216585 | 24.4 | 6.4 | 0.6 | ... | 15.1 | 4.9 | 2.4 | ... | ... | 18.2 | 45998 | 17.5 |
| Mexico | Cuidad De Mexico | 1998 | 6748731 | 20.6 | 3.8 | 0.5 | 21.2 | 4.8 | 7.1 | 2.4 | 6.7 | ... | 31.9 | 286055 | 4.1 |
| Mexico | Guadalajara | 1998 | 1490787 | 25.8 | 4.5 | 0.4 | 23.4 | 6.9 | 4.3 | 1.7 | 3.6 | ... | 28.8 | 47504 | 3.1 |
| Mexico | Monterrey | 1998 | 1315111 | 28.0 | 6.9 | 0.7 | 21.0 | 4.5 | 5.8 | 2.3 | 2.5 | ... | 28.0 | 37947 | 2.8 |
| Mexico | Puebla | 1998 | 583896 | 28.2 | 4.8 | 0.6 | 19.7 | 3.5 | 6.4 | 1.7 | 4.2 | ... | 28.3 | 13252 | 2.2 |
| Nicaragua | Managua | 1995 | 256261 | 12.5 | 5.7 | 0.9 | 25.9 | 4.5 | 5.9 | 1.6 | 6.6 | 4.8 | 9.1 | 52161 | 16.9 |
| Nicaragua | Jinotepe | 1995 | 6795 | 11.3 | 7.3 | 0.8 | 22.1 | 3.6 | 4.8 | 1.1 | 5.4 | 7.5 | 11.3 | 1577 | 18.8 |
| Nicaragua | Leon | 1995 | 34360 | 13.4 | 5.2 | 1.0 | 22.9 | 4.8 | 5.2 | 0.8 | 4.6 | 7.2 | 10.9 | 8190 | 19.2 |
| Nicaragua | Matagalpa | 1995 | 17525 | 7.8 | 8.0 | 0.6 | 25.6 | 4.3 | 5.9 | 0.9 | 4.2 | 4.1 | 7.9 | 3113 | 15.1 |

# TABLE B.7

*continued*

| | | | | | | | | | | | | | | | | |
|---|---|---|---|---|---|---|---|---|---|---|---|---|---|---|---|---|
| anama | Panama | 2000 | 149385 | 11.2 | 3.6 | 1.5 | 22.2 | 4.6 | 8.8 | 4.7 | 12.2 | 6.9 | 11.5 | 21771 | 12.7 |
| anama | Colon | 2000 | 16184 | 14.0 | 3.6 | 1.1 | 31.6 | 5.6 | 16.5 | 1.6 | 8.3 | 4.9 | 7.8 | 3140 | 16.2 |
| anama | David | 2000 | 32840 | 7.6 | 3.4 | 1.4 | 17.3 | 2.5 | 4.8 | 1.6 | 6.6 | 6.7 | 7.4 | 4807 | 12.8 |
| anama | San Miguelito | 2000 | 78966 | 15.3 | 7.3 | 1.6 | 23.3 | 4.6 | 8.3 | 2.7 | 12.6 | 6.2 | 9.2 | 14581 | 15.6 |
| uerto Rico | Bayamon | 1998 | 80400 | ... | ... | ... | ... | ... | ... | ... | ... | ... | ... | 7400 | 8.4 |
| uerto Rico | Ponce | 1998 | 50800 | ... | ... | ... | ... | ... | ... | ... | ... | ... | ... | 8900 | 14.9 |
| uerto Rico | Carolina | 1998 | 72800 | ... | ... | ... | ... | ... | ... | ... | ... | ... | ... | 7300 | 9.1 |
| ruguay | Montevideo | 1996 | 545301 | ... | ... | ... | ... | ... | ... | ... | ... | ... | ... | 64170 | 10.5 |
| ruguay | Paysandu | 1996 | 27203 | ... | ... | ... | ... | ... | ... | ... | ... | ... | ... | 2748 | 9.2 |
| ruguay | Rivera | 1996 | 23156 | ... | ... | ... | ... | ... | ... | ... | ... | ... | ... | 2133 | 8.4 |
| ruguay | Salto | 1996 | 31133 | ... | ... | ... | ... | ... | ... | ... | ... | ... | ... | 3600 | 10.4 |
| **NORTHERN AMERICA** | | | | | | | | | | | | | | | |
| ermuda | Hamilton | 1991 | 650 | 4.6 | 11.7 | 2.0 | 14.0 | 19.5 | 6.3 | ... | 8.5 | 8.0 | 2.6 | 69 | 9.6 |
| Canada | Calgary | 1996 | 441575 | 9.9 | 7.1 | 3.6 | 18.5 | 7.4 | 5.6 | 3.8 | 4.0 | 6.4 | 18.0 | 31265 | 6.6 |
| Canada | Montreal | 1996 | 1502380 | 18.9 | 4.5 | 4.0 | 20.2 | 6.4 | 4.6 | 4.6 | 5.3 | 7.5 | 19.5 | 190180 | 11.2 |
| Canada | Ottawa | 1996 | 502070 | 7.0 | 5.1 | 3.7 | 15.1 | 6.4 | 3.1 | 3.2 | 20.9 | 8.2 | 19.2 | 48685 | 8.8 |
| Canada | Toronto | 1996 | 2061615 | 17.8 | 5.2 | 3.9 | 19.3 | 6.3 | 3.8 | 6.7 | 4.0 | 6.7 | 17.4 | 207000 | 9.1 |
| United States | Houston | 1990 | 789635 | 11.7 | 7.7 | ... | 23.4 | ... | 7.4 | 7.6 | 2.8 | ... | 35.2 | 70369 | 8.2 |
| United States | Los Angeles | 1990 | 1673731 | 18.4 | 5.8 | ... | 20.1 | ... | 6.0 | 8.1 | 2.2 | ... | 37.6 | 125361 | 7.0 |
| United States | New York | 1990 | 3264303 | 11.4 | 4.1 | ... | 17.2 | ... | 9.3 | 12.3 | 4.8 | ... | 40.4 | 322125 | 9.0 |
| United States | Washington, DC | 1990 | 310077 | 4.2 | 4.1 | ... | 11.7 | ... | 6.6 | 7.4 | 18.6 | ... | 45.0 | 23442 | 7.0 |
| **OCEANIA** | | | | | | | | | | | | | | | |
| Guam | Dededo | 1990 | 14581 | ... | ... | ... | ... | ... | ... | ... | ... | ... | ... | 433 | 2.9 |
| Guam | Santa Rita | 1990 | 6884 | ... | ... | ... | ... | ... | ... | ... | ... | ... | ... | 150 | 2.1 |
| Guam | Tamuning | 1990 | 9489 | ... | ... | ... | ... | ... | ... | ... | ... | ... | ... | 247 | 2.5 |
| Guam | Yigo | 1990 | 7244 | ... | ... | ... | ... | ... | ... | ... | ... | ... | ... | 191 | 2.6 |

**Source:** United Nations, Human Settlements Statistics Questionnaire 1999.
For sources and footnotes, refer to technical notes.

## TABLE B.8

## Social Indicators, Selected Cities

| | | | Number of motor vehicles | Number of hospital establishments | Number of physicians | Number of schools | Number of telephone lines | Number of TV sets | Circulation of daily newspapers | Number of cinemas | Number of public parks |
|---|---|---|---|---|---|---|---|---|---|---|---|
| | | | | | (per 1000 people) | | (per 1000 people) | (per 1000 people) | (per 1000 people) | | |
| **AFRICA** | | | | | | | | | | | |
| Botswana | Gaberone | 1997 | 76579 | 27 | ... | 1042 | ... | ... | ... | ... | ... |
| Congo | Brazzaville | 1984 | ... | 4 | ... | ... | ... | ... | ... | ... | ... |
| Congo | Doligie | 1984 | ... | 2 | ... | ... | ... | ... | ... | ... | ... |
| Congo | Nkayi | 1984 | ... | 1 | ... | ... | ... | ... | ... | ... | ... |
| Congo | Pointe-Noire | 1984 | ... | 3 | ... | ... | ... | ... | ... | ... | ... |
| Gambia | Bakau | 1993 | ... | ... | ... | 8 | ... | ... | ... | ... | ... |
| Gambia | Banjul | 1993 | ... | 1 | 9 | 20 | ... | ... | ... | 2 | ... |
| Gambia | Kanifing | 1993 | ... | 3 | ... | 54 | ... | ... | ... | 2 | ... |
| Gambia | Serekunda | 1993 | ... | ... | ... | 34 | ... | ... | ... | 1 | ... |
| Mauritius | Port-Louis | 1999 | 222344 | ... | ... | ... | 2303.8 | 218700 | 6.0 | 29 | ... |
| Lesotho | Maseru | 1996 | ... | 3 | ... | ... | 72.5 | ... | ... | 2 | 1 |
| Seychelles | Port Victoria | 1998 | 9068 | 25 | 9.9 | 86 | 759.1 | 493.5 | ... | ... | ... |
| **ASIA** | | | | | | | | | | | |
| China, Hong Kong SAR | Hong Kong | 1998 | 500673 | 102 | 1.5 | 2800 | 596.3 | ... | ... | 188 | 1427 |
| China, Macau SAR | | 1996 | 82766 | 2 | 1.9 | ... | 389.9 | ... | 11.0 | 11 | ... |
| Cyprus | Larnaka | 1995 | ... | 20 | 3.5 | ... | 642.4[(1999)] | ... | ... | ... | ... |
| Cyprus | Limassol | 1995 | ... | 37 | 3.0 | ... | 766.1[(1999)] | ... | ... | ... | ... |
| Cyprus | Nicosia | 1995 | ... | 33 | 3.8 | ... | 812.6[(1999)] | ... | ... | ... | ... |
| Cyprus | Patos | 1995 | ... | 14 | 3.8 | ... | 859.9[(1999)] | ... | ... | ... | ... |
| Georgia | Batumi | 1999 | ... | ... | ... | 27 | ... | ... | 1.0 | ... | ... |
| Georgia | Kutaisi | 1999 | ... | ... | ... | 66 | ... | ... | ... | ... | ... |
| Georgia | Rustavi | 1999 | ... | ... | ... | 35 | ... | ... | ... | ... | ... |
| Israel | Haifa | 1995 | 88145 | ... | ... | ... | ... | ... | ... | ... | ... |
| Israel | Jerusalem | 1995 | 134030 | ... | ... | ... | ... | ... | ... | ... | ... |
| Israel | Rishon L'zion | 1995 | 60737 | ... | ... | ... | ... | ... | ... | ... | ... |
| Israel | Tel Aviv–Jaffa | 1995 | 210231 | ... | ... | ... | ... | ... | ... | ... | ... |
| Japan | Osaka | 1998 | 768189 | 213[(1997)] | 2.9[(1996)] | ... | ... | ... | 665.0 | ... | ... |
| Japan | Sapporo | 1998 | 811983 | 226[(1997)] | 2.6[(1996)] | ... | ... | ... | 791.3 | ... | ... |
| Japan | Tokyo | 1998 | 2473383 | 468[(1997)] | 3.1[(1996)] | ... | ... | ... | 607.5 | ... | ... |
| Japan | Yokohama | 1998 | 1228259 | 146[(1997)] | 1.6[(1996)] | ... | ... | ... | 458.4 | ... | ... |
| Kazakhstan | Astana | 1998 | 32699 | ... | ... | ... | ... | ... | ... | ... | ... |
| Kazakhstan | Karaganda | 1998 | 162685 | ... | ... | ... | ... | ... | ... | ... | ... |
| Kazakhstan | Ust-Kamenogorsk | 1998 | 144313 | ... | ... | ... | ... | ... | ... | ... | ... |
| Malaysia | Majlis Perbandaran Johor Bharu | 1999 | 1284960 | 46 | 2.8 | ... | 1158.3 | ... | 955.0 | 22 | ... |
| Malaysia | W.P Kuala Lumpur | 1999 | 1857055 | 44 | 3.7 | ... | 691.7 | ... | 466.4 | 32 | ... |
| Republic of Korea | Pusan | 1997 | 720614 | 2957 | 1.1 | ... | 486.6 | ... | ... | 26 | 397 |
| Republic of Korea | Seoul | 1997 | 2248567 | 9645 | 1.6 | ... | 533.8 | ... | ... | 173 | 1386 |
| Republic of Korea | Suweon | 1997 | 194892 | 553 | 1.4 | ... | 571.7 | ... | ... | 16 | 116 |
| Republic of Korea | Taegu | 1997 | 620111 | 2094 | 1.3 | ... | 476.6 | ... | ... | 27 | 313 |
| **EUROPE** | | | | | | | | | | | |
| Austria | Linz | | 109267 | 11 | 2.4 | 147 | ... | ... | 2.0 | 4 | 148 |
| Czech Republic | Praha | 1998 | 736458 | 89 | 6.0 | ... | 649.1 | 442209 | ... | ... | ... |
| Czech Republic | Brno | 1998 | 192165 | 34 | 15.6 | ... | 1136.6 | 139904 | ... | ... | ... |
| Czech Republic | Ostrava | 1998 | 131317 | 10 | 3.7 | ... | 346.2 | 114675 | ... | ... | ... |
| Czech Republic | Plzen | 1998 | 94628 | 10 | 3.6 | ... | 256.5 | 62593 | ... | ... | ... |
| Croatia | Osijek | 1991 | 32030 | 2 | 4.7 | ... | 431.0 | 339.0 | ... | 2 | 19 |
| Croatia | Rijeka | 1991 | 51991 | 2 | 4.2 | ... | 379.7 | 279.4 | ... | 3 | 20 |
| Croatia | Split | 1991 | 62581 | 3 | 3.9 | ... | 386.5 | 222.1 | ... | 6 | 5 |
| Croatia | Zagreb | 1991 | 264695 | 19 | 4.5 | ... | 519.6 | 317.4 | ... | 21 | 30 |
| Germany | Berlin | 1998 | 1386959[(1999)] | 73 | 2[6.5] | 1793 | ... | ... | ... | 242 | ... |
| Germany | Hamburg | 1998 | 856884[(1999)] | 35 | 2[6.6] | 889 | ... | ... | ... | 81 | ... |
| Hungary | Budapest | 1998 | 627504 | 42 | 6.1 | ... | 454.5 | 840810 | ... | 87 | 25547 |
| Hungary | Debrecen | 1998 | 55584 | 2 | 7.6 | ... | 347.8 | ... | ... | 21 | 2935 |
| Hungary | Miskolc | 1998 | 42788 | 5 | 4.9 | ... | 350.9 | ... | ... | 8 | 4457 |
| Hungary | Szeged | 1998 | 50409 | 4 | 7.1 | ... | 409.4 | ... | ... | 6 | 3991 |
| Latvia | Daugavpils | 1998 | 22641 | 31 | 3.3 | ... | ... | 2 | ... | 1 | ... |
| Latvia | Júrmala | 1998 | 15344 | 10 | 2.9 | ... | 329.3 | ... | ... | 4 | ... |
| Latvia | Liepája | 1998 | 18514 | 25 | 2.4 | ... | ... | 1 | 251.5 | 1 | ... |
| Latvia | Ríga | 1998 | 192863 | 170 | 5.6 | ... | 377.2 | 4 | 370.3 | 12 | ... |
| Norway | Bergen | 1998 | 106455 | 2 | 2.3 | ... | 556.6 | 399.2 | ... | ... | ... |
| Norway | Oslo | 1998 | 244026 | 11 | 3.3 | ... | 674.1 | 460.1 | 155.0 | 604 | ... |
| Norway | Stavanger | 1998 | 57766 | 1 | 2.8 | ... | 496.7 | 402.4 | ... | ... | ... |
| Norway | Trondheim | 1998 | 75045 | 1 | 3.2 | ... | 542.7 | 433.1 | ... | ... | ... |
| Portugal | Amandora | 1997 | ... | 2 | 5.1 | ... | ... | ... | ... | 1 | ... |
| Portugal | Lisboa | 1997 | ... | 40 | 10.6 | ... | 1.3 | 972 | 14.0 | 21 | ... |
| Portugal | Porto | 1997 | ... | 22 | 12.7 | ... | ... | ... | 5.0 | 12 | ... |
| Portugal | Setúbal | 1997 | ... | 2 | 4.5 | ... | ... | ... | ... | 3 | ... |
| Sweden | Goteborg | 1990 | ... | 1 | 3.7 | 206 | ... | ... | 2.0 | 46 | ... |
| Sweden | Malmo | 1990 | ... | 1 | 6.3 | 76 | ... | ... | 3.0 | 26 | ... |
| Sweden | Stockholm | 1998 | ... | 4 | 7.0 | 226 | ... | ... | 8.0 | 87 | ... |
| Sweden | Uppsala | 1998 | ... | 1 | 6.2 | 87 | ... | ... | 1.0 | 25 | ... |
| Yugoslavia | Beograd | 1998 | ... | 30 | 4.9 | 223 | ... | ... | ... | 38 | ... |
| Yugoslavia | Kragujevac | 1998 | ... | 1 | 3.5 | 29 | ... | ... | ... | 2 | ... |
| Yugoslavia | Nis | 1998 | ... | 4 | 5.4 | 50 | ... | ... | ... | 5 | ... |
| Yugoslavia | Novi Sad | 1998 | ... | 1 | 7.6 | 48 | ... | ... | ... | 2 | ... |

# TABLE B.8

## continued

### LATIN AMERICA

| | | | | | | | | | | | |
|---|---|---|---|---|---|---|---|---|---|---|---|
| Bahamas | Gr Bahama | 1996 | 25332 | 1 | ... | 30 | ... | ... | ... | 1 | ... |
| Bolivia | Cochabamba | 1997 | 86366 | 71 | ... | 145 | 161.9 | ... | ... | 4 | ... |
| Bolivia | La Paz | 1997 | 131713 | 152 | ... | 185 | 170.0 | ... | ... | 16 | ... |
| Bolivia | Oruro | 1997 | 22182 | 45 | ... | 130 | 87.5 | ... | ... | 5 | 15 |
| Bolivia | Santa Cruz De La Sierra | 1997 | 94519 | 118 | ... | 288 | 102.2 | ... | ... | 6 | 62 |
| Brazil | Belo Horizonte | 1998 | ... | ... | ... | 1500 | 139.3 | 355.4 | ... | 70 | ... |
| Brazil | Brasilia, Df | 1998 | ... | ... | ... | 851 | 184.5 | 353.4 | ... | 55 | ... |
| Brazil | Rio De Janeiro | 1998 | ... | ... | ... | 5443 | 100.1 | 381.3 | ... | 267 | ... |
| Brazil | Sao Paolo | 1998 | ... | ... | ... | 6063 | 138.3 | 391.5 | ... | 298 | ... |
| Colombia | Bogota | 1993 | ... | ... | ... | 4794 | ... | ... | ... | ... | ... |
| Colombia | Cali | 1993 | ... | ... | ... | 2137 | ... | ... | ... | ... | ... |
| Colombia | Medellin | 1993 | ... | ... | ... | 1321 | ... | ... | ... | ... | ... |
| Dominican Republic | Santo Domingo | 1993 | 1965670 | ... | ... | ... | 413.9 | ... | ... | ... | ... |
| Mexico | Cuidad De Mexico | 1997 | 3247208 | 1042 | 1.9 | ... | ... | ... | 176.7 | 265 | 1287 |
| Mexico | Guadalajara | 1997 | 700298 | 94 | 1.0 | ... | ... | 146.5 | 112.6 | 103 | 103 |
| Mexico | Monterrey | 1997 | 637339 | 169 | 1.5 | ... | 187.7 | ... | 369.5 | 121 | 121 |
| Mexico | Puebla | 1997 | 295877 | 127 | 0.7 | ... | ... | ... | 63.6 | 50 | 50 |
| Nicaragua | Jinotepe | 1995 | ... | 1 | 6.2 | ... | 171.9 | ... | ... | ... | ... |
| Nicaragua | Leon | 1995 | ... | 2 | 3.0 | ... | 60.7 | ... | ... | ... | ... |
| Nicaragua | Managua | 1995 | ... | 9 | 1.3 | ... | 98.4 | ... | ... | ... | ... |
| Nicaragua | Matagalpa | 1995 | ... | 1 | 4.8 | ... | 87.3 | ... | ... | ... | ... |
| Puerto Rico | Bayamon | 1998 | 163537 | 5 | 2.1 | ... | 464.3 | | 279.2 | 30 | 6 |
| Puerto Rico | Carolina | 1998 | 135791 | 1 | 1.7 | ... | 491.3 | | 304.3 | 41 | ... |
| Puerto Rico | Ponce | 1998 | 101190 | 12 | 3.2 | ... | 329.7 | | 181.9 | 9 | 28 |
| Puerto Rico | San Juan | 1998 | 330158 | 19 | 5.8 | ... | 505.3 | | 412.8 | 47 | 4 |
| Uruguay | Montevideo | 1996 | 382190 | 16 | 5.2 | ... | 811.5 | 303.4 | ... | 62 | 39 |
| Uruguay | Paysandu | 1996 | ... | 1 | 2.3 | ... | 502.0 | 265.3 | ... | 1 | 1 |
| Uruguay | Rivera | 1996 | ... | 1 | 1.7 | ... | 507.6 | 266.9 | ... | – | 2 |
| Uruguay | Salto | 1996 | 40928 | 1 | 2.1 | ... | 375.8 | 237.7 | ... | 1 | 4 |

### NORTHERN AMERICA

| | | | | | | | | | | | |
|---|---|---|---|---|---|---|---|---|---|---|---|
| United States | Houston | 1997 | ... | 74 | ... | ... | ... | ... | ... | 66 | ... |
| United States | Los Angeles | 1997 | ... | 140 | ... | ... | ... | ... | ... | 217 | ... |
| United States | New York | 1997 | ... | 156 | ... | ... | ... | ... | ... | 227 | ... |
| United States | Washington, DC | 1997 | ... | 63 | ... | ... | ... | ... | ... | 88 | ... |

### OCEANIA

| | | | | | | | | | | | |
|---|---|---|---|---|---|---|---|---|---|---|---|
| Pitcairn | Adamstown | 1999 | ... | 1 | 0.0 | | 1 | 21 | 0.0 | – | – |

**Source:** United Nations, Human Settlements Statistics Questionnaire 1999.

For sources and footnotes, refer to technical notes.

# INDEX